THE STRATEGY PROCESS
Concepts, Contexts, and Cases

James Brian Quinn
DARTMOUTH COLLEGE

Henry Mintzberg
McGILL UNIVERSITY

Robert M. James
UNIVERSITY OF CHICAGO

Englewood Cliffs, New Jersey 07632

Library of Congress Cataloging-in-Publication Data

QUINN, JAMES BRIAN, (date)
  The strategy process.

    Bibliography: p.
    Includes index.
    1. Strategic planning.   2. Strategic planning—Case
  studies.   I. Mintzberg, Henry.   II. James, Robert M.,
  (date).   III. Title.
  HD30.28.Q53 1988   658.4′012   87–1160
  ISBN   0–13–850892–5

Editorial/production supervision and interior design: JUDITH R. CORNWELL
Cover design: BEN SANTORA
Manufacturing buyers: BARBARA KITTLE, ED O'DOUGHERTY

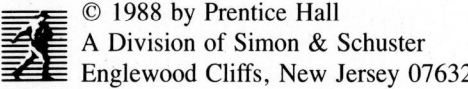 © 1988 by Prentice Hall
A Division of Simon & Schuster
Englewood Cliffs, New Jersey 07632

Printed in the United States of America

10   9   8   7   6   5   4   3   2   1

ISBN 0-13-850892-5 01

Prentice-Hall International (UK) Limited, *London*
Prentice-Hall of Australia Pty. Limited, *Sydney*
Prentice-Hall Canada Inc., *Toronto*
Prentice-Hall Hispanoamericana, S.A., *Mexico*
Prentice-Hall of India Private Limited, *New Delhi*
Prentice-Hall of Japan, Inc., *Tokyo*
Simon & Schuster Asia Pte. Ltd., *Singapore*
Editora Prentice-Hall do Brasil, Ltda., *Rio de Janeiro*

And to YVETTE

Small is the number of them that see with
their own eyes and feel with their
own hearts (Albert Einstein)

HENRY

To All Our Thoughtful Students
Past and Future

With Special Appreciation to
Our Wives,
ALLIE and LYNN

For their special kindness, patience,
beauty and intelligence.

BRIAN and BOB

CONTENTS

III.   CONTEXT

ACKNOWLEDGMENTS

We three authors have been involved in the teaching and practice of strategy formation since the 1960s. Individually we have written extensively in both book and article formats, though we have never before published a textbook with one another. What brought this book together was the firm belief by all three of us that the field badly needs a new kind of strategy text. We wanted a text that looked at process issues as well as analysis; one that was built around critical strategic concepts and contexts instead of the overworked dichotomy of formulation and implementation; and one that accomplished its goals with writing that was sophisticated, eclectic, and lively. We wanted to combine theory and practice, and description and prescription, in new ways that offered insights none could achieve alone. The writing process has been far longer and more difficult that we could have imagined. We hope all sophisticated students of management will think it worthwhile.

In any work of this scope, there are far too many people involved to thank each one individually. We would, however, like to acknowledge the special assistance given us by those who went far out of their way to be helpful. In the academic community, several people deserve special mention: Dean Colin Blaydon kindly arranged for time and funding support to develop the many complex cases contained in the book.

Mr. Bohdan Hawrylyshyn of the International Management Institute of Geneva, Switzerland generously contributed funding and contacts for cases made in Europe and Japan.

But the people who really make such a major project as this happen are the competent research associates and secretaries who undertake the major burden of the work. At the Amos Tuck School of Business Administration, Penny C. Paquette and Tammy Stebbins deserve special praise. Ms. Paquette was researcher and coauthor of many of the cases and reference notes in the book and oversaw the endless problems of coordinating clearances and production logistics for major portions of the book. Ms. Stebbins very professionally managed thousands of pages of original text and revisions with secretarial and computer skills that were invaluable.

At the University of Chicago, Raymond Friedman was very helpful as a researcher and collaborator. At McGill, Renee Mendelsohn helped in the early stages and later Jamal Shamsie was especially helpful in a variety of tasks, small and large, including the preparation of the bibliography. Zanette Kahn somehow rendered the cut and pasted articles into copy that the production people could deal with. At that point, Steve Anzovin took over in New Jersey and worked industriously to integrate the pieces into a comprehensive text, and then Judy Cornwell took charge of the production at Prentice Hall: no easy task but one she carried out with skill and diligence. But our experience at Prentice Hall started much earlier, with Alison Reeves, who championed this book since the beginning and then worked vigorously to see it through to publication. It may not always have been easy, but we are grateful. We'll not forget her efforts.

A special thanks must also be offered to those who worked with the book in its preliminary stages and offered invaluable feedback: in Montreal, those 1985–86 "guinea pig" McGill MBA students, likewise Pierre Brunet's class at Concordia in the summer of 1985. Bill Taylor of Concordia and Fritz Reiger at Windsor also provided useful comments on the text. Bill Joyce at Tuck and Bill Davidson at Colgate Darden made significant contributions through their sophisticated teaching of the cases on an experimental basis. At Rutgers University, John Voyer also used the book a number of times and provided feedback that had important influences on how the book turned out. We are particularly grateful to him not only for that feedback but for his capacity to get inside the book—to appreciate it for exactly what it is—and so to provide us with the first indication of what it might be able to accomplish.

Among those who provided invaluable help on individual cases were Charles H. Bell, James McGarland, Verne Johnson, and John Gerlach of General Mills, Inc.; Thomas Murphy, E. M. Estes, Henry Duncombe, and F. Alan Smith of General Motors Corporation; Alastair Pilkington, Lord Pilkington, and B. N. Tyler of Pilkington Bros. Ltd.; William Spoor, Jack Stafford, E. H. Wingate, and G. Dunkhowe of The Pillsbury Company; Helen Boehm of The Studios of Edward Marshall Boehm; Fred Middleton and Robert Swanson of Genentech, Inc.; Dr. Robert Noyce and Dr. Gordon Moore of Intel Corporation; Fred Smith, James Barksdale, and Thomas Oliver of Federal Express Corporation; Masaru Ibuka, Akoi Morita, Dr. Nobutoshi Kihara, and Dr. Makoto Kikuchi of Sony Corporation; Nobuhiko Kawamoto, Yasuhito Sato, T. Yashiki, and F. Kikuchi of Honda Motor Company, Ltd.; Bob O. Evans and Vincent Learson of IBM Corp.; Dr. Norton Belknap, Thomas Barrow, and George Piercy of Exxon Corp.; Dr. Richard Young, William McCune, I. M. Booth, and Peter Wensberg of Polaroid Corp.; Warren Bull, Rowland Frazee, and Alan Taylor of the Royal Bank of Canada; Stanley Feldberg, Sumner Feldberg, Maurice Segall, and Herschel Denker of Zayre Corporation; and Anthony Frank of First Nationwide Financial Corporation. To each person who kindly contributed valuable time to this project, we are deeply grateful.

One last word; this book is not "finished." Our text, like the subject of so much of its content, is an ongoing process, not a static statement. So much of this book is so different from conventional strategy textbooks that there are bound to be all kinds of opportunities for improvement. We would like to ask you to help us in this regard. We hope to revise the text soon, and to improve it to keep up with this exciting field. Please write to any of us with your suggestions on how to improve the readings, the cases, and the organization of the book at large and its presentation. Strategy making, we believe, is a learning process; we are also engaged in a learning process. And for that we need your feedback. Thank you and enjoy what follows.

James Brian Quinn

Henry Mintzberg

Robert M. James

PREFACE

". . . one must regard all analytical methodologies or structures . . . as mere intellectual frameworks and be very cautious about their overuse in detail. One should remember Von Clausewitz' wise counsel about the inadequacy of prescriptive systems when faced with the infinite resources of the mind and spirit. 'All theory can do is give . . . points of reference and standards of evaluation in specific areas of action, with the ultimate purpose of not telling one how to act but of developing his judgment.' " (James Brian Quinn, *Strategies for Change: Logical Incrementalism* [Richard D. Irwin, 1980], p. 206).

Each CEO (Chief Executive Officer) shares with all other CEOs the challenge of guiding his organization through the unfolding future of the world about him. Success will depend on his ability to perceive and understand his world in all its subtlety, inconsistency, bureaucracy and political maneuver as well as its rationality, in other words, in all of its *complexity*.

Because the picture facing each CEO is so complex, we will not take a simplistic approach to it, such as attempting to develop a single paradigm for forming strategies to deal with it, or only dwelling on certain aspects of implementing such strategies. Instead, we will be realists and embrace its *complexity* by using many different approaches, all of which may have varying degrees of usefulness depending on the circumstances. After all, an open-ended entrepreneurial situation calls for a much different set of skills and techniques than one locked in bureaucracy or politics. Strategy in an innovative or ad hoc situation varies widely from that in a slow-moving professional office or a large-scale military system. By our choice of readings and cases, we have tried to illustrate and enrich this complexity so that our students will approach the subject with the sophistication it deserves.

We think this perspective naturally leads to the selection of *good judgment* as the paramount attribute which enables leaders of business and industry to cope successfully with their complex environments. *Good judgment* must underlie every decision and action which any CEO takes. We do not denigrate the importance of leadership, skills of analysis or persuasion, integrity or dependability, compassion or humanity, flexibility or tenacity, or others. It is simply our conclusion that among all other attributes of managers, the most indispensable is *judgment* because it is the integrator which guides and controls all the others. Therefore, we are making it the central focal point for our book.

Large scale strategy deals not just with the uncertain, but with the unknowable. The strategist, therefore, is forced to go beyond mere analysis and rely somewhat on accummulated experience, on the "feel" of the situation, or on that marvelous bit of highest intellect often called intuition. All of these are parts of informed judgment, a skill we hope to inculcate in you.

To illustrate the need for this kind of judgment, look at some of the key decisions made by major executives in recent years.

In 1957, Tom Watson, Jr., only recently elevated to IBM's presidency because of his father's death, faced an incredibly difficult decision. Vacuum tubes were still the primary building blocks of computers, although transistors were finding their way into increasing military applications. IBM's Vice President and Chief Engineer was increasingly convinced that transistors would become less expensive than tubes and offer superior physical characteristics in performance and life. But whether this would happen, when it could happen, and at what costs if successful, were complete unknowns. Analyzing the conflicting technical assessments and forecasts available, the question was if, when, and how to make the transition. Tom Watson opted for a dramatic directive that simply stated, "Effective as of now, no new design for a computer or calculator populated with tubes instead of transistors will be released from development to production." As a result, IBM mobilized the experience and leadership in transistors that catapulted it to future success.

But Watson's decision was by no means a sure thing. How well transistors would work in computers was unknown. The cost of populating new computers and calculators with transistors appeared almost prohibitively expensive. Transistors even in small quantities for engineering purposes cost tens to hundreds of dollars each, orders of magnitude more than vacuum tubes. Future reductions in the cost of transistors for production purposes were promising, but still to be proven. Finally, the entire organization would have to deal with technologies in which it had less experience and confidence at the very time IBM was trying to press its commercial lead in the computer race. Success in using transistors could be a powerful strategic gain. But if the

move to transistors proved premature, it could perhaps have crippled IBM for years. History tells us that Watson's decision was timely and very effective. But one must remember that he did not make the decision alone. Nor could he have forced the organization to carry it out if either the laws of physics or the culture of his organization had been too hostile.

In the mid-1960s Reginald Jones, General Electric's Controller (and later CEO), recommended that GE terminate its involvement in the manufacture and sale of computers. His analysis indicated that GE wasn't going to be a significant factor in computers without a substantial increase in invested resources. Even then the probabilities were unclear. Again the decision was not Jones's alone. He had to convince GE's senior management and then lead an effort to find a buyer for GE's computer business at an acceptable price. Without these steps the strategy would have proved to be an interesting idea, but little else. Implementation and strategy formulation had to be intimately intertwined. And data analyses alone did not give unambiguous answers.

At the time Jones pressed his case in General Electric, its involvement in the computer world appeared to be at least as promising as that of RCA, Control Data, or Xerox—all of whom, while looking at the same data, waited several more years before making their costly choices.

Richard Gerstenberg, chairman and CEO of General Motors in the early 1970s, had commissioned a task force to look into the significance for GM of his chief economist's forecast that energy prices would rise during the remainder of the twentieth century due to declining world-wide oil reserves. The task force concluded that the cumulative, long-run effect on General Motors' automobiles would be very significant, but the timing of this impact was hard to judge. Faced with the question of what to do, Gerstenberg chose to leave the decision on the table to evolve at its own pace. The members of the task force represented virtually all of GM's automotive units, and had been carefully chosen for their ability to mold and shift opinion in the managerial ranks of their divisions and locations.

Gerstenberg would wait for the situation to develop, minds to open, and awareness and sensitivity to the issue of the cost of energy to trigger responses generated through natural management processes. Instead, GM merely built design options for fuel efficient cars in its international and advanced engineering groups.

When the actual crunch came in October 1973, it happened at a surprising speed. Perhaps because its management was better prepared psychologically to move, GM was the first American auto maker to respond to higher oil prices after the Arab oil embargo. Rather than a single dramatic move, GM's top management merely chose to speed up the rate of change.

The keys to strategy in GM were to maintain flexibility, not to make a mistake by moving too slowly or fast and thus risk the sales base of the country's largest company, yet to respond to the fickle demands of the American consumer who could shift purchasing preferences in weeks, while design and production changes might take years. Here good judgment said move incrementally, in a less dramatic, more controlled fashion. All the analysis in the world could not forecast precisely how all of the oil producing, oil using, competing countries and companies would interact in this situation. Almost 15 years later, the situation is still unclear. Again, judgment had to be exercised in light of the truly unknowable.

Steven Jobs, co-founder and Chairman of Apple Computer Company, found himself facing a substantially altered future. IBM at long last was making its entry into the world of personal computers. Under Jobs, Apple had become the darling of an industry which included such other great names and powerful competitors as Texas Instruments, Hewlett Packard, and Motorola along with a host of potentially aggressive Japanese firms and entrepreneurial startups. But none of these carried the potential threat of "Big Blue." Recognizing the importance of marketing and distribution—IBM's reputation as a sales and marketing machine was indisputable—Jobs added John Sculley to his executive team. Sculley came from the presidency of Pepsi Cola USA where his reputation as a marketer had been well established in the continuous competitive race with Coca Cola.

While no one could doubt Sculley's personal talent and his substantial marketing and distribution knowhow and experience, he was drawn from a non-technically oriented industry—consumer foods. Would he be accepted by Apple's marketing group which had already performed superbly in reaching individual consumers? Would his marketing experience and fresh approach to Apple's opportunities result in constructive new alternatives that would improve Apple's chances in the embryonic business market segment for PCs? Sculley quickly made significant contributions to Apple's marketing and management efforts and soon became CEO of Apple, actually ousting Jobs in the process. Was this a wise decision for Jobs? For Apple? Apple's ability to deal with IBM's challenge is yet to be determined, and involves much more complexity than any one person can comprehend.

In all of these cases management had to make its decisions based on *judgment*. Watson, Jones, Gerstenberg, and Jobs each had to deal with a future containing a fantastic range of external unknowns. Were transistors about to become less expensive than tubes? Would computers be essential in GE's product line? Would energy costs rise and would consumers buy smaller cars? Could even a marketing-oriented Apple respond successfully to IBM's entry into the PC market? Each management had to make its own judgment about factors it simply could not control.

Likewise, each had to make key judgments about unknowns *within* its own organization. Would IBM's engineers be willing and able to capture the promise of superior performance by transistors? Would General Electric's power structure permit the divestiture of such a major business unit? Could General Motors' designers and engineers eliminate features they themselves had created over the years, reduce weight, and improve engine efficiency? How would marketing and engineering groups be motivated to deal with the new effluent and safety regulations being imposed by government? Would Apple's entrepreneurial product and marketing managers accept Sculley and his ideas enthusiastically? Or would they see that nothing quite worked out?

Management judgments had to integrate external considerations about technologies, markets, competitors, resource limitations, suppliers' capabilities, and governmental and social attitudes—for each of which forecasts varied widely. Internally, they simultaneously had to deal with organizational structures, systems, resources, bureaucracies, existing and potential power bases, coalition realignments among these power bases, and potential individual responses of key people to each initiative. How all these would ultimately interact could not conceivably be handled in any analytical model. Successful action required considered judgment.

In order to influence the course of events or to bring about a desired change, a CEO must mediate between those aspects of his environment over which he has little real influence and those where his power or personality can make a difference. To do this he or she must realistically understand not just the mathematical forces at work, but the uses and limits of power, and the ways different interventions may assist or hinder desired change. Watson, Jones, Gerstenberg, and Jobs each had to gather and assess *all* of the relevant and significant factors in the situation and the likely reactions of all involved participants. No single issue could be isolated from its interrelationship with and, perhaps, contamination by all other facets of the firm and its world. Their choices were often highly qualitative in nature and not amenable to any easy or precise calculus.

Our hope is that the conceptual material in our text will help students comprehend the wide range of issues involved in strategy and that the complex cases will give them practice in developing and exercising judgment on strategic issues. While we recognize that experience is undoubtedly the best teacher of judgment, the cases and articles should serve as Link trainers or flight simulators do in shortening the time and reducing the expense of training airline pilots.

The readings were chosen to represent a wide range of issues and perspectives. The models and conceptual materials in each reading represent generalizations from common patterns and experiences in the business world. We hope that this combination will give the student enough "ammunition" to begin intelligent forays into the world of real business strategy and to improve the probability of being successful there. That is all any education can do. We believe none of the models provide any final "answers." The first payoff will come from applying these models and concepts to the more complex real world situations portrayed in our cases. Students can practice their judgment—think out and debate with others various possible responses to business problems. In this way, we hope they will develop an awareness of many complex and subtle issues common to the business world and a sensitivity to the small yet important signs that might otherwise be overlooked. Perhaps most important, this combination of experiences should help them recognize the limitations as well as the reasoning behind various theories and the serious problems caused by "standard" answers based on "conventional wisdom."

No single model or theory can incorporate all the factors that influence major business decisions, or all the possible combinations of these factors that could be faced. Nor can they anticipate the bizarre changes that occur in real world environments, or, even more important, the impacts of *your* own or others' creative innovations. Using food preparation as an analogy, we can liken the descriptions of business enterprises and the prescriptions of business writers to the cookbooks available for food preparers. The great chefs of the world—while knowing their content—disdain detailed use of cookbooks and depend upon their own skills in concocting new ways to please our palates. If you are daunted by the prospect of having to invent everything about your business, relax. There are many "cookbooks" available to help you. Simply remember that you are not limited to their recipes alone. And keep in mind that the world provides special rewards for successful innovators.

The authors of this book have set as their

goal placing you, the reader, on a path which will help you develop increasingly good judgment in business matters by helping you gain insights into various business situations from a series of differing perspectives. The purpose of developing these perspectives is to enable you to use your own judgment and creative instincts in finding new effective patterns for management. It is such judgments, we believe, that make the biggest differences in the business world. The decisions of Watson, Jones, Gerstenberg, and Jobs were bound to influence irrevocably their organizations for better or worse in a major way. If Watson's move to transistors had proved premature, IBM could have lost a whole generation of computers to its opponents. If a solid position in computers had turned out to be essential to GE not only as a profitable business but also as a key building block in its other businesses, it would have been at a distinct disadvantage for some time. If GM had taken premature action in improving the fuel efficiency of its automobiles, it could have found that it had moved beyond where its car-buying customers were willing to go, thereby irrevocably losing important markets, as Chrysler once did. If Sculley's influence on Apple's marketing efforts had turned out to be less productive than his predecessors', Apple and Jobs could have lost much, if not everything.

The key point we wish to impress upon you is that the strategic decision-making process is typically:

> ". . . characterized by novelty, complexity, and openendedness, by the fact that the organization usually begins with little understanding of the decision situation it faces or the route to its solution, and only a vague idea of what that solution might be and how it will be evaluated when it is developed. Only by groping through a recursive, discontinuous process involving many different steps and a host of dynamic factors over a considerable period of time is a final choice often made." (Mintzberg, et al., "The Structure of 'Unstructured' Decision Processes," *Administrative Science Quarterly,* 1976: 250–51).

INTRODUCTION

We have set out to produce a different kind of textbook in the field of business policy or, as it is now more popularly called, strategic management. We have tried to provide the reader with a richness of theory, a richness of practice, and a strong basis for linkage between the two. We have rejected the strictly case study approach, which leaves theory out altogether, or soft-pedals it, and thereby denies the accumulated benefits of many years of careful research and thought about management processes. We have also rejected an alternate approach that forces on readers a highly rationalistic model of how the strategy process *should* function. As authors with quite different backgrounds and outlooks, we have collaborated because we believe that in this complex world of organizations a range of concepts is needed to cut through and illuminate particular aspects of that complexity. There is no "one best way" to create strategy, nor is there "one best form" of organization. Quite different forms work well in particular contexts. We believe that exploring a fuller variety systematically will create a deeper and more useful appreciation of the strategy process.

This text, unlike most others, is therefore eclectic. Presenting published articles and portions of other books in their original form, rather than filtered through our minds and pens, is one way to reinforce this variety. Each author has his or her own ideas and his or her own best way of expressing them (ourselves included!). Summarized by us, these readings would lose a good deal of their richness.

We do not apologize for contradictions among the ideas of leading thinkers. The world is full of contradictions. The real danger lies in using pat solutions to a nuanced reality, not in opening perspectives up to different interpretations. The effective strategist is one who can live with contradictions, learn to appreciate their causes and effects, and reconcile them sufficiently for effective action. We have, nonetheless, ordered the readings by chapter to suggest some ways in which that reconciliation can be considered. Our own brief chapter introductions are also intended to assist in this task and to help place the readings themselves in perspective.

ON THEORY

A word on theory is in order. We do not consider theory a dirty word, nor do we apologize for making it a major component of this book. To some people, to be theoretical is to be detached, impractical. But a bright social scientist once said that "there is nothing so practical as a good theory." And every successful doctor, engineer, and physicist would have to agree: they would be unable to practice their modern work without theories. Theories are useful because they shortcut the need to store masses of data. It is easier to remember a simple framework about some phenomenon than it is to consider every detail you ever observed. In a sense, theories are a bit like cataloging systems in libraries: the world would be impossibly confusing without them. They enable you to store and conveniently access your own experiences as well as those of others.

One can, however, suffer not just from an absence of theories, but also from being dominated by them without realizing it. To paraphrase the words of John Maynard Keynes, most "practical men" are the slaves of some defunct theorist. Whether we realize it or not, our behavior is guided by the systems of ideas that we have internalized over the years. Much can be learned by bringing these out in the open, examining them more carefully, and comparing them with alternative ways to view the world—including ones based on systematic study (that is, research). One of our prime intentions in this book is to expose the limitations of conventional theories and to offer alternate explanations that can be superior guides to understanding and taking action in specific contexts.

Prescriptive Vs. Descriptive Theory

Unlike many textbooks in this field, we have tried to explain the world as it is, rather than as someone thinks it is *supposed* to be. Although there has sometimes been a tendency to disdain such *descriptive* theories, *prescriptive* (or normative) ones have often been the problem, rather than the solution, in the field of management. There is no one best way in management; no prescription works for all organizations. Even when a prescription seems effective in some context, it requires a sophisticated understanding of exactly what that context is and how it functions. In other words, one cannot decide reliably what should be done in a system as complicated as a contemporary organization without a genuine understanding of how that organization really works. In engineering, no student ever questions having

to learn physics; in medicine, having to learn anatomy. Imagine an engineering student's hand shooting up in a physics class: "Listen, prof, it's fine to tell us how the atom does work. But what we really want to know is how the atom *should* work." Why should a management student's similar demand in the realm of strategy or structure be considered any more appropriate? How can people manage systems they do not understand?

Nevertheless, we have not ignored prescriptive theory when it appears useful. A number of prescriptive techniques (industry analysis, portfolio analysis, experience curves, etc.) are discussed. But these are associated both with other readings and with cases that will help you understand the context and limitations of their usefulness. Both cases and readings offer opportunities to pursue the full complexity of strategic situations. You will find a wide range of issues and perspectives addressed. One of our main goals is to integrate a variety of views, rather than allow strategy to be fragmented into just "human issues" and "economics issues." The text and cases provide a basis for treating the full complexity of strategic management, regardless of what your particular starting background may be.

ON SOURCES

How were all the readings selected and edited? One popular textbook boasts that all of its readings were published since 1980 (except one dated 1979!). We make no such claim; indeed we would like to make quite a different boast: many of our readings have been around for a while, long enough to mature, like fine wine. Our criterion for selection was not the newness of the article so much as the quality of its insight—that is, its ability to explain some aspect of the strategy process better than any other article. Time does not age the really good articles. Quite the opposite—it distinguishes their quality (although it does bring us back to the old habits of masculine gender; we apologize to our female readers for this). We are, of course, not biased toward old articles either—just toward good ones. Hence, the materials in this book range from classics of the 1950s to some published just weeks before our final selection was made (as well as a few hitherto unpublished pieces). You will find articles from the most serious academic journals, the best practitioner magazines, books, and some very obscure sources. The best can sometimes be found in strange places!

We have opted to include many shorter readings rather than fewer longer ones, and we have tried to present as wide a variety of good ideas as possible while maintaining clarity. To do so we often had to cut within readings. We have, in fact, put a great deal of effort into the cutting in order to extract the key messages of each reading in as brief, concise, and clear a manner as possible. Unfortunately, our cutting sometimes forced us to eliminate interesting examples and side issues. (In the readings, as well as some of the case materials from published sources, dots . . . signify portions that have been deleted from the original, while square brackets [ ] signify our own insertions of minor clarifications into the original text.) We apologize to you, the reader, as well as to the authors, for having done this, but hope that the overall result has rendered these changes worthwhile.

We have also included a number of our own works. Perhaps we are biased, having less objective standards by which to judge what we have written. But we have messages to convey, too, and our own writings do examine the basic themes that we feel are important in policy and strategy courses today.

ON CASES

A major danger of studying the strategy process— probably the most enticing subject in the management curriculum, and at the pinnacle of organizational processes—is that students and professors can become detached from the basics of the enterprise. The "Don't bore me with the operating details; I'm here to tackle the really big issues" syndrome has been the death of many business

policy or strategy courses. The big issues *are* rooted in little details. We have tried to recognize this in both the readings and the cases. Effective strategy processes always come down to specifics. The cases and the industry reference notes provide a rich soil for investigating strategic realities. Their complexities always extend well below the surface. Each layer peeled back can reveal new insights and rewards.

As useful as they are, however, cases are not really the ideal way to understand strategy: involving oneself in the hubbub of life in a real organization is. We harbor no illusions that reading 20 pages on an organization will make you an expert. But cases remain the most convenient way to introduce practice into the classroom, to tap a wide variety of experiences, and to involve students actively in analysis and decision making. Our cases consciously contain both their prescriptive and descriptive aspects. On the one hand, they provide the data and background for making a major decision. Students can appraise the situation in its full context, suggest what future directions would be best for the organization in question, and discuss how their solutions can realistically be implemented. On the other hand, each case is also an opportunity to understand the dynamics of an organization—the historical context of the problems it faces, the influence of its culture, its probable reactions to varying solutions, and so on. Unlike many cases which focus on only the analytical aspects of a decision, ours constantly force you to consider the messy realities of arriving at decisions in large organizations and obtaining a desired response to any decision. In these respects, case study involves a good deal of descriptive *and* prescriptive analysis.

Linking Cases and Readings

The cases in this book are not intended to emphasize any particular theories, any more than the theoretical materials are included because they explain particular cases. Each case presents a slice of some specific reality, each reading a conceptual interpretation of some phenomenon. The readings are placed in particular groupings because they approach some common aspects or issues in theory.

We have provided some general guidelines for relating particular cases to sets of readings. But do not push this too far: analyze each case for its own sake. Cases are intrinsically richer than readings. Each contains a wide variety of issues—many awfully messy—in no particular order. The readings, in contrast, are usually neat and tidy, professing one or a few basic conceptual ideas, and providing some specific vocabulary. When the two connect—sometimes through direct effort, more often indirectly as conceptual ideas are recalled in the situation of a particular case—some powerful learning can take place in the form of clarification or, we hope, revelation.

Try to see how particular theories can help you to understand some of the issues in the cases and provide useful frameworks for drawing conclusions. Perhaps the great military theorist, Von Clausewitz, said it best over a century ago (to borrow a quotation from one of our readings of Chapter 1):

> All the theory can do is give the artist or soldier points of reference and standards of evaluation . . . with the ultimate purpose not of telling him how to act but of developing his judgment (1976:15).

In applying the theory to cases, please don't assume that it is only the readings cross referenced with the case that matter. We have designed the book so that the textual materials develop as the chapters unfold. Concepts introduced in earlier chapters become integrated in the later ones. And early cases tend to build knowledge for those appearing later. Problems and their organizational context move from the simple to the more complex. Space limitations and the structured nature of theories require some compartmentalization. But don't take that compartmentalization too literally. In preparing each case, use whatever concepts you find helpful both from chapters of this book and from your personal knowledge. The cases themselves deal with real people in real companies. The reality they present is enormously complicated; their dynamics extend to today's newspaper, and *Who's Who*, or any other reference you can imagine. Use any sound source of information that helps you to deal with them. Part of the fun of policy or strategy courses is understanding how major decisions happened to be made and their consequences—local, national, even international.

These are all living cases. In the strictest sense they have no beginning or end. They have been written in as lively a style as possible; we do not believe business school cases need be dull! Each case deals with a major transition point in the history of an enterprise. Each can be used in a variety of ways to emphasize a particular set of concepts at a particular time in the course. Many lend themselves to sophisticated financial, industry, portfolio, and competitive analyses as well as discerning organizational, behavioral, and managerial practice inquiries. And many contain entrepreneurial and technological dimensions rarely found in strategy cases. Trying to figure out what is going on should be challenging as well as fun!

Case Discussion

Management cases provide a concrete information base for students to analyze and share as they discuss management issues. Without this focus, discussions of theory can become quite confusing. You may have in mind an image of an organization or situation that is very different from that of all the other discussants. As a result, what appears to be a difference in theory will—after much argument—turn out to be simply a difference in choice of examples or perception of the realities surrounding these examples.

In this text we try to provide three levels of learning: *first*, a chance to share the generalized insights of leading theoreticians (in the readings); *second*, an opportunity to test the applicability and limits of these theories in specific (case) situations; *third*, the capacity to develop one's own special amalgam of insights based upon empirical observations and inductive reasoning (from case analyses). All are useful approaches; some students and professors will find one mix more productive for their special level of experience or mind set. Another will prefer a quite different mix. Hence, we include a wide selection of cases and readings.

The cases are not intended as *examples* of either weak or exceptionally good management practices. Nor, as we noted, do they provide *examples* of the concepts in a particular reading. They are discussion vehicles for probing the benefits and limits of various approaches. And they are analytical vehicles for applying and testing concepts and tools developed in your education and experience. Almost every case has its marketing, operations, accounting, financial, human relations, planning and control, external environmental, ethical, political, and quantitative dimensions. Each dimension should be addressed in preparations and classroom discussions, although some aspects will inevitably emerge as more important in one situation than another.

In each case you should look for several sets of issues. *First*, you should understand what went on in that situation. Why did it happen this way? What are the strong or weak features of what happened? What could have been changed to advantage? How? Why? *Second*, there are always issues of what should be done next. What are the key issues to be resolved? What are the major alternatives available? What outcomes could the organization expect from each? Which alternative should it select? Why? *Third*, there will almost always be "hard" quantitative data and "soft" qualitative data about each situation. Both deserve attention. Because the cases deal with real companies, and real people, in real situations, their data bases can be *extended* as far as students and professors wish. They only have to consult their libraries and daily newspapers.

But remember, no realistic strategy situation is *just* an organization behavior problem or *just* a financial or economic analytical one. Both sets of data should be massaged, and an *integrated* solution developed. Our cases are consciously constructed for this. Given their complexity we have tried to keep the cases as short as possible. And we have tried to capture some of the flavor

of the real organization. Moreover, we have sought to mix product and services cases, technological and "non-tech" cases, entrepreneurial, small company, and large enterprise situations. In this cross section, we have tried to capture some of the most important and exciting issues, concepts, and products of our times. We believe management is fun, and important. The cases try to convey this.

There is no "correct" answer to any case. There may be several "good" answers and many poor ones. The purpose of a strategy course should be to help you understand the nature of these "better" answers, what to look for, how to analyze alternatives, and how to see through the complexities of reaching solutions and implanting them in real organizations. A strategy course can only improve your probability of success, not ensure it. The total number of variables in a real strategy situation is typically beyond the control of any one person or group. Hence another caveat: don't rely on what a company actually did as a guide to effective action. The company may have succeeded or failed not because of its specific decisions, but because of luck, an outstanding personality, the bizarre action of an opponent, international actions over which it had no control, and so on. One of the products of a successful strategy course should be a little humility.

Case Study Guides

We have posed a few questions at the end of each case as discussion guides. Students have generally found these helpful in organizing their thinking about each case. If you answer these questions well, you can probably deal with anything that comes up in class. But each professor may conduct his class in a quite different fashion. The questions should help you see relevant issues, but they should not limit your thinking. From time to time there are intermediate "decision points" in a case. Work on the material up to that point just as you would a short case. The case materials immediately following these decision points consciously leave out much detail on what might have happened so that you can arrive at your own specific solutions. Later you can see them in the context of a longer time horizon, much like a mystery story unfolding in phases. Analyze the specific situations, consider alternatives, and arrive at specific conclusions— understanding that later events might have looked a bit different if your solution had been implemented. Like any good mystery story, a case provides many clues, never all, but, surprisingly, sometimes more than executives might have had time to absorb in the real situation.

Believing that no "canned approach" is viable for all strategic situations, we have selected cases that cut across a variety of issues and theoretical constructs. Almost any of these cases is so complex that it can be positioned at a number of different spots in a good strategy course. We have clustered them around the three major segments of the text for convenience to students and professors. But the cases could equally well be taught in a number of other sequences. We leave the final case selection to the style and wisdom of the professor and his or her students.

THIS BOOK'S STRUCTURE

Not Formulation, Then Implementation

This text offers a chapter format new to the policy or strategy field. Unlike most others, it has no specific chapter or section devoted to "implementation" per se. The assumption in other texts is that strategy is formulated and then implemented, with organizational structures, control systems, and the like following obediently behind strategy. In this text, as in reality, formulation and implementation are intertwined as complex interactive processes in which politics, values, organizational culture, and management styles determine or constrain particular strategic decisions. And strategy, structure, and systems mix together in complicated ways to influence outcomes. While strategy formulation and implementation may be separated in some situations—perhaps in crises, in some totally new ventures, as well as in organizations

facing predictable futures—these events are rare. We certainly do not believe in building a whole book (let alone a whole field) around this conceptual distinction.

But Concepts, Then Contexts

The text is divided roughly into two different parts. The first deals with *concepts*, the second with *contexts*. We introduce strategy and structure as well as power, culture, and several other concepts early in the text as equal partners in the complex web of ideas that make up what we call "the strategy process." In the second half of the text we weave these concepts together in a number of distinct situations, which we call *contexts*. A chapter on configuration stands as a bridge between these two halves and explains how concepts lead to contexts.

Our theme diagram illustrates this. Concepts, shown on top, are divided into two groups—strategy and organization—to represent the first two sections of the book. Configuration is in the center, drawing all these concepts together, giving rise to a variety of contexts—covered in the third section—which we consider the key ones in the field of strategy today (though hardly the only ones).

We will next review the outline of the text, chapter by chapter.

Section I. Strategy

The first section is called "*Strategy*"; it comprises five chapters (two introductory in nature, and three on the processes by which strategy making takes place). Chapter 1 introduces *the strategy concept* and probes the meaning of this important word to broaden your view of it. Here the pattern is set of challenging you to question conventional views, especially when these act to narrow perspectives. The themes introduced in this chapter carry throughout the book, and are worth care in understanding.

Chapter 2 introduces a very important character in the book, *the strategist* as general manager. This person may not be the only one who

STRATEGY PROCESS THEME DIAGRAM

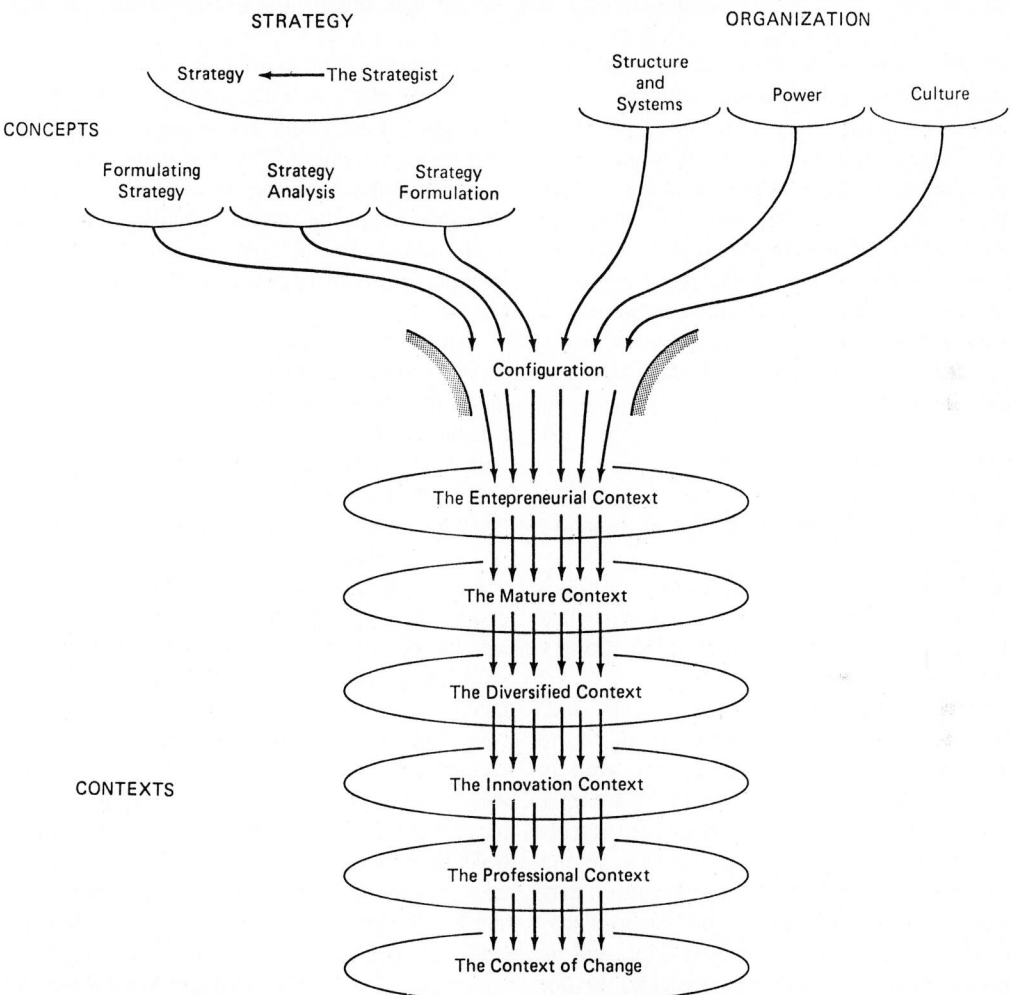

makes strategy in an organization, but he or she is clearly an important player. In examining the work of the general manager and the character of his or her job, we shall perhaps upset a number of widely accepted notions. We do this to help you understand the very real complexities and difficulties of making strategy and managing in contemporary organizations.

Chapters 3, 4, and 5 take up a theme that is treated extensively in the text—to the point of being reflected in its title: the development of an understanding of the *processes* by which

strategies are made. Chapter 3 looks at *formulating strategy*, specifically at some widely accepted prescriptive models for how organizations should go about developing their strategies. Chapter 4 extends these ideas to more formal ways of doing *strategy analysis* and considering what, if any, "generic" forms a strategy can take. While readings in later chapters will challenge some of these precepts, what will not be questioned is the importance of having to understand them. They are fundamental to understanding the strategy process today.

Chapter 5 switches from a prescriptive to a descriptive approach. Concerned with understanding *strategy formation*, it considers how strategies actually *do* form in organizations (not necessarily by being formulated) and *why* different processes may be effective in specific circumstances. This text takes an unconventional stand by viewing planning and other formal approaches as not the only—and often indeed not even the most desirable—ways to make strategy. You will find our emphasis on descriptive process—as an equal partner with the more traditional concerns for technical and analytical issues—is one of the unifying themes of this book (together with the notion of configuration).

Section II. Organization

In Section I, the readings introduced strategy, the strategist, and various ways in which strategy should be formulated and does in fact form. In Section II, entitled *Organization*, we introduce other concepts that constitute part of the strategy process.

In Chapter 6, we consider *structure and systems*, where particular attention is paid to the various forms that structure can take as well as the mechanisms that comprise them. In Chapter 7, *power* is the focus. We consider two aspects of power: first, the distribution of power among the various actors within the organization, and its links to political activity; second, the organization as a political entity in its own right, and its power to pursue its own ends, whether or not responsibly, in the face of opposing forces in society. Both aspects will be seen to influence significantly the processes by which strategies are formulated or form. In Chapter 8, we consider *culture*, especially how strong systems of beliefs, called "ideologies," impact on organizations and their strategies and so influence their effectiveness.

Section III. Context

Section III is called *Context*. We consider how all of the elements introduced so far—strategy, the processes by which it is formulated and gets formed, the strategist, structure, systems, power, and culture—combine to form "configurations" that appear to suit particular contexts. Chapter 9 discusses the issue of achieving configuration. It serves, as we noted above, as the bridge between the concepts of the first half of the book and the contexts of the second. After making "the case for configuration" and presenting some well-known types of configuration, we develop in depth six distinct contexts in the next six chapters.

Chapter 10 deals with the *entrepreneurial context*, where a rather simple organization comes under the close control of a strong leader, often a person with vision. Chapter 11 examines the *mature context*, one common to many large business and government organizations involved in the mass production or distribution of goods or services. Chapter 12 introduces the *diversified context*, and deals with organizations that have diversified their product or service lines and usually divisionalized their structures to deal with the greater varieties of environments they face.

Chapters 13 and 14 develop the *innovative context* and the *professional context*. In the former, the organization depends on high-powered expertise in project teams, under dynamic conditions, in order to innovate. The professional context also involves high expertise but in a more stable, if nonetheless, complex environment, leading to a different form of structure and different processes of strategy making. What these two contexts have in common, however, is that they act in ways that upset many of the widely accepted notions about the strategy process.

In considering each of these widely different contexts, we seek to discuss (where appropriate material is available) the situations in which each is most likely to be found, the structures most suited to it, the kinds of strategies that tend to be pursued, the processes by which these strategies tend to be formed and might be formulated, and the social issues associated with the context.

Chapter 15 is devoted not so much to a

specific context as to *managing the transition* between contexts, or major changes within a context (which we can, of course, characterize as the context of change). The major concerns are how organizations can cope with "turnarounds," significant shifts in their technologies, and new stages in their own life cycles or those of their key products.

The text ends on a lighter note, but one no less serious than the rest. Concerned with *thinking strategically*, the readings of Chapter 16 consider the "myth" of the well-educated manager, and probe the human brain to try to explain many of the unexpected findings of this book.

Well, there you have it. We have worked hard on this book, to get it right. We also tried to think things through from the basics. The result, we think, is a text that in style, format, and content is unusual for the field of policy or strategy. The final product may not be perfect, but we believe it's good, indeed better than any other text available. Now it's your turn to find out if you agree. Have fun doing so!

ONE

THE STRATEGY CONCEPT

We open this text on its focal point: strategy. The first section is called "Strategy," the first chapter, "the Strategy Concept." Section I describes the role of the general manager as strategist and considers the processes by which strategies get made from three perspectives: deliberate formulation, systematic analysis, and emergent formation. But in this opening chapter, we must first consider the central concept—strategy itself.

What is strategy anyway? There is no single, universally accepted definition. Different authors and managers use the term differently; for example, some include goals and objectives as part of strategy while others make firm distinctions between them. Our intention in including the following readings is not to promote any one view of strategy, but rather to clarify a number that seem useful. As will be evident throughout this text, our wish is not to narrow perspectives but to broaden them by trying to clarify issues. In pursuing these readings, it will be helpful to think about the meaning of strategy, to try to understand how different people have used the term, and, later, to see if certain definitions hold up better in particular contexts.

With these concerns in mind, we have selected three readings. They present different views, sometimes even contradictory ones, as they trace the major uses of the term.

The first reading, by James Brian Quinn

of the Amos Tuck Business School of Dartmouth College, provides a general overview by clarifying some of the vocabulary in this field and introducing a number of the themes that will appear throughout the text. In this reading from his book *Strategies for Change: Logical Incrementalism*, Quinn places special emphasis on the military uses of the term, and draws from this domain a set of essential "dimensions" or criteria for successful strategies. To derive these, he goes back to Philip and Alexander of Macedonia for his main example; he also provides a brief kaleidoscope of how similar concepts have influenced later military and diplomatic strategists. Discussion of the military aspects of strategy must surely be among the oldest continuous literatures in the world. In fact, the origins of the word "strategy" go back even farther than this experience in Macedonia, to the Greeks whom Alexander and his father defeated. As Quinn notes and Robert Evered, in another article, elaborates:

> Initially *strategos* referred to a role (a general in command of an army). Later it came to mean "the art of the general," which is to say the psychological and behavioral skills with which he occupied the role. By the time of Pericles (450 BC) it came to mean managerial skill (administration, leadership, oration, power). And by Alexander's time (330 BC) it re-

ferred to the skill of employing forces to overcome opposition and to create a unified system of global governance (1980:3).

The second reading from H. Igor Ansoff's well-known book *Corporate Strategy*, presents one of the earliest, but still most insightful, discussions of the strategy concept in business. Note the deliberate nature of the term, as in its military use. Ansoff, an American who wrote his book while teaching at the Carnegie-Mellon Graduate School of Industrial Administration before spending many years teaching and consulting in Europe, introduces various, now classic, forms of strategy. He was also responsible in this book for introducing to the management literature the notion of *synergy*, an indispensable concept today. As a result of Ansoff's work, management writers generally distinguish *corporate strategy* from *business strategy* (a parallel to the *grand* strategies and *battle* strategies Quinn develops). The former concerns the selection of what business (or more commonly today, what portfolio of businesses) to be in, the latter, how to compete or function in that business once selected. To this distinction, Astley and Fombrun [1983] have suggested the additional concept of *collective strategy*. This refers to the management of external relationships in non-competitive ways, particularly when the largest and most developed firms move beyond corporate strategy—and perhaps beyond competition itself—into the political domain. We return to this idea in our chapter on power.

The third reading, by Henry Mintzberg who teaches policy in the Faculty of Management at McGill University in Montreal, serves another purpose: to open up the concept of strategy to a view very different from those of traditional military or business writers (but suggested briefly in the Quinn reading). Mintzberg focuses on various distinct definitions of strategy—as a plan (as well as a ploy), a pattern, a position, and a perspective. He uses the first two of these definitions to take us beyond *deliberate* strategy—beyond the traditional planning-oriented view of the term—to the notion of *emergent* strategy. This introduces the idea that strategies can *form* in an organization without being consciously in-

tended, that is, without being *formulated*. This view may seem to run counter to the usual formal definition of the term—indeed to the whole thrust of the strategy literature—but Mintzberg argues that many people implicitly use the term this way even though they would not so define it. By presenting these quite different definitions of strategy, this reading seeks to flesh out the strategy concept in a practical way.

Upon completion of these readings, we hope that you will be less sure of *the* use of the word strategy, but ready to tackle the study of the strategy *process* with a broadened perspective and an open, enthusiastic mind. There are no universally right answers in this field (any more than there are in most other fields), but there are interesting and constructive orientations.

Several cases relate well to the concepts developed in this chapter. *The Guns of August* and *MacArthur and the Philippines* pick up the military and formally derived concepts of strategy discussed in the Quinn and Ansoff articles. Cases such as Boehm, Intel, and Genentech offer opportunities to consider the concept of strategy analytically, while IBM (A), Royal Bank of Canada (B), and MacArthur deal with the processes through which organizations arrive at strategies.

STRATEGIES FOR CHANGE*

by James Brian Quinn

SOME [USEFUL] DEFINITIONS

Because the words *strategy*, *objectives*, *goals*, *policy*, and *programs* . . . have different meanings to individual readers or to various organizational cultures, I [try] to use certain definitions consistently . . . For clarity—not pedantry—these are set forth as follows:

* Excerpted from James Brian Quinn, *Strategies for Change: Logical Incrementalism* (copyright © Richard D. Irwin Inc. 1980), chaps. 1 and 5; used by permission of the publisher.

A **strategy** is the *pattern* or *plan* that *integrates* an organization's *major* goals, policies, and action sequences into a *cohesive* whole. A well-formulated strategy helps to *marshal* and *allocate* an organization's resources into a *unique and viable posture* based on its relative *internal competencies* and *shortcomings*, anticipated *changes in the environment*, and contingent moves by *intelligent opponents*.

Goals (or **objectives**) state *what* is to be achieved and *when* results are to be accomplished, but they do not state *how* the results are to be achieved. All organizations have multiple goals existing in a complex hierarchy (Simon, 1964): from value objectives, which express the broad value premises toward which the company is to strive; through overall organizational objectives, which establish the intended *nature* of the enterprise and the *directions* in which it should move; to a series of less permanent goals that define targets for each organizational unit, its subunits, and finally all major program activities within each subunit. Major goals—those that affect the entity's overall direction and viability—are called *strategic goals*.

Policies are rules or guidelines that express the *limits* within which action should occur. These rules often take the form of contingent decisions for resolving conflicts among specific objectives. For example: ''Don't use nuclear weapons in war unless American cities suffer nuclear attack first'' or ''Don't exceed three months' inventory in any item without corporate approval.'' Like the objectives they support, policies exist in a hierarchy throughout the organization. Major policies— those that guide the entity's overall direction and posture or determine its viability—are called *strategic policies*.

Programs specify the *step-by-step sequence of actions* necessary to achieve major objectives. They express *how* objectives will be achieved within the limits set by policy. They ensure that resources are committed to achieve goals, and they provide the dynamic track against which progress can be measured. Those major programs that determine the entity's overall thrust and viability are called *strategic programs*.

Strategic decisions are those that determine the overall direction of an enterprise and its ultimate viability in light of the predictable, the unpredictable, and the unknowable changes that may occur in its most important surrounding environments. They intimately shape the true goals of the enterprise. They help delineate the broad limits within which the enterprise operates. They dictate both the resources the enterprise will have accessible for its tasks and the principal patterns in which these resources will be allocated. And they determine the effectiveness of the enterprise—whether its major thrusts are in the right directions given its resource potentials—rather than whether individual tasks are performed efficiently. Management for efficiency, along with the myriad decisions necessary to maintain the daily life and services of the enterprise, is the domain of operations.

Strategies versus Tactics

Strategies normally exist at many different levels in any large organization. For example, in government there are world trade, national economic, treasury department, military spending, investment, fiscal, monetary supply, banking, regional development, and local reemployment strategies—all related to each other somewhat hierarchically yet each having imperatives of its own. Similarly, businesses have numerous strategies from corporate levels to department levels within divisions. Yet if strategies exist at all these levels, how do strategies and tactics differ? Often the primary difference lies in the scale of action or the perspective of the leader. What appears to be a ''tactic'' to the chief executive officer (or general) may be a ''strategy'' to the marketing head (or lieutenant) if it determines the ultimate success and viability of his or her organization. In a more precise sense, tactics can occur at either level. They are the short-duration, adaptive, action-interaction realignments that opposing forces use to accomplish limited goals after their initial contact. Strategy defines a continuing basis for ordering these adaptations toward more broadly conceived purposes.

A genuine strategy is always needed when

the potential actions or responses of intelligent opponents can seriously affect the endeavor's desired outcome—regardless of that endeavor's organizational level in the total enterprise. This condition almost always pertains to the important actions taken at the top level of competitive organizations. However, game theorists quickly point out that some important top-level actions—for example, sending a peacetime fleet across the Atlantic—merely require elaborate coordinative plans and programs (Von Neumann and Morgenstern, 1944; Shubik, 1975; McDonald, 1950). A whole new set of concepts, a true strategy, is needed if some people or nations decide to oppose the fleet's purposes. And it is these concepts that in large part distinguish strategic formulation from simpler programmatic planning.

Strategies may be looked at as either a priori statements to guide action or a posteriori results of actual decision behavior. In most complex organizations . . . one would be hard pressed to find a complete a priori statement of a total strategy that actually is followed. Yet often the existence of a strategy (or strategy change) may be clear to an objective observer, although it is not yet apparent to the executives making critical decisions. One, therefore, must look at the actual emerging *pattern* of the enterprise's operant goals, policies, and major programs to see what its true strategy is (Mintzberg, 1972). Whether it is consciously set forth in advance or is simply a widely held understanding resulting from a stream of decisions, this pattern becomes the real strategy of the enterprise. And it is changes in this pattern—regardless of what any formal strategic documents may say—that either analysts or strategic decision makers must address if they wish to comprehend or alter the concern's strategic posture. . . .

THE CLASSICAL APPROACH [TO STRATEGY]

Military-diplomatic strategies have existed since prehistoric times. In fact, one function of the earliest historians and poets was to collect the accumulated lore of these successful and unsuc-

cessful life-and-death strategies and convert them into wisdom and guidance for the future. As societies grew larger and conflicts more complex, generals, statesmen, and captains studied, codified, and tested essential strategic concepts until a coherent body of principles seemed to emerge. In various forms these were ultimately distilled into the maxims of Sun Tzu (1963), Machiavelli (1950), Napoleon (1940), Von Clausewitz (1976), Foch (1970), Lenin (1927), Hart (1954), Montgomery (1958), or Mao Tse-Tung (1967). Yet with a few exceptions—largely introduced by modern technology—the most basic principles of strategy were in place and recorded long before the Christian era. More modern institutions primarily adapted and modified these to their own special environments.

Although one could choose any number of classical military-diplomatic strategies as examples, Philip and Alexander's actions at Chaeronea (in 338 B.C.) contain many currently relevant concepts (Varner and Ulger, 1978; Green, 1970). . . .

A CLASSICAL STRATEGY

A Grand Strategy

Philip and his young son, Alexander, had very *clear goals*. They sought to rid Macedonia of influence by the Greek city-states and to *establish dominance* over what was then essentially northern Greece. They also wanted Athens to *join a coalition* with them against Persia on their eastern flank. *Assessing their resources*, they *decided to avoid* the overwhelming superiority of the Athenian fleet and *chose to forego* attack on the powerful walled cities of Athens and Thebes where their superbly trained phalanxes and cavalry would not *have distinct advantages*.

Philip and Alexander *used an indirect approach* when an invitation by the Amphictyonic Council brought their army south to punish Amphissa. In a *planned sequence of actions and deceptive maneuvers*, they cut away from a direct line of march to Amphissa, *bypassed the enemy*, and *fortified a key base*, Elatea. They then took steps to *weaken their opponents politically and morally* by pressing restoration of the Phoenician communities earlier dispersed by the Thebans and by having Philip declared a champion of the Delphic gods. Then *using misleading messages* to make the enemy believe they had moved north to Thrace and also *using developed intelligence sources*, the Macedonians in a *surprise attack* annihilated the Greeks' positions near Amphissa. This *lured their opponents away from their defensive positions* in the nearby mountain passes to *consolidate their forces* near the town of Chaeronca.

There, *assessing the relative strengths* of their opponents, the Macedonians first *attempted to negotiate* to achieve their goals. When this was unsuccessful they had a *well-developed contingency plan* on how to *attack and overwhelm* the Greeks. Prior to this time, of course, the Macedonians had *organized* their troops into the famed phalanxes, and had *developed the full logistics* needed for their field support including a longer spear, which helped the Macedonian phalanxes penetrate the solid shield wall of the heavily massed Greek formations. *Using the natural advantages* of their grassy terrain, the Macedonians had developed cavalry support for their phalanxes' movements far beyond the Greek capability. Finally, using a *relative advantage*—the *command structure* their hierarchical social system allowed—against the more democratic Greeks, the Macedonian nobles had *trained their personnel* into one of the most *disciplined and highly motivated forces* in the world.

The Battle Strategy

Supporting this was the battle strategy at Chaeronea, which emerged as follows. Philip and Alexander first *analyzed their specific strengths and weaknesses and their opponents' current alignments and probable moves*. The Macedonian strength lay in their new spear technology, the *mobility* of their superbly disciplined phalanxes, and the powerful cavalry units led by Alexander. Their weaknesses were that they were badly outnumbered and faced—in the Athenians and the Theban Band—some of the finest foot troops in the world. However, their opponents had two weak points. One was the Greek left flank with lightly armed local troops placed near the Chaeronean Acropolis and next to some more heavily armed—but hastily assembled—hoplites bridging to the strong center held by the Athenians. The famed Theban Band anchored the Greek right wing near a swamp on the Cephissus River. (See map.)

Philip and Alexander *organized their leadership to command key positions*; Philip took over the right wing and Alexander the cavalry. They *aligned their forces* into *a unique posture* which *used their strengths* and *offset their weaknesses*. They decided on those spots at which they would *concentrate their forces*, what *positions to concede*, and what *key points* they *must take and hold*. Starting with their units angled back from the Greek lines (see map), they developed a *focused major thrust* against the Greek left wing and *attacked their opponents' weakness*—the troops near Chaeronea—with the most disciplined of the Macedonian units, the guards' brigade. After building up pressure and stretching the Greek line to its left, the guards' brigade abruptly began a *planned withdrawal*. This *feint* caused the Greek left to break ranks and rush forward, believing the Macedonians to be in full retreat. This *stretched the opponents' resources* as the Greek center moved left to *maintain contact* with its flank and to attack the "fleeing" Macedonians.

Then *with predetermined timing*, Alexander's cavalry *attacked the exposure* of the stretched line at the same moment Philip's phalanxes *re-formed as planned* on the high ground at the edge of the Heamon River. Alexander *broke through* and *formed a bridgehead* behind the Greeks. He *refocused his forces against a segment* of the opponents' line; his cavalry *surrounded and destroyed* the Theban Band as the *overwhelming power* of the phalanxes poured through the gap he had created. From its *secured position*, the Macedonian left flank then turned and *attacked the flank* of the Athenians. With the help of Philip's *planned counterattack*, the Macedonians *expanded their dominance and overwhelmed the critical target*, i.e., the Greek center. . . .

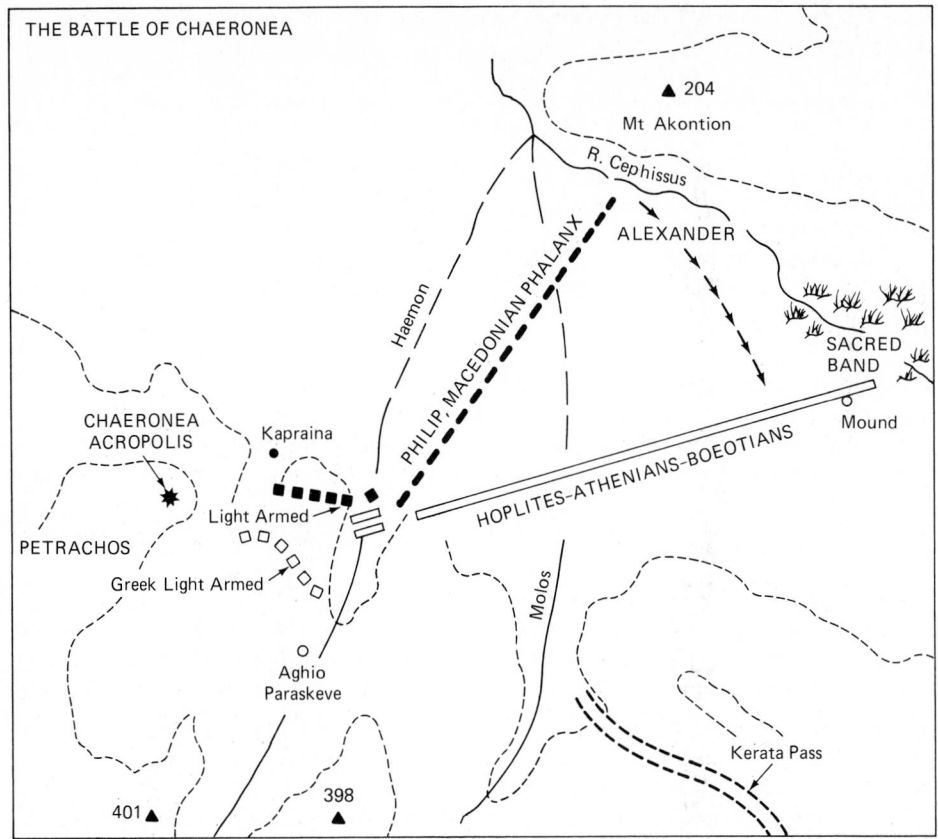

THE BATTLE OF CHAERONEA

Source: Modified with permission from P. Green, *Alexander the Great*, Praeger Publishers, New York, 1970.

Modern Analogies

Similar concepts have continued to dominate the modern era of formal strategic thought. As this period begins, Scharnhorst still points to the need to *analyze social forces and structures* as a basis for *understanding effective command styles* and *motivational stimuli* (Von Clausewitz, 1976:8). Frederick the Great proved this point in the field. Presumably based on such analyses, he adopted *training*, *discipline*, and *fast maneuvers* as the central concepts for a tightly disciplined German culture that had to be constantly ready to fight on two fronts (Phillips, 1940). Von Bülow (1806) continued to emphasize the dominant strategic roles of *geographical positioning* and *logistical*

support systems in strategy. Both Jomini (1971) and Von Bülow (1806) stressed the concepts of *concentration*, *points of domination*, and *rapidity of movement* as central strategic themes and even tried to develop them into mathematically precise principles for their time.

Still later Von Clausewitz expounded on the paramountcy of *clear major objectives* in war and on developing war strategies as a component of the nation's *broader goals* with *time horizons* extending beyond the war itself. Within this context he postulated that an effective strategy should be focused around a relatively *few central principles*, which can *create, guide, and maintain dominance* despite the enormous frictions that occur as one tries to position or maneuver large forces in war. Among these he included many of the concepts operant in Macedonian times: *spirit or morale, surprise, cunning, concentration in space, dominance of selected positions, use of strategic reserves, unification over time, tension and release*, and so on. He showed how these broad principles applied to a number of specific attack, defense, flanking, and retreat situations; but he always stressed the intangible of *leadership*. His basic positioning and organizational principles were to be mixed with boldness, perseverance, and genius. He constantly emphasized—as did Napoleon—the need for *planned flexibility* once the battle was joined.

Later strategic analysts adapted these classic themes for larger scale conflicts. Von Schlieffen linked together the huge numerical and production *strengths* of Germany and the vast *maneuvering capabilities* of Flanders fields to pull the nation's might together conceptually behind a *unique alignment of forces* (''a giant hayrake''), which would *outflank* his French opponents, *attack weaknesses* (their supply lines and rear), capture and *hold key political centers* of France, and *dominate or destroy* its weakened army in the field (Tuchman, 1962). On the other side, Foch and Grandmaison saw *morale* (''élan''), *nerve* (''cran''), and continuous *concentrated attack* (''attaque à outrance'') as *matching the values* of a volatile, recently defeated, and vengeful French nation, which had decided (for both moral and *coalition* reasons) to *set important limits* on its own actions in World War I—that is, not to attack first or through Belgium.

As these two strategies lost shape and became the head-on slaughter of trench warfare, Hart (1954) revitalized the *indirect approach*, and this became a central theme of British strategic thinking between the wars. Later in the United States, Matloff and Snell (1953) began to stress planning for *large-scale coalitions* as the giant forces of World War II developed. The Enigma group *moved secretly to develop the intelligence network* that was so crucial in the war's outcome (Stevenson, 1976). But once engaged in war, George Marshall still saw the only hope for Allied victory in *concentrating overwhelming forces*

against one enemy (Germany) first, then after *conceding early losses* in the Pacific, *refocusing Allied forces* in a gigantic *sequential coordinated movement* against Japan. In the eastern theater, MacArthur first *fell back, consolidated a base* for operations, *built up his logistics, avoided his opponent's strengths, bypassed* Japan's established defensive positions, and in a *gigantic flanking maneuver* was ready to invade Japan after *softening its political and psychological will* through saturation bombing (James, 1970).

All these modern thinkers and practitioners utilized classical principles of strategy dating back to the Greek era, but perhaps the most startling analogies of World War II lay in Patton's and Rommel's battle strategies, which were almost carbon copies of the Macedonians' concepts of planned concentration, rapid breakthrough, encirclement, and attack on the enemy's rear (Essame, 1964; Farago, 1964; Irving, 1971; Young, 1974).

Similar concepts still pervade well-conceived strategies—whether they are government, diplomatic, military, sports, or business strategies. What could be more direct than the parallel between Chaeroneá and a well-developed business strategy that first probes and withdraws to determine opponents' strengths, forces opponents to stretch their commitments, then concentrates resources, attacks a clear exposure, overwhelms a selected market segment, builds a bridgehead in that market, and then regroups and expands from that base to dominate a wider field? Many companies have followed just such strategies with great success. . . .

DIMENSIONS OF STRATEGY

Analysis of military-diplomatic strategies and similar analogies in other fields provides some essential insights into the basic dimensions, nature, and design of formal strategies.

First, effective formal strategies contain three essential elements: (*a*) the most important *goals* (or objectives) to be achieved, (*b*) the most significant *policies* guiding or limiting action, and (*c*) the major *action sequences* (or programs) that are to accomplish the defined goals within the limits set. Since strategy determines the overall direction and action focus of the organization, its formulation cannot be regarded as the mere generation and alignment of programs to meet predetermined goals. Goal development is an integral part of strategy formulation. . . .

Second, effective strategies develop around a *few key concepts and thrusts*, which give them cohesion, balance, and focus. Some thrusts are temporary; others are carried through to the end of the strategy. Some cost more per unit gain than others. Yet resources must be *allocated in patterns* that provide sufficient resources for each thrust to succeed regardless of its relative cost/gain ratio. And organizational units must be coordinated and actions controlled to support the intended thrust pattern or else the total strategy will fail. . . .

Third, strategy deals not just with the unpredictable but also with the *unknowable*. For major enterprise strategies, no analyst could predict the precise ways in which all impinging forces could interact with each other, be distorted by nature or human emotions, or be modified by the imaginations and purposeful counteractions of intelligent opponents (Braybrooke and Lindblom, 1963). Many have noted how large-scale systems can respond quite counterintuitively (Forrester, 1971) to apparently rational actions or how a seemingly bizarre series of events can conspire to prevent or assist success (White, 1978; Lindblom, 1959). . . .

Consequently, the essence of strategy—whether military, diplomatic, business, sports, (or) political . . .—is to *build a posture* that is so strong (and potentially flexible) in selective ways that the organization can achieve its goals despite the unforeseeable ways external forces may actually interact when the time comes.

Fourth, just as military organizations have multiple echelons of grand, theater, area, battle, infantry, and artillery strategies, so should other complex organizations have a number of hierarchically related and mutually supporting strategies (Vancil and Lorange, 1975; Vancil, 1976). Each such strategy must be more or less complete in itself, congruent with the level of decentralization intended. Yet each must be shaped as a cohesive element of higher level strategies. Although, for reasons cited, achieving total cohesion among all of a major organization's strategies would be a superhuman task for any chief executive officer, it is important that there be a systematic means for testing each component strategy and seeing that it fulfills the major tenets of a well-formed strategy.

The criteria derived from military-diplomatic strategies provide an excellent framework for this, yet too often one sees purported formal strategies at all organizational levels that are not strategies at all. Because they ignore or violate even the most basic strategic principles, they are little more than aggregates of philosophies or agglomerations of programs. They lack the cohesiveness, flexibility, thrust, sense of positioning against intelligent opposition, and other criteria that historical analysis suggests effective strategies must contain. Whether formally or incrementally derived, strategies should be at least intellectually tested against the proper criteria.

Criteria for Effective Strategy

In devising a strategy to deal with the unknowable, what factors should one consider? Although each strategic situation is unique, are there some common criteria that tend to define a good strategy? The fact that a strategy worked in retrospect is not a sufficient criterion for judging any strategy. Was Grant really a greater strategist than Lee? Was Foch's strategy better than Von Schlieffen's? Was Xerxes's strategy superior to that of Leonidas? Was it the Russians' strategy that allowed them to roll over the Czechoslovaks in 1968? Clearly other factors than strategy—including luck, overwhelming resources, superb or stupid implementation, and enemy errors—help determine ultimate results. Besides, at the time one formulates a strategy, he or she cannot use the criterion of ultimate success because the outcome is still in doubt. Yet one clearly needs some guidelines to define an effective strategic structure.

A few studies have suggested some initial criteria for evaluating a strategy (Tilles, 1963; Christensen et al., 1978). These include its clarity, motivational impact, internal consistency, compatibility with the environment, appropriateness in light of resources, degree of risk, match to the personal values of key figures, time horizon, and workability. . . . In addition, historical examples—from both business and military-diplomatic settings—suggest that effective strategies should at a minimum encompass certain other critical factors and structural elements. . . .

- Clear, decisive objectives: Are all efforts directed toward clearly understood, decisive, and attainable overall goals? Specific goals of subordinate units may change in the heat of campaigns or competition, but the overriding goals of the strategy for all units must remain clear enough to provide continuity and cohesion for tactical choices during the time horizon of the strategy. All goals need not be written down or numerically precise, but they must be understood and be decisive—i.e., if they are achieved they should ensure the continued viability and vitality of the entity vis-à-vis its opponents.

- Maintaining the initiative: Does the strategy preserve freedom of action and enhance commitment? Does it set the pace and determine the course of events rather than reacting to them? A prolonged reactive posture breeds unrest, lowers morale, and surrenders the advantage of timing and intangibles to opponents. Ultimately such a posture increases costs, decreases the number of options available, and lowers the probability of achieving sufficient success to ensure independence and continuity.

- Concentration: Does the strategy concentrate superior power at the place and time likely to be decisive? Has the strategy defined precisely what will make the enterprise superior in power—i.e., "best" in critical dimensions—in relation to its opponents. A distinctive competency yields greater success with fewer resources and is the essential basis for higher gains (or profits) than competitors. . . .

- Flexibility: Has the strategy purposely built in resource buffers and dimensions for flexibility and maneuver? Reserved capabilities, planned maneuverability, and repositioning allow one to use minimum resources while keeping opponents at a relative disadvantage. As corollaries of concentration and conces-

sion, they permit the strategist to reuse the same forces to overwhelm selected positions at different times. They also force less flexible opponents to use more resources to hold predetermined positions, while simultaneously requiring minimum fixed commitment of one's own resources for defensive purposes.

- Coordinated and committed leadership: Does the strategy provide responsible, committed leadership for each of its major goals? . . . [Leaders] must be so chosen and motivated that their own interests and values match the needs of their roles. Successful strategies require commitment, not just acceptance.

- Surprise: Has the strategy made use of speed, secrecy, and intelligence to attack exposed or unprepared opponents at unexpected times? With surprise and correct timing, success can be achieved out of all proportion to the energy exerted and can decisively change strategic positions. . . .

- Security: Does the strategy secure resource bases and all vital operating points for the enterprise? Does it develop an effective intelligence system sufficient to prevent surprises by opponents? Does it develop the full logistics to support each of its major thrusts? Does it use coalitions effectively to extend the resource base and zones of friendly acceptance for the enterprise? . . .

These are critical elements of strategy, whether in business, government, or warfare.

CONCEPT OF STRATEGY*

by H. Igor Ansoff

THE PROBLEM

During the past ten years the idea of strategy has received increasing recognition in management literature. Numerous papers have appeared

* Excerpted from H. Igor Ansoff, *Corporate Strategy* (copyright © McGraw-Hill Book Company, 1965), chap. 6; used by permission of McGraw-Hill.

dealing with product line strategy, marketing strategy, diversification strategy, and business strategy. This interest grew out of a realization that a firm needs a well-defined scope and growth direction, that objectives alone do not meet this need, and that additional decision rules are required if the firm is to have orderly and profitable growth. Such decision rules and guidelines have been broadly defined as *strategy* or, sometimes, as the *concept of the firm's business.* . . .

CONCEPT OF THE FIRM'S BUSINESS AND THE COMMON THREAD

. . . In seeking to [address this issue] it is useful to review how firms usually identify the nature of their business. Some firms are identified by the characteristics of their product line. Thus there are "transistor companies," "machine tool companies," and "automobile companies." Others are described by the technology which underlies the product line, such as "steel companies," "aluminum companies," and "glass companies." Each may sell a wide range of different products to different users, but a common thread is provided by a manufacturing and/or engineering technology. [The common thread is "a relationship between present and future product-markets which would enable outsiders to perceive where the firm is heading, and the inside management to give it guidance" (p. 105).]

Firms are also described in terms of their markets. Here it is useful to make a distinction between customers and missions. A *mission* is an existing product *need*; a *customer* is the actual *buyer* of the product: the economic unit (such as an individual, a family, a business firm) which possesses both the need and the money with which to satisfy it.

The usefulness of this distinction lies in the fact that sometimes the customer is erroneously identified as the common thread of a firm's business. In reality a given type of customer will frequently have a range of unrelated product missions or needs. He would not necessarily satisfy them through the same purchasing channels, nor

use the same approach to buying. Thus, the individual consumer fills his food needs at the supermarket and his entertainment needs at a television dealer's. Since the product technology, the distribution channels, and the customer motivation are different, no strong common thread is available to a firm which would attempt to sell both food and television sets. Similarly, the Department of Defense is a customer for a very wide range of missions. A company which supplies weapon systems for combat missions of the Army would have a better common thread in supplying control systems to industry than in selling replacement parts for Army trucks.

In selecting a useful range of missions of a particular customer, a firm needs to find a common thread either in product characteristics, technology, or similarity of needs. Thus agricultural machinery firms supply a range of needs of the farmer. All of these are related parts of his overall mission of tilling and harvesting the soil. Similarly, a home appliance manufacturer offers effort-saving products for the home which may range from washing machines to electronic irons.

In this perspective it is easy to see why the term "transportation business" fails to supply the common thread. First, the range of possible missions is very broad: intraurban, interurban, intracontinental, and intercontinental transportation; through the media of land, air, water, underwater; for moving passengers, and/or cargo. Second, the range of customers is wide: the individual, family, business firm, or government office. Third, the "product" varies: car, bus, train, ship, airplane, helicopter, taxi, truck. The number of practical combinations of the variables is large, and so is the number of common threads.

While such a concept of business is too broad to be useful, the traditional identification of a firm with a particular industry has become too narrow. Today a great many firms find themselves in a number of different industries. Furthermore, the boundaries of industries are continually changing, and new ones are being born. For example, radio, television, transistor, home appliance, and atomic energy are all industries which did not exist fifty years ago. The need is for a concept of business which on the one hand will give specific guidance for the firm and on the other hand will provide room for growth. We shall describe such a concept in the next section.

COMPONENTS OF STRATEGY

To the extent the respective objectives and goals are consonant with actual performance, they do provide an indirect description of a common thread. Thus, a firm which has shown a consistent rate of high growth is usually recognized by the investment community as a "growth firm," and a well-diversified one as a "broadly based" firm. Both of these descriptions can be constructively used by management as guidance in selecting new product-market areas.

However, this guidance is very weak and assures no common thread within the firm. Thus a "growth" firm may be simultaneously in pharmaceutics, banking, and industrial controls—areas which have no relationship to one another, except that they may all have attractive growth prospects.

A somewhat more positive specification of the common thread is arrived at through the use of the *product-market scope*. This specifies the particular industries to which the firm confines its product-market position and it has the advantage of focusing search on well-defined areas for which common statistics and economic forecasts are generally available. However, many industries offer a range of products, missions, technologies, and customers which is so broad as to make the common thread very tenuous. . . . To convey a common thread, description of the product-market scope frequently needs to be made in terms of subindustries which contain product-markets and technologies with similar characteristics.

Another useful specification of common thread is through the means of the *growth vector*, which indicates the direction in which the firm is moving with respect to its current product-market posture. This can be illustrated by means of a matrix shown in Table 1. *Market penetration* denotes a growth direction through the increase of market share for the present product-markets. In *market development* new missions are sought for the firm's products. *Product development* creates new products to replace current ones. Finally, *diversification* is distinctive in the fact that both products and missions are new to the firm. The common thread is clearly indicated, in the first three alternatives, to be either the marketing skills or product technology or both. In diversification the common thread is less apparent and is certainly weaker.

Specification of the common thread through the growth vector is complementary to the product-market scope, since it gives the directions *within* an industry as well as *across* industry boundaries which the firm proposes to pursue. . . .

A third way to see a common thread is to isolate characteristics of unique opportunities within the field defined by the product-market scope and the growth vector. This is the *competitive advantage*. It seeks to identify particular properties of individual product-markets which will give the firm a strong competitive position. Thus, a firm might seek acquisitions which are large enough to give it a commanding position in the new industry. Or it might insist on entries which enjoy strong patent protection. Or it might consider only "break-through" products which obsolete previously available products (just as the electric typewriter made the manual one obsolete and was in turn made obsolete by the IBM rotary head machine).

TABLE 1 GROWTH VECTOR COMPONENTS

Product ╲ Mission	Present	New
Present	Market penetration	Product development
New	Market development	Diversification

The triplet of specifications—the product-market scope, the growth vector, and the competitive advantage—describes the firm's product-market path in the *external environment*. . . .

There remains one other alternative for describing the common thread, and that is *synergy*. [From the preceding chapter, synergy is "a measure of joint effect." Ansoff elaborates: "It is concerned with the desired characteristics of fit between the firm and its new product-market entries. In business literature it is frequently described as the '2 + 2 = 5' effect to denote the fact that the firm seeks a product-market posture with a combined performance that is greater than the sum of its parts." Ansoff distinguishes "sales synergy" (when products use common distribution channels, warehousing, etc.), "operating synergy" (spreading overhead, common learning curves, etc.), "investment synergy" (joint use of plant, raw materials, etc.); and "management synergy" (using managerial expertise from one business in another). He also draws attention to "negative synergy" 2 + 2 = 3 (pp. 78–81).]
. . . Synergy is a measure of the firm's ability to make good on a new product-market entry. The common thread may be *aggressive,* requiring that new entries make use of an outstanding competence possessed by the firm (say, a nationwide chain of retail outlets or leadership in computer technology), or it may be *defensive*, requiring that new entries supply some key competence which the firm lacks. It may, of course, be both aggressive and defensive. Synergy is especially useful as the common thread in new growth areas where industry boundaries are ill-defined and changing. It is also a key variable in the choice of a diversification strategy.

The classification of common thread into product-market scope, growth vector, competitive advantage, and synergy is given added meaning when viewed in the light of the firm's search for profitability. The first triplet of specifications describes the firm's search for *inherently* profitable opportunities in the external environment. The first sets the scope for the search, the second the directions within the scope, and the third the characteristics of outstanding opportunities. The

firm may not realize the full profitability potential or may even lose money unless it has the capabilities required for success in the new ventures. This is provided by the fourth criterion, synergy.

The four characteristics are thus complementary, rather than mutually exclusive. We will call them, therefore, the *components of strategy*. In conjunction with its objectives the firm may choose one, two, or all of the strategy components. . . .

IS STRATEGY NECESSARY?

To define strategy is not to prove that it is necessary for each firm. The question of the usefulness of strategy as a management tool must, therefore, be examined. We will do this by first examining the alternative to strategy. This alternative is to have no rules beyond the simple decision to look for profitable prospects. Under these conditions the firm does not select formal objectives, performs no appraisals, formulates no search and evaluation rules. Instead, it would inform the business world . . . of its interest in "good" profitable opportunities; it would evaluate each new opportunity on the merits of its individual profitability.

Several reasons can be given in favor of this approach.

1. The firm would save the time, money, and executive talent which are required for a thorough strategic analysis. . . . such savings can be very considerable.

2. The field of potential opportunities will be in no way restricted. Objectives and strategy limit the field of its search. Since strategy is based on uncertain and incomplete knowledge, there is a chance that some attractive opportunities will be missed. An opportunistic firm takes no such chances.

3. The firm reaps the full advantage of the "delay principle." By delaying commitment until an opportunity is in hand, it is able to act on the basis of the best possible information.

Counterposed to these are some weighty disadvantages.

1. In the absence of strategy, there are no rules to guide the search for new opportunities, both inside and outside the firm. Internally, the research and development department has no guidelines for its contribution to diversification. The external acquisition department similarly lacks focus. Thus the firm as a whole either passively waits for opportunities, or pursues a "buckshot" search technique.

2. Project decisions will be of poorer quality than in firms with strategy. Without a focus for its efforts, the staff will lack the depth of knowledge in any particular area needed for competent analysis. Without strategy criteria, it will lack tools for recognizing outstanding opportunities. As a result managers acting on such advice will be forced into extreme forms of behavior. Conservatives will refuse to take what under better information might be reasonable risks; entrepreneurs will plunge without appreciation of potential costs and dangers.

3. The firm will have no formal provision for partial ignorance. No yardsticks will be available to judge whether a particular opportunity is a rare one, or whether much better ones are likely to develop in the future. Thus there will be a danger of either premature overcommitment of resources or of failure fully to utilize the resources available within a budget period.

4. Without the benefit of a periodic appraisal, the firm would have no assurance that its overall resource allocation pattern is efficient and that some product lines are not obsolete.

5. The firm will lack an internal ability to anticipate change. Without a strategy, managers will either do nothing or risk the danger of acting at cross-purposes. For example, the director of marketing could assume that the growth will be attained through adding new products to the existing product line. He will proceed to expand and strengthen the present marketing organization. At the same time, the director of engineering could assume that progress is to be made by eliminating the obsolete product line and diversi-fying into brand-new markets. He would, therefore, take appropriate action to curtail support of existing products and initiate developments for radically new missions. The potential result would be a marketing organization with no products to sell and a product line without a marketing capability.

To summarize, the advantages of not missing any bets and of not committing the firm's resources until the last moment are pitted against the disadvantages of inefficient search, enhanced risk of making bad decisions, and lack of control over the overall resource allocation pattern. . . .

OPENING UP THE DEFINITION OF STRATEGY*

by Henry Mintzberg

Marketing has its 4 P's (product, price, place, promotion). So why can't strategy do likewise, even go one better? But these P's pertain not to components of the field so much as to its most central concept, that of the nature of strategy itself.

Human nature is such that we tend to insist on *a* definition for every concept. But perhaps we fool ourselves, pretending that concepts such as strategy can be reduced to a single definition. In fact, the word is generally used in different ways, meaning that we *implicitly* accept various definitions even though we tend *formally* to quote only one. Let us, therefore, propose five formal definitions of strategy—as plan, ploy, pattern, position, and perspective—and then consider some of their interrelationships.

---

*   Abbreviated version of Chapter 1 of book in progress, entitled *Strategy Formation: Volume I, Schools of Thought,* to be published by Prentice-Hall, Inc.

STRATEGY AS PLAN

To almost anyone you care to ask, **strategy is a plan**—some sort of *consciously intended* course of action, a guideline (or set of them) to deal with a situation. A kid has a "strategy" to get over a fence, a corporation has one to capture a market. By this definition, strategies have two essential characteristics: they are made in advance of the actions to which they apply, and they are developed consciously and purposefully. Often they are also stated explicitly, in formal documents known as plans, but they may also remain formally unstated even though clear in someone's head. To Drucker, strategy is "purposeful action" (1974:104), to Moore "design for action" (1959:220), in essence, "conception preceding action." A host of definitions in a variety of fields reinforce this view. For example:

- in the military: strategy is concerned with "draft[ing] the plan of war. . . . shap[ing] the individual campaigns and within these, decid[ing] on the individual engagements" (Von Clausewitz, 1976:177).
- in Game Theory: strategy is "a complete plan: a plan which specifies what choices [the player] will make in every possible situation . . ." (Von Neumann and Morgenstern, 1944:79).
- in management: "strategy is a unified, comprehensive, and integrated plan designed to ensure that the basic objectives of the enterprise are achieved" (Glueck, 1980:9).
- and in the dictionary: strategy is (among other things) "a plan, method, or series of maneuvers or stratagems for obtaining a specific goal or result" (*Random House Dictionary*).

As plans strategies may be general or they can be specific. There is one use of the word in the specific sense that should be isolated here. As plan, **a strategy can be a ploy** too, really just a specific "maneuver" intended to outwit an opponent or competitor. The kid may use the fence as a ploy to draw a bully into his yard, where his Doberman Pincher waits for intruders. Likewise a corporation may threaten to expand plant capacity to stop a competitor from building a new plant. Here the real strategy (as plan, that is, the real intention) is the threat, not the expansion itself, and as such is a ploy.

STRATEGY AS PATTERN

But if strategies can be intended, surely they can also be realized. In other words, defining strategy as a plan in advance of taking action is not sufficient; we also need a definition that encompasses the resulting behavior, the strategies actually pursued through those actions. To put this another way, we need to understand the strategies organizations really have achieved, not just the ones they intend to pursue.

Thus we propose a third definition: **Strategy is a pattern**, specifically a pattern in a stream of actions (Mintzberg, 1972 and 1978; Mintzberg and Waters, 1985). By this definition, when Picasso painted blue for a time, that was a strategy, just as was the behavior of the Ford Motor Company when Henry Ford offered his Model T only in black. In other words, by this definition, strategy is *consistency* in behavior, *whether* or *not* intended.

This may sound like a strange definition for a word that has been so bound up with free will ("strategos" in Greek, the art of the army general). But while hardly anyone defines strategy in this way, many people seem at one time or another to so use it. Consider this quotation by a business executive:

> Gradually the successful approaches merge into a pattern of action that becomes our strategy. We certainly don't have an overall strategy on this . . . (quoted in Quinn, 1980:35).

This comment is inconsistent only if we restrict ourselves to one definition of strategy; what this man seems to be saying is that his firm has strategy as pattern, but not as plan. Or consider this comment in *Business Week* on a joint venture between General Motors and Toyota:

> The tentative Toyota deal may be most significant because it is another example

of how GM's strategy boils down to doing a little bit of everything until the market decides where it is going (October 31, 1983).

A journalist has inferred a pattern in the behavior of a corporation, and labelled it strategy.

Our point is that every time a journalist imputes a strategy to a corporation or to a government (some time ago it was Nixon's "southern strategy," because he made a series of decisions that favored Southern voters), and every time a manager does the same thing to a competitor or even to the senior management of his own firm, they are implicitly defining strategy as pattern in action—that is, inferring consistency in behavior and labelling it strategy. They may, of course, go further and impute intention to that consistency—that is, assume there is a plan behind the pattern. But that is an assumption, which may prove false.

Thus, our definitions of strategy as plan and pattern can be quite independent of each other: plans may go unrealized, while patterns may appear without preconceived plan. To paraphrase Hume (via Majone 1976–1977:206), strategies may result from human actions but not human designs. Now, if we label our first definition *intended* strategy and our second one *realized* strategy, as shown in Figure 1, then we can distinguish *deliberate* strategies, where intentions existed and

were then realized, from *emergent* strategies, where patterns developed in the absence of intentions, or despite them, which went *unrealized*.

For a strategy to be truly deliberate—that is, for a pattern to have been intended *exactly* as realized—would seem to be a tall order. Precise intentions would have had to be stated in advance by the leadership of the organization; these would have had to be accepted as is by everyone else, and then realized with no interference by market, technological, or political forces etc. Likewise, a truly emergent strategy is again a tall order, requiring consistency in action without any hint of intention. (No consistency means *no* strategy, or at least unrealized strategy.) Yet some strategies do come close enough to either form, while others—probably most—sit on the continuum that exists between the two, reflecting deliberate as well as emergent aspects. Table I lists various kinds of strategies along this continuum.

STRATEGY AS POSITION

Labelling strategies as plans or patterns (no matter how deliberate or emergent) still begs one basic question: *strategies about what*? An army may plan to reduce the number of nails in its shoes, or a corporation may realize a pattern of marketing only products painted black, but these hardly meet the lofty label "strategy." Or do they?

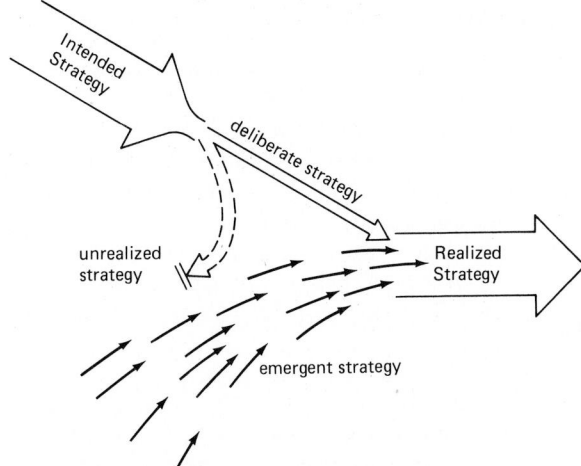

FIGURE 1   FORMS OF STRATEGY

TABLE I VARIOUS KINDS OF STRATEGIES, FROM RATHER DELIBERATE TO MOSTLY EMERGENT

Planned Strategy: precise intentions are formulated and articulated by a central leadership, and backed up by formal controls to ensure their surprise–free implementation in an environment that is benign, controllable, or predictable (to ensure no distortion of intentions); these strategies are highly deliberate.

Entrepreneurial Strategy: intentions exist as the personal, unarticulated vision of a single leader, and so are adaptable to new opportunities; the organization is under the personal control of the leader and located in a protected niche in its environment; these strategies are relatively deliberate but can emerge too.

Ideological Strategy: intentions exist as the collective vision of all the members of the organization, controlled through strong shared norms; the organization is often proactive vis-à-vis its environment; these strategies are rather deliberate.

Umbrella Strategy: a leadership in partial control of organizational actions defines strategic targets or boundaries within which others must act (for example, that all new products be high priced and at the technological cutting edge, although what these actual products are to be is left to emerge); as a result, strategies are partly deliberate (the boundaries) and partly emergent (the patterns within them); this strategy can also be called deliberately emergent, in that the leadership purposefully allows others the flexibility to maneuver and form patterns within the boundaries.

Process Strategy: the leadership controls the process aspects of strategy (who gets hired and so gets a chance to influence strategy, what structures they work within, etc.), leaving the actual content of strategy to others; strategies are again partly deliberate (concerning process) and partly emergent (concerning content), and deliberately emergent.

Disconnected Strategy: members or subunits loosely coupled to the rest of the organization produce patterns in the streams of their own actions in the absence of, or in direct contradiction to the central or common intentions of the organization at large; the strategies can be deliberate for those who make them.

Consensus Strategy: through mutual adjustment, various members converge on patterns that pervade the organization in the absence of central or common intentions; these strategies are rather emergent in nature.

Imposed Strategy: the external environment dictates patterns in actions, either through direct imposition (say by an outside owner or by a strong customer) or through implicitly preempting or bounding organizational choice (as in a large airline that must fly jumbo jets to remain viable); these strategies are organizationally emergent, although they may be internalized and made deliberate.

As the word has been handed down from the military, "strategy" refers to the important things, "tactics" to the details (more formally, "tactics teaches the use of armed forces in the engagement; strategy the use of engagements for the object of the war" [Von Clausewitz, 1976:128]). Nails in shoes, colors of cars: these are certainly details.

The problem with this is that in retrospect details sometimes prove "strategic." For an example we need look no further than the military, or at least its poetry: "For want of a Nail, the Shoe was lost; for want of a Shoe the horse was lost . . ." and so on through the rider perhaps to the battle, "all for want of Care about a Horseshoe Nail" (Franklin, 1977:280). Indeed, one of the reasons the first Henry Ford lost his war over market share with General Motors was that he refused to paint his cars anything but black.

Rumelt notes that "one person's strategy is another's tactics—that what is strategic depends on where you sit" (1979:197). It also depends on *when* you sit: what seems tactical today could prove strategic tomorrow. Our point is that these sorts of distinctions must be used with great care, that labels should not be used to imply that some issues are *inevitably* more important than others. There are times, as we shall see, when it pays to manage the details and let the strategies emerge for themselves. Thus, the answer to our question, strategy about what, is: potentially about anything—products and processes, customers and citizens, social responsibilities and self interests, control and color.

We must, nonetheless, single out some specific aspects of the content of strategies, because they are of particular importance and, accordingly, play major roles in the literature. For our fourth definition, **strategy is a position,** specifically a means of identifying where an organization (or an individual for that matter) locates itself in what is known in the management literature as an "environment," for a business firm, usually a market. By this definition, strategy becomes the mediating force—or "match" according to Hofer and Schendel (1978:4)—between organization and environment, that is, between the internal and the external context. In ecological terms, strategy by this definition is an environmental "niche"; in economic terms, a place that generates "rent"; in management terms, formally, a product-market "domain" (Thompson,1967), the place in the environment where resources are concentrated.

Note that our fourth definition of strategy can be compatible with either (or all) of the preceding ones: a position can be defined and aspired to through a plan (or ploy) and/or reached, perhaps even found, through a pattern of behavior.

Earlier we cited military and game theory definitions of strategy. In the military, strategy is generally used in the context of what the game theorists call a "two-person game," what is known in business as head-on competition (where ploys are especially common). The definition of strategy as position, however, implicitly allows us to open up the concept to so-called "n-person games" (that is, many players) and beyond. In other words, while we can always define position vis-à-vis a single competitor (in the military, of

course, we can take position literally, as the site chosen for battle), we can also consider it in the context of a number of competitors or even vis-à-vis markets or an environment at large. Since head-on competition is not always that common in business, management theorists have generally focussed on the n-person situation, although they have tended to retain the notion of economic competition (for example, Porter,1980, in his highly popular book *Competitive Strategy*). But strategy as position can extend beyond competition. Indeed, what is the meaning of the word "niche" but a position that is occupied to *avoid* competition.

Thus, we can move from the definition employed by General Ulysses Grant in the 1860s, "Strategy [is] the deployment of one's resources in a manner which is most likely to defeat the enemy," to that of Richard Rumelt in the 1980s, "Strategy is seeking and maintaining a sustainable advantage" (quoted at the Strategic Management Society Conference, Montreal, October 7, 1982), that is, any viable position, whether or not directly competitive.

Astley and Fombrun (1983), in fact, takes the next logical step by introducing the notion of "collective" strategy, strategy pursued to promote cooperation between organizations, sometimes would-be competitors (equivalent in biology, for example, to animals herding together for protection). Among the possible strategies of "collective action," these authors note a range "from informal arrangements and discussions to formal devices such as interlocking directorates, joint ventures, and mergers" (p. 577). In fact, looked at from a slightly different angle, these can sometimes be described as *political* strategies, that is, strategies to subvert what is legally or ethically expected to be an economically competitive situation.

STRATEGY AS PERSPECTIVE

While our last definition of strategy looked out, seeking to locate the organization in its external environment, our next looks inside the organization, indeed inside the heads of the collective strategist. Here, **strategy is a perspective,** its content consisting not just of a chosen position but of an ingrained way of perceiving the world. Some organizations, for example, are aggressive pacesetters, creating new technologies and exploiting new markets; others perceive the world as set and stable, and so sit back in long established markets and build protective shells around themselves, relying more on political influence than economic efficiency. There are organizations that favor marketing, and build a whole ideology around that (an IBM); others treat engineering in this way (a Hewlett-Packard); while still others concentrate on sheer productive efficiency (a McDonald's).

Strategy in this respect is to the organization what personality is to the individual. Indeed, one of the earliest and most influential writers on strategy (at least as his ideas have been reflected in more popular writings), Philip Selznick, wrote about the "character" of an organization, distinct and integrated "commitments to ways of acting and responding" that are built right into it (1957:47). A variety of concepts from other fields also capture this notion: psychologists refer to an individual's mental frame and cognitive structure, and a variety of other expressions for "relatively fixed patterns for experiencing [the] world" (Bieri,1971:78), anthropologists refer to the "culture" of a society and sociologists to its "ideology"; military theorists write of the "grand strategy" of armies, while management theorists have used terms such as the "theory of the business" (Drucker,1974) and its "driving force" (Tregoe and Zimmerman, 1980); behavioral scientists who have read Kuhn (1970) on the philosophy of science discuss the "paradigm" of a community of scholars; and Germans perhaps capture it best with their word *Weltanschauung*, literally "worldview," meaning collective intuition about how the world works.

This final definition suggests above all that strategy is a *concept*. An important implication of this is that all strategies are abstractions which exist only in the minds of interested people— those who pursue them, are influenced by that

pursuit, or care to observe either happening. It is important to remember that no one has ever seen a strategy or touched one; every strategy is an invention, a figment of someone's imagination, whether conceived of as intentions to regulate behavior before it takes place or inferred as patterns to describe behavior that has already occurred.

What is of key importance about this definition, however, is that the perspective is *shared*. As implied in the words *Weltanschauung*, culture, ideology, and paradigm, strategy is a perspective shared by the members of an organization (or group) through their intentions and/or by their actions. In effect, when we are talking of strategy in this context, we are entering the realm of the *collective mind*—individuals united by common intention and/or action. A major issue in the study of strategy formation becomes, therefore, how to read that collective mind—to understand how intentions diffuse through the system called organization to become shared and how action comes to be exercised on a collective yet consistent basis.

RELATING THE P'S OF STRATEGY

We have suggested above that strategy as perspective can be compatible within strategy as plan and/or strategy as pattern. The same can (and will) be shown for position. But in fact the relationships between these different definitions can be more involved than that. For example, while some consider perspective to *be* a plan, others describe it as *giving rise* to plans and/or patterns in some kind of implicit hierarchy. But the opposite can happen too.

Take the case of the Honda Company, which is described in one consulting report (Boston Consulting Group, 1975) as parlaying a particular perspective (being a low cost producer, seeking to attack new markets in aggressive ways) into a plan, in the form of an intended position (to capture the traditional motorcycle market in the United States and create a new one for small family motorcycles), which was realized through an integrated set of patterns (lining up distributorships, developing the appropriate advertising campaign of "You meet the nicest people on a Honda," etc.).

But a closer look at Honda's actual behavior indicates a very different story, that it did not go to America to sell small, family motorcycles at all; the company fell into that market almost inadvertently (Pascale, 1984, [his story of "The Honda Effect" is reprinted in Chapter 5]). But once it was clear to Honda executives that they had wandered into such a lucrative position, that became their plan. In other words, their strategy emerged, step by step, but once recognized, was made deliberate. Honda, if you like, developed its intentions through its actions, another way of saying that pattern evoked plan.

Of course, an overall perspective of Honda's way of doing things seems to have underlaid all this, but we may still ask how that perspective arose in the first place. Probably in a very similar way, through earlier experiences: the organization in its early years likely tried various things and gradually consolidated a perspective around what worked. In other words, organizations would appear to develop "character" much as people develop personality—by interacting with the world as they find it in terms of their innate skills and natural propensities. Thus pattern can form perspective too. And so can position. Witness Perrow's (1970:161) discussion of the "wool men" and "silk men" of the textile trade, people who develop an almost religious dedication to the fibers they happen to produce.

No matter how they derive, there is still an assumption that while plans and positions may be dispensable, perspectives are immutable. In other words, once they are established, perspectives become awfully difficult to change. Indeed, a perspective may become so deeply ingrained in behavior that the associated beliefs can become subconscious. When that happens, perspective can come to look more like pattern than like plan—in other words, it can be found more in consistency of behavior than in articulation of intention.

Of course, if perspective is immutable, then change in plan and position is feasible only when compatible with the existing perspective. In this regard, it is interesting to take up the case of Egg McMuffin. Was this new product—the American breakfast in a bun—a strategic change for the McDonald's fast food chain? Posed in MBA classes, this earth-shattering (or at least stomach-shattering) question inevitably evokes heated debate. Proponents (usually people sympathetic to fast food) argue that of course it was: it brought McDonald's into a new market, the breakfast one, extending the use of existing facilities. Opponents retort that this is nonsense, nothing changed but a few ingredients: this was the same old pap in a new package. Both sides are, of course, right . . . and wrong. It simply depends on how you define strategy. Position changed; perspective remained the same. Indeed—and this is our point—the position was changed so easily because it was compatible with the perspective. Egg McMuffin is pure McDonald's, not only in product and package but in production and propagation. But imagine a change of position at McDonald's that would require a change of perspective—say to introduce candlelight dining with personal service (your McMousse à l'orange cooked to order) to capture the late evening market. We needn't say more, except perhaps to label this the "Egg McMuffin syndrome."

All of this is to say that while various relationships exist among our definitions, no one relationship nor any single definition takes primacy over the others. In some ways, these definitions compete (in that they can substitute for each other), but in perhaps more important ways, they complement. Not all plans become patterns, nor are all the patterns that develop planned; some ploys are less than positions, while other strategies are more than positions yet less than perspectives. Each definition adds important elements to our discussion: plan introduces the notion of intention and emphasizes the role of conscious leadership; pattern focuses on action, reminding us that strategy is an empty idea without taking behavior into account, and introduces the notion that strategies can emerge; position introduces context, rooting strategy in external situation and encouraging us to consider competition and cooperation; and perspective reminds us that strategy is nothing more than a concept, and focuses our attention on the collective aspect of strategy. A good deal of the confusion in this field stems from contradic-tory and ill-defined uses of the term, as we just saw in the Egg McMuffin debate. By explicating and using various definitions we can avoid some of this confusion, and enrich our understanding of the strategy process.

TWO

THE
STRATEGIST

Every conventional strategy or policy textbook focuses on the job of the general manager as a main ingredient in understanding the process of strategy formation. The discussion of emergent strategy in the last chapter suggests that we do not take such a narrow view of the strategist. Anyone in the organization who happens to control key or precedent setting actions can be a strategist; the strategist can be a *collection* of people as well. Nevertheless, managers—especially senior general managers—are obviously prime candidates for such a role because their perspective is broader than any of their subordinates and because so much power naturally resides with them. Hence we focus in this chapter on the general manager as strategist.

We present two readings that describe the work of the manager. The one by Mintzberg challenges the conventional view of the manager as planner, organizer, coordinator, and controller. The point is not that managers do not do these things; it is that these words are too vague to capture the daily reality of managerial work. The image presented in this article is a very different one; a job characterized by pressure, interruption, orientation to action, oral rather than written communication, and working with outsiders and colleagues as much as with so-called subordinates. While the issue is not addressed at this point in any detail, one evident and important conclusion is that managers who work in such ways cannot possibly function as traditionally depicted strategists supposedly do—as leaders directing their organizations the way conductors direct their orchestras (at least the way it looks on the podium). We shall develop this point further in Chapter 5, when we consider how strategies really are formed in organizations.

The article by Edward Wrapp, of the University of Chicago and well-known in management development circles, provides at least one widely referenced model illustrating how this does happen in large organizations. He depicts managers as somewhat political animals, providing broad guidance, but facilitating or pushing through their strategies, bit by bit, in rather unexpected ways. They rarely state specific goals. They practice "the art of imprecision," trying to "avoid policy straightjackets," while concentrating on only a few really significant issues. They move whenever possible through "corridors of comparative indifference" to avoid undue opposition, at the same time they are trying to ensure that the organization has a cohesive sense of direction. Wrapp's observations challenge the more prescriptive views of strategy formulation, but elements of them can be observed in many of the cases, notably IBM (A), Pillsbury Co., Continental Group, and General Mills.

Philip Selznick, a famous Berkeley sociologist, offers another perspective on the manager as strategist in the third reading. It is not just his or her role in the *creation* of strategy so much as in its *institutionalization* that counts—the establishment of commitment among the people who make up the organization. In this reading, the full meaning of the view of strategy as perspective emerges—not as a calculated position but as a deep-rooted perspective. Selznick's brief but brilliant essay, written in the 1950s, introduced a number of concepts that subsequently became the foundation for much of our current thinking about business strategy (which, incidentally, both he and Wrapp refer to as "policy")—the selection of mission, the notion of distinctive competence, the definition of "organization character," and so on. Note also the differences between Selznick's and Wrapp's view of the managers, especially with regard to the articulation of purpose, or direction. Are they describing different contexts in which managers work? Might the two views sometimes be compatible in the same managerial job?

Selznick also discusses the role of values in managerial work, specifically the manager's role to "infuse [the organization] with value." Much strategy-making behavior is heavily influenced by values; individual managers looking at the same data may choose quite different strategies based on what they believe, i.e., their values. Values provide the perceptive screen or "prism" through which individual managers sift and weigh different options, opportunities, or threats. They provide the "utility system" of the economist and the expectations of desired or unacceptable behavior that become the "culture" of an organization.

We introduce some of these concepts in our brief excerpts from Selznick's book to try to capture in his words ideas that will recur throughout the remaining readings and cases. This reading is not always an easy one, and our editing of it may make it somewhat disjointed. But it is well worth your effort. The reading is brief, but it is an important premier statement on the role of leadership values in organizations. Peters

and Waterman, in their book *In Search of Excellence*, refer to this "often-overlooked" book as "beautifully describ[ing]" these and other traits "basic to the success of the excellent companies" (1982:85, 98).

The impact of values in strategic decision making shows up most clearly in the cases on Genentech, Sony, Pilkington, and Matsushita. But values issues pervade virtually all the cases, including the military strategies in *The Guns of August* and the diplomatic strategies in "Mountbatten and India." Be aware of them in any real life strategic situation.

THE MANAGER'S JOB:
Folklore and Fact*
by Henry Mintzberg

If you ask a manager what he does, he will most likely tell you that he plans, organizes, coordinates, and controls. Then watch what he does. Don't be surprised if you can't relate what you see to these four words.

When he is called and told that one of his factories has just burned down, and he advises the caller to see whether temporary arrangements can be made to supply customers through a foreign subsidiary, is he planning, organizing, coordinating, or controlling? How about when he presents a gold watch to a retiring employee? Or when he attends a conference to meet people in the trade? Or on returning from that conference, when he tells one of his employees about an interesting product idea he picked up there?

The fact is that these four words, which have dominated management vocabulary since the French industrialist Henri Fayol first intro-

---

* Originally published in the *Harvard Business Review* (July–August, 1975), and winner of the McKinsey prize for the best article in the *Review* in 1975; reprinted with deletions by permission of the *Harvard Business Review*.

duced them in 1916, tell us little about what managers actually do. At best, they indicate some vague objectives managers have when they work.

The field of management, so devoted to progress and change, has for more than half a century not seriously addressed *the* basic question: What do managers do? Without a proper answer, how can we teach management? How can we design planning or information systems for managers? How can we improve the practice of management at all? . . .

Somehow, in the rush to automate production, to use management science in the functional areas of marketing and finance, and to apply the skills of the behavioral scientist to the problem of worker motivation, the manager—that person in charge of the organization or one of its subunits—has been forgotten.

My intention in this article is simple: to break the reader away from Fayol's words and introduce him to a more supportable, and what I believe to be a more useful, description of managerial work. This description derives from my review and synthesis of the available research on how various managers have spent their time.

In some studies, managers were observed intensively (''shadowed'' is the term some of them used); in a number of others, they kept detailed diaries of their activities; in a few studies, their records were analyzed. All kinds of managers were studied—foremen, factory supervisors, staff managers, field sales managers, hospital administrators, presidents of companies and nations, and even street gang leaders. These ''managers'' worked in the United States, Canada, Sweden, and Great Britain. . . .

A synthesis of these findings paints an interesting picture, one as different from Fayol's classical view as a cubist abstract is from a Renaissance painting. In a sense, this picture will be obvious to anyone who has ever spent a day in a manager's office, either in front of the desk or behind it. Yet, at the same time, this picture may turn out to be revolutionary, in that it throws into doubt so much of the folklore that we have accepted about the manager's work.

SOME FOLKLORE AND FACTS ABOUT MANAGERIAL WORK

There are four myths about the manager's job that do not bear up under careful scrutiny of the facts.

1

Folklore: *The manager is a reflective, systematic planner*. The evidence on this issue is overwhelming, but not a shred of it supports this statement.

Fact: *Study after study has shown that managers work at an unrelenting pace, that their activities are characterized by brevity, variety, and discontinuity, and that they are strongly oriented to action and dislike reflective activities*. Consider this evidence:

- Half the activities engaged in by the five [American] chief executives [that I studied in my own research (Mintzberg, 1973a)] lasted less than nine minutes, and only 10% exceeded one hour. A study of 56 U.S. foremen found that they averaged 583 activities per eight-hour shift, an average of 1 every 48 seconds (Guest, 1956, 478). The work pace for both chief executives and foremen was unrelenting. The chief executives met a steady stream of callers and mail from the moment they arrived in the morning until they left in the evening. Coffee breaks and lunches were inevitably work related, and ever-present subordinates seemed to usurp any free moment.

- A diary study of 160 British middle and top managers found that they worked for a half hour or more without interruption only about once every two days (Stewart, 1967).

- Of the verbal contacts of the chief executives in my study, 93% were arranged on an ad hoc basis. Only 1% of the executives' time was spent in open-ended observational tours. Only 1 out of 368 verbal contacts was unrelated to a specific issue and could be called general planning. Another researcher finds that ''in *not one single case* did a manager report the obtaining of important external information from a general conversation or other undirected personal communication'' (Aguilar, 1967:102).

- No study has found important patterns in the way managers schedule their time. They seem to jump from issue to issue, continually responding to the needs of the moment.

Is this the planner that the classical view describes? Hardly. How, then, can we explain this behavior? The manager is simply responding to the pressures of his job. I found that my chief executives terminated many of their own activities, often leaving meetings before the end, and interrupted their desk work to call in subordinates. One president not only placed his desk so that he could look down a long hallway but also left his door open when he was alone—an invitation for subordinates to come in and interrupt him.

Clearly, these managers wanted to encourage the flow of current information. But more significantly, they seemed to be conditioned by their own work loads. They appreciated the opportunity cost of their own time, and they were continually aware of their ever-present obligations— mail to be answered, callers to attend to, and so on. It seems that no matter what he is doing, the manager is plagued by the possibilities of what he might do and what he must do.

When the manager must plan, he seems to do so implicitly in the context of daily actions, not in some abstract process reserved for two weeks in the organization's mountain retreat. The plans of the chief executives I studied seemed to exist only in their heads—as flexible, but often specific, intentions. The traditional literature notwithstanding, the job of managing does not breed reflective planners; the manager is a real-time responder to stimuli, an individual who is conditioned by his job to prefer live to delayed action.

2

Folklore: The effective manager has no regular duties to perform. Managers are constantly being told to spend more time planning and delegating, and less time seeing customers and engaging in negotiations. These are not, after all, the true tasks of the manager. To use the popular analogy,

the good manager, like the good conductor, carefully orchestrates everything in advance, then sits back to enjoy the fruits of his labor, responding occasionally to an unforeseeable exception. . . .

Fact: In addition to handling exceptions, managerial work involves performing a number of regular duties, including ritual and ceremony, negotiations, and processing of soft information that links the organization with its environment. Consider some evidence from the research studies:

- A study of the work of the presidents of small companies found that they engaged in routine activities because their companies could not afford staff specialists and were so thin on operating personnel that a single absence often required the president to substitute (Choran in Mintzberg, 1973a).
- One study of field sales managers and another of chief executives suggest that it is a natural part of both jobs to see important customers, assuming the managers wish to keep those customers (Davis, 1957; Copeman, 1963).
- Someone, only half in jest, once described the manager as that person who sees visitors so that everyone else can get his work done. In my study, I found that certain ceremonial duties—meeting visiting dignitaries, giving out gold watches, presiding at Christmas dinners—were an intrinsic part of the chief executive's job.
- Studies of managers' information flow suggest that managers play a key role in securing ''soft'' external information (much of it available only to them because of their status) and in passing it along to their subordinates.

3

Folklore: The senior manager needs aggregated information, which a formal management information system best provides. Not too long ago, the words *total information system* were everywhere in the management literature. In keeping with the classical view of the manager as that individual perched on the apex of a regulated, hierarchical system, the literature's manager was to receive all his important information from a giant, comprehensive MIS.

But lately, as it has become increasingly evident that these giant MIS systems are not working—that managers are simply not using them—the enthusiasm has waned. A look at how managers actually process information makes the reason quite clear. Managers have five media at their command—documents, telephone calls, scheduled and unscheduled meetings, and observational tours.

Fact: Managers strongly favor the verbal media—namely, telephone calls and meetings. The evidence comes from every single study of managerial work. Consider the following:

- In two British studies, managers spent an average of 66% and 80% of their time in verbal (oral) communication (Stewart, 1967; Burns, 1954). In my study of five American chief executives, the figure was 78%.

- These five chief executives treated mail processing as a burden to be dispensed with. One came in Saturday morning to process 142 pieces of mail in just over three hours, to "get rid of all the stuff." This same manager looked at the first piece of "hard" mail he had received all week, a standard cost report, and put it aside with the comment, "I never look at this."

- These same five chief executives responded immediately to 2 of the 40 routine reports they received during the five weeks of my study and to four items in the 104 periodicals. They skimmed most of these periodicals in seconds, almost ritualistically. In all, these chief executives of good-sized organizations initiated on their own—that is, not in response to something else—a grand total of 25 pieces of mail during the 25 days I observed them.

An analysis of the mail the executives received reveals an interesting picture—only 13% was of specific and immediate use. So now we have another piece in the puzzle: not much of the mail provides live, current information—the action of a competitor, the mood of a government legislator, or the rating of last night's television show. Yet this is the information that drove the managers, interrupting their meetings and rescheduling their workdays.

Consider another interesting finding. Managers seem to cherish "soft" information, especially gossip, hearsay, and speculation. Why? The reason is its timeliness; today's gossip may be tomorrow's fact. The manager who is not accessible for the telephone call informing him that his biggest customer was seen golfing with his main competitor may read about a dramatic drop in sales in the next quarterly report. But then it's too late.

To assess the value of historical, aggregated, "hard" MIS information, consider two of the manager's prime uses for his information—to identify problems and opportunities and to build his own mental models of the things around him (e.g., how his organization's budget system works, how his customers buy his product, how changes in the economy affect his organization, and so on). Every bit of evidence suggests that the manager identifies decision situations and builds models not with the aggregated abstractions an MIS provides, but with specific tidbits of data.

Consider the words of Richard Neustadt, who studies the information-collecting habits of Presidents Roosevelt, Truman, and Eisenhower:

> It is not information of a general sort that helps a President see personal stakes; not summaries, not surveys, not the *bland amalgams*. Rather . . . it is the odds and ends of *tangible detail* that pieced together in his mind illuminate the underside of issues put before him. To help himself he must reach out as widely as he can for every scrap of fact, opinion, gossip, bearing on his interests and relationships as President. He must become his own director of his own central intelligence (1960:153–154; italics added).

The manager's emphasis on the verbal media raises two important points:

First, verbal information is stored in the brains of people. Only when people write this information down can it be stored in the files of the organization—whether in metal cabinets or on magnetic tape—and managers apparently do not write down much of what they hear. Thus the strategic data bank of the organization is not in the memory of its computers but in the minds of its managers.

Second, the manager's extensive use of verbal media helps to explain why he is reluctant to delegate tasks. When we note that most of the manager's important information comes in verbal form and is stored in his head, we can well appreciate his reluctance. It is not as if he can hand a dossier over to someone; he must take the time to "dump memory"—to tell that someone all he knows about the subject. But this could take so long that the manager may find it easier to do the task himself. Thus the manager is damned by his own information system to a "dilemma of delegation"—to do too much himself or to delegate to his subordinates with inadequate briefing.

4

Folklore: *Management is, or at least is quickly becoming, a science and a profession.* By almost any definitions of *science* and *profession*, this statement is false. Brief observation of any manager will quickly lay to rest the notion that managers practice a science. A science involves the enaction of systematic, analytically determined procedures or programs. If we do not even know what procedures managers use, how can we prescribe them by scientific analysis? And how can we call management a profession if we cannot specify what managers are to learn? For after all, a profession involves "knowledge of some department of learning or science" (*Random House Dictionary*).

Fact: *The managers' programs—to schedule time, process information, make decisions, and so on—remain locked deep inside their brains.* Thus, to describe these programs, we rely on words like *judgment* and *intuition*, seldom stopping to realize that they are merely labels for our ignorance.

I was struck during my study by the fact that the executives I was observing—all very competent by any standard—are fundamentally indistinguishable from their counterparts of a hundred years ago (or a thousand years ago, for that matter). The information they need differs, but they seek it in the same way—by word of mouth. Their decisions concern modern technology, but the procedures they use to make them are the same as the procedures of the nineteenth-century manager. . . . In fact, the manager is in a kind of loop, with increasingly heavy work pressures but no aid forthcoming from management science.

Considering the facts about managerial work, we can see that the manager's job is enormously complicated and difficult. The manager is overburdened with obligations; yet he cannot easily delegate his tasks. As a result, he is driven to overwork and is forced to do many tasks superficially. Brevity, fragmentation, and verbal communication characterize his work. Yet these are the very characteristics of managerial work that have impeded scientific attempts to improve it. As a result, the management scientist has concentrated his efforts on the specialized functions of the organization, where he could more easily analyze the procedures and quantify the relevant information.

But the pressures of the manager's job are becoming worse. Where before he needed only to respond to owners and directors, now he finds that subordinates with democratic norms continually reduce his freedom to issue unexplained orders, and a growing number of outside influences (consumer groups, government agencies, and so on) expect his attention. And the manager has had nowhere to turn for help. The first step in providing the manager with some help is to find out what his job really is.

BACK TO A BASIC DESCRIPTION OF MANAGERIAL WORK

Now let us try to put some of the pieces of this puzzle together. Earlier, I defined the manager as that person in charge of an organization or one of its subunits. Besides chief executive officers, this definition would include vice presidents, bishops, foremen, hockey coaches, and prime ministers. Can all of these people have anything in common? Indeed they can. For an important starting point, all are vested with formal authority over an organizational unit. From formal authority comes status, which leads to various interpersonal relations, and from these comes access to information. Information, in turn, enables the manager to make decisions and strategies for his unit.

The manager's job can be described in terms of various "roles," or organized sets of behaviors identified with a position. My description, shown in Figure 1, comprises ten roles. As we shall see, formal authority gives rise to the three interpersonal roles, which in turn give rise to the three informational roles; these two sets of roles enable the manager to play the four decisional roles.

FIGURE 1
THE MANAGER'S ROLES

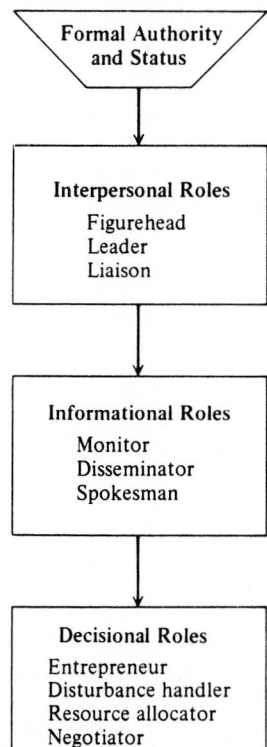

Interpersonal Roles

Three of the manager's roles arise directly from his formal authority and involve basic interpersonal relationships.

1. First is the *figurehead* role. By virtue of his position as head of an organizational unit, every manager must perform some duties of a ceremonial nature. The president greets the touring dignitaries, the foreman attends the wedding of a lathe operator, and the sales manager takes an important customer to lunch.

The chief executives of my study spent 12% of their contact time on ceremonial duties; 17% of their incoming mail dealt with acknowledgments and requests related to their status. For example, a letter to a company president requested free merchandise for a crippled schoolchild; diplomas were put on the desk of the school superintendent for his signature.

Duties that involve interpersonal roles may sometimes be routine, involving little serious communication and no important decision making. Nevertheless, they are important to the smooth functioning of an organization and cannot be ignored by the manager.

2. Because he is in charge of an organizational unit, the manager is responsible for the work of the people of that unit. His actions in this regard constitute the *leader* role. Some of these actions involve leadership directly—for example, in most organizations the manager is normally responsible for hiring and training his own staff.

In addition, there is the indirect exercise of the leader role. Every manager must motivate and encourage his employees, somehow reconciling their individual needs with the goals of the organization. In virtually every contact the manager has with his employees, subordinates seeking leadership clues probe his actions: "Does he approve?" "How would he like the report to turn out?" "Is he more interested in market share than high profits?"

The influence of the manager is most clearly seen in the leader role. Formal authority vests him with great potential power; leadership determines in large part how much of it he will realize.

3. The literature of management has always recognized the leader role, particularly those aspects of it related to motivation. In comparison, until recently it has hardly mentioned the *liaison* role, in which the manager makes contacts outside his vertical chain of command. This is remarkable in light of the finding of virtually every study of managerial work that managers spend as much time with peers and other people outside their units as they do with their own subordinates—and, surprisingly, very little time with their own superiors.

In Rosemary Stewart's diary study, the 160 British middle and top managers spent 47% of their time with peers, 41% of their time with people inside their unit, and only 12% of their time with their superiors. For Robert H. Guest's study of U.S. foremen, the figures were 44%, 46%, and 10%. The chief executives of my study averaged 44% of their contact time with people outside their organizations, 48% with subordinates, and 7% with directors and trustees.

The contacts the five CEOs made were with an incredibly wide range of people: subordinates; clients, business associates, and suppliers; and peers—managers of similar organizations, government and trade organization officials, fellow directors on outside boards, and independents with no relevant organizational affiliations. The chief executives' time with and mail from these groups is shown in Figure 2. . . .

As we shall see shortly, the manager cultivates such contacts largely to find information. In effect, the liaison role is devoted to building up the manager's own external information system—informal, private, verbal, but, nevertheless, effective.

Informational Roles

By virtue of his interpersonal contacts, both with his subordinates and with his network of contacts, the manager emerges as the nerve center of his organizational unit. He may not know everything,

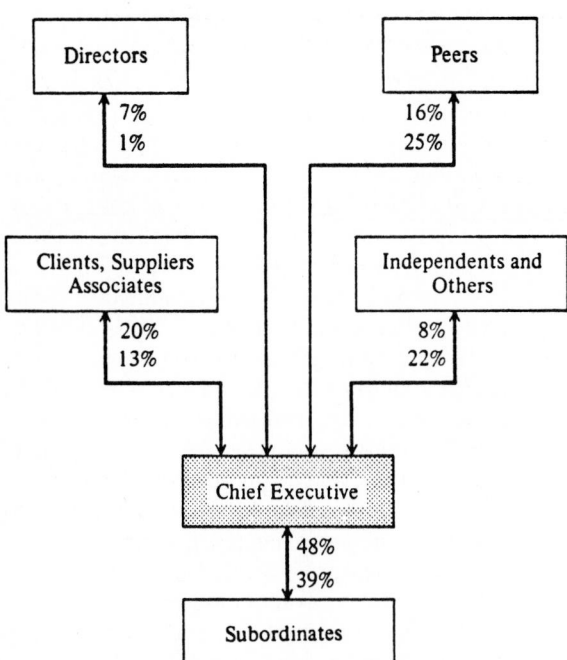

FIGURE 2
THE CHIEF EXECUTIVES' CONTACTS

but he typically knows more than any member of his staff.

Studies have shown this relationship to hold for all managers, from street gang leaders to U.S. presidents. In *The Human Group*, George C. Homans (1955) explains how, because they were at the center of the information flow in their own gangs and were also in close touch with other gang leaders, street gang leaders were better informed than any of their followers. And Richard Neustadt describes the following account from his study of Franklin D. Roosevelt:

> The essence of Roosevelt's technique for information-gathering was competition. "He would call you in," one of his aides once told me, "and he'd ask you to get the story on some complicated business, and you'd come back after a couple of days of hard labor and present the juicy morsel you'd uncovered under a stone somewhere, and *then* you'd find out he knew all about it, along with something else you *didn't* know. Where he got this information from he wouldn't mention, usually, but after he had done this to you once or twice you got damn careful about *your* information" (1960:157).

We can see where Roosevelt "got this information" when we consider the relationship between the interpersonal and informational roles. As leader, the manager has formal and easy access to every member of his staff. Hence, as noted earlier, he tends to know more about his own unit than anyone else does. In addition, his liaison contacts expose the manager to external information to which his subordinates often lack access. Many of these contacts are with other managers of equal status, who are themselves nerve centers in their own organization. In this way, the manager develops a powerful data base of information.

The processing of information is a key part of the manager's job. In my study, the chief executives spent 40% of their contact time on activities devoted exclusively to the transmission of information; 70% of their incoming mail was purely informational (as opposed to requests for action). The manager does not leave meetings or hang up the telephone in order to get back to work. In large part, communication *is* his work. Three roles describe these informational aspects of managerial work.

1. As *monitor*, the manager perpetually scans his environment for information, interrogates his liaison contacts and his subordinates, and receives unsolicited information, much of it as a result of the network of personal contacts he has developed. Remember that a good part of the information the manager collects in his monitor role arrives in verbal form, often as gossip, hearsay, and speculation. By virtue of his contacts, the manager has a natural advantage in collecting this soft information for his organization.

2. He must share and distribute much of this information. Information he gleans from outside personal contacts may be needed within his organization. In his *disseminator* role, the manager passes some of his privileged information directly to his subordinates, who would otherwise have no access to it. When his subordinates lack easy contact with one another, the manager will sometimes pass information from one to another.

3. In his *spokesman* role, the manager sends some of his information to people outside his unit—a president makes a speech to lobby for an organization cause, or a foreman suggests a product modification to a supplier. In addition, as part of his role as spokesman, every manager must inform and satisfy the influential people who control his organizational unit. For the foreman, this may simply involve keeping the plant manager informed about the flow of work through the shop.

The president of a large corporation, however, may spend a great amount of his time dealing with a host of influences. Directors and shareholders must be advised about financial performance; consumer groups must be assured that the organization is fulfilling its social responsibilities; and government officials must be satisfied that the organization is abiding by the law.

Decisional Roles

Information is not, of course, an end in itself; it is the basic input to decision making. One thing is clear in the study of managerial work: the manager plays the major role in his unit's decision-making system. As its formal authority, only he can commit the unit to important new courses of action; and as its nerve center, only he has full and current information to make the set of decisions that determines the unit's strategy. Four roles describe the manager as decision-maker.

1. As *entrepreneur*, the manager seeks to improve his unit, to adapt it to changing conditions in the environment. In his monitor role, the president is constantly on the lookout for new ideas. When a good one appears, he initiates a development project that he may supervise himself or delegate to an employee (perhaps with the stipulation that he must approve the final proposal).

There are two interesting features about these development projects at the chief executive level. First, these projects do not involve single decisions or even unified clusters of decisions. Rather, they emerge as a series of small decisions and actions sequenced over time. Apparently, the chief executive prolongs each project so that he can fit it bit by bit into his busy, disjointed schedule and so that he can gradually come to comprehend the issue, if it is a complex one.

Second, the chief executives I studied supervised as many as 50 of these projects at the same time. Some projects entailed new products or processes; others involved public relations campaigns, improvement of the cash position, reorganization of a weak department, resolution of a morale problem in a foreign division, integration of computer operations, various acquisitions at different stages of development, and so on.

The chief executive appears to maintain a kind of inventory of the development projects that he himself supervises—projects that are at various stages of development, some active and some in limbo. Like a juggler, he keeps a number of projects in the air; periodically, one comes down, is given a new burst of energy, and is sent back into orbit. At various intervals, he put new projects on-stream and discards old ones.

2. While the entrepreneur role describes the manager as the voluntary initiator of change, the *disturbance handler* role depicts the manager involuntarily responding to pressures. Here change is beyond the manager's control. He must act because the pressures of the situation are too severe to be ignored: a strike looms, a major customer has gone bankrupt, or a supplier reneges on his contract.

It has been fashionable, I noted earlier, to compare the manager to an orchestra conductor, just as Peter F. Drucker wrote in *The Practice of Management*:

> The manager has the task of creating a true whole that is larger than the sum of its parts, a productive entity that turns out more than the sum of the resources put into it. One analogy is the conductor of a symphony orchestra, through whose effort, vision and leadership individual instrumental parts that are so much noise by themselves become the living whole of music. But the conductor has the composer's score; he is only interpreter. The manager is both composer and conductor (1954:341–342).

Now consider the words of Leonard R. Sayles, who has carried out systematic research on the manager's job:

> [The manager] is like a symphony orchestra conductor, endeavouring to maintain a melodious performance in which the contributions of the various instruments are coordinated and sequenced, patterned and paced, while the orchestra members are having various personal difficulties, stage hands are moving music stands, alternating excessive heat and cold are creating audience and instrument problems, and the sponsor of the concert is insisting on irrational changes in the program (1964:162).

In effect, every manager must spend a good part of his time responding to high-pressure disturbances. No organization can be so well run, so standardized, that it has considered every contingency in the uncertain environment in advance. Disturbances arise not only because poor managers ignore situations until they reach crisis proportions, but also because good managers cannot possibly anticipate all the consequences of the actions they take.

3. The third decisional role is that of *resource allocator*. To the manager falls the responsibility of deciding who will get what in his organizational unit. Perhaps the most important resource the manager allocates is his own time. Access to the manager constitutes exposure to the unit's nerve center and decision-maker. The manager is also charged with designing his unit's structure, that pattern of formal relationships that determines how work is to be divided and coordinated.

Also, in his role as resource allocator, the manager authorizes the important decisions of his unit before they are implemented. By retaining this power, the manager can ensure that decisions are interrelated; all must pass through a single brain. To fragment this power is to encourage discontinuous decision making and a disjoined strategy. . . .

4. The final decisional role is that of *negotiator*. Studies of managerial work at all levels indicate that managers spend considerable time in negotiations: the president of the football team is called in to work out a contract with the holdout superstar; the corporation president leads his company's contingent to negotiate a new stock issue; the foreman argues a grievance problem to its conclusion with the shop steward. As Leonard Sayles puts it, negotiations are a "way of life" for the sophisticated manager.

These negotiations are duties of the manager's job; perhaps routine, they are not to be shirked. They are an integral part of his job, for only he has the authority to commit organizational resources in "real time," and only he has the nerve center information that important negotiations require.

The Integrated Job

It should be clear by now that the ten roles I have been describing are not easily separable. In the terminology of the psychologist, they form a gestalt, an integrated whole. No role can be pulled out of the framework and the job be left intact. For example, a manager without liaison contacts lacks external information. As a result, he can neither disseminate the information his employees need nor make decisions that adequately reflect external conditions. (In fact, this is a problem for the new person in a managerial position, since he cannot make effective decisions until he has built up his network of contacts.) . . . .

To say that the ten roles form a gestalt is not to say that all managers give equal attention to each role. In fact, I found in my review of the various research studies that

> . . . sales managers seem to spend relatively more of their time in the interpersonal roles, presumably a reflection of the extrovert nature of the marketing activity;
>
> . . . production managers give relatively more attention to the decisional roles, presumably a reflection of their concern with efficient work flow;
>
> . . . staff managers spend the most time in the informational roles, since they are experts who manage departments that advise other parts of the organization.

Nevertheless, in all cases the interpersonal, informational, and decisional roles remain inseparable. . . .

CONCLUSION

No job is more vital to our society than that of the manager. It is the manager who determines whether our social institutions serve us well or whether they squander our talents and resources. It is time to strip away the folklore about managerial work, and time to study it realistically so that we can begin the difficult task of making significant improvements in its performance.

GOOD MANAGERS
DON'T MAKE
POLICY DECISIONS *

by H. Edward Wrapp

The upper reaches of management are a land of mystery and intrigue. Very few people have ever been there, and the present inhabitants frequently send back messages that are incoherent both to other levels of management and to the world in general. This may account for the myths, illusions, and caricatures that permeate the literature of management—for example, such widely held notions as these:

- Life gets less complicated as a manager reaches the top of the pyramid.

- The manager at the top level knows everything that's going on in the organization, can command whatever resources he may need, and therefore can be more decisive.

- The general manager's day is taken up with making broad policy decisions and formulating precise objectives.

- The top executive's primary activity is conceptualizing long-range plans.

- In a large company, the top executive may be seen meditating about the role of his organization in society.

I suggest that none of these versions alone, or in combination, is an accurate portrayal of what a general manager does. Perhaps students of the management process have been overly eager to develop a theory and a discipline. As one executive I know puts it, "I guess I do some of the things described in the books and articles, but the descriptions are lifeless, and my job isn't."

What common characteristics, then, do suc-

cessful executives exhibit *in reality*? I shall identify five skills or talents which, in my experience, seem especially significant. . . .

KEEPING WELL INFORMED

First, each of my heroes has a special talent for keeping himself informed about a wide range of operating decisions being made at different levels in the company. As he moves up the ladder, he develops a network of information sources in many different departments. He cultivates these sources and keeps them open no matter how high he climbs in the organization. When the need arises, he bypasses the lines on the organization chart to seek more than one version of a situation.

In some instances, especially when they suspect he would not be in total agreement with their decision, his subordinates will elect to inform him in advance, before they announce a decision. In these circumstances, he is in a position to defer the decision, or redirect it, or even block further action. However, he does not insist on this procedure. Ordinarily he leaves it up to the members of his organization to decide at what stage they inform him.

Top-level managers are frequently criticized by writers, consultants, and lower levels of management for continuing to enmesh themselves in operating problems, after promotion to the top, rather than withdrawing to the "big picture." Without any doubt, some managers do get lost in a welter of detail and insist on making too many decisions. Superficially, the good manager may seem to make the same mistake—but his purposes are different. He knows that only by keeping well informed about the decisions being made can he avoid the sterility so often found in those who isolate themselves from operations. If he follows the advice to free himself from operations, he may soon find himself subsisting on a diet of abstractions, leaving the choice of what he eats in the hands of his subordinates. As Kenneth Boulding puts it: "The very purpose of a hierarchy is to prevent information from reaching higher layers. It operates as an information filter, and there are little wastebaskets all along the way'' (in *Business Week*, Feb. 18, 1967:202). . . .

FOCUSING TIME & ENERGY

The second skill of the good manager is that he knows how to save his energy and hours for those few particular issues, decisions, or problems to which he should give his personal attention. He knows the fine and subtle distinction between keeping fully informed about operating decisions and allowing the organization to force him into participating in these decisions or, even worse, making them. Recognizing that he can bring his special talents to bear on only a limited number of matters, he chooses those issues which he believes will have the greatest long-term impact on the company, and on which his special abilities can be most productive. Under ordinary circumstances he will limit himself to three or four major objectives during any single period of sustained activity.

What about the situations he elects *not* to become involved in as a decision maker? He makes sure (using the skill first mentioned) that the organization keeps him informed about them at various stages; he does not want to be accused of indifference to such issues. He trains his subordinates not to bring the matters to him for a decision. The communication to him from below is essentially one of: ''Here is our sizeup, and here's what we propose to do.'' Reserving his hearty encouragement for those projects which hold superior promise of a contribution to total corporate strategy, he simply acknowledges receipt of information on other matters. When he sees a problem where the organization needs his help, he finds a way to transmit his know-how short of giving orders—usually by asking perceptive questions.

PLAYING THE POWER GAME

To what extent do successful top executives push their ideas and proposals through the organization? The rather common notion that the ''prime

mover'' continually creates and forces through new programs, like a powerful majority leader in a liberal Congress, is in my opinion very misleading.

The successful manager is sensitive to the power structure in the organization. In considering any major current proposal, he can plot the position of the various individuals and units in the organization on a scale ranging from complete, outspoken support down to determined, sometimes bitter, and oftentimes well-cloaked opposition. In the middle of the scale is an area of comparative indifference. Usually, several aspects of a proposal will fall into this area, and *here is where he knows he can operate*. He assesses the depth and nature of the blocs in the organization. His perception permits him to move through what I call *corridors* of comparative indifference. He seldom challenges when a corridor is blocked, preferring to pause until it has opened up.

Related to this particular skill is his ability to recognize the need for a few trial-balloon launchers in the organization. He knows that the organization will tolerate only a certain number of proposals which emanate from the apex of the pyramid. No matter how sorely he may be tempted to stimulate the organization with a flow of his own ideas, he knows he must work through idea men in different parts of the organization. As he studies the reactions of key individuals and groups to the trial balloons these men send up, he is able to make a better assessment of how to limit the emasculation of the various proposals. For seldom does he find a proposal which is supported by all quarters of the organization. The emergence of strong support in certain quarters is almost sure to evoke strong opposition in others.

Value of Sense of Timing

Circumstances like these mean that a good sense of timing is a priceless asset for a top executive. . . . As a good manager stands at a point in time, he can identify a set of goals he is interested in, albeit the outline of them may be pretty hazy.

His timetable, which is also pretty hazy, suggests that some must be accomplished sooner than others, and that some may be safely postponed for several months or years. He has a still hazier notion of how he can reach these goals. He assesses key individuals and groups. He knows that each has its own set of goals, some of which he understands rather thoroughly and others about which he can only speculate. He knows also that these individuals and groups represent blocks to certain programs or projects, and that these points of opposition must be taken into account. As the day-to-day operating decisions are made, and as proposals are responded to both by individuals and by groups, he perceives more clearly where the corridors of comparative indifference are. He takes action accordingly.

THE ART OF IMPRECISION

The fourth skill of the successful manager is knowing how to satisfy the organization that it has a sense of direction *without ever actually getting himself committed publicly to a specific set of objectives*. This is not to say that he does not have objectives—personal and corporate, long-term and short-term. They are significant guides to his thinking, and he modifies them continually as he better understands the resources he is working with, the competition, and the changing market demands. But as the organization clamors for statements of objectives, these are samples of what they get back from him:

> "Our company aims to be number one in its industry."
> "Our objective is growth with profit."
> "We seek the maximum return on investment."
> "Management's goal is to meet its responsibilities to stockholders, employees, and the public."

In my opinion, statements such as these provide almost no guidance to the various levels of management. Yet they are quite readily accepted as objectives by large numbers of intelligent people.

Maintaining Viability

Why does the good manager shy away from precise statements of his objectives for the organization? The main reason is that he finds it impossible to set down specific objectives which will be relevant for any reasonable period into the future. Conditions in business change continually and rapidly, and corporate strategy must be revised to take the changes into account. The more explicit the statement of strategy, the more difficult it becomes to persuade the organization to turn to different goals when needs and conditions shift.

The public and the stockholders, to be sure, must perceive the organization as having a well-defined set of objectives and a clear sense of direction. But in reality the good top manager is seldom so certain of the direction which should be taken. Better than anyone else, he senses the many, many threats to his company—threats which lie in the economy, in the actions of competitors, and, not least, within his own organization.

He also knows that it is impossible to state objectives clearly enough so that everyone in the organization understands what they mean. Objectives get communicated only over time by a consistency or pattern in operating decisions. Such decisions are more meaningful than words. In instances where precise objectives are spelled out, the organization tends to interpret them so they fit its own needs.

Subordinates who keep pressing for more precise objectives are in truth working against their own best interests. Each time the objectives are stated more specifically, a subordinate's range of possibilities for operating are reduced. The narrower field means less room to roam and to accommodate the flow of ideas coming up from his part of the organization.

Avoiding Policy Straitjackets

The successful manager's reluctance to be precise extends into the area of policy decisions. He seldom makes a forthright statement of policy. He may be aware that in some companies there are executives who spend more time in arbitrating disputes caused by stated policies than in moving the company forward. The management textbooks contend that well-defined policies are the sine qua non of a well-managed company. My research does not bear out this contention. For example:

> The president of one company with which I am familiar deliberately leaves the assignments of his top officers vague and refuses to define policies for them. He passes out new assignments with seemingly no pattern in mind and consciously sets up competitive ventures among his subordinates. His methods, though they would never be sanctioned by a classical organization planner, are deliberate—and, incidentally, quite effective.

Since able managers do not make policy decisions, does this mean that well-managed companies operate without policies? Certainly not. But the policies are those which evolve over time from an indescribable mix of operating decisions. From any single operating decision might have come a very minor dimension of the policy as the organization understands it; from a series of decisions comes a pattern of guidelines for various levels of the organization.

The skillful manager resists the urge to write a company creed or to compile a policy manual. Preoccupation with detailed statements of corporate objectives and departmental goals and with comprehensive organization charts and job descriptions—this is often the first symptom of an organization which is in the early stages of atrophy.

The "management by objectives" school, so widely heralded in recent years, suggests that detailed objectives be spelled out at all levels in the corporation. This method is feasible at lower levels of management, but it becomes unworkable at the upper levels. The top manager must think out objectives in detail, but ordinarily some of the objectives must be withheld, or at least communicated to the organization in modest doses. A conditioning process which may stretch over months or years is necessary in order to prepare the organization for radical departures from what it is currently striving to attain.

Suppose, for example, that a president is convinced his company must phase out of the principal business it has been in for 35 years. Although making this change of course is one of his objectives, he may well feel that he cannot disclose the idea even to his vice presidents, whose total know-how is in the present business. A blunt announcement that the company is changing horses would be too great a shock for most of them to bear. And so he begins moving toward this goal but without a full disclosure to his management group.

A detailed spelling out of objectives may only complicate the task of reaching them. Specific, detailed statements give the opposition an opportunity to organize its defenses.

MUDDLING WITH A PURPOSE

The fifth, and most important, skill I shall describe bears little relation to the doctrine that management is (or should be) a comprehensive, systematic, logical, well-programmed science. Of all the heresies set forth here, this should strike doctrinaires as the rankest of all!

The successful manager, in my observation, recognizes the futility of trying to push total packages or programs through the organization. He is willing to take less than total acceptance in order to achieve modest progress toward his goals. Avoiding debates on principles, he tries to piece together particles that may appear to be incidentals into a program that moves at least part of the way toward his objectives. His attitude is based on optimism and persistence. Over and over he says to himself, "There must be some parts of this proposal on which we can capitalize."

Whenever he identifies relationships among the different proposals before him, he knows that they present opportunities for combination and restructuring. It follows that he is a man of wide-ranging interests and curiosity. The more things he knows about, the more opportunities he will have to discover parts which are related. This process does not require great intellectual brilliance or unusual creativity. The wider ranging his interests, the more likely that he will be able to tie together several unrelated proposals. He is skilled as an analyst, but even more talented as a conceptualizer.

If the manager has built or inherited a solid organization, it will be difficult for him to come up with an idea which no one in the company has ever thought of before. His most significant contribution may be that he can see relationships which no one else has seen. . . .

Contrasting Pictures

It is interesting to note, in the writings of several students of management, the emergence of the concept that, rather than making decisions, the leader's principal task is maintaining operating conditions which permit the various decision-making systems to function effectively. The supporters of this theory, it seems to me, overlook the subtle turns of direction which the leader can provide. He cannot add purpose and structure to the balanced judgments of subordinates if he simply rubberstamps their decisions. He must weigh the issues and reach his own decision. . . .

Many of the articles about successful executives picture them as great thinkers who sit at their desks drafting master blueprints for their companies. The successful top executives I have seen at work do not operate this way. Rather than produce a full-grown decision tree, they start with a twig, help it grow, and ease themselves out on the limbs only after they have tested to see how much weight the limbs can stand.

In my picture, the general manager sits in the midst of a continuous stream of operating problems. His organization presents him with a flow of proposals to deal with the problems. Some of these proposals are contained in voluminous, well-documented, formal reports; some are as fleeting as the walk-in visit from a subordinate whose latest inspiration came during the morn-

ing's coffee break. Knowing how meaningless it is to say, "This is a finance problem," or, "That is a communications problem," the manager feels no compulsion to classify his problems. He is, in fact, undismayed by a problem that defies classification. As the late Gary Steiner, in one of his speeches, put it, "He has a high tolerance for ambiguity."

In considering each proposal, the general manager tests it against at least three criteria:

1. Will the total proposal—or, more often, will some part of the proposal—move the organization toward the objectives which he has in mind?

2. How will the whole or parts of the proposal be received by the various groups and sub-groups in the organization? Where will the strongest opposition come from, which group will furnish the strongest support, and which group will be neutral or indifferent?

3. How does the proposal relate to programs already in process or currently proposed? Can some parts of the proposal under consideration be added on to a program already under way, or can they be combined with all or parts of other proposals in a package which can be steered through the organization? . . .

CONCLUSION

To recapitulate, the general manager possesses five important skills. He knows how to:

1. *Keep open many pipelines of information—* No one will quarrel with the desirability of an early warning system which provides varied viewpoints on an issue. However, very few managers know how to practice this skill, and the books on management add precious little to our understanding of the techniques which make it practicable.

2. *Concentrate on a limited number of significant issues—*No matter how skillful the manager is in focusing his energies and tal-

ents, he is inevitably caught up in a number of inconsequential duties. Active leadership of an organization demands a high level of personal involvement, and personal involvement brings with it many time-consuming activities which have an infinitesimal impact on corporate strategy. Hence this second skill, while perhaps the most logical of the five, is by no means the easiest to apply.

3. *Identify the corridors of comparative indifference*—Are there inferences here that the good manager has no ideas of his own, that he stands by until his organization proposes solutions, that he never uses his authority to force a proposal through the organization? Such inferences are not intended. The message is that a good organization will tolerate only so much direction from the top; the good manager therefore is adept at sensing how hard he can push.

4. *Give the organization a sense of direction with open-ended objectives*—In assessing this skill, keep in mind that I am talking about top levels of management. At lower levels, the manager should be encouraged to write down his objectives, if for no other reason than to ascertain if they are consistent with corporate strategy.

5. *Spot opportunities and relationships in the stream of operating problems and decisions*—Lest it be concluded from the description of this skill that the good manager is more an improviser than a planner, let me emphasize that he is a planner and encourages planning by his subordinates. Interestingly, though, professional planners may be irritated by a good general manager. Most of them complain about his lack of vision. They devise a master plan, but the president (or other operating executive) seems to ignore it, or to give it minimum acknowledgment by borrowing bits and pieces for implementation. They seem to feel that the power of a good master plan will be obvious to everyone, and its implementation automatic. But the general manager knows that even if the plan is sound and imaginative, the job has only begun. The long, painful task of implementation will depend on his skill, not that of the planner. . . .

LEADERSHIP IN ADMINISTRATION*

by Philip Selznick

The nature and quality of leadership, in the sense of statesmanship, is an elusive but persistent theme in the history of ideas. Most writers have centered their attention on *political* statesmen, leaders of whole communities who sit in the high places where great issues are joined and settled. In our time, there is no abatement of the need to continue the great discussion, to learn how to reconcile idealism with expediency, freedom with organization.

But an additional emphasis is necessary. Ours is a pluralist society made up of many large, influential, relatively autonomous groups. The United States government itself consists of independently powerful agencies which do a great deal on their own initiative and are largely self-governing. These, and the institutions of industry, politics, education, and other fields, often command large resources; their leaders are inevitably responsible for the material and psychological well-being of numerous constituents; and they have become increasingly *public* in nature, attached to such interests and dealing with such problems as affect the welfare of the entire community. In our society the need for statesmanship is widely diffused and beset by special problems. An understanding of leadership in both public and private organizations must have a high place on the agenda of social inquiry. . . .

The argument of this essay is quite simply stated: *The executive becomes a statesman as he makes the transition from administrative management to institutional leadership.* This shift entails a reassessment of his own tasks and of the needs of the enterprise. It is marked by a concern

* Excerpted from Philip Selznick, *Leadership in Administration: A Sociological Interpretation* (copyright © by Harper & Row, 1957); reprinted by permission of Harper & Row, Publishers, Inc.

for the evolution of the organization as a whole, including its changing aims and capabilities. In a word, it means viewing the organization as an institution. To understand the nature of institutional leadership, we must have some notion of the meaning and significance of the term "institution" itself.

ORGANIZATIONS
AND INSTITUTIONS

The most striking and obvious thing about an administrative organization is its formal system of rules and objectives. Here tasks, powers, and procedures are set out according to some officially approved pattern. This pattern purports to say how the work of the organization is to be carried on, whether it be producing steel, winning votes, teaching children, or saving souls. The organization thus designed is a technical instrument for mobilizing human energies and directing them toward set aims. We allocate tasks, delegate authority, channel communication, and find some way of co-ordinating all that has been divided up and parceled out. All this is conceived as an exercise in engineering; it is governed by the related ideals of rationality and discipline.

The term "organization" thus suggests a certain bareness, a lean, no-nonsense system of consciously co-ordinated activities (Barnard, 1938:73). It refers to an *expendable tool*, a rational instrument engineered to do a job. An "institution," on the other hand, is more nearly a natural product of social needs and pressures—a responsive, adaptive organism. This distinction is a matter of analysis, not of direct description. It does not mean that any given enterprise must be either one or the other. While an extreme case may closely approach either an "ideal" organization or an "ideal" institution, most living associations resist so easy a classification. They are complex mixtures of both designed and responsive behavior. . . .

In what is perhaps its most significant meaning, "to institutionalize" is to *infuse with value* beyond the technical requirements of the task at hand. The prizing of social machinery beyond its technical role is largely a reflection of the unique way in which it fulfills personal or group needs. Whenever individuals become attached to an organization or a way of doing things as persons rather than as technicians, the result is a prizing of the device for its own sake. From the standpoint of the committed person, the organization is changed from an expendable tool into a valued source of personal satisfaction. Some manifestations of this process are quite obvious; others are less easily recognized. It is a commonplace that administrative changes are difficult when individuals have become habituated to and identified with long-established procedures. For example, the shifting of personnel is inhibited when business relations become personal ones and there is resistance to any change that threatens rewarding ties. A great deal of energy in organizations is expended in a continuous effort to preserve the rational, technical, impersonal system against such counter-pressures. . . .

The test of infusion with value is *expendability*. If an organization is merely an instrument, it will be readily altered or cast aside when a more efficient tool becomes available. Most organizations are thus expendable. When value-infusion takes place, however, there is a resistance to change. People feel a sense of personal loss; the "identity" of the group or community seems somehow to be violated; they bow to economic or technological considerations only reluctantly, with regret. A case in point is the perennial effort to save San Francisco's cable cars from replacement by more economical forms of transportation. The Marine Corps has this institutional halo, and it resists administrative measures that would submerge its identity. . . .

To summarize: organizations are technical instruments, designed as means to definite goals. They are judged on engineering premises; they are expendable. Institutions, whether conceived as groups or practices, may be partly engineered, but they have also a "natural" dimension. They are products of interaction and adaptation; they become the receptacles of group idealism; they are less readily expendable. . . .

THE DEFAULT OF LEADERSHIP

When institutional leadership fails, it is perhaps more often by default than by positive error or sin. Leadership is lacking when it is needed; and the institution drifts, exposed to vagrant pressures, readily influenced by short-run opportunistic trends. This default is partly a failure of nerve, partly a failure of understanding. It takes nerve to hold a course; it takes understanding to recognize and deal with the basic sources of institutional vulnerability.

One type of default is the failure to set goals. Once an organization becomes a "going concern," with many forces working to keep it alive, the people who run it can readily escape the task of defining its purposes. This evasion stems partly from the hard intellectual labor involved, a labor that often seems but to increase the burden of already onerous daily operations. In part, also, there is the wish to avoid conflicts with those in and out of the organization who would be threatened by a sharp definition of purpose, with its attendant claims and responsibilities. Even business firms find it easy to fall back on conventional phrases, such as that "our goal is to make profit," phrases which offer little guidance in the formulation of policy.

A critique of leadership, we shall argue, must include this emphasis on the leader's responsibility to define the mission of the enterprise. This view is not new. It is important because so much of administrative analysis takes the goal of the organization as given, whereas in many crucial instances this is precisely what is problematic. We shall also suggest that the analysis of goals is itself dependent on an understanding of the organization's social structure. In other words, the purposes we have or can have depend on what we are or what we can be. In statesmanship no less than in the search for personal wisdom, the Socratic dictum—know thyself—provides the ultimate guide.

Another type of default occurs when goals, however neatly formulated, enjoy only a superficial acceptance and do not genuinely influence the total structure of the enterprise. Truly accepted values must infuse the organization at many levels, affecting the perspectives and attitudes of personnel, the relative importance of staff activities, the distribution of authority, relations with outside groups, and many other matters. Thus if a large corporation asserts a wish to change its role in the community from a narrow emphasis on profit-making to a larger social responsibility (even though the ultimate goal remains some combination of survival and profit-making ability), it must explore the implications of such a change for decision-making in a wide variety of organizational activities. We shall stress that the task of building special values and a distinctive competence into the organization is a prime function of leadership. . . .

Finally, the role of the institutional leader should be clearly distinguished from that of the "interpersonal" leader. The latter's task is to smooth the path of human interaction, ease communication, evoke personal devotion, and allay anxiety. His expertness has relatively little to do with content; he is more concerned with persons than with policies. His main contribution is to the efficiency of the enterprise. The institutional leader, on the other hand, *is primarily an expert in the promotion and protection of values*. The interpretation that follows takes this idea as a starting point, exploring its meaning and implications. . . .

It is in the realm of policy—including the areas where policy-formation and organization-building meet—that the distinctive quality of institutional leadership is found. Ultimately, this is the quality of statesmanship which deals with current issues, not for themselves alone but according to their long-run implications for the role and meaning of the group. Group leadership is far more than the capacity to mobilize personal support; it is more than the maintenance of equilibrium through the routine solution of everyday problems; it is the function of the leader-statesman—whether of a nation or a private association—to define the ends of group existence, to design an enterprise distinctively adapted to these ends, and to see that that design becomes a living reality. These tasks are not routine; they call for continuous self-appraisal on the part of the leaders; and they may require only a few critical decisions over a long period of time. "Mere speed, frequency, and vigor in coming to decisions may have little relevance at the top executive level, where a man's basic contribution to the enterprise may turn on his making two or three significant decisions a year" (Learned, Ulrich and Booz, 1951:57). This basic contribution is not always aided by the traits often associated with psychological leadership, such as aggressive self-confidence, intuitive sureness, ability to inspire. . . .

CHARACTER AS DISTINCTIVE COMPETENCE

In studying character we are interested in the *distinctive competence or inadequacy* that an organization has acquired. In doing so, we look beyond the formal aspects to examine the commitments that have been accepted in the course of adaptation to internal and external pressures. . . . Commitments to ways of acting and responding are built into the organization. When integrated, these commitments define the "character" of the organization. . . .

THE FUNCTIONS OF INSTITUTIONAL LEADERSHIP

We have argued that policy and administration are interdependent in the special sense that certain areas of organizational activity are peculiarly sensitive to policy matters. Because these areas exist, creative men are needed—more in some circumstances than in others—who know how to transform a neutral body of men into a committed polity. These men are called leaders; their profession is politics. . . .

Leadership sets goals, but in doing so takes account of the conditions that have already determined what the organization can do and to some extent what it must do. Leadership creates and molds an organization embodying—in thought and feeling and habit—the value premises of policy. Leadership reconciles internal strivings and environmental pressures, paying close attention to the way adaptive behavior brings about changes in organizational character. When an organization lacks leadership, these tasks are inadequately fulfilled, however expert the flow of paper and however smooth the channels of communication and command. And this fulfillment requires a continuous scrutiny of how the changing social structure affects the evolution of policy.

The relation of leadership to organizational character may be more closely explored if we examine some of the key tasks leaders are called on to perform:

1. *The definition of institutional mission and role.* The setting of goals is a creative task. It entails a self-assessment to discover the true commitments of the organization, as set by effective internal and external demands. The failure to set aims in the light of these commitments is a major source of irresponsibility in leadership.

2. *The institutional embodiment of purpose.* The task of leadership is not only to make policy but to build it into the organization's social structure. This, too, is a creative task. It means shaping the "character" of the organization, sensitizing it to ways of thinking and responding, so that increased reliability in the execution and elaboration of policy will be achieved according to its spirit as well as its letter.

3. *The defense of institutional integrity.* The leadership of any polity fails when it concentrates on sheer survival: institutional survival, properly understood, is a matter of maintaining values and distinctive identity. This is at once one of the most important and least understood functions of leadership. This area (like that of defining institutional mission) is a place where the intuitively knowledgeable leader and the administrative analyst often part company, because the latter has no tools to deal with it. The fallacy of combining agencies on the basis of "logical" association of functions is a characteristic result of the failure to take account of institutional integrity.

4. *The ordering of internal conflict.* Internal interest-groups form naturally in large-scale organizations, since the total enterprise is in one sense a polity composed of a number of sub-organizations. The struggle among competing interests always has a high claim on the attention of leadership. This is so because the direction of the enterprise as a whole may be seriously influenced by changes in the internal balance of power.

In exercising control, leadership has a dual task. It must win the consent of constituent units, in order to maximize voluntary co-operation, and therefore must permit emergent interest blocs a wide degree of representation. At the same time, in order to hold the helm, it must see that a balance of power appropriate to the fulfillment of key commitments will be maintained.

THREE

FORMULATING STRATEGY

Most of what has been published in this field deals with how strategy *should* be designed or consciously *formulated*. On the prescription of how this should be accomplished, there has been a good deal of consensus, although, as we shall see later, this is now eroding. Perhaps one should more properly say there have been two waves of consensus. The first, which developed in the 1960s, is presented in this chapter; the second, which emerged around 1980, did not challenge the first but rather built on it. This is presented in Chapter 4.

Ken Andrews of Harvard is the name most commonly associated with the first wave, although Bill Newman of Columbia wrote on some of these issues much earlier and Igor Ansoff simultaneously outlined very similar views while he was at Carnegie-Mellon. But the Andrews text became the best known, in part because it was so simply and clearly written, in part because it was embodied in a popular textbook (with cases) emanating from the Harvard Business School.

We reproduce parts of the Andrews text (as revised in its own publication in 1980, but based on the original 1965 edition). These serve to introduce the basic point that strategy, ultimately, requires the achievement of fit between the external situation (opportunities and threats) and internal capability (strengths and weaknesses). Note how the Andrews approach builds directly on some of the military concepts outlined earlier. Both seek to leverage the impact of resources by concentrating efforts within a defined zone of dominance while attempting to forestall disaster by anticipating the effects of potentially damaging or hostile external forces. In reading the Andrews excerpts, you may also be struck by the relationship in spirit—and indeed sometimes in detail—to the Selznick material of the last chapter.

As you read the Andrews text, a number of basic premises will quickly become evident. Among these are: The clear distinction made between strategy formulation and strategy implementation (in effect, between thinking and action); the belief that strategy (or at least intended strategy) should be made explicit; the notion that structure should follow strategy (in other words, be designed in accordance with it); and the assumption that strategy emanates from the formal leadership of the organization. Similar premises underlie most of the prescriptive side of the strategy formulation literature.

This model (if we can call it that) has proven very useful in many circumstances as a broad way to analyze a strategic situation and to think about making strategy. A careful strategist should certainly touch all the bases suggested in this approach. But in many circumstances the model cannot or should not be followed to the letter.

We shall call this approach into question in Chapter 4 and subsequent ones when we consider evidence on how strategies actually do form in organizations and why more systematic approaches sometimes break down in complex organizational situations.

The Rumelt reading elaborates on one element in this traditional model—the evaluation of strategies. While the Andrews text contains a similar discussion, Rumelt, a graduate of the Harvard Business School and policy professor at UCLA, develops it in a particularly elegant way, helping to round out this chapter on the classical view of formulating strategy.

A number of the cases allow us to apply and understand the value and limitations of this approach. The Boehm, Intel, and two Zayre cases provide particularly useful examples of where it has a high payoff.

THE CONCEPT OF CORPORATE STRATEGY*

by Kenneth R. Andrews

I. THE STRATEGY CONCEPT

What Strategy Is

Corporate strategy is the pattern of decisions in a company that determines and reveals its objectives, purposes, or goals, produces the principal policies and plans for achieving those goals, and defines the range of business the company is to pursue, the kind of economic and human organization it is or intends to be, and the nature of the economic and noneconomic contribution it intends to make to its shareholders, employees, customers, and communities. . . .

*   Excerpted from Kenneth R. Andrews, *The Concept of Corporate Strategy*, rev. ed. (copyright © by Richard D. Irwin, 1980), chap. 2 and 3; reprinted by permission of the publisher.

The strategic decision contributing to this pattern is one that is effective over long periods of time, affects the company in many different ways, and focuses and commits a significant portion of its resources to the expected outcomes. The pattern resulting from a series of such decisions will probably define the central character and image of a company, the individuality it has for its members and various publics, and the position it will occupy in its industry and markets. It will permit the specification of particular objectives to be attained through a timed sequence of investment and implementation decisions and will govern directly the deployment or redeployment of resources to make these decisions effective.

Some aspects of such a pattern of decision may be in an established corporation unchanging over long periods of time, like a commitment to quality, or high technology, or certain raw materials, or good labor relations. Other aspects of a strategy must change as or before the world changes, such as product line, manufacturing process, or merchandising and styling practices. The basic determinants of company character, if purposefully institutionalized, are likely to persist through and shape the nature of substantial changes in product-market choices and allocation of resources. . . .

It is important, however, not to take the idea apart in another way, i.e. to separate goals from the policies designed to achieve those goals. The essence of the definition of strategy I have just recorded is *pattern*. The interdependence of purposes, policies, and organized action is crucial to the particularity of an individual strategy and its opportunity to identify competitive advantage. It is the unity, coherence, and internal consistency of a company's strategic decisions that position the company in its environment and give the firm its identity, its power to mobilize its strengths, and its likelihood of success in the marketplace. It is the interrelationship of a set of goals and policies that crystallizes from the formless reality of a company's environment a set of problems an organization can seize upon and solve.

What you are doing, in short, is never meaningful unless you can say or imply what you are doing it for: the quality of administrative action and the motivation lending it power cannot be appraised without knowing its relationship to purpose. Breaking up the system of corporate goals and the character-determining major policies for attainment leads to narrow and mechanical conceptions of strategic management and endless logic-chopping. . . .

Summary Statements of Strategy

Before we proceed to clarification of this concept by application, we should specify the terms in which strategy is usually expressed. A summary statement of strategy will characterize the product line and services offered or planned by the company, the markets and market segments for which products and services are now or will be designed, and the channels through which these markets will be reached. The means by which the operation is to be financed will be specified, as will the profit objectives and the emphasis to be placed on the safety of capital versus level of return. Major policy in central functions such as marketing, manufacturing, procurement, research and development, labor relations, and personnel, will be stated where they distinguish the company from others, and usually the intended size, form, and climate of the organization will be included.

Each company, if it were to construct a summary strategy from what it understands itself to be aiming at, would have a different statement with different categories of decision emphasized to indicate what it wanted to be or do. . . .

Formulation of Strategy

Corporate strategy is an organization process, in many ways inseparable from the structure, behavior, and culture of the company in which it takes place. Nevertheless, we may abstract from the process two important aspects, interrelated in real life but separable for the purposes of analysis. The first of these we may call *formulation*, the second *implementation*. Deciding what strategy should be may be approached as a rational undertaking, even if in life emotional attachments . . . may complicate choice among future alternatives. . . .

The principal subactivities of strategy formulation as a logical activity include identifying opportunities and threats in the company's environment and attaching some estimate or risk to the discernible alternatives. Before a choice can be made, the company's strengths and weaknesses should be appraised together with the resources on hand and available. Its actual or potential capacity to take advantage of perceived market needs or to cope with attendant risks should be estimated as objectively as possible. The strategic alternative which results from matching opportunity and corporate capability at an acceptable level of risk is what we may call an *economic strategy*.

The process described thus far assumes that strategists are analytically objective in estimating the relative capacity of their company and the opportunity they see or anticipate in developing markets. The extent to which they wish to undertake low or high risk presumably depends on their profit objectives. The higher they set the latter, the more willing they must be to assume a correspondingly high risk that the market opportunity they see will not develop or that the corporate competence required to excel competition will not be forthcoming.

So far we have described the intellectual processes of ascertaining what a company *might do* in terms of environmental opportunity, of deciding what it *can do* in terms of ability and power, and of bringing these two considerations together in optimal equilibrium. The determination of strategy also requires consideration of what alternatives are preferred by the chief executive and perhaps by his or her immediate associates as well, quite apart from economic considerations. Personal values, aspirations, and ideals do, and in our judgment quite properly should, influence the final choice of purposes. Thus what the executives of a company *want to do* must be brought into the strategic decision.

Finally strategic choice has an ethical aspect—a fact much more dramatically illustrated in some industries than in others. Just as alternatives may be ordered in terms of the degree of risk that they entail, so may they be examined against the standards of responsiveness to the expectations of society that the strategist elects.

Some alternatives may seem to the executive considering them more attractive than others when the public good or service to society is considered. What a company *should do* thus appears as a fourth element of the strategic decision. . . .

The Implementation of Strategy

Since effective implementation can make a sound strategic decision ineffective or a debatable choice successful, it is as important to examine the processes of implementation as to weigh the advantages of available strategic alternatives. The implementation of strategy is comprised of a series of subactivities which are primarily administrative. If purpose is determined, then the resources of a company can be mobilized to accomplish it. An organizational structure appropriate for the efficient performance of the required tasks must be made effective by information systems and relationships permitting coordination of subdivided activities. The organizational processes of performance measurement, compensation, management development—all of them enmeshed in systems of incentives and controls—must be directed toward the kind of behavior required by organizational purpose. The role of personal leadership is important and sometimes decisive in the accomplishment of strategy. Although we know that organization structure and processes of compensation, incentives, control, and management development influence and constrain the formulation of strategy, we should look first at the logical proposition that structure should follow strategy in order to cope later with the organizational reality that strategy also follows structure. When we have examined both tendencies, we will understand and to some extent be prepared to deal with the interdependence of the formulation and implementation of corporate purpose. Figure 1 may be useful in understanding the analysis of strategy as a pattern of interrelated decisions. . . .

II. RELATING OPPORTUNITIES TO RESOURCES

Determination of a suitable strategy for a company begins in identifying the opportunities and risks in its environment. This [discussion] is concerned with the identification of a range of strategic alternatives, the narrowing of this range by recognizing the constraints imposed by corporate

FIGURE 1

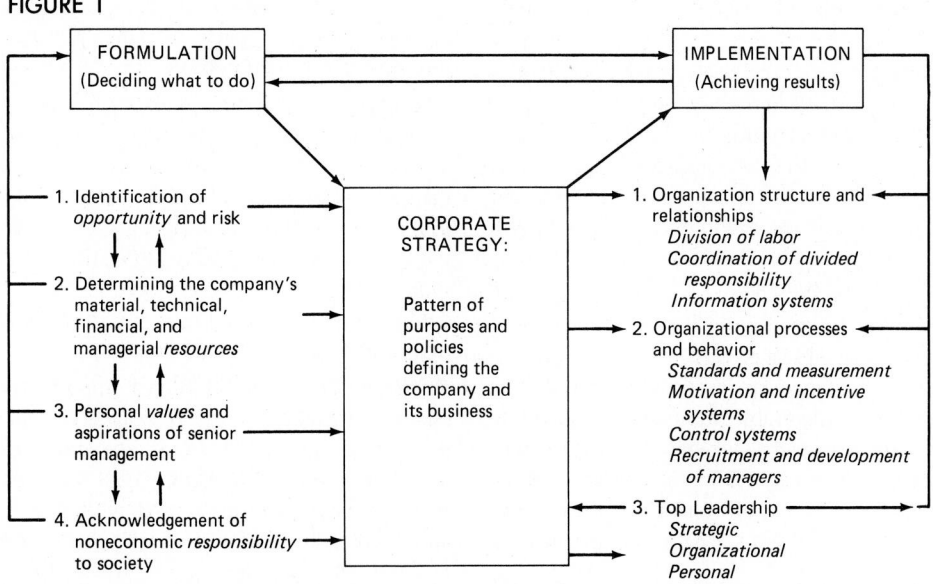

capability, and the determination of one or more economic strategies at acceptable levels of risk. . . .

The Nature of the Company's Environment

The environment of an organization in business, like that of any other organic entity, is the pattern of all the external conditions and influences that affect its life and development. The environmental influences relevant to strategic decision operate in a company's industry, the total business community, its city, its country, and the world. They are technological, economic, physical, social, and political in kind. The corporate strategist is usually at least intuitively aware of these features of the current environment. But in all these categories change is taking place at varying rates— fastest in technology, less rapidly in politics. Change in the environment of business necessitates continuous monitoring of a company's definition of its business, lest it falter, blur, or become obsolete. Since by definition the formulation of strategy is performed with the future in mind, executives who take part in the strategic planning process must be aware of those aspects of their company's environment especially susceptible to the kind of change that will affect their company's future.

Technology From the point of view of the corporate strategist, technological developments are not only the fastest unfolding but the most far-reaching in extending or contracting opportunity for an established company. They include the discoveries of science, the impact of related product development, the less dramatic machinery and process improvements, and the progress of automation and data processing. . . .

Ecology It used to be possible to take for granted the physical characteristics of the environment and find them favorable to industrial development. Plant sites were chosen using criteria like availability of process and cooling water, accessibility to various forms of transportation, and stability of soil conditions. With the increase in sensitivity to the impact on the physical environment of all industrial activity, it becomes essential, often to comply with law, to consider how planned expansion and even continued operation under changing standards will affect and be perceived to affect the air, water, traffic density, and quality of life generally of any area which a company would like to enter. . . .

Economics Because business is more accustomed to monitoring economic trends than those in other spheres, it is less likely to be taken by surprise by such massive developments as the internationalization of competition, the return of China and Russia to trade with the West, the slower than projected development of the Third World countries, the Americanization of demand and culture in the developing countries and the resulting backlash of nationalism, the increased importance of the large multinational corporations and the consequences of host-country hostility, the recurrence of recession, and the persistence of inflation in all phases of the business cycle. The consequences of world economic trends need to be monitored in much greater detail for any one industry or company.

Industry Although the industry environment is the one most company strategists believe they know most about, the opportunities and risks that reside there are often blurred by familiarity and the uncritical acceptance of the established relative position of competitors. . . .

Society Social developments of which strategists keep aware include such influential forces as the quest for equality for minority groups, the demand of women for opportunity and recognition, the changing patterns of work and leisure, the effects of urbanization upon the individual, family, and neighborhood, the rise of crime, the decline of conventional morality, and the changing composition of world population.

Politics The political forces important to the business firm are similarly extensive and complex—the changing relations between communist and noncommunist countries (East and West) and between the prosperous and poor countries (North and South), the relation between private enterprise and government, between workers and management, the impact of national planning on corporate planning, and the rise of what George Lodge (1975) calls the communitarian ideology. . . .

Although it is not possible to know or spell out here the significance of such technical, economic, social, and political trends, and possibilities for the strategist of a given business or company, some simple things are clear. Changing values will lead to different expectations of the role business should perform. Business will be expected to perform its mission not only with economy in the use of energy but with sensitivity to the ecological environment. Organizations in all walks of life will be called upon to be more explicit about their goals and to meet the needs and aspirations (for example, for education) of their membership.

In any case, change threatens all established strategies. We know that a thriving company— itself a living system—is bound up in a variety of interrelationships with larger systems comprising its technological, economic, ecological, social, and political environment. If environmental developments are destroying and creating business opportunities, advance notice of specific instances relevant to a single company is essential to intelligent planning. Risk and opportunity in the last quarter of the 20th century require of executives a keen interest in what is going on outside their companies. More than that, a practical means of tracking developments promising good or ill, and profit or loss, needs to be devised. . . .

For the firm that has not determined what its strategy dictates it needs to know or has not embarked upon the systematic surveillance of environmental change, a few simple questions kept constantly in mind will highlight changing opportunity and risk. In examining your own company or one you are interested in, these questions should lead to an estimate of opportunity and danger in the present and predicted company setting.

1. *What are the essential economic, technical, and physical characteristics of the industry in which the company participates?* . . .

2. *What trends suggesting future change in economic and technical characteristics are apparent?* . . .

3. *What is the nature of competition both within the industry and across industries?* . . .

4. *What are the requirements for success in competition in the company's industry?* . . .

5. *Given the technical, economic, social, and political developments that most directly apply, what is the range of strategy available to any company in this industry?* . . .

Identifying Corporate Competence and Resources

The first step in validating a tentative choice among several opportunities is to determine whether the organization has the capacity to prosecute it successfully. The capability of an organization is its demonstrated and potential ability to accomplish, against the opposition of circumstance or competition, whatever it sets out to do. Every organization has actual and potential strengths and weaknesses. Since it is prudent in formulating strategy to extend or maximize the one and contain or minimize the other, it is important to try to determine what they are and to distinguish one from the other.

It is just as possible, though much more difficult, for a company to know its own strengths and limitations as it is to maintain a workable surveillance of its changing environment. Subjectivity, lack of confidence, and unwillingness to face reality may make it hard for organizations as well as for individuals to know themselves. But just as it is essential, though difficult, that a maturing person achieve reasonable self-awareness, so an organization can identify approximately its central strength and critical vulnerability. . . .

To make an effective contribution to strategic planning, the key attributes to be appraised should be identified and consistent criteria established for judging them. If attention is directed to strategies, policy commitments, and past practices in the context of discrepancy between organization goals and attainment, an outcome useful to an individual manager's strategic planning is possible. The assessment of strengths and weaknesses associated with the attainment of specific objectives becomes in Stevenson's (1976) words a "key link in a feedback loop" which allows managers to learn from the success or failures of the policies they institute.

Although [a] study by Stevenson did not find or establish a systematic way of developing or using such knowledge, members of organizations develop judgments about what the company can do particularly well—its core of competence. If consensus can be reached about this capability, no matter how subjectively arrived at, its application to identified opportunity can be estimated.

Sources of Capabilities The powers of a company constituting a resource for growth and diversification accrue primarily from experience in making and marketing a product line or providing a service. They inhere as well in (1) the developing strengths and weaknesses of the individuals comprising the organization, (2) the degree to which individual capability is effectively applied to the common task, and (3) the quality of coordination of individual and group effort.

The experience gained through successful execution of a strategy centered upon one goal may unexpectedly develop capabilities which could be applied to different ends. Whether they should be so applied is another question. For example, a manufacturer of salt can strengthen his competitive position by offering his customers salt-dispensing equipment. If, in the course of making engineering improvements in this equipment, a new solenoid principle is perfected that has application to many industrial switching problems, should this patentable and marketable innovation be exploited? The answer would turn not only on whether economic analysis of the opportunity shows this to be a durable and profitable possibility, but also on whether the organization can muster the financial, manufacturing, and marketing strength to exploit the discovery and live with its success. The former question is likely to have a more positive answer than the latter.

In this connection, it seems important to remember that individual and unsupported flashes of strength are not as dependable as the gradually accumulated product and market-related fruits of experience.

Even where competence to exploit an opportunity is nurtured by experience in related fields, the level of that competence may be too low for any great reliance to be placed upon it. Thus a chain of children's clothing stores might well acquire the administrative, merchandising, buying, and selling skills that would permit it to add departments in women's wear. Similarly, a sales force effective in distributing typewriters might gain proficiency in selling office machinery and supplies. But even here it would be well to ask what *distinctive* ability these companies could bring to the retailing of soft goods or office equipment to attract customers away from a plethora of competitors.

Identifying Strengths The distinctive competence of an organization is more than what it can do; it is what it can do particularly well. To identify the less obvious or by-product strengths of an organization that may well be transferable to some more profitable new opportunity, one might well begin by examining the organization's current product line and by defining the functions it serves in its markets. Almost any important consumer product has functions which are related to others into which a qualified company might move. The typewriter, for example, is more than the simple machine for mechanizing handwriting that it once appeared to be when looked at only from the point of view of its designer and manufacturer. Closely analyzed from the point of view of the potential user, the typewriter is found to contribute to a broad range of information processing functions. Any one of these might have suggested an area to be exploited by a typewriter manufacturer. Tacitly defining a typewriter as a replacement for a fountain pen as a writing instrument rather than as an input-output device for word processing is the explanation provided by hindsight for the failure of the old-line typewriter companies to develop before

IBM did the electric typewriter and the computer-related input-output devices it made possible. The definition of product which would lead to identification of transferable skills must be expressed in terms of the market needs it may fill rather than the engineering specifications to which it conforms.

Besides looking at the uses or functions to which present products contribute, the would-be diversifier might profitably identify the skills that underlie whatever success has been achieved. The qualifications of an organization efficient at performing its long-accustomed tasks come to be taken for granted and considered humdrum, like the steady provision of first-class service. The insight required to identify the essential strength justifying new ventures does not come naturally. Its cultivation can probably be helped by recognition of the need for analysis. In any case, we should look beyond the company's capacity to invent new products. Product leadership is not possible for a majority of companies, so it is fortunate that patentable new products are not the only major highway to new opportunities. Other avenues include new marketing services, new methods of distribution, new values in quality-price combinations, and creative merchandising. The effort to find or to create a competence that is truly distinctive may hold the real key to a company's success or even to its future development. For example, the ability of a cement manufacturer to run a truck fleet more effectively than its competitors may constitute one of its principal competitive strengths in selling an undifferentiated product.

Matching Opportunity and Competence

The way to narrow the range of alternatives, made extensive by imaginative identification of new possibilities, is to match opportunity to competence, once each has been accurately identified and its future significance estimated. It is this combination which establishes a company's economic mission and its position in its environment. The combination is designed to minimize organizational weakness and to maximize strength. In every case, risk attends it. And when opportunity seems to outrun present distinctive competence, the willingness to gamble that the latter can be built up to the required level is almost indispensable to a strategy that challenges the organization and the people in it. Figure 2 diagrams the matching of opportunity and resources that results in an economic strategy.

Before we leave the creative act of putting together a company's unique internal capability and opportunity evolving in the external world, we should note that—aside from distinctive competence—the principal resources found in any company are money and people—technical and managerial people. At an advanced stage of economic development, money seems less a problem than technical competence, and the latter less critical than managerial ability. Do not assume that managerial capacity can rise to any occasion. The diversification of American industry is marked by hundreds of instances in which a company strong in one endeavor lacked the ability to manage an enterprise requiring different skills. The right to make handsome profits over a long period must be earned. Opportunism without competence is a path to fairyland.

Besides equating an appraisal of market opportunity and organizational capability, the decision to make and market a particular product or service should be accompanied by an identification of the nature of the business and the kind of company its management desires. Such a guiding concept is a product of many considerations, including the managers' personal values. . . .

Uniqueness of Strategy

In each company, the way in which distinctive competence, organizational resources, and organizational values are combined is or should be unique. Differences among companies are as numerous as differences among individuals. The combinations of opportunity to which distinctive competences, resources, and values may be applied are equally extensive. Generalizing about how to make an effective match is less rewarding than working at it. The effort is a highly stimulating and challenging exercise. The outcome will be unique for each company and each situation.

FIGURE 2   SCHEMATIC DEVELOPMENT OF ECONOMIC STRATEGY

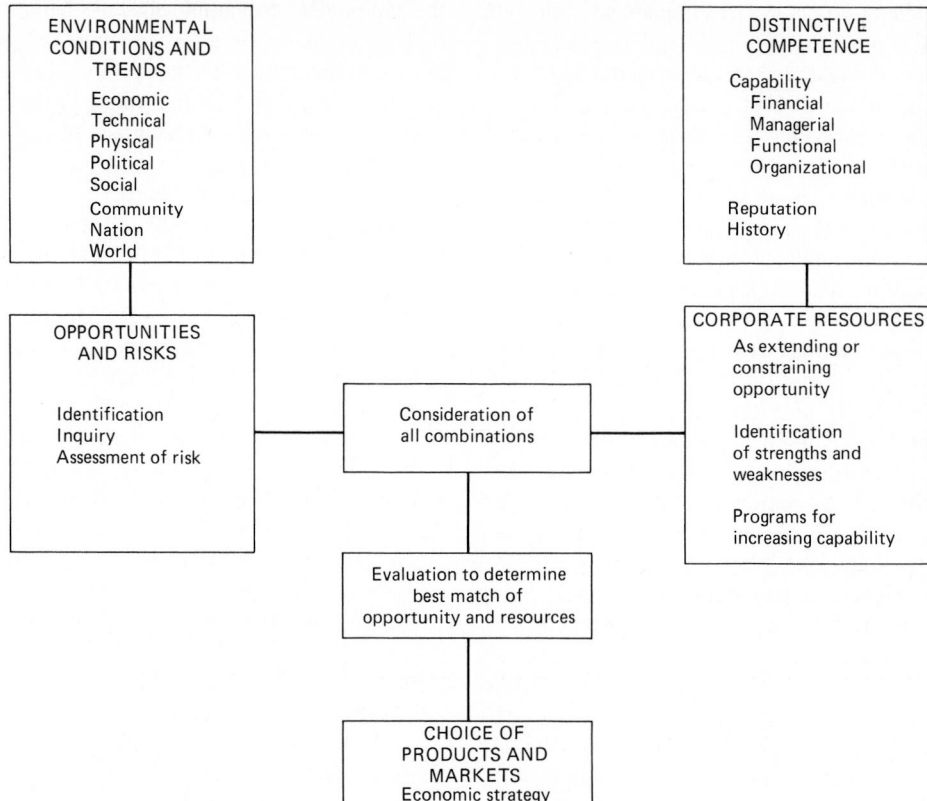

THE EVALUATION
OF BUSINESS STRATEGY*

by Richard Rumelt

Strategy can neither be formulated nor adjusted to changing circumstances without a process of strategy evaluation. Whether performed by an individual or as part of an organizational review procedure, strategy evaluation forms an essential step in the process of guiding an enterprise.

*   Originally published in William F. Glueck, *Business Policy and Strategic Management*, 3rd ed. (McGraw-Hill, 1980); reprinted with deletions by permission of the publisher.

For many executives strategy evaluation is simply an appraisal of how well a business performs. Has it grown? Is the profit rate normal or better? If the answers to these questions are affirmative, it is argued that the firm's strategy must be sound. Despite its unassailable simplicity, this line of reasoning misses the whole point of strategy—that the critical factors determining the quality of current results are often not directly observable or simply measured, and that by the time strategic opportunities or threats do directly affect operating results, it may well be too late for an effective response. Thus, strategy evaluation is an attempt to look beyond the obvious facts regarding the short-term health of a business and appraise instead those more fundamental factors and trends that govern success in the chosen field of endeavor.

THE CHALLENGE OF EVALUATION

However it is accomplished, the products of a business strategy evaluation are answers to these three questions:

1. Are the objectives of the business appropriate?
2. Are the major policies and plans appropriate?
3. Do the results obtained to date confirm or refute critical assumptions on which the strategy rests?

Devising adequate answers to these questions is neither simple nor straightforward. It requires a reasonable store of situation-based knowledge and more than the usual degree of insight. In particular, the major issues which make evaluation difficult and with which the analyst must come to grips are these:

- Each business strategy is unique. For example, one paper manufacturer might rely on its vast timber holdings to weather almost any storm while another might place primary reliance in modern machinery and an extensive distribution system. Neither strategy is "wrong" nor "right" in any absolute sense; both may be right or wrong for the firms in question. Strategy evaluation must, then, rest on a type of situational logic that does not focus on "one best way" but which can be tailored to each problem as it is faced.

- Strategy is centrally concerned with the selection of goals and objectives. Many people, including seasoned executives, find it much easier to set or try to achieve goals than to evaluate them. In part this is a consequence of training in problem solving rather than in problem structuring. It also arises out of a tendency to confuse *values*, which are fundamental expressions of human personality, with objectives, which are *devices* for lending coherence to action.

- Formal systems of strategic review, while appealing in principle, can create explosive conflict situations. Not only are there serious questions as to who is qualified to give an objective evaluation, the whole idea of strat-

egy evaluation implies management by "much more than results" and runs counter to much of currently popular management philosophy.

THE PRINCIPLES OF STRATEGY EVALUATION

. . . For our purposes a strategy is a set of objectives, policies, and plans that, taken together, define the scope of the enterprise and its approach to survival and success. Alternatively, we could say that the particular policies, plans, and objectives of a business express its strategy for coping with a complex competitive environment.

One of the fundamental tenets of science is that a theory can never be proven to be absolutely true. A theory can, however, be declared absolutely false if it fails to stand up to testing. Similarly, it is impossible to demonstrate conclusively that a particular business strategy is optimal or even to guarantee that it will work. One can, nevertheless, test it for critical flaws. Of the many tests which could be justifiably applied to a business strategy, most will fit within one of these broad criteria:

- *Consistency*: The strategy must not present mutually inconsistent goals and policies.

- *Consonance*: The strategy must represent an adaptive response to the external environment and to the critical changes occurring within it.

- *Advantage*: The strategy must provide for the creation and/or maintenance of a competitive advantage in the selected area of activity.

- *Feasibility*: The strategy must neither overtax available resources nor create unsolvable subproblems.

A strategy that fails to meet one or more of these criteria is strongly suspect. It fails to perform at least one of the key functions that are necessary for the survival of the business. Experience within a particular industry or other setting will permit the analyst to sharpen these criteria and add others that are appropriate to the situation at hand.

Consistency

Gross inconsistency within a strategy seems unlikely until it is realized that many strategies have not been explicitly formulated but have evolved over time in an ad hoc fashion. Even strategies that are the result of formal procedures may easily contain compromise arrangements between opposing power groups.

Inconsistency in strategy is not simply a flaw in logic. A key function of strategy is to provide coherence to organizational action. A clear and explicit concept of strategy can foster a climate of tacit coordination that is more efficient than most administrative mechanisms. Many high-technology firms, for example, face a basic strategic choice between offering high-cost products with high custom-engineering content and lower-cost products that are more standardized and sold at higher volume. If senior management does not enunciate a clear consistent sense of where the corporation stands on these issues, there will be continuing conflict between sales, design, engineering, and manufacturing people. A clear consistent strategy, by contrast, allows a sales engineer to negotiate a contract with a minimum of coordination—the trade-offs are an explicit part of the firm's posture.

Organizational conflict and interdepartmental bickering are often symptoms of a managerial disorder but may also indicate problems of strategic inconsistency. Here are some indicators that can help sort out these two different problems:

- If problems in coordination and planning continue despite changes in personnel and tend to be issue- rather than people-based, they are probably due to inconsistencies in strategy.

- If success for one organizational department means, or is interpreted to mean, failure for another department, the basic objective structure is inconsistent.

- If, despite attempts to delegate authority, operating problems continue to be brought to the top for the resolution of *policy* issues, the basic strategy is probably inconsistent.

A final type of consistency that must be sought in strategy is between organizational objectives and the values of the management group. Inconsistency in this area is more of a problem in strategy formulation than in the evaluation of a strategy that has already been implemented. It can still arise, however, if the future direction of the business requires changes that conflict with managerial values. The most frequent source of such conflict is growth. As a business expands beyond the scale that allows an easy informal method of operation, many executives experience a sharp sense of loss. While growth can of course be curtailed, it often will require special attention to a firm's competitive position if survival without growth is desired. The same basic issues arise when other types of personal or social values come into conflict with existing or apparently necessary policies: the resolution of the conflict will normally require an adjustment in the competitive strategy.

Consonance

The way in which a business relates to its environment has two aspects: the business must both match and be adapted to its environment and it must at the same time compete with other firms that are also trying to adapt. This dual character of the relationship between the firm and its environment has its analog in two different aspects of strategic choice and two different methods of strategy evaluation.

The first aspect of fit deals with the basic mission or scope of the business and the second with its special competitive position or "edge." Analysis of the first is normally done by looking at changing economic and social conditions over *time*. Analysis of the second, by contrast, typically focuses on the differences across firms at a given time. We call the first the "generic" aspect of strategy and the second "competitive" strategy. Exhibit 1 summarizes the differences between these concepts.

EXHIBIT 1   GENERIC VERSUS COMPETITIVE STRATEGY

	Generic	Competitive
Measure of success	Sales growth	Market share
Return to the firm	Value added	Return on investment
Function	Provision of value to the customer	Maintaining or obtaining a defensible position
Basic strategic tasks	Adapting to change and innovation	Creating barriers and deterring rivals
Method of expressing strategy	Product/market terms, functional terms	Policies leading to defensible position
Basic approach to analysis	Study of group of businesses over time	Comparision across rivals at a given time

The notion of consonance, or matching, therefore, invites a focus on generic strategy. The role of the evaluator in this case is to examine the basic pattern of economic relationships that characterize the business and determine whether or not sufficient value is being created to sustain the strategy. Most macroanalysis of changing economic conditions is oriented toward the formulation or evaluation of generic strategies. For example, a planning department forecasts that within 10 years home appliances will no longer use mechanical timers or logic. Instead, microprocessors will do the job more reliably and less expensively. The basic message here for the makers of mechanical timers is that their generic strategies are becoming obsolete, especially if they specialize in major home appliances. Note that the threat in this case is not to a particular firm, competitive position, or individual approach to the marketplace but to the basic generic mission.

One major difficulty in evaluating consonance is that most of the critical threats to a business are those which come from without, threatening an entire group of firms. Management, however, is often so engrossed in competitive thinking that such threats are only recognized after the damage has reached considerable proportions. . . .

The key to evaluating consonance is an understanding of why the business, as it currently stands, exists at all and how it assumed its current pattern. Once the analyst obtains a good grasp of the basic economic foundation that supports and defines the business, it is possible to study the consequences of key trends and changes. Without such an understanding, there is no good way of deciding what kinds of changes are most crucial and the analyst can be quickly overwhelmed with data.

Advantage

It is no exaggeration to say that competitive strategy is the art of creating or exploiting those advantages that are most telling, enduring, and most difficult to duplicate.

Competitive strategy, in contrast with generic strategy, focuses on the differences among firms rather than their common missions. The problem it addresses is not so much "how can this function be performed" but "how can *we* perform it either better than, or at least instead of, our rivals?" The chain supermarket, for example, represents a successful generic strategy. As a way of doing business, of organizing economic transactions, it has replaced almost all the smaller owner-managed food shops of an earlier era. Yet a potential or actual participant in the retail food business must go beyond this generic strategy and find a way of competing in this business. As another illustration, American Motors' early success in compact cars was generic—other firms soon copied the basic product concept. Once this happened, AMC had to try to either forge a strong competitive strategy in this area or seek a different type of competitive arena.

Competitive advantages can normally be traced to one of three roots:

- Superior resources
- Superior skills
- Superior position

The nature of the advantages produced by the first two are obvious. They represent the ability of a business to do more and/or do it better than its rivals. The critical analytical issue here is the question of which skills and resources represent advantages in which competitive arenas. The skills that make for success in the aerospace electronics industry, for instance, do not seem to have much to do with those needed in consumer electronics. Similarly, what makes for success in the early phases of an industry life cycle may be quite different than what ensures top performance in the later phases.

The idea that certain arrangements of one's resources can enhance their combined effectiveness, and perhaps even put rival forces in a state of disarray, is at the heart of the traditional notion of strategy. This kind of ''positional'' advantage is familiar to military theorists, chess players, and diplomats. Position plays a crucial role in business strategy as well. . . .

Positional advantage can be gained by foresight, superior skill and/or resources, or just plain luck. Once gained, a good position is defensible. This means that it (1) returns enough value to warrant its continued maintenance and (2) would be so costly to capture that rivals are deterred from full-scale attacks on the core of the business. Position, it must be noted, tends to be self-sustaining as long as the basic environmental factors that underlie it remain stable. Thus, entrenched firms can be almost impossible to unseat, even if their raw skill levels are only average. And when a shifting environment allows position to be gained by a new entrant or innovator, the results can be spectacular.

The types of positional advantage that are most well known are those associated with size or scale. As the scale of operations increases, most firms are able to reduce both the marginal and the total cost of each additional unit produced. Marginal costs fall due to the effects of learning and more efficient processes, and total costs per

unit fall even faster as fixed overheads are spread over a larger volume of activity. The larger firm can simply take these gains in terms of increased profitability or it can invest some of the extra returns in position-maintaining activities. By engaging in more research and development, being first to go abroad, having the largest advertising budget, and absorbing the costs involved with acting as an industry spokesman, the dominant business is rechanneling the gains obtained from its advantages into activities designed to maintain those advantages. This kind of positive feedback is the source of the power of position-based advantages—the policies that act to enhance position do not require unusual skills; they simply work most effectively for those who are already in the position in the first place.

While it is not true that larger businesses always have the advantages, it is true that larger businesses will tend to operate in markets and use procedures that turn their size to advantage. Large national consumer-products firms, for example, will normally have an advantage over smaller regional firms in the efficient use of mass advertising, especially network TV. The larger firm will, then, tend to deal in those products where the marginal effect of advertising is most potent, while the smaller firms will seek product/market positions that exploit other types of advantage.

Not all positional advantages are associated with size, although some type of uniqueness is a virtual prerequisite. The principal characteristic of good position is that it permits the firm to obtain advantage from policies that would not similarly benefit rivals without the position. For example, Volkswagen in 1966 had a strong, well-defined position as the preeminent maker of inexpensive, well-engineered, functional automobiles. This position allowed it to follow a policy of not changing its body styling. The policy both enhanced VW's position and reduced costs. Rivals could not similarly benefit from such a policy unless they could also duplicate the other aspects of VW's position. At the other end of the spectrum, Rolls-Royce employed a policy of deliberately limiting its output, a policy which enhanced its unique position and which could do so only because of that position in the first place. Mintzberg (1973b) calls strongly defensible positions and the associated policies ''gestalt strategies,'' recognizing that they are difficult to either analyze or attack in a piecemeal fashion.

Another type of positional advantage derives from successful trade names. These brands, especially when advertised, place retailers in the position of having to stock them which, in turn, reinforces the position and raises the barrier to entry still further. Such famous names as Sara Lee, Johnson & Johnson, and Kraft greatly reduce, for their holders, both the problems of gaining wide distribution for new products and obtaining trial use of new products by the buying public.

Other position-based advantages follow from such factors as:

- The ownership of special raw material sources or long-term supply contracts
- Being geographically located near key customers in a business involving significant fixed investment and high transport costs
- Being a leader in a service field that permits or requires the building of a unique experience base while serving clients
- Being a full-line producer in a market with heavy trade-up phenomena
- Having a wide reputation for providing a needed product or service trait reliably and dependably

In each case, the position permits competitive policies to be adopted that can serve to reinforce the position. *Whenever* this type of positive-feedback phenomena is encountered, the particular policy mix that creates it will be found to be a defensible business position. The key factors that sparked industrial success stories such as IBM and Eastman Kodak were the *early* and rapid domination of strong positions opened up by new technologies.

Feasibility

The final broad test of strategy is its feasibility. Can the strategy be attempted within the physical, human, and financial resources available? The financial resources of a business are the easiest to quantify and are normally the first limitation against which strategy is tested. It is sometimes forgotten, however, that innovative approaches to financing expansion can both stretch the ultimate limitations and provide a competitive advantage, even if it is only temporary. Devices such as captive finance subsidiaries, sale-leaseback arrangements, and tying plant mortgages to long-term contracts have all been used effectively to help win key positions in suddenly expanding industries.

The less quantifiable but actually more rigid limitation on strategic choice is that imposed by the individual and organizational capabilities that are available.

In assessing the organization's ability to carry out a strategy, it is helpful to ask three separate questions:

1. Has the organization demonstrated that it possesses the problem-solving abilities and/ or special competences required by the strategy? A strategy, as such, does not and cannot specify in detail each action that must be carried out. Its purpose is to provide structure to the general issue of the business' goals and approaches to coping with its environment. It is up to the members and departments of the organization to carry out the tasks defined by strategy. A strategy that requires tasks to be accomplished which fall outside the realm of available or easily obtainable skill and knowledge cannot be accepted. It is either infeasible or incomplete.

2. Has the organization demonstrated the degree of coordinative and integrative skill necessary to carry out the strategy? The key tasks required of a strategy not only require specialized skill, but often make considerable demands on the organization's ability to integrate disparate activities. . . .

3. Does the strategy challenge and motivate key personnel and is it acceptable to those who must lend their support? The purpose of strategy is to effectively deploy the unique and distinctive resources of an enterprise. If key managers are unmoved by a

strategy, not excited by its goals or methods, or strongly support an alternative, it fails in a major way. . . .

CONCLUSIONS

. . . In most medium- to large-size firms, strategy evaluation is not a purely intellectual task. The issues involved are too important and too closely associated with the distribution of power and authority for either strategy formulation or evaluation to take place in an ivory tower environment. In fact, most firms rarely engage in explicit formal strategy evaluation. Rather, the evaluation of current strategy is a continuing process and one that is difficult to separate from the normal planning, reporting, control, and reward systems of the firm. From this point of view, strategy evaluation is not so much an intellectual task as it is an organizational process.

As process, strategy evaluation is the outcome of activities and events which are strongly shaped by the firm's control and reward systems, its information and planning systems, its structure, and its history and particular culture. Thus, its performance is, in practice, tied more directly to the quality of the firm's strategic management than to any particular analytical scheme. In particular, organizing major units around the primary strategic tasks and making the extra effort required to incorporate measures of strategic success in the control system may play vital roles in facilitating strategy evaluation within the firm.

Ultimately, a firm's ability to maintain its competitive position in a world of rivalry and change may be best served by managers who can maintain a dual view of strategy and strategy evaluation—they must be willing and able to perceive the strategy within the welter of daily activity *and* to build and maintain structures and systems that make strategic factors the object of current activity.

## FOUR

STRATEGY ANALYSIS

As noted in the introduction to Chapter 3, there is a second prescriptive view, which developed in the 1980s, on the way strategy should be formulated. Its contribution is less as a new conceptual model—in fact it embraces most of the premises of the traditional model as its starting point— than in carefully structuring the kinds of formal analyses that should be undertaken to develop a successful strategy. One outcome of this more formal approach is that its adherents have come to see many strategies as fitting certain ''generic'' classifications—not being created so much individually as selected from a limited set of options based on systematic study of the firm and the industry conditions it faces. This approach has proved to be powerful and useful in many situations.

A leader of this approach is Michael Porter of the Harvard Business School, who studied at the doctoral level in Harvard's economics department. By building intellectual bridges between the fields of management policy and industrial organization—the latter a branch of economics concerned with the performance of industries as a function of their competitive characteristics— Porter elaborated on the earlier views of Andrews, Ansoff, Newman, et al. in three important ways.

First, he probed deeply into one specific aspect of their model—the assessment of the external environment, in particular the competitive situation the firm faces in its industry. In his highly successful 1980 book *Competitive Strategy*, Porter developed rather specific and detailed procedures for analyzing both competitors and industry structures in general. A summary of these (from a *Harvard Business Review* article) is presented in this chapter. Second, Porter also focused attention on a specific triad of generic strategies. He suggests—as can be seen in the second excerpt, from his 1985 book *Competitive Advantage*—that all competitive strategies can be reduced to three basic ones: (1) cost leadership, (2) differentiation, and (3) focus. Third, Porter developed several interesting views of how strategies tend to cluster: by type of industry, by groups within an industry, and so on. We present some of these basic ideas from Porter's writings in this chapter; some of his other concepts, on generic industry situations, appear in the ''Contexts'' section of the text.

The Porter readings present a number of useful concepts. But the reading by Gilbert and Strebel, two professors of strategy at the IMEDE business school in Lausanne, Switzerland, seems to knit them together in a unique way. Drawing on such Porter concepts as industry analysis, generic strategies, and strategic groups (including industry stage of development), Gilbert and Strebel suggest an integrated framework to formulate strategy. They also include in their article something akin to the value chain theme of Porter's 1985 book, which they label the "business system."

In some ways, the strategy analysis frameworks of this chapter parallel those of Andrews. But these authors add a number of new systematic and analytical elements, often creating a result that is less broad, more focused. You should consider which approach will be more effective, at least under specific circumstances.

You might also note one key divergence between Gilbert and Strebel's article and the Porter work. When Porter introduces his three generic strategies, he makes a specific case for not being "stuck in the middle," particularly between cost leadership and differentiation. Gilbert and Strebel, in contrast, introduce "outpacing" strategies designed to do just that—get the best of both these worlds. They believe that over time, through a "dynamic path," some truly successful firms manage to be both efficient in their delivery of low cost products and services and effective in their capacity to create high received value through differentiation. In reading the various cases, you may wish to consider this specific contradiction and these general views of strategy formulation, to help you decide for yourself which view better captures the realities of strategy, and under what specific circumstances each analytical approach is most useful.

The Financial Services Industry note offers an excellent opportunity for industry analysis. The Intel, General Motors, and the Royal Bank case is a powerful vehicle for competitive analysis. And the Exxon, AT&T, IBM, Matsushita, Sony, and Genetech cases raise many issues about the "value added chain" and "outpacing strategy" concepts. We hope these cases will teach you how to conduct such analysis, but at the same time will create some doubts about any specific analytical framework's capacity to capture the full richness of all major corporate strategies.

HOW COMPETITIVE FORCES SHAPE STRATEGY*
by Michael E. Porter

The essence of strategy formulation is coping with competition. Yet it is easy to view competition too narrowly and too pessimistically. While one sometimes hears executives complaining to the contrary, intense competition in an industry is neither coincidence nor bad luck.

Moreover, in the fight for market share, competition is not manifested only in the other players. Rather, competition in an industry is rooted in its underlying economics, and competitive forces exist that go well beyond the established combatants in a particular industry. Customers, suppliers, potential entrants, and substitute products are all competitors that may be more or less prominent or active depending on the industry.

The state of competition in an industry depends on five basic forces, which are diagrammed in Figure 1. The collective strength of these forces determines the ultimate profit potential of an industry. It ranges from *intense* in industries like tires, metal cans, and steel, where no company earns spectacular returns on investment, to *mild* in industries like oil field services and equipment, soft drinks, and toiletries, where there is room for quite high returns.

In the economists' "perfectly competitive" industry, jockeying for position is unbridled and entry to the industry very easy. This kind of industry structure, of course, offers the worst prospect for long-run profitability. The weaker the forces collectively, however, the greater the opportunity for superior performance.

Whatever their collective strength, the cor-

FIGURE 1   ELEMENTS OF INDUSTRY STRUCTURE

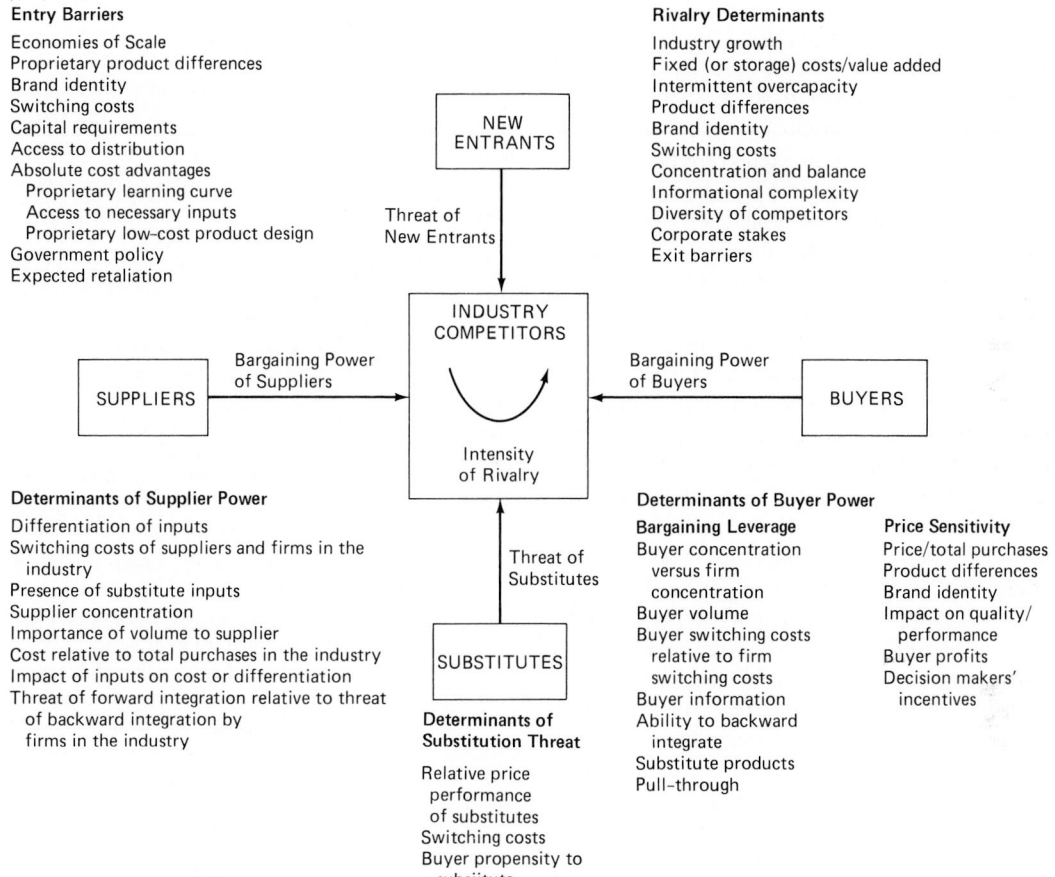

Entry Barriers

Economies of Scale
Proprietary product differences
Brand identity
Switching costs
Capital requirements
Access to distribution
Absolute cost advantages
  Proprietary learning curve
  Access to necessary inputs
  Proprietary low-cost product design
Government policy
Expected retaliation

Rivalry Determinants

Industry growth
Fixed (or storage) costs/value added
Intermittent overcapacity
Product differences
Brand identity
Switching costs
Concentration and balance
Informational complexity
Diversity of competitors
Corporate stakes
Exit barriers

Determinants of Supplier Power

Differentiation of inputs
Switching costs of suppliers and firms in the
  industry
Presence of substitute inputs
Supplier concentration
Importance of volume to supplier
Cost relative to total purchases in the industry
Impact of inputs on cost or differentiation
Threat of forward integration relative to threat
  of backward integration by
  firms in the industry

Determinants of Buyer Power

Bargaining Leverage	Price Sensitivity
Buyer concentration versus firm concentration	Price/total purchases
	Product differences
	Brand identity
Buyer volume	Impact on quality/performance
Buyer switching costs relative to firm switching costs	Buyer profits
	Decision makers' incentives
Buyer information	
Ability to backward integrate	
Substitute products	
Pull-through	

Determinants of Substitution Threat

Relative price
  performance
  of substitutes
Switching costs
Buyer propensity to
  subsiitute

Source: Excerpted with permission of The Free Press, a Division of Macmillan, Inc. from *Competitive Strategy: Techniques for Analyzing Industries and Competitors* by Michael E. Porter. Copyright © 1980 by The Free Press. [used in place of article's Figure 1 as it contains more detail]

porate strategist's goal is to find a position in the industry where his or her company can best defend itself against these forces or can influence them in its favor. The collective strength of the forces may be painfully apparent to all the antagonists; but to cope with them, the strategist must delve below the surface and analyze the sources of each. For example, what makes the industry vulnerable to entry? What determines the bargaining power of suppliers?

Knowledge of these underlying sources of competitive pressure provides the groundwork for a strategic agenda of action. They highlight the critical strengths and weaknesses of the company, animate the positioning of the company in its industry, clarify the areas where strategic changes may yield the greatest payoff, and highlight the places where industry trends promise to hold the greatest significance as either opportunities or threats. Understanding these sources also proves to be of help in considering areas for diversification.

CONTENDING FORCES

The strongest competitive force or forces determine the profitability of an industry and so are of greatest importance in strategy formulation. For example, even a company with a strong position in an industry unthreatened by potential entrants will earn low returns if it faces a superior or a lower-cost substitute product—as the leading manufacturers of vacuum tubes and coffee percolators have learned to their sorrow. In such a situation, coping with the substitute product becomes the number one strategic priority.

Different forces take on prominence, of course, in shaping competition in each industry. In the ocean-going tanker industry the key force is probably the buyers (the major oil companies), while in tires it is powerful OEM buyers coupled with tough competitors. In the steel industry the key forces are foreign competitors and substitute materials.

Every industry has an underlying structure, or a set of fundamental economic and technical characteristics, that gives rise to these competitive forces. The strategist, wanting to position his company to cope best with its industry environment or to influence that environment in the company's favor, must learn what makes the environment tick.

This view of competition pertains equally to industries dealing in services and to those selling products. To avoid monotony in this article, I refer to both products and services as "products." The same general principles apply to all types of business.

A few characteristics are critical to the strength of each competitive force. I shall discuss them in this section.

Threat of Entry

New entrants to an industry bring new capacity, the desire to gain market share, and often substantial resources. Companies diversifying through acquisition into the industry from other markets often leverage their resources to cause a shake-up, as Philip Morris did with Miller beer.

The seriousness of the threat of entry depends on the barriers present and on the reaction from existing competitors that the entrant can expect. If barriers to entry are high and a newcomer can expect sharp retaliation from the entrenched competitors, obviously he will not pose a serious threat of entering.

There are six major sources of barriers to entry:

1. *Economies of scale*—These economies deter entry by forcing the aspirant either to come in on a large scale or to accept a cost disadvantage. Scale economies in production, research, marketing, and service are probably the key barriers to entry in the mainframe computer industry, as Xerox and GE sadly discovered. Economies of scale can also act as hurdles in distribution, utilization of the sales force, financing, and nearly any other part of a business.

2. *Product differentiation*—Brand identification creates a barrier by forcing entrants to spend heavily to overcome customer loyalty. Advertising, customer service, being first in the industry, and product differences are among the factors fostering brand identification. It is perhaps the most important entry barrier in soft drinks, over-the-counter drugs, cosmetics, investment banking, and public accounting. To create high fences around their businesses, brewers couple brand identification with economies of scale in production, distribution, and marketing.

3. *Capital requirements*—The need to invest large financial resources in order to compete creates a barrier to entry, particularly if the capital is required for unrecoverable expenditures in up-front advertising or R&D. Capital is necessary not only for fixed facilities but also for customer credit, inventories, and absorbing start-up losses. While major corporations have the financial resources to invade almost any industry, the huge capital requirements in certain fields, such as computer manufacturing and mineral extraction, limit the pool of likely entrants.

4. *Cost disadvantages independent of size*—Entrenched companies may have cost advantages not available to potential rivals, no matter what their size and attainable economies of scale. These advantages can

stem from the effects of the learning curve (and of its first cousin, the experience curve), proprietary technology, access to the best raw materials sources, assets purchased at preinflation prices, government subsidies, or favorable locations. Sometimes cost advantages are legally enforceable, as they are through patents. . . . [Editors' note: See Chapter 11 of this text for a discussion of the experience curve.]

5. *Access to distribution channels*—The new boy on the block must, of course, secure distribution of his product or service. A new food product, for example, must displace others from the supermarket shelf via price breaks, promotions, intense selling efforts, or some other means. The more limited the wholesale or retail channels are and the more that existing competitors have these tied up, obviously the tougher that entry into the industry will be. Sometimes this barrier is so high that, to surmount it, a new contestant must create its own distribution channels, as Timex did in the watch industry in the 1950s.

6. *Government policy*—The government can limit or even foreclose entry to industries with such controls as license requirements and limits on access to raw materials. Regulated industries like trucking, liquor retailing, and freight forwarding are noticeable examples; more subtle government restrictions operate in fields like ski-area development and coal mining. The government also can play a major indirect role by affecting entry barriers through controls such as air and water pollution standards and safety regulations.

The potential rival's expectations about the reaction of existing competitors also will influence its decision on whether to enter. The company is likely to have second thoughts if incumbents have previously lashed out at new entrants or if:

■ The incumbents possess substantial resources to fight back, including excess cash and unused borrowing power, productive capacity, or clout with distribution channels and customers.

■ The incumbents seem likely to cut prices because of a desire to keep market shares or because of industrywide excess capacity.

■ Industry growth is slow, affecting its ability to absorb the new arrival and probably causing the financial performance of all the parties involved to decline.

Changing Conditions From a strategic standpoint there are two important additional points to note about the threat of entry.

First, it changes, of course, as these conditions change. The expiration of Polaroid's basic patents on instant photography, for instance, greatly reduced its absolute cost entry barrier built by proprietary technology. It is not surprising that Kodak plunged into the market. Product differentiation in printing has all but disappeared. Conversely, in the auto industry economies of scale increased enormously with post-World War II automation and vertical integration—virtually stopping successful new entry.

Second, strategic decisions involving a large segment of an industry can have a major impact on the conditions determining the threat of entry. For example, the actions of many U.S. wine producers in the 1960s to step up product introductions, raise advertising levels, and expand distribution nationally surely strengthened the entry roadblocks by raising economies of scale and making access to distribution channels more difficult. Similarly, decisions by members of the recreational vehicle industry to vertically integrate in order to lower costs have greatly increased the economies of scale and raised the capital cost barriers.

Powerful Suppliers and Buyers

Suppliers can exert bargaining power on participants in an industry by raising prices or reducing the quality of purchased goods and services. Powerful suppliers can thereby squeeze profitability out of an industry unable to recover cost increases in its own prices. By raising their prices, soft drink concentrate producers have contributed to the erosion of profitability of bottling companies because the bottlers, facing intense competition from powdered mixes, fruit drinks, and other beverages, have limited freedom to raise *their* prices accordingly. Customers likewise can force down prices, demand higher quality or more service, and play competitors off against each other—all at the expense of industry profits.

The power of each important supplier or buyer group depends on a number of characteristics of its market situation and on the relative importance of its sales or purchases to the industry compared with its overall business.

A *supplier* group is powerful if:

- It is dominated by a few companies and is more concentrated than the industry it sells to.

- Its product is unique or at least differentiated, or if it has built up switching costs. Switching costs are fixed costs buyers face in changing suppliers. These arise because, among other things, a buyer's product specifications tie it to particular suppliers, it has invested heavily in specialized ancillary equipment or in learning how to operate a supplier's equipment (as in computer software), or its production lines are connected to the supplier's manufacturing facilities (as in some manufacture of beverage containers).

- It is not obliged to contend with other products for sale to the industry. For instance, the competition between the steel companies and the aluminum companies to sell to the can industry checks the power of each supplier.

- It poses a credible threat of integrating forward into the industry's business. This provides a check against the industry's ability to improve the terms on which it purchases.

- The industry is not an important customer of the supplier group. If the industry *is* an important customer, suppliers' fortunes will be closely tied to the industry, and they will want to protect the industry through reasonable pricing and assistance in activities like R&D and lobbying.

A *buyer* group is powerful if:

- It is concentrated or purchases in large volumes. Large-volume buyers are particularly

potent forces if heavy fixed costs characterize the industry—as they do in metal containers, corn refining, and bulk chemicals, for example—which raise the stakes to keep capacity filled.

- The products it purchases from the industry are standard or undifferentiated. The buyers, sure that they can always find alternative suppliers, may play one company against another, as they do in aluminum extrusion.

- The products it purchases from the industry form a component of its product and represent a significant fraction of its cost. The buyers are likely to shop for a favorable price and purchase selectively. Where the product sold by the industry in question is a small fraction of buyers' costs, buyers are usually much less price sensitive.

- It earns low profits, which create great incentive to lower its purchasing costs. Highly profitable buyers, however, are generally less price sensitive (that is, of course, if the item does not represent a large fraction of their costs).

- The industry's product is unimportant to the quality of the buyers' products or services. Where the quality of the buyers' products is very much affected by the industry's product, buyers are generally less price sensitive. Industries in which this situation obtains include oil field equipment, where a malfunction can lead to large losses, and enclosures for electronic medical and test instruments, where the quality of the enclosure can influence the user's impression about the quality of the equipment inside.

- The industry's product does not save the buyer money. Where the industry's product or service can pay for itself many times over, the buyer is rarely price sensitive; rather, he is interested in quality. This is true in services like investment banking and public accounting, where errors in judgment can be costly and embarrassing, and in businesses like the logging of oil wells, where an accurate survey can save thousands of dollars in drilling costs.

- The buyers pose a credible threat of integrating backward to make the industry's product. The Big Three auto producers and major buyers of cars have often used the threat of self-manufacture as a bargaining lever.

But sometimes an industry engenders a threat to buyers that its members may integrate forward.

Most of these sources of buyer power can be attributed to consumers as a group as well as to industrial and commercial buyers; only a modification of the frame of reference is necessary. Consumers tend to be more price sensitive if they are purchasing products that are undifferentiated, expensive relative to their incomes, and of a sort where quality is not particularly important.

The buying power of retailers is determined by the same rules, with one important addition. Retailers can gain significant bargaining power over manufacturers when they can influence consumers' purchasing decisions, as they do in audio components, jewelry, appliances, sporting goods, and other goods.

Strategic Action A company's choice of suppliers to buy from or buyer groups to sell to should be viewed as a crucial strategic decision. A company can improve its strategic posture by finding suppliers or buyers who possess the least power to influence it adversely.

Most common is the situation of a company being able to choose whom it will sell to—in other words, buyer selection. Rarely do all the buyer groups a company sells to enjoy equal power. Even if a company sells to a single industry, segments usually exist within that industry that exercise less power (and that are therefore less price sensitive) than others. For example, the replacement market for most products is less price sensitive than the overall market.

As a rule, a company can sell to powerful buyers and still come away with above-average profitability only if it is a low-cost producer in its industry or if its product enjoys some unusual, if not unique, features. In supplying large customers with electric motors, Emerson Electric earns high returns because its low cost position permits the company to meet or undercut competitors' prices.

If the company lacks a low cost position or a unique product, selling to everyone is self-defeating because the more sales it achieves, the more vulnerable it becomes. The company may have to muster the courage to turn away business and sell only to less potent customers.

Buyer selection has been a key to the success of National Can and Crown Cork & Seal. They focus on the segments of the can industry where they can create product differentiation, minimize the threat of backward integration, and otherwise mitigate the awesome power of their customers. Of course, some industries do not enjoy the luxury of selecting "good" buyers.

As the factors creating supplier and buyer power change with time or as a result of a company's strategic decisions, naturally the power of these groups rises or declines. In the ready-to-wear clothing industry, as the buyers (department stores and clothing stores) have become more concentrated and control has passed to large chains, the industry has come under increasing pressure and suffered falling margins. The industry has been unable to differentiate its product or engender switching costs that lock in its buyers enough to neutralize these trends.

Substitute Products

By placing a ceiling on prices it can charge, substitute products or services limit the potential of an industry. Unless it can upgrade the quality of the product or differentiate it somehow (as via marketing), the industry will suffer in earnings and possibly in growth.

Manifestly, the more attractive the price-performance trade-off offered by substitute products, the firmer the lid placed on the industry's profit potential. Sugar producers confronted with the large-scale commercialization of high-fructose corn syrup, a sugar substitute, are learning this lesson today.

Substitutes not only limit profits in normal times; they also reduce the bonanza an industry can reap in boom times. In 1978 the producers of fiberglass insulation enjoyed unprecedented demand as a result of high energy costs and severe winter weather. But the industry's ability to raise prices was tempered by the plethora of insulation substitutes, including cellulose, rock wool, and styrofoam. These substitutes are bound to become an even stronger force once the current round of plant additions by fiberglass insulation producers has boosted capacity enough to meet demand (and then some).

Substitute products that deserve the most attention strategically are those that (a) are subject to trends improving their price-performance trade-off with the industry's product, or (b) are produced by industries earning high profits. Substitutes often come rapidly into play if some development increases competition in their industries and causes price reduction or performance improvement.

Jockeying for Position

Rivalry among existing competitors takes the familiar form of jockeying for position—using tactics like price competition, product introduction, and advertising slugfests. Intense rivalry is related to the presence of a number of factors:

- Competitors are numerous or are roughly equal in size and power. In many U.S. industries in recent years foreign contenders, of course, have become part of the competitive picture.

- Industry growth is slow, precipitating fights for market share that involve expansion-minded members.

- The product or service lacks differentiation or switching costs, which lock in buyers and protect one combatant from raids on its customers by another.

- Fixed costs are high or the product is perishable, creating strong temptation to cut prices. Many basic materials businesses, like paper and aluminum, suffer from this problem when demand slackens.

- Capacity is normally augmented in large increments. Such additions, as in the chlorine and vinyl chloride businesses, disrupt the industry's supply-demand balance and often lead to periods of overcapacity and price cutting.

- Exit barriers are high. Exit barriers, like very specialized assets or management's loyalty to a particular business, keep companies competing even though they may be earning low or even negative returns on investment. Excess capacity remains functioning, and the profitability of the healthy competitors suffers as the sick ones hang on. If the entire industry suffers from overcapacity, it may seek government help—particularly if foreign competition is present.

- The rivals are diverse in strategies, origins, and "personalities." They have different ideas about how to compete and continually run head-on into each other in the process. . . .

While a company must live with many of these factors—because they are built into industry economics—it may have some latitude for improving matters through strategic shifts. For example, it may try to raise buyers' switching costs or increase product differentiation. A focus on selling efforts in the fastest-growing segments of the industry or on market areas with the lowest fixed costs can reduce the impact of industry rivalry. If it is feasible, a company can try to avoid confrontation with competitors having high exit barriers and can thus sidestep involvement in bitter price cutting.

FORMULATION OF STRATEGY

Once the corporate strategist has assessed the forces affecting competition in his industry and their underlying causes, he can identify his company's strengths and weaknesses. The crucial strengths and weaknesses from a strategic standpoint are the company's posture vis-à-vis the underlying causes of each force. Where does it stand against substitutes? Against the sources of entry barriers?

Then the strategist can devise a plan of action that may include (1) positioning the company so that its capabilities provide the best defense against the competitive force; and/or (2) influencing the balance of the forces through strategic moves, thereby improving the company's position; and/or (3) anticipating shifts in the factors underlying the forces and responding to them, with the hope of exploiting change by choosing a strategy appropriate for the new competitive balance before opponents recognize it. I shall consider each strategic approach in turn.

Positioning the Company

The first approach takes the structure of the industry as given and matches the company's strengths and weaknesses to it. Strategy can be viewed as building defenses against the competitive forces or as finding positions in the industry where the forces are weakest.

Knowledge of the company's capabilities and of the causes of the competitive forces will highlight the areas where the company should confront competition and where avoid it. If the company is a low-cost producer, it may choose to confront powerful buyers while it takes care to sell them only products not vulnerable to competition from substitutes. . . .

Influencing the Balance

When dealing with the forces that drive industry competition, a company can devise a strategy that takes the offensive. This posture is designed to do more than merely cope with the forces themselves; it is meant to alter their causes.

Innovations in marketing can raise brand identification or otherwise differentiate the product. Capital investments in large-scale facilities or vertical integration affect entry barriers. The balance of forces is partly a result of external factors and partly in the company's control.

Exploiting Industry Change

Industry evolution is important strategically because evolution, of course, brings with it changes in the sources of competition I have identified. In the familiar product life-cycle pattern, for example, growth rates change, product differentiation is said to decline as the business becomes more mature, and the companies tend to integrate vertically.

These trends are not so important in themselves; what is critical is whether they affect the sources of competition. . . .

Obviously, the trends carrying the highest priority from a strategic standpoint are those that affect the most important sources of competition in the industry and those that elevate new causes to the forefront. . . .

The framework for analyzing competition that I have described can also be used to predict the eventual profitability of an industry. In long-range planning the task is to examine each competitive force, forecast the magnitude of each underlying cause, and then construct a composite picture of the likely profit potential of the industry. . . .

The key to growth—even survival—is to stake out a position that is less vulnerable to attack from head-to-head opponents, whether established or new, and less vulnerable to erosion from the direction of buyers, suppliers, and substitute goods. Establishing such a position can take many forms—solidifying relationships with favorable customers, differentiating the product either substantively or psychologically through marketing, integrating forward or backward, establishing technological leadership.

GENERIC COMPETITIVE STRATEGIES*

by Michael E. Porter

[A] central question in competitive strategy is a firm's relative position within its industry. Positioning determines whether a firm's profitability is above or below the industry average. A firm that can position itself well may earn high rates of return even though industry structure is unfavorable and the average profitability of the industry is therefore modest.

The fundamental basis of above-average performance in the long run is *sustainable competitive advantage*. Though a firm can have a myriad of strengths and weaknesses vis-à-vis its competitors, there are two basic types of competitive advantage a firm can possess: low cost or differentiation. The significance of any strength or weakness a firm possesses is ultimately a function of its impact on relative cost or differentiation. Cost advantage and differentiation in turn stem from industry structure. They result from a firm's ability to cope with the five forces better than its rivals.

The two basic types of competitive advantage combined with the scope of activities for which a firm seeks to achieve them lead to three *generic strategies* for achieving above-average performance in an industry: cost leadership, differentiation, and focus. The focus strategy has two variants, cost focus and differentiation focus. The generic strategies are shown in Figure 1.

Each of the generic strategies involves a fundamentally different route to competitive advantage, combining a choice about the type of competitive advantage sought with the scope of the strategic target in which competitive advantage is to be achieved. The cost leadership and differentiation strategies seek competitive advantage in a broad range of industry segments, while focus strategies aim at cost advantage (cost focus) or differentiation (differentiation focus) in a narrow segment. The specific actions required to implement each generic strategy vary widely from industry to industry, as do the feasible generic strategies in a particular industry. While selecting and implementing a generic strategy is far from simple, however, they are the logical routes to competitive advantage that must be probed in any industry.

The notion underlying the concept of generic strategies is that competitive advantage is at the heart of any strategy, and achieving competitive advantage requires a firm to make a choice—if a firm is to attain a competitive advantage, it must make a choice about the type of competitive advantage it seeks to attain and the scope within which it will attain it. Being "all things to all people" is a recipe for strategic mediocrity and below-average performance, because it often means that a firm has no competitive advantage at all.

COST LEADERSHIP

Cost leadership is perhaps the clearest of the three generic strategies. In it, a firm sets out to become *the* low-cost producer in its industry. The firm has a broad scope and serves many industry segments, and may even operate in related indus-

COMPETITIVE ADVANTAGE

	Lower Cost	Differentiation
Broad Target	1. Cost Leadership	2. Differentiation
Narrow Target	3A. Cost Focus	3B. Differentiation Focus

COMPETITIVE SCOPE

FIGURE 1
THREE GENERIC STRATEGIES

tries—the firm's breadth is often important to its cost advantage. The sources of cost advantage are varied and depend on the structure of the industry. They may include the pursuit of economies of scale, proprietary technology, preferential access to raw materials, and other factors. . . In TV sets, for example, cost leadership requires efficient size picture tube facilities, a low-cost design, automated assembly, and global scale over which to amortize R&D. In security guard services, cost advantage requires extremely low overhead, a plentiful source of low-cost labor, and efficient training procedures because of high turnover. Low-cost producer status involves more than just going down the learning curve. A low-cost producer must find and exploit all sources of cost advantage. Low-cost producers typically sell a standard, or no-frills, product and place considerable emphasis on reaping scale or absolute cost advantages from all sources.

If a firm can achieve and sustain overall cost leadership, then it will be an above-average performer in its industry provided it can command prices at or near the industry average. At equivalent or lower prices than its rivals, a cost leader's low-cost position translates into higher returns. A cost leader, however, cannot ignore the bases of differentiation. If its product is not perceived as comparable or acceptable by buyers, a cost leader will be forced to discount prices well below competitors' to gain sales. This may nullify the benefits of its favorable cost position. Texas Instruments (in watches) and Northwest Airlines (in air transportation) are two low-cost firms that fell into this trap. Texas Instruments could not overcome its disadvantage in differentiation and exited the watch industry. Northwest Airlines recognized its problem in time, and has instituted efforts to improve marketing, passenger service, and service to travel agents to make its product more comparable to those of its competitors.

A cost leader must achieve *parity* or *proximity* in the bases of differentiation relative to its competitors to be an above-average performer, even though it relies on cost leadership for its competitive advantage. Parity in the bases of differentiation allows a cost leader to translate its cost advantage directly into higher profits than competitors.[1] Proximity in differentiation means that the price discount necessary to achieve an acceptable market share does not offset a cost leader's cost advantage and hence the cost leader earns above-average returns.

The strategic logic of cost leadership usually requires that a firm be *the* cost leader, not one of several firms vying for this position. Many firms have made serious strategic errors by failing to recognize this. When there is more than one aspiring cost leader, rivalry among them is usually fierce because every point of market share is viewed as crucial. Unless one firm can gain a cost lead and "persuade" others to abandon their strategies, the consequences for profitability (and long-run industry structure) can be disastrous, as has been the case in a number of petrochemical industries. Thus cost leadership is a strategy particularly dependent on preemption, unless major technological change allows a firm to radically change its cost position.

DIFFERENTIATION

The second generic strategy is differentiation. In a differentiation strategy, a firm seeks to be unique in its industry along some dimensions that are widely valued by buyers. It selects one or more attributes that many buyers in an industry perceive as important, and uniquely positions itself to meet those needs. It is rewarded for its uniqueness with a premium price.

The means for differentiation are peculiar to each industry. Differentiation can be based on the product itself, the delivery system by which it is sold, the marketing approach, and a broad range of other factors. In construction equipment, for example, Caterpillar Tractor's differentiation is based on product durability, service, spare parts availability, and an excellent dealer network. In cosmetics, differentiation tends to be based more

---

Parity implies either an identical product offering to competitors, or a different combination of product attributes that is equally preferred by buyers.

on product image and the positioning of counters in the stores. . . .

A firm that can achieve and sustain differentiation will be an above-average performer in its industry if its price premium exceeds the extra costs incurred in being unique. A differentiator, therefore, must always seek ways of differentiating that lead to a price premium greater than the cost of differentiating. A differentiator cannot ignore its cost position, because its premium prices will be nullified by a markedly inferior cost position. A differentiator thus aims at cost *parity* or *proximity* relative to its competitors, by reducing cost in all areas that do not affect differentiation.

The logic of the differentiation strategy requires that a firm choose attributes in which to differentiate itself that are *different* from its rivals'. A firm must truly be unique at something or be perceived as unique if it is to expect a premium price. In contrast to cost leadership, however, there can be more than one successful differentiation strategy in an industry if there are a number of attributes that are widely valued by buyers.

FOCUS

The third generic strategy is focus. This strategy is quite different from the others because it rests on the choice of a narrow competitive scope within an industry. The focuser selects a segment or group of segments in the industry and tailors its strategy to serving them to the exclusion of others. By optimizing its strategy for the target segments, the focuser seeks to achieve a competitive advantage in its target segments even though it does not possess a competitive advantage overall.

The focus strategy has two variants. In *cost focus* a firm seeks a cost advantage in its target segment, while in *differentiation focus* a firm seeks differentiation in its target segment. Both variants of the focus strategy rest on *differences* between a focuser's target segments and other segments in the industry. The target segments must either have buyers with unusual needs or else the production and delivery system that best serves the target segment must differ from that of other industry segments. Cost focus exploits differences in cost behavior in some segments, while differentiation focus exploits the special needs of buyers in certain segments. Such differences imply that the segments are poorly served by broadly-targeted competitors who serve them at the same time as they serve others. The focuser can thus achieve competitive advantage by dedicating itself to the segments exclusively. Breadth of target is clearly a matter of degree, but the essence of focus is the exploitation of a narrow target's differences from the balance of the industry.[2] Narrow focus in and of itself is not sufficient for above-average performance.

A good example of a focuser who has exploited differences in the production process that best serves different segments is Hammermill Paper. Hammermill has increasingly been moving toward relatively low-volume, high-quality specialty papers, where the larger paper companies with higher volume machines face a stiff cost penalty for short production runs. Hammermill's equipment is more suited to shorter runs with frequent setups.

A focuser takes advantage of suboptimization in either direction by broadly-targeted competitors. Competitors may be *underperforming* in meeting the needs of a particular segment, which opens the possibility for differentiation focus. Broadly-targeted competitors may also be *overperforming* in meeting the needs of a segment, which means that they are bearing higher than necessary cost in serving it. An opportunity for cost focus may be present in just meeting the needs of such a segment and no more.

If a focuser's target segment is not different from other segments, then the focus strategy will

[2]   *Overall differentiation and differentiation focus are perhaps the most often confused strategies in practice. The difference is that the overall differentiator bases its strategy on widely valued attributes (e.g., IBM in computers), while the differentiation focuser looks for segments with special needs and meets them better (e.g., Cray Research in computers).*

not succeed. In soft drinks, for example, Royal Crown has focused on cola drinks, while Coca-Cola and Pepsi have broad product lines with many flavored drinks. Royal Crown's segment, however, can be well served by Coke and Pepsi at the same time they are serving other segments. Hence Coke and Pepsi enjoy competitive advantages over Royal Crown in the cola segment due to the economies of having a broader line.

If a firm can achieve sustainable cost leadership (cost focus) or differentiation (differentiation focus) in its segment and the segment is structurally attractive, then the focuser will be an above-average performer in its industry. Segment structural attractiveness is a necessary condition because some segments in an industry are much less profitable than others. There is often room for several sustainable focus strategies in an industry, provided that focusers choose different target segments. Most industries have a variety of segments, and each one that involves a different buyer need or a different optimal production or delivery system is a candidate for a focus strategy. . . .

STUCK IN THE MIDDLE

A firm that engages in each generic strategy but fails to achieve any of them is "stuck in the middle." It possesses no competitive advantage. This strategic position is usually a recipe for below-average performance. A firm that is stuck in the middle will compete at a disadvantage because the cost leader, differentiators, or focusers will be better positioned to compete in any segment. If a firm that is stuck in the middle is lucky enough to discover a profitable product or buyer, competitors with a sustainable competitive advantage will quickly eliminate the spoils. In most industries, quite a few competitors are stuck in the middle.

A firm that is stuck in the middle will earn attractive profits only if the structure of its industry is highly favorable, or if the firm is fortunate enough to have competitors that are also stuck in the middle. Usually, however, such a firm

will be much less profitable than rivals achieving one of the generic strategies. Industry maturity tends to widen the performance differences between firms with a generic strategy and those that are stuck in the middle, because it exposes ill-conceived strategies that have been carried along by rapid growth.

Becoming stuck in the middle is often a manifestation of a firm's unwillingness to make *choices* about how to compete. It tries for competitive advantage through every means and achieves none, because achieving different types of competitive advantage usually requires inconsistent actions. Becoming stuck in the middle also afflicts successful firms, who compromise their generic strategy for the sake of growth or prestige. A classic example is Laker Airways, which began with a clear cost focus strategy based on no-frills operation in the North Atlantic market, aimed at a particular segment of the traveling public that was extremely price-sensitive. Over time, however, Laker began adding frills, new services, and new routes. It blurred its image, and suboptimized its service and delivery system. The consequences were disastrous, and Laker eventually went bankrupt.

The temptation to blur a generic strategy, and therefore become stuck in the middle, is particularly great for a focuser once it has dominated its target segments. Focus involves deliberately limiting potential sales volume. Success can lead a focuser to lose sight of the reasons for its success and compromise its focus strategy for growth's sake. Rather than compromise its generic strategy, a firm is usually better off finding new industries in which to grow where it can use its generic strategy again or exploit interrelationships. . . .

The concept of generic strategies is based on the premise that there are a number of ways in which competitive advantage can be achieved, depending on industry structure. If all firms in an industry followed the principles of competitive strategy, each would pick different bases for competitive advantage. While not all would succeed, the generic strategies provide alternate routes to superior performance. Some strategic planning concepts have been narrowly based on only one route to competitive advantage, most notably cost. Such concepts not only fail to explain the success of many firms, but they can also lead all firms in an industry to pursue the same type of competitive advantage in the same way—with predictably disastrous results. . . .

DEVELOPING COMPETITIVE ADVANTAGE*

by Xavier Gilbert and Paul Strebel

Different industries offer different competitive opportunities and, as a result, successful strategies vary from one industry to another. Identifying which strategies can lead to competitive advantages in an industry may be done in three main steps:

1. *Industry Definition*: This involves defining the boundaries of the industry, learning its rules of the game and identifying the other players.

2. *Identification of Possible Competitive Moves*: Competitive moves exploit the possible sources of competitive advantages in the industry. Their degree of effectiveness evolves with the industry life cycle and is influenced by the moves of other competitors.

3. *Selecting Among Generic Strategies*: Successful strategies rely on a sequence of competitive moves. There are only a few such successful sequences corresponding to different industry situations.

We shall discuss each of these steps in turn.

*   This article was prepared especially for this book, and was also published with modifications in *The Handbook of Business Strategy: 1986–1987 Year Book*, William D. Guth (ed.), (Warrer, Gorham and Lamont, 1986), used with the permission of Xavier Gilbert and Paul Strebel.

INDUSTRY DEFINITION

The arena of competition within which an industry member should fight will be described in terms of its boundaries, its rules of the game, and its players.

Identifying the Boundaries of the Industry

In identifying what constitutes the industry, we must take into account all the activities that are necessary to deliver a product or service that meets the expectations of a market. In this regard, many definitions of a company's business, or of its industry, have been too narrow: there is more to its business than a product, a process and a market; there is in fact an entire chain of activities, from product design to product utilization by the final customer, that must be mobilized to meet certain market expectations.

The most commonly accepted term to designate this chain of activities is the *business system*. The concept, or some variation of it, has been used frequently under different names, such as ''industry dynamics'' or ''value chain''; the term ''business system'' was coined in the Seventies by the consulting firm McKinsey & Company, from whom we borrow it. Some examples will illustrate why it is important to take into account the entire chain of activities represented by the business system when deciding how to compete.

The first example is provided by the personal computer industry (Figure 1). The business system of the personal computer industry includes a wide range of activities: product design, component manufacturing, different stages of assembly, software development, marketing, selling, distribution, service and support to the customer, and the utilization of the product by the customer. Each of these activities is expected to add value to the product so that it meets the needs of the customer. A view of all the activities necessary to serve customer expectations, as provided by the industry's business system, is thus the starting point of industry analysis.

Different competitors have made different

FIGURE 1 THE PC INDUSTRY

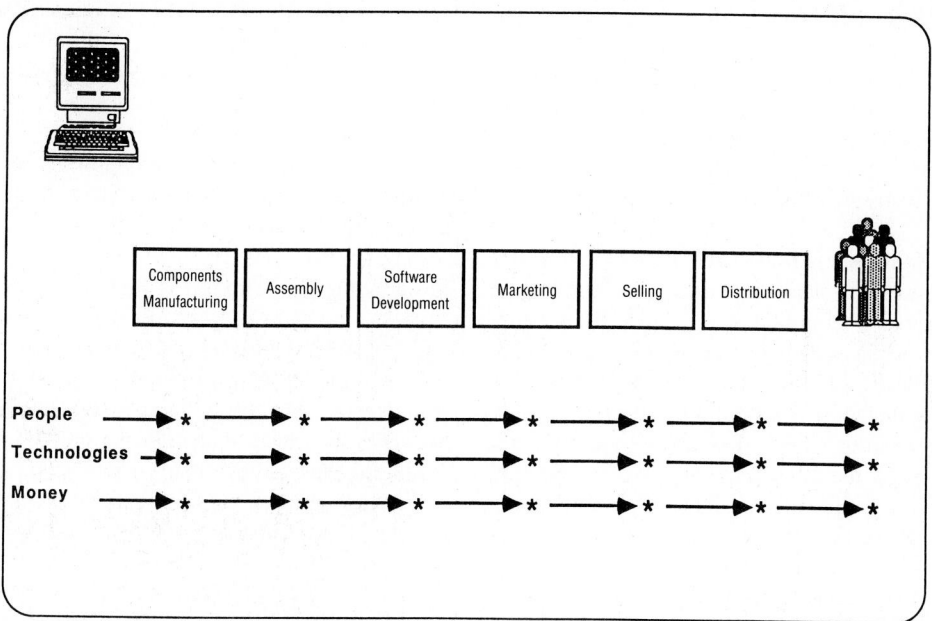

choices with respect to how these activities should be dealt with. Some have designed their product around the "IBM industry standard" in order to have access to software, while others have been using a proprietary operating system. Some are designing their own components, while others are finding sources for them outside. Some have selectively authorized dealers to sell their products, while others use mass-retailing channels and others again sell directly to the final customer. This shows that there may be different ways to use the activities in the business system to provide value to the final customer.

Rather than considering the company as competing *in an industry*, it should thus be seen as competing *within a business system*, in the same way as a chess player uses the resources of a chessboard. A chess player does not try to win by asking simply, "How do I win at chess?" Instead, the player asks, "How should I use my pawns, my rooks, my knights, my bishops, my queen, and even my king?" Similarly, each personal computer company should see itself as competing with other companies on design, on compo-

nent manufacturing, on assembly of specific configurations, on software development, on marketing, on selling, on distribution, and on service support to the customer, and not simply as competing "in the personal computer industry."

Learning the Rules of the Game

Each activity in the business system adds perceived value to the product or service. Value,[1] for the customer, is the perceived stream of benefits that accrue from obtaining the product or service. Price is what the customer is willing to pay for that stream of benefits. If the price of a good or service is high, it must provide high value, otherwise it is driven out of the market. If the value of a good or service is low, its price must be low, otherwise it is also driven out of the market. Hence, in a competitive situation, and over a period of time, the price customers are willing to pay for a good or service is a good proxy measure of its value.

[1] *"Value" is used here with the meaning it is given by economists in the utility theory.*

The "game" is to create a disequilibrium between the perceived value offered and the price asked by either increasing the former or by reducing the latter. This modifies the terms of competition and potentially drives competitors out of the market. Competitors will have to respond by either offering more perceived value for the same price, or by offering the same value at a lower price.

At the same time, each activity in the business system is performed at a cost. Getting the stream of benefits that accrue from the good or service to the customer is thus done at a certain "delivered cost" which sets a lower limit to the price of the good or service if the business system is to remain profitable. Decreasing the price will thus imply that the delivered cost be first decreased by adjusting the business system. As a result, the rules of the game may also be described as providing the highest possible perceived value to the final customer, at the lowest possible delivered cost.

In addition, the intrinsic logic of the business system must also be taken into account. This logic is dictated by the fact that the business-system activities must be coordinated to provide a specific final product. This requirement is best examined at the level of the resources needed for each activity: people, technologies and money.

The personal computer industry again illustrates the point. Among the resources needed to perform the various activities of the business system, the technologies will be used as an example. First, the final customers are not supposed to be computer experts. Their technological know-how might be in the areas of financial analysis, accounting or text processing, not in programming or establishing communication protocols with peripherals. This implies technological choices at the level of product and software design that will make the machine user-friendly. It also implies that the technology required to service the machine and to assist customers, also selected at the time of product design, be compatible with the technology available in the distribution channels.

Similar consistency requirements could be observed with respect to the other resources: people and money. If these rules of the game were not respected, the business system could not deliver a product or service of desired perceived value. Laying out the activities of the business system and the resources required by each of them is thus necessary before the game can be played effectively.

Identifying the Other Players

"Players" in a business system do not consist only of competitors; they may be other participants in the business system that perform vital activities. For the provider of a product or service, managing the business system can be complicated by players up- and down-stream in the system. By playing an optimal game from their perspective, these other participants may suboptimize the whole business system and put pressure on other activities.

Consider for example the Swiss watch industry (Figure 2). As long as competition was limited, the Swiss watch manufacturers, who were essentially fragmented assemblers, enjoyed satisfactory margins, even though their value added was small relative to the entire business system. But the industry experienced intense global competition during the Seventies and Eighties, leading to sharp price decreases. The first reaction was to believe that competition among watchmakers was the source of these difficulties. Attempts were made to restructure the Swiss watch industry so as to obtain economies of scale similar to those of global competitors.

However, the business system shows clearly that competition among watchmakers was not the biggest problem. Producing cheaper watches was necessary, but not sufficient. The Swiss watchmakers were competing fiercely for the consumers' money with costly distribution channels whose added value was questionable for a fast growing mass market. Developing a watch which would not only be inexpensive, but could also be sold through low-margin distribution channels with no service, such as the Swatch,

FIGURE 2   THE SWISS WATCH INDUSTRY

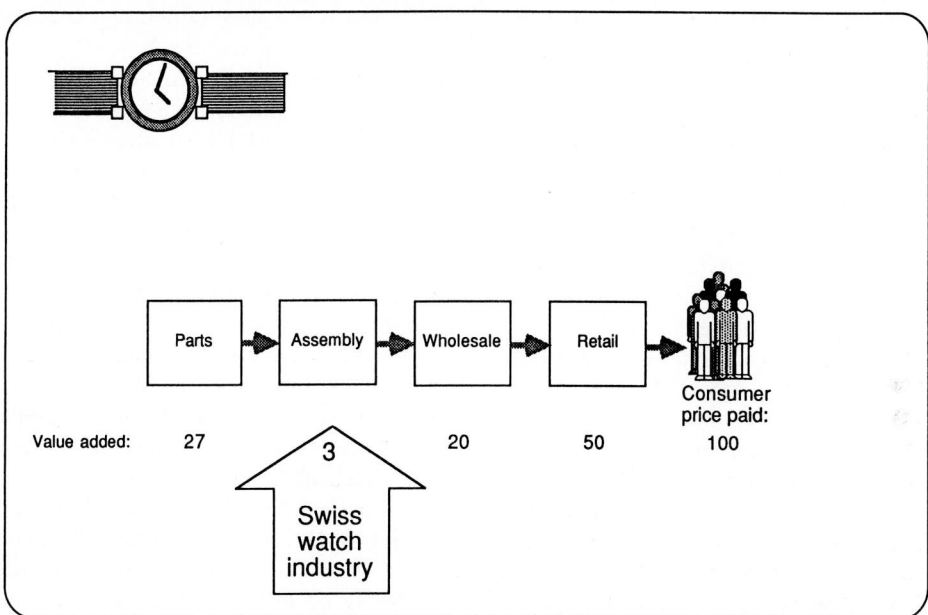

Value added: 27   3   20   50   100

Parts → Assembly → Wholesale → Retail → Consumer price paid:

Swiss watch industry

was the way to effectively circumvent this form of competition.

COMPETITIVE MOVES

Competitive advantages are built on the ability to utilize the business system to provide final customers with the desired perceived value, at the lowest delivered cost. However, not all the activities of a business system offer the same potential to build these competitive advantages. In addition, their choice is affected by the stage of development of the industry as well as by the moves of other competitors. This leads to the identification of a limited number of generic moves to gain competitive advantages.

Competitive Advantages Offered by the Business System

Superior profitability requires either higher perceived value and/or lower delivered cost than the competition. This is achieved either through superior performance in at least one of the busi-

ness-system activities, or through a creative and innovative combination of several activities. Such *competitive formulas* are the basis of all successful strategies.

For example, in the watch industry the main activities of the business system include design, manufacturing of movement parts, movement assembly, case manufacturing and assembly, wholesaling, and retail. Each of these activities can be performed to maximize the perceived value for the final user, or to minimize the delivered cost. Design, for example, can emphasize luxury and elegance, or it can ensure low cost manufacturing. Traditional distribution channels through wholesalers and specialty stores will provide more perceived value, while mass distribution directly through low-margin outlets will contribute to a low delivered cost. A range of competitive formulas can thus be developed, combining the various activities of the business system in a manner that will provide the desired perceived value at the desired delivered cost.

Two observations, however, suggest that this range of possible competitive formulas is not very wide. The first one is that there is an internal logic to each business system. The balance between perceived value and delivered cost cannot be established for one activity independently of the others. For example, it is not possible to use traditional distribution channels to distribute the Swatch. Because of the high distribution margins and of the limited volume the delivered cost would be higher than the perceived value. This is indeed what is meant by a competitive formula. The various activities of the business system must combine high perceived value and low delivered cost in a coherent manner.

The second observation, is that high perceived value and low delivered cost constitute the only possible generic competitive moves. Experience shows that there are no other possibilities. There are only variations around these two main themes, as allowed by the expectations of different market segments. Strategic advantages are obtained by combining them in a sequence, one being implemented preferably in a way that prepares the implementation of the other at a later time.

Many failures have been caused by the inability to put together coherent business systems, with respect to low delivered cost and high perceived value. This was exactly how the Swiss watch industry got into trouble, trying to compete in markets expecting low delivered cost with a business system designed for high perceived value. When the promoters of the Swatch saw that the biggest revolution in the industry was not a technological one, but a distribution one, they engineered a fine-tuned competitive formula in which each business-system activity contributed to delivering a watch for less than SFr50 (about $25). Even though the Swatch is very precise and carries an element of snobbish appeal, the move was quite clearly a low-delivered-cost one, with a formula that provided maximum perceived value within the low-delivered-cost constraint.

Stage of Development of the Industry

Although it would be theoretically feasible to choose either of these two moves—high-perceived-value or low-delivered-cost—at any point in time, the actual possibilities are in fact strongly influenced by the stage of industry development. The personal computer industry will be used as an example of the inferences that can be drawn from an industry life cycle to assist in the diagnosis of potential competitive advantages.

Consider first the personal computer industry in the second half of the seventies. The characteristics of the product were in a state of flux, with many competing versions. The manufacturing process was not yet a matter of real concern, as the technology was still evolving. The business system of the industry had not stabilized. Competition was restricted to product innovation and development. These characteristics are typical of an *emerging industry* offering *high perceived value* to a limited market (Figure 3).

Consider now the personal computer industry after IBM's entry. Even though IBM's product was not regarded by seasoned users as particularly innovative on the technological side, it had the perhaps unintended advantage of embodying an acceptable common denominator of characteristics desired by a wide cross section of the market. Not the least of these characteristics was the image of IBM's reliability. The IBM PC was soon perceived as the industry standard.

Standardization marks the first important transition to another phase of industry evolution during which competitive advantages shift to *low delivered cost*. This new phase is characterized by *rapid market development*. The personal computer industry was no exception as it moved into a period of very rapid growth in unit sales. Attention had to be shifted to the production process, while most manufacturers were adopting the "IBM standard." Rather than further product development, resources were now directed towards the entire business system: process technology, market positioning and distribution efficiency were key.

When IBM and others began to use prices strategically, many of the early competitors could not follow. Those who did survive had joined the industry-standard bandwagon and had the necessary resources to invest in the manufacturing process. The key competitors were now large,

FIGURE 3   INDUSTRY LIFE CYCLE

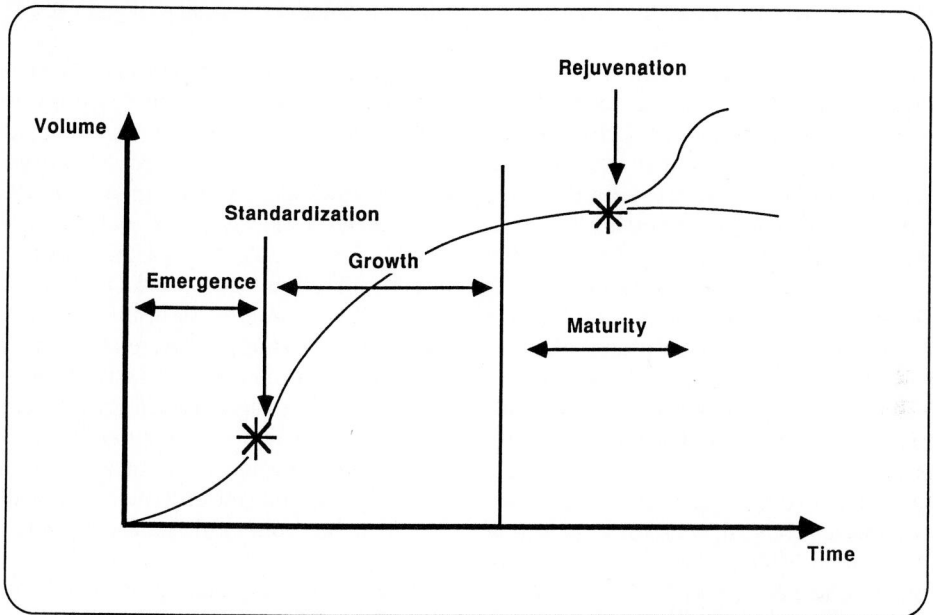

professional firms which followed a similar, low-delivered-cost industry discipline.

At the end of 1984 and in 1985, however, a new turn took place in the industry. Signs of *industry maturity* were appearing in the U.S., while activity was starting again on the side of product improvement. IBM itself launched its PC-AT and the need for networks was receiving increasing attention from competitors. Such renewed interest in the perceived value of the product is typical at this stage of an industry's evolution, often called rejuvenation (Figure 3). However, the entire process that made the business system work was still getting much attention. Resources were now channelled both to the process and to a new product generation: integrated computer networks. These developments were in the hands of a few large competitors who could be active on two fronts, process and product.

In a *maturing industry*, *rejuvenation* is the second important evolutionary transition. It marks the shift to product differentiation and innovation, in addition to cost reduction and process efficiency. At this stage, competitive advantages

must be maintained on two fronts: *low delivered cost* and, again, *high perceived value*. As a result of this combination, however, perceived-value advantages can only be marginal and shortlived. This is a time when marketing activity is at its peak.

The effectiveness of high-perceived-value and low-delivered-cost advantages thus varies with the stage of development of the industry. The two generic moves that lead to these advantages must be implemented at the right stage of development of the industry, either to accelerate its evolution, or to follow it.

Identifying Strategic Groups

The competitors in an industry can be positioned according to which generic moves they are making at a given time. The resulting mapping may be examined for signs of strategic groups of competitors.

Identifying strategic groups can serve several purposes. An important one is to assess how the moves of competitors may affect the evolution of the industry. The life cycle of an industry is not only pulled by changes in market expectations. It is also pushed by the move of some of the competitors. For example, IBM's entry in the personal computer industry accelerated the transition to market development. Subsequently, IBM's low-delivered-cost move accompanied with decreasing prices accelerated the transition to maturity. As we have seen, assessing the industry evolution is an important input in deciding which competitive move to implement next.

In addition, the identification of strategic groups can serve two other purposes. First, by observing how the key competitors are playing the business system to obtain their competitive advantages, it is possible to develop a better understanding of the business system and of the possible competitive advantages it offers. Second, identifying which competitive positions are occupied and by whom helps decide which competitors may be confronted or avoided.

Although the movements of competitors can be assessed quantitatively, since both perceived value and delivered cost can be measured, an example of how it can be done qualitatively will

be provided here. This example is based on the personal computer industry (Figure 4).

Three main groups could be identified in early 1986. The first group included the industry-standard competitors, of course led by IBM. A low-delivered-cost obsession was clear with this group, as indicated by the price decreases that marked 1985 and were continuing in 1986. In addition to IBM, the group included Compaq, Zenith, for example in the U.S., Sharp, Epson and Toshiba from Japan, and Olivetti from Europe. All were offering basically the same commodity-like product. All were seeing low price as a necessary condition to stay in the game. However, and this is characteristic of a mature industry, all were also trying to offer something else in addition to low price, such as more speed, more capacity, more user-friendliness, wider distribution. But none of these features could yield a lasting advantage.

There was a second group that was trying to exploit the fact that the rules of the game could perhaps be changed. If networking of personal computers, with each other and with mainframes, became critical, which seemed to be the

FIGURE 4   STRATEGIC GROUPS: THE PC INDUSTRY

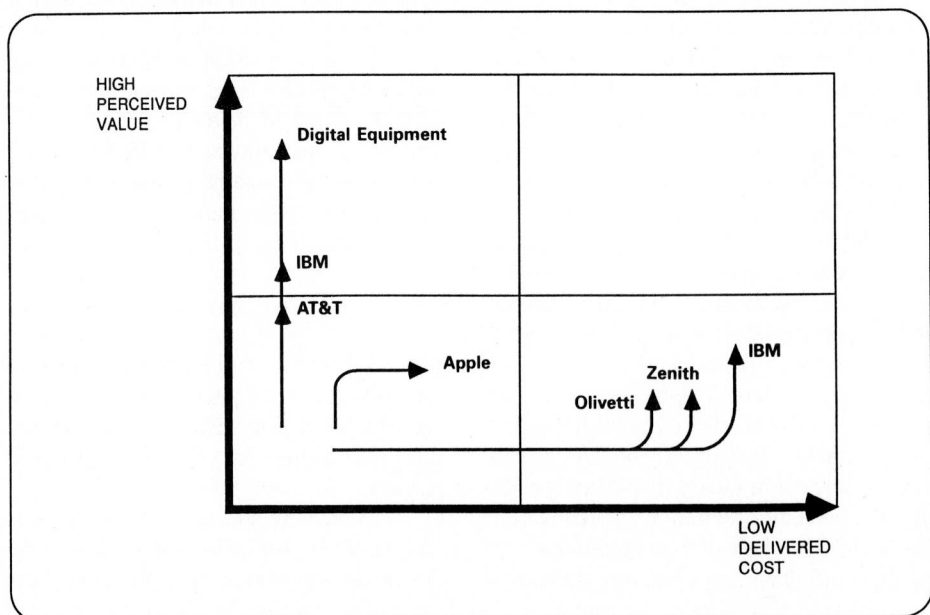

case, the personal computer would become a standard work-station in a decentralized data processing system. It would no longer be the "force de frappe" and future competitive advantages would accrue from the ability to provide communication hardware and software.

Among the companies competing effectively in this direction were Digital Equipment and other mini-computer vendors, who had traditionally networked their machines. IBM was also trying to compete on this front, with its usual follower approach, but it was hampered by its traditionally centralized approach to data processing. AT&T and other telecommunication companies were other credible contenders. The strategies in this group were clearly on the side of high perceived value. The battle of communication standards that was taking place at that time was characteristic of these strategies.

There was finally a third group of those who were beginning to look as if they had missed the boat. Apple was still its most successful member, fighting with low prices and product uniqueness, but a uniqueness of increasingly questionable relevance. However, Apple's statements of intention concerning a future compatibility of the Macintosh with IBM's personal-computer standard and with Digital Equipment's network architecture, demonstrated some understanding of the emerging new rules of the game.

GENERIC STRATEGIES

Two generic moves, leading either to high-perceived-value, or to low-delivered-cost advantages, have been identified and their relevance at different stages of evolution of an industry has been discussed. Successful competitors, however, appear to be combining these moves within overall strategies that allow them to maintain a superior competitive position throughout the evolution of their industry. Two types of generic strategies can be identified:

> One-dimensional strategies, either high-perceived-value, or low-delivered-cost.

Outpacing strategies, either pre-emptive or proactive.

One-dimensional Strategies

One-dimensional strategies rely on the continued repetition of one move, either a high-perceived-value one, or low-delivered-cost one. The situations where this seems possible are not numerous. Only in industries with very short life cycles, like fashion, is it possible to pursue indefinitely a high-perceived-value strategy. Only in industries with very long life cycles, like commodities, is it possible to stick continuously to a low-delivered-cost strategy. In other instances, one-dimensional strategies often hide an inability to implement a new move at the right time and lead to disasters.

The Japanese entry into Western automobile markets is an illustration. In the Sixties, Western manufacturers were pursuing high-perceived-value strategies. In the U.S., this led to yearly model changes. In Europe, ingenious, over-engineered small cars were being produced with rather primitive processes. In the late sixties, Japanese manufacturers began to sell basic and very inexpensive cars thanks to their highly efficient way of playing the business system, of which the manufacturing process was only a part. Success was almost immediate. Western manufacturers failed to see the need for a radical change in their competitive thrust and several were never able to respond.

However, this was not the end of the story. Both the price umbrella offered by Western manufacturers and the superior productivity of the Japanese allowed the latter to reinvest their cash-flow into product improvements and to offer more value for the same price. In Europe, this shift towards higher perceived value was welcomed because it brought new attraction to a standardizing product entering the maturity stage. In the U.S., it essentially met an unsatisfied need for a lower-value, lower-price car to which U.S. manufacturers could never respond. This is evidenced by the instant success achieved by Hyundai by providing the same value as a Japanese car maker, but for less money.

Outpacing Strategies

The example of the automobile industry showed clearly that the formulation of a successful strategy rarely relies on the repeated implementation of the same move to maintain a static position. Successful strategies generally consist of a planned sequence of moves from one position to another, at the right time. The sequential implementation of competitive moves should not be seen as strategy changes. It must be planned, one move creating the conditions for the implementation of the next. The dynamic nature of successful strategies is reflected in their description as *outpacing* strategies (Figure 5). Outpacing strategies can be pre-emptive or pro-active.

A pre-emptive strategy is needed by an industry leader to prevent the occurrence of a situation such as the one in the automobile industry. If successful, this strategy will shift the industry life cycle from the emergence stage to the growth stage. Its purpose is to prevent followers from developing secure low-price positions. This is achieved by shifting at the right time from a high-perceived-value position to a low-delivered-cost

one. This implies the establishment of a product standard and the development of a *pricing reserve*.

Establishing a standard is not only a matter of technology, as was well demonstrated by the IBM Personal Computer. It is rather a question of business system: establishing a formula that meets the expectations of a larger number of potential customers than do other competitive formulas. It is the desired outcome of a high-perceived-value move.

Developing a pricing reserve simply means investing in process improvements to enable the shift to a low-delivered-cost strategy, as soon as a standard is accepted. Experience shows that very few companies can make this shift effectively. It is nevertheless the condition for the tactical use of prices to prevent followers from generating the cashflow that will be necessary to go through the next industry transition, from low delivered cost, back to high perceived value, when the industry matures, if not to discourage them from entering at all. Such a strategy was followed by IBM, immediately after the IBM PC was accepted as a standard.

FIGURE 5   OUTPACING STRATEGIES

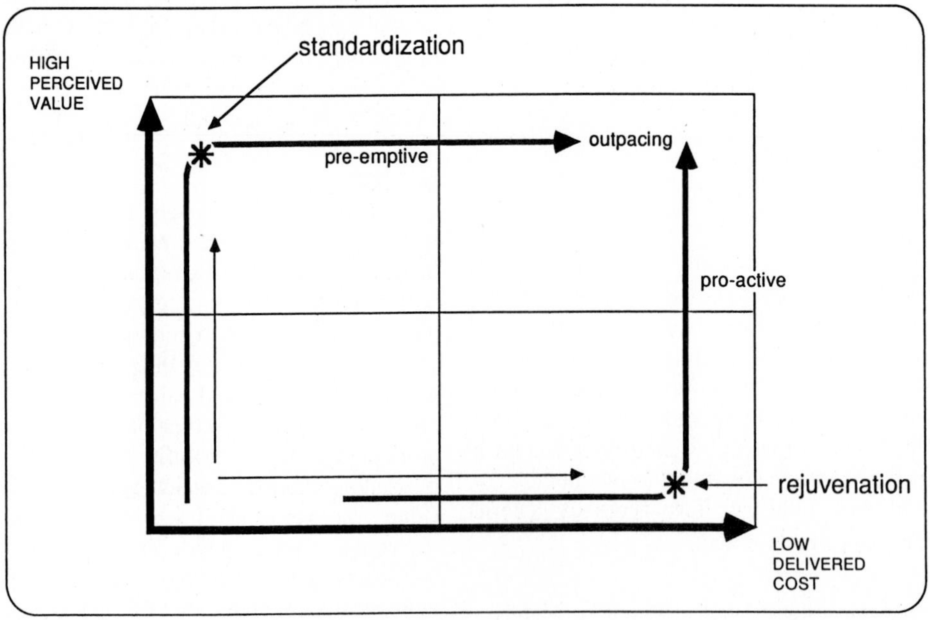

The timing of a pre-emptive, outpacing strategy is clearly critical. Launched too early, considerable investments in process improvement will be started before the formula is accepted as a standard. Should another standard emerge rapidly, the company will not be able to write off its previous process investments. Launched too late, further investments will have been made into product improvements which the market will not be willing to pay for. This will make it difficult to defend market share against the lower priced standards and will waste resources that would otherwise be needed for process investments.

Pro-active, outpacing strategies are required after the industry transition to lower growth and maturity. Their purpose is to escape the stalemate of maturity, so characteristic of many industries, where price wars often equate with self destruction. Often implemented by followers, they consist in building a solid low-delivered-cost position from which to launch a high-perceived-value move. While a pre-emptive strategy focuses on a mass market, a proactive one focuses on selected market segments to which more perceived value can be offered through a range of possibilities, from simple formula differentiation to rejuvenation of the industry. All these possibilities imply essentially the same approach: changing the rules of the game of the business system.

This is done by "un-bundling" the perceived value added by each activity of the business system: what does each activity really provide to the selected market segment, and at what cost? The process of unbundling will identify elements of perceived value that are not worth their delivered cost. Then additional elements of perceived value, desirable for the market segment, can be included in the formula at an acceptable cost.

An example of this approach is the way in which the Swedish firm, IKEA, redesigned its business system in order to compete effectively in furniture mass distribution. IKEA eliminated or modified the activities that increased the delivered cost and did not add essential perceived value from the consumer point of view. Carefully monitored sub-contracting of production to specialized manufacturers ensured quality at a lower cost.

The furniture was no longer assembled, but flat-packed. It was not displayed in city-center stores, but in hyper-stores, outside cities. A trade-off was made between minimum inventories, to decrease the delivered cost, and immediate availability. Furthermore, by doing its own product design, IKEA could insure a low-delivered cost consistency throughout its business system.

On the other hand, perceived value was added where this could be done for a low delivered cost. A very wide range of home products was offered under the same roof and could be looked at and tried by the consumer in the display section of the stores, rather than only seen in different stores or in catalogues. The furniture was normally available immediately and could be taken back home by car. Doing its own design, Ikea could offer an homogenous, modular product range. The desirable image of Scandinavian furniture was skillfully exploited to add perceived value. Last but not least, by redesigning its entire business system, IKEA built an additional powerful competitive advantage: the know-how necessary to operate this formula.

DEVELOPING COMPETITIVE ADVANTAGE: AN INTRINSIC PART OF CORPORATE STRATEGY

Analysis of competitive advantage is thus an intrinsic part of strategic management, rather than a separate exercise, as it is often presented. Indeed, it cannot be performed linearly in a way that leads to one end product, the "knowledge of the industry." It is performed through an iterative process, leading to hypotheses concerning possible strategies, testing them against the company's capabilities and against the positions of competition, and going back to the drawing board to assess other possibilities. This iterative process is the foundation on which each move can lead to sustainable competitive advantages by being part of an overall strategy to fight in the dynamic battlefield of an industry. Bringing this iterative process to life is a permanent responsibility of the general manager of a business unit.

FIVE

STRATEGY FORMATION

The readings of the last two chapters described how strategies are supposed to be made and thereby illustrated the *pre*scriptive side of the field. This chapter presents readings that describe how strategies really do seem to be made, the *de*scriptive side. We title this chapter ''Strategy Formation'' to emphasize the point introduced in Chapter 1 that strategies can *form* implicitly as well as be *formulated* explicitly.

The preceding chapters may seem to deal with an unreachable utopia, this one with an imperfect reality. But, there may be a better conclusion: that *pre*scription offers useful guidelines for thinking about ends and how to order physical resources efficiently to achieve them, while *de*scription provides a useful frame of reference for considering how this must be related to real-world patterns of behavior in organizations. Another way to say this is that while the analytical tools and models prescribed earlier are vital to thinking about strategy intelligently, they must also be rooted in a genuine understanding of the realities of organizations. Unfortunately, management writers, especially in traditional strategy textbooks, have often been quick to prescribe without offering enough appreciation of why managers and organizations act in the ways they do.

The Mintzberg reading sets the stage by discussing three broad views, or ''modes,'' by which the strategy-making process has been conceived in the literature. As he points out, the popular view of strategy making is as a planning process. This is reflected, sometimes implicitly, sometimes explicitly, in the readings of the previous chapters. But successful strategies need not be developed in this way, as this same article makes clear—there are entrepreneurial and adaptive approaches to effective strategy making as well. Each, it is argued, is suited to its own particular set of conditions, leading us in subsequent chapters into what is popularly called a *contingency* approach: The type of strategy-making process best used in an organization depends on the situation at hand.

The next article takes a deeper look inside the planning mode of making strategy, but not so much prescriptively as descriptively. It discusses what planning really can do. Written by Brian Loasby, an Englishman, in 1967, and aptly titled ''Long-range Formal Planning in Perspective,'' it remains one of the most sensible assessments of the capabilities and weaknesses of the planning mode. It is not easy reading, but it is well worth the effort. Loasby directly addresses the important conflict between planning and remaining flexible, drawing the interesting conclusion that planning is ''something [firms] should try to avoid,'' while recognizing that it is nonetheless something they must necessarily do ''a good deal of.''

We do not discuss Mintzberg's second mode, entrepreneurial strategy, here. (That is in Chapter 10.) Instead, the other readings of this chapter probe into the third mode, strategy formation as an adaptive process. The Quinn reading is drawn from his book *Strategies for Change, Logical Incrementalism*, which developed a particular view of the strategy making process based on intensive interviews in some of America's and Europe's best known corporations. Planning does not capture the essence of strategy formation, according to Quinn, although it did play an important role in developing new data and in confirming strategies derived in other ways. The traditional view of incrementalism (as outlined in the adaptive mode of this chapter's first reading) did not fit observed behavior patterns either. The processes Quinn observed seemed incremental on the surface, but a powerful logic underlay them. And, unlike the other incremental processes, these were not so much *re*active as subtly *pro*active. Executives used incremental approaches to deal simultaneously with the informational, motivational, and political aspects of creating a strategy.

Above all, Quinn depicts strategy formation as a managed interactive *learning* process in which the chief strategist gradually works out strategy in his own mind and orchestrates his organization's acceptance of it. In emphasizing the role of a central strategist—or small groups managing "subsystems" of strategy—Quinn often seems close to Andrews's view. But the two differ markedly in other important respects. In his emphasis on the political and motivational dimensions of strategy, Quinn may be closer to Wrapp whose managers "don't make policy decisions." In fact, Quinn attempts to integrate his views with the traditional one, noting that while the strategies themselves "emerge" from an incremental process, they have many of the characteristics of the highly deliberate ones of Andrews's strategists. In these and other readings, you will see the appearance of clear and rather distinct themes in the literature as well as attempts to reconcile some of the seeming anomolies. A number of the cases, notably those on IBM (A), General Motors, Pillsbury, MacArthur, and Continental Group, offer opportunities to investigate the interaction of analytical and incremental processes in strategy formation.

In this chapter that challenges many of the accepted notions about how strategy should be made, the next reading may be the most upsetting of all. In it Richard Pascale, a well-known consultant, writer, and lecturer at Stanford Business School, challenges head-on not only the whole approach to competitive strategy as practiced by the Boston Consulting Group (one of the better known "strategy boutiques" whose ideas will be discussed in Chapters 11 and 12), but also the very concept of strategy formulation itself.

As his point of departure, Pascale describes a BCG study carried out for the British government to explain how manufacturers in that country lost the American motorcycle market to the Japanese, and to the Honda Company in particular. The analysis seems impeccable, and eminently logical: The Japanese were simply more clever, by thinking through a brilliant strategy before they acted. But then Pascale flew to Japan and interviewed those clever executives who pulled off this coup. We shall save the story for Pascale, who tells it with a great deal of color, except to note here its basic message: An openness to learning and a fierce commitment to an organization and its markets may count for more in strategy making than all the brilliant analysis one can imagine. (Ask yourself while reading these accounts, how the strategic behavior of the British motorcycle manufacturers who received the BCG report might have differed if they had instead received Pascale's second story.) Pascale in effect takes the arguments for incrementalism and strategy making as a learning process to their natural conclusions (or one of them, at least).

No one who reads Pascale's account can ever feel quite so smug about rational strategy analysis again. We include this reading, however, not to encourage rejection of that type of analysis, or the very solid thinking that has gone into the works of Porter, Ansoff, and others. Rather, we wish to balance the message conveyed in so much of the strategy literature with the practical lessons from the field. The point is that successful strategists can no more rely exclusively on such analysis than they can do without it. Effective strategy formation, one must conclude from all these readings, is a sometimes deceptive and multi-faceted affair, its complexity never to be underestimated.

STRATEGY-MAKING
IN THREE MODES*

by Henry Mintzberg

How do organizations make important decisions and link them together to form strategies? So far, we have little systematic evidence about this important process, known in business as *strategy-making* and in government as *policy-making*. The literature of management and public administration is, however, replete with general views on the subject. These fall into three distinct groupings or "modes." In the *entrepreneurial* mode, found in the writings of some of the classical economists and of many contemporary management writers, one strong leader takes bold, risky actions on behalf of his organization. Conversely, in the *adaptive* mode, described by a number of students of business and governmental decision-making, the organization adapts in small, disjointed steps to a difficult environment. Finally, the proponents of management science and policy science describe the *planning* mode, in which formal analysis is used to plan explicit, integrated strategies for the future.

I shall begin by describing each mode as its proponents do, in simple terms and distinct from the other two. Considered in this way, each may appear to be a naive reflection of the complex reality of strategy-making. But taken as a set of three, as I shall do in subsequent sections, to be combined and alternated by managers acting under different conditions, these modes constitute

*   Originally published in the *California Management Review* XVI, no. 2 (Winter 1973), pp. 44–53. Copyright © 1973 by the Regents of the University of California; reprinted by permission of the Regents.

a realistic and useful description of the strategy-making process. . . . Finally, I shall discuss some important implications for strategic planning.

THE ENTREPRENEURIAL MODE

The entrepreneur was first discussed by early economists as that individual who founded enterprises. His roles were essentially those of innovation, of dealing with uncertainty, and of brokerage. The entrepreneur found capital which he brought together with marketing opportunity to form, in the words of Joseph Schumpeter, the well known Harvard economist, "new combinations."

In a . . . book called *The Organization Makers*, Orvis Collins and David Moore present a fascinating picture of those independent entrepreneurs, based on a study of 150 of them. The authors trace the lives of these men from childhood, through formal and informal education, to the steps they took to create their enterprises. Data from psychological tests reinforce their analysis. What emerges are pictures of tough, pragmatic men driven from early childhood by a powerful need for achievement and independence. At some point in his life, each entrepreneur faced disruption ("role determination"), and it was here that he set out on his own:

> What sets them apart is that during this time of role deterioration they interwove their dilemmas into the projection of a business. In moments of crisis, they did not seek a situation of security. They went on into deeper insecurity . . . (Collins and Moore, 1970:134).

A number of management writers view the entrepreneurial mode of strategy-making not only in terms of creating new firms but in terms of the running of ongoing enterprises. Typical of these is Peter Drucker, who writes . . .

> Central to business enterprise is . . . the entrepreneurial act, an act of economic

risk-taking. And business enterprises is an entrepreneurial institution . . . Entrepreneurship is thus central to function, work and performance of the executive in business (Drucker, 1970:10).

What are the chief characteristics of the entrepreneurial mode of strategy-making as described by economists and management writers? We can delineate four:

1. *In the entrepreneurial mode, strategy-making is dominated by the active search for new opportunities.*—The entrepreneurial organization focuses on opportunities; problems are secondary. Drucker writes: "Entrepreneurship requires that the few available good people be deployed on opportunities rather than frittered away on 'solving problems' " (p. 10). . . .

2. *In the entrepreneurial organization, power is centralized in the hands of the chief executive.*—Collins and Moore write of the founder-entrepreneur: "The entrepreneurial personality . . . is characterized by an unwillingness to 'submit' to authority, an inability to work with it, and a consequent need to escape from it" (p. 45). In the entrepreneurial mode, power rests with one man capable of committing the organization to bold courses of action. He rules by fiat, relying on personal power and sometimes on charisma. Consider this description of an Egyptian firm:

The great majority of Egyptian-owned private establishments . . . are organized closer to the pattern of the Abboud enterprises. Here the manager is a dominant individual who extends his personal control over all phases of the business. There is no charted plan of organization, no formalized procedure for selection and development of managerial personnel, no publicized system of wage and salary classifications.
. . . authority is associated exclusively with an individual . . .
Abboud is the kind of person most people have in mind when they discuss the successful Egyptian entrepreneur (Harbison and Myers, 1959:40–41).

But while there may be "no charted plan of organization," typically one finds instead that strategy is guided by the entrepreneur's own vision of direction for his organization—his personalized plan of attack. Drucker writes:

Every one of the great business builders we know of—from the Medici and the founders of the Bank of England down to IBM's Thomas Watson in our days—had a definite idea, indeed a clear 'theory of the business' which informed his actions and decisions (p. 5).

3. *Strategy-making in the entrepreneurial mode is characterized by dramatic leaps forward in the face of uncertainty.*—Strategy moves forward in the entrepreneurial organization by the taking of large, bold decisions. The chief executive seeks out and thrives in conditions of uncertainty, where his organization can make dramatic gains. The entrepreneurial mode is probably most alive in the popular business magazines such as *Fortune* and *Forbes* which each month devote a number of articles to the bold actions of manager-entrepreneurs. The theme that runs through these articles is what has been referred to as the "bold stroke," the courageous move that succeeds against all the odds and all the advice.

4. *Growth is the dominant goal of the entrepreneurial organization.*—According to psychologist David McClelland, the entrepreneur is motivated above all by his need for achievement. Since his organization's goals are simply the extension of his own, we can conclude that the dominant goal of the organization operating in the entrepreneurial mode is growth, the most tangible manifestation of achievement. *Fortune* magazine came to this conclusion in a 1956 article about the Young Presidents' Organization entitled "The Entrepreneurial Ego":

Most of the young presidents have the urge to build rather than manipulate. "Expansion is a sort of disease with us," says one president. "Let's face it," says another. "We're empire builders. The tremendous compulsion and obsession is not to make money, but to build an empire." The opportunity to keep on pushing ahead is, indeed, the principal advantage offered by the entrepreneurial life (Klaw, 1956:143).

In summary, we can conclude that the organization operating in the entrepreneurial mode suggests by its actions that the environment is malleable, a force to be confronted and controlled.

THE ADAPTIVE MODE

The view of strategy-making as an adaptive process has gained considerable popularity since the publication of two complimentary books in 1963. Charles Lindblom and David Braybrooke wrote *A Strategy of Decision* about policy-making in the public sector, while Richard Cyert and James March published *A Behavioral Theory of the Firm* based on empirical studies of decision-making.

Lindblom first called this approach "the science of 'muddling through (1959)'," later "disjointed incrementalism" (with Braybrooke, 1963). The term "adaptive" is chosen here for its simplicity. As described by Lindblom, the adaptive policy-maker accepts as given a powerful status quo and the lack of clear objectives. His decisions are basically remedial in nature, and he proceeds in small steps, never moving too far from the given status quo. In this way, the policy-maker comes to terms with his complex environment.

Cyert and March's strategy-maker, although working in the business firm, operates in much the same fashion. Again, his world is complex and he must find the means to cope with it. Cyert and March suggest that he does so in a number of ways. He consciously seeks to avoid uncertainty, sometimes solving pressing problems instead of developing long-run strategies, other times "negotiating" with the environment (for example, establishing cartels). Furthermore, because the organization is controlled by a coalition of disparate interests, the strategy-maker must make his decisions so as to reduce conflicts. He does this by attending to conflicting goals sequentially, ignoring the inconsistencies:

Just as the political organization is likely to resolve conflicting pressures to 'go left' and 'go right' by first doing one and then the other, the business firm is likely to resolve conflicting pressures to 'smooth production' and 'satisfy customers' by first doing one and then the other (1963:118).

Four major characteristics distinguish the adaptive mode of strategy-making:

1. *Clear goals do not exist in the adaptive organization; strategy-making reflects a division of power among members of a complex coalition.*—the adaptive organization is caught in a complex web of political forces. Unions, managers, owners, lobby groups, government agencies, and so on, each with their own needs, seek to influence decisions. There is no one central source of power, no one simple goal. The goal system of the organization is characterized by bargaining among these groups, with each winning some issues and losing others. Hence, the organization attends to a whole array of goals sequentially, ignoring the inconsistencies among them. The organization cannot make decisions to "maximize" any one goal such as profit or growth; rather it must seek solutions to its problems that are good enough, that satisfy the constraints.

2. *In the adaptive mode, the strategy-making process is characterized by the "reactive" solution to existing problems rather than the "proactive" search for new opportunities.*—The adaptive organization works in a difficult environment that imposes many problems and crises. Little time remains to search out opportunities. And even if there were time, the lack of clear goals in the organization would preclude a proactive approach:

. . . if [the strategy-makers] cannot decide with any precision the state of affairs they want to achieve, they can at least specify the state of affairs from which they want to escape. They deal more confidently with what is wrong than with what in the future may or may not be right (Lindblom, 1968:25).

Furthermore, the adaptive organization seeks conditions of certainty wherever possible, otherwise it seeks to reduce existing uncertainties. It establishes cartels to ensure markets, negotiates long-term purchasing arrangements to stabilize sources of supply, and so on.

3. *The adaptive organization makes its decisions in incremental, serial steps.*—Because its environment is complex, the adaptive organization finds that feedback is a crucial ingredient in strategy-making. It cannot take large decisions for fear of venturing too far into the unknown. The strategy-maker focuses first on what is familiar, considering the convenient alternatives and the ones that differ only slightly from the status quo. Hence, the organization moves forward in incremental steps, laid end to end in serial fashion so that feedback can be received and the course adjusted as it moves along. As Lindblom notes, ". . . policy making is typically a never-ending process of successive steps in which continual nibbling is a substitute for a good bite" (1968:25).

4. *Disjointed decisions are characteristic of the adaptive organization.*—Decisions cannot be easily interrelated in the adaptive mode. The demands on the organization are diverse, and no manager has the mental capacity to reconcile all of them. Sometimes it is simply easier and less expensive to make decisions in disjointed fashion so that each is treated independently and little attention is paid to problems of coordination. Strategy-making is fragmented, but at least the strategy-maker remains flexible, free to adapt to the needs of the moment.

Lindblom provides us with an apt summary of the adaptive mode:

Man has had to be devilishly inventive to cope with the staggering difficulties he faces. His analytical methods cannot be restricted to tidy scholarly procedures. The piecemealing, remedial incrementalist or satisficer may not look like an heroic figure. He is nevertheless a shrewd, resourceful problem-solver who is wrestling bravely with a universe that he is wise

enough to know is too big for him (1968:27).

THE PLANNING MODE

In [his book on planning], Russell Ackoff isolates the three chief characteristics of the planning mode:

1. Planning is something we do in advance of taking action; that is, it is *anticipatory decision-making.* . . .

2. Planning is required when the future state that we desire involves a set of interdependent decisions; that is, a *system of decisions.* . . .

3. Planning is a process that is directed toward producing one or more future states which are desired and which are not expected to occur unless something is done (1970: 2–5).

Formal planning demands rationality in the economist's sense of the term—the systematic attainment of goals stated in precise, quantitative terms. The key actor in the process is the analyst, who uses his scientific techniques to develop formal, comprehensive plans.

The literature of planning is vast. . . . Much of the early writing concerned "operational planning"—the projecting of various budgets based on the given strategies of the organization. [Later], attention has turned to the planning of organizational strategies themselves, the more significant and long-range concerns of senior managers. . . .

We can delineate three essential features of the planning mode:

1. *In the planning mode, the analyst plays a major role in strategy-making.*—The analyst or planner works alongside the manager, and assumes major responsibility for much of the strategy-making process. His role is to apply the techniques of management science and policy analysis to the design of long-range strategies. A U.S. Senator notes the reasons for this:

I am convinced that we never will get the kind of policy planning we need if we expect the top-level officers to participate actively in the planning process. They simply do not have the time, and in any event they rarely have the outlook or the talents of the good planner. They cannot explore issues deeply and systematically. They cannot argue the advantages and disadvantages at length in the kind of give-and-take essential if one is to reach a solid understanding with others on points of agreement and disagreement (quoted in Anthony, 1965:46–47).

2. *The planning mode focuses on systematic analysis, particularly in the assessment of the costs and benefits of competing proposals.*—Formal planning involves both the active search for new opportunities and the solution of existing problems. The process is always systematic and structured. As one business planner [has written]:

No doubt much of top-level management is unscientific. But by applying a systematic, structured approach to these problems, we have a better basis for analyzing them. We may identify more specifically the challenges and needs in the situation and see how they are interrelated (Cantley, 1969:19).

Formal planning follows a stepwise procedure in which particular attention is paid to the cost-benefit evaluation of proposals, where the planning methodology is best developed. The planner tests proposals for feasibility, determines their efficiency (or economic value), and relates them to each other. The planner deals best with conditions known to the management scientist as "risk"—where the uncertainty can be expressed in statistical terms. Conditions of certainty require no planning; those of pure uncertainty cannot be subjected to analysis.

3. *The planning mode is characterized above all by the integration of decisions and strategies.*—Ackoff notes that "the principal complexity in planning derives from the interrelatedness of decisions rather than from the decisions themselves" (p. 3). But this interrelatedness is the key element in planning. An organization plans in the belief that decisions made together in one systematic process will be less likely to conflict and more likely to complement each other than if they were made independently. For example, planning can ensure that the decision to acquire a new firm complements (or at least does not conflict with) the decision to expand the product line of an existing division. Thus, strategic planning is a process whereby an organization's strategy is designed essentially at one point in time in a comprehensive process (all major decisions made are interrelated). Because of this, planning forces the organization to think of global strategies and to develop an explicit sense of strategic direction.

To conclude, the planning mode is oriented to systematic, comprehensive analysis and is used in the belief that formal analysis can provide an understanding of the environment sufficient to influence it.

The upper part of Table I presents in summary form the characteristics of the three modes of strategy-making, while Figure 1 depicts these three modes in graphic form. The first figure shows the taking of bold steps consistent with the entrepreneur's general vision of direction. In the second figure, we see a purely adaptive organization taking incremental steps in reaction to environmental forces, while the third figure indicates a precise plan with a specific, unalterable path to one clear end point.

THE DETERMINATION OF MODE

What conditions drive an organization to favor one mode of strategy-making over the others? We may delineate a number of characteristics of the organization itself, such as its size and the nature of its leadership, and features of its environment, such as competition and stability. These are discussed below and are summarized in the lower portion of Table I.

The *entrepreneurial* mode requires that strategy-making authority rest with one powerful individual. The environment must be yielding,

TABLE 1   CHARACTERISTICS AND CONDITIONS OF THE THREE MODES

Characteristic	Entrepreneurial Mode	Adaptive Mode	Planning Mode
Motive for Decisions	Proactive	Reactive	Proactive & Reactive
Goals of Organization	Growth	Indeterminate	Efficiency & Growth
Evaluation of Proposals	Judgmental	Judgmental	Analytical
Choices made by	Entrepreneur	Bargaining	Management
Decision Horizon	Long Term	Short Term	Long Term
Preferred Environment	Uncertainty	Certainty	Risk
Decision Linkages	Loosely Coupled	Disjointed	Integrated
Flexibility of Mode	Flexible	Adaptive	Constrained
Size of Moves	Bold Decisions	Incremental Steps	Global Strategies
Vision of Direction	General	None	Specific
Condition for Use			
Source of Power	Entrepreneur	Divided	Management
Objectives of Organization	Operational	Non-Operational	Operational
Organizational Environment	Yielding	Complex, Dynamic	Predictable, Stable
Status of Organization	Young, Small or Strong Leadership	Established	Large

the organization oriented toward growth, the strategy able to shift boldly at the whim of the entrepreneur. Clearly, these conditions are most typical of organizations that are small and/or young. Their sunk costs are low and they have little to lose by acting boldly. Young organizations in particular have set few precedents for themselves and have made few commitments. The way is

FIGURE 1   PATHS OF THE THREE MODES

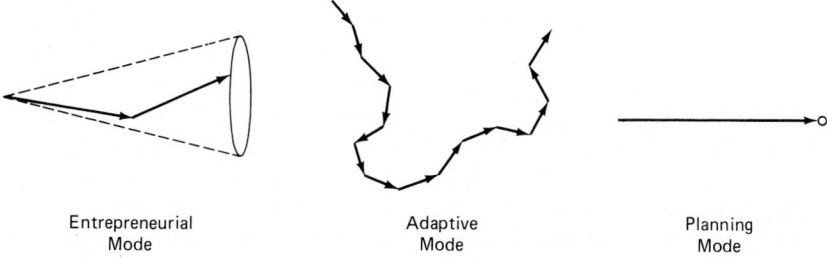

Entrepreneurial Mode   Adaptive Mode   Planning Mode

open for them to bunch a number of key decisions at an early stage and take them in entrepreneurial fashion. This behavior may also be characteristic of the organization in trouble—it has little to lose by acting boldly, indeed this may be its only hope. . . .

To satisfy the condition of centralized power, the organization must be either a business firm (often with the owner as chief executive), or an institutional or governmental body with a powerful leader who has a strong mandate. The entrepreneurial mode is often found with charismatic leadership. . . .

Use of the *adaptive* mode suggests that the organization faces a complex, rapidly changing environment and a divided coalition of influencer forces. Goals cannot be agreed upon unless they are in "motherhood" form and non-operational (they cannot be quantified). Here we have a clear description of the large established organization with great sunk costs and many controlling groups holding each other in check. This is typical of most universities, of many large hospitals, of a surprising number of large corporations, and of many governments, especially those in minority positions or composed of coalitions of divergent groups. Indeed, the American system of government has been expressly designed to create conditions of divided power, and it is, therefore, not surprising that Charles Lindblom, the chief proponent of the adaptive approach, is a student of the U.S. public policy-making process.

In order to rely on the *planning* mode, an organization must be large enough to afford the costs of formal analysis, it must have goals that are operational, and it must face an environment that is reasonably predictable and stable. (This last point inevitably raises the comment that planning is most necessary when the environment is difficult to understand. This may be true, but the costs of analyzing a complex environment may be prohibitive and the results may be discouraging. As one Latin American chief executive commented: "Planning is great. But how can you plan—let alone plan long-term—if you don't know what kind of government you'll have next year?" [quoted in Stieglitz, 1969:46–47)].

The above conditions suggest that formal comprehensive planning will generally be found in business firms of reasonable size that do not face severe and unpredictable competition and in government agencies that have clear, apolitical mandates. . . . The communist form of government with its five year plan is [a] good example. The power system is hierarchical, goals can be made operational, the home environment can be controlled and made more or less stable and predictable (at least as long as the crops are good). . . .

[Of course, organizations can mix these modes in various ways. We can find adaptive entrepreneurs and also organizations where marketing is more entrepreneurial and production more planning oriented, others where the corporate headquarters plans while some divisions below muddle through (though the opposite would not work easily, since it is difficult to plan at the whim of a controlling force that is adaptive).]

IMPLICATIONS FOR STRATEGIC PLANNING

What can we conclude from this description of strategy-making? One point merits special emphases. *Planning is not a panacea for the problems of strategy-making.* As obvious as this seems, there is little recognition of it in planning books or by planners. Instead, one finds a focus on abstract, simple models of the planning process that take no cognizance of the other two modes of strategy-making. Little wonder then that one finds so much frustration among formal planners. Rather than seeking panaceas, we should recognize that the mode used must fit the situation. . . .

Some situations require no planning, others only limited planning. Often the planning mode can be used only when mixed with the others. Most important, planners must recognize the need for the manager to remain partially in the adaptive mode at all times. Crises and unexpected events are an important part of every strategy-maker's reality. Conventional planning requires operational goals which managers cannot always provide (the coalition may simply not agree on anything specific). Furthermore, it must be recognized that good planning is expensive, it often requires unrealistic stability in the environment, and, above all, it is the least flexible of the strategy-making modes. All this is not to conclude that planning is useless; rather, it suggests that the planner must become more realistic about the limitations of his science. . . .

LONG-RANGE FORMAL PLANNING IN PERSPECTIVE*

by Brian J. Loasby

Planning has become a fashionable subject in American management literature, and shows some signs of becoming a fashionable managerial preoccupation in Britain. But the word 'planning' is currently used in so many and various senses that it is in some danger of degenerating into an emotive noise. . . . instead of succumbing to the slogan that 'The Future is Planning',[1] let us attempt to restore some content to the idea by examining the purposes of a formal procedure for long-range planning. . . .

ADVANTAGES OF FORMAL PLANNING

The basic question in considering any sort of planning is: why should a firm attempt to look into the future? Why not wait until it arrives? There seem to be three basic reasons.

The first reason for looking into the future

in a systematic way is to understand the future implications of present decisions. What must a firm be prepared to do next year in order to gain the full advantage from what it decides to do now; what will be the effect of its current choice on the range of options available to it in the future; what problems may be created later on by choosing a particular course of action now? These questions need to be asked on a project-by-project basis; but the major advantage of a systematic procedure is that it also requires various projects to be looked at simultaneously. This is important if individual projects have important 'external effects,' i.e., if one project is likely to assist or impede another—whether by their combined effects on the demand for the firm's resources (or the efficiency with which they are used), or by their effects outside the firm. The process by which two or more projects assist each other has been christened synergy (Ansoff, 1965:75); perhaps the opposite process by which they impede each other could be called allergy. It is hard to imagine a situation in which such effects are completely absent; if they are significant, then the agenda for considering one project is not wide enough unless it includes the implications of competitive or complementary projects. A formal procedure, by informing various levels and various sections of the firm of what other levels and other sections are proposing to do, and requiring such information to be taken into account when decisions are made, may be the most effective way of securing the necessary width.

The second reason for looking into the future in a systematic way is in a sense the obverse of the first. As well as considering the future implications of present decisions, it is necessary to examine the present implications of future events. The question here is: 'What needs to be decided now in order to be prepared for what is expected to happen later on?' If the first question is concerned with the width of the agenda, the second is concerned with its length. When James P. McFarland of General Mills says that 'effective long-range planning will probably be more useful in making problems apparent than in solving

---

*   Originally published in *The Journal of Management Studies* (October, 1967); used by permission of the publishers.
[1]   *"The Past is History . . . The Future is Planning"* is the title of an article (Rickard, 1965).

them'[2] he is pointing to the second purpose of looking into the future in a formal kind of way. The systematic attempt to forecast the future should help to reveal problems in time to anticipate them.

The future implications of present decisions and the present implications of future events cannot, obviously, be thoroughly considered every day; but without some specific motivation and mechanism they may never be adequately considered at all. The third reason for looking into the future in a systematic way is to provide such motivation and such a mechanism. The formal planning process should require an explicit review of the assumptions which underlie the limited agendas which are necessarily used for day-to-day decisions, in order to reduce the danger that 'what look like rational decisions under limited agendas . . . (may) turn out to be disastrous' (Boulding, 1966:167).

Too many major issues, though obviously important, seem easily postponable in favour of immediate minor problems; they are therefore liable to be postponed either until they are decided by default, or, at best, until they have to be resolved by improvisation instead of by thoughtful and wide-ranging study. The formal planning process should ensure an adequate commitment of management resources to these issues, and a commitment in time to allow such study. It should encourage the proper exploration of a range of genuine options, not merely a single proposal. A time to make choices is a time to offer alternatives: the final decision-maker, of course, has the power of veto, but the power of veto is a very limited form of the power to choose.

It is not always easy for a manager to combine efficient day-to-day operation of a system with the review and redesign of that system; that he should be encouraged and assisted to combine them is clearly desirable for the reasons already given. There is another reason: this exercise of both widening and lengthening his agenda is the part of a manager's job that is most relevant to

the requirements of a higher position, and is thus particularly useful in preparing him for greater responsibilities and in indicating his capacity to undertake them.

POTENTIAL DANGERS OF FORMAL PLANNING

It should be emphasized that the purposes identified so far all relate to present decisions for present action. ('I use long-range planning,' says a senior I.C.I. manager, 'to decide what to do tomorrow.') They imply no commitment to any future action, and do not in themselves require any planning document to be kept after the immediate decisions have been made. Short-term plans will presumably be prepared in the normal budgeting process, and performance will be evaluated against these. Why should managers be required to make decisions now about action to be taken in the future?

One obvious reason is that a comparison of performance with plan may be useful in revealing possible problems or opportunities—in other words as a means of getting topics on the agenda. This is clearly useful in itself, though one must remember the danger with any incomplete automatic warning system—that it tends to divert attention from the danger that it does not signal.

Another possible reason is to secure a manager's commitment to an objective. But one must be very careful here. Commitment to making a proper job of today's decisions, based on careful and imaginative evaluation of their future implications, is certainly desirable. Some commitment to next year's plans may be desirable too—but not unquestioning commitment, because conditions may change. It is far from clear that any commitment that is at all precise is desirable beyond that. The fact that a firm should not, for example, start to develop a new product unless it is, at the time of the decision, prepared to launch a marketing effort at the appropriate time does not mean that it should decide now to launch that future effort. The attempt to develop a new product may fail; and even if it succeeds, the situation may have so changed by the time the decision to market needs to be taken that it may be best not to market. Just as by then the costs

2   McFarland, James P., "Planning and Control at General Mills" (unpublished lecture notes), (Harvard Business School).

of development are sunk costs, so the earlier intention to market is a bygone intention; and sunk costs and bygone intentions are a poor basis for present decisions.

The third reason why a firm might want managers to make decisions now about future actions is to provide a basis for evaluation of their performance. This reason is subject to the same criticism as that advanced against commitment, that action in accordance with a plan prepared long beforehand may well not be the action that is best for the firm.

It is not surprising that some companies should make the apparently natural progression for the annual budget to the 'five-year forward look.' It is not surprising, but it is dangerous. Any attempt to use a long-term plan for control purposes is liable to frustrate the valuable purposes of the planning process. Budgetary control is intended to ensure, by a system of rewards and penalties, the attainment of forecast results. As the penalty for failure is usually greater than the reward for success, the control system motivates a manager to promise no more than he is confident of performing.

This is quite the wrong apparatus for securing the advantages of formal planning. These advantages lie in the stimulus to fresh thought and imaginative ideas; but imaginative ideas involve risk, and risk implies the possibility of failure. To ask a man to commit himself, under threat of penalty, to the success of his proposed action is to ask him never to take a risk. It is therefore quite natural that, as Charles O. Rossotti (n.d.) observes, 'one objection to action planning is that it makes an insufficient contribution to, or even hinders, the vital process of generating proposals for major policy changes and new opportunities' (p. 6). The allure of an integrated planning and control system should be resisted.

The fourth reason for requiring managers to decide now what they will do at specific points in the future is that it facilitates future decision-making in other groups where external effects are important. Short-term decisions are made on the basis of two kinds of assumptions: one kind is about the outside world, the other is about what is happening in other parts of the organiza-

tion. Whether the first kind of assumption turns out to be right or wrong cannot be controlled by the firm; but it does have the power to ensure that the assumptions of the second kind are right, by insisting that they be spelled out well in advance and adhered to. Thus the assurance which may be given in an action plan of what other parts of the organization will be doing helps to narrow the agenda for other decisions. It does not improve communications between parts of the organization; it eliminates the need for them. It makes it possible to allocate responsibilities in a pretty watertight way. This kind of planning is not an aid, but an alternative, to good communications.

Of course, the price of improving the compatibility between a decision made in one part of an organization and simultaneous decisions made elsewhere may be the reduction of compatibility between the decision and the outside environment. One way of dealing with this is to draw up a set of contingency plans, or conditional decisions, based on several different sets of assumptions; provided that the facts fit one set reasonably well, it is necessary only to make sure that everyone knows which set they are all to use. In some circumstances this may be a good method. But just how necessary is it to secure this co-ordination in advance? If these conditional decisions are to be intelligently prepared, with due regard for the interaction between various sections of the business, then while they are being prepared there has to be close contact between the sections (unless, of course, as may be the case, there really is very little cross-effect, in which case this reason for decisions about future action disappears). Why, then, should one design a system which appears to postulate very little contact in the intervals between the formulation of these decisions? Might one not get both better-integrated decision-making and better-co-ordinated response to changing conditions by abandoning compartmentalization and not specifying responsibility so narrowly?

The apparent need to improve (but in fact to dispense with) communication and co-ordination is likely to be associated with what has been called a 'mechanistic system of management'

(Burns and Stalker, 1961), that is a system characterized by a well-ordered hierarchy of clearly-defined responsibilities, so that everyone knows precisely what is—and also what is not—his business. In a situation where the inter-relationships ignored by this formal structure are nevertheless important, the structure may appear to require equally formal planning procedures; and these procedures may appear to be facilitated by the structure. But instead of using formal planning procedures to reconcile the organization structure to the real needs of the company, it might be better to encourage the growth of a network structure of relationships, in which the active contacts at any time are determined by the task in hand, instead of being specified in advance. Such an 'organic system' (Burns and Stalker, 1967) will be more responsive to changing circumstances, and might well produce better results for the organization than an attempt to predetermine future decisions.

An important virtue of a systematic look into the future is that it forces a company to make its forecasts more explicit. But even this virtue is not without its accompanying dangers. It is often argued that to make better decisions we need better information. Now it is certainly true that information can be improved. To take two examples: few firms apparently attempt to improve the accuracy of their forecasts by analyzing the reasons for past forecasting errors—even when the errors are as notorious as those made by American television manufacturers in the early days of color television; and few firms do as much as they could to assess the impact of known technological change. Better information is both desirable and obtainable. But—and here is a major source of error—better information does not necessarily mean more precise information. The demand for better information is often a demand for false certainty; and the institution of formal procedures for looking into the future may encourage this demand. Certainly one cannot make sensible decisions in ignorance; but uncertainty is not ignorance—it is knowledge. A seemingly-precise forecast hides uncertainties, and therefore actually provides less information than a forecast which shows a range of possible values.

Thus the search for more information may be perverted into a search for false certainty. This is particularly likely if managers are asked to commit themselves to results at all far ahead. Such a pervasion may have two unfortunate consequences. Decisions may be made that do not properly reflect the possibility of error in the forecasts on which they are based; and over-confidence may produce excessive commitment to future action, and therefore a reluctance to take new decisions in the light of new information—indeed sometimes a reluctance even to notice new information.

The risk of domination by sophisticated techniques is serious. As a consequence of the emphasis on perfection of calculations, 'computerized data processing rather than planning has (sometimes) become the major concern. Figures (have been) accepted without sufficient questioning' (Little, Inc., 1966). At least one major British company has rejected the use of discounted cash flow for investment calculations because of the fear that its use will divert resources and attention from improving the quality of the basic data.

But these dangers are not inevitable. Instead of attempting to produce an optimum solution under given assumptions, formal procedures can be designed to force a 'broadening of the planning agenda, . . . giving a means for exploring the meaning of changed assumptions and effects of changes in policy' (Magee, 1966). Its power to compel a systematic search, in situations where sequential search procedures may be inadequate, or even disastrous, is perhaps the most important virtue of the 'decision tree' as an aid to management (Magee, 1964).

FORMAL PLANNING AND THE MANAGEMENT SYSTEM

Even if planning procedures are properly designed, however, there remains a deeper danger. Improving the quality of information is not the only way of improving the quality of decisions. If one asks what information is needed now to make the decisions that must be made now, one sometimes finds that some of the desired information is not really necessary. Some decisions are made too soon, even within the management system that a firm has at present. Others could be made later if the system were changed. Rossotti's statement that 'the more efficiently . . . information is made available, presumably the more flexible the organization can be in adapting to it quickly' (p. 13) is precisely the reverse of the truth. Rossotti is confusing the speed of response with its timing. If reliable information is available well in advance, the organization can start to prepare well in advance. If one sets out early, one doesn't need to go very fast. Flexibility is not the result of good early warning, it is an alternative to it.

If one looks at the whole sequence between the emergence of information and the fruition of decisions, one may well see greater possibilities in reducing the delays in the system than in improving the quality of information. The Industrial Dynamics Group at M.I.T., investigating a successful company that was worried about the problem of predicting success for a new product, found not only that there were ways of reducing the interval between ordering equipment and getting it into production, but that half the total lapse of time between information and production was consumed in the decision process itself. In another instance, a company's production scheduling was improved by making more frequent but less accurate forecasts. A consulting team from Arthur D. Little, Inc., found a complex PERT chart, prepared for a highway agency, which showed a lead time of ten years between the results of a traffic survey and the engineering drawings for the road; and not one input during that ten years represented any further information about traffic. A formal procedure which is directed at producing more information for earlier decisions is liable to channel efforts into refining forecasts and elaborating future action which could be better used in other ways.

The dangers of formal procedures outlined in the previous section may be summarized in two points: they may reduce the organization's flexibility (or in other words inhibit the initiation of a new decision-process and reduce the speed with which new decisions can be made), and

they may divert attention away from recognizing the need for flexibility. Perhaps the best way for firms to approach formal long-range planning is as something they should try to avoid. This does not mean as something they should try to dodge: it means so arranging the way they do things that as little as possible needs to be decided in advance. Of course, 'as little as possible' will still be a good deal; but if, instead of asking how they can more accurately foresee future events and thus make better decisions further ahead, firms were to ask first what they can do to avoid the need to decide so far ahead, they might be led to discover important ways of improving their performance.

What is needed is not action planning but system planning: the question at issue is not only the adequacy of formal procedures but also the effectiveness (and especially the speed) of the decision-process: these are by no means the same. The effectiveness of the decision-process depends on information and organization. In assembling information, more emphasis should be placed on surveillance rather than sophistication. The valid arguments for sophistication should not be ignored, but nor should it be forgotten that effective monitoring is more useful than elaborate manipulation of data which is out-of-date before the manipulation is complete.

. . . the real problem is to design an organization that can cope with the amount of uncertainty that is inherent in its situation. To deal effectively with this problem requires a shift of emphasis for organizational structure to the decision-process . . . It is easy to become so absorbed in the details of devising an elaborate planning procedure as to forget that redesign of the information flow and of the management system may be more effective ways of achieving some of the objectives of formal long-range planning.

THE PLACE OF FORMAL PLANNING

This article has been concerned with the purposes of formal planning, not with techniques. The great value of formal procedures—and their value can be very great—is in the raising and broadening of important issues that are liable otherwise to be inadequately considered. Much of this value can, however, be lost if these formal procedures are at all closely connected with the conflicting objective of controlling managerial performance. Planning procedures should be designed to illuminate, rather than obscure, the existence and implications of uncertainty. Finally, planning procedures should not concentrate on management action at the expense of the management system, and in particular should not be used to reconcile organization structure with the real situation: the design of a management system which facilitates quicker and more direct responses can be a better answer to some of the problems for which formal procedures offer only a second-best solution.

STRATEGIC CHANGE: "LOGICAL INCREMENTALISM"*

by James Brian Quinn

"When I was younger I always conceived of a room where all these [strategic] concepts were worked out for the whole company. Later I didn't find any such room. . . . The strategy [of the company] may not even exist in the mind of one man. I certainly don't know where it is written down. It is simply transmitted in the series of decisions made." Interview quote.

When well-managed major organizations make significant changes in strategy, the approaches they use frequently bear little resemblance to the rational-analytical systems so often touted in the planning literature. The full strategy is rarely written down in any one place. The processes used to arrive at the total strategy are typically fragmented, evolutionary, and largely intuitive. Al-

* Excerpted from an article originally published in *Sloan Management Review* I, no. 20 (Fall 1978), pp. 7–21. Copyright © 1978 by Sloan Management Review; reprinted by permission of the Review.

though one can usually find embedded in these fragments some very refined *pieces* of formal strategic analysis, the real strategy tends to *evolve* as internal decisions and external events flow together to create a new, widely shared consensus for action among key members of the top management team. Far from being an abrogation of good management practice, the rationale behind this kind of strategy formulation is so powerful that it perhaps provides the normative model for strategic decision making—rather than the step-by-step "formal systems planning" approach so often espoused.

THE FORMAL SYSTEMS PLANNING APPROACH

A strong normative literature states what factors *should* be included in a systematically planned strategy and how to analyze and relate these factors step-by-step. The main elements of this "formal planning approach" include: (1) analyzing one's own *internal situation:* strengths, weaknesses, competencies, problems; (2) *projecting* current product lines, profits, sales, investment needs into the future; (3) analyzing selected *external environments* and opponents' actions for opportunities and threats; (4) establishing *broad goals* as targets for subordinate groups' plans; (5) *identifying the gap* between expected and desired results; (6) communicating *planning assumptions* to the divisions; (7) requesting *proposed plans* from subordinate groups with more specific target goals, resource needs, and supporting action plans; (8) occasionally asking for *special studies of alternatives, contingencies,* or longer-term opportunities; (9) *reviewing and approving* divisional plans and summing these for corporate needs; (10) developing *long-term budgets* presumably related to plans; (11) *implementing* plans; and (12) *monitoring and evaluating* performance (presumably against plans, but usually against budgets).

While this approach is excellent for some purposes, it tends to focus unduly on measurable quantitative factors and to under-emphasize the vital qualitative, organizational, and power-behavioral factors which so often determine strategic success in one situation versus another. In practice, such planning is just one building block in a continuous stream of events that really determine corporate strategy.

THE POWER-BEHAVIORAL APPROACH

Other investigators have provided important insights on the crucial psychological, power, and behavioral relationships in strategy formulation. Among other things, these have enhanced understanding about: the *multiple goal structures* of organizations, the *politics* of strategic decisions, executive *bargaining* and *negotiation* processes, *satisficing* (as opposed to maximizing) in decision making, the role of *coalitions* in strategic management, and the practice of "*muddling*" in the public sphere. Unfortunately, however, many power-behavioral studies have been conducted in settings far removed from the realities of strategy formulation. Others have concentrated solely on human dynamics, power relationships, and organizational processes and ignored the ways in which systematic data analysis shapes and often dominates crucial aspects of strategic decisions. Finally, few have offered much normative guidance for the strategist.

THE STUDY

Recognizing the contributions and limitations of both approaches, I attempted to document the dynamics of actual strategic change processes in some ten major companies as perceived by those most knowledgeably and intimately involved in them. These companies varied with respect to products, markets, time horizons, technological complexities, and national versus international dimensions. . . .[1]

[1]   *Cooperating companies included: General Motors Corp., Chrysler Corp., Volvo (AB), General Mills, Pillsbury Co., Xerox Corp., Texas Instruments, Exxon, Continental Group, and Pilkington Brothers.*

SUMMARY FINDINGS

Several important findings have begun to emerge from these investigations.

- Neither the "power-behavioral" nor the "formal systems planning" paradigm adequately characterizes the way successful strategic processes operate.

- Effective strategies tend to emerge from a series of "strategic subsystems," each of which attacks a specific class of strategic issue (e.g., acquisitions, divestitures, or major reorganizations) in a disciplined way, but which is blended incrementally and opportunistically into a cohesive pattern that becomes the company's strategy.

- The logic behind each "subsystem" is so powerful that, to some extent, it may serve as a normative approach for formulating these key elements of strategy in large companies.

- Because of cognitive and process limits, almost all of these subsystems—and the formal planning activity itself—must be managed and linked together by an approach best described as "logical incrementalism."

- Such incrementalism is not "muddling." It is a purposeful, effective, proactive management technique for improving and integrating *both* the analytical and behavioral aspects of strategy formulation.

This article will document these findings, suggest the logic behind several important "subsystems" for strategy formulation, and outline some of the management and thought processes executives in large organizations use to synthesize them into effective corporate strategies. Such strategies embrace those patterns of high leverage decisions (on major goals, policies, and action sequences) which affect the viability and direction of the entire enterprise or determine its competitive posture for an extended time period.

CRITICAL STRATEGIC ISSUES

Although certain "hard data" decisions (e.g., on product-market position or resource allocations) tend to dominate the analytical literature

(Ansoff, 1965; Katz, 1970), executives identified other "soft" changes that have at least as much importance in shaping their concern's strategic posture. Most often cited were changes in the company's:

1. Overall organizational structure or its basic management style;
2. Relationships with the government or other external interest groups;
3. Acquisition, divestiture, or divisional control practices;
4. International posture and relationships;
5. Innovative capabilities or personnel motivations as affected by growth;
6. Worker and professional relationships reflecting changed social expectations and values;
7. Past or anticipated technological environments.

When executives were asked to "describe the processes through which their company arrived at its new posture" vis-à-vis each of these critical domains, several important points emerged. First, few of these issues lent themselves to quantitative modeling techniques or perhaps even formal financial analyses. Second, successful companies used a different "subsystem" to formulate strategy for each major class of strategic issues, yet these "subsystems" were quite similar among

FIGURE 2

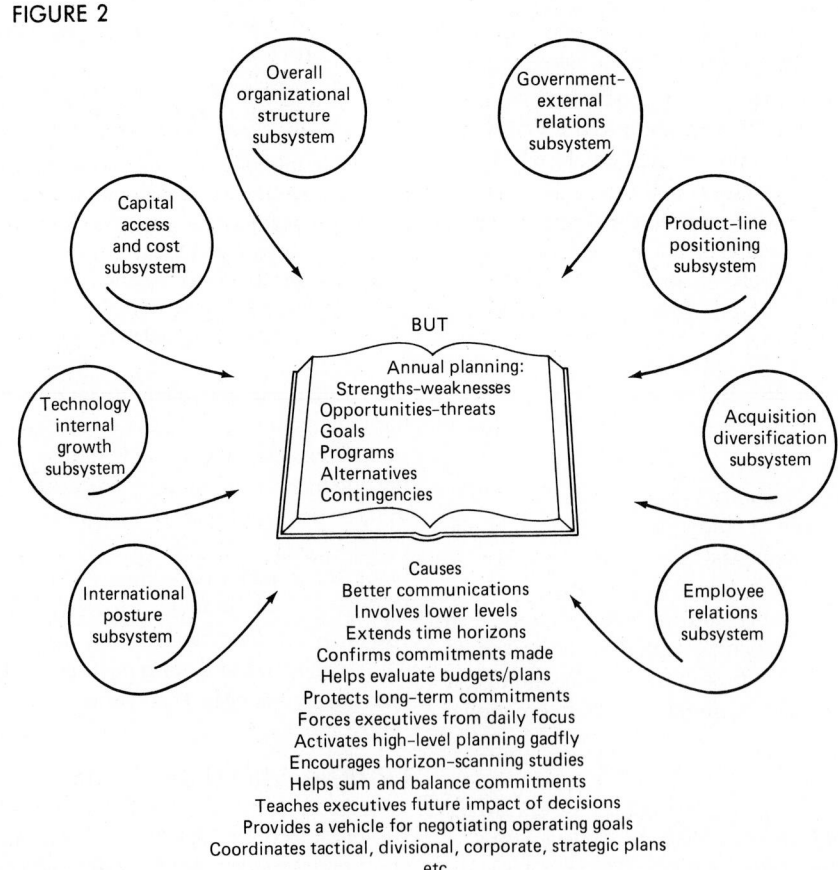

companies even in very different industries (see Figure 2). Finally, no single formal analytical process could handle all strategic variables simultaneously on a planned basis. Why?

Precipitating Events

Often external or internal events, over which managements had essentially no control, would precipitate urgent, piecemeal, interim decisions which inexorably shaped the company's future strategic posture. One clearly observes this phenomenon in: the decisions forced on General Motors by the 1973–74 oil crisis, the shift in posture pressed upon Exxon by sudden nationalizations, or the dramatic opportunities allowed for Haloid Corporation and Pilkington Brothers, Ltd. by the unexpected inventions of xerography and float glass.

In these cases, analyses from earlier formal planning cycles did contribute greatly, as long as the general nature of the contingency had been anticipated. They broadened the information base available (as in Exxon's case), extended the options considered (Haloid-Xerox), created shared values to guide decisions about precipitating events in consistent directions (Pilkington), or built up resource bases, management flexibilities, or active search routines for opportunities whose specific nature could not be defined in advance (General Mills, Pillsbury). But no organization— no matter how brilliant, rational, or imaginative— could possibly foresee the timing, severity, or even the nature of all such precipitating events. Further, when these events did occur there might be neither time, resources, nor information enough to undertake a full formal strategic analysis of all possible options and their consequences. Yet early decisions made under stress conditions often meant new thrusts, precedents, or lost opportunities that were difficult to reverse later.

An Incremental Logic

Recognizing this, top executives usually consciously tried to deal with precipitating events in an incremental fashion. Early commitments were kept broadly formative, tentative, and sub-ject to later review. In some cases neither the company nor the external players could understand the full implications of alternative actions. All parties wanted to test assumptions and have an opportunity to learn from and adapt to the others' responses. Such behavior clearly occurred during the 1973–74 oil crisis; the ensuing interactions improved the quality of decisions for all. It also recurred frequently in other widely different contexts. For example:

Neither the potential producer nor user of a completely new product or process (like xerography or float glass) could fully conceptualize its ramifications without interactive testing. All parties benefited from procedures which purposely delayed decisions and allowed mutual feedback. Some companies, like IBM or Xerox, have formalized this concept into "phase program planning" systems. They make concrete decisions only on individual phases (or stages) of new product developments, establish interactive testing procedures with customers, and postpone final configuration commitments until the latest possible moment.

Similarly, even under pressure, most top executives were extremely sensitive to organizational and power relationships and consciously managed decision processes to improve these dynamics. They often purposely delayed initial decisions, or kept such decisions vague, in order to encourage lower-level participation, to gain more information from specialists, or to build commitment to solutions. Even when a crisis atmosphere tended to shorten time horizons and make decisions more goal oriented than political, perceptive executives consciously tried to keep their options open until they understood how the crisis would affect the power bases and needs of their key constituents. . . .

INCREMENTALISM IN STRATEGIC SUBSYSTEMS

One also finds that an incremental logic applies in attacking many of the critical subsystems of corporate strategy. Those subsystems for considering diversification moves, divestitures, major reorganizations, or government-external relations are typical and will be described here. In each case, conscious incrementalism helps to: (1) cope with both the cognitive and process limits on each major decision, (2) build the logical-analytical framework these decisions require, and (3) create the personal and organizational awareness, understanding, acceptance, and commitment needed to implement the strategies effectively.

The Diversification Subsystem

Strategies for diversification, either through R&D or acquisitions, provide excellent examples. The formal analytical steps needed for successful diversification are well documented (Mace and Montgomery, 1962). However, the precise directions that R&D may project the company can only be understood step-by-step as scientists uncover new phenomena, make and amplify discoveries, build prototypes, reduce concepts to practice, and interact with users during product introductions. Similarly, only as each acquisition is sequentially identified, investigated, negotiated for, and integrated into the organization can one predict its ultimate impact on the total enterprise.

A step-by-step approach is clearly necessary to guide and assess the strategic fit of each internal or external diversification candidate. Incremental processes are also required to manage the crucial psychological and power shifts that ultimately determine the program's overall direction and consequences. These processes help unify both the analytical and behavioral aspects of diversification decisions. They create the broad conceptual consensus, the risk-taking attitudes, the organizational and resource flexibilities, and the adaptive dynamism that determine both the timing and direction of diversification strategies. Most important among these processes are:

■ *Generating a genuine, top-level psychological commitment to diversification.* General Mills, Pillsbury, and Xerox all started their major diversification programs with broad analytical studies and goal-setting exercises designed both to build top-level consensus

around the need to diversify and to establish the general directions for diversification. Without such action, top-level bargaining for resources would have continued to support only more familiar (and hence apparently less risky) old lines, and this could delay or undermine the entire diversification endeavor.

■ *Consciously preparing to move opportunistically.* Organizational and fiscal resources must be built up in advance to exploit candidates as they randomly appear. And a "credible activist" for ventures must be developed and backed by someone with commitment power. All successful acquirers created the potential for "profit centered" divisions within their organizational structures, strengthened their financial-controllership capabilities, took action to create low-cost capital access, and maintained the shortest possible communication lines from the "acquisitions activist" to the resource-committing authority. All these actions integrally determined which diversifications actually could be made, the timing of their accession, and the pace they could be absorbed.

■ *Building a "comfort factor" for risk taking.* Perceived risk is largely a function of one's knowledge about a field. Hence well-conceived diversification programs should anticipate a trial-and-error period during which top managers reject early proposed fields or opportunities until they have analyzed enough trial candidates to "become comfortable" with an initial selection. Early successes tend to be "sure things" close to the companies' past (real or supposed) expertise. After a few successful diversifications, managements tend to become more confident and accept other candidates—farther from traditional lines—at a faster rate. Again the way this process is handled affects both the direction and pace of the actual program.

■ *Developing a new ethos.* If new divisions are more successful than the old—as they should be—they attract relatively more resources and their political power grows. Their most effective line managers move into corporate positions, and slowly the company's special competency and ethos change. Finally, the concepts and products which once dominated the company's culture may decline in importance or even disappear. Acknowledging these ultimate consequences to the organization at the beginning of a diversification program would clearly be impolitic, even if the manager both desired and could predict the probable new ethos. These factors must be handled adaptively, as opportunities present themselves and as individual leaders and power centers develop.

Each of the above processes interacts with all others (and with the random appearance of diversification candidates) to affect action sequences, elapsed time, and ultimate results in unexpected ways. Complexities are so great that few diversification programs end up as initially envisioned. Consequently, wise managers recognize the limits to systematic analysis in diversification, and use formal planning to build the "comfort levels" executives need for risk taking and to guide the program's early directions and priorities. They then modify these flexibly, step-by-step, as new opportunities, power centers, and developed competencies merge to create new potentials.

The Divestiture Subsystem

Similar practices govern the handling of divestitures. Divisions often drag along in a less-than-desired condition for years before they can be strategically divested. In some cases, ailing divisions might have just enough yield or potential to offer hoped-for viability. In others, they might represent the company's vital core from earlier years, the creations of a powerful person nearing retirement, or the psychological touchstones of the company's past traditions.

Again, in designing divestiture strategies, top executives had to reinforce vaguely felt concerns with detailed data, build up managers' comfort levels about issues, achieve participation in and commitment to decisions, and move opportunistically to make actual changes. In many cases, the precise nature of the decision was not clear at the outset. Executives often made seemingly unrelated personnel shifts or appointments which changed the value set of critical groups,

or started a series of staff studies which generated awareness or acceptance of a potential problem. They might then instigate goal assessment, business review, or "planning" programs to provide broader forums for discussion and a wider consensus for action. Even then they might wait for a crisis, a crucial retirement, or an attractive sale opportunity to determine the timing and conditions of divestiture. In some cases, decisions could be direct and analytical. But when divestitures involved the psychological centers of the organization, the process had to be much more oblique and carefully orchestrated. For example:

When General Rawlings became president at General Mills, he had his newly developed Staff (Corporate Analysis) Department make informal presentations to top management on key issues. Later these were expanded to formal Management Operating Reviews (MORs) with all corporate and divisional top managers and controllers present. As problem operations were identified (many "generally known for a long time"), teams of corporate and divisional people were assigned to investigate them in depth. Once needed new data systems were built and studies came into place, they focused increasing attention on some hasty post-World War II acquisitions. . . .

Careful incrementalism is essential in most divestitures to disguise intentions yet create the awareness, value changes, needed data, psychological acceptance, and managerial consensus required for such decisions. Early, openly acknowledged, formal plans would clearly be invitations to disaster.

The Major Reorganization Subsystem

It is well recognized that major organizational changes are an integral part of strategy (Chandler, 1962). Sometimes they constitute a strategy themselves, sometimes they precede and/or precipitate a new strategy, and sometimes they help to implement a strategy. However, like many other important strategic decisions, macro-organizational moves are typically handled incrementally *and* outside of formal planning processes. Their effects on personal or power relationships preclude discussion in the open forums and reports of such processes.

In addition, major organizational changes have timing imperatives (or "process limits") all their own. In making any significant shifts, the executive must think through the new roles, capabilities, and probable individual reactions of the many principals affected. He may have to wait for the promotion or retirement of a valued colleague before consummating any change. He then frequently has to bring in, train, or test new people for substantial periods before he can staff key posts with confidence. During this testing period he may substantially modify his original concept of the reorganization, as he evaluates individuals' potentials, their performance in specific roles, their personal drives, and their relationships with other team members.

Because this chain of decisions affects the career development, power, affluence, and self-image of so many, the executive tends to keep close counsel in his discussions, negotiates individually with key people, and makes final commitments as late as possible in order to obtain the best matches between people's capabilities, personalities, and aspirations and their new roles. Typically, all these events do not come together at one convenient time, particularly the moment annual plans are due. Instead the executive moves opportunistically, step-by-step, selectively moving people toward a broadly conceived organizational goal, which is constantly modified and rarely articulated in detail until the last pieces fit together.

Major organizational moves may also define entirely new strategies the guiding executive cannot fully foresee. For example:

When Exxon began its regional decentralization on a worldwide basis, the Executive Committee placed a senior officer and board member with a very responsive management style in a vaguely defined "coordinative role" vis-à-vis its powerful and successful European units. Over a period of two years this man sensed problems and experimented with voluntary coordinative possibilities on a pan-European basis. Only later, with greater understanding by both corporate and divisional officers, did Exxon move to a more formal "line" relationship for what became Exxon Europe. Even then the move had to be coordinated in other areas of the world. All of these changes together led to an entirely new internal power balance toward regional and non-U.S. concerns and to a more responsive worldwide posture for Exxon. . . .

In such situations, executives may be able to predict the broad direction, but not the precise nature, of the ultimate strategy which will result. In some cases, such as Exxon, the rebalance of power and information relationships *becomes* the strategy, or at least its central element. In others, organizational shifts are primarily means of triggering or implementing new strategic concepts and philosophies. But in all cases, major organizational changes create unexpected new stresses, opportunities, power bases, information centers, and credibility relationships that can affect both previous plans and future strategies in unanticipated ways. Effective reorganization decisions, therefore, allow for testing, flexibility, and feedback. Hence, they should, and usually do, evolve incrementally.

The Government-External Relations Subsystem

Almost all companies cited government and other external activist groups as among the most important forces causing significant changes in their strategic postures during the periods examined. However, when asked "how did your company arrive at its own strategy vis-à-vis these forces?" it became clear that few companies had cohesive strategies (integrated sets of goals, policies, and programs) for government-external relations, other than lobbying for or against specific legislative actions. To the extent that other strategies did exist, they were piecemeal, ad hoc, and had been derived in a very evolutionary manner. Yet there seemed to be very good reasons for such incrementalism. The following is one of the best short explanations of the way these practices develop:

We are a very large company, and we understand that any massive overt action on our part could easily create more public antagonism than support for our viewpoint. It is also hard to say in advance exactly what public response any particular action might create. So we tend to test a number of different approaches on a small scale with only limited or local company identification. If one approach works, we'll test it further and amplify its use. If another bombs, we try to keep it from being used again. Slowly we find a series of advertising, public relations, community relations actions that seem to help. Then along comes another issue and we start all over again. Gradually the successful approaches merge into a pattern of actions that becomes our strategy. We certainly don't have an overall strategy on this, and frankly I don't think we devote enough [organizational and fiscal] resources to it. This may be our most important strategic issue. . . .

In this realm, uncontrollable forces dominate. Data are very soft, often can be only subjectively sensed, and may be costly to quantify. The possible responses of individuals and groups to different stimuli are difficult to determine in advance. The number of potential opponents with power is very high, and the diversity in their viewpoints and possible modes of attack is so substantial that it is physically impossible to lay out probabilistic decision diagrams that would have much meaning. Results are unpredictable and error costs extreme. Even the best intended and most rational-seeming strategies can be converted into disasters unless they are thoroughly and interactively tested. . . .

For such reasons, companies will probably always have to derive major portions of their government-external relations strategies in an experimental, iterative fashion. But such incrementalism could be much more proactive than it often has been in the past. Favorable public opinion and political action take a long time to mold. There is a body of knowledge about how to influence political action. There are also methods of informal and formal analyses which can help companies anticipate major political movements and adjust their goals or policies in a timely fashion. Once potential approaches are experimentally derived (without destroying needed flexibilities), more cohesive planning can ensure that the resources committed are sufficient to achieve the desired goals, that all important polities are included in plans, and that rigorous and adaptive internal controls maintain those high performance, attitude, service, and image qualities that lend credibility to the strategy. But again, one sees logical incrementalism as the essential thread linking together information gathering, analysis, testing, and the behavioral and power considerations in this strategic subsystem.

FORMAL PLANNING IN CORPORATE STRATEGY

What role do classical formal planning techniques play in strategy formulation? All companies in the sample do have formal planning procedures embedded in their management direction and control systems. These serve certain essential functions. In a process sense, they:

Provide a discipline forcing managers to take a careful look ahead periodically;

Require rigorous communications about goals, strategic issues, and resource allocations;

Stimulate longer-term analyses than would otherwise be made;

Generate a basis for evaluating and integrating short-term plans;

Lengthen time horizons and protect longterm investments such as R&D;

Create a psychological backdrop and an information framework about the future against which managers can calibrate short-term or interim decisions.

In a decision-making sense, they:

Fine tune annual commitments;

Formalize cost reduction programs;

Help implement strategic changes once decided

on (for example, coordinating all elements of Exxon's decision to change its corporate name);

Finally, "special studies" had high impact at key junctures for specific decisions.

Formal Plans Also "Increment"

Although individual staff planners were often effective in identifying potential problems and bringing them to top management's attention, the annual planning process itself was rarely (if ever) the initiating source of really new key issues or radical departures into new product/market realms. These almost always came from precipitating events, special studies, or conceptions implanted through the kinds of "logical incremental" processes described above.

In fact, formal planning practices actually institutionalize incrementalism. There are two reasons for this. *First*, in order to utilize specialized expertise and to obtain executive involvement and commitment, most planning occurs "from the bottom up" in response to broadly defined assumptions or goals, many of which are longstanding or negotiated well in advance. Of necessity, lower-level groups have only a partial view of the corporation's total strategy, and command only a fragment of its resources. Their power bases, identity, expertise, and rewards also usually depend on their existing products or processes. Hence, these products or processes, rather than entirely new departures, should and do receive their primary attention. *Second*, most managements purposely design their plans to be "living" or "ever green." They are intended only as "frameworks" to guide and provide consistency for future decisions made incrementally. To act otherwise would be to deny that further information could have a value. Thus, properly formulated formal plans are also a part of an incremental logic.

Special Studies

Formal planning was most successful in stimulating significant change when it was set up as a "special study" on some important aspect of corporate strategy. For example:

In 1958, when it became apparent that Pilkington's new float glass process would work, the company formed a Directors Flat Glass Committee consisting of all internal directors associated with float glass "to consider the broad issues of flat glass [strategy] in both the present and the future." The Committee did not attempt detailed plans. Instead, it tried to deal in broad concepts, identify alternate routes, and think through the potential consequences of each route some ten years ahead. Of some of the key strategic decisions Sir Alastair later said, "It would be difficult to identify an exact moment when the decision was made. . . . Nevertheless, over a period of time a consensus crystallized with great clarity.". . .

In each case there were also important precursor events, analyses, and political interactions, and each was followed by organizational, power, and behavioral changes. But interestingly, such special strategic studies also represent a "subsystem" of strategy formulation distinct from both annual planning activities and the other subsystems exemplified above. Each of these develops some important aspect of strategy, incrementally blending its conclusions with those of other subsystems, and it would be virtually impossible to force all these together to crystallize a completely articulated corporate strategy at any one instant.

Total Posture Planning

Occasionally, however, managements do attempt very broad assessments of their companies' total posture. An example follows:

Shortly after becoming CEO of General Mills, Mr. James McFarland decided that his job was "to take a very good company and move it to greatness," but that it was up to his management group, not himself alone, to decide what a great company was and how to get there. Consequently he took some thirty-five of the company's topmost managers away for a three day management retreat. On the first day, after agreeing to broad financial goals, the group broke up into units of six to eight people. Each unit was to answer the question, "what is a great company?" from the viewpoints of stockholders, employees, suppliers, the public, and society. Each unit reported back at the end of the day, and the whole group tried to reach a consensus through discussion.

On the second day the groups, in the same format, assessed the company's strengths and weaknesses relative to the defined posture of "greatness." The third day focused on how to overcome the company's weaknesses and move it toward a great company. This broad consensus led, over the next several years, to the surveys of fields for acquisition, the building of management's initial "comfort levels" with certain fields, and the acquisition-divestiture strategy that characterized the McFarland era at General Mills. . . .

Yet even such major endeavors were only portions of a total strategic process. Values which had been built up over decades stimulated or constrained alternatives. Precipitating events, acquisitions, divestitures, external relations, and organizational changes developed important segments of each strategy incrementally. Even the strategies articulated left key elements to be defined as new information became available, polities permitted, or particular opportunities appeared (like Pilkington's Electro-float invention or Xerox's Daconics acquisition). Major product thrusts (like Pilkington's TV tubes or Xerox's computers) proved unsuccessful. Actual strategies therefore evolved as each company overextended, consolidated, made errors, and rebalanced various thrusts over time. And it was both logical and expected that this would be the case.

LOGICAL INCREMENTALISM

All of the above suggest that strategic decisions do not lend themselves to aggregation into a single massive decision matrix where all factors can be treated relatively simultaneously in order to arrive at a holistic optimum. Many have spoken of the "cognitive limits" (March and Simon, 1958) which prevent this. Of equal importance are the "process limits"—i.e., the timing and sequencing imperatives necessary to create aware-

ness, build comfort levels, develop consensus, select and train people, etc.—which constrain the system, yet ultimately determine the decision itself. Unlike the preparation of a fine banquet, it is virtually impossible for the manager to orchestrate all internal decisions, external environmental events, behavioral and power relationships, technical and informational needs, and actions of intelligent opponents so that they come together at any precise moment.

Can the Process Be Managed?

Instead, the executive usually deals with the logic of each "subsystem" of strategy formulation largely on its own merits and usually with a different subset of people. He tries to develop or maintain in his own mind a consistent pattern among the decisions made in each subsystem. Knowing his own limitations and the unknowability of the events he faces, he consciously tries to tap the minds and psychic drives of others. He often purposely keeps questions broad and decisions vague in early stages to avoid creating undue rigidities and to stimulate others' creativity. Logic, of course, dictates that he make final commitments *as late as possible* consistent with the information he has.

Consequently, many a successful executive will initially set only broad goals and policies which can accommodate a variety of specific proposals from below, yet give a sense of guidance to the proposers. As they come forward the proposals automatically and beneficially attract the support and identity of their sponsors. Being only proposals, the executive can treat these at less politically charged levels, as specific projects rather than as larger goal or policy precedents. Therefore, he can encourage, discourage, or kill alternatives with considerably less political exposure. As events and opportunities emerge, he can incrementally guide the pattern of escalated or accepted proposals to suit his own purposes without getting prematurely committed to any rigid solution set which unpredictable events might prove wrong or which opponents find sufficiently threatening to coalesce against.

A Strategy Emerges

Successful executives link together and bring order to a series of strategic processes and decisions spanning years. At the beginning of the process it is literally impossible to predict all the events and forces which will shape the future of the company. The best executives can do is to forecast the most likely forces which will impinge on the company's affairs and the ranges of their possible impact. They then attempt to build a resource base and a corporate *posture* that are so strong in selected areas that the enterprise can survive and prosper despite all but the most devastating events. They consciously select market/technological/product segments which the concern can "dominate" given its resource limits, and place some "side bets" (Ansoff, 1965) in order to decrease the risk of catastrophic failure or to increase the company's flexibility for future options.

They then proceed incrementally to handle urgent matters, start longer-term sequences whose specific future branches and consequences are perhaps murky, respond to unforeseen events as they occur, build on successes, and brace up or cut losses on failures. They constantly reassess the future, find new congruencies as events unfurl, and blend the organization's skills and resources into new balances of dominance and risk aversion as various forces intersect to suggest better— but never perfect—alignments. The process is dynamic, with neither a real beginning nor end. . . .

CONCLUSION

Strategy deals with the unknowable, not the uncertain. It involves forces of such great number, strength, and combinatory powers that one cannot predict events in a probabilistic sense. Hence logic dictates that one proceed flexibly and experimentally from broad concepts toward specific commitments, making the latter concrete as late as possible in order to narrow the bands of uncertainty and to benefit from the best available information. This is the process of "logical incrementalism."

"Logical incrementalism" is not "muddling," as most people use that word. It is conscious, purposeful, proactive, good management. Properly managed, it allows the executive to bind together the contributions of rational systematic analyses, political and power theories, and organizational behavior concepts. It helps the executive achieve cohesion and identity with new directions. It allows him to deal with power relationships and individual behavioral needs, and permits him to use the best possible informational and analytical inputs in choosing his major courses of action. . . .

THE HONDA EFFECT*
by Richard T. Pascale

At face value, "strategy" is an innocent noun. Webster defines it as the large-scale planning and direction of operations. In the business context, it pertains to a process by which a firm searches and analyzes its environment and resources in order to 1) select opportunities defined in terms of markets to be served and products to serve them, and 2) makes discrete decisions to invest resources in order to achieve identified objectives (Bower, 1970: 7–8).

But for a vast and influential population of executives, planners, academics, and consultants, strategy is more than a conventional English noun. It embodies an implicit model of how organizations should be guided and consequently, proconfigures our way of thinking. Strategy formulation 1) is generally assumed to be driven by senior management whom we expect to set strategic direction; 2) has been extensively influenced by empirical models and concepts; and 3) is often associated with a laborious strategic planning pro-

* Excerpted from an article originally entitled "Perspectives on Strategy: The Real Story Behind Honda's Success," *California Management Review XXVI,* no. 3, pp. 47–72. Copyright © 1984 by the Regents of the University of California. Reprinted by permission of the Regents.

cess that, in some companies, has produced more paper than insight.

A $500-million-a-year "strategy" industry has emerged in the United States and Europe comprised of management consultants, strategic planning staffs, and business school academics. It caters to the unique emphasis that American and European companies place upon this particular aspect of managing and directing corporations.

Words often derive meaning from their cultural context. *Strategy* is one such word and nowhere is the contrast of meanings more pronounced than between Japan and the United States. The Japanese view the emphasis we place on "strategy" as we might regard their enthusiasm for Kabuki or sumo wrestling. They note our interest not with an intent of acquiring similar ones but for insight into our peculiarities. The Japanese are somewhat distrustful of a single "strategy" for in their view any idea that focuses attention does so at the expense of peripheral vision. They strongly believe that *peripheral vision* is essential to discerning changes in the customer, the technology or competition, and is the key to corporate survival over the long haul. They regard any prospensity to be driven by a single-minded strategy as a weakness.

The Japanese have particular discomfort with strategic concepts. While they do not reject ideas such as the experience curve or portfolio theory outright they regard them as a stimulus to perception. They have often ferreted out the "formula" of their concept-driven American competitors and exploited their inflexibility. In musical instruments, for example, (a mature industry facing stagnation as birthrates in the U.S. and Japan declined), Yamaha might have classified its products as "cash cows" and gone on to better things (as its chief U.S. competitor, Baldwin United, had done). Instead, beginning with a negligible share of the U.S. market, Yamaha plowed ahead and destroyed Baldwin's seemingly unchallengeable dominance. YKK's success in zippers against Talon (a Textron division) and Honda's outflanking of Harley-Davidson (a former AMF subsidiary) in the motorcycle field provide parallel illustrations. All three cases involved American conglomerates, wedded to the portfolio concept, that had classified pianos, zippers, and motorcycles as mature businesses to be harvested rather than nourished and defended. Of course, those who developed portfolio theory and other strategic concepts protest that they were never intended to be mindlessly applied in setting strategic direction. But most would also agree that there is a widespread tendency in American corporations to misapply concepts and to otherwise become strategically myopic—ignoring the marketplace, the customer, and the problems of execution. This tendency toward misapplication, being both prevasive and persistent over several decades, is a phenomenon that the literature has largely ignored [for recent exceptions, see Hayes and Abernathy, 1980:67; Hayes and Garvin 1982:71]. There is a need to explicitly identify the factors that influence how we conceptualize strategy—and which foster its misuse.

HONDA: THE STRATEGY MODEL

In 1975, Boston Consulting Group [BCG] presented the British government its final report: *Strategy Alternatives for the British Motorcycle Industry*. This 120-page document identified two key factors leading to the British demise in the world's motorcycle industry:

- market share loss and profitability declines, and
- scale economy disadvantages in technology, distribution, and manufacturing.

During the period 1959 to 1973, the British share of the U.S. motorcycle industry had dropped from 49 percent to 9 percent. Introducing BCG's recommended strategy (of targeting market segments where sufficient production volumes could be attained to be price competitive) the report states:

> The success of the Japanese manufacturers originated with the growth of their domestic market during the 1950s. As

recently as 1960, only 4 percent of Japanese motorcycle production was exported. By this time, however, the Japanese had developed huge production volumes in small motorcycles in their domestic market, and volume-related cost reductions had followed. This resulted in a highly competitive cost position which the Japanese used as a springboard for penetration of world markets with small motorcycles in the early 1960s (BCG, 1975:xiv).

The BCG study was made public by the British government and rapidly disseminated in the United States. It exemplifies the necessary (and I argue, insufficient) strategist's perspective of

- examining competition primarily from an intercompany perspective,
- at a high level of abstraction,
- with heavy reliance on micro-economic concepts (such as the experience curve).

Case writers at Harvard Business School, UCLA, and the University of Virginia quickly condensed the BCG report for classroom use in case discussions. It currently enjoys extensive use in first-term courses in Business Policy.

Of particular note in the BCG study, and in the subsequent Harvard Business School rendition, is the historical treatment of Honda.

The mix of competitors in the U.S. motorcycle market underwent a major shift in the 1960s. Motorcycle registrations increased from 575,000 in 1960 to 1,382,000 in 1965. Prior to 1960 the U.S. market was served mainly by Harley-Davidson of U.S.A., BSA, Triumph and Norton of U.K. and Moto-Guzzi of Italy. Harley was the market leader with total 1959 sales of $16.6 million. After the second world war, motorcycles in the U.S.A. attracted a very limited group of people other than police and army personnel who used motorcycles on the job. While most motorcyclists were no doubt decent people, groups of rowdies who went around on motorcycles and called themselves by such names as "Hell's An-

gels," "Satan's Slaves" gave motorcycling a bad image. Even leather jackets which were worn by motorcyclists as a protective device acquired an unsavory image. A 1953 movie called "The Wild Ones" staring a 650cc Triumph, a black leather jacket and Marlon Brando gave the rowdy motorcyclists wide media coverage. The stereotype of the motorcyclist was a leather-jacketed, teenage troublemaker.

Honda established an American subsidiary in 1959—American Honda Motor Company. This was in sharp contrast to other foreign producers who relied on distributors. Honda's marketing strategy was described in the 1963 annual report as "With its policy of selling, not primarily to confirmed motorcyclists but rather to members of the general public who had never before given a second thought to a motorcycle. . . ." Honda started its push in the U.S. market with the smallest, lightweight motorcycles. It had a three-speed transmission, an automatic clutch, five horsepower (the American cycle only had two and a half), an electric starter and step through frame for female riders. And it was easier to handle. The Honda machines sold for under $250 in retail compared with $1,000–$1,500 for the bigger American or British machines. Even at that early date Honda was probably superior to other competitors in productivity.

By June 1960 Honda's Research and Development effort was staffed with 700 designers/engineers. This might be contrasted with 100 engineers/draftsmen employed by . . . (European and American competitors). In 1962 production per man-year was running at 159 units, (a figure not reached by Harley-Davidson until 1974). Honda's net fixed asset investment was $8170 per employee . . . (more than twice its European and American competitors). With 1959 sales of $55 million Honda was already the largest motorcycle producer in the world.

Honda followed a policy of developing the market region by region. They started on the West Coast and moved eastward over a period of four-five years. Honda sold 2,500 machines in the U.S.

in 1960. In 1961 they lined up 125 distributors and spent $150,000 on regional advertising. Their advertising was directed to the young families, their advertising theme was "You Meet the Nicest People on a Honda." This was a deliberate attempt to dissociate motorcycles from rowdy, Hell's Angels type people.

Honda's success in creating demand for lightweight motorcycles was phenomenal. American Honda's sales went from $500,000 in 1960 to $77 million in 1965. By 1966 the market share data showed the ascendancy of Japanese producers and their success in selling lightweight motorcycles. [Honda had 63% of the market.] . . . Starting from virtually nothing in 1960, the lightweight motorcycles had clearly established their lead (Purkayastha, 1981: 5, 10, 11, 12).

QUOTING FROM THE
BCG REPORT:

The Japanese motorcycle industry, and in particular Honda, the market leader, present a [consistent] picture. The basic philosophy of the Japanese manufacturers is that high volumes per model provide the potential for high productivity as a result of using capital intensive and highly automated techniques. Their marketing strategies are therefore directed towards developing these high model volumes, hence the careful attention that we have observed them giving to growth and market share.

The overall result of this philosophy over time has been that the Japanese have now developed an entrenched and leading position in terms of technology and production methods. . . . The major factors which appear to account for the Japanese superiority in both these areas are . . . (specialized production systems, balancing engineering and market requirements, and the cost efficiency and reliability of suppliers) (BCG, pp. 59, 40).

As evidence of Honda's strategy of taking position as low cost producer and exploiting economies of scale, other sources cite Honda's construction in 1959 of a plant to manufacture 30,000 motorcycles per month well ahead of existing demand at the time. (Up until then Honda's most popular models sold 2,000–3,000 units per month.) (Sakiya, 1982:119)

The overall picture is depicted by the quotes above exemplifies the "strategy model." Honda is portrayed as a firm dedicated to being the low price producer, utilizing its dominant market position in Japan to force entry into the U.S. market, expanding that market by redefining a leisure class ("Nicest People") segment, and exploiting its comparative advantage via aggressive pricing and advertising. Richard Rumelt, writing the teaching note for the UCLA adaptation of the case states: "The fundamental contribution of BCG is not the experience curve per se but the ever-present assumption that differences in cost (or efficiency)

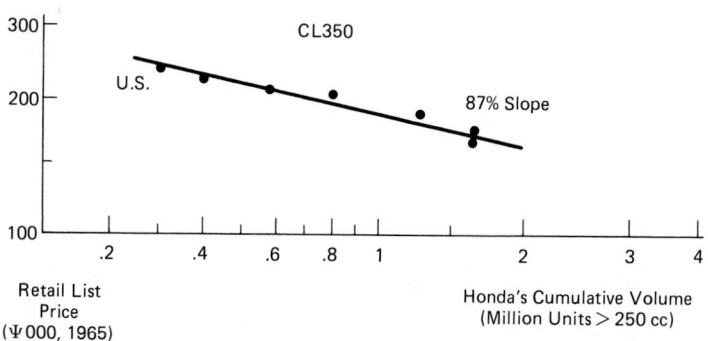

Source: BCG (1975) "Strategy Alternatives for the British Motorcycle Industry."

are the fundamental components of strategy''
(Rumelt, 1980:2).

THE ORGANIZATIONAL PROCESS
PERSPECTIVE

On September 10, 1982, the six Japanese executives responsible for Honda's entry into the U.S.
motorcycle market in 1959 assembled in Honda's
Tokyo headquarters. They had gathered at my
request to describe in fine grain detail the sequence
of events that had led to Honda's ultimate position
of dominance in the U.S. market. All were in
their sixties; three were retired. The story that
unfolded, greatly abbreviated below, highlights
miscalculation, serendipity, and organizational
learning—counterpoints to the streamlined ''strategy'' version related earlier.

Any account of Honda's successes must
grasp at the outset the unusual character of its
founder, Sochiro Honda and his partner, Takeo
Fujisawa. Honda was an inventive genius with
a large ego and mercurial temperament, given
to bouts of ''philandering'' (to use his expression)
(Sakiya, 1979). In the formative stages of his
company, Honda is variously reported to have
tossed a geisha out a second-story window,
climbed inside a septic tank to retrieve a visiting
supplier's false teeth (and subsequently placed the
teeth in his mouth), appeared inebriated and in
costume before a formal presentation to Honda's
bankers requesting financing vital to the firm's
survival (the loan was denied), hit a worker on
the head with a wrench, and stripped naked before
his engineers to assemble a motorcycle engine
(interview, and Sakiya, 1979, 1982).

Post-war Japan was in desperate need of
transportation. Motorcycle manufacturers proliferated, producing clip-on engines that converted
bicycles into makeshift ''mopeds.'' Honda was
among these but it was not until he teamed up
with Fujisawa in 1949 that the elements of a
successful enterprise began to take shape. Fujisawa provided money as well as financial and
marketing strengths. In 1950 their first D type
motorcycle was introduced. They were, at that

juncture, participating in a fragmented industry
along with 247 other manufacturers. Other than
its sturdy frame, this introductory product was
unnoteworthy and did not enjoy great commercial
success (Sakiya, 1979, 1982).

Honda embodied a rare combination of inventive ability and ultimate self-confidence. His
motivation was not primarily commercial. Rather,
the company served as a vehicle to give expression
to his inventive abilities. A successful company
would provide a resource base to pursue, in Fujisawa's words, his ''grandiose dream.'' Fujisawa
continues, ''There was no end to his pursuit of
technology'' (Sakiya, 1982).

Fujisawa, in an effort to save the faltering
company, pressed Honda to abandon their noisy
two-stroke engine and pursue a four-stroke design. The quieter four-stroke engines were appearing on competitive motorcycles, therefore threatening Honda with extinction. Mr. Honda balked.
But a year later, Honda stunned Fujisawa with
a breakthrough design that doubled the horsepower of competitive four-stroke engines. With
this innovation, the firm was off and putting,
and by 1951 demand was brisk. There was no
organization, however, and the plant was chaotic
(Sakiya, 1982). Strong demand, however, required early investment in a simplified mass production process. As a result, *primarily* due to
design advantages, and secondarily to production
methods, Honda became one of the four or five
industry leaders by 1954 with 15 percent market
share (data provided by company).

For Fujisawa, the engine innovation meant
increased sales and easier access to financing.
For Mr. Honda, the higher horsepower engine
opened the possibility of pursuing one of his central ambitions in life—to race his motorcycle and
win. Winning provided the ultimate confirmation
of his design abilities. Racing success in Japan
came quickly. As a result, in 1959 Honda raised
his sights to the international arena and committed
the firm to winning at Great Britain's Isle of
Man—the ''Olympics'' of motorcycle racing.
Again, Honda's inventive genius was called into
play. Shifting most of the firm's resources into
this racing effort, Honda embarked on studies

of combustion that resulted in a new configuration of the combustion chamber that doubled horsepower and halved weight. Honda leapfrogged past European and American competitors—winning in one class, then another, winning the Isle of Man manufacturer's prize in 1959 and sweeping the first five positions by 1961 (Sakiya, 1979).

Fujisawa, throughout the fifties, sought to turn Honda's attention from his enthusiasm with racing to the more mundane requirements of running an enterprise. By 1956, as the innovations gained from racing had begun to pay off in vastly more efficient engines, Fujisawa pressed Honda to adapt this technology for a commercial motorcycle (Sakiya, 1979, 1982). Fujisawa had a particular segment in mind. Most motorcyclists in Japan were male and the machines were used primarily as an alternative form of transportation to trains and buses. There were, however, a vast number of small commercial establishments in Japan that still delivered goods and ran errands on bicycles. Trains and buses were inconvenient for these activities. The pursestrings of these small enterprises were controlled by the Japanese wife—who resisted buying conventional motorcycles because they were expensive, dangerous, and hard to handle. Fujisawa challenged Honda: Can you use what you've learned from racing to come up with an inexpensive, safe-looking motorcycle that can be driven with one hand (to facilitate carrying packages) (Sakiya, 1982).

In 1958, the Honda 50cc Supercub was introduced—with an automatic clutch, three-speed transmission, automatic starter, and the safe, friendly look of a bicycle (without the stigma of the outmoded mopeds). Owing almost entirely to its high horsepower but *lightweight 50cc engine* (not to production efficiencies), it was affordable. Overnight, the firm was overwhelmed with orders. Engulfed by demand, they sought financing to build a new plant with a 30,000 unit per month capacity. "It wasn't a speculative investment," recalls one executive. "We had the proprietary technology, we had the market, and the demand was enormous." (The plant was completed in mid-1960.) Prior to its opening, demand was met through makeshift, high cost, company-owned assembly and farmed-out assembly through subcontractors. By the end of 1959, Honda had skyrocketed into first place among Japanese motorcycle manufacturers. Of its total sales that year of 285,000 units, 168,000 were Supercubs.

Fujisawa utilized the Supercub to restructure Honda's channels of distribution. For many years, Honda had rankled under the two-tier distribution system that prevailed in the industry. These problems had been exacerbated by the fact that Honda was a late entry and had been carried as secondary line by distributors whose loyalties lay with their older manufacturers. Further weakening Honda's leverage, all manufacturer sales were on a consignment basis.

Deftly, Fujisawa had characterized the Supercub to Honda's distributors as "something much more like a bicycle than a motorcycle." The traditional channels, to their later regret, agreed. Under amicable terms Fujisawa began selling the Supercub directly to retailers—and primarily through bicycle shops. Since these shops were small and numerous (approximately 12,000 in Japan), sales on consignment were unthinkable. A cash-on-delivery system was installed, giving Honda significantly more leverage over its dealerships than the other motorcycle manufacturers enjoyed.

The stage was now set for exploration of the U.S. market. Mr. Honda's racing conquests in the late fifties had given substance to his convictions about his abilities. While still heavily occupied by the Isle of Man, success fueled his quest for new and different challenges.

To the onlooker from Japan, the American market was vast, untapped, and affluent. In addition, Honda had experimented with local Southeast Asian markets in 1957–58 with little success. With little disposable income and poor roads, total Asian exports had reached a meager 1,000 units in 1958. The European market, while larger, was heavily dominated by its own name brand manufacturers, and the popular mopeds dominated the low price, low horsepower end. Spurred in part by ambition and in part by a process of deduction, Fujisawa and Honda focused attention on the United States.

Two Honda executives—the soon-to-be named president of American Honda, Kihachiro Kawashima, and his assistant—arrived in the U.S. in late 1958. Their itinerary: San Francisco, Los Angeles, Dallas, New York, and Columbus. Mr. Kawashima recounts his impressions:

My first reaction after travelling across the United States was: How could we have been so stupid as to start a war with such a vast and wealthy country! My second reaction was discomfort. I spoke poor English. We dropped in on motorcycle dealers who treated us discourteously and in addition, gave the general impression of being motorcycle enthusiasts who, secondarily, were in business. There were only 3,000 motorcycle dealers in the United States at the time and only 1,000 of them were open five days a week. The remainder were open on nights and weekends. Inventory was poor, manufacturers sold motorcycles to dealers on consignment, the retailers provided consumer financing; after-sales service was poor. It was discouraging.

My other impression was that everyone in the United States drove an automobile—making it doubtful that motorcycles could ever do very well in the market. However, with 450,000 motorcycle registrations in the U.S. and 60,000 motorcycles imported from Europe each year it didn't seem unreasonable to shoot for 10 percent of the import market. I returned to Japan with that report.

In truth, we had no strategy other than the idea of seeing if we could sell something in the United States. It was a new frontier, a new challenge, and it fit the "success against all odds" culture that Mr. Honda had cultivated. I reported my impressions to Fujisawa—including the seat-of-the-pants target of trying, over several years, to attain a 10 percent share of U.S. imports. He didn't probe that target quantitatively. We did not discuss profits or deadlines for breakeven. Fujisawa told me if anyone could succeed, I could and authorized $1 million for the venture.

The next hurdle was to obtain a currency allocation from the Ministry of Finance. They were extraordinarily skeptical. Toyota had launched the Toyopet in the U.S. in 1958 and had failed miserably. "How could Honda succeed?" they asked. Months went by. We put the project on hold. Suddenly, five months after our application, we were given the go-ahead—but at only a fraction of our expected level of commitment. "You can invest $250,000 in the U.S. market," they said, "but only $110,000 in cash." The remainder of our assets had to be in parts and motorcycle inventory.

We moved into frantic activity as the government, hoping we would give up on the idea, continued to hold us to the July 1959 start-up timetable. Our focus, as mentioned earlier, was to compete with the European exports. We knew our products at the time were good but not far superior. Mr. Honda was especially confident of the 250cc and 305cc machines. The shape of the handlebar on these larger machines looked like the eyebrow of Buddha, which he felt was a strong selling point. Thus, after some discussion and with no compelling criteria for selection, we configured our start-up inventory with 25 percent of each of our four products—the 50cc Supercub and the 125cc, 250cc, and 305cc machines. In dollar value terms, of course, the inventory was heavily weighted toward the larger bikes.

The stringent monetary controls of the Japanese government together with the unfriendly reception we had received during our 1958 visit caused us to start small. We chose Los Angeles where there was a large second and third generation Japanese community, a climate suitable for motorcycle use, and a growing population. We were so strapped for cash that the three of us shared a furnished apartment that rented for $80 per month. Two of us slept on the floor. We obtained a warehouse in a run-down section of the city and waited for the ship to arrive. Not daring to spare our funds for equipment, the three of us stacked the motorcycle crates three high—by hand, swept the floors, and built and maintained the parts bin.

We were entirely in the dark the

first year. We were not aware the motor-cycle business in the United States occurs during a seasonable April-to-August win-dow—and our timing coincided with the closing of the 1959 season. Our hard-learned experiences with distributorships in Japan convinced us to try to go to the retailers direct. We ran ads in the motorcycle trade magazine for dealers. A few responded. By spring of 1960, we had forty dealers and some of our inventory in their stores—mostly larger bikes. A few of the 250cc and 305cc bikes began to sell. Then disaster struck.

By the first week of April 1960, reports were coming in that our machines were leaking oil and encountering clutch failure. This was our lowest moment. Honda's fragile reputation was being de-stroyed before it could be established. As it turned out, motorcycles in the United States are driven much farther and much faster than in Japan. We dug deeply into our precious cash reserves to air freight our motorcycles to the Honda testing lab in Japan. Throughout the dark month of April, Pan Am was the only enterprise in the U.S. that was nice to us. Our testing lab worked twenty-four-hour days bench testing the bikes to try to replicate the failure. Within a month, a redesigned head gasket and clutch spring solved the problem. But in the meantime, events had taken a surprising turn.

Throughout our first eight months, following Mr. Honda's and our own in-stincts, we had not attempted to move the 50cc Supercubs. While they were a smash success in Japan (and manufactur-ing couldn't keep up with demand there), they seemed wholly unsuitable for the U.S. market where everything was bigger and more luxurious. As a clincher, we had our sights on the import market—and the Europeans, like the American manufacturers, emphasized the larger ma-chines.

We used the Honda 50s ourselves to ride around Los Angeles on errands. They attracted a lot of attention. One day we had a call from a Sears buyer. While persisting in our refusal to sell through an intermediary, we took note of Sear's interest. But we still hesitated to push the 50cc bikes out of fear they might harm our image in a heavily macho market. But when the larger bikes started break-ing, we had no choice. We let the 50cc bikes move. And surprisingly, the retail-ers who wanted to sell them weren't mo-torcycle dealers, they were sporting goods stores.

The excitement created by the Honda Supercub began to gain momen-tum. Under restrictions from the Japanese government, we were still on a cash basis. Working with our initial cash and inven-tory, we sold machines, reinvested in in-ventory, and sunk the profits into addi-tional inventory and advertising. Our advertising tried to straddle the market. While retailers continued to inform us that our Supercub customers were normal everyday Americans, we hesitated to tar-get toward this segment out of fear of alienating the high margin end of our busi-ness—sold through the traditional motor-cycle dealers to a more traditional "black leather jacket" customer.

Honda's phenomenal sales and share gains over the ensuing years have been previously re-ported. History has it that Honda *"redefined"* the U.S. motorcycle industry. In the view of American Honda's start-up team, this was an in-novation they backed into—and reluctantly. It was certainly not the strategy they embarked on in 1959. As late as 1963, Honda was still working with its original Los Angeles advertising agency, its ad campaigns straddling all customers so as not to antagonize one market in pursuit of another.

In the spring of 1963, an undergraduate advertising major at UCLA submitted, in fulfill-ment of a routine course assignment, an ad cam-paign for Honda. Its theme: You Meet the Nicest People on a Honda. Encouraged by his instructor, the student passed his work on to a friend at Grey Advertising. Grey had been soliciting the Honda account—which with a $5 million a year budget was becoming an attractive potential client. Grey purchased the student's idea—on a tightly kept nondisclosure basis. Grey attempted to sell the idea to Honda.

Interestingly, the Honda management team,

which by 1963 had grown to five Japanese executives, was badly split on this advertising decision. The President and Treasurer favored another proposal from another agency. The Director of Sales, however, felt strongly that the Nicest People campaign was the right one—and his commitment eventually held sway. Thus, in 1963, through an inadvertent sequence of events, Honda came to adopt a strategy that directly identified and targeted that large untapped segment of the marketplace that has since become inseparable from the Honda legend.

The Nicest People campaign drove Honda's sales at an even greater rate. By 1964, nearly one out of every two motorcycles sold was a Honda. As a result of the influx of medium income leisure class consumers, banks and other consumer credit companies began to finance motorcycles—shifting away from dealer credit, which had been the traditional purchasing mechanism available. Honda, seizing the opportunity of soaring demand for its products, took a courageous and seemingly risky position. Late in 1964, they announced that thereafter, they would cease to ship on a consignment basis but would require cash on delivery. Honda braced itself for revolt. While nearly every dealer questioned, appealed, or complained, none relinquished his franchise. In one fell swoop, Honda shifted the power relationship from the dealer to the manufacturer. Within three years, this would become the pattern for the industry.

THE "HONDA EFFECT"

The preceding account of Honda's inroads in the U.S. motorcycle industry provides more than a second perspective on reality. It focuses our attention on different issues and raises different questions. What factors permitted two men as unlike one another as Honda and Fujisawa to function effectively as a team? What incentives and understandings permitted the Japanese executives at American Honda to respond to the market as it emerged rather than doggedly pursue the 250cc and 305cc strategy that Mr. Honda favored? What

decision process permitted the relatively junior sales director to overturn the bosses' preferences and choose the Nicest People campaign? What values or commitment drove Honda to take the enormous risk of alienating its dealers in 1964 in shifting from a consignment to cash? In hindsight, these pivotal events all seem ho-hum common sense. But each day, as organizations live out their lives without the benefit of hindsight, few choose so well and so consistently.

The juxtaposed perspectives reveal what I shall call the "Honda Effect." Western consultants, academics, and executives express a preference for oversimplifications of reality and cognitively linear explanations of events. To be sure, they have always acknowledged that the "human factor" must be taken into account. But extensive reading of strategy cases at business schools, consultants' reports, strategic planning documents as well as the coverage of the popular press, reveals a widespread tendency to overlook the process through which organizations experiment, adapt, and learn. We tend to impute coherence and purposive rationality to events when the opposite may be closer to the truth. How an organization deals with miscalculation, mistakes, and serendipitous events *outside its field of vision is often crucial to success over time*. It is this realm that requires better understanding and further research if we are to enhance our ability to guide an organization's destiny. . . .

An earlier section has addressed the shortcomings of the narrowly defined microeconomic strategy model. The Japanese avoid this pitfall by adopting a broader notion of "strategy." In our recent awe of things Japanese, most Americans forget that the original products of the Japanese automotive manufacturers badly missed the mark. Toyota's Toyopet was square, sexless, and mechanically defective. It failed miserably, as did Datsun's first several entries into the U.S. market. More recently, Mazda miscalculated badly with its first rotary engine and nearly went bankrupt. Contrary to myth, the Japanese did not from the onset embark on a strategy to seize the high-quality small car market. They manufactured what they were accustomed to building in

Japan and tried to sell it abroad. Their success, as any Japanese automotive executive will readily agree, did not result from a bold insight by a few big brains at the top. On the contrary, success was achieved by senior managers humble enough not to take their initial strategic positions too seriously. What saved Japan's near-failures was the cumulative impact of "little brains" in the form of salesmen and dealers and production workers, all contributing incrementally to the quality and market position these companies enjoy today. Middle and upper management saw their primary task as guiding and orchestrating this input from below rather than steering the organization from above along a predetermined strategic course.

The Japanese don't use the term "strategy" to describe a crisp business definition or competitive master plan. They think more in terms of "strategic accommodation," or "adaptive persistence," underscoring their belief that corporate direction evolves from a incremental adjustment to unfolding events. Rarely, in their view, does one leader (or a strategic planning group) produce a bold strategy that guides a firm unerringly. Far more frequently, the input is from below. It is this ability of an organization to move information and ideas from the bottom to the top and back again in continuous dialogue that the Japanese value above all things. As this dialogue is pursued, what in hindsight may be "strategy" evolves. In sum, "strategy" is defined as "all the things necessary for the successful functioning of organization as an adaptive mechanism." . . .

EDWARD MARSHALL
BOEHM, INC.

Edward Marshall Boehm—a farmer, veterinarian, and nature lover living near New York City— was convinced by his wife and friends to translate some of his clay animal sculptures into pieces for possible sale to the gift and art markets. Boehm recognized that porcelain was the best medium for portraying his creations because of its translucent beauty, permanence, and fidelity of color as well as form. But the finest of the porcelains, hard paste porcelain, was largely a secret art about which little technical literature existed. Boehm studied this art relentlessly, absorbing whatever knowledge artbooks, museums, and the few U.S. ceramic factories offered. Then after months of experimentation in a dingy Trenton (N.J.) basement, Boehm and some chemist friends developed a porcelain clay equal to the finest in the world.

Next Boehm had to master the complex art of porcelain manufacture. Each piece of porcelain sculpture is a technical as well as artistic challenge. A 52-step process is required to convert a plasticine sculpture into a completed porcelain piece. For example, one major creation took 509 mold sections to make 151 parts, and consumed 8 tons of plaster in the molds. Sculptural detail included 60,000 individually carved feather barbs. Each creation had to be kiln-fired to 2400° where heat could change a graceful detail into a twisted mass. Then it had to be painted, often in successive layers, and perhaps fired repeatedly to anneal delicate colors. No American had excelled in hard paste porcelains. And when Boehm's creations first appeared no one understood the quality of the porcelain or even believed it was hard paste porcelain.

Case Copyright © 1976 by James Brian Quinn. The generous cooperation of Edward Marshall Boehm, Inc. is gratefully acknowledged.

But Boehm began to create in porcelain what he knew and loved best, nature—particularly the more delicate forms of animals, birds, and flowers. In his art Boehm tried "to capture that special moment and setting which conveys the character, charm, and loveliness of a bird or animal in its natural habitat." After selling his early creations for several years during her lunch hours, his talented wife, Helen, left an outstanding opthalmic marketing career to "peddle" Boehm's porcelains full time. Soon Mrs. Boehm's extraordinary merchandising skills, promotional touch, and sense for the art market began to pay off. People liked Boehm's horses and dogs, but bought his birds. And Boehm agreeably complied, striving for ever greater perfection on ever more exotic and natural bird creations.

By 1968 some Boehm porcelains (especially birds) had become recognized as collectors items. An extremely complex piece like "Fondo Marino" might sell for $28,500 at retail, and might command much more upon resale. Edward Marshall Boehm, then 55—though flattered by his products' commercial success—considered his art primarily an expression of his love for nature. He felt the ornithological importance of portraying vanishing species like U.S. prairie chickens with fidelity and travelled to remote areas to bring back live samples of rare tropical birds for study and later rendering into porcelain. A single company, Minton China, was the exclusive distributor of Boehm products to some 175 retail outlets in the U.S. Boehm's line included: (1) its "Fledgling" series of smaller somewhat simpler pieces, usually selling for less than $100, (2) its profitable middle series of complex sculptures like the "Snowy Owl" (see picture) selling from $800 to $5,000, and (3) its special artistic pieces (like "Fondo Marino" or "Ivory Billed

SNOWY OWL

Courtesy of Edward Marshall Boehm, Inc.

Woodpeckers'') which might sell initially for over $20,000.

Individual Boehm porcelains were increasingly being recognized as outstanding artistic creations and sought by some sophisticated collectors. Production of such designs might be sold out for years in advance, but it was difficult to anticipate which pieces might achieve this distinction. Many of the company's past policies no longer seemed appropriate. And the Boehms wanted to further position the company for the long run. When asked what they wanted from the company, they would respond, ''to make the world aware of Mr. Boehm's artistic talent, to help world wildlife causes by creating appreciation and protection for threatened species, and to build a continuing business that could make them comfortably wealthy, perhaps millionaires.'' No one goal had great precedence over the others.

QUESTIONS

1. What strategy should the Boehms follow?
2. Why?

GENENTECH, INC. (A)

In January 1976, Robert Swanson, a venture capitalist with Kleiner and Perkins in San Francisco called Dr. Herbert Boyer at the University of California (San Francisco) to discuss the potentials of commercializing recombinant DNA technology. The cold call—triggered by one of Boyer's papers that Swanson had read—resulted in a 20 minute planned meeting, which extended into a four-hour conversation over several beers in a nearby tavern. What emerged from that meeting stands as one of the most exciting partnerships in recent years between entrepreneur and scientist. Their company, Genentech, achieved a number of important technical firsts in the application of genetic technologies for useful purposes. Then in October 1980, when it offered its shares publicly, Genentech's stock exploded within minutes from an initial offering price of $35 to a peak of $89 before subsiding to $71.25 a share—making both Swanson (32) and Boyer (44) millionaires many times over. How did this large scale venture come into being? What would its role be in this "industry of the future?"

THE PARTNERSHIP

Swanson, a graduate of M.I.T. with a Bachelor's Degree in Chemistry and a Master's in Management, had worked with Citicorp Venture Capital Ltd. before joining Kleiner and Perkins in 1975. Out of a number of technologies he was actively following, recombinant DNA most intrigued his imagination. He had tried unsuccessfully to interest private biological laboratories in industrial

Case copyright © 1982 by James Brian Quinn. Research assistant—Allie J. Quinn. The generous support of the Adolf H. Lundin Professorship at the International Management Institute, Geneva, Switzerland is gratefully acknowledged, as is the generous cooperation of Genentech, Inc.

prospects for the technology. They thought it would take at least five years to develop the earliest products, too long when compared to their other priorities. Swanson had also canvassed many academic scientists who were leaders in the field. They too felt the newly emerging science was far from the marketplace. Dr. Boyer was the only eminent scientist who at that time believed the technology was ripe for commercial application. Based upon their mutual interests, Swanson and Boyer formed a partnership soon after their first meeting, each putting up $500 of capital to pursue prospects further. Their backgrounds provided an interesting contrast.

Gene Splicing Begins

In high school Herb Boyer, the scientific half of the team—had played football, served as class president, and dabbled in drama. Presciently perhaps, in his senior yearbook, he had stated his goal in life as: "to become a successful businessman." The young Boyer had studied science, primarily because his football coach taught it. But the exposure took. Taking a Ph.D. in bacteriology from University of Pittsburgh and a postdoctoral fellowship at Yale, Boyer joined the faculty of the University of California Medical Center in San Francisco in 1966. His true interest was research into DNA, the helix shaped molecule which carries the genetic information determining hereditary characteristics of all living things.

Boyer's work led to another chance meeting in November 1972. After listening to papers all day at a Hawaii scientific conference, Boyer and Stanley Cohen of Stanford met at a delicatessen for a late snack. As they munched on corned beef sandwiches they discovered that their research merged in a unique way. Cohen had been looking for a way to insert foreign genetic material into an *E. coli* bacterium. He had been experimenting with *E. coli*'s plasmids which contained genetic information in simpler structures than its chromosomes. Boyer had found some restriction enzymes that could cut free DNA structures precisely at predetermined points, leaving some "sticky ends" of the DNA molecule to which (the two reasoned) specific genes similarly cut from other structures might attach themselves. The twin breakthroughs—Cohen's understanding of bacterial plasmids and Boyer's enzymes—soon opened a new era.

In 1973 Dr. Boyer's and Dr. Cohen's teams became the first to perfect the technique called "gene splicing" or "Recombinant DNA Technique." They transplanted a gene from a South African toad into a bacterium, which then reproduced the toad gene. This confirmed the possibility of transferring specific genes from other living systems into bacteria and using the bacteria as factories for reproducing that genetic material.

Being academic scientists, Drs. Cohen and Boyer quickly published their results in a refereed journal for the science community to scrutinize. Only many months later, just in time to avert the one year prior-publication limit on U.S. patent applications, did Stanford's patent expert (Niel Reimers) get Boyer and Cohen to apply for a U.S. patent with Stanford as the holding agent. Even then, their early publication of results prohibited patenting in most foreign countries, where any prior (nonpatent) publication normally precludes patentability. Boyer and Cohen assigned their rights to royalties in their initial patents to their respective universities.

During this period of basic research Dr. Boyer, like many other biochemists, was thoroughly absorbed by the fascinating frontiers of his complex science. He even named his Siamese cats Watson and Crick after James Watson and Francis Crick who shared the 1962 Nobel prize for their revelations on the structure of the DNA molecule. Before Swanson approached him about forming a company, Dr. Boyer had reportedly "never considered such a possibility." In fact, he even had to borrow the initial $500 for his share of the partnership. Although well established in academic and professional circles, Boyer

was virtually unknown to the public or investment community until Genetech's stock underwent its spectacular opening. Even then he preferred a low profile role, rarely agreeing to press interviews.

The Seed Capital Era

Between January and April 1976, Boyer and Swanson made more detailed investigations of specific technological and market opportunities. Swanson continued to be supported by Kleiner and Perkins on an informal basis during this period. Then on April 7th Swanson and Boyer incorporated Genentech, each taking 25,000 common shares[*] in return for the cash and assets of their partnership. Kleiner and Perkins agreed to provide some $200,000 of seed capital in return for 20,000 shares[**] of A Series convertible preferred stock. During this period Swanson and Boyer worked out a detailed business plan which became the basis of Genentech's early technical development and financial expansion.

> *Decision Point*: What should have been the critical considerations in Kleiner and Perkins' strategy at this time? What specific actions should Boyer and Swanson take within the limits of the $200,000 seed capital? What should their early strategy be? Why?

THE BUSINESS PLAN

The business plan Swanson and Boyer drew up called for more extensive financing than the initial seed capital could provide. Initially Genentech had authorized capital of 1,000,000 shares of common stock (2¢ par value) and 100,000 shares of convertible preferred (2¢ par). The plan called

---

[*]   *Later the initial common split 10 for 1.*

[**]   *Each then convertible for 1 common share, later 4 shares before the common split.*

for a secondary financing of $500,000 in convertible preferred stock (at $50 per share for 10,000 shares, or 11% of the company). The resulting financial structure (assuming total dilution) was to be:

Name	Shares
Boyer	25,000
Swanson	25,000
Riggs and Itakura[a]	10,000
Kleiner and Perkins	20,000
New Partner	10,000
TOTAL	90,000

[a] *Scientists attracted to work with Genentech.*

Source: Company records.

The money was to carry Genentech through the development of its first commercial product. At that time more capital would be raised to finish the development of the second product and to establish production facilities. The Plan read, "With the following sales and earnings estimates for 1980, investors are offered an investment opportunity with more than a 79% compound growth rate."

1980 Estimates Sales	$15,000,000
1980 Estimated Profits	3,140,000

The financing was expanded to $850,074 with negotiations completed in March 1977 for a private placement of 29,496 Class A Preferred Shares to five venture capital groups plus Kleiner and Perkins.

Goals for Genentech

The Plan further stated, "It is Genentech's goal to select products that are in great demand and to specifically engineer microorganisms to produce those products. We expect to be the first company to commercialize the technology, and we plan to build a major profitable corporation by manufacturing and marketing needed products

that benefit mankind. . . . It is Genentech's initial strategy to design microorganisms that will synthesize products for which there is a large existing market and where economies of production will give the company very substantial cost advantages. . . . The future uses of genetic engineering are far reaching and many. With Genentech's technology, microorganisms could be engineered to produce protein to meet world food needs or to produce antibodies to fight viral infections. Any product produced by a living organism is eventually within the company's reach."

The Plan also provided: a detailed explanation of the recombinant DNA technology itself,* a schedule for the development of products, a broad description of the market opportunity, and more detailed descriptions of the intended first two products (somatostatin and insulin). A copy of Genentech's daring development schedule appears as Exhibit 2.

Initial Products

Mr. Fred Middleton, one of the first 8 members of the Genentech team and later Chief Financial Officer of Genentech, said, "One of the challenges of this field is that there are so many different sorts of applications. It is time consuming and all encompassing to work on any particular protein. With limited resources you must be sure that you strategically pick the right things to do." Somatostatin, a relatively small and simple protein was selected as the first targeted product, and human insulin as the second. Somatostatin was a naturally occurring brain hormone with possible uses in a variety of disorders. Insulin—a much more complex structure—was essential to the treatment of diabetes.

In seeking these products, Mr. Swanson repeatedly affirmed Genentech's determination "to build one of the finest scientific teams in this field in the world." Genentech's policy was to remain "a part of the scientific community with responsibilities to both its own scientists and to science at large." Mr. Swanson stressed

---

*   *For a simpler description see Exhibit 1.*

a philosophy of integrating science and business. Genentech was not to be "just an innovative research and development organization that coordinates major research projects," he said. That might be profitable in its own right, but short-sighted. "We were determined to be a fully integrated business organization."

OPERATIONS BEGIN

Then in August 1977, little more than a year after the company was founded, Genentech scientists "cloned" DNA in a bacteria culture to produce somatostatin. Somatostatin was the first useful product produced by the recombinant DNA technology. In testimony before the Congress of the United States, Dr. Philip Handler, President of the National Academy of Sciences, hailed the achievement as a "scientific triumph of the first order." Production of somatostatin was to begin in February 1978. Genentech's somatostatin would initially be sold only for use in laboratory research. But its potential markets were very large, including possible uses in the treatment of diabetes, gastric bleeding, and various hormonal disorders. The FDA had already cleared somatostatin produced by other techniques as a

chemical for clinical trials. Competitors' somatostatin was selling for between $30,000 and $55,000 per gram in small amounts. Genetech sought to supply large quantities of somatostatin with production costs of under $30 per gram.

In November 1977 Genentech scientists began to work on methods for bacterial production of human insulin. In February 1978 the company leased space in South San Francisco for its headquarters and laboratories for its scientists' experiments aimed at human insulin expression. To complete the second phase of its physical plant expansion program, and also to fund the insulin project, Genentech raised additional equity capital of $950,000 also through private placements.

At the end of the offering, there were also 758,976 shares of common stock owned by the founders, Genentech's employees, and consultants. Boyer and Swanson each owned 250,000 shares after the 10:1 common split. Wilmington Securities (of Pittsburgh) was the lead group in this third offering. Exhibit 3 provides a summary of all other Genentech financings.

Human Insulin Achieved

In August 1978 Genentech and City of Hope National Medical Center at Duart, California,

CLASS A PREFERRED STOCK*

Name	Seed Shares	Capital $	March 1977 Shares	March 1977 $	April 1978 Shares	April 1978 $
Kleiner and Perkins	20,000	100,000	3,470	100,000	—	—
Inco Securities			13,880	400,000	—	—
Innoven			4,338	125,000	2,500	200,000
Mayfield II			4,338	125,000	1,250	100,000
Sofinnova			1,735	50,000	1,000	80,000
Venture Assoc.			1,735	50,000	—	—
Wilmington Securities			—	—	6,250	500,000
Others			—	—	875	70,000
			29,496	850,000	11,875	950,000

* All shares convertible at 4:1 before Genentech's 10:1 common stock split.

Source: Company records.

jointly announced that they had produced human insulin by recombinant DNA technology. The announcement said, "This achievement may be the most significant advance in the treatment of diabetes since the development of animal insulin for human use in the 1920s. The insulin synthesis is the first laboratory production of a significant widely needed human hormone using recombinant DNA technology." The contributions of Drs. Crea, Itakura, and Riggs at the City of Hope, as well as Drs. Goeddel and Cleid at Genentech, were specifically cited. The announcement noted that approximately 1.5 million diabetics took injections of expensive insulin every day. The new process would permit ample quantities of a product "chemically identical to human insulin" to be produced at substantially lower costs than existing processes. This laboratory success followed a remarkably rapid development of the technology:[1]

- May 1977: Rat insulin gene incorporated in E. coli at University of California, San Francisco, with no gene expression occurring.

- November 1977: Stanford University reports E. coli takes up DNA from higher cells.

- November 1977: University of California at San Francisco fuses clinically synthesized gene for somatostatin to an E. coli enzyme gene; gene expression obtained.

- June 1978: Joslin Diabetes Foundation announces rat insulin gene fused to another gene and incorporated into E. coli. The combined protein was excreted from bacteria.

- August 1978: Genentech achieves successful laboratory production of insulin from recombinant DNA technology.

If successfully produced in quantity Genentech's insulin would be "human insulin," with a chemical structure exactly like the insulin naturally occurring within the human body. Unlike bovine or porcine insulin, "human insulin" was not expected to cause allergic reactions in certain individuals. Insulin represented a large existing market (more than $100 million worldwide, with over half the market in the United States). Eli Lilly Co. held over 80% of the domestic market,

which at that time was growing at about 6% annually. The existing source for insulin was animal pancreas glands. As the market grew, these were coming into increasingly short supply and were very expensive to process.

Bovine and porcine pancreases had increased in price from 40¢ per pound in 1972 to over $1.25 per pound in 1978. Ten thousand pounds of pancreas were needed for one pound of insulin. Then, large scale and complicated chemical processing techniques were needed to obtain purified insulin. Genentech's production process was expected to take place in a standard 750 liter laboratory fermentation vessel. A little over $800 worth of growth medium would produce approximately 15 kilograms (net weight) of bacterial cells coded for insulin within an 8 hour shift, and the process could be speeded so that cell mass doubled every 20 minutes. Early estimates were that about 30% of the total protein would be insulin. This would yield approximately one pound of purified insulin per production run.

However, Mr. Swanson cautioned "the technology is a long way from being ready for commercial production. We've set up a pilot manufacturing facility for fermentation and extraction. We have hired key personnel to work on the scale-up process. And we have filed patent applications for the present technology. But the fate of these patents cannot be predicted at this time." Nevertheless, in Swanson's view "the procedure was similar to having the process to make a semiconductor when everyone else was using vacuum tubes."[2]

Development and scale up costs would be "several million dollars" for each product. Clinical tests would require $3–20 million more. (See Exhibit 4 for the typical sequence of steps involved.) Few pharmaceutical products then reached the market with less than $8–10 million in investment, with delays of 3–4 years being common. Even then Genentech would have to meet other potential genetic competitors, existing products in the market, and an unreliable world patent structure in which many countries did not recognize product patents on products for human health. To complicate things further Genentech was supporting other laboratory work which could lead to a highly diverse set of end products. But the company could not be sure which products could ultimately be achieved in the laboratory or cleared for commercial use. Nor did it know the precise sequence in which these events would occur. Against this background, Genentech had to decide the next stage of its strategy. In December 1978 Genentech, whose scientific team had increased to 26 including 12 Ph.D.s, added three laboratories and six new offices to its facilities. A second business plan was developed which projected a doubling of staff and facilities in 1978, a $1.3 million needed capital expansion, and a

fully integrated product program for the "post-insulin era."

QUESTIONS

1. What should the venture capitalists' strategy have been with their first $100–200,000 investment? Why is the company financed the way it is?
2. What are the major strategic options facing Genentech at the end of the case? What strategy should it follow? Why?
3. Answer the questions interspersed in the case.

EXHIBIT 1   REDESIGNING BACTERIA

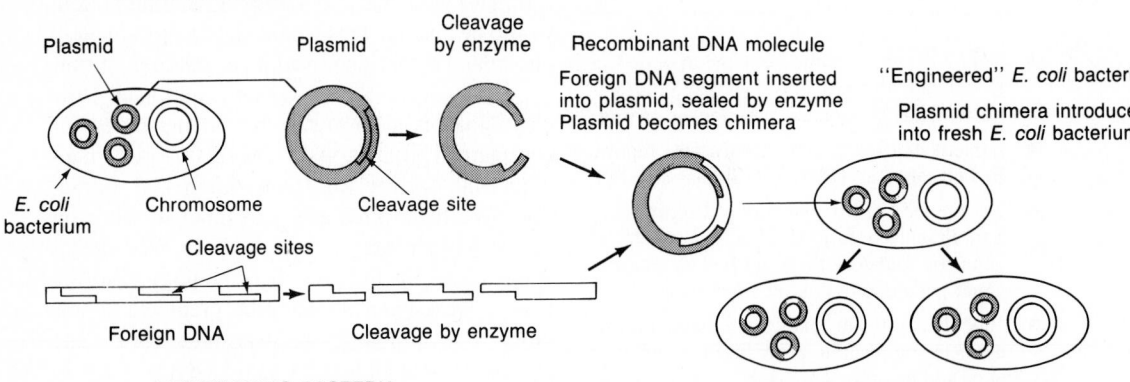

REDESIGNING BACTERIA

Source: "Tinkering With Life," *Time,* April 18, 1977. Copyright © 1977 Time, Inc. All rights reserved. Reprinted by permission from *Time.*

The development of the recombinant DNA technique ushered in a new era of genetic engineering—with all of its promise and possible peril. The lowly organism that currently plays the largest role in the process is the *E. coli* bacterium. This microbe—a laboratory derivative of a common inhabitant of the human intestine—lends itself to being engineered because its genetic structure has been so well studied. In the first step of the process, scientists place the bacterium

in a test tube with a detergent-like liquid. This dissolves the microbe's outer membrane, causing its DNA strands to spill out in a disorderly tangle. Most of the DNA is included in the bacterium's chromosome, in the form of a long strand containing thousands of genes. The remainder is found in several tiny, closed loops called plasmids, which have only a few genes each and are the most popular vehicles for the recombinant technique.

After the plasmids are separated from the chromosomal DNA in a centrifuge, they are placed in a solution with a chemical catalyst called a restriction enzyme. This enzyme cuts through the plasmids' DNA strips at specific points. It leaves overlapping, mortise-type breaks with "sticky" ends. The opened plasmid loops are then mixed in a solution with genes—also removed by the use of restriction enzymes—from the DNA of a plant, animal, bacterium or virus. In the solution is another enzyme called a DNA ligase, which cements the foreign gene into place in the opening of the plasmids. The result of these unions are new loops of DNA called plasmid chimeras because, like the Chimera—the mythical lion-goat-serpent after which they are named—they contain the components of more than one organism.

Finally, the chimeras are placed in a solution of cold calcium chloride containing normal *E. coli* bacteria. When the solution is suddenly heated, the membranes of the *E. coli* become permeable, allowing the plasmid chimeras to pass through and become part of the microbes' new genetic structure. When the *E. coli* reproduce, they create carbon copies of themselves, new plasmids—and DNA sequences—and all. Thus they become forms of life potentially different from what they had been before—imbued with characteristics dictated not only by their own *E. coli* genes, but also by genes from an entirely different species.

EXHIBIT 2 DEVELOPMENT SCHEDULE

	1976				1977						1978	
	Nov.	Dec.	Jan.	Feb.	Mar.	Apr.	May	June	3Q	4Q	1Q	2Q

Sequencing Development
Enzyme Technique Dev.
Plasmid Development
Nucleotide Protection
Somatostatin
"A" fragment
"A" fragment stitched and characterized
Assay Development
Gene purified
Gene stitched
Gene Characterized
Production of Protein
Insulin
B Chain
Fragment 1
Fragment 2
Complete Chain
A Chain
Stitching and Characterization
Coupling Reagent
Assays and Tests
Begin Government Approval
Move to new facilities
Financing complete
2nd round
3rd round

Personnel

	Nov.	Dec.	Jan.	Feb.	Mar.	Apr.	May	June
Management and Administration	1	1	1	2	2	2	2	2
Development	7	8	9	9	9	9	9	9
Manufacturing					1	3	3	3
Total	8	9	10	11	12	14	14	14

▶ = *Actual results*

Source: Company records.

EXHIBIT 3   STATEMENT OF SHAREHOLDERS' EQUITY

	Preferred Stock	Common Stock	Series B Restricted Stock	Series C Restricted Stock	Capital in Excess of Par Value	Retained Earnings (Deficit)	Less Notes Receivable Sale of Stock	Total Shareholders' Equity
Balance at December 31, 1978	$1,227	$ 14,465	—	—	$ 1,937,580	$(888,368)	$ (24,749)	$ 1,040,155
Issuance of Preferred Stock (25,000 shares)	500	—	—	—	9,999,500	—	—	10,000,000
Issuance of Common Stock (45,726 shares)	—	915	—	—	29,678	—	(20,500)	10,093
Stock issuance costs	—	—	—	—	(11,000)	—	—	(11,000)
Repurchase of Common Stock (3,750 shares)	—	(75)	—	—	(1,050)	—	—	(1,125)
Ten-for-one conversion of Preferred Stock (863,710 shares)	(1,727)	17,274	—	—	(15,547)	—	—	—
Payments on notes receivable	—	—	—	—	—	—	9,954	9,954
Net income	—	—	—	—	—	116,336	—	116,336
Balance at December 31, 1979	—	32,579	—	—	11,939,161	(772,032)	(35,295)	11,164,413
Four-for-one conversion of Common Stock (4,885,134 shares)	—	97,702	—	—	(97,702)	—	—	—
Issuance of Common Stock (1,124,608 shares)	—	22,493	—	—	39,209,596	—	—	39,232,089
Issuance of Series B Restricted Stock (224,250 shares)	—	—	$4,485	—	342,015	—	(301,330)	45,170
Stock issuance costs	—	—	—	—	(2,945,579)	—	—	2,945,579
Repurchase of Common Stock (48,236 shares)	—	(965)	—	—	(15,875)	—	—	(16,840)
Payments on notes receivable	—	—	—	—	—	—	20,182	20,182
Donated equipment	—	—	—	—	36,450	—	—	36,450
Tax benefit from employee stock plan	—	—	—	—	10,998	—	—	10,998
Net income	—	—	—	—	—	236,292	—	236,292
Balance at December 31, 1980	—	151,809	4,485	—	48,479,064	(535,740)	(316,443)	47,783,175
Issuance of Common Stock (163,684 shares)	—	3,274	—	—	5,047,378	—	—	5,050,652
Issuance of Series B Restricted Stock (71,980 shares)	—	—	1,440	—	358,460	—	(317,250)	42,650
Issuance of Series C Restricted Stock (69,500 shares)	—	—	—	$1,390	241,860	—	(200,150)	43,100
Stock issuance costs	—	—	—	—	(328,800)	—	—	(328,800)
Repurchase of Common Stock (7,903 shares)	—	(158)	—	—	(10,558)	—	—	(10,716)
Conversion of Series B Restricted Stock (296,230 shares)	—	5,925	(5,925)	—	—	—	—	—
Payments on notes receivable	—	—	—	—	—	—	26,680	26,680
Tax benefit from employee stock plan	—	—	—	—	23,000	—	—	23,000
Net income	—	—	—	—	—	503,010	—	503,010
Balance at December 31, 1981	—	$160,850	—	$1,390	$53,810,404	$ (32,730)	$(807,163)	$53,132,751

See accompanying notes provided in company's annual report.

Source: Genentech, Inc., *Annual Report,* 1981.

EXHIBIT 4   THE PRODUCT DEVELOPMENT PROCESS

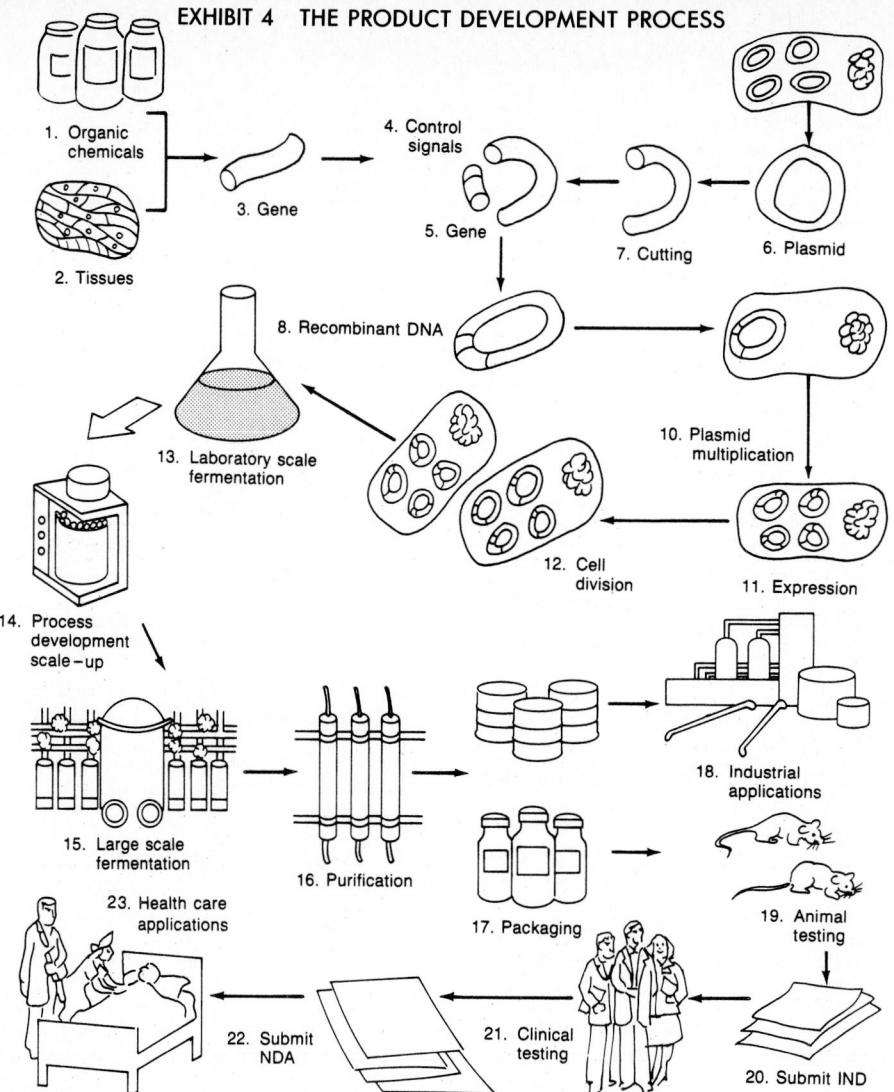

1. Organic chemicals
2. Tissues
3. Gene
4. Control signals
5. Gene
6. Plasmid
7. Cutting
8. Recombinant DNA
10. Plasmid multiplication
11. Expression
12. Cell division
13. Laboratory scale fermentation
14. Process development scale-up
15. Large scale fermentation
16. Purification
17. Packaging
18. Industrial applications
19. Animal testing
20. Submit IND
21. Clinical testing
22. Submit NDA
23. Health care applications

The development process begins by obtaining DNA either through organic synthesis (1) or derived from biological sources such as tissues (2). The DNA obtained from one or both sources is tailored to form the basic "gene" (3) which contains the genetic information to "code" for a desired product, such as human interferon or human insulin. Control signals (4) containing instructions are added to this gene (5). Circular DNA molecules called plasmids (6) are isolated from micro-organisms such as E. coli, cut open (7) and spliced back (8) together with genes and control signals to form "recombinant DNA" molecules. These molecules are then introduced into a host cell (9).

Each plasmid is copied many times in a cell (10). Each cell then translates the information contained in these plasmids into the desired product, a process called "expression" (11). Cells divide (12) and pass on to their offspring the same genetic information contained in the parent cell.

Fermentation of large populations of genetically engineered micro-organisms is first done in shaker flasks (13), and then in small fermenters (14) to determine growth conditions, and eventually in larger fermentation tanks (15). Cellular extract obtained from the fermentation process is then separated, purified (16), and packaged (17) either for industrial use (18) or health care applications.

Health care products are first tested in animal studies (19) to demonstrate a product's pharmacological activity and safety. In the United States, an investigational new drug application (IND) (20) is submitted to begin human clinical trials to establish safety and efficacy. Following clinical testing (21), a new drug application (NDA) (22) is filed with the Food and Drug Administration (FDA). When the NDA has been reviewed and approved by the FDA the product may be marketed in the United States (23).

Source: Genentech, Inc.

EXHIBIT 5   POTENTIAL MARKETS FOR THE GENE-SPLICERS

Product category	Number of compounds	Current market value	Selected compound or use	Time needed to implement genetic production
AMINO ACIDS	9	$1,703,000,000	Glutamate Tryptophan	5 years 5 years
VITAMINS	6	667,700,000	Vitamin C Vitamin E	10 years 15 years
ENZYMES	11	217,700,000	Pepsin	5 years
STEROID HORMONES	6	367,800,000	Cortisone	10 years
PEPTIDE HORMONES	9	269,700,000	Human growth hormone Insulin	5 years 5 years
VIRAL ANTIGENS	9	N/A	Hoof-and-mouth disease virus Influenza viruses	5 years 10 years
SHORT PEPTIDES	2	4,400,000	Aspartame	5 years
MISCELLANEOUS PROTEINS	2	300,000,000	Interferon	5 years
ANTIBIOTICS	4*	4,240,000,000	Penicillins Erthromycins	10 years 10 years
PESTICIDES	2*	100,000,000	Microbial Aromatics	5 years 10 years
METHANE	1	12,572,000,000	Methane	10 years

ALIPHATICS
(Other than methane)
	24	2,737,500,000	Ethanol
			Ethylene
			  glycol
			Propylene
			  glycol
			Isobutylene
				5 years
				
				5 years
				
				10 years
				10 years

AROMATICS	10	1,250,900,000	Aspirin Phenol	5 years 10 years
INORGANICS	2	2,681,000,000	Hydrogen Ammonia	15 years 15 years
MINERAL LEACHING	5	N/A	Uranium Cobalt Iron	
BIODEGRADATION	N/A	N/A	Removal of organic phosphates	

N/A = not available
* Number indicates classes of compounds, rather than number of compounds.
Source: Industry Week, September 7, 1981.

EXHIBIT 5 *(Continued)*
APPLICATIONS OF GENETIC ENGINEERING TECHNOLOGIES ENCOMPASS PRODUCTS
IN MANY AREAS

Microbial Product or Process	End Use	Microbial Product or Process	End Use
AGRICULTURE		**FOOD PROCESSING**	
Amino acids, vitamins	Feed additives (e.g., lysine)	Amino acids, vitamins	Food enrichment and flavoring agents
Antibiotics	Feed additives and prophylactics	Aromatic compounds	Food additives
		Aliphatic compounds	Food additives
Short peptides	Feed additives and growth promoters	Short peptides	Artificial sweeteners
		Enzymes	Manufacturing processes
Viral Antigens	Vaccines	Cellulose conversion	Sugar production
Insecticides	Pest control	**PHARMACEUTICALS**	
Nitrogen fixation	Fertilizer and legume inoculants	Amino acids, vitamins	Intravenous solutions
		Aromatic compounds	Analgesics, narcotics, etc.
Biodegradation	Organic phosphate removal	Steroid hormone modification	Various therapeutics and prophylactics
CHEMISTRY		Antibiotics, antibiotic modification	Control of infectious diseases
Aromatic compounds	Chemical intermediates		
Aliphatic compounds	Chemical intermediates	Short peptides	Control of hemoglobin disorders
Enzymes	Manufacturing processes		
Biodegradation	Organic phosphate and arylsulfonate removal	Peptide hormones	Control of metabolic disorders
Mineral leaching	Metal extraction	Enzymes	Various diagnostic (e.g., glucose oxidase) and therapeutic (e.g., urokinase) procedures
ENERGY			
Enzymes	Manufacturing processes		
Biodegradation	Petroleum by-products removal	Viral antigens	Vaccines (e.g., hepatitis vaccine)
Sewage conversion	Methane production		
Cellulose conversion	Alcohol production	Other proteins	Various therapeutics (e.g., interferon, human serum albumin)
Mineral leaching	Uranium concentration		
Coal conversion	Methane production		
Biophotolysis	Hydrogen production	Gene preparations	Control of hereditary disorders

Source: Genex Corporation in *Chemical & Engineering News*, March 17, 1980, p. 23.

THE GUNS OF AUGUST: GERMAN AND FRENCH STRATEGY IN 1914

THE GERMAN VIEW

Count Alfred von Schlieffen, Chief of the German General Staff from 1891 to 1906 was, like all German officers, schooled in Clausewitz's precept, "The heart of France lies between Brussels and Paris." It was a frustrating axiom because the path it pointed to was forbidden by Belgian neutrality, which Germany, along with the other four major European powers, had guaranteed in perpetuity. Believing that war was a certainty and that Germany must enter it under conditions that gave her the most promise of success, Schlieffen determined not to allow the Belgian difficulty to stand in Germany's way. Of the two classes of Prussian officer, the bullnecked and the wasp-waisted, he belonged to the second. Monocled and effete in appearance, cold and distant in manner, he concentrated with such single-mindedness on his profession that when an aide, at the end of an all-night staff ride in East Prussia, pointed out to him the beauty of the river Pregel sparkling in the rising sun, the General gave a brief, hard look and replied, "An unimportant obstacle." So too, he decided, was Belgian neutrality.

The Belgian Question

A neutral and independent Belgium was the creation of England, or rather of England's ablest

Reprinted with permission of Macmillan Publishing Company and Russell & Volkening, as agents for the author, from *The Guns of August* by Barbara W. Tuchman. Copyright © 1962 by Barbara W. Tuchman. Subheadings and questions at end inserted by James Brian Quinn to aid students.

Foreign Minister, Lord Palmerston. Belgium's coast was England's frontier; on the plains of Belgium, Wellington had defeated the greatest threat to England since the Armada. Thereafter England was determined to make that patch of open, easily traversible territory a neutral zone and, under the post-Napoleon settlement of the Congress of Vienna, agreed with the other powers to attach it to the Kingdom of the Netherlands. Resenting union with a Protestant power, burning with the fever of the nineteenth century nationalism, the Belgians revolted in 1830, setting off an international scramble. The Dutch fought to retain their province; the French, eager to reabsorb what they had once ruled, moved in; the autocratic states—Russia, Prussia, and Austria—bent on keeping Europe clamped under the vise of Vienna, were ready to shoot at the first sign of revolt anywhere.

Lord Palmerston outmaneuvered them all. He knew that a subject province would be an eternal temptation to one neighbor or another and that only an independent nation, resolved to maintain its own integrity, could survive as a safety zone. Through nine years of nerve, of suppleness, of never swerving from his aim, of calling out the British fleet when necessary, he played off all contenders and secured an international treaty guaranteeing Belgium as an "independent and perpetually neutral state." The treaty was signed in 1839 by England, France, Russia, Prussia, and Austria.

Ever since 1892, when France and Russia had joined in military alliance, it was clear that four of the five signatories of the Belgian treaty would be automatically engaged—two against two—in the war for which Schlieffen had to plan. Europe was a heap of swords piled as delicately as jackstraws; one could not be pulled out without moving the others. Under the terms of the Austro-German alliance, Germany was obliged to support Austria in any conflict with Russia. Under the terms of the alliance between France and Russia, both parties were obliged to move against Germany if either became involved in a "defensive war" with Germany. These arrangements made it inevitable that in any war in which she engaged, Germany would have to fight on two fronts against both Russia and France.

What part England would play was uncertain; she might remain neutral; she might, if given cause, come in against Germany. That Belgium could be the cause was no secret. In the Franco-Prussian War of 1870, when Germany was still a climbing power, Bismarck had been happy enough, upon a hint from England, to reaffirm the inviolability of Belgium. Gladstone had secured a treaty from both belligerents providing that if either violated Belgian neutrality, England would cooperate with the other to the extent of defending Belgium, though without engaging in the general operations of the war. Although there was something a little impractical about the tail of this Gladstonian formula, the Germans had no reason to suppose its underlying motive any less operative in 1914 than in 1870. Nevertheless, Schlieffen decided, in the event of war, to attack France by way of Belgium.

France First

His reason was "military necessity." In a two-front war, he wrote, "the whole of Germany must throw itself upon *one* enemy, the strongest, most powerful, most dangerous enemy, and that can only be France." Schlieffen's completed plan for 1906, the year he retired, allocated six weeks and seven-eighths of Germany's forces to smash France while one-eighth was to hold her eastern frontier against Russia until the bulk of her army could be brought back to face the second enemy. He chose France first because Russia could frustrate a quick victory by simply withdrawing within

her infinite room, leaving Germany to be sucked into an endless campaign as Napoleon had been. France was both closer at hand and quicker to mobilize. The German and French armies each required two weeks to complete mobilization before a major attack could begin on the fifteenth day. Russia, according to German arithmetic, because of her vast distances, huge numbers, and meager railroads, would take six weeks before she could launch a major offensive, by which time France would be beaten.

The risk of leaving East Prussia, hearth of Junkerdom and the Hohenzollerns, to be held by only nine divisions was hard to accept, but Frederick the Great had said, "It is better to lose a province than split the forces with which one seeks victory," and nothing so comforts the military mind as the maxim of a great but dead general. Only by throwing the utmost numbers against the West could France be finished off quickly. Only by a strategy of envelopment, using Belgium as a pathway, could the German armies, in Schlieffen's opinion, attack France successfully. His reasoning, from the purely military point of view, appeared faultless.

The German Army of a million and a half that was to be used against France was now six times the size it had been in 1870, and needed room to maneuver. French fortresses constructed along the frontiers of Alsace and Lorraine after 1870 precluded the Germans from making a frontal attack across the common border. A protracted siege would provide no opportunity, as long as French lines to the rear remained open, of netting the enemy quickly in a battle of annihilation. Only by envelopment could the French be taken from behind and destroyed. But at either end of the French lines lay neutral territory—Switzerland and Belgium. There was not enough room for the huge German Army to get around the French armies and still stay inside France. The Germans had done it in 1870 when both armies were small, but now it was a matter of moving an army of millions to outflank an army of millions. Space, roads, and railroads were essential. The flat plains of Flanders had them. In Belgium there was both room for the outflanking maneuver which was

Schlieffen's formula for success as well as a way to avoid the frontal attack which was his formula for disaster.

Clausewitz, oracle of German military thought, had ordained a quick victory by "decisive battle" as the first object in offensive war. Occupation of the enemy's territory and gaining control of his resources was secondary. To speed an early decision was essential. Time counted above all else. Anything that protracted a campaign Clausewitz condemned. "Gradual reduction" of the enemy, or a war of attrition, he feared like the pit of hell. He wrote in the decade of Waterloo, and his works had been accepted as the Bible of strategy ever since.

The New Cannae

To achieve decisive victory, Schlieffen fixed upon a strategy derived from Hannibal and the Battle of Cannae. The dead general who mesmerized Schlieffen had been dead a very long time. Two thousand years had passed since Hannibal's classic double envelopment of the Romans at Cannae. Field gun and machine gun had replaced bow and arrow and slingshot, Schlieffen wrote, "but the principles of strategy remain unchanged. The enemy's front is not the objective. The essential thing is to crush the enemy's flanks . . . and complete the extermination by attack upon his rear." Under Schlieffen, envelopment became the fetish and frontal attack the anathema of the German General Staff.

Schlieffen's first plan to include the violation of Belgium was formulated in 1899. It called for cutting across the corner of Belgium east of the Meuse. Enlarged with each successive year, by 1905 it had expanded into a huge enveloping right-wing sweep in which the German armies would cross Belgium from Liège to Brussels before turning southward, where they could take advantage of the open country of Flanders, to march against France. Everything depended upon a quick decision against France, and even the long way around through Flanders would be quicker than laying siege to the fortress line across the common border.

Schlieffen did not have enough divisions for a double envelopment of France à la Cannae. For this he substituted a heavily one-sided right wing that would spread across the whole of Belgium on both sides of the Meuse, sweep down through the country like a monstrous hayrake, cross the Franco-Belgian frontier along its entire width, and descend upon Paris along the Valley of the Oise. The German mass would come between the capital and the French armies which, drawn back to meet the menace, would be caught, away from their fortified areas, in the decisive battle of annihilation. Essential to the plan was a deliberately weak German left wing on the Alsace-Lorraine front which would tempt the French in that area forward into a "sack" between Metz and the Vosges. It was expected that the French, intent upon liberating their lost provinces, would attack here, and it was considered so much the better for the success of the German plan if they did, for they could be held in the sack by the German left wing while the main victory was obtained from behind. In the back of Schlieffen's mind always glimmered the hope that, as battle unfolded, a counterattack by his left wing could be mounted in order to bring about a true double envelopment—the "colossal Cannae" of his dreams. Sternly saving his greatest strength for the right wing, he did not yield to that vaulting ambition in his plan. But the lure of the left wing remained to tempt his successors.

Thus the Germans came to Belgium. Decisive battle dictated envelopment, and envelopment dictated the use of Belgian territory. The German General Staff pronounced it a military necessity; Kaiser and Chancellor accepted it with more or less equanimity. Whether it was advisable, whether it was even expedient in view of the probable effect on world opinion, especially on neutral opinion, was irrelevant. That it seemed necessary to the triumph of German arms was the only criterion. Germans had imbibed from 1870 the lesson that arms and war were the sole source of German greatness. They had been taught by Field Marshal von der Goltz, in his book *The Nation in Arms,* that "We have won our position through the sharpness of our sword, not through the sharpness of our mind.'' The decision to violate Belgian neutrality followed easily.

National Character

Character is fate, the Greeks believed. A hundred years of German philosophy went into the making of this decision in which the seed of self-destruction lay embedded, waiting for its hour. The voice was Schlieffen's, but the hand was the hand of Fichte who saw the German people chosen by Providence to occupy the supreme place in the history of the universe, of Hegel who saw them leading the world to a glorious destiny of compulsory *Kultur*, of Nietzsche who told them that Supermen were above ordinary controls, of Treitschke who set the increase of power as the highest moral duty of the state, of the whole German people, who called their temporal ruler the "All-Highest." What made the Schlieffen plan was not Clausewitz and the Battle of Cannae, but the body of accumulated egoism which suckled the German people and created a nation fed on "the desperate delusion of the will that deems itself absolute."

The goal, decisive battle, was a product of the victories over Austria and France in 1866 and 1870. Dead battles, like dead generals, hold the military mind in their dead grip, and Germans, no less than other peoples, prepare for the last war. They staked everything on decisive battle in the image of Hannibal, but even the ghost of Hannibal might have reminded Schlieffen that though Carthage won at Cannae, Rome won the war.

Old Field Marshal Moltke in 1890 foretold that the next war might last seven years—or thirty—because the resources of a modern state were so great it would not know itself to be beaten after a single military defeat and would not give up. His nephew and namesake who succeeded Schlieffen as Chief of Staff also had moments when he saw the truth as clearly. In a moment of heresy to Clausewitz, he said to the Kaiser in 1906, "It will be a national war which will not be settled by a decisive battle but by a long wearisome struggle with a country that will not be overcome until its whole national force is bro-

ken, and a war which will utterly exhaust our own people, even if we are victorious." It went against human nature, however—and the nature of General Staffs—to follow through the logic of his own prophecy. Amorphous and without limits, the concept of a long war could not be scientifically planned for as could the orthodox, predictable, and simple solution of decisive battle and a short war. The younger Moltke was already Chief of Staff when he made his prophecy, but neither he nor his Staff, nor the Staff of any other country, ever made any effort to plan for a long war. Besides the two Moltkes, one dead and the other infirm of purpose, some military strategists in other countries glimpsed the possibility of prolonged war, but all preferred to believe, along with the bankers and industrialists, that because of the dislocation of economic life a general European war could not last longer than three or four months. One constant among the elements of 1914—as of any era—was the disposition of everyone on all sides not to prepare for the harder alternative, not to act upon what they suspected to be true.

Schlieffen, having embraced the strategy of "decisive battle," pinned Germany's fate to it. He expected France to violate Belgium as soon as Germany's deployment at the Belgian frontier revealed her strategy, and he therefore planned that Germany should do it first and faster. "Belgian neutrality must be broken by one side or the other," his thesis ran. "Whoever gets there first and occupies Brussels and imposes a war levy of some 1,000 million francs has the upper hand."

Indemnity, which enables a state to conduct war at the enemy's expense instead of its own, was a secondary object laid down by Clausewitz. His third was the winning of public opinion, which is accomplished by "gaining great victories and possession of the enemy's capital" and which helps to bring an end to resistance. He knew how material success could gain public opinion; he forgot how moral failure could lose it, which too can be a hazard of war.

It was a hazard the French never lost sight of, and it led them to the opposite conclusion from the one Schlieffen expected. Belgium was their pathway of attack too, through the Ardennes if not through Flanders, but their plan of campaign prohibited their armies from using it until after the Germans had violated Belgium first. To them the logic of the matter was clear: Belgium was an open path in either direction; whether Germany or France would use it depended on which of the two wanted war the more. As a French general said, "The one that willed war more than the other could not help but will the violation of Belgian neutrality."

Schlieffen and his Staff did not think Belgium would fight and add its six divisions to the French forces. When Chancellor Bülow, discussing the problem with Schlieffen in 1904, reminded him of Bismarck's warning that it would be against "plain common sense" to add another enemy to the forces against Germany, Schlieffen twisted his monocle several times in his eye, as was his habit, and said: "Of course. We haven't grown stupider since then." But Belgium would not resist by force of arms; she would be satisfied to protest, he said.

German confidence on this score was due to placing rather too high a value on the well-known avarice of Leopold II, who was King of the Belgians in Schlieffen's time. Tall and imposing with his black spade beard and his aura of wickedness composed of mistresses, money, Congo cruelties, and other scandals, Leopold was, in the opinion of Emperor Franz Josef of Austria, "a thoroughly bad man." There were few men who could be so described, the Emperor said, but the King of the Belgians was one. Because Leopold was avaricious, among other vices, the Kaiser supposed that avarice would rule over common sense, and he conceived a clever plan to tempt Leopold into [an] alliance with an offer of French territory. Whenever the Kaiser was seized with a project he attempted instantly to execute it, usually to his astonishment and chagrin when it did not work. In 1904 he invited Leopold to visit him in Berlin, spoke to him in "the kindest way in the world" about his proud forefathers, the Dukes of Burgundy, and offered to re-create the old Duchy of Burgundy for him out of Artois, French Flanders, and the French Ardennes. Leopold gazed at him "openmouthed," then, at-

tempting to pass it off with a laugh, reminded the Kaiser that much had changed since the fifteenth century. In any event, he said, his Ministers and Parliament would never consider such a suggestion.

That was the wrong thing to say, for the Kaiser flew into one of his rages and scolded the King for putting respect for Parliament and Ministers above respect for the finger of God (with which William sometimes confused himself). "I told him," William reported to Chancellor von Bülow, "I could not be played with. Whoever in the case of a European war was not with me was against me." He was a soldier, he proclaimed, in the school of Napoleon and Frederick the Great who began their wars by forestalling their enemies, and "so should I, in the event of Belgium's not being on my side, be actuated by strategical considerations only."

This declared intent, the first explicit threat to tear up the treaty, dumbfounded King Leopold. He drove off to the station with his helmet on back to front, looking to the aide who accompanied him "as if he had had a shock of some kind."

Although the Kaiser's scheme failed, Leopold was still expected to barter Belgium's neutrality for a purse of two million pounds sterling. When a French intelligence officer, who was told this figure by a German officer after the war, expressed surprise at its generosity, he was reminded that "the French would have had to pay for it." Even after Leopold was succeeded in 1909 by his nephew King Albert, a very different quantity, Belgium's resistance was still expected by Schlieffen's successors to be a formality. It might, for example, suggested a German diplomat in 1911, take the form of "lining up her army along the road taken by the German forces."

"Brush the Channel"

Schlieffen designated thirty-four divisions to take the roads through Belgium, disposing on their way of Belgium's six divisions if, as seemed to the Germans unlikely, they chose to resist. The Germans were intensely anxious that they should not, because resistance would mean destruction

of railways and bridges and consequent dislocation of the schedule to which the German Staff
was passionately attached. Belgian acquiescence,
on the other hand, would avoid the necessity of
tying up divisions in siege of the Belgian fortresses and would also tend to silence public disap-
proval of Germany's act. To persuade Belgium
against futile resistance, Schlieffen arranged that
she should be confronted, prior to invasion, by
an ultimatum requiring her to yield "all fortresses,
railways and troops" or face bombardment of
her fortified cities. Heavy artillery was ready to
transform the threat of bombardment into reality,
if necessary. The heavy guns would in any case,
Schlieffen wrote in 1912, be needed further on
in the campaign. "The great industrial town of
Lille, for example, offers an excellent target for
bombardment."

Schlieffen wanted his right wing to reach
as far west as Lille in order to make the envelopment of the French complete. "When you march
into France," he said, "let the last man on the
right brush the Channel with his sleeve." Furthermore, counting on British belligerency, he wanted
a wide sweep in order to rake in a British Expedi-
tionary Force along with the French. He placed
a higher value on the blockade potential of British
sea power than on the British Army, and therefore
was determined to achieve a quick victory over
French and British land forces and an early decision of the war before the economic consequences
of British hostility could make themselves felt.
To that end everything must go to swell the right
wing. He had to make it powerful in numbers
because the density of soldiers per mile determined the extent of territory that could be covered.

Employing the active army alone, he would
not have enough divisions both to hold his eastern
frontier against a Russian breakthrough and to
achieve the superiority in numbers over France
which he needed for a quick victory. His solution
was simple if revolutionary. He decided to use
reserve units in the front line. According to prevailing military doctrine, only the youngest men,
fresh from the rigors and discipline of barracks
and drill, were fit to fight; reserves who had finished their compulsory military service and re-

turned to civilian life were considered soft and
were not wanted in the battle line. Except for
men under twenty-six who were merged with
the active units, the reserves were formed into
divisions of their own, intended for use as occupation troops and for other rear duty. Schlieffen
changed all that. He added some twenty reserve
divisions (the number varied according to the
year of the plan) to the line of march of the
fifty or more active divisions. With this increase
in numbers his cherished envelopment became
possible.

After retiring in 1906 he spent his last years
still writing about Cannae, improving his plan,
composing memoranda to guide his successors,
and died at eighty in 1913, muttering at the end:
"It must come to a fight. Only make the right
wing strong."

Von Moltke

His successor, the melancholy General von
Moltke, was something of a pessimist who lacked
Schlieffen's readiness to concentrate all his
strength in one maneuver. If Schlieffen's motto
was "Be bold, be bold," Moltke's was, "But
not too bold." He worried both about the weakness of his left wing against the French and about
the weakness of the forces left to defend East
Prussia against the Russians. He even debated
with his Staff the advisability of fighting a defensive war against France, but rejected the idea
because it precluded all possibility of "engaging
the enemy on his own territory." The Staff agreed
that the invasion of Belgium would be "entirely
just and necessary" because the war would be
one for the "defense and existence of Germany."
Schlieffen's plan was maintained, and Moltke
consoled himself with the thought, as he said in
1913, that "We must put aside all commonplaces
as to the responsibility of the aggressor. . . .
Success alone justifies war." But just to be safe
everywhere, each year, cutting into Schlieffen's
dying request, he borrowed strength from the
right wing to add to the left.

Moltke planned for a German left wing of
8 corps numbering about 320,000 men to hold

the front in Alsace and Lorraine south of Metz. The German center of 11 corps numbering about 400,000 men would invade France through Luxembourg and the Ardennes. The German right wing of 16 corps numbering about 700,000 men would attack through Belgium, smash the famed gateway fortresses of Liège and Namur which held the Meuse, and fling itself across the river to reach the flat country and straight roads on the far side. Every day's schedule of march was fixed in advance. The Belgians were not expected to fight, but if they did the power of the German assault was expected to persuade them quickly to surrender. The schedule called for the roads through Liège to be open by the twelfth day of mobilization, Brussels to be taken by M-19, the French frontier crossed on M-22, a line Thionville-St. Quentin reached by M-31, Paris and decisive victory by M-39.

The plan of campaign was as rigid and complete as the blueprint for a battleship. Heeding Clausewitz's warning that military plans which leave no room for the unexpected can lead to disaster, the Germans with infinite care had attempted to provide for every contingency. Their staff officers, trained at maneuvers and at war-college desks to supply the correct solution for any given set of circumstances, were expected to cope with the unexpected. Against that elusive, that mocking and perilous quantity, every precaution had been taken except one—flexibility.

While the plan for maximum effort against France hardened, Moltke's fears of Russia gradually lessened as his General Staff evolved a credo, based on a careful count of Russian railway mileage, that Russia would not be "ready" for war until 1916. This was confirmed in German minds by their spies' reports of Russian remarks "that something was going to begin in 1916."

In 1914 two events sharpened Germany's readiness to a fine point. In April, England had begun naval talks with the Russians, and in June, Germany herself had completed the widening of the Kiel Canal, permitting her new dreadnoughts direct access from the North Sea to the Baltic. On learning of the Anglo-Russian talks, Moltke said in May during a visit to his Austrian opposite

number, Franz Conrad von Hötzendorff, that from now on "any adjournment will have the effect of diminishing our chances of success." Two weeks later, on June 1st, he said to Baron Eckhardstein, "We are ready, and the sooner the better for us."

THE FRENCH VIEW

General de Castelnau, Deputy Chief of the French General Staff, was visited at the War Office one day in 1913 by the Military Governor of Lille, General Lebas, who came to protest the General Staff's decision to abandon Lille as a fortified city. Situated ten miles from the Belgian border and forty miles inland from the Channel, Lille lay close to the path that an invading army would take if it came by way of Flanders. In answer to General Lebas' plea for its defense, General de Castelnau spread out a map and measured with a ruler the distance from the German border to Lille by way of Belgium. The normal density of troops required for a vigorous offensive, he reminded his caller, was five or six to a meter. If the Germans extended themselves as far west as Lille, de Castelnau pointed out, they would be stretched out two to a meter.

"We'll Cut Them in Half"

"We'll cut them in half!" he declared. The German active Army, he explained, could deploy some twenty-five corps, about a million men, on the Western Front. "Here, figure it out for yourself," he said, handing Lebas the ruler. "If they come as far as Lille," he repeated with sardonic satisfaction, "so much the better for us."

French strategy did not ignore the threat of envelopment by a German right wing. On the contrary, the French General Staff believed that the stronger the Germans made their right wing, the correspondingly weaker they would leave their center and left where the French Army planned to break through. French strategy turned its back to the Belgian frontier and its face to the Rhine. While the Germans were taking the long way around to fall upon the French flank, the French planned a two-pronged offensive that would smash through the German center and left on either side of the German fortified area at Metz and by victory there, sever the German right wing from its base, rendering it harmless. It was a bold plan born of an idea—an idea inherent in the recovery of France from the humiliation of Sedan.

The Shadow of Sedan

Under the peace terms dictated by Germany at Versailles in 1871, France had suffered amputation, indemnity, and occupation. Even a triumphal march by the German Army down the Champs Elysées was among the terms imposed. It took place along a silent, black-draped avenue empty of onlookers. At Bordeaux, when the French Assembly ratified the peace terms, the deputies of Alsace-Lorraine walked from the hall in tears, leaving behind their protest: "We proclaim forever the right of Alsatians and Lorrainers to remain members of the French nation. We swear for ourselves, our constituents, our children and our children's children to claim that right for all time, by every means, in the face of the usurper."

The annexation, though opposed by Bismarck, who said it would be the Achilles' heel of the new German Empire, was required by the elder Moltke and his Staff. They insisted, and convinced the Emperor, that the border provinces with Metz, Strasbourg, and the crest of the Vosges must be sliced off in order to put France geographically forever on the defensive. They added a crushing indemnity of five billion francs intended to hobble France for a generation, and lodged an army of occupation until it should be paid. With one enormous effort the French raised and paid off the sum within three years, and their recovery began.

The memory of Sedan remained, a stationary dark shadow on the French consciousness. "*N'en parlez jamais*; *pensez-y toujours*" (Never speak of it; think of it always) had counseled Gambetta. For more than forty years the thought of "Again" was the single most fundamental factor of French policy. In the early years after 1870, instinct and military weakness dictated a fortress strategy. France walled herself in behind a system of entrenched camps connected by forts. Two fortified lines, Belfort-Epinal and Toul-Verdun, guarded the eastern frontier, and one, Maubeuge-Valenciennes-Lille, guarded the western half of the Belgian frontier; the gaps between were intended to canalize the invasion forces.

Behind her wall, as Victor Hugo urged at his most vibrant: "France will have but one thought: to reconstitute her forces, gather her energy, nourish her sacred anger, raise her young generation to form an army of the whole people, to work without cease, to study the methods and skills of our enemies, to become again a great France, the France of 1792, the France of an idea with a sword. Then one day she will be irresistible. Then she will take back Alsace-Lorraine."

Through returning prosperity and growing empire, through the perennial civil quarrels—royalism, Boulangism, clericalism, strikes, and the culminating, devastating Dreyfus Affair—the sacred anger still glowed, especially in the army. The one thing that held together all elements of the army, whether old guard or republican, Jesuit or Freemason, was the *mystique d'Alsace*. The eyes of all were fixed on the blue line of the Vosges. A captain of infantry confessed in 1912 that he used to lead the men of his company in secret patrols of two or three through the dark pines to the mountaintops where they could gaze down on Colmar. "On our return from those clandestine expeditions our columns reformed, choked and dumb with emotion."

Originally neither German nor French, Alsace had been snatched back and forth between the two until, under Louis XIV, it was confirmed to France by the Treaty of Westphalia in 1648. After Germany annexed Alsace and part of Lorraine in 1870 Bismarck advised giving the inhabitants as much autonomy as possible and encouraging their particularism, for, he said, the more Alsatian they felt, the less they would feel French. His successors did not see the necessity. They

took no account of the wishes of their new subjects, made no effort to win them over, administered the provinces as *Reichsland*, or "Imperial
territory," under German officials on virtually
the same terms as their African colonies, and
succeeded only in infuriating and alienating the
population until in 1911 a constitution was granted
them. By then it was too late. German rule exploded in the Zabern Affair in 1913 which began,
after an exchange of insults between townspeople
and garrison, when a German officer struck a
crippled shoemaker with his saber. It ended in
the complete and public exposure of German policy in the *Reichsland*, in a surge of anti-German
feeling in world opinion, and in the simultaneous
triumph of militarism in Berlin where the officer
of Zabern became a hero, congratulated by the
Crown Prince.

For Germany 1870 was not a final settlement. The German day in Europe which they
thought had dawned when the German Empire
was proclaimed in the Hall of Mirrors at Versailles
was still postponed. France was not crushed; the
French Empire was actually expanding in North
Africa and Indo-China; the world of art and beauty
and style still worshiped at the feet of Paris. Germans were still gnawed by envy of the country
they had conquered. "As well off as God in
France," was a German saying. At the same
time they considered France decadent in culture
and enfeebled by democracy. "It is impossible
for a country that has had forty-two war ministers
in forty-three years to fight effectively," announced Professor Hans Delbrück, Germany's
leading historian. Believing themselves superior
in soul, in strength, in energy, industry, and national virtue, Germans felt they deserved the dominion of Europe. The work of Sedan must be
completed.

"Élan Vital"

Living in the shadow of that unfinished business,
France, reviving in spirit and strength, grew
weary of being eternally on guard, eternally exhorted by her leaders to defend herself. As the
century turned, her spirit rebelled against thirty

years of the defensive with its implied avowal
of inferiority. France knew herself to be physically weaker than Germany. Her population was
less, her birth rate lower. She needed some
weapon that Germany lacked to give herself confidence in her survival. The "idea with a sword"
fulfilled the need. Expressed by Bergson it was
called *élan vital*, the all-conquering will. Belief
in its power convinced France that the human
spirit need not, after all, bow to the predestined
forces of evolution which Schopenhauer and Hegel had declared to be irresistible. The spirit of
France would be the equalizing factor. Her will
to win, her *élan*, would enable France to defeat
her enemy. Her genius was in her spirit, the spirit
of *la gloire*, of 1792, of the incomparable "Mar-
seillaise," the spirit of General Margueritte's heroic cavalry charge before Sedan when even Wil-
helm I, watching the battle, could not forbear
to cry, "*Oh, les braves gens!*"

Belief in the fervor of France, in the *furor
Gallicae*, revived France's faith in herself in the
generation after 1870. It was that fervor, unfurling
her banners, sounding her bugles, arming her
soldiers, that would lead France to victory if the
day of "Again" should come.

Translated into military terms Bergson's
élan vital became the doctrine of the offensive.
In proportion as a defensive gave way to an offensive strategy, the attention paid to the Belgian
frontier gradually gave way in favor of a progressive shift of gravity eastward toward the
point where a French offensive could be launched
to break through to the Rhine. For the Germans
the roundabout road through Flanders led to Paris;
for the French it led nowhere. They could only
get to Berlin by the shortest way. The more the
thinking of the French General Staff approached
the offensive, the greater the forces it concentrated
at the attacking point and the fewer it left to
defend the Belgian frontier.

The doctrine of the offensive had its fount
in the Ecole Supérieure de la Guerre, or War
College, the ark of the army's intellectual elite,
whose director, General Ferdinand Foch, was the
molder of French military theory of his time.
Foch's mind, like a heart, contained two valves:

one pumped spirit into strategy; the other circulated common sense. On the one hand Foch preached a *mystique* of will expressed in his famous aphorisms, "The will to conquer is the first condition of victory," or more succinctly, "*Victoire c'est la volonté*," and, "A battle won is a battle in which one will not confess oneself beaten."

In practice this was to become the famous order at the Marne to attack when the situation called for retreat. His officers of those days remember him bellowing "Attack! Attack!" with furious, sweeping gestures while he dashed about in short rushes as if charged by an electric battery. Why, he was later asked, did he advance at the Marne when he was technically beaten? "Why? I don't know. Because of my men, because I had a will. And then—God was there."

Though a profound student of Clausewitz, Foch did not, like Clausewitz's German successors, believe in a foolproof schedule of battle worked out in advance. Rather he taught the necessity of perpetual adaptability and improvisation to fit circumstances. "Regulations," he would say, "are all very well for drill but in the hour of danger they are no more use. . . . You have to learn to think." To think meant to give room for freedom of initiative, for the imponderable to win over the material, for will to demonstrate its power over circumstance.

But the idea that morale alone could conquer, Foch warned, was an "infantile notion." From his flights of metaphysics he would descend at once, in his lectures and his prewar books *Les Principes de la Guerre* and *La Conduite de la Guerre*, to the earth of tactics, the placing of advance guards, the necessity of *sureté*, or protection, the elements of firepower, the need for obedience and discipline. The realistic half of his teaching was summed up in another aphorism he made familiar during the war, "*De quoi s'agit-il?*" (What is the essence of the problem?)

Eloquent as he was on tactics, it was Foch's *mystique* of will that captured the minds of his followers. Once in 1908 when Clemenceau was considering Foch, then a professor, for the post of Director of the War College, a private agent whom he sent to listen to the lectures reported back in bewilderment, "This officer teaches metaphysics so abstruse as to make idiots of his pupils." Although Clemenceau appointed Foch in spite of it, there was, in one sense, truth in the report. Foch's principles, not because they were too abstruse but because they were too attractive, laid a trap for France. They were taken up with particular enthusiasm by Colonel Grandmaison, "an ardent and brilliant officer" who was Director of the Troisième Bureau, or Bureau of Military Operations, and who in 1911 delivered two lectures at the War College which had a crystallizing effect.

"Offensive à Outrance"

Colonel Grandmaison grasped only the head and not the feet of Foch's principles. Expounding their *élan* without their *sureté*, he expressed a military philosophy that electrified his audience. He waved before their dazzled eyes an "idea with a sword" which showed them how France could win. Its essence was the *offensive à outrance*, offensive to the limit. Only this could achieve Clausewitz's decisive battle which "exploited to the finish, is the essential act of war" and which "once engaged, must be pushed to the end, with no second thoughts, up to the extremes of human endurance." Seizure of initiative is the *sine qua non*. Preconceived arrangements based on a dogmatic judgment of what the enemy will do are premature. Liberty of action is achieved only by imposing one's will upon the enemy. "All command decisions must be inspired by the will to seize and retain the initiative." The defensive is forgotten, abandoned, discarded; its only possible justification is an occasional "economizing of forces at certain points with a view to adding them to the attack."

The effect on the General Staff was profound, and during the next two years was embodied in new Field Regulations for the conduct of war and in a new plan of campaign called Plan 17, which was adopted in May, 1913. Within a few months of Grandmaison's lectures, the President of the Republic, M. Fallières, announced: "The offensive alone is suited to the temperament of French soldiers. . . . We are determined to march straight against the enemy without hesitation."

The new Field Regulations, enacted by the government in October, 1913, as the fundamental document for the training and conduct of the French Army, opened with a flourish of trumpets: "The French Army, returning to its tradition, henceforth admits no law but the offensive." Eight commandments followed, ringing with the clash of "decisive battle," "offensive without hesitation," "fierceness and tenacity," "breaking the will of the adversary," "ruthless and tireless pursuit." With all the ardor of orthodoxy stamping out heresy, the Regulations stamped upon and discarded the defensive. "The offensive alone," it proclaimed, "leads to positive results." Its Seventh Commandment, italicized by the authors, stated: *Battles are beyond everything else struggles of morale. Defeat is inevitable as soon as the hope of conquering ceases to exist. Success comes not to him who has suffered the least but to him whose will is firmest and morale strongest.*

Nowhere in the eight commandments was there mention of matériel or firepower or what Foch called *sureté*. The teaching of the Regulations became epitomized in the favorite word of the French officer corps, *le cran*, nerve, or less politely, guts. Like the youth who set out for the mountaintop under the banner marked "Excelsior!" the French Army marched to war in 1914 under a banner marked "*Cran.*"

Over the years, while French military philosophy had changed, French geography had not. The geographical facts of her frontiers remained what Germany had made them in 1870. Germany's territorial demands, William I had explained to the protesting Empress Eugénie, "have no aim other than to push back the starting point from which French armies could in the future attack us." They also pushed forward the starting point from which Germany could attack France. While French history and development after the turn of the century fixed her mind upon the offensive, her geography still required a strategy of the defensive.

General Michel

In 1911, the same year as Colonel Grandmaison's lectures, a last effort to commit France to a strategy of the defensive was made in the Supreme War Council by no less a personage than the Commander in Chief designate, General Michel. As Vice President of the Council, a post which carried with it the position of Commander in Chief in the event of war, General Michel was then the ranking officer in the army. In a report that precisely reflected Schlieffen's thinking, he submitted his estimate of the probable German line of attack and his proposals for countering it. Because of the natural escarpments and French fortifications along the common border with Germany, he argued, the Germans could not hope to win a prompt decisive battle in Lorraine. Nor would the passage through Luxembourg and the near corner of Belgium east of the Meuse give them sufficient room for their favored strategy of envelopment. Only by taking advantage of "the whole of Belgium," he said, could the Germans achieve that "immediate, brutal and decisive" offensive which they must launch upon France before the forces of her Allies could come into play. He pointed out that the Germans had long yearned for Belgium's great port of Antwerp, and this gave them an additional reason for an attack through Flanders. He proposed to face the Germans along a line Verdun-Namur-Antwerp with a French army of a million men whose left wing—like Schlieffen's right—should brush the Channel with its sleeve.

Not only was General Michel's plan defensive in character; it also depended upon a proposal that was anathema to his fellow officers. To match the numbers he believed the Germans would send through Belgium, General Michel proposed to double French front-line effectives by attaching a regiment of reserves to every active regiment. Had he proposed to admit Mistinguette to the Immortals of the French Academy, he could hardly have raised more clamor and disgust.

"*Les réserves, c'est zéro!*" was the classic dogma of the French officer corps. Men who had finished their compulsory training under universal service and were between the ages of twenty-three and thirty-four were classed as reserves. Upon mobilization the youngest classes filled out the regular army units to war strength; the others were formed into reserve regiments, brigades, and divisions according to their local geographical districts. These were considered fit only for rear duty or for use as fortress troops, and incapable, because of their lack of trained officers and NCOs, of being attached to the fighting regiments. The regular army's contempt for the reserves, in which it was joined by the parties of the right, was augmented by dislike of the principle of the "nation in arms." To merge the reserves with the active divisions would be to put a drag on the army's fighting thrust. Only the active army, they believed, could be depended upon to defend the country.

The left parties, on the other hand, with memories of General Boulanger on horseback, associated the army with *coups d'état* and believed in the principle of a "nation in arms" as the only safeguard of the Republic. They maintained that a few months' training would fit any citizen for war, and violently opposed the increase of military service to three years. The army demanded this reform in 1913 not only to match an increase in the German Army but also because the more men who were in training at any one time, the less reliance needed to be placed on reserve units. After angry debate, with bitterly divisive effect on the country, the Three-Year Law was enacted in August, 1913.

Disdain of the reserves was augmented by the new doctrine of the offensive which, it was felt, could only be properly inculcated in active troops. To perform the irresistible onslaught of the *attaque brusquée*, symbolized by the bayonet charge, the essential quality was *élan*, and *élan* could not be expected of men settled in civilian life with family responsibilities. Reserves mixed with active troops would create "armies of decadence," incapable of the will to conquer.

Similar sentiments were known to be held

across the Rhine. The Kaiser was widely credited with the edict "No fathers of families at the front." Among the French General Staff it was an article of faith that the Germans would not mix reserve units with active units, and this led to the belief that the Germans would not have enough men in the front line to do two things at once: send a strong right wing in a wide sweep through Belgium west of the Meuse and keep sufficient forces at their center and left to stop a French breakthrough to the Rhine.

When General Michel presented his plan, the Minister of War, Messimy, treated it "*comme une insanité.*" As chairman of the Supreme War Council he not only attempted to suppress it but at once consulted other members of the council on the advisability of removing Michel.

Messimy, an exuberant, energetic, almost violent man with a thick neck, round head, bright peasant's eyes behind spectacles, and a loud voice, was a former career officer. In 1899 as a thirty-year-old captain of Chasseurs, he had resigned from the army in protest against its refusal to reopen the Dreyfus case. In that heated time the officer corps insisted as a body that to admit the possibility of Dreyfus's innocence after his conviction would be to destroy the army's prestige and infallibility. Unable to put loyalty to the army above justice, Messimy determined upon a political career with the declared goal of "reconciling the army with the nation." He swept into the War Ministry with a passion for improvement. Finding a number of generals "incapable not only of leading their troops but even of following them," he adopted Theodore Roosevelt's expedient of ordering all generals to conduct maneuvers on horseback. When this provoked protests that old so-and-so would be forced to retire from the army Messimy replied that that was indeed his object. He had been named War Minister on June 30, 1911, after a succession of four ministers in four months and the next day was met by the attack of the German gunboat *Panther* on Agadir precipitating the second Moroccan crisis. Expecting mobilization at any moment, Messimy discovered the generalissimo-designate, General Michel, to be "hesitant, indecisive and crushed by the weight of the duty that might at any moment devolve upon him.'' In his present post Messimy believed he represented a ''national danger.'' Michel's ''insane'' proposal provided the excuse to get rid of him.

Michel, however, refused to go without first having his plan presented to the Council whose members included the foremost generals of France: Gallieni, the great colonial; Pau, the one-armed veteran of 1870; Joffre, the silent engineer; Dubail, the pattern of gallantry, who wore his kepi cocked over one eye with the ''*chic exquis*'' of the Second Empire. All were to hold active commands in 1914 and two were to become Marshals of France. None gave Michel's plan his support. One officer from the War Ministry who was present at the meeting said: ''There is no use discussing it. General Michel is off his head.''

Whether or not this verdict represented the views of all present—Michel later claimed that General Dubail, for one, had originally agreed with him—Messimy, who made no secret of his hostility, carried the Council with him. A trick of fate arranged that Messimy should be a forceful character and Michel should not. To be right and overruled is not forgiven to persons in responsible positions, and Michel duly paid for his clairvoyance. Relieved of his command, he was appointed Military Governor of Paris where in a crucial hour in the coming test he was indeed to prove ''hesitant and indecisive.''

Messimy having fervently stamped out Michel's heresy of the defensive, did his best, as War Minister, to equip the army to fight a successful offensive but was in his turn frustrated in his most-cherished prospect—the need to reform the French uniform. The British had adopted khaki after the Boer War, and the Germans were about to make the change from Prussian blue to field-gray. But in 1912 French soldiers still wore the same blue coats, red kepi, and red trousers they had worn in 1830 when rifle fire carried only two hundred paces and when armies, fighting at these close quarters, had no need for concealment. Visiting the Balkan front in 1912, Messimy saw the advantages gained by the dull-colored Bulgarians and came home determined to make

the French soldier less visible. His project to clothe him in gray-blue or gray-green raised a howl of protest. Army pride was as intransigent about giving up its red trousers as it was about adopting heavy guns. Army prestige was once again felt to be at stake. To clothe the French soldier in some muddy, inglorious color, declared the army's champions, would be to realize the fondest hopes of Dreyfusards and Freemasons. To banish ''all that is colorful, all that gives the soldier his vivid aspect,'' wrote the *Echo de Paris*, ''is to go contrary both to French taste and military function.'' Messimy pointed out that the two might no longer be synonymous, but his opponents proved immovable. At a parliamentary hearing a former War Minister, M. Etienne, spoke for France.

''Eliminate the red trousers?'' he cried. ''Never! *Le pantalon rouge c'est la France*!''

''That blind and imbecile attachment to the most visible of all colors,'' wrote Messimy afterward, ''was to have cruel consequences.''

In the meantime, still in the midst of the Agadir crisis, he had to name a new prospective generalissimo in place of Michel. He planned to give added authority to the post by combining with it that of Chief of the General Staff and by abolishing the post of Chief of Staff to the War Ministry, currently held by General Dubail. Michel's successor would have all the reins of power concentrated in his hands.

Messimy's first choice was the austere and brilliant general in pince-nez, Gallieni, who refused it because, he explained, having been instrumental in Michel's dismissal he felt scruples about replacing him. Furthermore he had only two years to go before retirement at sixty-four, and he believed the appointment of a ''colonial'' would be resented by the Metropolitan Army—''*une question de bouton*,'' he said, tapping his insignia. General Pau, who was next in line, made it a condition that he be allowed to name generals of his own choice to the higher commands which, as he was known for his reactionary opinions, threatened to wake the barely slumbering feud between rightist army and republican nation. Respecting him for his honesty, the government refused his condition. Messimy consulted Gallieni, who suggested his former subordinate in Madagascar, "a cool and methodical worker with a lucid and precise mind." Accordingly the post was offered to General Joseph-Jacques-Césaire Joffre, then aged fifty-nine, formerly chief of the Engineer Corps and presently Chief of the Services of the Rear.

Massive and paunchy in his baggy uniform, with a fleshy face adorned by a heavy, nearly white mustache and bushy eyebrows to match, with a clear youthful skin, calm blue eyes and a candid, tranquil gaze, Joffre looked like Santa Claus and gave an impression of benevolence and naïveté—two qualities not noticeably part of his character. He did not come of a gentleman's family, was not a graduate of St. Cyr (but of the less aristocratic if more scientific Ecole Polytechnique), had not passed through the higher training of the War College. As an officer of the Engineer Corps, which dealt with such unromantic matters as fortifications and railways, he belonged to a branch of the service not drawn upon for the higher commands. He was the eldest of the eleven children of a petit bourgeois manufacturer of wine barrels in the French Pyrénées. His military career had been marked by quiet accomplishment and efficiency in each post he filled: as company commander in Formosa and Indo-China, as a major in the Sudan and Timbuktu, as staff officer in the Railway Section of the War Ministry, as lecturer at the Artillery School, as fortifications officer under Gallieni in Madagascar from 1900 to 1905, as general of a division in 1905, of a corps in 1908, and as Director of the Rear and member of the War Council since 1910.

General Joffre

He had no known clerical, monarchist, or other disturbing connections; he had been out of the country during the Dreyfus Affair; his reputation as a good republican was as smooth as his well manicured hands; he was solid and utterly phlegmatic. His outstanding characteristic was a habitual silence that in other men would have seemed self-deprecatory but, worn like an aura over Joffre's great, calm bulk, inspired confidence. He had still five years to go before retirement.

Joffre was conscious of one lack: he had had no training in the rarefied realms of staff work. On a hot July day when doors in the War Ministry on the Rue St. Dominique were left open, officers glancing out of their rooms saw General Pau holding Joffre by a button of his uniform. "Take it, *cher ami*," he was saying. "We will give you Castelnau. He knows all about staff work—everything will go of itself."

Castelnau, who was a graduate both of St. Cyr and of the War College, came, like D'Artagnan, from Gascony, which is said to produce men of hot blood and cold brain. He suffered from the disadvantage of family connections with a marquis, of associating with Jesuits, and of a personal Catholicism which he practiced so vigorously as to earn him during the war the name of *le capucin botté*, the Monk in Boots. He had, however, long experience on the General Staff. Joffre would have preferred Foch but knew Messimy to have an unexplained prejudice against him. As was his habit, he listened without comment to Pau's advice, and promptly took it.

"Aye!" complained Messimy when Joffre asked for Castelnau as his Deputy Chief. "You will rouse a storm in the parties of the left and make yourself a lot of enemies." However, with the assent of the President and Premier who "made a face" at the condition but agreed, both appointments were put through together. A fellow general, pursuing some personal intrigue warned Joffre that Castelnau might displace him. "Get rid of me! Not Castelnau," Joffre replied, unruffled. "I need him for six months; then I'll give him a corps command." As it proved, he found Castelnau invaluable, and when war came gave him command of an army instead of a corps.

Joffre's supreme confidence in himself was expressed in the following year when his aide, Major Alexandre, asked him if he thought war was shortly to be expected.

"Certainly I think so," Joffre replied. "I have always thought so. It will come. I shall fight it and I shall win. I have always succeeded in whatever I do—as in the Sudan. It will be that way again."

"It will mean a Marshal's baton for you," his aide suggested with some awe at the vision.

"Yes." Joffre acknowledged the prospect with laconic equanimity.

Plan 17

Under the aegis of this unassailable figure the General Staff from 1911 on threw itself into the task of revising the Field Regulations, retraining the troops in their spirit, and making a new plan of campaign to replace the now obsolete Plan 16. The staff's guiding mind, Foch, was gone from the War College, promoted and shifted to the field and ultimately to Nancy where, as he said, the frontier of 1870 "cuts like a scar across the breast of the country." There, guarding the frontier, he commanded the XXth Corps which he was soon to make famous. He had left behind, however, a "chapel," as cliques in the French Army were called, of his disciples who formed Joffre's entourage. He had also left behind a strategic plan which became the framework of Plan 17. Completed in April, 1913, it was adopted without discussion or consultation, together with the new Field Regulations by the Supreme War Council in May. The next eight months were spent reorganizing the army on the basis of the plan and preparing all the instructions and orders for mobilization, transport, services of supply, areas and schedules of deployment and concentration. By February, 1914, it was ready to be distributed in sections to each of the generals of the five armies into which the French forces were divided, only that part of it which concerned him individually going to each one.

Its motivating idea, as expressed by Foch, was, "We must get to Berlin by going through Mainz," that is, by crossing the Rhine at Mainz, 130 miles northeast of Nancy. That objective, however, was an idea only. Unlike the Schlieffen plan, Plan 17 contained no stated over-all objective and no explicit schedule of operations. It was not a plan of operations but a plan of deployment with directives for several possible lines of attack for each army, depending on circum-

stances, but without a given goal. Because it was in essence a plan of response, of riposte to a German attack, whose avenues the French could not be sure of in advance, it had of necessity to be, as Joffre said, "a posteriori and opportunist." Its intention was inflexible: Attack! Otherwise its arrangements were flexible.

A brief general directive of five sentences, classified as secret, was all that was shown in common to the generals who were to carry out the plan, and they were not permitted to discuss it. It offered very little for discussion. Like the Field Regulations it opened with a flourish: "Whatever the circumstance, it is the Commander in Chief's intention to advance with all forces united to the attack of the German armies." The rest of the general directive stated merely that French action would consist of two major offensives, one to the left and one to the right of the German fortified area of Metz-Thionville. The one to the right or south of Metz would attack directly eastward across the old border of Lorraine, while a secondary operation in Alsace was designed to anchor the French right on the Rhine. The offensive to the left or north of Metz would attack either to the north, or, in the event the enemy violated neutral territory, to the northeast through Luxembourg and the Belgian Ardennes, but this movement would be carried out "only by order of the Commander in Chief." The general purpose, although this was nowhere stated, was to drive through to the Rhine, at the same time isolating and cutting off the invading German right wing from behind.

To this end Plan 17 deployed the five French armies along the frontier from Belfort in Alsace as far as Hirson, about a third of the way along the Franco-Belgian border. The remaining two-thirds of the Belgian frontier, from Hirson to the sea, was left undefended. It was along that stretch that General Michel had planned to defend France. Joffre found his plan in the office safe when he succeeded Michel. It concentrated the center of gravity of the French forces to this extreme left section of the line where Joffre left none. It was a plan of pure defense; it allowed for no seizing of initiative; it was, as Joffre decided after careful study, "foolishness."

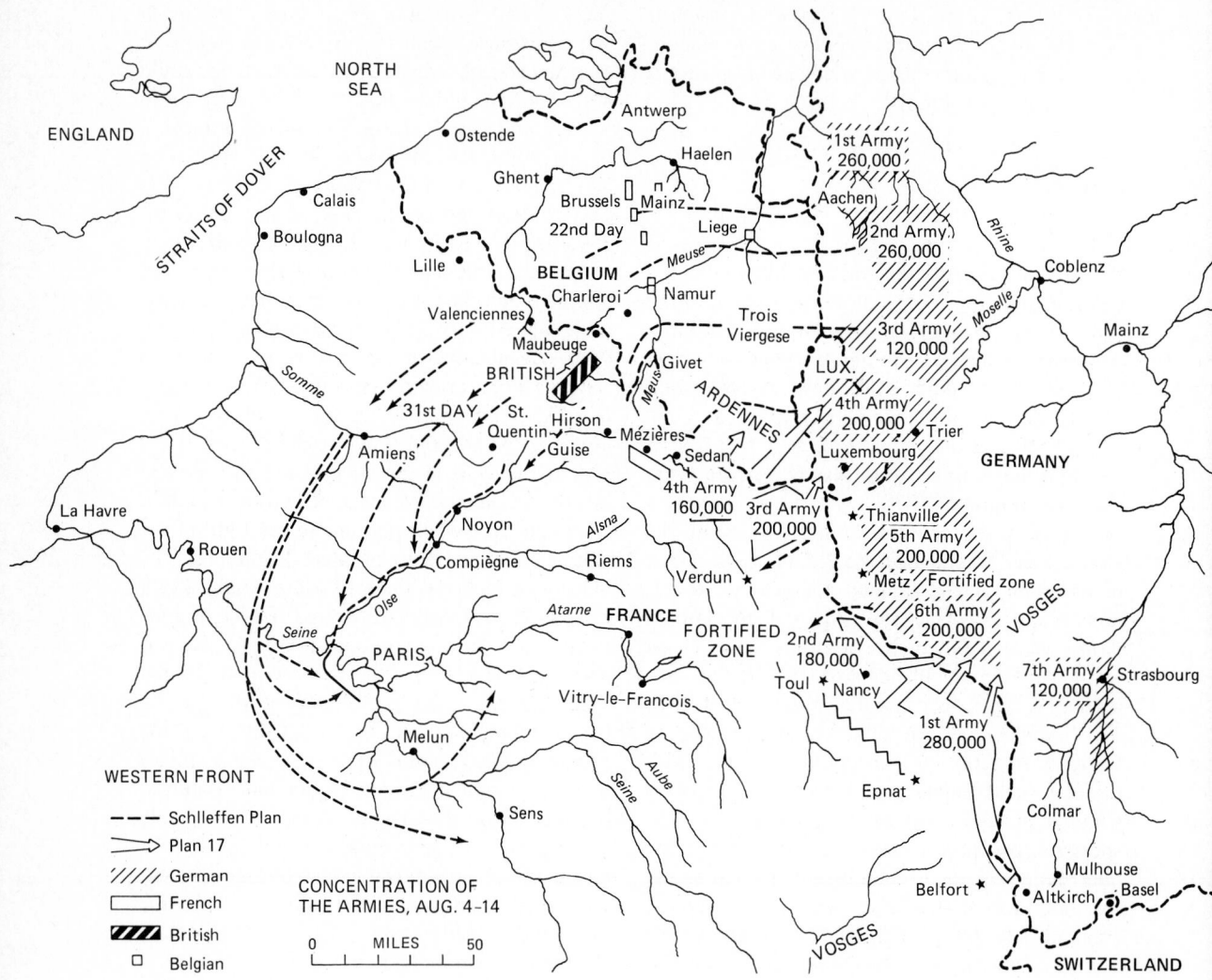

ENGLAND

NORTH SEA

STRAITS OF DOVER

Ostende

Calais

Boulogna

Lille

Valenciennes

Maubeuge

BRITISH

Amiens

La Havre

Rouen

Noyon

Compiègne

Somme

PARIS

Melun

Seine

Olse

Sens

Ghent

Brussels

22nd Day

BELGIUM

Charleroi

Givet

St. Quentin

Guise

Hirson

Méziéres

Sedan

Alsna

Riems

Verdun

Atarne

FRANCE

Vitry-le-Francois

Antwerp

Haelen

Mainz

Liege

Meuse

Namur

Meus

Trois Viergese

ARDENNES

4th Army
160,000

3rd Army
200,000

FORTIFIED ZONE

Aachen

1st Army
260,000

2nd Army
260,000

3rd Army
120,000

Rhine

Moselle

Coblenz

Mainz

4th Army
200,000

LUX.

Luxembourg

Trier

GERMANY

Thianville

5th Army
200,000

Metz   Fortified zone

6th Army
200,000

VOSGES

2nd Army
180,000

Toul

Nancy

1st Army
280,000

Epnat

7th Army
120,000

Strasbourg

Colmar

Mulhouse

Belfort

Altkirch

Basel

VOSGES

SWITZERLAND

WESTERN FRONT

- - - - Schlleffen Plan
———▷ Plan 17
////// German
☐ French
▨ British
☐ Belgian

CONCENTRATION OF
THE ARMIES, AUG. 4-14

0   MILES   50

31st DAY

QUESTIONS

1. What were the major characteristics (or dimensions) of the French and German strategies in World War I?

2. What were the strong points in these strategies? Weak points? What should have been done differently? Why?

3. What principles of strategy do the success and failures of each side suggest?

ROBIN HOOD

It was early in the spring of the second year of his insurrection against the High Sheriff of Nottingham that Robin Hood took a walk in Sherwood forest. As he walked he pondered the progress of the campaign, the disposition of his forces, his opposition's moves, and the options that confronted him.

The revolt against the Sheriff began as a personal crusade. It erupted out of Robin's own conflict with the Sheriff and his administration. Alone, however, he could accomplish little. He therefore sought allies, men with personal grievances, and a deep sense of justice. Later he took all who came without asking too many questions. Strength, he believed, lay in numbers.

The first year was spent in forging the group into a disciplined band—a group united in enmity against the Sheriff, willing to live outside the law as long as it took to accomplish their goals. The band was simply organized. Robin ruled supreme, making all important decisions. Specific tasks were delegated to his lieutenants. Will Scarlett was in charge of intelligence and scouting. His main job was to keep tabs on the movements of the Sheriff's men. He also collected information on the travel plans of rich merchants and abbots. Little John kept discipline among the men, and saw to it that their archery was at the high peak that their profession demanded. Scarlock took care of the finances, paying shares of the take, bribing officials, converting loot to cash, and finding suitable hiding places for surplus gains. Finally, Much the Miller's Son had the difficult task of provisioning the ever increasing band.

The increasing size of the band was a source of satisfaction for Robin, but also a subject of much concern. The fame of his Merrymen was

spreading, and new recruits were pouring in. Yet the number of men was beginning to exceed the food capacity of the forest. Game was becoming scarce, and food had to be transported by cart from outlying villages. The band had always camped together. But now what had been a small gathering had become a major encampment that could be detected miles away. Discipline was also becoming harder to enforce. "Why?" Robin reflected, "I don't know half the men I run into these days."

While the band was getting larger, their main source of revenue was in decline. Travelers, especially the richer variety, began giving the forest a wide berth. This was costly and inconvenient to them, but it was preferable to having all their goods confiscated by Robin's men. Robin was therefore considering changing his past policy to one of a fixed transit tax.

The idea was strongly resisted by his lieutenants who were proud of the Merrymen's famous motto: "Rob from the rich and give to the poor." The poor and the townspeople, they argued, were their main source of support and information. If they were antagonized by transit taxes they would abandon the Merrymen to the mercy of the Sheriff.

Robin wondered how long they could go on keeping to the ways and methods of their early days. The Sheriff was growing stronger. He had the money, the men, and the facilities. In the long run he would wear Robin and his men down. Sooner or later, he would find their weaknesses and methodically destroy them. Robin felt that he must bring the campaign to a conclusion. The question was how this could be achieved?

Robin knew that the chances of killing or capturing the Sheriff were remote. Besides, killing the Sheriff might satisfy his personal thirst for revenge, but would not change the basic problem. It was also unlikely that the Sheriff would be removed from office. He had powerful friends at court. On the other hand, Robin reflected, if the district was in a perpetual state of unrest, and the taxes went uncollected, the Sheriff would fall out of favour. But on further thought, Robin reasoned, the Sheriff might shrewdly use the unrest to obtain more reinforcements. The outcome depended on the mood of the regent Prince John. The Prince was known as vicious, volatile and unpredictable. He was obsessed by his unpopularity among the people, who wanted the imprisoned King Richard back. He also lived in constant fear of the barons who were growing daily more hostile to his power. Several of these barons had set out to collect the ransom that would release King Richard the Lionheart from his jail in Austria. Robin had been discreetly asked to join, in return for future amnesty. It was a dangerous proposition. Provincial banditry was one thing, court intrigue another. Prince John was known

for his vindictiveness. If the gamble failed he would personally see to it that all involved were crushed.

The sound of the supper horn startled Robin from his thoughts. There was the smell of roasting venison in the air. Nothing had been resolved or settled. Robin headed for camp promising himself that he would give these problems first priority after tomorrow's operation.

QUESTIONS

1. What are Robin's key problems? How are they related to each other? Trace their emergence.
2. Which problems should Robin tackle first?
3. Develop a new strategy for Robin Hood. Pay close attention to implementation as well as formulation.

MacARTHUR AND THE
PHILIPPINES

The Americans never came. *They never came.*
Month after month the embattled garrison awaited
a blow in vain. . . . Truk was being devastated
by Nimitz's carrier planes, but the sky over Rabaul was serene, and sentinels posted to sound
the alarm when Allied patrols approached over-
land from Cape Gloucester and Arawe stared out
at a mocking green silence. All they wanted was
an opportunity to sell their lives dearly before
they were killed or eviscerated themselves in hon-
orable seppuku. They believed that they were
entitled to a Nipponese gotterdammerung. . . .
MacArthur was denying them it, and they were
experiencing a kind of psychological hernia.[1]

Here they were, commanding an army
larger than Napoleon's at Waterloo or Lee's at
Gettysburg—or Wellington's or Meade's, for that
matter—which was spoiling for a fight. Their
sappers had thrown up ramparts, revetments, par-
apets, barbicans, and ravelins. Hull-down tanks
were in position. Mines had been laid, Hotchkiss-
type guns sited, Nambus cunningly camouflaged.
Mortarmen had calculated precise ranges. Crack
troops, designated to launch counterattacks,
lurked in huge bunkers behind concertinas of
barbwire. And there they remained, in an agony
of frustration, for the rest of the war. . . . (335–
36)

Case compilation copyright © 1980 by James Brian Quinn.
All sections from *American Caesar: Douglas MacArthur
1880–1964* by William Manchester, copyright 1978 by
William Manchester; reproduced by permission of Little,
Brown and Company. All rights reserved to original copyright holders. Subheadings and questions at end added
by James Brian Quinn. Numbers in parentheses indicate
the page number of the quotation in the Dell Books 1978
edition of the book. Footnotes at end are from the book
itself.

"BYPASS" OR "ISLAND HOP?"

This phenomenon was not confined to Rabaul. . . . Exactly who first suggested the
strategem is unclear. MacArthur himself has been
widely credited with it, largely on the basis of
his own recollections and those of the men around
him. In *Reminiscences* he writes:

> To push back the Japanese perimeter of
> conquest by direct pressure against the
> mass of enemy-occupied islands would
> be a long and costly effort. My staff wor-
> ried about Rabaul and other strongpoints.
> . . . I intended to envelop them, inca-
> pacitate them, apply the "hit 'em where
> they ain't—let 'em die on the vine" phi-
> losophy. I explained that this was the very
> opposite of what was termed "island-hop-
> ping," which is the gradual pushing back
> of the enemy by direct frontal pressure,
> with the consequent heavy casualties
> which would certainly be involved. There
> would be no need for storming the mass
> of islands held by the enemy. (336)

According to Huff, Willoughby, and Kenney,
the General first unveiled this concept at a council
of war attended by, among others, Halsey,
Krueger, and Australia's Sir Thomas Blamey.
Gesturing at the map, one of the conferees said,
"I don't see how we can take these strongpoints
with our limited forces." Tapping his cigarette
on an ashtray, MacArthur said in a slow deliberate
voice: "Well, let's just say that we don't take
them. In fact, gentlemen, I don't want them."
Turning to Kenney [head of Allied air forces in
the area], he said: "You incapacitate them . . ."
He told the airman: "Starve Rabaul! The jungle!
Starvation! They're my allies."[2] (337)

But the notion that the isolation of Rabaul was the General's inspiration just won't wash. Apparently the first references to the possibility of such a bypass were made in March of 1943, during Washington talks which were attended by Sutherland, Kenney, and Stephen J. Chamberlin, the General's operations officer. If they mentioned it to MacArthur on their return, he was unimpressed. Eight months earlier the Joint Chiefs had instructed him to take Rabaul and Kavieng. He hadn't protested then, and he didn't now. Indeed, when the Chiefs sounded him out in June, informing him that some Pentagon officers thought that Rabaul could be cut off and left to rot, he objected. He needed "an adequate forward naval base" there, he said, to protect his right flank; without it, his westward drive along the back of New Guinea's plucked buzzard "would involve hazards rendering success doubtful." (337–38)

"THE STRATEGY WE HATED MOST"

The issue was resolved in August, at the Quadrant conference in Quebec. Ironically, this boldest stratagem of the Pacific war was decided, not on its merits, but because the Anglo-American Combined Chiefs were searching for a compromise. The British wanted more U.S. troops and more landing craft in the European theater. They didn't see why the American offensive against Japan couldn't be mounted on a single front— Nimitz's, in the central Pacific—and U.S. admirals were inclined to agree with them. Roosevelt and his political advisers demurred, however. They had to reckon with MacArthur's popularity at home. . . . In the end FDR sided with MacArthur's strongest supporter at the conference— George Marshall. MacArthur never acknowledged Marshall's strong support at Quebec and elsewhere, and it is possible that he never knew of it. . . . (338)

However, the fact remains that MacArthur transformed the bypass maneuver into the war's most momentous strategic concept. Here the most impressive testimony comes from the Japanese. After the war Colonel Matsuichi Juio, a senior intelligence officer who had been charged with deciphering the General's intentions, told an interrogator that MacArthur's swooping envelopment of Nipponese bastions was "the type of strategy we hated most." The General, he said, repeatedly, "with minimum losses, attacked and seized a relatively weak area, constructed airfields and then proceeded to cut the supply lines to [our] troops in that area. . . . Our strongpoints were gradually starved out. The Japanese Army preferred direct [frontal] assault, after the German fashion, but the Americans flowed into our weaker points and submerged us, just as water seeks the weakest entry to sink a ship. We respected this type of strategy . . . because it gained the most while losing the least."[3] (338)

Yet, while GIs would proudly identify themselves as members of his army, they disparaged their commander in chief, or rather the image of himself he had created. Distrust of great commanders by their troops is nothing new; the British rank and file loathed Wellington, and during the American Revolution, as Gore Vidal has pointed out, "the private soldiers disliked Washington as much as he disdained them." In MacArthur's case it was ironical, however, for had his bitter men understood the consequences of the General's strategy they would have taken a very different view. For every Allied serviceman killed, the General killed ten Japanese. Never in history, John Gunther wrote, had there been a commander so economical in the expenditure of his men's blood. In this respect certain comparisons with European Theater Operations campaigns are staggering. During the single Battle of Anzio, 72,306 GIs fell. In the Battle of Normandy, Eisenhower lost 28,366. Between MacArthur's arrival in Australia and his return to Philippine waters over two years later, his troops suffered just 27,684 casualties.[4] (339)

THE HAWAIIAN CONFERENCE

The one great Pacific issue confronting American strategists that summer [1944] was where to strike next. MacArthur wanted to reconquer the Philippines. Admiral King recommended bypassing the archipelago and invading Formosa instead; he saw no reason to risk becoming mired in the great land masses of the islands. The dispute had been almost a year in the making. The previous October Eichelberger [field Commander of American Forces] had heard in Hawaii that once MacArthur had reached the equator, the admirals wanted the war against Japan to be "their show and no one else's." The decision could be deferred no longer.[5] (364)

They needed each other, and the President, the more flexible of the two, recognized that. Therefore he decided, after MacArthur had dropped out of the presidential race, to meet him in Hawaii. The Joint Chiefs—to their discomfiture—would be left in Washington. Nimitz would represent the navy. The three of them, as power brokers, would hammer out the wisest way to defeat the Japanese, who, despite the vicissitudes of quadrennial politics, were after all, the real enemy.[6] (363)

Roosevelt's military advisers were sharply divided on the subject. MacArthur was at one end of the spectrum; King at the other. Field commanders of all services in the Pacific tended to agree with the General, while George Marshall (chief of staff) and Hap Arnold leaned toward King, though individuals changed their minds from week to week. By the week of the Honolulu conference, Marshall was beginning to side with MacArthur. Hap Arnold, eager for B-29 bases on Formosa, continued to support King. Admiral Nimitz, wavering, instructed his staff to draw up plans for assaults on all possible objectives, including the Japanese homeland. (364)

If Roosevelt was already familiar with the Pentagon's views, vacillating as they were, he knew those of MacArthur and Nimitz, too. . . . The blunt fact is that he was running for a fourth term, and being photographed with MacArthur and Nimitz would be more impressive to his constituents than pictures of him politicking at the Democratic National Convention.

A Great Entrance

Roosevelt knew how to make a great entrance; a huge crowd of Hawaiians, who had been alerted to his approach, cheered as the *Baltimore* docked

at 3:00 P.M. on Wednesday, July 26, and fifty high-ranking military officers, led by Nimitz and Lieutenant General Robert C. Richardson, the commander of Nimitz's ground forces, mounted the gangboard. But MacArthur could be dramatic, too. Though [MacArthur's] B-17 had landed an hour earlier, . . . , he would be the last officer to board the cruiser. . . . Roosevelt had just asked Nimitz if he knew the General's whereabouts when "a terrific automobile siren was heard, and there raced on to the dock and screeched to a stop a motorcycle escort and the longest open car I have ever seen. . . . The car traveled some distance around the open space and stopped at the gangplank. When the applause died down, the General strode rapidly to the gangplank all alone."[7] (365)

[Later the President] led MacArthur, Nimitz, and Leahy into [a large] room, one wall of which was covered by a huge map of the Pacific. Picking up a long bamboo pointer, the President touched the islands with it and suddenly spun his wheelchair around to face the General. "Well, Douglas," he said challengingly, "Where do we go from here?" MacArthur shot back, "Mindanao, Mr. President, then Leyte—and then Luzon."[8] (368)

He and Nimitz took turns at the map arguing their cases forcefully while the President listened intently, interrupting now and then to ask a question or suggest another line of reasoning. Leahy thought he was "at his best as he tactfully steered the discussion from one point to another and narrowed down the areas of disagreement between MacArthur and Nimitz." Despite his earlier misgivings, the General found himself thoroughly enjoying the session. The President, he said afterward, had conducted himself as a "chairman," and had remained "entirely neutral," while Nimitz displayed a "fine sense of fair play.". . . [But Nimitz] lacked the General's eloquence. He was arguing King's case, not his own; under FDR's skillful questioning he conceded that Manila Bay would be useful to him, and admitted that an attack on Formosa, instead of Luzon, would succeed only if anchorages and fighter strips had been established in the central and southern Philippines. Finally, he was unprepared or unwilling to discuss the political problems which would arise if the archipelago were bypassed.[9]

Here MacArthur was his most trenchant. The Filipinos, he said, felt that they had been betrayed in 1942—he did not add that he had shared the feeling, but FDR knew it—and they would not forgive a second betrayal. "Promises must be kept," he said forcefully, meaning his own vow to return at the head of an army of liberation, a pledge which, he believed, had committed the United States. . . . In the postwar world all Asian eyes would be on the emerging Philippine republic. If its people thought they had been sold out, the reputation of the United States would be sullied with a stain that could never be removed.[10] (368–69)

Again and again he used the words "ethical" and "unethical," "virtue" and "shame." As Barbey later wrote, "General MacArthur approached the matter from a different point of view" than the Joint Chiefs; "he felt it was as much a moral issue as a military one." In addition, however, "He did not think the military conquest of the Philippines would be as costly, lengthy, or difficult as the conquest of Formosa, and yet the same military purposes would be accomplished." . . . (369)

The Greater Prize?

Luzon was a greater [strategic] prize than Formosa . . . the Filipinos, unlike the Formosans, would provide the Americans with powerful guerrilla support. Last—and here Leahy thought he saw Nimitz nod—Luzon couldn't be enveloped. It was too big. Rabaul and Wewak could be bypassed because their land masses were smaller. Attempting to detour around Luzon would expose U.S. flanks to crippling attacks from the enemy's bomber bases there.[11] (369)

Newspapers and even some correspondence of that summer support the premise that the issue had been resolved at Waikiki. After MacArthur had left Hickam Field, FDR told reporters that "we are going to get the Philippines back, and without question General MacArthur will take a

part in it." There was more to it than that, however. Under the Constitution Roosevelt's power over the Pentagon was absolute, but in practice he couldn't act without the support of the military advisers who hadn't accompanied him to Hawaii. In effect, he, MacArthur, and Leahy had formed a coalition, the object of which was the conversion of the Joint Chiefs. (370–71)

The Joint Chiefs continued the Luzon-or-Formosa debate through August and September. Leahy had briefed them on the Waikiki talks and told them that both he and Roosevelt were impressed by MacArthur's political and moral arguments. The Chiefs weren't. They insisted that the matter be decided wholly on the grounds of military merit. They agreed to a Leyte landing, but added that a "decision as to whether Luzon will be occupied before Formosa will be made later." King still wanted to land in southern Formosa, supported by American aircraft using Chiang Kai-shek's bases. . . . [Then over] the last weekend in September, Nimitz convinced him. The two admirals met in San Francisco, and Nimitz, pointing to recent Japanese successes against Chiang's troops, said the United States could no longer rely on his airdromes. An attack on Formosa, Nimitz said, would now be impossible unless Luzon were seized first. And back in Washington, King withdrew his objections to MacArthur's Philippine plans. (371–72)

The Invasion Timetable

MacArthur, meanwhile, had been contemplating a continuation of his steady advance northward, with each amphibious thrust providing airfields for the next, so that Kenney could always fill the skies over the beaches with friendly fighters and bombers. Under this principle their schedule had called for vaults into Morotai (September 15), Mindanao (November 15), and Leyte (December 20). Then, in the waning days of summer, even before King's capitulation, Admiral Halsey gave the General a tremendous lift by proposing that the timetable be scrapped for a bolder leap.[12] (372)

Halsey had been cruising off the Philippines, launching carrier strikes at Japanese bases. One of his pilots had been shot down over Leyte, the archipelago's midrib. Parachuting to safety and rescued by a submarine, he had reported that Leyte was held by far fewer Japanese troops than the Americans had thought. All week the admiral had noticed that his fleet was rarely challenged by land-based enemy aircraft. The rescued flier seemed to confirm his suspicion that, in his words, the central Philippines were "a hollow shell, with weak defense and skimpy facilities. In my opinion, this was the vulnerable belly of the imperial dragon.". . . Finally on Wednesday, September 13, 1944, he radioed Nimitz in Pearl Harbor, suggesting that assaults on the Talauds, Mindanao, and the Palaus be canceled. In their place he urged the swift seizure of Leyte.[13] (372)

At that moment two U.S. invasion convoys were at sea. MacArthur, aboard the cruiser *Nashville*, was bound for Morotai, the northeasternmost island of the Molucas, which would be needed to launch any blow at the Philippines. . . . Halsey's proposals were forwarded to Quebec, where the Combined Chiefs were attending a formal dinner as guests of Prime Minister W. L. Mackenzie King. As Hap Arnold later wrote, "Admiral Leahy, General Marshall, Admiral King, and I excused ourselves, read the message, and had a staff officer prepare an answer which naturally was in the affirmative." There was one small difficulty. MacArthur's approval was needed, and he couldn't be reached; the *Nashville*, in enemy waters, was observing radio silence. Thus the momentous message from Canada was handed to Sutherland [MacArthur's chief of staff]. That normally impassive officer's hands trembled; he was, Kenney later recalled, "worried about what the General would say about using his name and making so important a decision without consulting him." After a long, tense pause, the chief of staff radioed back an endorsement in MacArthur's name.[14] (372–73)

The General had gone ashore on Morotai after the first wave had hit the beach. His Higgins boat had grounded on a rock, and when he stepped off the ramp he found the water was chest deep,

. . . [but] if his clothes were damp, his mood wasn't. The landing was unopposed; without losing a man, he had anchored his right flank for the next amphibious bound. By now he had evaded 220,000 enemy troops and was within three hundred miles of the Philippines. On hearing the news from Sutherland, he instantly approved. (373)

THE PHILIPPINE INVASION

In the fall of 1944 the Philippines were inhabited by about 18,160,000 Filipinos, 80 percent of whom worshiped the Roman Catholic God, and some 400,000 Japanese soldiers, all of whom venerated their emperor and could imagine no greater honor than to die for him in battle. The twain seldom met. Except for chronic food shortages and the repressive regime, life in the thousand-mile chain of islands had for the most part been unaffected by enemy rule, now approaching the end of its third year. The hulk of [the giant island fortress of] Corregidor lay dead in the slate-gray waters of Manila Bay. . . . An unwary stranger might have concluded that it was a land finished with fiery deeds, was now slumbering, indolent, indifferent. But the General knew better. He understood that the flames of ardor needed only a spark of hope to be rekindled. He had a better grasp of the Philippines than of the United States. It was his second homeland, and in some ways it was a metaphor of his intricate personality: dramatic, inconsistent, valiant, passionate, and primitive.[15] (374)

No sparrow fell there but MacArthur knew of it; his files held everything from the transcripts of executive sessions in Malacanan to the guest lists of the Manila Hotel. His submarines brought the guerrillas equipment, technicians, transmitters, and commando teams, and he personally interviewed each partisan who escaped into his lines. . . . The resistance grew and grew. . . . The strategic information the partisans sent southward was priceless. Their eagerness to provide it was an index of their enthusiasm for the U.S. cause and their devotion was translated into loy-

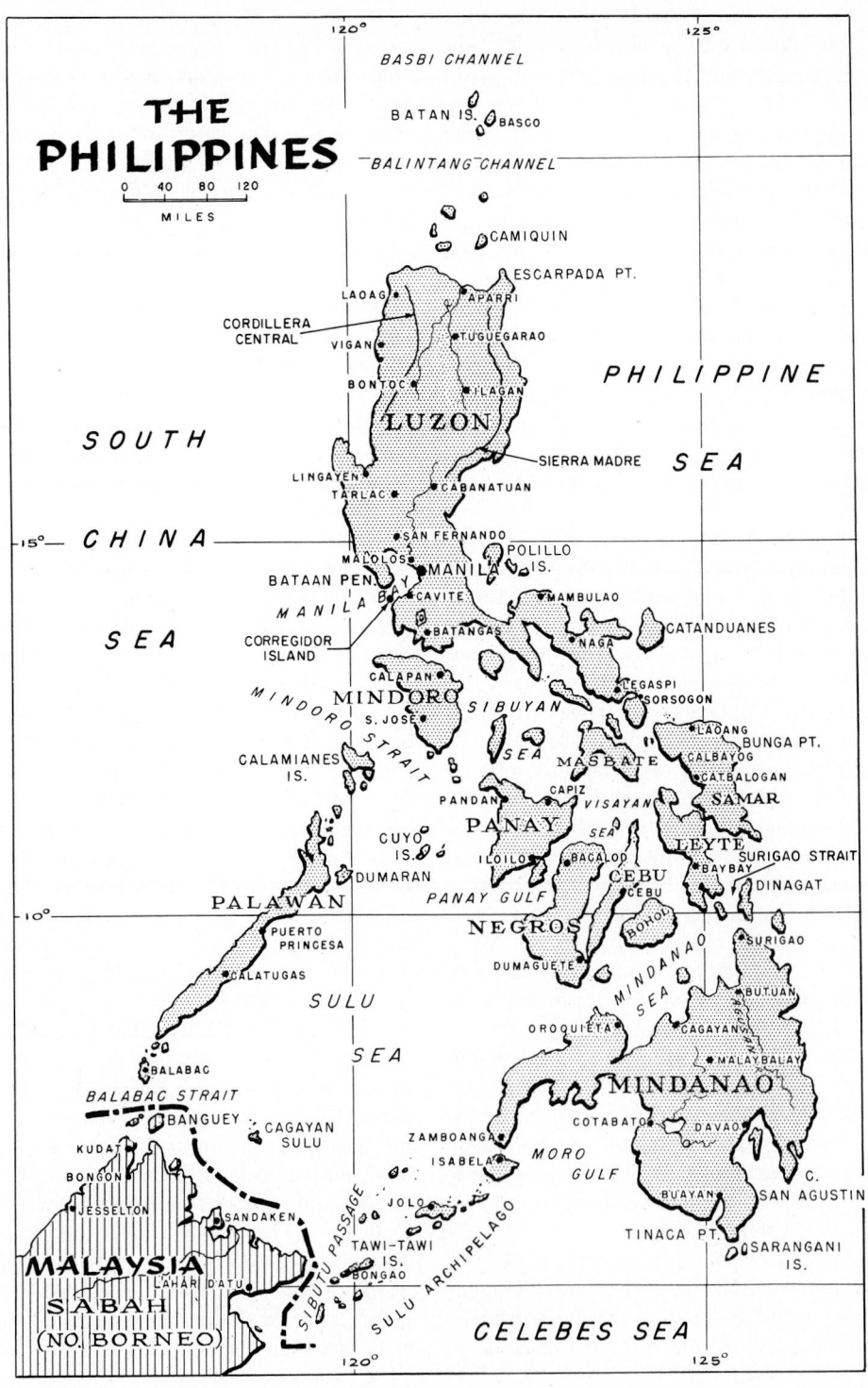

THE PHILIPPINES

0   40   80   120
MILES

BASBI CHANNEL

BATAN IS. ○BASCO

BALINTANG CHANNEL

●CAMIQUIN

●ESCARPADA PT.

LAOAG● ●APARRI

CORDILLERA
CENTRAL

VIGAN● ●TUGUEGARAO

BONTOC● ●ILAGAN

LUZON

PHILIPPINE

SIERRA MADRE

SEA

LINGAYEN● ●CABANATUAN
TARLAC●

SOUTH

CHINA

15° ●SAN FERNANDO

MALOLOS● POLILLO
BATAAN PEN. MANILA IS.
●CAVITE ●MAMBULAO
MANILA BAY ●BATANGAS
CORREGIDOR ●NAGA ●CATANDUANES
ISLAND

SEA

MANILA

CALAPAN●

MINDORO SIBUYAN ●LEGASPI
●SORSOGON
MINDORO STRAIT S. JOSE● SEA

CALAMIANES ●LAOANG
IS. MASBATE ●CALBAYOG ●BUNGA PT.
●CAT.BALOGAN
PANDAN● CAPIZ● VISAYAN SAMAR
CUYO● SEA
IS. PANAY BACALOD● LEYTE
DUMARAN● ILOILO● CEBU BAYBAY● SURIGAO STRAIT
●DINAGAT

PALAWAN PANAY GULF CEBU●

10° NEGROS BOHOL●

PUERTO ●SURIGAO
PRINCESA DUMAGUETE● MINDANAO
●CALATUGAS SEA ●BUTUAN

SULU OROQUIETA● ●CAGAYAN

SEA ●MALAYBALAY

●BALABAC MINDANAO

BALABAC STRAIT COTABATO●
●BANGUEY CAGAYAN ●DAVAO
KUDAT● SULU ZAMBOANGA●
BONGON● ISABELA● MORO C.
GULF ●SAN AGUSTIN
●JESSELTON ●SANDAKEN ●JOLO ●BUAYAN
TAWI-TAWI TINACA PT. ●SARANGANI
MALAYSIA IS. IS.
LAHAR DATU● BONGAO●
SABAH
(NO. BORNEO) SULU ARCHIPELAGO

CELEBES SEA

120° 125°

alty to two men, MacArthur and Quezon. When Quezon died of tuberculosis at Saranac, New York, the day after the General returned from his Hawaii conference with Roosevelt, MacArthur became their sole idol. He was, quite simply, the symbol of their hopes for a better postwar world. American GIs ridiculed him. Filipinos didn't. Carlos Romulo wrote: "To me he represents America."[16] (375–76)

Leyte —The Giant Molar

Leyte Gulf, the chief anchorage in the central islands, is approachable through only two major entrances. Surigao Strait to the southwest and San Bernardino Strait to the northwest. These tropical waters were about to become the scene of the greatest naval battle in history, for the Japanese were now desperate. If they were unable to prevent MacArthur from retaking the Philippine archipelago, they knew they would no longer have access to the Indies' oil, the lifeblood of their generals and admirals.[17] (381)

Imperial Japanese headquarters in Tokyo had drawn up a do-or-die plan encoded "Sho-Go," or "Operation Victory." Everything would be thrown into an attempt to prevent the General from establishing a foothold in the islands. . . . There would be no sense in saving the fleet at the expense of the loss of the Philippines. (381)

When word reached [the Japanese] that a seven-hundred-ship, hundred-mile-long American armada was steaming toward Surigao Strait between Dinagat and Homonhon islands, they brimmed with confidence. Lieutenant General Sosaku Suzuki, commander of the Thirty-fifth Army in the Visayan Islands, the central Philippines, told his staff: "We don't even need all the reinforcements they are sending us." His only worry, he said, was that the American leader might attempt to surrender just the troops participating in this operation: "We must demand the capitulation of MacArthur's entire forces, those in New Guinea and other places as well as the troops on Leyte."[18] (381–82)

The most cheerful news, for many Japanese, was the identity of the new overall com-

mander of Philippine defenses. He was Lieutenant General Tomoyuki Yamashita, the legendary "Tiger of Malaya" of the war's opening weeks. Jealous of his fame, Tojo had shunted him off to minor posts, but now Tojo was out of office, and Koiso needed someone in Manila in whom the country had faith. Tamashita seemed to be just the man; his appointment as MacArthur's adversary meant that two gifted generals, each at the height of his powers, would be pitted against each other. . . . (382–83)

Guns at Leyte

Leyte at that moment was under the awesome guns of two U.S. fleets, Halsey's Third and Tom Kinkaid's Seventh. Kinkaid was subordinate to MacArthur, but Halsey—whose force was faster and far more powerful—was answerable only to Nimitz in Honolulu. The split command worried MacArthur. He repeatedly urged the Joint Chiefs to designate one commander in chief, and had even offered to step down if they thought that necessary. They didn't believe he was serious, and they were probably right. In any event, shunting a national idol aside in the middle of a presidential campaign was unthinkable, especially when he belonged to the party out of power. George Marshall wouldn't agree to an admiral as supreme commander, so the flawed command structure remained. Presently it would lead the Allied cause in the Pacific to the brink of disaster.[19] (383)

[MacArthur] had perfected a battle plan which he considered his best yet. After the war Vincent Sheean agreed: "His operations towards the end . . . were extremely daring, more daring and far more complicated than those of Patton in Europe, because MacArthur used not infantry alone but also air and seapower in a concerted series of jabbing and jumping motions designed to outflank and bypass the Japanese all through the islands. The operation in which he jumped from Hollandia to Leyte will remain, I believe, the most brilliant strategic conception and tactical execution of the entire war."[20] (383–84)

He knew that his reputation was as imperiled as the lives of his men. Kenney had pointed out one glaring flaw in the plan—until Japanese landing strips had been captured, they would be fighting five hundred miles beyond the range of their fighter cover. Kenney recalls: "He stopped pacing the floor and blurted out, 'I tell you I'm going back there this fall if I have to paddle a canoe with you flying cover for me with that B-17 of yours.' "[21] (384)

At daybreak, the U.S. warships opened fire on the beach. The General stood on the bridge. The shore was dimly visible through an ominous, rising haze shot with yellow flashes; inland, white phosphorus crumps were bursting among the thick, ripe underbrush of the hills. The light of the rising sun spread rapidly across the smooth green water of the gulf. . . . Halsey had been misinformed; the enemy was nowhere as weak as the admiral had thought. Imperial General Headquarters had been holding back, waiting until MacArthur committed himself. Even more alarming, Kenney would discover before the day was out that because of the island's unstable soil, airfields there were unusable during the rainy season, which had just begun. U.S. air support would be limited to carrier planes through most of the coming engagement.[22] (385–86)

After lunch the General reappeared on deck wearing a freshly pressed khaki uniform, sunglasses, and his inimitable cap. He stood, arms akimbo, watching the diving enemy planes zooming overhead; then he looked shoreward, where the sand pits, palms, thick underbrush, and tiny grass-thatched huts were obscured by the bursts of exploding shells and tall columns of black smoke. (386)

In his *Reminiscences* he writes that he went in with the third assault wave. Actually the invasion was four hours old when he descended a ladder to a barge; his staff and war correspondents followed him aboard . . . Then, fifty yards from shore, they ran aground. . . . The General, impatient and annoyed, ordered the barge ramp lowered, stepped off into knee-deep brine, and splashed forty wet strides to the beach, destroying the neat creases of his trousers. A newspaper photographer snapped the famous picture of this.

His scowl, which millions of readers interpreted as a reflection of his steely determination, was actually a wrathful glare at the impertinent naval officer. When MacArthur saw a print of it, however, he instantly grasped its dramatic value, and the next day he deliberately waded ashore for cameramen on the 1st Cavalry Division's White Beach. By then the shore was safe there, and troopers watching him assumed that he had waited until Japanese snipers had been cleared out. Later, seeing yesterday's photography, they condemned it as a phony. Another touch had been added to his antihero legend.[23] (386–387)

"Sir, There Are Snipers Over There"

[But the facts were very different.] On Red Beach that first afternoon there were plenty of snipers, tied in trees or huddled in takotsubo —literally, "octopus traps," the Nipponese equivalent of foxholes. In his braided cap, pausing to relight his corncob from time to time, he once more made a conspicuous target. A Nambu opened up. He didn't even duck. As he strolled about, inspecting four damaged landing craft and looking for the 24th Division's command post, Kenney heard the General murmur to himself: "This is what I dreamed about." Kenney thought it was more like a nightmare. He could hear the taunts of enemy soldiers, speaking that broken English which was so familiar to soldiers and marines in the Pacific. . . .

The airman heard a GI crouched behind a coconut log gasp: "Hey, there's General MacArthur!" Without turning to look, the GI beside him drawled, "Oh, yeah? And I suppose he's got Eleanor Roosevelt along with him.". . . Hearing heavy fire inland, he strolled in that direction, jovially asked an astonished fire team of the 24th, "How do you find the Nip?" and, seeing several fresh Japanese corpses, kicked them over with his wet toe to read their insignia. He said with deep satisfaction: "The Sixteenth Division. They're the ones that did the dirty work on Bataan." (387)

Back at the shore, he sat on a coconut log by four wrecked Higgins boats, his back to the surf. A nervous lieutenant pointed toward a nearby grove and said, "Sir, there are snipers over there." The General seemed not to have heard him. He continued to stare entranced at the Leyte wilderness. (388)

[Sitting there] MacArthur scrawled a letter to President Roosevelt.[24] Granting the Filipinos independence swiftly, he predicted, would "place American prestige in the Far East at the highest pinnacle of all times." On "the highest plane of statesmanship" the General urged "that this great ceremony be presided over by you in person;" such a step would "electrify the world and rebound immeasurably to the credit and honor of the United States for a thousand years." . . .

[But] Roosevelt's failing health, his global command responsibilities, and his campaign for reelection prevented him from agreeing to broadcast an address to the Filipinos, so their first vivid recollection of their liberation was the two-minute address which the General had edited on the *Nashville* and was now prepared to deliver. (388)

"I Have Returned"

"People of the Philippines: I have returned," he said. His hands were shaking, and he had to pause to smooth out the wrinkles in his voice. He then continued, "By the grace of Almighty God, our forces stand again on Philippine soil— soil consecrated in the blood of our two peoples. . . . At my side is your President, Sergio Osmena, a worthy successor of that great patriot, Manuel Quezon. . . . The seat of your government is now, therefore, firmly re-established on Philippine soil. The hour of your redemption is here. . . . Rally to me. Let the indomitable spirit of Bataan and Corregidor lead on. As the lines of battle roll forward to bring you within the zone of operations, rise and strike. Strike at every favorable opportunity. For your homes and hearths, strike! For future generations of your sons and daughters, strike! In the name of your sacred dead, strike! Let no heart be faint. Let every arm be steeled. The guidance of Divine God points the way. Follow

in His name to the Holy Grail of righteous victory."[25]

Next Osmena and then Romulo spoke briefly into the hand-held mike. That ended the little ceremony, and a small cluster of Filipinos, who had been trapped here since the beginning of Kinkaid's bombardment, cheered. (388–89)

Later Kenney wanted to inspect an old Japanese airfield nearby. MacArthur decided to join him. Kenney recalled that "my enthusiasm cooled when I found that the west end of the field was being used as a firing range by the Japs on one side and our troops on the other . . . We had to halt a couple of times on the way, once until a Jap sniper had been knocked out of a tree about 75 yards off the road and again when we had to wait for about twenty minutes until a Jap tank headed in our direction had been hit and the crew disposed of. We passed the burning tank on the way to the airdrome."

Once there, MacArthur paced around the strip, asking Kenney how quickly it could be made operational. Ricochets of enemy bullets were whining around them. The airman afterward remembered, "I told him I'd like to look at it under more favorable conditions, when I could inspect all of it at the same time. I added that I would feel much better at that moment if I were inspecting the place from an airplane. MacArthur laughed and said it was good for me to find out 'how the other half of the world lives.' "[26] (390)

Surigao Straits

Now that MacArthur had committed himself to Leyte, now that over 200,000 troops of Krueger's Sixth Army were pouring ashore, the Japanese navy made its great move. Admiral Toyoda, flying his flag on Formosa, had hatched a brilliant plan. His main fleet, led by seven battleships, thirteen heavy cruisers, and three light cruisers, was racing up from Singapore under Vice Admiral Takeo Kurita. Kurita was instructed to divide this force in two, with the smaller detachment, under Vice Admiral Teji Nishamura, entering Leyte Gulf through Surigao Strait while the main body commanded by Kurita himself knifed through San Bernardino Strait. Both jaws would then converge on MacArthur's troop transports and Kinkaid's obsolescent warships. Banzai.

Halsey's Task Force 34, the backbone of his Third Fleet, was guarding San Bernardino Strait. To divert him, a third Nipponese flotilla of four overage carriers and two battleships converted into carriers was steaming down from the Japanese homeland. The mission of its commander, Vice Admiral Jisaburo Ozawa, was to entice Task Force 34 away from Leyte Gulf. (391)

On the night of Monday, October 23, 1944, two U.S. submarines, the *Darter* and the *Dace*, sighted Kurita's main force off the coast of Borneo. At first light Tuesday morning, they torpedoed three of his cruisers, sinking two of them, and warned Halsey and Kinkaid that trouble was on its way. . . . Ozawa, the decoy commander, learned of this development and tried to draw Halsey toward him by sending out uncoded messages. Halsey didn't pick up the signals, however, and his reconnaissance planes missed Ozawa because they were all flying westward, looking for Kurita's vanguard. Finding it, U.S. planes hit the massive *Musashi* thirty-six times, thereby sending to the bottom a vessel that the Japanese thought unsinkable. . . . Kurita turned his fleet away from Leyte Gulf, intending to sail beyond reach of U.S. naval planes until dark, when he could return. Halsey concluded that he was retreating and could now be ignored. But the American admiral noted that no enemy carriers had been sighted. Believing that there must be some in the vicinity, he sent up reconnaissance planes on broader searches. At 5:00 P.M. they finally discovered Ozawa's bait. Halsey went for it leaving San Bernardino Strait wide open.[27]

Tuesday night, under a roving moon, Admiral Nishimura, commanding Kurita's southern unit, entered the narrow waters of Surigao Strait. Rear Admiral Jesse Oldendorf, USN, had the strait corked. As the enemy vessels came through one by one, Oldendorf "crossed their T"—raked them viciously with broadsides from all his ships. Nishimura drowned and his force was wiped out; at dawn there would be nothing left of it but wreckage and streaks of oil. . . . Now, to his horror, [Kinkaid, who was guarding the San Bernardino Strait learned that the returning] Kurita was almost upon him, and that the Japanese force was intact except for the sunken *Musashi*. Kurita had passed through San Bernardino Strait and was already training his mammoth guns on part of Kinkaid's fleet, six escort carriers and a group of destroyers covering MacArthur's beachheads. The fox was among the chickens.

At 8:30 A.M. Kinkaid radioed Halsey: "Urgently need fast battleships Leyte Gulf at once." There was no response. . . . At this point there occurred one of the most remarkable episodes in the history of naval warfare. Kurita was less than thirty miles from his objective. All that stood between his guns and Kinkaid's carriers was a screen of destroyers and [antisubmarine] escorts . . . The destroyers counterattacked Kurita's battleships, and then their gallant little escorts sprang toward the huge Japanese armada, firing their small-bore guns and launching torpedoes. Kurita's Goliaths milled around in confusion as the persistent Davids, some of them sinking, made dense smoke. Kinkaid's carriers sent up everything that could fly, and Kurita, with the mightiest Nipponese fleet since Midway, hesitated.[28] (391–93)

"Where Is Task Force 34?"

[Halsey] had gone so far in chasing the decoy that [his fleet] could not arrive until the next morning. By all the precedents of naval warfare but one, Kurita had won the battle. The exception was confusion. . . . He intercepted and misread two of Kinkaid's messages to Halsey. Believing that Halsey was approaching rapidly, and that he would soon bolt the door of San Bernardino Strait, Kurita turned tail. He passed through the strait a few minutes before 10:00 P.M.—unaware that Halsey's leading ships would not reach it for another three hours.

Thus ended the Battle of Leyte Gulf. It had involved 282 warships, compared with 250 at Jutland in 1916, until then the greatest naval engagement in history. And unlike Jutland, which neither side had won, this action had been decisive. The Americans had lost one light carrier, two escort carriers, and three destroyers. They had sunk four carriers, three battleships, six heavy cruisers, three light cruisers and eight destroyers. Except for sacrificial kamikaze fliers, who made their debut in this battle, Japanese air and naval strength would never again be serious instruments in the war.

"Leave the Bull Alone"

Thursday evening MacArthur was sitting down to dinner in the restored Price house when he heard staff officers at the other end of the table making recriminatory remarks about Halsey's action 'in abandoning us' while he went after the Jap northern 'decoy' fleet. The General slammed his bunched fist on the table. "That's enough!" he roared. "Leave the Bull alone! He's still a fighting admiral in my book." (393–94)

[On the land] MacArthur had achieved strategic surprise. The troops of Shiro Makino's 16th Division were being slowly pushed back on Leyte's Highway 2, toward an eminence which American GIs had christened Breakneck Ridge . . . At the time MacArthur seemed to be just inching along. Unlike commanders of marines and Australians, the two other infantry forces in the Pacific, the General preferred to pause at enemy strongpoints, waiting until his artillery had leveled the enemy's defenses. When American newspapers fretted over this . . . MacArthur said, "If I like I can finish Leyte in two weeks, but I won't! I have too great a responsibility to the mothers and wives in America to do that to their men. I will not take by sacrifice what I can achieve by strategy.[29]

His greatest problem . . . was the weather, which erased the margin that superior naval and air power should have given him. He had called Leyte a springboard, but he was discovering that it could be a very soggy one. In forty days, thirty-four inches of rain fell, turning the island into one vast bog. The steady, drenching tropical monsoon made runway grading impossible. . . . Finally a new strip was built on relatively solid ground at Tanauan, nine miles south of Tacloban, and P-38s began flying in and out, but Leyte never became the air base the General needed.[30] (395–96)

THE COMMAND STYLE

[MacArthur's] staff continued to seethe and churn with plots, counterplots, and intrigues which would have been more appropriate in Medicean Florence. Dr. Egeberg and Laurence E. "Larry" Bunker, like most survivors of it, blame Sutherland; "he divided the Gs—[G-1, administration; G-2, intelligence; G-3, operations; G-4, quartermaster]—against each other." But the chief of staff could hardly have pitted officers against one another without the knowledge, and even the encouragement, of the ironhanded commander in chief. What is extraordinary is the degree to which MacArthur convinced them that he knew nothing of the turmoil. . . . (400)

MacArthur, like Roosevelt, was exploiting his position at the center of the staff. Kenney noted how "in a big staff meeting, or in conversation with a single individual, MacArthur has a wonderful knack of leading a discussion up to the point of a decision that each member present believes he himself originated. I have heard officers say many times, 'The Old Man bought my idea,' when it was something that weeks before I had heard MacArthur decide to do. . . . As a salesman, MacArthur had no superior and few equals." In other conferences, the General would identify a military target and invite suggestions on how it might be seized. Each officer would reply, he would ask broad questions, say "Thank you very much, gentlemen," and go off to ponder the problem himself. (401)

Often an aide recalls "he would ask me questions and then answer them. From some of these interchanges I got a clear picture of the connection between chess and war. He might say, 'Now if we do this, which Steve suggested, they might do this, or if they were clever, they might do that. Now if they do this, we should answer them in one of three ways,' and he would outline the other alternative, and then he would go to the Japanese answer to the six or seven possibilities. By the time he had done this for a day or a week, he would call his staff, establish the strategy which was amazingly frequently the opposite from the feeling of the majority, and which would seem always to have been right."[31] (401–402)

He never lost an opportunity to remind his staff that while they were talking, other, younger men were dying. Before leaving Hollandia, each of the headquarters officers had chipped in twenty dollars apiece to buy liquor. The shipment had arrived after they had left for Leyte, and it could not be forwarded without the General's permission. They chose Dick Marshall as their spokesman. After mess that evening, he cleared his throat and explained the problem. MacArthur asked, "What about the men? Have they got anything?" Marshall explained that they had beer. The General thought awhile and then said: "If beer is good enough for the enlisted men, it's good enough for the officers."[32] (402)

THE LAST STEPPINGSTONE

Altogether [at Luzon] MacArthur would command nearly a thousand ships, accompanied by three thousand landing craft, many of them new arrivals from Normandy, and 280,000 men— more than Eisenhower's U.S. strength in the campaigns of North Africa, Italy, or southern France; more than the total Allied force in the conquest of Sicily. But Yamashita was lying in wait for him with 275,000 men, the largest enemy army to be encountered in the Pacific campaigns. . . . (406)

Although [Yamashita] had thirty-six thousand men on the Lingayen beaches, he withdrew them, having concluded that American firepower made resistance at the shoreline pointless, and that with Halsey roaming the seas the best he could do was to prolong the struggle for the island, tying up MacArthur to buy time for the Japanese now furiously digging in on the home islands of Dai Nippon. (406)

Walk on Water

Before dawn on Wednesday, January 10, the Americans lay to off the landing beaches, and a thousand anchors plummeted into the gulf. It was a calm sea; there was less surf than anyone could remember. A typhoon had darted away at the last moment, and the different reactions of Americans and Filipinos to that lucky circumstance says much about their views of the General. U.S. war correspondents wondered whimsically whether he would walk on the water. To the Filipinos it was no laughing matter; many of them believed then, and believe to this day, that the gentle waves lapping the white sands were a consequence of divine intervention. MacArthur was the last man to disillusion them. He knew the power of myth in the minds of islands' people. If they thought him capable of miracles, their conviction added a powerful weapon to his arsenal, one which his showmanship would polish. (407–409)

After Krueger's first four divisions had splashed ashore, the commander in chief followed in his Higgins boat. In his memoirs he writes: "As was getting to be a habit with me, I picked a boat that took too much draft to reach the beach, and I had to wade in. . . ." It should be added that a group of peasants watching on the shore cheered lustily and hurried inland to spread the word of his second coming. That, of course, was precisely what he wanted them to do.[33] (409)

"Get to Manila"

The General had told Eichelberger that he wanted him to "undertake a daring expedition against Manila with a small mobile force," using tactics which "would have delighted Jeb Stuart." The implication was that such a maneuver was too difficult for Krueger, and while MacArthur was doubtless playing his two fighting generals against one another—as Napoleon did with his marshals, and as Stalin would soon do in encouraging Zhukov and Konev to race each other to Berlin— the General clearly regarded his senior field commander as unenterprising, and even timid.[34] (409–410)

The amphitheater in which they were maneuvering, the island's central plain, is about 40 miles wide and 110 miles deep. . . . Though MacArthur had shown the defensive potential of Bataan and Corregidor, south of Manila, Yamashita preferred to withdraw the main body of his troops into the mountains to the east. And MacArthur somehow knew this. He was so sure of it that he saw no need to guard his left flank. "Get to Manila!" he told his field commanders. "Go around the Japs, bounce off the Japs, save your men, but get to Manila! Free the internees at Santo Tomas! Take Lalacanan and the legislative buildings!" But Krueger was haunted by the nightmare of a quarter-million Japanese driving in his flank pickets, cutting him off from the gulf, and "slicing him up like a pie." He wanted to spend two or three weeks consolidating his gains before advancing behind heavy artillery barrages toward the capital, which he assumed would be strongly defended.[35] (410)

The General vehemently disagreed. Those, he said, were the tactics which had destroyed the flower of a generation in the trenches of World War I. Moreover, he pointed out, in his words . . . "I knew every wrinkle of the terrain, every foot of the topography." He saw no reason why flying columns shouldn't move swiftly down the fine roads leading southward between the rice paddies and neat little towns to Manila, which he believed would be undefended. MacArthur and Krueger [often] had words over this . . . Yet MacArthur never pulled rank on him. Sutherland had frequently urged that Krueger be "sent home"—Sutherland wanted to lead the Sixth Army himself—and others wondered why he wasn't. The likeliest explanation was that the General knew his plodding subordinate was a useful counterweight to his own bravura.[36] (410)

Control the Strategy

[George Marshall wrote in an official report to the secretary of war] "Yamashita's inability to cope with MacArthur's swift moves" and "his desired reaction to the deception measures" combined "to place the Japanese in an impossible situation." The enemy "was forced into a piecemeal commitment of his troops.". . . "They were unable to conduct an orderly retreat, in classic fashion, to fall back on inner perimeters with forces intact for a last defense. . . . It was a situation unique in modern war. Never had such large numbers of troops been so outmaneuvered, . . . and left tactically impotent to take an active part in the final battle for their homeland."[37]

While Krueger was investing Clark Field, his commander in chief was dazzling Yamashita with a series of lightning thrusts elsewhere. . . . Without losing a man, an expedition captured the invaluable port of Olangapo. Then he put a regiment ashore at Mariveles, on the peninsula's lower tip. Trapped in a double envelopment, Yamashita's Bataan garrison was isolated and impotent; the peninsula was taken in just seven days.[38] (410–411)

The only remaining stronghold in the bay itself was Corregidor. In 1942 the Japanese had lost twice their landing force—several thousand men—to the gallant marines on the Rock's beaches. Now, with 5,200 enemy defenders in superb condition and provided with enormous stocks of ammunition, the fortress seemed far more formidable. MacArthur landed a regiment of airborne troops on Topside while an infantry battalion, with exquisite timing, leaped from Higgins boats to storm the Bottomside shore. After losing 1,500 men in a ten-day battle, the enemy commander holed up with the rest in Malinta Tunnel, where they committed suicide spectacularly by igniting a huge mass of explosives and blowing themselves up. The Americans' losses had been 210 men, 50 of them killed in that final blowup. (411)

In Personal Command

What makes [these events] all the more remarkable is that [MacArthur] was leaving his staff every morning to race around in his five-star jeep like a man forty years younger. "The Chief wanted to be in *personal* command," Eichelberger wrote, "and apparently he has done so." Willoughby wrote afterward: "Constantly on the front line—at times well ahead of it—his sheer physical endurance and his reckless exposure of himself excited the native population and even his own forces to a pitch of effort that became the dismay of the enemy.''. . . He was everywhere, doing everything but digging the foxholes and loading the machine-gun belts. He watched the airborne drops from a B-17 overhead. On the central plain, he climbed on tanks to observe enemy patrols through field glasses. On Bataan he ventured five miles beyond American lines, hoping for a glimpse of Corregidor, and was almost strafed by a squadron of Kenney's fighters. He stood erect at an enemy roadblock, and when a nearby Nambu opened up and an American lieutenant said, "We're going after those fellows, but please get down sir; we're under fire," MacArthur replied crisply, without moving, "I'm not under fire. Those bullets are not intended for me."[39] (411–412)

In late January he was inspecting the 161st Infantry when the regiment was struck by a tank-led counterattack. The American lines buckled, and MacArthur personally rallied the men. When Stimson heard about it, the General was awarded his third Distinguished Service Cross. (412)

On another occasion, just north of Manila, his jeep halted at a blown bridge. . . . Shortly thereafter, he made what he called a "personal reconnaissance" inside the enemy-held city itself, touring the Malacanan Palace grounds and returning to report, like a scout, that he believed GIs "could cross the river and clear all southern Manila with a platoon.". . . As MacArthur had predicted, Yamashita had withdrawn his troops from the city, declaring that "the capital of the republic and its law-abiding inhabitants should not suffer from the ravages of war." MacArthur's headquarters informed senior U.S. officers that plans were being made "for a great victory parade à la Champs Elysees." (412–13)

"Destruction Is Imminent"

At 6:00 P.M. on Saturday, February 3, patrols of the 1st Cavalry entered the city limits. Three days later, on Tuesday, MacArthur's communi-

que announced: "Our forces are rapidly clearing the enemy from Manila. Our converging columns . . . entered the city and surrounded the Jap defenders. Their complete destruction is imminent." (413)

Although the American public was unaware of the fact—the General's censors told correspondents they couldn't expose his victory communique as a lie—the fall of the capital was a month away . . . Eichelberger wrote on February 21, "the big parade has been called off." That was a shattering understatement. . . . The devastation of Manila was one of the great tragedies of World War II. Of Allied cities in those war years, only Warsaw suffered more. Seventy percent of the utilities, 75 percent of the factories, 80 percent of the southern residential district, and 100 percent of the business district were razed. Nearly 100,000 Filipinos were murdered by the Japanese. Hospitals were set afire after their patients had been strapped to their beds. The corpses of males were mutilated, females of all ages were raped before they were slain, and babies' eyeballs were gouged out and smeared on walls like jelly. (413)

MacArthur blamed the holocaust on [Yamashita] but the guilt lay elsewhere. Yamashita's orderly evacuation into the hills had left about thirty thousand Japanese sailors and marines under Rear Admiral Sanji Iwabuchi . . . Either Iwabuchi had not received the order from Yamashita declaring the capital an open city, or he chose to ignore it. Once he had decided to defend Manila, the atrocities began, and the longer the battle raged, the more the Japanese command structure deteriorated, until the uniforms of Nipponese sailors and marines were saturated with Filipino blood. (414)

"The Islands Are Liberated"

[Yet] the contrast between [MacArthur's] casualties and those of the enemy is, in fact, extraordinary. In his Philippine operations after Luzon he lost 820 GIs, while over 21,000 Japanese were slain. On July 5 he could announce: "The entire Philippine Islands are now liberated . . . The Japanese during the operations employed twenty three divisions, all of which were practically anni-hilated. Our forces comprised seventeen divi-sions. This was one of the rare instances when in a long campaign a ground force superior in numbers was entirely destroyed by a numerically inferior opponent.'' (430)

In these battles he continued to expose him-self to danger at the front. At Brunei Bay and Balikpapan, he insisted on going in with the as-sault waves. . . . Ashore at Brunei Bay he walked along a road paralleling the beach, about a quarter of a mile inland, with the sound of snipers' shots and machine guns on both sides. Kenney remembers beginning ''to feel all over again as I had when we landed in the Philippines at Leyte.''. . . A tank lumbered by, and fifty yards ahead, atop a small rise, a rifleman and a machine gunner exchanged bursts of fire. MacAr-thur walked there to see what was happening. Two dead Japanese lay in a ditch . . . An Austra-lian army photographer appeared, hoping to take a picture of the General and the bodies. MacAr-thur refused, and the cameraman squared away to snap the two corpses. Just as his bulb flashed, the photographer fell with a sniper's bullet in his shoulder.[40] (432–33)

ON TO JAPAN

[MacArthur] looked forward to Soviet entry into the Pacific war. By engaging a million Japanese and taking the sting out of their air force, he reckoned, Stalin would distract the enemy and save thousands of lives. (431)

Meanwhile Hirohito's generals, grimly pre-paring for the invasion [of Japan] had not aban-doned hope of saving their homeland. Although a few strategic islands had been lost, they told each other, most of their conquests, including the Chinese heartland, were firmly in their hands, and the bulk of their army was undefeated. Even now they could scarcely believe that any foe would have the audacity to attempt landings in Japan itself. Allied troops, they boasted, would face the fiercest resistance in history. Over ten thousand kamikaze planes were readied for ''Ketsu-Go,'' Operation Decision. Behind the

beaches, enormous connecting underground caves had been stocked with caches of food and thousands of tons of ammunition. Manning the nation's ground defenses were 2,350,000 regular soldiers, 250,000 garrison troops, and 32,-000,000 civilian militiamen—a total of 34,-600,000, more than the combined armies of the United States, Great Britain, and Nazi Germany. All males aged fifteen to sixty, and all females aged seventeen to forty-five, had been con-scripted. Their weapons included ancient bronze cannon, muzzle-loading muskets, bamboo spears, and bows and arrows. Even little children had been trained to strap explosives around their waists, roll under tank treads, and blow them-selves up. They were called ''Sherman carpets.'' (436)

Fanatics or Doves?

This was the enemy the Pentagon had learned to fear and hate—a country of fanatics dedicated to hara-kiri, determined to slay as many invaders as possible as they went down fighting. But there was another Japan, and MacArthur was one of the few Americans who suspected its existence. He kept urging the Pentagon and the State Depart-ment to be alert for conciliatory gestures. Kenney notes that the General predicted that ''the break would come from Tokyo, not from the Japanese army.''. . . A dovish coalition was forming in the Japanese capital, and it was headed by Hiro-hito himself, who had concluded in the spring of 1945 that a negotiated peace was the only way to end his nation's agony. Beginning in early May a six-man council of Japanese diplomats explored ways to accommodate the Allies. (436–37)

Had Roosevelt been alive, his fine political antennae might have sensed the possibilities here. But Truman, new in office and less flexible in diplomacy, was swayed by such advisers as Dean Acheson, Archibald MacLeish, and Hopkins who believed that negotiations were pointless; that un-less Hirohito was unthroned, the war would have been in vain. The upshot was the Potsdam declara-tion in July, demanding that Japan surrender un-conditionally or face ''prompt and utter destruction.'' MacArthur was appalled. He knew that the Japanese would never renounce their emperor, and that without him an orderly transition to peace would be impossible anyhow, because his people would never submit to Allied occupation unless he ordered it. Ironically, when the surrender did come, it was conditional, and the condition was a continuation of the imperial reign. Had the General's advice been followed, the resort to atomic weapons at Hiroshima and Nagasaki might have been unnecessary.[41] (437)

In an implacable mood then, successive versions of ''Downfall,'' the code word for the invasion of Dai Nippon, were drafted in Washington and revised in Manila. . . . ''Downfall'' would begin with ''Operation Olympic,'' a frontal assault on Kyushu by 766,700 Allied troops under Krueger on November 1, 1945, whose purpose would be to secure, in the General's words ''airfields to cover the main assault on Honshu.'' The second phase ''Operation Coronet,'' the landing on Honshu, would follow on March 1, 1946. He himself probably with Eichelberger as his chief of staff would lead that.[42]

He had no illusions about the savagery that lay ahead—he told Stimson that Downfall would ''cost over a million casualties to American forces alone''—but he was confident that with the tanks from Europe he could outmaneuver the defenders on the great Kanto Plain before Tokyo. (437–38)

The Atomic Bomb

With each passing day the General felt surer that peace was very near. Two weeks before Hiroshima he told Kenney that he believed the enemy would surrender ''by September 1 at the latest and perhaps even sooner.'' On Sunday, August 5, a courier arrived from Washington with word that an atomic bomb would be dropped ''on an industrial area south of Tokyo the following day.''. . . Three days later President Truman suspended B-29 raids on Japan; three days after that, on Wednesday, August 15, Hirohito ordered an end to all hostilities at 4:00 P.M. Tokyo time, telling his people that they must ''endure the unendurable and suffer the insufferable.'' Tru-

man, with the approval of Clement Attlee, Stalin, and Chiang Kai-shek, appointed MacArthur Supreme Commander for the Allied Powers (SCAP). (439)

THE OCCUPATION

One of his first acts, he told Bonner Fellers, would be to give women the vote. ''The Japanese men won't like it,'' said Fellers, and indeed, as events would prove, many of them regarded it as worse than sexual assault. The General said, ''I don't care. I want to discredit the military. Women don't like war.'' It was part of his enigmatic temperament that although he could be ungenerous toward American admirals and uncivil toward his superiors in Washington, he was an imaginative, magnanimous conqueror. He intended, he said, to ''use the instrumentality of the Japanese government to implement the occupation.'' Sitting in front of a Quonset hut and puffing on his pipe, he told an aide that woman suffrage was only one point in his seven-point plan for Japan. The others were disarming Japanese soldiers, sending them home, dismantling war industry, holding free elections, encouraging the formation of labor unions, and opening all schools with no check on instruction except the elimination of military indoctrination and the addition of courses in civics.[43] (440)

''Of All the Amazing Deeds''

Later Winston Churchill said: ''Of all the amazing deeds in the war, I regard General MacArthur's personal landing at Atsugi [Japan] as the bravest of the lot.'' John Gunther wrote: ''Professors who studied Japan all their lives, military experts who knew every nook and cranny of the Japanese character, thought that ''MacArthur was taking a frightful risk.'' In Manila Sutherland remonstrated: ''My God, General, the emperor is worshipped as a real god, yet they still tried to assassinate him. What kind of target does that make you?'' MacArthur replied that he believed the reported attempt on Hirohito's life was spurious—he was right, although there was no way of knowing it then—and when his C-54, with "Bataan" emblazoned on its nose, touched down for a brief stop on Okinawa, and he noticed that Kenney and the others were strapping on pistols in shoulder holsters, he said, "Take them off. If they intend to kill us, sidearms will be useless. And nothing will impress them like a show of absolute fearlessness. If they don't know they're licked, this will convince them."[44] (444)

The General knew that word of everything he said and did would quickly spread throughout the country. He was determined that the occupation be benign from the outset. Moreover, remembering his tour of duty in Germany after the 1918 Armistice, he realized that in a war-torn, defeated country, food would be at a premium. . . . When the commander of the 11th Airborne ruefully reported that his division had searched all night and found exactly one egg for the Supreme Commander's breakfast, MacArthur immediately issued an order at odds with the whole history of conquering armies in Asia. Occupation troops were forbidden to consume local victuals; they would eat only their own rations. An hour later, he canceled the martial law and curfew decrees Eichelberger had imposed on the city. The first step in the reformation of Japan, he said, would be an exhibition of generosity and compassion by the occupying power.[45]

That evening he was sitting down to dinner in the hotel when an aide reported that he had a visitor outside: Lieutenant General Jonathan M. Wainwright. Liberated from his Manchurian prisoner-of-war camp by the Russians four days earlier . . . was the man the General had left in command [at Corregidor] in 1942. . . . [Wainwright] was haggard and aged. . . . He walked with difficulty and with the help of a cane. His eyes were sunken and there were pits in his cheeks. His hair was snow white and his skin looked like old shoe leather. . . . For three years he had imagined himself in disgrace for having surrendered Corregidor. He believed he would never again be given an active command. This shocked MacArthur. "Why, Jim," he said, "Your old corps is yours when you want it."[46]

Wainwright said, "General . . ." Then his voice wavered and he burst into tears. (448)

The Final Ceremony

Early Sunday morning, two days later, a destroyer took Wainwright out to the slate-gray, forty-five thousand ton battleship *Missouri*, on Tokyo Bay. . . . (448)

[At the ceremony, MacArthur's] stance was a portrait of soldierly poise. Only his hand trembled slightly as he held a single sheet of paper before him and said: "We are gathered here, representatives of the major warring powers, to conclude a solemn agreement whereby peace may be restored. . . . Both the conquerors and the conquered must rise to that higher dignity which alone befits the sacred purposes we are about to serve. . . . To the Pacific basin has come the vista of a new emancipated world. Today, freedom is on the offensive, democracy is on the march. Today, in Asia, as well as in Europe, unshackled peoples are tasting the full sweetness of liberty, the relief from fear." He concluded: "And so, my fellow countrymen, today I report to you that your sons and daughters have served you well and faithfully with the calm, deliberate, determined fighting spirit of the American soldier and sailor. . . . Their spiritual strength and power has brought us through to victory. They are homeward bound—take care of them."[47] (452–454)

QUESTIONS

1. What were the most important components of the Allies' strategy in the South Pacific? Why were these strategies chosen?
2. Were better strategies available? If so, what were they? Why?
3. What do you think of the way in which the Allies' strategy was arrived at? What made Douglas MacArthur a good (or poor) strategist?
4. What characteristics of a good military strategy have application in the business world? What "principles of strategy" can you derive from this case?

INTEL CORPORATION

In 1968 Robert N. Noyce (age 40) and Gordon E. Moore (39) broke away from Fairchild Semiconductor to form Intel Corporation. They concentrated on semiconductor memory components for the computer industry. When Intel started, no market existed for its principal product. By the late 1970s Intel's trailblazing technologies had irrevocably restructured the electronics, computer and communications industries. In the 1980s semiconductors were effecting social changes many believed would be as profound as those of the industrial revolution. Not without cause did CEO Moore say, "We're in the business of revolutionizing society."[1] Opportunities seemed boundless. But in the early '80s continuing technological advances and Japan's massive competitive capabilities presented strategic challenges without precedent for this relatively new and small company in a world of industrial giants.

BUDDING ENTREPRENEURS

Noyce and Moore made an unusual team. Although the future of this revolutionary technology was unknown at that time, Noyce—an inveterate young tinkerer from a small Iowa town—headed for MIT to study about the new field only to find it had no courses on semiconductors. Taking his Ph.D. (in electron physics) at the top of his class, Noyce had joined Philco's semiconductor division. Two and a half years later, he got a call from William Shockley, the inventor of the transistor, who was starting a new semiconductor company in Palo Alto (California). Noyce and Moore, a Ph.D. chemist from Cal Tech, arrived there the same day.[2] Thus began one of the most successful technical partnerships of modern times.

Fairchild Semiconductor

The imaginative Shockley had assembled a group of bright young scientists, but the operation fell apart when eight of them left only a year later. Shockley's managerial shortcomings had totally alienated them.[3] Even while with Shockley the group had looked upon Noyce as a leader. His enthusiasm—and his approach to everything with the idea that it was going to work— easily infected people. One of the members of the group wrote to a friend of his family who worked for Hayden Stone, the New York investment firm. Hayden Stone soon arranged to finance the new semiconductor company the young entrepreneurs wanted to organize. The eight young founders contributed about $500 apiece . . . But most of the start-up money came from Fairchild Camera and Instrument Corporation which also received an option to buy the group's budding company, known as Fairchild Semiconductor. (2,147)

Big Company Blues

The company, which started in a rented building in Mountain View, California, grew fast. By 1968 Noyce was supervising nearly 15,000 employees in the United States and abroad. Both he and Moore achieved major technical advances in semiconductor technology at Fairchild (including the first planar integrated circuit and the first stable MOS transistor).* But both men had begun to

Case Copyright © 1985 by James Brian Quinn. The generous support of the Adolf H. Lundin Professorship at the International Management Institute, Geneva, Switzerland is gratefully acknowledged. The generous cooperation of Intel Corporation is gratefully acknowledged. Numbers in parentheses indicate the reference and page number for material from a previously footnoted source.

*   *All technical terms are defined in Appendix A.*

find big-company life less and less satisfying.

When Fairchild Camera had exercised its option to buy out Fairchild Semiconductor in 1959 and make it into an operating division, the originators each got about $250,000 worth of stock in Fairchild Camera. But Noyce and Moore began to feel that a company as big as Fairchild could not easily expand into new areas of semiconductor technology. Noyce said, "Fairchild was getting big and clumsy. LSI had been talked about a good deal, but there was no commitment behind it."[4] New ventures in such a complex field initially lose money—sometimes a lot of it—and it is often difficult to justify big losses to directors and stockholders. Moore and Noyce finally left Fairchild Semiconductor (in the summer of 1968). But not before they had built the company into a $150 million enterprise, one of the Big Three in its field along with Texas Instruments and Motorola.

A NEW COMPANY

"We figured LSI (Large Scale Integration) was the kind of business we'd be interested in. We both had started in technology, not in computers or finance. It would be fun for us," said Noyce. Noyce and Moore decided that their new company should try to establish itself as a specialist and leader in the computer memory field, a field where semiconductors had had very little impact and no larger companies were present. As Moore explains, "It's very tempting for a little company to run in all directions. We went the other way. It was our objective to dominate any market in which we participated."

Venture Capital

The pair knew they would need quite a bit of money to start up. Fortunately, Noyce had already had considerable personal exposure to the investment community. Among his acquaintances was Arthur Rock, who had helped to arrange the original financing for Fairchild Semiconductor while he was at Hayden Stone. Later Rock had become a successful venture capitalist in San Francisco and had helped start Teledyne and Scientific Data Systems. In fact, Rock was among the premier venture capitalists in high technology. (2,149) His major coup was arranging to sell SDS, which he had helped to start with $1 million, to Xerox for $900 million worth of stock. Rock makes it a point not to master the intricate technologies of the companies he backs. He fears that would interfere with his judgment of people as managers. (2,65)

"It was a very natural thing to go to Art and say, 'Incidentally, Art, do you have an extra $2.5 million you would like to put on the crap table?' " said Noyce. Rock had long before become convinced of Noyce's abilities as a manager. But he also knew that men who run big companies for others don't necessarily make good entrepreneurs. So Rock, a cautious man, grilled Noyce on his goals and his emotional and financial commitment to the idea. "My way with people who want to start companies is to talk to them until they are exhausted—and then talk to them some more," said Rock. "Finally, I get an impression what their real objectives are, whether they have integrity, whether they are interested in running a big company, whether their goals are big enough. One of the things I'm interested in is whether the management puts a limit on the company they want. If they do, I get fearful." (2,149) Noyce wanted to grow to $100 million in 10 years.[3] Rock was pleased with Noyce's response and by the fact that both Noyce and Moore were willing to invest substantial amounts of their own money, about $250,000 each.

Intel (a contraction of "integrated electronics") started in the enviable position of having so many would-be investors that it could choose those it preferred. "People had known Bob and were kind of lined up to invest in the company," said Rock. Rock purchased $300,000 worth of convertible debentures and brought in other investors who took an additional $2.2 million. Later Intel sold 154,000 shares of common stock in private placements for $2.2 million. The common was immediately oversubscribed.[5] Ultimately, paid-in capital for Intel amounted to about $17.5

million. But after its initial debenture issues, Intel did not find it necessary to borrow or to use its line of bank credit. During this period the company owned almost all its facilities.

Total sales growth of integrated circuits (I /Cs) in the 1970s was expected to average 20% per year.[6] I /Cs were expected to have even more impact on electronics than transistors had, although no one knew precisely when or how. It cost millions to develop initial technologies, to build facilities, and to make the first successful chips. But production bugs made yields a miserable 1–5% of each run. Over 100 steps had to be performed perfectly in sequence. (See Semiconductor Industry Note.) With tolerances of a few microns (millionths of a meter) required, a fleck of dust would cause a faulty device. And reliability testing of the circuits had to be meticulous, a million or more tests for each chip. Nevertheless, this miraculous technology, if mastered, could drive the cost of transistors down ten-thousand fold or more. (2,151–152) Older vacuum tube companies couldn't cope with these uncertainties.[7] And customers, so-called "systems houses," were often afraid of trusting their design secrets to outside I /C suppliers.[8] This was the business Intel set its cap for.

A Complex Technology

Semiconductor memory chips at that time had only highly specialized, limited applications in computers. They were too slow for main memories where tiny ferrite ringlets (or cores) had to be tediously and expensively hand strung on fine wire networks. In 1970 memory could occupy half the CPU and be 60% of its cost, but memory demand was growing faster than computer demand.[9] If one could succeed, the opportunity could be great. In theory, chips could be mass produced rather than hand assembled; and their compact structures could allow more flexible computer designs and much faster operation with lower electrical power.

To invade the main-frame computer market Noyce and Moore decided to leapfrog existing memories and drive for a 1000 bit (4000 transis-tor) chip no larger than the 200 bit chips then in service. Intel soon had plenty of competition—all small fry. But many failed or sold out to larger companies. Intel was the first small concern to focus specifically on semiconductor memory and concentrated more talent on memories than any of its rivals, including such giants as Texas Instruments.

Intel engineers began work on novel memory chips that utilized a brand-new concept, the so-called "silicon-gate" approach. Before Intel's pioneering, aluminum electrode gates were built into semiconductors. But the use of metal made the manufacturing process so delicate and tricky that only 5 percent of the devices manufactured were usable. Noyce and Moore decided to substitute polysilicon for metal in the gate, and they were vindicated when they got yields of 10 percent on their first memory chip.

"They Just Bowled Us Over"

But it was their second MOS product that became famous. The 1103 memory chip held more than 1,000 bits, or more than 4,000 transistors. Intel wasn't the first with a 1,000-bit chip. Advanced Memory Systems (AMS) had started delivery of a similar chip a few months earlier in 1970. But Intel's 1103 quickly grabbed the major share of the market. It became not only the industry standard but also the largest-selling semiconductor component in the world. A crucial element in the acceptance of the 1103 as the industry standard was the cooperation of a Honeywell computer team in testing the device to get rid of hidden bugs and in devising circuit specifications that suited makers of computers.

The 1103 attracted so much attention and looked so promising that Texas Instruments, Fairchild, and almost everyone else in the semiconductor industry initially sought to become a "second source" for the chip. The AMS device was buried in this avalanche. "We had a better design," said Robert H.F. Lloyd, former chairman of AMS. "But Intel just bowled us over with their prestige, salesmanship, and the publicity their device got." Soon Intel drew so far ahead of its competition that most rivals decided it wouldn't be worthwhile to copy the 1103. Even Texas Instruments finally chose not to commit to the 1,000-bit memory-device race. It started working, instead, on an even denser chip.

Meantime, Intel established its own second source. For a $2 million fee, it licensed a Montreal company, Microsystems International, Ltd. (MIL), and taught its engineers how to make the 1103. Royalties came from MIL at a propitious time for Intel. The market for semiconductors slumped in the spring of 1970, but Intel escaped much of the impact because it was not yet in volume production. And Noyce and Moore even convinced their skeptical directors that construction should not be halted on a much needed $2.3 million headquarters and production expansion in Santa Clara.

Nightmares and Jelly Beans

Success was not easy or straightforward. Two months after the 1103 was introduced, a complex reliability problem cropped up. An excess electrical charge on the surface tended to erase data stored within the chip. Recognizing that the company's whole future might be at stake, Intel's engineers worked at a panicky pace for two months to identify the cause of the problem, and six more to clear it up. How it was done remains a company secret. "This place was a madhouse," recalls Andrew S. Grove, then vice president and director of operations.

"The 1103 was a brand-new circuit-design concept, it brought about a brand-new systems approach to computer memories, and its manufacturing required a brand-new technology," added Grove. "Yet it became, over the short period of one year, a high-volume production item—high volume by any standards in this industry." Making the 1103 concept work at the technology level, at the device level, and at the systems level and successfully introducing it into high-volume manufacturing required . . . a fair measure of orchestrated brilliance. Everybody from technologists to designers to reliability experts had to work to the same schedule toward a differ-

ent aspect of the same goal, interfacing simultaneously at all levels over quite a long period of time . . . Yet I would wake up at night, reliving some of the fights that took place during the day on how to accomplish various goals." (2,155)

"The operating style that evolved at Intel was based on the recognition of our own identify," said Grove. "The semiconductor industry consisted of companies that typically fell into one of two extremes: technology leaders and manufacturing leaders. Neither of these types of leadership would accomplish what we wanted to do. We wanted to capitalize on new technology and we wanted to sell our technology and our engineering over and over again. This meant high volume. We regarded ourselves as essentially a manufacturer of *high-technology jelly beans*."

Early Organization

"A manufacturer of high-technology jelly beans needs a different breed of people. The wild-eyed, bushy-haired, boy geniuses that dominate the think tanks and the solely technology-oriented companies will never take their technology to the jelly-bean stage. Similarly, the other stereotype—the straight-laced, crewcut, and moustache-free manufacturing operators of conventional industry—will never generate the technology in the first place." A key question was how to find and mix the two talents. There weren't many experienced engineering or manufacturing people, and top young graduates were sought after by everyone. "In engineering we needed to orient toward market areas and specialized customer needs—such as computer mainframe memories, increasingly sophisticated peripheral capabilities, general purpose I/Cs, and timing circuits." Engineering had to come through *first* with a workable design for what the customer would need most.

But in manufacturing Intel needed to standardize as much as possible. In production, said Grove, "We actually borrowed from a very successful manufacturer of medium technology jelly beans—MacDonalds Hamburgers. When you thought about their standardized process and standardized module approach, it had much to offer in our technology.'' But there was also a sociological reason for what became known as the ''MacIntel'' approach. Noyce was convinced that the day of the huge production unit was gone, that modern workers performed better in smaller, more informal production units. And by 1975 Intel had such units in various Santa Clara towns as well as in Oregon, the Philippines, and Malaysia. In each area Grove introduced perhaps the toughest quality control and monitoring systems in the industry and a system of rewards to match Intel's production philosophy.

Finally Intel realized that reliable delivery was perhaps the most important single issue in marketing its chips. Intel quickly evolved its well known motto, ''Intel Delivers.'' But these words had to be backed by careful practices and dramatic policies to be credible to a skeptical market place. For example, at one point early in its history, Intel convinced Honeywell to give it a contract for a custom memory device. Honeywell had already placed contracts with six semiconductor manufacturers including Texas Instruments and Fairchild. ''We started about six months later than the others,'' recalls Grove, ''and we were the only ones to deliver the device, about a year later.'' (2,158)

Living on the Brink of Disaster

''This business lived on the brink of disaster,'' explained Moore. ''As soon as you could make a device with high yield, you calculated that you could decrease costs by trying to make something four times as complex, which brought your yield down again.'' Overeager technologists could easily miscalculate future yields and pledge deliveries they could not meet or set prices that turned out to be below their costs. Said Noyce, ''If you look at our stuff and melt it down for silicon, that's a small fraction of cost—the rest is mistakes. Yet we chose to work on the verge of disaster because that meant doing the job with finesse, not brute strength.'' Early entry allowed Intel quick recovery of development costs through high prices for unique products. It also meant

''experience curve'' advantages in costs over those who entered later. Volumes were growing so rapidly that future plant space was a necessity, but the technology was moving so fast that one never knew two years ahead what products would be made in the plants. Still plant construction might easily take more than two years for planning and implementation.

The conflicting strategic requirements of production, engineering, marketing (plus international operations) required some unique policy and organizational solutions for the young Intel. Intel had an insatiable need for skilled personnel and tried some imaginative ways of meeting it. The company hired new employees for its wafer-processing facility at Livermore months before that plant went into operation and bused the employees thirty-five miles each way daily to Santa Clara to train them. To hang on to skilled people, Grove used a technique that he called ''Peter Principle recycling.''* Instead of firing foremen and other managers who flopped when promoted to more demanding jobs, he split their tasks, giving them smaller responsibilities. Some of these ''recycled'' men again advanced to higher positions; only a few left.

Middle managers at Intel were monitored carefully but had considerable operational freedom. ''Lots of guys starting new companies are interested in keeping their fingers in every part of the pie,'' said Moore. ''I think Bob and I were relatively willing to relinquish day-to-day details.'' For example, Intel had streamlined purchasing to the point where the engineer in charge of a project could buy a $250,000 tester, or whatever he needed, by simply signing for it—provided it was in his budget . . .'' ''(In a big company) you would need seven different signatures on a piece of paper to spend any money,'' said Moore. Noyce and Moore also tried to keep operations as informal as they could. Spaces in the huge Intel parking lot were not marked with

---

*   The Peter Principle said that an organization kept on promoting its people until they reached a level beyond their competency, where they were held. Thus managements of all organizations became incompetent.

officials' names. . . . "If Bob gets to work late," said Moore, "he parks way out in the corner of the lot. I think this will continue. Sometimes it's a pain in the neck. But the other problem is, once you start marking parking spaces, where do you stop." (2,189–190) The rule still held in the 1980s.

> *Decision Point*: What are the key factors for success in each functional area? What specific policies should Intel develop to meet the conflicting requirements of manufacturing, engineering, and the market? What specific organizational form should Intel undertake in its early years?

AN EXPLODING MARKET

In 1973, just as the 1103 reached its production peak, the trade press dubbed it the "DC-3" of the chip field. The 4000 bit (or 4K) chip had arrived, but it was possible for two or three 4K devices to dominate different market segments. Thus, Mostek, TI, Fairchild, and some ten other companies went after the new market. Intel announced its 4K chip a month before TI, but later found its circuitry slower than TI's—fast enough for peripherals, but not the big main-frame market. Intel countered by making a chip "compatible" with TI's and hammering away at volume production and reliability to take market share. About then Gordon Moore came up with "Moore's Law"—a recognition that the number of components one could put on a chip doubled every year. (See Semiconductor Industry Note.) This set implicit targets for future LSI programs.

The Microprocessor

Among the more exciting potentials of the mid-1970s was the emerging impact of another Intel invention—the microprocessor. By 1972 a number of LSI chips capable of significant computa-

tion had been produced or were in design for small calculators or intelligent terminals. A Japanese calculator company, Busicom, asked Intel to develop a 12 chip set for a high-performance programmable calculator series. ROM—read only memory— chips would customize each model for specific uses. As he worked on the problem, Intel's M.E. "Ted" Hoff concluded that Busicom's design was too complex to be cost effective. Hoff had been utilizing a DEC PDP8 and was struck by its lean architecture versus the complexity of the Busicom design. With a relatively primitive instruction set, the PDP8 could perform highly complex control and arithmetic functions because of its large program memory. Hoff proposed to Intel management a program to design a simpler, more general purpose, more powerful single chip processor. If successful, such a device might have applications well beyond just calculators.

Intel's management responded quickly and enthusiastically. A small team soon defined a 3 chip design: a 4 bit CPU, a ROM program memory, and a RAM (Random Access Memory) data memory. This design was vastly aided by the concurrent invention of the EPROM (Erasable Programmable Read Only Memory) by Dov Frohman at Intel. But it still languished for lack of staffing until Federico Faggin—later co-founder of Zilog—arrived from Fairchild in early 1970. Faggin worked furiously on the silicon design, and in only nine months produced working samples of the chips that would become the MCS-4 microprocessor, the world's first "micro" computer.

In some complex negotiations with Busicom, Intel won the right to sell the MCS-4 chips to others for non-calculator applications. The marketing department saw microprocessors as possibly a 10% slice of the minicomputer market, then at 20,000 units per year. While Intel management thought it might obtain as much as 90% of this market in its early stages, there was considerable debate at the Board level as to whether and how the company should exercise this option. There was widespread skepticism about the microprocessor in the industry. Many saw it as too slow and small to be of much use. But Intel went ahead. As the market finally opened, competitors grew rapidly—to 54 by 1976. And TI, a late entry with its TMW-1000, actually became the leading producer of 4 bit processors.

About that time other fields of application for I/Cs had begun to loom as interesting possible areas of diversification. A trap Noyce wanted to avoid was becoming so engrossed in existing profitable products that Intel neglected new opportunities. The company looked carefully at Microma, Inc., a manufacturer of electronic watches using Intel chips. This looked like "a unique opportunity for electronics to supplant another technology." And there were a myriad of other application possibilities on the horizon. Eventually, the company bought Microma for $2.8 million. This began a complex of longer term developments that intimately shaped the Intel of the early 1980s.

Even as Intel was working on the MSC-4, a parallel development was underway that would lead to its first 8 bit processor, the 8008. Then in 1974 Intel introduced its much more powerful 8080, which quickly became accepted as the 8 bit standard and was widely second sourced. Faggin, Hoff, and Mazor carefully designed the 8080 to be compatible in software with the earlier 8008. This policy of upward compatibility has been followed for all Intel machines thereafter. The 8080 was the first Intel microprocessor announced before it was actually available, "to give customers lead time to design the part into new products." Now things were moving fast. In only three years, microcomputers had exceeded the population of both minis and mainframe computers combined. (2,189–190) The first 8 bit single chip computer (CPU, I/O, RAM, and ROM) was Intel's 8048, introduced in 1976. With it a whole new era of computers and automation began.

The 16 Bit Era

Originally, a 16 bit processor had been considered a mini, and all smaller ones were micros. But this distinction began to fade as National Semi-

conductor introduced its one chip, 16 bit, Pace microprocessor series. Although other entrants were earlier, Intel hit the market in 1978 with its powerful 8086 which had 10 times the throughput and 16 times the memory (one megabyte) of its earlier 8080. By 1979, 75 million microprocessors had been shipped, with an annual compound growth rate of 188% since 1975.

By 1982 microprocessors had created a whole new market for intelligent, user-friendly instruments unavailable 10 years previously. Electronic games and toys had become by far the largest current market—suddenly surpassing the sales of any other single form of entertainment in the U.S. and Japan. Arthur D. Little expected this market to grow sixfold by 1987. But others saw microprocessors and VLSI chips of other sorts restructuring a variety of industries and services in the 1980s. Microprocessors could already be built on a single chip to be as powerful as the room-sized IBM machines of the late 1960s. (See Table 1 later in text.) And a 64 bit microprocessor—with even more inherent address and accuracy capabilities than the most powerful mainframes—seemed probable in the not too distant future.

Cost and Performance

Intel's most radical new offering was its iAPX432 which had a 16 megabyte physical address space and a virtual address of one trillion bytes. This 3 chip processor was designed for critical on-line data base management, networking, and switching system management and control. (2,189–190)

The iAPX432 characterized other major changes in the industry. The rule of thumb through the 1970s was that every 10 years one could buy ten times more computing power for the same cost as a decade before. It was also common for LSI and VLSI chip costs to drop 25% yearly. And the early '80s seemed unlikely to decrease this rate of change. But development costs were also soaring. The 4004 microprocessor was designed by one man in nine months. In contrast the iAPX432 took 6 years and 100 man years

TABLE 1   MICROPROCESSOR FUNCTIONAL CLASSES

Micro System Class	Level of Functionality	Typical Price	Performance Relative to Microcontroller		Memory	
			CPU	I/O	Typical Size (Bytes)	Management
Micromainframe	32 bit	$400–$3,600	20–70	6–45	256K–8M	dynamic addressing, segmented or paged; adaptive virtual support
Micromaxi	16 or 32 bit	$100–$500	25	12	128K–1M	structured addressing, segmented or paged; virtual support
Micromini	16 bit	$20–$150	8–10	6	32K–256K	static addressing, segmented or paged
Microcomputer	8 or 16 bit	$10–$50	1–5	3–5	4K–64K	segmented or direct
Microcontroller	8 bit	$2–$20	1	1	1K–2K	direct or absolute

Source: "Intel Takes Aim at the '80's," *Electronics*, February 28, 1980. Copyright © 1980, McGraw-Hill Inc. All rights reserved.

of engineering. Intel—through 1981—had already spent some $100 million to design its next generation of computers. In the late 1970s it had cost only about $100,000 to produce a typical first LSI (Large Scale Integrated) chip and the marginal cost of a millionth good chip was close to zero. But as VLSI (Very Large Scale Integrated) chips in the early 1980s became more complex, the first chip might cost more than $10–20 million—and later chips were correspondingly expensive. A whole new plant for complex VLSI chips might cost $100–200 million alone.

By 1981 over 100,000 products already had microprocessors built into them. And the quantity and complexity of applications were growing exceedingly rapidly, with virtually every industry and household a potential user. Yet the number of computer programmers to develop these applications was not. In 1980 Andy Grove, then president of Intel, noted, "If the computer industry keeps growing at its current rate, by 1990 it will take a million more qualified programmers to provide the needed software."[10] University output was only in the tens of thousands. In addition, the amount of software for new systems had risen dramatically. Typical customer software for major new applications in the 1970s might have

ranged from $250,000 to $300,000. By the mid-1980s similar applications might cost $1–5 million.[11] The cost of marketing a new system had become as expensive as its initial development.

The computer world of the 1980s would be peculiar. Replacing all of IBM's 360s with 8086 micros would occupy only a few days production at Intel. Yet Intel was projecting a growth of 33% per year and was investing over $150 million in capital per year in an industry where domestic competition was popping all around, where the Japanese had targeted national priorities to dominate semiconductors in the 1980s, and where European governments were ready to put up $½ billion to insure their companies a future in the field.

The Japanese Challenge

In 1979 the U.S. still commanded 67% of the world market for semiconductors, while the Japanese had only 22%. But, led by its large integrated companies—NEC, Fujitsu, and Hitachi—the Japanese moved strongly into the 16K and 64K RAM markets.[12] By 1979 they had 40% of the 16K RAM market. Although Intel had been earlier than the Japanese in introducing its 64K RAM, the company ran into trouble producing it in quantity. Meanwhile the Japanese introduced and perfected production on a 64K RAM that was not as densely packed as the American 64K RAM— i.e. it had larger overall dimensions—and shipped some 85% of that market in 1981. By early 1982 Motorola and Intel had solved their problems with 64K chips that had some potential advantages in speed and packaging over the Japanese. But the Japanese were well down the experience curve on their chips and cut prices severely to discourage the entry of others. As a result various sources estimated that the total profit from 64K chips in 1982 would be only $20 million worldwide.

A number of factors made the Japanese challenge upsetting to the U.S. industry. Almost all the basic research and early technical work on semiconductors had been done by U.S. companies. Many claimed that the early Japanese entries in I/Cs had simply copied U.S. designs relying on the U.S. courts' notoriously lax attitudes on patent enforcement to keep them out of legal troubles. Others noted that the Japanese government through its MITI (Ministry for International Trade and Industry) had given Japanese companies some $200 million in development support to invade the semiconductor and computer markets. And Japanese banks financed these entrants with a level of debt that would not be considered prudent—or perhaps legal—in the U.S. or Europe. Because of high savings rates and low inflation, interest rates were very low (5–6%) in Japan; and satisfactory net profits could thus be correspondingly lower, i.e. 1–2% on sales in NEC. The Japanese did not have to carry the overhead burden of a military establishment. And because of post World War II recovery and high investment rates their suppliers' plants were relatively modern.

In addition to these structural advantages no one denied that a highly disciplined, well educated, and strongly motivated Japanese worker-manager pool was also at the heart of the Japanese challenge. In fact, Japanese management, worker security, and worker cooperation practices were widely admired. But many resented the overt and covert trade barriers that protected the Japanese market, allowing domestic manufacturers to build volume—and lower costs—without foreign competition. Prior to 1975 semiconductor imports into Japan were reportedly controlled by an informal quota system in which MITI would "suggest" that an importer "consider" a domestic source before MITI would approve an import license. Japan's NT&T (the government-controlled telecommunications company) refused to allow foreigners to bid on its contracts, and so on.[12] The fact that Japan's biggest semiconductor producers (Hitachi, NEC, Fujitsu) were also among the biggest component users compounded the market control problem. Unknown internal transfer pricing practices made it difficult to substantiate Silicon Valley's claims that the Japanese were "dumping" 16K chips on the U.S. market at half the Japanese price. See Exhibits I and II for data on the Japanese semiconductor industry.

Acknowledging many of these points in a January 1982 speech, Bob Noyce noted, "The Japanese are smart, patient, and hard working people. And that's unfair competition. We must do something about it. . . . But on the whole to date they are still very much followers in microelectronics. They have yet to produce an innovation in microprocessors."

PRACTICES ATTUNED TO THE TIMES

How could Intel adapt to these challenges? The company had grown larger and more complex in the 1970s. But it had also worked hard to keep its management systems attuned to the times. A few key elements in its approach follow.

The Top Team

By 1982 Intel's "two headed monster"—Noyce and Moore—had become a three headed "executive office." Chairman Moore—pensive and more reserved in his habits—was the company's long range thinker, charting overall product strategies. The more gregarious Noyce, now vice chairman, had become Intel's Mr. Outside and was increasingly recognized as one of the industry's major spokesmen. Andy Grove (age 45), who had headed Fairchild's metal oxide semiconductor (MOS) research and joined Intel at its startup, was president and chief operating officer. Although less visible than Noyce and Moore in the early years, Grove was increasingly recognized as the personality driving Intel's internal affairs. "Grove has to be the world's most organized guy," said an admiring Moore. "He sees problems developing much sooner than other people, and he's interested in the people and people interactions needed to solve them."

The three worked well together, respecting each other's technical abilities, and arguing openly and without rancor when they disagreed. To maintain a close touch with the organization each man was in a separate area of Intel's Santa Clara complex. Their offices were indistinguishable from all the other cubicles that secretaries and junior executives worked in. All office walls in Intel were only shoulder high partitions, there were no doors on any offices (including Moore's), no limousines, and no executive dining rooms. Any of the top three was likely to plop down at a table in their building's cafeteria and join in a lunch chat with whomever was there. Said one group of employees, "It's exciting to know you may see and talk to the very top guy at any time. You feel a real part of things."

Councils and Confrontation

Intel had tried hard to avoid communications barriers and structural bureaucracies. While the company was decentralized into relatively small operating units, people might still have several bosses, depending on the problems at hand. Virtually all staff functions—purchasing, operating procedures, employee compensation, etc.—were handled by "councils" of line managers. There were usually several dozen—ninety were once counted—of such councils operating at one time. On the councils all people participated as equals, with new members free to openly challenge top managers. "The idea," said Grove,

"is to remove authority from an artificial spot at the top and place it where the most knowledgeable people are. . . . I can't pretend to know the shape of the next generation of silicon or computer technology any more. People like me need information from those closest to the technology. We can't afford the hierarchical barriers to the exchange of ideas that so many corporations have. The technology is moving too fast."

This free exchange of ideas was reinforced by a policy of "constructive confrontation." Each member of a team was expected to challenge *ideas* openly and aggressively, but never to attack an individual's motives for presenting an idea. Employees said, "Things can get very rough in a meeting. You'd be surprised at the things people can say. But if you are seeking a solution, it's OK." Grove himself set the tone. "When he walks into the room, things can get electric. . . . I've seen him listen to a carefully prepared report for a while and shatter the room with 'I've never heard so much bullshit in my life.' " The company has courses on "constructive confrontation" for all its rising executives and includes the concept in its early training of people in Intel's philosophy.

The World of High Achievers

Like all other groups and individuals in Intel, the councils were required to set performance objectives and be measured against them. Assignments were set by the council and agreed to by each employee and his supervisor. Grove said, "This takes a lot of time but everyone knows exactly whom they report to on each item—and so do their supervisors. We can't afford to leave anything to chance as we grow larger." Performance measurement pervaded everything. When Noyce had joined Shockley, he had said, "I had to test myself, to know if I could hold my own with the best." In 1982 the attitude persisted: "We are seeking high achievers. And high achievers love to be measured because otherwise they can't prove to themselves that they're achieving. Measuring them says that you care about them. . . . (But it must be an honest review.)

Many people have never had an honest review before. They've been passed along by school systems and managements that don't want to tell people when they don't measure up. We tell them, 'Here are the things you did poorly. And here are the things you did well.'"

Intel had MBO (management by objectives) everywhere. Each person had multiple objectives. All employees wrote down what they were going to do, got their bosses' agreements and reviewed how well they performed with both their management *and* peer groups. This made the review a communication device among various groups as well. A key to the system was the "one on one" meetings between a supervisor and subordinate. The meeting belonged to the subordinate who went to the boss, provided the agenda, told the boss what he was doing, and saw whether there was any assistance the boss could offer. These meetings were required for everyone on a regular basis. They might occur weekly for newcomers, but they were seldom less than monthly for anyone. In any meeting at Intel problems were put forward first, and everyone dug in to solve them.[13]

Formal Organization

There was no large corporate staff in the usual sense. Instead the top division managers formed the "executive staff" whose job was to worry about the whole business, not just their individual portions of it. Expectedly, Intel was leery of formal organization charts. But Exhibit III gives some sense of the matrix of management that guided Intel in 1982.

The basic product group organization included: (1) *Components Group* —RAM's, EPROM's, bubble memories, memory products, and all component manufacturing, wafer processing, and assembly; (2) *Microcomputers Group* — microprocessors, microcontrollers, development systems, telecommunication circuits, and military products; (3) *Systems Group* —single board computers, integrated systems, OEM and end user memory systems, commercial software, commercial microsystems operations, and systems manufacturing. But within this structure "flexibility"

still dominated. Teams were formed for special problems. And planning was performed across all divisions toward a selected set of Strategic Business Segments (SBSs), Intel's version of the strategic business units (SBUs) used in other companies. Noyce said, "Strategic planning is imbedded into the organization. It is one of the primary functions of line managers. They buy into the program. They carry it out. They're determining their own future."[14]

An interesting example of this was the bubble memory group established as a separate entrepreneurial division within Intel. In 1970 Bell Laboratories discovered that in certain materials, it was possible to create small densely packed magnetic bubbles whose location and polarity could be controlled to store enormous quantities of information in a very small space. Although greeted with enthusiasm at first, the technology was difficult to reduce to practice, and most larger companies gave up on it in the late 1970s. A few small entrepreneurial concerns persisted, however; and in 1978 one of these came to Intel with a promising approach ready for scale up and possible introduction. Intel brought the company in as a separate division with a very unusual incentive program to maintain its management's enthusiasm and entrepreneurial flair. In 1982, Intel bubble memories with 1 million bits per chip capacity were commercial and a 4 million bit chip was announced for release late in the year.

An Innovative Year

Despite the deep recession in 1981, Intel had introduced a chain of impressive new products. Its 64K RAM seemed destined to take back a share of this market where the Japanese had surged to dominance. Intel used a "cell redundancy" design that cost 15–20% in chip area but gave a 2 to 3X yield gain. Rothschild, Unterberg, Towbin estimated Intel's direct chip costs as perhaps the U.S.'s lowest ($8–$9 in 1981) in a market where Hitachi was selling 64K chips for $8–$9 in quantity. Volume production could bring Intel's costs down to $4.50–$4.00 in the future. Other competitors' cost estimates follow:

64K PRODUCER COST AND PRODUCTION ESTIMATES

Manufacturer	Est. Average 1981 Production Per Month	Est. Average 1981 Unit Cost
Intel	75,000	$ 8–9
Motorola	150,000	10–12
Texas Instruments	40,000	12–16
Fujitsu	150,000	9–11
Hitachi	200,000	9–11
NEC	150,000	10–12
AMD	0	—
National Semiconductor	0	—
Mostek	70,000	12–16

Source: Rothschild, Unterberg, Towbin, *Intel Research Report*, August 25, 1981.

Other significant new products were a 64K EPROM (fastest available), the i432X microprocessor (with power equal to IBM's 370/158 main-frame), and the revolutionary E²PROM (Electrically Erasable Programmable Read Only Memory). The micro-mainframe market could be over $½ billion in the mid 1980s. And Intel thought E²PROMs could replace all EPROM applications in time and open vast new possibilities. E²PROMs could be reprogrammed without removing the chip from its setting and destroying its old programs with ultraviolet light as EPROMs required. These were but a few of the 85–90 new products Intel introduced in 1981, a disaster year for the industry caused by severe price competition and general economic conditions. As a result Rothschild, Unterberg, Towbin was forecasting Intel's growth at 35% per year to 1985 with profit margins of 15–17%. They forecast Intel's overall financials as shown in Tables 2 and 3.

But Intel could meet this competition with some powerful strengths. Processing technology at Intel was perhaps unmatched in the industry. The density of components on a chip was defined by so called "design rules" which set the minimum spacings which could be reliably met between components. Intel's technology (H-MOS III) was perhaps the most powerful in the industry for this purpose. But the Japanese were pushing hard on this gap. Some comparisons follow:

PROCESS TECHNOLOGY COMPARISON

Company	New Process Name	Minimum New Process Design Rule	Current Process Design Rule u = microns	New Process Status
Intel	H-MOS II H-MOS III*	2–3 u 1–2 u*	2–4 u	Stable
Motorola	H-MOS II H-MOS III*	2–2½ u 1.4–1.8 u*	2½–5 u	Stable
Texas Instruments	S-MOS	3 u	3½–5 u	Improving
National Semi.	X-MOS	2–3 u	3½–5 u	Development
Advanced Micro Devices	N/S 8	2–3 u	3⅓–4 u	Improving
Mostek	SP 5	2.5–2.7 u	4 u	Improving
Nippon Electric	N.A.	N.A.	3½–4 u	Stable

* Planned.
Source: Rothschild, Unterberg, Towbin, *Intel Research Report*, August 25, 1981.

TABLE 2   INTEL FINANCIAL ESTIMATES

($ Millions, except per share data)

Sales	1979	1980	1981E	1982E
Memory:				
1K, 4K Dynamic	$ 41	$ 32	$ 10	$ 5
16K Dynamic	49	86	80	45
64K Dynamic	—	6	20	55
1K, 4K, 16K Static	66	95	65	90
PROM, EPROM, EEPROM	120	153	100	165
Total Memory	$276	$372	$275	$ 360
Microprocessor:				
Memory	70	94	85	105
CPU	60	86	125	195
Peripheral	30	49	60	90
Total Micro	$160	$229	$270	$ 390
Board Level	30	37	30	40
Develop. System	95	125	140	160
Memory System	100	92	85	115
Total Sales	$663	$855	$800	$1,065

Pretax Income/Margin				
Memory	$54/19%	$61/16%	$(18)/—%	$30/8%
Microprocessor	53/33	76/33	43/16	91/23
Develop. System	29/30	36/29	27/19	35/22
Other	13/10	10/8	7/6	12/8
Total	$149/22.5%	$183/21.4%	$ 59/7%	$168/16%
TAX RATE	47.8%	47.8%	44.4%	44%
NET INCOME	$ 78	$ 95.5	$ 33	$ 94
E.P.S. (43.5 million shares)	$ 1.80	$ 2.21	$.50 –1.00	$ 2.15

Source: Rothschild, Unterberg, Towbin, *Intel Research Report*, August 25, 1981.

THE INTEL CULTURE

Many observers felt that the "Intel culture" would be a major determinant of its success in the wild world of the '80s. This "culture" was an odd mixture of discipline and flexibility that pervaded the company. So important was this "culture" that all employees were put through a course on it soon after they arrived. This was especially important in a company like Intel where half of the people might have been present only a year or less. The top three executives consistently taught in this course as they did in the complex of other courses set up to maintain Intel's competitiveness for the 1980s. Grove said, "Management must teach to have the courses believed. . . . It takes a lot of time. But nothing could be more important than understanding how we operate and what makes Intel unique. Intel is a complete philosophy not just a job."

At Intel people were expected to be disciplined, to work hard. There are clocks and "sign in sheets" for all people who arrived after the rigorous 8:00 AM starting hour. Even top executives followed this rule. Someone once said, "Intel is the only place I've ever seen where 8 AM meetings start at 8." Many people don't like the demands Intel makes and its lack of structure.

TABLE 3   INTEL FINANCIAL ESTIMATES

Funds Flow	1979	1980	1981E	1982E	1983E	1984E	1985E
SOURCES:							
Net Income	$ 77.8	$ 96.7	$ 33	$ 94	$130	$170	$230
Depreciation	40.4	49.0	70	85	100	135	170
Deferred Taxes	6.8	8.0	2	8	10	14	20
Equity Sales	19.8	32.9	25	35	45	55	65
Debt Financing	—	150.0	—	—	—	—	—
Total	$144.8	$336.7	$130.0	$222.0	$285	$374	$485
USES:							
Capital Spending	$ 96.7	$152.2	$150	$110.0	$145	$225	$300
Funds Required for Working Capital	52.0	39.0	(11)	53	75	100	135
Funds Provided/ (Required)	$ (3.9)	$145.4	$ 9	$ 59	$ 65	$ 49	$ 50
Return on Average Equity	30.6%	26.3%	7.5%	17.7%	19.0%	19.3%	20.1%

Source: Rothschild, Unterberg, Towbin, *Intel Research Report*, August 25, 1981.

Some employees said, "Some people can't understand that no one will tell them what to do. They have to define what they are going to do and then live up to it. We've seen lots of people quit in the first month because they can't take the pressure." But those who stay like the atmosphere. "It's great to say you work at Intel. You know you're the best. . . . I guess it's a real pride in being first, in being on the frontier. You know you're really a part of something very big— very important." At Intel employees had put over $60 million of their own money into its stock, which had never paid a dividend.[10] Perhaps this was why Intel was able to meet the 1981 downturn with its "20% solution." Under this program many of the professional staff agreed to work an extra day a week—without extra pay—to get out new products and to break production bottlenecks as necessary. Many participated in the 7 month campaign, which was an outstanding success, allowing Intel to rocket out of the recession with a momentum of new products and processes few enjoyed.

"Quality Circles," Total Quality Control, and Quality Assurance programs had long been present in Intel, along with a monthly cash bonus system for quantity and quality of production out-put. The latter was announced at a monthly bonus meeting in which performance, suggestions, and solutions were discussed directly with the people doing the job on the production line. But noted Noyce, "In a larger organization there is a frustration. It takes longer to see the results of what you're doing. You push on one thing a year and see some movement. In a small organization you can turn on a dime and change direction. With 10,000 people, you break the organization into small manageable units, so you can change the direction of one unit at a time. . . ."

"But in development you can't afford that. You have to move fast, to be first. But you're in a realm where no one has done before what you're trying to do. You have to measure absolutely everything, so when something goes wrong, you have some idea of what went wrong. You don't change something unless you've proved it on a pilot basis first, so that it won't louse up something else. . . . Yet you have to compete against other people who may not know this—and get lucky. You also have to compete against the massive capacities of the large Japanese companies to change the whole market place if they make a right decision and you don't. None of us—no one—has managed a company in this kind of technology and this competition before. We have to write the book for the future. It's quite a challenge.''

Moore stated the ultimate challenge in these terms, ''We intend to be the outstandingly successful company in this industry. And we intend to continue to be a leader in the revolutionary technology that is changing the way the world is run.''[1] The question was how to do this in an era in which many saw the once almost mystically high technology chip business moving into a commodity era.

Said Noyce, ''A company with 16,000 employees and $800 million in sales can't fail to be different than the start up company we were 13 years ago. But in the past we have been first with major innovations like the silicon gate MOS,

LSI memory, microprocessor, E^2PROM, HMOS, megabit bubbles, and 32 bit microprocessor. . . . To be recognized as the technological leader in those areas we pursue is still a goal. . . . This and our other stated goals (see Exhibit IV) remain guideposts for our future.''

QUESTIONS

1. Evaluate the past strategy of Intel. What criteria should one use in evaluating a strategy?
2. What new problems do you see for Intel's future? What should it do about these?
3. How should it organize to support its strategy?

EXHIBIT I   PRELIMINARY ESTIMATED 1981 VERSUS 1980 WORLDWIDE SEMICONDUCTOR SHIPMENT COMPARISONS (Millions of Dollars)

Company	1980	1981	Annual Growth Percent
Texas Instruments	$ 1,580	$ 1,295	(18.0)
Motorola	1,100	1,185	7.7
Nippon Electric	769	928	20.7
Hitachi	658	824	25.2
Toshiba	629	768	22.1
National Semiconductor	770	730	(5.2)
Fairchild	566	505	(10.8)
Intel	575	500	(13.0)
Fujitsu	419	482	15.0
Philips*	558	480	(14.0)
Matsushita	300	379	21.3
Signetics	384	375	(2.3)
Siemens**	423	337	(20.3)
Mitsubishi	254	308	26.3
RCA	322	293	(9.0)
AMD	282	277	(1.8)
General Instrument	244	264	8.2
Mostek	330	255	(22.7)
Sanyo	180	216	20.0

EXHIBIT I (*Continued*)

Company	1980	1981	Annual Growth Percent
ITT	241	200	(17.0)
SGS-ATES	170	178	4.7
Harris	185	165	(10.8)
Thomson-CSF	179	156	(12.8)
AEG-Telefunken	180	141	(21.7)
American Microsystems	117	130	11.1
General Electric	137	122	(10.9)
Hewlett-Packard	95	90	(5.3)
International Rectifier	90	90	0.0
Intersil	106	88	(17.0)
Synertek	60	72	20.0
Unitrode	70	70	0.0
Rockwell	70	70	0.0
Total of Above Companies	$12,043	$11,973	(0.6%)

*Excludes Signetics subsidiary.
**Excludes U.S. subsidiaries.
Source: DATAQUEST, Inc., March 1982.

EXHIBIT II COMPARISON U.S. VS. JAPAN

Producer	Year	Plant & Equipment Expenditure	Sales	Percent
U.S.A.	1979	$ 980 mil.	$6,600 mil.	14.8%
	1980	1,275 mil.	8,400 mil.	15.1
	1981	1,150 mil.	8,900 mil.	12.9
Japan	1979	$ 555 mil.	$3,284 mil.	16.9%
	1980	829 mil.	4,592 mil.	18.1
	1981	900 mil.	5,165 mil.	17.4

Source: Rothschild, Unterberg, Towbin, *Intel Research Report,* August 25, 1981.

EXHIBIT III   INTEL'S ORGANIZATION 1982

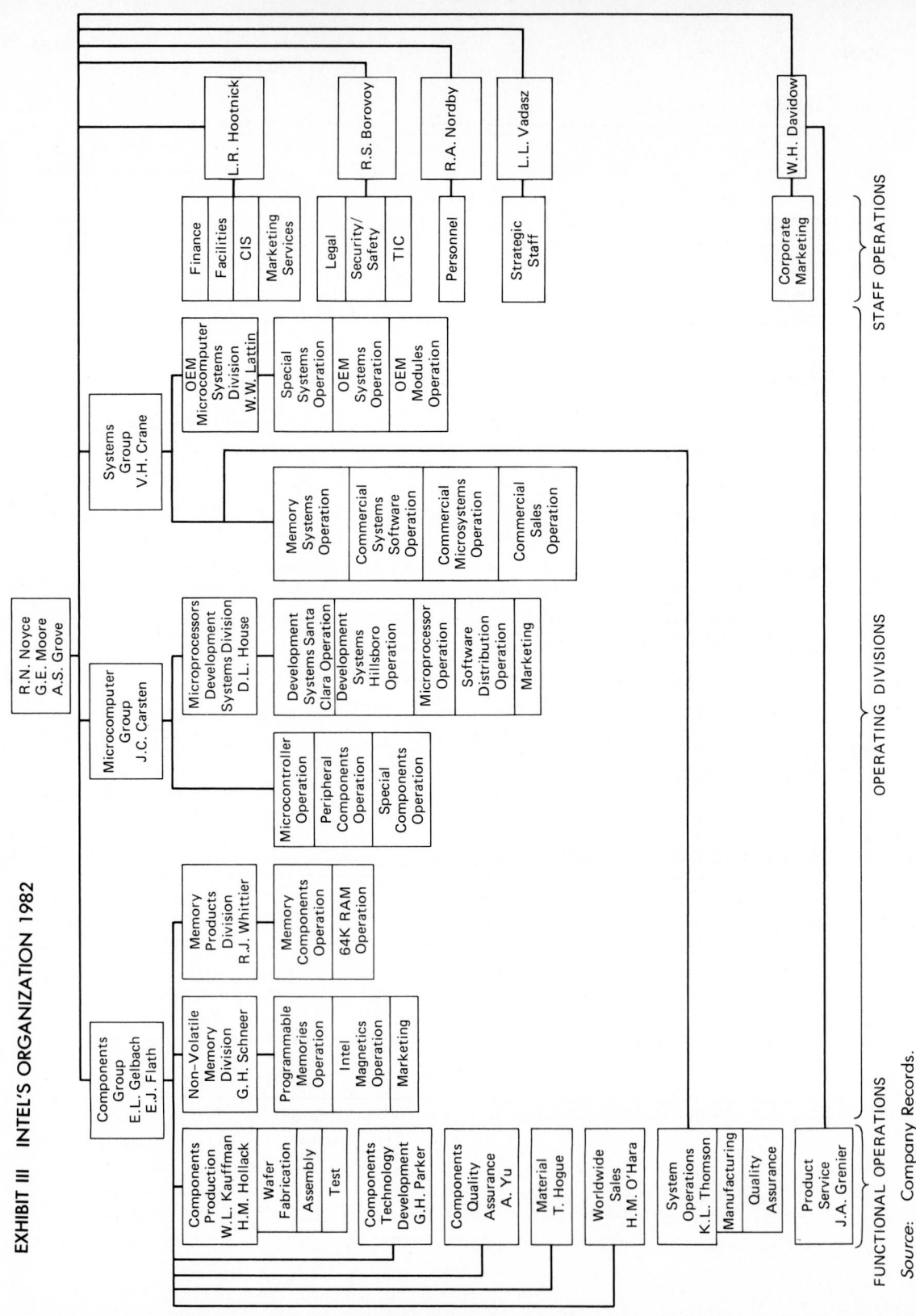

FUNCTIONAL OPERATIONS

OPERATING DIVISIONS

STAFF OPERATIONS

Source: Company Records.

EXHIBIT IV   INTEL CORPORATION CORPORATE OBJECTIVES

Intel's basic objective is to be an outstandingly successful business over the long term. We have become accustomed to excellence in everything we undertake. This overall objective can be divided into series of more specific objectives:

1. To grow to a minimum of 250 million dollars in after-tax earnings by 1985 while maintaining an average of at least 10% after-tax margin and, at all times, the highest margins of major companies in our industry.

2. To concentrate on those areas of business where we can have a commanding position (either #1 or #2) and in which our combination of capabilities result in uniquely strong competitive advantages; to maintain a position in other business areas only if it is important to develop or support the commanding positions.

3. To be and be recognized as the technological leader in those areas we pursue.

4. To be and be recognized as the leader in meeting our customers' needs for delivery, reliability, quality and service.

5. To minimize the effects of disruptive fluctuations caused by business cycles and capricious competitors so that our long term commitments to people and programs can be maintained.

6. To seek out, attract and retain the best people possible at all levels and provide them with challenging jobs, training and opportunities for personal growth so that they may share in Intel's success.

7. To conduct our business with customers and vendors and in our internal activities with integrity and professionalism.

8. Be an asset to the countries and communities in which we operate.

Source: Company Records, May 8, 1981.

EXHIBIT V   COMPETITOR PROFILES

The worldwide non-captive market for semiconductors approximated $13.8 billion in 1980. Discrete devices constituted a large portion of the market and accounted for $4.3 billion or 31% of all semiconductors sold. Integrated circuits, which consist of bipolar and MOS devices, amounted to $9.5 billion or 69% of industry sales. MOS memory devices accounted for the largest portion of integrated circuit sales and comprised about 18% of all semiconductor device sales. Bipolar logic circuits at $2.2 billion and linear devices at $1.8 billion accounted for the next largest portions of the industry.

MOTOROLA

Motorola appears to have the strongest position in the semiconductor industry. It has the best product balance of all the suppliers and is well-positioned in leading-edge, rapidly growing products. The company is the world's largest supplier of discrete devices with a 10% market share. Within the discrete category, Motorola dominates the market for power devices. It is the largest factor in power transistors, rectifiers and zener diodes, and second to General Electric in thyristors. The company should also become a major force in power MOS/FETs, an emerging market. The discrete business is highly profitable, very stable, and provides funds which can be invested in faster growing integrated circuit lines.

In bipolar logic, Motorola has emerged as the dominant supplier of high speed emitter coupled logic (ECL), which is used in high performance computers. It also offers a line of ECL gate arrays. The company is one of the top three bipolar linear producers, and appears to be gaining position in this market. . . . Motorola has the broadest range of processors and peripherals next to the industry leader, Intel. In memories, Motorola is the current domestic leader in 64K-bit

EXHIBIT V (*Continued*)

RAM production and a leading factor in static RAMs, EPROMs and EEPROMs. Finally, as the dominant factor in CMOS, the most important technology for the second half of this decade, the company offers a broad line of CMOS logic circuits and several CMOS microprocessor families.

INTEL

Intel garners the second-place award because of its dominant position in microprocessors and specialty memory products. Intel literally invented the microprocessor in 1971 and exploited its position by continually upgrading its processor and peripheral and support capabilities. The company is unsurpassed in the 8-bit market and is expected to share the top spot with Motorola's 68000 in the 16-bit market. Furthermore, the company was the first to introduce a 32-bit processor, the iAPX-432, which will be available for customer sampling in 1982. Intel also pioneered many new memory products such as the static RAM, EPROM and EEPROM. The company still maintains its leadership position in these rapidly growing product lines, but is not expected to achieve the dominance of these markets that it did during the 1970s.

ADVANCED MICRO DEVICES

AMD is rapidly emerging as a major force in the integrated circuit market. The company emphasizes proprietary products which account for 40–50% of its revenues and a larger portion of its profits. It pioneered and now dominates the 4-bit slice bipolar microprocessor market, which is used for high speed computation applications, and followed this product with a 16-bit line aimed at the high speed controller market. The company is also a leading factor in high performance bipolar RAMs and PROMs. Key thrusts for the future include a line of MOS and linear telecommunica-

tions chips and Ethernet controller circuits. In addition, the company was recently designated as the official domestic second source for Intel's 8086 16-bit microprocessor line.

TEXAS INSTRUMENTS (TI)

This company was once perceived as the premier semiconductor company. Its position has slipped because of the glittering performances of Intel and Advanced Micro Devices combined with its relatively poor performance in 8-bit and 16-bit microprocessors and CMOS development. We sense that TI is regrouping and preparing for a market onslaught in the 1982–86 period. It intends to protect its dominant position in digital bipolar markets through extensions of the advanced low power Shottky (ALS) line and expanded gate array offerings. In the MOS memory area, TI has become a major factor in EPROMs, and is the second largest domestic supplier, next to Motorola, in the 64K-bit dynamic RAM. The company is the leading supplier of 4-bit microprocessors, which are principally used in toys, games and appliances. Its 8-bit effort has stalled, but new thrusts are being made in the single-chip processor area. A very fast, 24-MHz version of the 9900 16-bit microprocessor was recently announced. While this part is the fastest on the market, we do not expect it to be overwhelmingly successful due to its rather turgid, outdated architecture. CMOS is receiving lots of development attention and we would expect numerous product introductions to unfold over the next few years. TI must offer a broad line of CMOS logic circuits in order to protect its flanks in the bipolar logic market.

NATIONAL SEMICONDUCTOR

National is perhaps the most maligned of the semiconductor companies. It is viewed as a strong production house with little technology and thin

EXHIBIT V (*Continued*)

management. This latter point has been further emphasized by the recent departures of several corporate officers. In our opinion, National is a much better company than is generally perceived. It is the third largest domestic semiconductor company and one of the top five independent vendors in the world. The company offers a very broad product line ranging from discrete devices to high performance integrated circuits. National is one of the leaders in bipolar logic with a strong position in Shottky and ALS, and will soon broaden its bipolar memory participation through the introduction of high speed ECL RAMs. In addition, the company will offer ECL Macrocell arrays. National is the dominant factor in the linear circuit area and has probably introduced more innovative linear devices than all competitors combined. This product line is highly profitable and can be viewed as a cash cow.

National's other strength is CMOS, where it offers a line of logic devices, gate arrays and microprocessors. Moreover, the company has developed several CMOS digital/analog converters and three proprietary telecommunications chips. The company is a leading participant in MOS memories but has not distinguished itself in this area. National's weakest area is MOS microprocessors, where its only success to date has been in the 4-bit processor. The company has not participated heavily in the 8-bit market and is now sampling its 16-bit proprietary processor, the NS16000.

MONOLITHIC MEMORIES

Monolithic Memories is the second largest supplier of bipolar, programmable read-only memories (PROMs). These devices are used in minicomputer, military electronics and microprocessor applications. The company pioneered this product in the early 1970s and has retained a leadership position. The company was late in developing higher density versions of the PROM, but has made excellent progress in developing the next generation of product in an attempt to overtake the competition. The 16K-bit family will shortly be available in two configurations: 2K × 8 and 4K × 4. A registered version of the 16K-bit part will be available next year along with a 32K-bit device. Furthermore, faster versions of low density devices have been introduced, such as a 256-bit part with an access time of 17 nanoseconds, and will secure the company's leadership position at the low end of the market.

Source: Hambrecht & Quist Incorporated, *Research Report*, November 1981.

EXHIBIT VI   SEMICONDUCTOR SCORECARD ($ Millions)

	Discretes	Bipolar Logic	Bipolar Memory	Linear	MOS Memories	MOS Micro-processors	CMOS	Total
Texas Instruments	$200	$530 LS	$50	$180	$300 64K DRAM EPROM	$90	$10	$1,360
Motorola	$420 Power	$170 ECL	$20	$165	$155	$75 6800 68000	$175	$1,180
National Semiconductor	$50	$250	$30	$205	$130	$30	$80 p^2 process	$775
Intel	—	$5	$30	—	$355 EPROM EEPROM	$220 8080 8086	$5	$615
Advanced Micro Devices	—	$80 Bit Slice	$40 RAM PROM	$30	$90	$50	—	$290
Monolithic Memories	—	$20 PAL	$68 PROM	—	—	—	—	$88
Other Major Competitors	Phillips $310 Toshiba $275 NEC $260 Hitachi $250	Fairchild $300 Signetics $250 Fujitsu $125 RCA $100	Signetics $95 Fairchild $70 Harris $50 Fujitsu $25	Fairchild $90 RCA $85 Analog $80 Signetics $70	Mostek $260 Fujitsu $230 NEC $180 Hitachi $150	NEC $75 Hitachi $40 Zilog $30 Fairchild $30	RCA $100 Harris $60 AMI $40 Intersil $30	$3,660
Total	$4,300	$2,200	$600	$1,800	$2,500	$800	$600	$13,800

Source: Hambrecht & Quist Incorporated, *Research Report*, November 1981.

EXHIBIT VII FINANCIAL STATEMENTS—INTEL CORPORATION

CONSOLIDATED STATEMENT OF INCOME (Thousands—except per share amounts)

Three Years ended December 31, 1981	1981	1980	1979
NET REVENUES	**$788,676**	**$854,561**	**$660,984**
Cost of sales	458,308	399,438	313,106
Research and development	116,496	96,426	66,735
Marketing, general and administrative	184,293	175,577	131,974
Operating costs and expenses	759,097	671,441	511,815
Income before interest and other and taxes on income	29,579	183,120	149,169
Interest and other	(10,655)	(2,209)	121
Income before taxes on income	**40,234**	**185,329**	**149,048**
Taxes on income	12,875	88,588	71,244
NET INCOME	**$ 27,359**	**$ 96,741**	**$ 77,804**
Earnings per capital and capital equivalent share	**$ .61**	**$ 2.21**	**$ 1.85**
Capital shares and equivalents	**44,700**	**43,720**	**42,145**

CONSOLIDATED STATEMENT OF SHAREHOLDERS' EQUITY (Thousands)

Three Years ended December 31, 1981	1981 Capital Stock		1980	1979
	Number of Shares	*Amount*	*Retained Earnings*	*Total*
Balance at December 31, 1978	**39,832**	**$ 70,618**	**$134,444**	**$205,062**
Proceeds from sales of shares through employee stock plans and tax benefit thereof	1,180	19,869	—	19,869
Acquisition of MRI, Inc.	372	4,562	(4,108)	454
Net income	—	—	77,804	77,804
Balance at December 31, 1979	**41,384**	**95,049**	**208,140**	**303,189**
Proceeds from sales of shares through employee stock plans and tax benefit thereof	1,352	32,930	—	32,930
Net income	—	—	96,741	96,741
Balance at December 31, 1980	**42,736**	**127,979**	**304,881**	**432,860**
Proceeds from sales of shares through employee stock plans and tax benefit thereof	1,030	27,598	—	27,598
Net income	—	—	27,359	27,359
Balance at December 31, 1981	**43,766**	**$155,577**	**$332,240**	**$487,817**

See accompanying notes provided in company's annual report.

Source: Intel Corporation, *Annual Report,* 1981.

EXHIBIT VII (*Continued*)
INTEL CORPORATION CONSOLIDATED BALANCE SHEET (Dollars in Thousands)

December 31, 1981 and 1980	1981	1980
ASSETS		
Current assets:		
Cash and short-term investments at cost, which approximates market	$115,260	$127,681
Accounts receivable, net of allowance for doubtful accounts of $3,878 ($4,296 in 1980)	179,604	195,644
Inventories	97,452	91,401
Prepaid taxes on income and other assets	67,454	31,883
Total current assets	**459,770**	**446,609**
Property, plant and equipment:		
Land and buildings	215,519	165,831
Machinery and equipment	279,676	222,140
Construction in progress	80,269	48,417
Equipment leased to others	15,478	10,546
	590,942	446,934
LESS Accumulated depreciation	179,195	126,375
Property, plant and equipment, net	**411,747**	**320,559**
TOTAL ASSETS	**$871,517**	**$767,168**
LIABILITIES AND SHAREHOLDERS' EQUITY		
Current liabilities:		
Notes payable	$ 31,889	$ 11,844
Accounts payable	41,700	30,350
Deferred income on shipments to distributors	52,683	46,033
Accrued liabilities	45,705	39,902
Profit sharing retirement plan accrual	—	15,250
Income taxes payable	—	3,892
Total current liabilities	**171,977**	**147,271**
7% Convertible subordinated debentures	**150,000**	**150,000**
Deferred taxes on income	**44,019**	**23,266**
Unamortized investment tax credits	**17,704**	**13,771**
Shareholders' equity:		
Capital stock, no par value, 75,000,000 shares authorized	155,577	127,979
Retained earnings	332,240	304,881
Total shareholders' equity	**487,817**	**432,860**
TOTAL LIABILITIES AND SHAREHOLDERS' EQUITY	**$871,517**	**$767,168**

See accompanying notes provided in company's annual report.

Source: Intel Corporation, *Annual Report*, 1981.

EXHIBIT VII (*Continued*)

INTEL CORPORATION FINANCIAL SUMMARY (Thousands—except per share amounts)

Ten years ended December 31, 1981

| | Net Investment In Plant & Equip. | Total Assets | Long-Term Debt | Shareholders' Equity | Working Capital Provided By: | | Working Capital Used for Net Additions To Plant & Equip. |
					Operations	Employee Stock Plans	
1981	$411,747	$871,517	$150,000	$487,817	$115,021	$27,598	$154,164
1980	320,559	767,168	150,000	432,860	153,751	32,930	152,151
1979	217,391	500,093	—	303,189	124,961	19,869	96,681
1978	160,140	356,565	—	205,062	78,025	12,025	104,157
1977	80,117	221,246	—	148,942	49,777	7,766	44,881
1976	51,069	156,568	—	109,460	38,018	10,073	32,073
1975	28,474	102,719	—	74,173	24,232	7,100	11,169
1974	22,186	75,410	—	50,799	25,515	3,135	12,783
1973	13,015	50,567	—	27,888	12,402	1,278	9,113
1972	5,376	21,944	—	17,396	3,552	684	2,104

| | Net Revenues | Cost of Sales | Research & Development | Other Costs & Expenses, Net | Net Income | |
					Total	Per Share
1981	$788,676	$458,308	$116,496	$186,513	$27,359	$ .61
1980	854,561	399,438	96,426	261,956	96,741	2.21
1979	660,984	313,106	66,735	203,339	77,804	1.85
1978	399,390	196,376	41,360	117,340	44,314	1.08
1977	282,549	143,979	27,921	78,933	31,716	.80
1976	225,979	117,193	20,709	62,863	25,214	.63
1975	136,788	67,649	14,541	38,324	16,274	.42
1974	134,456	67,909	10,500	36,271	19,776	.53
1973	66,170	35,109	4,565	17,282	9,214	.25
1972	23,417	12,425	3,442	4,466	3,084	.09

Source: Intel Corporation, *Annual Report,* 1981.

Bit	Contraction for binary digit. A bit is a 0 or 1. Bits are usually grouped together to form bytes (8 bits) or words (4, 8, 16, or 32 etc. bits).
Byte	A group of 8 bits.
CMOS	Complementary metal-oxide-semiconductor technology. CMOS offers the advantages of very low power consumption and high noise immunity. CMOS uses both n-channel and p-channel transistors and has speed and density characteristics between NMOS and PMOS.
CPU	The central processing unit. The part of the computer responsible for fetching, decoding, and executing instructions. The CPU contains the control unit, arithmetic logic unit and related support facilities such as clocks, drivers, and registers.
Dynamic RAM	(DRAM) A dynamic read/write memory. Each data bit is stored as a charge on a single MOS transistor. This design permits high circuit densities, but the charge "leaks" away. Therefore, in a typical dynamic memory the data must be "refreshed" (recharged) every 2 milliseconds. This process requires additional refresh logic, usually external to the chip. Dynamic memory chips are less espensive than static ones and are frequently preferred for memory sizes over 16K.
EEPROM	(or "E-square PROM") A read-only memory that can be electrically reprogrammed in the field (a limited number of times) after the entire memory is erased by an electric field.
EPROM	Erasable programmable read-only memory. An EPROM can be reprogrammed several times. EPROM typically refers to an erasable PROM in which all data can be erased by exposing the chip to a powerful ultraviolet light source for several minutes. The IC can then be reprogrammed (by the user) with a PROM-programmer and will retain its data contents for several years. EPROMs that can be erased with electricity are called EEPROMs.
IC	Integrated circuit. A device that incorporates a circuit of several electronic components in a single package. The number of components, typically transistors, can range from 2 to several hundred thousand.
Linear (Analog)	Having a continuous variable signal as in a radio wave, TV transmission, or telephone signal. Linear ICs accept and manipulate analog signals.
LSI	Large-scale integration (incorporating 500 to 10,000–20,000 transistors/chip).
MOS	Metal-oxide semiconductor technology. A semiconductor process technology named for the three successive layers of materials used. MOS is used to fabricate most high density (LSI and VLSI) devices such as microprocessors and memories.
PROM	A programmable read-only memory (ROM). PROMs may be programmed by the user. PROM programmers are typically external devices used to write bit patterns into the user-programmable ROM. PROMs, like all ROMs, are non-volatile.
RAM	Random-access memory. A memory device allowing the repeated storage and retrieval of information (sometimes called "read/write" memory). RAMs are usually volatile, i.e. all data are lost when power is removed.
ROM	Read-only memory. ROMs include mask-type ROMs, PROMs, EPROMs, and EEPROMs. All ROMs retain their data without power.
SLSI	Super-large-scale integration (or ULSI) technology incorporating over 500,000 transistors per IC.
Static RAM	Read/write memories not requiring dynamic refresh. Static RAMs offer lower densities but similar speeds to dynamic RAMs (DRAMs). Like dynamic memories, static RAMs retain data only as long as power is supplied.
VLSI	Very-large-scale integration incorporating approximately 10,000 to 50,000 —100,000 transistors per chip.
Wafer	A round slice of silicon ingot upon which integrated circuits are fabricated. The ICs on a wafer (dice) are tested, cut into chips, packaged, further tested, and then sold as finished ICs.

IBM (A):
THE SYSTEM/360
DECISION

The decision by the management of the International Business Machines Corp. to produce a new family of computers, called the System /360, was one of the most crucial and portentous—as well as perhaps the riskiest—business judgments of recent times. The decision committed IBM to laying out money in sums that read like the federal budget—some $5 billion over a period of four years. To launch the 360, IBM was forced into sweeping organizational changes, with executives rising and falling with the changing tides of battle. The very character of this large and influential company was significantly altered by the ordeal of the 360, and the way it thinks about itself changed, too. Bob Evans, the line manager who had the major responsibility for designing this gamble of a corporate lifetime, was only half joking when he said: "We called this project 'You bet your company.' "

Evans insisted that the 360 "was a damn good risk, and a lot less risk than it would have been to do anything else, or to do nothing at all," and there is a lot of evidence to support him. . . . A long stride ahead in the technology of computers in commercial use was taken by the 360. So sweeping were the implications that it required ten years before there was enough

data to evaluate the wisdom of the whole undertaking.

The new System /360 was intended to obsolete virtually all other existing computers—including those being offered by IBM itself. Thus, the first and most extraordinary point to note about this decision was that it involved a challenge to the marketing structure of the computer industry—an industry that the challenger itself had dominated overwhelmingly for nearly a decade. It was roughly as though General Motors had decided to scrap its existing makes and models and offer in their place one new line of cars, covering the entire spectrum of demand, with a radically redesigned engine and an exotic fuel. . . .

[In 1966] there were perhaps 35,000 computers in use, and it was estimated that there would be 85,000 by 1975. IBM sat astride this exploding market, accounting for something like two-thirds of the worldwide business—i.e., the dollar value of general-purpose computers then installed or on order. IBM's share of this market [in 1965] represented about 77 percent of the company's $3.6 billion gross revenues [and $477 million of profits].

Several separate but interrelated steps were involved in the launching of System /360. Each one of the steps involved major difficulties, and taking them all meant that IBM was accepting a staggering challenge to its management capabilities. First, the 360 depended heavily on microcircuitry, an advanced technology in the field of computers. In a 1952 vacuum-tube model of IBM's first generation of computers, there were about 2,000 components per cubic foot. In a sec-

Case compilation copyright © 1983 by James Brian Quinn. All sections drawn from a two-part series: T.A. Wise, "IBM's $5 Billion Gamble," and "The Rocky Road to the Marketplace," *Fortune*, September–October 1966. Copyright © 1966 Time, Inc. All rights reserved to original copyright holder. Reproduced by permission. Questions at end added by Professor Quinn. Verb tenses have been edited to clarify time relationships. Minor sections have been deleted (. . .) when peripheral.

ond-generation machine, which used transistors instead of tubes, the figure was 5,000 per cubic foot. The System /360 model 75 computer, using hybrid microcircuitry, involved 30,000 components per cubic foot. The old vacuum-tube computer could perform approximately 2,500 multiplications per second; the 360 model 75 was designed to perform 375,000 per second. The cost of carrying out 100,000 computations on the first-generation model was $1.38; the 360 reduced the cost to $3\frac{1}{2}$ cents.

The second step was the provision for compatibility—that is, as the users' computer requirements grew they could move up from one machine to another without having to discard or rewrite already existing programs. Limited compatibility had already been achieved by IBM, and by some of its competitors too, for that matter, on machines of similar design but different power. But it had never been achieved on a broad line of computers with a wide range of powers, and achieving this compatibility depended as much on developing compatible programs or "software" as it did on the hardware. All the auxiliary machines—"peripheral equipment" as they are called in the trade—had to be designed so that they could feed information into or receive information from the central processing unit; this meant that the equipment had to have timing, voltage, and signal levels matching those of the central unit. In computerese, the peripheral equipment was to have "standard interface." The head of one competing computer manufacturing company acknowledges that at the time of the System /360 announcement he regarded the IBM decision as sheer folly and doubted that IBM would be able to produce or deliver a line that was completely compatible.

Finally—and this was the boldest and most perilous part of the plan—it was decided that six main units of the 360 line, originally designated models 30, 40, 50, 62, and 70, should be announced and made available simultaneously. (Models at the lower and higher ends of the line were to be announced later.) This meant that all parts of the company would have to adhere to a meticulous schedule.

UP IN MANUFACTURING, DOWN IN CASH

The effort involved in the program was enormous. IBM spent over half a billion dollars on research and development programs associated with the 360. This involved a tremendous hunt for talent: by the end of 1966, one-third of IBM's 190,000 employees had been hired since the new program was announced. Between that time, April 7, 1964, and the end of 1967, the company opened five new plants in the U.S. and abroad and had budgeted a total of $4.5 billion for rental machines, plant, and equipment. Not even the Manhattan Project, which produced the atomic bomb in World War II, cost so much (the government's costs up to Hiroshima are reckoned at $2 billion), nor, probably, had any other privately financed commercial project in history.

Such an effort changed IBM's nature in several ways:

> The company, which was essentially an assembler of computer components and a business-service organization, became a major manufacturing concern as well. It became the world's largest maker of integrated circuits, producing an estimated 150 million of the hybrid variety annually in the late 1960s.

> After some ambivalence, IBM abandoned any notion that it was simply another American company with a large foreign operation. The view now is that IBM is a fully integrated international company, in which the managers of overseas units are presumed to have the same capabilities and responsibilities as those in the U.S. The company's World Trade subsidiary stopped trying to develop its own computers; instead, it marketed the 360 overseas, and helped in the engineering and manufacturing of the 360.

> The company's table of organization was restructured significantly at least three times during the 360's development cycle. Several new divisions and their executives emerged, while others suffered total or partial eclipse. An old maxim of the IBM organization was that few men rose to line executive positions unless they had spent some time selling. A new group of technically oriented executives came to the forefront for

the first time, diluting some of the traditional power of the marketing men in the corporation.

The Missionaries and the Scientists

Oddly enough, the upheaval at IBM went largely unnoticed. The company was able to make itself over more or less in private. It was able to do so partly because IBM is so widely assumed to be an organization in which the unexpected simply doesn't happen. Outsiders viewing IBM presume it to be a model of rationality and order—a presumption related to the company's products which are, of course, instruments that enable (and require) their users to think clearly about management.

This image of IBM, moreover, had been furthered over the years by the styles of the two Watsons. Tom Watson, Sr., combined an intense devotion to disciplined thinking with formal, rather Victorian attitudes about conduct, clothes, and courtesy. The senior Watson's hostility toward drinking, and his demand that employees dedicate themselves totally to the welfare of the corporation, created a kind of evangelical atmosphere. When Tom Watson, Jr., took over from his father in 1956, the manner and style shifted somewhat, but the missionary zeal remained— now overlaid by a new dedication to the disciplines of science. The overlay reinforced the image of IBM as a chillingly efficient organization, one in which plans were developed logically and executed with crisp efficiency. It was hard to envision the company in a gambling role.

The dimensions of the 360 gamble are difficult to state precisely. The company's executives, who are men used to thinking of risks and payoffs in hard quantitative terms, insist that no meaningful figure could ever be put on the gamble—i.e., on the odds that the program would be brought off on schedule, or on the costs involved if it failed.

Outsailing the Boss

At the time, it scarcely seemed that any gamble at all was necessary. IBM was way out ahead of the competition, and looked as if it could continue smoothly in its old ways forever. Below the surface, though, IBM's organization didn't fit the changing markets so neatly anymore, and there really was, in Evans' phrase, a risk involved in doing nothing.

No one understood this more thoroughly, or with more sense of urgency, than one of the principal decision makers of the company, T. Vincent Learson. His entire career at IBM, which began in 1935, had been concerned with getting new products to market. In 1954 he was tapped by young Tom Watson as the man to spearhead the company's first big entry into the commercial computer field—with the 702 and 705 models. His success led to his promotion to vice president and group executive in 1956. In 1959 he took over both of the company's computer development and manufacturing operations, the General Products Division and the Data Systems Division.

Learson stood six foot six and was a tough and forceful personality. When he was managing any major IBM program, he tended to be impatient with staff reports and committees, and to operate outside the conventional chain of command; if he wanted to know why a program was behind schedule, he was apt to call directly on an executive at a much lower level who might help him find out. But he often operated indirectly, too, organizing major management changes without his own hand's being visible to the men involved. Though he lacked the formal scientific background that is taken for granted in many areas of IBM, Learson had a reputation as a searching and persistent questioner about any proposals brought before him; executives who had not done their homework might find their presentations falling apart under his questions— and might also find that he would continue the inquisition in a way that made their failure an object lesson to any spectators. And Learson was the most vigorous supporter of the company's attitude that a salesman who had lost an order without exhausting all the resources the company had to back him up deserved to be drawn and quartered.

At IBM, Learson was known as demanding, domineering, and direct—given to calling people anywhere in the company to find out firsthand what was going on. But Learson was also known as a friendly and whimsical man who was IBM's No. 1 cheerleader. He delighted in showing up unannounced, whether in a hospital to cheer up one of his sick secretaries or at a retirement dinner in Boston for a lady who ran a course in keypunching there when Learson was a young salesman. For all the diverging views of Learson, the man, as a top executive the degree of loyalty that Learson inspired was remarkable. Said one former executive, who was forced out of IBM: "I admire the man. He's like General Patton—someone you follow into battle."

Learson's personal competitiveness was something of a legend at IBM. It was significantly demonstrated in the Newport-to-Bermuda yacht race, in which Learson entered his own boat, the *Thunderbird*. He boned up on the history of the race in past years, and managed to get a navigator who had been on a winning boat three different times. He also persuaded Bill Lapworth, the famous boat designer, to be a crewman. Learson traveled personally to California to get one of the best spinnaker men available. All these competitive efforts were especially fascinating to the people at IBM because Tom Watson, Jr., also had an entry in the Bermuda race; he'd, in fact, been competing in it for years. Before the race Watson good-humoredly warned Learson at a board meeting that he'd better not win if he expected to stay at IBM. Learson's answer was not recorded. But Learson won the race. Watson's *Palowan* finished twenty-fourth on corrected time.

When Learson took over the computer group he found himself supervising two major engineering centers that had been competing with each other for some time. The General Products Division's facility in Endicott, New York, produced the low-priced 1401 model, by far the most popular of all IBM's computers—or of anyone else's to that date; something like 10,000 of them had been installed by the mid-1960s. Meanwhile, the Data Systems Division in Poughkeepsie made the more glamorous 7000 series, of which the 7090 was the most powerful. Originally, IBM had intended that the two centers operate in separate markets, but as computer prices came down in the late 1950s and as more versions of each model were offered, their markets came to overlap—and they entered a period in which they were increasingly penetrating each other's markets, heightening the feeling of rivalry. Each had its own development program, although any decision to produce or market a new computer, of course, had to be ratified at corporate headquarters. The rivalry between the two divisions was to become an element in, and be exacerbated by, the decision to produce the 360.

Both the 1401 and the 7000 series were selling well in 1960. But computer engineers and architects are a restless breed; they are apt to be thinking of improvements in design or circuitry five minutes after the specifications of their latest machines are frozen. In the General Products Division, most such thinking in 1960 and 1961 was long term; it was assumed that the 1401 would be on the market until about 1968. The thinking at the Data Systems Division concerned both long-range and more immediate matters.

A $20 Million Stretch

One of the immediate matters was the division's "Stretch" computer, which was already on the market but having difficulties. The computer had been designed to dwarf all others in size and power, and it was priced around $13,500,000. But it never met more than 70 percent of the promised specifications, and not many of them were sold. In May, 1961, Tom Watson made the decision that the price of Stretch should be cut to $8 million to match the value of its performance—at which level Stretch was plainly uneconomic to produce. He had to make the decision, it happened, just before he was to fly to California and address an industry group on the subject of progress in the computer field.

Before he left for the coast, an annoyed Watson made a few tart remarks about the folly of getting involved in large and overambitious projects that you couldn't deliver on. In his speech, he admitted that Stretch was a flop. ''Our greatest mistake in Stretch,'' he said, ''is that we walked up to the plate and pointed at the left-field stands. When we swung, it was not a homer but a hard line drive to the outfield. We're going to be a good deal more careful about what we promise in the future.'' Soon after he returned the program was quietly shelved; only seven of the machines were ultimately put in operation. IBM's overall loss on the program was about $20 million.

The Stretch fiasco had two consequences. One was that the company practically ignored the giant-computer field during the next two years—and thereby enabled Control Data to get a sizeable headstart in the market. Customers were principally government and university research centers, where the most complex scientific problems are tackled and computers of tremendous power are required. Eventually, in 1963, Watson pointed out that his strictures against overambitious projects had not been meant to exclude IBM from this scientific market, and the company later tried to get back into it. Its entry was to be the 360–90, the most powerful machine of the new line.

A second consequence of the Stretch fiasco was that Learson and the men under him, especially those in the Data Systems Division, were under special pressure to be certain that the next big project was thought out more carefully and that it worked exactly as promised. As it happened, the project the division had in mind in 1960–61 was a fairly ambitious one: it was for a line of computers, tentatively called the 8000 series, that would replace the 7000 series, and would also provide a limited measure of compatibility among the four models projected. The 8000 series was based on transistor technology, and therefore still belonged to the second generation; however, there had been so much recent progress in circuitry design and transistor performance that the series had considerably more capability than anything being offered by IBM at that time.

The principal sponsor of the 8000 concept was Fred Brooks, head of systems planning for the Poughkeepsie division. An imaginative, enthusiastic twenty-nine year old North Carolinian with a considerable measure of southern charm, Brooks became completely dedicated to the concept of the new series, and beginning in late 1960 he began trying to enlist support for it. He had a major opportunity to make his case for the 8000 program at a briefing for the division's management, which was held at Poughkeepsie in January 1961.

By all accounts, he performed well: he was relaxed, confident, informed on every aspect of the technology involved, and persuasive about the need for a change. Data Systems' existing product line, he argued, was a mixed bag. The capability of some models overlapped that of others, while still other capabilities were unavailable in any model. The 8000 series would end all this confusion. One machine was already built, cost estimates and a market forecast had been made, a pricing schedule had been completed, and Brooks proposed announcing the series late that year or early in 1962. It could be the division's basic product line until 1968, he added. Most of Brooks' auditors found his case entirely persuasive.

Enter the Man from Headquarters

Learson, however, was not ready to be sold so easily. The problems with Stretch must have been on his mind, and probably tended to make him look hard at any big new proposals. Beyond that, he was skeptical that the 8000 series would minimize the confusion in the division's product line, and he wondered whether the concept might not even *contribute* to the confusion. Learson had received a long memorandum from his chief assistant, Don Spaulding, on the general subject of equipment proliferation. Spaulding argued that there were already too many different computers in existence, and that they required too many supporting programs and too much peripheral equipment; some drastic simplification of the industry's merchandise was called for.

With these thoughts in mind, Learson was not persuaded that Brooks' concept was taking

IBM in the right direction. Finally, he was not persuaded that the company should again invest heavily in second-generation technology. Along with a group of computer users, he had recently attended a special course on industrial dynamics that was being given at the Massachusetts Institute of Technology. Much of the discussion had been over his head, he later recalled; but from what his classmates were saying he came away with the clear conviction that computer applications would soon be expanding rapidly, and that what was needed was a bold move away from "record keeping" and toward more sophisticated business applications.

There was soon direct evidence of Learson's skepticism about the 8000 series. Shortly after the briefing Bob Evans, who was then manager of processing systems in the General Products Division, was dispatched to Poughkeepsie as head of Data Systems' planning and development. He brought along a number of men who had worked with him in Endicott. Given the rivalry between the two divisions, it is not very surprising that he received a cool welcome. His subsequent attitude toward the 8000 concept ensured that his relations with Brooks would stay cool.

Evans made several different criticisms of the concept. The main one was that the proposed line was "non-homogeneous"—that is, it was not designed throughout to combine scientific and business applications. Further, he contended that it lacked sufficient compatibility within the line. It would compound the proliferation problem. He also argued that it was time to turn to the technologies associated with integrated circuits.

Blood on the Floor

For various reasons, including timing, Brooks was opposed, and he and Evans fought bitterly for several months. At one point Evans called him and quietly mentioned that Brooks was getting a raise in salary. Brooks started to utter a few words of thanks when Evans said flatly, "I want you to know I had nothing to do with it."

In March 1961, Brooks had a chance to make a presentation to the corporate management committee, a group that included Tom Watson, his brother, A.K. Watson, who headed the World Trade Corp., Albert Williams, who was then president of the corporation (later chairman of the executive committee), and Learson. Brooks made another effective presentation, and for a while he and his allies thought that the 8000 might be approved after all.

But early in May it became clear that Evans was the winner. His victory was formalized in a meeting, at the Gideon Putnam Hotel in Saratoga, of all the key people who had worked on the 8000. There, on May 15, Evans announced that the 8000 project was dead and that he now had the tough job of reassigning them all to other tasks. In the words of one participant, "There was blood all over the floor."

Evans now outlined some new programs for the Data Systems Division. His short-term program called for an extension of the 7000 line, both upward and downward. At the lower end of the line there would be two new models, the 7040 and the 7044. At the upper end there would be a 7094 and a 7094 II. This program was generally non-controversial, except for the fact that the 7044 had almost exactly the same capabilities as a computer called Scamp, which was being proposed by another part of IBM. It would obviously make no sense to build both computers; and, as it happened, Scamp had some powerful support.

Scamp was a small scientific computer developed originally for the European market. Its principal designer was John Fairclough, a young man (he was then thirty) working in the World Trade Corp.'s Hursley Laboratory, sixty miles southwest of London. The subsidiary had a sizable stake in Scamp. It had been trying for many years to produce a computer tailored to the needs of its own markets, but had repeatedly failed, and had therefore been obliged to sell American-made machines overseas.

But Scamp looked especially promising, and the subsidiary's executives, including Fairclough and A.K. Watson, were confident that it would meet American standards. It had previously tested well and attracted a fair amount of attention in IBM's American laboratories. Evans himself came to Hursley to look at it, and was impressed. But its similarity to the 7044 finally took Fairclough and some associates to the U.S. to test their machine against a 7044 prototype.

Mere Equality Won't Do

As things turned out, Scamp did about as well as the 7044—but, also as things turned out, that wasn't good enough. Evans and Learson were resolved to stretch out the 7000 line, but opposed to anything that would add to proliferation. In principle, A.K. Watson, who had always run World Trade as a kind of personal fiefdom, could have stepped in and ordered the production of Scamp on his own authority. In practice, he decided the argument against proliferation was a valid one. And so, in the end, he personally gave the order to drop Scamp. Fairclough got the news one day soon after he had returned to England, and he found himself with a sizable staff that had to be reassigned. He says that he considered resigning, but instead worked off his annoyance by sipping Scotch and brooding much of the night.

Evans and Learson had also agreed that Data Systems should try its hand at designing a computer line that would blanket the market. The General Products Division was asked to play a role in the new design, but its response was lukewarm, so the bulk of the work at this stage fell to Data Systems. The project was dubbed NPL, for new product line; the name System /360 was not settled on until much later. To head the project, Evans selected his old adversary Brooks— a move that surprised a large number of IBM executives, including Brooks himself.

Still smarting over the loss of the 8000 project, and suspicious that the NPL was just a "window-dressing" operation, Brooks accepted the job only tentatively. To work with him, and apparently to ensure the NPL did not end up as the 8000 under a new name, Evans brought Gene Amdahl, a crack designer whom the company had called on to work on several earlier computers. However, Amdahl's influence was offset by that of another designer, Gerrit Blaauw, a veteran

and past supporter of the 8000 project. Brooks' group received enough money to show that the company took NPL seriously (the first-year appropriation was $3,800,000), but Amdahl and Blaauw disagreed on design concepts, and the project floundered until November of 1961.

Even to the trained eye IBM's main divisions appeared to be in excellent health in the summer of 1961. The General Products Division, according to Evans, was "fat and dumb and happy" in the lower end of the market, selling the 1401 at a furious rate, and still feeling secure about its line through about 1968. The World Trade Corp. was growing rapidly, although it had suffered its third major setback on getting a computer line of its own. The Data Systems Division was extending its old 7000 line to meet the competition, and working on the NPL.

THE PROLIFERATING PRODUCTS

But it was around this time that Tom Watson and Learson—then a group executive vice president, and nominally at least working under Albert Williams, the company president— developed several large concerns. There was the absence of any clear, overall concept of the company's product line; fifteen or twenty different engineering groups scattered throughout the company were generating different computer products, and while the products were in most cases superior, the proliferation was putting overwhelming strains on the company's ability to supply programming for customers. The view at the top was that IBM required some major changes if it expected to stay ahead in the computer market when the third generation came along.

Between August and October, 1961, Watson and Learson initiated a number of dialogues with their divisional lieutenants in an effort to define a strategy for the new era. By the end of October, though, neither of them believed that any strategy was coming into focus. At this point Learson made a crucial decision. He decided to set up a special committee, composed of representatives from every major segment of the company, to formulate some policy guidance. The committee was called SPREAD—an acronym for systems programming, research, engineering, and development. Its chairman was John Haanstra, then a vice president of the General Products Division. There were twelve other members, including Evans, Brooks, and Fairclough.

The SPREAD Committee —Fall 1961

The SPREAD Committee was conducted informally, but with a good amount of spirited discussion. For the same purposes it broke up into separate committees, such as one on programming capability. Haanstra, as one member put it, acted as a hammer on the committee anvil, forcing ideas into debate and demanding definitions. Still, there was some feeling that Haanstra was bothered by the fact that the group was heavily represented by "big machine" oriented men.

The progress of the committee during November was steady, but it was also, in Learson's view, "hellishly slow." Suddenly Haanstra found himself promoted to the presidency of the General Products Division and Bob Evans took over as chairman of SPREAD. The committee meetings were held in the New Englander Motor Hotel, just north of Stamford, Connecticut. In effect, although not quite literally, Learson locked the doors and told the members that they couldn't get out until they had reached some conclusions.

While Evans accelerated the pace of the sessions somewhat, Fred Brooks increasingly emerged as the man who was shaping the direction of the committee recommendations. This was not very surprising, for he and his group had had a headstart in thinking out many of the issues. By December 28, 1961, the SPREAD Committee had hammered out an eighty page statement of its recommendations. On January 4, 1962, the committee amplified the report for the benefit of the fifty top executives of the corporation.

Brooks was assigned the role of principal speaker on this occasion. The presentation was split into several parts and took an entire day. The main points of the report were:

There was a definite need for a single, compatible family of computers ranging from one with the smallest existing core memory, which would be below the 1401 line, to one as powerful as IBM's biggest—at that time the 7094. In fact, the needs were said to extend beyond the IBM range, but the report expressed doubt that compatibility could be extended that far.

The new line should not be aimed simply at replacing the popular 1401 or 7000 series, but at opening up whole new fields of computer applications. At that time compatibility between those machines and the new line was not judged to be of major importance, because the original timetable on the appearance of the various members of the new family of computers stretched out for several years.

The System/360 must have both business and scientific applications. This dual purpose was a difficult assignment because commercial machines accept large amounts of data but have little manipulative ability, while scientific machines work on relatively small quantities of data that are endlessly manipulated. To achieve duality the report decided that each machine in the new line would be made available with core memories of varying sizes. In addition, the machine would provide a variety of technical and esoteric features to handle both scientific and commercial assignments.

Information input and output equipment, and all other peripheral equipment, must have "standard interface"—so that various types and sizes of peripheral equipment could be hitched to the main computer without missing a beat. This too was to become an important feature of the new line.

Learson recalled the reaction when the presentation ended. "There were all sorts of people up there and while it wasn't received too well, there were no real objections. So I said to them, 'All right, we'll do it.' The problem was, they thought it was too grandiose. The report said we'd have to spend $125 million on programming the system at a time when we were spending only about $10 million a year for programming. Everybody said you just couldn't spend that amount. The job just looked too big to the marketing people, the financial people, and the engineers. Everyone recognized it was a gigantic task that would mean all our resources were tied up in one project—and we knew that for a long time we wouldn't be getting anything out of it.''

APRIL 1964—PUBLIC ANNOUNCEMENT

When Tom Watson, Jr., made what he called "the most important product announcement in the company's history," he created quite a stir. International Business Machines is not a corporation given to making earth-shaking pronouncements casually, and the declaration that it was launching an entirely new computer line, the System /360, was headline news. The elaborate logistics that IBM worked out in order to get maximum press coverage—besides a huge assembly at Poughkeepsie, IBM staged press conferences on the same day in sixty-two cities in the U.S. and in fourteen foreign countries—underscored its view of the importance of the event. And the fact that the move until then had been a closely guarded secret added an engaging element of surprise. . . . In the scattered locations where IBM plans, builds, and sells its products, there was, on that evening of April 7, 1964, a certain amount of dancing in the streets. . . .

But the managerial and organizational changes that were brought about by the company's struggle to settle on, and then to produce and market, the new line [had very long term] effects. In each of these several aspects, past, present, and future were closely intertwined.

The Rising Cost of Asking Questions

No part of the whole adventure of launching System /360 was as tough, as stubborn, or as enduring as the programming. Early in 1966, talking to a group of IBM customers, Tom Watson, Jr., said ruefully: "We are investing nearly as much in System /360 programming as we are in the entire development of System /360 hardware. A few months ago the bill for 1966 was going to be $40 million. I asked Vin Learson last night before

I left what he thought it would be for 1966 and he said $50 million. Twenty-four hours later I met Watts Humphrey, who is in charge of programming production, in the hall here and said, 'Is this figure about right? Can I use it?' He said it's going to be $60 million. You can see that if I keep asking questions we won't pay a dividend this year.''

Watson's concern about programming went back to the beginnings of the System /360 affair. By late 1962 he was sufficiently aware of the proportions of the question to invite the eight top executives of IBM to his ski lodge in Stowe, Vermont, for a three-day session on programming. The session was conducted by Fred Brooks, the corporate manager for the design of the 360 project, and other experts; they went into the programming in considerable detail. While the matter can become highly technical, in general IBM's objective was to devise an "operating system" for its computer line, so that the computers would schedule themselves, without manual interruption, and would be kept working continuously at or near their capacity. At the time it announced System /360, IBM promised future users that it would supply them with such a command system.

Delivery on that promise was agonizingly difficult. Even though Tom Watson and the other top executives knew the critical importance of programming, the size of the job was seriously underestimated. The difficulty of coordinating the work of hundreds of programmers was enormous. The operating system IBM was striving for required the company to work out many new ideas and approaches; as one company executive said, "We were trying to schedule inventions, which is a dangerous thing to do in a committed project." Customers came up with more extensive programming tasks than the company had expected, and there were inevitable delays and slowdowns. The difficulties of programming prevented some users from getting the full benefits from their new machines for years. The company didn't have most of the bugs out of the larger systems' programming until at least mid-1967—well behind its expectations.

The Cold Realities of Choice

In technology, IBM was also breaking new ground. During the formative years of the decisions about the technology of System /360, a lengthy report on the subject was prepared by the *ad hoc* Logic Committee, headed by Erich Bloch, a specialist in circuitry for IBM. Eventually, the Logic Committee report led to the company's formal commitment to a new hybrid kind of integrated-circuit technology—a move that, like many other aspects of the 360 decision, is still criticized by some people in the computer industry, both inside and outside of IBM.

The move, though, was hardly made in haste. The whole computer industry had raced through two phases of electronic technology—vacuum tubes and transistors—between 1951 and 1960. By the late 1950s it was becoming apparent that further technological changes of sweeping importance were in the offing. At that time, however, IBM was not very much of a force in scientific research, its strengths lying in the assembling and marketing of computers, not in their advanced concepts. The company's management at the time had the wit to recognize the nature of the corporate deficiency, and to see the importance of correcting it. In 1956, IBM hired Dr. Emanuel Piore, formerly chief scientist of U.S. naval research. Piore became IBM's director of research and a major figure in the technological direction that the company finally chose for its System /360.

In the end, the choice narrowed to two technologies. One was monolithic integrated circuitry: putting all the elements of a circuit—transistors, resistors, and diodes—on one chip at one time. The other was hybrid integrated circuitry—IBM rather densely termed it "solid logic technology"—which means making transistors and diodes separately and then soldering them into place. In 1961 the Logic Committee decided that the production of monolithic circuits in great quantities would be risky, and in any case would not meet the schedule for any new line of computers to be marketed by 1964.

There was little opposition to this recommendation initially, except among a few engineering purists. Later, however, the opposition strengthened. The purists believed that monolithic circuits were sure to come, and that the company in a few years would find itself frozen into a technology that might be obsolete before the investment could be recovered. However, the Logic Committee's recommendation on the hybrid approach was accepted; since that time, Watson has referred to the acceptance as "the most fortunate decision we ever made."

THE SECRETS CIRCUITS HIDE

The decision to move into hybrid integrated technology accelerated IBM's push into component manufacturing, a basic change in the character of the company. In the day of vacuum tubes and transistors, IBM had designed the components for its circuits, ordered them from other companies (a principal supplier: Texas Instruments), then assembled them to its own specifications. But with the new circuitry, those specifications would have to be built into the components from the outset. "Too much proprietary information was involved in circuitry production," said Watson. "Unless we did it ourselves, we could be turning over some of the essentials of our business to another company. We had no intention of doing that." In addition, of course, IBM saw no reason why it should not capture some of the profit from the manufacturing that it was creating on such a large scale.

The company's turn to a new technology jibed neatly with a previous decision made in 1960 by Watson at the urging of the man who was then IBM president, Al Williams, that the company should move into component manufacturing. By the time the decision to go into hybrid circuits was made, IBM already had started putting together a component manufacturing division. Its general manager was John Gibson, a Johns Hopkins Ph.D. in electrical engineering. Under Gibson, the new division won the authority, hitherto divided among other divisions of the company, to designate and to buy the components for computer hardware, along with a new authority to manufacture them when Gibson thought it appropriate.

This new assignment of responsibility was resented by managers in the Data Systems and General Products divisions, since it represented a limitation of their authority. Also, they protested that they would be unable to compare the price and quality of inhouse components with those made by an outside supplier if they lost their independence of action. But Vincent Learson, then group executive vice president, feared that if they kept their independence they would continue to make purchases outside the company, and that IBM as a consequence would have no market for its own component output. He therefore put the power of decision in Gibson's hands. IBM's board, in effect, ruled in Gibson's favor when, in 1962, it authorized the construction of a new manufacturing plant, and the purchase of its automatic equipment, at a cost of over $100 million.

Systems Design: Worldwide

While IBM was making up its corporate mind about the technology for System /360, the delegation of specific responsibilities was going ahead. Learson designated Bob Evans, now head of the Federal Systems Division, to manage the giant undertaking. Under Evans, Fred Brooks was put in charge of all the System /360 work being done at Poughkeepsie, where four of the original models were designed; he was also made manager of the overall design of the central processors. The plant at Endicott was given the job of designing the model 30, successor to the popular 1401, which had been developed there. And John Fairclough, a systems designer at World Trade, was assigned to design the model 40 at the IBM lab at Hursley, England.

Out of the Hursley experience came an interesting byproduct that had significant implications for IBM's future. With different labs engaged in the 360 design, it was vital to provide for virtually instant communication between them. IBM therefore leased a special transatlantic line between its home offices and the engineers

in England, and later in Germany. The international engineering group was woven together with considerable effectiveness, giving IBM the justifiable claim that the 360 computer was probably the first product of truly international design.

In a Tug-of-War, Enough Rope to Hang Yourself

Even in a corporation inured to change, people resist change. By 1963, with the important decisions on the 360 being implemented, excitement about the new product line began to spread through the corporation—at least among those who were privy to the secret. But this rising pitch of interest by no means meant that the struggle inside the company was settled. The new family of computers cut across all the old lines of authority and upset all the old divisions. The System / 360 concepts plunged IBM into an organizational upheaval.

Resistance came in only a mild form from the World Trade Corp., whose long-time boss was A.K. Watson, Tom's brother. World Trade managers always thought of European markets as very different from those in the U.S., and as requiring special considerations that U.S. designers would not give them. Initially they had reservations about the concept of a single computer family, which they thought of as fitted only to U.S. needs. But when IBM laboratories in Europe were included in the formulation of the design of some of the 360 models, the grumblings from World Trade were muted. Later A.K. Watson was made vice chairman of the corporation and Gilbert Jones, formerly the head of domestic marketing of computers for the company, took over World Trade. These moves further integrated the domestic and foreign operations, and gave World Trade assurance that its voice would be heard at the top level of the corporation.

The General Products Division, for its part, really bristled with hostility. Its output, after all, accounted for two-thirds of the company's revenues for data processing. It had a popular and profitable product in the field, the 1401, which the 360 threatened to replace. The executive in charge of General Products, John Haanstra, fought against some phases of the 360 program. Haanstra thought the new line would hit his division hard. He was concerned, from the time the System /360 program was approved, about the possibility that it would undermine his division's profits. Specifically, he feared that the cost of providing compatibility in the lower end of the 360 line (which would be General Products' responsibility) might price the machines out of the market. Later he was to develop some more elaborate arguments against the program.

Long after the company's SPREAD Committee had outlined the System /360 concept, and it had been endorsed by IBM's top management, there were numerous development efforts going on inside the company that offered continuing alternatives to the concept—and they were taken seriously enough, in some cases, so that there were fights for jurisdiction over them. Early in 1963, for example, there was a row over development work at IBM's San Jose Laboratory, which belonged to the General Products Division. It turned out that San Jose—which had been explicitly told to stop the work—was still developing a low-power machine similar to the one being worked on in World Trade's German lab. When he heard about the continuing effort, A.K. Watson went to the lab, along with Emanuel Piore, and seems to have angrily restated his demand that San Jose cut it out. Some people from San Jose were then transferred to Germany to work on the German machine, and the General Products effort was stopped. In the curious way of organizations, though, things turned out well enough in the end; the German machine proved to be a good one, and the Americans who came into the project contributed a lot to its salability. With some adaptations, the machine was finally incorporated into the 360 line, and, as the model 20 it later sold better than probably any other in the series.

TOP MANAGEMENT SHIFTS

In the fall of 1963, Tom Watson . . . made some new management assignments that reflected the impact of the 360 program on the corporation.

Learson was shifted away from supervising product development and given responsibility for marketing, this being the next phase of the 360 program. Gibson took over Learson's former responsibilities. The increasing development of IBM into a homogeneous international organization was reflected in the move up of A.K. Watson from World Trade to corporate vice chairman. He was succeeded by Gilbert Jones, former head of domestic marketing. Piore became a group vice president in charge of research and several other activities.

One reason for Watson's interest in speeding up the 360 program in late 1963 was an increasing awareness that the IBM product line was running out of steam. The company was barely reaching its sales goals in this period. Some of this slowdown, no doubt, was due to mounting rumors about the new line. But there was another, critical reason for the slowdown: major customers were seeking ways of linking separate data-processing operations on a national basis, and IBM had limited capability along that line. Finally, IBM got a distinctly unpleasant shock in December 1963, when the Honeywell Corp. announced a new computer. Its model 200 had been designed along the same lines as the 1401—a fact Honeywell cheerfully acknowledged—but it used newer, faster, and cheaper transistors than the 1401 and was therefore priced 30 percent below the IBM model. To make matters worse, Honeywell's engineers had figured out a means by which customers interested in reprogramming from an IBM 1401 to a Honeywell 200 could do so inexpensively. The vulnerability of the 1401 line was obvious, and so was the company's need for the new line of computers.

It was around this time that some IBM executives began to argue seriously for simultaneous introduction of the whole 360 family. There were several advantages to the move. One was that it would have a tremendous public-relations impact and demonstrate the distinctive nature of IBM's new undertaking. Customers would have a clear picture of where and how they could grow with the computer product line, and so would be more inclined to wait for it. Finally, there might be an antitrust problem in introducing the various

360 models sequentially. The Justice Department might feel that an IBM salesman was improperly taking away competitors' business if he urged customers not to buy their products because of an impending announcement of his own company's new model. IBM had long had a company policy under which no employee was allowed to tell a customer of any new product not formally announced by the management. (Several employees have, in fact, been fired or disciplined for violating the rule.) Announcing the whole 360 line at once would dispose of the problem.

Learson Stages a Shoot-Out

Beginning in late 1963, then, the idea of announcing and marketing the 360 family all at once gained increasing support. At the same time, by making the 360 program tougher to achieve, the idea gave Haanstra some new arguments against the program. His opposition now centered on two main points. First, he argued that the General Products manufacturing organization would be under pressure to build in a couple of years enough units of the model 30 to replace a field inventory of the 1401 that had been installed over a five-year period. He said that IBM was in danger of acquiring a huge backlog, one representing perhaps two or three years' output, and that competitors, able to deliver in a year or less, would steal business away.

But Haanstra's argument was countered to some extent by a group of resourceful IBM engineers. They believed that the so-called "read-only" storage device could be adapted to make the 360–30 compatible with the 1401. The read-only technique, which involved the storing of permanent electronic instructions in the computer, could be adapted to make the model 30 act like a 1401 in many respects: the computer would be slowed down, but the user would be able to employ his 1401 programs. IBM executives had earlier been exposed to a read-only device by John Fairclough, the head of World Trade's Hursley Laboratory in England, when he was trying (unsuccessfully) to win corporate approval for his Scamp computer.

Could the device really be used to meet

Haanstra's objections to the 360–30? To find out, Learson staged a "shoot-out" in January 1964, between the 1401-S and the model 30. The test proved that the model 30, "emulating" the 1401, could already operate at 80 percent of the speed of the 1401-S—and could improve that figure with other adaptations. That was good enough for Learson. He notified Watson that he was ready to go, and said that he favored announcing the whole System/360 family at once.

"Going . . . Going . . . Gone!"

Haanstra was still not convinced. He persisted in his view that his manufacturing organization probably could not gear up to meet the production demand adequately. On March 18 and 19, a final "risk-assessment" session was held at Yorktown Heights to review once again every debatable point of the program. Tom Watson, Jr., President Al Williams, and thirty top executives of the corporation attended. This was to be the last chance for the unpersuaded to state their doubts or objections on any aspect of the new program — patent protection, policy on computer returns, the company's ability to hire and train an enormous new work force in the time allotted, etc. Haanstra himself was conspicuously absent from this session. In February he had been relieved of his responsibilities as president of the General Products Division and assigned to special duty— monitoring a project to investigate the possibility of IBM's getting into magnetic tape. (He later became a vice president of the Federal Systems Division.) At the end of the risk-assessment meeting, Watson seemed satisfied that all the objections to the 360 had been met. Al Williams, who had been presiding, stood up before the group, asked if there were any last dissents, and then, getting no response, dramatically intoned, "Going . . . going . . . gone!"

The April 7, 1964 announcement of the program unveiled details of six separate compatible computer machines; their memories would be interchangeable, so that a total of nineteen different combinations would be available. The peripheral equipment was to consist of forty different input and output devices, including printers, optical scanners, and high-speed tape drives. Delivery of the new machines would start in April 1965.

The Nature of the Risk

The basic announcement of the new line brought a mixed reaction from the competition. The implication that the 360 line would make obsolete all earlier equipment was derided and minimized by some rival manufacturers, who seized every opportunity to argue that the move was less significant than it appeared . . . [or claimed it was unfeasible or uneconomic for customers].

But some of the competition was concerned enough about the System /360 to respond to its challenge on a large scale. During the summer of 1964, General Electric announced that its 600 line of computers would have time-sharing capabilities. The full import of this announcement hit IBM that fall, when MIT, prime target of several computer manufacturers, announced that it would buy a G.E. machine. IBM had worked on a time-sharing program back in 1960 but had abandoned the idea when the cost of the terminals involved seemed to make it uneconomic. G.E.'s success caught IBM off base and in 1964 and 1965 it was scrambling madly to provide the same capability in the 360 line. Late in 1964, RCA announced it would use pure monolithic integrated circuitry (i.e., as opposed to IBM's hybrid circuitry) in some models of its new Spectra 70 line. This development probably led to a certain amount of soul-searching at IBM.

In the end, . . . the company felt that the turn to monolithic circuitry did not involve capabilities that threatened the 360 line; furthermore, if and when monolithic circuitry ever did prove to have decisive advantages over IBM's hybrid circuitry, the company was prepared—the computers themselves and some three-quarters of the component manufacturing equipment could be adapted fairly inexpensively to monolithics. As for time-sharing, any anxieties IBM had about that were eased in March 1965, when Watts Humphrey, a systems expert who had been given the assignment of meeting the time-sharing challenge, got the job done. . . .

IBM announced additions to the 360 line in 1964 and 1965. One was the model 90, a supercomputer type, designed to be competitive with Control Data's 6800. Another was the 360 – 44, designed for special scientific purposes. Also, there was the 360 – 67, a large time-sharing machine. Another, the 360 –20, represented a pioneering push into the low end of the market. None of these were fully compatible with the models originally announced, but they were considered part of the 360 family.

System /360 underwent many changes after the concept was originally brought forth back in 1962 and even after Watson's announcement in 1964. More central processors were later offered in the 360 line; some of them had memories that were much faster than those originally offered. The number of input-output machines [increased several times]. . . .

"Major Reshufflements"

IBM had several managers trying to keep the 360 program on track in 1964 –65. Gibson, who had succeeded Learson in the job, was replaced late in 1964. His successor, Paul Knaplund, lasted about another year. . . . In 1965 there was one item of unalloyed bad news: the company had suffered heavy setbacks at the high end of the 360 line—i.e., in its efforts to bring forth a great supercomputer in the tradition of Stretch. In 1964 it wrote off $15 million worth of parts and equipment developed specifically for the 360 –90.

There were signs at about this time that the 360 program was still generating other reshufflements of divisions and personnel. Dr. Piore had been freed from operational duties and responsibilities and given a license to roam the company checking on just about all technical activities. Some of his former duties were placed in a division headed by Eugene Fubini, a former Assistant Secretary of Defense and the Pentagon's deputy director of research and engineering before he joined IBM in 1965. Fubini was one of the first outsiders ever brought into the company at such a high executive level. Another change represented a comeback for Stephen Dunwell, who had managed the Stretch program and had been made the goat for its expensive failure to perform as advertised. When IBM got into the 360 program, its technical group discovered that the work done on Stretch was immensely valuable to them; and Watson personally gave Dunwell an award as an IBM fellow (which entitled him to work with IBM backing, for five years, on any project of his choosing).

In 1971 58-year-old Tom Watson, Jr., slowed by poor health, turned over the chairmanship of the company to T. Vincent Learson. While Learson was taking on the top job, computer makers were rattled by a recession and shaken by a series of corporate crises. 1970–72 saw General Electric Co. and RCA withdraw from the field, cutting the number of U.S. computer makers from nine to seven. The industry was struck by a backlash from oversold customers, a new generation of computers, and a switch in government expenditures away from R&D and toward social services. Customers became sales resistant and cost conscious.

Business Week commented:

> The Learson era in the computer business promises to be vastly different from the preceding two decades of frantic growth, during which IBM's yearly revenues increased more than thirty-fold—from $226 million in 1951 to $8.2 billion this year. The outlook for the industry is for a lower rate of growth from a bigger base. But the growth will still be a very healthy 10% to 12% annually, depending on the state of the general economy. If IBM merely holds its present share of the market, this pace of growth would mean annual increments in its revenues of around half a billion dollars. . . .

On his 60th birthday in 1972, T.V. Learson surprised nearly everyone by announcing his retirement after only 18 months as chairman. Said Learson, "We believe very strongly that in a business as technical and competitive as this, the interests of IBM will be best served by management teams of younger upcoming men and women. . . ." Learson's successor as chairman, 52 year old Frank Cary, was a quieter and more amiable executive, yet few observers felt the management shuffle heralded any significant departure from the vigorous marketing oriented practices of the Learson era.

QUESTIONS

1. What stimulated the change in strategy at the time of the 360? Evaluate the process by which change was brought about.
2. Evaluate Mr. Learson as a change manager. Why does he act this way?
3. How could other companies have taken advantage of IBM's 360 strategy? What should IBM do about these?

FINANCIAL SERVICES INDUSTRY
REFERENCE NOTE

INTRODUCTION

If an industry is defined as a group of companies whose products are largely substitutable, the Financial Services Industry, per se, did not exist prior to the mid 1970s. Before that, each type of financial intermediary or institution was considered by consumers, regulators, and the institutions themselves to constitute a distinct, separate industry which had only minimal competition from other types of intermediaries. However, all types of financial intermediaries are basically similar because their (asset) portfolios consist of primary securities (claims against businesses and individuals) and their liabilities consist of secondary securities (claims against financial intermediaries).

The differences among intermediaries principally arose from the laws and regulations which (1) required some of them to invest in particular types of primary securities and (2) restricted the types of secondary securities they could issue.[1] The bulk of these laws and regulations, especially those separating commercial and investment banking were passed as a response to the collapse of the country's financial system during the Great Depression. Legislators believed that if they limited the powers of depository institutions and surrounded them with protective regulations, the overall banking system would be much safer.

A NEW WORLD

The period from 1973 to 1985 was a traumatic one for all of the major financial intermediaries.

Case copyright © 1985 by James Brian Quinn. Case prepared by Penny C. Paquette under the supervision of Professor Quinn.

They all found they suddenly were operating in a changed and constantly evolving environment. This note concentrates on the commercial banking and investment banking segments of the industry. However, other financial intermediaries experienced many of the same changes. Table 1 shows the major asset restructuring which occurred during this dramatic decade.

TRENDS

1973 saw an end to the fixed currency exchange rates which had long been used in international transactions. Then, as governments sought to control inflation by controlling money supply and worried less about money's price (interest rates), huge exchange rate fluctuations began taking place. With few exchange controls, differences in interest rates between countries were magnified into exchange rate shifts by movements of capital seeking higher returns. In the mid 1980s more than $200 billion of foreign exchange was traded every day.[2] Then another shock hit the monetary community. From the end of 1973 through the end of 1982 the U.S. inflation rate, stimulated by the oil price shocks of 1973/74 and 1979/80, was never less than 5%, ranging from $5\frac{3}{4}\%$ to over 15% (See Table 2).

Suddenly, interest rates capped by the government's Regulation Q at 5% for savings accounts made no sense. During the peak inflation period of 1978–1982 savings deposits fell by 25% while money market mutual funds grew by 152%, reaching a peak of $233 billion in November of 1982.[3] And on the average, paper assets failed to preserve their owners' wealth, let alone make them richer. From 1968 to 1980, the average

TABLE 1   ASSETS OF FINANCIAL INTERMEDIARIES (Billions $)

	1973	%	1983	%
Commercial Banks	832.7	46.5	2,341.8	41.6
Savings and Loan Assns.	264.4	14.8	806.5	14.3
Mutual Savings Banks	106.7	6.0	193.5	3.4
Credit Unions	18.9	1.1	82.0	1.5
Life Insurance Cos.	252.4	14.1	654.9	11.6
Other Insurance Cos.	25.7	1.4	249.1	4.4
Private Pension Funds	126.5	7.1	607.8	10.8
Finance Cos.	73.2	4.1	202.7	3.6
Securities Brokers & Dealers	22.6	1.3	214.8	3.8
Mutual Funds	46.5	2.6	113.6	2.0
Money Market Mutual Funds	—		162.5	2.9
Real Estate Investment Trusts	19.9	1.1	7.6	0.0
TOTAL	1,789.5		5,629.0	

Source: Statistical Information on the Financial Services Industry, 3rd ed., 1984. © American Bankers Association. Reprinted with permission. All rights reserved.

change in CPI was 8%. Common stocks, as measured by the S&P 500 Index, returned about the same %, and so did short-term money market instruments. Long-term high-quality corporate bonds actually lost 4% of their value each year in real terms. Real estate, on the other hand, increased in value by 250% from 1970 to 1980 while the CPI rose only 112%. Individuals consequently increased their mortgage debt half again as fast as they raised their total assets. Between 1970 and 1980 tangible assets as a % of total householder assets rose from 30 to 40%. Adjusted for inflation, householders' direct holdings of stocks fell 30% over the same period.[4] (See Table 3 at end of this section for statistics on ownership of various financial instruments in 1983.)

As the federal debt rose along with federal spending (from $243 billion in 1960 to $1.63 trillion by 1983[5]) all segments of the financial services industry were obliged to increase their proportion of total assets represented by government securities. The existence of huge federal deficits also brought greater uncertainty about the future to financial markets in general, further increasing upward pressures on money costs. Monetary policy makers struggled with problems of

TABLE 2   INFLATION RATES

	(1st Quarter)								
	'74	'75	'76	'77	'78	'79	'80	'81	'82
% Change in U.S. Consumer Price Index (CPI)	10	11	6.5	5.8	6.5	9.5	14.5	11.3	7.5

Source: Statistical Information on the Financial Services Industry, 3rd Ed., 1984. © American Bankers Association. Reprinted with permission. All rights reserved.

TABLE 3   OWNERSHIP OF VARIOUS FINANCIAL INSTRUMENTS, 1983 (*Estimated Values in Billions of Dollars*)

Institution	Total Assets	Common Stocks Amount	%	Corporate Bonds Amount	%	Mortgages Amount	%	U.S. Treasury/Agency Bonds Amount	%	Municipal Bonds Amount	%	Open Market Paper Amount	%	Loans Amount	%
Mutual savings banks	193	3	—	22	4	99	8	34	3	2	1	7	3	6	1
Savings and loans	814	—	—	—	—	531	40	125	10	—	—	9	4	26	2
Credit unions	106	—	—	—	—	6	1	32	3	—	—	—	—	52	5
Life insurance companies	654	70	3	226	37	151	11	51	4	11	2	29	11	—	—
Property/casualty insurance	230	50	2	26	4	—	—	30	2	89	19	—	—	—	—
Corporate pensions	419	265	12	69	11	5	—	64	5	—	—	—	—	—	—
State/local pensions	319	69	3	119	19	16	1	88	7	3	1	—	—	—	—
Endowments	98	75	4	16	3	2	—	3	—	—	—	2	1	—	—
Municipal bond funds	87	—	—	—	—	—	—	—	—	87	18	—	—	—	—
Mutual funds	125	73	3	12	2	—	—	7	—	—	—	5	2	—	—
Money market funds	161	—	—	—	—	—	—	30	2	—	—	72	29	—	—
REIT/mortgage banks	26	—	—	—	—	20	2	—	—	—	—	—	—	—	—
Broker/dealers	50	3	—	4	1	—	—	10	1	2	—	—	—	—	—
Foreign investors	370	131	6	38	6	—	—	168	13	—	—	33	13	—	—
Commercial banks	1,636	—	—	11	2	333	25	270	21	164	35	16	6	806	69
Households	4,652	1,413	66	76	12	157	12	494	38	113	24	46	18	—	—
State/local governments	78	—	—	—	—	—	—	88	7	—	—	—	—	—	—
Finance companies	247	—	—	—	—	—	—	—	—	—	—	—	—	225	19
Business corporations	114	—	—	—	—	—	—	17	1	—	—	35	14	61	5
Totals	10,379	2,151	100	618	100	1,320	100	1,511	100	471	100	254	100	1,175	100

Source: From *Inside Investment Banking* by Robert C. Perez. Copyright © 1984 by Praeger Publishers. Reprinted by permission of Praeger Publishers.

defining M1 (the basic money supply indicator including all checkable deposits) let alone controlling it as capital markets became increasingly volatile and global in nature. The demand deposit turnover rate in New York City rose from 243 in 1973 to approximately 1200 in 1982 and the income velocity of M1 rose from 5.02 to 6.39 over the same period.[6] Since quasi-checks could now be written on deposits in mutual funds, some believed they should be included in the calculation of M1. Money could be transferred easily into and out of Eurodollars by commercial banks, raising further questions about the nature of money supplies and their control by governments.

Interest and currency exchange rates were so volatile that a new financial futures market opened which operated like a commodities futures market and allowed both speculation and hedging. By 1981 financial intermediaries and others were writing 8 million interest rate futures contracts and more than 5 million currency exchange rate contracts per year.

Technology Changes

Technologically, the financial services world had changed dramatically. Computer and memory costs and performance improved so rapidly that electronics technologies spread quickly from back-room operations to products with which the customer interacted directly—such as Automatic Teller Machines (ATMs) and International Cash Management systems on corporate treasurers' desks. Advances in technology made it possible for a group of banks in the New York Clearing House to create CHIPS (Clearing House International Payments System) and handle 20 million transfers worth $60 trillion annually with same day settlements.[7] Electronics also made it possible for the National Association of Securities Dealers to create their automatic quotation and electronic national market system which in 1983 handled an annual volume of 3.7 million trades of 4.4 billion shares from multiple market makers.[8] Electronic communications integrated the world's capital markets into a single global system, and electronic funds transfer (EFT) systems increased

the flow of funds, the complexity, and the velocity of financial world transactions to the point where the use of electronic technology in all financial services sectors became a necessity.

Demographic Changes

Demographically, the 1970s and early '80s witnessed the coming of age of the "baby boom" generation and the beginning of the so-called "graying" of America as the number of people over 65 rose dramatically in comparison with those under 20. Two-income families became the norm and education levels in the general population rose steadily.

These demographic changes along with high rates of inflation in the late '70s/early '80s forced individuals and corporations to become much more sophisticated and value conscious financially. Individuals moved their money from low yield savings accounts and insurance policies into newly created money market funds whose returns exceeded inflation. And corporations hired highly trained financial staffs to explore alternatives to high cost external financial services. They began self-insuring for certain risks, setting up or acquiring their own financial subsidiaries, preparing their own securities issues, using EFT to maintain zero-balance checking accounts, and issuing commercial paper and tapping the Eurobond market rather than relying on bank loans.

Deregulation and New Competitors

In 1977 Merrill Lynch introduced its revolutionary Cash Management Account (CMA) which provided consumers with the services of a checking account, money market fund, and credit card as well as those of a traditional securities trading account. CMA typified both the consumer's growing sophistication and demands for convenience, and the development of "hybrid" money instruments which cut across the regulatory barriers between different segments of the financial services industry. Providers of financial services began invading each other's turf wherever a loophole or ambiguity in the laws permitted. There was a growing recognition that many of the barriers, especially geographic ones, established in the past had been made irrelevant by electronic funds transfer technologies, communications advances (like satellites and 800 numbers), the unregulated Euromarket, extensive private and business use of credit cards, and the ingenuity of companies both within and outside the industry to find chinks in the old regulatory armor.

Commercial banks and savings and loans were unable to respond effectively to the new competitive environment because of various regulations limiting (1) the interest rates they could pay on deposits, (2) the types of assets they could hold, and (3) their geographic markets. (Insurance companies and investment banks while regulated were not hampered by such limitations.) In the mid 1970s prompted by soaring inflation, regulators began a gradual process of "deregulation." Major milestones in that process included the Depository Institutions Deregulation and Monetary Control Act of 1980, the Garn-St. Germain Depository Institutions Act of 1982, and the July 1985 Supreme Court decision upholding the legality of regional interstate banking. (See the section on Commercial Banking for more details.)

In their efforts to compete in new areas many formerly specialized financial firms acquired or merged with firms already in those markets, creating "financial supermarkets" such as the Sears Financial Network, Shearson/Lehman/ American Express, and Prudential/Bache. Although many people questioned their ability to gain the benefits of synergy, these large, diversified financial service companies became formidable competitors. Competition among financial service providers was no longer based on old perceptions about a particular institution's or intermediary's traditional role, but on the quality of its products and services, its efficiency in pricing, its innovative use of technology, and its convenience and rendering of personal support services.[9] The following sections offer some pertinent facts about major segments of the new industry.

Keeping Up with Inflation?

Inflation and interest rates have enormous impact on pension funds. High inflation rates rapidly erode the purchasing power of fixed retirement benefits. For example, a 9% inflation rate could drop the value of a retiree's benefits by 58% at age 75 and by 82% at age 85.[10] Approximately 70% of all companies surveyed by the *Institutional Investor* in November 1983 said they had upgraded benefits to help retirees keep up with inflation, but they could make no promises for the future. More than 70% had raised their actuarial assumptions to reflect higher inflation and interest rates, but less than 50% said that the total return on their pension fund investments had kept up with the inflation rate over the past decade.[11] Pension funds increasingly acquired such inflation hedged assets as real estate and guaranteed investment contracts. Through the early 1980s, inflation driven salary increases as well as ERISA requirements had led to rapidly rising pension costs for companies. However, by 1983 these costs began leveling off.

COMMERCIAL BANKING

Commercial banks made up the largest segment of the Financial Services Industry with assets of $2.25 trillion in January 1985.[12] Although their share of deposits relative to other depository institutions had not changed much since 1973, their share of total financial assets had dropped while that of insurance companies, pension funds, finance companies, real estate investment trusts, open-ended investment companies, money market funds, and securities brokers and dealers grew.

The structure of commercial banking changed substantially from 1970–1983. Although the number of banks grew only moderately (13,976 in 1973 to 14,473 in 1983), average assets per bank soared. More importantly, the Bank Holding Company (BHC) became the dominant form of banking organization. (See Table 4.) Although small banks dominated the number of in-

TABLE 4 COMPARATIVE STATISTICS —HOLDING COMPANIES 1969–1980

	1969	1980
% of total domestic assets held by subs of BHCs		
Total	19.0	74.1
Multi-Bank	—	35.7
One-Bank	—	38.4
# of Multi-Bank Holding Cos.	86	361
# of banks controlled by Multi-Bank Holding Cos.	723	2,426
# of One-Bank Holding Cos.	1,352	2,544

Source: "Developments in Banking Structure, 1970–1981," Federal Reserve Bulletin, February 1982.

stitutions, the largest banks dominated the banking system. In 1980, those BHCs with consolidated assets of over $1 billion had 41.3% of all branches, 60.3% of all employees, and 69.2% of all assets.[13]

A BHC form of organization has many advantages. Perhaps the most significant are: (1) certain tax-related benefits, (2) the ability to supplement funds through sale of commercial paper, and (3) the capacity through subsidiaries to engage in nonbank activities on an interstate basis. In 1985 one-bank holding companies were permitted in all states. Three states prohibited multi-bank holding companies, and 15 others placed restrictions on them. The nonbank activities of BHCs were regulated by the Fed under the proviso that such activities must be "so closely related to banking . . . as to be a proper incident thereto." As of 1983, there were more than 10,000 interstate nonbank subsidiaries of BHCs and the largest BHCs operated in as many as 40 states.

Other changes in the banking structure included a tendency for states to liberalize their branching laws—allowing county-wide if not state-wide branching. Partly as a result of liberalized branching laws and partly in an effort to collect low-cost deposits, banks steadily expanded their branch networks, increasing the average number of branch offices from 1.91 in 1973 to 2.82 in 1983.

Bank Regulation

Commercial banks, like S&Ls, had a dual system of regulation—federal regulators overseeing federally chartered national banks and state regulators overseeing state chartered banks. In addition, the Federal Deposit Insurance Corporation (FDIC) examined member banks (which held 99% of all bank deposits and included many state chartered banks). The Federal Reserve Board regulated BHCs and the activities of state chartered banks that were held by BHCs. National banks, granted a charter by the Office of the Controller of the Currency (OCOC), were required to be members of the Federal Reserve System while state banks might elect not to be. The Federal Reserve System (Fed) was made up of a Board of Governors and 12 Federal Reserve Banks of which member banks were shareholders. (See Exhibit 1.)

The Fed's primary activities were the management of monetary policy and the supervision and regulation of its members. Member banks were required to deposit with the Fed "reserves" which were specified minimum percentages of each bank's demand and time deposits. No interest was paid on these funds but they could be used to provide a secondary source of liquidity for member banks in the form of "discount paper." The level of these reserve requirements

EXHIBIT 1   THE FEDERAL RESERVE SYSTEM: RELATIONSHIPS TO INSTRUMENTS
OF CREDIT POLICY

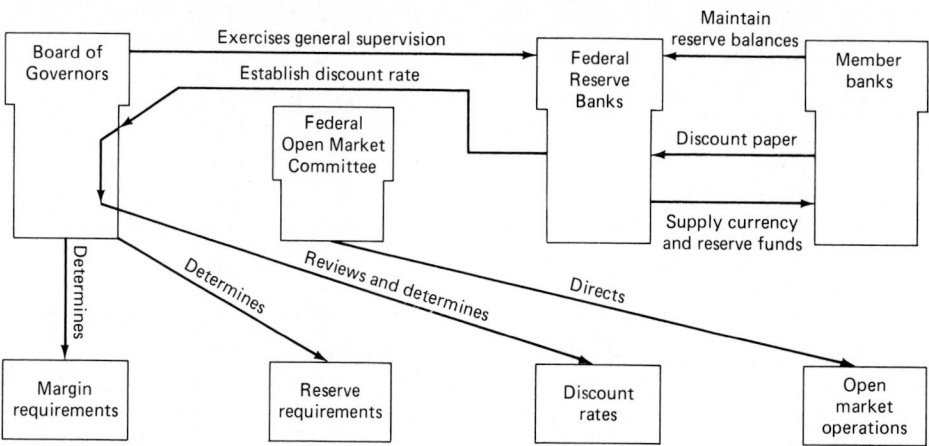

Source: Benton E. Gup, *Financial Intermediaries: An Introduction*, Houghton-Mifflin Co. 1976.

determined how far member banks could "expand" credit to their customers.

Membership in the Fed provided a bank with free access to the check clearing and collection, wire transfer, and securities storage systems run by the Fed as well as access to its low-rate discount funds. Non-member banks could obtain access to some of these services through relations with a "correspondent" member bank. However, since state non-member banks were often subject to less onerous reserve requirements, there were certain disincentives to membership. In fact, over the decade of the '70s the number of member banks had fallen steadily. The Fed felt that this hindered its conduct of monetary policy, despite the fact that the Fed could "create" money through the banks or withdraw it from circulation through its Open Market Operations.

The Depository Institutions Deregulation and Monetary Control Act of 1980 (DIDMCA) changed many of these relationships. It made all depository institutions (banks, S&Ls, savings banks, and credit unions) whether members or not, subject to the Fed's reserve requirements (although these were reduced from past levels). It then required the Fed to charge for all its services at full market rates and to offer them to

all depository institutions. The Fed had to compete with major banks and other enterprises for its share of those services—like clearing—which were not its exclusive domain. By mid 1985 a subsidiary of General Electric, Automatic Data Processing, Inc., GM's Electronic Data Systems, and NCR were competing with the Fed in processing payments between banks—automated clearinghouse businesses.[14]

Deregulation

During the period 1980 to 1985 there were three areas of banking which underwent "deregulation." The DIDMCA mandated the gradual removal of interest rate ceilings which allowed banks to compete more effectively for deposits during periods of high inflation/high interest rates. The Act also put banks and other depository institutions on a par in terms of reserve requirements.

Then, faced with increasing competition from nonbank competitors, major BHCs began to press vigorously on the Fed to loosen its definition of allowable "non-banking" activities. In 1982 the Bank of America applied for and received permission to acquire a discount brokerage firm, and in 1983 it acquired 24.9% of an insurance company. Citicorp tried but failed to obtain permission for a specialized securities subsidiary but was successful in winning approval for a data processing-oriented subsidiary. State banking commissions went even further in expanding permissible activities. In 1985, some states allowed banks to enter certain non-banking activities including: real estate development (13 states), travel agencies (12 states), management consulting (10 states), insurance underwriting (8 states), and various areas of investment banking (4 states).[15]

Finally, there was an inexorable movement towards some form of interstate banking. In May 1983, the Chairman of the Federal Reserve Board himself stated that "interstate banking exists de facto for everything but that portion of retail banking and other services that require a building."[16] But for BHCs to expand beyond the highly competitive business of lending to large corporations into consumer and small business banking they needed to be able to offer full-service banking. And the increasing use of technology requiring huge systems and investments demanded a large customer support base. Other competitors such as brokerage firms could sell services on a national level. The Bank Holding Company Act of 1970 allowed a state to permit an interstate bank acquisition/merger if it saw fit. By September 1985,

22 states had passed legislation allowing interstate mergers in specific circumstances. (See Table 5.)

In June 1985 the Court unanimously ratified interstate banking on a regional basis and thereby "unleashed a process of consolidation that makes nationwide banking a virtual certainty by the end of the decade."[17] In response, the House Banking Committee approved legislation to permit nationwide interstate banking after a five-year transition period. The bill would prohibit mergers that would result in one institution controlling more than 1% of the nation's deposits and mergers among the nation's 25 largest banks in terms of assets. The Senate Banking Committee had not acted but was unlikely to go along with the House bill.

The dual system of bank regulation was threatened by worries that (1) individual states might be too liberal in defining allowable bank activities and geographic expansion limits, and (2) individual states would be regulating entities that crossed state lines.

Reregulation

While federal and state regulators generally pursued a course of deregulation, the regulations which remained were more strictly enforced and

TABLE 5   STATES ALLOWING INTERSTATE BANK MERGERS

Circumstances	States	
National, nonreciprocal	Alaska Arizona	Maine
National, reciprocal	New York	Washington
Regional, nonreciprocal	Oregon	
Regional reciprocal with national trigger	Kentucky Nevada	Ohio Rhode Island
Regional, reciprocal with no national trigger	Connecticut Florida Georgia Idaho Indiana Maryland	Massachusetts North Carolina South Carolina Tennessee Utah Virgina

Source: "Banking Deregulation Benefits Many People But Stirs Some Worry," Wall Street Journal, September 30, 1985. With permission of the Wall Street Journal.

bank supervision was increased overall. In addition, there were two instances where regulation was increased and loopholes closed. The Fed had permitted BCHs to offer discount brokerage services, but in July 1985 the SEC extended its regulations to cover those services. It required banks to segregate those activities in separate subsidiaries and register them with the SEC. And the existence of so-called "limited-service" or "nonbank" banks was jeopardized by moves to close the loopholes which had enabled them to arise. A "limited-service" bank was a bank which either made commercial loans or accepted deposits but not both. Such banks fell outside of the legal definition of a commercial bank and thus were exempt from the BHC Act or other federal regulations which prohibited bank ownership across state lines or ownership by non-banking companies. More than 100 such banks had been chartered by BCHs and other non-bank competitors.

Payments Systems

In the mid '80s banks, which had maintained a virtual hegemony over third-party payments (check clearing and collection) systems, faced new competitors. Savings and Loan Associations, Savings Banks, and credit unions (the so-called "Thrifts") in 1980 began offering checking account services through NOW Accounts and share-draft accounts. Money market funds and brokerage firms (through their Cash Management Accounts) also began to offer checking and other financial transaction services. Initially, all these financial intermediaries chose to handle transactions through commercial banks. However, the Thrifts had direct access to the Fed's check collection and clearing services if they so choose.

Should the banks' pricing of payment services make it economical, new competitors could also enter this business. The volume of check processing handled by banks and by the Fed had grown from 59 billion in 1973 to almost 86 billion in 1983.[7] Domestic interbank transfers via the Fed's wire system had also grown significantly from 14.8 million transfers worth $30.8 trillion in 1977 to 38 million transfers worth $89.5 trillion in 1983.[7] The emergence of telephone bill paying, home banking, preauthorized payments, Automated Clearing House transactions (such as direct payroll deposits), and direct debit or point-of-sale systems—and their possible control by non-bank competitors—would also influence the future of the payments system. The development of direct debit systems would particularly affect bank credit card systems (like Master Card and Visa) which were currently paper-based systems. These systems embraced 132.5 million cards used at 4.2 million merchant outlets for a gross volume of $83.7 billion in 1983 (up from 55.8 million cards, 2.2 million outlets, and $13.9 billion in 1973).[7]

Cheap Funds?

With cheap funds from deposits readily available, bankers used to focus primarily on the loan aspects of their businesses. The 1970s quickly changed that view. Funds for loans were not necessarily easily accessible, especially at low prices. "The volatile behavior of interest rates, combined with the increasing sensitivity of both corporate and retail customers to interest rate changes made accurate control of both sides of a bank's balance sheet indispensable."[18] Asset-liability management emerged as a critical banking activity. Even with NOW Accounts and the removal of Regulation Q rate ceilings, banks had to compete hard for funds against many new competitors—both other depository institutions and other types of intermediaries. Banks' cost of funds had risen significantly—interest-free checking deposits fell from more than 17% of all funds raised in 1978 by the five largest BCHs to just over 9% in 1982.[19] (See Table 6.)

And obtaining deposits became ever more costly. Inflation drove up banks' operating costs, and they had to make major investments in new technologies to compete. The cost of maintaining large branch networks often became a burden as electronic funds transfer (EFT) systems increasingly offered economies both for front and back office operations. (See Exhibit 2.)

TABLE 6   ASSETS AND LIABILITIES OF FDIC-INSURED COMMERCIAL BANKS

	1973		1983	
Distribution of Assets (%)				
Commercial and Industrial Loans		19.1		22.4
Cash and Due from Deposit.				
Institutions		14.0		14.6
Real Estate Loans		14.3		14.4
Loans to Individuals		12.1		9.6
State/Local Securities		11.0		6.8
U.S. Treasury Securities		6.6		7.2
Federal Funds and RPs		4.1		4.0
Other U.S. Gov't Agency and				
Corporate Securities		3.3		3.3
Other Assets		15.6		17.9
Total Assets		$832.7		$2,341.8
Distribution of Liabilities (%)				
Deposits				
Demand	37.1		16.6	
Savings	—		19.7	
Time	44.7		29.1	
Total Domestic		81.9		65.5
In Foreign Offices		—		13.2
Total		81.9		78.7
Other Liabilities and				
Subordinated Notes and				
Debentures		11.8		15.3
Equity Capital		6.4		6.0

Perhaps most importantly, all financial intermediaries had to deal with the fact that interest rates (and therefore their cost of funds) had become extremely difficult to predict. The average cost of deposits (and thus the relative attractiveness of any specific deposit product) depends on (a) anticipated inflation rates, (b) the desire and will of the government to control monetary supply, (c) individual corporate appetites for debt financing, (d) the level of anticipated federal deficits, (e) interactions with trade deficits and the relative economic performance of other economies hence the attractiveness of other countries' currencies, (f) the performance of other financial markets, etc.

Less Lending/More Guarantees

The joint trends of internationalization and securitization of capital markets had changed the world of commercial banking dramatically. As the *Economist* commented, most of the banks' large customers, especially those with good credit ratings, had discovered ways to raise money preferable to fixed-priced bank loans. Since the early 1970s, such companies have increasingly chosen to issue commercial paper (selling their own securities directly to investors, cutting out the "turn" made by bankers). By 1985 the market for commercial paper was worth over $230 billion. The unregulated Eurobond market, in which "blue-

EXHIBIT 2   ECONOMIES OF SCALE

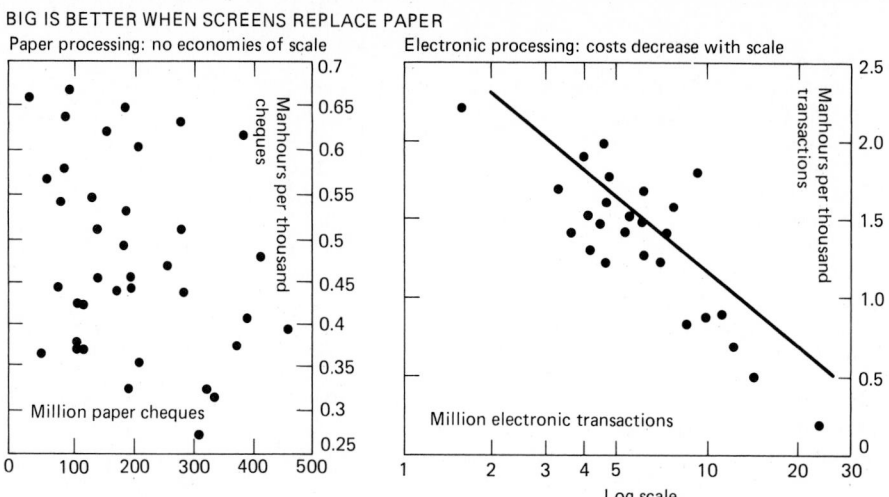

BIG IS BETTER WHEN SCREENS REPLACE PAPER

Source: Boston Consulting Group in " A New Awakening: Survey of International Bank-ing," *Economist*, March 24, 1984.

chip'' borrowers could raise money at lower rates than the American treasury pays on treasury bonds, was taking away other loan customers. The annual compound growth rate in Eurodollar bonds from 1979 to 1983 was 32.2% with total volume going from $12.6 billion to $38.4 bil-lion— exceeding the total value of bonds issued in the U.S.[20] Back in 1980, new bank loans far outstripped the volume of new bond offerings. But the Organization for Economic Cooperation and Development (OECD) recently estimated that for the first half of 1985 new international bond issues would total $80.1 billion and new interna-tional bank credits only $44.6 billion.[21]

Even companies with lower-quality credit ratings found alternatives to high-cost bank loans and private placement bonds. In the growing ''junk'' or high-yield bond market, companies with credit ratings from B to BBB could issue and readily sell bonds with compensatingly higher yields. Inflation and the realization that even on a risk-adjusted basis their yields may be higher have made junk bonds popular with high risk investors. In the U.S., some $14 billion of junk bonds were issued in 1984,[22] when they became

an especially popular instrument for use in hostile takeovers.

As banks found fewer opportunities to make profitable commercial loans and became locked in to their huge loans to LDCs (see discussion later), they began ''guaranteeing'' more through standby loans, Note Issuance Facilities (NIF), and swaps. NIFs are medium-term loans financed by selling short-term paper. Underwriting banks guaranteed the availability of funds to the bor-rower by buying any unsold notes at each roll-over date or by providing a stand-by credit line. NIFs were significantly less profitable than ordi-nary stand-by loans. In 1983 use of this device totaled $2.7 billion but by the first half of 1985 it had soared to $23 billion.[23] By 1982 volatile interest and currency exchange rates had led to the creation of the swaps market. In a swap two companies obtain financing in the market in which they are best rated and then swap their interest obligations, splitting the interest savings. For ex-ample, a medium sized U.S. company that wanted fixed rate funds might find them very expensive in this country, while a large foreign corporation might be happy with cheaper U.S. floating-rate money at costs below its domestic wholesale money markets. In effect, instead of borrowing long-term fixed-rate money from its U.S. banks, the medium sized company would borrow at floating rates (much less profitable for the banks) and use the proceeds to perform a swap with the foreign company.[22] In a swap, banks must cover lost interest but not the principal, if someone defaults. *Euromoney* estimated that close to $20 billion of long-term currency and interest rate swaps were completed in 1983, and the *Economist* stated that over 80% of Eurobond issues had a swap transaction linked to them. By the end of 1984, swaps amounted to about $80 billion.[23]

Competitive pressures forced down bank fees for such "guarantees" and often margins became extremely thin. Since this type of business did not count as assets on banks' balance sheets, many of them used it as a way to grow without having to add capital. Regulations requiring banks to set aside capital for off-balance-sheet business seemed likely.

INTERNATIONAL BANKING

International banking, both by U.S. banks and by their foreign competitors, had been greatly affected by (1) some countries' moves to allow foreign institutions a bigger role in their domestic financial markets, (2) the growth of international markets, such as the Eurocurrency markets, and (3) increases in the integration of domestic markets with international markets.

Foreign Operations of U.S. Banks

In an attempt to provide services to their largest customers (who were increasingly international or multinational in scope) and to expand their sources of funds and profits, U.S. banks looked more and more to international operations. By the early 1980s, 30 – 40% of all bank profits came from these operations, with the figure for many of the biggest money center banks exceeding 50%. International banking in the U.S. had its origins in the 1919 Edge Act which "permitted

banks to establish Edge Act Corporations (EACs) to engage in international banking activities and to acquire foreign banks by the establishment of subsidiary EACs."[24] EACs were used not only to move overseas but also to establish interstate networks of international banking services within the U.S., a trend which was accelerated by a 1979 ruling of the Fed explicitly excluding EACs from interstate branching rules. By 1983 there were 168 interstate EAC offices majority owned by U.S. banks.[7]

Although the aggregate impact of U.S. banks' overseas operations is very significant, only about 1% of U.S. banks have overseas branches or affiliates. By 1983 163 banks had 900 overseas units holding $476.2 billion in assets. However, ownership of more than 80% of these overseas branches and affiliates and 90% of all overseas banking assets was held by only 20 U.S. banks.[24] Nevertheless, many banks participated in international syndicated loans and in the interbank lending market. While U.S. banks went international primarily to service their U.S.-based customers, they soon diversified their foreign lending to include loans to foreign local firms, foreign banks, and foreign governments. And because their overseas EAC subsidiaries were not covered by the Glass-Steagall regulations which prohibited investment banking activities, U.S. banks became quite active in the Eurobond market and the capital markets of some foreign countries.

As world oil prices increased in the late 1970s, loans to Less Developed Countries (LDCs) by U.S. banks grew from $47 billion in 1977 to nearly $100 billion by 1982 with close to 50% of that amount in loans to only 3 countries (Mexico, Brazil, Argentina).[24] Non-OPEC LDCs' international bank debt also rose to 125% of their total exports.[7] Several large U.S. banks loaned more to LDCs than their total equity. As oil prices fell, an international debt crisis developed which was still being resolved in the mid 1980s. Although actual default had been avoided, the implications for participating U.S. banks were enormous. Their original and later work-out agreements locked them into continuing participation in LDC loans which might not ever be repaid. And the ensuing crisis brought new disclosure requirements and increased regulatory scrutiny in this area of banking.

International Banking in the U.S.

As foreign banks followed their own multinationals into the U.S. market, U.S. assets held by foreign banks grew from $24 billion in 1972 to more than $300 billion in 1983.[7] In the mid 1980s over 300 foreign banks had offices in various states. Prior to the passage of the International Banking Act (IBA) of 1978 foreign banks were only regulated by the states that chartered them; consequently they could offer many services their U.S. competitors could not. The IBA made all branches, agencies, and commercial lending subsidiaries of foreign banks subject to the U.S. Bank Holding Company Act—and thus to federal regulation and supervision (although many ongoing activities were "grandfathered").

On U.S. banks' home turf, Japanese, Australian, British, West German, Canadian and other foreign rivals grabbed big portions of the corporate loan market at least in part because they were willing to compete on a price basis. U.S. offices of foreign banks had made $12.8 billion of loans to companies in the U.S. in 1973 or 7.6% of total U.S. business loans. By 1983 they had made $84.5 billion of loans, capturing 18.3% of the total.[25] In addition, foreign banks helped drive down fees on standby letters of credit guaranteeing municipal-bond issues and guarantees of commercial paper.

In an effort to discourage further development of "offshore" banking operations, as of 1981 any U.S. depository institution, EAC, or U.S. office of a foreign bank was permitted to establish—through a relatively simple segregation on its books—an International Banking Facility (IBF). These units could accept foreign-source deposits and make overseas loans with the same freedom as an overseas subsidiary. By 1983 there were 400 IBFs having aggregate assets of almost $160 billion.[24] And in response to the Japanese trading companies success, the 1982 Export Trad-

ing Company (ETC) Act allowed banks to own and finance ETCs with approval from the Fed. Bank-owned ETCs were permitted to engage in all aspects of international trade, including financing, marketing coordination, order processing, and providing transportation support services. These support activities were especially useful to the "middle market companies" banks were assiduously trying to woo as loan customers, as these companies ventured more into international markets.

The Banks Respond

As banks lost much of the lending business they used to do with major U.S. and multinational companies, they had begun to market heavily to the next hierarchical level—the "middle market." Success in this market required a different type of relationship management. And since only the "lead" bank was likely to make good returns, ability to provide full-service banking was essential.

Another development in commercial lending was the creation of a genuine secondary market for loans. Banks wanting to increase equity-to-loan ratios transferred (sold) loans to a bank that needed something to do with its money. Corporate bonds and corporate loans thus became very similar, although bonds were still a more liquid, tradeable instrument. As the secondary market grew, it became ever harder to distinguish between lending for resale and underwriting corporate bonds, an activity forbidden to commercial banks by the Glass-Steagall Act of 1933.

As commercial banks' opportunities to earn profits from lending out cheap deposited funds steadily decreased, they were caught in another squeeze. Non-interest costs rose by an average of nearly 15% a year in 1979–82. By contrast, net interest income increased by an annual average of only 10.6% in the same period despite high inflation rates.[18] Fee income became an increasing percentage of banks' profits. Part of the apparent increase in fee income came from explicit charges for services which had been cross-subsidized in the past—such as check and credit card processing costs. Most fee business, however, was based on highly specialized skills or on offering the customer something new and different rather than on the continuing relationships banks were used to. Increasingly the push for fee income coincided with another trend—i.e., measuring bank performance on the basis of return on assets (which can be ballooned by fee income) rather than return on equity (which is most effectively fueled by asset growth).

Increasingly, commercial banks have pushed into obviously profitable investment banking activities. They began (1) participating fully in the Euromarket and other capital markets through Edge Act Corporations; (2) acting as agents in the "private placement" of commercial paper and "shelf-registered" corporate securities (see *Investment Banking* below); (3) offering retail discount brokerage services; (4) offering "corporate finance" advice and specialized services in areas like mergers and acquisitions, venture capital, and leveraged buyouts; (5) participating in Euromarket foreign exchange hedging and underwriting; (6) trading in interest rate futures and mortgage-backed securities, and (7) managing such stock related programs as dividend reinvestment and employee or payroll stock purchase plans. Glass-Steagall, however, continued to bar commercial banks from both major corporate securities underwriting and the high-volume industrial revenue bond business. Thus it was still impossible for a U.S. bank to offer a complete product and service system to corporate clients.

INVESTMENT BANKING

Investment banks' primary public capital-raising services are: (1) originating and managing a new financing issue; (2) underwriting (contracting to purchase an issuer's securities at a fixed price, thus assuming market risks); (3) distributing securities to institutional and individual investors. Related services and activities include corporate financial services such as consulting on corporate capital structures, advising on mergers and acquisitions, and handling certain secondary-market

activities like brokerage, market making, and arbitrage. Many investment banks also provide private placement services and offer some venture capital potentials. Recently, investment banks have also begun offering consumer-oriented products like Cash Management Accounts, mutual funds, or deferred annuities through their retail brokerage outlets.

The Way It Was

In the early 1970s corporations felt dependent on their primary investment banker for financial and market expertise and tended to maintain a long-term relationship with one firm—a partner of which often sat on their Boards of Directors. Capital markets tended to be local or national (rather than international) in scope due to communications and other structural limitations. The secondary securities market was dominated by the New York Stock Exchange (NYSE) whose members maintained fixed commission rates on trades and were prohibited from trading outside of the exchange. Investment banks were almost entirely organized as partnerships and as such had limited and unpredictable levels of capital. The majority of investment banks' revenues came from commissions (66% in 1972).[26]

The industry was broken down into three major segments: originators, regionals, and national distributors. Originators normally had small, elitist professional staffs, low overhead, and a minimal presence in the secondary markets. They tended to maintain long-term, stable relationships with corporate clients. For the latter, they designed securities issues, handled the registration and regulatory hurdles of the SEC, negotiated a gross spread from which they took a 20% management fee, and syndicated regional and national distribution firms to underwrite and sell those securities not sold directly to large institutional investors. Distributors had regional or national networks of retail outlets to deal with many small or local investors. They played major roles in secondary markets, handled very little (if any) origination, and were dependent upon originators for supplies of newly issued securities. The entire industry was regulated by the SEC, with membership in the exchanges and the National Association of Securities Dealers (NASD) involving additional restraints.

The bull market of the '60s with its high volume of trading on the secondary markets offered distributors expanded opportunities. Some of them began to integrate vertically and to "manufacture" by developing their own mutual funds, real estate deals, and tax shelters. As their staffs grew, they began to compete on the origination of new issues. Eventually many of the larger distributors converted from partnerships to corporations and sold their stock to the public. This gave them the capital base they needed to aggressively compete in other areas.

Open competition for underwriting developed, and firms began locating professionals in regional offices to call on current or potential corporate clients. Many active large corporations came to realize that their bankers, particularly originators, were dependent on them—rather than the other way around. They began to develop their own internal financial and market expertise and to shop around for investment counselors when needed. Dividend reinvestment programs and the trend toward stock-for-stock corporate mergers (versus registered secondary offerings) also increased corporate clients' independence.

"May Day" and Its Aftermath

The Securities Industries Amendments Act of 1975 increased competition further by mandating an end to fixed commission rates on May 1, 1975—"May Day." The Act also eliminated the NYSE rules that prohibited members from using other exchanges and mandated the creation of an electronic network to form a national market. The Act, particularly the national market notion ("a linking of all markets . . . through communications and data-processing facilities"), was designed to: foster efficiency, enhance competition, increase the availability of market information, and facilitate the offsetting and execution of investors' orders.[27]

The unfixing of commission rates led to dramatic changes in U.S. capital markets. The NYSE's portion of total shares traded fell from 65% to 50% between 1975 and 1983; its percentage of share values traded dropped from 75% to 70% over the same period.[28] NASD's Automatic Quotation System (NASDAQ) garnered market share with its introduction in 1982 of an electronic National Market System which utilized multiple market makers rather than specialists for each stock traded. NYSE contributed to a more national marketplace by introducing a Composite Quotation System (consolidated tape) and by participating in the national clearance and settlement system started in 1980. Finally an Intermarket Trading System was introduced to permit orders received in any market to be displayed instantaneously with orders in the same stock on all of the other markets and NASD's Computer Assisted Execution System was connected up to the NYSE's Intermarket Trading System in May 1982.

Negotiated commissions led to huge cuts of up to 75% in the rates for large institutional trades. Turnover of institutional portfolios rose dramatically pushing average daily shares traded on the NYSE from 18.5 million to 102 million by 1984. Able to negotiate lower commission rates and unencumbered by tax considerations, pension fund managers sought to lock in short-term profits often because of the greater scrutiny of their performance created by ERISA. A growing proportion of individual savings were being channeled through institutions such as life insurance companies, pension funds and mutual funds. And as institutional trading increased, so did the dominance of institutional investors in the market. By 1984 50% of all NYSE trades involved 10,000 shares or more and were made primarily by institutional investors.[29] The exchanges could handle the greater volume only because of the application of new technologies and the development of block trading mechanisms off the trading floors and off the specialists' books.

This increased portfolio turnover among institutions changed many corporations' attitudes about having their shares held mainly by institutions. Large block trades could cause big short term swings in a company's stock price. And desires for short-term stock gains made some institutions impatient about longer term investments and eager to accept tender offers in takeover situations. Corporate clients' disenchantment with institutional investors for equity issues often forced old style originators to co-manage new issues with a distribution firm that could reach the retail market.

New Retail Products

While the institutional brokerage business was less attractive, it was still essential. Institutions still purchased over 90% of all debt offerings. Many investment firms, however, began looking more closely at their retail customers who had suddenly become relatively more profitable. The emergence of ''discount brokerage'' firms who cut retail commission rates by offering only trade execution services increased competition for retail customers. By 1984 these discount brokerages had captured a 20% share of the retail market. Studies revealed that 1% of all households produced 45% of all retail brokerage revenues and that these customers viewed themselves as having a relationship with their particular broker, not the firm.[30] Full-line investment houses began to exploit this relationship by developing and mar-

keting new products like Merrill Lynch's Cash Management Account (CMA) and money market mutual funds. By 1981 broker/dealer money-market funds held the largest share of total fund assets with about $90 billion.[31]

These products helped diversify firms away from commission revenues. Other new products helped to bolster sagging commission incomes. Stock options which were first traded in 1973 had mushroomed to 55 million contracts by 1981. The market for commodities futures and later financial futures also grew rapidly, and by 1981 commissions on these products made up 20% of larger firms' commission revenues.[32] Some insurance related products (like deferred annuities or even term insurance) were added to enhance the commissions needed to give distributors a national presence and a competitive advantage over other financial service providers.

Changing Revenue Mix

In addition to shrinking commissions, investment banks were faced with other changes in their revenue bases. (See Tables 7a and 7b.)

Underwriting revenues were cut by high inflation rates. Tax considerations and high inflation made debt more attractive to corporations than equity issues. In 1979 79% of all underwrit-

TABLE 7a   CHANGES IN INVESTMENT BANKING REVENUES

Mix of Revenues (%)

	1970	1974	1980
Commissions	48	48	36
Trading and Investment	19	15	23
Underwriting	12	10	8
Margin Interest	8	12	13
Other	13	15	20
Total ($ billions)	$4.8	$5.1	$16.0

Source: Based on material from Paul A. Masson, *Report No. 696, Trends in Corporate Financial Services.* Copyright © 1984 by Business Intelligence Program, SRI International.

TABLE 7b   CHANGES IN INVESTMENT BANKING REVENUES

Revenue Growth Index

	1973	1977
Public Underwriting	100	199
Private Placement	100	251
Mergers & Acquisitions and other fees	100	391
Municipal Financing	100	290

Source: Reprinted by permission of the Harvard Business Review. An exhibit from "The Transformation of Investment Banking," by Samuel L. Hayes III (January/February 1979.) Copyright © by the President and Fellows of Harvard College; all rights reserved.

ten public offerings were bonds— only 15% were equities. Margins on underwriting major debt issues were only 25% of those for equity issues.

As finance costs shifted and more creative instruments became available, the fastest growing revenue source for investment bankers became Merger and Acquisition (M&A) activities. In 1973 dollar values of acquisitions were $16.7 billion; by 1983 they had soared to $73.1 billion.[33] In 1984 they were $120 billion, but the actual number of mergers had only risen from 2,300 in 1975 to 2,550 in 1984.[34] Investment banks earned fees for arranging mergers, fighting off mergers, arranging divestitures, arbitraging, or establishing fair prices for friendly transactions of this sort. Fees were normally based on a % of the deal's dollar value and could run as high as 5% on a single transaction. Although there was heavy competition for M&A services, corporations tended to be somewhat price insensitive in such a vital strategic area. Since M&A business involved no capital risk, large commercial banks and even several public accounting firms became competitors for this business. But investment banks had some competitive advantages, and with their combination of analytical staffs and traders they were able to engage in profitable—but risky—arbitrage or trading activities whenever they were not being retained by either of the parties involved.

Another growing source of revenues was municipal underwriting. The bulk of profits in this field came not from underwriting general obligation bonds—which faced thin margins and highly competitive commercial bidding—but from underwriting negotiated revenue bond issues which, like other tax-exempt bond financings, were growing rapidly.

The private placement market also became a more important part of investment bankers' portfolios as the SEC eased its rigid (Regulation A) requirements for such securities in the late 1970s and early '80s. Private placements do not have to follow the costly and time consuming procedures of a public offering, but must be presented to only a few knowledgeable and financially competent investors as defined by SEC rules. In the

mid 1980s, 70% of all private placements used a financial intermediary—93% of the time an investment bank. However, since fees for private placements compared favorably with those for management of public bond underwritings and involved no capital risk, commercial banks began competing for this business with corresponding pressures on margins. On the buyers side, life insurance companies dominated the private placement bond market. However, in recent years, insurance companies had sought the more liquid portfolios that publicly traded bonds offer. And the supply of private placements bonds had been held down by the surge in publicly traded junk bonds issued by companies who otherwise might have used the private market.

The internationalization of the world's capital markets brought other, dramatic changes to the economics of investment banking.

Internationalization

In the world's capital markets, borders had begun to be irrelevant. Computerized quotes and satellite communications had made global markets possible. Big institutional investors had increased their overseas involvement in search of fresh investments. Savvy corporate treasurers had discovered that by tapping foreign markets they could often lower their capital costs and broaden their investor base. In 1985 some 500 companies were listed on at least one stock exchange outside their home country and international markets like the Eurobond markets were booming.

Interconnections among capital markets meant that innovations or changes in one market were gradually being reflected in others. The Eurobond market offered companies both lower costs and new ways of doing business which allowed them to decrease the time required to arrange and present a new financing issue— critical because of the growing volatility of interest rates and capital markets in general. Corporate treasurers could dispense with the time and expense of formal underwriting procedures. Instead, banks bid competitively to buy an issue, with the successful bank taking the whole issue directly onto its books and reselling pieces of it as quickly and as profitably as possible. This was known as a "bought deal." The SEC gradually changed key requirements to make the U.S. capital markets more attractive. In 1978, the SEC: (1) instituted abbreviated registration statements that allowed large companies to disclose information in a prospectus by reference to other publicly available documents (10Ks, etc.) and (2) provided for "selective SEC review" of certain documents which cut clearance times from several weeks down to 48 hours. Large companies, which had strong enough internal finance staffs to design and register issues using this abbreviated process, began pressing investment banks to bid for their business on the same competitive "bought deal" basis they used in the Eurobond market.

SEC Rule 415 in March 1982 accelerated this process further. Rule 415 allowed large, well capitalized companies to register all the securities they planned to issue over the following two years at one time, and then sell some or all of them "off the shelf" as funds needs or market conditions dictated. From 1982 to 1984, 50–60% of all debt issues and 10% of all equity issues used this technique. Rule 415 meant that a company did not have to choose a managing underwriter before registering an issue; it could simply list a number of acceptable possible managers and encourage those firms to bid for its business, often on a bought deal basis. The advent of shelf registration heated up competition in the capital markets since commercial banks could place shelf registered issues without actually underwriting them, and some corporations were even contemplating doing their own private placements.

The negotiated rates of the U.S. markets were being forced on exchanges in other countries by powerful institutional investors—as evidenced by the unfixing of commission rates in London and Australia. To compete with the Eurobond markets the U.S. removed the withholding requirements for foreign purchasers of U.S. bonds. The result was an increasingly comparability in rates for Eurodollar bonds and U.S. Treasurys.

Abroad— especially in the fast growing unregulated Euromarket—investment banks faced both new foreign competitors and large U.S. commercial banks free from Glass-Steagall restrictions. But currency volatilities and the internationalization which meant increased foreign trading and ownership of U.S. securities made it imperative for investment banks to operate on a global level both to serve their corporate clients and to take advantage of arbitrage opportunities for their own account. As foreign exchanges in London and Tokyo opened up their memberships and let foreign brokerages in, major U.S. investment firms were faced with difficult decisions about how fast and where they should expand their operations.

Resulting Structural Changes

As bought deals became more common and negotiated spreads shrank, the underwriting side of investment banking became highly concentrated. Only certain firms had the capital base, distribution, and trading systems to handle bought deals. By 1984 two-thirds of all new issues were underwritten by 5 firms.[34] Syndicate sizes shrank along with spreads and regional firms were increasingly squeezed out of underwriting, which they wanted badly because of its higher profit potentials. Regional distributors were also forced to automate their back-offices to deal with the high trading volumes and growing array of new products. Many either merged with national firms or went out of business. This heightened the competition between old style originators and national distributors.

Trading gained in relative importance and the nature of corporate/banker relationships shifted away from long-term stable ties and toward a transaction basis. The banks competed by developing innovative financing techniques and many new firms (boutiques) emerged pursuing niche or specialist strategies. Specialists and traders gained more power within investment banks. As competition increased in underwriting and other activities proliferated, investment banks rapidly expanded the size of their professional staffs. From 1966 to 1977 while revenues grew by 135% on an inflation adjusted basis, staffs grew by 345%.[35]

Many of these changes were reflected in the balance sheets of investment banks. (See Table 8.)

TABLE 8 ASSETS AND LIABILITIES OF NEW YORK STOCK EXCHANGE MEMBER FIRMS*

	1973	1978	1983
Distribution of Assets (%)			
Long Positions in Securities and Commodities	37.6	54.6	67.6
Receivables from Customers and Partners	37.1	29.8	15.4
Receivables from Other Brokers and Dealers	12.9	9.5	11.4
Bank Balances, Cash and Other Deposits	4.3	1.8	1.4
Land and Other Fixed Assets	1.1	0.6	0.9
Secured Demand Notes	1.9	0.5	0.1
Exchange Memberships	0.7	0.2	0.1
Other Assets	4.4	3.1	3.1
Total ($ billions)	$22.6	$53.9	$214.8
Distribution of Liabilities (%)			
Money Borrowed	38.8	47.8	48.7
Short Positions in Securities and Commodities	4.8	12.3	18.0
Payables to Other Brokers and Dealers	11.5	8.7	9.5
Other Accrued Expenses and Accounts Payable	7.4	9.5	8.0
Capital	16.6	8.1	6.6

* NYSE Member firms account for over 90% of total industry assets.

Source: Statistical Information on the Financial Services Industry, 3rd ed., 1984, pp. 121 and 164. © American Bankers Association. Reprinted with permission. All rights reserved.

THE ROYAL BANK OF CANADA (B)

The Royal Bank of Canada (RBC) was founded (as the Merchants Bank) in 1894 to fund the Nova Scotian fishing trade. In 1985 it was the largest chartered bank in Canada, with operations in many other areas of the world. Although Canada is very large geographically (the second largest country in the world), it is sparsely settled in many areas, with its population concentrated along the Great Lakes–St. Lawrence waterways and in a few large western cities. Historically the western provinces have been especially strong raw material, energy, and agricultural producers, while the eastern provinces have dominated the manufacturing, retailing, financial, and service sectors of the economy. Significantly, however, Ontario produces 40% of Canada's minerals, and Quebec is noted for its extensive hydropower and forestry resources. Though similar to the U.S. banking system, Canada's structure differs in certain significant dimensions (see Appendix A). Its total domestic banking market is about the size of California's.

From 1961–1977 the Royal Bank was led by Mr. W. Earle McLaughlin. When Mr. McLaughlin took over in 1961, the Bank had assets of just over $4 billion*; by 1977 its assets were $34 billion. Many changes, in addition to growth, occurred during the McLaughlin era. In 1967 the Bank Act of Canada was revised and among other things, eliminated the interest rate ceiling on bank loan charges and eased the restrictions on residential mortgage lending by banks.

Although the chartered banks vigorously pursued both deposits and consumer as well as commercial lending opportunities, "the near banks" grew slightly faster than the banks.**

For the Royal Bank, the decade 1967–77 brought asset growth of 340% and the addition of some 50 new services. RBC became a large scale residential mortgage lender; moved firmly into consumer loans; developed specialized financial services for fishermen, farmers, professionals, and small businessmen; and took major steps in automation and international banking. In 1970, RBC was one of the founding partners of Orion Bank (with Chase Manhattan and others) formed to handle the growing consortium Euro-dollar lending business. Orion eventually became RBC's main focus for merchant banking activities.

In June 1977, Mr. Rowland Frazee became President and heir apparent to Mr. McLaughlin and began the process of adjusting the Bank's organization, culture, and strategy to cope with the massive changes in the world of banking.

1980 BANK ACT CHANGES

In 1980, after three extensions, the decennial revisions to the Canadian Bank Act passed, taking effect in January 1981. And in 1981–82, Canadian banks underwent a full-scale parliamentary hearing into "obscene" bank profits. Said *U.S. Banker*: "The view of Canadians prior to the

---

Case copyright © 1986 by James Brian Quinn. Case prepared by Penny C. Paquette under the supervision of Professor Quinn. The generous cooperation of the Royal Bank of Canada is gratefully acknowledged.

* *Note: All dollar figures are Canadian dollars unless otherwise indicated.*

** *These include: trust companies, credit unions, some mortgage loan companies, and certain other institutions such as the Montreal City and District Savings Bank, the Province of Ontario Savings Office, and the Province of Alberta Treasury Branches.*

Bank Act was that banking was being controlled by a handful of entities. That was more apparent than real."[1] Nevertheless, the Bank Act did open Canada to increased competition from foreign banks. There was a continuing need for foreign capital to develop Canada's natural resources and economic potentials. But the Foreign Investment Review Act of 1974 (FIRA), and other factors had led to a drop in net foreign direct investment in Canada. In 1980 the government passed the National Energy Program (NEP) designed to foster greater Canadian control over its gas and oil activities. Under NEP Canada subsidized its own energy companies and was exerting increasing pressures to ensure a Canadian position—if not dominance—in oil and gas discoveries. These trends resulted in "an increasingly acrimonious relationship with the United States," yet Canada's economy was strongly hitched to that of its southern neighbor.

Perhaps partially in response in these pressures, the 1980 revisions to the Bank Act increased the flexibility of the Canadian financial system. It also substantially increased potential competition in the industry. In summary, the new Act: (1) increased competition by providing a less complicated procedure for obtaining a license to operate as a bank; (2) permitted foreign banks to establish subsidiaries subject to specific terms and conditions, including reciprocal treatment for Canadian banks and making it difficult for them to operate as non-banks as many had in the past; (3) extended banks' business powers to include direct participation in financial leasing, factoring, and venture capital; (4) clarified (and restricted) the business powers of the banks in areas like data processing and underwriting of corporate securities; (5) established a new Canadian Payments Association which would operate a national payments clearing system and allow direct access to that system for banks and other deposit accepting institutions.[2]

The immediate response to the Bank Act changes was an increase in the number of foreign banks with offices or operations in Canada. Few foreign bank subsidiaries planned to enter the "retail market." However, many expected to expand their competition in the "wholesale market"— corporate loans funded largely through the short term paper market. While the Bank Act required more detailed reporting of certain activities, it opened the possibility for various financial institutions to increasingly penetrate each other's primary markets. (See Appendix A for information concerning the financial structure of Canada.)

EARLY 1980s ISSUES

By 1981, the Royal Bank had grown to $85 billion Canadian or U.S. $71 billion in assets at prevailing exchange rates, ranking it fourth in North America. One third of its assets were foreign based. And its profits had grown at 16% compounded for the past five years. Income from international operations was growing at 26% compounded. Its international profits growth at 21.5% was better than twice the increase of Bank of America and four times that of Citicorp. As Canada's largest bank, RBC boasted a coast to coast retail network of 1,522 branches and held about $18 billion in secure retail deposits. This was twice the volume of Citicorp and almost half again as many branches as Bank of America.

The Bank enjoyed a good reputation internationally, but was still not considered "a first tier" bank. Domestically, it was strong in cash management and energy financing. Internationally, it was well known as a sound correspondent banker and merchant banker (through its Orion group). It had excellent funding strength in dollars and strong foreign exchange capabilities, especially in the $U.S./$Canadian and $U.S./Stirling markets. However, the whole world banking situation was changing rapidly. As the U.S. economy began to weaken in late 1981–82, and the "energy shortage" faded, a variety of pressures developed for the world banking community. Most notable among these was the LDC debt crisis. Many U.S. banks had lent sums in excess of their total reserves to developing countries. The Royal Bank's exposure in this area is shown in the next table. Because of U.S. inflation, interest rates had risen to all time highs in 1979–80, placing intolerable debt burdens on many LDCs. The strong U.S.

INTERNATIONAL OPERATIONS DISTRIBUTION OF ASSETS
BY COUNTRY CLASSIFICATION*

($ Billions at October 31)	1982	%	1981	%
Industrialized Countries	$21.3	66.4%	$21.2	67.7%
Centrally Planned Countries	0.8	2.6	0.9	2.9
Oil Exporting Countries	1.2	3.7	1.0	3.2
Developing Countries:				
High Income	1.3	4.0	1.4	4.5
Upper Middle Income	3.6	11.1	3.6	11.5
Intermediate Middle Income	3.0	9.5	2.4	7.7
Lower Middle Income	0.7	2.1	0.6	1.9
Low Income	0.2	0.6	0.2	0.6
Total Earning Assets	$32.1	100.0%	$31.3	100.0%

* Based on International Bank for Reconstruction and Development classifications of per capita income.

Source: RBC internal report.

dollar and depressed world prices for raw materials made these debts increasingly difficult to repay as the decade of the 1980s developed.

1983–85 SITUATION

By 1983, the organization of the Royal Bank of Canada had slowly mutated to the form shown in Exhibit 1. Profiles of the key players are provided in Exhibit 2. In 1983–85 the U.S. began to recover from its early 1980s recession, pulling the world economy up with it. Oil prices began to sag, offering the hope for a stronger long-term world growth pattern—but with some very great uncertainties facing the entire financial world. Mr. Frazee and his top management group began to work through the next important steps necessary to position the Royal Bank for its long term future. As they looked forward, they saw the following as the most important near-term and long-term changes in the Royal Bank's environment.

Deregulation Begins

By 1985, Canada would emerge from the severe recession of 1982 into an era of slower, but more evenly distributed regional growth. The National

Energy Program had "backfired substantially" and raised serious doubts as to the merits of formalized sector planning. Loan demand sagged reaching such low levels at this time that some banks decreased their deposit interest rates below the market rate offered by other institutions. The Progressive Conservative Party successfully pinpointed "unrestrained government interventionism" as the cause of Canada's faltering growth prospects. The country had elected a new government headed by a Progressive Conservative, Brian Mulroney; and prospects for improved relations and possibly even a free trade zone with the United States were fostered by a pulling back from some aspects of the Foreign Investment Review Act. An articulate internationalist constituency (including leading bankers) began to stress the concept of reciprocity versus that of "Canadianization."

The movement toward "constitutional reform" was put on a back burner, but provincial-federal rivalry over jurisdiction of the financial services industry continued. Quebec separatism had faded somewhat—key aspects of Bill 101 had been overturned by the Supreme Court of Canada, and Montreal was making a bid to recapture its position as a major international financial center. After the October Crisis of 1970 when some extremists set off bombs in Montreal, the financial industry had fled to Toronto and the Toronto Stock Exchange had boomed.

As the separatists' power receded, Quebec's Finance Minister, Jacques Parizeau pushed hard to enhance the Province's financial markets. In Canada, bank regulation is federal, stock brokers are regulated by the Provinces, while insurance and trust companies can choose between the two. Parizeau allowed brokers to diversify into other financial activities. He permitted insurance companies to own brokerages and to move into other areas as well. Similar legislation for trusts was expected in 1985, high taxes and death duties having driven away pension funds and trusts from the Province. In 1985 further legislation on these issues seemed possible.

Euromoney noted that "deregulation is in the air in Canada; Canada's more adventurous banks are beginning to test the legal barriers that keep the main financial functions apart."[3] And pressure was building for changes in legislation governing the financial services industry as a whole. The Mulroney government, which had stressed cooperation versus rivalry between federal and provincial regulators, issued a White Paper in the Spring of 1985 laying out a plan (1) to allow holding companies to own banks as well as investment dealers if provincial legislation permitted, and (2) to allow insurance and trust companies to make commercial loans. If this became policy, it would cast aside Canada's long standing "Four Pillars" concept—see Appendix A—and pit the big banks against large financial conglomerates, several of which (Trilon, Laurentian Group, Power Financial Corp.) were already in operation.

Such financial holding companies could already both sell stocks and perform some banking activities. But these companies would not be limited to the 10% ownership maximum imposed on other individual shareholders in banks. Trilon (owned by the Bronfman family) already controlled Canada's largest trust company, a number of real estate companies, and an insurance company. Through a subsidiary it had moved into merchant banking in a partnership with Merrill Lynch and Canadian Imperial Bank of Commerce

(CIBC). The Government's White Paper would also permit life insurance and trust companies to make commercial loans—previously the exclusive domain of the banks. The Mulroney government was said to be "eager to bring free competition into the system, to lower borrowing costs, and to help spur lagging capital investment in the country."[4]

The Banks Respond

But the chartered banks were also responding. By purchasing Harris Trust in September 1984, the Bank of Montreal not only gained a foothold in the U.S. market, but created an opportunity to circumvent the Canadian law that prevented commercial banks from entering the trust business. No regulation forbade Harris Trust from managing Canadian pension fund money. CIBC used a loophole to arrange a $100 million convertible preferred private placement deal for Canadian Pacific. Toronto Dominion Bank had been in the stock brokerage business since 1983, after the Ontario Securities Commission allowed banks to register as brokers (but not to trade on the exchanges). For its part, the Royal Bank had opened an Orion Royal Bank representative office in Toronto, but its existence was being threatened by possible changes in Ontario Security Commission regulations.

As of late 1984, in Canada there were 13 "Schedule A" banks and 59 "Schedule B" banks, all of which were foreign based. (See Appendix A.) The foreign Schedule Bs soon introduced Canadian corporate treasurers to the "cost of funds" lending concept, which Canadian banks had successfully resisted until then. By early 1985 over 50% of the Schedule Bs loans were on this cost-plus basis. The Schedule Bs had also driven down the price on bankers' acceptances, letters of credit, and stand-by lines of credit. Yet several of the Schedule Bs had achieved high ROAs and were going after more potentially lucrative or fee-based activities like factoring, venture capital, foreign exchange, and money-market transactions. The following table shows the Royal Bank's fee-based income.

FEE-BASED INCOME ($ millions)

	1984	1983	Percent Change
Service charges	$212	$185	14.6%
Visa fees	98	84	16.7
Loan and commitment fees	105	108	(2.8)
Securities commissions	38	44	(13.6)
Foreign exchange revenue	101	93	8.6
Bankers' acceptances, letters of credit and guarantee fees	69	72	(4.2)
Sundry	86	81	6.2
Total	$709	$667	6.3%

Source: Royal Bank of Canada, Annual Report, 1984.

Merrill Lynch's Canadian subsidiary, although it was constrained to some extent by capital restrictions imposed in 1972, had been moving aggressively to regain a top position in Canada's capital markets. And new rules proposed by the Ontario government would allow additional foreign brokers to set up shop under similar capital restrictions, or to buy as much as 30% of a Canadian securities dealer—this would definitely heat up competition in the industry.[5] To complicate matters further, new electronics technologies were changing the financial services industry enormously. Non-banks were increasingly involved in banking type services. Credit cards had proliferated in retailing and similar institutions. Automated teller machines (ATMs) made it possible to obtain cash virtually anywhere. And in the U.S., retail operations—like Sears Roebuck, JC Penney, and others—were offering cash, insurance, and financial services through their retail outlets, a trend which might well spread to Canada.

THE ROYAL BANK IN 1985

From the Royal Bank Annual Report of 1984 and its March 1985 presentation to bank analysts, certain summary dimensions could be derived about RBC's internal operations. By mid 1985, The Royal Bank had grown to over $88 billion in assets, of which more than one third were international. However, the severe recession of 1981–83 and the LDC debt crisis had taken their toll on RBC's profits. The following tables give details of RBC's loan losses and non-performing loans. (See Exhibit 3 for summary RBC financials.) RBC's prominent position as lender to major Canadian energy companies and to Latin American countries and corporations had put the bank in the uncomfortable position of having the highest loan loss experience on these accounts among the major Canadian banks. Profit margins had been squeezed by the competitive pressures outlined above (see Exhibit 4 for comparative data on RBC and other Canadian Banks). But RBC continued to invest heavily in computer and automation equipment.

On the positive side, the Royal Banks's non-interest expenses (NIE) had increased by less than the inflation rate during 1984, and RBC ranked second best of the majors in NIE as a percent of income. Exhibit 3 shows the composition of RBC's NIE.

RBC had $16 billion in domestic consumer loans in Canada, representing a 25% market share for installment loans, mortgages, and credit card debt. Because of innovative new mortgage options and pricing structures, RBC's share of new commitments in mortgages was growing and was currently 29%. The Bank's retail distribution network was made up of 1,440 branches and 750 automatic teller machines, representing the largest block of ATMs in Canadian banking. RBC's $28

DETAIL OF LOAN LOSSES ($ millions)

	1984	1983	1982	1981	1980
Loan Loss Experience					
Domestic					
Consumer installment, Visa,					
mortgages and other personal					
loans	$ 48	$ 92	$ 77	$ 43	$ 34
Agriculture and independent					
business	84	104	84	37	29
Large commercial and corporate	248	258	369	64	28
	380	454	530	144	91
International					
Asia Pacific	22	14	—	3	2
Europe, Middle East and Africa	48	85	57	31	19
Latin America and Caribbean	123	45	18	27	28
U.S.A.	169	174	75	14	7
	362	318	150	75	56
Total	$ 742	$ 772	$ 680	$ 219	$ 147
Eligible Loans					
Domestic	$45,476	$44,726	$47,178	$41,632	$29,568
International	21,281	20,529	20,904	19,222	12,706
Total	$66,757	$65,255	$68,082	$60,854	$42,274
Loss Experience as a Percent of					
Eligible Loans					
Domestic	.84%	1.01%	1.12%	.35%	.31%
International	1.70	1.55	.72	.39	.44
Total	1.11%	1.18%	1.00%	.36%	.35%
Provision for Loan Losses					
(five-year average)					
Domestic	$ 327	$ 309	$ 258	$ 135	$ 90
International	208	143	86	51	34
Total	$ 535	$ 452	$ 344	$ 186	$ 124

Source: Royal Bank of Canada, *Annual Report,* 1984.

billion in personal deposits comprised a 24.5% share of those held by chartered banks. And RBC's $4 billion in independent business loans represented a market share of 25%, up 300 basis points since 1982. The Bank had $3.5 billion in agricultural loans to some 80,000 farmers, but about 5% of these were said to be in some difficulty because of the serious agricultural situation in Canada. In addition, the Bank had $19 billion in commercial loans to some 8,000 large clients, including those managed by the National Ac-counts Division, and Global Energy and Minerals (GEM).

RBC enjoyed the largest customer base of any financial services concern in Canada. However, competition was increasing faster than the total size of the market. By 1985 more than 60% of RBC's personal clients dealt with other financial service providers as well, and it was more and more important to provide a full array of products and services to retain their basic deposit business. These clients were also being heavily

NON-PERFORMING LOANS (net of provisions for losses)

As at October 31 ($ Millions)	1984	1983	1982	1981	1980
Domestic					
Atlantic Provinces	$ 9	$ 13	$ 30	$ 9	$ 7
Quebec	90	87	53	26	21
Ontario	126	145	155	61	48
Manitoba and Saskatchewan	93	79	68	28	22
Alberta	567	681	377	42	33
British Columbia	522	627	369	50	40
	1,407	1,632	1,252	216	171
Of which:					
Consumer installment loans, mortgages and other personal loans	77	133	174	48	38
Agriculture and independent business	279	255	231	99	73
Large commercial and corporate	1,051	1,244	847	69	60
	1,407	1,632	1,252	216	171
International					
Asia Pacific	40	40	5	—	—
Europe, Middle East and Africa	127	216	140	—	—
Latin America and Caribbean	832	486	460	12	33
U.S.A.	277	464	183	—	—
	1,276	1,206	788	12	33
Total	$2,683	$2,838	$2,040	$228	$204

Source: Royal Bank of Canada, *Annual Report*, 1984.

marketed by new competitors using careful niching strategies. These factors became of increasing importance as domestic margins were being squeezed on both fixed rate and prime-related business, due to a reduced differential between money market and prime rates. The foreign Schedule B banks, as noted above, were compressing margins in order to build market share during this period. And this pressure had increased in 1984 when the Schedule Bs allowable asset ceiling was raised to 16% of total banking assets.

Technology was also eroding the competitive advantages of traditional branch networks. Mr. Frazee noted in a 1984 interview that, "RBC does not make money on its depositors directly." ATMs could be easily installed at specific locations by competitors, near banks and non-banks. It was becoming increasingly difficult for RBC to support a full service branch network as well as a growing ATM network. There was even some question as to whether RBC's traditional banking markets offered sufficient potential to utilize its extensive available distribution system.

International Operations

In the international realm, RBC had completed the purchase of Orion in 1981 and changed the name to Orion Royal Bank. Orion was in a lead or co-managed position in approximately 200 issues worth some $U.S. 38 billion or 50% of the total Euromarket. In Euro-Canadian and Euro-Australian dollar bonds, Orion Royal had 70% of the action on the Euromarket. Orion Royal Pacific managed the 10 largest syndicated credits in the Asian market. For the period January 1983 to May 1985, *Euromoney* lists Orion Royal Bank as the No. 1 bookrunner for private sector Canadian issues in the Eurobond market, as No. 8 for public sector Canadian issues, and as No. 4 for all Canadian issues combined. Only in the Eurocredits market did the other large Canadian banks factor heavily in the competition. The Bank of Montreal is ranked as the No. 2 lead manager to Canadian borrowers by a narrow margin over RBC-Orion Royal Bank as No. 3. Bank of Montreal also edged out RBC-Orion Royal Bank as the No. 1 Canadian lead manager to all borrowers in the Euromarkets.[6]

The total international division held over $18 billion in assets, managed over 5,000 correspondent relationships and employed some 6,000 people. RBC's international business was shifting from loan oriented products toward a full array of capital market products. (See Financial Services Industry Note.) The increasing interconnectedness among the world's capital markets was leading many of RBC's competitors to offer more extended global trading services and to provide their multinational clients access to all major capital markets as well as global account management services. In addition, as international trade balances and growth patterns changed, the positioning of RBC's extensive international distribution network became an issue. (See map—Exhibit 5.) One area of long term concern had been RBC's strategy for the United States. The U.S. offered a huge market in which RBC had the advantage of a common language, cultural understanding, business contacts, and extensive market knowledge. However, the option of entering the U.S. market through a large acquisition was becoming increasingly unattractive due to the high cost and small number of appropriate candidates.

Organizational Issues

Despite a growing familiarity with its relatively new matrix organization, difficulties still arose for RBC in coordinating the efforts of its commercial and merchant bankers, especially on the international scene. Commercial bankers were increasingly being asked to "concept sell' complex capital market products such as interest and exchange rate swaps, note issuance facilities, and Eurobonds which were delivered by the merchant banking group as well as selling and managing the delivery of bread-and-butter banking products such as short term commercial loans, letters of credit, stand-by lines of credit, and international cash management services.

In a time of rapidly changing business environments and extremely tight operating margins, innovation and flexibility were essential to the Royal Bank. However, its very size and complexity created significant barriers to communications and serious concerns for top management. Executives in RBC's far flung operations often complained of the complexity and length of time it took to make decisions and commitments. The Bank had conducted numerous experiments to understand changing customer patterns and how specific services would be received by its customers. But top management did not feel that it had found ultimate solutions to these complex problems in 1985. There was widespread discussion of the appropriate degree of decentralization needed by the bank. A crucial question was how this decentralization could be accomplished, yet maintain the essential controls required both by the banking laws and by prudent management.

Over the last decade differences in culture had become apparent between domestic bankers operating in the more restricted and conservative environment of Canada and international bankers, many of whom operated in markets where fewer barriers existed between the various segments of the financial services industry. There were also inherent differences in outlook between commercial bankers with a lending orientation and traders or merchant bankers with the more flamboyant style often required in the fast-paced capital markets. Although there were advantages (improved communications and support systems) to grouping each speciality together, such groupings also led to communication problems and potential value conflicts between groups with slightly different goals and quite different operating styles.

Values for the New Era

In dealing with the wide variety of issues facing the Royal Bank in 1985, its top management had developed a preliminary statement of values to serve as guidelines for any proposed solutions. The following statement seemed to meet with wide acceptance among key managers although it was under continuing review:

Our Values:

- The customer comes first.
- Integrity forms the foundation of our business.
- Trust, respect, and openness strengthen our relationships with customers and with each other.
- Quality and excellence are central to all that we do.
- Innovation and creativity give us the power to renew our business.
- Teamwork, we pull together for greater effectiveness.
- Community involvement strengthens our awareness and reputation.
- With our global presence we hope to build a strong Canada, competitive in a world economy.

Our Objectives:

- To be a consistent leader in providing customers with services and counseling of quality and value.
- To be viewed with respect and to be the leading financial services enterprise in Canada and the Canadian leader abroad.
- To be an enlightened employer known for quality of leadership and quality of people.
- To be one of the most profitable major financial enterprises in Canada and to have a top credit rating.

In summarizing the Bank's aspirations in 1985 Mr. Frazee endorsed the following statement.

From our modest beginning in 1864 in Halifax, we have become a world scale international bank. We succeeded by "serving the customer" well. We followed ships at sea and rails across continents. We pioneered with the pioneers. Since 1941 we have remained Canada's largest and most successful bank. This is our history as a bank.

Let's turn to our future as a financial services enterprise. We have already entered a new era—an era which requires us to pioneer as never before in a world fast being reinvented. We will have to meet the changing needs of our customers quicker than ever before. We will continue to follow telecommunications to the perimeters of space. We will need to segment our markets, to serve our customers better, and to outpace our competitors—both new and old. If we actively seize every opportunity to serve our clients better, we will make more money, keep our jobs challenging, create new jobs for others, and be able to invest even more in improving our services to Canada and the world.

QUESTIONS

1. In 1985, what are the most critical factors which will determine the Royal Bank's future success in its changing environments?
2. Given the trends and changes indicated in the case and in the Financial Services Industry Note, if RBC is allowed to diversify into other financial services, which should be given highest priority? Why? How can RBC use its unique strengths and capabilities to maximum advantage?
3. What key thrusts should it undertake in its strategies for the future?
4. How should the Bank redeploy its resources to meet its future challenges? Specifically, how should it restructure its total organization to accomplish this effectively?

EXHIBIT 1   RBC ORGANIZATION JANUARY 1982

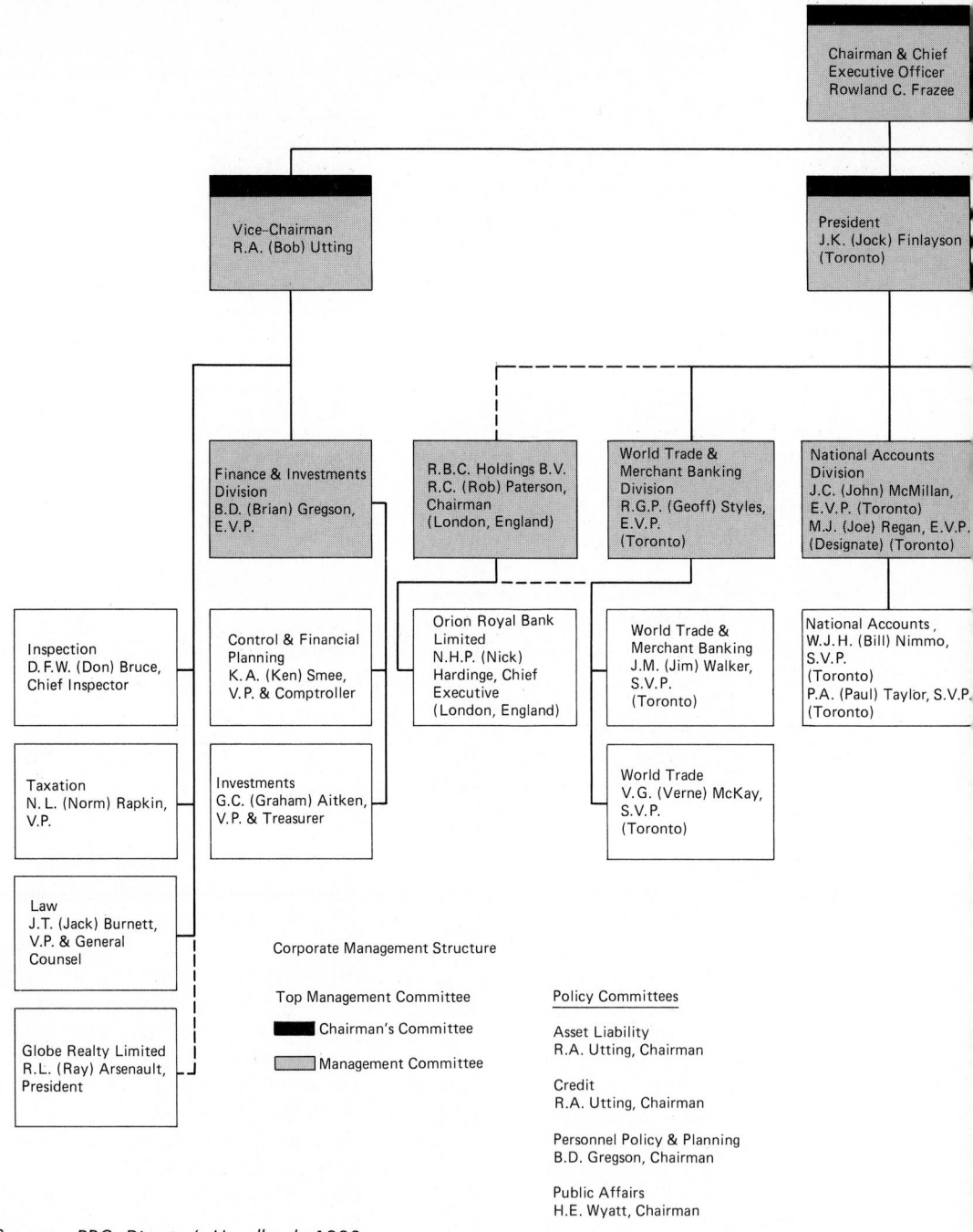

Source: RBC, *Director's Handbook*, 1982.

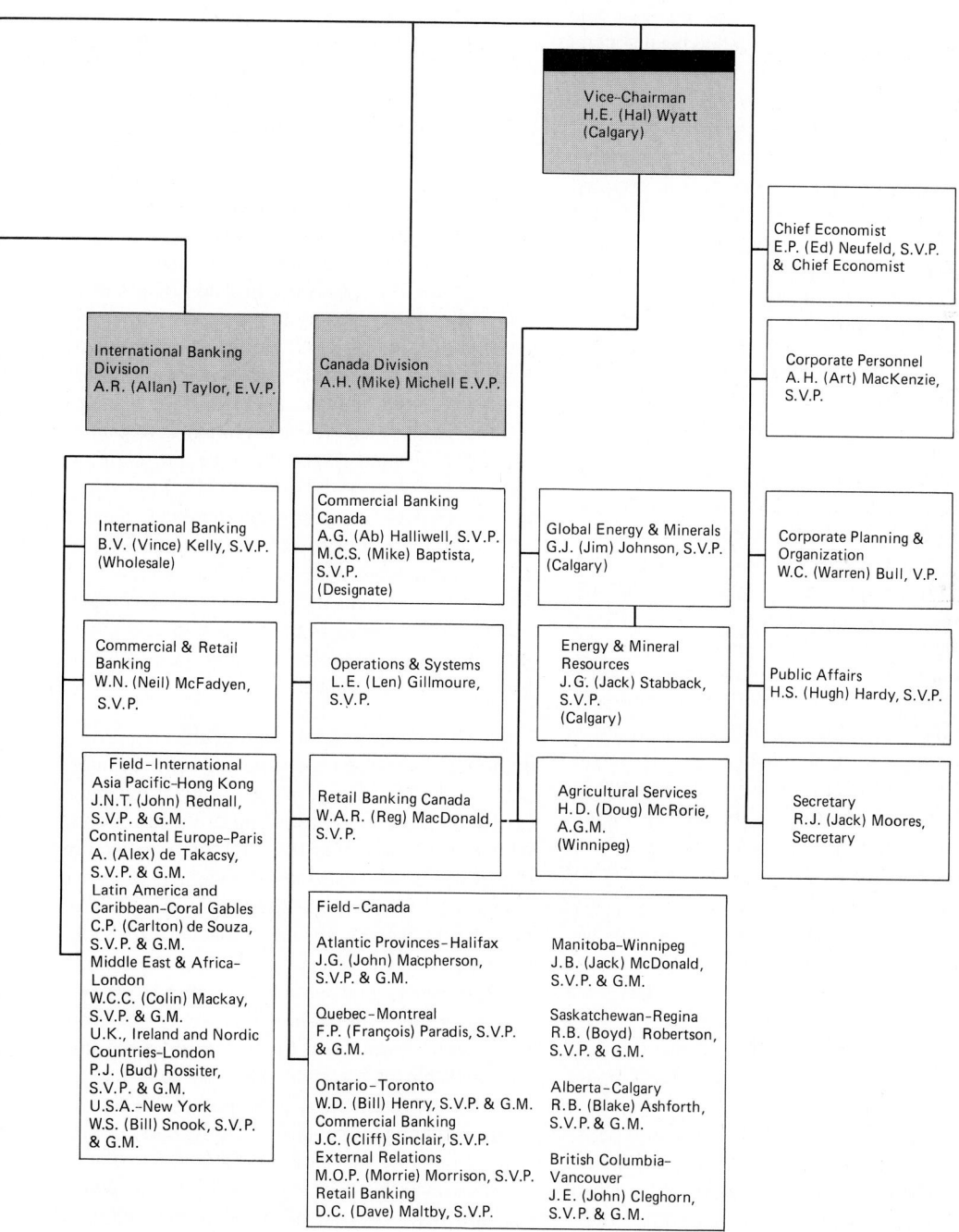

Vice-Chairman
H.E. (Hal) Wyatt
(Calgary)

Chief Economist
E.P. (Ed) Neufeld, S.V.P.
& Chief Economist

Corporate Personnel
A. H. (Art) MacKenzie,
S.V.P.

International Banking
Division
A.R. (Allan) Taylor, E.V.P.

Canada Division
A.H. (Mike) Michell E.V.P.

International Banking
B.V. (Vince) Kelly, S.V.P.
(Wholesale)

Commercial Banking
Canada
A.G. (Ab) Halliwell, S.V.P.
M.C.S. (Mike) Baptista,
S.V.P.
(Designate)

Global Energy & Minerals
G.J. (Jim) Johnson, S.V.P.
(Calgary)

Corporate Planning &
Organization
W.C. (Warren) Bull, V.P.

Commercial & Retail
Banking
W.N. (Neil) McFadyen,
S.V.P.

Operations & Systems
L.E. (Len) Gillmoure,
S.V.P.

Energy & Mineral
Resources
J.G. (Jack) Stabback,
S.V.P.
(Calgary)

Public Affairs
H.S. (Hugh) Hardy, S.V.P.

Field – International
Asia Pacific–Hong Kong
J.N.T. (John) Rednall,
S.V.P. & G.M.
Continental Europe–Paris
A. (Alex) de Takacsy,
S.V.P. & G.M.
Latin America and
Caribbean–Coral Gables
C.P. (Carlton) de Souza,
S.V.P. & G.M.
Middle East & Africa–
London
W.C.C. (Colin) Mackay,
S.V.P. & G.M.
U.K., Ireland and Nordic
Countries–London
P.J. (Bud) Rossiter,
S.V.P. & G.M.
U.S.A.–New York
W.S. (Bill) Snook, S.V.P.
& G.M.

Retail Banking Canada
W.A.R. (Reg) MacDonald,
S.V.P.

Agricultural Services
H.D. (Doug) McRorie,
A.G.M.
(Winnipeg)

Secretary
R.J. (Jack) Moores,
Secretary

Field – Canada

Atlantic Provinces–Halifax
J.G. (John) Macpherson,
S.V.P. & G.M.

Quebec–Montreal
F.P. (François) Paradis, S.V.P.
& G.M.

Ontario–Toronto
W.D. (Bill) Henry, S.V.P. & G.M.
Commercial Banking
J.C. (Cliff) Sinclair, S.V.P.
External Relations
M.O.P. (Morrie) Morrison, S.V.P.
Retail Banking
D.C. (Dave) Maltby, S.V.P.

Manitoba–Winnipeg
J.B. (Jack) McDonald,
S.V.P. & G.M.

Saskatchewan–Regina
R.B. (Boyd) Robertson,
S.V.P. & G.M.

Alberta–Calgary
R.B. (Blake) Ashforth,
S.V.P. & G.M.

British Columbia–
Vancouver
J.E. (John) Cleghorn,
S.V.P. & G.M.

EXHIBIT 2   BRIEF PERSONAL PROFILES OF KEY EXECUTIVES

Mr. Brian Gregson had been named Executive Vice President of Finance and Investments in September 1980. A line banker, he had come up through the Canada Bank and had been general manager of the large Toronto division and other central branches. Mr. Gregson was described as "having good business instincts, a good deal maker, and a skilled negotiator." He was known for his decisiveness and his directness in personal relationships. He tended to cut through to the core of issues and "to see things in clear terms." Friendly and distinguished in appearance, he took pains to get out of his office, to meet his people, and to work with them.

Mr. "Mike" Michell was a brawny, cigar-smoking analytical executive with a phenomenal appetite for numbers. He was highly respected as "a tremendously energetic person, who works 18 hour days, 8 day weeks." Mr. Michell had worked his way up through the ranks to become Executive Vice President of the Canada Division in 1978. Although he tended to manage from his office in a somewhat formal style, he was superb in one-on-one situations. He had a strong commitment to financial planning, drove himself hard in pursuit of objectives and had firm expectations of others. More formal than Mr. Gregson, he was known for his meticulous preparations for public appearances and his capacity to run his highly diverse empire in a manner totally dedicated and supportive of top management's goals. He had been a champion of the long-term development of RBC's electronic technology programs.

Mr. "Rob" Paterson had risen through various line positions in the domestic bank and a short stint in the New York unit of RBC. He then moved into the Bank's head office investment department and rose to its top. From there he became Executive Vice President of the Finance and Investments Division. In 1980 he was posted to London as Chairman, RBC Holdings B.V. He had spent most of his banking life in the money markets and investments side of the Royal Bank. A cultured, sophisticated man with an inter-national perspective, Mr. Paterson had a trader's instincts for how money markets operated and an ability to see the bank's actions from the viewpoint of investors and depositors. On the personal level, he was said to have "a good sense of the market, what makes it tick. . . . Rob has a strong belief in people's willingness to perform. . . . His style is tolerant, helpful, not dictatorial."

Mr. "Joe" Regan's career had been primarily in the international area, dealing with "big ticket" loans and large clients. He had been involved in the U.S., Carribbean, and London markets and had been deputy to the head of the international division of RBC. He was a soft spoken, witty man of few words who had a distaste for those who might pontificate. In 1979 he was appointed Senior Vice President National Accounts, and 1982 became Executive Vice President of the National Accounts Division. Mr. Regan was an experienced corporate-international banker who could think in non-traditional terms. He had headed up a bank-wide task force on trends in the financial services industry and had developed a deep understanding of the fundamental changes occurring in this environment and their implications for the Royal Bank.

Mr. "Geoff" Styles was a tall, gregarious, outgoing, comfortable person who was very international in his viewpoint. He had represented the Royal Bank at the founding of its Orion unit. Although he was an ardent "internationalist" in his viewpoint, he had moved back and forth between the European and Montreal units perhaps more than anyone in the upper levels in the bank. He was often described as "a visionary, very entrepreneurial, and perhaps the bank's best sponsor of the merchant-banking, investment-banking viewpoint." He tended to be very informal and approachable in his style. He was described as "a good communicator, encouraging freedom in thinking among his people." Despite his entrepreneurial flair, he was said "to have good balance sheet instincts and to be very effective with outside constituencies because of his deep knowledge of

EXHIBIT 2 (*Continued*)

international banking and his dialoguing capabilities.'' He had been appointed Executive Vice President of the World Trade and Merchant Banking Division in June of 1980.

Mr. Allan Taylor was a very warm, open person. He had an extraordinarily high energy level, persistence, and an orderly mind that enabled him to digest the essence and dynamics of a complex issue and deal with it forthrightly. After working his way up the line in the domestic bank, Mr. Taylor spent three years in New York before returning to Montreal where he became the head of the International Division in 1977

and an Executive Vice President in 1978. Colleagues said, ''Al Taylor relentlessly pursues his homework. Al says what he means and means what he says. He is known for his articulate, well prepared, careful phrasings in public forums.'' Internally, he paid careful attention to details and expected clear commitments and carefully worked out plans from his subordinates. He was dedicated to the planning process, with accountability and commitment of individuals behind it. And his experiences had given him a well balanced view of both Canadian and international operations.

Source: Author's interviews with various RBC executives.

EXHIBIT 3 SUMMARY OF ROYAL BANK OF CANADA FINANCIAL HISTORY 1977–1984
CONSOLIDATED STATEMENT OF INCOME

For the Year Ended October 31 (in thousands of dollars)	1984	1983	1982	1981	1980	1979	1978	1977
Interest Income								
Loans	$6,967,533	$7,008,683	$ 9,360,648	$ 8,193,495	$5,006,165	$3,649,193	$2,532,891	$2,071,257
Lease financing	64,572	71,093	75,426	41,316	33,778	22,069	21,089	9,387
Securities	718,337	663,882	788,414	776,790	613,836	501,004	320,344	244,808
Deposits with banks	1,267,152	1,138,627	1,860,323	1,738,799	1,114,410	640,722	364,927	262,181
	9,017,594	8,882,285	12,084,811	10,750,400	6,768,189	4,812,988	3,239,251	2,587,633
Interest Expense								
Deposits	6,605,067	6,513,404	10,150,744	8,952,226	5,350,810	3,601,352	2,095,151	1,626,124
Bank debentures	120,217	126,699	128,506	71,659	49,476	44,894	33,764	27,933
Other	38,610	39,318	40,293	14,780	9,739	4,857	4,628	5,072
	6,763,894	6,679,421	10,319,543	9,038,665	5,410,025	3,651,103	2,133,543	1,659,129
Net Interest Income	2,253,700	2,202,864	1,765,268	1,711,735	1,358,164	1,161,885	1,105,708	928,504
Provision for loan losses	535,000	452,000	344,000	185,601	124,430	106,021	96,544	83,710
Net Interest Income After Provision for Loan Losses	1,718,700	1,750,864	1,421,268	1,526,134	1,233,734	1,055,864	1,009,164	844,794
Other income	708,792	667,037	582,874	500,410	377,647	321,292	270,480	244,747
Net Interest and Other Income	2,427,492	2,417,901	2,004,142	2,026,544	1,611,381	1,377,156	1,279,644	1,089,541
Non-Interest Expenses								
Salaries	1,014,353	976,905	944,545	783,894	664,310	575,217	493,650	443,714
Pension and other staff benefits	91,546	98,129	91,516	78,668	73,783	64,780	54,059	49,055
Premises and equipment, including depreciation	293,954	273,264	255,852	203,029	176,886	157,975	151,387	132,747
Other	403,659	397,459	381,961	318,425	274,650	212,963	180,492	159,562
	1,803,512	1,745,757	1,673,874	1,384,016	1,189,629	1,010,935	879,588	785,078
Net Income Before Income Taxes	623,980	672,144	330,268	642,528	421,752	366,221	400,056	304,463
Income taxes	173,000	191,000	(28,000)	160,219	60,876	60,557	135,651	114,289
Net Income Before Minority Interests	450,980	481,144	358,268	482,309	360,876	305,664	264,405	190,174
Minority interests in subsidiaries	895	1,151	620	4,133	12,844	15,973	3,300	2,218
Net Income	$ 450,085	$ 479,993	$ 357,648	$ 478,176	$ 348,032	$ 289,691	$ 261,105	$ 187,956
Income Per Share								
Basic	**$4.25**	$5.03	$3.87	$5.75	$4.74	$3.96	$3.57	$2.57
Fully diluted	**$3.87**	$4.58	$3.68	$5.71	$4.74	$3.96	$3.57	$2.57

Source: Royal Bank of Canada, *Annual Report*, 1984.

EXHIBIT 3 (Continued)

NET INTEREST INCOME ON AVERAGE ASSETS AND LIABILITIES ($ Millions)

	1984			1983			1982			1981		
	Average Balances	Interest	Average Rate	Average Balances	Interest	Average Rate	Average Balances	Interest	Average Rate	Average Balances	Interest	Average Rate
Assets												
Earning Assets												
Deposits with other banks	**$13,182**	**$1,267**	**9.61%**	$12,126	$1,138	9.38%	$13,765	$1,860	13.51%	$11,794	$1,739	14.74%
Securities—Issued or guaranteed by Canada, provinces and municipal or school												
corporations	**2,873**	**317**	**11.03**	2,673	302	11.30	2,236	316	14.13	2,613	386	14.77
Other	**4,402**	**622**	**14.13**	4,551	587	12.90	4,590	805	17.54	4,008	677	16.89
	7,275	**939**	**12.91**	7,224	889	12.31	6,826	1,121	16.42	6,621	1,063	16.05
Loans—												
Mortgages	**8,866**	**1,064**	**12.00**	7,806	1,013	12.98	7,288	921	12.64	7,559	927	12.26
Installment loans	**4,860**	**720**	**14.81**	4,396	701	15.95	4,636	812	17.52	4,252	655	15.40
Other loans in Canadian currency	**22,437**	**2,663**	**11.87**	24,190	2,781	11.50	25,223	4,225	16.75	20,877	3,945	18.90
Other loans in foreign currencies	**22,637**	**2,586**	**11.42**	22,642	2,585	11.42	22,330	3,478	15.58	16,072	2,708	16.85
	58,800	**7,033**	**11.96**	59,034	7,080	11.99	59,477	9,436	15.86	48,760	8,235	16.89
Total earning assets	**79,257**	**9,239**	**11.66**	78,384	9,107	11.62	80,068	12,417	15.51	67,175	11,037	16.43
Other Assets	**7,405**			8,309			8,464			6,313		
Total Assets	**$86,662**	**$9,239**	**10.66%**	$86,693	$9,107	10.50%	$88,532	$12,417	14.03%	$73,488	$11,037	15.02%

EXHIBIT 3 (*Continued*)

Liabilities

	Bal.	Int.	Rate	Bal.	Int.	Rate	Bal.	Int.	Rate	Bal.	Int.	Rate
Interest-Bearing Deposits —												
Demand deposits	$ 5,661	$ 138	2.44%	$ 6,028	$ 154	2.55%	$ 5,973	$ 253	4.24%	$ 5,778	$ 229	3.96%
Deposits by banks	19,804	1,977	9.98	19,605	1,984	10.12	21,306	2,976	13.97	16,348	2,518	15.40
Term deposits in Canadian currency	15,450	1,526	9.88	16,872	1,725	10.22	19,486	2,916	14.96	16,759	2,501	14.92
Other deposits in Canadian currency	16,502	1,113	6.74	15,479	1,025	6.62	13,421	1,555	11.59	11,896	1,541	12.95
Term deposits in foreign currencies	16,592	1,726	10.40	15,950	1,542	9.67	16,437	2,346	14.27	12,928	2,037	15.76
Other deposits in foreign currencies	2,407	125	5.19	2,304	83	3.60	1,920	105	5.47	2,889	126	4.36
	76,416	6,605	8.64	76,238	6,513	8.54	78,543	10,151	12.92	66,598	8,952	13.44
Liabilities of subsidiaries other than deposits	342	39	11.40	340	39	11.47	312	40	12.82	163	15	9.20
Bank debentures	1,115	120	10.76	1,121	127	11.33	1,054	129	12.24	657	72	10.96
Total interest-bearing	77,873	6,764	8.69	77,699	6,679	8.60	79,909	10,320	12.91	67,418	9,039	13.41
Other Liabilities	5,260			5,923			5,745			3,601		
Capital and Reserves	2,529			3,071			2,878			2,469		
Total Liabilities	$86,662	$6,764	7.80%	$86,693	$6,679	7.70%	$88,532	$10,320	11.66%	$73,488	$ 9,039	12.30%
Total Assets/Net Interest Income	$86,662	$2,475	2.86%	$86,693	$2,428	2.80%	$88,532	$ 2,097	2.37%	$73,488	$ 1,998	2.72%

Source: Royal Bank of Canada, *Annual Report,* 1984.

EXHIBIT 3 (*Continued*)

RETURN ON ASSETS (% OF AVERAGE ASSETS)

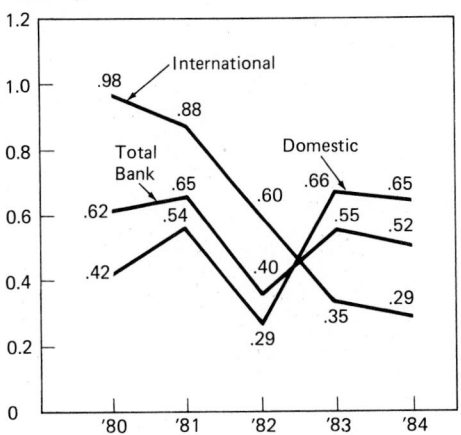

NET INTEREST MARGIN (% OF AVERAGE ASSETS)

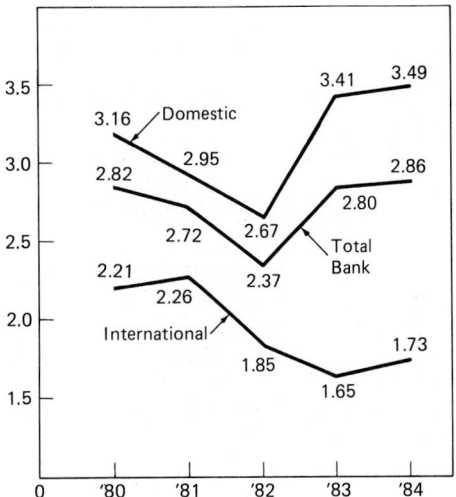

COMPOSITION OF AVERAGE DOMESTIC DEPOSITS ($ BILLIONS)

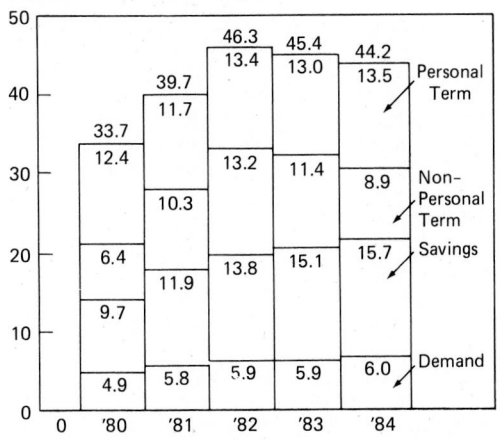

FIXED RATE LENDING PORTFOLIO YIELD VERSUS PORTFOLIO COST OF PERSONAL TERM DEPOSITS (INCLUDING RESERVE COSTS) (PER CENT)

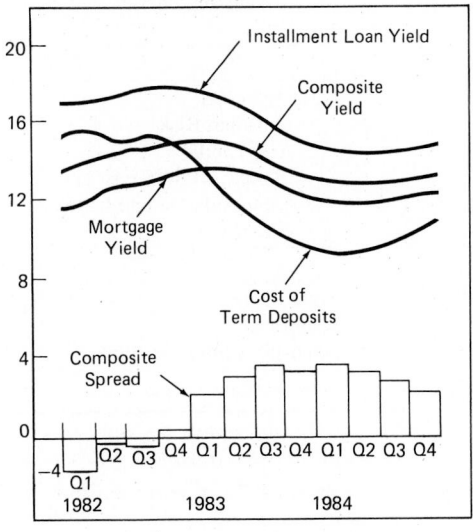

Source: Royal Bank of Canada, *Annual Report*, 1984.

EXHIBIT 3 (*Continued*)

BREAKDOWN OF EARNING ASSETS*

As at September 30 ($ Millions)	1984	Percent	1983	Percent
Loans				
Domestic				
Atlantic Provinces	$ 2,562	6.1%	$ 2,394	6.0%
Quebec	5,203	12.5	4,540	11.5
Ontario	13,070	31.3	11,968	30.3
Manitoba and Saskatchewan	4,862	11.6	4,327	11.0
Alberta	8,633	20.7	8,784	22.2
British Columbia	7,411	17.8	7.521	19.0
	41,741	100.0	39,534	100.0
Of which:				
Mortgages	8,990	21.5	8,004	20.2
Loans to individuals	8,343	20.0	7,682	19.4
Agricultural	2,240	5.4	2,262	5.7
Financial institutions	2,866	6.9	2,446	6.2
Merchandisers	2,857	6.8	2,553	6.5
Manufacturing	3,704	3.9	4,108	10.4
Construction	1,959	4.7	2,359	6.0
Mining and energy	4,023	9.6	3,964	10.0
Other	6,759	16.2	6,156	15.6
	41,741	100.0	39,534	100.0
International				
Canadian Risk	659	3.7	739	4.1
Asia Pacific	2,169	12.0	1,911	10.7
Europe, Middle East and Africa	5,227	28.9	5,927	33.3
Latin America and Caribbean	5,907	32.7	5,372	30.1
U.S.A.	4,102	22.7	3,874	21.8
	13,064	100.0	17,823	100.0
Total Loans	59,805	74.0	57,357	75.2
Securities	6,867	8.5	7,092	9.3
Deposits with Other Banks	14,126	17.5	11,851	15.5
Total Earning Assets	$80,798	100.0%	$76,300	100.0%

* *Earning assets are defined as all assets except cash and deposits with Bank of Canada, acceptances, land, buildings and equipment and other assets.*

Source: Royal Bank of Canada, *Annual Report*, 1984.

EXHIBIT 3 (*Continued*)

COMPARATIVE STATISTICS FOR THE FIVE LARGEST CANADIAN BANKS

Asset Growth Rates (1980–84 Compound Average)

Toronto-Dominion Bank	9.8%
Royal Bank of Canada	9.4
Bank of Nova Scotia	8.7
Bank of Montreal	8.6*
Canadian Imperial Bank of Canada (CIBC)	5.9

* *Excludes assets acquired with Harris Trust. Including Harris assets the rate is 12.6%.*

Pre-Tax Profits (as % shareholders' funds plus own account borrowing, 1980–84 average)

Toronto-Dominion Bank	20.1
Bank of Nova Scotia	16.7
Royal Bank of Canada	14.6
CIBC	13.2
Bank of Montreal	13.2

Return on Assets (1980–1984 average —%)

	Domestic	International	Combined
Toronto-Dominion	0.74	0.73	0.73
CIBC	0.40	0.56	0.56
Royal Bank of Canada	0.51	0.62	0.55
Bank of Montreal	0.50	0.50	0.50
Bank of Nova Scotia	0.43	0.70	0.45

Lending as % of Deposits (1980–84 average)

CIBC	83.1
Toronto-Dominion	82.1
Bank of Montreal	77.3
Royal Bank of Canada	75.7
Bank of Nova Scotia	73.2

Source: "An End to the Monopoly?" *Euromoney*, Supplement, July 1985.

EXHIBIT 3 (*Continued*)

Distribution of Domestic Lending by Category of Borrower (*%, at Sept. 30, 1984*)

	RBC	BOM	CIBC	BNS	TD
Personal Loans	20.0	20.6	21.9	28.3	19.0
Residential Mortgages	21.5	20.0	24.6	22.1	22.2
Primary Producers	15.0	21.9	11.5	24.0	21.5
Trade & Fin. Services	13.7	24.1	16.7		
Manufacturing	8.9		11.0	12.0	19.2
Construction and Real Estate	4.7	13.4	7.3	13.6	7.2
Other	16.2	—	7.0	—	10.9
	100.0	100.0	100.0	100.0	100.0

Distribution of Geographical Risk (*% as of Sept. 30, 1984*)

	RBC	BOM	CIBC	BNS	TD
North America					
Canada	61.8	55.0	70.2	48.1	65.6
USA	9.7	20.9	9.8	16.4	12.8
Europe, Middle East, Africa					
UK	4.9	3.4	2.1	4.5	1.8
France	1.7	1.3	0.9	3.1	1.4
Other	8.4	4.6	4.8	9.0	6.3
Latin America and Caribbean					
Mexico	1.8	2.3	1.4	2.0	2.1
Brazil	1.6	2.4	1.4	1.7	1.9
Other	4.6	2.2	2.2	7.5	2.1
Asia and Pacific					
Japan	2.3	5.5	1.1	4.2	2.7
Other	3.2	2.4	2.3	3.5	3.3

Source: "An End to the Monopoly?" *Euromoney*, Supplement, July 1985.

EXHIBIT 4   COMPETITIVE SUMMARY—FINANCIAL ($ Millions)

	1981					1984				
	RBC	CIBC	BOM	BNS	TD	RBC	CIBC	BOM	BNS	TD
Total Interest Income	11037.1	9047.8	8713.6	6639.5	6007.9	9238.6	7233.3	7720.7	6014.4	4985.4
of Which: Loans	8193.5	7370.1	7028.3	4660.2	4934.9	6967.5	5988.0	5767.6	4328.2	3954.0
Securities	776.8	573.4	601.7	369.0	429.6	718.3	488.7	852.3	414.5	465.8
Bank Deposits	1738.8	884.8	823.2	1448.7	476.1	1267.2	594.1	901.1	1148.6	407.5
Total Interest Expense	9038.7	7408.8	7133.4	5549.6	4977.1	6763.9	5435.1	5961.9	4623.3	3624.9
of Which: Deposits	8952.2	7337.1	7005.7	5500.2	4943.8	6605.1	5321.6	5769.9	4547.4	3584.5
Debentures	71.7	53.1	68.3	37.7	28.4	120.2	110.6	111.4	74.3	39.0
Tax Equiv. Spread	1998.4	1639.0	1580.2	1089.9	1030.8	2474.7	1798.2	1758.8	1391.1	1360.5
Loan Loss Provision	185.6	215.2	196.3	81.2	74.4	535.0	431.2	375.0	241.5	199.2
Other Income	500.4	378.1	288.4	268.3	209.9	708.8	522.8	499.3	309.4	333.6
Net Revenue	2313.2	1801.9	1672.3	1277.0	1166.3	2648.5	1889.8	1883.1	1459.0	1494.9
Total Non-Interest Exp.	1384.0	1175.1	1000.7	832.8	664.4	1803.5	1355.2	1384.2	1005.2	833.5
of Which: Staff Costs	862.6	730.9	602.5	514.4	408.8	1105.8	840.0	777.6	611.0	512.6
Premises	203.0	199.9	184.7	144.6	114.7	294.0	233.7	287.8	190.0	154.5
Other Oper.	318.4	244.3	213.5	173.8	140.9	403.7	281.5	318.8	204.2	166.4
Net Income Before Tax	929.2	626.8	671.6	444.2	501.9	845.0	534.6	498.9	453.8	661.4
Net Income	478.2	320.1	352.9	244.1	285.4	405.1	282.3	283.4	271.7	355.9
Average Assets	73,488	59,752	54,980	45,241	38,605	86,662	68,279	66,714	56,512	44,517
Total Assets	85,360	65,698	62,374	49,067	43,249	88,003	68,118	76,491	59,124	46,597

Source: Competitive Summary by RBC's Control and Financial Planning Group, November 1984.

EXHIBIT 5

R.B.C. Global Network

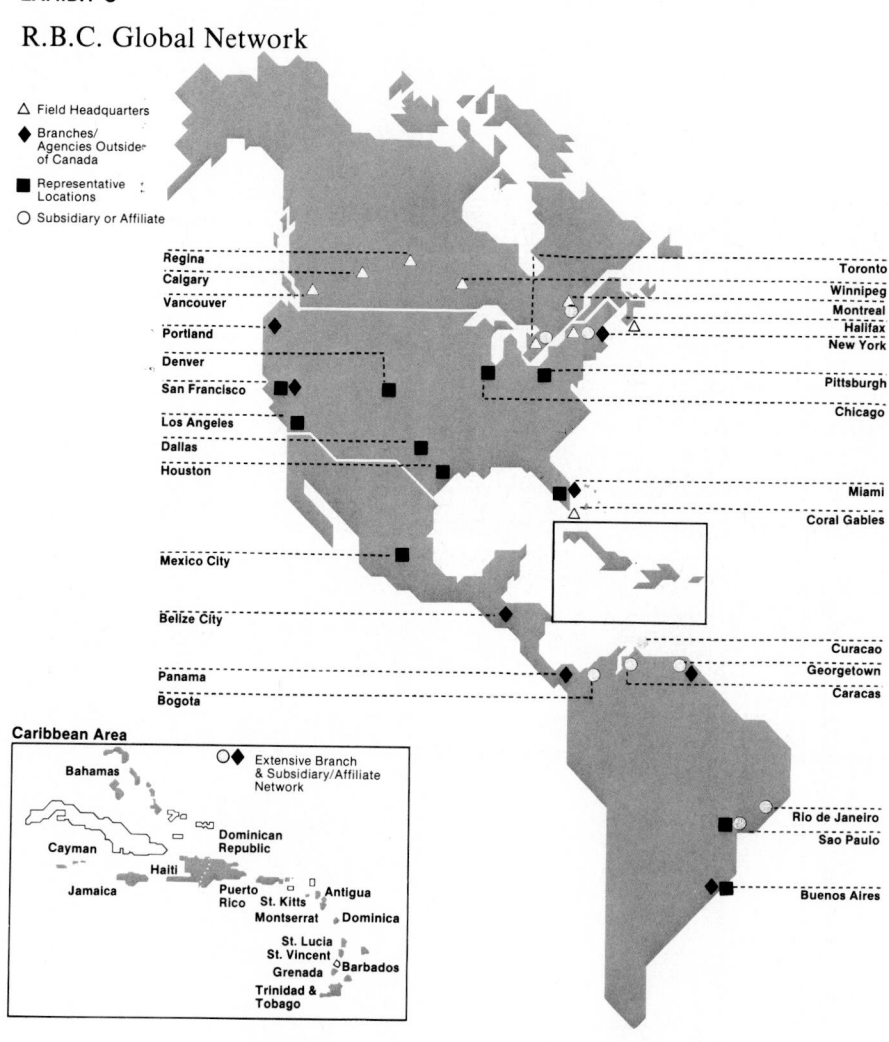

△ Field Headquarters

◆ Branches/
Agencies Outside
of Canada

■ Representative
Locations

○ Subsidiary or Affiliate

Regina
Calgary
Vancouver
Portland
Denver
San Francisco
Los Angeles
Dallas
Houston

Mexico City

Belize City

Panama
Bogota

Toronto
Winnipeg
Montreal
Halifax
New York
Pittsburgh
Chicago

Miami
Coral Gables

Curacao
Georgetown
Caracas

Rio de Janeiro
Sao Paulo

Buenos Aires

Caribbean Area

○◆ Extensive Branch
& Subsidiary/Affiliate
Network

Bahamas

Cayman

Jamaica

Haiti

Dominican
Republic

Puerto
Rico

St. Kitts

Montserrat

Antigua

Dominica

St. Lucia
St. Vincent
Grenada ○Barbados

Trinidad &
Tobago

Source: RBC *Director's Handbook,* 1984.

EXHIBIT 5 (*Continued*)

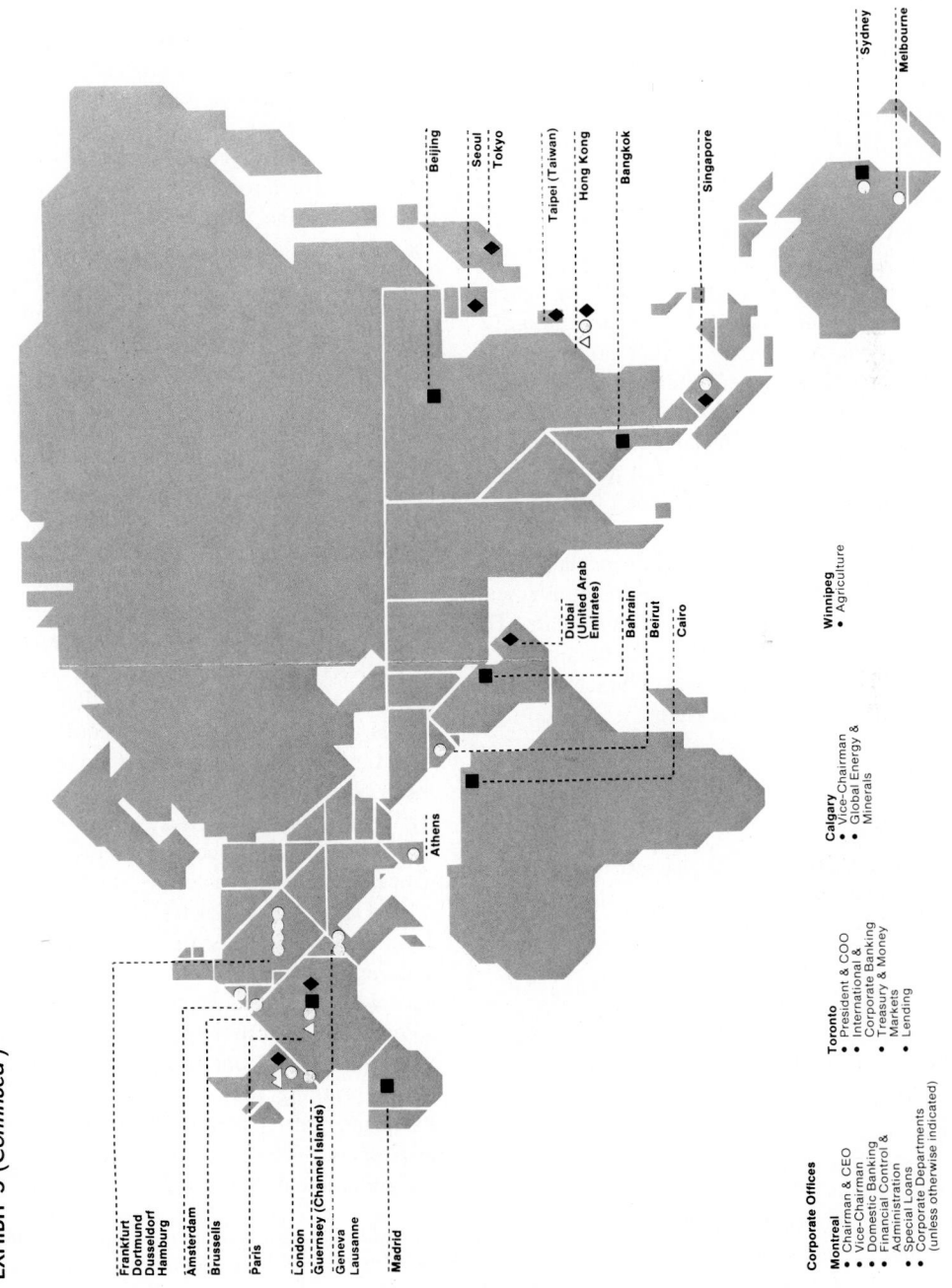

Frankfurt
Dortmund
Düsseldorf
Hamburg

Amsterdam
Brussels

Paris

London
Guernsey (Channel Islands)
Geneva
Lausanne

Madrid

Athens

Dubai (United Arab Emirates)
Bahrain
Beirut
Cairo

Beijing
Seoul
Tokyo
Taipei (Taiwan)
Hong Kong
Bangkok
Singapore

Sydney
Melbourne

Corporate Offices

Montreal
• Chairman & CEO
• Vice-Chairman
• Domestic Banking
• Financial Control & Administration
• Special Loans
• Corporate Departments (unless otherwise indicated)

Toronto
• President & COO
• International & Corporate Banking
• Treasury & Money Markets Lending

Calgary
• Vice-Chairman
• Global Energy & Minerals

Winnipeg
• Agriculture

APPENDIX A-Canada's Financial Services Industry

Competition and the Four Pillars "The Canadian regulatory tradition has been to maintain institutional barriers around the 'core functions' performed by each of the four pillars of the Canadian financial system, primarily to prevent the conflicts of interest which can arise if these functions are combined under one roof."[1] The four pillars and their "core functions" are (1) the banks (chartered and regulated on the federal level) for commercial and consumer lending; (2) trust companies (chartered either on the federal or a provincial level) performing fiduciary activities; (3) insurance companies (chartered either on the federal or a provincial level) for insurance underwriting; and (4) investment dealers, (chartered and regulated on a provincial level) underwriting corporate securities.

Despite this tradition, the Canadian financial services industry is quite competitive with considerable overlap among the four pillars. The various key players have the following shares of total 1983 financial industry assets, using a global corporate asset measure:

Chartered Banks	61.1%
Life Insurance Companies	11.8
Trust Companies	8.7
Credit Unions/Caisses Populaires	6.2
Investment Dealers	1.4
Other Financial Corps., etc.	10.8
	100.0%

Source: Where's the Power in the Financial Services Industry?" *Canadian Banker*, June, 1985.

These statistics overstate the banks' dominance within Canada because they include the foreign currency assets which make up more than 40% of banks' assets, and they exclude trust and insurance companies' administered assets. They also fail to take into account the fact that many trust and life insurance companies are actually divisions of large financial conglomerates, some of which are larger than the banks. The combined assets of the 6 largest financial holding companies total $142 billion while those of the 6 largest banks (excluding foreign currency assets) total $185 billion.[2] If one examines competition on a market by market basis, the banks held a 44% share of the personal savings market, 33% of mortgages outstanding, and 67% of consumer loans at the end of 1983.

The chartered banks compete to varying degrees with the "near banks" for deposits and for mortgages and loan (primarily consumer but some commercial) business. Banks compete with investment dealers in a more limited way. They can be members of selling groups for debt and equity securities and operate fully in the money market, but they can underwrite only certain government and bank related debt securities. More recently, many banks have pushed into private placements and one into discount brokerage while investment dealers have begun offering consumer banking services with Merrill Lynch-like cash management accounts. Banks compete with life insurance companies for mortgage and Registered Retirement Savings Plan (RRSP, the equivalent of an IRA) business and by selling credit-related life insurance. Trust companies, insurance companies, and investment dealers compete for pension fund management but trust companies are the only ones permitted to act in a fiduciary capacity. Banks compete directly with consumer loan companies on consumer loans and with sales finance, leasing, and factoring companies on sales-related and other commercial loans. Finally, there are a growing number of "merchant banking"* and venture capital firms in Canada which compete with the banks (and investment dealers in some areas) in: providing foreign exchange services, financing and facilitating international trade, bringing together buyers and sellers of listed and unlisted companies, providing financial advisory services, arranging long-term financing for governments and multinational corporations,

* *Note: Merchant banking is a term used primarily in Great Britain and Europe to define the activities of such firms as Rothschilds which combine investment banking and parts of commercial banking as they have traditionally been practiced in the U.S.*

and funding and nurturing of entrepreneurial enterprises.

Chartered Banking Canada, unlike the U.S., permits nationwide branch banking in the British tradition, and thus has relatively few banks. There are five large banks with national branch systems which together hold 85% of all bank assets and have close to 7,000 branches—The Royal Bank of Canada, the Canadian Imperial Bank of Commerce, the Bank of Nova Scotia, the Bank of Montreal, and the Toronto Dominion Bank. In addition, there are other Schedule A banks which either have regional or specialized businesses, and 59 Schedule B banks chartered since the 1980 revisions to the Bank Act. Schedule A banks are widely held. No one interest can hold more than 10% of the voting shares. Schedule B banks can be closely held and are subsidiaries of foreign banks.

Foreign Schedule B banks have significant restrictions imposed on them by the Bank Act. They must obtain specific approval to operate from the Minister of Finance, based on their contribution to banking in Canada and reciprocity for Canadian banks in their home countries. Their license to operate is granted on an annual basis, and the Minister must approve their authorized capital. The domestic assets of any individual foreign B bank cannot exceed 20 times its authorized capital and the combined assets of Schedule Bs as a group cannot exceed 16% of all Canadian domestic banking assets. Only 17 of the 59 Bs offer any retail service. Nevertheless, the Bs represent a powerful competitive force since they have all the powers of Schedule A banks, most of them are subsidiaries of the largest banks in the world, and the 14 largest Bs account for 66% of Schedule B assets and 85% of Schedule B net income. In fact, B bank profits (excluding losses of Can. $2.5 million) increased by 14.4% in 1984 while the A banks had a fall of 7.7%.[3]

Given the scope of their operations, Canada's five big banks resemble the large New York City banks except that they have more extensive retail operations. The Canadian banks' international operations account for more than 40% of their total assets, and their role in relation to international financial markets is greater than that of Canada in relation to the world economy.[4] Domestic competition for commercial loan business is intense and until 1982 (when a 50% of equity limit was set) there was no legal lending limit. A single bank could, and often did, supply a large company with all its loans. All banks are members of the Canadian and/or Quebec Deposit Insurance Corporations and are subject to both primary cash reserve requirements set by the Bank Act and secondary reserve requirements set by the Bank of Canada. The chartered banks (and the Montreal City and District Savings Bank chartered under the Quebec Savings Bank Act) are the only institutions subject to such reserve requirements.

The Canadian payments system has one of the most efficient and effective check clearing systems in the world, making possible same-day credit and overnight clearing across a nation which covers six time zones. Prior to the 1980 establishment of the Canadian Payments Association, the banks controlled and operated the payments system with the Bank of Canada holding clearing accounts and making final inter-bank settlements. Now, other check-issuing institutions can gain direct access to the payments system through the Association, or continue to handle transactions through a clearing bank. The degree of internal automation and cooperation among the banks allows them to handle high value corporate payments, payrolls, and dividend credits on magnetic tape without intermediaries like automated clearing houses or Fed Wire. This also enables them to offer national cash management systems to corporations.

The Inspector General of Banks is responsible to the Minister of Finance for the administration of the Bank Act, including supervision of the banking system. He is assisted by and cooperates with the Canadian Deposit Insurance Corporation and the central bank, the Bank of Canada. The Bank of Canada's primary function is to formulate and execute monetary policy. In addition, the Bank holds the cash reserves of the banks, acts as fiscal agent for the federal government, provides liquidity for the banks, and acts as lender of last resort for the banks and investment dealers.

Trust Companies At the end of 1982 there were 67 trust companies in Canada, about 25 of which were federally incorporated. While trusts have no reserve requirements per se, the Province of Ontario (in which most of them operate) requires them to have liquid assets equal to 20% of deposits. Most, if not all, trusts are members of the Canadian and/or Quebec Deposit Insurance Corporations. However, since most of their deposits are either non-checkable or have low turnover rates, few trusts maintain direct access to the payments system. The trusts' fiduciary business includes administration of estates and personal trust funds, management of pension funds, and administration of corporate funds set aside to repay bonded debt. As financial intermediaries, trusts operate much like Savings and Loan Associations in the U.S., having the vast majority of their liabilities in the form of term deposits and the majority of their assets in the form of mortgages.

Credit Unions/Caisses Populaires Credit unions and their Quebec style counterparts, Caisses Populaires, are cooperative, non-profit seeking firms with autonomous local, normally (but not exclusively) single-office operations accepting deposits and lending money to members only. Overall, more than 32% of Canadians belong to a credit union and while much of their growth since the 1930s has been outside Quebec, Quebec's credit unions still represented 53% of all members and 46% of combined assets in 1975. There are many more Caisses Populaires than bank offices in Quebec, while in the rest of Canada bank offices outnumber credit unions 4 to 3. Credit unions tend to operate as mutual consumer loan societies where Caisses Populaires operate more like relatively conservative savings banks with more of their assets being in mortgages and "productive" loans to small independent proprietorships. Both types, because of their organizational form, can offer higher rates than banks on savings (or membership shares) while lending at low rates.

Credit unions have no reserve requirements, and except in Quebec, their deposits are not insured. While each credit union is independent in its operating policies, they almost all belong to a provincial federation or league which provides technical assistance, educational and public relations services, and a central credit society serving as a kind of central bank for its members. At present, no national link exists among the credit unions. However, the formation of shared ATM networks and syndicates for making commercial loans may be a step in that direction.

Life Insurance Companies Canada's life insurance industry is made up of some 170 companies. But it is highly concentrated with more than 85% of all assets in 1980 being held by only 16 companies. Although insurance companies can be chartered by the provinces, more than 90% of all policies are written by federally registered companies. More than half of these companies are foreign based, and a third of Canada's life insurance policies are written by foreign companies. On the other hand, Canadian insurance companies (like the banks) have significant international operations with about 25% of their policies being written outside of Canada.

As in the U.S. the importance of life insurance as a savings vehicle has waned because of high inflation and bank interest rates. But the industry has expanded its products and services to include mortgage loans, RRSPs, mutual funds, computer services, portfolio management, investment advice, and (through segregated funds) variable annuities, higher yield life contracts, individual and group pension plans. Policy holders still invest 76% of their dividends in life insurance companies; and the industry finances 13% of all mortgages, 30% of all Canadian corporate bonds, and 10% of the Government of Canada's market securities.

Investment Dealers and Canada's Capital Markets Canada has about 100 investment houses most of which are fully integrated, acting as brokers, dealers, and underwriters. With Canadian commission rates only unfixed in 1983, the investment houses still receive 56% of their in-

PROFILE OF THE FINANCIAL SERVICES INDUSTRY IN CANADA
FINANCIAL INFORMATION 1977–83 ($ Billions)

Financial Institution	June 1983			December 1981			December 1977	
	Assets	Market Share	Dec./81–June/83 Compound Annual Growth	Assets	Market Share	1977–1981 Compound Annual Growth	Assets	Market Share
Chartered Banks Sch. A (Total)	368.7	45.2%	3.6%	349.7	47.3%	23.4%	150.5	46.7%
(Cdn. $ Assets)	213.5		3.7	202.3		18.4	102.8	
Insurance Companies[1]	85.7	18.1	12.5	71.8	16.8	14.1	42.4	19.4
Trust Companies and	52.8	11.2	8.2	46.9	11.0	14.5	27.3	12.4
Mortgage Loan Companies (excludes Mortgage and Loan Companies associated with chartered banks)	94.4 (Adm.)		16.5	75.1 (Adm.)			N/A	
Credit Unions[2]	41.9	8.9	4.4	39.3	9.2	13.4	23.8	10.8
Other Financial Corp.[3]	30.7	6.5	(16.0)	39.9	9.3	35.0	12.0	5.4
Chartered Banks Sch. B	20.1	4.3	108.0	6.7	1.6	24.4	2.8	1.3
Investment Funds[4]	18.1	3.8	23.4	13.2	3.1	38.4	3.6[5]	1.6
Investment Dealers	9.5	2.0	17.1	7.5	1.7	9.6	5.2	2.4
Total[6]	$472.3	100%	6.9%	$427.6	100%	24.6%	$219.9	100%

Notes: Information for all financial institutions is on a consolidated basis.

In terms of compound annual growth Chartered Banks Schedule A had the smallest positive growth rate during the period 1981–83; other financial corporations experienced a negative compound annual growth for the same period; Chartered Banks Schedule B experienced the greatest growth.

[1] Includes life, accident and sickness, and property and casualty insurance companies.

[2] Includes credit union centrals.

[3] Includes acceptance, consumer loans, leasing, factoring, venture capital, term financing and merchant banking companies.

[4] Includes closed end funds, mutual funds, and segregated funds managed by insurance companies.

[5] Excludes segregated funds—information for that period not available.

[6] Excludes Banks—Schedule A (Total) Assets, and Trust Companies and Mortgage Loan Companies administered total assets. Assets as at October 31, 1983 for Chartered Banks: Sch. A (Total)—$368.7; Schedule A (Cdn. $ Assets)—$217.6; Schedule B—$22.3.

Source: RBC internal report.

come from brokerage compared to 32% from underwriting and trading. Competition in this sector is increasing substantially; discount brokers have sprung up and one bank now offers discount brokerage services. Competition for underwriting business has also increased rapidly, with investment dealers now targeting older Canadians (and those with high net worths) for money and cash management services. Despite some recent mergers, most investment dealers are thinly capitalized and are viewed by many as being too weak and reactionary to cope with the growing competition and internationalization in world capital markets.

Foreign dealer involvement in Canada's capital market peaked in 1971. In 1972 regulations were established which limited foreign shareholding in any Ontario-registered Securities Dealer to 10% for any one foreign shareholder and 25% for foreign shareholders in aggregate. At that time there were 26 affiliates of overseas firms in Canada with shareholdings in excess of the new rules. They were allowed to continue to do business subject to restrictions on the rate at which they could expand their business. In 1985 only three of the 26 affiliates were still in business, including a subsidiary of Merrill Lynch.[5] In February 1985 the Ontario Securities Commission proposed to allow additional foreign brokers to set up shop under similar restrictions, or to buy as much as 30% of a Canadian securities dealer.[6]

Canada has five stock exchanges— one in Toronto which accounts for nearly 80% of all trading, one in Montreal, and smaller exchanges trading mostly local stocks in Winnipeg, Calgary, and Vancouver. There is also an extensive Over-The-Counter market in which all bonds and many stocks are traded. The combination of the five exchanges, the OTC market, and the nationwide branches of some of the investment houses provides Canada with something approaching a national capital market. However, private placements are very common and relatively few companies "go public" to raise equity capital. Only 9% of Canadians (as opposed to 22% of Americans) own shares directly; and the widespread use of non-voting shares has led to 80% of the companies in the Toronto Stock Exchange's 300 Index being controlled by a small (half dozen or so) group of investors.[7] The Montreal Stock Exchange, having dropped to only 8% of the share value traded in 1981, had increased its share by 1985 to more than 20%, by encouraging the number of Quebec companies going public to grow, by adding new products such as options and futures, and by attempting to become a connection point for the main international money centers.[8] Toronto is Canada's largest stock exchange and in the forefront of computer developments worldwide. Montreal is the innovator, introducing a widening range of new investment products. Vancouver for some years now has been carving out for itself a special niche as the market for new companies at an earlier stage of development than would qualify them for a listing on staider markets.[9]

COMPARATIVE PLANNING SYSTEMS: LITTON INDUSTRIES AND TEXAS INSTRUMENTS

Following are brief descriptions of the planning and control systems in several diversified companies. Each has been heralded as an important example of the planning act. The student should evaluate the merits and demerits of each system. What are the functions and components of a well formed planning system? What are the elements of strategic control, management control, and operational control? What determines which planning and control system is most appropriate to an individual company? Are there any generalizations applicable to all companies?

LITTON INDUSTRIES, INC.

"In the late summer of 1953, three young men quit their high paying jobs with Hughes Aircraft (where they had helped push sales from $2 million to $200 million in just five years) to strike out on their own in the electronics business. Charles "Tex" Thornton had been Vice President and

Case copyright © 1985 by James Brian Quinn. Major sections of the Litton Industries segment of case excerpted from the Litton Industries (AR), (BR) cases prepared by R. Hanna under the supervision of Kenneth R. Andrews. Copyright © 1968 by the President and Fellows of Harvard College. Used by permission of the Harvard Business School. Materials for the Texas Instruments segment of case derived largely from studies by Edgar Barrett[12], Mariann Jelinek[13], and R.F. Vancil[14]. All materials used by permission of copyright holder indicated in footnote. Verb tenses occasionally changed to maintain continuity. At the end of each major quote appears a footnote indicating the page number within a major source, e.g., (7, xx) indicates the appropriate page in the Litton Industries (BR) case.

Assistant General Manager at Hughes; Hugh Jamieson, a Research Scientist turned engineer and businessman, had been one of the two chiefs of Hughes' large radar-development group. Roy Ash had been Hughes' Assistant Controller. The oldest, Thornton, was 40 . . . . They were probably worth $200,000 —about enough money to go into business in a loft. . . . By late November 1953, however, Thornton had talked [sic] Lehman Brothers into raising $1.5 million with which the three bought a small microwave tube company in San Carlos, California, owned by an engineer names Charles Litton."[1]

"The way to sell [government electronics], Thornton thought, was to build a company loaded with brainy [people] who could come up with new weapons. . . . Lehman Brothers, by one insider's count, had "dozens" of similar propositions to choose among at the time Thornton made his pitch. What made Lehman back Thornton and reject so many others? "We were impressed by Thornton himself . . . he spoke our language.

The original financing consisted of the following securities:"[2]

525,000 shares of $0.10 par value common stock:	$ 52,500
2,500 shares of $100 par value preferred stock:	250,000
$1,200,000 of five year 5% sub. income debentures:	1,200,000
	$1,502,500

Almost immediately the corporation embarked on a program of research, development and acquisitions in three distinct areas: computers and control systems, radar systems, and navigational systems. The R&D program was made possible by the high rate of cash generation coming from the San Carlos tube plant. The acquisition program soon extended to companies in other phases of electronics.[3]

Continued Acquisition Growth

Through the late 1960s, Litton grew at an annual rate of 36%, half by acquisition and half by internal growth. *Fortune* commented as follows:

> What sticks out all over . . . is not just diversification— everybody does that— but a superb sense of timing. Litton's secret is that it has made a practice of doing what other companies are not doing, and of *not* doing what everybody else is doing. From its very beginning, when almost all industry was scrambling after contracts for military systems, Litton walked the other way and concentrated on electronic components, the profitable hardware of the advanced sciences. When others . . . went after the glamorous missile market, Litton shot for manned military planes, which turned out to be a far bigger market than anyone supposed. . . . Other companies were lured into marketing big general purpose computers; Litton . . . stayed out of that, . . . , and instead developed a promising business in small inexpensive computers. . . .[4]

Through 1967, Litton's acquisitions were largely electronics related. Even Ingalls Shipyard was looked upon as an application of electronics to submarines. The same rationale was applied to the acquisition of Stouffer Foods which "coupled closely with Litton's capabilities in electronic cooking technology."[5] However, by the late 60s *Business Week* described Litton as:

> . . . A giant conglomerate in technology. . . . Increasingly, . . . it is performing a myriad of professional and business services—store design, computer preparation of income tax forms, design of educational curricula, . . . and

broad economic studies, such as one . . . for the Greek government, on how to best develop the Island of Crete and the Peloponnesus Peninsula. A former Litton officer [said] Litton now is something like a Fourth of July skyrocket. First, ten stars burst. Then each of them burst into ten others.[6]

Litton became a darling of the stock markets and one of the fastest growing companies of the booming late 60s and early 70s. By 1984 Litton Industries had grown into a $5 billion company and it was among the most profitable and stable of the "multimarket" companies during the 1981–83 recession.

OPPORTUNITY PLANNING

Line Planning

During this period Litton coined the term "opportunity planning." Planning was considered to be a line and not a staff activity. Division managers, group vice presidents, and the president were each actively concerned with planning at their levels. The genesis of the majority of Litton's plans took place at the division level, at least once a year, and possibly more frequently.* With some of the larger divisions, the division manager was required to submit to his group VP a description of what he wanted his division to do during the coming 12-month period. Mr. Ash, the president, described the process as follows: (7,1)

> [Each division head must first] assess the strengths and weaknesses of his division in detail. Then he must look at the world around him. He knows his own industry best and he is expected to determine niches, opportunities or whatever you like to call them that his division could possibly exploit. In addition, he must examine each of his existing products to see where he could do better, what he could perhaps

---

* *The frequency was determined by need rather than formal schedules.*

dispense with and how he plans to take the appropriate action. In effect, he progressively narrows in on a match between the world around him and his own division's capabilities.

. . . We dislike the word planning here because it tends to suggest staff activities, and also implies a sense of neatness of approach. Because of this we have substituted the word ''opportunity.'' This has more of the flavor we want—it suggests innovation and new ways of doing things. We want, wherever possible, major steps forward—not just successive refinements. It's with this in mind that we push our division managers very hard to really identify the opportunities and to be creative in doing so.

Using this basic approach, the division manager created his own opportunity or business plan. At this stage there was no great emphasis on financial data, although in broad terms the projected revenue, profit and capital required for the various opportunities had to be identified. The emphasis was on the logic of the proposals and how well thought-out the various alternatives were. In addition, a missed or unidentified opportunity was as catastrophic as a poorly supported or overly ambitious proposal.

At the group level, the division opportunity plans were evaluated, discussed and modified as appropriate. A Group VP stated that he . . . acted as a sounding board which allowed the division manager to test and try out new ideas and suggestions. In the final analysis, however, the Group VP felt that he had to reach some agreement with the division manager's proposals and to check them for consistency with the other divisions of his group. The relationship was one of cooperation, with both the group and division managers trying to arrive at the most advantageous final solution. The process at this stage was described by another Group VP as follows:

The development of an opportunity plan is not a financial rigamarole. Basically, I try to look at what assets we have, what are the opportunities that exist and what are the risks and rewards that could result.

Each opportunity is evaluated as a complete package, considering what we can get out of it and whether we can make a go of it. If we think the best route to exploiting the opportunity is the acquisition of another company, then we will recommend which one and why. (7,2)

The Corporate Level Presentation

The third and final major step in the opportunity planning process was the presentation of the division plans to the company's president. . . . Each division had a separate opportunity session which was attended by approximately five people: the division manager, probably one divisional marketing executive, one divisional technical expert, the appropriate group vice president and [the president]. At this session the *division manager* presented his opportunity plan for the coming year. The president commented:

Our evaluation of opportunities is systematized, not formalized. We try to emphasize the analysis aspect of the opportunity session rather than the formal presentation side of things. *Everybody digs in.* I bring to the meeting a company-wide perspective yet the least detailed knowledge, while the division manager brings the most intimate knowledge with his special perspective and, of course, the group VP is somewhere in between with both perspective and knowledge. We attempt to hammer out strategies as distinct from tactics. If the proposals seem a bit weak or data is missing we will send them back to the drawing board and have the division manager try again. There is no satisfactory technique that suits all divisions. We don't set goals that they have to meet. Some divisions, by the nature of their business, will grow faster than the corporation as a whole, while others will be slower or perhaps even be temporarily static. The real question we ask ourselves is, have we made the very most of the opportunities that are available to us in each environment as the division group managers and I see it. Of course, the group VP has done most of his own soul-searching before he comes to these sessions.

One group vice president commented on the meetings:

> . . . To my knowledge there has never been an occasion when a good project or opportunity has been held up for lack of funds. It is not really a matter of having a certain size pie and trying to equitably share this out among all the competing claims. That's just a textbook notion of how things *should* go. (7,3)

Long Range Financial Plans

Once the opportunity session had been successfully completed, the division manager then generated a set of detailed and interlocking financial plans that reflected the decisions taken in the meetings. These plans contained profit and loss statements, balance sheets and supporting data for the coming 12-month period on a month-by-month basis. Financial data were also included for a 24-month period on a quarterly basis and for a 36-month period on a yearly basis. The financial plans were developed on a "running-year" system and were submitted ultimately to the corporate financial VP. Once checked for accuracy they were returned to the divisions as a "charter" for the coming year's operations. . . . Opportunity planning and review was completely independent of financial planning and review. . . . [But] it was the opportunity sessions that formed the basis upon which the financial plans were developed. . . . (7,3)

In the opportunity review sessions [the president] relied upon at least two other "inputs" to help him relate each division's activities to those of the corporation as a whole. These two inputs were: 1) an overall plan for Litton as a corporation, and 2) the identification of opportunities outside existing corporate group activities. These latter were developed by a corporate staff planning function at company headquarters.

The Corporate Plan

Litton's overall plan was something about which very little was publicly said. As [Chairman] Thornton [commented], "We do not disclose the details of our plan because we feel that this could be viewed as a promotion. We are more interested in replacing words and pseudo-promises with results." Although it was clear that the plan involved financial considerations, the opportunity aspects of it were embodied in a chart of the form shown in Figure 1. . . . The "relative" environment had been divided into basic areas which were then further subdivided into more specific product groupings. The format was highly flexible and the completion of any one part could occur at any time. (7,4)

Generally speaking, the responsibility for consummating an acquisition was placed on the source that recommended it. [If recommended by group or division managers], negotiations and details were their responsibility after it had been determined with corporate management (1) that such an acquisition was desirable and (2) what range of terms and conditions were allowable. Division heads were expected to be the driving force behind their proposed acquisitions, although they were also expected to call upon headquarters for needed professional and technical assistance. Possible acquisitions that came from other sources were usually handled by the corporate planning staff. Whenever possible a member of the corporate planning staff was assigned to such newly acquired company to ensure that it was properly integrated into the total Litton structure.

Acquisition Criteria

The company did not have a single set of specific acquisition criteria except with regard to the overall opportunity plan shown in Figure 1 and in relation to anti-trust considerations, where great care was taken to ensure than no anti-trust regulations were violated. Each acquisition was examined in the light of its ability to fulfill an opportunity potential. (7,6)

Mr. Ash elaborated on some of the guidelines which influenced the company's search for acquisition candidates:

Our acquisition criteria are not explicitly listed, but generally speaking there are certain attributes against which we evaluate each potential acquisition. For instance, we do not want to become involved with companies or industries that are dependent for their future growth upon the growth of the economy as a whole or, put in another way, each opportunity must have a growth potential in its own right. Most suitable acquisitions will ideally be greater than a certain critical mass, that is, the acquisition shouldn't be of such a size that it has become dependent on the economy for growth, neither should it be so small that it has to struggle for survival. Apart from these factors, we also try to avoid getting into situations where we are just selling brain power. We want to obtain some leverage on our skills by selling an end product and not

FIGURE 1   A REPRESENTATION OF LITTON'S OVER-ALL OPPORTUNITY PLAN*

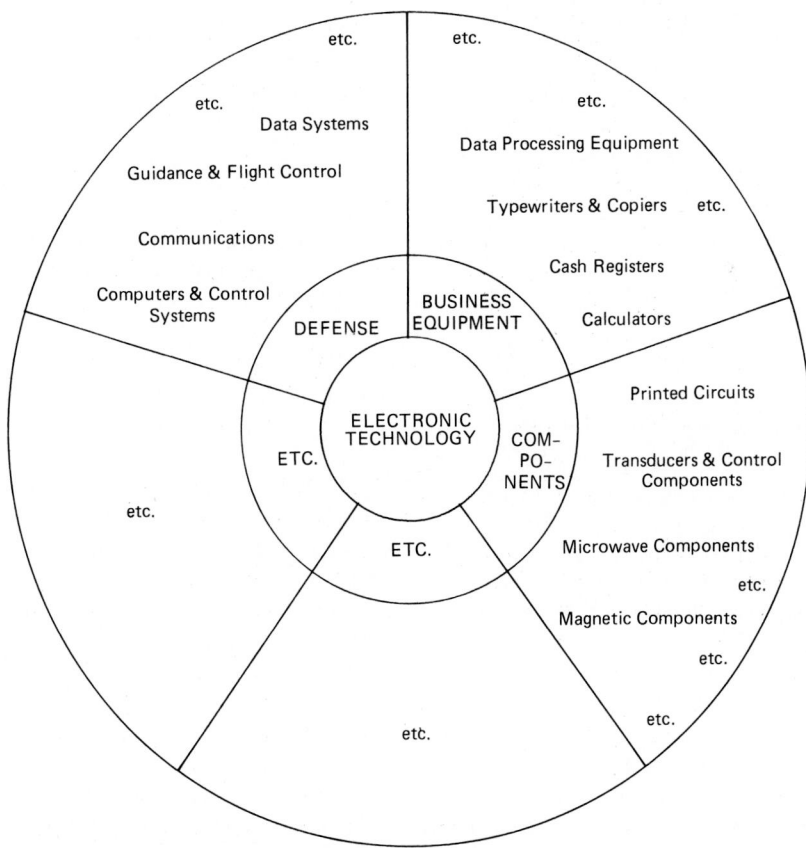

*   *The above diagram is representative of the structure of Litton's plan. As was explained in the text, the actual details were not released by the company.*

Source: Company records.

just the skill itself. In addition to these guidelines there are certain industries which have characteristics that we feel are not suited to our particular business philosophy. As an example we are not interested in acquiring financial companies or in becoming involved with retailing. (7,7)

Organization

One basic tenet upon which the Litton organization was built was the importance attached to the line as distinct from the staff organization. . . . In the Litton system, the key role was played by the division manager. He was responsible for the day-to-day operations of the company and for the generation of revenue within the organization. Because he was such an important link in the chain, the company provided him with a great deal of autonomy and freedom to operate his own division.[8] As one division manager put it:

> We ultimately have only three responsibilities. First, we are checked that our return on gross assets is reasonable and that it does in fact represent a worthwhile use of the capital employed. Second, we are expected to make an operating profit that is in line with the nature of the opportunities in our particular business. Both of these measures, of course, are expected to show improvement over time, that is, we have to grow. The only other requirement they place upon us is that we stay out of jail. Very simple really. (7,10)

In actual practice the division managers were not quite as free as the above quotation would suggest. Although the aim was to keep the organization decentralized at the division level and to have each of these operate as true profit centers, there were several activities over which the division manager had little control. Figure 2 lists the responsibilities reserved for corporate headquarters. These responsibilities were not listed anywhere in the company, nor was there any one person who could (or perhaps would)

quote more than a few of those included. The list was compiled by the researcher from information supplied by nine separate executives at various levels within the organization. (7,10)

There was very little sense of imposition by headquarters on a division's freedoms. The feeling was more one of how do we (at corporate) let the divisions make the most of their opportunities? This feeling of freedom from interference was also shared by the division managers who were interviewed. One division manager commented: . . . "As a division manager you are certainly master of your own show. . . ."

Another division manager, when discussing line, staff relationships, said: . . .

> In actual practice we almost have more freedom than if we owned the show ourselves. In effect, I feel I make all the important decisions here—sure we have to check some things with corporate and we have certain financial targets we aim to meet—but what business doesn't? In fact, it's better running this business now than it was as an independent. I have a really skilled staff I can call on for help and yet, thank goodness, they are never down here poking around. Because we pay a fixed management fee, I have no hesitation in calling them in. They are essentially free. (7,12)

All the mandatory interaction in the organization was vertical, the horizontal interaction developed on the mutual self-interest of each division. . . . The prerogative was purely in their own hands. There was *no* attempt to interfere with divisions on the basis of centralized planning efficiencies. The increase in individual motivation provided by this delegation of responsibility and autonomy was felt to outweigh any advantages that could be gained by imposing centralized "slide-rule" efficiencies from the corporate office. The company possessed no organization chart, nor did it possess any policy manuals at the corporate level, except for a manual detailing the company's accounting practices. (7,13)

[There was a] qualified stock option plan "to aid the corporation in retaining its key em-

FIGURE 2 ACTIVITIES OUTSIDE THE CONTROL OF THE DIVISION MANAGERS

1. Pension funding

2. Most insurance work had become centralized at corporate headquarters

3. Legal work. Although Divisions could and did have legal groups, these were under the control of the corporate level. Items specifically reserved for the corporate legal staff were: acquisition legal work; tax planning; S.E.C.; anti-trust and litigation

4. Every year division managers had to report conflicts of interest, private dealings with customers or suppliers, equity transactions and dealings

5. All real estate was handled at headquarters

6. The raising of capital

7. Each division had to meet the performance requirements of their financial plan. This was checked by headquarters.

8. The payment of an annual management fee

9. Reporting on a monthly basis

10. Cash control was at corporate headquarters

11. Salary or wage changes had to be approved by the supervisor and the supervisor's su-

pervisor. Salaries greater than $30,000 were approved by Ash.

12. There were 17 basic accounting policies that the divisions were required to follow

13. The divisions were subjected to an internal audit

14. The division managers could not go outside the company for management consulting help without concurrence

15. Some aspects of the acquisition procedure, notably legal, final price and integration of the acquired company were corporate responsibilities

16. Opportunities were subject to review and acceptance in the opportunity sessions

17. Indiscriminate use of the Litton name was not permitted

18. The divisions did not report independently to financial and credit services

19. Stockholder relations were reserved for corporate

20. Loss pricing, or unusual risk-taking such as fixed price research and development bids.

Source: Company Interviews (7,11).

ployees and the key employees of companies acquired by the corporation and to assist the corporation in attracting additional key employees." The main incentive[s] in the total organization, however, appeared to be the opportunities for advancement provided by the continuous growth of Litton, as well as by the fact that many top executives over the years had moved out of Litton to assume high-ranking positions in other companies. Commenting on this movement of executives, Ash said:

> We aim to keep a continuous upward spiralling of our best talent. We will move people across the organization from say a controllership of a large division to the managership of a smaller one. Staff people will move into line positions and line people may move into staff roles at head-

quarters. But, in all our moves, the aim is to take the person up, not just across. We are also finding that many of our top people leave us after a period of years. This is mainly because they are dynamic individuals who want to be at the top of the tree—when they meet a block here, their inclination is to move to areas where they can go higher. We feel this is probably a good thing. It helps us to keep moving people up and thus the organization stays young. (7,14)

The Control System

The crux of the control system was the financial plan generated by each division once a year and updated as required. . . . The plan was on a running year basis and included projections for

12 months on a monthly basis. . . . Each plan consisted of a full balance sheet and a profit and loss statement for the appropriate period coupled with complete supporting data. The original plans were approved by headquarters and updated quarterly. . . . Divisions returned to headquarters a monthly report showing actual performance. This was compared to the plan and significant deviations noted and explanations sought. The corporate controller, . . . said:

> . . . We realize here that when we receive a report, it is past history. We expect divisions to call up if anything is out of line and not wait to send in the report. We probably make as many mistakes in this company as in any other company, but our reaction time is fast enough to catch them before they get out of control. . . .
> . . . To help us in this regard, we travel to many of the divisions and try to get a feeling for what they are up to. I would guess that I spend about a third of my time keeping up with the products we make and the types of markets we sell to. (7,15)

Another form of control was that exercised over cash. The treasurer's office at corporate headquarters acted as the company's banker and all cash generated by the divisions, apart from any local compensating balances, was wire transferred to headquarters on a daily basis. Similarly, requests for cash from divisions were attended to on a daily basis. . . .*

Any discussion of control would be incomplete without a mention of several indirect controls. First of these was the corporate real estate staff which approved all site elections, oversaw lease negotiations, and reviewed all economic analyses for land purchases, construction, or asset disposals. Second was the corporate consulting

group which, when called in, could highlight areas of gross negligence. Third, all legal work was under corporate control. Fourth was the internal audit function. Litton had a *highly* developed internal auditing staff which, as well as being responsible for auditing, was also available to divisions managers for special surveys. It was another of the many lines of communication that extended between the corporate headquarters and the divisions. (7,16)

Internal Communications

One particularly distinguishing feature of Litton was its emphasis on direct communication between personnel. . . .

> The most effective means of contact—providing both communication and understanding—is personal conversation. Litton's corporate management has recognized that the improved technology of today's communication industry allows a company to be controlled through extensive personal contact. Therefore, Litton's main tool of communication and understanding, i.e., control, is personal contact within its management, made possible by extensive use of telephones and jet aircraft.[9]
> Litton executives hate memos. They substitute personal visits and long-distance phone calls. "We spend millions,"[10] conceded Ash. "It's our lifeblood." Doors are nearly always open, and people move in and out with a bustle that sometimes makes Litton on Monday morning resemble a war room. If a big deal arises, the wheels really spin, often far into the night. But the company can move fast; it decided to buy Hewitt-Robins Inc. $2\frac{1}{2}$ hours after the chance arose. . . .[11]

The emphasis was on continuing personal contact for all levels of discussion. Telephone meetings were a common method of discussing

---

* *This procedure did not apply to foreign subsidiaries. However, there was at headquarters a foreign currency specialist who was responsible for hedging soft currencies, moving money between foreign divisions, and for the borrowing of capital outside of the U.S.*

mutual problems and providing information. Apart from these meetings, the company had only two other committees. One was the executive committee of the board, which never met in scheduled formal sessions but had the authority to act as needed between board meetings. The other was a committee of trustees that supervised the pension fund. Decision-making was assigned to individuals and not to groups. . . .

Chairman Thornton summarized this philosophy as follows:

> Our organizational purpose is to motivate the individual manager. We believe in placing responsibility on people and not on groups, and having given a person responsibility, we like to provide an environment in which he can truly exercise his own judgment. We think that the increase in motivation or "individual efficiency" that results from this approach enhances the over-all organization's effectiveness. We may not have the most efficient organization, but we certainly have a very effective one. . . . (7,18)

Problems of the 1980s

After the booming 1960s era in which Litton grew at a 36% annual rate, it settled down to a more conservative pattern in the 1970s. It began to divest some of its less technological divisions, including Stouffer Corp., its Great Lakes cargo vessels and shipbuilding facilities, its medical supply, industrial rubber products, refrigeration equipment, medical supplies, and printing businesses. But it also continued to acquire related companies and product lines, including Itek Corp. In 1984 it still had plants in 81 cities and 30 states. Its major product groups and lines of business were:

Advanced Electronic Systems: Electronic and communications systems for government and commercial customers, inertial navigation systems, digital data processing systems, mission control, fire control and monitoring systems, microelectronic digital data converting equipment.

Business Systems: Office machines and equipment, electronic display devices, printing calculators, programmable calculators, microcomputers, special purpose minicomputers, automated business systems, point of sale systems, electronic cash registers, electronic label printing systems, credit terminals, fine paper for speciality purposes, office design and planning services.

Electronic and Electrical Products: Computer and microwave components, integrated circuits, specialized motors and drives, electronic and mechanical components, avionic instruments, night vision devices, electronic and microwave cooking equipment, medical electronic instrumentation and optical surgical equipment.

Industrial Systems and Services: Materials handling systems and equipment, engineering and construction of material handling systems, computer controlled machine tools and accessories, hand tools and related metal products, seismic exploration and data processing systems, geophysical and exploration systems.

Marine Engineering and Production: Commercial and defense shipbuilding, production and overhaul of military and commercial vessels, oil drilling platforms, industrial products for commercial customers.

The breakdown of sales and profits among these lines of business was:

	Percent of Total Sales	Percent of Total Profits
Industrial systems & services	21%	24%
Business systems	17	−5
Advanced electronic systems	28	37
Electronic & electrical products	19	22
Marine engineering & production	15	22

Source: Litton Industries, *Annual Report*, 1984.

EXHIBIT I KEY FINANCIAL DATA (*$ Millions, except per share data*)

Year	Revenues	Oper. Income	Capital Expense	Depr.	Net Income	Cash	Total Assets	Long Term Debt	Common Equity
1983	4,720	515	179	203	232	1,243	3,999	214	1,779
1982	4,933	584	296	155	315	1,178	3,837	211	1,627
1981	4,936	586	291	127	312	1,248	3,688	229	1,371
1980	4,242	556	209	106	291	1,008	3,264	263	1,084
1979	4,086	442	158	105	189	724	2,854	371	829
1978	3,651	306	149	92	(91)	93	2,279	514	651
1977	3,441	249	99	82	56	73	2,064	550	745
1976	3,351	220	100	79	28	66	2,057	604	691
1975	3,430	212	104	76	35	76	2,186	630	676
1974	3,028	221	88	70	(15)	71	2,214	643	644

	1984	1983	1982	1981	1980	1979	1978	1977	1976	1975
Earnings/Share	N/A	5.41	7.39	7.31	6.85	4.41	(2.35)	1.21	0.54	0.72
Prices—										
High	$74\frac{1}{4}$	$71\frac{1}{2}$	$58\frac{3}{8}$	$86\frac{3}{4}$	$83\frac{3}{4}$	$39\frac{1}{2}$	$25\frac{7}{8}$	$13\frac{3}{8}$	15	$7\frac{1}{2}$
Low	$56\frac{1}{4}$	$47\frac{1}{2}$	$34\frac{1}{2}$	$46\frac{1}{4}$	$36\frac{5}{8}$	$17\frac{7}{8}$	12	10	$5\frac{7}{8}$	$2\frac{1}{2}$

Source: Data drawn from Standard & Poor's, *Stock Reports*, various years.

EXHIBIT II   A COMPENDIUM OF CONGLOMERATES

Conglomerate 1983 Sales in Millions	Return on Stockholders' Equity, 1978–83			
	Median	*High*		*Low*
Teledyne $2,979	**24.4%**	**29.2%** 1979		**11.5%** 1983
Minnesota Mining & Manufacturing $7,039	**20.1**	**22.2**	1979	**17.8** 1982
Chesebrough-Pond's $1,685	**19.8**	**20.0**	1982	**17.8** 1978
Litton Industries $4,719	**19.6**	**24.9**	1980	**Loss** 1978
American Standard $2,182	**19.3**	**24.7**	1980	**5.8** 1982
Emerson Electric $3,475	**19.3**	**19.7**	1981	**17.8** 1983
Northwest Industries $1,976	**19.2**	**41.1**	1981	**Loss** 1983
Lear Siegler $1,464	**18.6**	**20.9**	1979	**13.3** 1983
Marmon Group $1,467	**18.6**	**25.1**	1979	**10.6** 1983
General Electric $26,797	**18.3**	**19.1**	1979	**17.8** 1982
Gillette $2,183	**17.3**	**19.3**	1983	**16.1** 1978
Emhart $1,686	**16.5**	**18.2**	1978	**12.9** 1979
TRW $5,493	**16.3**	**16.9**	'78–'79	**12.7** 1983
Parker Hannifin $1,038	**16.0**	**17.5**	1979	**6.5** 1983
Perkin-Elmer $1,015	**16.0**	**17.9**	1980	**9.8** 1983
Rockwell International $8,098	**16.0**	**17.0**	1979	**13.0** 1978
Dresser Industries $3,473	**15.9**	**16.6**	1978	**0.3** 1983
Tenneco $14,353	**15.6**	**17.4**	1980	**12.3** 1983
Colt Industries $1,576	**15.2**	**21.3**	1983	**Loss** 1982
Ogden $1,918	**14.6**	**15.5**	1978	**10.8** 1982
W. R. Grace $6,220	**14.4**	**17.5**	1981	**7.3** 1983
United Technologies $14,669	**13.9**	**15.3**	1982	**13.0** 1979
Honeywell $5,753	**13.6**	**15.9**	1979	**10.0** 1983
Gulf & Western $5,072	**13.2**	**15.3**	1980	**Loss** 1983
Borg-Warner $3,542	**13.1**	**14.4**	1979	**10.9** 1980
Brunswick $1,216	**13.0**	**52.8**	1982	**5.3** 1980
Kidde $2,330	**13.0**	**14.6**	1979	**Loss** 1983
Signal Companies $6,151	**12.9**	**17.2**	1979	**3.9** 1983
North American Philips $3,800	**12.6**	**14.3**	1979	**9.4** 1982
FMC $3,498	**11.6**	**13.4**	1978	**10.8** 1981
ITT $14,155	**11.3**	**14.3**	1980	**6.8** 1979
SCM $1,813	**10.8**	**11.8**	1980	**4.8** 1983
National Distillers & Chemical $2,267	**10.7**	**14.9**	1979	**6.8** 1983
Crane $1,003	**10.6**	**14.8**	1979	**Loss** '82–'83
Textron $2,980	**10.0**	**16.5**	1978	**6.9** 1982
American Can $3,346	**9.5**	**12.0**	1979	**Loss** 1982
IC Industries $3,864	**8.8**	**14.4**	1979	**4.2** 1982
U.S. Industries $1,076	**8.2**	**9.7**	1979	**Loss** 1981
Williams Companies $2,167	**7.0**	**14.4**	1980	**1.8** 1978

Who's hot and who's not among conglomerates is illustrated by the 39 listed above, chosen from the 295 FORTUNE *500 industrial companies with $1 billion or more in 1983 sales.* FORTUNE *defines conglomerates as companies engaged in at least four different businesses, none accounting for more then 50% of sales—which eliminates some, like Raytheon, often considered conglomerates. Also excluded are co-ops and companies that weren't on the 500 list all six years.*

EXHIBIT III RETURN ON STOCKHOLDERS'
EQUITY (Median rates of return)

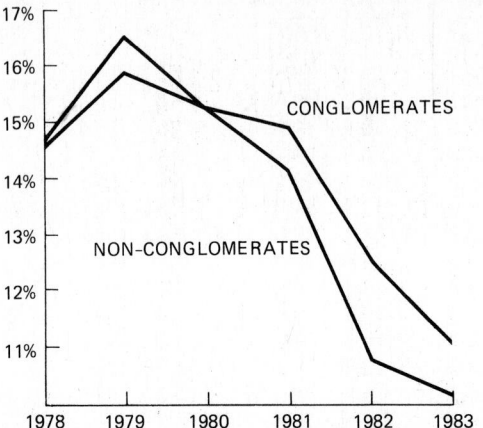

Source: "Conglomerates are Doing Better Than You Think," *Fortune,* copyright © 1984 by Royal Little, Time, Inc. All rights reserved. Adapted from a drawing by Karl Hartig.

TEXAS INSTRUMENTS INCORPORATED

Texas Instruments (TI) is a multinational corporation producing a wide variety of products having some tie to the electronics industry. In addition to its U.S. plants, TI maintains facilities in Canada, Latin America, Europe, Australia, and the Far East. TI's growth has been based on innovations as opposed to acquisitions. The company grew at an average rate of approximately 25% per year until 1980. At that time its sales growth slowed. 1980 sales of $4.1 billion grew to only $4.6 billion in 1983. In the early 1980s the company's line management structure was divided into six groups: semiconductor products, distributed computing, consumer electronics, materials and electrochemicals, government electronics, and geophysical exploration services. In charge of each group was a senior manager who reported directly to the president. These top level managers were responsible for worldwide strategic direction of their businesses as well as for the regular daily management functions. Each group was further

divided into divisions which were in turn broken down into product customer centers (PCCs).

By 1980, there were some 80 PCCs in the company. (12,81) A PCC was considered to be a complete business unit responsible for a particular family of products or services targeted at a specific market segment. The structure had come into being because of the interrelationships between divisions and groups. Many of the groups within TI were natural customers for each other. Further, the development of any new product or service to be marketed by TI was likely to require the coordinated cooperation of several of these six groups.

The PCCs were the focal point of operations, embodying the TI philosophy that the company "exists to create, make and market useful products and services to satisfy the needs of its customers." Each PCC was to "create," "make," and "market" products and services for a specific set of customers. The number and orientation of these basic operating units changed as TI's businesses evolved. When possible, PCCs with common markets, technologies, or customers were clustered together into divisions within the operating groups. (13,3) However, this was not always possible. PCCs varied in size from a few million dollars to some 80 million dollars in sales. PCCs performance was evaluated on the basis of profits, return on assets, and current operating plans.

The OST System

The OST system was a conscious attempt by TI's management to understand its early successes and to manage the processes of innovation based upon those successes. In its early history, TI had found out that with very limited resources it could outmaneuver large laboratories (like Bell Labs., RCA, GE, etc.). In the words of Patrick Hagerty, President and later CEO of TI, "This worked because we'd just go out and try to *do* something, rather than keep it in the laboratory. We might not understand all the reasons why it worked, we may have had to do some of it just empirically; but we'd try to make something real out of it."

Hagerty believed in setting aggressive goals—"to make the organizations strive for something, to push and motivate people." Hagerty described the OST system as "an attempt to make explicit the company's longer range goals, strategic objectives, and shorter term tactics to achieve them. Unless someone is paying attention to this kind of planning, day to day crises consume all a manager's attention." (12,4)

Mr. S.T. Harris, Officer of the Board, said:

> To handle growth and increasing complexity, the organization decentralizes into groups, divisions, departments, and branches. The total job becomes divided up and cut into sized pieces that a good administrative manager can get his arms around. This is logical and good management practice. But unless the general managers understand their jobs thoroughly, the company is in danger of becoming no more than the sum total of its decentralized parts. . . . Although the organization as a whole might have far more of the tools, opportunity, and skilled people needed for innovation, the perspective of any one manager can be restricted. He can simply fail to see larger opportunities and to solve problems of the right scale for the whole corporation. (14,2)

Objectives

Mr. Grant A. Dove, Vice President for Corporate Development of Texas Instruments, described the OST system in the following terms:[15]

> The OST system amounted to a statement of goals and the plans for achieving those goals at the appropriate level in the organization. The goals expressed in OST formed a structure, or hierarchy, beginning with the corporate objective and extending downward to Business Objectives and Strategies and finally Tactics. (See Figure 1)
>
> Our Corporate Objective states the economic purposes, the reasons for existence of the organization. It also states in broad terms, our product, market, and

technical goals. It defines our responsibilities to our employees, our shareholders, our community, and society as a whole. And it establishes the financial goals by which we measure our contribution to the economic development of society.

> The Corporate Objective is supported by a set of Business Objectives. Each of these is expressed in terms of (1) a business charter, which establishes the boundaries of the business, (2) an appraisal of the potential opportunities we perceive in this business, (3) a study of the technical and marketing trends, and (4) the overall competitive structure of the industries serving this business.

The Corporate Objective tended to look out 5–10 years in a challenging fashion. Expectations for the first two years were broken down into quarters, the others were in annual terms. (12,81) Mr. Dove continued:

> We carefully evaluate the competition, the threats and contingencies we might have to meet, market shifts we might anticipate, and attempt to evaluate what we must make happen in order to achieve success of the Objective. The ranking of these key factors provides a priority list for future management attention. We expect the Objective to be challenging enough, even shocking enough, to force a radical rethinking of all the Strategies and Tactics [supporting it]. . . . Any time we have enough well defined Strategies to give us a high confidence level in exceeding the goals stated in a Business Objective, then that Business Objective is probably not ambitious enough, and the probability of truly innovative strategic thinking is likely to be low. (14,4)

Business Objectives focus on a limited field of opportunity, its potential technical and market trends, and the competitive industry structure associated with it. Performance measures at this level are specific goals for financial factors—like sales, market share, profit, and return on assets—for 5 and 10 years out. Any Business Objective must be consistent and compatible with the Corporate Objective and with the underlying philosophy it represents. For each Business Objective there was a Business Objective Manager. (13,5)

Strategies and Tactics

Following is a composite view of the remainder of the OST system derived from various sources. At the next level in the structure was a Strategy Statement. The Strategy described in detail the environment of the business opportunity to be pursued in support of the Objective. Normally there would be several strategies supporting each Objective. For example, if TI had an Objective to achieve certain goals in the automobile market, it might have one Strategy involving automobile electronics, one involving material applications, and perhaps others for safety systems, control systems, etc. The Strategy looked ahead for a number of years—normally 5–10—and established intermediate checkpoints to provide milestones against which to judge progress. Progress measurement is an element of a Strategy not included at the Objectives level. But the contribution of a Strategy to the overall Objective was defined in quantitative measures and a critique was formulated to assign a success probability to the Strategy. (14,4) Each strategy was assigned to a Strategy Manager. (12,82)

Next in the goal hierarchy, was the Tactical Action Program or TAP. A TAP was a detailed action plan of the steps necessary to reach the major long range checkpoints defined by the Strategies. It was normally short run, covering 6–18 months. For each TAP, a "responsible individual" was designated, a start and finish schedule established and the required resources defined. (14,5) Within the TAP specific individuals were defined as responsible for achieving each milestone. Figure 3 diagrams the relationship among objectives, strategies, tactics, and milestones.

One way to visualize this complex structure was as a matrix with the traditional organizational units across the top and the OST structure along the left margin. (See Figure 4) However, unlike the typical matrix organization, the OST system

expressed a relationship between a strategic mode and an operating mode within the same organization. (14,6)

One of the roles of a Strategy Manager was to identify the TAPs required to accomplish the Strategy (represented by the Xs in the matrix) and to pull these together across the company into a coordinated strategic plan. Many times the Strategic Manager was also the manager of a PCC especially if one PCC would have a dominant role in the strategy. Nearly always, the Strategy or Tactic Manager would also have an operating role to play. Only in rare cases would the Strategy Manager or Tactic Manager have that job as his full time assignment. Frequently, an Objective Manager would also be a Division Manager—although this was not always the case. (14,6) Said Mr. Dove:

> This provides a goal structure for strategic as well as operating activities. Not only can we measure profit and loss performance operationally, we can also allocate resources through the OST structure and measure our progress toward the Strategic goals. Now, new ideas have a home. They can be given resources for further development, and if progress warrants, heavier support later. . . . New ideas can be clearly a part of the OST structure and be recognized and supported by deliberate choice. They do not have to be bootlegged, nor can they be dropped completely through a crack. . . . The strategic mode gives us a mechanism for large scale opportunities or those requiring combinations of resources not found in a single unit. It gives us a mechanism for planning and controlling our investments for the future and for making sure that we do achieve the desired balance of priorities between short term and long term activities.[15]

Strategic expenditures were discretionary as far as the current year's business went. They were project—rather than level-of-effort oriented—and had a long term emphasis. All OST programs and funding were intended to make a definite change in TI's business. OST programs

FIGURE 3 TEXAS INSTRUMENTS' OST SYSTEM

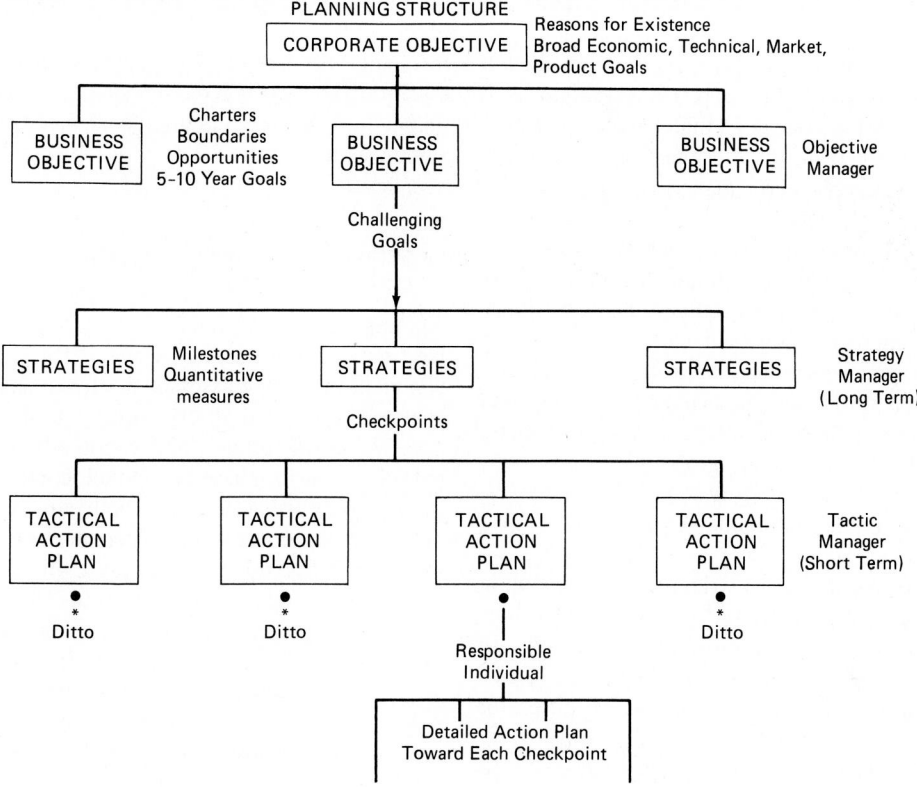

Source: Texas Instruments Incorporated: Management Systems (14,5).

FIGURE 4 MATRIX OF PLANS

O	S	T	Group 1			Group 2					6 Groups
			Div. A		Div. B	Div. C		Div. D		Div. E	20 Divisions
			PCC	PCC	PCC	PCC	PCC	PCC	PCC	PCC	80 Product Customers Centers
1	A	1	X		X		X				
		2	X			X			X		
		3		X			X	X			
		4				X				X	
	B	1			X		X				
		2		X	X	X		X			
		3	X			X			X		

Source: Texas Instruments Incorporated: Management Systems (14,5).

had definite directions, beginning, intermediate milestones, and ends. TI's internal accounting treated OST expenditures apart from ordinary operating expenditures. Managers were evaluated on both their operating responsibilities and OST responsibilities. Because funds were separated and earmarked with milestones, targets, dates (etc.), "strategic performance could be readily assessed." (12,82)

OST programs were approved yearly by the Growth Committee at the top level of the organization. This occurred at a Strategic Planning Conference each year when some 500 top TI managers from around the world came together for a week of strategic planning. The Growth Committee had some 13 permanent members, including the president, group vice presidents, and other officers reporting at the corporate level. The Committee met about 18 times a year for a full day, in addition to the annual meeting. At each meeting there was a rigorous reexamination of at least one Business Objective, or consideration of a major new business opportunity. In addition, managers of key strategies or tactics frequently met with the Growth Committee for progress reviews or reports. (14,8 and 13) In the early 1980s TI tended to have some 9–10 Business Objectives, some 50–60 Strategies, and more than 250 TAP's. (12,81)

In essence, TI had two budgets for the year, one for OST funds and the other for operating expenses. Expenditures associated with each category appeared as separate distinct lines on the P/L statement for each unit. Zero based budgeting was applied to the operating segments of each unit. The OST package was allocated among objectives, then to Strategies and to TAPs. The balance between OST expenses and operating expenses was a top level, long term/short term tradeoff. The key principle was that operating profit, as measured before OST expenditures, had to meet certain standards for each business. The size of the OST pot was influenced strongly by the expected total operating profit. (14,11) The entire OST pool was not allocated to Objective Managers at the beginning of the year. The Growth Committee retained approximately 10% of it as a fund for subsequent use and for new

opportunities. The use of OST funds could also be modified during the year by managers at any of the 3 key levels. A TAP Manager was permitted to change the nature of his activity on his own discretion as long as it did not change the tactical goal which he was committed to achieve. The same was true at the Strategy or Objective Manager level. (14,12)

Incentive Compensation System

An important part of the OST system was the Key Personnel Analysis (KPA). KPA made an annual comparative assessment of individual executives. It divided all executives into five comparative rating groups and eventually made a paired comparison based upon their contributions during the current year for both strategic and operational purposes. Each person was placed into one of five comparative rating groups, containing 20% of his total organization. The process began at departmental levels and continued to Division and Group Levels. Within each 20% group, individuals were compared with other individuals in that group, and rank ordered on the basis of their relative performance and contribution. Incentive bonuses and rewards were based on the rankings which resulted. The KPA systems created a competitive environment within the company which executives thought was constructive. Many different executives within the individuals' group would rank them on the basis of both their strategic and operating performance each year. Both annual bonuses and participation in stock option plans was related to this rating. In contrast to operating expenses, it was often considered desirable to have spent the full amount of the budgeted Strategic expense category, indicating adequate attention to the future. (14,7–8)

People and Asset Effectiveness

Starting in the early 1970s, TI established its P&AE program. These were set up much like OST programs—with specific objectives, strategies, and tactics to achieve them. P&AE programs focused attention and funding on efficiency improving activities for all company resources. Each Business Objective had its own funds and money was allocated within the Objective to P&AE programs that were unique to that Business Objective. A central P&AE Committee allocated monies to programs that could have corporate-wide impact across all Business Objectives—such as energy conservation, management information systems, or manufacturing automation programs important to virtually every Business Objective Manager. The OST program took care of growth, new products, and market positioning, while P&AE programs provided for the innovations needed to improve the productivity of people or assets in the business. TI had Intra Company Objectives for "people and asset effectiveness" and managed these activities just as it did other growth ventures. TI measured productivity as a percentage return on assets per person employed and aimed for a 10–12% goal. Increasing capital investment was seen as a major productivity-maximizing strategy to compete with lower labor costs elsewhere in the world. Investments in automated design and manufacturing capabilities were a major focus.[16]

The IDEA System

An IDEA (Identify, Develop, Expose, Action) program provided opportunities for initial feasibility demonstration of concepts that did not fit within immediate OST thrusts. The IDEA system was regarded as "a supplement to OST."

As TI grew in size, its top management felt an increasing distance between potential innovators and the decision makers who could commit resources to make their innovations into realities. The IDEA system was designed to forge a missing link into the innovation chain. Its acronym represented the process TI saw as necessary to turn a raw idea into a commercial innovation. *Identify* the idea as having potential commercial value. *Develop* the idea far enough to provide sufficient information on which a management commitment could be based. *Expose* the developed idea directly to a group that had the authority to commit necessary resources. *Initiate Action* by feeding the newly funded idea into the OST system for

development and eventual commercialization. (17,5)

Although most IDEA projects were technically oriented, they could encompass any facet of the business. But IDEA projects had to be oriented toward step advances rather than evolutionary improvements. An IDEA project was intended to be only 4–6 months in span and require very limited funding. The funding was to be used by the originator only for buying the necessary services and materials to demonstrate the project. The IDEA originator could not charge his own time to the project. The originator was asked to prepare a memorandum proposing the approach, impact, or application of the idea, an estimate of project expenditures and their designated use; the estimated time for accomplishing the task; and what its end result would be (demonstration model, paper analysis, etc.). IDEA executives were designated in each division. However, the originator could take his concept to the IDEA person in *any* division or even contact more than one IDEA person for support. If the IDEA person thought the idea had merit, (s)he merely called Corporate Development to coordinate whether (1) the project was similar to others in Texas Instruments and (2) it fit the general business interests of the corporation. Once cleared, Corporate Development could release funds for the project almost immediately. And a follow up procedure was developed directly with the responsible IDEA person. (17,6–7)

By 1984, TI's management systems were often referred to as examples for other companies. However, TI's own management readily admitted the complexities of operating with these systems and was looking for even better solutions.

QUESTIONS

1. Why is Litton's system an "opportunity planning" system? What are its strengths and weaknesses?

2. How well does TI's system fit its needs? What are its strengths and weaknesses?

3. At the end of the case, what should be changed in each company's organization planning system and control system? How?

EXHIBIT IV   TEXAS INSTRUMENTS INC. CONSOLIDATED FINANCIAL STATEMENTS

In millions of dollars, except per share amounts

	For the year ended December 31		
	1983	*1982*	*1981*
Income and Retained Earnings			
Net sales billed	**$4,579.8**	$4,326.6	$4,206.0
Operating costs and expenses			
Cost of goods and services sold	**3,908.4**	3,343.6	3,238.7
General, administrative and marketing	**901.0**	699.6	674.1
Employees' retirement and profit sharing plans	**58.5**	47.7	40.3
Total	**4,867.9**	4,090.9	3,953.1
Profit (loss) from operations	**(288.1)**	235.7	252.9
Other income (expense) net	**.9**	10.5	(36.6)
Interest on loans	**(36.0)**	(33.1)	(41.3)
Income (loss) before provision (credit) for income taxes	**(323.2)**	213.1	175.0
Provision (credit) for income taxes	**(177.8)**	69.1	66.5
Net income (loss)	**(145.4)**	144.0	108.5
Retained earnings at beginning of year	**1,167.1**	1,070.3	1,008.8
Cash dividends declared on common stock ($2.00 per share in 1983, 1982 and 1981)	**(47.8)**	(47.2)	(47.0)
Retained earnings at end of year	**$ 973.9**	$1,167.1	$1,070.3
Earnings (loss) per common share (average outstanding during year)	**$ (6.09)**	$ 6.10	$ 4.62
Changes in Financial Position			
Sources of cash			
Net income (loss)	**$ (145.4)**	$ 144.0	$ 108.5
Depreciation	**351.4**	338.5	333.3
Net decrease in working capital (excluding cash and short-term investments, loans payable and current portion long-term debt, and dividends payable)	**123.9**	118.1	42.9
Provided from operations	**329.9**	600.6	484.7
Net change in total long-term debt	**11.0**	1.8	.9
Sales and other common stock transactions	**35.0**	6.7	41.2
Other	**(42.8)**	24.1	7.9
	333.1	633.2	534.7
Uses of cash			
Additions (net) to property, plant and equipment	**454.1**	329.3	341.4
Decrease (increase) in loans payable	**12.1**	(16.3)	138.0
Dividends paid on common stock	**47.6**	47.2	46.9
Increase (decrease) in deferred charges	**54.4**	.1	(8.8)
Purchase of common stock of the company for employee stock option and incentive plans	**—**	2.9	7.0
	568.2	363.2	524.5
Increase (decrease) in cash and short-term investments	**$ (235.1)**	$ 270.0	$ 10.2

See accompanying notes provided in company's annual report.

Source: Texas Instruments Inc., *Annual Report*, 1983.

EXHIBIT IV (*Continued*)

TEXAS INSTRUMENTS INCORPORATED AND SUBSIDIARIES BALANCE SHEET ($ Millions)

	December 31 1983	December 31 1982
Assets		
Current assets		
Cash and short-term investments	$ 184.9	$ 420.0
Accounts receivable, less allowance for losses of $159.2 in 1983 and $72.7 in 1982	664.6	641.7
Inventories (net of progress billings)	335.6	360.0
Prepaid taxes and expenses	266.6	105.2
Total current assets	1,451.7	1,526.9
Property, plant and equipment at cost	2,266.3	2,083.8
Less accumulated depreciation	(1,067.3)	(987.5)
Property, plant and equipment (net)	1,199.0	1,096.3
Other assets and deferred charges	62.6	8.2
Total assets	$2,713.3	$2,631.4
Liabilities and Stockholders' Equity		
Current liabilities		
Loans payable and current portion long-term debt	$ 37.3	$ 49.5
Accounts payable and accrued expenses	1,050.8	784.0
Income taxes payable	77.2	68.8
Accrued retirement contribution	53.2	44.6
Dividends payable	12.0	11.8
Total current liabilities	1,230.5	958.7
Deferred liabilities and credits		
Long-term debt	225.1	214.0
Incentive compensation payable in future years	3.8	6.8
Deferred credits and other liabilities	51.2	91.1
Total deferred liabilities and credits	280.1	311.9
Stockholders' equity (common shares outstanding at year-end: 1983—24,027,538; 1982—23,652,416)	1,202.7	1,360.8
Total liabilities and stockholders' equity	$2,713.3	$2,631.4

See accompanying notes provided in company's annual report.

Source: Texas Instruments Inc., *Annual Report*, 1983.

```
┌─ SIX ──────────────────────────────────────┐
│  ┌────────────────────────────────────────┐ │
│  │                                        │ │
│  │            DEALING                     │ │
│  │                                        │ │
│  │       WITH STRUCTURE                   │ │
│  │                                        │ │
│  │        AND SYSTEMS                     │ │
│  │                                        │ │
│  └────────────────────────────────────────┘ │
└─────────────────────────────────────────────┘
```

DEALING WITH STRUCTURE AND SYSTEMS

Chapter 5 has completed Section I which introduced the concepts related to our central theme, strategy—what it is, how it should and does get made, and the nature of the work of one of its key makers, the general manager. Chapter 6 introduces Section II which deals with another set of concepts that every student of general management must come to understand. We group these under the title "*Organization*" because they all pertain to the basic design and running of the organization. In this chapter we examine the design of organizational *structure* and the development of *systems* for coordination and control. In Chapter 7, we turn to the questions of *power*—how it flows within the organization and how the organization uses it in its external environment. In Chapter 8, we consider *culture*, that ideological glue that holds organizations together, enhancing their ability to pursue strategies on one hand, but sometimes impeding strategic change on the other.

Structure, in our view, no more follows strategy than the left foot follows the right in walking. The two exist *inter*dependently, each influencing the other. There are certainly times when a structure is redesigned to carry out a new strategy. But the choice of any new strategy is likewise influenced by the realities and potentials of the existing structure. Indeed, the classical model of strategy formulation (discussed in Chap-

ter 3) implicitly recognizes this by showing the strengths and weaknesses of the organization as an input to the creation of strategies. Surely these are deeply rooted within the existing structure, indeed often part and parcel of it. Hence, we introduce here structure and the associated administrative systems which make it work as essential factors to consider in the strategy process. Later when we present the various contexts within which organizations function, we shall ponder the different ways in which strategy and structure may interact.

All of the readings of this chapter reinforce these points. The Waterman, Peters, and Phillips article originally published under the title "Structure is Not Organization," introduces the well-known "7-S" framework that was developed at the McKinsey consulting firm where all three authors were when this article was published. (This framework was, in fact, one of the antecedents of the best-selling management book *In Search of Excellence* by two of these authors.) This framework explicitly considers how structure, systems, style, and other organizational factors interrelate with strategy; as such many practicing executives and students have found this a most valuable construct in thinking about organizations. (Note that what the authors call "superordinate goals" were renamed "shared values" in the *Excellence* book. We discuss them in some depth under the label "culture" in Chapter 8, noting that these were first introduced in the Selznick reading of Chapter 2.)

The second reading, excerpted from Mintzberg's book *The Structuring of Organizations*, probes the design of organizational structures, including their formal systems. A number of basic dimensions of structure are introduced—mechanisms used to coordinate the work in organizations, parameters to consider in designing structures, and contingency factors which influence choices among the design parameters. The text provides a somewhat lengthy discussion especially of the design parameters, which should be helpful for those who have not yet had a course on organization theory; others may wish to scan this discussion for review purposes. This reading also introduces a somewhat novel, but useful, way to depict organizations, not as the usual organizational chart or cybernetic flow process, but as a funny conceptual diagram showing the six critical parts of a typical organization.

This reading concludes by clustering these various dimensions into a set of *configurations*, or distinct types of organizations, with specific characteristics. The theme diagram, altered in different ways, graphically depicts these types. They are briefly introduced at this point in the text, with in-depth discussion of them reserved for Section III where they serve as the framework for our discussion of context. There we discuss at length the structure of each configuration (except for one, which is discussed in Chapter 8), its external situation, its strategies and the processes by which these are and can be made.

The third reading more closely approaches conventional concepts of strategy and its relationship to structure. But it does so in an unconventional way. In his article "Strategy and Organization Planning," Jay Galbraith, an ex-MIT and Wharton Business School professor who now writes from his experiences as a management consultant, also views structure broadly as encompassing support systems of various kinds. Building on concepts like "driving force" and "center of gravity," Galbraith links various strategies (of vertical integration and diversification, "generic"

in their own ways) to forms of structure, ranging from the functional to the increasingly diversified. Galbraith covers a wide body of important literature in the field, and uses visual imagery, but of a different kind, to make his points. The result is one of the best articles in print on the relationship between the strategy of diversification and the structure of divisionalization.

A number of cases allow students to probe the particular ramifications of these concepts. Those which bring out most clearly the issues Galbraith raises are: Polaroid, Royal Bank (B), Pillsbury, General Mills, Exxon, and Matsushita. But as you will see, these issues are present in all complex strategy situations.

THE 7–S FRAMEWORK*

by Robert H. Waterman, Jr.,
Thomas J. Peters, and
Julien R. Phillips

The Belgian surrealist René Magritte painted a series of pipes and titled the series *Ceci n'est pas une pipe*: this is not a pipe. The picture of the thing is not the thing. In the same way, a structure is not an organization. We all know that, but like as not, when we reorganize what we do is to restructure. Intellectually all managers and consultants know that much more goes on in the process of organizing than the charts, boxes, dotted lines, position descriptions, and matrices can possibly depict. But all too often we behave as though we didn't know it; if we want change we change the structure. . . .

Our assertion is that productive organization change is not simply a matter of structure, although structure is important. It is not so simple as the interaction between strategy and structure, although strategy is critical too. Our claim is that effective organizational change is really the relationship between structure, strategy, systems, style, skills, staff, and something we call superordinate goals. (The alliteration is intentional: it serves as an aid to memory.)

Our central idea is that organization effectiveness, stems from the interaction of several factors—some not especially obvious and some underanalyzed. Our framework for organization change, graphically depicted in [Figure 1], suggests several important ideas:

- First is the idea of a multiplicity of factors that influence an organization's ability to change and its proper mode of change. Why pay attention to only one or two, ignoring the others? Beyond structure and strategy, there are at least five other identifiable elements. The division is to some extent arbitrary, but it has the merit of acknowledging the complexity identified in the research and segmenting it into manageable parts.

- Second, the diagram is intended to convey the notion of the interconnectedness of the variables—the idea is that it's difficult, perhaps impossible, to make significant progress in one area without making progress in the others as well. Notions of organization change that ignore its many aspects or their interconnectedness are dangerous.

- In a recent article on strategy, *Fortune* commented that perhaps as many as 90 percent of carefully planned strategies don't work. If that is so, our guess would be that the failure is a failure in execution, resulting from inattention to the other S's. Just as a logistics bottleneck can cripple a military strategy, inadequate systems or staff can make paper tigers of the best-laid plans for clobbering competitors.

- Finally, the shape of the diagram is significant. It has no starting point or implied hierarchy. A priori, it isn't obvious which of the seven factors will be the driving force in changing a particular organization at a particular point in time. In some cases, the

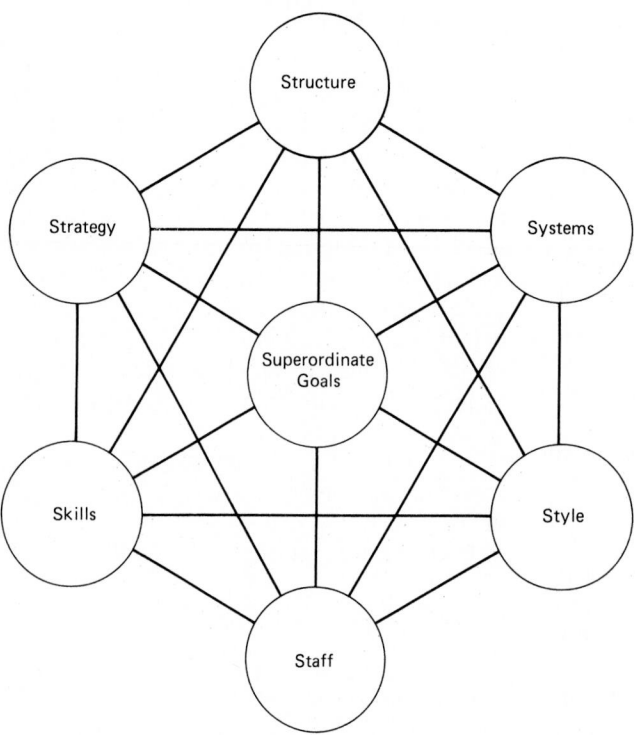

FIGURE 1
A NEW VIEW OF ORGANIZATION

critical variable might be strategy. In others, it could be systems or structure.

STRUCTURE

To understand this model of organization change better, let us look at each of its elements, beginning—as most organization discussions do—with structure. What will the new organization of the 1980s be like? If decentralization was the trend of the past, what is next? Is it matrix organization? What will "Son of Matrix" look like? Our answer is that those questions miss the point. . . .

The central problem in structuring today . . . is not the one on which most organization designers spend their time—that is, how to divide up tasks. It is one of emphasis and coordination—how to make the whole thing work. The challenge lies not so much in trying to comprehend all the possible dimensions of organization structure as in developing the ability to focus on those dimensions which are currently important to the organization's evolution—and to be ready to refocus as the crucial dimensions shift.

STRATEGY

If structure is not enough, what is? Obviously, there is strategy. It was Alfred Chandler (1962) who first pointed out that structure follows strategy, or more precisely, that a strategy of diversity forces a decentralized structure. Throughout the past decade, the corporate world has given close attention to the interplay between strategy and structure. Certainly, clear ideas about strategy make the job of structural design more rational.

By "strategy" we mean those actions that a company plans in response to or anticipation of changes in its external environment—its customers, its competitors. Strategy is the way a company aims to improve its position vis-a-vis competition—perhaps through low-cost production or delivery, perhaps by providing better value to the customer, perhaps by achieving sales and service dominance. It is, or ought to be, an organi-

zation's way of saying: "Here is how we will create unique value."

As the company's chosen route to competitive success, strategy is obviously a central concern in many business situations—especially in highly competitive industries where the game is won or lost on share points. But "structure follows strategy" is by no means the be-all and end-all of organization wisdom. We find too many examples of large, prestigious companies around the world that are replete with strategy and cannot execute any of it. There is little if anything wrong with their structures; the causes of their inability to execute lie in other dimensions of our framework. When we turn to nonprofit and public-sector organizations, moreover, we find that the whole meaning of "strategy" is tenuous—but the problem of organizational effectiveness looms as large as ever.

Strategy, then, is clearly a critical variable in organization design—but much more is at work.

SYSTEMS

By systems we mean all the procedures, formal and informal, that make the organization go, day by day and year by year: capital budgeting systems, training systems, cost accounting procedures, budgeting systems. If there is a variable in our model that threatens to dominate the others, it could well be systems. Do you want to understand how an organization really does (or doesn't) get things done? Look at the systems. Do you want to change an organization without disruptive restructuring? Try changing the systems.

A large consumer goods manufacturer was recently trying to come up with an overall corporate strategy. Textbook portfolio theory seemed to apply: Find a good way to segment the business, decide which segments in the total business portfolio are most attractive, invest most heavily in those. The only catch: Reliable cost data by segment were not to be had. The company's management information system was not adequate to support the segmentation. . . .

[One] intriguing aspect of systems is the way they mirror the state of an organization. Consider a certain company we'll call International Wickets. For years management has talked about the need to become more market oriented. Yet astonishingly little time is spent in their planning meetings on customers, marketing, market share, or other issues having to do with market orientation. One of their key systems, in other words, remains *very* internally oriented. Without a change in this key system, the market orientation goal will remain unattainable no matter how much change takes place in structure and strategy.

To many business managers the word "systems" has a dull, plodding, middle-management sound. Yet it is astonishing how powerfully systems changes can enhance organizational effectiveness—without the disruptive side effects that so often ensue from tinkering with structure.

STYLE

It is remarkable how often writers, in characterizing a corporate management for the business press, fall back on the word "style." . . . The trouble we have with style is not in recognizing its importance, but in doing much about it. Personalities don't change, or so the conventional wisdom goes.

We think it is important to distinguish between the basic personality of a top-management team and the way that team comes across to the organization. Organizations may listen to what managers say, but they believe what managers do. Not words, but patterns of actions are decisive. The power of style, then, is essentially manageable.

One element of a manager's style is how he or she chooses to spend time. As Henry Mintzberg (1975) has pointed out managers don't spend their time in the neatly compartmentalized planning, organizing, motivating, and controlling modes of classical management theory. Their days are a mess—or so it seems. There's a seeming infinity of things they might devote attention to. No top executive attends to all of the demands on his time; the median time spent on any one issue is nine minutes.

What can a top manager do in nine minutes? Actually, a good deal. He can signal what's on his mind; he can reinforce a message; he can nudge people's thinking in a desired direction. Skillful management of his inevitably fragmented time is, in fact, an immensely powerful change lever. . . .

Another aspect of style is symbolic behavior. [Companies most successful in finding mineral deposits] typically have more people on the board who understand exploration or have headed exploration departments. Typically they fund exploration more consistently (that is, their year-to-year spending patterns are less volatile). They define fewer and more consistent exploration targets. Their exploration activities typically report at a higher organizational level. And they typically articulate better reasons for exploring in the first place.

STAFF

Staff (in the sense of people, not line/staff) is often treated in one of two ways. At the hard end of the spectrum, we talk of appraisal systems, pay scales, formal training programs, and the like. At the soft end, we talk about morale, attitude, motivation, and behavior.

Top management is often, and justifiably, turned off by both these approaches. The first seems too trivial for their immediate concern ("Leave it to the personnel department"), the second too intractable ("We don't want a bunch of shrinks running around, stirring up the place with more attitude surveys").

Our predilection is to broaden and redefine the nature of the people issue. What do the top-performing companies do to foster the process of developing managers? How, for example, do they shape the basic values of their management cadre? Our reason for asking the question at all is simply that no serious discussion of organization can afford to ignore it (although many do). Our reason for framing the question around the development of managers is our observation that the superbly performing companies pay extraordinary attention to managing what might be called the socialization process in their companies. This applies especially to the way they introduce young recruits into the mainstream of their organizations and to the way they manage their careers as the recruits develop into tomorrow's managers. . . .

Considering people as a pool of resources to be nurtured, developed, guarded, and allocated is one of the many ways to turn the "staff" dimension of our 7–S framework into something not only amenable to, but worthy of practical control by senior management.

We are often told, "Get the structure 'right' and the people will fit" or "Don't compromise the 'optimum' organization for people considerations." At the other end of the spectrum we are earnestly advised, "The right people can make any organization work." Neither view is correct. People do count, but staff is only one of our seven variables.

SKILLS

We added the notion of skills for a highly practical reason: It enables us to capture a company's crucial attributes as no other concept can do. A strategic description of a company, for example, might typically cover markets to be penetrated or types of products to be sold. But how do most of us characterize companies? Not by their strategies or their structures. We tend to characterize them by what they do best. We talk of IBM's orientation to the marketplace, its prodigious customer service capabilities, or its sheer market power. We talk of Du Pont's research prowess, Procter & Gamble's product management capability, ITT's financial controls, Hewlett-Packard's innovation and quality, and Texas Instruments' project management. These dominating attributes, or capabilities, are what we mean by skills.

Now why is this distinction important? Because we regularly observe that organizations facing big discontinuities in business conditions must do more than shift strategic focus. Frequently

they need to add a new capability, that is to say, a new skill. . . . These dominating capability needs, unless explicitly labeled as such, often get lost as the company "attacks a new market" (strategy shift) or "decentralizes to give managers autonomy" (structure shift).

Additionally, we frequently find it helpful to *label* current skills, for the addition of a new skill may come only when the old one is dismantled. Adopting a newly "flexible and adaptive marketing thrust," for example, may be possible only if increases are accepted in certain marketing or distribution costs. Dismantling some of the distracting attributes of an old "manufacturing mentality" (that is, a skill that was perhaps crucial in the past) may be the only way to insure the success of an important change program. Possibly the most difficult problem in trying to organize effectively is that of weeding out old skills—and their supporting systems, structures, etc.—to ensure that important new skills can take root and grow.

SUPERORDINATE GOALS

The word "superordinate" literally means "of higher order." By superordinate goals, we mean guiding concepts—a set of values and aspirations, often unwritten, that goes beyond the conventional formal statement of corporate objectives.

Superordinate goals are the fundamental ideas around which a business is built. They are its main values. But they are more as well. They are the broad notions of future direction that the top management team wants to infuse throughout the organization. They are the way in which the team wants to express itself, to leave its own mark. Examples would include Theodore Vail's "universal service" objective, which has so dominated AT&T; the strong drive to "customer service" which guides IBM's marketing. . . .

In a sense, superordinate goals are like the basic postulates in a mathematical system. They are the starting points on which the system is logically built, but in themselves are not logically derived. The ultimate test of their value is not their logic but the usefulness of the system that ensues. Everyone seems to know the importance of compelling superordinate goals. The drive for their accomplishment pulls an organization together. They provide stability in what would otherwise be a shifting set of organization dynamics.

Unlike the other six S's, superordinate goals don't seem to be present in all, or even most, organizations. They are, however, evident in most of the superior performers.

To be readily communicated, superordinate goals needs to be succinct. Typically, therefore, they are expressed at high levels of abstraction and may mean very little to outsiders who don't know the organization well. But for those inside, they are rich with significance. Within an organization, superordinate goals, if well articulated, make meanings for people. And making meanings is one of the main functions of leadership.

CONCLUSION

We have passed rapidly through the variables in our framework. What should the reader have gained from the exercise?

We started with the premise that solutions to today's thorny organizing problems that invoke only structure—or even strategy and structure—are seldom adequate. The inadequacy stems in part from the inability of the two-variable model to explain why organizations are so slow to adapt to change. The reasons often lie among our other variables: systems that embody outdated assumptions, a management style that is at odds with the stated strategy, the absence of a superordinate goal that binds the organization together in pursuit of a common purpose, the refusal to deal concretely with "people problems" and opportunities.

At its most trivial, when we merely use the framework as a checklist, we find that it leads into new terrain in our efforts to understand how organizations really operate or to design a truly comprehensive change program. At a minimum, it gives us a deeper bag in which to collect our experiences.

More importantly, it suggests the wisdom of taking seriously the variables in organizing that have been considered soft, informal, or beneath the purview of top management interest. We believe that style, systems, skills, superordinate goals can be observed directly, even measured—if only they are taken seriously. We think that these variables can be at least as important as strategy and structure in orchestrating major change; indeed, that they are almost critical for achieving necessary, or desirable change. A shift in systems, a major retraining program for staff, or the generation of top-to-bottom enthusiasm around a new superordinate goal could take years. Changes in strategy and structure, on the surface, may happen more quickly. But the pace of real change is geared to all seven S's.

At its most powerful and complex, the framework forces us to concentrate on interactions and fit. The real energy required to redirect an institution comes when all the variables in the model are aligned. One of our associates looks at our diagram as a set of compasses. "When all seven needles are all pointed the same way," he comments, "you're looking at an *organized* company."

THE STRUCTURING OF ORGANIZATIONS*

By Henry Mintzberg

The "one best way" approach has dominated our thinking about organizational structure since the turn of the century. There is a right way and a wrong way to design an organization. This approach is best captured in Colonel Urwick's famous principle of the 1930s that "no supervisor

* Excerpted from an unpublished draft chapter by this title and from Henry Mintzberg, "A Typology of Organizational Structure" in D. Miller and P. Friesen, eds., *Organizations: A Quantum View* (Prentice-Hall), which themselves are excerpted from Henry Mintzberg, *The Structuring of Organizations: A Synthesis of the Research* (Prentice-Hall, 1979). Used with permission of the publishers.

can supervise directly the work of more than five, or at the most, six subordinates whose work interlocks" (Urwick, 1956:41). But "one best way" thinking continues to the present day, for example in the activities of consultants who believe that every organization needs MBO, or LRP, or OD.

A variety of failures, however, has made it clear that organizations differ, that long-range planning systems or organizational development programs are good for some but not others. Just as it would be foolish to restrict a foreman to a span of control of six assembly-line workers whose work interlocks, so too is there little sense in forcing formal planning on a firm that must remain highly flexible in an unpredictable market (as many firms discovered during the early days of the energy crisis).

And so recent management theory has moved away from the "one best way" approach, toward an "it all depends" approach, formally known as "contingency theory." Structure should reflect the organization's situation—for example, its age, size, type of production system, the extent to which its environment is complex and dynamic. To cite some of the more established relationships, larger organizations need more formalized structures—more rules, more planning, tighter job descriptions; so do those in stable environments and those in mass production. Organizations in more complex environments need higher degrees of decentralization; those diversified in many markets need divisionalized instead of functional structures.

This [reading] argues that the "it all depends" approach does not go far enough, that structures are rightfully designed on the basis of a third approach, which might be called the "getting it all together" or, "configuration" approach. Spans of control, types of formalization and decentralization, planning systems, and matrix structures should not be picked and chosen independently, the way a shopper picks vegetables at the market or a diner a meal at a buffet table. Rather, these and other parameters of organizational design should logically configure into internally consistent groupings. Like most phenomena—atoms, ants, and stars—characteristics

of organizations appear to fall into natural clusters, or configurations.

We can, in fact, go a step farther and include in these configurations not only the design parameters but also the so-called contingency factors. In other words, the organization's type of environment, its production system, even its age and its size, can in some sense be "chosen" to achieve consistency with the elements of its structure. The important implication of this conclusion, in sharp contrast to that of contingency theory, is that organizations can select their situations in accordance with their structural designs just as much as they can select their designs in accordance with their situations. Diversified firms may divisionalize, but there is also evidence that divisionalized firms have a propensity to further diversify (Rumelt, 1974: 76–77; Fouraker and Stopford, 1968). Stable environments may encourage the formalization (bureaucratization) of structure, but bureaucracies also have a habit of trying to stabilize their environments. And in contrast, entrepreneurial firms, which operate in dynamic environments, need to maintain flexible structures. But such firms also seek out and try to remain in dynamic environments in which they can outmaneuver the bureaucracies. In other words, no one factor—structural or situational—determines the others; rather, all are often logically formed into tightly knit configurations.

When the enormous amount of research that has been done on organizational structuring is looked at in the light of this conclusion, much of its confusion falls away, and a convergence is evident around several configurations, which are distinct in their structural designs, in the situations in which they are found, and even in the periods of history in which they first developed.

To understand these configurations, we must first understand each of the elements that make them up. Accordingly, the first four sections of this [reading] discuss the basic parts of organizations, the mechanisms by which organizations coordinate their activities, the parameters they use to design their structures, and their contingency, or situational, factors. The final section of this reading introduces the structural configuration [Editors' note: which will be developed at length in the last section of this text.]

A. SIX BASIC PARTS OF THE ORGANIZATION

Different parts of the organization play different roles in the accomplishment of work and of these forms of coordination. Our framework introduces six basic parts of the organization, shown in Figure 1 and listed below:

The *operating core* is where the basic work of producing the organization's products and services gets done, where the workers assemble automobiles and the surgeons remove appendices.

The *strategic apex* is the home of top management, where the organization is managed from a general perspective.

The *middle line* comprises all those managers who stand in direct line relationship between the strategic apex and the operating core.

The *technostructure* includes the staff analysts who design the systems by which work processes and outputs of others in the organization are formally designed and controlled.

The *support staff* comprises all those specialists who provide support to the organization outside of its operating workflow—in the typical manufacturing firm, everything from the cafeteria staff and the mailroom to the public relations department and the legal counsel.

The *ideology* forms the sixth part, a kind of halo of beliefs and traditions that surrounds the whole organization.

B. SIX BASIC COORDINATING MECHANISMS

Six mechanisms of coordination seem to describe the fundamental ways in which organizations coordinate their work. Two are ad hoc in nature; the other four involve various forms of standardization.

1. *Mutual adjustment* achieves coordination of work by the simple process of informal communication. The people who do the work interact with one another to coordinate, much as two canoeists in the rapids adjust to

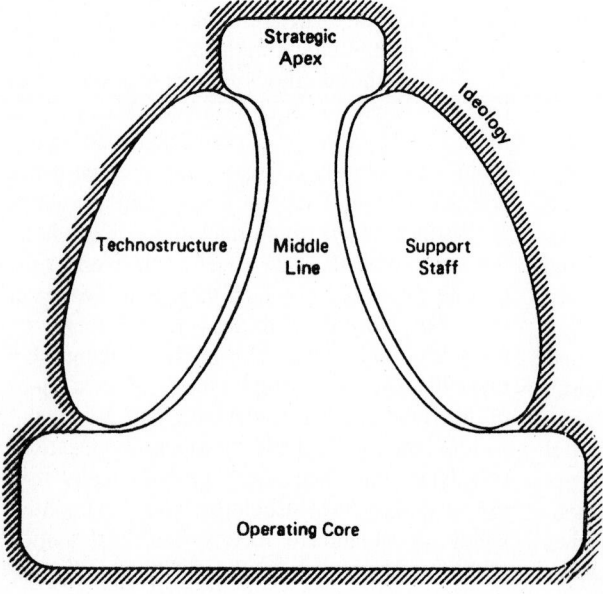

FIGURE 1
THE SIX BASIC PARTS
OF THE ORGANIZATION

one another's actions. Figure 2a shows mutual adjustment in terms of an arrow between two operators. Mutual adjustment is obviously used in the simplest of organizations—it is the most obvious way to coordinate. But, paradoxically, it is also used in the most complex, because it is the only means that can be relied upon under extremely difficult circumstances, such as trying to figure out how to put a man on the moon for the first time.

2. *Direct supervision* in which one person coordinates by giving orders to others, tends to come into play after a certain number of people must work together. Thus, fifteen people in a war canoe cannot coordinate by mutual adjustment; they need a leader who, by virtue of his instructions, coordinates their work, much as a football team requires a quarterback to call the plays. Figure 2b shows the leader as a manager with his instructions as arrows to the operators.

Coordination can also be achieved by *standardization*—in effect, automatically—by virtue of standards that predetermine what people do and so ensure that their work is coordinated. We can consider four forms—the standardization of the work processes themselves, of the outputs of the work, of the knowledge and skills that

serve as inputs to the work, or of the norms that more generally guide the work.

3. *Standardization of work processes* means the specification—that is, the programming—of the content of the work directly, the procedures to be followed, as in the case of the assembly instructions that come with many children's toys. As shown in Figure 2c, it is typically the job of the analyst to so program the work of different people in order to coordinate it tightly.

4. *Standardization of outputs* means the specification not of what is to be done but of its results. In that way, the interfaces between jobs is predetermined, as when a machinist is told to drill holes in a certain place on a fender so that they will fit the bolts being welded by someone else, or a division manager is told to achieve a sales growth of 10% so that the corporation can meet some overall sales target. Again, such standards generally emanate from the analyst, as shown in Figure 2d.

5. *Standardization of skills*, as well as knowledge, is another, though looser way to achieve coordination. Here, it is the worker rather than the work or the outputs that is standardized. He or she is taught a body of knowledge and a set of skills which are

FIGURE 2   THE BASIC MECHANISMS OF COORDINATION

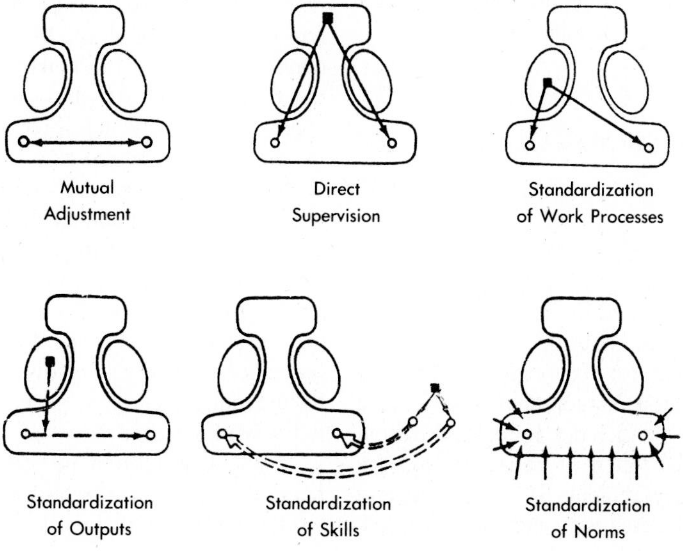

Mutual
Adjustment

Direct
Supervision

Standardization
of Work Processes

Standardization
of Outputs

Standardization
of Skills

Standardization
of Norms

subsequently applied to the work. Such standardization typically takes place outside the organization—for example in a professional school of a university before the worker takes his or her first job—indicated in Figure 2e. In effect, the standards do not come from the analyst; they are internalized by the operator as inputs to the job he takes. Coordination is then achieved by virtue of various operators' having learned what to expect of each other. When an anesthetist and a surgeon meet in the operating room to remove an appendix, they need hardly communicate (that is, use mutual adjustment, let alone direct supervision); each knows exactly what the other will do and can coordinate accordingly.

6. *Standardization of norms* means that the workers share a common set of beliefs and can achieve coordination based on it, as implied in Figure 2d. For example, if every member of a religious order shares a belief in the importance of attracting converts, then all will work together to achieve this aim.

Bear these six coordinating mechanisms in mind; we shall be returning to them repeatedly. Every organization must divide up its work among individuals (known as "division of labor") to get it done. These coordinating mechanisms, as the basic means to knit together the divided labor of the organization, serve as the most basic elements of structure—the glue that holds the organization together.

C. THE ESSENTIAL PARAMETERS OF DESIGN

In the structuring of organizations, design means turning those knobs that influence the division of labor and coordination. In this section we shall be discussing ten such knobs or "design parameters," which fall into four basic groups. The first deals with the design of individual positions in the organization and includes the specialization of jobs, the formalization of behavior, and the establishment of requirements for the training and indoctrination associated with each job. The sec-

ond concerns the design of the "superstructure," or skeleton of the organization, and includes the determination of the bases on which positions and units are grouped, as well as etablishment of the size of units. The third deals with the design of lateral linkages to flesh out the superstructure, and includes two design parameters called planning and control systems and liaison devices. The last concerns the design of the decision making system in the organization, and includes the design parameters we call vertical decentralization and horizontal decentralization.

Job Specialization

The first order of business in organizational design is to decide what each person will do. Key here is the determination of how specialized each job is to be—how many distinct tasks it is to contain—and how much control over those tasks the person who does the job should have. In determining these aspects of job specialization, the organization designer is essentially establishing the division of labor in the organization.

Jobs that have few and "narrow" tasks are generally referred to as *horizontally specialized,* those with many and "broad" ones as *horizontally enlarged.* A worker bolts on a bumper every few seconds all day long; a maintenance man nearby is a jack-of-all-trades, shifting from one problem to another. Jobs that involve little control by those who do them—carried out without thinking how or why—are called *vertically specialized*; those which are thoroughly controlled by the worker are referred to as *vertically enlarged.* Thus the student who must copy lecture notes and parrot them back in an exam has a vertically specialized job to do; the one who carries out a field study does more vertically enlarged work. (And jobs that have been enlarged in both the vertical and horizontal dimensions are sometimes referred to as having been "enriched," the movement to do so in general known as "quality of working life.")

Jobs must often be specialized vertically because they are specialized horizontally: the work is so narrow that worker control of it would preclude the necessary coordination. These are generally *unskilled* jobs. On the other hand, many so-called *professional* jobs are horizontally specialized yet vertically enlarged—the worker has a narrow repertoire of programs, but because these are highly complex, he must have a good deal of control over them.

Behavior Formalization

The next issue in the design of individual positions is the determination of the extent to which the work content of tasks will be specified—in other words, the behavior or the job "formalized."

Organizations formalize the behavior of their workers in order to reduce its variability, ultimately to predict and control it. Thus behavior formalization is also a means to achieve specialization in the vertical direction. A prime motive for formalizing behavior is, of course, to coordinate work very tightly, specifically through the mechanism we have called standardization of work processes. Airline pilots, for example, cannot figure out emergency landing procedures when the need arises and then coordinate by mutual adjustment with the ground staff; those have to be very carefully prescribed in advance.

Organizations that rely primarily on the formalization of behavior to achieve coordination are generally referred to as "bureaucracies," a word that has become highly charged in everyday speech. We shall, however, use a neutral definition here. A structure is *bureaucratic* to the extent that it relies on standardization for coordination. Note that this definition includes any form of standardization, not just that of work processes. *Organic* is the label generally given to the opposite type of structure, in our terms, ones relatively absent of standardization.

One final point: a high degree of formalization of the operators' jobs "institutionalizes" the job of their manager, the first line supervisor— that is, reduces his or her ability to coordinate the work directly through supervision—and puts the power instead into the bureaucratic systems designed by the analysts. So the analysts, above all, gain power at the expense of lower level managers to the extent that behavior is formalized in the operating core. Indeed, to the extent that behavior formalization permeates the entire organization, it is the analysts—those who design the rules—who gain at everyone else's expense.

Training

The behavior required of some tasks is too complex to be rationalized and then formalized directly by the analysts of the technostructure. And so the people who are to do the tasks must be extensively trained before they begin their work. In other words, they must acquire some standardized body of knowledge and set of skills. Such training can, of course, be designed in the organization itself, but more often it must take place in some formal institution (unless it must be learned under an apprenticeship system, as a craft). And so this third aspect of position design entails deciding what formal training the organization will require in its different positions and then selecting the appropriately trained "professionals" to fill them (or establishing its own training programs where it can).

We noted above that formalization and training are basically substitutes for one another. Typically the organization has to choose one or the other (or something else), not both, depending on the complexity of the work in question (Hall, 1968, 1972:121). Both are designed to program the work of the individual, but one focuses on unskilled work, while the other is oriented toward complex, professional work. And herein lies the essential difference between the two, for while one takes power from the worker and puts it into the technostructure, the other takes power from all the other parts of the organization and puts it into the hands of the professional workers themselves. In other words, professional tasks must be controlled by those who actually perform them.

Yet we have also seen that professional work can be highly standardized work, the professionals carrying out routinely applied, well-established programs, as in the case of the surgeon who removes two or three appendices each day.

In other terms, an organization of professionals can be a highly bureaucratic one, but with one marked difference from that form of bureaucracy discussed under behavior formalization: here the control of the work rests largely with the workers themselves. The implication, to which we shall return, is that there are two distinct types of bureaucracies, one for professional, the other for unskilled work.

Indoctrination

Socialization "refers to the process by which a new member learns the value system, the norms, and the required behavior patterns of the society, organization, or group which he is entering" (Schein, 1968:3). A good deal of socialization takes place informally and unofficially in the organization, as new members interact with old. But some also takes place more formally, for the organization's own benefit, through the process known as *indoctrination*. As a parameter in the design of individual positions, indoctrination resembles training in many ways. It too takes place largely outside the job—often before it begins—and is also designed for the internalization of standards. But the standards differ. They relate not to formal bodies of knowledge and sets of skills, but to the norms of the organization itself—its values, beliefs, manners of doing things, what is generally referred to as its internal "culture." And because these standards are unique to each organization, indoctrination must take place within its own walls under full control of its own personnel.

Indoctrination is important to any organization that has a strong system of beliefs—often called an *ideology*. It is imperative that every member share the beliefs so as to be able to act in accordance with them. Indoctrination is also particularly important for jobs that are sensitive and remote, in other words, where the individual must act in accordance with the organization's norms, yet cannot be controlled directly—the ambassador sent to a remote nation, the Mountie off in the far North, the manager transferred to a foreign subsidiary.

Unit Grouping

Given a set of positions duly designed in terms of specialization, formalization, training, and indoctrination, the next issue in organization design relates to the establishment of a managerial "superstructure" to knit it all together. In other words, positions are grouped into units, each under its own manager, and units clustered into ever larger units under their own managers, until the whole organization comes under a single manager—the chief executive officer at the strategic apex. Thus, a hierarchy of authority is constructed through which flows the *formal* power to control decisions and actions.

That hierarchy is generally represented by an organizational chart, what we shall call (borrowing from the French) an *organigram* (as can be seen in Figures 3 and 4 ahead). The organigram is a much maligned document, rejected by many as an inadequate picture of what really takes place in organizations. True enough, since it represents the flow of official power—formal authority—which is often superseded by informal power. Yet the organigram is inevitably the first thing asked for by anyone interested in the organization, and for good reason: like a map, it is a useful portrayal of certain surface features of the organization and their linkages. In particular, it tells at a glance how labor is divided into positions in the organization, who fills these positions, how they are grouped into units, and how formal authority flows among these units.

Two major questions arise in the design of the superstructure which are dealt with by our next two design parameters. First, on what basis are positions and units grouped into larger units, and second, what size should each of the units be?

Grouping is not simply a convenience for the sake of creating an organigram, a handy way to keep track of everyone who works for the organization. Rather, it is a fundamental way to coordinate work in the organization, for four reasons: (a) it establishes a system of common supervision among positions and units, (b) it typically requires positions and units to share common resources and (c) to be assessed on common measures of performance (i.e., output standards), and (d) as a result of the tendency to put the members of given units into close physical proximity with one another, it encourages mutual adjustment among them.

Positions and units can be grouped on at least six different bases:

- by *knowledge and skill*, as in a hospital that puts surgeons in one department and anesthetists in another,

- by *work process and function*, as in the classic grouping of a manufacturing firm into manufacturing, marketing, engineering, and so on,

- by *time*, as in shifts in a factory,

- by *output*, as when a corporation establishes different divisions for different product lines,

- by *client*, as in the insurance firm that sets up one marketing department to sell individual policies, another to sell group policies,

- by *place*, as in the supermarket chain that establishes one division for its Quebec stores, another for its Ontario stores.

For convenience, we can reduce all these bases of grouping to two fundamental ones—by *function* (including knowledge, skill, work process work function), and by *market* (output, client, and place).[1] In one we have grouping by *means*, by the intermediate functions the organization uses to produce or support the production of its final outputs, in the other, grouping by *ends*, by the features of the markets served by the organization—the products or services it markets, the clients it serves, the places where it serves them.

The question that now arises is: on what criteria should the choice of a basis for grouping be made? First, there is the consideration of workflow linkages, or "interdependencies." Obviously, the more tightly linked are positions or

Grouping by time can fall into either category.

units in the workflow, the more desirable that they be grouped together to facilitate their coordination. Second is the consideration of process interdependencies—for example, across people doing the same kind of work but in different workflows (such as maintenance men working on different machines). It sometimes makes sense to group them together to facilitate their sharing of equipment or ideas, for encouraging the improvement of their skills, and so on. Third is the question of scale interdependencies. For example, all maintenance people in a factory may have to be grouped together because no single department has enough maintenance work for one person. Finally, there are the social interdependencies, the need to group people together for social reasons, as in coal mines where mutual support under dangerous working conditions can be a factor in deciding how to group people.

Grouping by function is illustrated in Figure 3, the case of a cultural center. Clearly, it is favored by process and scale interdependencies, and to a lesser extent by social interdependencies (in the sense that people who do the same kind of job often tend to get along better). Grouping by function also encourages specialization, for example, by allowing specialists to come together under the supervision of one of their own kind. The problem with functional grouping is that it narrows perspectives, encouraging a focus on means instead of ends—the way to do the job instead of the reason for doing the job in the first place. It also cuts arbitrarily across workflows, providing no built-in mechanism for that kind of coordination. Since different managers supervise different portions of the workflow, mutual adjustment is impeded across the workflow, as is direct supervision. The organization is forced to rely on some other mechanism of coordination. In fact, bureaucratic structures for unskilled operators tend to group on the basis of function and then coordinate across functions on the basis of formalization.

The market bases for grouping—shown in Figure 4 as the example of the two-tier regional structure of the Canadian Post Office—tends to

FIGURE 3   GROUPING BY FUNCTION: A CULTURAL CENTER

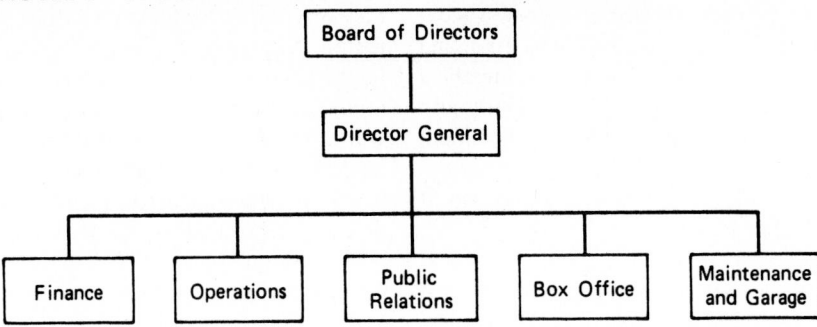

favor coordination in the workflow at the expense of process and scale specialization. Here, by favoring mutual adjustment and direct supervision as the mechanisms for coordination, there is a certain tendency to reduce the degree of bureaucratization. In general, market grouping reduces the ability to do a specialized or repetitive task well and is more wasteful, being less able to take advantage of economies of scale and often requiring the duplication of resources. But it can do more tasks and change its tasks more easily to serve the organization's end markets. And so if the workflow interdependencies are the important ones and if the organization cannot easily handle them by standardization, then it will tend to favor the market bases for grouping in order to encourage mutual adjustment and direct supervision. But if the workflow is irregular (as in a "job shop"), if standardization can easily contain the important workflow interdependencies, or if the process or scale interdependencies are the important ones, then the organization will be inclined to seek the advantages of specialization and group on the basis of function instead.

In designing the superstructure, the question is often not so much *which* basis of grouping, but in what *order*. Much as fires are built by stacking logs first one way and then the other, so too are superstructures often built by varying the different bases for grouping to take care of various interdependencies.

Unit Size

On the question of the size of units—historically described in terms of the "span of control" of their managers—the classical literature was clear: As we quoted Urwick earlier, "No supervisor can supervise directly the work of more than five or, at the most, six subordinates whose work interlocks." Yet effective units containing dozens—sometimes even hundreds—of people or subunits have been reported. The problem as we shall see, seems to stem from the assumption in the classical literature that coordination was synonymous with direct supervision, in other words, that mutual adjustment and the various forms of standardization did not exist as coordinating mechanisms. Thus, the focus was on the span of "control" of the manager, instead of the size of the unit, as if managerial control were the only factor in determining the size of units.

When we turn to an analysis of the coordinating mechanisms other than direct supervision, we get the clearest explanation of variation in unit size. Two relationships in particular explain a good deal. First, the greater the use of standardization (of any kind) for coordination, the larger the size of the work unit. It stands to reason that the more coordination within a unit can be achieved by standardization—in effect, automatically, without direct managerial intervention—the less time its manager need spend on direct

FIGURE 4 GROUPING BY MARKET: THE CANADIAN POST OFFICE

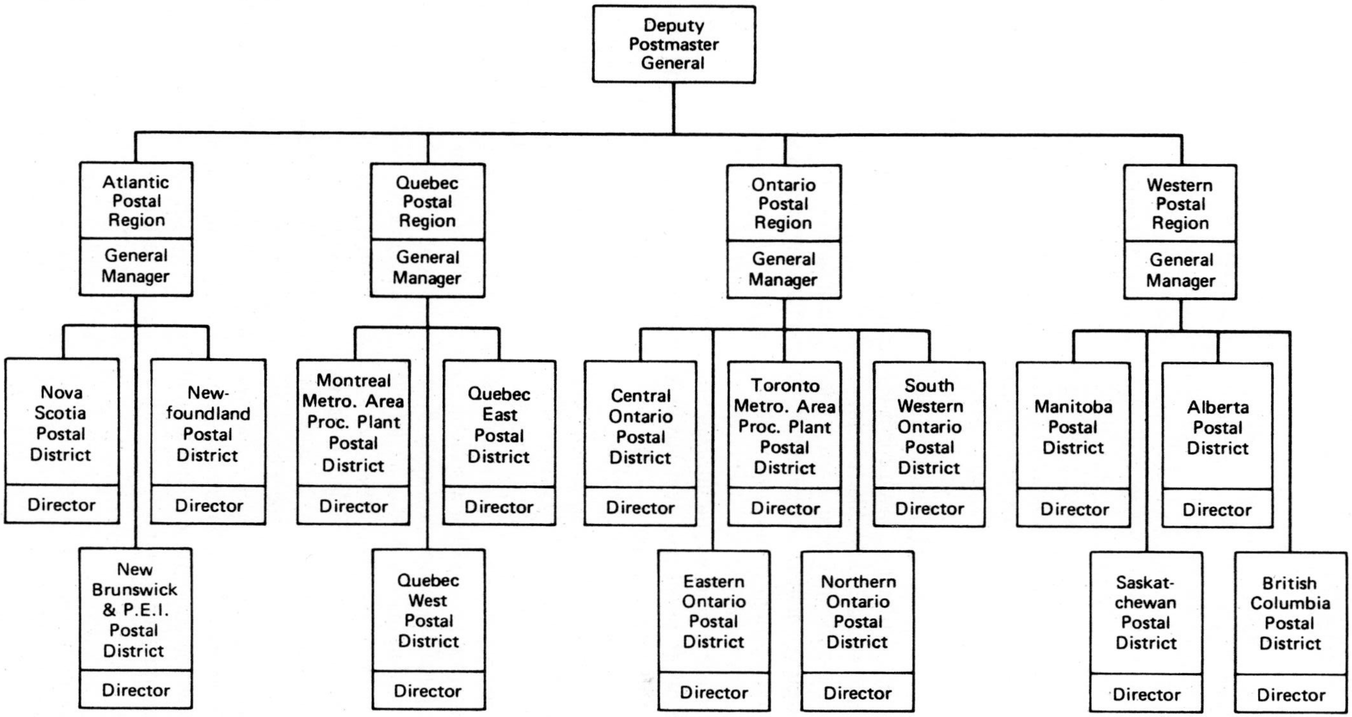

* Headquarter staff groups deleted.

supervision and so the greater the number of employees that can report to him. Thus we find examples of 50 and 100 assembly line workers reporting to a single foreman; similarly, I report together with fifty colleagues directly to one dean.

The second relationship is that the greater the need for mutual adjustment, the smaller must be the size of the work unit. When tasks are rather complex yet tightly coupled, neither direct supervision nor any form of standardization suffices to effect the necessary coordination. The specialists who perform the various tasks must coordinate by virtue of informal, face-to-face communication among themselves. As we noted at the very outset of this [reading], mutual adjustment is the favored coordinating mechanism for the most complex of endeavors, like putting a man on the moon for the first time. Now, what effect does reliance on mutual adjustment have on unit size? For mutual adjustment to work effectively, the work unit must be small enough to encourage convenient, frequent, and informal interaction among all its members—typically less than ten people and often of the order of five, six, or seven (Filley et al., 1976:417–418).[2]

An important conclusion emerges here, one that will reappear later in our discussion. Since complex work is professional work, there seem to be two fundamentally different kinds of professional work, requiring very different structures. One, loosely coupled, can rely on the standardization of skills for coordination, and so it allows the professionals to work relatively autonomously in large units. The other, tightly coupled, requires the tighter coordination of mutual adjustment, and so necessitates the grouping of the professionals into small, face-to-face work units. The first is bureaucratic by virtue of its reliance on a form of standardization for coordination, the second organic by virtue of its non-reliance on standardization.

---

[2] Interestingly, since each unit has a manager, we can conclude that the span of control must be narrow despite the relative absence of direct supervision. (The manager may just be a member of the unit named to represent it externally.) That is the trouble with using the term "span of control": unit size has little to do with "control" here.

Planning and Control Systems

With the establishment of positions and the construction of the superstructure, we have the skeleton of the organizational structure. But the design is still not complete. We need other parameters to flesh it out, to create other kinds of linkages among the component parts. Specifically, we need planning and control systems to standardize outputs and liaison devices to encourage mutual adjustment.

The purpose of formal planning is to specify—standardize—outputs ahead of time, and the purpose of formal control is to determine later whether or not the standards have in fact been met. The two go together, like the proverbial horse and carriage. Nevertheless, we can distinguish *action planning systems*—which focus on before-the-fact determination of outputs—from *performance control systems*—which are more oriented to after-the-fact monitoring of results. Shown in Figure 5, one seeks to guide specific actions ("The holes should be drilled 1.108 centimeters wide"), the other to measure general results of a whole series of actions ("Fifty holes should be drilled per hour"; "the profit of the division should increase to 10% next quarter").

Action planning, by focusing on specific actions, like behavior formalization, tends to be used to coordinate work across functional structures, but often at a higher level in the hierarchy. Performance control, in contrast, is less tightly regulating, more respectful of unit autonomy. Thus, whereas it says "Increase sales by 10% this year (in any way you care to)," action planning specifies who, when, where. Thus, performance control tends to be associated with the market bases for grouping, to control the performance of self-contained units while leaving the details of how to do so to each of them.

Many organizations use extensive hierarchies of both these systems. For example, action planning can begin with broad strategic plans which are elaborated into specific programs, which in turn get detailed as schedules and operating specifications. And performance control can begin as quantitative objectives for the entire organ-

FIGURE 5 THE RELATIONSHIPS BETWEEN DECISIONS AND ACTION
PLANNING AND PERFORMANCE CONTROL

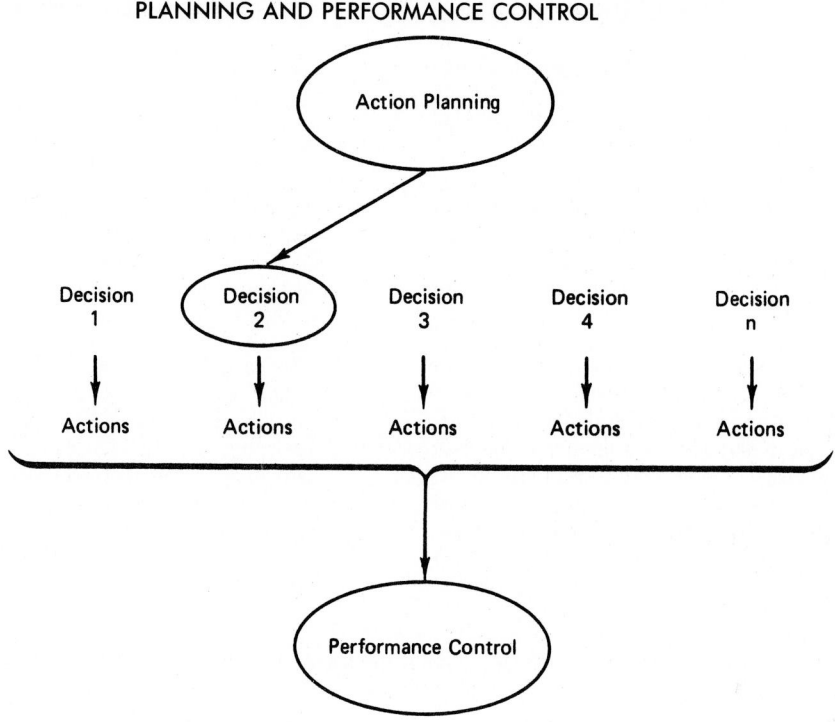

ization, which are divided into subobjectives, budgets, and other standards for upper-level units, which finally emerge as operating budgets, etc. for the lowest-level units in the hierarchy.

Liaison Devices

Mutual adjustment may occur naturally in the small, face-to-face work unit. But how to encourage it across units, when grouping has the known tendency to discourage *inter*unit communication even as it encourages *intra*unit communication? In the past, the resolution of this problem was left to chance. But in recent years, as it has become more and more serious, a whole series of what we shall call *liaison devices*—formal parameters of structural design—have developed to stimulate mutual adjustment across units. These, in fact, represent the most significant—perhaps the only significant—development in structural

design in the past fifteen or twenty years. Four are of particular importance, presented in ascending order of their capacity to encourage mutual adjustment.

- *Liaison positions* are jobs created to coordinate the work of two units directly, without having to pass through vertical, managerial channels. They carry no formal authority per se; rather, those who serve in them must use their powers of persuasion, negotiation, etc. to bring the two sides together. Typical liaison positions are the purchasing engineer who sits between purchasing and engineering or the sales liaison person who mediates between the sales force and the factory.

- *Task forces and standing committees* are institutionalized forms of meetings which bring members of a number of different units together on a more intensive basis, in the first case to deal with a temporary issue, in the second, in a more permanent and regular way to discuss issues of common interest. Thus a task force may be formed of engineering, sales, and production personnel to redesign a given product and then disband, while line and technocratic personnel may form a standing committee to meet weekly to plan production.

- *Integrating managers*—essentially liaison personnel with formal authority—provide for stronger coordination by mutual adjustment than either of the first two devices. These "managers" are not given authority over the units they link—each of these still has its own manager. But they are given authority over something important to those units, for example, approval of certain of their decisions or control over their budgets. One example is the unit manager in the hospital, responsible for integrating the efforts of doctors, nurses, and support staff in a particular ward; another is the brand manager in a consumer goods firm who is responsible for a certain product but who must negotiate its

production and marketing with different functional departments.

- *Matrix structure* carries liaison to its natural conclusion. No matter what the bases of grouping at one level in an organization, some interdependencies always remain. Functional groupings pose workflow problems; market-based ones impede contacts among like specialists. Standardization may help, but problems often remain. As shown in Figure 6, we have seen three ways to deal with the "residual interdependencies": a different type of grouping can be used at the next level in the hierarchy; staff units can be formed next to line units to advise on the problem; or one of the liaison devices already discussed can be overlaid on the grouping. But in each case, one basis of grouping is favored over the others. The concept of matrix structure is to balance two (or more) bases of grouping, for example functional with market (or for that matter, one kind of market with another—say, re-

FIGURE 6   STRUCTURES TO DEAL WITH RESIDUAL INTERDEPENDENCIES

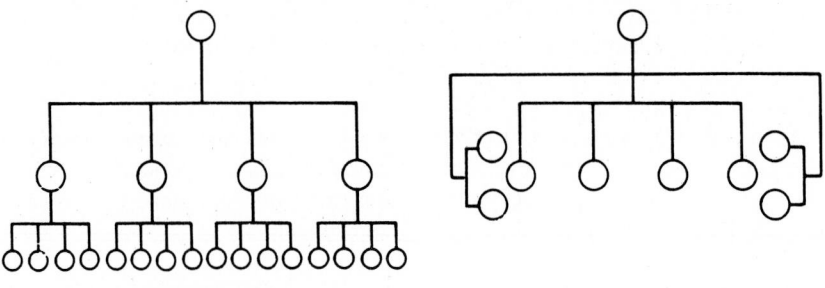

(a) Hierarchical Structure   (b) Line and Staff Structure

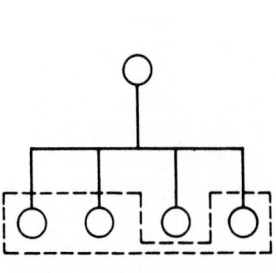

(c) Liaison Overlay Structure
(e.g., Task Force)

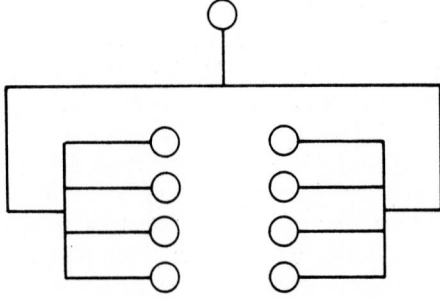

(d) Matrix Structure

gional with product). This is done by the creation of a dual authority structure—two (or more) managers, units, or individuals are made jointly and equally responsible for the same decisions. We can distinguish a *permanent* form of matrix structure, where the units and the people in them remain more or less in place, as shown in the example of a whimsical multinational firm in figure 7, and a *shifting* form, suited to project work, where the units and the people in them move around frequently. Shifting matrix structures are common in high technology industries, which group specialists in functional departments for housekeeping purposes (process interdependencies, etc.) but deploy them from various departments in project teams to do the work, as shown in Figure 8.

How do these liaison devices relate to the other design parameters we have already discussed? One point seems clear. As means to encourage mutual adjustment, these are most logically used with work that is: (a) horizontally specialized, since specialization impedes natural coordination, (b) complex, in other words, professional, and (c) interdependent, so that coordination is in fact necessary. Thus, the liaison devices—especially the stronger ones, such as task forces, integrating managers and matrix struc-

ture—seem most appropriate to the second kind of professional work we discussed earlier, where the professionals must work together in small units. These liaison devices, as agents of mutual adjustment instead of standardization, are obviously associated with organic structures—indeed, in overriding formal authority or bifurcating it, they tend to destroy bureaucratic priority.

Vertical and Horizontal Decentralization

Finally we come to the most extensively discussed yet least understood of the parameters of structural design, those related to *decentralization*. What does the word really mean? To some, it describes the physical location of facilities: a library is "centralized" in one location or "decentralized" to many. To others, it describes the delegation of formal power down the hierarchy of authority. We shall use a broader definition than the second one, but different from the first, associating the term with the sharing of decision making power. When all the power rests at a single point in the organization, we shall call the structure centralized; to the extent that the power is dispersed among many individuals, we shall call the structure relatively decentralized. Notice that our defi-

FIGURE 7   A PERMANENT MATRIX STRUCTURE IN AN INTERNATIONAL FIRM

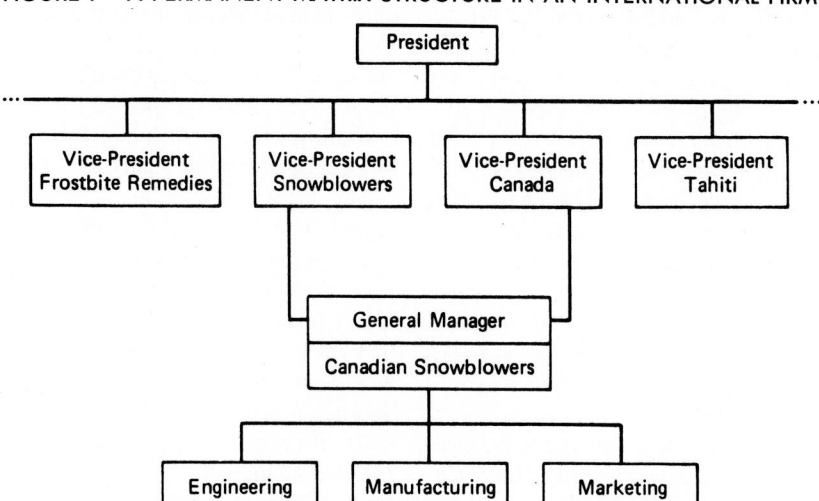

FIGURE 8   SHIFTING MATRIX STRUCTURE IN THE NASA WEATHER
            SATELLITE PROGRAM

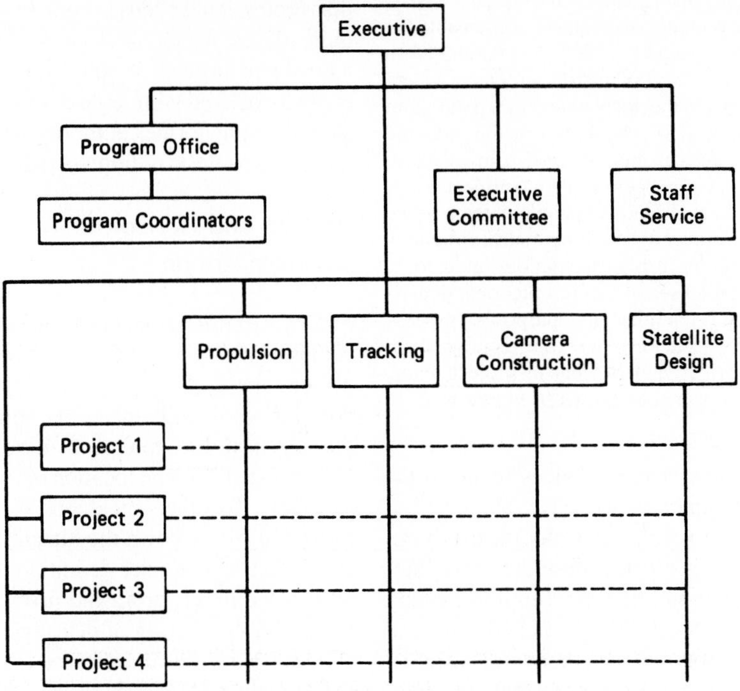

Source: Modified from Delbecq and Filley, 1974:16.

nition of decentralization is not restricted to formal power. In fact we shall distinguish *vertical decentralization*—the delegation of *formal* power down the hierarchy to line managers—from *horizontal decentralization*—the extent to which *formal or informal* power is dispersed out of the line hierarchy to non-managers (operators, analysts, and support staffers). We also introduce another distinction: between *selective* decentralization—the dispersal of power over one or a few kinds of decisions to the same place in the organization—from *parallel* decentralization—the dispersal of power for many kinds of decisions to the same place.

Centralization has one great advantage in the organization. By keeping all the power in one place, it ensures the very tightest form of coordination.

All the decisions are made in one head, and then implemented through direct supervision. So then why bother to decentralize? Primarily because one brain is often not big enough. It cannot understand all that must be known. Also, decentralization allows the organization to respond quickly to local conditions in many different places, and it can serve as a stimulus for motivation, since capable people require considerable room to maneuver if they are to perform at full capacity.

How do organizations decentralize vertically? In functional structures, it has been found that when organizations decentralize extensively, they do so selectively, delegating power for each decision process to that level in the line hierarchy where the necessary information can best be accumulated. In market-based structures, in contrast—especially those grouped on the basis of products and services—the tendency is to decentralize in parallel, delegating to each market-based unit the power to make most of the decisions that affect its own operations. In this way, the unit—generally called "division"—is allowed to operate in quasi-autonomous fashion, coordinated, as noted earlier, only by performance control systems. But does this constitute "decentralization"? Not necessarily at all. All the power may go to the division chief and stop there. That hardly constitutes the wide sharing of power.

Horizontal decentralization—the sharing of power to make decisions by non-managers—can assume a variety of forms, since we have different kinds of non-managers in the organization. The most limited form of horizontal decentralization occurs when most of the power remains in the line structure, but because the organization relies for coordination on the systems of standardization designed by the analysts of the technostructure, they gain some degree of informal power. As noted earlier, the analysts tend to gain this power at the expense of the operators—whose work is most susceptible to such standardization—and of their immediate supervisors, whose jobs become "institutionalized," technocratic standardization replacing their capacity to use direct supervision. Note two results here. First, many operators and some managers lose power to a small number of analysts—that is why we call this form of horizontal decentralization "limited." And second, because lower level managers tend to lose power relative to those higher up—on whose behalf the systems of standardization are designed—the result of this form of horizontal decentralization is vertical *centralization*.

A second form of horizontal decentralization occurs when an organization is dependent on specialized knowledge, and so must pass a good deal of its power to its experts or professionals, notably in its operating core and/or support staff. This is a more extensive form of horizontal decentralization, for two reasons. First, there will tend to be more experts in this case than analysts in the last. And second, here the non-managers tend to gain power primarily at the expense of the line managers.

Earlier we discussed two kinds of professionals, one who tends to work autonomously, coordinating by standardized skills (such as doctors in hospitals), the other who works in small groups, coordinating by mutual adjustment (such as researchers in a space agency). In the first case, we tend to have a more thorough form of horizontal decentralization, parallel in nature, since the professionals—who tend to be found in the operating core—have more or less complete control of their own work. In the second, horizontal decentralization tends to be more selective in nature. This is because different decisions tend to be made not only by different groups but also by different combinations within each group of line managers, staff and operating experts.

The third and final form of horizontal decentralization occurs when all members of the organization share power equally because all have been socialized to share the same ideology. By our definition, this is its most extreme form. As a result, all can be trusted to make decisions on a more or less equal basis. Thus, the most ideological organizations, which distribute their power not on the basis of knowledge or position but on the basis of membership—the religious sect or Israeli kibbutz, for example—tend to be the most decentralized (and egalitarian).

To summarize this discussion, let us consider decentralization in terms of the six coordinating mechanisms because, as we shall see, each inherently leads to a different form and a different degree of decentralization. By considering them all together, in the context of our preceding discussion, we can derive six basic types of decentralization.

Direct supervision clearly constitutes full horizontal centralization, since all the power rests with the managers. In fact, it also constitutes vertical centralization since a dependence on direct supervision for coordination means that each manager tightly controls those below him such that all the power eventually rises to the top of the hierarchy, where it rests in the hands of the chief executive at the strategic apex. What we call *Centralization*—in effect, horizontal and vertical as well as parallel—is shown as Type I decen-

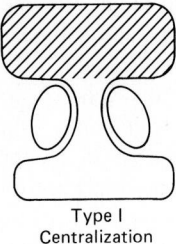

Type I
Centralization
(direct supervision)

Type II
Limited Horizontal
Decentralization
(Selective)
(standardization of
work processes)

Type III
Limited Vertical
Decentralization
(Parallel)
(standardization of
outputs)

Type IV
Horizontal
Decentralization
(Parallel)
(standardization
of skills)

Type V
Selective Horizontal
and Vertical
Decentralization
(mutual adjustment)

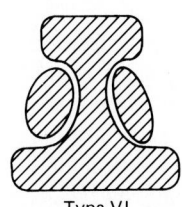

Type VI
Decentralization
(standardization
of norms)

**FIGURE 9
SIX TYPES
OF DECENTRALIZATION**

tralization in Figure 9 (where the size of the shaded parts designate their influence in decision making).

The various forms of standardization can, as we have seen, lead to different degrees of decentralization. When the organization relies on the standardization of work processes for coordination, as we have seen, the unskilled operators and lower level line managers lose power to the managers higher up in the hierarchy, and also to some extent to the analysts of the technostructure who design the systems of behavior formalization that control others. The result is centralization in the vertical dimension, with a limited and selective degree of decentralization in the horizontal dimension (to the analysts, who control only the design of the systems of standardization). What we call *Limited Horizontal Decentralization* (Selective) is shown as Type II in Figure 9.

We have also seen that a reliance on standardization of output goes with the delegation of

power over many decisions to the managers of market-based units. This is a form of vertical decentralization, but as we noted earlier, only a very limited form, since a few division managers can retain the lion's share of the power. Thus our Type III decentralization is referred to as *Limited Vertical Decentralization (Parallel)*. (Some power is shown in the technostructure, because it is the analysts who design the planning and control systems to standardize outputs.)

Next, we have decentralization based on the two kinds of professional work. Because, as noted earlier, experts who do complex work must control it to a large degree, these represent—in contrast to our first three types—rather extensive forms of decentralization.

In the first, the standardization of skills (based on extensive training) is relied upon for coordination. As a result, the professionals can work rather autonomously in large units, relatively free of the control of line managers and in control of most of the decisions that affect their work directly. In other words, here we have an extreme form of *Horizontal Decentralization (Parallel)*, shown as Type IV in Figure 9, with much of the power residing at the bottom of the hierarchy. Note that we have in Types II and IV our two kinds of bureaucracies, the first relatively centralized, the second relatively decentralized.

In the second kind of professional work, the experts work in small units and coordinate by mutual adjustment (encouraged by use of the liaison devices), which gives them a good deal of power. Here we have a combination, in both cases selective, of vertical decentralization—delegation to work groups at different levels in the hierarchy—and horizontal decentralization—a varying distribution of power within each group, of managers and non-managers, with the different decisions being controlled by whoever happens to have the necessary expertise. We end up with *Selective Horizontal and Vertical Decentralization*, Type V in Figure 9. Note that in Types I and V we have essentially two kinds of organic structures, one based on direct supervision for coordination, the other on mutual adjustment.

Finally, we come to the form of decentralization dictated by a reliance on the standardization of norms for coordination. As noted earlier, when an organization socializes and indoctrinates its members to believe in its strong ideology, it can then allow them considerable freedom to act, since they will in fact act in accordance with the prevailing norms. The result can be the purest form of decentralization—in one sense, the most democratic form of structure. Everyone shares power more or less equally—manager, staff person, operator—hence we have just plain *Decentralization*.

D. THE SITUATIONAL FACTORS

A number of contingency or situational factors influence the choice of these design parameters, and vice versa. These include the age and size of the organization; its technical system of produc-

tion; various characteristics of its environment, such as stability and complexity; and its power system, for example, whether or not it is tightly controlled from the outside. Some of their influences on the design parameters as found in an extensive body of research are summarized below as hypotheses.

Age and Size

Five hypotheses seem to cover a good deal of the findings in the research on the effects of the age and size of the organization itself on its own structure.

H1. The older the organization, the more formalized its behavior. What we have here is the "we've-seen-it-all-before" syndrome. As organizations age, they tend to repeat their behaviors; as a result, these become more predictable and so more amenable to formalization.

H2. The larger the organization, the more formalized its behavior. Just as the older organization formalizes what it has seen before, so the larger organization formalizes what it sees often. ("Listen mister, I've heard that story at least five times today. Just fill in the form like it says.")

H3. The larger the organization, the more elaborate its structure; that is, the more specialized its tasks, the more differentiated its units, and the more developed its administrative components. As organizations grow in size, they are able to specialize their tasks more finely. (The big barbershop can afford a specialist to cut children's hair; the small one cannot.) As a result, they can also specialize—or "differentiate"—the work of their units more extensively. This leads to greater homogeneity of work within units, but greater diversity between them, which necessitates more efforts at coordination. And so the larger organization tends also to enlarge its hierarchy to effect direct supervision or its technostructure to coordinate by standardization, or to include more liaison or integrating positions to encourage coordination by mutual adjustment.

H4. The larger the organization, the larger the size of its average unit. This finding relates to the previous two, the size of units growing larger as organizations themselves grow larger because: (a) as behavior becomes more formalized, and (b) as the work of each unit becomes more homogeneous, managers are able to supervise more employees.

H5. Structure reflects the age of founding of the industry. This is a curious finding, but one that we shall see holds up remarkably well, Organizational structure seems to reflect not just the age of the organization itself, but the age of the industry in which it operates, no matter what its own age. Industries that predate the industrial revolution seem to favor one kind of structure, those of the age of the early railroads another, and so on. We should obviously expect different structures in different periods; the surprising thing is that these structures seem to carry through to new periods, old industries remaining relatively unaffected by innovations in structural design.

Technical System

Technical system refers to the instruments used in the operating core to produce the outputs. (This should be distinguished from ''technology,'' which refers to the knowledge base of the organization.) Three hypotheses are especially important here.

H6. The more regulating the technical system—that is, the more it controls the work of the operators—the more formalized the operating work and the more bureaucratic the structure of the operating core. Technical systems that regulate the work of the operators—for example, mass production assembly lines—render that work highly routine and predictable, and so encourage its specialization and formalization, which in turn create the conditions for bureaucracy in the operating core.

H7. The more complex the technical system, the more elaborate the administrative structure, especially the larger and more professional the support staff, the greater the selective decentralization (to that staff), and the greater the use of liaison devices to coordinate the work of that staff. Essentially, if an organization is to use complex machinery, it must hire staff experts who can understand that machinery—who have the capability to design, select, and modify it. And then it must give them considerable power to make decisions concerning that machinery, and encourage them to use the liaison devices to ensure mutual adjustment among them.

H8. The automation of the operating core transforms a bureaucratic administrative structure into an organic one. When unskilled work is coordinated by the standardization of work processes, we get bureaucratic structure. But it is not only the operating core that gets bureaucratized. The whole organization tends to take on characteristics of bureaucracy, because an obsessive control mentality pervades the system. But when the work of the operating core gets automated, social relationships change. Now it is machines, not people, that are regulated. So the obsession with control disappears—machines do not need to be watched over—and with it go many of the managers and analysts who were needed to control the operators. In their place come the support specialists, to look after the machinery. And they, as described in the last hypothesis, gain a good deal of power and coordinate by mutual adjustment. In other words, the result of automation is a reduction of line authority in favor of staff expertise and a tendency to rely less on standardization for coordination, more on mutual adjustment. Thus, ironically, organizations tend to get humanized by the automation of their operating work.

Environment

Environment is a catch-all term that has been used in the literature to describe the general conditions that surround an organization. We shall discuss five hypotheses here, each one dealing with a different condition.

H9. The more dynamic the environment, the more organic the structure. It stands to reason that in a stable environment—when nothing changes—an organization can predict its future conditions and so, all other things being equal, can easily rely on standardization for coordination. But when conditions become dynamic—when sources of supply are uncertain, the need for product change frequent, labor turnover high, political conditions unstable—the organization cannot standardize, but must instead remain flexible through the use of direct supervision or mutual adjustment for coordination. In other words, it must have organic structure. Thus, for example, armies, which tend to be highly bureaucratic institutions in peacetime, can become rather organic when engaged in highly dynamic, guerrilla-type warfare.

H10. The more complex the environment, the more decentralized the structure. We saw earlier that the prime reason to decentralize a structure is that all the information needed to make decisions cannot be comprehended in one head. For example, when the operations of the organization are based on a complex body of technical knowledge (as in a hospital), then the organization must engage professionals (the physicians) and grant them a good deal of power over their own work. Note that Hypotheses 9 and 10 are independent of one another. A simple environment can be stable or dynamic (the manufacturer of dresses faces a simple environment yet cannot predict style from one season to another). A complex one likewise can be stable or dynamic (the specialist in perfected open heart surgery faces a complex task, yet knows exactly what to expect).

H11. The more diversified the organization's markets, the greater the propensity to split it into market-based units, or divisions, given favorable economies of scale. When an organization can identify distinct markets—geographical regions, clients, but especially products and services—it will be predisposed to split itself into high-level units on that basis, and to give each a good deal of control over its own operations (that is, to use what we called "limited vertical decentralization"). In

simple terms, diversification breeds divisionalization. In this way, the organization can reduce the coordination needed across units: each has all the functions associated with its own markets. But this assumes favorable economies of scale. If the operating core cannot be divided (as in the case of an aluminum smelter), or if some critical function must be centrally coordinated (as in purchasing in a retail chain), then full divisionalization may simply be impossible.

H12. Extreme hostility in its environment drives any organization to centralize its structure temporarily. Evidence from the social psychological laboratory suggests that when threatened by extreme hostility in its environment, the tendency for groups (and, presumably, organizations) is to centralize power, in other words, to fall back on the tightest coordinating mechanism they know, direct supervision. Here a central leader can ensure fast and highly coordinated response to the threat (at least temporarily).

H13. Disparities in the environment encourage the organization to decentralize selectively to differentiated work constellations. When an organization faces very different kinds of environments—one dynamic, requiring organic structure, another stable, requiring bureaucratic structure, and so on—the natural tendency is to differentiate the structure, to create different pockets, or "work constellations," to deal with each. Each constellation is given the power to make the decisions related to its own "subenvironment," with the result that the structure becomes decentralized selectively.

Power

Our fourth set of situational factors relates to power. The impact of external control of the organization, the power needs of the members, and fashion are discussed below.

H14. The greater the external control of the organization, the more centralized and formalized its structure. This important hypothesis claims that to the extent that an organization is controlled externally—for example, by a parent firm or a government—it tends to centralize power at the strategic apex and to formalize its behavior. The reason is that the two most effective ways to control an organization from the outside are to hold its chief executive officer responsible for its actions and to impose clearly defined standards on it. Moreover, external control forces the organization to be especially careful about its actions; because it must justify its behaviors to outsiders, it tends to formalize them. Finally, external control can further formalize the structure when it imposes special demands for rationalization, for example, when a parent firm insists that all its subsidiaries use a common set of purchasing procedures. The important point about this hypothesis is that the centralization of power in society—as independent organizations lose their power to larger systems—means centralization of power at the organizational level, and bureaucratization in the use of that power.

H15. The power needs of the members tend to generate structures that are excessively centralized. All members of the organization—operators, support staffers, analysts, managers—seek to enhance their own power, or at least to keep others from having power over them. But the dice are loaded in this game, the line managers and especially those at the strategic apex being favored by the existence of an authority structure that aggregates formal power up the hierarchy of command. And so we would expect that to the extent that the members seek personal power, excessively centralized structures would tend to be the most common result.

H16. Fashion favors the structure of the day, (and of the culture), sometimes even when inappropriate. Ideally, the design parameters are chosen according to the dictates of age, size, technical system, and environment. In fact, however, fashion seems to play a role too, encouraging many organizations to adopt currently popular design parameters that are inappropriate for themselves. Paris has its salons of haute couture; likewise New York has its offices of "haute structure," the consulting firms that

sometimes tend to oversell the latest in structural fashion.

E. THE CONFIGURATIONS

This completes our discussion of the elements of structure. So far—and especially in our presentation of the situational factors—we have tended to look at structure the way a diner looks at a buffet table. But in fact these elements seem to cluster naturally in a certain number of ways, which we have called configurations. A number may have been evident to the reader in the discussion. In particular, we have six basic parts of the organization, six basic mechanisms of coordination, six basic types of decentralization. These in fact all fit together, to describe the essence of six basic configurations, as can be seen in Table 1, which also lists the design parameters and situational factors associated with each configuration.

We can explain this correspondence by considering the organization as being pulled in six different directions, one by each of its parts, as shown in Figure 10. When conditions favor one of these pulls over the others, a particular organization is drawn to structure itself as one of the configurations, as described below.

The Simple Structure

The name tells it all. And Figure 11 shows it all. The structure is simple, not much more than one large unit consisting of one or a few top managers, one of whom dominates by the pull to centralize, and a group of operators who do the basic work. Little of the behavior in the organization is formalized and minimal use is made of planning, training, or the liaison devices. The absence of standardization means that the structure is organic and has little need for staff analysts. Likewise there are few middle line managers because so much of the coordination is handled at the top. Even the support staff is minimized, in order to keep the structure lean, the organization flexible.

The organization must be flexible because it operates in a dynamic environment, often by choice since that is the only place where it can outsmart the bureaucracies. But that environment must be simple, as must the production system, or else the chief executive could not for long hold on to the lion's share of the power. The organization is often young, in part because time drives it toward bureaucracy, in part because the vulnerability of simple structures causes many of them to fail. And many are often small, since size too drives the structure toward bureaucracy. Not infrequently the chief executive purposely keeps the organization small in order to retain his personal control.

The classic simple structure is of course the entrepreneurial firm, controlled tightly and personally by its owner. Sometimes, however, under the control of a very clever autocratic leader who refuses to let go of the reins, a simple structure can grow large. Sometimes under crisis conditions, large organizations also revert temporarily to simple structures to allow forceful leaders to try to save them.

The Machine Bureaucracy

The machine bureaucracy is the offspring of the Industrial Revolution, when jobs became highly specialized and work became highly standardized. As can be seen in Figure 12, in contrast to simple structure, the machine bureaucracy elaborates its administration. First, it requires a large technostructure to design and maintain its systems of standardization, notably those that formalize its behaviors and plan its actions. And by virtue of the organization's dependence on these systems, the technostructure gains a good deal of informal power, resulting in a limited amount of horizontal decentralization, reflecting the pull to standardize. A large hierarchy of middle line managers emerges to control the highly specialized work of the operating core. But that middle line hierarchy is usually structured on a functional basis all the way up to the top, where the real

power of coordination lies. So the structure tends to be rather centralized in the vertical sense.

To enable the top managers to maintain centralized control, both the environment and the production system of the machine bureaucracy must be fairly simple, the latter regulating the work of the operators but not itself automated. In fact, machine bureaucracies fit most naturally with mass production. Indeed it is interesting that this structure is most prevalent in industries that date back to the period from the Industrial Revolution to the early part of this century.

The Professional Bureaucracy

There is another bureaucratic configuration, but because this one relies on the standardization of skills rather than of work processes or outputs for its coordination, it emerges as dramatically different from the machine bureaucracy. Here the pull to professionalize dominates. In having to rely on trained professionals—people highly specialized, but with considerable control over their work, as in hospitals or universities—to do its operating tasks, the organization surrenders a good deal of its power not only to the professionals themselves but also to the associations and institutions that select and train them in the first place. So the structure emerges as highly decentralized horizontally; power over many decisions, both operating and strategic, flows all the way down the hierarchy, to the professionals of the operating core.

Above the operating core we find a rather unique structure, as can be seen in Figure 13. There is little need for a technostructure, since the main standardization occurs as a result of training that takes place outside the organization. Because the professionals work so independently, the size of operating units can be very large, and few first line managers are needed. The support staff is typically very large too, in order to back up the high priced professionals.

Professional bureaucracy is called for whenever an organization finds itself in an environment that is stable yet complex. Complexity requires

TABLE 1 BASIC DIMENSIONS OF THE SIX CONFIGURATIONS

	Simple Structure	Machine Bureaucracy
Key coordinating mechanism	Direct Supervision	Standardization of work
Key part of organization	Strategix apex	Technostructure
Design parameters:		
Specialization of jobs	Little specialization	*Much horiz. and vert. spec.*
Training	Little	Little
Indoctrination	Little	Little
Formalization of behavior, bureaucratic/organic	Little formalization, *organic*	*Much formalization, bureaucratic*
Grouping	Usually functional	*Usually functional*
Unit size	Wide	Wide at bottom, narrow elsewhere
Planning and control systems	Little pl. and control	Action planning
Liaison devices	Few liaison devices	Few liaison devices
Decentralization	*Centralization*	*Limited horizontal decent.*
Situational factors:		
Age and size	Typically young and small (first stage)	Typically old and large (second stage)
Technical system	Simple, not regulating	Regulating but not automated, not very sophisticated
Environment	Simple and dynamic; sometimes hostile	Simple and stable
Power	Chief executive control; often owner-managed; not fashionable	Technocratic and external control; not fashionable

*Italic type designates key design parameter.

Professional Bureaucracy	Divisionalized Form	Adhocracy	Missionary
Standardization of skills	Standardization of outputs	Mutual adjustment	Standardization of norms
Operating core	Middle line	Support staff	Ideology
Much horiz. spec.	Some horiz. and vert. spec. (between divisions and HQ)	*Much horiz. spec.*	Little specialization
Much	Little	Much	Little
Little	Some of div. managers	Some	*Much*
Little formalization, *bureaucratic*	Much formalization (within divisions), bureaucratic	Little formalization, *organic*	Little formal, bureaucratic
Functional and market	*Market*	*Functional and market*	Market
Wide at bottom, narrow elsewhere	Wide (at top)	*Narrow throughout*	Wide (in enclaves of limited size)
Little pl. and control	*Much perf. control*	Limited action pl.	Little pl. and control
Liaison devices in administration	Few liaison devices	*Many liaison devices throughout*	Few liaison devices
Horizontal decent.	*Limited vertical decent.*	*Selective decent.*	*Decentralization*
Varies	Typically old and very large (third stage)	Often young	Typically neither very young nor very old; large only through many small enclaves
Not regulating or sophisticated	Divisible, otherwise typically like Mach. Bur.	Very sophisticated, often automated, or else not regulating or sophisticated	Simple, not regulating
Complex and stable	Relatively simple and stable; diversified markets (esp. products and services)	Complex and dynamic; sometimes disparate	Simple and usually stable
Professional operator control; fashionable	Middle-line control; fashionable (esp. in industry)	Expert control; very fashionable	Ideological control; coming fashion?

FIGURE 10   SIX PULLS ON THE ORGANIZATION

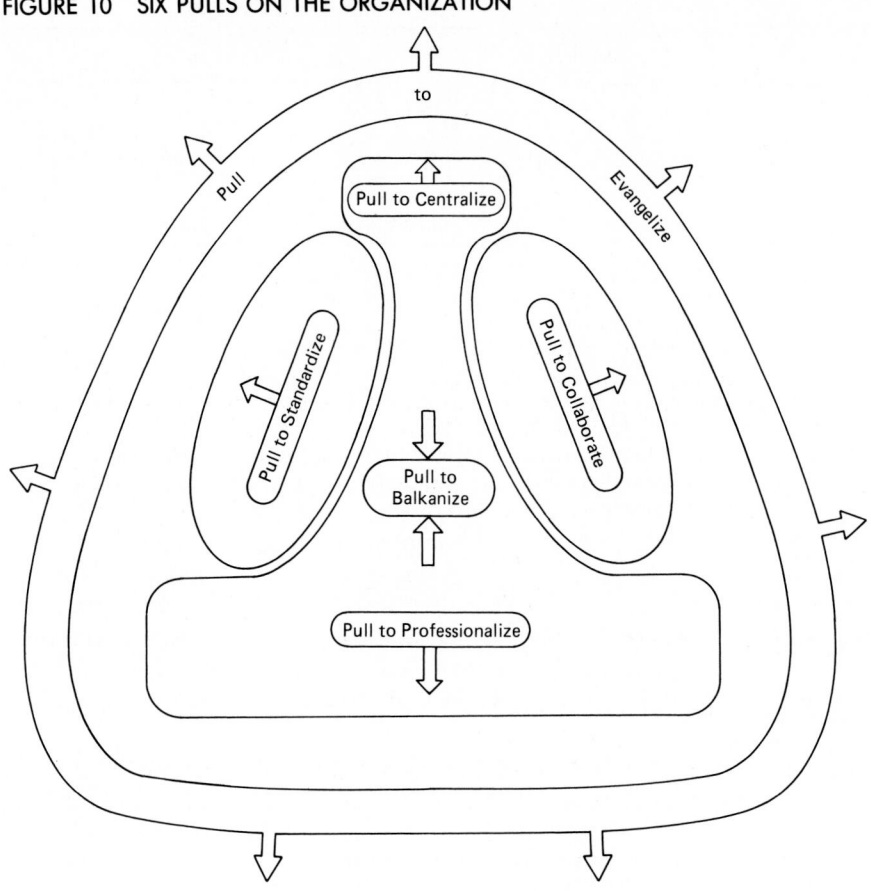

FIGURE 11   THE SIMPLE STRUCTURE

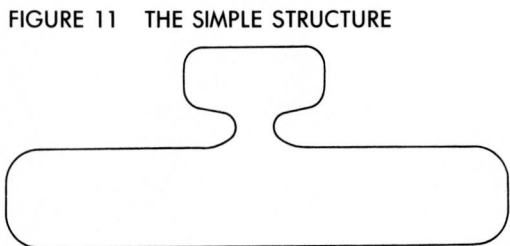

FIGURE 12   THE MACHINE BUREAUCRACY

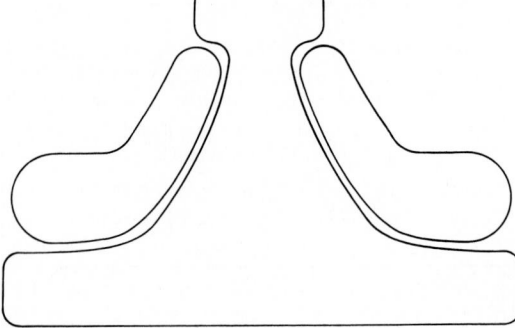

FIGURE 13   THE PROFESSIONAL BUREAUCRACY

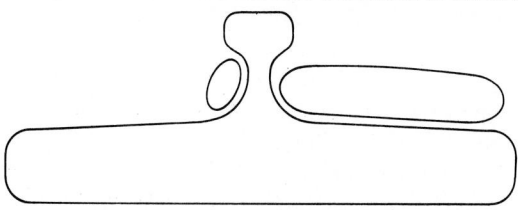

decentralization to highly trained individuals, and stability enables them to apply standardized skills and so to work with a good deal of autonomy. To ensure that autonomy, the production system must be neither highly regulating, complex, nor automated.

The Divisionalized Form

Like the professional bureaucracy, the divisionalized form is not so much an integrated organization as a set of rather independent entities coupled together by a loose administrative structure. But whereas those entities of the professional bureaucracy are individuals, in the divisionalized form they are units in the middle line, generally called "divisions," exerting a dominant pull to Balkanize. The divisionalized form differs from the other four configurations in one central respect: it is not a complete structure, but a partial one superimposed on others. Each division has its own structure.

An organization divisionalizes for one reason above all, because its product lines are diversified. And that tends to happen most often in the largest and most mature organizations, the ones that have run out of opportunities—or have become bored—in their traditional markets. Such diversification encourages the organization to replace functional by market-based units, one for each distinct product line (as shown in Figure 14), and to grant considerable autonomy to each to run its own business. The result is a limited form of decentralization down the chain of command.

How does the central headquarters maintain a semblance of control over the divisions? Some direct supervision is used. But too much of that interferes with the necessary divisional autonomy. So the headquarters relies on performance control systems, in other words the standardization of outputs. To design these control systems, headquarters creates a small technostructure. This is shown in Figure 14, across from the small central support staff that headquarters sets up to provide certain services common to the divisions such as legal counsel and public relations.

The Adhocracy

None of the structures so far discussed suits the industries of our age, industries such as aerospace, petrochemicals, think tank consulting, and film making. These organizations need above all to innovate in very complex ways. The bureaucratic structures are too inflexible, and the simple structure too autocratic. These industries require "project structures," structures that can fuse experts drawn from different specialties into

FIGURE 14   THE DIVISIONALIZED FORM

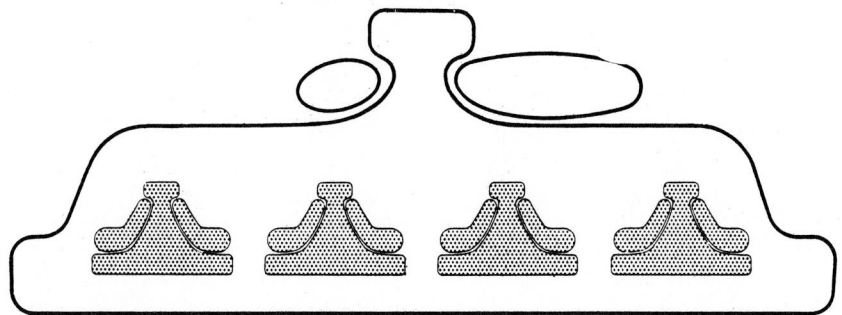

smoothly functioning creative teams. That is the role of our fifth structural configuration, adhocracy, dominated by the experts' pull to collaborate.

Adhocracy is an organic structure that relies for coordination on mutual adjustment among its highly trained and highly specialized experts, which it encourages by the extensive use of the liaison devices—integrating managers, standing committees, and above all task forces and matrix structure. Typically the experts are grouped in functional units for housekeeping purposes but deployed in small market based project teams to do their work. To these teams, located all over the structure in accordance with the decisions to be made, is delegated power over different kinds of decisions. So the structure becomes decentralized selectively in the vertical and horizontal dimensions, that is, power is distributed unevenly, all over the structure, according to expertise and need.

All the distinctions of conventional structure disappear in the adhocracy, as can be seen in Figure 15. With power based on expertise, the line-staff distinction evaporates. With power distributed throughout the structure, the distinction between the strategic apex and the rest of the structure blurs.

Adhocracies are found in environments that are both complex and dynamic, because those are the ones that require sophisticated innovation, the type of innovation that calls for the cooperative efforts of many different kinds of experts. One type of adhocracy is often associated with a production system that is very complex, sometimes and so requires a highly skilled and influential support staff to design and maintain the technical system of the operating core. (The dotted lines of Figure 15 designate the separation of the operating core from the adhocratic administrative structure.) Here the projects take place in the administration to bring new operating facilities on line (or when a new complex is designed in a petrochemical firm). Another type of adhocracy produces its projects directly for its clients (as in a think tank consulting firm or a manufacturer of engineering prototypes). Here, as a result, the operators also take part in the projects, bringing their expertise to bear on them; hence the operating core blends into the administrative structure (as indicated in Figure 15 above the dotted line). This second type of adhocracy tends to be young on average, because with no standard products or services, many tend to fail while others escape their vulnerability by standardizing some products or services and so converting themselves to a form of bureaucracy.*

The Missionary

Our sixth configuration forms another rather distinct combination of the elements we have been discussing. When an organization is dominated by the pull to evangelize, its members are encouraged to pull together, and so there tends to be a loose division of labor, little job specialization as well as a reduction of the various forms of differentiation found in the other configurations—of the strategic apex from the rest, of staff from line or administration from operations, between operators, between divisions, and so on.

What holds the missionary together—that is, provides for its coordination—is the standard-

FIGURE 15   THE ADHOCRACY

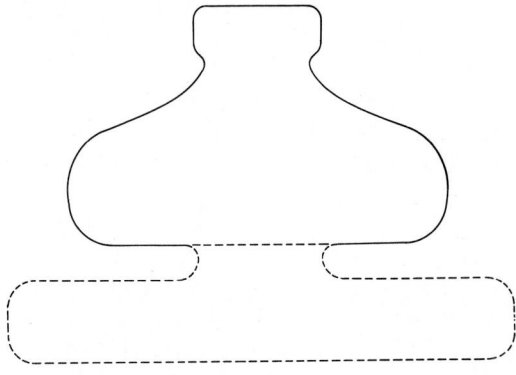

---

*[Editors' note: We shall clarify in a later text reading these two basic types of Adhocracies. Toffler (1970) employed the term Adhocracy is his popular book *Future Shock*, but it can be found in print at least as far back as 1964 (Bennis and Slater, 1964).]

ization of norms, the sharing of values and beliefs among all its members. And the key to ensuring this is their socialization, effected through the design parameter of indoctrination. Once the new member has been indoctrinated into the organization—once he or she identifies strongly with the common beliefs—then he or she can be given considerable freedom to make decisions. Thus the result of effective indoctrination is the most complete form of decentralization. And because other forms of coordination need not be relied upon, the missionary formalizes little of its behavior as such and makes minimal use of planning and control systems. As a result, it has virtually no technostructure. Likewise, external professional training is not relied upon, because that would force the organization to surrender a certain control to external agencies.

Hence, the missionary ends up as an amorphous mass of members, with little specialization as to job, differentiation as to part, division as to status. Beyond a certain size, however, as indicated in Figure 16, it tends to divide itself, like the amoeba, into smaller units, best thought of as "enclaves," with perhaps a nominal headquarters in one of the enclaves—a loose strategic apex to serve as the depository of the official manifestations of the ideology (the "archives").

Missionaries tend not to be very young organizations—it takes time for a set of beliefs to become institutionalized as an ideology. Many missionaries do not get a chance to grow very old either (with notable exceptions, such as certain long-standing religious orders). Size, as we saw, is also not very clear-cut. On one hand, there is a clear limit to the size of each enclave; on the other hand, nothing stops the organization from spinning off enclave after enclave, since each is a rather independent entity. Neither the environment nor the technical system of the missionary can be very complex, because that would require the use of highly skilled specialists, who would hold a certain power and status over others and thereby serve to differentiate the structure. Nor can the technical system be regulating, because that would lead to the formalizing of the operating work. Thus we would expect to find the simplest technical systems in missionaries, usually hardly any at all, as in religious orders or in the primitive farm cooperatives. And the environment of the missionary, in addition to being simple, can also typically be described as stable, in that the organization tends to function in a placid environment that makes few demands on it.

This completes a rather lengthy discussion of the structuring of organizations. As we have seen, what appears to be an enormously complex subject—comprising organizational parts, coordinating mechanisms, design parameters, and situational factors—can be made manageable by considering how all these many dimensions cluster to form distinct types of organizations. This may seem like an artificial reduction of the complexity, but in important ways it is far more realistic than trying to consider all of the permutations and combinations of these dimensions (an impossible, or at least awfully confusing task, in any event), or of giving up and dealing with this material in a fragmented way (as has been done in much of the traditional academic literature).

In fact, a good deal of experience with this "typology" (the common label for a set of types developed logically) in both university teaching and business practice has suggested much use for it. In no way do all organizations fit one type or another. But having the set of them as a conceptual framework can help enormously to cut through, not only the complexities of structure, but of strategy and power and almost any other factor associated with organizations. [Editor's note: We shall see this in Section III, where five of these six configurations serve as the basis

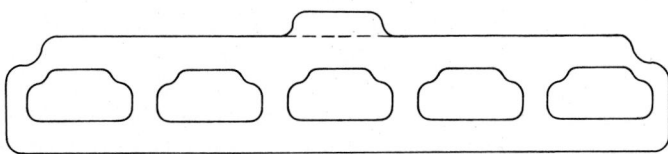

FIGURE 16   THE MISSIONARY

to develop contexts there; in Chapter 9 a reading by Miller and Mintzberg probes the "case for configuration," while in Chapter 15, a further reading from Mintzberg's work on structuring considers using this framework to understand unusual combinations of these configurations and broader uses of the framework at large.]

STRATEGY AND ORGANIZATION PLANNING*

by Jay R. Galbraith

. . . There has been a great deal of progress in the knowledge base supporting organization planning in the last twenty-five years. Modern research on corporate structures probably started with Chandler's *Strategy and Structure*. Subsequent research has been aimed at expanding the number of attributes of an organization beyond that of just structure. I have used the model shown in Figure 1 to indicate that organization consists of structure, processes that cut the structural lines like budgeting, planning, teams, and so on, reward systems like promotions and compensation, and finally people practices like selection and development (Galbraith, 1977). The trend lately is to expand to more attributes like the 7's (Waterman, 1980) and to "softer" attributes like culture.

All of these models are intended to convey the same ideas. First organization is more than just structure. And second, all of the elements must "fit" to be in "harmony" with each other. The effective organization is one that has blended its structure, management practices, rewards, and people into a package that in turn fits with its strategy. However, strategies change and therefore the organization must change.

*   Originally published in *Human Resource Management*, 22, no. 1/2 (Spring/Summer 1983), pp. 64–77; Copyright © 1983 John Wiley & Sons, Inc. Reprinted with deletions by permission of John Wiley & Sons, Inc.

FIGURE 1   MODEL OF ORGANIZATION STRUCTURE

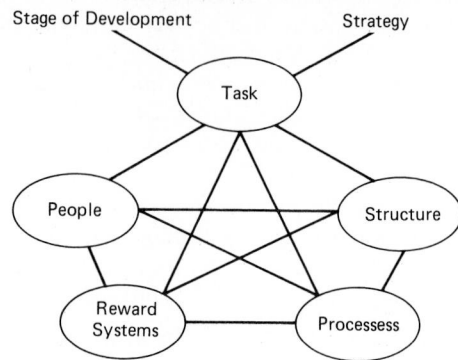

The research of the past few years is creating some evidence by which organizations and strategies are matched. Some of the strategies are proving more successful than others. One of the explanations is organizational in nature. Also the evidence shows that for any strategy, the high performers are those who have achieved a fit between their strategy and their organization.

These findings give organization planning a base from which to work. The organization planner should become a member of the strategic team in order to guide management to choose the appropriate strategies for which the organization is developed or to choose the appropriate organization for the new strategy.

In the sections that follow, the strategic changes that are made by organizations are described. Then the strategy and organization evidence is presented. Finally the data on economic performance and fit is discussed.

I. STRATEGY AND ORGANIZATION

There has been a good deal of recent attention given to the match between strategy and organization. Much of this work consists of empirical tests of Chadler's ideas presented in *Strategy and Structure* (1962). Most of this material is reviewed elsewhere (Galbraith and Nathanson, 1978). However, some recent work and ideas hold out considerable potential for understanding how different patterns of strategic change lead to different organization structures, management systems, and company cultures. In addition, some good relationships with economic performance are also attained.

The ideas rest on the concept of an organization having a center of gravity or driving force (Tregoe and Zimmerman, 1980). This center of gravity arises from the firm's initial success in the industry in which it grew up. Let us first explore the concept of center of gravity, then the patterns of strategic change that have been followed by American enterprises.

The center of gravity of a company depends on where in the industry supply chain the company started. In order to explain the concept, manufacturing industries will be used. Figure 2 depicts the stages of supply in an industry chain. Six stages are shown here. Each industry may have more or less stages. Service industries typically have fewer stages.

The chain begins with a raw material extraction stage which supplies crude oil, iron ore, logs, or bauxite to the second stage of primary manufacturing. This second stage is a variety-reducing stage to produce a standardized output (petrochemicals, steel, paper pulp, or aluminum ingots). The next stage fabricates commodity products from this primary material. Fabricators produce polyethylene, cans, sheet steel, cardboard cartons, and semiconductor components. The next stage is the product producers who add value, usually through product development, patents, and proprietary products. The next stage is the marketer and distributor. These are the consumer branded product manufacturers and various distributors. Finally, there are the retailers who have the direct contact with the ultimate consumer.

The line splitting the chain into two segments divides the industry into upstream and downstream halves. While there are differences between each of the stages, the differences between the upstream and downstream stages are striking. The upstream stages add value by reducing the variety of raw materials found on the earth's surface to a few standard commodities. The purpose is to produce flexible, predictable raw materials and intermediate products from which an increasing variety of downstream products are made. The downstream stages add value through producing a variety of products to meet varying customer needs. The downstream value is added through advertising, product positioning, marketing chennels, and R&D. Thus, the upstream and downstream companies face very different business problems and tasks.

The reason for distinguishing between upstream and downstream companies is that the factors for success, the lessons learned by managers, and the organizations used are fundamentally different. The successful, experienced manager has been shaped and formed in fundamentally different ways in the different stages. The management processes are different, as are the dominant functions. In short, the company's culture is shaped by where it began in the industry chain. Listed below are some fundamental differences that illustrate the contrast.

Upstream	Downstream
Standardize/homogenize	Customize/segment
Low cost producer	High margins/proprietary positions
Process Innovation	Product Innovation
Capital Budget	R&D/Advertising Budget

FIGURE 2   SUPPLY STAGES IN AN INDUSTRY CHAIN

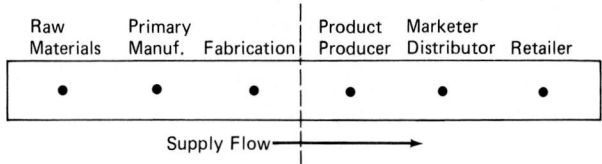

Upstream	Downstream
Technology/Capital Intensive	People Intensive
Supply/Trader/ Engineering	R&D/Marketing Dominated
Line Driven	Line/Staff
Maximize End Users	Target End Users
⋮	⋮
Sales Push	Market Pull

The mind set of the upstream manager is geared toward standardization and efficiency. They are the producers of standardized commodity products. In contrast, downstream managers try to customize and tailor output to diverse customer needs. They segment markets and target individual users. The upstream company wants to standardize in order to maximize the number of end users and get volume to lower costs. The downstream company wants to target particular sets of end-users. Therefore, the upstreamers have a divergent view of the world based on their commodity. For example, the cover of the 1981 annual report of Intel (a fabricator of commodity semiconductors) is a listing of the 10,000 uses to which microprocessors have been put. The downstreamers have a convergent view of the world based on customer needs and will select whatever commodity will best serve that need. In the electronics industry there is always a conflict between the upstream component types and the downstream systems types because of this contrast in mind sets.

The basis of competition is different in the two stages. Commodities compete on price since the products are the same. Therefore, it is essential that the successful upstreamer be the low-cost producer. Their organizations are the lean and mean ones with a minimum of overheads. Low cost is also important for the downstreamer, but it is proprietary features that generate high margins. That feature may be a brand image, such as Maxwell House, a patented technology, an endorsement (such as the American Dental Association's endorsement of Crest toothpaste), customer service policy, and so on. Competition revolves around product features and product po-

sitioning and less on price. This means that marketing and product management sets prices. Products move by marketing pull. In contrast, the upstream company pushes the product through a strong sales force. Often sales people negotiate prices within limits set by top management.

The organizations are different as well. The upstream companies are functional and line driven. They seek a minimum of staff, and even those staffs that are used are in supporting roles. The downstream company with multiple products and multiple markets learns to manage diversity early. Profit centers emerge and resources need to be allocated across products and markets. Larger staffs arise to assist top management in priority setting across competing product/market advocates. Higher margins permit the overhead to exist.

Both upstream and downstream companies use research and development. However, the upstream company invests in process development in order to lower costs. The downstream company invests primarily in product development in order to achieve proprietary positions.

The key managerial processes also vary. The upstream companies are driven by the capital budget and have various capital appropriations controls. The downstream companies also have a capital budget but are driven by the R&D budget (product producers) or the advertising budget (marketers). Further downstream it is working capital that becomes paramount. Managers learn to control the business by managing the turnover of inventory and accounts receivable. Thus, the upstream company is capital intensive and technological "know-how" is critical. Downstream companies are more people intensive. Therefore, the critical skills revolve around human resources management.

The dominant functions also vary with stages. The raw material processor is dominated by geologists, petroleum engineers, and traders. The supply and distribution function which searches for the most economical end use is powerful. The manufacturers of commodities are dominated by engineers who come up through manufacturing. The downstream companies are dominated first by technologists in research and product development. Farther downstream, it is marketing and then merchandising that emerge as the power centers. The line of succession to the CEO usually runs through this dominant function.

In summary, the upstream and downstream companies are very different entities. The differences, a bit exaggerated here because of the dichotomy, lead to differences in organization structure, management processes, dominant functions, succession paths, management beliefs and values or, in short, the management way of life. Thus, companies can be in the same industry but be very different because they developed from a beginning at a particular stage of the industry. This beginning, and the initial successes, teaches management the lessons of that stage. The firm develops an integrated organization (structure, processes, rewards, and people) which is peculiar to that stage and forms the center of gravity.

II. STRATEGIC CHANGE

The first strategic change that an organization makes is to vertically integrate within its industry. At a certain size, the organization can move backward to prior stages to guarantee sources of supply and secure bargaining leverage on vendors. And/or it can move forward to guarantee markets and volume for capital investments and become a customer to feed back data for new products. This initial strategic move does not change the center of gravity because the prior and subsequent stages are usually operated for the benefit of the center-of-gravity stage.

The paper industry is used to illustrate the concepts of center of gravity and vertical integration. Figure 3 depicts five paper companies which operate from different centers of gravity. The first is Weyerhauser. Its center of gravity is at the land and timber stage of the industry. Weyerhauser seeks the highest return use for a log. They make pulp and paper rolls. They make containers and milk cartons. But they are a timber company. If the returns are better in lumber, the

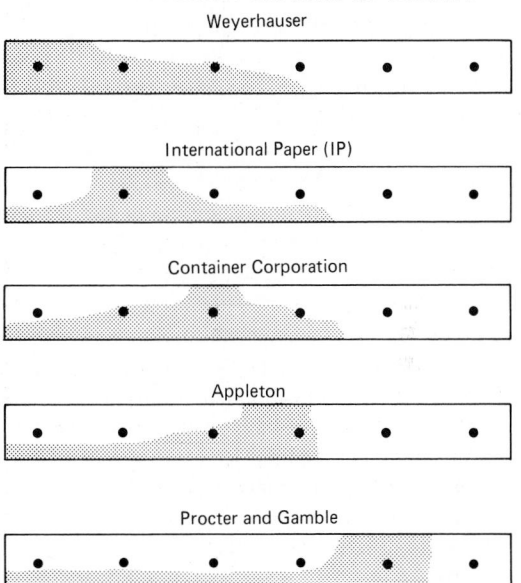

FIGURE 3   EXAMPLES OF FIVE PAPER COMPANIES OPERATING AT DIFFERENT CENTERS OF GRAVITY

Weyerhauser

International Paper (IP)

Container Corporation

Appleton

Procter and Gamble

pulp mills get fed with sawdust and chips. International Paper (the name of the company tells it all), by contrast, is a primary manufacturer of paper. It also has timber lands, container plants, and works on new products around aseptic packaging. However, if the pulp mills ran out of logs, the manager of the woodlands used to be fired. The raw material stage is to supply the manufacturing stage, not seek the highest return for its timber. The Container Corporation (again, the name describes the company) is the example of the fabricator. It also has woodlands and pulp mills, but they are to supply the container making operations. The product producer is Appleton. It makes specialty paper products. For example, Appleton produces a paper with globules of ink imbedded in it. The globules burst and form a letter or number when struck with an impact printer.

The last company is Procter and Gamble. P&G is a consumer products company. And, like the other companies, it operates pulp mills and owns timber lands. However, it is driven by the advertising or marketing function. If one wanted to be CEO of P&G, one would not run a pulp mill or the woodlands. The path to CEO is through the brand manager for Charmin or Pampers.

Thus, each of these companies is in the paper industry. Each operates at a number of stages in the industry. Yet each is a very diferent company because it has its center of gravity at a different stage. The center of gravity establishes a base from which subsequent strategic changes take place. That is, as a company's industry matures, the company feels a need to change its center of gravity in order to move to a place in the industry where better returns can be obtained, or move to a new industry but use its same center of gravity and skills in that industry, or make some combination of industry and center of gravity change. These options lead to different patterns of corporate developments.

A. Byproducts Diversification

One of the first diversification moves that a vertically integrated company makes is to sell byproducts from points along the industry chain. Figure 4 depicts this strategy. These companies appear to be diversified if one attributes revenue to the various industries in which the company operates. But the company has changed neither its industry nor its center of gravity. The company is behaving intelligently by seeking additional sources of revenue and profit. However, it is still psychologically committed to its center of gravity and to its industry. Alcoa is such a firm. Even though they operate in several industries, their output varies directly with the aluminum cycle. They have not reduced their dependence on a single industry, as one would with real diversification.

B. Related Diversification

Another strategic change is the diversification into new industries but at the same center of gravity. This is called "related diversification." The firm diversifies into new businesses, but they are all related. The relationship revolves around the company's center of gravity. Figure 5 depicts the diversification moves of Procter and Gamble. After beginning in the soap industry, P&G vertically integrated back into doing its own chemical processing (fatty acids) and seed crushing. Then, in order to pursue new growth opportunities, it has been diversifying into paper, food, beverages, pharmaceuticals, coffee, and so on. But each move into a new industry is made at the company's center of gravity. The new businesses are all consumer products which are driven out of advertising by brand managers. The 3M Company also follows a related diversification strategy, but theirs is based on technology. They have 40,000 different products which are produced by some seventy divisions. However, 95% of the products are based on coating and bonding technologies. Its center of gravity is a product producer, and it adds value through R&D.

C. Linked Diversification

A third type of diversification involves moving into new industries and operating at different centers of gravity in those new industries. However, there is a linkage of some type among various businesses. Figure 6 depicts Union Camp as following this pattern of corporate development.

FIGURE 5   RELATED DIVERSIFICATION

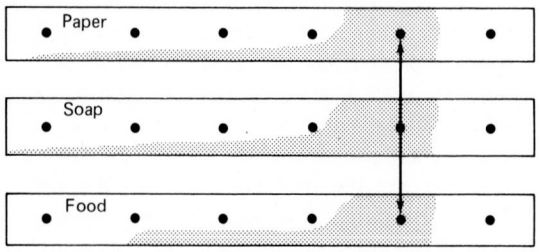

Procter and Gamble

FIGURE 4   BYPRODUCT DIVERSIFICATION

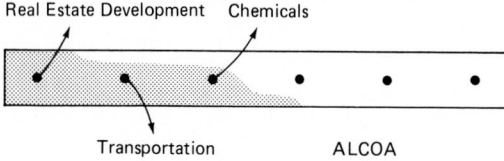

FIGURE 6   LINKED DIVERSIFICATION

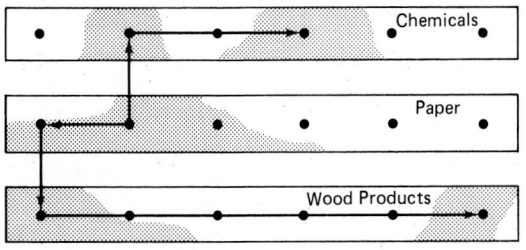

Union Camp

Union Camp is a primary producer of paper products. As such, it vertically integrated backwards to own woodlands. From there, it moved downstream within the wood products industry by running sawmills and fabricating plants. However, they recently purchased a retail lumber business.

They also moved into the chemical business by selling byproducts from the pulping process. This business was successful and expanded. Recently, Union Camp was bidding for a flavors and fragrances (F & F) company. The F&F company is a product producer which adds value through creating flavors and fragrances for mostly consumer products companies.

Thus, Union Camp is an upstream company that is acquiring downstream companies. However, these new companies are in industries in which the company already diversified from its upstream center of gravity. But these new acquisitions are not operated as vertically integrated entities. They are not operated for the benefit of the center of gravity but are standalone profit centers.

D. Unrelated Diversification

The final type of strategic change is to diversify into unrelated businesses. Like the linked diversifiers, unrelated diversifiers move into new industries often at different centers of gravity. They almost always use acquisition, while related and linked companies will use some acquisitions but rely heavily on internal development. There is often very little relation between the industries into which the unrelated company diversifies.

Textron and Teledyne have been the paradigm examples. They operate in industrial equipment, aerospace, consumer products, insurance, and so on. Others have spread into retailing, services, and entertainment. The purpose is to insulate the company's earnings from the uncertainties of any one industry or from the business cycle.

E. Center of Gravity Change

Another possibility is for an organization to stay in the same industry but change its center of gravity in that industry. Recent articles describe the attempts of chemical companies to move downstream into higher margin, proprietary products. They went to move away from the overcapacity/undercapacity cycles of commodity businesses with their low margins and high capital intensity. In aerospace, some of the system integration houses are moving backward into making electronic components. For example, there are going to be fewer airplanes and more effort on the avionics, radars, weapons, and so on that go into airplanes. In either case, it means a shift in the center of gravity of the company.

In summary, several patterns of strategic change can occur in a company. These involve changes to the company's industry of origination, changes to the center of gravity of the company, or some combination of the two. For some of the strategic changes there are appropriate organizations and measures of their economic performance.

III. STRATEGY, ORGANIZATION, AND PERFORMANCE

For a number of years now, studies have been made of strategy and structure of the Fortune 500. Most of these were conducted by the Harvard Business School. These studies were reviewed in previous work (Galbraith and Nathanson, 1978). The current view is illustrated in Table I. If one samples the Fortune 500 and categorizes them by strategy and structure, the following relationships hold.

TABLE I

Strategy	Structure
Single business	Functional
Vertical byproducts	Functional with P & Ls
Related businesses	Divisional
Linked businesses	Mixed structures
Unrelated businesses	Holding company

One can still find organizations staying in their same original business. Such a single business is Wrigley Chewing Gum. These organizations are run by centralized functional organizations. The next strategic type is the vertically integrated byproduct seller. Again, these companies have some diversification but remain committed to their industry and center of gravity. The companies are also functional, but the sequential stages are often operated as profit and loss divisions. The companies are usually quite centralized and run by collegial management groups. The profit centers are not true ones in being independent to run their own businesses. These are almost all upstream companies.

The related businesses are those that move into new industries at their center of gravity. Usually these are downstream companies. They adopt the decentralized profit center divisions. However, the divisions are not completely decentralized. There are usually strong corporate staffs and some centralized marketing, manufacturing, and R&D. There may be several thousand people on the corporate payroll.

The clearest contrast to the related diversifier is the unrelated business company. These companies enter a variety of businesses at several centers of gravity. The organization they adopt is the very decentralized holding company. Their outstanding feature is the small corporate staff. Depending on their size, the numbers range between fifty and two hundred. Usually these are support staffs. All of the marketing, manufacturing, and R&D is decentralized to the divisions. Group executives have no staffs and are generally corporate oriented.

The linked companies are neither of these extremes. Often linked forms are transitory. The

organizations that they utilize are usually mixed forms that are not easily classified. Some divisions are autonomous, while others are managed out of the corporate HQ. Still others have strong group executives with group staffs. Some work has been done on classifying these structures (Allen, 1978).

There has been virtually no work done on center of gravity changes and their changes in structure. Likewise, there has been nothing done on comparisons for economic performance. But for the other categories and structures, there is emerging some good data on relative economic performance.

The studies of economic performance have compared the various strategic patterns and the concept of fit between strategy and organization. Both sets of results have organization design implications. The economic studies use return on equity as the performance measure. If one compares the strategic categories listed in Table I, there are distinct performance differences. The high performers are consistently the related diversifiers (Rumelt, 1974; Galbraith and Nathanson, 1978; Nathanson and Cassano, 1982; Bettis, 1981; Rumelt, 1982). There are several explanations for this performance difference. One explanation is that the related diversifiers are all downstream companies in businesses with high R&D and advertising expenditures. These businesses have higher margins and returns than other businesses. Thus, it may not be the strategy but the businesses the relateds happen to be in. However, if the unrelateds are good acquirers, why do they not enter the high return businesses?

The other explanation is that the relateds learn a set of core skills and design an organization to perform at a particular center of gravity. Then, when they diversify, they take on the task of learning a new business, but at the same center of gravity. Therefore, they get a diversified portfolio of businesses but each with a system of management and an organization that is understood by everyone. The management understands the business and is not spread thin.

The unrelateds, however, have to learn new industries and also how to operate at a different center of gravity. This latter change is the most difficult to accomplish. One upstream company diversified via acquisition into downstream companies. They consistently encountered control troubles. They instituted a capital appropriation process for each investment of fifty thousand dollars or more. They still had problems, however. The retail division opened a couple of stores with leases for forty thousand dollars. They didn't use the capital process. The company got blindsided because the stores required forty million dollars in working capital for inventory and receivables. Thus, the management systems did not fit the new downstream businesses. It appears that organizational fit makes a difference. . . .

One additional piece of evidence results from the studies of economic performance. This result is that the poorest performer of the strategic categories is the vertically integrated byproduct seller (Rumelt, 1974). Recall these companies are all upstream, raw material, and primary manufacturers. They make up a good portion of "Smokestack America." In some respects, these companies made their money early in the century, and their value added is shifting to lesser developed countries in the natural course of industrial development. However, what is significant here is their inability to change. It is no secret to anyone that they have been underperformers, yet they have continued to put money back into the same business.

My explanation revolves around the center of gravity. These previously successful companies put together an organization that fit their industry and stage. When the industry declined, they were unable to change as well as the downstream companies. The reason is that upstream companies were functional organizations with few general managers. Their resource allocation was within a single business, not across multiple products. The management skill is partly technological know-how. This technology does not transfer across industries at the primary manufacturing center of gravity. The knowledge of paper making does not help very much in glass making. Yet both might be combined in a packaging company. Also, the capital intensity of these industries limits

the diversification. Usually one industry must be chosen and capital invested to be the low-cost producer. So there are a number of reasons why these companies have been notoriously poor diversifers.

In addition, it appears to be very difficult to change centers of gravity no matter where an organization is along the industry chain. The reason is that a center of gravity shift requires a dismantling of the current power structure, rejection of parts of the old culture, and establishing all new management systems. The related diversification works for exactly the opposite reasons. They can move into new businesses with minimal change to the power structure and accepted ways of doing things. Changes in the center of gravity usually occur by new start-ups at a new center of gravity rather than a shift in the center of established firms. . . .

There are some exceptions that prove the rule. Some organizations have shifted from upstream commodity producers to downstream product producers and consumer product firms. General Mills moved from a flour miller to a related diversified provider of products for the homemaker. Over a long period of time they shifted downstream into consumer food products from their cake mix product beginnings. From there, they diversified into related areas after selling off the milling operations, the old core of the company. . . . [In these cases], however, new management was brought in and acquisition and divestment used to make the transition. So, even though vestiges of the old name remain, these are substantially different companies. . . .

The vast majority of our research has examined one kind of strategic change—diversification. The far more difficult one, the change in center of gravity, has received far less [attention]. For the most part, the concept is difficult to measure and not publicly reported like the number of industries in which a company operates. Case studies will have to be used. But there is a need for more systematic knowledge around this kind of strategic change.

II. ORGANIZATION

## SEVEN

DEALING

WITH

POWER

The readings to this point have, for the most part, dealt with organizations as rather rational instruments. Strategies, whether formulated analytically or allowed to emerge in some kind of learning process, have nonetheless served for the good of the organization at large in a purely economic and competitive sense, as have the associated structures and systems. True, Wrapp's and Quinn's managers, for example, have consciously considered and dealt with potential resistance in creating and implanting their strategies. In doing so, they may have been forced to think in political terms. But the overt use of power and organized political action has largely been absent from our discussion.

An important group of thinkers in the field, however, have come to view strategy formation as essentially an interplay of power processes, sometimes highly politicized ones. Rather than assuming that organizations are consistent and coherent systems, tightly integrated to pursue certain traditional ends (namely the delivery of their products and services in the pursuit of profit, at least in the private sector), these writers start with quite different premises. They believe that organizations' goals and directions are determined primarily by the power needs of those who populate them. Their analyses raise all kinds of interesting and unsettled questions, such as: For whom does the organization really exist? For what purposes? If the organization is truly a political entity, how does one manage effectively in it? And so on.

No work in the literature sets this into perspective better than the famous study of the United States' response to the Cuban Missile Crisis by Graham Allison of Harvard's Kennedy School of Government. The context may be public, but Allison's message—indeed his full analysis—applies equally well to large complex organizations in any setting, business or otherwise. Allison believes that our conception of how decision making proceeds in organizations can be considered from three perspectives: a "rational actor" model (which is the concept he believes the American leaders had of the Soviets); an "organizational process" model; and a "bureaucratic politics" model (both of which Allison thinks could have been used as well to improve America's understanding of the Soviets' behavior). All are models of power. In one model, power is embedded in a relatively rational and calculating center of action. In the second, it is entrenched in various organizational departments, each using power to further its own particular purposes. In the third model, "politics" comes into full play as individuals and groups exercise their influence to determine outcomes for their own benefits. We present the Allison models by themselves because unfortunately, our space limitations preclude inclusion of the links he makes in the original article to the Cuban Missile crisis.

The Allison reading serves two critical roles for us. First, it conveys the very important message that how you see the world depends on what set of lenses you put on. Very different predictions of the behavior of organizations result from these three models. Not that any one view is wrong: Allison makes clear that all are right, though only partially so. And he suggests that the clearest vision belongs to those who can change lenses with ease—those who can see the different sides of an issue. This is a prime message of this text, too, and we are indebted to Allison for stating it so eloquently.

Second, each of the models is important in its own right, and merits full coverage in a book on the strategy process. The first model— rational actor—is really the closest to the prescriptive approach to strategy formulation presented in Chapters 3 and 4. We have already considered it in some depth. The second model depicts the organization as a complex system of bureaucratic units within which its power is lodged. Since each unit protects its own people and standard procedures, the whole system is retarded by bureaucratic inertia and is slow to change its strategies. Allison's depiction of this model provides an excellent review of an important theme in the management literature that first developed at Carnegie-Mellon's Graduate School of Industrial Administration in the 1950s and 1960s in the writings of Herbert Simon (who won a Nobel Prize for his efforts), and Richard Cyert and James March, especially in their books *Administration Behavior* and *A Behavioral Theory of the Firm*.

Allison's third model depicts the organization as a fully politicized system, and drives home the notion of strategy making as a political process in a most powerful way. This is probably the best and most concise presentation of it anywhere in print. To the extent that the process does become so politicized, one must cease to think in terms of clear, crisp strategies and begin to look instead for an outpouring of decision compromises. Managers, of course, then have to learn to manage in this kind of negotiated political atmosphere.

Up to this point we have considered power and politics inside organizations in terms of the maneuverings of the different actors within the system. But there is another perspective on power issues that is just as important, namely political maneuvers by organizations themselves as entities. To some observers, organizations are not just instruments to produce goods and services for society, but also political systems in their own right, out to enhance their own power in a world of organizations. This might be called a "macro political" perspective, in contrast to Allison's third model, which might be labelled "micro politics."

We mentioned this theme in Chapter 1 in reference to "collective strategies," in which organizations join forces to pursue some common strategic purposes, replacing competition by cooperation. This is a very real aspect of strategy making in a world increasingly dominated by large organizations, corporate and government coalitions, worldwide "partnering," and multinational companies who encounter host country politics. The reading by Jeffrey Pfeffer, a Stanford Business School professor and perhaps the researcher most identified with the perspective of organizations as power entities, goes further. It considers not only such legal, cooperative alignments, but also overt political behaviors for ends such as market collusion.

Note that Pfeffer is writing about *generic* strategies too, indeed some of the very same ones introduced earlier as competitive strategies (such as mergers and joint ventures). But here they appear as *political* devices. Pfeffer's work, in some respects, can be viewed as a mirror image of Porter's. Perhaps you may want to go back to Chapter 4 and reread Porter, this time between the lines, about barriers to entry, bargaining power of suppliers, and so on—from Pfeffer's perspective. You may discover that "political" and "competitive" actions are not so distinct as they might have seemed at first.

You may not agree with Pfeffer who challenges some of the most cherished precepts about business. But it is difficult to deny the need to consider his point of view, which serves at the very least to balance what is often an overstatement of the economic and competitive point of view. Pfeffer's views also deserve attention because they lie at the heart of many people's fears and concerns about business and the need to regulate the behavior of large entities.

The third reading introduces another major theme about power, perhaps one that is really a composite of the issues raised in the other articles: For whom does or should the large business corporation exist? Mintzberg proposes a whole portfolio of answers around a "conceptual horseshoe." In so doing, he perhaps helps to reconcile some basic differences between those who view organizations as agents of economic competition and those who consider them to be instruments of the public will, or as political systems in their own right. This reading also discusses the concept of *social responsibility,* one of the traditional topics covered in policy or strategy courses. But here the subject is treated not in a philanthropic or ethical sense, but in a managerial or organizational one. Mintzberg also reviews the issues of corporate democracy, of regulation and pressure campaigns, of "freedom" as described by Milton Friedman, and so on.

In discussing the power that various "influencers" can have over the large corporation under different circumstances, Mintzberg concludes on a contingency note: A corporation can exist for different people under different circumstances. It can be political and it can be competitive, in a variety of different ways. Society will have to determine what is most appropriate to achieve its desired mix of economic output, psychic satisfaction, and political freedom.

While no case deals solely with issues of power, many involve aspects of the concepts developed in these readings. Arcop deals with the interface between personal power needs and the potentials for a cohesive strategy. IBM (A), Pillsbury, Mountbatten, and MacArthur show how certain executives manage power relationships. General Motors-Downsizing, Exxon, Continental Group, and Genentech raise questions about the relationship of corporations to outside sources having significant power to affect their actions. Almost all the cases implicitly require that students deal with issues of personal power, organizationally entrenched power, and the power of opposing forces. Throughout the text, we emphasize that coping with power is one of the constant elements in any real life strategic situation.

CONCEPTUAL MODELS IN DECISION MAKING*

by Graham T. Allison

. . . This study proceeds from the premise that marked improvement in our understanding of [major] events depends critically on more self-consciousness about what observers bring to the analysis. What each analyst sees and judges to be important is a function not only of the evidence about what happened but also of the "conceptual lenses" through which he looks at the evidence. The principal purpose of this essay is to explore some of the fundamental assumptions and categories employed by analysts in thinking about problems of governmental behavior, especially in foreign and military affairs.

The general argument can be summarized in three propositions:

> 1. Analysts think about problems of foreign and military policy in terms of largely implicit conceptual models that have significant consequences for the content of their thought.

. . . The first proposition is that clusters of . . . related assumptions constitute basic frames of reference or conceptual models in terms

---

* Originally published under the title "Conceptual Models and the Cuban Missle Crisis" in *The American Political Science Review* (September, 1969). Reprinted with deletions by the permission of *The American Political Science Review.*

of which analysts both ask and answer the questions: What happened? Why did the event happen? What will happen? . . . Conceptual models both fix the mesh of the nets that the analyst drags through the material in order to explain a particular action or decision and direct him to cast his net in select ponds, at certain depths, in order to catch the fish he is after.

> 2. Most analysts explain (and predict) the behavior of national governments in terms of various forms of one basic conceptual model, here entitled the Rational Policy Model (Model I).

In terms of this conceptual model, analysts attempt to understand happenings as the more or less purposive acts of unified national governments. For these analysts, the point of an explanation is to show how the nation or government could have chosen the action in question, given the strategic problem that it faced. For example, in confronting the problem posed by the Soviet installation of missiles in Cuba, rational policy model analysts attempt to show how this was a reasonable act from the point of view of the Soviet Union, given Soviet strategic objectives.

> 3. Two "alternative" conceptual models, here labeled an Organizational Process Model (Model II) and a Bureaucratic Politics Model (Model III) provide a base for improved explanation and prediction.

Although the standard frame of reference has proved useful for many purposes, there is powerful evidence that it must be supplemented, if not supplanted, by frames of reference which focus upon the large organizations and political actors involved in the policy process. Model I's implication that important events have important causes, i.e., that monoliths perform large actions for big reasons, must be balanced by an appreciation of the facts (a) that monoliths are black boxes covering various gears and levers in a highly differentiated decision-making structure, and (b) that large acts are the consequences of innumerable and often conflicting smaller actions by individuals at various levels of bureaucratic organizations in the service of a variety of only partially compatible conceptions of national goals, organizational goals, and political objectives. Recent developments in the field of organization theory provide the foundation for the second model. According to this organizational process model, what Model I categorizes as "acts" and "choices" are instead *outputs* of large organizations functioning according to certain regular patterns of behavior. . . . The third model focuses on the internal politics of a government. Happenings in foreign affairs are understood, according to the bureaucratic politics model, neither as choices nor as outputs. Instead, what happens is categorized as *outcomes* of various overlapping bargaining games among players arranged hierarchically in the national government. . . . a Model III analyst displays the perceptions, motivations, positions, power, and maneuvers of principal players from which the outcome emerged.

A central metaphor illuminates differences among these models. Foreign policy has often been compared to moves, sequences of moves, and games of chess. If one were limited to observations on a screen upon which moves in the chess game were projected without information as to how the pieces came to be moved, he would assume—as Model I does—that an individual chess player was moving the pieces with reference to plans and maneuvers toward the goal of winning the game. But a pattern of moves can be imagined that would lead the serious observer, after watching several games, to consider the hypothesis that the chess player was not a single individual but rather a loose alliance of semi-independent organizations, each of which moved its set of pieces according to standard operating procedures. For example, movement of separate sets of pieces might proceed in turn, each according to a routine, the king's rook, bishop, and their pawns repeatedly attacking the opponent according to a fixed plan. Furthermore, it is conceivable that the pattern of play would suggest to an observer that a number of distinct players, with distinct objectives but shared power over the pieces, were determining the moves as the resultant of collegial bargaining. For example, the black rook's move might contribute to the loss of a black knight with no comparable gain for the black team, but with the black rook becoming the principal guardian of the "palace" on that side of the board.

The space available does not permit full development and support of such a general argument. Rather, the sections that follow simply sketch each conceptual model, articulate it as an analytic paradigm . . .

MODEL I: RATIONAL [ACTOR]

. . . What is striking about [many] examples from the literature of foreign policy and international relations are the similarities among analysts of various styles when they are called upon to produce explanations. Each assumes that what must be explained is an action, i.e., the realization of some purpose or intention. Each assumes that the actor is the national government. Each assumes that the action is chosen as a calculated response to a strategic problem. For each, explanation consists of showing what goal the government was pursuing in committing the act and how this action was a reasonable choice, given the nation's objectives. This set of assumptions characterizes the rational policy model. . . .

Most contemporary analysts (as well as laymen) proceed predominantly—albeit most often implicitly—in terms of this model when attempting to explain happenings in foreign affairs. Indeed, that occurrences in foreign affairs are the *acts* of *nations* seems so fundamental to thinking about such problems that this underlying model has rarely been recognized: to explain an occurrence in foreign policy simply means to show how the government could have rationally chosen that action. . . .

1. Basic Unit of Analysis: Policy as National Choice

Happenings in foreign affairs are conceived as actions chosen by the nation or national government. Governments select the action that will maximize strategic goals and objectives. These "solutions" to strategic problems are the fundamental categories in terms of which the analyst perceives what is to be explained.

II. Organizing Concepts

A. National Actor. The nation or government, conceived as a rational, unitary decisionmaker, is the agent. This actor has one set of specified goals (the equivalent of a consistent utility function), one set of perceived options, and a single estimate of the consequences that follow from each alternative.

B. The Problem. Action is chosen in reponse to the strategic problem which the nation faces. Threats and opportunities arising in the "international strategic market place" move the nation to act.

C. Static Selection. The sum of activity of representatives of the government relevant to a problem constitutes what the nation has chosen as its "solution." Thus the action is conceived as a steady-state choice among alternative outcomes (rather than, for example, a large number of partial choices in a dynamic stream).

D. Action as Rational Choice. The components include:

1. *Goals and Objectives.* National security and national interests are the principal categories in which strategic goals are conceived. Nations seek security and a range of further objectives. . . .

2. *Options.* Various courses of action relevant to a strategic problem provide the spectrum of options.

3. *Consequences.* Enactment of each alternative course of action will produce a series of consequences. The relevant consequences constitute benefits and costs in terms of strategic goals and objectives.

4. *Choice.* Rational choice is value-maximizing. The rational agent selects the alternative whose consequences rank highest in terms of his goals and objectives.

III. Dominant Inference Pattern

This paradigm leads analysts to rely on the following pattern of inference: if a nation performed a particular action, that nation must have had ends towards which the action constituted an optimal means. The rational policy model's explanatory power stems from this inference pattern. . . .

MODEL II: ORGANIZATIONAL PROCESS

For some purposes, governmental behavior can be usefully summarized as action chosen by a unitary, rational decisionmaker: centrally controlled, completely informed, and value maximizing. But this simplification must not be allowed to conceal the fact that a "government" consists of a conglomerate of semi-feudal, loosely allied organizations, each with a substantial life of its own. Government leaders do sit formally, and to some extent in fact, on top of this conglomerate. But governments perceive problems through organizational sensors. Governments define alternatives and estimate consequences as organizations process information. Governments act as these organizations enact routines. Government behavior can therefore be understood according to a second conceptual model, less as deliberate choices of leaders and more as *outputs* of large organizations functioning according to standard patterns of behavior.

To be responsive to a broad spectrum of problems, governments consist of large organizations among which primary responsibility for particular areas is divided. Each organization attends to a special set of problems and acts in quasi-independence on these problems. But few important problems fall exclusively within the domain of a single organization. Thus government behavior relevant to any important problem reflects the independent output of several organizations, partially coordinated by government leaders. Government leaders can substantially disturb, but not substantially control, the behavior of these organizations.

To perform complex routines, the behavior of large numbers of individuals must be coordinated. Coordination requires standard operating procedures: rules according to which things are done. Assured capability for reliable performance of action that depends upon the behavior of hundreds of persons requires established "programs." Indeed, if the eleven members of a football team are to perform adequately on any particular down, each player must not "do what he thinks needs to be done" or "do what the quarterback tells him to do." Rather, each player must perform the maneuvers specified by a previously established play which the quarterback has simply called in this situation.

At any given time, a government consists of *existing* organizations, each with a *fixed* set of standard operating procedures and programs. The behavior of these organizations—and consequently of the government—relevant to an issue in any particular instance is, therefore, determined primarily by routines established in these organizations prior to that instance. But organizations do change. Learning occurs gradually, over time. Dramatic organizational change occurs in response to major crises. Both learning and change are influenced by existing organizational capabilities. . . .

I. Basic Unit of Analysis: Policy as Organizational Output

The happenings of international politics are in three critical senses, outputs of organizational processes. First, the actual occurrences are organizational outputs. . . . Second, existing organizational routines for employing present physical capabilities constitute the effective options open to government leaders confronted with any problem. . . . Third, organizational outputs structure the situation within the narrow constraints of which leaders must contribute their "decision" concerning an issue. Outputs raise the problem, provide the information, and make the initial moves that color the face of the issue that is turned to the leaders. As Theodore Sorensen has observed: "Presidents rarely, if ever, make decisions—particularly in foreign affairs—in the sense of writing their conclusions on a clean slate. . . . The basic decisions, which confine their choices, have all too often been previously made'' (Sorensen, 1967). If one understands the structure of the situation and the face of the issue—which are determined by the organizational outputs— the formal choice of the leaders is frequently anti-climactic.

II. Organizing Concepts

A. Organizational Actors. The actor is not a monolithic ''nation'' or ''government'' but rather a constellation of loosely allied organizations on top of which government leaders sit. This constellation acts only as component organizations perform routines.

B. Factored Problems and Fractionated Power. Surveillance of the multiple facets of foreign affairs requires that problems be cut up and parcelled out to various organizations. To avoid paralysis, primary power must accompany primary responsibility. But if organizations are permitted to do anything, a large part of what they do will be determined within the organization. Thus each organization perceives problems, processes information, and performs a range of actions in quasi-independence (within broad guidelines of national policy). . . .

C. Parochial Priorities, Perceptions, and Issues. Primary responsibility for a narrow set of problems encourages organizational parochialism. These tendencies are enhanced by a number of additional factors: (1) selective information available to the organization, (2) recruitment of personnel into the organization, (3) tenure of individuals in the organization, (4) small group pressures within the organization, and (5) distribution of rewards by the organization. Clients . . . , government allies . . . and extra-national counterparts . . . for . . . galvanize this parochialism. Thus organizations develop relatively stable propensities concerning operational priorities, perceptions, and issues.

D. Action as Organizational Output. The preeminent feature of organizational activity is its programmed character: the extent to which behavior in any particular case is an enactment of preestablished routines. In producing outputs, the activity of each organization is characterized by:

1. *Goals: Constraints Defining Acceptable Performance.* The operational goals of an organization are seldom revealed by formal mandates. Rather, each organization's operational goals emerge as a set of constraints defining acceptable performance. Central among these constraints is organizational health, defined usually in terms of bodies assigned and dollars appropriated. The set of constraints emerges from a mix of expectations and demands of other organizations in the government, statutory authority, demands from citizens and special interest groups, and bargaining within the organization. . . .

2. *Sequential Attention to Goals.* The existence of conflict among operational constraints is resolved by the device of sequential attention. As a problem arises, the subunits of the organization most concerned with that problem deal with it in terms of the constraints they take to be most important. When the next problem arises, another cluster of subunits deals with it, focusing on a different set of constraints.

3. *Standard Operating Procedures.* Organizations perform their ''higher'' functions, such as attending to problem areas, monitoring information, and preparing relevant responses for likely contingencies, by doing ''lower'' tasks, for example, preparing budgets, producing reports, and developing hardware. Reliable performance of these tasks requires standard operating procedures (hereafter SOPs). Since procedures are ''standard'' they do not change quickly or easily. Without these standard procedures, it would not be possible to perform certain concerted tasks. But because of standard procedures, organizational behavior in particular instances often appears unduly formalized, sluggish, or inappropriate.

4. *Programs and Repertoires*. Organizations must be capable of performing actions in which the behavior of large numbers of individuals is carefully coordinated. Assured performance requires clusters of rehearsed SOPs for producing specific actions; e.g., fighting enemy units or answering an embassy's cable. Each cluster comprises a "program" (in the terms both of drama and computers) which the organization has available for dealing with a situation. The list of programs relevant to a type of activity, e.g., fighting, constitutes an organizational repertoire. The number of programs in a repertoire is always quite limited. When properly triggered, organizations execute programs; programs cannot be substantially changed in a particular situation. The more complex the action and the greater the number of individuals involved, the more important are programs and repertoires as determinants of organizational behavior.

5. *Uncertainty Avoidance*. Organizations do not attempt to estimate the probability distribution of future occurrences. Rather, organizations avoid uncertainty. By arranging a *negotiated environment*, organizations regularize the reactions of other actors with whom they have to deal. The primary environment, relations with other organizations that comprise the government, is stabilized by such arrangements as agreed budgetary splits, accepted areas of responsibility, and established conventional practices. The secondary environment, relations with the international world, is stabilized between allies by the establishment of contracts (alliances) and "club relations." . . . Where the international environment cannot be negotiated, organizations deal with remaining uncertainties by establishing a set of *standard scenarios* that constitute the contingencies for which they prepare. . . .

6. *Problem-directed Search*. Where situations cannot be construed as standard, organizations engage in search. The style of search and the solution are largely determined by existing routines. Organizational search for alternative courses of action is problem-oriented: it focuses on the atypical discomfort that must be avoided. It is simple-minded: the neighborhood of the symptom is searched first; then, the neighborhood of the current alternative. Patterns of search reveal biases which in turn reflect such factors as specialized training or experience and patterns of communication.

7. *Organizational Learning and Change*. The parameters of organizational behavior mostly persist. In response to non-standard problems, organizations search and routines evolve, assimilating new situations. Thus learning and change follow in large part from existing procedures. But marked changes in organizations do sometimes occur. Conditions in which dramatic changes are most likely include: (1) Periods of budgetary feast . . . if committed to change, leaders who control the budget can use extra funds to effect changes. (2) Periods of prolonged budgetary famine . . . prolonged famine forces major retrenchment. (3) Dramatic performance failures. Dramatic change occurs (mostly) in response to major disasters. Confronted with an undeniable failure of procedures and repertoires, authorities outside the organization demand change, existing personnel are less resistant to change, and critical members of the organization are replaced by individuals committed to change.

E. Central Coordination and Control.

Action requires decentralization of responsibility and power. But problems lap over the jurisdictions of several organizations. Thus the necessity for decentralization runs headlong into the requirement for coordination. . . . Each organization's propensities and routines can be disturbed by government leaders' intervention. Central direction and persistent control of organizational activity, however, is not possible. . . .

Intervention by government leaders does sometimes change the activity of an organization in an intended direction. But instances are fewer than might be expected. As Franklin Roosevelt, the master manipulator of government organizations, remarked:

> The Treasury is so large and far-flung and ingrained in its practices that I find it is almost impossible to get the action

and results I want. . . . But the Treasury is not to be compared with the State Department. You should go through the experience of trying to get any changes in the thinking, policy, and action of the career diplomats and then you'd know what a real problem was. But the Treasury and the State Department put together are nothing compared with the Na-a-vy. . . . To change anything in the Na-a-vy is like punching a feather bed. You punch it with your right and you punch it with your left until you are finally exhausted, and then you find the damn bed just as it was before you started punching (Eccles, 1951:336). . . .

F. Decisions of Government Leaders. Organizational persistence does not exclude shifts in governmental behavior. For government leaders sit atop the conglomerate of organizations. Many important issues of governmental action require that these leaders decide what organizations will play out which programs where. Thus stability in the parochialisms and SOPs of individual organizations is consistent with some important shifts in the behavior of governments. The range of these shifts is defined by existing organizational programs.

III. Dominant Inference Pattern

If a nation performs an action of this type today, its organizational components must yesterday have been performing (or have had established routines for performing) an action only marginally different from this action. At any specific point in time, a government consists of an established conglomerate of organizations, each with existing goals, programs, and repertoires. The characteristics of a government's action in any instance follows from those established routines, and from the choice of government leaders—on the basis of information and estimates provided by existing routines—among existing programs. The best explanation of an organization's behavior at t is $t - 1$; the prediction of $t + 1$ is t. Model II's explanatory power is achieved by uncovering the organizational routines and repertoires that pro-

duced the outputs that comprise the puzzling occurrence. . . .

MODEL III: BUREAUCRATIC POLITICS

The leaders who sit on top of organizations are not a monolithic group. Rather, each is, in his own right, a player in a central, competitive game. The name of the game is bureaucratic politics: bargaining along regularized channels among players positioned hierarchically within the government. Government behavior can thus be understood according to a third conceptual model not as organizational outputs, but as outcomes of bargaining games. In contrast with Model I, the bureaucratic politics model sees no unitary actor but rather many actors as players, who focus not on a single strategic issue but on many diverse intra-national problems as well, in terms of no consistent set of strategic objectives but rather according to various conceptions of national, organizational, and personal goals, making government decisions not by rational choice but by the pulling and hauling that is politics. . . .

Men share power. Men differ concerning what must be done. The differences matter. This milieu necessitates that policy be resolved by politics. What the nation does is sometimes the result of the triumph of one group over others. More often, however, different groups pulling in different directions yield a resultant distinct from what anyone intended. . . .

. . . Hundreds of issues compete for players' attention every day. Each player is forced to fix upon his issues for that day, fight them on their own terms, and rush on to the next. Thus the character of emerging issues and the pace at which the game is played converge to yield government "decisions" and "actions" as collages. . . .

I. Basic Unit of Analysis: Policy as Political Outcome

The decisions and actions of governments are essentially intra-national political outcomes: outcomes in the sense that what happens is not chosen as a solution to a problem but rather results from compromise, coalition, competition and confusion among government officials who see different faces of an issue; political in the sense that the activity from which the outcomes emerge is best characterized as bargaining. Following Wittgenstein's use of the concept of a "game," national behavior in international affairs can be conceived as outcomes of intricate and subtle, simultaneous, overlapping games among players located in positions, the hierarchical arrangement of which constitutes the government. These games proceed neither at random nor at leisure. Regular channels structure the game. Deadlines force issues to the attention of busy players. The moves in the chess game are thus to be explained in terms of the bargaining among players with separate and unequal power over particular pieces and with separable objectives in distinguishable subgames.

II. Organizing Concepts

A. Players in Positions. The actor is neither a unitary nation, nor a conglomerate of organizations, but rather a number of individual players. Groups of these players constitute the agent for particular government decisions and actions. Players are men in jobs.

Individuals become players in the national security policy game by occupying a critical position in an administration [and include "Chiefs," "Staffers," "Ad Hoc Players" from the press, special interest groups, etc.]. . . . Positions define what players both may and must do. The advantages and handicaps with which each player can enter and play in various games stems from his position. So does a cluster of obligations for the performance of certain tasks. . . . All of these obligations are his simultaneously. His performance in one affects his credit and power in the others. . . .

For players are also people. Men's metabolisms differ. The core of the bureaucratic politics mix is personality. How each man manages to stand the heat in his kitchen, each player's basic operating style, and the complementarity or contradiction among personalities and styles in the inner circles are irreducible pieces of the policy blend. Moreover, each person comes to his position with baggage in tow, including sensitivities to certain issues, commitments to various programs, and personal standing and debts with groups in the society.

B. Parochial Priorities, Perceptions and Issues. Answers to the questions: "What is the issue?" and "What must be done?" are colored by the position from which the questions are considered. For the factors which encourage organizational parochialism also influence the players who occupy positions on top of (or within) these organizations. To motivate members of his organization, a player must be sensitive to the organization's orientation. . . .

C. Interests, Stakes, and Power. Games are played to determine outcomes. But outcomes advance and impede each player's conception of the national interest, specific programs to which he is committed, the welfare of his friends, and his personal interests. These overlapping interests constitute the stakes for which games are played. Each player's ability to play successfully depends upon his power. Power, i.e., effective influence on policy outcomes, is an elusive blend of at least three elements: bargaining advantages (drawn from formal authority and obligations, institutional backing, constituents, expertise, and status), skill and will in using bargaining advantages, and other players' perceptions of the first two ingredients. Power wisely invested yields an enhanced reputation for effectiveness. Unsuccessful investment depletes both the stock of capital and the reputation. Thus each player must pick the issues on which he can play with a reasonable probability of success. But no player's power is sufficient to guarantee satisfactory outcomes. Each player's needs and fears run to many other players. What ensues is the most intricate and subtle of games known to man.

D. The Problem and the Problems. "Solutions" to strategic problems are not derived by detached analysts focusing coolly on *the* problem. Instead, deadlines and events raise issues in games, and demand decisions of busy players in contexts that influence the face the issue wears. The problems for the players are both narrower and broader than *the* strategic problem. For each player focuses not on the total strategic problem but rather on the decision that must be made now. But each decision has critical consequences not only for the strategic problem but for each player's organizational, reputational, and personal stakes. Thus the gap between the problems the player was solving and the problem upon which the analyst focuses is often very wide.

E. Action-Channels. Bargaining games do not proceed randomly. Action-channels, i.e., regularized ways of producing action concerning types of issues, structure the game by pre-selecting the major players, determining their points of entrance into the game, and distributing particular advantages and disadvantages for each game. Most critically, channels determine "who's got the action," that is, which department's Indians actually do whatever is chosen. . . .

F. Action as Politics. Government decisions are made and government actions emerge neither as the calculated choice of a unified group nor as a formal summary of leaders' preference. Rather the context of shared power but separate judgments concerning important choices, determines that politics is the mechanism of choice. Note the *environment* in which the game is played: inordinate uncertainty about what must be done, the necessity that something be done and crucial consequences of whatever is done. These features force responsible men to become active players. The *pace of the game*—hundreds of issues, numerous games, and multiple channels—compels players to fight to "get other's attention," to make them "see the facts," to assure that they "take the time to think seriously about the broader issue." The *structure of the game*—power shared by individuals with separate responsibilities—validates each player's feeling that "others don't see my problem," and "others must be persuaded to look at the issue from a less parochial perspective." The *rules of the game*—he who hesitates loses his chance to play at that point, and he who is uncertain about his recommendation is overpowered by others who are sure—pressures players to come down on one side of a 51–49 issue and play. The *rewards of the game*—effectiveness, i.e., impact on outcomes, as the immediate measure of performance—encourages hard play. Thus, most players come to fight to "make the government do what is right.". . .

G. Streams of Outcomes. Important government decisions or actions emerge as collages composed of individual acts, outcomes of minor and major games, and foul-ups. Outcomes which could never have been chosen by an actor and would never have emerged from bargaining in a single game over the issue are fabricated piece by piece. Understanding of the outcome requires that it be disaggregated.

III. Dominant Inference Pattern

If a nation performed an action, that action was the *outcome* of bargaining among individuals and groups within the government. That outcome included *results* achieved by groups committed to a decision or action, *resultants* which emerged from bargaining among groups with quite different positions and *foul-ups*. Model III's explanatory power is achieved by revealing the pulling and hauling of various players with different perceptions and priorities, focusing on separate problems, which yielded the outcomes that constitute the action in question. . . .

CONCLUSION

This essay has obviously bitten off more than it has chewed. For further developments and synthesis of these arguments the reader is referred to the larger study (Allison, 1971). In spite of the limits of space, however, it would be inappropriate to stop without spelling out several implications of the argument and addressing the question of relations among the models and extensions of them to activity beyond explanation.

. . . formulation of alternative frames of reference and demonstration that different analysts, relying predominantly on different models, produce quite different explanations should encourage the analyst's self-consciousness about the nets he employs. The effect of these "spectacles" in sensitizing him to particular aspects of what is going on—framing the puzzle in one way rather than another, encouraging him to examine the problem in terms of certain categories rather than others, directing him to particular kinds of evidence, and relieving puzzlement by one procedure rather than another—must be recognized and explored. . . .

THE INSTITUTIONAL FUNCTION OF MANAGEMENT*

by Jeffrey Pfeffer

Theory, research, and education in the field of organizational behavior and management have been dominated by a concern for the management of people *within* organizations. The question of how to make workers more productive has stood as the foundation for management theory and practice since the time of Frederick Taylor. Such an emphasis neglects the institutional function of management. While managing people within organizations is critical, managing the organization's relationships with other organizations such as competitors, creditors, suppliers, and governmental agencies is frequently as critical to the firm's success.

Parsons (1960) noted that there were three levels in organizations: (a) the technical level, where the technology of the organization was used to produce some product or service; (b) the

*   Originally published as "Beyond Management and the Worker: The Institutional Function of Management," in the *Academy of Management Review* (April 1976); copyright © *Academy of Management Review*. Reprinted with deletions by the permission of the *Academy of Management Review* and the author.

administrative level, which coordinated and supervised the technical level; and (c) the institutional level, which was concerned with the organization's legitimacy and with organization-environment relations. Organization and management theory has primarily concentrated on administrative level problems, frequently at very low hierarchical levels in organizations.

Practicing managers and some researchers do recognize the importance of the institutional context in which the firm operates. There is increasing use of institutional advertising, and executives from the oil industry, among others, have been active in projecting their organizations' views in a variety of contexts. Mintzberg (1973a) has identified the liaison role as one of ten roles managers fill. Other authors explicitly have noted the importance of relating the organization to other organizations (Pfeffer and Nowak, n.d., Whyte, 1955).

Saying that the institutional function is important is different from developing a theory of the organization's relationships with other organizations, a theory which can potentially guide the manager's strategic actions in performing the function of institutional management. Such a theory is needed, and data are accumulating to construct such a theory.

The purposes of this article are: (a) to present evidence of the importance of the institutional function of management, and (b) to review data consistent with a model of institutional management. This model argues that managers behave as if they were seeking to manage and reduce uncertainty and interdependence arising from the firm's relationships with other organizations. Several strategic responses to interorganizational exchange, including their advantages and disadvantages, are considered.

INSTITUTIONAL PROBLEMS OF ORGANIZATIONS

Organizations are open social systems, engaged in constant and important transactions with other organizations in their environments. Business firms transact with customer and supplier organizations, and with sources of credit; they interact on the federal and local level with regulatory and legal authorities which are concerned with pollution, taxes, antitrust, equal employment, and myriad other issues. Because firms do interact with these other organizations, two consequences follow. First, organizations face uncertainty. If an organization were a closed system so that it could completely control and predict all the variables that affected its operation, the organization could make technically rational, maximizing decisions and anticipate the consequences of its actions. As an open system, transacting with important external organizations, the firm does not have control over many of the important factors that affect its operations. Because organizations are open, they are affected by events outside their boundaries.

Second, organizations are interdependent with other organizations with which they exchange resources, information or personnel, and thus open to influence by them. The extent of this influence is likely to be a function of the importance of the resource obtained, and inversely related to the ease with which the resource can be procured from alternative sources (Jacobs, 1974; Thompson, 1967). Interdependence is problematic and troublesome. Managers do not like to be dependent on factors outside their control. Interdependence is especially troublesome if there are few alternative sources, so the external organization is particularly important to the firm.

Interdependence and uncertainty interact in their effects on organizations. One of the principal functions of the institutional level of the firm is the management of this interdependence and uncertainty.

tHE IMPORTANCE
OF INSTITUTIONAL MANAGEMENT

Katz and Kahn (1966) noted that organizations may pursue two complementary paths to effectiveness. The first is to be as efficient as possible, and thereby obtain a competitive advantage with respect to other firms. Under this strategy, the firm succeeds because it operates so efficiently that it achieves a competitive advantage in the market. The second strategy, termed ''political,'' involves the establishment of favorable exchange relationships based on considerations that do not relate strictly to price, quality, service, or efficiency. Winning an order because of the firm's product and cost characteristics would be an example of the strategy of efficiency; winning the order because of interlocks in the directorates of the organizations involved, or because of family connections between executives in the two organizations, would illustrate political strategies.

The uses and consequences of political strategies for achieving organizational success have infrequently been empirically examined. Hirsch (1975) has . . . compared the ethical drug and record industries, noting great similarities between them. Both sell their products through gatekeepers or intermediaries—in the case of pharmaceuticals, through doctors who must write the prescriptions, and in the case of records, through disc jockeys who determine air time and, consequently, exposure. Both sell products with relatively short life cycles, and both industries place great emphasis on new products and product innovation. Both depend on the legal environment of patents, copyrights, and trademarks for market protection.

Hirsch noted that the rate of return for the average pharmaceutical firm during the period 1956–1966 was more than double the rate of return for the average firm in the record industry. Finding no evidence that would enable him to attribute the striking differences in profitability to factors associated with internal structural arrangements. Hirsch concluded that at least one factor affecting the relative profitability of the two industries is the ability to manage their institutional environments, and more specifically, the control over distribution, patent and copyright protection, and the prediction of adoption by the independent gatekeepers.

In a review of the history of both industries, Hirsch indicated that in pharmaceuticals, control over entry was achieved by (a) amending the patent laws to permit the patenting of naturally occurring substances, antibiotics, and (b) instituting a long and expensive licensing procedure required before drugs could be manufactured and marketed, administered by the Food and Drug Administration (FDA). In contrast, record firms have much less protection under the copyright laws; as a consequence, entry is less controlled, leading to more competition and lower profits. While there are other differences between the industries, including size and expenditures on research and development, Hirsch argued that at least some of the success of drug firms derives from their ability to control entry and their ability to control information channels relating to their product through the use of detail personnel and advertising in the American Medical Association Journals. Retail price maintenance, tariff protection, and licensing to restrict entry are other examples of practices that are part of the organization's institutional environment and may profoundly affect its success.

MANAGING UNCERTAINTY AND INTERDEPENDENCE

The organization, requiring transactions with other organizations and uncertain about their future performance, has available a variety of strategies that can be used to manage uncertainty and interdependence. Firms face two problems in their institutional relationships: (a) managing the uncertainty caused by the unpredictable actions of competitors; and (b) managing the uncertainty resulting from non-competitive interdependence with suppliers, creditors, government agencies, and customers. In both instances, the same set of strategic responses is available: merger, to completely absorb the interdependence and resulting uncertainty; joint ventures; interlocking directorates, to partially absorb the interdependence; the movement and selective recruiting of executives and other personnel, to develop interorganizational linkages; regulation, to provide government enforced stability; and other political activity to reduce competition, protect markets and sources of supply, and otherwise manage the organization's environment.

Because organizations are open systems, each strategy is limited in its effect. While merger or some other interorganizational linkage may manage one source of organizational dependence, it probably at the same time makes the organizations dependent on yet other organizations. For example, while regulation may eliminate effective price competition and restrict entry into the industry (Jordan, 1973; Pfeffer, 1974a; Posner, 1975), the regulated organizations then face the uncertainties involved in dealing with the regulatory agency. Moreover, in reducing uncertainty for itself, the organization must bargain away some of its own discretion (Thompson 1967). One can view institutional management as an exchange process—the organization assures itself of needed resources, but at the same time, must promise certain predictable behaviors in return. Keeping these qualifications in mind, evidence on use of the various strategies of institutional management is reviewed.

Merger

There are three reasons an organization may seek to merge—first, to reduce competition by absorbing an important competitor organization; second, to manage interdependence with either sources of input or purchasers of output by absorbing them; and third, to diversify operations and thereby lessen dependence on the present organizations with which it exchanges (Pfeffer, 1972b). While merger among competing organizations is presumably proscribed by the antitrust laws, enforcement resources are limited, and major consolidations do take place. . . .

The classic expressed rationale for merger has been to increase the profits or the value of the shares of the firm. In a series of studies beginning as early as 1921, researchers have been unable to demonstrate that merger active firms are more profitable or have higher stock prices following the merger activity. This literature has been summarized by Reid (1968), who asserts that mergers are made for growth, and that growth is sought because of the relationship between firm size and managerial salaries.

Growth, however, does not provide information concerning the desired characteristics of the acquired firm. Under a growth objective, any merger is equivalent to any other of the same size. Pfeffer (1972b) has argued that mergers are undertaken to manage organizational interdependence. Examining the proportion of merger activity occurring within the same 2-digit SIC industry category, he found that the highest proportion of within-industry mergers occurred in industries of intermediate concentration. The theoretical argument was that in industries with many competitors, the absorption of a single one did little to reduce competitive uncertainty. At the other extreme, with only a few competitors, merger would more likely be scrutinized by the antitrust authorities and coordination could instead be achieved through more informal arrangements, such as price leadership.

The same study investigated the second reason to merge: to absorb the uncertainty among organizations vertically related to each other, as in a buyer-seller relationship. He found that it was possible to explain 40 percent of the variation in the distribution of merger activity over industries on the basis of resource interdependence, measured by estimates of the transactions flows between sectors of the economy. On an individual industry basis, in two-thirds of the cases a measure of transactions interdependence accounted for 65 percent or more of the variation in the pattern of merger activity. The study indicated that it was possible to account for the industry of the likely merger partner firm by considering the extent to which firms in the two industries exchanged resources.

While absorption of suppliers or customers will reduce the firm's uncertainty by bringing critical contingencies within the boundaries of the organization, this strategy has some distinct costs. One danger is that the process of vertical integration creates a larger organization which is increasingly tied to a single industry.

The third reason for merger is diversification. Occasionally, the organization is confronted by interdependence it cannot absorb, either because of resource or legal limitations. Through diversifying its activities, the organization does not reduce the uncertainty, but makes the particular contingency less critical for its success and well-being. Diversification provides the organization with a way of avoiding, rather than absorbing, problematic interdependence.

Merger represents the most complete solution to situations of organizational interdependence, as it involves the total absorption of either a competitor or a vertically related organization, or the acquisition of an organization operating in another area. Because it does involve total absorption, merger requires more resources and is a more visible and substantial form of interorganizational linkage.

Joint Ventures

Closely related to merger is the joint venture: the creation of a jointly owned, but independent organization by two or more separate parent firms. Merger involves the total pooling of assets by two or more organizations. In a joint venture, some assets of each of several parent organizations are used, and thus only a partial pooling of resources is involved (Bernstein, 1965). For a variety of reasons, joint ventures have been prosecuted less frequently and less successfully than mergers, making joint ventures particularly appropriate as a way of coping with competitive interdependence.

The joint subsidiary can have several effects on competitive interdependence and uncertainty. First, it can reduce the extent of new competition. Instead of both firms entering a market, they can combine some of their assets and create a joint subsidiary to enter the market. Second, since joint subsidiaries are typically staffed, particularly at the higher executive levels, with personnel drawn from the parent firms, the joint subsidiary becomes another location for the management of competing firms to meet. Most importantly, the joint subsidiary must set price and output levels, make new product development and marketing decisions and decisions about its advertising policies. Consequently, the parent organizations are brought into association in a setting in which exactly those aspects of the competitive relationship must be jointly determined.

In a study of joint ventures among manufacturing and oil and gas companies during the period 1960–71, Pfeffer and Nowak (1976a, 1976b) found that 56 percent involved parent firms operating in the same two-digit industry. Further, in 36 percent of the 166 joint ventures studied, the joint subsidiary operated in the same industry as both parent organizations. As in the case of mergers, the proportion of joint venture activities undertaken with other firms in the same industry was related to the concentration of the firm's industry being intermediate. The relationship between concentration and the proportion of joint ventures undertaken within the same industry accounted for some 25 percent of the variation in the pattern of joint venture activities.

In addition to considering the use of joint ventures in coping with competitive interdependence, the Pfeffer and Nowak study of joint ventures examined the extent to which the creation of joint subsidiaries was related to patterns of transaction interdependence across industries. While the correlations between the proportion of transactions and the proportion of joint ventures undertaken between industry pairs were lower than in the case of mergers, statistically significant relationships between this form of interorganizational linkage activity and patterns of resource exchange were observed. The difference between mergers and joint ventures appears to be that mergers are used relatively more to cope with buyer–seller interdependence, and joint ventures are more highly related to considerations of coping with competitive uncertainty.

Cooptation and Interlocking Directorates

Cooptation is a venerable strategy for managing interdependence between organizations. Cooptation involves the partial absorption of another organization through the placing of a representative of that organization on the board of the focal organization. Corporations frequently place bankers on their boards; hospitals and universities offer trustee positions to prominent business leaders; and community action agencies develop advisory boards populated with active and strong community political figures. . . .

Interlocks in the boards of directors of competing organizations provide a possible strategy for coping with competitive interdependence and the resulting uncertainty. The underlying argument is that in order to manage interorganizational relationships, information must be exchanged, usually through a joint subsidiary or interlocking directorate. While interlocks among competitors are ostensibly illegal, until very recently there was practically no prosecution of this practice. In a 1965 study, a subcommittee of the House Judiciary Committee found more than 300 cases in which direct competitors had interlocking boards of directors (House of Representatives, 1965). In a study of the extent of interlocking among competing organizations in a sample of 109 manufacturing organizations, Pfeffer and Nowak (n.d.) found that the proportion of directors on the board from direct competitors was higher for firms operating in industries in which concentration was intermediate. This result is consistent with the result found for joint ventures and mergers as well. In all three instances, linkages among competing organizations occurred more frequently when concentration was in an intermediate range.

Analyses of cooptation through the use of boards of directors have not been confined to business firms. Price (1963) argued that the principal function of the boards of the Oregon Fish and Game Commissions was to link the organizations to their environments. Zald (1967) found that the composition of YMCA boards in Chicago matched the demography of their operating areas, and affected the organizations' effectiveness, particularly in raising money. Pfeffer (1973) examined the size, composition, and function of hospital boards of directors, finding that variables of organizational context, such as ownership, source of funds, and location, were important explanatory factors. He also found a relationship between cooptation and organizational effectiveness. In 1972, Pfeffer (1972a) found that regulated firms, firms with a higher proportion of debt in their capital structures, and larger firms tended to have more outside directors. Allen (1974) also found that size of the board and the use of cooptation was predicted by the size of the firm, but did not replicate Pfeffer's earlier finding of a relationship between the organization's capital structure and the proportion of directors from financial institutions. In a study of utility boards, Pfeffer (1974b) noted that the composition of the board tended to correlate with the demographics of the area in which the utility was regulated.

The evidence is consistent with the strategy of organizations using their boards of directors to coopt external organizations and manage problematic interdependence. The role of the board of directors is seen not as the provision of management expertise or control, but more generally as a means of managing problematic aspects of an organization's institutional environment.

Executive Recruitment

Information also is transferred among organizations through the movement of personnel. The difference between movement of executives between organizations and cooptation is that in the latter case, the person linking the two organizations retains membership in both organizations. In the case of personnel movement, dual organizational membership is not maintained. When people change jobs, they take with themselves information about the operations, policies, and values of their previous employers, as well as contacts in the organization. In a study of the movement of faculty among schools of business, Baty, et al. (1971) found that similar orientations and curricula developed among schools exchanging personnel. The movement of personnel is one method by which new techniques of management and new marketing and product ideas are diffused through a set of organizations.

Occasionally, the movement of executives between organizations has been viewed as intensifying, rather than reducing, competition. Companies have been distressed by the raiding of trade secrets and managerial expertise by other organizations. While this perspective must be recognized, the exchange of personnel among organizations is a revered method of conflict *reduction* between organizations (Stern, Sternthal and Craig, 1973). Personnel movement inevitably involves sharing information among a set of organizations.

If executive movement is a form of interfirm linkage designed to manage competitive relationships, the proportion of executives recruited from within the same industry should be highest at intermediate levels of industrial concentration. Examining the three top executive positions in twenty different manufacturing industries, the evidence on executive backgrounds was found to be consistent with this argument (Pfeffer and Leblebici, 1973). The proportion of high level executives with previous jobs in the same industry but in a different company was found to be negatively related to the number of firms in the industry. The larger the number of firms, the less likely that a single link among competitors will substantially reduce uncertainty, but the larger the available supply of external executive talent. The data indicated no support for a supply argument, but supported the premise that interorganizational linkages are used to manage interdependence and uncertainty.

The use of executive movement to manage non-competitive interorganizational relationships is quite prevalent. The often-cited movement of personnel between the Defense Department and major defense contractors is only one example, because there is extensive movement of personnel between many government departments and industries interested in the agencies' decisions. The explanation is frequently proposed that organizations are acquiring these personnel because of their expertise. The expertise explanation is frequently difficult to separate from the alternative that personnel are being exchanged to enhance interorganizational relationships. Regardless of the motivation, exchanging personnel inevitably involves the transfer of information and access to the other organization.

Regulation

Occasionally, institutional relationships are managed through recourse to political intervention. The reduction of competition and its associated uncertainty may be accomplished through regulation. Regulation, however, is a risky strategy for organizations to pursue. While regulation most frequently benefits the regulated industry (Jordan, 1972; Pfeffer, 1974a), the industry and firms have no assurance that regulatory authority will not be used against their interests. Regulation is very hard to repeal. Successful use of regulation requires that the firm and industry face little or no powerful political opposition, and that the political future can be accurately forecast.

The benefits of regulation to those being regulated have been extensively reviewed (Posner, 1974; Stigler, 1974). Regulation frequently has been sought by the regulated industry. . . . Estimates of the effects of regulation on prices in electric utilities, airlines, trucking, and natural gas have indicated that regulation either increases price or has no effect.

The theory behind these outcomes is still unclear. One approach suggests that regulation is created for the public benefit, but after the initial legislative attention, the regulatory process is captured by the firms subject to regulation. Another approach proposes that regulation, like other goods, is acquired subject to supply and demand considerations (Posner, 1974). Political scientists, focusing on the operation of interest groups, argue that regulatory agencies are "captured" by organized and well-financed interests. Government intervention in the market can solve many of the interdependence problems faced by firms. Regulation is most often accompanied by restriction of entry and the fixing of prices, which tend to reduce market uncertainties. Markets may be actually allocated to firms, and with the reduction of risk, regulation may make access to capital easier. Regulation may alter the organization's relationships with suppliers and customers. One theory of why the railroads were interested in the creation of the Interstate Commerce Commission (ICC) in 1887 was that large users were continually demanding and winning discriminatory rate reductions, disturbing the price stability of railroad price fixing cartels. By forbidding price discrimination and enforcing this regulation, the ICC strengthened the railroads' position with respect to large customers (MacAvoy, 1965).

Political Activity

Regulation is only one specific form of organizational activity in governmental processes. Business attempts to affect competition through the operation of the tariff laws date back to the 1700's (Bauer et al., 1968). Epstein (1969) provided one of the more complete summaries of the history of corporate involvement in politics and the inevitability of such action. The government has the power of coercion, possessed legally by no other social institution. Furthermore, legislation and regulation affect most of our economic institutions and markets, either indirectly through taxation, or more directly through purchasing, market protection or market creation. For example, taxes on margarine only recently came to an end. Federal taxes, imposed in 1886 as a protectionist measure for dairy interests, were removed in 1950, but a law outlawing the sale of oleo in its colored form lasted until 1967 in Wisconsin.

As with regulation, political activities carry both benefits and risks. The risk arises because once government intervention in an issue on behalf of a firm or industry is sought, then political intervention becomes legitimated, regardless of whose interests are helped or hurt. The firm that seeks favorable tax legislation runs the risk of creating a setting in which it is equally legitimate to be exposed to very unfavorable legislation. After an issue is opened to government intervention, neither side will find it easy to claim that further government action is illegitimate.

In learning to cope with a particular institutional environment, the firm may be unprepared for new uncertainties caused by the change of fundamental institutional relationships, including the opening of price competition, new entry and the lack of protection from overseas competition.

CONCLUSION

. . . Considering its probable importance to the firm, the institutional function of management has received much less concern than it warrants. It is time that this aspect of management receives the systematic attention long reserved for motivational and productivity problems associated with relationships between management and workers.

WHO SHOULD CONTROL THE CORPORATION?*

by Henry Mintzberg

Who should control the corporation? How? And for the pursuit of what goals? Historically, the corporation was controlled by its owners—through direct control of the managers if not through direct management—for the pursuit of economic goals. But as shareholding became dispersed, owner control weakened; and as the corporation grew to very large size, its economic actions came to have increasing social consequences. The giant, widely held corporation came increasingly under the implicit control of its managers, and the concept of social responsibility—the voluntary consideration of public social goals alongside the private economic ones—arose to provide a basis of legitimacy for their actions.

To some, including those closest to the managers themselves, this was accepted as a satisfactory arrangement for the large corporation. "Trust it" to the goodwill of the managers was their credo; these people will be able to achieve an appropriate balance between social and economic goals.

* Originally published in the *California Management Review* XXVII, no. 1 (Fall 1984), pp. 90–115, based on a section of Henry Mintzberg, *Power in and Around Organizations* (Prentice-Hall, 1983). Copyright © 1984 by The Regents of the University of California. Reprinted with deletions by permission of The Regents.

But others viewed this basis of control as fundamentally illegitimate. The corporation was too large, too influential, its actions too pervasive to be left free of the direct and concerted influence of outsiders. At the extreme were those who believed that legitimacy could be achieved only by subjecting managerial authority to formal and direct external control. "Nationalize it," said those at one end of the political spectrum, to put ultimate control in the hands of the government so that it will pursue public social goals. No, said those at the other end, "restore it" to direct shareholder control, so that it will not waiver from the pursuit of private economic goals.

Other people took less extreme positions. "Democratize it" became the rallying cry for some, to open up the governance of the large, widely held corporation to a variety of affected groups—if not the workers, then the customers, or conservation interests, or minorities. "Regulate it" was also a popular position, with its implicit premise that only by sharing their control with government would the corporation's managers attend to certain social goals. Then there were those who accepted direct management control so long as it was tempered by other, less formal types of influence. "Pressure it," said a generation of social activists, to ensure that social goals are taken into consideration. But others argued that because the corporation is an economic instrument, you must "induce it" by providing economic incentives to encourage the resolution of social problems.

Finally, there were those who argued that this whole debate was unnecessary, that a kind of invisible hand ensures that the economic corporation acts in a socially responsible manner. "Ignore it" was their implicit conclusion.

This article is written to clarify what has become a major debate of our era, *the* major debate revolving around the private sector: Who should control the corporation, specifically the large, widely held corporation, how, and for the pursuit of what goals? The answers that are eventually accepted will determine what kind of society we and our children shall live in. . . .

As implied earlier, the various positions

of who should control the corporation, and how, can be laid out along a political spectrum, from nationalization at one end to the restoration of shareholder power at the other. From the managerial perspective, however, those two extremes are not so far apart. Both call for direct control of the corporation's managers by specific outsiders, in one case the government to ensure the pursuit of social goals, in the other case the shareholders to ensure the pursuit of economic ones. It is the moderate positions—notably, trusting the corporation to the social responsibility of its managers—that are farthest from the extremes. Hence, we can fold our spectrum around so that it takes the shape of a horseshoe.

Figure 1 shows our "conceptual horseshoe," with "nationalize it" and "restore it" at the two ends. "Trust it" is at the center, be-cause it postulates a natural balance of social and economic goals. "Democratize it," "regulate it," and "pressure it" are shown on the left side of the horseshoe, because all seek to temper economic goals with social ones. "Induce it" and "ignore it," both of which favor the exclusive pursuit of economic goals, are shown on the right side.

This conceptual horseshoe provides a basic framework to help clarify the issues in this important debate. We begin by discussing each of these positions in turn, circling the horseshoe from left to right. Finding that each (with one exception) has a logical context, we conclude—in keeping with our managerial perspective—that they should be thought of as forming a portfolio from which society can draw to deal with the issue of who should control the corporation and how.

FIGURE 1   THE CONCEPTUAL HORSESHOE

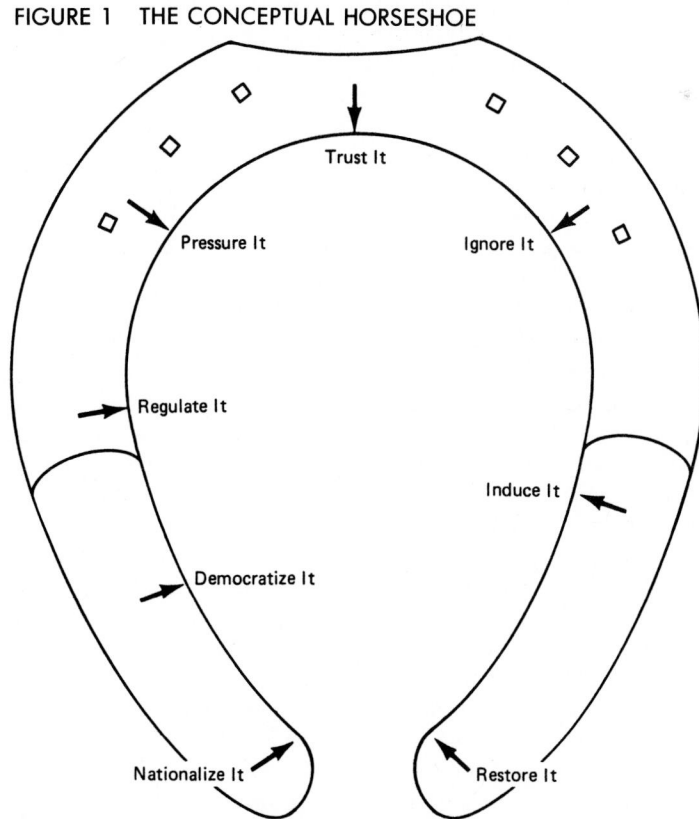

"NATIONALIZE IT"

Nationalization of the corporation is a taboo subject in the United States—in general, but not in particular. Whenever a major corporation runs into serious difficulty (i.e., faces bankruptcy with possible loss of many jobs), massive government intervention, often including direct nationalization, inevitably comes up as an option. This option has been exercised: U.S. travellers now ride on Amtrak; Tennessee residents have for years been getting their power from a government utility; indeed, the Post Office was once a private enterprise. Other nations have, of course, been much more ambitious in this regard.

From a managerial and organizational perspective, the question is not whether nationalization is legitimate, but whether it works—at least in particular, limited circumstances. As a response to concerns about the social responsibility of large corporations, the answer seems to be no. The evidence suggests that social difficulties arise more from the size of an organization and its degree of bureaucratization than from its form of ownership (Epstein, 1977; Jenkins, 1970). On the other hand, contrary to popular belief in the United States, nationalization does not necessarily harm economic efficiency. Over the years, Renault has been one of the most successful automobile companies outside Japan; it was nationalized by the French government shortly after World War II. . . . When people believe that government ownership leads to interference, politicization, and inefficiency, that may be exactly what happens. However, when they believe that nationalization *has* to work, then state-owned enterprises may be able to attract the very best talent in the country and thereby work well.

But economic efficiency is no reason to favor nationalization any more than is concern about social responsibility. Nationalization does, however, seem to make sense in at least two particular circumstances. The first is when a mission deemed necessary in a society will not be provided adequately by the private sector. That is presumably why America has its Amtrak [and why Third World nations often create state enterprises]. . . . The second is when the activities of an organization must be so intricately tied to government policy that it is best managed as a direct arm of the state. The Canadian government created Petrocan to act as a "window" and a source of expertise on the sensitive oil industry.

Thus, it is not rhetoric but requirement that should determine the role of this position as a solution to who should control the corporation. "Nationalize it" should certainly not be embraced as a panacea, but neither should it be rejected as totally inapplicable.

"DEMOCRATIZE IT"

A less extreme position—at least in the context of the American debate—is one that calls for formal devices to broaden the governance of the corporation. The proponents of this position either accept the legal fiction of shareholder control and argue that the corporation's power base is too narrow, or else they respond to the emergent reality and question the legitimacy of managerial control. Why, they ask, do stockholders or self-selected managers have any greater right to control the profound decisions of these major institutions than do workers or customers or the neighbors downstream.

This stand is not to be confused with what is known as "participative management." The call to "democratize it" is a legal, rather than ethical one and is based on power, not generosity. Management is not asked to share its power voluntarily; rather, that power is to be reallocated constitutionally. That makes this position a fundamental and important one, *especially* in the United States with its strong tradition of pluralist control of its institutions.

The debate over democratization of the corporation has been confusing in part because many of the proposals have been so vague. We can bring some order to it by considering, in organizational terms, two basic means of democratization and two basic constituencies that can be involved. As shown in Table 1, they suggest four possible

GROUPS INVOLVED

		Internal Employees	External Interest Groups
FOCUS OF ATTENTION	Board of Directors	Worker Representative Democracy (European style, e.g., "co-determination" or worker ownership)	Pluralistic Representative Democracy (American style, e.g., "public interest" directors)
	Internal Decision-Making Process	Worker Participatory Democracy (e.g., works councils)	Pluralistic Participatory Democracy (e.g., outsiders on new product committees)

TABLE 1
FOUR BASIC FORMS
OF CORPORATE DEMOCRACY

forms of corporate democracy. One means is through the election of representatives to the board of directors, which we call *representative democracy*. The other is through formal but direct involvement in internal decision making processes, which we call *participatory democracy*. Either can focus on the *workers* . . . or else on a host of outside interest groups, the latter giving rise to a *pluralistic* form of democracy. These are basic forms of corporate democracy in theory. With one exception, they have hardly been approached—let alone achieved—in practice. But they suggest where the "democratize it" debate may be headed.

The European debate has focused on worker representative democracy. This has, in some sense, been achieved in Yugoslavia, where the workers of all but the smallest firms elect the members of what is the equivalent of the American board of directors. In Germany, under the so-called *Mitbestimmung* ("co-determination"), the workers and the shareholders each elect half of the directors.

The evidence on this form of corporate democracy has been consistent, and it supports neither its proponents nor its detractors. Workers representation on the board seems to make relatively little difference one way or the other. The worker representatives concern themselves with wage and welfare issues but leave most other questions to management. Worker-controlled firms (not unlike the state-owned ones) appear

to be no more socially responsible than private ones. . . .

On the other hand, worker representative democracy may have certain positive benefits. German Chancellor Helmut Schmidt is reported to have said that "the key to [his] country's postwar economic miracle was its sophisticated system of workers' participation" (in Garson, 1977:63). While no one can prove this statement, co-determination certainly does not seem to have done the German economy much harm. By providing an aura of legitimacy to the German corporation and by involving the workers (at least officially) in its governance, co-determination may perhaps have enhanced the spirit of enterprise in Germany (while having little real effect on how decisions are actually made). More significantly, co-determination may have fostered greater understanding and cooperation between the managers and the union members who fill most of the worker seats on the boards. . . .

. . . the embryonic debate over representative democracy in the United States has shown signs of moving in a different direction. Consistent with the tradition of pluralism in America's democratic institutions, there has been increasing pressure to elect outside directors who represent a wide variety of special interest groups—i.e., consumers, minorities, environmentalists, and so on. . . .

Critics . . . have pointed out the problems of defining constituencies and finding the means to hold elections. "One-person, one-vote" may be easily applied to electing representatives of the workers, but no such simple rule can be found in the case of the consumer or environmental representatives, let alone ones of the "public interest." Yet it is amazing how quickly things become workable in the United States when Americans decide to put their collective mind to it. Indeed, the one case of public directors that I came across is telling in this regard. According to a Conference Board report, the selection by the Chief Justice of the Supreme Court of New Jersey of 6 of the 24 members of the board of Prudential Insurance as public directors has been found by the company to be "quite workable" (Bacon and Brown, 1975:48). . . .

Despite its problems, representative democracy is crystal clear compared with participatory democracy. What the French call "auto-gestion" (as opposed to "co-gestion," or co-determination) seems to describe a kind of bottom-up, grassroots democracy in which the workers participate directly in decision making (instead of overseeing management's decisions from the board of directors) and also elect their own managers (who then become more administrators than bosses). Yet such proposals are inevitably vague, and I have heard of no large mass production or mass service firm—not even one owned by workers or a union—that comes close to this. . . .

What has impeded worker participatory democracy? In my opinion, something rather obvious has stood in its way; namely, the structure required by the very organizations in which the attempts have been made to apply it. Worker participatory democracy—and worker representative democracy too, for that matter—has been attempted primarily in organizations containing large numbers of workers who do highly routine, rather unskilled jobs that are typical of most mass production and service—what I have elsewhere called Machine Bureaucracies. The overriding requirement in Machine Bureaucracy is for tight coordination, the kind that can only be achieved by central administrators. For example, the myriad of decisions associated with producing an automobile at Volvo's Kalmar works in Sweden

cannot be made by autonomous groups, each doing as it pleases. The whole car must fit together in a particular way at the end of the assembly process. These decisions requre a highly sophisticated system of bureaucratic coordination. That is why automobile companies are structured into rigid hierarchies of authority. . . .

Participatory democracy *is* approached in other kinds of organizations . . . the autonomous professional institutions such as universities and hospitals, which have very different needs for central coordination. . . . But the proponents of democracy in organizations are not lobbying for changes in hospitals or universities. It is the giant mass producers they are after, and unless the operating work in these corporations becomes largely skilled and professional in nature, nothing approaching participative democracy can be expected.

In principal, the pluralistic form of participatory democracy means that a variety of groups external to the corporation can somehow control its decision-making processes directly. In practice, of course, this concept is even more elusive than the worker form of participatory democracy. To fully open up the internal decision-making processes of the corporation to outsiders would mean chaos. Yet certain very limited forms of outside participation would seem to be not only feasible but perhaps even desirable. . . . Imagine telephone company executives resolving rate conflicts with consumer groups in quiet offices instead of having to face them in noisy public hearings.

To conclude, corporate democracy—whether representative or participatory in form—may be an elusive and difficult concept, but it cannot be dismissed. It is not just another social issue, like conservation or equal opportunity, but one that strikes at the most fundamental of values. Ours has become a society of organizations. Democracy will have decreasing meaning to most citizens if it cannot be extended beyond political and judicial processes to those institutions that impinge upon them in their daily lives—as workers, as consumers, as neighbors. This is why we shall be hearing a great deal more of "democratize it."

"REGULATE IT"

In theory, regulating the corporation is about as simple as democratizing it is complex. In practice, it is, of course, another matter. To the proponents of "regulate it," the corporation can be made responsive to social needs by having its actions subjected to the controls of a higher authority—typically government, in the form of a regulatory agency or legislation backed up by the courts. Under regulation, constraints are imposed externally on the corporation while its internal governance is left to its managers.

Regulation of business is at least as old as the Code of Hammurabi. In America, it has tended to come in waves. . . .

To some, regulation is a clumsy instrument that should never be relied upon; to others, it is a panacea for the problems of social responsibility. At best, regulation sets minimum and usually crude standards of acceptable behavior; when it works, it does not make any firm socially responsible so much as stop some from being grossly irresponsible. Because it is inflexible, regulation tends to be applied slowly and conservatively, usually lagging public sentiment. Regulation often does not work because of difficulties in enforcement. The problems of the regulatory agencies are legendary—limited resources and information compared with the industries they are supposed to regulate, the cooptation of the regulators by industries, and so on. When applied indiscriminately, regulation either fails dramatically or else succeeds and creates havoc.

Yet there are obvious places for regulation. A prime one is to control tangible "externalities"—costs incurred by corporations that are passed on to the public at large. When, for example, costly pollution or worker health problems can be attributed directly to a corporation, then there seems to be every reason to force it (and its customers) to incur these costs directly, or else to terminate the actions that generate them. Likewise, regulation may have a place where competition encourages the unscrupulous to pull all firms down to a base level of behavior, forcing even the well-intentioned manager to ignore the social consequences of his actions. Indeed, in such cases, the socially responsible behavior is to encourage sensible regulation. "Help us to help others," businessmen should be telling the government. . . .

Most discouraging, however, is Theodore Levitt's revelation some years ago that business has fought every piece of proposed regulatory or social legislation throughout this century, from the Child Labor Acts on up. In Levitt's opinion, much of that legislation has been good for business—dissolving the giant trusts, creating a more honest and effective stock market, and so on. Yet, "the computer is programmed to cry wolf" (Levitt, 1968:83). . . .

In summary, regulation is a clumsy instrument but not a useless one. Were the business community to take a more enlightened view of it, regulation could be applied more appropriately, and we would not need these periodic housecleanings to eliminate the excesses.

"PRESSURE IT"

"Pressure it" is designed to do what "regulate it" fails to do: provoke corporations to act beyond some base level of behavior, usually in an area that regulation misses entirely. Here, activists bring ad hoc campaigns of pressure to bear on one or a group of corporations to keep them responsive to the activists' interpretation of social needs. . . .

"Pressure it" is a distinctively American position. While Europeans debate the theories of nationalization and corporate democracy in their cafés, Americans read about the exploits of Ralph Nader et al. in their morning newspapers. Note that "pressure it," unlike "regulate it," implicitly accepts management's right to make the final decisions. Perhaps this is one reason why it is favored in America.

While less radical than the other positions so far discussed, "pressure it" has nevertheless proved far more effective in eliciting behavior sensitive to social needs . . . [activist groups] have pressured for everything from the dismemberment of diversified corporations to the development of day care centers. Of special note is the class action suit, which has opened up a whole new realm of corporate social issues. But the effective use of the pressure campaign has not been restricted to the traditional activist. President Kennedy used it to roll back U.S. Steel price increases in the early 1960s, and business leaders in Pittsburgh used it in the late 1940s by threatening to take their freight-haulage business elsewhere if the Pennsylvania Railroad did not replace its coal burning locomotives to help clean up their city's air.

"Pressure it" as a means to change corporate behavior is informal, flexible, and focused; hence, it has been highly successful. Yet it is irregular and ad hoc, with different pressure campaigns sometimes making contradictory demands on management. Compared to the positions to its right on the horseshoe, "pressure it," like the other positions to its left, is based on confrontation rather than cooperation.

"TRUST IT"

To a large and vocal contingent, which parades under the banner of "social responsibility," the corporation has no need to act irresponsibly, and therefore there is no reason for it to either be nationalized by the state, democratized by its different constituencies, regulated by the government, or pressured by activists. This contingent believes that the corporation's leaders can be trusted to attend to social goals for their own sake, simply because it is the noble thing to do. (Once this position was known as *nobelesse oblige,* literally "nobility obliges.")

We call this position "trust it," or, more exactly, "trust the corporation to the goodwill of its managers," although looking from the outside in, it might just as well be called "socialize it." We place it in the center of our conceptual horseshoe because it alone postulates a natural balance between social and economic goals—a balance which is to be attained in the heads (or

perhaps the hearts) of responsible businessmen. And, as a not necessarily incidental consequence, power can be left in the hands of the managers; the corporation can be trusted to those who reconcile social and economic goals.

The attacks on social responsibility, from the right as well as the left, boil down to whether corporate managers should be trusted when they claim to pursue social goals; if so, whether they are capable of pursuing such goals; and finally, whether they have any right to pursue such goals.

The simplest attack is that social responsibility is all rhetoric, no action. E. F. Cheit refers to the "Gospel of Social Responsibility" as "designed to justify the power of managers over an ownerless system" (1964:172). . . .

Others argue that businessmen lack the personal capabilities required to pursue social goals. Levitt claims that the professional manager reaches the top of the hierarchy by dedication to his firm and his industry; as a result, his knowledge of social issues is highly restricted (Levitt, 1968:83). Others argue that an orientation to efficiency renders business leaders inadept at handling complex social problems (which require flexibility and political finesse, and sometimes involve solutions that are uneconomic). . . .

The most far reaching criticism is that businessmen have no right to pursue social goals. "Who authorized them to do that?", asks Braybrooke (1967:224), attacking from the left. What business have they—self-selected or at best appointed by shareholders—to impose *their* interpretation of the public good on society. Let the elected politicians, directly responsible to the population, look after the social goals.

But this attack comes from the right, too. Milton Friedman writes that social responsibility amounts to spending other people's money—if not that of shareholders, then of customers or employees. Drawing on all the pejorative terms of right-wing ideology, Friedman concludes that social responsibility is a "fundamentally subversive doctrine," representing "pure and unadulterated socialism," supported by businessmen who are "unwitting puppets of the intellectual forces that have been undermining the basis of a free society these past decades.'' To Friedman, ''there is one and only one social responsibility of business—to use its resources and engage in activities designed to increase its profits so long as it stays within the rules of the game'' (1970). Let businessmen, in other words, stick to their own business, which is business itself.

The empirical evidence on social responsibility is hardly more encouraging. Brenner and Molander, comparing their 1977 survey of *Harvard Business Review* readers with one conducted fifteen years earlier, concluded that the ''respondents are somewhat more cynical about the ethical conduct of their peers'' than they were previously (1977:59). Close to half the respondents agreed with the statement that ''the American business executive tends not to apply the great ethical laws immediately to work. He is preoccupied chiefly with gain (p. 62).'' Only 5% listed social responsibility as a factor ''influencing ethical standards'' whereas 31% and 20% listed different factors related to pressure campaigns and 10% listed regulation. . . .

The modern corporation has been described as a rational, amoral institution—its professional managers ''hired guns'' who pursue ''efficiently'' any goals asked of them. The problem is that efficiency really means measurable efficiency, so that the guns load only with goals that can be quantified. Social goals, unlike economic ones, just don't lend themselves to quantification. As a result, the performance control systems—on which modern corporations so heavily depend—tend to drive out social goals in favor of economic ones (Ackerman, 1975). . . .

In the contemporary large corporation, professional amorality turns into economic morality. When the screws of the performance control systems are turned tight . . . economic morality can turn into social immorality. And it happens often: A *Fortune* writer found that ''a surprising number of [big companies] have been involved in blatant illegalities'' in the 1970s, at least 117 of 1,043 firms studied (Ross, 1980:57). . . .

How, then, is anyone to ''trust it''?

The fact is that we have to trust it, for two reasons. First, the strategic decisions of large organizations inevitably involve social as well as economic consequences that are inextricably intertwined. The neat distinction between economic goals in the private sector and social goals in the public sector just doesn't hold up in practice. Every important decision of the large corporation—to introduce a new product line, to close an old plant, whatever—generates all kinds of social consequences. There is no such thing as purely economic decisions in big business. Only a conceptual ostrich, with his head deeply buried in the abstractions of economic theory, could possibly use the distinction between economic and social goals to dismiss social responsibility.

The second reason we have to ''trust it'' is that there is always some degree of discretion involved in corporate decision making, discretion to thwart social needs or to attend to them. Things could be a lot better in today's corporation, but they could also be an awful lot worse. It is primarily our ethics that keep us where we are. If the performance control systems favored by diversified corporations cut too deeply into our ethical standards, then our choice is clear; to reduce these standards or call into question the whole trend toward diversification.

To dismiss social responsibility is to allow corporate behavior to drop to the lowest level, propped up only by external controls such as regulation and pressure campaigns. Solzhentisyn, who has experienced the natural conclusion of unrestrained bureaucratization, warns us (in sharp contrast to Friedman) that ''a society with no other scale but the legal one is not quite worthy of man. . . . A society which is based on the letter of the law and never reaches any higher is scarcely taking advantage of the high level of human possibilities'' (1978:B1).

This is not to suggest that we must trust it completely. We certainly cannot trust it unconditionally by accepting the claim popular in some quarters that only business can solve the social ills of society. Business has no business using its resources without constraint in the social sphere—whether to support political candidates or to dictate implicitly through donations how non-profit institutions should allocate their efforts. But where business is inherently involved, where its decisions have social consequences, that is where social responsibility has a role to play: where business creates externalities that cannot be measured and attributed to it (in other words, where regulation is ineffective); where regulation would work if only business would cooperate with it; where the corporation can fool its customers, or suppliers, or government through superior knowledge; where useful products can be marketed instead of wasteful or destructive ones. In other words, we have to realize that in many spheres we must trust it, or at least socialize it (and perhaps change it) so that we can trust it. Without responsible and ethical people in important places, our society is not worth very much.

"IGNORE IT"

"Ignore it" differs from the other positions on the horseshoe in that explicitly or implicitly it calls for no change in corporate behavior. It assumes that social needs are met in the course of pursuing economic goals. We include this position in our horseshoe because it is held by many influential people and also because its validity would preempt support for the other positions. We must, therefore, investigate it alongside the others.

It should be noted at the outset that "ignore it" is not the same position as "trust it." In the latter, to be good is the right thing to do; in the present case, "it pays to be good." The distinction is subtle but important, for now it is economics, not ethics, that elicits the desired behavior. One need not strive to be ethical; economic forces will ensure that social needs fall conveniently into place. Here we have moved one notch to the right on our horseshoe, into the realm where the economic goals dominate. . . .

"Ignore it" is sometimes referred to as "enlightened self-interest," although some of its proponents are more enlightened than others. Many a true believer in social responsibility has used the argument that it pays to be good to ward off the attacks from the right that corporations have no business pursuing social goals. Even Milton Friedman must admit that they have every right to do so if it pays them economically. The danger of such arguments, however—and a prime reason "ignore it" differs from "trust it"—is that they tend to support the status quo: corporations need not change their behavior because it already pays to be good.

Sometimes the case for "ignore it" is made in terms of corporations at large, that the whole business community will benefit from socially responsible behavior. Other times the case is made in terms of the individual corporation, that it will benefit directly from its own socially responsible actions. . . . Others make the case for "ignore it" in "social investment" terms, claiming that socially responsible behavior pays off in a better image for the firm, a more positive relationship with customers, and ultimately a healthier and more stable society in which to do business.

Then, there is what I like to call the "them" argument: "If we're not good, *they* will move in"—"they" being Ralph Nader, the government, whoever. In other words, "Be good or else." The trouble with this argument is that by reducing social responsibility to simply a political tool for sustaining managerial control of the corporation in the face of outside threats, it tends to encourage general pronouncements instead of concrete actions (unless of course, "they" actually deliver with pressure campaigns). . . .

The "ignore it" position rests on some shaky ground. It seems to encourage average behavior at best; and where the average does not seem to be good enough, it encourages the status quo. In fact, ironically, "ignore it" makes a strong case for "pressure it," since the whole argument collapses in the absence of pressure campaigns. Thus while many influential people take this position, we question whether in the realities of corporate behavior it can really stand alone.

"INDUCE IT"

Continuing around to the right, our next position drops all concern with social responsibility per se and argues, simply, "pay it to be good," or, from the corporation's point of view, "be good only where it pays." Here, the corporation does not actively pursue social goals at all, whether as ends in themselves or as means to economic ends. Rather, it undertakes socially desirable programs only when induced economically to do so—usually through government incentives. If society wishes to clean up urban blight, then let its government provide subsidies for corporations that renovate buildings; if pollution is the problem, then let corporations be rewarded for reducing it.

"Induce it" faces "regulate it" on the opposite side of the horseshoe for good reason. While one penalizes the corporation for what it does do, the other rewards it for doing what it might not otherwise do. Hence these two positions can be direct substitutes: pollution can be alleviated by introducing penalties for the damage done or by offering incentives for the improvements rendered.

Logic would, however, dictate a specific role for each of these positions. Where a corporation is doing society a specific, attributable harm—as in the case of pollution—then paying it to stop hardly seems to make a lot of sense. If society does not wish to outlaw the harmful behavior altogether, then surely it must charge those responsible for it—the corporation and, ultimately, its customers. Offering financial incentives to stop causing harm would be to invite a kind of blackmail—for example, encouraging corporations to pollute so as to get paid to stop. And every citizen would be charged for the harm done by only a few.

On the other hand, where social problems exist which cannot be attributed to specific corporations, yet require the skills of certain corporations for solution, then financial incentives clearly make sense (so long, of course, as solutions can be clearly defined and tied to tangible economic rewards). Here, and not under "trust it," is where

the "only business can do it" argument belongs. When it is true that only business can do it (and business has not done it to us in the first place), then business should be encouraged to do it. . . .

"RESTORE IT"

Our last position on the horseshoe tends to be highly ideological, the first since "democratize it" to seek a fundamental change in the governance and the goals of the corporation. Like the proponents of "nationalize it," those of this position believe that managerial control is illegitimate and must be replaced by a more valid form of external control. The corporation should be restored to its former status, that is, returned to its "rightful" owners, the shareholders. The only way to ensure the relentless pursuit of economic goals—and that means the maximization of profit, free of the "subversive doctrine" of social responsibility—is to put control directly into the hands of those to whom profit means the most.

A few years ago this may have seemed to be an obsolete position. But thanks to its patron saint Milton Friedman . . . , it has recently come into prominence. Also, other forms of restoring it, including the "small is beautiful" theme, have also become popular in recent years.

Friedman has written:

> In a free-enterprise, private-property system, a corporate executive is an employee of the owners of the business. He has direct responsibility to his employers. That responsibility is to conduct the business in accordance with their desires, which generally will be to make as much money as possible while conforming to the basic rules of the society, both those embodied in law and those embodied in ethical custom (1970:33).

Interestingly, what seems to drive Friedman is a belief that the shift over the course of this century from owner to manager control, with its concerns about social responsibility, represents an unstoppable skid around our horseshoe. In the opening chapter of his book *Capitalism and Freedom,* Friedman seems to accept only two possibilities— traditional capitalism and socialism as practiced in Eastern Europe. The absence of the former must inevitably lead to the latter.

> The preservation and expansion of freedom are today threatened from two directions. The one threat is obvious and clear. It is the external threat coming from the evil men in the Kremlin who promise to bury us. The other threat is far more subtle. It is the internal threat coming from men of good intentions and good will who wish to reform us (1962:20).

The problem of who should control the corporation thus reduces to a war between two ideologies—in Friedman's terms, "subversive" socialism and "free" enterprise. In this world of black and white, there can be no middle ground, no moderate position between the black of "nationalize it" and the white of "restore it," none of the grey of "trust it." Either the owners will control the corporation or else the government will. Hence: " 'restore it' or else." Anchor the corporation on the right side of the horseshoe, Friedman seems to be telling us, the only place where "free" enterprise and "freedom" are safe.

All of this, in my view, rests on a series of assumptions—technical, economic, and political—which contain a number of fallacies. First is the fallacy of the technical assumption of shareholder control. Every trend in ownership during this century seems to refute the assumption that small shareholders are either willing or able to control the large, widely held corporation. The one place where free markets clearly still exist is in stock ownership, and that has served to detach ownership from control. When power is widely dispersed—among stockholders no less than workers or customers—those who share it tend to remain passive. It pays no one of them to invest the effort to exercise their power. Hence, even if serious shareholders did control the boards of widely held corporations (and one survey of all the directors of the *Fortune 500* in 1977 found that only 1.6% of them represented significant

shareholder interests, [Smith, 1978], the question remains open as to whether they would actually try to control the management. (This is obviously not true of closely held corporations, but these— probably a decreasing minority of the *Fortune 500*—are "restored" in any event.)

The economic assumptions of free markets have been discussed at length in the literature. Whether there exists vibrant competition, unlimited entry, open information, consumer sovereignty, and labor mobility is debatable. Less debatable is the conclusion that the larger the corporation, the greater is its ability to interfere with these processes. The issues we are discussing center on the giant corporation. It is not Luigi's Body Shop that Ralph Nader is after, but General Motors, a corporation that employs more than half a million people and earns greater revenues than many national governments.

Those who laid the foundation for conventional economic theory—such as Adam Smith and Alfred Marshall—never dreamed of the massive amounts now spent for advertising campaigns, most of them designed as much for affect as for effect; of the waves of conglomeration that have combined all kinds of diverse businesses into single corporate entities; of chemical complexes that cost more than a billion dollars; and of the intimate relationships that now exist between giant corporations and government, as customer and partner not to mention subsidizer. The concept of arm's length relationships in such conditions is, at best, nostalgic. What happens to consumer sovereignty when Ford knows more about its gas tanks than do its customers? And what does labor mobility mean in the presence of an inflexible pension plan, or commitment to a special skill, or a one-factory town? It is an ironic twist of conventional economic theory that the worker is the one who typically stays put, thus rendering false the assumption of labor mobility, while the shareholder is the mobile one, thus spoiling the case for owner control.

The political assumptions are more ideological in nature, although usually implicit. These assumptions are that the corporation is essentially amoral, society's instrument for producing goods and services, and, more broadly, that a society is "free" and "democratic" so long as its governmental leaders are elected by universal suffrage and do not interfere with the legal activities of businessmen. But many people—a large majority of the general public, if polls are to be believed— seem to subscribe to one or more assumptions that contradict these "free enterprise" assumptions.

One assumption is that the large corporation is a social and political institution as much as an economic instrument. Economic activities, as noted previously, produce all kinds of social consequences. Jobs get created and rivers get polluted, cities get built and workers get injured. These social consequences cannot be factored out of corporate strategic decisions and assigned to government.

Another assumption is that society cannot achieve the necessary balance between social and economic needs so long as the private sector attends only to economic goals. Given the pervasiveness of business in society, the acceptance of Friedman's prescriptions would drive us toward a one-dimensional society—a society that is too utilitarian and too materialistic. Economic morality, as noted earlier, can amount to a social immorality.

Finally, the question is asked: Why the owners? In a democratic society, what justifies owner control of the corporation any more than worker control, or consumer control, or pluralistic control? Ours is not Adam Smith's society of small proprietors and shopkeepers. His butcher, brewer, and baker have become Iowa Beef Packers, Anheuser-Bush, and ITT Continental Baking. What was once a case for individual democracy now becomes a case for oligarchy. . . .

I see Friedman's form of "restore it" as a rather quaint position in a society of giant corporations, managed economies, and dispersed shareholders—a society in which the collective power of corporations is coming under increasing scrutiny and in which the distribution between economic and social goals is being readdressed.

Of course, there are other ways [than Friedman's] to "restore it." "Divest it" could return

the corporation to the business or central theme it knows best, restoring the role of allocating funds between different businesses to capital markets instead of central headquarters. Also, boards could be restored to positions of influence by holding directors legally responsible for their actions and by making them more independent of managers (for example, by providing them with personal staffs and by precluding full-time managers from their ranks, especially the position of chairman). We might even wish to extend use of "reduce it" where possible, to decrease the size of those corporations that have grown excessively large on the basis of market or political power rather than economies of scale, and perhaps to eliminate certain forms of vertical integration. In many cases it may prove advantageous, economically as well as socially, to have the corporation trade with its suppliers and customers instead of being allowed to ingest them indiscriminately.[1]

I personally doubt that these proposals could be any more easily realized in today's society than those of Friedman, even though I believe them to be more desirable. "Restore it" is the nostalgic position on our horseshoe, a return to our fantasies of a glorious past. In this society of giant organizations, it flies in the face of powerful economic and political forces.

CONCLUSION: IF THE SHOE FITS . . .

I believe that today's corporation cannot ride on any one position any more than a horse can ride on part of a shoe. In other words, we need to treat the conceptual horseshoe as a portfolio of positions from which we can draw, depending on circumstances. Exclusive reliance on one position will lead to a narrow and dogmatic society, with an excess concentration of power. . . . the use of a variety of positions can encourage the

[1] *A number of these proposals would be worthwhile to pursue in the public and parapublic sectors as well, to divide up overgrown hospitals, school systems, social service agencies, and all kinds of government departments.*

pluralism I believe most of us feel is necessary to sustain democracy. If the shoe fits, then let the corporation wear it.

I do not mean to imply that the eight positions do not represent fundamentally different values and, in some cases, ideologies as well. Clearly they do. But I also believe that anyone who makes an honest assessment of the realities of power in and around today's large corporations must conclude that a variety of positions have to be relied upon [even if they themselves might tilt to the left, right or center of our horseshoe]. . . .

I tilt to the left of center, as has no doubt been obvious in my comments to this point. Let me summarize my own prescriptions as follows, and in the process provide some basis for evaluating the relevant roles of each of the eight positions.

First "Trust It," or at Least "Socialize It."

Despite my suspicions about much of the rhetoric that passes for social responsibility and the discouraging evidence about the behavior of large contemporary organizations (not only corporations), I remain firmly convinced that without honest and responsible people in important places, we are in deep trouble. We need to trust it because, no matter how much we rely on the other positions, managers will always retain a great deal of power. And that power necessarily has social no less than economic consequences. The positions on the right side of our horseshoe ignore these social consequences while some of those on the left fail to recognize the difficulties of influencing these consequences in large, hierarchical organizations. Sitting between these two sets of positions, managers can use their discretion to satisfy or to subvert the wishes of the public. Ultimately, what managers do is determined by their sense of responsibility as individual members of society.

Although we must "trust it," we cannot *only* "trust it." As I have argued, there is an

appropriate and limited place for social responsibility—essentially to get the corporation's own house in order and to encourage it to act responsibly in its own sphere of operations. Beyond that, social responsibility needs to be tempered by other positions around our horseshoe.

Then "Pressure It," Ceaselessly

As we have seen, too many forces interfere with social responsibility. The best antidote to these forces is the ad hoc pressure campaign, designed to pinpoint unethical behavior and raise social consciousness about issues. The existence of the "pressure it" position is what most clearly distinguishes the western from the eastern "democracies." Give me one Ralph Nader to all those banks of government accountants.

In fact, "pressure it" underlies the success of most of the other positions. Pressure campaigns have brought about necessary new regulations and have highlighted the case for corporate democracy. As we have seen, the "ignore it" position collapses without "pressure it". . . .

After That, Try to "Democratize It"

A somewhat distant third in my portfolio is "democratize it," a position I view as radical only in terms of the current U.S. debate, not in terms of fundamental American values. Democracy matters most where it affects us directly—in the water we drink, the jobs we perform, the products we consume. How can we call our society democratic when many of its most powerful institutions are closed to governance from the outside and are run as hierarchies of authority from within?

As noted earlier, I have no illusions about having found the means to achieve corporate democracy. But I do know that Americans can be very resourceful when they decide to resolve a problem—and this is a problem that badly needs resolving. Somehow, ways must be found to open the corporation up to the formal influence of the constituencies most affected by it—employees, customers, neighbors, and so on—without weakening it as an economic institution. At stake is nothing less than the maintenance of basic freedoms in our society.

Then, Only Where Specifically Appropriate, "Regulate It" and "Induce It"

Facing each other on the horseshoe are two positions that have useful if limited roles to play. Regulation is neither a panacea nor a menace. It belongs where the corporation can abuse the power it has and can be penalized for that abuse—notably where externalities can be identified with specific corporations. Financial inducements belong, not where a corporation has created a problem, but where it has the capability to solve a problem created by someone else.

Occasionally, Selectively, "Nationalize It" and "Restore It," But Not in Friedman's Way

The extreme positions should be reserved for extreme problems. If "pressure it" is a scalpel and "regulate it" a cleaver, then "nationalize it" and "restore it" are guillotines.

Both these positions are implicitly proposed as alternatives to "democratize it." One offers public control, the other "shareholder democracy." The trouble is that control by everyone often turns out to be control by no one, while control by the owners—even if attainable—would remove the corporation even further from the influence of those most influenced by it.

Yet, as noted earlier, nationalization sometimes makes sense—when private enterprise cannot provide a necessary mission, at least in a sufficient or appropriate way, and when the activities of a corporation must be intricately tied in to government policy.

As for "restore it," I believe Friedman's particular proposals will aggravate the problems of political control and social responsibility, strengthening oligarchical tendencies in society and further tilting what I see as the current imbalance between social and economic goals. In response to Friedman's choice between "subversive" socialism and "free" enterprise, I say "a pox on both your houses." Let us concentrate our efforts on the intermediate positions around the horseshoe. However, other forms of "restore it" are worth considering—to "divest it" where diversification has interfered with capital markets, competition, and economic efficiency; to "*dis*integrate it" vertically where a trading network is preferable to a managerial hierarchy; to strengthen its board so that directors can assess managers objectively; and to "reduce it" where size represents a power game rather than a means to provide better and more efficient service to the public. I stand with Friedman in wishing to see competitive markets strengthened; it is just that I believe his proposals lead in exactly the opposite direction.

Finally, Above All, Don't "Ignore It"

I leave one position out of my portfolio altogether, because it contradicts the others. The one thing we must not do is ignore the large, widely held corporation. It is too influential a force in our lives. Our challenge is to find ways to distribute the power in and around our large organizations so that they will remain responsive, vital, and effective.

EIGHT

DEALING
WITH
CULTURE

Culture arrived on the management scene in the 1980s like a typhoon blowing in from the Far East. It suddenly became fashionable in consulting circles to sell culture like some article of organizational clothing, much as "management by objectives" or "total information systems" were once sold. What gave this subject most impetus was Peters's and Waterman's book *In Search of Excellence*. This depicted successful organizations as being rich in culture—permeated with strong and sustaining systems of beliefs, often called ideologies. In our view—as in theirs—culture is not an article of fashion, but an intrinsic part of a deeper organizational "character," as Selznick described it (in Chapter 2). To draw on definitions introduced earlier, strategy is not just an arbitrarily chosen *position*, nor an analytically developed *plan*, but a deeply entrenched *perspective* which influences the way the organization develops new ideas, considers and weights options, and responds to changes in its environment.

Culture thus permeates many critical aspects of strategy making. But perhaps the most crucial realm is the way people are chosen, developed, nurtured, interrelated, and rewarded in the organization. The kinds of people attracted to an organization and the way they can most effectively deal with problems and each other are largely a function of the culture a company builds—and the practices and systems which support it. In some organizations, the culture may become so strong that it is best referred to as an "ideology" that dominates all else—as in the "missionary" configuration introduced in Mintzberg's "Structuring of Organizations" reading in Chapter 6. But because its culture can be a powerful factor in any organization, no matter what overall form it may take, we now introduce the concept along with structure, systems, and power, the other elements of "organization" which significantly affect the human interactions in an organization. In a way, culture may be considered the mirror opposite of power exercised as politics. While the latter focuses on self interest and the building of one's own power base through individual initiative, culture concentrates on the collective interest and the building of a unified organization, through shared systems of beliefs, habits, and traditions.

The readings in this chapter tend to focus on rich cultures—really ideologies—and how these may promote "excellence" in certain situations. Later we shall consider how these, and other, imbedded cultures can discourage excellence by making organizations resistant to strategic change.

The first reading, drawn from two chapters of Mintzberg's book *Power in and Around Organizations*, traces how ideologies evolve through three stages: their rooting in a sense of mission, their development through traditions and sagas, and their reinforcement through various forms of identifications. Mintzberg then briefly considers the missionary type organization introduced in Chapter 6, and shows how business firms may sometimes superimpose some of its characteristics on their more conventional ways of operating.

The Pucik and Hatvany reading focuses on the well-known example of the norm-driven Japanese business firm. The authors first investigate this much discussed organization's particular ways of functioning, its management practices and techniques. Pucik and Hatvany then show how such a company's favored objectives and strategies—for example, its emphasis on market share, internal growth, and longer term returns—grow directly out of its culture.

This chapter is supported by a number of case examples that give the reader a sense of the wide variety of cultures that can promote excellence. One should note the compatabilities and the contrasts between the Japanese cultures in Sony and Matsushita, the highly innovative cultures of Intel and AT&T Bell Labs, and the powerful competitive cultures of IBM and Pillsbury. Each case offers an opportunity to investigate the important relationships among strategy, structure, systems, and style—four of the 7S's—that create and sustain a culture.

IDEOLOGY AND THE MISSIONARY ORGANIZATION*

by Henry Mintzberg

Simple mathematics tells us that $2 + 2 = 4$. But general systems theory, under the concept *synergy*, suggests that it can also equal 5. A flashlight and batteries add up to so many pieces of hardware; together they form a working system. So also an organization is more than just the sum of its parts, more than a collection of people

*   Adapted from Henry Mintzberg, Power In and Around Organizations (copyright © Prentice-Hall, 1983), chaps. 11 and 21; used by permission of the publisher.

and machines. The behavior of the group cannot be predicted solely from an understanding of the personality of each of its members. Various social processes intervene. From some of these, the group develops a "mood," an "atmosphere"; it is said to have some kind of "chemistry." In the context of the organization, we talk of a "style," a "culture," a "character." One senses something unique when one walks into an office of IBM; the Canadian Broadcasting Corporation just does not feel like CBS or NBC; the chemistry of the Harvard Business School is simply not the same as that of the MIT Sloan School, serving the same mission on the other side of the Charles River. It is all of these phenomena—intangible yet very real, over and above all of the concrete components of the organization—that we here refer to as *organizational ideology*. Specifically, organizational ideology is taken here to mean a system of beliefs about the organization, shared by its members, that distinguishes it from other organizations.

The key feature of an ideology (the adjective "organizational" will be assumed from here on), for our purposes, is its unifying power. An ideology ties the individual to the organization; it generates an "esprit de corps," a "sense of mission," in effect, an integration of individual and organizational goals. . . .

The development of an organizational ideology will be discussed here in three stages. The roots of the ideology are planted when a group of individuals band together around a leader and through a sense of mission, to found an organization. The ideology then develops over time through the establishment of traditions. And finally, an existing ideology is reinforced through the identification of new members with the organization and its system of beliefs.

STAGE 1: THE ROOTING OF AN IDEOLOGY IN A SENSE OF MISSION

Typically an organization is founded when a single prime mover (an "entrepreneur") identifies a mission—some product to be produced or service to be rendered in a special way—and collects a group around him to accomplish it. Sometimes one organization is founded by another, as when a new agency is created by a government or a subsidiary by a corporation. But the basic ingredients remain the same—a founding leader, a unique mission to be accomplished, and the establishment of a group.

These individuals do not come together at random, but coalesce because they share some norms associated with the fledgling organization. At the very least they see something in it for themselves. But in some cases, in addition to the mission there is the "sense of mission," that is, a feeling that the group has banded together to create something new and exciting. This is common in new organizations for a number of reasons. First, unbounded by procedure and tradition, new organizations offer wide latitude for maneuver. Second, they tend to be small, enabling the members to establish personal relationships. Third, the founding members often share some strong basic beliefs, perhaps a sense that they wish to work together. Fourth, a sense of "charisma" is often associated with the founder of a new organization. Charisma, as Weber used the term, means a sense of "personal devotion" to the leader for the sake of his personal qualities rather than his formal position (1969:12). People join and remain with the organization because of a sense of dedication to the leader and what he seeks to accomplish. All of this contributes to the sense of mission, the esprit de corps established at the outset. Thus the roots of an organizational ideology are planted in the founding of the organization.

STAGE 2: THE DEVELOPMENT OF THE IDEOLOGY THROUGH TRADITIONS AND SAGAS

As the organization establishes itself, it makes decisions and takes actions which serve as commitments and establish precedents that reinforce themselves over time. Actions become infused with value. When these forces are strong enough, ideology begins to emerge. Furthermore, stories

—sometimes called "myths"—develop around important events and the actions of great leaders in the organization's past. Gradually the organization develops a history of its own. All of this—the precedents, habits, myths, history— form a common data base of tradition which the members of the organization share. Over time, this tradition influences behavior, and that behavior in turn reinforces the tradition. Eventually, an ideology may become established.

As this happens, in Selznick's terms, the organization is converted from an expendible "instrument" for the accomplishment of externally imposed goals into an "institution," a system with a life of its own— ". . . it acquires a self, a distinctive identity" (1957:21). . . .

Perhaps the best illustration of this process in the research literature on organizations comes from Burton Clark's study of the "distinctive college" (1970, 1972). In discussing the strong ideologies of these institutions, Clark introduces the notion of an "organizational saga . . . a collective understanding of a unique accomplishment based on historical exploits. . . . Believers give loyalty to the organization and take pride and identity from it" (1972:178). The saga, "embellished through retelling and rewriting" links the organization's present with its past, and "turns a formal place into a beloved institution, to which participants may be passionately devoted" (p. 178).

Clark studied the organizational sagas of three "distinctive colleges"—highly regarded private, liberal arts colleges in the United States— Reed, Antioch, and Swarthmore. He distinguishes two stages in the development of the saga: initiation, which takes place during a short time, and fulfillment which is more enduring. At Reed, initiation took the form of an autonomous new organization wherein its first president, "a high-minded reformer," could escape what he believed to be the "corrupt" Eastern universities; at Reed, he felt he could build "an academically pure college, Balliol for America" (p. 180). At Antioch, "a crisis of decay" caught "the attention of the reformer looking for opportunity" (p. 180), opportunity to change a system of beliefs. And in the case of Swarthmore, it was simply ready for evolutionary change by another new charismatic leader. . . .

While the conditions of initiation seemed to vary in these three institutions, those of the second stage, fulfillment, appeared to be more consistent. As Clark describes it, the leader initiates the changes, but these emerge in an organizational saga only if, once he is gone, the important members of the organization become committed to them, and conserve and perpetuate them. . . .

The saga manifests itself in the form of various practices of the organization which stand out as unique, "that things had been done differently, and so much against the mainstream, and often against imposing odds. . . ." Supporting such practices are various symbols and rituals, "invested with meaning." These are recorded in written histories and current catalogs, "even in an 'air about the place' " (all above quotes from Clark 172:182). Finally, Clark notes that the organizational saga serves as a powerful force to integrate the goals of the individual with those of the institution:

> The most important characteristic and consequence of an organization saga is the capturing of allegiance, the committing of staff to the institution. Emotion is invested to the point where many participants significantly define themselves by the central theme of the organization. . . . Deep emotional investment binds participants as comrades in a cause. . . . An organizational saga turns an organization into a community, even a cult. (1970:235)

STAGE 3: THE REINFORCEMENT OF THE IDEOLOGY THROUGH IDENTIFICATIONS

Our description to this point makes it clear that an individual entering an organization does not join a random collection of individuals but rather a living system with its own distinct history and tradition—its own ideology, whether weak or strong. He may come with his own preformulated goals, but there is little doubt that the ideology

of the organization can weigh heavily on the behavior he will exhibit once inside of it. We say that the individual develops an *identification* with, or a *loyalty* to, the organization. This identification develops for a number of reasons—a natural attraction, the result of selection procedures, specific organizational attempts to evoke it, and the calculated cultivation of it by the individual.

Natural Identification

The simplest type of identification occurs when the new member gets attracted to the ideology of the organization he has joined—to use the vernacular, he gets "caught up" with it. . . .

In his book, *Administrative Behavior*, Herbert Simon discusses a pointed example of two very different forms of identification: "Two soldiers sit in a trench opposite a machine-gun nest. One of them stays under cover. The other, at the cost of his life, destroys the machine-gun nest with a grenade. Which is rational?" (1957:76). Obviously Simon's question is not meant to be answered. What can be said is that under the circumstances one individual opted for his personal goals while the other exhibited a strong identification with those of his organization. . . .

As Simon notes (p. 205), a member of an organization may also identify with its leader, or even with the organization itself as an entity distinct from its purpose. Simon suggests that this last form of identification leads to very different behavior than does identification with mission or goals. In one case, the individual will support "opportunistic changes" in mission to enable the organization to survive and grow; in the other, he will resist them and may even leave to express his discontent. . . .

Selected Identification: Recruitment and Promotion

Many organizations cannot rely solely on identification that develops naturally. Their needs for loyalty are too great. And so they must take steps to influence the process of identification. This is most obviously done in the selection process:

The organization chooses job candidates not only for their ability to do the work, but also for the match of their values with its ideology. As is so often heard, "Will he fit in here?" Recruiting becomes a device to reinforce identification with the organization's ideology.

But selection is a two-sided process, and just as the organization is careful to select the right candidates, so too are the candidates careful to select the right organization. They do not arrive at random, nor solely to negotiate material inducements for their contributions. "As Schallschneider has written, the members of the American League to Abolish Capital Punishment are not active in that group's work because they expect to be hanged" (Lindblom 1965:224). People often seek to join organizations because they already identify with the ideologies they perceive to exist there. Thus at Antioch College, Clark reports that "Public image . . . grew strong and sharp, directing liberals and radicals to the college and conservatives to other places" (1972:183).

The initial job interview often serves as the screening device for both parties; this is followed by an implicit or explicit trial period during which the graft of the new individual onto the existing organization is tested. Where it does not take, the individual is rejected (or leaves voluntarily), as is foreign tissue from the human body.

Those who stay may enter into a new phase of selection, that for positions in the hierarchy. When an organization's ideology is strong, it is those most committed to it who rise, because such organizations can afford to have only the most ideologically committed in positions of formal power. This applies increasingly as one climbs the heirarchy so that at the top, the chief executive tends to exhibit the strongest identification with the organization's ideology. The CEO is the person, as noted earlier, who "embodies" the ideology.

Evoked Identification: Socialization and Indoctrination

In many cases, natural and selected identification do not satisfy the organization's needs for loyalty. Also because the decisions to join and to leave an organization are, in Soelberg's words, "non-symmetrical"—that is, people "will be predisposed toward staying with whatever organizations they have chosen to work for" (1967:28)—they often stay despite an absence of natural or selected identification with the organization. The organization may, therefore, try to *evoke* the necessary identification, and at the same time to reduce outside identifications that might interfere with the employee's ability to serve it. In this regard, two processes can be relied upon, an explicit one called *indoctrination* and an implicit one called *socialization*.

The term *indoctrination* encompasses that set of formal techniques used by organization to develop identifications on the part of their members. Indoctrination can take extreme forms, as in the use of "brainwashing" by the Chinese forces during the Korean War to break the resistance of captured American pilots and get them to identify with Communist ideology. But most techniques of indoctrination are less extreme, if not always less subtle:

> Beatrice [Foods Corporation] tries to keep its managers fired up by what might be called "cheerleading." Each of the fourteen divisions holds a convention every year, and the company uses these occasions to pump enthusiasm and pride into its managers. At a recent dairy-division meeting in Nashville, 700 employees joined lustily in the chorus of a song led from the podium. "We're Number One," they sang, thrusting their fingers into the air . . . (Martin 1976:126).

Organizations in need of strong loyalty—for example, those whose members are sent off alone to distant, difficult assignments, as in certain religious orders, spy agencies, and police forces—put their new recruits through extensive courses where they learn not only skills and knowledge but also ideology. Many business firms also use programs of indoctrination: They, too, require loyalty, but their utilitarian nature often impedes its natural development. Few rely on "lusty" choruses of "We're Number One," but many publish internal magazines, stage retreats, distribute company ties, publicize their credos, hand out gold watches for long service. Large corporations make extensive use of job rotation, which some writers see as a means of uprooting local identifications in place of ones with the corporation. . . .

Socialization is an implicit, and therefore more subtle, means of evoking identification. As such, however, it may ultimately be more powerful. The individual is subjected to a host of informal pressures, all of which carry one message: "Conform to the ideology." Gradually the values of the organization "become 'internalized' and are incorporated into the psychology and attitudes of the individual participant. He acquires an attachment or loyalty to the organization that automatically—i.e., without the necessity for external stimuli—guarantees that his decisions will be consistent with the organization objectives"; in this way, he "acquires an 'organization personality' rather distinct from his personality as an individual" (Simon 1957:198). . . .

Calculated Identification

But what of the individual who runs the gauntlet of all these forms of identification and remains at the end firmly commited to his own goals? He has no natural identification with the organization, its mission, or its leadership; somehow he successfully passed all of the selection procedures; and he has been able to resist all of the pressures of indoctrination and socialization. He remains a private person, self-serving to the core. Must we assume that his personal interests put this person into opposition with the organization's established ideology? Not at all. This may be the very person who finds that his self-interest can best be served by an identification . . . with the organization's ideology. In other words, it may be in his very best interests to accept the organization's ideology. . . .

Every person interested in his own welfare has all kinds of obvious reasons to cooperate with the organization that employs him. He may simply get pleasure from his work and so wish to support the system that provides him with it; he may get psychological rewards from belonging to a social group; he may take pride in the success and reputation of the organization and the fact that his work contributes to those ends. [In addition he knows that he can get a variety of rewards—from harmonious working relationships and better pay to promotion—for cooperating with the rest of the organization.]. . . .

Calculated identification is clearly the weakest of the forms of loyalty, and differs from the others in that the identification is not really internalized by the individual. He identifies with the organization only because—and only so long as—it is in his best interests to do so. His identification, being calculated, is fragile. . . .

THE MISSIONARY ORGANIZATION

. . . While some degree of ideology can be found in virtually every organization, that degree can vary considerably. At one extreme are those organizations, such as religious orders or radical political movements, whose ideologies are very strong and whose identifications are primarily natural and selected. Edwards (1977) refers to organizations with strong ideologies as "stylistically rich," Selznick (1957) as "institutions." It is the presence of such an ideology that enables an organization to have "a life of its own," to emerge as "a living social institution" (Selznick 1949:10). At the other extreme are those organizations with relatively weak ideologies, "stylistically barren," in many cases business organizations with strongly utilitarian reward systems. History and tradition have no special value in these organizations. In the absence of natural forms of identification on the part of their members, these organizations sometimes try to rely on the process of indoctrination to integrate individual and organizational goals. But usually they have to fall back on calculated identifications and especially . . . formal controls. . . .

We can refer to "stylistically rich" organizations as *Missionaries*, because they are somewhat akin in their beliefs to the religious organizations by that name. Mission counts above all—to preserve it, extend it, or perfect it. As a result of their attachment to its mission, the members of the organization resist strongly any attempt to change it, to interfere with tradition. The mission and the rest of the ideology must be preserved at all costs.

As for their own rewards, these are primarily collective and psychic in nature, deriving from participation in a system that has its own accomplishments. And this allows members to work with a minimum of interference. Once selected, socialized, and indoctrinated as necessary, they are firmly wedded to the organization's ideology and so need not be closely supervised. To take a pointed example:

> St. Augustine once gave as the only rule for Christian conduct, "Love God and do what you like." The implication is, of course, that if you truly love God, then you will only ever want to do things which are acceptable to Him. Equally, Jesuit priests are not constantly being rung up, or sent memos, by the head office of the Society. The long, intensive training over many years in Rome is a guarantee that wherever they go afterwards, and however long it may be before they even see another Jesuit, they will be able to do their work in accordance with the standards of the Society. (Jay 1970:70)

The contrast between the conventional hierarchial organization and the missionary type comes out clearly in the following chart, which uses the classic Israeli kibbutz as its example:

Principles of Bureaucratic Organization	Principles of Kibbutz Organization
1. Permanency of office.	Impermanency of office.
2. The office carries with it impersonal, fixed privileges and duties.	The definition of office is flexible—privileges and duties are not formally fixed and often depend on the personality of the official.
3. A hierarchy of functional authorities	A basic assumption of the equal value of all
expressed in the authority of the officials.	functions without a formal hierarchy of authority.
4. Nomination of officials is based on formal objective qualifications.	Officials are elected, not nominated. Objective qualifications are not decisive, personal qualities are more important in election.
5. The office is a full-time occupation.	The office is usually supplementary to the full-time occupation of the official.

Source: From Rosner, 1969, p. 38.

In fact, this classic missionary form is difficult to maintain, as many of the Israeli kibbutzim have found out. On one side is the danger of isolation—of growing too inward, around an obsession with the mission. On the other side, is the danger of assimilation—of being too connected to the rest of the world, where hierarchy and calculated identification often count for more than unique beliefs and rich ideologies.

But there is another, perhaps more common form, and that is the conventional organization that nonetheless manages to maintain a good dose of missionary fervor. We can see this, for example, in business firms that have a special uniqueness and enthusiasm, reflected in a rich culture and a good deal of natural identification. The mission may sometimes seem ordinary—serving hamburgers, selling computers—but it is performed in a special way, perhaps because a charismatic leader in the past left the organization with a strong vision and set of beliefs that subsequently created a distinguished history.

Ouchi and Jaeger (1978) show how the influence of [national] culture can drive business firms toward the missionary [form]. In the table reproduced below, they contrast the typical large American corporation with its Japanese counterpart:

Type A (American)	Type J (Japanese)
Short-term employment	Lifetime employment
Individual decision-making	Consensual decision-making
Individual responsibility	Collective responsibility
Rapid evaluation and promotion	Slow evaluation and promotion
Explicit, formalized control	Implicit, informal control
Specialized career path	Nonspecialized career path
Segmented concern	Holistic concern

Source: From Ouchi and Jaeger 1978, p. 308.

Every characteristic of what these authors call the Type J firm is consistent with . . . the missionary. The personal relationship between the individual and the organization, the collective nature of responsibility and choice, the holistic concern instead of specialization, the discouragement of formal controls in favor of implicit (presumably normative) ones, all of these point to loyalty and a strong ideology as the central elements in the power [system]. Ouchi and Jaeger present one example in which [these two forms] meet head on, which highlights a fundamental difference between them:

> . . . during one of the author's visits to a Japanese bank in California, both the Japanese president and the American vice-presidents of the bank accused the other of being unable to formulate objectives. The Americans meant that the Japanese president could not or would not give them explicit, quantified targets to attain over the next three or six months, while the Japanese meant that the Americans could not see that once they understood the company's philosophy, they would be able to deduce for themselves the proper objective for any conceivable situation. (p. 309)

In a related empirical study, Ouchi and Johnson (1978) contrast a typical American corporation with one that resembles in certain of its characteristics the Japanese form (although it was American owned).[1] In the latter, they found many of the characteristics of the Missionary—greater loyalty, a strong collective orientation, less specialization, and a greater reliance on informal controls. Here, for example, ''a new manager will be useless for at least four or five years. It takes that long for most people to decide whether the new person really fits in, whether they can really trust him.'' This was in sharp contrast to the ''auction market'' atmosphere of the other firm: ''. . . it is almost as if you could open up the doors each day with 100 executives and engineers who had been randomly selected from the county, and the organization would work just as well as it does now'' (p. 302).

MANAGEMENT PRACTICES IN JAPAN AND THEIR IMPACT ON BUSINESS STRATEGY*

by Vladimir Pucik and Nina Hatvany

. . . THE ORGANIZATIONAL PARADIGM

. . . we propose that a basic organizational paradigm in large Japanese organizations is the *focus on human resources*. Our understanding of this paradigm follows Kuhn's (1970) definition of it as an amalgamation of shared rules and common intuitions. The focus on human resources in Japanese firms reflects an explicit preference for the

[1]   *They describe it as "an American version of the prototypical Japanese organization" (p. 293) and label it "Type Z," Ouchi (1981) subsequently wrote a widely marketed book called* Theory Z: How American Business Can Meet the Japanese Challenge.

*   Orginally published in *Advances in Strategic Management*, Vol. 1 (JAI Press, Inc., 1983), pp. 103–131. Copyright © 1983 by JAI Press, Inc. Reprinted with deletions by permission of JAI Press, Inc.

maximum utilization of available human assets as well as an implicit understanding of how an organization ought to be managed.

This paradigm translates into the three main interrelated strategic thrusts. First, an internal labor market is created to secure a labor force of the desired quality and to induce employees to remain with the firm (Pucik, 1979). Second, a company philosophy is articulated that expresses concern for employee needs and emphasizes cooperation and teamwork in a "unique" environment (Ouchi and Jaeger, 1978). Third, close attention is given both to hiring people who will fit well with the values of the particular company and to integrating employees into the company at all stages of their working life (Rohlen, 1974). These general strategies are expressed in specific management techniques. Open communication is encouraged, supported, and rewarded. Emphasis is placed on continuous development of employee skills; formal promotion is of secondary importance, at least during the initial career stages. Employees are evaluated on a multitude of criteria, often including group performance results, rather than on individual "bottom-line" contribution. The work is structured in such a way that it may be carried out by groups operating with a great deal of autonomy. Information about pending decisions is circulated to all before the decisions are actually made. Active, observable concern for each and every employee is expressed by supervisory personnel (e.g., Rohlen, 1974; Clark, 1979). (See Figure 1.) These strategies and techniques apply to both blue-collar and white-collar workers. . . .

STRATEGIES

A. The Organization as an Internal Labor Market

As a rule, large Japanese companies hire a male employee just after graduation from high school or university with the expectation of retaining him for the rest of his working life (Yoshino, 1968). The policy of lifetime employment is not extended to females, who are generally expected to leave the company and the job market once they are married. The temporary nature of the female work force, as well as the use of part-time workers, gives employers flexibility in ad-

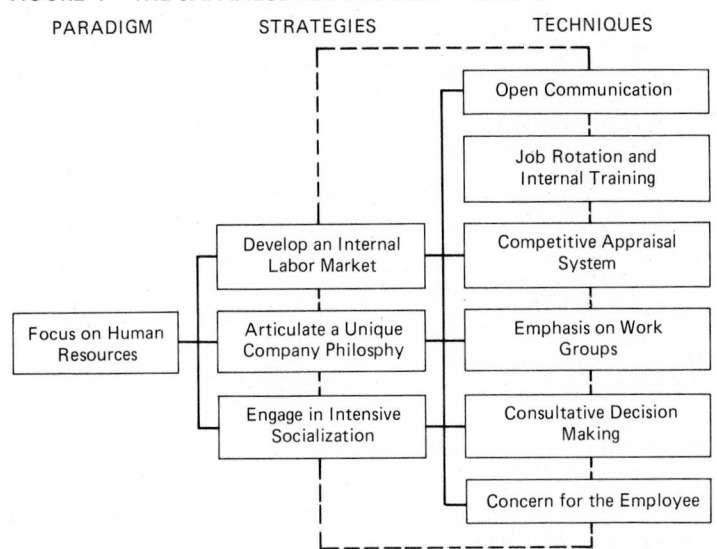

FIGURE 1   THE JAPANESE MANAGEMENT SYSTEM

justing the size of their work force to adapt to current economic conditions and still maintain employment for regular workers. The widespread use of subcontracting serves a similar purpose. Even during the recession in the mid-1970s, lay-offs and terminations of regular workers were exceptional (Rohlen, 1979).

Such a set of employment practices that price and allocate labor according to intraorganizational rules and procedures rather than according to external demand and supply conditions is described in the economic literature as an internal labor market (ILM) (Doeringer and Piore, 1971). ILMs often develop in response to a scarcity of specific skills on the open labor market, and this indeed occurred in Japan as rapid industrialization took place in the 1920s, with a limited pool of skilled workers available (Taira, 1970; Dore, 1973). Firms had to invest a great deal in training and naturally then attempted to discourage turnover by offering premium wages to senior workers. . . .

The maintenance of a stable ILM requires that sufficient training is provided within the firm so that the company does not have to hire outside to satisfy its need for qualified personnel. Yet, when skills are learned on the job, they are largely "company specific," the employee cannot realize their full value outside the firm, and inter-firm mobility is again discouraged (Becker, 1964).

The guarantee of job security implicit in an ILM is a marked departure from conventional American managerial assumptions about the need to retain flexibility in the size of the work force so as to respond effectively to cyclical variations in demand. It is also often thought that institutionalized labor security deprives the manager of the ultimate weapon with which to control subordinates' behavior—the threat of firing. However, other more subtle forms of control are still available in an ILM such as placement in a dead-end position or one of low centrality. Moreover, job security has advantages for the organization. One, for example, is the reduction of employee hostility to the introduction of labor-saving technology or to organizational changes (Vogel, 1979). Employees know that they may be transferred to new jobs but do not fear losing their jobs altogether. Another advantage, suggested by Hall (1976) and Salancik (1977), is that long tenure is positively associated with commitment to the organization. . . .

B. Articulated and Unique Company Philosophy

A philosophy that is both articulated and enacted may facilitate [the transformation of commitment to the organization into a productive effort] as it presents a clear picture of the organization's goals, norms, and values. Familiarity with the goals of an organization provides direction for individuals' actions, sets constraints on their behavior, and enhances their motivation (Scott, 1966). In fact, the strategy of disseminating an articulated company philosophy has been adopted by a number of American companies as well. As Peters (1978) points out, the biographies of many industrial leaders stress their quest to give operational force and meaning to their goals.

The personnel departments of large Japanese firms as well as many chief executives are actively engaged in promoting their company's philosophy of work and management (Rohlen, 1974). These philosophies frequently describe the firm as a family, unique and distinct from any other firm. This "family" is a social group into which one is carefully selected, but which, as in a real family, one is not supposed to leave, even if one becomes dissatisfied with this or that aspect of "family" life. The cultivation of a sense of "uniqueness" may provide an ideological justification of the limited possibilities for inter-firm mobility.

At the same time, the articulation of concepts, such as "the family" embedded in a company philosophy, may change over time in order to fit the shifting values of a broader social environment. For example, loyalty to the company, once heavily emphasized, has taken a second place to the stress on individual responsibility to fellow workers for doing one's best toward the common goal based on a common fate (e.g., Rohlen, 1974; Clark, 1979).

Among the norms of company life, *wa* (harmony), is still the single most popular component in company philosophies. The concept of *wa* expresses a "quality of relationship, particularly within working groups and it refers to the cooperation, trust, sharing, warmth, morale, and hard work of efficient, pleasant and purposeful fellowship. Teamwork comes to mind as a suitable approximation" (Rohlen, 1974:74). *Wa* is the watchword for developing the group consciousness of the employees and enhancing cooperation within the work group. The ideal is to integrate two objectives: pursuit of profits and perpetuation of the company as a primary social group. The employees are asked to devote substantial effort to the company's well-being, and in return the company is expected to avoid layoffs and to contribute generously to its employees' welfare. Without reasonable employment security, the fostering of team spirit and cooperation would be a nearly impossible task.

The understanding of shared meanings and beliefs expressed in the company philosophy binds the individual to the collectivity (Pfeffer, 1979b) and at the same time stimulates the emergence of goals that are shared within an organization. This goal congruence provides one of the principal defenses against opportunistic behavior on the part of those members who, endowed with special skills, might be inclined to bargain for special rewards (Ouchi, 1980). Accordingly, managing the myths and symbols that form the basis of a company philosophy may be regarded as an elegant informational device that provides a form of control at once all-pervasive and effective, as it presents a basic theory of how the firm should be managed that a manager can use for guidance in any situation.

C. Intensive Socialization

The benefits of an articulated company philosophy are lost, however, if not properly communicated to employees or if not visibly supported in management's behavior. Therefore, ensuring that em-ployees have understood the philosophy and have seen it in action is one of the primary functions of the company's socialization effort.

The development of cohesiveness within the firm, based on the acceptance of common goals and values, is a major focus of personnel policies in a Japanese firm throughout the whole working life of an employee. In the initial screening process, young graduates are not favored solely because of their acceptance of low salaries or because of structural features of the internal labor market in the firm. "Virgin work forces are preferred for the reason that they can be readily assimilated into each company's unique environment as a community" (Hazama, 1978:148). The basic criteria for hiring are moderate views and a harmonious personality. Ability on the job is obviously also a requirement, but at the same time applicants may be eliminated during the selection process if they arouse suspicion that they cannot get along with people, possess radical views, or come from an unfavorable home environment (Rohlen, 1974). It is only natural that, when employees are expected to remain in the firm for most of their working lives, even top executives become intimately involved in the interviewing and assessment of new hires. To encourage recruitment into the company, employees' referrals are often actively solicited.

The socialization process begins with the initial training program, which is geared toward familiarizing new employees with the company, sometimes for as long as six months. During the course of the program the recruits learn about the business philosophy of the company and experience work on the factory floor as well as in the sales offices, disregarding their final vocational specialization. They are expected to assume the identity of a "company man," and in such a case their specialization becomes of secondary importance. Both careful screening and introductory training are designed to develop the homogeneity of the people in the firm.

In addition to this initial socialization, a "resocialization" (Katz, 1980) takes place each time the employee enters a new position, as he has to familiarize himself with a new set of people and tasks. Employees are transferred for two main reasons. First, they are assigned to new positions to learn additional skills in on-the-job training programs. Second, transfers are part of a long-range experience-building program, through which the organization grooms its future managers, which usually takes the form of periodic, lateral, interdepartmental transfers (Yoshino, 1968). While employees rotate semilaterally from job to job, they become increasingly socialized into the organization, immersed in the company's philosophy and culture, as well as bound to a set of shared goals. It should be noted that such transfers are the prerogative of management, and unions are usually not involved. . . .

TECHNIQUES

The basic management orientation and strategies are closely interrelated with [the following] management techniques used in Japanese firms. . . .

A. Open Communication

If we had to stress one technique . . . it would be management's commitment to developing a climate of trust in the corporation, through sharing information across departmental boundaries. The emphasis on team spirit embodied in corporate philosophies and the network of contacts that employees develop during their long socialization in the organization encourage the extensive face-to-face communication reported in several studies involving Japanese companies (e.g., Pascale, 1978). Frequent and open communication is also an inherent part of the Japanese work setting. Work spaces are crowded with individuals at different levels of the hierarchy. Subordinates can do little that the supervisor is not aware of and vice versa. Even high-ranking office managers seldom have separate private offices. Partitions, cubicles, and small side rooms are used to set off special areas for conferences with visitors or for small discussions within the staff. In factory situations, the foreman is constantly on the floor discussing problems, helping with pieces of work,

talking to outsiders, and instructing the inexperienced. Even senior plant managers spend as much time as possible on the shop floor.

Open communication is not limited to vertical exchanges. Periodic job rotation is instrumental in building extensive informal lateral communication networks across departmental boundaries. . . .

Extensive communication is also an important component of the total control system. It supports a high degree of information-processing capability within the organization, which permits the firm to take on tasks of great complexity without resorting to complicated and inflexible formal rules and structure (Thompson, 1967). . . .

B. Job Rotation, Slow Promotion, and Internal Training

Under conditions of lifetime employment the hierarchical structure of organizations makes vacancies in higher positions emerge sequentially as each cohort moves a step closer toward retirement. Promotion is thus unlikely to be rapid unless an organization is expanding dramatically. This limited upward mobility is another element that encourages lateral job rotation in Japanese organizations. Although formal promotion is slow, early informal identification of the "elite" is not unusual (Rohlen, 1974), and carefully planned lateral job transfers thereafter may add substantial flexibility to job reward and recognition (Ono, 1976). Not all jobs at the same hierarchical level are equal in their centrality or importance to the organization's activity (Schein, 1971). By assigning individuals to jobs that are at the same level but vary in their centrality, the organization can de facto discriminate in terms of both promotion and demotion among individuals who, within the formal system, share the same status, salary, and privileges (Rohlen, 1974). This informal recognition system has the effect of providing or withholding opportunities to learn skills required for future formal promotions. . . .

Furthermore, as indicated earlier, job rotation facilitates the development of informal communication networks which help in coordinating the flow of work across functional areas and in the speedy resolution of problems (Tushman, 1977; Roberts and O'Reilly, 1979). Finally, job rotation "unfreezes" an individual from being unresponsive to the demands of his job (Katz, 1980). . . .

An additional feature adding flexibility to the promotion system is the emergence of a dual promotion system in many Japanese companies (Haitani, 1978). Promotion in "status" is based on the results of past evaluations and seniority within the firm; promotion in "position" is based on evaluation results and the availability of vacancies in the level above. Therefore, even if immediate upper-level positions are blocked by a cohort of seniors, promotion in status will provide an employee with more respect and money. Delegation of authority is also frequent, so a position of responsibility can be assigned to an outstanding employee who does not fulfill the seniority requirements for promotion in status (Tsurumi, 1977). . . .

Besides its relevance for promotion, job rotation is also facilitated by the inhouse training typical of an internal labor market. This training is usually on the job, which is in most cases highly economical; it does not require great administrative expense, and the employee learns skills that are largely relevant only to the production process (Williamson, 1975). The exception is, of course, when the skills are not available in the firm to begin with. Then, learning on the job becomes more of a "trial-and-error" effort which at times might be rather costly to the organization.

The emphasis on job rotation creates an environment in which an employee becomes a "generalist," rather than a "specialist" in any functional area. These general skills are, however, for the most part, still unique to the firm (Hazama, 1978). And yet, the specificity of a particular skill is not limited to its task content. It also includes the familiarity with an appropriate "information map" that indicates where to obtain necessary job-related information, how to process it, and to whom it should be forwarded. Job manu-

als in Japanese companies are seldom well developed (Tsurumi, 1977), and many jobs cannot be performed by a relative newcomer who lacks the knowledge of the relevant information exchange norms (Pucik, 1979).

C. Competitive Appraisal System

Employee evaluations in Japanese firms are usually conducted on an annual or semiannual basis. The evaluation criteria include not only "bottom-line" individual performance measures but also various desirable personality traits and behaviors, such as creativity, emotional maturity, and cooperation with others. Team "bottom-line" performance results are, however, often assessed (Hazama, 1978). Especially for white-collar workers, personality and behavior, rather than output, are the key criteria (Ouchi and Jaeger, 1978), yet the difference is often merely symbolic. Output measures may be easily "translated" into attributes such as leadership skills, technical competence, relations with others, and judgment. In this way, the employee is not made to feel that the "bottom-line," which may sometimes be beyond his control, is the key dimension of evaluation. Occasional mistakes, particularly for lower-level employees, are considered part of the learning process (Tsurumi, 1977).

At the same time, evaluations do clearly discriminate among employees, as each employee is compared to other members of an appropriate group (in age and status); and the competition is keen. Year after year, all managers at a given level are ranked according to their performance and future potential. This is done by the personnel department based on raw scores submitted by line superiors. For each manager, the scores from at least two superiors are required to assure objectivity, but the scores seldom differ substantially to begin with.

A future- rather than a past-oriented evaluation system serves, however, as a powerful check in divisive competitiveness. What is rewarded is the credibility and ability to get things done in cooperation with others. Thus, the focal point of competition is building cooperative networks with the same people who are rivals for future promotions (Pucik, 1981a). . . .

As group performance is also a focus of evaluation, peer pressure on an individual to contribute sufficiently to the group performance becomes an important mechanism of performance control. Long tenure, friendship ties, and informal communication ntworks enable both superiors and peers to have a very clear sense of the employee's performance and potential relative to others. Moreover, basing evaluation and rewards on work group performance, such that all group members share the consequences of their efforts, tends to increase productivity as well as the level of mutual aid and tutoring (Wodarski et al., 1973).

D. The Emphasis on Work Groups

Not only evaluation but many other company policies revolve around groups. Tasks are assigned to groups rather than individuals (Rohlen, 1974). Group cohesion is stimulated by the delegation of responsibility to work groups as well as by other job design features such as job rotation and group-based performance feedback. Acknowledging the enormous impact of groups, both directly by the enforcement of norms and indirectly by affecting the beliefs and values of the members (Hackman, 1976), the organization devotes far more attention to structural factors that enhance group motivation and cooperation than to the motivation of individuals.

Work-group autonomy is enhanced by not using experts to solve operational problems for specific groups. This would be regarded as outside interference, and the result would be to undermine morale and leadership (Rohlen, 1974). One widely used group-based technique is Quality Control (QC) circles (Cole, 1979). A QC circle has as its major function the uncovering and solving of a particular workshop's problem. However, fostering motivation by direct participation in the design of the work process is also a major consideration in the introduction of QC circles and similar activities to the factory floor. In principle, participation is voluntary, but in practice refusal to participate is unusual. The team operates autonomously, with an emphasis on self-improvement activities that will help the achievement of group goals. . . .

E. Consultative Decision Making

The extensive face-to-face communication observed in Japanese companies is often confused with participative decision making. However, data from Pascale's (1978) study indicate that the extent of face-to-face communication bears no relationship to employees' perceptions of their level of participation in decision making. The usual procedure is that a formal proposal will be initiated by a middle manager, but often under the directive of top management (Hattori, 1977). Some observers of the Japanese decision-making process argue, contrary to the popular belief expressed in numerous papers (e.g., Yoshino, 1968; Drucker, 1975), that this process is not "bottom-up" but rather a top-down or interactive consultative process, especially when long-term planning and strategy are concerned (Kono, 1980).

The middle manager will usually engage in informal discussion and consultation about the decisions with his subordinates, peers, and supervisors. When all are familiar with the proposal, a request for a decision is made formally at an appropriate level, and because of the earlier discussions it is almost inevitably ratified, often in a ceremonial group meeting or through the *ringi* procedure. All this does not imply unanimous approval of the proposed decision, but it does imply consent to its implementation.

This kind of decision making is not "participative" in the Western sense of the word, which includes ideas of negotiations and bargaining between a manager and his subordinates. In the Japanese context the negotiations are primarily lateral, between the departments concerned with the decision. Within the work group, the emphasis is on inclusion of all group members in the process of decision making rather than on a consensus about the alternatives. However, the manager will usually not state his position "until others who will be affected have had sufficient time to offer their views, feel that they have been fairly heard, and are willing to support the decision even though they may not feel that it is the best one'' (Rohlen, 1974:308).

Those outside the core of the decision-making group merely express their acknowledgment of the proposed course of action. They do not participate; they do not feel ownership of the decision. On the other hand, early communication of the proposed changes helps to reduce uncertainty in the organization (Thompson, 1967). In addition, prior information on upcoming decisions provides employees with an opportunity to rationalize and accept the outcomes (Janis and Mann, 1977). . . .

A frequently mentioned consequence of decision making in Japan is the avoidance of identifying responsibility for eventual mistakes (Yoshino, 1968; Tsuji, 1968). However, Clark (1979) calls this ''misleading,'' citing the large number of Japanese firms managed by a strong and powerful chief executive. It follows from this fact that the avoidance of individual responsibility is far from being an inherent psychological trait of Japanese people, as is often claimed (e.g., Yoshino, 1968). . . .

F. Concern for the Employee

Informal communication not only facilitates decision making but it also forms a channel to express management concern for the well-being of employees. Managers invest a great deal of time in talking to employees about everyday matters (Cole, 1971), and the quality of their relationships with subordinates is also an important part of their evaluation. They thus develop a feeling for their employees' personal needs and problems, as well as their performance. Obviously this intimate knowledge of each employee is facilitated by the employees' long tenure, but managers do consciously and explicitly attempt to get to know their employees and place a premium on having time to talk.

Deepening the company's involvement with employees' lives is the sponsoring of various cultural, athletic, and other recreational activities. There is usually a heavy schedule of company social affairs. These activities are ostensibly voluntary, but virtually all members participate. Rohlen (1974) describes an annual calendar of office events: it typically includes two overnight trips, monthly Saturday afternoon recreation, and an average of six office parties, all at company expense. At these events a great deal of drinking goes on and much good fellowship is expressed. Discussion in an informal atmosphere is also characteristic of evening social activities of the work team which are often subsidized by the manager's budget.

Finally, the company allocates substantial financial resources to pay for benefits that are given all employees such as a family allowance and commuting and other job-related allowances. Furthermore, there are various welfare systems that ''penetrate every crack of workers' lives'' (Hazama, 1978:43). These range from company housing, dormitories, and housing loans through company nurseries and company scholarships for employees' children, to credit extension, savings, and insurance. Thus, employees perceive their own welfare and the financial welfare of their company as being identical (Tsurumi, 1977). . . .

The reciprocal relationship between the employee and the organization is especially crucial. The system that we have described is based on the understanding that, in return for the employee's contribution toward the company's growth and well-being, the profitable firm will provide him with a stable and secure work environment and protect his welfare even during a period of economic slowdown. However, there is nothing uniquely Japanese in this exchange. On the contrary, the following observation about employees' behavior in Japanese firms may well be made in any American organization: ''The behavior for the company which may appear to others as self-sacrificing is not a sacrificing for the benefits of others at all, it is for the benefit of his own self '' (Hazama, 1978:115).

DISCUSSION

We have proposed an alternative model of the Japanese management system that fully rests on elements and relationships observable in other cultures. Our position is empirically supported by several recent studies that indicate the existence of similar operational patterns in Western companies (e.g., Tsurumi, 1977; Ouchi and Jaeger, 1978; Ouchi, 1981; Pascale and Athos, 1981), as well as by the relative ease with which the "imported" management techniques are introduced in Japanese subsidiaries abroad (Johnson and Ouchi, 1974; Takamiya, 1981). Several of the companies in the former category are among the largest of American corporations, with records of innovation, growth, and high employee morale.

There are indeed many cultural differences between people in Japan and Western countries. However, this should not distract our attention from the fact that people in any country also have a lot in common. In the workplace, they value decent treatment, security, and an opportunity for emotional fulfillment. It goes to the credit of Japanese managers that they have developed organizational systems which, even though far from perfect, respond to these needs to a great extent.

The strategies and techniques we have reviewed constitute a remarkably well-integrated system. The management practices are highly congruent with the way tasks are structured, with the goals of individual members, and with the climate of the organization. Such a "fit" is expected to result in a high degree of organizational effectiveness or productivity (Nadler and Lawler, 1977). . . .

There are, however, [certain] contingencies that may limit the applicability of [these] techniques. As we have indicated, the practices described and the resulting efficiency can be observed primarily in large Japanese manufacturing corporations. In the service industries, even among large firms as well as in parts of the public sector, the effectiveness of the system is markedly lower. This brings up an important question, namely, to what extent is the system's effectiveness facilitated by such factors as the dominant technology of the firm or patterns of control and ownership?

The system also implicitly assumes the near equality of rights between the employees, man-

agement, and owners. The institutional arrangements in some countries may in fact operate against such equality. Moreover, general economic conditions are also obviously an important additional intervening variable. During recessions the system's stability in many Japanese firms relies to some degree on a reduction in a "buffer" labor force, be it women, reemployed retirees, or subcontractors. This pattern may be difficult to replicate in other countries, but, as the evidence shows, that does not preclude the emergence of the ILM structure (Doeringer and Piore, 1971). In addition, less overtime, hiring freezes, reduced bonuses, and temporary transfers are other effective and often used measures protecting basic job security while keeping labor costs flexible (Rohlen, 1979).

We have also pointed out several areas where the implementation of some of the techniques may invite unwanted consequences. The most critical are probably the quality of evaluations, the speed of decision making, the rigidity of promotion, and the effectiveness of on-the-job training programs. . . .

IMPLICATIONS FOR BUSINESS STRATEGY

So far we have focused primarily on the relationship between Japanese human resource management practices and employee commitment and productivity. However, several important organizational characteristics directly tied to the area of business strategy are also heavily influenced by the management style described in detail above. Therefore, an assessment of how Japanese management practices influence strategy formulation and implementation would provide a fitting conclusion to our discussion.

A. Competitive Spirit

First of all, the long-term socialization of employees in combination with the articulated "distinct" company philosophy is conducive to the development of organizational culture emphasizing competition. The world outside of the firm is perceived in terms of foes and friends, markets to be captured or defended. The purpose of the organization is to survive as a group, a task possible only through besting its current and potential rivals, both in Japan and overseas.

Japanese managers are brought up in an atmosphere of a competitive rivalry that gradually permeates every action and decision they make. The activities of the firm are continuously scrutinized with respect to its impact on its major competitors (Ohmae, 1982). Intensive defensive and offensive scouting is built into all external operations, and gathered intelligence is distributed widely throughout the organization, accompanied by summaries pointing out its consequences for future market battles (Tsurumi, 1977).

Contrary to the popular image of "Japan, Inc." where the government and the private industry support each other in an oligopolistic collusion, competition in Japan is very keen. Often the foreign market strategies of Japanese firms are products of the competitive circumstances at home. For example, the heavy emphasis on export by relative newcomers in their respective fields, such as Sony on consumer electronics and Honda in automobiles, was to a large degree made imperative by the difficulties encountered in competition with the established domestic producers. At the same time, the ignorance of the competitive nature of the Japanese market so far has prevented most foreign firms from recognizing conflicting interests among their Japanese counterparts and building successful alliances for the penetration of markets in Japan.

B. Long-Term Perspective

It is not, as often thought, superior planning that enables the Japanese to execute consistent business strategies. Rather, it is the absence of short-term incentives that may otherwise distract managers from pursuing long-term corporate objectives. Although bonuses are usually tied to current performance, the fact that one cannot escape the consequences of one's decisions, as most employees are expected to remain in the organization for most of their working lives, tends to minimize the danger of taking advantage of the current circumstances at the expense of future goals.

In addition, the reliance on future company well-being to provide for individual welfare, coupled with the future-oriented appraisal system, makes it easier to incorporate long-term strategic objectives into the management of everyday operations, with a minimum of formality and complexity. There is no need for "sophisticated" reporting systems which attempt to use complex formulas to direct executives and managers in a proper direction. In this respect, "perseverance" and "commitment" are equal to "harmony" and "team spirit" in the arsenal of desired, and rewarded, corporate values.

The impact of a long-term strategic perspective is clearly visible in the way the Japanese on the one hand, and many Western firms on the other, view joint ventures and other kinds of technological and marketing tie-ups. Japanese perceive such relationships as a temporary arrangement to rectify some of their competitive weakness, and that should, in the long run, lead to their dominance in the partnership; the foreign firms are generally content with short-term gains from such endeavors, without considering the long-term competitive consequences. This perceptual difference does not mean that a long-term mutually advantageous relationship with Japanese partners is impossible. It can be done, but only so long as long-term competitive parity is maintained.

C. Emphasis on Market Share

It has been asserted that Japanese firms' desire to maintain stable employment, combined with a heavy dependence on debt financing, increases the "real" fixed costs of production. It follows that in times of business retrenchment it is more advantageous to slash prices and keep output high than to follow the strategy typical of Western firms and attempt to protect margins by trimming output and consequently employment.

However, it was pointed out recently that the high debt/equity ratio in Japan, relative to other industrialized countries, is more a reflection of different accounting practices and definitions, and if market values of debt and equities are used for calculations the difference is much smaller than commonly thought (Kuroda and Oritani, 1980). In the same manner there is evidence to demonstrate that in recessions, while employment holds steady in Japan, actual labor costs show more flexibility than those in the United States (Shimada, 1980). It seems, therefore, that the rationale for the market share orientation of Japanese business strategies must be sought elsewhere.

In this respect a market share orientation fits well into the system of Japanese management practices, as it provides an objective measure of competitive standing, independent of current investment and research-and-development (R&D) strategies, or changes in depreciation and tax rules, clear and understandable to anyone in the organization. At the same time, it has been shown that market share over the long run is a good predictor of corporate performance expressed in more traditional financial terms (Buzzell, Gale, and Sultan, 1975).

For most Japanese firms, driven by their competitive orientation, market share is ultimately a worldwide concept. To retreat from a market territory or product segment under challenge from a Japanese competitor will therefore do nothing more than buy time before the remaining markets also fall under siege. Just as self-defeating is attempting to piggyback onto Japanese manufacturing prowess and use them as OEM (original equipment manufacturer) suppliers for domestically well-established brands. Sooner or later they will go independent, with only crumbs left for their former partner. Again, maintaining competitive parity is the only way to ensure fruitful long-term cooperation.

D. Internal Growth

The value system of Japanese managers and executives places a premium on maintaining the corporation as a semipermanent group of individuals tied together with lasting bonds. For that reason,

divestitures, mergers, and acquisitions, especially affecting unrelated firms, are unusual in Japan, and hostile takeovers are for all practical purposes next to impossible (Clark, 1979).

This might be detrimental to the efficiency of resource allocation in the economy to some degree, but once it is clearly established that the only way to grow is from internal competitive strength, the strategic implications are clear: there is no shortcut, no other way, than concentrating on making a product which fits customers' needs and is cheaper and of better quality than the competitors'.

Under such conditions it is natural that production becomes a major strategic concern, resulting in an emphasis on continuous product and process innovation, on upgrading quality, and on lowering costs (Wheelwright, 1981). The production area is viewed as a key to corporate survival in the long run and is staffed by high-quality managers with good chances of advancing eventually to top executive positions.

Usually top management is also closely involved with production, and their staff are free from spending their time planning takeover strategies or putting together defenses against them. Given the limits on executive time, a constrast with the Japanese suggests that the acquisition route to growth may suffer from rather substantial opportunity costs.

In addition the focus on internal growth permits the organization to pursue strategic changes incrementally, so they can be more easily absorbed by the organization. The ''logical incrementalism'' advocated by Quinn (1980) is a concept familiar in practice to managers in many Japanese firms. Moreover, internal growth allows the organization to satisfy the career aspirations of many employees by opening additional vacancies in new areas of business to be staffed from within.

E. Aggressive Innovation

It was pointed out earlier that the nature of the competitive appraisal system in Japanese firms and the rapid reception and dissemination of new ideas possible in an "organic" firm should encourage innovation. This notion is contrary to the stereotypical image of the Japanese as poor innovators constrained in the exploration of new frontiers by a group desire to maintain consensus and harmony (Lohr, 1982). In this respect the evidence is clear: Japanese do innovate, and probably as fast, if not faster, than most businesses in other countries (Moritani, 1981).

One reason for the discrepancy between the stereotype and the reality is the misunderstanding of innovation processes in the organization. It is not only the bright idea that counts, it is also the process of bringing the product based on the new idea to market. In terms of winning the competitive game, the origin of the idea is often secondary. After all, computers, jet engines, or scanners were not invented in the United States. It is in the implementation process that the Japanese have an advantage with their carefully built worldwide monitoring systems on the outside, and high level of interface, coordination, and teamwork on the inside, which involve all those concerned with development, design, and manufacturing.

Second, it is widely believed that a lack of venture capital in Japan limits incentives for innovation, as it is very difficult for research-and-development (R&D) personnel to quit their employers and strike out on their own, a pattern common in the United States (*Business Week*, December 14, 1981). However, a closer look at the problem reveals this also to be to the advantage of the Japanese.

With their stable research teams shielded from the temptation of windfall profits as independent entrepreneurs, Japanese companies are well poised to capitalize quickly on newly acquired knowledge. Rather than working in the secrecy of the family garage, the Japanese engineer is working on a new invention in the corporate laboratory, in regular communication with those responsible for its future commercial adaptation. Then, once an innovative idea is proven to be potentially promising, the organization can move on very quickly to the adoption phase, as everyone

concerned is already familiar with the new product's characteristics.

The close cooperation and communication between the research engineers on the one side, and production and market personnel on the other, built into the Japanese management system, greatly facilitates the commercialization of new innovations and assures the integration of research and development with other critical corporate functions. A steady feedback of market information to the research personnel makes it more likely that research and development result in products that will meet market needs. Participation of production engineers in the development process increases the likelihood that the newly designed product can be built efficiently with available production technologies or that new technologies will be available shortly. Thus, rather than remaining an exclusive domain of R&D professionals, the innovation process is diffused widely throughout the organization, enlarging the strategic alternatives available to the firm, especially in the high-technology area.

VII. CONCLUSIONS

In many countries it is possible to observe firms as committed as the Japanese to growth through a superior product and process innovation. Well-run U.S. firms use management practices to a large degree similar to those we have pointed out as typical for the Japanese. What make the Japanese special, but by no means unique, is their concentrated effort to develop systemic solutions to managerial problems, to match cultural, organizational, and strategic imperatives in an integrated management system.

During the 1980s the Japanese will be facing new challenges. Their economic growth is sluggish, compared to the past, unemployment levels are creeping up, while savings rates critical to new investment are falling. Rising protectionism abroad will make it difficult to continue stimulating the economy by exports. The changing age structure of the labor force may result in an explosion of welfare expenditures in the near future, further straining the deficit-ridden public finance (Drucker, 1982).

However, in our opinion, the built-in competitive drive on the corporate level will strengthen Japan's ability to tackle these problems. Some setbacks might occur, but, by and large, the Japanese will remain the principal challengers of any Western firm serious about world markets. There is no shortcut other than to meet this challenge. No concession bargaining, marketing gimmicks, or shuffling of assets through acquisitions will do more than provide a bit of breathing space. In the long run the only feasible response is to do better what the Japanese are doing well already—developing management systems that motivate employees from the top to the bottom to pursue growth-oriented, innovation-focused competitive strategies.

ARCOP

Many people live without changing their circumstances. We try different things. That is our strength. Once we get institutionalized, organized, paragraphed, that's when we are dead. The most important considerations for us are the preservation of our spirit . . . and the preservation of our quality.

This was the manner in which Fred Lebensold, one of the partners of ARCOP, described the firm that had surged to prominence in Canadian architecture during the 1960s. ARCOP ("Architects in Co-Partnership") had won several competitions for significant public buildings across Canada and received awards for many of the buildings that it had completed. Yet, there were underlying concerns about the ability of ARCOP to maintain the success that it had attained. Some of the partners wondered about the dramatic manner in which the volume of work seemed to grow and decline (see Exhibit 2) and about the strength and continuity of their partnership.

EVOLUTION OF THE PARTNERSHIP

The origins of ARCOP can be traced back to a group of aspiring young architects: Ray Affleck, Guy Desbarats, Hasen Size and Jean Michaud. The four of them had met each other through the architecture department at McGill University, where they had been teaching on a part-time basis. They first began to pool resources in 1953 with the intention of working independently on their own jobs. They started off sharing an office in the basement of a building in suburban Montreal. They also jointly employed a secretary and a draftsperson to assist them with their work.

At the outset, each partner obtained and conducted his own work, mostly in the form of small jobs. However, two larger jobs created the possibility of sharing work between them. Ray and Jean worked together on a post office building in a suburb of Montreal. Concurrently, Guy and Hasen jointly undertook the work on a service facility in centrally located Mont Royal Park, overlooking downtown Montreal. These joint efforts resulted in buildings that quickly gained recognition for excellence in architecture. The completed post office subsequently became the first public building to receive a prestigious Canadian award for architecture.

These jobs also led these four individual architects to think about the possibility of all collaborating closely on a challenging job. In the meantime, they had come to know Fred Lebensold who was similarly teaching at McGill University and through him, Dimi Dimakopoulos who had been developing some preliminary drawings for a theatre as part of his student course work. The six of them joined forces to prepare a submission for a national competition for a theatre complex in Vancouver. The group described their joint entry into the competition: "We tried to capture the timeless quality of civic building at the same time creating the delight, contrast and visual excitement that is part of the experience of going to the theatre."[1]

The resulting design was awarded first place in the competition from over sixty submissions, some of which came from other larger firms that had already established themselves in Canada. However, the award confronted the group with the need to create an organization that could be contracted to carry out the job on the buildings

Case copyright © 1986 Jamal Shamsie, McGill University. Material is partly adapted from H. Mintzberg, Suzane Otis, Jamal Shamsie, and James Waters, "Strategy of Design: A Study of 'Architects in Co-partnership'", in J. Grant, ed., *Strategic Management Frontiers* (JAI Press, 1987).

to be known as the Queen Elizabeth and the Play-house Theatres. As Fred noted: "We suddenly realized that it wasn't just a competition . . . it was a real job. We had never done a job of that size before . . . never."

Consequently, all of the six individuals formed a partnership that would be responsible for this single large job. The group also moved to larger premises and began hiring several architects and draftsmen to assist them in their work on the theatres.

Shortly afterwards, the developing organization received some visitors from I.M. Pei and Associates, a large U.S. architectural firm that was looking for help with the work on a major commercial complex that they had been designing for Montreal. Dimi recollected their meeting: "They came to see us in our building . . . We had quickly fixed the office up, put pictures on the walls, tried to look proper . . . While we were sitting around the conference table, I.M. Pei leaned back and one of the pictures we had stuck on the wall fell off and landed on his head . . . There was a grim silence for a moment or two, then we all burst out laughing spontaneously . . . It seemed to clinch the job."

The buildings, later called Place Ville Marie, consisted of a 50 story central tower surrounded by smaller office blocks that were all linked to each other by a shopping concourse at the lower levels. The project was centrally located in Montreal and became a driving force in the revitalization of the downtown core.

By 1958, the partners moved to a large office in downtown Montreal and decided to expand their partnership agreement to cover all their jobs. At this point, some questions were raised about the inclusion of Jean. Jean had been useful in bringing in some of the early work through his contacts, but he tended to be less active in the actual work. Guy commented: "We never saw him . . . He would be away for months on end. But he was collecting full salary as a partner. We were all getting so busy we couldn't tolerate a partner that wasn't delivering anything." As a result, the partnership was reduced to five full fledged architects by 1960.

A DYNAMIC PARTNERSHIP

All of the partners that constituted ARCOP shared a common enthusiasm for the modern movement in architecture which had only taken root in Canada in the 1950s. Each of them aspired to design buildings that would be unique and exciting. In an early promotional brochure, the partners expressed the objective of their firm as follows: "above all, to develop the utmost social and artistic values that represent the highest contribution of architecture to our civilization."

Their strong convictions led these budding architects to place a particularly strong emphasis on commitment to design excellence. Furthermore, all of the partners firmly believed that they could generate better designs through a collaborative problem solving approach to architecture as originally developed by Walter Gropius at the Bauhaus during the 1920s. An article in a leading U.S. architectural journal described them as follows:

> As their names suggest, the partners are of varied cultural backgrounds and share five languages among them. The firm's cosmopolitanism, and its juxtaposition of Turks, young and not so young, may account for the special quality of its work, which is marked by avoidance of fashionable cliches and scorn for the creation of monuments to individual self-expression—in favor of an emphasis upon inventive control of materials and construction processes, and fine detailing.[2]

The firm adopted the name ARCOP which stood for "Architects in Co-Partnership." It emphasized the values of equality and collaboration in the partnership. This ran contrary to most established architectural firms where the names of the partners identified the firm and the order of listing of the names represented the hierarchy of the status of the different partners. Furthermore, the partners decided that all of the work that they carried out would be attributed to their firm as a whole.

To their dismay, the partners discovered

that the provincial laws governing professional practice required listing the names of the partners. Consequently, it was decided to place the names in alphabetical order to denote lack of hierarchy. Nevertheless, there were serious concerns about the possibility that the alphabetical order would not be recognized, leading clients to believe that those listed first represented the senior partners.

Acquisition of Work

The real impetus for ARCOP's growth came from the many different architectural competitions that were being organized all across Canada during these early years to support the development of domestic talent. Starting in 1958, the firm entered six competitions and won four of them.

The success of ARCOP in these competitions resulted in significant work on public buildings all across Canada. Some of these developed directly out of winning the competitions, while others came to the firm on the basis of the reputation that it was acquiring.

In particular, the firm was able to build up a string of jobs on civic complexes (see Exhibit 1). An early commission that came right on the heels of the job on the Queen Elizabeth Theatre was for a major concert hall as the first phase of a Place des Arts complex in Montreal.

Another major job resulted from a national competition for a complex of buildings that would commemorate the confederation of Canada. This complex was to be called the Confederation Centre and was located in Charlottetown on Prince Edward Island, off the eastern coast of Canada. It included a theatre, a museum and a library and was to have as its focal point the 1847 building which was the meeting place for the representatives who met to confederate the Canadian provinces.

Finally, ARCOP was asked to submit a design for the National Arts Centre in Ottawa. This led to a commission for the work on this prestigious building that was to consist of an opera house, a regular and an experimental theatre by the side of the Rideau Canal in the capital city of Canada.

In commenting on this type of work, an architectural critic wrote about the competition for the Confederation building:

> In the design of the . . . Confederation Memorial building, the architect has an opportunity, rare in any generation, of designing a building for centuries. The competitor is wasting his time who thinks of this building as anything but a national shrine to which Canadians will forever pay homage as the birthplace of their nation.[3]

Besides this type of work on public buildings, ARCOP was also building recognition in multi-use commercial complexes through its involvement in Place Ville Marie. The firm's best known job resulted from a subsequent collaboration with some developers. Ray recalled the events that led up to the job: "I remember seeing an advertisement asking developers to submit proposals for this property on Lagauchetiere and University Streets. I looked at it . . . we're not developers of course. A day or two later one of the developers who was involved with Place Ville Marie . . . asked if we would work with them in making a proposal. I was so busy with other things . . . somehow the whole idea didn't appeal to me tremendously . . . I don't know why, because it turned out to be one of the most fascinating jobs I have ever done. I must say they had an extremely imaginative proposal for building on that site. We put it together . . . our design and their concept . . . submitted it . . . and there was no contest."

This building, Place Bonaventure, was primarily a merchandise mart, the first of its kind in Canada. But it also contained a retail shopping concourse, an exhibition hall and a 400 room roof garden courtyard hotel. It generated the following comments:

> Place Bonaventure has no real plaza at all. One of the largest buildings in the world and relatively low in comparison to surrounding office and hotel towers, it is a dense monolith which almost completely covers its 6-acre site. As a building

type it has no counterpart anywhere. As a prototype for the dense, multi-use urban complex of the future, Place Bonaventure's brilliant and unusual parti deserves careful study.[4]

Other significant types of work came to the firm through the personal contacts of the various partners. These included several educational buildings, among them the Leacock Social Sciences building and the Student Union building, both for McGill University. The firm also got involved in the design of some of the theme buildings for the world exhibition, Expo, that was slated to open in Montreal in 1967.

In 1967, ARCOP returned to competitions to try and generate new jobs, the first such effort since 1962. However, none of the partners showed much interest in either of the two competitions that were pursued and there was little effort to collaborate in a manner that had earlier been so successful. Much of the work was actually handled by some of the associates. As Guy put it: "We lost because we did not have our hearts in it."

Execution of Work

The partners quickly discovered that, with so many partners, someone had to take formal charge of each project or job, whether or not the work was shared. Moreover, they found that the clients usually preferred dealing with a single partner as primary contact. Hence there was an understanding that a single partner would take overall responsibility for each job and that the allocation of jobs would be worked out between the partners on an informal basis.

At the same time, an integral part of ARCOP's philosophy called for a close relationship between client, architect and contractor during the execution of jobs. This meant that the partner in charge had to personally get involved with the client and the contractor relatively early in the design stage. It signified a radical departure on the part of this firm away from the traditional practice of architecture where projects

were passed from clients to architects to contractors in a sequential manner.

Ray elaborated upon the benefits of this method of working at length:

An architect who is some sort of an isolated expert is a Don Quixote galloping around on a steed against windmills that aren't there. We really are nothing if we are not able to communicate with a great variety of people who are in many ways much more skilled in the areas in which we claim to be skilled. One of the great bogeymen that we must continually fight against . . . is the fragmented professional who sits in one area, is an expert in this and somebody else who sits in another area is an expert in that and both work in water-tight compartments. In today's world this will get us absolutely nowhere . . .

Basically it is important . . . to get all the significant entities, professionals, and otherwise involved together in the decision-making process and involved in a situation of simultaneity and not in a situation of linear sequence. It means bringing people together at the same time to collide with each other. One of the very important elements of this process is the exposure of conflict—conflicts between technically oriented people, esthetically oriented people and people who are experts at measuring things like money and time.

A great deal of stalemate in creative work occurs when these diverse people do not interact soon enough. They collide when it is too late—they see each other in court or go behind each other's backs. This unfortunately is the traditional relationship between architect and contractor and often architect and client. If the conflicts aren't brought out in a controlled area of communication they will come up sooner or later to the detriment of action, rather than to its benefit. As we all know, in any dialectic process it is around the conflict that the real creative activity occurs. The exposure of conflict is a key thing.

The process demands of the architect that he vacates his age old formalist prison and begins to perceive form as process, and accept that in dealing with extremely complex problems, . . . solutions—good ideas—can come from almost any source and are not locked into the narrow confines of the traditional professional disciplines. In our experience, this method has been an extremely rapid, often unpredictable but most creative mode of clarifying problems and finding solutions.[5]

However, this type of approach suggested that the partner in charge had to have sufficient control over the job so as to be able to engage in this creative problem solving process with the other parties. The collaboration between the partners on ongoing jobs began to depend upon the ability of the partner in charge of a project to draw in the other partners from time to time to consult on specific problems or issues.

Furthermore, the clients considered the partner that had worked with them as being primarily responsible for the final product. A problem with this occurred in 1963 when a plaque appeared at the completed Place des Arts building specifically crediting Fred, instead of the firm as a whole, as the architect. Although this plaque was subsequently removed, it created some tensions about the concept and role of the partner in charge, leading to an increase in lobbying for prestigious jobs within the partnership. In response to this growing conflict, Guy finally attempted to develop some formal criteria for the appointment of a partner in charge on new jobs, emphasizing rotation among the partners, depending upon their current workloads.

Another aspect of the job that was handled by the partner in charge was the organization of staff into teams that would undertake the job. The overall team on each job was headed by a project manager, whose principal responsibilities lay in the coordination and administration of the entire job. Additionally, larger jobs were broken down into sections based upon the actual physical parts of the structure as well as certain functional divisions of the work. Each of these sections was placed in the hands of a group of architects

and draftsmen that was headed by a job captain.

Over time, the different partners also began to favor working with certain members of the staff, particularly those who acted as project managers and job captains. This led to occasional conflicts when another partner would want to use staff that had not previously worked with him. It is believed that on one occasion, a job was lost because a partner would not release a particular staff member who was requested by the potential client.

Growth and Organization

The team approach to job execution allowed the different partners to delegate a great deal of responsibility and provide tremendous challenge to the best young architectural talent that they had been hiring out of McGill University. Two of these were elevated to the position of associates of the partnership by 1961.

By 1963, ARCOP's billings had reached close to $1 million and the level of staff had risen to almost 60 members. A form of profit sharing plan was introduced by the partners for the associates and the senior staff. The firm also moved into a building that had been designed by the partners for the needs of their business.

With continued growth of work, the partnership also began to hire individuals with expertise in different areas such as design, drafting, graphics, specifications, field supervision and interior design. In something of a matrix management approach, individuals from these various areas worked closely with each other on job teams, coordinated by a project manager. Ray described the creation of the interior design group: "We got some young ladies . . . they had a little corner . . . They were not architects, they were specialists in furnishings, colors."

The firm's rapid growth also required increased attention to the management of the overall practice. The partners began to create some administrative management positions. A production manager was handed responsibility for scheduling and supervising the staff on the various jobs. The costing and accounting functions were vested in another position that was termed business manager. Finally, a construction manager was appointed to assist the supervision staff with the construction phase of jobs.

As the mid-1960s approached, the firm experienced its greatest spurt of growth, the result of the simultaneous occurrence of several very large jobs. The combination of these jobs resulted in a rise of billings to slightly over $3 million and a growth in staff to almost 150 people by 1966. The number of associates was increased to eight to handle the management of these jobs.

At the same time, the firm continued to add staff to fill in the various functional areas. This eventually forced the partners to make the role of these specialists clearer. The interior design group, in particular, began to lobby for a more independent practice. Its members wanted to take several steps, which included the possibility of setting themselves up in a separate location, that would allow them to solicit work for themselves. Guy most strongly favored the seeking of different kinds of work by these different areas, but Ray felt equally strongly that work should only be solicited by the firm as a whole. After much discussion, the partners eventually turned down the demands of the interior designers for a more autonomous operation.

But with the phenomenal rise in the volume of work, there was a growing belief among the managers and the associates that the firm was making insufficient profits and even losing money on the big jobs. Ray commented: "There was a feeling that we were inefficient . . . We should be making more money. Everything should be going like clockwork." This led to frequent complaints from the associates and the managers whose bonuses were tied to the overall profitability of the practice. In order to deal with this growing dissatisfaction, the partners created another organization within their partnership that was controlled by the senior staff. This organization negotiated separately with the partners over fees that it charged for the work that it carried out on the jobs of the partnership. As such, it was also allowed to distribute among its employees any of the profits that it made on this work.

At around the same time, the partners asked the senior staff, mostly associates, to form a management committee to deal with the administration of the firm. The committee was headed by Roger Marshall, a senior associate who was appointed executive director. Roger was also pledged extensive powers to manage the daily operations. Under his direction, subcommittees were also established to deal with specific aspects of management such as reviewing job contracts, administering budgets, creating job descriptions and reviewing salaries.

However, the various partners differed radically in their enthusiasm for this growth in management structure. This was reflected in the following responses to the appointment of Roger Marshall as executive director. Ray: "It was a terrible disfavour we did to him. I found that he was trying to coordinate the uncoordinable." Guy: "It was a giant leap forward towards the possibility of setting up a properly managed firm."

The senior staff questioned the usefulness or effectiveness of the steps that had been taken. There were growing concerns about the relative indifference of most of the partners to issues other than their own jobs. One of the associates recollected later: "All of the partners were becoming decreasingly tolerant of any organizational decisions that would infringe upon their personal involvement with their own jobs."

Underlying all of this was a growing disagreement between Guy and Ray in particular on the kind of organization that was desirable. Guy pushed for a larger tighter organization with increased formal controls, whereas Ray preferred a smaller looser organization with greater personal control. Dimi remarked of this growing confrontation: "Guy and Ray found themselves in boxes . . . with no windows or doors open."

THE LA CITE JOB

By 1968, the partnership had begun to show increasing signs of disintegration. The partners had started to hold some weekend retreats away from the office to try to recreate the earlier atmosphere. As Guy noted: "The more successful we were, the more tensions we created."

Subsequently, Guy chose to increase his teaching commitments at the University of Montreal and reduce his involvement with ARCOP. Hasen Size was retired from the partnership, though he continued to receive some benefits from the practice as his settlement.

The office was moved to another downtown location as the remaining partners decided to move out of the ARCOP-designed building, which was subsequently sold off.

In 1968, the partnership was approached regarding a job involving a multipurpose commercial development in downtown Montreal. The complex that was being designed included separate buildings for offices, retail, a hotel and apartments. However, it involved the demolition of several blocks of housing and consequently generated organized protests from the residents of the area that were being forced out. The clients for the job were the developers who had worked with ARCOP on Place Bonaventure. Ray recalled his involvement with the project as follows: "It started as an interesting job . . . the notion of a great big development in an existing urban fabric. It involved a fair amount of demolition and of pushing people out. That kind of thing I don't think any developer would even try to do today. I attempted for quite a while to involve the citizens in the decision making. It ended up in quite a clash of values that I found myself very much caught in. I eventually resigned because I was pretty much divided in my loyalties. I couldn't perform with integrity and commitment, particularly with respect to the client." Dimi disagreed strongly with Ray and recalled his feelings: "I felt it was our duty to examine the situation properly. I think Ray abandoned the job without examining all the possibilities . . . it was easier pulling out."

Torn between this sense of commitment to client as well as to community, Dimi took over the job as Ray withdrew his services. The confrontation over the job on La Cite created more tensions in the partnership. As a result,

the future of ARCOP was increasingly placed in doubt by late 1969, as the partners tried to seek a way out of their conflicts.

Through all of this, the level of work continued to decline with billings for 1969 almost dropping to $1 million. By the end of 1969, there were just over 30 people remaining with the firm. Most of the associates also left the firm during these years, and several of them were talented designers who subsequently started their own firms or became partners in already established competing firms. Yet, none of the partners, apart from Guy, seriously considered inviting any of these associates to join the partnership. Dimi justified this decision: "We had an element that made us successful . . . The same magic could not be reproduced. We could not consider the associates to fill our ranks."

> *Decision Point*: What are the critical issues that underlie the growing conflict in ARCOP? How can they be effectively addressed?

STARTING OVER

Ray Affleck and Fred Lebensold decided to continue working together after the decision was made to terminate the earlier partnership agreement. Two of the four associates remaining with the firm, Art Nichol and Ramesh Khosla, were also promoted to the status of new partners. Art had been the first associate appointed in the firm but Ramesh had only recently been hired and made an associate. As a result, Ray and Fred were viewed as the senior partners while Art and Ramesh were, in a sense, feeling their way into the partnership role. This move away from equality was clearly indicated by Fred's negotiated listing of his name first in the new partnership.

The immediate concern of all the partners was with the generation of work for their newly reorganized practice. Most of the new jobs obtained by ARCOP in the 1970s involved working with other architectural firms on multi-use commercial buildings (see Exhibit 2).

The search for more work also led the partners to think about opening another office in a different location, possibly Toronto. This move was made possible in 1973 when Paul Hughes, an established architect, approached ARCOP to open a separate office in Toronto under their name. Paul recalls, "I felt it would be more interesting, more challenging to practice with a firm that was already established . . . perhaps with a Montreal firm that I knew very well . . . I began talking to Ray about opening an office in Toronto . . . As it developed, there was a mutual interest in doing so." The new office in Toronto basically operated in an independent manner, obtaining and working on its own jobs.

Subsequently, both Paul and Ramesh spearheaded the effort to pursue more work for the two offices. Fred commented, "We all had to really look for work. We are not very good at that. We never did much of it. Work came to us . . . We never had to chase work."

The firm began to increasingly seek jobs in the U.S. as well as in more distant overseas locations. Paul explained, "It seemed that the only way to survive was to go where the action was. We ended up having to go far afield to get to the action."

By 1975, the new partnership had built up enough work to generate close to $2 million in billings and the number of staff had increased to 70 employees, of which 45 were located in Montreal. But the partners had clearly moved away from hiring staff that were specialized in areas other than design or drafting. Ray explained the reasons for this change: "Our experience has been that the types of work we get has always been erratic . . . Sometimes we get something to do requiring specifications or interiors, sometimes we don't."

The partners also tried to stay clear of the organizational issues which had created such conflict during the 1960s. Art, who had been substantially involved in administrative work even as an associate, assumed responsibility for most of the overall management functions. The partners continued to appoint project managers that took charge of individual jobs and to organize groups around the execution of work on these jobs. But they carefully avoided the recreation of the administrative management structure that had been previously developed. Ray justified this choice, "Managers tend to be too administratively oriented. They are not close enough to the work."

In 1976, ARCOP decided to enter a national competition, their first since the reorganization of their partnership. It was decided that the design work for this competition should be done in collaboration with another Montreal based firm that had francophone partners. Art recalled the nature in which work progressed on the competition: "It was a great opportunity. There was a great desire for everyone to get involved. However, there were sharp differences in the approaches of Fred and Ray to the job. Things went from bad to worse. Each partner pulled in his favorite staff members. It ended up as a competition within the office. Ray's design finally won out, but there was a great deal of bitterness created in the process. Needless to say, we lost the competition."

Meanwhile, annual billings for ARCOP dropped again to well below $1 million in 1977 resulting in the first loss ever registered by the partnership. The level of staffing was reduced to only 20 people distributed between the two offices at the start of 1978.

QUESTIONS

1. What kind of strategy did ARCOP pursue? What led to its early success?
2. What kind of conflicts did ARCOP face? Could these conflicts have been better resolved?
3. How were power and control exercised by the partners? by the associates? by the management staffs? by the departments?
4. Did the new firm effectively resolve the issues faced by the earlier partnership?

EXHIBIT 1   LIST OF SIGNIFICANT WORK

The jobs that represented the bulk of ARCOP's work over the years are listed below by the year in which work was started. Most jobs typically took three to five years to complete.

Name of Job	Location	Type of Work
1955 Queen Elizabeth Theatre	Vancouver	performing arts center
1958 Place Ville Marie*	Montreal	office, retail complex
1958 Place des Arts	Montreal	performing arts center
1961 McGill Leacock Building	Montreal	university building
1961 Confederation Center	P.E.I.	theatre, library, museum complex
1962 McGill Student Union	Montreal	university building
1962 Provincial Buildings	P.E.I.	office complex
1963 Place Bonaventure	Montreal	merchandise mart, retail, hotel complex
1964 National Arts Center	Ottawa	performing arts center
1964 Arts and Culture Centre	St. Johns, Newfoundland	performing arts center
1964 Expo Theme Buildings	Montreal	exhibition buildings
1966 Polyvalente School	Montreal	high school buildings
1968 Dalhousie Life Sciences Building	Halifax	university building
1968 La Cite Complex**	Montreal	residential, office, retail complex
1970 Onondaga County Centre	Syracuse	theatre, offices, retail complex
1970 World Trade Centre*	New York	office, retail complex
1972 Museum of Fine Arts	Montreal	art museum building
1972 Waterfront Study	Halifax	master development plan for area
1973 Winnipeg Square	Winnipeg	office, retail, hotel complex
1973 Sheraton Centre	Montreal	hotel building
1973 Centrum Centre**	Los Angeles	office, retail, hotel complex
1974 Harborfront Study	Toronto	master development plan for area
1975 La Chaudiere	Ottawa/Hull	office, retail, hotel complex
1977 Adeola-Odeku Centre	Nigeria	shopping centre

* represents work carried out on parts of building
** represents preliminary study and design work only

Source: ARCOP records.

EXHIBIT 2 FINANCIAL DATA IN THOUSANDS OF DOLLARS

	Billings	Salaries*	Expenses**	Overhead***	Profit
1958	85	8	7	45	25
1959	285	105	3	71	106
1960	692	299	52	129	212
1961	609	328	36	119	126
1962	970	389	247	175	159
1963	975	387	274	230	84
1964	1411	465	467	314	165
1965	2151	888	369	417	477
1966	3085	1137	867	483	598
1967	2001	707	482	341	471
1968	1602	529	442	314	317
1969	1134	480	261	230	163
1970	953	418	171	198	166
1971	913	453	147	200	113
1972	985	457	141	227	160
1973	1472	630	92	276	474
1974	1449	681	118	349	301
1975	1951	1035	111	367	438
1976	1324	697	124	341	162
1977	904	483	148	324	−51

* *covers architectural salaries applicable to jobs*
** *covers fees of consultants used that were not charged to client*
*** *covers general and administrative expenses*

Source: ARCOP records.

EXHIBIT 3 THE ARCHITECTURAL INDUSTRY

PRACTICE

Architects must be registered by provincial boards to be able to practice on their own in Canada. An individual architect is required to undergo a training period with practicing architects and to pass a board examination before he or she can be registered. An architect may, however, work with another firm under registered architects without obtaining registration.

Most Canadian architectural firms exist as individual proprietorships or as partnerships because most provinces do not allow incorporation. There were 57% individual proprietorships, 31% partnerships and 10% incorporated companies among architectural firms in Canada in 1977.

Incorporation has recently been permitted in some Canadian provinces, but an estimated 16% of firms in the other provinces have set up incorporated service companies to which they transferred all of the non-registered architectural staff.

EXHIBIT 3 (*Continued*)

FIRMS

The number of architectural firms has generally increased since the late 1950s and has doubled since the late 1960s. There were 1,707 firms registered in 1977, but only 1,283 firms were actually in operation. Architectural firms have grown in all provinces, although in 1977, Quebec and Ontario still accounted for 63% and British Columbia and Alberta accounted for 26% of architectural firms in Canada.

The relative distribution of establishments in 1977 by volume of billings is indicated below:

Less than $100,000	646 firms	50.3%
$100,000–$999,999	580 firms	45.2%
$1,000,000 and over	57 firms	4.5%

The firms in the smallest category generally employ less than five people, whereas those in the largest category usually carry more than thirty-five staff.

STAFF

Over two-thirds of the staff in architectural firms is generally evenly distributed between architects and drafting or technical people. The remainder of the staff carry out office and administrative functions. Staff are hired and laid off, for the most part, depending upon the volume and pressure of work. It is not uncommon for firms to hire certain people intermittently to help out during busy periods.

WORK

Architectural work is typically carried out in stages. In some instances, preliminary studies and planning work can be undertaken before any designs are produced. Otherwise, the work actually starts with the conceptual design stage, during which the basic design is developed in accordance with the client's needs and financial constraints. It subsequently moves into working drawings, which include all technical specifications that are necessary for construction. The final stage requires supervision of construction to ensure that it proceeds in accordance with the drawings.

CONTRACTED SERVICES

Architectural firms frequently hire external consultants from different areas during the course of work on jobs. For example, acoustical engineers can assist a firm with the design of an auditorium or theatre. Part of the cost of these consultants can be recovered from the client in addition to the regular fees for the architectural firm. The use of external consultants does, however, generally reduce the profits that can be made on a job. Nevertheless, most architectural firms do not carry in-house specialists because of their high salary expense and the fluctuating demand for their services.

MARKETING

Architectural firms acquire most of their work through the reputation that is generated as a result of their completed buildings. Nevertheless, this reputation can be built up and supported by a variety of marketing efforts. Firms can engage in promotional activities that are geared towards cultivating and maintaining contacts with prospective clients. Speculative work can also be done at minimal or no cost to the client on the understanding that if the client decides to proceed, further work at full cost will come to the firm. Finally, architectural firms can enter official competitions when these are announced to bid for work on specific jobs.

EXHIBIT 3 (*Continued*)

FEE STRUCTURE

Billings for a job are generally on a fixed fee basis, usually determined as a percentage of cost of construction, if construction activity is involved. It is sometimes charged on a cost plus basis, with an upset price determining the upper limit.

Profit margins have generally declined in the industry with average profits running from 11% to 17% of annual fees in 1977. These declines have occurred because of decline in larger jobs, tighter fee structures and increased client demands.

INDUSTRY BILLINGS

Overall billings in the Canadian architectural industry have shown periods of strong growth as indicated in the figures below:

1961	81 million	1970	186 million
1962	94 million	1971	185 million
1963	112 million	1972	181 million
1964	136 million	1973	194 million
1965	147 million	1974	233 million
1966	153 million	1975	291 million
1967	159 million	1976	324 million
1968	181 million	1977	326 million
1969	188 million	1978	329 million

Sources: (1) "Offices of Architects 1977," *Statistics Canada*, Department of Industry Trade and Commerce, 1979. (2) P. Bernard Associates, "Survey of Canadian Architects' Services," Department of Industry, Trade and Commerce, 1979.

CASE II – 2

POLAROID CORPORATION

Polaroid started as an inventor's story on the classical model.[1] A superbly gifted inventor and scientist, Edwin Land, created Polaroid in 1937 and remained its chairman and director of research until 1982, when he stepped aside to pursue his research interests full time and be available as a consultant to Polaroid. Mr. William McCune, CEO since 1980 and a long time colleague and friend of Dr. Land, had to reposition the company in light of some powerful new competitive forces.

EARLY HISTORY

Edwin Land never graduated from Harvard, preferring to form a company with one of his professors. His doctorate was honorary. But his attachment to research and invention was inseparable and ultimately led to his acquiring over 500 patents. Dr. Land's innovative mind caused one associate to claim, in reference to Land's original instant photography work: "100 Ph.D.'s would not have been able to duplicate Land's feat in ten years of uninterrupted work."[2] Yet Land developed the basic physical elements of this process within six months. Polaroid was actually founded on Land's invention of a light-polarizing sheet material, which filtered out all light except that vibrating in a single plane. Normally light waves vibrate in myriad planes as they emanate from a source. By crossing these planes two polarized sheets could eliminate light or glare as desired.

Land's early efforts concentrated on manufacturing easily marketed products like sunglasses and scientific products. And almost from the beginning, his company earned a profit. (2,154)

In 1937 Land incorporated the company, selling common stock to the Rothschilds and Baron Schroder under an unusual agreement that allowed him to maintain control. The agreement gave Land power over a trust that held the majority of the stock. (1,116) With this unusual beginning, Polaroid issued no long term debt for years, financing itself internally and through stock issues. Among other innovations, Polaroid was one of the first public companies to consciously adopt a "low dividend" policy, offering its stockholders the opportunity of taking almost all their profits as capital gains. The company grew rapidly through the World War II period when it was a government supplier of specialized optical products.

But Land hoped to design his product into automobile headlights and windshields to reduce night driving glare. (2,157) With windshields polarized in one direction and headlights in another, each driver would have a full view of the road ahead with no glare from oncoming lights. In 1947 although Detroit had successfully tested the headlight polarizing system, the automakers turned them down. (2,157) The industry saw no practical way to equip the 33 million cars then on the roads and was concerned that owners of those vehicles might be handicapped by the somewhat brighter headlights needed on filter equipped cars.

INSTANT PHOTOGRAPHY

1947 started as a dismal year, but all that changed in February when Land disclosed his now famous sixty-second photographic process. Land's inspiration came one day during World War II, as he was taking pictures of his daughter. She had asked impatiently why she could not see the finished picture right away. The question triggered Land's fertile imagination. And he soon conceptualized the basic idea for his revolutionary product. But he worked three long years before the process produced a sufficiently acceptable result. The secret lay in a self developing film packet. Once he achieved initial success with this, Land moved quickly (in 1947) to design a camera to handle the film. William McCune, then a Polaroid engineer, and several associates contributed a series of important early inventions to support Land's work. (2,157) But this was only the beginning of a decades-long quest to develop improved films and cameras for instant photography.

The full requirements of the camera and film were beyond the financial capabilities of the young Polaroid Corporation, and it turned to outside contractors for much of its production. Protected by over 1000 patents, Polaroid ultimately had Bell & Howell and U.S. Time manufacture the camera, while Kodak supplied the negative film. Polaroid produced only the unique instant positive film and used its remaining manpower to market the camera.[3]

Sales grew from $1.5 million in 1947 to nearly $100 million by 1960. During this period Polaroid offered only black and white film—but vastly improved the quality of both its cameras and the film. It stayed strictly in the high (over $100) end of the camera market, while most of its potential competitors, including Kodak, scoffed at the idea of a large instant picture market. (2,125) In fact, Kodak worked with Polaroid, helping the growing fledgling introduce the world's first instant color film in 1963. This technological achievement spurred Polaroid's sales in the mid-sixties as Polaroid rode a burgeoning amateur photography market along with Kodak and its Instamatic line.

By 1963 Polarod completely dominated the high priced "instant" camera field and began to eye the much larger inexpensive segment controlled by Kodak. The Polaroid Swinger—a black and white camera selling under $20—introduced in the fall of 1965 was an immediate success.[4] Polaroid soon expanded its presence with the Big Swinger (in 1968) and Colorpak II in 1969. In each case, the new camera, priced within $5 of its predecessor overwhelmed the former model, and large inventories of the older cameras were often sold below cost to discount houses.[4]

SX-70 AND SHOCKWAVES

Still, in this period Polaroid began to face some ominous problems. Its original patents for instant photography started to expire in 1965. While newer patents prevented immediate competition, other companies would be able to enter the instant picture market by 1970. And Polaroid's successful forays into the low price camera market had stimulated Kodak's interest in instant photography.[4]

In the early sixties, Dr. Land began organizing a project team to revolutionize instant photography and leapfrog past his competition into another fortress of patents. As Land's project team pushed both film technology and the camera design art (Land called it forced evolution) Polaroid became involved in such seemingly unrelated fields as integrated circuits and batteries. Polaroid's new products had such demanding standards that they required significant design and manufacturing cooperation with suppliers. During this period, talented Polaroid engineers often "lived" with vendors to help them achieve new and rigorous design and production specifications. Virtually all of this project's work was performed without any market research except Polaroid's own confidence in knowing its customers' needs.[5]

Polaroid felt market research was only valid as a method of delineating an existing market, not for evaluating an entirely new concept. Land always held that Polaroid's product created the market, rather than the market dictating the product. This was in part why he could withstand the knee buckling skepticism and delays that accompanied the introduction of the revolutionary SX-70 line. He later scoffed at those who "couldn't see the potential of a $600 camera value marketed in the $100 range."[6]*

In 1972, this project ("Aladdin") bore its professed creation, the SX-70. The camera offered startling improvements over previous models. Its color film literally developed before the customer's eyes. The distasteful refuse layers generated by the old "peel apart" process were eliminated. And the camera itself was a marvel of optical engineering. The SX-70's development costs had been staggering; some estimates were as high as $600 million (including buildings) over its full duration.

Polaroid initiated another important shift along with the introduction of the SX-70. Because of the camera's sophistication and Kodak's impending instant camera introduction, Polaroid decided to manufacture and assemble the major components of the camera "in house," as well as produce the negatives for its film. This decision not only required substantial investments in plant and equipment (over $200 million) between 1968 and 1972, but it strained the organization to adapt its highly unstructured management style to the routine operations of an assembly line.[7] The gamble also sent shockwaves down Wall Street, with many analysts doubting Polaroid's ability to maintain respectable earnings growth during this period. (3,125)

In fact, the SX-70's introduction was plagued with bad luck. The national introduction was delayed until late 1973, while engineers scrambled to solve its problems. Production difficulties caused product shortages in most locales. The 1974 recession cut deeply into the SX-70's potential sales, as its high price ($180) kept it from the volume markets. At the same time there were complaints about the quality of the SX-70's innovative self developing pictures, and the sale of other Polaroid models fell off more than expected. Profits for 1974 dropped to $28.4 million, down $23.4 million from the previous year.

Land Changes Roles

In January, 1975 Dr. Land stepped aside as President. Land wanted to get out of daily operations to concentrate on one of his favorite projects—instant movies—and he saw the need for a full-time operations manager. Wiliam McCune, who took over the presidency, was experienced in all phases of engineering and manufacturing and had spearheaded the project which removed Polaroid's color negative manufacturing from Kodak's benevolent control. "Bill" McCune had a warm, calm, and relaxed manner even in crisis situations. Slim and graying, McCune understood the unique Polaroid organization and Dr. Land's style well. He preferred to operate through consensus, but he was also demanding and wanted problems addressed. Said one executive at the time:

> "He has known for years that certain things needed to be done around here, and now that he's got the charter he's doing them. . . . We had been trying to get certain product decisions for as long as two years before Bill became president," the executive added. "The routine had been that one top guy thought this and another top guy thought that and the boss (Mr. Land) was waffling. So we'd go back and get more data and do it all over again. Now Bill just says, 'Okay, do it.' "[8]

McCune also removed some of the centralizing aura of Dr. Land's style from operating decisions.

> McCune's orders are usually clear, but if they aren't I can say, 'Bill, what are you trying to tell me? Exactly what do you want me to do?' I would never dare ask Land that.[8]

A NEW ERA BEGINS

Polaroid faced its first direct competitor in 1975. Pint-sized Berkey Photo introduced an instant picture camera which used SX-70 film.[9] Polaroid's reaction was prompt and predictable; it immediately filed a patent infringement suit against Berkey. Despite this unexpected intruder into its domain, Polaroid rebounded to near record profits of $62.5 million in 1975. But the prospects of a much bloodier battle seemed in prospect when Kodak marketed its entry in April, 1976. Instead, the entire instant photo market exploded. Even with Kodak initially grabbing 25% of the market, Polaroid's sales grew to $950 million with record profits of $79.7 million by the end of 1976.

But the threat from the Rochester giant was lethal; and Polaroid, armed with its vast patent portfolio, pursued an injunction against Kodak to cease and desist from further manufacture of instant cameras and film. Similar actions in Canada and the United Kingdom temporarily prevented Kodak from offering its product, but Kodak's lawyers soon found a way out from each injunction.[9] Still, counterpunching effectively with Kodak, Polaroid's sales and profits grew while Kodak's instant camera division operated in the red.[10] Then from the east, a third challenger, Fuji Photo of Japan, reared its head and began its tentative probing of what had been Polaroid's exclusive domain only two years before.

As a partial counter to these entries, in 1977 Polaroid introduced instant movies. Dr. Land had been determined to provide a moving picture complement to his instant still pictures. But the initial product entry, Polavision, was expensive ($699) and was positioned at the high end of a stagnant home movie market, representing only 10% of the total photography market. Unlike SX-70, the camera and hardware were manufactured outside Polaroid. With his characteristic optimism, Dr. Land entered the new field hoping to generate the same response that occurred 30 years before. (9,45) As he had so many times before, Dr. Land made the announcement of this new product dramatically at the 1976 stockholders meeting (April 1977), a year before the product was to be fully available in the marketplace.

Unfortunately, Polavision was a striking failure in both technology and marketing—the very areas in which the company had been so strong,[11] and it was financially costly with three years of "substantial" operating losses and a $68.5 million write off in 1979. But *Fortune* also noted:

> Polavision began in the late 1960s as part of Project Sesame, the code name the company used for experiments with film that is designed to be viewed by shining light through it (as opposed to film designed to produce printed pictures). One consolation for Polaroid is that Polavision is merely the first of the products that can be expected to grow out of Project Sesame . . . Polaroid may have discovered a way to reduce the cost of manufacturing all instant color film . . . In any case, there is an obvious application of the Polavision technology—instant slides.[11]

New Competitive Forces

Instant cameras reached a peak of 41% of the still photographic market in 1978, with Polaroid selling a record 9.4 million cameras worldwide. Confident of future growth, it launched an extensive capital expenditure program to increase production of SX-70 cameras and film worldwide.[12] In 1979, after a 4 year growth of 41%, the U.S. camera market dropped 3%.[13] Polaroid's unit sales plummeted more than 22% just as its capital expansion projects neared completion. The worldwide recession of the following several years hurt the whole photographic industry, but even more so the instant cameras and films which had always sold to lower income groups than those who bought conventional cameras.[14]

Polaroid fought to maintain and survive on its $\frac{2}{3}$ share of the declining instant market. It introduced sonar automatic focusing, Time Zero Supercolor film, the Sun (light management system) cameras, and high speed 600 ASA instant color film. Kodak's share dropped from 40% in 1978 to 30% in 1982. But by 1982 Polaroid's instant still sales had fallen to an estimated 4 million units annually.

Fuji Photo's instant system was doing well in its Japanese home market, and Eastman upgraded its somewhat deficient instant line in 1982. In addition Kodak's new disc system had proved an immediate novelty and consumer success. Nimslo International had introduced a three dimensional still process, but its market was generally considered a novelty.[15] Sony too had announced its all electronic Mavica camera and system, but in 1982 this required several cabinets of complex backup equipment to manipulate and display its images. Other important market trends are shown in Exhibits II–VII.

Diversification Efforts

Polaroid had for years marketed photographic products in non-consumer markets—such as instant cameras for use in hospitals and labs, microphotography cameras, panorama cameras, studio films, passport and drivers license photo equipment and special event cameras.[16] As the amateur market for instant photography declined, the company began to devote more of its energies toward expanding such markets and breaking into well-established (non-photography related) fields with spinoffs from its instant photographic and optical technology (such as a wafer thin battery, a filter for video display terminal screens, a curing agent for polyurethene, an anti-counterfeit labeling material, a sonar transducer, and precision optical devices).[16]

These diversification efforts were beginning to bear fruit by mid 1982. Sales of such products constituted a growing percentage of Polaroid's revenues; although not yet the 50% that represented the goal that *Business Week* had earlier reported.[17] Intensified development efforts in these areas were also paying off. The company's 1982 *Annual Report* stated:

> The new 35mm Autoprocess color and black and white rapid access slide film system adds a new dimension to 35mm photography and marks the first time Polaroid will be marketing products in a conventional film format for use in existing cameras and instruments. [Our prototype of a new low-cost business graphics system for use with the Apple II and IBM Personal Computers] consists of a menu-driven software program (supplied on a diskette) and a tri-color videoprinter which can produce 4x5 inch format color prints and 35mm rapid-access color and black and white slides. These new Polaroid tabletop imaging and processing systems make Polaroid instant photography a part of the flow of immediate informa-

tion in the office and laboratory. In their design, these self-contained systems become logical extensions of their host electronic imaging systems, and in operation they expand and complement the functions of those systems.

The graphics hardcopy system was an offshoot of Polaroid's 23% stake in a small company, Image Resource Corp. But these endeavors did not remedy the decline of Polaroid's primary market and the failure of its Polavision product. Polaroid saw its EPS drop from a high of $3.60 in 1978 to $0.95 in 1981. In the same period, return on assets fell from 9.3% to 2.2% and pretax profits as a percent of sales went from 14.1% down to 4.4%.

MANAGEMENT AND ORGANIZATIONAL CHANGES

In April 1980, Bill McCune took over as CEO, and Land became Chairman of the Board and Consulting Director of Basic Research in Land Photography. Soon after he took office, Mr. McCune began to change Polaroid's unique organization. *Business Week* had summarized some of the key philosophies under Dr. Land as follows:

> Seldom, if ever, has a large American company so faithfully reflected the substance and style of one man as does Polaroid Corp. under Dr. Edwin H. Land . . . Land thrives on informality; thus, Polaroid has no organization chart. Land is almost compulsively secretive; so is Polaroid. Land believes manufacturing is an extension of research; Polaroid employees often follow such projects as the new SX-70 camera from laboratory to factory floor. Land works prodigious hours; so do key employees, who are resigned to taking phone calls from Land anytime.[18]

Other philosophies of Dr. Land were still important factors in Polaroid's 1982 culture. (See Appendix A) Under Dr. Land, Polaroid's commitment to research and development had dominated the organization's structure and approach. By providing exceptional work flexibility, Dr. Land attempted to create an innovative atmosphere where the corporate structure did not interfere with employees' motivation. Major divisions were organized simply along functional lines (i.e. marketing, manufacturing, etc.). The heart of the corporation's creative capability was the research division headed by Dr. Land. The manufacturing and operating divisions were coordinated by Mr. McCune. A Management Executive Committee (M.E.C.), comprised of Land, McCune, Julius Silver (corporate attorney) and the heads of the major divisions, served as a forum to discuss key aspects of corporate policy and to exchange information about major operating decisions.

McCune had coordinated the functional operations of the company. However, not being a detail man, he preferred to delegate to his young, aggressive divisional managers, who in turn assumed firm control over their areas and promoted strong divisional loyalties and even some degree of proprietary control over divisional information. All the division and senior managers were long time Polaroid employees. And, although McCune could act as an effective coordinator and buffer, all understood that Land's word had been final on crucial issues, especially those associated with product offerings. In fact, Land had held strategic direction strictly to himself, and often preempted decisions or overturned operating management's consensus on issues of particular interest to him. Although no official organization chart existed prior to 1980, published information and informed outside observers estimated key relationships to be as shown in Exhibit X. Some details about each major activity and player follow.

Manufacturing Division

Under the direction of I.M. "Mac" Booth, this division had responsibility for domestic camera and film pack production as well as all negative film coatings. Labor intensive operations such as the camera assembly were separated from the highly automated coating facilities for the negative and positive film production.

Polaroid had decided against consolidating all Boston area facilities into one giant Cambridge industrial complex, preferring to keep things in relatively smaller locations in Norwood, Needham, New Bedford, Freetown, and Waltham, Mass. It wanted to keep things more on a human and manageable scale, with workers having a greater opportunity to feel an integral part of what was happening. This dispersal also raised the company's profile in each community the way a single large Cambridge complex could not. (6,191)

In 1980 Booth, 49, was a rising star at Polaroid. Tough, hard nosed, and inquiring, he often became the "devil's advocate" in top level discussions. Booth had the difficult task of planning and operating the bulk of Polaroid's complex manufacturing facilities and coordinating them with the vagaries of the consumer marketplace and the magnificent spurts of inventiveness coming from Research. Booth believed in running a tight ship, was willing to experiment with new management techniques and prided himself on his capacities to select people. Booth had become the senior vice-president of manufacturing after successfully developing and operating the company's new negative film manufacturing facilities. He had earlier served as an assistant to McCune and enjoyed excellent relationships with the president.

Marketing Division

Since the company's early beginnings, its marketing division had always played an important role. Polaroid's innovative product line had required an aggressive and intelligent marketing program which Edwin Land personally supported. In 1980 the division was headed by youthfully graying, dapper, soft spoken, Peter Wensberg (52) who had become senior vice-president in 1971. More philosophical than "Mac" Booth in many ways, Wensberg liked to talk about the long term market positioning and management needs of Polaroid amidst a collection of historical instruments and nautical devices that artistically decorated his office. Nevertheless, within his division Wensberg was known as a hard driver. Along with Richard

Young, head of Polaroid's International Division, Wensberg had been considered one of the three likely successors to Land, before McCune was named to the position. (6,216) He had complete control over marketing and was a powerful force throughout the corporation. However, his non-technical background limited the depth of his influence in the more technical divisions.

The marketing division was responsible for all domestic marketing including advertising, customer service, and marketing/sales. The marketing/sales department was divided into a consumer and an industrial product group with a separate sales force for each. Consumer products were distributed directly to large retail, department, and discount stores and through selected wholesalers to smaller retail outlets. Polaroid's sales force handled both cameras and film supplied within their regional territories. Industrial products—designed for commercial photographers and industrial, scientific, or medical applications—were sold through an industrial sales force or independent industrial agents. In addition, the marketing division also had its own market research, marketing planning, advertising, promotion, order processing, internal bookkeeping, (etc.) groups.

Research Divisions

Since its inception Polaroid had been dominated by its research activities. And under Dr. Land's leadership research continued to be a major focal point of the corporation. No absolute delineation existed between applied and pure research; however, separate divisions had been set up to specialize in those two functions. The applied research division, referred to as the technology division, carried most new products or product improvements into production. It occasionally was responsible for manufacturing new products which either needed further design changes or whose market demand was not sufficient to justify transferring them to the huge manufacturing division. Dr. Sheldon Buckler (49), who had originally worked in pure research and had participated in a number of Land's entrepreneurial projects, had served as the division's manager since 1972. Dr. Land's great technical abilities and strong personality

made this both a difficult and a highly rewarding role.

The research division worked primarily on more basic research projects and had fostered many major technological improvements in films and coatings. The division's close relations to Dr. Land gave it extremely high level support in dealing with other divisions. In fact, some claimed that Research often had the controlling hand in such relationships. President McCune had also had a long association with research. When Land had come up with his early inventions McCune had been the one who followed up and built them. (6,216) In addition to McCune, research had served as an incubation ground for other senior managers, with three present members of the M.E.C.—Drs. Young, Buckler, and Bloom—each having at one time been Land's assistant director of research.

Land had philosophically conceptualized Polaroid as an extension of the scientific laboratory. He wanted to move the concept of scientific experimentation into the industrial sphere, with the same absence of guilt attached to business as to laboratory failures. In fact the company's success really came back to continual experiments and recombinations of technical work and business ventures that at many points in time had indeed been stopped, or looked like failures. (6,184–5) Hence R&D teams were formed, dissolved and reformed with scientists and engineers fluidly following projects into development or production and then returning to the labs again.

Land believed in a strong relationship between the laboratory and the factory. In a manner reminiscent of Mao sending the intellectuals to the rice fields, he sometimes had research people "operating machines." He felt this exposure would give them a greater practical feel for their own theoretical work. In Land's vision, production was just a continuation of research and development, with McCune and Land participating (for example) in the design of machinery and components for SX-70. (6,190)

International Division

Dr. Richard Young, 54, had managed the International division with an independence and feistiness sometimes envied by the domestic managers. His entrepreneurial talents were put to work in the division when he was appointed its president in 1969 after a very successful career in the research division. By early 1980 international sales had grown to nearly 40% of total corporate revenues and the division controlled all manufacturing and marketing outside the United States. The manufacturing capabilities of the division included positive film coating operations, camera and film pack assembly, and sunglass production. It relied on the U.S. operation for batteries, negative film and other proprietary items but used local contractors for other components. International had three manufacturing facilities—in Scotland, in Ireland, and The Netherlands. The facilities in Scotland and the Netherlands were involved with most phases of production, whereas the plant in Ireland was strictly for film pack assembly. No research had been conducted by the division. Almost all of its products had been first introduced in the U.S. And its product line had been essentially the same as the domestic unit's, with some local adaptations to accommodate metric measures, special market conditions, or local regulations.

In 1980 International marketed the full line of Polaroid products directly through wholly-owned subsidiaries in some 20 countries.[19] It hired independent distributors in most other areas of the world. The sales force also had a line of sunglasses which was marketed along with its other products; otherwise the sales organization operated in a manner similar to the domestic group's.

International was reportedly the only profit center within Polaroid in 1980. With this distinction, it seemed to operate somewhat more independently and aggressively within the corporation. Financial controls for all divisions were maintained by McCune and the finance division. Financial allocations had generally been based largely on the presentations of each functional group as reviewed by the finance division and the M.E.C. With the exception of major new products there had been little attempt to interrelate capital programs between divisions. And there had been significant reluctance to develop integrated five year plans among the divisions because of the entrepreneurial nature of the company and the uncertainty of the marketplace.

Staff Divisions

The remaining divisions represented specialized staff activities which supported the line manufacturing, research, and marketing divisions. The largest were the engineering, finance, and legal divisions—although there were also personnel, planning, systems analysis, and public relations specialists at the corporate level. The company's accounting and financial controls tended to follow functional lines, with each division handling the bulk of its own detailed bookkeeping, systems development, and data generation internally. Of course, the finance division specified the records and reports needed for corporate purposes and coordinated all contracts with outside capital sources.[20]

A Smorgasbord of Talent

Dr. Land had used his flexible and creative organization as a "smorgasbord of talent." By selecting individuals with specific skills from any area in the corporation, Land could quickly assemble the highly diverse talents needed to handle desired tasks. For example, when he was confronted with an enormous project like "Aladdin" (SX-70), Land would reach into all his functional groups to gather the necessary people available within Polaroid. Then he would fill any gaps with outside specialists.

In such circumstances, Land reportedly maintained complete control over the project team's R&D activities, even to the information going to and from his team. Secrecy would often shroud his group's activities, and team members might purposely be kept isolated from nonessential contact with other groups in Polaroid. Land himself might be the only individual intimately aware of the entire project's work. (6,210) He would call for additional support work as necessary, and tried to make sure that each research task was the responsibility of a particular individual, rather than diffused as "an organizational responsibility."

As the project's concept crystallized into more definite shape, moved into development, or began scale-up, Dr. Land transferred his attention increasingly to marketing the evolving product. Individual technical team members usually followed their element of the project through full scale-up and debugging before returning to their former jobs. But occasionally, a team researcher or engineer ended up managing manufacturing for the developed component.

Under Land's care and feeding the Polaroid organization responded dynamically—and somewhat amorphously—to changing conditions. Teams formed and reformed around problems. (6,198) From the beginning Polaroid had encouraged employees to participate in decisions affecting their areas. In fact, innovation in organization and corporate human relations was a stated goal of the company. Employees were encouraged to take courses and advanced degrees at company expense. And many of Polaroid's more productive engineers were high school graduates or technicians who had never taken full time university training. Formal organizational constraints and authority relationships were kept to a minimum, and inconsistencies in managerial styles and even the corporation's functional setup were frequent. For example, digressions often arose when a development project moved into manufacturing or commercialization stages. At that point, the responsibility for the project's completion usually reverted to the team leader's division regardless of its function. Consequently, an applied research or engineering division might house manufacturing operations or a small commercial unit for some time. Eventually, however, the misplaced unit would be relocated to its proper functional area or occasionally operated as a small division more or less on its own.

Knowledgeable observers referred to the Polaroid organization as a "moving target." The arrangement at any moment seemed to evolve naturally from the unstructured operational environment, and further adjustments might soon change any existing situation. The attached organizational charts indicate only those broad relationships which one could define from published data and external contacts with the company. And

even these might change quickly with circumstances. There seemed to be substantial participation in decision making among affected parties *within* a division. But such participation *between* divisions was reportedly less common, and of course major interdivisional decisions had to be made at the very top level if substantial disagreements occurred.

The 1980 Reorganization

In October, 1980, Mr. McCune began to restructure the top level activities of Polaroid, although many of its *operating* philosophies remained unchanged. He stated:

> Our goals are fourfold: to understand better our total potential; to encourage expanding fields such as our technical and industrial photographic businesses; to explore fields which are new for Polaroid such as batteries and the commercial chemical business; and to establish clear cut areas of responsibility for growth in both sales and profits.[21]

The Office of the President was enlarged by the creation of four Executive Vice Presidents. These were Drs. Buckler and Young, and Messrs. Booth and Wensberg. Major departments were consolidated on a worldwide basis to recognize global needs more fully in such areas as marketing, finance, manufacturing, and materials management.[21] This was widely recognized as the beginning of several phased moves which would ensure Polaroid's competitiveness and continued innovativeness in the 1980s. Mr. McCune wanted to be ready to announce his final organization concept in 1982.

QUESTIONS

1. In light of its changing competitive situation, what should Polaroid's strategy be in 1982? Why?

2. Design an organization suited to support this strategy. Draw an organization chart showing critical relationships down through the departmental level. Who should occupy each position at the division level or above? Why?

3. What control system is needed to make your strategy and organization effective? Define key measures at each level down to departments.

4. What other steps are necessary to implement your strategy?

APPENDIX A

Polaroid Corporation Philosophy & Culture

In May 1967, Dr. Land wrote down some key points of the Polaroid philosophy. These were still widely accepted in Polaroid in 1982.

> We have two basic products at Polaroid: (1) Products that are genuinely unique and useful, excellent in quality, made well and efficiently, so that they present an attractive value to the public and an attractive profit to the Company; (2) A worthwhile working life for each member of the Company—a working life that calls out the member's best talents and skills—in which he or she shares the responsibilities and the rewards.
>
> These two products are inseparable. The Company prospers most, and its members find their jobs most worthwhile, when its members are contributing their full talents and efforts to creating, producing, and selling products of outstanding merit. (6,183)

In amplifying this Dr. Land was quoted as saying,

> "What we're after in America is an industrial society where a person maintains at work the full dignity he has at home. I don't mean that they will all be happy. They'll be unhappy—but in new, exciting, and important ways. [At Polaroid, people] would work happy for that time." Polaroid eliminated the time clock, provided extensive educational opportunities inside and outside the company, and allowed employees to "try out" for other jobs if they thought they would be more satisfying. (6,188–9)

In a *Harvard Business Review* article Dr. Land further stated his philosophies:

> I think whether outside science or within science there is no such thing as *group* originality or *group* creativity or *group* perspicacity.
>
> I do believe wholeheartedly in the individual capacity for greatness, in one way or another in almost any healthy human being under the *right* circumstances; but being part of a group is, in my opinion, generally the *wrong* circumstance. Profundity and originality are attributes of single, if not singular, minds. Two minds may sometimes be better than one, provided that each of the two minds is working separately while the two are working together; yet three tend to become a crowd.[22]

Dr. Land believed in mutual trust and commitment between employees and management; and he expected his people to actively participate in this opportunity.

> I don't regard it as normal for a human being to have an eight-hour day, with two long coffee breaks, with a martini at lunch, with a sleepy period in the afternoon and a rush home to the next martini. I don't think that can be dignified by calling it working, and I don't think people should be paid for it.[23]

In 1977 Dr. Land reaffirmed his commitment to a high corporate ethic in Polaroid's Annual Report.

> A company has as many aspects to its character as a person has, seeking fulfillment and self expression, power, friendship, creativity, immediate recognition and ultimate significance. It has a conscience and high purpose and moral standards and vulnerability. It can sin, feel guilty and repent, it can love and it can hate, it can build and it can destroy. . . . Recognition of the analogs of human characteristics in corporate life will in my opinion rejuvenate the economy, regenerate national self-respect, initiate an intellectual renaissance, and reward us all with a vast family of blessings which in our blindness we hold stubbornly at arm's length. (9,3)

EXHIBIT I   POLAROID CORPORATION AND SUBSIDIARY COMPANIES TEN YEAR
             FINANCIAL SUMMARY (Unaudited)

Years Ended December 31
(Dollar Amounts in Millions, Except Per Share Data)

	1981	1980	1979
Consolidated Statement of Earnings			
Net sales:			
United States	$ 817.8	$ 791.8	$ 757.2
International	601.8	659.0	604.3
Total net sales	1,419.6	1,450.8	1,361.5
Cost of goods sold	855.4	831.1	876.8
Marketing, research, engineering and administrative expenses	520.8	483.9	449.4
Total costs	1,376.2	1,315.0	1,326.2
Profit from operations	43.4	135.8	35.3
Other income	49.2	25.4	13.3
Interest expense	29.9	17.0	12.8
Earnings before income taxes	62.7	144.2	35.8
Federal, state and foreign income taxes (credit)	31.6	58.8	(.3)
Net earnings	$ 31.1	$ 85.4	$ 36.1
Earnings per share	$ .95	$ 2.60	$ 1.10
Cash dividends per share	$ 1.00	$ 1.00	$ 1.00
Average number of shares (in millions)	32.9	32.9	32.9
Selected Balance Sheet Information			
Working capital*	$ 749.5	$ 721.9	$ 535.9
Net property, plant and equipment	332.9	362.2	371.6
Total assets*	1,434.7	1,404.0	1,253.7
Long-term debt	124.2	124.1	—
Stockholders' equity*	958.2	960.0	907.5
Other Statistical Data			
Additions to property, plant and equipment	$ 42.5	$ 68.1	$ 134.6
Depreciation	$ 69.2	$ 62.7	$ 51.7
Payroll and benefits	$ 550.5	$ 497.3	$ 464.1**
Number of employees, end of year	16,784	17,454	18,416
Return on equity* (two point average)	3.2%	9.1%	4.0%

* Years 1972 through 1980 have been restated to reflect implementation of Financial Account-
ing Standards Board Statement No. 43 "Accounting for Compensated Absences."
** Restated.

Source: Polaroid Corporation, *Annual Report*, 1981.

1978	1977	1976	1975	1974	1973	1972
$ 817.4	$ 645.8	$ 586.7	$ 495.6	$ 487.3	$ 493.1	$ 417.5
559.2	416.1	363.3	317.1	270.0	192.4	141.8
1,376.6	1,061.9	950.0	812.7	757.3	685.5	559.3
778.3	575.7	511.8	467.9	485.2	358.0	260.1
418.2	337.3	294.9	237.0	239.3	251.6	236.7
1,196.5	913.0	806.7	704.9	724.5	609.6	496.8
180.1	148.9	143.3	107.8	32.8	75.9	62.5
20.3	19.0	14.4	16.8	13.4	14.2	13.5
5.9	6.4	3.3	1.3	1.1	.3	(.8
194.5	161.5	154.4	123.3	45.1	89.8	75.2
76.1	69.2	74.7	60.7	16.7	38.0	32.7
$ 118.4	$ 92.3	$ 79.7	$ 62.6	$ 28.4	$ 51.8	$ 42.5
$ 3.60	$ 2.81	$ 2.43	$ 1.91	$ .86	$ 1.58	$ 1.30
$ .90	$ .65	$ .41	$ .32	$ .32	$ .32	$ .32
32.9	32.9	32.9	32.9	32.9	32.9	32.8
$ 609.5	$ 589.6	$ 546.4	$ 475.1	$ 402.0	$ 380.1	$ 341.7
294.8	225.9	198.2	203.3	224.3	228.3	224.5
1,276.0	1,076.7	959.0	843.7	777.8	751.0	661.2
—	—	—	—	—	—	—
904.3	815.5	744.6	678.4	626.3	608.4	566.2
$ 115.0	$ 68.7	$ 33.9	$ 21.8	$ 40.0	$ 40.3	$ 44.6
$ 43.0	$ 39.5	$ 38.3	$ 39.1	$ 39.6	$ 35.3	$ 32.0
$ 421.4**	$ 332.2**	$ 289.6**	$ 231.8**	$ 223.2	$ 191.3	$ 160.2
20,884	16,394	14,506	13,387	13,019	14,227	11,998
13.8%	11.8%	11.2%	9.6%	4.6%	8.8%	7.7%

EXHIBIT II   COMPARATIVE INSTANT CAMERA AND FILM DATA—1982 (Dollars in Millions)

	Polaroid 1982			Kodak 1982
	Total	*Nonamateur*	*Amateur*	*All Amateur*
Sales	$1,294	$390	$904	$425
Cost of goods	741	211	530	264
% of Sales	57.3%	54.0%	58.6%	62.0%
S & A.	473	128	345	162
% of Sales	36.6%	32.8%	38.2%	38.2%
Operating profit	$ 80	$ 51	$ 29	$ (1)
Margins	6.2%	13.1%	3.2%	—

Source: Donaldson, Lufkin & Jenrette, *Research Bulletin*, Sept. 28, 1983.

EXHIBIT III   U.S. MANUFACTURERS' SHIPMENTS OF PHOTOGRAPHIC EQUIPMENT AND SUPPLIES ($ Millions)

	1977		1978		1979		1980		1981		1982	
	$	%	$	%	$	%	$	%	$	%	$	%
Sensitized Film and Paper	$3,874.1	39.0%	$ 4,489.7	39.0%	$ 5,288.7	39.5%	$ 6,706.7	42.3%	$ 7,186.4	42.4%	$ 7,652.9	41.3
Prepared Photographic Chemicals	695.6	7.0	805.4	7.0	937.2	7.0	1,030.6	6.5	1,033.9	6.1	1,080.4	5.8
Micrographic Equipment	298.1	3.0	345.2	3.0	401.7	3.0	539.1	3.4	793.2	3.5	948.5	4.0
Motion Picture Equipment	198.7	2.0	230.1	2.0	267.8	2.0	269.5	1.7	220.3	1.3	298.3	1.6
Still Picture Equipment	993.7	10.0	1,150.6	10.0	1,405.9	10.5	1,442.8	9.1	1,271.2	7.5	1,466.5	7.9
Reprographic Equipment	3,876.8	39.0	4,485.0	39.0	5,087.7	38.0	5,866.3	37.0	6,644.0	39.2	7,310.4	39.4
Total	$9,937.0	100.0%	$11,506.0	100.0%	$13,389.0	100.0%	$15,855.0	100.0%	$16,949.0	100.0%	$18,557.0	100.0
Yr. to Yr. Change	15.8%		15.8%		16.4%		18.4%		6.9%		9.5%	

Source: Lehman Brothers Kuhn Loeb, *The Photographic Products Market*, August 4, 1983.

EXHIBIT IV U.S. IMPORTS AND EXPORTS OF PHOTOGRAPHIC EQUIPMENT AND SUPPLIES

ESTIMATED PRODUCT BREAKDOWN ($ Millions)

	1979			1980			1981			1982		
	Exports	Imports	Net	Exports	Imports	Net	Exports	Imports	Net	Exports	Imports	Net
Sensitized Film and Paper	$1,074.2	$ 390.7	$683.5	$1,349.9	$ 532.7	$817.2	$1,346.1	$ 567.1	$779.0	$1,234.9	$ 607.7	$627.2
Prepared Photographic Chemicals	133.9	6.7	127.2	137.8	9.1	128.7	133.3	9.5	123.8	135.6	8.0	127.6
Micrographic Equipment	77.3	1.6	75.7	90.9	1.9	89.0	110.0	5.0	105.0	86.1	2.7	83.4
Motion Picture Equipment	82.7	68.3	14.4	99.1	69.4	29.7	99.3	45.5	53.8	85.9	32.3	53.6
Still Picture Equipment	420.5	731.7	(311.2)	450.3	644.5	(194.2)	457.7	798.9	(341.2)	491.3	783.4	(292.1)
Reprographic Equipment	358.4	358.3	0.1	331.7	497.0	(165.3)	361.5	721.1	(359.6)	423.6	676.4	(252.8)
Total	$2,147.0	$1,557.3	$589.7	$2,459.7	$1,754.6	$705.1	$2,507.9	$2,147.1	$360.8	$2,457.4	$2,110.5	$346.9

Source: Lehman Brothers Kuhn Loeb, *The Photographic Products Market*, August 4, 1983.

EXHIBIT IV (Continued)

ESTIMATED REGIONAL BREAKDOWN ($ Millions)

	1979				1980				1981				1982			
	Exports		Imports		Exports		Imports		Exports		Imports		Exports		Imports	
	$	%	$	%	$	%	$	%	$	%	$	%	$	%	$	%
Europe	$ 972.6	45.3%	$ 294.3	18.9%	$,116.7	45.4%	$ 352.7	20.1%	$ 969.4	38.7%	$ 329.7	15.3	$1,069.7	43.5%	$ 373.2	17.7%
Canada	255.5	11.9	73.2	4.7	275.5	11.2	119.3	6.8	271.2	10.8	113.9	5.3	316.5	12.9	102.8	4.9
Latin America	188.9	8.8	1.6	0.1	206.6	8.4	1.8	0.1	376.2	15.0	1.8	0.1	287.5	11.7	3.0	.1
Asia	298.5	13.9	1,175.7	75.5	332.1	13.5	1,272.1	72.5	491.9	19.6	1,669.9	77.8	529.8	21.6	1,622.0	76.9
Other	431.5	20.1	12.5	0.8	528.8	21.5	8.7	0.5	399.2	15.9	31.9	1.5	253.9	10.3	9.5	.4
Total	$2,147.0	100.0%	$1,557.3	100.0%	$2,459.7	100.0%	$1,754.6	100.0%	$2,507.9	100.0%	$2,147.1	100.0%	$2,457.4	100.0%	$2,110.5	100.0%

Source: Lehman Brothers Kuhn Loeb, *The Photographic Products Market*, August 4, 1983.

EXHIBIT V   ESTIMATED BREAKDOWN OF STILL PICTURES TAKEN BY U.S. CONSUMERS (Millions of Units)

	1977		1978		1979		1980		1981		1982	
	Units	% Chg.	Units	% Chg.	Units	% Chg.	Units	% Chg.	Units	% Chg.	Units	% Chg.
Color Print (Negative)	4,805	17.8%	6,010	25.1%	6,295	4.7%	6,645	5.6%	7,300	9.9%	7,950	8.9%
Slides (Positive)	1,495	(4.4)	1,585	6.0	1,530	(3.5)	1,540	0.7	1,350	(12.3)	1,250	(7.4)
Instant	1,370	5.4	1,675	22.3	1,550	7.5	1,500	(3.3)	1,450	(3.3)	1,250	(13.8)
Black & White	660	(10.0)	600	(9.1)	575	(4.2)	565	(1.7)	525	(7.1)	500	(4.8)
Total	8,330	8.5%	9,870	18.5%	9,950	0.8%	10,250	3.0%	10,625	3.7%	10,950	3.1%

Source: Lehman Brothers Kuhn Loeb, The Photographic Products Market, August 4, 1983.

EXHIBIT VI ESTIMATED U.S. CONSUMER PURCHASES OF FILM, BY TYPE
(Millions of Units)

Film Type	1978	1979	1980	1981	1982	Change
Instant B&W	18.8	12.8	7.9	5.8	4.4 *	(24.1)%
Instant Color	119.6	124.1	124.2	126.0	110.9	(12.0)
35mm B&W	26.7	21.2	25.3	23.0	18.6	(19.1)
35mm Color Slide	61.3	56.2	55.3	57.0	52.0	(8.8)
35mm Color Print	84.8	98.5	119.9	137.0	146.8	7.2
110 Cartridge B&W	16.1	18.4	14.0	10.0	13.9	39.0
110 Cartridge Color		170.7	182.3	193.0	196.5	1.8
126 Cartridge B&W	221.6	14.3	9.2	8.0	9.0	12.5
126 Cartridge Color		104.2	103.1	105.0	90.0	(14.3)
Disc					21.0	
Other Still B&W	20.0	8.2	6.9	6.7	6.5	(3.0)
Other Still Color	44.4	17.8	13.4	15.0	13.2	(12.0)
Movie	35.3	27.5	26.8	22.0	19.0	(13.6)
Total	648.6	673.9	688.3	708.5	701.8	(0.9)%

Source: Lehman Brothers Kuhn Loeb, *The Photographic Products Market*, August 4, 1983.

EXHIBIT VI (*Continued*)
ESTIMATED BREAKDOWN OF U.S. CONSUMER CAMERA SALES (Thousands of Units)

	1974	1975	1976	1977	1978
Cartridge*	8,590	8,630	9,050	9,250	10,200
35mm (All Types)	825	708	980	1,560	2,300
Instant	3,300	3,900	4,500	6,600	8,200
8mm Movie	636	392	450	609	525
Other†	12	15	20	22	24
Total	13,363	13,645	15,000	18,041	21,249

	1979	1980	1981	1982	Change
Cartridge*	8,800	7,500	7,000	2,800	(60)%
Disc	—	—	—	3,900	—
35mm (All Types)	2,600	2,900	3,400	3,700	8.8
Instant	6,600	5,700	5,000	4,500	(10.0)
8mm Movie	300	230	180	100	(44.4)
Other†	30	33	36	35	(2.8)
Total	18,330	16,363	15,616	15,035	(3.7)%

* 110 and 126 combined.
† Roll and large format.

Source: Lehman Brothers Kuhn Loeb, *The Photographic Products Market*, August 4, 1983.

EXHIBIT VII   POLAROID CORP. COMPARATIVE DATA ($ Millions, # Millions)

	1977	1978	1979	1980	1981	1982
Sales						
Worldwide ($)	1,061.9	1,376.6	1,361.5	1,450.8	1,419.6	1,293.9
U.S.	645.8	817.4	757.2	791.8	817.8	752.5
Europe	274.2	364.9	383.3	436.8	369.2	333.2
Rest of World						
including Asia	141.9	194.3	220.9	222.2	232.6	208.2
Worldwide (# Units)						
Cameras	7.0+[2]	9.4	7.3	6.6	5.6	4.0
Film Packs	n/a	200+	205[1]	198[1]	194[1]	n/a
Tech/Ind Photo						
as % of Total $	n/a	n/a	n/a	25.30%	30%	33%
Financials ($)						
EPS	2.81	3.60	1.10	2.60	.95	.73
Dividends/share	.65	.90	1.00	1.00	1.00	1.00
R&D Expense	88.9	86.5	109.6	114.0	121.4	118.4
Capital Expense	68.9	115.0	134.7	68.1	42.5	31.5
Advertising Expense	70.8	101.1	105.0	101.4	106.6	96.4
Return on Assets	8.6%	9.3%	2.9%	6.1%	2.2%	1.8%
# Employees	16,394	20,884	18,416	17,454	16,784	14,540

[1] *Merrill Lynch Securities Research Report, May 17, 1982, p. 3.*
[2] *The Wall Street Journal, September 5, 1980.*

Source: All data not otherwise noted drawn from Polaroid Corporation, *Annual Report*, 1978–1982.

EXHIBIT VIII   POLAROID EXECUTIVE OFFICERS—1981

Name	Office	Age
Edwin H. Land	Chairman of the Board	72
William J. McCune, Jr.	President and Chief Executive Officer	66
I.M. Booth	Executive Vice President	50
Sheldon A. Buckler	Executive Vice President	50
Peter Wensberg	Executive Vice President	53
Richard W. Young	Executive Vice President	55
Milton S. Dietz	Senior Vice President	50
Charles Mikulka	Senior Vice President	68
Howard G. Rogers	Senior Vice President and Director of Research	66
Harvey H. Thayer	Senior Vice President, Finance	54
Richard F. deLima	Vice President and Secretary	51
Julius Silver	Vice President and Chairman Executive Committee	81
Edward R. Bedrosian	Treasurer	49

Dr. Land, founder of the Company, served as Chairman of the Board, Chief Executive Officer and Director of Research from 1937 to 1980. In 1980, Dr. Land was reelected Chairman of the Board and assumed the new position of Consulting Director of Basic Research in Land Photography. He is the inventor of synthetic sheet polarizer for light and of one-step photography. He is the holder of numerous honorary degrees and has been the recipient of many awards from various professional societies.

Mr. McCune joined the Company in 1939

EXHIBIT VIII (*Continued*)

and has been a Director since 1975. He was elected Vice President, Engineering in 1954, Vice President, Assistant General Manager in 1963, Executive Vice President in 1969, President and Chief Operating Officer in 1975 and to his present positions as President and Chief Executive Officer in 1980.

Mr. Booth joined the Company in 1958. He was elected Assistant Vice President and Assistant to the President in 1975, Vice President and Assistant to the President in 1976, Senior Vice President in 1977, and to his present position as Executive Vice President in 1980.

Dr. Buckler joined the Company in 1964. He was elected Assistant Vice President in 1969, Vice President, Research Division in 1972, Group Vice President in 1975, Senior Vice President in 1977 and to his present position as Executive Vice President in 1980.

Mr. Wensberg joined the Company in 1958. He was elected Assistant Vice President, Advertising in 1966, Vice President, Advertising in 1968, Senior Vice President in 1971 and to his present position as Executive Vice President in 1980.

Dr. Young joined the Company in 1962. He was elected Vice President, Assistant Director of Research in 1963, Senior Vice President in 1969 and to his present position as Executive Vice President in 1980.

Mr. Dietz joined the Company in 1955.

He was elected Assistant Vice President in 1975. Vice President, Engineering in 1977 and to his present position as Senior Vice President in 1980.

Mr. Mikulka joined the Company in 1942. He was elected Vice President, Patents in 1960 and to his present position as Senior Vice President in 1975.

Mr. Rogers joined the Company in 1937. He was elected Vice President and Senior Research Fellow in 1968. Vice President, Senior Research Fellow and Associate Director of Research in 1975, Senior Vice President and Associate Director of Research in 1979 and to his present positions as Senior Vice President and Director of Research in 1980.

Mr. Thayer joined the Company in 1956. He was elected Treasurer in 1970, Vice President and Treasurer in 1971, Vice President, Finance and Treasurer in 1977 and to his present position as Senior Vice President, Finance in 1980.

Mr. deLima joined the Company as Secretary in 1972. He was elected to his present positions as Vice President and Secretary in 1975.

Mr. Silver, a Director and Vice President since 1937 and Chairman of the Executive Committee, is also a partner in the firm of Silver & Solomon, the Company's general counsel.

Mr. Bedrosian joined the Company in 1965. He was elected Assistant Treasurer in 1975 and to his present position as Treasurer in 1980.

Source: Polaroid Corporation, *10K*, 1981.

EXHIBIT IX   POLAROID CORPORATION PRODUCTION
FACILITIES AS OF 1981

Location	Function
Domestic	
Norwood, Mass.	polarizer sheet production
Norwood, Mass.	transparency film production
Norwood, Mass.	camera assembly[1]
Waltham, Mass.	battery assembly
Waltham, Mass.	chemical production
Waltham, Mass.	film pack production
Waltham, Mass.	positive film production
Freetown, Mass.	chemical production
Foreign	
Dumbarton, Scotland	camera assembly, film pack assembly, positive film production, sunglass production
Enschede, Netherlands	film pack assembly, positive film production, sunglass production
Newbridge, Ireland	film pack assembly

[1] *Highly labor intensive.*

Source: Compiled from various annual reports.

EXHIBIT X   POLAROID CORPORATION—1980

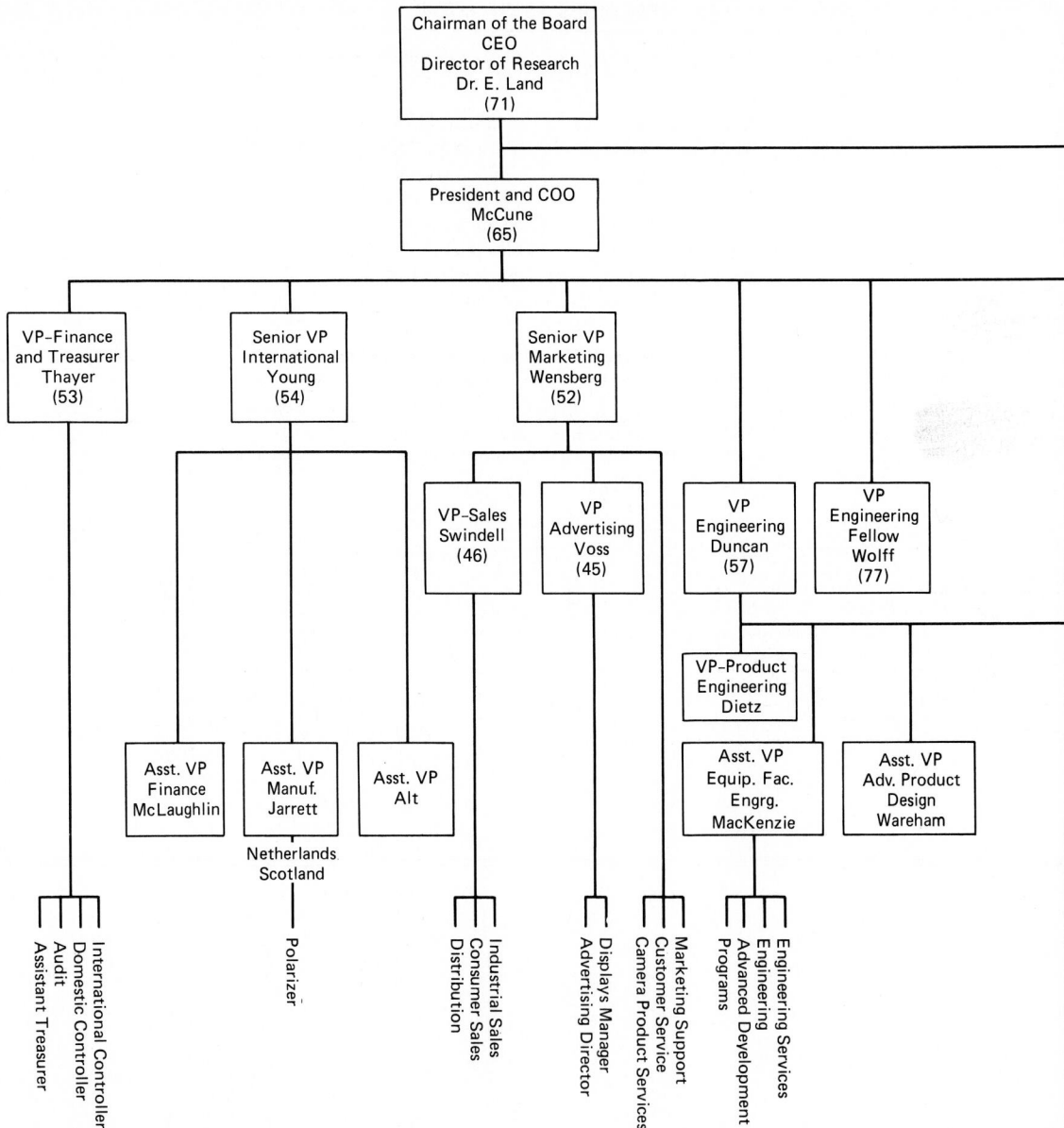

Note: Numbers in parentheses indicate the ages of the various executives.

Source: Approximate 1980, pre-reorganization, organizational chart drawn from various secondary sources. company does not have an official organization chart.

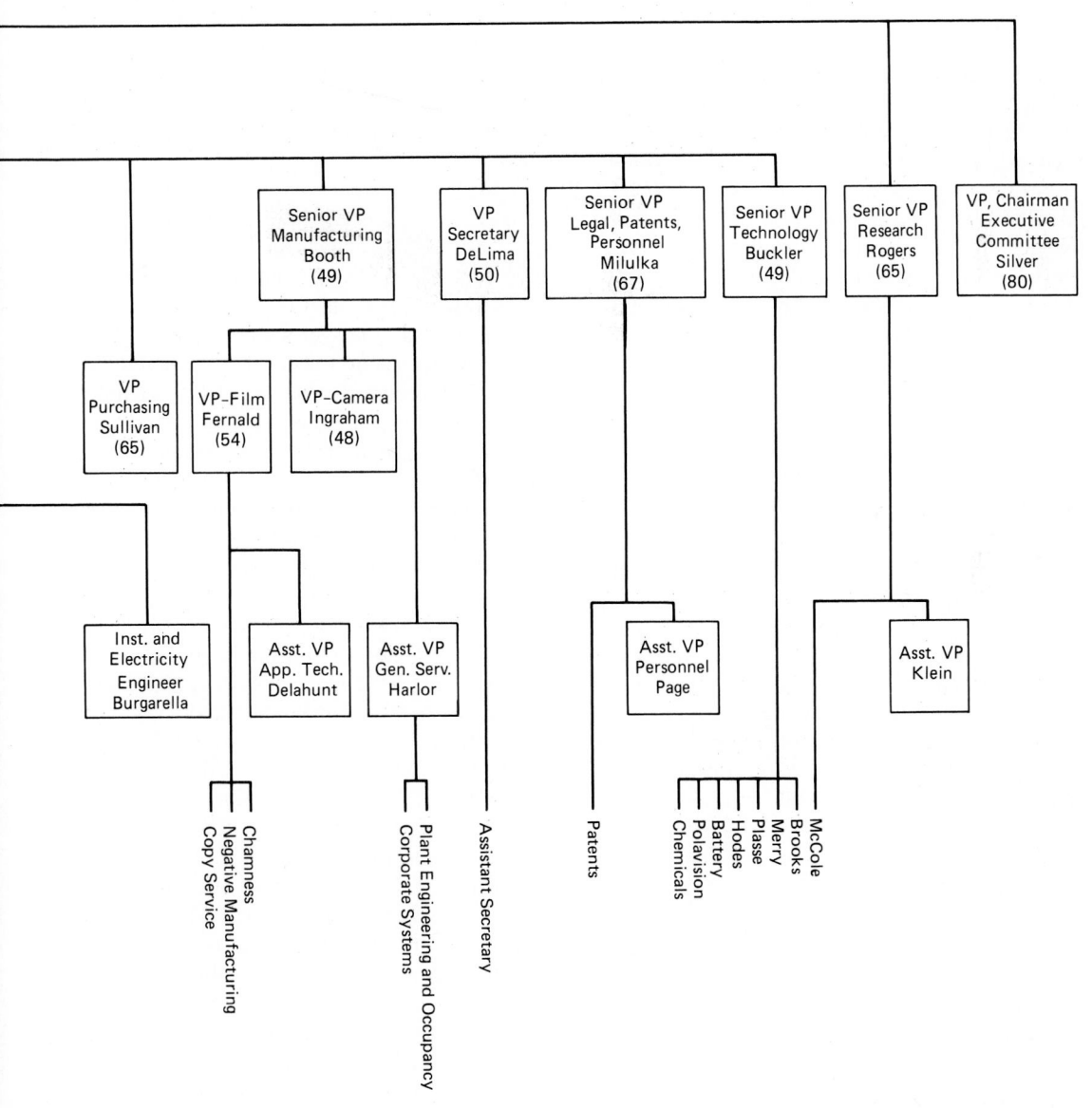

THE PILLSBURY COMPANY

"We laughed at Pillsbury ten years ago," said a General Mills executive as the 1980s began. "But now for better or for worse, Pillsbury seems to be getting all the action."[1] With fine performances by both companies over the preceding decade, this was rare praise in one of the strongest crosstown rivalries in the whole business world. What caused the spectacular turnaround at Pillsbury? What could be learned from these events? In May 1985, Mr. William Spoor, the man most associated with the changes at Pillsbury would step down as CEO and turn this authority over to his President, Jack Stafford. What actions should Stafford take to ensure the company's continuing success? And what should Pillsbury's-strategies be for the late 1980s and early 1990s?

EARLY HISTORY AND BACKGROUND

Both companies had grown up in the burgeoning grain and flour markets of the mid 1800s. Both had headquarters in Minneapolis. And both began to diversify away from their stagnating flour milling activities in the early 1950s. In contrast to General Mills which moved into electronics, chemicals, and appliances (see General Mills, Inc. case), Pillsbury concentrated on flour, grains, baking mixes, and dough products through the 1950s. And it remained primarily a U.S. based company.

Under President Paul S. Gerot, Pillsbury expanded in the 1960s into powdered drink mixes, calcium cyclamate, and poultry.[2] And it made

some small related acquisitions in Canada and Latin America.[3] But earnings remained unstable; and when 1966 earnings dropped 3% despite a 9% sales growth, a new management team was named.

Robert J. Keith—who had engineered the company's 1940s entry into consumer baking mixes and 1950s expansion into refrigerated dough products—moved from president of the Consumer Division to chief executive officer. And Terrance Hanold, a lawyer with computer expertise, became president. Messrs. Keith and Hanold diversified Pillsbury further. In 1967, Call-A-Computer, a computer time sharing subsidiary, was formed; but more importantly, Burger King, a $12 million Miami restaurant chain, was acquired. Burger King expanded rapidly, growing by 150 restaurants in FY 1969 alone, to a total of 850 in 1972, when with less than $\frac{1}{6}$ of Pillsbury's sales it began to provide more than $\frac{1}{4}$ of total earnings.[4] In 1969, Pillsbury acquired majority interest in Poppin' Fresh Pie Shops. In 1970, J–M Poultry Packing was acquired, as were Pemton, Inc. (a residential and community developer of experimental housing),[5] Bon Appetit, (a gourmet foods magazine) and Bon Voyage (travel services). In 1971, Bachman's European Flower Markets (retail outlets for cut flowers, plants, and accessories) were added. In 1972, the company acquired: Mallory Restaurants; Souverain Cellars, a California vintner; and Moline, Inc.

Messrs. Keith and Hanold, also decentralized Pillsbury's organization, establishing Consumer Products, Agri-Products, Pillsbury Farms (poultry operations), Burger King, Food Service (commercial foods), and International as "free standing businesses." But company-wide profit margins hovered between 4.7% and 5.8% from 1967 to 1972 while rival General Mills achieved 7.8% to 11.4%. Consumer food sales stagnated at $267–$272 million for three years. And Pills-

Case copyright © 1985 by James Brian Quinn. Material is partly adapted from an earlier case written by James Brian Quinn and Mariann Jelinek. Research associates— Penny C. Paquette and Allie J. Quinn. The generous cooperation of the Pillsbury Company is gratefully acknowledged.

bury was a slow third behind General Mills (Betty Crocker) and P&G's (Duncan Hines) brands in the crucial cake mix field.[6]

THE PILLSBURY DREAM

About this time (early 1972) CEO, Robert Keith, named an executive team to consider new goals and strategies for Pillsbury. As William Spoor, then vice president and general manager of international operations, recalls:

> The process kind of evolved in a natural way. I was talking to Bob Keith. I said, "You know, Bob, this is the fifth year of my stock options and they're all under water." He responded, "Bill, if you're dissatisfied with the results of the company, why don't you develop an alternate strategy?" I said, "Are you serious?" And he said, "Yes! You're free to use anyone you want in the company." So I got the general managers together and we agreed to meet 2–3 times a month to put together a preliminary plan.

A New Management Team

But Mr. Keith did not live to see the results of these deliberations. At the age of 59, he developed cancer, resigned in December 1972, and died only a few months later. In a move surprising to most outsiders, Mr. Hanold "stepped aside for youth." Bill Spoor (49), a tough numbers oriented executive with acquisitions and overseas experience, was named Chairman and CEO. James R. Peterson (45), a fast-rising grocery products and marketing executive, became president. Both had been hand-selected by Mr. Keith as potential contenders for the top job.

Mr. Spoor's strategy group had met over an eight month period in 1972, before the seriousness of Mr. Keith's illness was known. In November, when Mr. Keith's condition worsened, Spoor and Peterson were asked to prepare a strategy presentation for the Board. They were given thirty days. Mr. Peterson, on vacation, reportedly added a few comments to the draft Mr. Spoor worked up with the help of inside and outside experts. The presentation was a distillation of the general managers' strategy deliberations, what the new team would do with the company, Mr. Spoor's philosophy, and a bit about proposed management style.

One executive who saw this document noted: "It talked about the kind of teamwork they were going to develop, the kind of company they would try to build, the kind of people they would try to acquire. It was on a high plane. It didn't say we were going to be $\frac{1}{3}$ restaurants, $\frac{1}{3}$ consumer, $\frac{1}{3}$ agri. It talked about the approach to the business, the strengthening of our staff, attracting stronger people through aggressive compensation, and good business planning . . . about the use of the executive committee as kind of the conscience and central nervous system of the company. It was seen on an informal basis—pieces of it—by senior management inside the company . . . [in addition to the Board's nominating committee]."

As a portion of drawing up the statement, Mr. Spoor asked each outside board member to identify the company's strengths and weaknesses and why each thought the company's performance had been so lackluster. He also asked twelve outside analysts both these questions and why Pillsbury wasn't more attractive to the investing public. Said Spoor:

> If you put them all together they said basically the same thing: inconsistent performance in earnings per share growth, poor profit record, a shotgun approach to our portfolio [without] the necessary resources to support all our businesses, the failure to make acquisitions in support of our basic businesses, which were then Agri-Products and Consumer Products. And last was a simple observation that we had some businesses making money, but too many that were losing money. [With this in mind] we sat down and laid out a plan that we knew would have the

support of the general managers because, after all, they helped create it.

Setting Goals for a New Era

A portion of the process was the examination of other companies in the food business. Each member of the general managers' strategy group took 3–4 companies in the foods business and analyzed why they were successful. How they got there? What their performance measures were? Why they were great? Why the investors and analysts liked them? And so on. The general managers next extracted a composite of concepts they thought made attractive goals for Pillsbury and some things they were convinced the company really could do. Then, Mr. Spoor said:

> We laid out the key objectives of what we called "the Pillsbury dream." We said we wanted a five-year record of consistent growth in sales and earnings per share. We wanted more than anything else, credibility, not only with our Board and ourselves, but with the investing public. We needed quality earnings, consistent, repetitive, growing. We wanted an average 10% growth per year in sales, minimum 10% growth in EPS, an ROE of 16%, an ROI on total capital employed of 20%, and a P/E ratio in the upper $\frac{1}{3}$ of the leading food companies. We felt if we had a record of performance [like that] the stock price would follow. We said that recruiting, development, and motivation of people was key. We wanted to be a quality company, first class in all respects—in our people, our products, our facilities, and our business conduct.

After almost a year of discussion there was a strong consensus. Of the goals, Mr. Spoor said, "There was no issue at all. The big issue became how do we know we're going to do it? What are our plans?" The next steps were unique. "We decided to really put ourselves on the spot. I suggested to the Board that we go public with our objectives, really lay the company out. . . . They said, 'Why? Why don't you just wait?' So we waited until the May Board meeting; then we laid out [for the Board] the presentation we

wanted to take to the New York security analysts." Two months later (on July 19, 1973) Spoor, Peterson, and Arthur Rosewall (CEO of Burger King) publicly announced certain key strategies and objectives at a meeting of the New York Society of Security Analysts. Highlights are included in Exhibit I. Mr. Spoor said, "I think people understood this was a different group [of managers] with different aspirations. But they still had doubts we could achieve what we said."

The Changeover

Certain actions were already under way. Organizationally, most of the operations now reported directly to Spoor: Wallin in Agriproducts, Elston (whom Spoor brought in from McKinsey) in International, Rosewall in Burger King, and most corporate staff units. Although Peterson had the title of President, he was not Chief Operating Officer. His role was more that of group vice president over the consumer business. Spoor quickly started "Monday morning staff meetings" attended by these top line people and ultimately a few staff people. He made it clear that the style of Pillsbury had changed. He was going to be involved. He would call the shots. He would listen to people, but he was going to make the decisions. As one executive said, "Peterson didn't get to make many decisions—very aggravating to Jimmy," a man who had been considered a genuine candidate for the top spot.

According to some, "Pillsbury had become a bit inbred at this time." There was an inside Board with many Minneapolis people on it. The tenor of the company was described as "hold things the way they were." Sales growth had been largely through inflation. Relationships at the top level had been "very gentlemanly." In this milieu Spoor's style created a new driving force. His style was described as follows:

> He's a challenger. He really takes nothing at face value, even after you've worked with him for a long time. I'm as liable as ever to go up to his office and be really grilled. He's not doing it to grill me, but to really penetrate, to see how carefully an idea has been thought through, how

ready it is to be hatched—and how strongly I believe it. He may oppose me and disguise his reason for opposition, just to see how deeply I feel about a thing. He's a challenger, a questioner. He's an options open kind of guy. . . . But he has very strong opinions on things. [To change an opinion] you just have to tackle him and break his shoulder.

He's also very much a scorecard guy. He says, ''I keep a scorecard, good and bad.'' Each time the Board meets, he says this is what I said I was going to do. This is what we've done. This is what we haven't done. This is what we're going to do the next period. And this is how I'll come to you to measure my and the corporation's performance. He has said, ''I'm on this stage for awhile; then somebody else is going to have it. Some people have stayed here too long. I'm not going to. . . . I expect to be taken care of if I do a good job here, but don't keep me here a month longer than I am really contributing.'' He means it.

He's not a gentle, caring, warm, human being. He's fun. He likes to have a drink, to tell a good story, to laugh. But he's an intensive, inward guy—very performance oriented. Unfortunately, there's a lot of fear of Bill Spoor too. Sometimes it costs him in terms of some people's willingness to really say where they are on issues. He seeks a lot of input, listens to people he respects and trusts, thinks. He doesn't make a decision until he has to. I don't mean that he procrastinates. He keeps every option open, whether it's who he'll have lunch with, who he'll name to the Board, or what organizational form he'll use. He doesn't commit his mind to a course of action until he has everything he can learn about it. He's a very bright guy, and a very clear thinker, especially on paper. Yet he's very low on self ego, very unselfish in his management style.

THE CHICKEN IS THE EGG

The first real test of the new management team was in stabilizing earnings. A key element in this had to be Pillsbury Farms' chicken business.

Two years before Mr. Spoor's accession, *Financial World* had pointed out:

> [In 1971] Pillsbury's first half sales rose 4% from those in the corresponding period of fiscal 1969–70, but common share earnings fell from $2.34 to $1.30. This sharp drop would be startling enough even in a company dependent mainly on the badly depressed broiler market; but Pillsbury Farms, the chicken division, brought in only 16% of the sales in fiscal 1969–70, so it's obvious that the chicken impact is really staggering.[7]

The Biggest Question

According to Mr. G.M. Donhowe, Vice President and Treasurer at the time,

> Bill knew before he took the job that the biggest question he'd have to face was to stay in or get out of chickens. [Within a few months after taking over] he asked a number of people who he knew were protagonists on one side or the other for whatever memoranda or position papers they had in their files on the subject. Then he invited any member of senior management who wanted to present a position paper to do so. He got papers from Terry Hanold, who was a strong advocate of the chicken business; Dean McNeal, who was on the Board and had formerly run our Agricultural Products group which included chickens; and Mike Harper, who had run the operation trying to sell branded chickens (fresh and frozen) and frozen processed chickens . . . I was a chief protagonist for getting rid of it. I was joined in that position substantially by Paul Kelsey, the controller. Just about everyone else was sitting in the wings. . . .

Spoor had purposely commissioned two papers on each side of the issue: Hanold and McNeal for retention, Harper and Donhowe for divestiture. But the decision was not easy. As Mr. Spoor said later, ''Poultry was some $140 million of our [roughly] $700 million in sales, and in that particular year it was on an up cycle. In the last full year of our ownership, poultry made $6 million.'' Management was split on the issue. And to complicate matters, Mr. Hanold, the past president who had been largely responsible for the chicken business concept, was still on the Board and was Chairman of the Executive Committee.

Debate and Decision

With the position papers as background management debated the issue for twelve months ''very hotly and under difficult circumstances.'' Spoor and Donhowe visited Ralston Purina which had recently made a similar divestiture. They invited consultants to look at the issue. And they asked Lehman Brothers what Pillsbury Farms' real value was. Lehman responded that they could sell it to a potential European buyer at a price higher ''by some healthy margin'' than the present value of the division's then projected five year cash flows. Finally this information, the position papers, and management's own recommendation to divest went to the Board. The Board continued the debate for some months. When the issue finally came to a vote, only Mr. Hanold voted against divestiture. According to some, this signaled Mr. Hanold's ''break with management.'' And shortly afterward at his own request Hanold ''went onto special assignment.'' Mr. Spoor later commented very sympathetically, ''A very brilliant man! A shame, but that's just the way it went.''

Following the Board's vote on March 6, 1974, Pillsbury Farms was sold to Imperial Group, Ltd. for over $20 million. Mr. Spoor later noted: ''This really taught everyone a lesson—that anything that wasn't performing, that didn't have good long-range plans and prospects, was in trouble.'' But in his public announcement of the decision, he emphasized that:

> Pillsbury Farms is a good business directed by sound management. Our decision to sell is based on strategic fit and price—not inadequate performance. . . .
> To remain with Farms would call for a significant reinvestment program. . . .
> We do not believe that selection of broiler

chickens for growth investments meets the corporate objectives we outlined to you in our meeting with the New York Society last July.[8]

The divested division had made $3 million net in fiscal 1974 before its sale.[9] In the next year, it reportedly lost money for its new owners; and in the words of one executive, ''Spoor became an overnight hero. He gained a lot of ground with the Board.''

A FOODS COMPANY

''By then, after a year,'' said Mr. Spoor, ''we had decided that we wanted to be a foods company. As we looked back, that was the only thing that we'd really made money on. Once we'd agreed on that . . . we got rid of all the sideshows. We dumped housing, timesharing, the gourmet magazine, wines, and fresh flowers— all after careful study. But you have to give people a rationale—a truthful rationale—as to why you do these things. So we said, we want to be a foods company. We've agreed to that. This [or that division or business] doesn't fit, besides which it is losing money.''

For example, housing had lost a lot of money. And, according to one major participant, ''top management really didn't even know the vocabulary of the business.'' Time sharing had been created because the company had excess computer capacity and the former president—who was interested in computer applications[10]—had pushed the opportunity. This business clearly did not fit well into the ''foods'' concept. On the other hand, Spoor later said, ''We should have been able to make *Gourmet* magazine go, but I couldn't find anyone who would take the challenge. That was an easy sale [because the business could have been made profitable].''

Out of Wine

Souverain Cellars was much more complicated because it involved big losses. In 1972 Pillsbury had bought Souverain in California's Napa Valley and had pumped in some $8 million to boost production from 12,000 cases toward 1978 goals of 570,000 cases. But the total industry overexpanded to an extent that it outran both consumer demand and its own storage facilities. By mid 1975 Souverain had lost money for two consecutive years, and its near term future looked just as bleak.[11] Pillsbury tried several management teams in an attempt to turn the company around, but with little success. Finally Mr. Spoor asked the president of Souverain, "How much money could we make if every case was sold for margin." The president responded, "$2 million before taxes." At that time Pillsbury had already lost $6 million on Souverain. Shortly thereafter Souverain's president came back to Spoor and recommended, himself, that Pillsbury leave the wine business.

Several rationales presented themselves for this action in 1975. First, Souverain was a losing operation. Second, certain states prohibited alcoholic beverage producers from selling alcohol in their own restaurants. This would have prevented Burger King from ever selling beer. And it would have precluded an attractive potential acquisition, Steak and Ale, which suddenly appeared. But executives noted the divestiture decision was really underway much earlier. "We had a 1½% market share and no real ability—without just mammoth investments—to become major. . . . Also, remember, Bill Spoor wants to be big and recognizable in anything he does, whether it's hitting a tennis ball or business. Steak and Ale just accelerated the decision. We had enormous earnings in 1975 so we could afford to take the bath then."

Of this early period, Mr. Spoor said:

> I used to do quiet things at night. I was convinced if we could just turn off these loss divisions, we could really make some money. We were draining the company for no purpose at all. I've always got hedges in the back of my mind. I'm never overcommitted [to a business] unless I *know* there's something back there. I get surprised sometimes. But I knew if we got rid of all these, we'd have a better

income later. Maybe that could give us 3–4% of our 10% target profit growth.

Mr. Spoor also noted that in this divestiture period:

> In several cases the people who were directly involved in the management of troubled divisions—for example the president of Souverain—came in with recommendations that theirs were businesses we ought to get out of. In Souverain's case it was a major problem area. We had proven we couldn't manage it. We had made lots of fundamental managerial mistakes in terms of how we ran it.
>
> But essentially the same thing occurred in the European Flower Markets. In its final year as a part of Pillsbury, that reported to me. I'd told the general manager that I'd like to have his recommendation for the future of the business. . . . And his recommendation was to get out of it. He has a very important role elsewhere in Pillsbury now.

Reinvestment and Diversification

With the cash freed up by divestitures, Pillsbury began to reinvest in growth opportunities. Primary among these, at the time, was Burger King. As Spoor said, "With cake mix you could only grow two ways—by a new product expanding the total market or by increasing your market share. But with Burger King we could grow these two ways, or we could grow geographically. Burger King was the throttle on our growth. [With care we could open it up a little or close it down] to control our growth rate and credibility." Another advantage of restaurants was that they could, in part, finance themselves without impairing the capital access of the rest of the company. All debt and lease obligations of the restaurant subsidiaries were obtained on the basis of their own credits and not guaranteed by the parent company. Eventually the company carried some 65% of its combined restaurant capitalization as debt or debt equivalent.[12]

In 1975 Pillsbur began another important

entry into the restaurant field. As Mr. Spoor re-calls:

> I got a call from an outside director, John Whitehead, on Steak and Ale Restaurants of America. They were being courted and were almost [at the point of being] ac-quired by Ralston Purina . . . We were not looking [at Steak and Ale] at all. John Whitehead had just picked up [signals about it informally] . . . So I called Norm Brinker, who was a co-founder of Steak and Ale, and he and I talked very quietly. We hit it off. We talked the same way, we were trying to do the same things in life, and we had a similar upbringing . . . We just clicked. [Finally, during later negotiations, Brinker] said, "Bill, if we can put this thing together, I'll go with Pillsbury. But I have one condition. I will only report to you."

It seems another top Pillsbury executive, after spending days looking at Steak and Ale Restaurants, had given up around 10:30 one night while Spoor had hung on for as long as Brinker wanted. Spoor said, "He was a nondrinker, so it was pretty dry at times. . . . But a sensitive guy like that is selling his life's blood. He wants to know he's loved, accepted, part of the organiza-tion. . . . Little things like that make a big differ-ence."

Mr. Walter Scott, Chief Financial Officer of Pillsbury, later noted:

> At that stage we were not particularly out looking for new acquisitions in the restaurant business. We were concentrat-ing our efforts on consumer products com-panies. [Nevertheless] through our acqui-sitions department we looked at the particular sector in which Steak and Ale was operating to determine whether (on a long-term basis) it looked like an inter-esting aspect of the restaurant business and what it would do for Pillsbury—posi-tive and negative. We commissioned some outside studies to try to help us in developing a conviction as to whether we were on the right track. [All this] was orchestrated by the acquisition department

with lots of plug-ins from other parts of the company.

By the end of 1976 the company had begun to assume a new shape. Pillsbury had pared off all its non food-related lines and some of its smaller food lines overseas. In addition to Pills-bury Farms, *Bon Apetit*, Pemton, Standard Com-puter, Souverain, and European Flower Markets, Pillsbury had divested McLaren's (Canadian-pickles and olives), Lara (Mexican-cookies), Cal-gary Mills (Canadian-flour), and Gringoire-Brossard (French bakery products). Spoor began to say publicly: "I'm only interested in busi-nesses that fall into three categories . . . con-sumer foods, foods-away-from-home, and agri-products."[13]

The Consumer Group

Of these, Pillsbury's consumer foods activities posed special problems for Mr. Spoor. *Fortune* described some of the key issues this way:

> In picking Pillsbury's new chief, Spoor's predecessor sidestepped his own protege, James R. Peterson, whose management skills were much admired by many Pills-bury executives despite the lackluster per-formance of the consumer group he headed. When Spoor was appointed CEO, Peterson was named President with con-tinuing responsibility for consumer prod-ucts.
>
> It soon became apparent that nei-ther man was too comfortable working with the other. Spoor gradually began to limit Peterson's role. Peterson sensed ero-sion in the high level support he was used to in previous jobs—and subordinates found him more difficult to work for. Ulti-mately, Peterson was forced out by pres-sures from above and below. In De-cember, 1975, one of his ranking subordinates, George Masko, resigned. Using this resignation along with state-ments of dissatisfaction from another vet-eran consumer products executive, Ray-mond V. Kimrey, Spoor argued to the Board that Peterson's subordinates were up in arms. Confronted with an unappeal-ing choice—the departure of the President

or his two top lieutenants—the directors opted to get rid of Peterson.[14]*

When Mr. Peterson left in April 1976 (as executive vice president and director of R.J. Reynolds) Pillsbury's Consumer Group, which provided some 36% of FY1976 profits, included: Grocery Products, Refrigerated Products (largely dough), Frozen Foods (principally pizza), Wilton Enterprises (cake and party decorations), and Pillsbury's international consumer activities. According to *Fortune* the group "had seldom developed exciting new products or provided consistent marketing support for the winners it had."[14] To wake up the operation Spoor went after a new top man and recruited Raymond F. Good, who as its president had restored Heinz' domestic foods operations to profitability.

Each of the Consumer Group's divisions had its own problems. The Grocery Division was mired into cake mixes, flour, potatoes (etc.) with declining markets in which it held only a number 2 or 3 position. It had to accept price levels set by the leaders, but lacked their modern facilities and scale. The refrigerated dough business, where Pillsbury's market share was high, also appeared to be in a long-term declining industry. The only bright spot in Consumer was frozen foods; Totino's[15] pizza brand—acquired in 1975—was on its way to a strong second-place market share. Although frozen foods in general were declining, frozen pizzas were booming. Said the *Wall Street Journal*:

> Totino's is the market leader almost everywhere it competes. The frozen pizza market is growing rapidly and is already larger than the cake mix or refrigerated dough markets, previously Pillsbury's major consumer food areas.[16]

Good had a choice of two overall strategies: (a) put up the long-term massive advertising necessary to gain first-place penetration for more of his products or (b) manage the declining prod-

ucts for cash and build future businesses in other growth markets. Wishing to avoid the negative profit impact of the former course, Good chose the latter. He commissioned a McKinsey & Company study, which suggested positive consumer trends toward convenience foods, natural foods, more nutritious foods, snacks, and "foods-to-match-changing-lifestyles" where the sit-down family meal was becoming the exception rather than the rule. At Spoor's request Good presented the complete plan for Consumer's redevelopment to the Board. "You could have heard a pin drop. . . . It was so good," said Spoor soon afterwards.

Good brought in Edgar Mertz, a former Heinz executive vice president as his number two man and pressed hard on cost cutting programs to yield savings of 2–3% of sales. Then he plowed the margins into Totino's and selected acquisitions like Speas Farm (apple juice and vinegar) and American Beauty (macaroni). For a while these things seemed to work. By late 1978, however, company veterans were complaining about the new Consumer team's management style, and Good's relations with Spoor seemed to deteriorate. According to *Fortune* Spoor became progressively more insistent that Good clean up "the mess in grocery," show some dramatic financial improvements, and deal with Mertz's abrasive style which was becoming a "time bomb" about to explode the consumer operation.[14] When Spoor needed money to make up shortfalls elsewhere, Good grudgingly cut back on Consumer's advertising and promotional activities and slashed marketing budgets to meet short-term profit goals. On the other hand, while Spoor wanted more profits from Consumer, he was reportedly reluctant to back away from its traditional baking products. So the division in 1979 began to press hard to increase its market share on those lines—with all that implied.[14]

Agri-Products

Agri-Products had provided the remaining quarter of Pillsbury's sales and earnings. Agri—which included mainly Industrial Foods (flour milling, baking mix, hydro-processing), Commodity Merchandising (of grain and feed ingredients), Food Service (volume feeding to institutions), and Export—had been the foundation of Pillsbury's original foods business. But by the late 1970's these activities were declining in relative importance to Pillsbury. In boom years Agri fared well as its grain merchandising and flour milling activities responded to industry cycles. But even as the largest flour producer, Pillsbury found it hard to maintain acceptable margins in bad years.

Nevertheless, Agri was one of the world's largest grain merchandising operations, and enjoyed gross sales of over $3 billion in 1983. Only gross margins from these operations appeared in consolidated sales. The industries on which Agri was based (especially grain production and feed ingredients) were huge and growing at some 3% per year. In summary, in 1983 Agri-Products was: (1) the nation's largest flour miller, (2) its eighth largest rice miller, (3) its largest feed ingredient merchandiser, (4) its largest flour exporter, (5) among the top 5 in grain and oilseed origination, and (6) a major producer of bakery mixes.

Phase Two

In 1976–1977 Pillsbury entered phase two of its overall plan. Most of its divestitures were complete, and a new management team was coming into place. About this time Spoor started to talk about becoming "a truly great corporation." How was this to be measured? "We have 12 foods companies we measure ourselves against—like General Mills, General Foods, Kraft, Ralston Purina. We want our P/E ratio to be in the upper $\frac{1}{3}$ of these food companies," said Spoor. But he also wanted to have "the best management" of these companies and "to be number one or number two in every product category we compete in." Spoor continued, "I also want to leave the next management with the same kind of growth vehicle we inherited."[17]

The latter idea became known throughout the company as Spoor's "superbox." Anticipating that in a decade or so the fast food market would be saturated, Spoor was planting the seeds

for a totally new opportunity further down the road. "It can be almost anything—food, non food, or food related." This was the first official break with the "foods" concentration that had emerged from the divestiture period. In 1976–77 Spoor allocated some $350,000 to an open ended search for "superbox." The concept was not clearly specified—only that it was to be a large move and one that would provide the basis for growth in the late 1980's. Said Spoor at the time:

> "I deal in dreams. You can't deal just in the hard facts in this kind of job. Somebody's got to dream. And then you get some smart people to put meat on the dreams. . . ."[17] He observed: "We broke the initial Pillsbury Dream into submissions. We started out with the spirit of '76. We said by 1976, the 200th anniversary of our company, we can break $1 billion in sales and have a $5 EPS. We had things to talk about, magic things, because people need handles. We talked about the 'spirit of '76' first, which was a dream. And we hit that about a year in advance. That then let us push forward the financial dream. We wanted to split the shares, call the converts, clean up the balance sheet, and really get a powerful balance sheet for the first time—all of which we did . . . zap! The next dream is superbox."

ORGANIZATION CHANGES

Mr. Spoor later said, "In terms of everything that's happened at Pillsbury, it's the people that made the big difference." The people changes began shortly after Spoor took office, and seven years later they were still a dramatic portion of Pillsbury's activities. Along with the early divestitures outlined above, Mr. Spoor quickly began to modify the company's overall organizational structure. He said:

> We inherited the "free standing business" concept which I felt was hurting the company more than anything we could have done organizationally. We took great

strengths and fragmented them. So one of the early ideas was to pull the company back together. [The idea of what specifically to do] wasn't too far advanced at that time. . . . I couldn't just go to a [lower level unit] and get anything [coordinated] done. I'd have to talk to Grocery or Refrigerated and so forth first. . . . [Among other things the former management] had delegated acquisitions to each of the businesses, but no one had made an acquisition. . . . And so on. The company was very split up; a "this is mine, that's your's idea" prevailed. We were really going to have to change the culture [to get needed coordination].

Consolidation and Acquisition

Spoor immediately had most operations report directly to him: Rosewall of Burger King, Wallin in Agri-Products, Elston (whom Spoor brought in from McKinsey) in International, and Peterson in Consumer Products. In addition, the various corporate staff units reported to Spoor. Most important among these were Personnel and Finance where Spoor recruited two high powered heads from outside the company—Walter D. Scott, and Edwin H. Wingate. Both were top candidates from extensive head hunts. Like many others recruited later, both were reportedly extremely well paid and offered "the opportunity to fulfill their career objectives" with Pillsbury. In short order Spoor also brought in Philip D. Aines from Procter & Gamble to head up research and Jerry W. Levin to handle mergers and acquisitions. Most agree that these were all outstanding people, extremely talented. Commentary like that used about Mr. Scott would apply to many of these executives:

> Wally Scott was a gifted man—not just good—he was gifted. He had given up two years of his life [at about one tenth of his industrial income] to make his government better. He was then at OMB. He liked the Pillsbury Dream we had started by then and saw the challenge. [At the time he was interviewed] the head hunters said "These final two men are

great men, but we think you'll find Mr. Scott head and shoulders above."

After Mr. Wingate had been aboard a short time, Spoor asked him to "Think about the kinds of businesses we are in, how we ought to be structured." With substantial impact from Mr. Willys H. Monroe, a Board member, the three began to discuss how to organizationally restructure Pillsbury. From the first, it was abundantly clear that we were in three businesses. Win Wallin had the agribusiness, Jimmy Peterson had the consumer business, and Arthur Rosewall had the restaurants (which was really Burger King at that time). The key questions then were: "How do we take best advantage of these businesses, use the people we've got, and develop succession management?" In response to these questions Wingate and Monroe wrote up "white papers" for Spoor. Finally the three men, working largely from the Monroe document, designed the basic outlines of the new organization. Mr. Wingate noted:

> These papers weren't done in a vacuum. They were reviewed with Spoor often and we'd test different thoughts. It's hard to say which day it really happened. . . . There was talk even a year earlier in the consumer companies that some day it would be possible to take advantage of synergies that undoubtedly existed in production, sales, marketing, and research— to restructure activities so that this body of knowledge could be focused against the whole retail market.

Distron—which was part of Burger King and was the second largest food distribution system in the U.S.—could service 2–5 restaurant chains. Davmor, a manufacturer of kitchen equipment and furniture for restaurants, could also apply staff across the board. Real Estate could work across the various businesses. There was a lot of construction in the groups. And so on. Mr. Wingate later said:

> In developing the final format there were many discussions with corporate level

people before the new organization could be officially put on paper. . . . There were extensive interchanges and seminar activities on "how this or that would work?" before anything was done. . . . There evolved a consensus understanding—if not a consensus agreement— on where we were heading. . . . Individuals might not even recall who articulated the concept to them or when. People simply gained an appreciation and were able to internalize the fact that some organization changes were going to take place. They knew what was being considered and could project how they would be affected.

In the area of what became the new senior management committee, there was serious opposition from the heads of the "free standing businesses" and staff people who would not be on that committee any more. The new group was line, just seven people: Spoor, Scott, Powell, and the four line executive vice presidents—instead of the fifteen general managers who had previously funneled into the executive office. Most of these now reported to the executive VPs as staff heads or heads of individual product or activity centers. Support activities for each unit were consolidated at the group level whenever possible. Some of the very senior people reportedly found this quite hard to swallow. Nevertheless, by mid 1976 the new structure was largely in place. But it kept evolving over the next several years as pieces of Peterson's former activities were split between Spoor and Scott.

Changes at the Top

Meanwhile Spoor kept up his search for first-rate talent to run his line operations. As was noted, Ray Good had taken over Consumer Products. In 1977 Spoor hired Donald N. Smith (then 36 and McDonalds' third ranking executive) as CEO of Burger King; and the talented newcomer began to bring that diverse enterprise under more effective operating control. But Burger King had an uphill profitability fight against McDonalds' larger distribution system and outlet size

($200,000 per year greater sales than the average Burger King unit.)

Then unfortunately, after a glowing few years, Ray Good's relationship with Spoor began to deteriorate seriously as Consumer profit performance lagged and it developed internal management problems. When Spoor suddenly picked the much liked head of Agri-Products, Winston R. Wallin, to be president, both Good and "Wally" Scott were deeply unsettled. In the process of selection the Board's nominating committee reviewed all the top line and staff people. Mr. Spoor later described events this way:

I went to the Board in March (1978) and said, "We need a president of this company." They were absolutely aghast. They said, "But things are going so well. Why rush into naming a president now and risk losing all those top candidates you brought in? The reason they're good is they're scrambling for that open slot." I answered, "Because the company could be run more effectively." They replied, "Let us think about it." And basically they turned me down.

In May I went back and I was irate. . . . I said, "I want to set up the time this company can be managed more effectively; and frankly it can be. There's something called the concentration of power—in me. [Everybody] listens [too] carefully to what I say—and I'm not that good—it becomes 'Spoor said this, and Spoor said that.' I know what I can do and what I can't do within reason. . . . If you want to put this company at risk, just let me go on like this for another couple of years.". . . Zap! [The situation] changed in two seconds. We announced Wallin as president in June.

A few years before, Spoor and Wallin had participated in an encounter group at the National Training Laboratories. There they had spent a lot of time together and had gotten to know each other quite well. Spoor said, "Win has a marvelous sense of humor. He is very slow on the draw and will let people speak their piece. But when he comes out, he has a point of view that is absolutely spectacular. I have built up extreme confidence in Win.''

The Green Giant Arrives

Then in late 1978 Spoor began negotiations with Green Giant Company, a large well established foods company headed by Thomas H. Wyman, formerly second in command at Polaroid. Before the merger, Spoor reportedly told visitors, ''No one at Pillsbury can run Green Giant.'' And Wyman—who was considered one of the rising stars of the U.S. executive world—was assured like other talented managers that his ''career expectations could be fulfilled at Pillsbury.''[14]

On completion of the merger, Wyman personally received a windfall of almost $1 million in salary, bonuses, and benefits. The question then became where to put Wyman in the Pillsbury structure. The solution was an Executive Office—with Wallin as President, Wyman as Vice Chairman, and Scott as Executive Vice President. Explained Spoor, ''I had to offer [Wyman] the top job to keep him and to make the merger work.''[18] Discouraged by these events, Good left the company in July 1979 and became president of Munsingwear in October of that year. When asked why he was willing to sacrifice Good, Spoor replied bluntly, ''Tom's better.''[19]

By March 1980 Spoor could report to analysts that Pillsbury had ''the finest management team in the foods industry.'' Then began a series of high level defections that staggered the company. In early May, Wally Scott resigned to head Investors Diversified Services, Inc. Then shortly thereafter Don Smith left for the top spot at PepsiCo, Inc. *Business Week* noted however that: ''Spoor had created an atmosphere of intense competition among the top officers, luring each initially with the promise of succession.'' But perhaps the biggest jolt came on May 23 when Tom Wyman agreed to become president and chief executive of CBS. While upset by the turmoil, Spoor responded philosophically, ''There were solid reasons behind each of the moves. Tom Wyman couldn't turn down the offer CBS made him . . . [reportedly a $1 million bonus

and $800,000 per year guaranteed salary] . . . And we would have destroyed our pay structures trying to meet the offers.''[20]

One consolation for Spoor was that along with Wyman, Pillsbury got Jack Stafford, Green Giant's Chief Operating Officer. Stafford's background seemed ideal for Pillsbury. In addition to his success at Green Giant, he had spent 12 years in consumer advertising at Leo Burnett and had risen to Senior Vice President-Marketing at Kentucky Fried Chicken Corporation. Stafford was named an Executive Vice President at Pillsbury in 1979, became head of Consumer Foods in 1981, and joined the board of directors in 1983.

CONTINUED PERFORMANCE

Despite the turmoil, Pillsbury's financial performance continued to be exceptionally strong. (See Exhibits II–IV). And the departed executives had all left their own positive imprints. Before leaving, Don Smith had brought a new discipline to Burger King. He had expanded menus and increased sales in real terms during a period when McDonalds' and Wendy's real sales declined. Green Giant's Stafford had moved into the top slot at Consumer; and Spoor claimed ''the company could now market in the league with Kraft and General Mills.''

The company also continued both to acquire and divest operations in keeping with its extraordinary goals.

ACQUISITIONS AND DIVESTMENTS
FISCAL 1974–1983

Divestments	Acquisitions
Pillsbury Farms (Poultry)	Wilton Enterprises (Cake Decorating)
Pemtom (Housing Development)	Totino's Finer Foods (Frozen Pizza)
Standard Computer (Timesharing)	Steak & Ale Restaurants of America
Lara (Mexican Cookie Manufacturer)	American Beauty Macaroni Company
Bon Appetit (Gourmet Magazine)	Fox Deluxe Pizza

Divestments	Acquisitions
Souverain Wine	Green Giant
European Flower Markets	Wickes Agricultural
Calgary Flour Mill	Pioneer Rice
Wilson Enterprises	B & B Mushrooms
Poppin Fresh Pie Shops	Jokish
	Hoffman Meuü
	Hammonds
	Häagen-Dazs

The company had changed in important qualitative dimensions as well. At the time the Pillsbury Dream was first drawn up, the management group had decided it wanted to share its proposed successes with all important constituencies, including stockholders, the board of directors, employees, customers, suppliers, and especially the communities where the company operated. The management group set general goals in each area and resolved to monitor progress against these. As profits grew, the company multiplied its contributions to community causes to $3.5 million in 1983. Pillsbury occasionally bought out the remaining tickets to the Minnesota Vikings games and gave them to United Way so local people could see games which would have been blacked out on TV. During the Vietnam refugee crisis, company officers went to Washington to see what Pillsbury could do to help and gave every person in the company who would "adopt" a Vietnamese family $1,000 — or a year's supply of food for the family.

In addition, top management engaged Survey Research, Inc. to do a series of employee attitude surveys to see how people at all levels regarded Pillsbury in terms of compensation, supervisory practices, planning, communications, etc. The company had changed a number of employee practices: better explaining each individual's compensation and role in the total enterprise, posting and allowing bidding for all internal openings, improving the house medium *The Pillsbury Reporter* to explain where the company was going, the progress it was making, and the reasons things were being done. Top executives noted, "Recruiting is a lot easier than it was. We have people coming to us now—good people—saying they hear what's happening here and want to be a part of it."

1985 AND BEYOND

In 1984–85 Mr. Spoor announced a new set of goals for Pillsbury. These were: annual growth rates of 12–15% for EPS, 25% for ROI, and 18% for ROE. How this should be accomplished was an open question. Mr. Spoor had told analysts and public audiences that Pillsbury wished to remain dominantly a foods company. But to achieve its goals it would consider: making tactical acquisitions, joining in major mergers where Pillsbury was the surviving entity, and entering non-foods fields where Pillsbury could add significant value through use of its skills and resources. In keeping with this Pillsbury had recently acquired Häagen Dazs (a quality ice cream producer and distributor); Sedutto Ice Creams (for the food service market); Azteca Corn Products (refrigerated tortillas); Apollo Foods (high quality ethnic foods); and Van de Kamps (frozen foods).

In June 1983, it had attempted to acquire Stokley-Van Camp Inc. for a $62 per share tender offer. When the target company's management fought the offer and Quaker Oats put in a "friendly" tender of $77 per share, Pillsbury withdrew with a pre-tax gain of over $6 million.[21] A similar scenario occurred when Pillsbury made a bid for the Joan of Arc Co., a closely-held producer of specialty canned goods.[22]

Summary financial data for Pillsbury's major divisions are included in Exhibit II. Burger King continued to be the most significant contributor to 1984 gains in sales (20%) and operating profit (60%). Its system wide sales rose to $3.43 billion. Over the preceding two years, operating profit had increased 74% while return on invested capital had increased from 18% to nearly 26%. By year end Burger King had 3,827 restaurants worldwide, with 14% operating as company owned units. While experiencing losses during fiscal 1984, Burger King's international operations improved substantially over the preceding year, and it was making substantial progress with its institutional franchise program. By the end of fiscal 1984, Häagen Dazs had a total of 316 units located in 32 states. Steak & Ale Restaurants numbered 32, with average restaurant sales increasing to $1.5 million. Bennigan's, the popular fern bar, continued its growth with average unit sales of $2.3 million and instituted a number of programs to offer non-alcoholic drinks and to discourage intoxicated individuals from driving. By year end it had 148 units. J.J. Muggs, a gourmet hamburger restaurant concept that began in fiscal 1983, showed strong consumer acceptance and had been expanded to 5 units.

Pillsbury's Foods Group included Consumer Foods and Agri-Products. Overall sales increased 10% to $2.4 billion and operating profits rose 16% to $181 million. Agri-Products, aided by a large sale of flour to Egypt and the movement of grain as part of the government's Payment-in-Kind program to support farm prices, showed an increase of 111% over the preceding year's depressed profit levels. However, profits for fiscal 1984 remained below acceptable levels in barge transportation, grain exporting, rice milling, and edible beans.[23]

Consumer Foods 1984 performance was led by strong profit gains from Refrigerated Foods and Häagen Dazs with important volume growth in Frozen Foods. Partially due to the attention given to EDB, the Dry Grocery business experienced a marginal year with profits and volume somewhat below fiscal 1983. Häagen Dazs sales increased 22% during 1984, and Refrigerated Foods set new records for profits and sales. Within the Foods Group, all of International's wholly-owned businesses finished fiscal 1984 ahead of the preceding year in their local currencies. However, the strength of the U.S. dollar resulted in operating profits below fiscal 1983.

Pillsbury's capital spending increased dramatically during fiscal 1984 to $282 million, a 16% increase over 1983. Restaurant expansion was the primary focus of investment, with other major capital projects supporting Häagen Dazs' major new production facilities and some tactical acquisitions domestically and abroad.

In his last two years as CEO, Mr. Spoor had emphasized both internal development of Pillsbury's three basic businesses (see Exhibit IV) and an aggressive acquisition program. He had formed a venture capital unit within Pillsbury to help it investigate and take positions in promising new areas and had commissioned studies by Stanford Research Institute (SRI) and Hudson Institute to define promising areas for future growth.

In early 1984 when Pillsbury announced that Jack Stafford (46) was moving up to president, replacing Win Wallin who became vice chairman, the press suggested that Spoor had identified his successor.[24] At that time Stafford took over responsibility for all foods operations while Wallin managed the restaurant businesses. Agri-Products was broken up into Commodities Marketing under Mr. Coonrod and Industrial Foods overseen by Kent Larson, who was responsible for the Dry Grocery portion of Consumer Foods.

As Mr. Stafford assumed the role of CEO, he faced a strong and much different Pillsbury than that of the early 1970s. Analysts, both within and outside the company, were wondering what he would make the hallmarks of his era. Mr. Spoor had worked hard to create a "superbox" for his successor, but what it should be and how Pillsbury should change its overall structure and portfolio to meet the opportunities and challenges of the late '80s and '90s were still unclear.

QUESTIONS

1. Evaluate Mr. Spoor's handling of the early stages in his strategy changes at Pillsbury? Why were these steps taken in this sequence? What could have been improved? How?

2. What do you think of the way Pillsbury's acquisition-expansion program was planned? Implemented? What changes would you have made? Why?

3. What should Mr. Stafford's strategy be for the late 1980s? Why? What should he do to implement it? What should Pillsbury's "superbox" be? How would you identify it? Implement it?

EXHIBIT I   HIGHLIGHTS OF A PRESENTATION BY THE PILLSBURY COMPANY TO THE NEW YORK
SOCIETY OF SECURITY ANALYSTS JULY 19, 1973

Strategic Posture (Mr. Spoor)

I believe I can best outline our strategic posture by simply stating a group of propositions about the kind of company we intend to be:

- We are and will continue to be a market and marketing oriented company.
- We will be international in scope.
- We will be diversified beyond our food base.
- We will be dominated by our brand oriented businesses serving rapidly growing consumer needs.
- There remains an important place for the basic commodity oriented enterprises in Pillsbury, provided earnings can be demonstrated to meet corporate standards for volatility.

We selected this kind of company over other alternates for two reasons. First, this posture represents a natural extension of what we are and what we know how to do best. Secondly, we believe there are an ample number of investment opportunities available within this definition to satisfy our objectives. . . .

Corporate Objectives

In the general category:

- We know that we must have a consistent record of growth in sales and earnings.
- We are hopeful of a price/earnings ratio in the upper one-third of a selected sample of food-based companies.
- We intend to continue our dividend policy.

If we can manage ourselves like that, in fiscal 1976 our sales would exceed $1 billion and earnings per share $5.00.

Applied against the base of fiscal 1973 results, this means we will have to grow at a compounded annual rate of 10% in both sales and earnings per share.

We recognize that these are demanding objectives, particularly for a company that historically has not operated at these levels. . . .

Agri-Products

The oldest business function of Pillsbury is our Agri-Products group, led by flour milling. Producing flour and selling it to the baker is a thoroughly mature business. We happen to be number one in this industry, and I think in more ways than capacity. Nonetheless we have in the past and will continue to employ a very disciplined allocation of capital for reinvestment in this business. Our objective is to sustain the most satisfactory earnings stream from flour milling on a constant or modestly declining capital base. . . .

International

Our International operations finished a fine year. Jim Peterson will comment on the momentum in our consumer businesses in Europe, all of which are healthy and growing. Economic nationalism in Latin America, however, points to some difficult times ahead. We do not intend to walk away from these investment areas which have been very good to us. However, the desire for local government participation in several of our businesses and the recent adoption of Andean Pact legislation in Venezuela suggest a reduction rather than expansion of our developing country investments. . . .

Pillsbury Farms

Finally, I want to report to you on Pillsbury Farms, our broiler poultry business. First, you should understand that after the pruning and redirection of the business, which was begun two years ago, and included our recent withdrawal from further processed and micro-wave operations, Farms has become a healthy business. Aided by a strong price level, Farms turned in

EXHIBIT I (*Continued*)

a record performance last year, delivering in excess of $5 million profit before tax. There is no doubt in my mind that this is an extremely well-run business with a management team second to none.

The question that we have been wrestling with is whether or not this well-run and profitable business fits the strategy we have laid out for Pillsbury. This is not an easy question to answer because one does not, with haste, decide to dispose of a major source of earnings per share where the likelihood for replacement is through internal development. . . .

So, at this point we are not prepared to make a definite statement as to what the answer to the question on Farms will be other than to say that all options remain open. . . .

Consumer Strategies (Mr. Peterson)

1. The importance of our consumer business in size, as well as in quality of earnings, identifies the fundamental need for accelerated growth here first if we are to move the total company.

2. The retail food industry with sales of over $100 billion in 1972 represents a broad array of opportunities for the mass marketing of branded consumer food products and an increasing opportunity in the '70s for the mass marketing of non-food products.

3. We are keenly aware that to be a leader in our industry and to maintain the leverage that will insure premium profitability, we must be both a leader in the markets in which we participate or plan to enter and that we must generate a growing share of retail grocery sales.

4. One's ability to grow in today's highly competitive food business and the rapidly emerging non-food areas of the supermarket depends on one's understanding of the consumer environment with its ever more rapidly increasing levels of personal income (both here and abroad), resulting in demands for ever-increasing levels of quality and convenience in both products and services.

We finally stated that we felt our plans for the future of our consumer businesses were soundly based on these principles, that they represented a balanced program, and a continuing opportunity for premium growth.

Our four point strategy was stated as follows:

1. We are committed to a larger share of market in our current business areas. We will continue to place the investment of resources behind our fundamental consumer businesses to continue their share growth.

2. We believe that internal growth from new products can continue to be a source of increased earnings even in our mature areas.

3. The third part of our strategy involves the internal development of new businesses in areas that we are not in currently.

4. We will increase our acquisition activities and this will be a primary accountability of the executive office.

In February, I emphasized the importance of the development of brand franchises through the application of our marketing skills. We are giving great priority to the acceleration of this process. . . .

Consumer Orientation

As I stated earlier, we have based our consumer products efforts on the belief that the consumer is demanding rapidly increasing levels of quality and convenience and that this rate of change, fueled by increasing levels of personal income, provides an excellent opportunity for premium growth for those food companies that have the insight to identify the desired changes and are organized to commercialize them. We have reorganized our new products' teams to do both.

In each of the consumer business areas that I have discussed, branded products of high quality and convenience, keyed to contemporary life styles and value systems, clearly dominate our strategy. How we apply this philosophy to in-

EXHIBIT I (*Continued*)

crease our share of market in our basic businesses, to accelerate our new product program, to develop products for new areas, and to acquire new consumer businesses will, in our view, determine our record in the months ahead. . . .

Burger King Restaurants (Mr. Rosewall)

Looking ahead for fiscal 1974 through fiscal 1977, our present planning horizon:

1. The fast food industry is expected to grow at a compound rate of 11% per year, increasing from present annual sales of $5.9 billion to $9.9 billion.
2. The number of Burger King restaurants is expected to increase at a rate of 18% per year.
3. Total Burger King restaurant sales are expected to increase at a rate of 27% per year.

Attainment of these objectives would result in the number of restaurants increasing from the

Source: Company records.

982 in operation at the end of fiscal 1973 to 1,930. Company operated units would increase from 278 to 670, or to about 35% of the total.

Total restaurant sales would increase from last year's $338 million to $891 million, with average sales per store, for comparable stores, moving from fiscal 1973's $376,000 to $492,000.

We want to continue to be Pillsbury's major investment opportunity.

Social Responsibility (Mr. Spoor)

This discussion of our business performance would not be complete without reporting on that broad and important topic "social responsibility." We are convinced that excellence in performance in these areas is a requirement our customers, employees and stockholders expect if we intend to compete successfully in the marketplace. This is not an extra-curricular activity, but rather an integral part of the practice of management. . . .

EXHIBIT II   SALES (Billions)

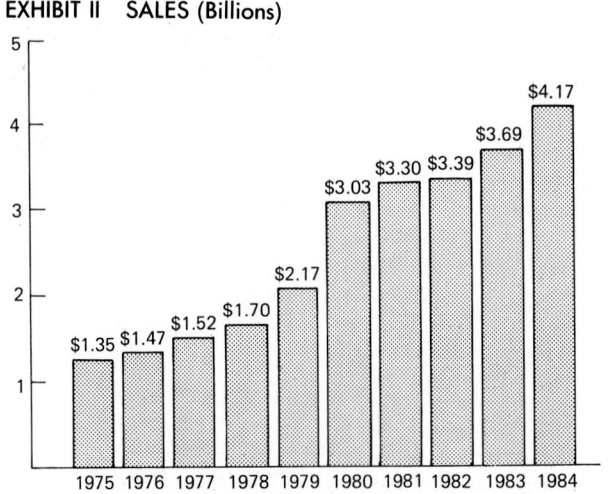

Source: The Pillsbury Company, *Annual Report*, 1975–84.

EXHIBIT II (*Continued*)
NET EARNINGS (Millions)

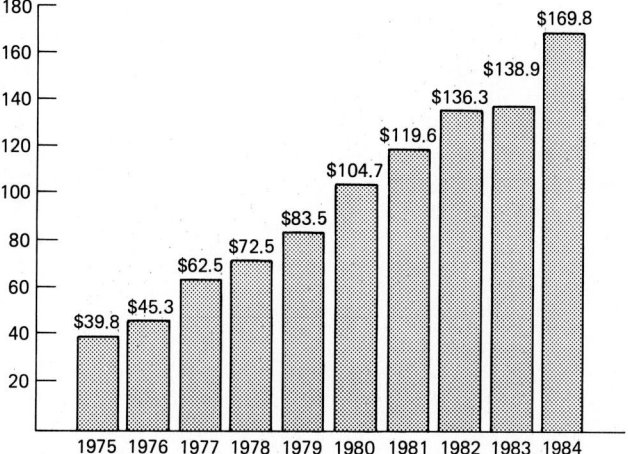

Source: The Pillsbury Company, *Annual Report*, 1975–84.

EXHIBIT II (*Continued*)
CASH DIVIDENDS (Per Share)

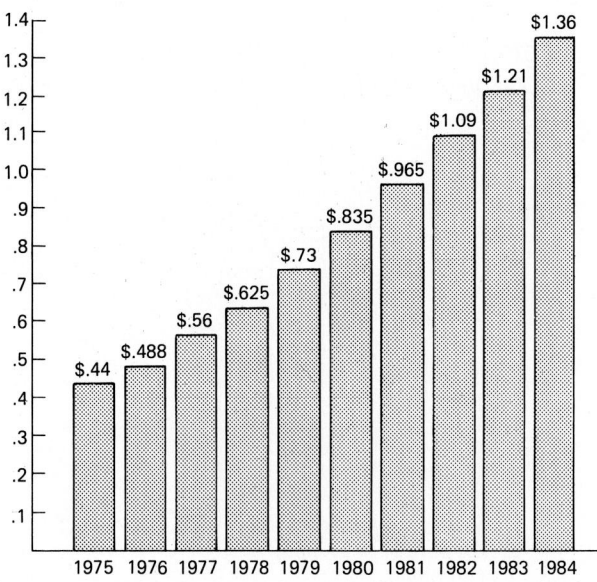

Source: The Pillsbury Company, *Annual Report*, 1975–84.

EXHIBIT II (*Continued*)
THE PILLSBURY COMPANY, CHARITABLE CONTRIBUTIONS (Millions)

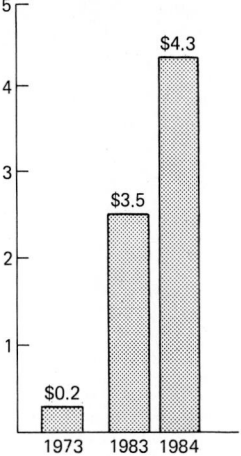

Source: The Pillsbury Company, *Annual Report*, 1973, 1983, 1984.

EXHIBIT II (*Continued*)
CONSUMER FOODS OPERATING PROFIT (Millions)

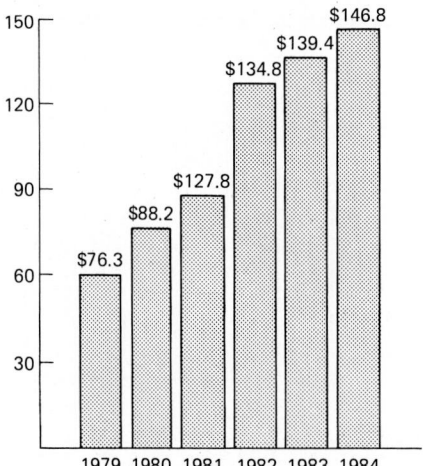

Source: The Pillsbury Company, *Annual Report*, 1979–84.

EXHIBIT II (*Continued*)
RESTAURANT OPERATING PROFIT (Millions)

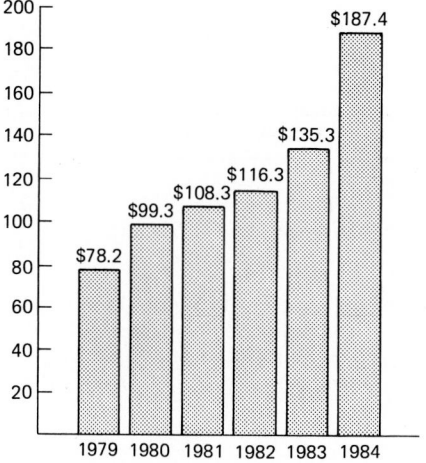

Source: The Pillsbury Company, *Annual Report*, 1979–84.

EXHIBIT II (*Continued*)
AGRI PRODUCTS OPERATING PROFIT (Millions)

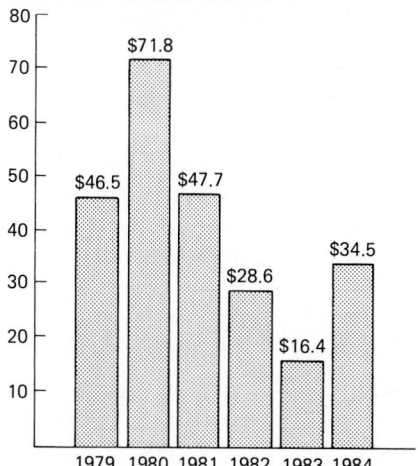

Source: The Pillsbury Company, *Annual Report*, 1979–84.

EXHIBIT III   THE PILLSBURY COMPANY AND SUBSIDIARIES
CONSOLIDATED BALANCE SHEETS

	May 31	
	1984	*1983*
	(In Millions)	
Assets		
Current assets:		
Cash and equivalents	**$ 142.5**	$ 129.6
Receivables, less allowance for doubtful accounts of $11.5 million and $12.9 million, respectively	**355.8**	350.6
Inventories:		
Grain	**75.5**	52.9
Finished products	**214.1**	204.1
Raw materials, containers and supplies	**150.6**	133.7
	440.2	390.7
Advances on purchases	**107.7**	128.4
Prepaid expenses	**25.6**	22.3
Total current assets	**1,071.8**	1,021.6
Property, plant and equipment (Notes 4, 6 and 8):		
Land and improvements	**199.2**	179.3
Buildings and improvements	**885.1**	788.2
Machinery and equipment	**692.5**	600.3
	1,776.8	1,567.8
Less accumulated depreciation	**583.8**	514.6
	1,193.0	1,053.2
Net investment in direct financing leases (Note 9)	**184.0**	178.7
Intangibles	**83.2**	21.6
Investments and other assets	**76.3**	91.5
	$2,608.3	$2,366.6

See Summary of Significant Accounting Policies and Notes to Consolidated Financial Statements provided in company's annual report.

Source: The Pillsbury Company, *Annual Report,* 1984.

EXHIBIT III (*Continued*)

	May 31	
	1984	*1983*
	(*In Millions*)	
Liabilities and Stockholders' Equity		
Current liabilities:		
Notes payable (Note 5)	$ **17.3**	$ 10.5
Current portion of long-term debt (Note 6)	**94.3**	32.8
Trade accounts payable	**369.2**	279.6
Advances on sales	**136.0**	136.7
Employee compensation	**83.8**	72.4
Taxes on income	**16.5**	20.8
Other liabilities	**169.3**	152.1
Total current liabilities	**886.4**	704.9
Long-term debt, noncurrent portion (Notes 6, 7 and 8)	**503.1**	572.4
Deferred taxes on income	**149.3**	108.5
Other deferrals	**22.3**	24.4
Stockholders' equity (Notes 6 and 11):		
Preferred stock, without par value, authorized 500,000 shares, no shares issued		
Common stock, without par value, authorized 80,000,000 shares, issued 43,516,019 shares and 43,462,156 shares, respectively	**306.2**	284.1
Common stock in treasury at cost, 322,785 shares and 180,318 shares, respectively	**(11.7)**	(4.6)
Accumulated earnings retained and used in the business	**792.4**	704.9
Accumulated foreign currency translation	**(40.7)**	(28.0)
Total stockholders' equity	**1,046.2**	956.4
	$2,608.3	$2,366.6

See Summary of Significant Accounting Policies and Notes to Consolidated Financial Statements provided in company's annual report.

Source: The Pillsbury Company, *Annual Report*, 1984.

EXHIBIT IV

SUMMARY BY INDUSTRY SEGMENT
THE PILLSBURY COMPANY AND SUBSIDIARIES

	Year ended May 31		
	1984	1983	1982
	(In Millions)		
Net sales:			
Consumer Foods	$1,793.9	$1,652.1	1,635.7
Restaurants	1,768.7	1,494.6	1,279.3
Agri-Products	694.8	627.5	568.6
Less Agri-Products intersegment sales	(85.1)	(88.3)	(98.5)
Total	4,172.3	3,685.9	3,385.1
Operating profit:			
Consumer Foods	146.8	139.4	134.8
Restaurants	187.4	135.3	116.3
Agri-Products	34.5	16.4	28.6
Total	368.7	291.1	279.7
General corporate expense, net	(20.8)	(21.5)	(12.4)
Interest expense, net	(44.2)	(39.4)	(39.3)
Earnings before taxes on income	303.7	230.2	228.0
Identifiable assets:			
Consumer Foods	836.3	725.4	747.9
Restaurants	1,191.2	1,025.7	993.3
Agri-Products	498.2	486.1	536.6
Corporate	82.6	129.4	150.5
Total	2,608.3	2,366.6	2,428.3
Capital expenditures:			
Consumer Foods	59.4	48.7	50.0
Restaurants	197.4	164.0	126.8
Agri-Products	13.8	20.9	15.8
Corporate	11.8	10.3	15.9
Total	282.4	243.9	208.5
Depreciation expense:			
Consumer Foods	36.1	33.0	30.3
Restaurants	59.5	54.7	48.6
Agri-Products	14.2	13.6	11.5
Corporate	4.8	4.2	2.4
Total	114.6	105.5	92.8
Foreign operations included in the above categories are as follows:			
Net sales	355.5	360.1	357.9
Operating profit	16.2	18.0	22.8
Identifiable assets	241.8	212.8	241.8
Capital expenditures	20.4	16.3	22.6
Depreciation expense	9.7	10.3	8.8

Pillsbury is a diversified international food company operating in three major segments of the food industry. Net sales by segment include both sales to unaffiliated customers, as reported in the consolidated statements of earnings, and intersegment sales made on the same basis as sales to unaffiliated customers. Operating profit of reportable segments is net sales less operating expenses. In computing operating profit, none of the following items has been included: interest income and expense; general corporate income and expenses; equity in net earnings (losses) of unconsolidated affiliates; and income taxes.

Source: The Pillsbury Company, *Annual Report,* 1984.

EXHIBIT V 10 YEAR COMPARISONS IN FOODS INDUSTRY 1973–1983

Company Name	Annual Growth EPS	Annual Growth Net Sales	10 Year Change in ROE	10 Year Change in ROIC*
Pillsbury Co.	17.7%	17.0%	115.4%	76.8%
Heinz (J.J.) Co.	15.5	15.1	69.8	85.4
General Mills Inc.	14.7	15.8	31.9	48.7
Kellogg Co.	13.5	13.3	25.2	5.4
Carnation Co.	12.8	11.9	10.4	6.0
CPC International Inc.	12.5	11.6	35.3	41.0
Quaker Oats Co.	12.4	14.4	20.7	21.9
Ralston Purina Co.	11.6	11.6	9.1	22.8
Beatrice Foods Co.	10.2	17.0	(7.6)	(2.5)
General Foods Corp.	8.0	11.2	5.8	7.2

Return on Invested Capital (Pre Tax)

Source: Prepared Foods, Sept. 1983.

MATSUSHITA ELECTRIC INDUSTRIAL COMPANY

In the mid 1980's Matsushita Electric Industrial Co. was often cited as one of the premier examples of the management practices and style that had made Japan into an industrial power, with a GNP second only to the United States. Matsushita's own brand names, Quasar, National, Panasonic, Victor (JVC), and Technic, were known around the world. Matsushita was Japan's largest producer of electric and electronic products and one of the world's largest firms in these fields. Why did its management practices work so well? To what extent were they applicable to other companies? What could be adopted outside Japan?

EARLY HISTORY

Matsushita (generally pronounced Mat*SOOSH*-'ta) was started in 1918 by Mr. Konosuke Matsushita, one of Japan's now legendary entrepreneurs. In 1911, Mr. Matsushita had joined the Osaka Electric Light Company (at age 15), convinced that electricity had a great future in Japan. Seven years later, then the youngest inspector on Osaka's payroll, he resigned to form his own company.

At that time the few wired Japanese homes

Case copyright © 1985 by James Brian Quinn. Research assistants–Penny C. Paquette and Allie J. Quinn. Major sources for case were company interviews; company published records; and (1) T. Kono, *Strategy and Structure of Japanese Enterprises* (M.E. Sharpe, Armonk, N.Y., 1985); (2) J. Cruikshank, "Matsushita," *Harvard Business School Bulletin*, February 1983; and (3) R. Pascale and A. Athos, *The Art of Japanese Management* (Simon and Schuster, N.Y., 1981). Footnotes (x,xx) indicate cited references and page numbers in these sources. The generous cooperation of Matsushita Electric is gratefully acknowledged.

typically had only one circuit, and that usually emerged inconveniently from the center of the ceiling in one room. To light another room or to use electricity meant using an awkward extension cord, dangling from the ceiling fixture. And the resident still had only one room lit. Mr. Matsushita, a tinkerer from his early days in his father's bicycle shop, conceived of a double ended attachment for the outlet that permitted the main room to be lighted while a swivel socket allowed an extension cord to be guided elsewhere without tangling. When he offered his idea to Osaka Electric the company was not interested. Consequently, Mr. Matsushita took about $50 in savings and severance pay and—with his wife and brother-in-law—began manufacturing his unique multiple socket in his own home. By using recycled light bulb bases, Matsushita was soon able to cut his already low costs (and prices) by some 30%, discouraging larger competitors from entering his market.

His next product was a bicycle lamp to replace the unreliable battery lamps (or in many cases small metal boxes with candles) then used by Japanese for cycling at night. Matsushita developed an improved battery, mounted his lamps in well styled wooden casings, and left samples burning in Osaka's shop windows over weekends to prove that his lights would burn 10 times longer than competitors'. From these humble beginnings began a great consumer electric products line. Matsushita became a public company in 1935. The National brand was registered in 1925; the first National radios were produced in 1930; washing machines, refrigerators, and televisions appeared in the post World War II era; and a full range of high fidelity electronics products in the 1960s through 1980s. In the 1960s and '70s Matsushita added industrial equipment, communications devices, and measuring systems. Matsushita began producing television receivers in 1952, exported its first TVs to Thailand in 1956, and completed its 75 millionth set in 1985. A breakdown of its 1985 product line and summary financials appear in Exhibit I.

A 250 Year Strategy

In 1932 Konosuke Matsushita noticed a tramp drinking water from a water tap on the street. He later said, ''I began to think about abundance. And I decided that the task of an industrialist was to make his products widely available at the lowest possible cost to bring a better living to the people of the world.'' (2,63) This became his exhortation to his employees on the company's 14th anniversary in 1932—and the cornerstone of the company's ''250 year corporate strategy.'' Exemplifying this philosophy was an incident in the early 1930s. There was a Japanese inventor/ investor who then controlled most of the patents for radio circuitry, which was moving from the crystal set era toward the speaker radio. Mr. Matsushita approached this man—who intended to monopolize the new industry—and after lengthy negotiations bought out his patents for a huge price. Matsushita then opened the patents to the entire industry ''so that everyone could manufacture in a more efficient way.''

Mr. Matsushita's 250 Year Plan to eliminate poverty is divided into ten 25 year segments. In May 1982, Matsushita Company began the third 25 Year Plan which was to include ''the true internationalization of the Matsushita Industrial Electric Company.''(2,75) Shortly before Mr. Matsushita had noted in his book, *Japan at the Brink*, that ''the Japanese miracle itself was on the verge of capsizing, politically, economically, and spiritually.'' He outlined problems of inflation, disaffected youth, what he called ineffective government, and a national lack of philosophical bearings. Among his many startling recommendations was the suggestion that Japan should abolish half of its universities. He felt much of the education was not worthwhile and that Japan's needs could be better provided by other institutions.

Selling off the assets of Tokyo University (the nation's most prestigious university) alone would save the country some $500 million per year.

These incidents suggest the creative quality which Mr. Matsushita has lent to his company. When General MacArthur's advisors decided to eliminate the *zaibatsu* (or ''financial clique'') which had controlled Japanese industry prior to World War II, they removed Mr. Matsushita as head of his company. Numerous delegations of workers approached the authorities, saying Matsushita represented the very entrepreneurial spirit which the Americans were professing. While tolerated by the *zaibatsu*, they said Matsushita was distinctly not a part of it. He had welcomed a union in the post war era, reiterating his conviction that labor and management must work together for a greater good. But the American authorities refused to listen to these supplications, and for four years during Mr. Matsushita's enforced exile, his company shrank from 20,000 to 3,800 employees, with many divisions closing permanently. Only when he was reinstated in 1951 did the company begin to return to its former strength.

Japan's Industry Structure

In this period, Japan was a nation still emerging from feudalism and a military system gone berserk. Its industrial infrastructure had been destroyed, its youth decimated, and its illusions of military conquest dashed. The nation had no significant energy resources, few natural resources, a small land mass relative to its population, and a very poorly paid labor force. Many ordinary amenities had disappeared and its social system verged on breakdown or revolution. But for 300 years, its dominant feudal and religious (Confucion and Shinto) groups had emphasized devotion to one's family and organization. Personal courtesy had been ingrained in numerous rituals and was a necessity for a large population living on a small land mass. But respect for laborers had not been a widely held value, nor had wealth been widely distributed.

In the disillusioned and labor-short post war era, more democratic values began to appear. There began a concerted national effort to improve the ordinary Japanese person's standard of living. Through its Ministry for International Trade and Industry (MITI) the government targeted certain industries for expansion and assisted them in developing their own technologies and in importing foreign technologies. To stabilize the society large Japanese companies began to emphasize lifetime employment (to age 55) and to take over many of the social roles other institutions provide in western countries. Companies often provided employee housing, recreation facilities, and a focal point for sports activities. Even today the Japanese government provides few unemployment or retirement benefits to workers. Instead, it attempts to stabilize price levels, manages the economy to maintain employment and offers supplementary employment opportunities only when necessary— through the national railroad system, public works, and public service (sanitary, groundskeeping, etc.) activities. Income and social security taxes are low. In most large companies employees are considered partners in the enterprise, not interchangeable parts of production; and in recession times employment is continued at the sacrifice of profits or dividends. Japanese executives often say that since maintaining sales and profit levels is management's responsibility—not that of factory workers—management (not workers) should take the brunt of any layoffs which are unavoidable.

Another unique feature of Japanese industry has been its financial structures. Large Japanese companies are heavy users of loan capital, with an equity ratio of only 20% being average. The largest equity shareholders, however, are also banks and insurance companies, which are forbidden individually to own more than 10% of a given company. They hold stock to secure a long term relationship more than to reap current profits. Other shareholders tend to be important suppliers or buyers from the companies. Only some 30% of all stock is held by individuals. Some typical financial ratios are illustrated below.

CORPORATE PROFITS IN FOUR COUNTRIES—AVERAGE RETURN ON PROFITS FOR MANUFACTURING FIRMS IN THE UNITED STATES, THE UNITED KINGDOM, WEST GERMANY, AND JAPAN

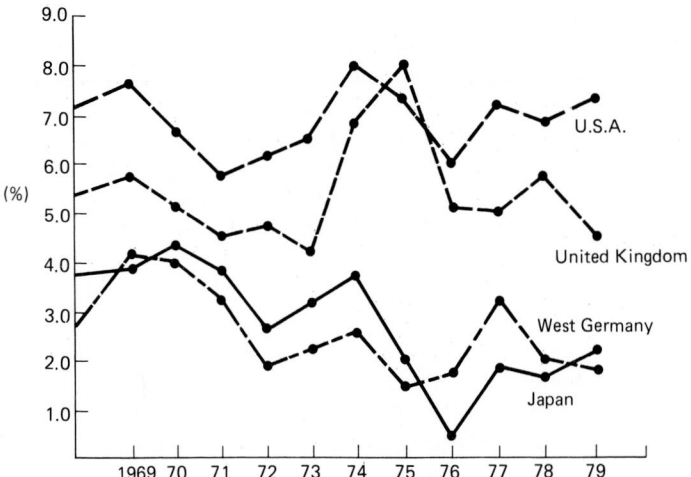

Source: From *Sekai no Kigyo no Keiei Bunseki*. Industrial Policy Bureau, MITI, Tokyo, 1980, p. 20 in William H. Davidson, *The Amazing Race*, copyright © 1984 John Wiley & Sons, Inc. Reprinted by permission of John Wiley & Sons, Inc.

FINANCIAL RATIOS FOR SELECTED U.S. AND JAPANESE FIRMS (1978)

Company	Debt-Equity Ratio	Profit/Sales	Inventory Turn Ratio
Burroughs	.538	10.46%	4.24
IBM	.538	14.76	6.24
NCR	.923	12.18	4.23
Control Data	.786	4.65	4.38
DEC	.639	9.90	3.58
Hitachi	2.99	2.56	5.45
Toshiba	5.08	1.52	3.56
Fujitsu	2.68	2.37	4.77
NEC	5.18	1.09	4.10
Oki	17.05	0.57	3.8
Mitsubishi Electric	5.67	1.71	3.78
Matsushita	1.01	3.34	16.47
Sanyo	2.02	1.93	21.32
Ricoh	1.43	4.15	12.10
Casio	1.60	3.54	7.82
Sony	.923	4.35	5.65
Sharp	2.125	2.76	9.64

Source: *Sekai no Kigyo no Keiei Bunseki*, Industrial Policy Bureau, MITI, Tokyo, 1980, p. 29 in *William H. Davidson, The Amazing Race*, copyright © 1984 John Wiley & Sons, Inc. Reprinted by permission of John Wiley & Sons, Inc.

A COMPARISON OF PRODUCTIVITY-ADJUSTED LABOR COSTS IN THE UNITED STATES AND JAPAN (1970–1980)

Year	Average Annual Japanese Wages in Manufacturing[a]	÷	Japanese Output per Labor Hour Divided by U.S. Output per Labor Hour[b]	=	Adjusted Japanese Labor Cost	U.S. Labor Cost[c]
1970	$ 1,787		0.508		$ 3,517	$ 7,439
1972	2,693		0.580		4,643	8,719
1974	4,224		0.649		6,508	9,947
1976	5,633		0.701		8,036	11,780
1978	10,009		0.782		12,799	14,063
1980	10,724		0.918		11,682	15,008

[a] *These data cover the contracted cash payments to workers in manufacturing firms with 29 or more employees. From* Economic Statistics Annual, *Research and Statistics Department, Bank of Japan, 1981, pp. 293–294.*
[b] *This variable is created by dividing the average output per labor hour for Japanese industries by the average output in U.S. industries. Data are taken from the U.S. Department of Labor, Bureau of Labor Statistics.*
[c] *From Bureau of Labor Statistics,* Monthly Labor Review, *for manufacturing only.*

Source: William H. Davidson, *The Amazing Race*, copyright © 1984 John Wiley & Sons, Inc. Reprinted by permission of John Wiley & Sons, Inc.

LEADING WORLD SEMICONDUCTOR COMPANIES' SALES

(Discrete and Integrated Devices, 1982)

Company	Total ($ Million)
Motorola	1310
Texas Instruments	1227
Nippon Electric	1220
Hitachi	1000
Toshiba	810
National Semiconductor	690
Intel	610
Philips[a]	558
Fujitsu	475
Siemens[a]	420
Matsushita	340
Signetics (Philips)	384
Mitsubishi	380
Mostek	335
Advanced Micro Devices (Siemens)	282
Sanyo	260
AEG	196
Thomson-CSF	190
Sharp	155
SGS-ATES	150
Oki	125

[a] *Not including U.S. affiliates.*

Source: Annual Reports, Hambrecht and Quist "The Japanese Semiconductor Industry" in William H. Davidson, *The Amazing Race*, copyright © 1984 John Wiley & Sons, Inc. Reprinted by permission of John Wiley & Sons, Inc.

COMPANY PHILOSOPHY

Within this general framework, Matsushita Company has developed its own unique and extraordinarily powerful philosophy. Matsushita's stated mission is "to contribute to the well being of mankind by providing reasonably priced products and services in sufficient quantities to achieve peace, happiness, and prosperity for all." This is supported by "5 Principles": (1) Growth through mutual benefit between the company and the consumer, (2) Profit as a result of contributions to society, (3) Fair competition in the marketplace, (4) Mutual benefit between the comapny, its suppliers, dealers, and shareholders, (5) Participation by all employees.

"Seven Spirits" then provide the code of behavior for employees to follow in making decisions. (1,50) They are the:

- Spirit of Service through Industry
- Spirit of Fairness and Faithfulness
- Spirit of Harmony and Cooperation
- Spirit of Struggle for Betterment
- Spirit of Courtesy and Humility
- Spirit of Adaptation and Assimilation
- Spirit of Gratitude

Exercises and Discussions

Every morning at Matsushita's plants in Japan (and in most areas throughout the world) every employee attends a "morning meeting" at which the Matsushita creed, principles, and/or spirits are recited aloud. Only a skeleton force of telephone operators, guards, process controllers, etc. is not present. In Japan the meeting begins with prearranged exercises learned in early grade school. Then in "relaxation exercises" each person massages and pounds the back of another person, and then both turn around to give or receive similar benefits. Following the Company Song and these recitations, a discussion leader—a task rotated daily—poses a question for the group to discuss and try to resolve. This can be an operating problem, a new opportunity, an important philosophical issue (etc.) designed to promote interest. After 15 minutes or so, everyone goes off to work. At work stations the exercise routine is repeated for 5 minutes at the end of each hour and for 10–15 minutes at mid-morning and afternoon.

In the company's early years, Mr. Matsushita used to interview all employees himself. This is no longer possible. But annually he and his wife host a gathering of newlywed employees. There are announcements and awards on "Adults Day" every January 15th to celebrate trainees becoming full employees. And there are constant company messages in each employee's paycheck to personalize the company-individual relationship. Mr. Niwa, chairman of Matsushita Electric Works, says, "We try to develop the supportive idea that 'we are always with you' psychologically."(2,65) Within most plants is a "trophy area" where individual and plant awards for outstanding performance are displayed. Much emphasis is given to company awards and to the performance of company sports teams competing with those of other companies.

Mr. Kosaka, head of Matsushita's Overseas Training Center says, "We feel you must create a spirit in which everyone can share. . . . It's not a theory, formulated after reading other people's books, but something based on *experience* itself. Once the philosophy is clear, it talks to every individual, and all communication in the company can be based on it." (2,63) In Matsushita's Japan operations virtually all employees wear company provided blue uniforms with white tennis shoes. Overseas the company provides the uniforms, but the choice is up to individuals.

AN ORGANIZED MAVERICK

Despite what appears to be conformity and regimentation in its philosophy, Matsushita has consistently been a maverick in Japanese industry. From the first, Matsushita violated the usual rules used by Japanese and American companies of the era. Rather than attempting to recoup investments as rapidly as possible, Matsushita has consistently cut its prices quickly and sought profits in the long run. While other companies used manufacturers representatives to reach established retail channels, Matsushita set up its own distribution networks and went directly to retailers. Instead of an arms length transaction with retailers, Matsushita offered innovative trade financing for them and pioneered the use of installment sales and point-of-purchase advertising in Japan. Rather than using the Matsushita name, the company promoted its National, Victor, and Panasonic brands.

A Decentralization Pioneer

In the mid 1930s, paralleling DuPont's pioneering efforts with a decentralized divisional structure, Matsushita and his talented controller, Takahashi, developed a similar concept with only 1,600 employees at the time. Matsushita was attracted not only to the organizational clarity and control the system offered, but to its motivational advantages as well. He wanted to keep things small, entrepreneurial, and market oriented in the rapidly emerging radio and small consumer appliance fields the company was in.

This decentralized divisional concept still dominates today's organization. But, recognizing the inherent disadvantages of this system, Matsushita also centralized four key functions which remain so to the present. First, he created a cadre of controllers reporting directly to headquarters and a centralized accounting system across the company. Second, he institutionalized a company "bank" into which 60% of all divisional profits flowed and from which divisions have to seek funds for capital improvements. Divisions have no bank accounts except for day-to-day transactions. Divisions' "float" must be cleared monthly, and borrowings beyond this are charged out at prime plus 2%. Third, Matsushita centralized the personnel function; no employee is hired without a central prescreening, and all management promotions are reviewed and monitored by headquarters. Fourth, he centralized the company's training system with its heavy emphasis on the values described above. Each university level employee goes through an approximately eight month training cycle to inspire them with the company's goals and philosophies, as well as to provide them with essential technical skills.

A Product Group Matrix

This basic organization has since oscillated back and forth with more (or less) autonomy given to the divisions depending on external economic or competitive conditions. In 1953 Matsushita introduced Product Groups with division heads reporting vertically to the President and horizontally to Group Vice Presidents, who serve as specialists with detailed knowledge of a whole family of similar products. (3,33) This innovation was some 10 years ahead of the widespread use of matrix organizations in the U.S. Matsushita tried not to take its formal organization charts too seriously and to "humanize" some of the inherent conflicts in the matrix structure. Controllers were called "coordinators" and housed directly in the factories they served. (3,35) To relieve some of the resistance to this matrix concept, Matsushita constantly reminded executives that everyone grew up with two bosses (a mother and a father) a situation that generally seemed quite tolerable. Even at the top level Matsushita established a three-person Executive Council to handle major decisions. He then slowly withdrew himself into a strategic role as chairman, although in times of crisis he reserved the right to reemerge to assume direct control.

Competition and Cooperation

Japanese corporations compete intensively with companies in the same line of business, but often cooperate extensively with other companies in a complementary relationship. For example, Matsushita has 120 "fully controlled" wholesalers selling only its products. It has 20% or more equity interest in all these distributors and serves them and other retailers through 100 sales offices which provide management assistance, showroom facilities, and other services to Matsushita's Japanese distribution network. Retailers include 25,000 National Shops, where Matsushita products account for 80% of sales and another 25,000 National Stores where its products exceed 50% of sales.

Matsushita does not hold shares in these retailers, but controls them by long term contracts and the special services it provides: management training, classes on new technologies, shared advertising, and some special rebates. Typically, products are sold at list in these channels, but they may have to meet the prices of the discount stores now becoming more common in Japan. Other separate channels exist for: (1) industrial and non-industrial construction products, and (2) commercial, industrial, and government customers. Marketing for Matsushita is controlled from headquarters. Each product division can sell directly to its wholesalers or large customers like the government, but under rules established at headquarters. Export sales are handled by an independent subsidiary, Matsushita Trading Co., which has worldwide sales branches for all products.

TECHNOLOGY AND MANUFACTURING

Matsushita is heavily integrated on the components side. It produces its own batteries, vacuum tubes, integrated circuits, circuit boards, condensors, transformers, speakers, tuners, magnetic heads, etc. But it buys standard raw materials (wire, steel, aluminum sheet, etc.) outside. Purchases from subsidiaries amount to about 80% of the value of all purchased materials. The company also sells components to outside groups. It only consumes about 50% of its component production, and is the largest single component manufacturer in Japan, with Y386 billion sales in 1983. The manufacturing divisions are all profit centers, able to buy components outside if they so choose. These manufacturing divisions sell through the marketing channels described above. Products are sold by divisional salesmen, shipped directly to distributors or retailers, and transferred to Marketing at internal transfer prices. The Central Marketing group handles sales planning, marketing coordination, and promotional functions.

Although Matsushita started with two innovative products, it has rarely pioneered entirely new technologies. (3,30) Instead, it emphasizes quality and price. Its experience with video tape recorders (VTR's) is perhaps typical. SONY was generally acknowledged as the real pioneer of

VTR technology with its Umatic and Betamax formats. While Matsushita had also done excellent early work on the technology, it took a license under SONY's early VHS-like format and turned its several divisions loose on improving the device for the marketplace. Discovering that customers wanted a 2–4 hour recording capacity (as opposed to SONY's 1 hour format), Matsushita designed this into a more compact VTR that was highly reliable and could be priced 10–15% below SONY. When SONY came up with its superior quality Beta format, Matsushita stayed with its well developed VHS concept, got other major Japanese and U.S. firms to adopt its preferred format, and by the late 1970s manufactured $\frac{2}{3}$ of all VTR's sold.

"FIGURE OUT HOW TO DO IT BETTER"

Matsushita consistently invested some 4% of sales in R&D, much of which went into production engineering. The company had some 20 production engineering laboratories equipped with the latest available technology. Most of these were attached to individual product divisions. But Matsushita's Central Production Engineering Laboratory at corporate level was one of the world's outstanding units. The company also had a Central (basic) Research Laboratory, Wireless Research Laboratory, and Research Institute Tokyo (which operated on an independent basis and conducted research for both company and outside groups). In addition, there were a Corporate Product Development Division, Corporate Quality Assurance Division, and Corporate Patent and Legal Division under the Central Engineering structure.

The company's focus in R&D was said to be "to analyze competing products and figure out how to do the job better."(3,31) Its Engineering and Research Laboratories were backed up by one of the world's most awesome production line suggestion systems. Matsushita processed some 460,000 employee generated suggestions or improvements per year. The company's motto

was "Matsushita produces capable people before it produces products." Thus Matsushita's eight month training for all university graduates involved: 3 weeks of headquarters training classes; 3 months in retail stores; one month in the factory; one month in cost accounting; and two months in marketing lectures and activities. Lesser time, but equal attention went into training rank and file workers. Job rotation was common throughout all ranks; 5% of all employees (comprised of $\frac{1}{3}$ managers, $\frac{1}{3}$ supervisors, and $\frac{1}{3}$ workers) rotated from one division to another each year, and some 80% of all employees participated in quality circle activities. About 15% of all suggestions were accepted and formally implemented, others were simply implemented by informal agreement among supervisors and employees.(1,304) Of these about 35 "super suggestions" occurred each year. These won coveted awards. And sponsors of patentable suggestions could receive patents and monetary awards in their own names.(2,71)

"Manage From Goodwill"

Not only could workers suggest improvements, they could stop the production line if they were not satisfied with quality. Production plants tended to be spotlessly clean. Cleanliness standards were dictated from headquarters and were not subject to interpretation anywhere in the world. Work stations were typically separated by 8–10 feet, aisles were extremely wide (15–30 feet), noise levels were relatively low around work stations, and the production line itself moved more slowly than was typical in western plants. A substantial amount of small scale automation was generally visible at individual work stations. Individual workers were directly responsible for quality results at their own stations, but heavily automated quality control and test facilities were in evidence all along electronics and consumer products lines. Employee turnover in Japan was of course extremely low, but even overseas plants tended to have $\frac{1}{4}$ the turnover of comparable plants in their host countries—and often they rejected local unions.

Matsushita managers attributed this to the attempt to "manage from goodwill" and to "foster a homey, family atmosphere. We are first interested in nurturing a relationship of trust between management and labor. Once we achieve that goal, we can develop other things like suggestion systems, quality circles, and so on." North American employees responded, "You're not under a lot of pressure here; it's a comfortable place to work. You do the best you can. Everyone understands we're all here to help each other, and to put out the best product we can."(2,86) In 1974 Matsushita Electric Company of American (MECA) had bought a 25 year old Westinghouse heavy equipment plant near Toronto. Although 7 of the 12 competitors in the market then had left by 1983, MECA had the highest growth rate in its industry in Canada over the decade.

PLANNING AND CONTROL SYSTEMS

Matsushita had derived its planning system from Phillips (NV), the Dutch electronics giant. On New Years day some 7,000 managers assembled to hear the chairman and president declare the basic policy for the year. This contained some key dimensions and figures, but more broadly it presented the important elements to be emphasized in the company during the year. These strategic directions were later conveyed to all employees through the company magazine.

Every six months each division manager presented three plans. The first was a long term (five year) plan, updated as new technologies and environmental events occurred. Second was a two year (mid-term) plan which stated how the division would translate its long-term plan into such things as plant capacity or specific new products. Neither was extensively reviewed by top line management, but each was scrutinized heavily by the product group side of the organization matrix.(3,36)

Most attention was given to the Six Month Operating Plan. Here the division stated its monthly forecasts of sales, market share, profits, inventories, accounts receivable, capital expenditures, head count, quality targets (etc.). When variances occurred the division manager and his controller had to be prepared to explain them. Particular attention was given to market share, return on sales, asset turnover, and actual versus budgeted costs, since these were considered to be under the division managers' control. Matsushita had rigorous standards for collections from its customers and payments to its suppliers—normally both less than 30 days—but the corporation could extend long term credit to build sales channels, develop new markets, or meet special competitive needs.

Everyone understood that key variables would be tracked monthly and reviewed scrupulously. Figures were available within a few days after the end of each month and were widely shared in Matsushita's "open information system." (3,39) Performance was judged and rewards made on the basis of actual versus planned results. Reviews were performed by three groups: corporate line officers, corporate staff, and "peer review" by the heads of other divisions. Matsushita expected every division to be completely self sustaining within 5 years and strongly resisted subsidizing losing divisions.

The 60% of each division's profits paid to headquarters covered Product Group Management, R&D, Production Engineering, and an equity return. The remaining 40% belonged to the divisions for facilities updating, production engineering, and new product development. But the funds were held at corporate and earned interest for the division. Matsushita expected each division to make sure its current and future product lines were healthy and did not use "portfolio" concepts favored in U.S. companies.

Performance Reviews

Corporate headquarters was kept deliberately lean, with only 1.5% of the company's total personnel there (excluding the Engineering Research Laboratories). However, each month the division manager spent several days at headquarters, going over each performance item and variance in detail with the Finance Office and with senior management. Key criteria were: (1) the ability to stay on plan, and (2) whether the division's management was "doing its best" and "as well as anyone in the market." If not, poor performers might be quickly transferred to other areas, "where their talents better fit circumstances." (3,37) In the "peer review" process (quarterly), summary operating results were shared before all divisions. Divisions were grouped A, B, C, or D; the A (outstanding) groups made their presentations first, D's last. Though individuals or divisions were not singled out for embarrassment, each group's relative performance was clear to all.

Matsushita's sales force and executives were monitored through exacting prospect lists and yield statistics. And the salesforce was backed by the largest advertising budget in Japan. Senior sales executives were expected to visit retail outlets regularly and to seek group level help when they needed it. To support its strong sales channels, Matsushita also operated an elaborate network of "customer clubs" to keep informed about its users' needs and to solicit ideas for improvement of products or services. Even top executives, like Mr. Matsushita and Mr. Yamashita (president), were expected to spend most of their time out of their offices and with customers. At various times both had gone into the field to solve specific crisis situations themselves. And in a 1970 recession, even assembly line workers were shifted to door-to-door selling to cut inventories and to bring costs into line.

Overseas Operations

Overseas, Matsushita operated 46 production facilities in 27 countries and 34 sales companies in 28 countries. In addition to marketing through its own affiliates, Matsushita also produced for private label distribution of OEM's abroad. In addition, it had a series of licensing arrangements with foreign companies, notably RCA (non exclusive) and Phillips (exclusive) with the latter own-ing a minority position in Matsushita Electric Company. Matsushita had a variety of ownership arrangements in various host countries from full ownership to joint ventures, but never had less than a 50% board position.

Overseas units were almost always headed by a Japanese, and many middle managers were Japanese. Almost all managerial people—whether Japanese or not—were put through Matsushita's Overseas Training Center in Osaka, which offered specialized training in English, in overseas operations, in company policy, and in the company's value system. Because of scales of operation, tariff barriers, distances from Japan, (etc.), the specific organization of each subsidiary might be quite different. For example the Malaysian subsidiary had a small local market, was close to Japan, was heavily protected by tariffs, and had to deal with significant "local content" rules. The UK and Canadian plants were bound by few such rules, but served huge domestic markets. Because of the company's size, its stock was traded on several of the world's stock markets (including the U.S.) and it often raised funds locally.

A Pragmatic Approach

Matsushita had a pragmatic approach to all problems. The heart of its style was "to get to the problem and fix it." (3,43) There was much latent conflict between its competing divisions, its matrix units, and in its "Venture Capital Fund," administered from the corporation's 60% of profits. Divisions made proposals asking the Fund's managers to support new products or concepts which did not fit normal capital allocation processes well. Yet Matsushita executives expressed surprise when asked if there was much interdivisional fighting. They said, "We conflict without conflicting. Our underlying premise is that in life we make adjustments. . . . We presuppose that parties will fundamentally strive to pull together rather than push apart."(3,43)

Employees were not viewed as "participating in management" but their opinions were sought. The company's books were open to the union, and the union was consulted directly as each division prepared its long term and six month plans. Matsushita encouraged long term managerial continuity in its divisions with 5–7 years in key spots being common. But the Central Personnel group also tracked the top several performers in each division and consciously moved these people to openings as they occurred. Matsushita's maxim was "extraordinary results from ordinary people."(3,47) It did not make particular efforts to hire from the elite schools, and was willing to jump younger people over dozens of their seniors if their performance warranted. Another maxim was, "If you make an honest mistake, the company will be very forgiving. Treat it as a training experience and learn from it. You will be severely criticized [a euphemism for dismissed] however if you deviate from the company's basic principles."(3,51)

QUESTIONS

1. What is Japan's basic industrial strategy? Why has it chosen this strategy? How does it keep capital costs so low? What are the potential weaknesses in this strategy?
2. What is Matsushita's basic strategy? What are the most important policies involved in its implementation? Why were these chosen? What issues do they pose?
3. Based on the information in the case, draw an organization chart of Matsushita. What issues does this pose? How would you measure performance for each major unit? How should overseas operations be organized? Why?
4. What functions does Matsushita's elaborately developed value system perform? What problems does it pose?

EXHIBIT I   MATSUSHITA'S MAJOR PRODUCTS—1983

The Company is engaged in production and sales of electric and electronic products. For revenue reporting purposes, the Company classified its products into the following categories.

VIDEO EQUIPMENT

Matsushita produces video tape recorders and related products (cameras, tapes, etc.) for home and professional use. For the year ended November 20, 1983, sales of video tape recorder products increased rapidly and accounted for Y1,045 billion or 26% of total Company sales.

The Company manufactures a broad range of color and black-and-white television receivers designed to meet the demands of all segments of the Japanese and overseas markets. The Company manufactures color and black-and-white television receivers with screens ranging from $1\frac{1}{2}$ to 25 inches and $1\frac{1}{2}$ to 19 inches, respectively, measured diagonally. The Company also manufactures large screen color projection TV systems. For the year ended November 20, 1983, sales of television receivers accounted for Y399 billion or 10% of total sales of the Company for that period.

AUDIO EQUIPMENT

The Company produces a large variety of audio equipment, ranging from radio receivers, tape recorders and radio cassette combination models to stereo radio phonographs, hi-fi components and digital audio equipment. It also produces electronic organs. For the fiscal year 1983, total audio

EXHIBIT I (*Continued*)

equipment sales represented Y481 billion or 12% of the Company total.

HOME APPLIANCES

The major products in this category include: refrigerators and freezers; home laundry equipment such as washing machines and dryers; cooking equipment such as microwave and other ovens, blenders, juicers, food processors and rice cookers; air conditioners and electric fans; electric and kerosene heaters; vacuum cleaners and electric irons. For fiscal 1983, total home appliance sales amounted to Y596 billion or 15% of total sales of the Company.

COMMUNICATION AND INDUSTRIAL EQUIPMENT

This category covers two-way communication equipment, including push-button telephones, community telephone systems and mobile communication equipment; broadcasting equipment, including radio and television broadcasting installations, broadcast television cameras and CATV systems; measuring instruments, including oscilloscopes and ultrasonic diagnostic systems; automotive accessories, including car radios and stereos; business equipment, including facsimile equipment, personal computers, word processors and plain paper copiers; and other products, including hearing aids, electronic calculators, traffic control systems, electronic educational systems, point-of-sale systems and professional audio equipment. It also includes electric motors, micro motors, welding equipment, industrial robots, power distribution equipment, power transformers and capacitors, anti-pollution equipment, TLD irradiation measuring systems, vending machines and other electric and electronic industrial devices.

Sales of this product category were Y588 billion, representing 15% of the Company total, in 1983.

ENERGY AND KITCHEN-RELATED PRODUCTS

This category includes many types of batteries, among them manganese, nickel-cadmium, mercury, alkaline, silver oxide, lithium and air wet cells, storage batteries for automotive use, fuel cell batteries primarily for marine use, and solar cells. It also encompasses various battery appliances, gas appliances, kitchen sinks and cabinets, and solar energy equipment. Sales of these products as a whole reached Y187 billion or 5% of the Company's 1983 total.

ELECTRONIC COMPONENTS

This category includes a wide variety of transistors, diodes, ICs (integrated circuits) and LSIs (large scale integrated circuits), as well as television picture tubes, other cathode ray tubes, image pickup tubes and magnetrons, for use by the Company and other manufacturers. The Company also manufactures a comprehensive line of incandescent, fluorescent, mercury and sodium lamps, speakers, audio accessories, TV tuners, resistors, capacitors, ceramic components, printed circuits, sensing devices and other parts. Total electronic components sales amounted to Y386 billion or 9% of the Company total for 1983.

OTHERS

This category includes phonograph records, prerecorded tapes, electric pencil sharpeners, bicycles, and photographic products, including cameras and flash units. Total sales of these miscellaneous products totaled Y307 billion and accounted for 8% of total 1983 sales of the Company.

Source: Matsushita Electric, SEC Form 20–F, November 20, 1983.

EXHIBIT I (*Continued*)   MAIN PRODUCTS

Consumer Electronics

TV receivers
  color
  monochrone
  industrial
Transistor radios
  portables
  clock radios
Headphones
Radio cassette recorders
Cassette recorders
Car audio
Transceivers
Music centers
Hi-fi components
  turntables
  tape decks
  amplifiers
  receivers
  tuners
  speaker systems
Video tape recorders
Video cameras
Video projection systems
Video tape printers
Video editing machines
Video mixing apparatus
Electronic organs
Hearing aids

Industrial Equipment

Welding machines
  light beam
  electron beam
  arc
  automatic CO_2
Component insertion machines
  (PANASERT*)
Automatic riveting machines
Automatic screw feeding and
  driving machines
High voltage transformers
Power capacitors
Power distribution equipment
Circuit breakers
TLD (Thermoluminescent
  dosimeter)
Medical equipment
  (PANAVISTA*)
Vending machines
Refrigerated showcases
Card readers

Measuring equipment
Elevators
Escalators
Anti-pollution equipment

Business Machines

Small business computers
Facsimile equipment
Plain paper copiers
Word processors
Electronic cash registers
Electronic calculators
Key telephones
Intercom systems
Automatic slide processors
Pencil sharpeners
Staplers
Letter openers

Home Appliances

Refrigerators
Microwave ovens
Gas and electric ovens
Rice cookers
Toasters
Blenders
Food processors
Coffee makers
Tempura-fondue cookers
Joy Cook (Induction heating
  cooker)
Kitchen units
Water heaters
Dish washers
Disposers
Pumps
Washing machines
Dryers
Vacuum cleaners
Polishers
Electric fans
Ventilating fans
Air and water purifiers
Water coolers
Electric irons
Electric blankets
Air conditioners
Heating and cooling systems
  electric
  gas
  kerosene
Dehumidifiers and humidifiers
Hair setters

Bicycles
Flash units
Clocks

Lighting Equipment

Incandescent lamps
Fluorescent lamps
Mercury discharge lamps
Metal halide lamps
Sodium lamps
Infrared ray lamps
Halogen lamps
Lighting fixtures

System Products

LL (Learning laboratory) systems
Broadcasting systems
Sound systems
Traffic control systems
Tunnel systems
Disaster alert systems
Hotel service systems
Dam control systems
Meteorological robot buoy systems
CATV systems
POS (Point of sale) systems
POSTA (Post office service total
  automation) systems
Lighting systems
Surveillance systems
Public address systems
Mobile telephone systems

Electronic Components

Transistors
Diodes
ICs
LSIs
Thyristors
Cathode ray tubes
Image pickup tubes
  (NEWVICON*)
Receiving and transmitting tubes
Indicator tubes
Magnetrons
Hybrid microcircuits (Hi-MIC*)
Capacitors
Resistors
Ceramics (PCM*, ZNR*)
Printed circuit boards
Transformers

EXHIBIT I (*Continued*)

Coils	Coreless motors	Lithium batteries
Switches	Flat motors	Mercury batteries
Connectors	Fan motors	Silver oxide batteries
Sensors	Blower motors	Air batteries
Display and graphic devices	Capacitor motors	Paper-thin batteries
System modules	Hermetically-sealed motors	Lead-acid batteries
Tuners	Clutch motors	car batteries
Speakers	Needle positioning motors	storage batteries
Tape heads (HPF*)	Shaded pole motors	PANALLOID* batteries
Microphones	Synchronous motors	Nickel-cadmium batteries
Antennas	Geared motors	Battery chargers
	General purpose motors	Solar batteries
Motors	Universal motors	Fuel cells
		Carbon electrodes
DC motors	**Batteries**	Battery operated golf carts and other appliances
Micro motors		
Transistor motors	Manganese dioxide batteries	
Stepping motors	Alkaline manganese batteries	
Servo motors		

* *Trademark of Matsushita Electric.*

Source: Matsushita Electric, *Annual Report*, 1983.

EXHIBIT I (*Continued*)   **SALES BREAKDOWN BY PRODUCTS AND GEOGRAPHIC AREAS** (Billions of Yen)

	Year Ended November 20					
	1981		1982		1983	
Video equipment	Y 1,109	(32%)	Y 1,329	(36%)	Y 1,444	(36%)
Audio equipment	543	(16)	485	(13)	481	(12)
Home appliances	591	(17)	590	(16)	596	(15)
Communication and industrial equipment	429	(12)	464	(13)	588	(15)
Energy and kitchen-related products	166	(5)	181	(5)	187	(5)
Electronic components	313	(9)	310	(9)	386	(9)
Others	300	(9)	291	(8)	307	(8)
Total	Y 3,451	(100%)	Y 3,650	(100%)	Y 3,989	(100%)

	Year Ended November 20					
	1981		1982		1983	
Japan	Y 1,872	(54%)	Y 1,965	(54%)	Y 2,128	(53%)
North America (United States and Canada)	640	(19)	670	(18)	842	(21)
Others	939	(27)	1,015	(28)	1,019	(26)
Total	Y 3,451	(100%)	Y 3,650	(100%)	Y 3,989	(100%)

Source: Matsushita Electric, *SEC Form 20–F*, November 20, 1983.

EXHIBIT I (*Continued*)   SELECTED FINANCIAL DATA (Billions of Yen, Except Per Share Amounts and Yen Exchange Rates)

| | Year Ended November 20 | | | | |
	1979	1980	1981	1982	1983
Net sales	Y 2,363	2,916	3,451	3,650	3,989
Net income	98	125	157	157	183
Per common share:					
Net income	69.54	87.13	101.48	100.79	116.29
Dividends	8.26	8.26	9.09	10.00	12.50
	($0.036)	($0.038)	($0.038)	($0.041)	($0.053)
Net working capital	Y 495	548	615	676	768
Total assets	2,139	2,478	2,946	3,174	3,451
Long-term indebtedness	68	59	35	49	40
Minority interests	200	242	302	339	377
Stockholders' equity	922	1,092	1,275	1,435	1,602
Yen exchange rates per U.S. dollar:					
Year-end	246.20	213.70	218.65	257.85	235.95
Average	213.94	231.79	220.74	245.55	239.58
High	193.95	206.50	199.05	214.20	226.75
Low	247.00	261.40	246.10	277.65	257.05

Notes: 1.   *Per share amounts have been appropriately adjusted for free distributions of shares.*

2.   *Dividends per share are those declared with respect to the income for each fiscal year and dividends charged to retained earnings are those actually paid.*

Source: Matsushita Electric, *SEC Form 20–F*, November 20, 1983.

EXHIBIT I (*Continued*) MATSUSHITA ELECTRIC INDUSTRIAL CO., LTD. AND CONSOLIDATED SUBSIDIARIES

Consolidated Balance Sheets November 20, 1983 and 1982

Assets	Yen (Millions)	
	1983	1982
Current assets:		
Cash (note 4)	553,988	492,509
Marketable securities, at cost, which approximates market	212,762	120,028
Trade receivables (note 4):		
Related companies (note 3)	75,321	78,044
Notes	118,386	112,186
Accounts	365,761	343,061
Allowance for doubtful receivables	(14,582)	(15,040)
Net trade receivables	544,886	518,251
Inventories (notes 2 and 4)	528,529	556,953
Other current assets (note 5)	179,179	158,577
Total current assets	2,019,344	1,846,318
Investments and advances (note 3):		
Nonconsolidated subsidiaries	164,281	169,235
Associated companies	76,054	71,762
Other investments and advances	590,942	508,061
Total investments and advances	831,277	749,058
Property, plant and equipment (note 4):		
Land	73,584	66,926
Buildings	330,193	308,874
Machinery and equipment	642,789	568,098
Construction in progress	22,168	17,540
	1,068,734	961,438
Less accumulated depreciation	603,709	508,942
Net property, plant and equipment	405,025	452,496
Other assets (note 5)	134,947	125,848
	3,450,593	3,173,720

Liabilities and Stockholders' Equity	Yen (Millions)	
	1983	1982
Current liabilities:		
Short-term bank loans (note 4)	195,011	245,929
Current portion of long-term debt (note 4)	1,200	1,413
Trade payables:		
Related companies (note 3)	36,959	32,991
Notes	82,325	75,101
Accounts	243,263	213,401
Total trade payables	362,547	321,493
Accrued income taxes (note 5)	161,253	113,187
Accrued payroll	114,892	104,918
Other accrued expenses	198,375	173,324
Deposits and advances from customers	76,956	75,536
Employees' deposits	83,107	76,374
Other current liabilities	58,453	57,725
Total current liabilities	1,251,794	1,169,899
Long-term debt (note 4)	40,405	49,158
Retirement and severance benefits	179,247	180,340
Minority interests:		
Capital stock	39,273	38,082
Surplus	337,800	300,928
Total minority interests	377,073	339,010
Stockholders' equity:		
Common stock of Y50 par value (notes 4 and 6): Authorized—2,700,000,000 shares; issued—1,589,239,462 shares (1982—1,576,298,513 shares)	79,462	78,815
Capital surplus (note 6)	216,719	205,797
Legal reserve (note 7)	30,011	27,831
Retained earnings (notes 3, 4, 6 and 7)	1,282,536	1,117,689
Cumulative translation adjustments (note 1(d))	(3,820)	12,237
	1,606,908	1,442,369
Less cost of 7,005,397 shares (1982—16,641,324 shares) of common stock held by consolidated subsidiaries	2,834	7,056
Total stockholders' equity	1,602,074	1,435,313
Commitments and contingent liabilities (note 9)		
	3,450,593	3,173,720

See accompanying notes to consolidated financial statements provided in company's 20-F.

Source: Matsushita Electric, *SEC Form 20-F*, Nov. 1983.

EXHIBIT I (*Continued*)   MATSUSHITA ELECTRIC INDUSTRIAL CO., LTD. AND CONSOLIDATED
SUBSIDIARIES

Consolidated Statements of Income
Years Ended November 20, 1983, 1982 and 1981

	Yen (Millions)		
	1983	*1982*	*1981*
Net sales:			
Related companies (note 3)	Y 958,972	772,326	732,492
Other	3,029,547	2,877,245	2,718,847
Total net sales	3,988,519	3,649,571	3,451,339
Cost of sales (note 3)	2,571,006	2,354,189	2,230,116
Gross profit	1,417,513	1,295,382	1,221,223
Selling, general and administrative expenses	990,987	917,552	848,483
Operating profit	426,526	377,830	372,740
Other income (deductions):			
Interest and dividend income	92,405	80,716	75,372
Equity in earnings of nonconsolidated subsidiaries and associated companies (note 3)	17,106	14,515	17,590
Interest expense	(50,257)	(54,958)	(44,742)
Other, net	12,294	10,830	10,969
	71,548	51,103	59,189
Income before income taxes	498,074	428,933	431,929
Provision for income taxes (note 5):			
Current	276,984	242,265	265,318
Deferred	(8,493)	(14,450)	(33,526)
	268,491	227,815	231,792
Income before minority interests	229,583	201,118	200,137
Minority interests	46,835	43,997	43,410
Net income	Y 182,748	157,121	156,727
Net income per depositary share, each representing 10 shares of common stock (note 1(i)):			
Assuming no dilution	Y 1,163	1,008	1,015
Assuming full dilution	1,138	979	982

See accompanying notes to consolidated financial statements provided in company's 20–F.

Source: Matsushita Electric, *SEC Form 20–F*, November 20, 1983.

GENERAL MOTORS CORPORATION:
THE DOWNSIZING DECISION

In his book, *My Years with General Motors*,[1] Alfred P. Sloan, Jr. describes in detail the crucial policy shifts of the 1920s and 1930s that made General Motors Corporation the leading automobile manufacturer in the world. Emma Rothschild later summarized these shifts rather colorfully as follows:

> Ford in the early 1920s made about half of all cars sold in America, and General Motors about one quarter; by the middle of the 1930s the position was reversed. The transition from Ford leadership to GM leadership can stand for the transformation of the industry. Henry Ford wrote passionately about the 1920s, about industrial and engineering expansion, about the falling prices of his Model T's. . . . Alfred Sloan of GM wrote with similar rapture about his company's expansion in the 1930s, about the development and elaboration of the car market, about the rising quality and rising prices of GM cars, their bright colors and sculptured lines.[2]

GM had developed a complete spectrum of automobiles, consisting of five well known lines. Each line had several models, occupied a specified price-quality niche, changed its styles annually, and competed not just with other manufacturers but also—at the margin—with other GM lines. This basic posture continued through the 1950s and well into the 1960s. Each line fulfilled a designated portion of GM's goal "to supply a car for every purse and every purpose." The

Case copyright © 1985 by James Brian Quinn. Research assistants—Mrs. W.L. Baldwin and Allie J. Quinn. The generous cooperation of General Motors Corporation is gratefully acknowledged.

late 1960s brought changes that would slowly alter the whole strategic posture of General Motors, then the largest industrial corporation in the world.

HIGHWAY SAFETY

In 1965, reportedly motivated by his outrage over a small girl's unnecessary death in an automobile accident, Ralph Nader wrote *Unsafe at Any Speed*, a scathing indictment of the whole automobile industry. One of the targets he picked out for special treatment was GM's first serious entry into the U.S. small car field, the Corvair. Although acclaimed by engineers for its innovative design, the Corvair's rear suspension system became a focal point of Nader's attack. With the Nader book and testimony as a catalyst—and with a televised furor over GM's lawyers' having detectives tail Nader—Congress passed the National Traffic and Motor Vehicle Safety Act of 1966.[3]

This Act led to the issuance of a number of initial safety standards, covering such items as seat belts, energy absorbing instrument panels, lights, energy absorbing steering columns, etc. for all automobiles sold in the U.S.

Automotive Safety Engineering

At first a number of automobile designers felt confused, insulted, or genuinely hurt. They had spent their lives as professionals trying to create safe vehicles that customers would buy. Now they were being told by regulators with a lot less expertise how their cars must perform. Some were not too keen about the idea or too impressed with many of the regulatory proposals. But as one member of GM's Auto Safety Engineering said:

> Despite resistance on both sides, we tried to walk the government regulators patiently through the details of what we could and could not do. At the beginning of the Safety Act the regulatory people were not always very technically expert in the automotive field. We tried to go through each proposed change slowly and carefully so they could understand the issues and how complex any change in this industry is. And we tried to explain the purpose of the regulations to our managers and designers. At first the government people were leery of this, and some of our design people were quite impatient. In time both responded more and more.

Later, some of Nader's allegations about the 1960–63 Corvair were investigated by the National Highway Safety Bureau, which concluded that the Corvair's "handling and stability performance is at least as good as the performance of some contemporary vehicles both domestic and foreign."[4] Nevertheless, the production of Corvair ended in May 1969, partly because of the bad press the car had received from Nader's book and partly because of changed consumer preferences. At that time GM had not lost a single final court case on the Corvair.[5]

The Basic Dilemma

Over the years the Department of Transportation (DOT) and its National Highway Traffic Safety Administration (NHTSA) have developed numerous safety standards and regulations, affecting many aspects of auto safety performance and design.[6] The industry accepted many regulations as reasonable or inevitable. Others—like air bags and 5 mph shock resistant bumpers favored by individuals within DOT or NHTSA—were severely questioned as expensive, fuel consuming, experimental, or ineffective in meeting the needs of automobile safety. As an experiment, GM volunteered to install air bags as optional equipment

(but only some 10,000 cars so equipped were sold over a 3-year period).

It was theoretically possible to design a car that very few people would be killed in. But several GM spokesmen expressed the company's basic dilemma concerning product safety. "Such a car would be an elaborate and prohibitively expensive tank, and no one would buy it. We also know that eliminating potentially unsafe drivers, requiring people to use their safety belts and more thorough driver training and law enforcement would save many more lives less expensively. But we feel very uncomfortable recommending mandatory actions in these areas. After all, such things impinge upon the personal freedom of our customers, their values, and their choices."

AIR QUALITY CONCERNS

By the late 1960s the public had begun to voice serious concerns about the impact of the automobile on air quality. The problem first emerged in the 1950s smogs of Los Angeles when studies began to indicate that sunlight broke down trapped automotive exhaust gases into eye stinging ozone and nitrous oxide compounds. At first, top GM officials were skeptical that their product was to blame. At this stage GM contributed limited amounts of scientific talent, primarily to see whether the automobile was in fact a major contributor to smog. Once Dr. Arie J. Haagen-Smit of Cal. Tech. had identified the composition of photochemical smog and the mechanisms through which the automobile contributed to it,[7] the company made a determined technical effort to reduce emissions drastically. By 1966 all new cars sold in California had crankcase (1961) and exhaust control (1966) devices which reduced emissions of some hydrocarbon and carbon monoxide pollutants by about 40%. Under the Clean Air Act Amendments of 1965 these became standard on all new U.S. cars in 1968. GM also test-marketed a kit to reduce older cars' pollution some 30–50%. But in the smog-prone Phoenix (Arizona) area—despite an intensive promotional campaign—only 528 of an estimated 334,000 potential customers were willing to pay the approximately $20 for such a retrofit.[8]

The 1970 Clean Air Act Amendments

In 1970 the Department of Health, Education and Welfare proposed tighter exhaust standards for 1975 cars to reduce hydrocarbons 97%, carbon monoxide 91%, and nitrogen oxide effluents 85% below uncontrolled levels.[9] Then in a sudden move, led by Senator Muskie of Maine, Congress passed the Clean Air Act Amendments of 1970, cutting these permissible effluent levels essentially in half. Although no specific cost benefit studies suggested the new standards as optimum, the Senate passed the "Muskie Bill" with a close to unanimous vote. Mr. E.N. Cole, then GM's President, had earlier said the Muskie standards "simply aren't attainable . . . with existing technology" and had proposed an alternate set based upon GM's own calculations.[10]

Nevertheless, General Motors now had to meet the new standards. A variety of options existed including the stratified charge engine, catalytic converters, or entirely new engines—like the Wankel rotary design. All had their proponents and opponents inside and outside the company. Because of the importance of this and other similar decisions, GM formed a Research Policy Committee consisting of top level technical, operating, and financial people to weigh the alternatives. GM took a license on the Wankel engine, reportedly prepared to spend some $50 million on its development.[11] Many engineers preferred the stratified charge engine—which was satisfactorily demonstrated on small cars and later successfully scaled up by Honda for a demonstration 6-cylinder Chevrolet-sized engine. But GM's decision eventually favored the catalytic converter approach.

Although requiring use of completely non-leaded fuel, the catalytic converter: (1) provided the ability for better gasoline mileage than some alternative approaches; (2) allowed GM to use its existing engine manufacturing facilities; (3) could immediately be adapted to all engines regardless of size; (4) could be guaranteed to meet effluent standards for 50,000 miles (while radically redesigned engines might fail to meet standards if they wore differentially during this period); (5) avoided extensively retraining dealers, mechanics, customers, service stations, and the full infra-structure necessary to maintain redesigned engines. Even before Congress passed the Clean Air Amendments of 1970, GM was urging the oil companies to reconstitute fuels to eliminate lead and sulphur and reduce other toxic components.[12] But the 1970 standards required a crash program to get large scale catalytic converter production underway in the fall of 1974.[13]

Damned If You Do or Don't

Many GM executives referred to the high risk of this decision. A $100 million plant had to be constructed and put into operation in 3 years. It had to produce an entirely new product to work continuously and safely on millions of vehicles for at least 50,000 miles. The new plant had to proceed into early construction stages while researchers were still trying to find a proper blend of sufficiently effective and available catalysts to make this solution realistic.

One GM executive later said, "Frankly we got lucky. The converters worked better than we ever expected. We actually improved on gas mileage. Then we found ourselves in the incongruous position of losing credibility by performing better than we thought we could. Our earlier statements about the difficulty or 'impossibility' of the standards were thrown in our faces. We were accused of lying or foot dragging. You are damned if you do and damned if you don't."

The company was frequently stumped in finding an effective way to present its case to the public. During the 1960s California smog crisis, it found that careful technical discussions about the unknowns of air chemistry provided no answer to emotional campaigns using simplistic slogans like: "smog kills," "you're destroying the lungs of millions," or "GM is the worst polluter in the world." Complex arguments about economic tradeoffs were useless against simple statistics comparing auto fatalities to war casualties or gory photographs of accident victims.

These culminated in Ralph Nader's 1970 "Campaign GM" attack. At the May stockholders meeting he put forward a proposal "to add three representatives of the public"[14] to GM's Board. This was overwhelmingly defeated at the meeting. But the company did appoint a "Public Policy Committee" of directors later that year. Soon thereafter it established a Science Advisory Committee of distinguished independent scientists to insure that GM responded properly to developing evidence about the impact of its products on the environment.

SMALL CARS AND FUELS

About this same time two other major issues began to achieve prominence—the invasion of foreign car imports into the U.S. market and a projected rise in fuels costs. In March 1969 *Fortune* pointed out that foreign cars' share of the U.S. market had risen from below 5% in 1962 to more than 10% in 1968. And that share was expected to increase to 14% in 1970.[15] *Fortune* chided the industry noting that:

> The perennial ability of the U.S. auto industry to sell by the millions a product so complex and expensive as the motorcar is one of the marvels of commercial history. But for the last dozen years the feat has been blemished by the industry's repeated failure to grasp the true nature of the minority market for small cars. . . . [In the early 1960s, American compacts had achieved] an initial stunning success. . . . By 1962 they had won a market of almost 1,800,000 cars a year . . . and had cut U.S. sales of imported cars to little more than half the 1959 level. But as the compacts grew in size and price, their sales declined and imports rebounded.[16]

GM spent about $100 million for design and manufacturing techniques to produce its new compact, Vega, in fall 1970. It assembled the Vega in an automated plant in Lordstown, Ohio. The plant was designed in part to eliminate some of the more onerous jobs on older assembly lines. Both the plant and the Vega later ran into significant problems. After a short strike in March 1972, the Lordstown plant settled down and became an efficient operation. But Vega's higher than expected price and early quality problems—overheating aluminum engine block, body rust, and three safety recalls—held sales well below its expected 400,000 sales level in 1971. Meanwhile Volkswagen led in small car sales with 520,000 in units sold.[17]

Fuel Efficiency

In the early 1970s there was still a glut in world oil supplies. Nevertheless, analyses in the GM Chief Economist's Office began to project a developing U.S. dependency on foreign oil and the likelihood of higher future oil prices. These concerns led the board in 1972 to create an ad hoc energy task force headed by David C. Collier, then Treasurer, later head of GM of Canada and then the Buick Division. Collier's group included people from manufacturing, research, design, finance, industry-government relations, and the economics staff. In May of 1973 the task force went to the board with three conclusions: (1) there was a developing energy problem, (2) the government had no particular plan to deal with it, (3) energy costs would have a profound effect on GM's business. Collier's report created a good deal of discussion around the company in the ensuing months. "We were trying to get other people to think about the issue," said Richard C. Gerstenberg, then chairman of GM.[18]

"There was not a good feel as to when all this would come to a head, and no complete strategy was worked out to cope with it," said one of the executives involved. Nevertheless GM initiated work on two fuel-efficient car designs in the U.S. and in Germany. These became known as the "K Body" (later Seville) and "T Body" (later Chevette). And the board asked Collier's group to report back in October 1973 with an analysis of the company's overall product program. GM also began to experiment with stack gas scrubbers and to convert some of its own internal power plants from oil to coal. Mr. Gerstenberg even got blistered by some of the utilities for suggesting that electric power be produced with coal, not oil.

GM sales had reached highs in both 1972 and early '73. Throughout the industry, mid-1973 production was near maximum capacity, slowed only by delays in parts deliveries.[19] Everyone expected the Nixon Administration's dollar devaluation to halt the steady rise in imports. It did not. But no one expected the oil embargo that multiplied oil prices from $2.59 in May to $11.56 per barrel in December 1973.

The Embargo

The October 1973 oil embargo hit GM hard. The company shut down 16 of its 24 assembly plants in December 1973 and cut its first quarter '74 schedules 15–20%. And the company stopped construction projects at one Oldsmobile and two Buick plants because of declining large car sales.[20]

While GM moved to expand its small car production, it was not ready to abandon its traditional interest in larger lines. Some 75% of its late 1973 cars had V-8 engines. Still GM expanded its smaller engine plants in 1974 and bought back tooling for a V-6 line it had sold to AMC in 1968. After GM's annual meeting in May 1974, Chairman Gerstenberg announced, "In 1975 we will offer a new small car in every GM division . . .[21] GM was also "speeding programs to first lighten—and eventually shrink—all its big cars."[22]

These were among the first public announcements of the most momentous shift in GM's product posture since Alfred Sloan's restructuring of the 1920s. They were made against a backdrop of great uncertainty about which direction customer preferences would take. Mr. Gerstenberg predicted "the family car will continue

to command a major if somewhat lesser share of the market." Richard L. Terrell, then GM's Executive Vice President, said, "Some see 50–60% small cars (in the near future) . . . but we see the possibility of it swinging the other way."[23]

Some Drastic Revisions

Mr. Elliott M. (Pete) Estes, later President of GM, described the way these corporate decisions were reached. "We had done a lot of talking and thinking about how to modify our line to meet developing fuel economy, environmental, and customer demands. In October 1973 the Middle East War broke out, the embargo came on the 22nd, and the curtain came down on auto sales. This led us to discuss our reactions in somewhat more of a 'panic mode' than we would have liked. We concluded: (1) we should have a car smaller than Vega, (2) we needed a smaller luxury car. The members of the executive committee essentially arrived at a consensus on these approaches during its regular daily work sessions at the lunch hour. GM had to introduce these cars faster than ever before. We had always operated with the GM committee system which was very slow. We knew we would have to bypass our usual procedures. The decisions on these two cars were basically made in October–December 1973."

Fortunately the company had been designing smaller cars for years. The executive committee had agreed that the new subcompact car "had to be number one in fuel economy." None of the domestic designs would do this. The corporation therefore reached across the Atlantic to pick up its "T car"—a car that had originally been designed in Germany, introduced in Brazil, contained an engine produced in Brazil, and was being restyled in Britain. Britain had a "three door design," larger than a standard small car, with a modern look, and more storage space because of the rear door. The executive committee wanted an available car which would do the best job and be flexible for future changes. On January 23, 1974, the decision was to go ahead and introduce the ''T car''—soon-to-be Chevette—to the U.S. in an unprecedented eighteen months. As Estes later said, ''We flew a team to Germany to pick up the drawings for the Chevette. We even stayed with the metric system to simplify our problems in debugging the car over here.''

The search for a fuel efficient luxury car disclosed that GM had a design that was partially completed in engineering. But the vehicle had never been fully developed because people had perceived the car as having a marketing appeal primarily limited to the relatively few customers who traditionally bought Mercedes class cars. The clay models were finished, and many parts were already being made in the U.S. Mr. Estes said, ''We made the decision to kick off the [Cadillac] Seville on January 23rd too. We wanted production on the Seville by March 27, 1975, and the Chevette by August 18, 1975. The luxury car had to have a formal look. It had to come out at the top of the line. Previously big was good, and bigger was better. Now we had to put a smaller car, at a higher price, at the top of the line.''

DOWNSIZING THE LINE

By themselves, these two decisions would have been simply the introduction of two new models— common enough for an auto company. But they were made in the context of other events, which ultimately led to the downsizing of the total GM line.

A New Concept for GM?

How did this concept come into being? Mr. Gail Smith, General Director of GM Advertising and Merchandising, said, ''Downsizing was a part of a recognition that fuel economy would be an important factor in the marketplace. Our market research showed many foreign car buyers made very different tradeoffs from big-car customers. They discounted comfort heavily in favor of maneuverability or gas mileage.'' Another executive said, ''In the early 1970s, there was a distinct awareness of a conservation—or economy— ethic. This contributed to the early 1971–72 concepts of what became the Cadillac Seville. But our conclusions were really at the conversational level: that the big car trend was nearing its end. At that time there was certainly no tendency to go whole hog in emphasizing economy-conservation factors. We were not at all sure sufficient numbers of large car buyers were ready to move to dramatically smaller-lighter cars. We were dreadfully aware of how Chrysler had been hurt by moving too soon to smaller cars in earlier years.'' The company was then thinking in terms of a relatively modest downsizing to be followed by successive and more drastic product changes in later years.

It is difficult to pinpoint the precise time when these ''decisions''—or many other major decisions—in General Motors were actually made. Well prior to the presentation of matters at formal sessions of GM's governing committees and policy groups, a broad consensus is generally obtained among members of senior management. Part of this occurs as members of the executive committee sit along with other key staff and operating executive on various policy groups—subcommittees of the executive committee—where important topics are discussed. In addition, all top executives receive continuing input on significant matters from various levels of the organization outside of the formal setting of policy group meetings.

Informal Discussions

Another executive described the decision process as follows: ''There were a lot of informal discussions going on among different people and small groups around the company. Even at the top level I don't think there was an attempt to get everybody together to analyze this as a momentous issue. At the Product Policy Group level a lot of discussion always occurs before a formal meeting. From this perhaps 6–7 key people will convince themselves—for a variety of reasons—that something must be done. That is where the crucial decisions are really made. In an organization as big as this, it is very important that the major decision makers appear to be together when a big decision is reached. They don't even want too much difference in viewpoint within the meeting as to the sense of direction their comments may convey. Otherwise there could be a lot of confusion throughout the design process. The major conceptual decisions are really thoroughly discussed and reviewed before the formal meeting.

"The formal meeting is just to make sure everything gets looked at. One is forced to listen to a complete rationale. We get clear cost estimates and a thoroughly worked out plan for a given product line. Everybody feels much more comfortable about the decisions after they have been discussed in a forum like that. More importantly, the line people know how we are planning to get where we are going. The more they understand this, the more they know what to do on their own as the program progresses.

"There is a lot of moving out of channels in this organization. Product Planning knows in advance what is acceptable. People are involved in a lot of presentations at multiple levels. Everybody knows everyone. And the top decision makers have actually had a chance to meet and deal with a number of people on a person to person basis. We try to keep these key decision makers informed about the marketplace and who to go to for detailed information, and also bring to bear their own considerable experience garnered from a lifetime career in the transportation business."

The Project Center

An important change in the design process occurred in early 1973. Prior to this time, most major components of the car had been assigned to a specific division as "lead group" for its design; for example air conditioning went to Pontiac, frames to Chevrolet, brakes to Buick, etc. This had been begun in 1964 to promote commonality in parts and resultant scale economies. Previously each car division had designed the entire car minus the Fisher Body. Slowly more and more parts and systems were brought under a

lead division's control. The corporation tried to get as many common parts as possible to insure efficiency without impairing marketability. But the car divisions maintained control over those aspects which lent individual difference—grilles, bumpers, trim, dashboards, ride, handling characteristics, etc.—and marketability to their lines.

In April 1973 a 10 year product plan had been presented to corporate top management. In each division there had traditionally been 5 year plans. These had to be extended and revised to reflect a 10 year horizon. Mr. Estes said, "This is the first such 10 year presentation I can remember. Fuel costs were likely to rise and fuel economy appeared saleable. So we set an initial target of reducing weight by 400 pounds. This figure had two merits: (1) we couldn't figure out how to get out more weight than that, (2) it would give us one more mile per gallon in fuel economy. But we needed to do this without decreasing the comfort level, baggage capability, or six-person capacity of the cars."

Mr. Estes continued, "Rather than just turn this over to the divisions we formed a Project Center to coordinate the task.[24] We wanted to get most of the advantages of a centralized engineering group without losing the advantages of divisionalization. Pontiac's assistant chief engineer, Bill Collins, was brought in to be project manager. The development engineers were on a loan basis from all divisions. Typically we would take an engineering manager from the lead division on each major component involved. We wanted a new design that would give each section of the car as much compatibility as possible across the full GM line."

Collins had certain general guidelines for the cars. The car designers had "packaged" the external features of the car. And management had approved that package. Mr. R.L. Dorn, Chief Engineer, Corporate Car Programs, said, "The Project Center group had a feeling for the kind of car they wanted. The objective was basically a B/C (regular car) space interior with an A body (intermediate) exterior. It was to have an A car weight, but perform functionally for the same sized people, number of people, and use patterns as then current B/C cars. The project group was to optimize the efficiency of the design. At first we only assumed we were making a car for a B/C price. We knew there would still be A cars on the market. And in engineering we also had a feeling for the cost and volume figures. But we didn't work out these figures specifically. That is the province of the finance group. As we moved forward we understood more and more what the target economic specifications for the car would be.''

In April 1973 the Project Center took over system interface negotiations that had previously occurred at the divisional level—i.e. when component, subsystem, or marketing-design conflicts affected two or more divisions. But a Project Manager could not force a car division to accept a standardized part. The general manager and chief engineer of each car division had to be satisfied with the change for it to be implemented. The Project Center concept augmented rather than replaced, the lead division concept. Its success rested on the same delicate balance of persuasion and direction that underlay the rest of GM's complex system of coordinated decentralization. (See Appendix A.)

Downsizing Goals

Mr. Dorn said, ''When I came to the Project Center in November 1973, the original goals for downsizing had not been modified very much. But the embargo had caused a major sales loss and a lot of rethinking of the approved program content for the redesign of the large car lines. We began to bring up and address other design alternatives, with the result that the car sizes were cut a bit more. Shortly thereafter (December 1973), the Product Policy Committee posed a lot of 'what if' objectives. What if we gave you this—or that—weight objective? We pointed out that we could meet different objectives, but at a cost—of aluminum, tooling, structural materials, etc.''

The Product Policy Committee soon decided that the 10 year plan had to be drastically revised. From a product policy viewpoint the goal became ''to get approximately 3 mpg improve-

ment.'' This meant removing some 800–1000 pounds of vehicle weight for most cars. Estes again said, ''We had found by then that taking weight out of one area had an additive effect. A pound out of the body lightened the chassis; both lightened the engine, which helped the chassis some more—and so on. The target of 3 miles per gallon (800–1000 pounds) improvement was intended as a challenge. . . . It was arrived at as a seat of the pants judgment. But everyone agreed it *was* a challenge. . . . We wanted to accomplish this while maintaining six passenger seating capacity, the same luggage space, and equal or greater comfort characteristics in the vehicle.''

Key Thrusts and Increments

A marketing executive said, ''Strategy formulation here tends to be pretty amorphous, but with a few key threads. For example, there was some discussion as to whether we should drop full sized cars altogether. But this was not long or drawn out. There was substantial psychological commitment to total market coverage, hence little serious thought that we should serve only selected functions in the marketplace. . . . The strategy really evolved in a series of incremental steps. As one of my colleagues says: when I was younger I always conceived of a room where all these concepts were carefully worked out for the whole company. Later I didn't find any such room. . . .

''In this company there is a real competition of ideas. We thrive on the adversary process. Anyone with a good idea can get heard. The top people have been around a long time. They know each other and their way down in the organization very well. They have had many opportunities to appraise people's actions, their capabilities, their judgments. In this kind of organization, there are rarely single instants of decision. I frequently don't know precisely when a decision is made in General Motors. I don't remember being in a committee meeting when things came to a vote. Usually someone will simply summarize a developing position. Everyone else either nods or states his particular terms of consensus.''

The December 23rd Meeting

A crucial meeting on product strategy occurred on December 23, 1973. The Executive Committee (GM's seven top officials) met in the Technical Center's design dome to review various proposals of the car divisions and the Product Policy Committee (The Engineering Policy Group at that time). Discussion was lively, intense, but not prolonged. Whenever there was a choice between a division's view and corporate's, Mr. Gerstenberg listened carefully to both viewpoints, and generally sided with the divisions. For example, there was some inclination within the executive committee not to have Buick and Oldsmobile in the small car field. Gerstenberg backed the divisions' desire to have a full range of automobiles for their dealers. Mr. Cole preferred a larger (though scaled down) Cadillac. But the division had designed the Seville and preferred it. Again Gerstenberg chose the division's viewpoint.

One of the executives present said, "So much of the December 23 discussion was really instinct, there were strong feelings, rather than studies or data, that said every division should have a small car in its line. Some board members had been very vocal in pressing Gerstenberg for smaller cars. The Olds and Buick groups were influenced primarily by concern for the competitive position of their dealers. The Cadillac Division staff saw they needed a smaller car. And Chevrolet felt it needed a car still smaller than its Vega to offer its dealers. The decision process was highly unstructured." In February 1974, the executive committee instructed the engineers to make the final modifications on small cars for each line and to complete the pending plans for substantial reductions in the 1977 big cars. The Chevrolet small car was the Nova, Pontiac's was the Ventura, Oldsmobile's the Omega and Buick's the Skylark. Oldsmobile also offered the Starfire, and Pontiac got the Astra, a Vega size car. These were to support each division's dealer body in light of the plummeting 1973–74 sales of large cars.

GM could not afford to downsize all its line at once. Mr. Estes said, "Our real job was to move our customers over to a fuel economic car without taking anything from them. It was very important for us to maintain our customers. One of the big problems was to get the dealers to realize the full potential of these newly designed cars. From the start, we emphasized that the downsized regular car would not sacrifice the interior space, comfort, or value of the 'regular' car, and was not a 'compact' or 'smaller' car. Many reporters at first thought the resized line would be a disaster and said so. But when people actually saw the new cars standing by themselves they looked big enough. I said the only difference the customer would notice was that he had more room to walk around it in his garage."

Discipline and "Plastic Cars"

In mid-1974 the Environmental Protection Agency (EPA) came forth with its proposed methods for measuring the mileage and exhaust characteristics of automobiles. Cars would be tested according to weight classes, with all cars in a given class measured in terms of the midpoint of their weight class. For example, all cars in the 3750–4250 pound weight band would be tested with a 4000 pound dynamometer load. Mr. Dorn said, "As these standards became clear, the Product Policy Committee decided to put all the B cars into the 4000 pound EPA weight class. All C body cars would go into the 4500 pound class, and so on. These became the real design objectives, not a specific weight reduction per se. They really dictated the move from the initial target weight reduction of 400 pounds to what became 700–1000 pound reductions for specific models.

"Each car's weight had crept up—incremented by minor design changes. But if we didn't watch the EPA standards carefully we paid a great penalty both on emissions and on dynamometer mileage ratings. In our early planning, we built in a 3% reserve below our target weight to allow for errors in estimating and other miscellaneous contingencies. Then as the program got further along in its evolution, we might weed out some of the most costly weight reducing features and still not suffer heavy penalties in meeting the EPA weight category.

"Initially, we proposed a program using a lot of aluminum and substitute materials to meet the new 'mass' targets. But this would have meant a very high cost, and would have strained our suppliers' aluminum capacity. However when we presented this program to management, they said, 'Okay, if necessary, we'll do it.' They didn't back down. We began to understand then that they were dead serious. Feeling that the company would spend the money was critical to the success of the entire mass reduction effort. Fortunately, the divisions assigned topflight people to the Project Center. We had only about 20 people in the Project Center to coordinate this whole project. Consequently, the real credit belongs to the divisional people who did the design work and to the division managements that were willing to change some of their prior practices. This was also the first real participation by the GM Assembly Division in a whole new car."

Set up in 1965 "to tighten and revamp assembly operations that GM believed had become seriously deficient under car divisional direction," General Motors Assembly Division had taken over all but 4 of GM's 22 assembly plants by early 1972.[25] The shift was seen as a centralizing move to cut costs and eliminate duplication. John DeLorean, then General Manager of Chevrolet, had noted, "It became illogical to put a B Chevrolet, an A Chevrolet (Chevelle) and an F Chevrolet in the same plant because they weren't built the same way . . . It became more logical to put a B Chevrolet, Pontiac, and Oldsmobile in the same plant. Then if the plant made more cars for other divisions than Chevrolet, why should Chevrolet control the plant?"[26]

ORGANIZATION CHANGES

In October–November 1974 both GM's Chairman (Gerstenberg) and President (Cole) retired mandatorily at age 65. Thomas A. Murphy, who like Gerstenberg had a finance background, became Chairman and CEO. Elliott M. ("Pete") Estes, an operating man with substantial international experience, replaced engineer Cole as President and Chief Operating Officer.[27]

An earlier action now began to influence events. In response to an early 1974 Federal Energy Administration (FEA) inquiry about what GM could do to improve fuel economy, a GM task force produced a report, *Comments by the General Motors Corporation to the Federal Energy Administration on Passenger Car Fuel Economy*, dated August 1974. GM indicated that it "had committed itself to an all out effort" to meet or exceed the 18.7 mpg fleet goal (or 50% improvement) by 1980. GM pointed out in the letters that emission standards more stringent than the 1975 levels and weight added to meet future safety standards could adversely affect its ability to reach the goal. These letters became the "voluntary agreement" with President Ford in early 1975.

One of the Industry-Government Relations Staff described an event which took place just after the new management team took over: "In early December, 1974, I was preparing a draft statement of a possible GM position on auto fuel economy for presentation at December 10, 1974, hearings by the Senate Commerce Committee. I had finished the first draft on about December 1st, the day Mr. Gerstenberg retired. In this draft, the position I was proposing was hinged on technical matters—what was technologically possible. But in mid-stream the decision was made that the emphasis in our position should be oriented not just to what was technologically feasible but more toward what was practicable from the standpoint of economics. Our Chief Economist, Henry Duncombe, made the presentation to the Commerce Committee and became GM's principal spokesman on fuel economy issues. Now we were pointing out that fuel economy was essentially an economic issue. We questioned whether it was good public policy to require the production of vehicles that might not be acceptable to the public."

When asked how policy on such matters comes about, the same executive said: "For the most part the policy simply evolves. In meetings, people say things that do or don't hold up to argument. Slowly everyone begins to sort out a sensible position from all of this. . . . We may write this position into testimony or a speech writer will put it into a draft speech for one of our corporate officers. After an initial review by the principal, we will then circulate the draft to all the appropriate staffs for comment. . . . The top people are very open to critiques of this sort. The ideas tend to flush upward so the top level can adopt them as they see a consensus emerging. If there is a major policy question, the executive may take the statement to the Executive Committee for comment or approval. Mr. Murphy will nearly always comment on any important issue. Once a corporate officer has spoken publicly on an issue there is a tendency to give his statements weight and wide circulation.''

The New Team

Although viewpoints on personalities might differ widely, various people used the following terms to describe the new management team which was to have such impact on GM's future. *Wall Street Journal* reported:

> Known as a stern and sometimes demanding boss to insiders, Mr. Murphy swept past a number of other GM officials [in 1972] to become vice chairman and the clear front runner for the top job. A dyed-in-the-wool finance man, he had spent all but four of his years at GM on the finance staff.[28]

GM executives said: ''Mr. Murphy is basically a finance guy.'' . . . ''He always has a briefcase jammed full of papers. . . . He has to be the most prodigious reader of internal documents in the place. He has always done his homework, and any memorandum to him is likely to come back with questions or comments for its originators or any recipients.'' . . . ''He always appears distinguished, formal, a bit distant in a group setting. But one-on-one he's very friendly, warm, perceptive. His door is always open to people here at headquarters.''

Of President, ''Pete'' Estes, GM executives reported: ''Estes is an engineer, a manufacturing guy. He's held in unbelievable awe by the organization. He is very effective as an operating man. He will be excellent and responsible in ensuring

that the product meets all the requirements of the customer and the government.'' . . . ''Estes has a kind of humble midwestern charm. People find him easy to talk to. He comes across as honest, straightforward, not flashy, but very competent.''

Of other executives: ''Roger Smith [Chief Financial Officer] is similar in many ways to Mr. Murphy. He also represents the buck in GM. To him the name of the game is profit.'' . . . ''Mr. F.J. McDonald runs 35 divisions. He's very competent, but with this responsibility it's hard to see how he could do much more than operations. Mr. H.H. Kehrl has to stay on top of the entire corporation's technology and Mr. Jensen has his hands full with overseas operations. In essence, all these are very effective operating guys.'' . . .

Disappointment and Rebounding Morale

For General Motors the first quarter of 1975 turned out to be the worst since 1946.[29] Faced with declining profits and determined to make changes in virtually all its cars, GM reduced its quarterly dividend and in March 1975 floated $600 million of new debt. This was the largest fixed income financing by an industrial company in history. However, Mr. Estes said, ''By spring 1975 we knew our product program was very right. . . . We thought we could be two years ahead of anyone else with our strategy. In March or April, Tom Murphy and I began talking around the organization that things were getting better. At the same time people at Ford were saying 'things are in a heck of a mess.' But we went ahead with a 10 year plan for the downsizing of *intermediate* cars. In March 1975 we decided to remove 700 pounds from these to gain approximately 3 mpg for their introduction in 1977 (1978 models).''[30] In December Congress passed the Energy Act of 1975 converting President Ford's voluntary agreements into law and further mandating each manufacturer to meet fleet fuel economy averages of 20 mpg by 1980 and $27\frac{1}{2}$ mpg by 1985. Said Estes, ''Our financial forecasts still said we couldn't meet even reduced dividend targets. But Tom and I started boosting our idea that 1975 was not going to be a loss year. By late 1975 you could feel the morale coming up.''

International Changes

An important decision of this era was to take a joint ownership position in Isuzu. Historically GM had insisted on 100% ownership in overseas units. But the company began to realize that this policy might exclude it from major growth markets. The areas where it had positions would account for an increasingly small share of the world market. In 1972 GM ranked as only the fifth automaker overseas with only 9% of total sales outside North America. But total auto sales abroad were growing twice as fast as in the U.S.[31]

GM's 1972 Annual Report noted austerely: "General Motors sees an important part of its future in the rapidly growing overseas market. . . . [But] the realization of these opportunities depends to an important degree on the ability of GM and other American business enterprises to trade and invest throughout the world without undue restrictions. Protectionist measures like the Burke-Hartke Bill . . . import quotas, limits on further investments overseas and restrictions on the overseas use of patents and licenses could cause trade retaliation at a time when our national purpose is to draw the nations of the world closer together . . ."[32]

SUCCESS AND FAILURES

Then to the tune of "It's About Time," GM introduced the internationally designed, U.S. modified, Chevette in fall 1975. It was 16.7″ shorter and 629 pounds lighter than the Vega. Its automatic transmission was 35 pounds lighter than other GM models but—in keeping with GM's standardization program—could be mated to engines large enough for the Buick Electra.[33] Another version of the Chevette "World Car" came into the Buick line as "Opel by Isuzu." The Isuzu car was similar to the (German GM) Opel Kadett. Versions of this car were being built in Britain, Brazil, and Australia.[34]

By the end of 1975 GM's share of American made cars had rebounded to 54%, profitability had improved, and reports said the company was aiming, unofficially, at 60%.[35] 1976 saw record sales of $47.2 billion and earnings of $10.08 per share. But the fickle public was shifting its taste in new cars. As gasoline supplies became more plentiful and less expensive, people moved up to larger cars more rapidly than expected. Less than a year after its highly successful introduction, Chevette's production plans had to be cut 50% below anticipated levels.[36] GM resumed expansion of its Lansing, Michigan, Oldsmobile plant—a project which it had halted in 1974.[37]

In introducing its 1977 standard cars GM found itself countering advanced press comments about the "downsized" cars.[38] It also had to hold off Ford's campaign for large cars, "Welcome to the home of the Whopper."[39] For the first time Ford was making the biggest cars across its full line, but GM was betting that its new models would make its competition seem "over the hill, like men with middle aged spread."[40] In the spring of 1979 GM planned to execute the third round of its automobile shrinkage. GM's compacts would be replaced by its X body design—a half ton lighter than 1977 compacts, with the same interior space, and powered by a transverse mounted front wheel drive engine. Further into the 1980s GM forecast a new "minicar," further shrinkage of its big cars and intermediates, and replacement of virtually all its V-8 engines with 4 to 6 cylinder engines.[41] $27\frac{1}{2}$ mpg was the mandated target for 1985. The problem was to choose something the customer would like and be willing to buy.

The costs of overhauling the GM product line would be enormous. Annual R&D expenditures were running over $1 billion, and in 1980 GM estimated it would invest $50 billion in safety, emissions control, and downsizing by 1985. In 1979 GM seemed to have successfully worked its way out of the crises of 1973–74. Not the least of these was, as *Fortune* said, "a revivified sense of purpose and a much sharper understanding of the outside world."[42] By the late 1970s GM's Headquarters was confident and optimistic. Its new aggressive spirit was perhaps best exemplified in Mr. Murphy's statements that he would not be satisfied "until we sell every car that's sold."[43]

CHALLENGES FOR THE FUTURE

Then the roof caved in. The combination of imported cars, high interest rates, and a world economic depression hammered GM sales and profits. Sales dropped from $66 billion in 1979 to $58 billion in 1980, and GM lost $762 million in perhaps its worst year in history. A new management team, headed by Roger B. Smith from GM's powerful corporate finance group, took over control for the new era. Despite strong internal measures to restore profitability, sales of both passenger cars and trucks dropped further in both 1981 and 1982. Slowly, the U.S. auto industry began to realize the cause behind the steadily growing penetration of Japanese cars in the U.S. A Presidential commission estimated Japanese cost advantages for a subcompact car at $1,500–$2,000 delivered to the U.S. west coast.

While GM's subcompact J car and its intermediate A car had fared better than its X body series, quality problems plagued the GM line in the early 1980s. In terms of recalls,* GM was second only to Subaru in the 1978–82 period as a percent of cars produced. Approximate percentages were:[44]

1978–1982
% OF SALES RECALLED

Subaru	97%
General Motors	86%
Chrysler	47%
Ford	45%
Volkswagen	38%
Honda	35%
Nissan	20%
Toyota	20%

---

* *A recall does not mean each car is defective. Hundreds or thousands may be investigated to find the few defectives.*

QUESTIONS

1. What were the key steps in the decision processes leading to GM's new strategy? What aspects of the process appear strong? Weak?
2. What should GM have done? When?
3. What should it do at the end of the case?
4. What national policy issues does this situation pose?

APPENDIX A

The General Motors Style

Several executives described GM's style in approaching complex strategy issues as follows:

Mr. Estes, President: "Every day you have a problem at the top of the list. My approach is to discuss it with everyone. I also try to hang on and not make a decision until I have all possible inputs. Then I decide what *ought* to be. After that I go out and try to sell it. When you arrive at your conclusions, you hope it is a majority opinion, but it may not be. Mr. Murphy and I may have discussed a problem to the point where we understand that we really do disagree. But when the chips are down, we must put forward a unified front.

"Many decisions are crystal clear when you get all the facts together. That is why one seeks out all possible information on major issues first. The tough ones are when such clarity does not come about. Then all you can do is get the facts together, close the door, and kick it around. You may come out of the meeting with a whole list of questions to be answered. But ultimately after several sessions like that, you all come out of the door together.

"We do not try to tell people how to get there from this level of the organization. We try to give them the broad concepts we are trying to achieve. We operate through questioning and fact gathering. Strategy is a state of mind you go through. When you think about a little problem, your mind begins to think how it will affect all the different elements in the total situation. Once you have had all the jobs that you need to qualify for this position, you can see the problem from a variety of viewpoints. But you don't try to ram your conclusions down people's throats. We try to persuade people what has to be done and provide confidence and leadership for them.''

Mr. J.N. Stewart, Director-Marketing Staff: ''Finally, we don't go on line with our goals. This would make for too much rigidity. Around here, if it is written down, it is out of date. [Our goals] are well understood throughout the organization. The decision process tends to work within these broad concepts. And the concept itself is molded by a series of incremental decisions made in response to particular opportunities or problems. We certainly don't want to stop thinking about options because we've written something down. The people who have a commitment to writing things down find themselves very frustrated as to how the company really does operate. Instead, things work up through a series of screens. A fundamental change is worked out long before it reaches the Finance Committee. Virtually nothing gets to the Finance Committee that is turned down. Sure, there may be changes in programs, amounts, or timing. But our management wouldn't put forward something the board wouldn't countenance. Individual board members are, of course, asked for their advice ahead of time.''

F. Alan Smith, Vice President-Finance: ''An important dimension of change has been our response to issues like equal employment and quality of work life movements in the U.S. We have developed a Quality of Work Life Program with the union. It is a joint exercise with employees—a bottom up sort of thing. In the past we tried a number of 'Volvo operations.' They simply didn't work. We tried to move people around and expand their job scope. They said to heck with it, let me do a job I know how. Now we have a number of special task groups on environmental affairs. As an extension of our staff concept, they are available directly to the divisions on demand . . .

''The data is rarely clear on which way to go in these or other major decisions. Each data set presented to management is persuasive, if you believe it. But at least some part of each major decision is intuitive. You have to judge the credibility of data sources and their basic assumptions. In addition there is no way you can say precisely what customers will want 3 years—and especially more—in the future. However, each division has its goals and forward business programs and product plans five years ahead . . . But there are no explicit fixed overall corporate goals in a formal sense. We use an iterative process to make a series of tentative decisions on the way we think the market will go. As we get more data we modify these continuously. It is often difficult to say who decided something, when—or even who originated a decision.''

APPENDIX B   GENERAL MOTORS CORPORATION FINANCIAL STATEMENTS 1982

Statement of Consolidated Income

For the Years Ended December 31, 1982, 1981 and 1980
(Dollars in Millions Except Per Share Amounts)

	1982	1981	1980
Net Sales (Note 2)	$60,025.6	$62,698.5	$57,728.5
Costs and Expenses			
Cost of sales and other operating charges, exclusive of items listed below	51,548.3	55,185.2	52,099.8
Selling, general and administrative expenses	2,964.9	2,715.0	2,636.7
Depreciation of real estate, plants and equipment	2,403.0	1,837.3	1,458.1
Amortization of special tools	2,147.5	2,568.9	2,719.6
Total Costs and Expenses	59,063.7	62,306.4	58,914.2
Operating Income (Loss)	961.9	392.1	(1,185.7)
Other income less income deductions—net (Note 4)	476.3	367.7	348.7
Interest expense (Note 1)	(1,415.4)	(897.9)	(531.9)
Income (Loss) before Income Taxes	22.8	(138.1)	(1,368.9)
United States, foreign and other income taxes (credit) (Note 6)	(252.2)	(123.1)	(385.3)
Income (Loss) after Income Taxes	275.0	15.0	(983.6)
Equity in earnings of nonconsolidated subsidiaries and associates (dividends received amounted to $412.7 in 1982, $189.7 in 1981 and $116.8 in 1980)	687.7	348.4	221.1
Net Income (Loss)	962.7	333.4	(762.5)
Dividends on preferred stocks	12.9	12.9	12.9
Earnings (Loss) on Common Stock	$ 949.8	$ 320.5	($ 775.4)
Average number of shares of common stock outstanding (in millions)	307.4	299.1	292.4
Earnings (Loss) Per Share of Common Stock (Note 7)	$3.09	$1.07	($2.65)

Reference should be made to notes on pages 20 and 26 in company's annual report.

Source: General Motors Corporation, *Annual Report*, 1982.

453

APPENDIX B (*Continued*)

Consolidated Balance Sheet

December 31, 1982 and 1981
(Dollars in Millions Except Per Share Amounts)

Assets	1982	1981
Current Assets		
Cash	$ 279.6	$ 204.1
United States Government and other marketable securities and time deposits—at cost, which approximates market of $2,835.5 and $1,086.3	2,846.6	1,116.6
Total cash and marketable securities	3,126.2	1,320.7
Accounts and notes receivable (including GMAC and its subsidiaries—$312.0 and $636.2)—less allowances	2,864.5	3,643.3
Inventories (less allowances) (Note 1)	6,184.2	7,222.7
Prepaid expenses and deferred income taxes	1,868.2	1,527.1
Total Current Assets	14,043.1	13,713.8
Equity in Net Assets of Nonconsolidated Subsidiaries and Associates (principally GMAC and its subsidiaries—Note 8)	4,231.1	3,369.5
Other Investments and Miscellaneous Assets—at cost (less allowances)	1,550.0	1,783.5
Common Stock Held for the Incentive Program (Note 3)	35.2	71.5
Property		
Real estate, plants and equipment—at cost (Note 9)	37,687.2	34,811.5
Less accumulated depreciation (Note 9)	18,148.9	16,317.4
Net real estate, plants and equipment	19,538.3	18,494.1
Special tools—at cost (less amortization)	2,000.1	1,546.6
Total Property	21,538.4	20,040.7
Total Assets	$41,397.8	$38,979.0

Liabilities and Stockholders' Equity

	1982	1981
Current Liabilities		
Accounts payable (principally trade)	$ 3,600.7	$ 3,699.7
Loans payable (principally overseas) (Note 11)	1,182.5	1,727.8
Accrued liabilities (Note 10)	7,601.8	7,127.5
Total Current Liabilities	12,385.0	12,555.0
Long-Term Debt (Note 11)	4,452.0	3,801.1
Capitalized Leases	293.1	242.9
Other Liabilities (including GMAC and its subsidiaries—$876.0 and $424.0)	4,259.8	3,092.7
Deferred Credits (including investment tax credits—$1,158.7 and $1,111.1)	1,720.8	1,566.2
Stockholders' Equity (Notes 3 and 12)		
Preferred stocks ($5.00 series, $183.6; $3.75 series, $100.0)	283.6	283.6
Common stock (issued, 312,363,657 and 304,804,228 shares)	520.6	508.0
Capital surplus (principally additional paid-in capital)	1,930.4	1,589.5
Net income retained for use in the business	15,552.5	15,340.0
Total Stockholders' Equity	18,287.1	17,721.1
Total Liabilities and Stockholders' Equity	$41,397.8	$38,979.0

Reference should be made to notes on pages 20 through 26 provided in company's annual report.
Certain amounts for 1981 have been reclassified to conform with 1982 classification.

Source: General Motors Corporation, *Annual Report, 1982.*

APPENDIX B (*Continued*)

Summary Financial Statistics

1982

	United States	Canada	Europe	Latin America	All Other	Total
Net Sales:						
Outside	$45,650.1	$2,621.9	$7,150.5	$2,699.5	$1,903.6	$60,025.6
Interarea	4,673.8	5,350.7	234.3	310.2	192.9	—
Total net sales	$50,323.9	$7,972.6	$7,384.8	$3,009.7	$2,096.5	$60,025.6
Net Income (Loss)	$ 1,079.3	($ 33.5)	$ 6.2	($ 16.5)	($ 63.2)	$ 962.7
Total Assets	$29,227.4	$2,299.0	$5,952.3	$2,973.3	$1,063.5	$41,397.8
Net Assets	$15,756.0	$ 774.7	$ 803.3	$ 894.3	$ 170.7	$18,287.1
Average Number of Employes (in thousands)	441	34	114	38	30	657

1981

	United States	Canada	Europe	Latin America	All Other	Total
Net Sales:						
Outside	$47,022.4	$4,099.2	$6,585.2	2,730.0	$2,261.7	$62,698.5
Interarea	5,731.1	4,747.2	265.6	129.9	128.1	—
Total net sales	$52,753.5	$8,846.4	$6,850.8	$2,859.9	$2,389.8	$62,698.5
Net Income (Loss)	$ 763.3	($ 35.6)	($ 426.7)	($ 62.6)	$ 129.2	$ 333.4
Total Assets	$27,510.8	$2,772.8	$5,208.5	$2,642.8	$ 980.3	$38,979.0
Net Assets	$15,608.7	$ 832.6	$ 505.5	$ 640.7	$ 247.3	$17,721.1
Average Number of Employes (in thousands)	522	39	113	38	29	741

Source: General Motors Corporation, *Annual Report,* 1982.

EXXON CORPORATION

With total sales in 1981 of $113.7 billion, Exxon Corp. was the largest oil company in the world. It held interests in a number of enterprises, mainly in the oil, gas, energy, and chemical industries. In most of its affiliates—with the notable exception of Aramco which was substantively controlled by Saudi Arabia—Exxon was the majority or sole shareholder. Exxon was a worldwide entity, with exploration activities on all continents, 54 refineries in 28 countries, and marketing activities in nearly 100 countries. Six million motorists stopped at its 65,000 service stations each day. In 1981, Exxon's holdings outside the U.S. comprised 55% of its assets; it obtained 4 times more oil from foreign than U.S. sources, and its overseas affiliates refined and sold twice its U.S. volume. Within the non communist world Exxon sold some 4.6 million barrels per day (BPD) of petroleum products or 9.75% of the world's 47.1 million BPD demands.[1] The company's ownership was widely dispersed, with some 776,000 shareholders in many different countries throughout the world.

ORGANIZATION AND PHILOSOPHY

As a truly multinational company, Exxon attempted to decentralize operations as much as possible to its divisions and affiliates. These units were responsible for maintaining adequate returns on corporate investments in them. Since corporate policy was to staff each subsidiary with nationals of its host countries, it was rare to find more than a few Americans in any non U.S. subsidiary. Wherever possible, the boards, CEOs, and key executives of each unit were also nationals of the host country.

The corporation maintained some centralized units to help allocate overall corporate resources and to coordinate activities of operating groups where necessary. Whenever possible, raw materials, supplies, intermediate products, and services were transferred among divisions at market prices. When these could not be readily determined, negotiated transfer prices were used. The corporation's policy was to transfer materials and services "at arm's length"—with divisions allowed to purchase outside the corporation if they so desired. Purchasing from and trading with other companies was common.

Certain major decisions were of course reserved to corporate headquarters. Operating heads were expected to clear major policy decisions having corporate-wide significance with their "contact member" on the Board of Directors or with the appropriate major Board committee. No single listing of such decisions existed in the corporation.

Exxon also had its own $7 billion Exxon Chemicals operation producing and supplying chemicals worldwide. Coordination between successive operations in both (petroleum and chemicals) groups was very important. Efficient plant sizes in either group were so large that their outputs could easily exceed the demands of smaller countries in which production occurred. Since petro-chemicals and plastics were important inputs for many secondary and fabricating industries, it was common to find large chemical-industrial complexes growing up around refineries or petro-chemical plants—located even in the most remote areas of individual countries.

Exxon's size and complexity inevitably exposed the company to a variety of different national policies, nationalistic pressures, and risks of retaliation or expropriation by host countries.

As a mature and progressive company, Exxon's management had given considerable attention to the problem of host country relationships. Its expressed policy was: "To perform as a responsible and desirable corporate citizen in all host countries . . . (since) Exxon's interests are inextricably linked to the interests of our host countries throughout the world. . . ." The company had purposely not tried to refine this broad policy into rigid rules, binding on all its affiliates.

RECENT HISTORY

Crude oil prices had been steady at less than $2 per barrel through the 1960s, reflecting a general surplus supply balance. They had crept up very slowly to approximately $3 per barrel when, in October 1973, Arab oil producing nations imposed a total ban on petroleum exports to Israel, the U.S., and other "supporters" of Israel in the 1973 Arab-Israeli War. Posted prices leapt to $10 per barrel (BBL) during January-February 1974, with some oil auctioned in the spot markets for $17. Nevertheless, after the initial 1973–74 crisis subsided, oil prices increased only nomi-

nally until 1978. Inflationary pressures actually forced the real price of oil to drop some 10–15% during this period.

The next major jolt came on October 31, 1978 when oil workers in Iran went on strike—cutting production from 5.3 million barrels per day (BPD) to 2 million BPD. The workers demanded higher wages and an end to martial law. In December, OPEC ended an 18 month price freeze on crude oil by announcing increases that would boost the price from $12.70/BBL to $14.54/BBL by October 1979. Iran announced price increases to $16.50/BBL. Saudi Arabia supported these prices by limiting its oil production in April to the ceiling of 8.5 million BPD imposed before the Iranian revolution. As production limits forced prices up, OPEC raised the posted price to $20/BBL in June 1979, approximately double the preceding year's prices. And a new era in oil began.

In 1978, Exxon's sales were $63.9 billion with profits of $2.7 billion reported. Sales had been growing at 9.1% per year rate and profits at 3.8%. The company and its affiliates accounted for about 9% of the industry's crude runs. Exxon expected its sales growth in the early 1980s to

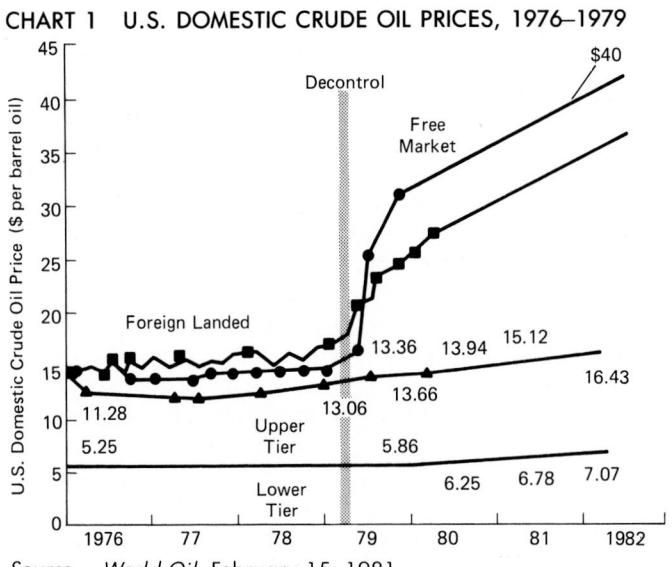

CHART 1   U.S. DOMESTIC CRUDE OIL PRICES, 1976–1979

Source: *World Oil*, February 15, 1981.

at least match industry averages and to be slightly above recent levels. The company deployed total assets of $41.5 billion against which it charged $1.7 billion in depreciation per year. Its announced proved reserves were 23 billion barrels of crude, offering it an 11.9 year coverage in terms of 1978 refinery runs. Chase Econometrics and industry sources estimated that the industry would invest over $1.5 trillion worldwide in the next decade to replace existing facilities and develop needed new resources.

Through 1980–81 there had been no significant shifts in expected growth rates of oil use throughout the world. Most observers continued to forecast growth at 4–5% per year through the year 2000. Despite extensive exploration by oil companies and ministries throughout the world, only a few large new finds were developed between 1974–81. Most publicized of these were the North Slope (Alaska), North Sea (Europe), and Mexican fields. North Slope (Canada-Alaska) fields were thought to contain some 20–50 billion barrels of ultimately exploitable oil. Because of price increases Mexico's estimated reserves expanded dramatically to some 200–300 billion barrels of petroleum liquids. Nevertheless most writers projected long term shortages of crude at high prices. (See Charts 1 and 2.) Exxon's own reserves are described in Appendix A.

By October 1981, Chase Econometrics and major banking institutions[2] were estimating that the industry would have to invest $2–3 trillion worldwide in the next decade to meet forecast demands. Each country had its own special interests in the developing worldwide energy situation. The differing postures of some example countries and areas are briefly described below. Appendix A summarizes their crude reserves and gives some brief economic comparisons.

EUROPE DISCOVERS OIL —THE NORTH SEA

Northeastern Europe had very limited oil and gas resources until November 10, 1969, when the *Oil and Gas Journal* noted: "Phillips confirmed the first huge oil discovery in the North Sea off Norway in field #2, Block 4, with its #2 Ekofisk well flowing high gravity oil from tertiary sand at approximately 5,500 feet. The well—which produces highly desirable, low sulfur, crude—lies in an area with little open acreage around it, inside Norwegian territorial waters." Within a few months other finds and geological assessments indicated the probability of a very large play extending across both British and Norwegian waters. (See Map.) But costs of developing these

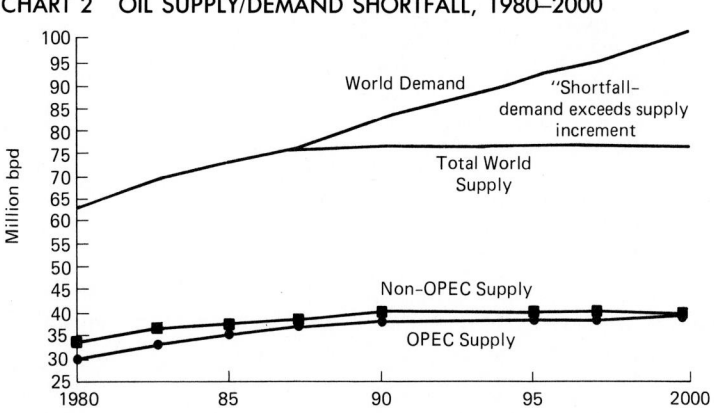

CHART 2   OIL SUPPLY/DEMAND SHORTFALL, 1980–2000

Source: The Journal of Energy and Development, Autumn 1979 in *World Oil*, February 15, 1981.

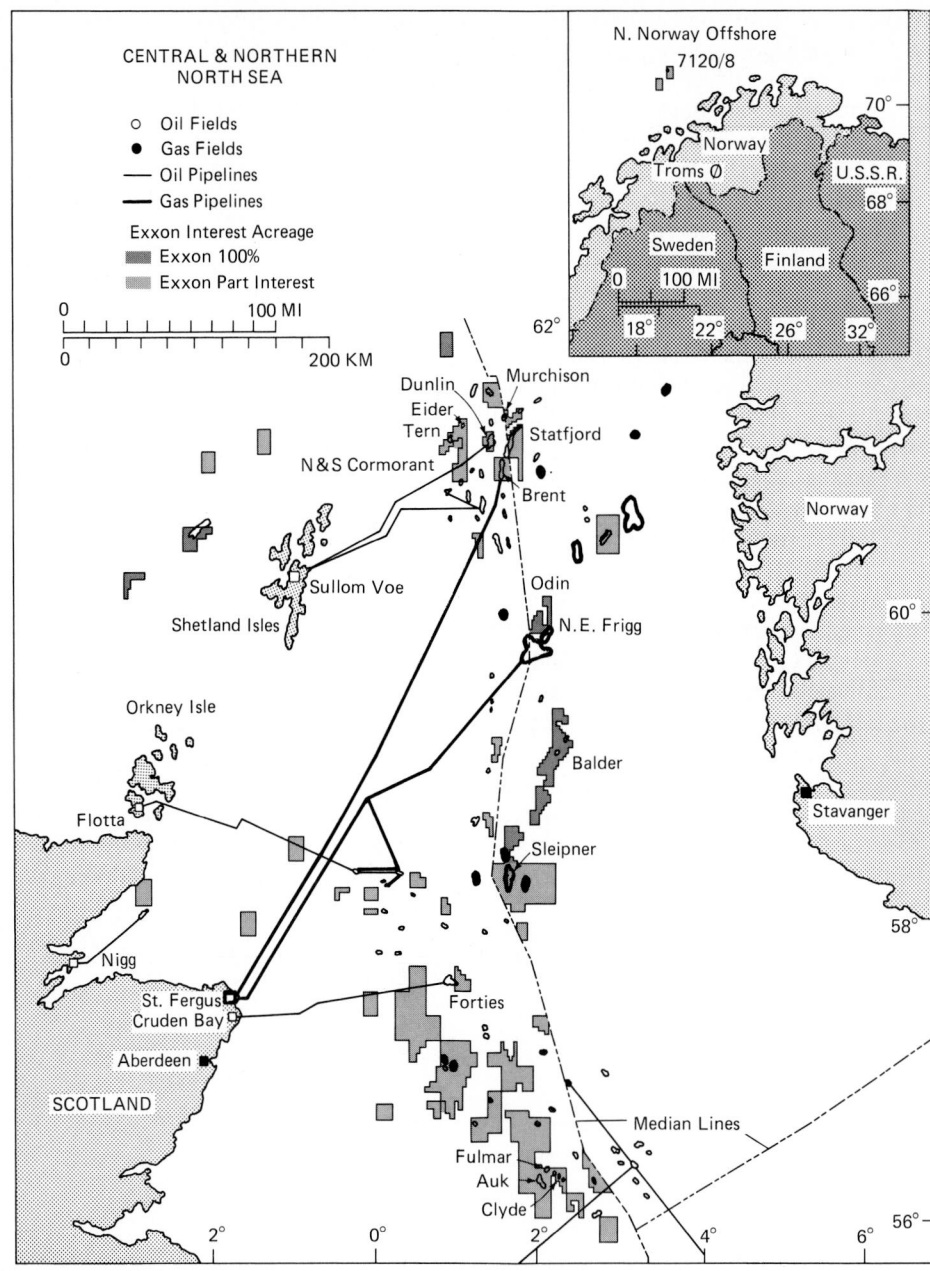

CENTRAL & NORTHERN
NORTH SEA

○   Oil Fields
●   Gas Fields
—   Oil Pipelines
━   Gas Pipelines
Exxon Interest Acreage
▓   Exxon 100%
░   Exxon Part Interest

0   100 MI
0   200 KM

N. Norway Offshore
7120/8
Norway
Troms
Sweden   Finland
U.S.S.R.
70°
68°
66°
0   100 MI
18°   22°   26°   32°

Murchison
Dunlin
Eider
Tern
Statfjord
N & S Cormorant
Brent
Sullom Voe
Odin
N.E. Frigg
Shetland Isles
62°
Orkney Isle
Balder
Flotta
Sleipner
Nigg
60°
St. Fergus
Cruden Bay
Forties
Aberdeen
SCOTLAND
Median Lines
Fulmar
Auk
Clyde
Norway
Stavanger
58°
56°
2°   0°   2°   4°   6°

Source: Exxon Corporation, *Financial and Statistical Supplement to the Annual Report*, 1981.

fields was exceptionally high. The North Sea was one of the worst areas in the world for construction work. And the technical problems of laying, protecting, and inspecting underwater pipelines several hundred miles long were substantial.

THE NORWEGIAN SITUATION

North Sea oil led to wide ranging discussions in Norway about how to best exploit its resources in the national interest. Norway had essentially no domestic oil industry prior to the North Sea find. Abundant hydroelectric sources had fulfilled most central power needs, while imported oil and gas had met transportation and other demands. Norway's highly dispersed population of 4.1 million did not represent a major—or concentrated—market for petroleum products. In fact, a large modern refinery would have a throughput vastly in excess of the sales any company could reasonably expect in Norway.

Independence and Wealth

Government officials wanted to see the country's North Sea resources exploited in ways which improved Norway's balance of payments and offered flexibility in dealing with its major trading partners. The government was also concerned about the percentage of industry owned by foreigners. For centuries Norway had been controlled by Denmark and Sweden, and it had suffered severely during the Nazi occupation of World War II. When the North Sea find was announced, over 60% of Norway's large manufacturing industry was foreign held.

Government policy makers wanted to shift exports away from the basic (wood products, mechanical products, electro-metallurgical, shipbuilding and ship operating) industries which had dominated the past and into the "knowledge industries" of the future. Norway's technical schools and institutions had been expanded in recent years, but were small by international standards. And petroleum engineering and petrochemical research and curricula were either non-existent or quite underdeveloped when oil was found. To coordinate its oil activities, Norway formed a government owned company, Den Norske Stats Okjeselscap (called Statoil). Statoil was to take over operation of the Norwegian portion of all concession rights and be solely responsible for drilling north of the 62nd parallel "in order to preserve relationships with Russia," which bordered Norway on the North and only had access to its year round Port of Murmansk through this area.

A Unique Quality of Life

Norwegians were fiercely proud of their national identity, their beautiful natural surroundings, and their "unique quality of life." No slums existed in the major cities, and full employment had been a policy for decades. To control the impact of North Sea oil, the government set a ceiling of 1.8 million BPD on production and set out on massive infrastructure investments to modernize the more remote areas of the country. By 1981 oil and gas accounted for 15% of GDP, as much as all other manufactures combined. Some predicted they would reach 20–25% by the mid 1990s.[3] With revenues from these sources, the government hoped to repay the enormous debts it had incurred earlier, when it had continued its planned high social investments despite the fact that oil revenues had been slow in materializing due to difficulties in developing the North Sea.[4]

By the late 1970s Norway had changed its initial concession rights. Statoil's 50% interest could be increased to 80%, if so desired. And starting with block 34/10 in 1978 it began its "Norwegian Solution." Only three companies—Statoil (100% government owned), Norsk Hydro (51% government owned), and Saga Petroleum (100% Norwegian privately owned)—could hold equity positions. Foreign companies could serve as "technical advisors" in exchange for access to petroleum.[5] In 1980, the Ministry of Petroleum and Energy issued a Parliamentary Report, outlining tax proposals to increase the government's share of oil revenues to levels which industry leaders said "would make Norway's tax laws onerous to a degree unparalleled in the world."[6]

As elections approached in the fall of 1981, Norway faced some difficult decisions. During the past two years substantial new discoveries had been made, which if exploited efficiently would result in production beyond the 1.8 million BPD ceiling.[7] In addition the three Norwegian companies allowed to explore north of the 62nd parallel had found enough recoverable reserves to support production at current rates for 25 years.[8] But only one tenth of the continental shelf had yet been explored.

THE BRITISH SITUATION

Realizing that exploiting Britain's North Sea oil would require considerable cash and expertise, the government had awarded its first blocks to large companies for fast exploitation. But in 1974 as prices rose above $10/BBL the Wilson government actively discussed nationalizing the whole North Sea area. Instead it "restructured" the terms of earlier leases, calling for both majority government interest in *existing* concessions and a controlling interest in blocks *already* leased. It also formed the British National Oil Corporation (BNOC) to act as the vehicle for exercising the government's participation rights.

Britain's initial interest was to get the North Sea explored and producing as soon as possible because of its weak balance of payments situation. However, despite predictions of 2–3 million BPD production rates in the early 1980s, actual production by 1981 was only 1.5 million BPD.[9] In summer 1979, British motorists had suffered a shortage of gasoline while 45% of all production was being exported to the U.S. and Western Europe. This was partly a function of Britain's need for exports and partly the fact that private oil companies controlled refining activities.[10] At one point in 1980, Britain "found itself in the strange position of charging $30/BBL for its oil while Saudi Arabia's was pegged at $24/BBL."[11]

The Conservative (Thatcher) government tried to "privatize" some of BNOC's activities in 1980, but was thwarted by other political interests which feared a massive oil boom in the 1980s followed by an abrupt reentry to importation in the 1990s.[12] By mid 1980, 25 fields had been discovered in the U.K. North Sea. (See Map.) Predictions were that subsequent fields would be smaller and costs of developing them (excluding taxes and dry holes) soon would move from $11/BBL to over $15/BBL.[13] Shell Oil Co. estimated that to achieve full North Sea potentials would require £115 billion over the next 10–15 years.[14] But *Oil & Gas Journal* noted that proposed British tax actions would "raise the government's share of all revenues from U.K. North Sea oil production to more than 90%."[15] Fortunately, rising oil prices had changed the economics of developing smaller fields and could support the tertiary recovery necessary to keep old fields in action.

JAPAN

Japan, with its powerful national economy, had very limited fossil fuel supplies. When the Iranian turmoil cut off 17% of this crucial supply in 1978, the government formed the Japan National Oil Company (JNOC), and MITI pressed for Japanese controlled oil sources to equal 30% of imports by 1985 (versus 8.5% in 1978). Nippon Oil, one of Japan's major refiners, boosted prices 15% immediately in response to government pressures, although Exxon's prices went up only 1–2%. Japan solved its immediate shortfall by going to the spot market and by direct "government-to-government" purchase agreements with exporting countries.[16]

For its longer term needs, it started a joint venture with China to develop oil in the latter's Bohai Sea and stepped up its financial and technical aid to poorer oil exporting nations, notably Mexico and Indonesia.[17] Because of its tight pollution standards Japan became the world's largest user (60% of all supplies) of liquified natural gas (LNG)—for central power production and for propane in automobiles.[18] Exxon's *Energy Outlook* (*1980*) predicted Japan would still be dependent on outside sources for 74% of its energy needs in the year 2000, despite its strong conservation and nuclear power programs.

RECENTLY DEVELOPED COUNTRIES

China The size of the People's Republic of China's petroleum resources was largely unknown, although for over 25 years Peking (Beijing) had force fed the country's oil industry with funds and technical manpower. Knowledgeable observers, as reported in *Wall Street Journal*, thought there could be several hundred billion barrels of potential oil in the China Sea. Other sources estimated some 40 billion more on shore. But there were severe financial, technological, and structural constraints on China's developing these reserves itself.

After a brief spurt (+11%) in 1978 production, China's oil and gas output rose at only a disappointing 1–2% per year. But China hoped to have 8 to 10 giant new fields opened by 1985. Its internal economic plans, however, keyed on doubling coal output to 1 billion tons/year in the late 1980s and to twice that in the 1990s. Oil was intended primarily as an export to generate capital needed for China's gigantic "Four Modernizations" programs. The world community's most serious concerns were that China might increasingly "press for its share" of world oil imports or come into conflict with its neighbors who were already developing oil in the very large coastal zone claimed by China.[19]

Indonesia Indonesia had a population of some 150 million people, about half of OPEC's total. Despite increased oil revenues in recent years, Indonesia's $488 per person annual income in 1980 ranked it as one of Asia's poorest countries. About 50 million of its people subsisted on less than $100 per year. Its recent oil and economic history had been chaotic. The Sukarno regime of the 1960s had created inflation rates of 650% per year which it took successor regimes almost 10 years to bring under control. Then in 1975 a series of disastrous ($10.5 billion) tanker deals by General Ibn Sutowo—head of the state oil company, Pertomina—brought on a late 1970s debt and currency crisis which was only handled by the "inspired management"[20] of the country's well trained civil servants. By 1981 they had managed to balance the budget, increase capital spending, and increase GDP by some 40%.

Nevertheless, Indonesia faced the prospect of declining oil revenues as its big fields like Minas shifted to secondary recovery, and domestic energy needs grew at 13% per year.[21] The country's ambitious Five Year Plan (1979–84) relied on "increased investment by local and foreign businessmen" to reduce the country's precarious dependence on oil and raw materials exports and to make a dent in its massive unemployment.[22] By mid 1980 the future looked brighter than ever as exploration picked up and the U.S. and Indonesia implemented new agreements, allowing dollar for dollar credits for U.S. companies on taxes paid to Indonesia for oil production.

Venezuela Venezuela's oil had been originally developed by international oil companies. However, Venezuela nationalized substantially all of its very large oil resources in the mid-1970s. Its proved crude reserves of 18.0 billion barrels made it third in the western hemisphere. But it was well known that Venezuela also had "trillions" of barrels of heavy oil in identified formations. Estimates of ultimately exploitable potentials varied from 2 to 3 trillion BBL. This oil required an infusion of heat (or heat and chemicals) to make it flow through its sustaining formations. It also contained extraneous chemicals which had to be removed in a "pre-processing" stage before refining. By 1981 new refining methods increasingly allowed heavy oils to be processed competitively versus many crudes.

Venezuela had the largest refining capacity in Latin America, but its facilities had been built largely to supply the U.S. East Coast with fuel oil. During the early 1980s Venezuela planned to invest some $25 billion to upgrade these facilities for gasoline and other "high end" products and to develop new capabilities for heavy oils.[23]

As the Venezuelan government put together its Sixth Plan (in 1980–81) it was running large deficits in its 200-odd government businesses. And the Sixth Plan's emphasis on hospitals, schools, and housing (rather than industrial growth) seemed likely to create even larger deficits and international debts—despite an oil production rate of 2.2 million BPD and prices reaching $47/BBL.[24] Venezuela had the largest "steam flood" field in the world for processing heavy oil and was among the leaders in developing new heavy crude processing technologies. Observers said that, "Despite the politicization, corruption, and general lack of efficiency elsewhere, the oil industry is kept out of politics and is well run in Venezuela."[25]

Nigeria Through the 1970s Nigeria had become second only to Saudi Arabia in its exports of oil to the U.S. But Nigerian economic fortunes took a sudden reversal in 1978 when oil payments, which formed 85% of total government income, dropped to only 3/4 of 1977's levels. Nigeria's economy crashed, its trade balances went into deficit for the first time since the oil boom, and there were rumblings about maladministration of $ billions in the Nigerian National Petroleum Corp. (NNPC).[26]

Experts considered Nigeria "one of the best oil provinces in the world" with a superb sulfur free crude and potentials of up to 5 million BPD possible for export in the mid 1980s. Because of high quality and good location, Nigeria often priced its oil at premiums over other OPEC crudes.[27] And Nigeria faced further confrontations with some OPEC countries (particularly Iran) over their oil exports to South Africa.[28] In fact, the government had nationalized all the Nigerian assets of BP in retaliation for that company's breaking sanctions against South Africa.[29]

Although bribery remained a fact of life in Nigeria and getting money out of the country was difficult, foreign investors continued to participate there because, "This is a real free enterprise country." In 1980 foreign companies were invited to submit proposals for over 120,000 square miles of exploration, with much of the

rich Niger basin and offshore areas yet to be explored. Although the latter was reserved for NNPC, it was widely recognized that NNPC lacked the resources for the task. And like other new or replacement supplies throughout the world these areas would cost considerably more than the ($.30–$.50 per barrel) finding and lifting costs then encountered in many Middle Eastern areas.

EXXON'S CURRENT OPERATIONS

In 1981, Exxon was the largest industrial company in the world, excluding certain Japanese banking and holding complexes. Key financial and operating data about the company are included as Appendix B. Exxon managed the world's largest tanker fleet, aggregating over 21 million tons. The company's own tankers were built to its specifications in shipyards throughout the world. In addition, Exxon owned or shared in the ownership of an extensive network of pipelines. Some of these carried crude from underdeveloped areas to coastlines. Some were undersea. Some carried chemical intermediates; others took finished products to distribution centers. Because of the size and complexity of its worldwide operations, Exxon had been forced to develop extremely sophisticated techniques for long-range planning, fleet operations and control, plant production allocation decisions, cost and management control, communications, data handling, (etc.).

Exxon Research and Engineering (ER&E) was responsible for Exxon's long term technological activities worldwide. Its laboratories performed research, engineering, and technical service activities in close coordination with the operating companies they supported. Royalty income received was deducted from the total cost of ER&E's operations to obtain a "net cost" which was allocated to affiliates roughly in proportion to their sales at point of manufacture. ER&E tried to allocate specific corporate R&D tasks to those laboratories in various countries which could most effectively perform on behalf of the total corporation. Whenever possible,

ER&E tried to staff its research centers throughout the world with scientists and engineers representing many nationalities—not just those of the host country.

For almost a decade prior to 1973 Exxon's return on total assets had remained below 8%. But the 1970s had changed all that. 1981 was a banner year for Exxon. Over the past five years its sales had grown at an average 14.5% rate to $113 billion and profits at 18.5% rates to $5.5 billion. Total assets had grown from $38.4 billion in 1978 to $62.9 billion in 1981—and employees from 127,000 to 180,000 in the same period. Exxon's own proved reserves of oil had dropped from some 45 billion barrels in 1972 to about 7 billion barrels in 1981, largely due to nationalizations. But its coal (10.6 billion tons) and uranium holdings were also substantial, and it had attempted to diversify into energy devices (Reliance Electric Co.) and other areas through Exxon Enterprises, Inc.

In late 1981, a worldwide recession began, triggered by high U.S. interest rates, disastrous U.S. trade balances, and widespread layoffs in a less competitive U.S. manufacturing base. Some expected a strong recovery by 1983–84, others dismally predicted a continuing long term world stagflation. Most agreed that world GDP growth to the end of the century would be less than the 5% per year experienced through the 1960s and mid 1970s, but published estimates placed real GDP growth at between 2.7% and 3.6% per year to the year 2000. However, China's sudden real growth at 7–8% per year (planned and actually experienced in 1978–'81) was pushing estimates upward. Since modernized agriculture and rapidly industrializing countries throughout the world called for substantially increased uses of energy, energy forecasts in 1981 usually indicated a ''shortfall'' of energy for the late 1980s and 1990s. (See Chart 2.) Combined with higher replacement costs for reserves and host governments' strong political interests in maintaining prices, many forecasters foresaw energy demand and prices significantly outpacing GNP growth through the mid 1990s.

QUESTIONS

1. Why should any of the above host countries allow Exxon to participate in their markets or the development of their resources? What are the most significant potential conflicts between Exxon's interests and those of these host countries?

2. What should have been the principal strategic concerns of Exxon from 1978–1982? What should its strategy have been in response to these? How should Exxon have dealt with its potential conflicts with host countries in this era?

3. How should Exxon's 1978–82 strategy be modified for the future? What specific actions should be taken? Why? How should Exxon be organized for the future?

APPENDIX A　WORLD SUPPLY AND DATA SITUATION

POPULATION AND GROSS DOMESTIC
PRODUCT BY COUNTRY

Country	Population (Thousands)		Gross Domestic Product ($ Billion U.S.)	
	1977	1981	1977	1980
Algeria	17,910	19,590	16.5[2]	31.4[4]
China	865,677	1,007,760	N/A	N/A
Indonesia	143,282	150,520	45.9	69.8
Iran	34,274	39,320	66.7[2]	52.6[3]
Japan	113,863	117,650	564[2]	1,036.2
Mexico	64,594	71,190	74.2	121.3[4]
Nigeria	66,628	79,680	25.1[1]	35.1[1]
Norway	4,042	4,100	35.6	57.4
Saudi Arabia	9,522	9,320	56.8[2]	73.1
Sweden	8,255	8,320	78.3	123.7
United Kingdom	55,852	55,830	244.5	523.3
United States	216,817	229,810	1,878.8	2,587.0
Venezuela	12,737	14,310	35.6	60.0

[1] 1975
[2] 1976
[3] 1978
[4] 1979

Source:　U.N. Statistical Yearbook, 1978 and 1981 Monthly Bulletin of Statistics U.N., February 1983.

APPENDIX A (*Continued*)

WORLD OIL PRODUCTION AND PROVED RESERVES: 1978 VERSUS 1980

	1978		1980	
	Prod. (*Million bpd*)	*Reserves* (*Billion bbls*)	*Prod.* (*Million bpd*)	*Reserves* (*Billion bbls*)
Western Hemisphere				
Total	14.8	75.7	15.7	102.3
U.S.	8.7	28.5	8.7	26.4
*Venezuela	2.2	18.0	2.2	18.0
Mexico	1.3	16.0	2.0	44.0
Canada	1.3	6.0	1.5	6.4
Western Europe				
Total	1.8	24.0	2.4	23.1
U.K.	1.1	16.0	1.6	14.8
Norway	0.4	5.9	0.5	5.5
Middle East				
Total	18.2	362.1	20.8	370.0
*Saudi Arabia	7.8	165.7	9.6	165.0
*Kuwait	1.9	66.2	1.4	64.9
*Iran	5.3	59.0	1.3	57.5
*U.A.E.	1.9	31.3	1.8	30.4
*Iraq	2.5	32.1	2.6	30.0
Africa				
Total	6.1	57.9	6.0	55.1
*Libya	2.1	24.3	1.8	23.0
*Nigeria	1.8	18.2	2.1	16.7
*Algeria	1.3	6.3	1.0	8.2
Asia-Pacific				
Total	2.8	20.0	2.7	19.6
*Indonesia	1.7	10.2	1.6	9.5
India	0.2	2.9	0.2	2.6
Australia	0.4	2.1	0.4	2.4
Malaysia	0.2	2.8	0.3	3.0
OPEC	29.4	438.5	26.2	428.4
Non-Communist World	46.2	547.6	45.1	562.2
Total World	60.0	641.6	59.7	648.5

* *OPEC Members.*

Source: *Oil & Gas Journal*, Dec. 25, 1978 and Dec. 29, 1980.

APPENDIX A (Continued)

INTERNATIONAL PETROLEUM SUPPLY AND DISPOSITION, 1979
(Thousand barrels per day)

	Crude Oil Prod.[1]	Crude Oil Imports	Refined Product Imports	Crude Oil Exports	Refined Product Exports	Apparent Consumption[2]
United States	10,136	6,519	1,937	235	236	18,513
Mexico	1,611	0	27	533	68	904
Brazil	171	1,026	19	5	22	1,175
Venezuela	2,436	0	2	1,412	618	279
France	46	2,555	242	0	434	2,385
West Germany	95	2,187	828	0	137	3,073
Italy	36	2,215	231	0	437	2,003
Norway	443	129	77	382	25	219
United Kingdom	1,613	1,157	286	796	272	1,930
Eastern Europe and USSR	12,176	2,020	184	2,603	1,015	10,762
Algeria	1,294	7	15	1,082	71	104
Libya	2,132	0	47	1,979	85	85
Nigeria	2,302	0	91	2,210	24	161
Middle East	22,045	531	158	19,311	1,173	1,774
China	2,122	0	1	190[3]	0[3]	1,851
Indonesia	1,631	52	39	1,233	108	367
Japan	8	4,834	770	0	16	5,480

[1] Data includes lease condensate and natural gas plant liquids.
[2] Data represents apparent consumption, which includes domestic consumption, refinery fuel and loss, and international bunkering.
[3] Estimated

Source: U.S. Department of Energy, 1981 Annual Report to Congress, May 1982, pp. 75–77.

APPENDIX A (*Continued*)

OPEC: AVERAGE CRUDE OIL OFFICIAL SALES PRICE[1]

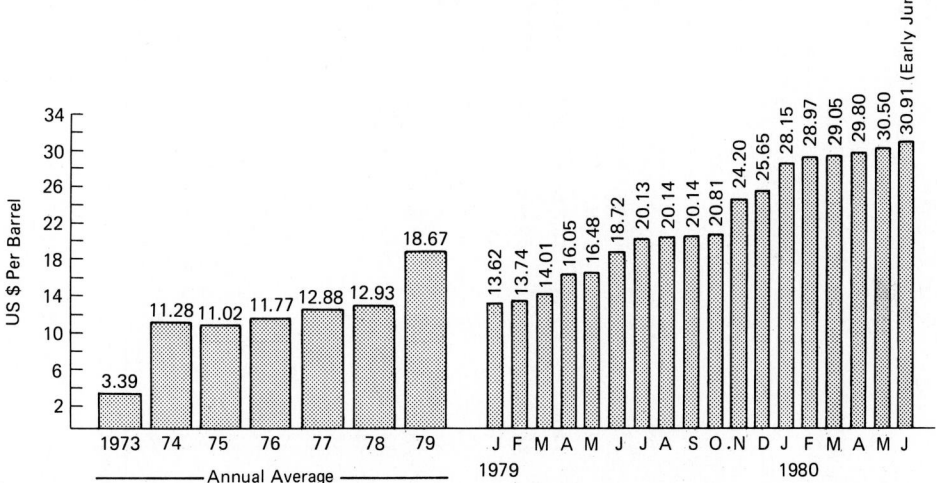

[1] *Pre-1974 prices are derived from posted prices and are not official sales prices.*

Source: CIA in *World Oil*, August 15, 1980.

PRICE—LANDED COST OF CRUDE OIL IMPORTS FROM SELECTED COUNTRIES[1]

Dollars per Barrel

		Algeria	Canada	Indonesia	Iran	Libya	Mexico	Nigeria	Saudi Arabia	United Arab Emirates	United Kingdom	Venezuela
1975	**AVERAGE**	**12.72**	**12.72**	**13.79**	**12.21**	**12.35**	**NA**	**12.62**	**12.30**	**12.87**	**NA**	**11.65**
1976	**AVERAGE**	**13.81**	**13.57**	**13.82**	**12.82**	**13.58**	**NA**	**13.80**	**13.04**	**13.30**	**NA**	**11.80**
1977	**AVERAGE**	**15.20**	**14.21**	**14.63**	**13.80**	**14.87**	**13.75**	**15.25**	**13.61**	**14.04**	**NA**	**13.13**
1978	**AVERAGE**	**14.91**	**14.50**	**14.64**	**13.88**	**14.72**	**13.54**	**14.86**	**13.92**	**14.39**	**NA**	**12.83**
1979	**AVERAGE**	**21.90**	**20.43**	**20.69**	**25.02**	**23.68**	**20.86**	**22.96**	**19.15**	**21.90**	**22.16**	**18.18**
1980	January	35.32	27.73	31.03	30.37	37.10	30.18	33.03	27.85	32.35	32.14	26.25
	February	35.28	28.60	32.95	NA	36.98	32.38	35.25	28.15	32.71	34.07	25.91
	March	38.54	30.75	33.04	(2)	37.18	31.17	36.93	28.26	30.96	35.73	24.97
	April	38.52	30.31	33.81	(2)	36.57	30.77	37.41	29.14	32.29	35.34	25.10
	May	38.54	31.16	33.73	(2)	37.36	31.22	37.53	30.30	34.06	35.82	25.93
	June	38.71	31.26	34.51	(2)	38.09	31.43	38.15	30.16	34.96	37.41	26.42
	July	39.60	31.31	34.81	(2)	38.39	32.60	38.23	30.04	NA	37.25	25.47
	August	38.60	31.44	34.81	(2)	38.38	32.62	37.77	31.24	NA	36.20	26.37
	September	38.28	30.97	34.64	(2)	38.30	31.93	37.60	31.86	NA	36.35	25.47
	October	38.77	29.22	33.65	(2)	38.53	31.96	37.75	31.73	NA	36.82	23.92
	November	38.41	28.81	34.55	(2)	38.22	32.42	37.97	32.86	NA	36.62	27.75
	December	38.63	32.72	34.64	(2)	39.04	33.76	38.11	33.40	NA	36.31	27.66
	AVERAGE	**37.90**	**30.47**	**33.92**	**(2)**	**37.72**	**31.80**	**37.05**	**30.02**	**NA**	**35.88**	**25.86**
1981	January	41.25	34.26	38.08	(2)	41.81	36.81	41.55	34.06	NA	39.90	33.80

1. Landed cost of imported crude oil from selected countries does not represent the total cost of all imported crude.
2. No crude oil was imported.

Source: U.S. Department of Energy, Energy Information Administration, *Monthly Energy Review*, October 1982.

SUMMARY FINANCIAL DATA FOR EXXON CORP: COMPARATIVE FINANCIAL DATA

Company	Sales		Net Income		Return on Equity		Return on Net Assets	
	1978	1981	1978	1981	1978	1981	1978	1981
Exxon	60.3	108.1	2.8	5.6	13.7	19.5	6.7	8.8
Royal Dutch Shell Group	44.0	82.3	2.1	3.6	12.8	14.4	4.9	5.6
Mobil	34.7	64.5	1.1	2.4	12.6	16.6	5.0	7.0
General Motors	63.2	62.7	3.5	0.3	20.0	1.9	11.5	1.0
Texaco	28.6	57.6	0.9	2.3	9.0	16.8	4.2	8.4
British Petroleum	27.4	52.2	0.8	2.1	11.1	13.9	3.2	4.3
Standard Oil of Calif.	23.2	44.2	1.1	2.4	13.4	18.7	6.6	10.1
Ford Motor	42.8	38.2	1.6	(1.1)	16.4	(14.4)	7.2	(4.6)
Standard Oil of Indiana	15.0	29.9	1.1	1.9	15.1	18.0	7.6	8.4
Gulf Oil	18.1	28.3	0.8	1.2	12.0	12.3	5.3	6.0

Source of Raw Data: Fortune 500 Listings of 1978–81.

APPENDIX B (*Continued*)

CONSOLIDATED BALANCE SHEET AT YEAR-END
(Millions of Dollars)

	1972	1973	1974	1975	1976	1977	1978	1979	1980	1981
Assets										
Current assets										
Cash	482	563	939	876	1,279	1,598	1,993	2,516	2,762	2,479
Marketable securities	1,211	2,525	3,819	3,773	3,795	3,086	2,763	1,991	2,164	1,404
Notes and accounts receivable	3,328	4,063	5,282	5,098	5,354	5,708	6,726	9,011	9,849	9,665
Inventories										
Crude oil	251	446	1,172	1,229	1,337	1,250	1,190	1,214	1,438	1,623
Products and merchandise	1,301	1,615	2,597	2,368	2,458	2,606	2,537	3,576	4,175	4,341
Materials and supplies	199	206	375	399	440	479	570	691	937	1,620
Prepaid taxes and expenses	333	424	603	262	389	605	590	1,479	2,134	2,716
Total current assets	7,105	9,842	14,787	14,005	15,052	15,332	16,369	20,478	23,459	23,840
Investments and advances	1,277	1,295	954	1,523	1,578	1,592	1,533	1,475	1,459	1,575
Property, plant & equipment, at cost, less accumulated depreciation and depletion	12,645	13,462	14,846	16,115	18,593	20,491	22,806	26,293	30,311	36,094
Other assets										
Deferred charges	163	139	193	262	275	316	274	246	221	581
Special deposits and funds	224	197	299	515	627	559	361	277	331	297
Intangibles and other assets	86	99	93	393	155	147	188	721	796	536
Total assets	21,500	25,034	31,172	32,813	36,280	38,437	41,531	49,490	56,577	62,931

Liabilities

Current liabilities										
Notes and loans payable	1,161	1,127	1,729	1,598	1,860	1,385	1,401	1,868	1,537	**3,032**
Accounts payable	1,877	2,998	4,597	5,288	6,315	6,764	7,234	9,183	9,557	**9,536**
Accrued liabilities	857	996	1,307	1,198	1,399	1,586	1,881	2,662	2,925	**3,183**
Income taxes payable	812	1,187	1,913	1,261	947	978	1,525	2,170	2,865	**1,993**
Total current liabilities	4,707	6,308	9,546	9,345	10,521	10,713	12,041	15,883	16,884	**17,744**
Long-term debt										
U.S. dollars—Exxon Corporation	725	601	702	735	786	772	684	683	697	**627**
U.S. dollars—consolidated subsidiaries	833	978	1,177	1,554	1,697	1,640	2,085	2,574	3,052	**3,356**
Other currencies—consolidated subsidiaries	1,059	1,092	1,173	1,162	1,214	1,458	980	1,001	968	**1,170**
Total long-term debt	2,617	2,671	3,052	3,451	3,697	3,870	3,749	4,258	4,717	**5,153**
Annuity and other reserves	499	551	640	609	647	807	1,100	1,414	1,892	**2,041**
Deferred income tax credits	750	1,076	1,890	1,987	2,516	3,036	3,437	4,385	6,218	**7,959**
Deferred income	105	90	83	78	72	69	95	105	139	**144**
Equity of minority shareholders in affiliated companies	538	598	666	705	769	821	880	893	1,314	**1,373**
Total liabilities	9,216	11,294	15,877	16,175	18,222	19,316	21,302	26,938	31,164	**34,414**
Shareholders' equity										
Capital stock	2,637	2,595	2,578	2,583	2,608	2,572	2,389	2,136	1,695	**1,826**
Earnings reinvested	9,647	11,145	12,717	14,055	15,450	16,549	17,840	20,416	23,718	**26,691**
Total shareholders' equity	12,284	13,740	15,205	16,638	18,058	19,121	20,229	22,552	25,413	**28,517**
Total liabilities and shareholders' equity	21,500	25,034	31,172	32,813	36,280	38,437	41,531	49,490	56,577	**62931**

Source: Exxon Corporation, *Financial and Statistical Supplement to the Annual Report,* 1981.

APPENDIX B (*Continued*)

CONSOLIDATED STATEMENT OF INCOME

(Millions of Dollars)

	1972	1973	1974	1975	1976	1977	1978	1979	1980	1981
Revenue										
Sales and other operating revenue										
Petroleum and natural gas										
Petroleum products, including excise taxes	16,072	20,681	31,597	33,040	36,867	40,739	45,216	59,458	77,910	79,674
Crude oil	3,177	3,985	8,488	9,548	8,474	9,628	10,340	11,968	14,784	17,117
Natural gas	646	748	903	1,262	1,509	1,791	2,123	2,517	3,034	3,167
Other	744	872	991	979	1,106	1,225	1,429	2,219	2,546	2,429
Total	20,639	26,286	41,979	44,829	47,956	53,383	59,108	76,162	98,274	102,387
Chemical products*	1,258	1,563	2,787	2,594	3,238	3,578	4,034	5,807	6,936	7,126
Other	174	173	255	373	432	568	754	1,586	3,239	3,684
Total sales and operating revenue	22,071	28,022	45,021	47,796	51,626	57,529	63,896	83,555	108,449	113,197
Earnings from equity interests and other revenue**	365	454	775	968	966	931	1,191	1,412	1,932	1,951
Total revenue	22,436	28,476	45,796	48,764	52,592	58,460	65,087	84,967	110,381	115,148
Costs and other deductions										
Crude oil and product purchases	6,022	7,456	18,607	21,702	26,776	29,274	34,677	45,746	60,915	64,324
Operating expenses	3,009	3,855	4,246	4,347	4,658	5,378	6,395	8,482	10,872	11,698
Selling, general and administrative expenses	2,104	2,277	2,439	2,628	2,719	2,955	3,640	4,292	5,461	5,231
Depreciation and depletion	1,059	1,136	1,231	1,471	1,392	1,494	1,678	2,027	2,282	2,948
Exploration expenses										
Dry holes	133	108	191	239	267	321	378	594	504	811
Other	132	147	240	246	260	321	397	458	648	842
Total exploration expenses	265	255	431	485	527	642	775	1,052	1,152	1,653

Income, excise and other taxes

Income taxes, U.S. Federal	279	417	649	938	960	842	1,063	1,155	1,762	**1,407**
Income taxes, other	2,066	3,322	7,205	6,347	4,222	4,801	1,634	2,547	3,666	**2,803**
Total income taxes	2,345	3,739	7,854	7,285	5,182	5,643	2,697	3,702	5,428	**4,210**
Excise taxes	1,761	2,298	2,959	2,931	2,995	3,403	3,561	4,449	5,306	**5,089**
Other taxes and duties	3,989	4,558	4,460	5,116	5,323	6,545	8,190	10,184	12,474	**14,025**
Total taxes	8,095	10,595	15,273	15,332	13,500	15,591	14,448	18,335	23,208	**23,324**
Interest expense	251	280	366	385	396	399	425	494	728	**843**
Foreign exchange translation loss/(gain)**	(11)	44	82	(165)	(105)	186	186	103	(82)	**(575)**
Income applicable to minority interests	83	127	126	123	114	98	100	141	195	**135**
Total deductions	20,877	26,025	42,801	46,308	49,977	56,017	62,324	80,672	104,731	**109,581**
Net income	1,559	2,451	2,995	2,456	2,615	2,443	2,763	4,295	5,650	**5,567**
*		70	72	(50)	45	72	130	35	(112)	*(135)*
**			476	449	503	610	619	878	1,292	*1,323*

* Chemical products supplied to petroleum affiliates not included above.

** Foreign exchange loss/(gain) related to equity companies included in "Earnings from equity interests and other revenue."

Source: Exxon Corporation, Financial and Statistical Supplement to the Annual Report, 1981.

RETURN ON AVERAGE CAPITAL EMPLOYED BY BUSINESS SEGMENT (Percent)

	1977	*1978*	*1979*	*1980*	**1981**
Energy operations					
Petroleum & natural gas					
United States					
Exploration & production	20.2	20.5	22.6	29.2	**24.8**
Refining & marketing	10.0	10.7	4.0	7.9	**3.5**
Foreign					
Exploration & production	25.9	25.7	30.5	36.7	**37.0**
Refining & marketing	8.9	10.5	24.1	22.6	**11.6**
International marine	1.0	—	—	2.4	**0.2**
Coal mining and development	—	—	—	0.8	**2.7**
Uranium mining and nuclear fuel fabrication	—	—	—	—	**—**
Other energy	8.7	5.2	4.9	2.5	**3.7**
Total energy operations	14.7	15.3	20.2	23.5	**18.4**
Chemical operations					
United States	18.0	14.6	16.1	8.7	**7.5**
Foreign	7.1	9.8	20.4	20.5	**8.9**
Total chemical operations	11.5	12.1	18.2	14.3	**8.1**
Reliance Electric Co. operations	—	—	—	—	**2.0**
Minerals mining and development	—	—	—	—	**—**
Other operations	4.8	—	—	—	**—**
Total operations	14.2	14.6	18.7	20.5	**15.7**
Corporate total	11.9	12.5	16.6	18.4	**14.4**

Source: Exxon Corporation, *Financial and Statistical Supplement to the Annual Report*, 1981.

APPENDIX B (Continued)

PETROLEUM PRODUCT SALES, NATURAL GAS SALES, EUROPEAN PETROLEUM PRODUCT PRICE INDICES

	1972	1973	1974	1975	1976	1977	1978	1979	1980	1981
Petroleum product sales* (thousands of barrels daily)										
Market sales										
Aviation fuels	318	329	277	266	285	298	309	320	311	294
Motor gasolines, naphthas	1,201	1,328	1,221	1,184	1,215	1,258	1,333	1,362	1,282	1,188
Heating oils, kerosene, diesel oils	1,211	1,322	1,087	1,034	1,154	1,160	1,192	1,200	1,110	1,047
Heavy fuels	1,487	1,543	1,392	1,168	1,212	1,143	1,131	1,089	946	836
Specialty petroleum products	441	479	429	396	408	408	396	405	378	355
Total market sales	4,658	5,001	4,406	4,048	4,274	4,267	4,361	4,376	4,027	3,720
Supply sales	1,043	1,177	1,099	942	1,079	999	1,029	943	926	881
Total market and supply sales	5,701	6,178	5,505	4,990	5,353	5,266	5,390	5,319	4,953	4,601
Natural gas sales** (millions of cubic feet daily)										
United States	5,952	5,758	5,312	4,937	4,673	4,476	4,348	4,007	3,729	3,364
Canada	423	477	419	410	376	361	343	367	314	299
Other Western Hemisphere	68	91	104	104	41	50	54	76	84	87
Europe										
Netherlands	2,319	2,814	3,409	3,579	3,807	3,756	3,505	3,630	3,396	3,127
West Germany	552	643	727	692	689	783	1,021	1,079	1,061	1,193
United Kingdom	367	398	477	502	613	515	486	456	362	443
Other	3	3	2	3	2	3	3	3	5	16
Total Europe	3,241	3,858	4,615	4,776	5,111	5,057	5,015	5,168	4,824	4,779
Other Eastern Hemisphere										
Libya	173	237	208	253	286	304	367	346	232	128
Australia	54	84	117	141	167	194	190	171	196	256
Other	12	12	17	24	24	46	51	46	83	67
Total other Eastern Hemisphere	239	333	342	418	477	544	608	563	511	451
Worldwide	9,923	10,517	10,792	10,645	10,678	10,488	10,368	10,181	9,462	8,980
European petroleum product price indices*** (1980 = 100)										
Gasoline	17	21	40	45	46	47	51	69	100	102
Distillate	12	18	34	36	38	41	45	70	100	101
Fuel oil	12	14	35	41	40	46	47	66	100	110
Total product barrel (major fuels)	13	19	36	40	41	44	47	69	100	103

* Petroleum product sales include 100 percent of the sales of Exxon and majority-owned affiliates. Market sales are sales to service station dealers, consumers (including government and military), jobbers and small resellers. Supply sales are sales to large oil marketers, large unbranded resellers and other oil companies.

** Natural gas sales include 100 percent of the sales of Exxon and majority owned affiliates and Exxon's ownership percentage of sales by companies owned 50 percent or less. Natural gas sales for the Netherlands and West Germany have been restated for the years 1972–1975 to include Exxon's ownership share of sales by two additional companies owned less than 50 percent.

*** The European product price index is the ratio of U.S. dollar realization per unit volume (excluding excise tax) from company sales to that obtained in the 1980 base period.

Source: Exxon Corporation, *Financial and Statistical Supplement to the Annual Report*, 1981.

PROVED RESERVES AND SUPPLIES OF LIQUIDS (Millions of Barrels at Year-End)

	1972	1973	1974	1975	1976	1977	1978	1979	1980	1981
Net proved developed and undeveloped reserves										
United States	4,679	4,401	4,298	4,030	3,823	3,751	3,435	2,997	2,854	2,822
Canada	1,119	1,084	769	728	734	685	669	629	574	489
Other Western Hemisphere	6,226	6,463	7,045	47	40	34	30	26	21	36
Europe	331	490	734	878	791	991	972	1,157	1,765	1,646
Middle East and Africa	1,174	536	479	447	413	389	426	398	377	7**
Australia and Far East	652	758	845	801	788	751	981	1,088	1,139	1,157
Total consolidated affiliates	14,181	13,732	14,170	6,931	6,589	6,601	6,513	6,295	6,730	6,157
Proportional interest in reserves of equity companies	26,089	20,435	10,768	11,149	11,246	11,193	83*	67*	75	80
Supplies available under long-term agreements with foreign governments	4,570	3,965	2,966	1,859	1,702	1,565	1,255	608	593	544**
Oil sands reserves—Canada	—	—	—	—	—	—	355	295****	303	294
Total worldwide	44,840	38,132	27,904	19,939	19,537	19,359	8,206	7,265	7,701	7,075
Net proved developed reserves included above										
United States					2,836	2,965	2,900	2,347***	2,281	2,185
Canada					700	632	599	565	490	408
Other Western Hemisphere					36	30	26	23	20	19
Europe					131	139	192	273	316	470
Middle East and Africa					397	387	420	392	276	3**
Australia and Far East					518	589	595	599	551	551
Total consolidated affiliates					4,618	4,742	4,732	4,199***	3,934	3,636
Proportional interest in reserves of equity companies					7,612	7,511	70*	62*	71	66
Supplies available under long-term agreements with foreign governments					1,651	1,532	1,142	608	593	544**
Oil sands reserves—Canada					—	—	355	295****	249	240
Total worldwide	N.A.	N.A.	N.A.	N.A.	13,881	13,785	6,299	5,164	4,847	4,486

* Aramco data not included.

** Under the terms of an agreement effective December 1, 1981, Exxon assigned its rights, assets and properties in Libya to the National Oil Corporation. Consequently, no reserves for Libya are included in the year-end 1981 data.

*** 291 million barrels of proved reserves, classified as developed in the 1979 data, were reclassified as undeveloped in the 1979 information.

**** During 1979, the Alberta Energy Company Ltd. exercised its option to purchase 20 percent of the participating interests in the Syncrude project. As a result, Imperial Oil Limited's interest was reduced from 31.25 percent to 25 percent.

Source: Exxon Corporation, Financial and Statistical Supplement to the Annual Report, 1981.

PROVED RESERVES AND SUPPLIES OF NATURAL GAS (Billions of Cubic Feet at Year-End)

	1972	1973	1974	1975	1976	1977	1978	1979	1980	1981
Net proved developed and undeveloped reserves										
United States	28,656	26,040	24,061	22,655	20,696	19,489	18,170	17,200	16,687	16,924
Canada	2,590	2,426	2,021	1,909	1,513	1,361	1,338	1,495	1,358	1,293
Other Western Hemisphere	15,653	16,581	17,078	375	346	343	329	324	309	280
Europe	5,847	5,848	5,908	5,922	5,261	4,908	4,790	4,411	6,271	5,998
Middle East and Africa	3,238	1,528	1,467	1,311	1,240	1,160	1,459	1,382	1,322	5**
Australia and Far East	3,687	3,034	3,470	3,084	3,237	2,856	3,173	3,297	3,294	3,285
Total consolidated affiliates	59,671	55,457	54,005	35,256	32,293	30,117	29,259	28,109	29,241	27,785
Proportional interest in reserves of equity companies	34,289	30,647	25,798	25,650	24,771	24,041	17,231*	17,000*	16,194	16,067
Supplies available under long-term agreements with foreign governments	20,202	7,562	5,113	5,033	1,753	1,657	1,976	1,881	1,809	—**
Total worldwide	114,162	93,666	84,916	65,939	58,817	55,815	48,466	46,990	47,244	43,852
Net proved developed reserves included above										
United States					15,164	17,814	16,628	15,766	16,133	15,886
Canada					989	909	872	1,191	1,094	1,021
Other Western Hemisphere					279	272	257	252	238	208
Europe					3,124	2,759	3,241	2,944	3,006	3,097
Middle East and Africa					757	1,099	1,403	1,325	1,216	5**
Australia and Far East					2,262	2,108	2,238	1,981	2,035	2,689
Total consolidated affiliates					22,575	24,961	24,639	23,459	23,722	22,906
Proportional interest in reserves of equity companies					21,177	20,996	16,140*	15,938*	15,492	15,071
Supplies available under long-term agreements with foreign governments					1,753	1,657	1,976	1,881	1,809	—**
Total worldwide	N.A.	N.A.	N.A.	N.A.	45,505	47,614	42,755	41,278	41,023	37,977

* Aramco data not included.

** Under the terms of an agreement effective December 1, 1981, Exxon assigned its rights, assets and properties in Libya to the National Oil Corporation. Consequently, no reserves for Libya are included in the year-end 1981 data.

Source: Exxon Corporation, Financial and Statistical Supplement to the Annual Report, 1981.

GENERAL MILLS, INC.

In 1866, Mr. C.C. Washburn constructed a flour mill on the banks of the Mississippi River near Minneapolis. From these beginnings grew General Mills, the premier flour miller in the United States until it voluntarily sold approximately half its milling capacity in the mid 1960s. By the mid 1980s this and other strategic shifts had changed General Mills into a highly diversified consumer products company on the *Fortune* 100 list. How did these events occur? And what did they portend for the future of this once conservative, middle western, flour milling enterprise?

EARLY HISTORY

In 1928 Washburn Crosby's President, James Ford Bell, began to realize that the network of grain and flour mills he had merged to become General Mills was not going to have the kind of profitability he wanted for the company's future. He began to focus General Mills on more controllable, high-margin, consumer items, starting one of the country's first research operations dedicated to new product development. Bisquick, the nation's first prepared mix, grew from this effort in 1931, as did Cheerios, the world's first ready-to-eat oat cereal in 1941. By then major marketing efforts had made General Mills into the largest flour miller in the U.S. and its trade names—Wheaties (cereals), Gold Medal (flour), and Betty Crocker (mixes)—into household words.

Case copyright © 1985 by James Brian Quinn. Research associates—Penny C. Paquette and Allie J. Quinn. Material is partly drawn from an earlier case written by James Brian Quinn and Mariann Jelinek. The generous cooperation of General Mills, Inc. is gratefully acknowledged.

The War, Electronics, and Chemicals

Then during World War II, General Mills diversified almost by accident into any field—lens coatings, sandbags, electronics, materials testing equipment, and torpedo direction devices—that helped support the war effort while keeping its own highly skilled technical teams intact. After the war it tried to use these same skills in small consumer appliances and started a line of coffee makers, toasters, pressure cookers, and steam irons in 1946. But, General Mills soon discovered that it lacked the marketing ability and the trade outlets to compete with larger companies like GE and Westinghouse. And consumer appliances were sold off in 1954. Despite some other diversifications—like an attempt to convert soybeans into chemical specialties—flour milling dominated General Mills' 1950s activities.

NEW DIRECTIONS

At about this time, a new management team joined the company, headed by General Edwin W. Rawlings, a dynamic, forceful man who had risen rapidly in the wartime Army Air Force to become one of the youngest four star generals in the nation's history.

The Changes Begin—Close Outs and Divestitures

Rawlings began to probe many of the areas that had concerned his predecessors—notably the commodity nature of the company's businesses and the wild and unpredictable swings caused by its dependency on grains and milling. At first he did this through a series of informal presentations. Later these became more formalized Management Operations Reviews—MOR's as they were called—to reevaluate all aspects of the company's businesses. Based upon a Controllership Department's presentation the group raised questions, and made assignments when information was sketchy or answers were incomplete. Some person or group would be asked to report back on these matters at a specified time.

One of the first areas to be highlighted was formula feeds for livestock and poultry. The business had been started as a way to improve the profits of the basic milling operation. Various nutrients were added to mill feed, and the mix was concentrated for cattle, turkey, chicken, and broiler feeds. General Mills had established large, centrally located, heavily automated plants, serving a wide area. But the industry—and a now dominant competitor, Ralston—had gone the other way. Ralston's small, "crossroads" or "neighborhood" type mills had stayed closer to the growers and producers.

On the basis of an MOR study, first the corporate officers and then the Board of Directors decided to get out of the formula feeds business in late 1962. A staff officer close to the process observed: "It was a traumatic experience for a few people. But I don't think there was a real heavy philosophical commitment to the feed business, like there was to the flour business. This was a fairly easy one—particularly since we were losing so much money in it—to start with." A total termination loss of $15.5 million ($4.4 million, A.T.), was ultimately charged to retained earnings. Because of the high inventory and receivables commitments of the business, however, the move freed up working capital for other operations.

This became a model for other shutdowns. In short order, General Mills sold off its Magnaflux Division to Champion Spark Plug Co., closed selected foods operations in Mexico and England (major soybean plants, various oil seed operations), and—perhaps most importantly—got out of the electronics business in 1964. A staff officer observed, "We weren't making much money in electronics, and it was something I don't think our directors felt very comfortable with because

it was so different from our usual businesses. The person in charge of electronics—at the administrative level—in the early stages had been administrative assistant to the Controller and the President. And the person directly in charge when the division was divested was also from the finance area. Neither had strong emotional attachments to the electronics business, so they could approach it quite objectively."

The Commodity Flour Decision

All of this was backdrop for the most traumatic decision in General Mills' history. By the early 1960s worldwide overcapacity in flour milling was rampant. But the company had a strong internal need for flour, both for its institutional customers and for its consumer products like layer cakes and Bisquick. Family flour and the branded products supported by the mills showed adequate returns in the early 1960s. But there was a growing concern, frustration, and discontent concerning the commodity aspects of the business. Managers felt they were at the mercy of a volatile marketplace and, in the long run, in a losing situation.

Eventually, General Mills did not leave commodity (bakery) flour entirely. The consumer flour business was profitable enough to keep, but quite seasonal. Therefore the company maintained enough of a presence in bakery flour to even out the peaks and valleys of flour production and demand. The decision made in 1964 took the better part of a year and struck at the very heart of General Mills—no longer to be the world's largest flour miller. Emotional attachments to the company's century-old basic business were deep seated.

Consumer Products

As milling capacity decreased to half its former size, the company's product mix changed markedly. And packaged foods soon provided some 75% of General Mills' total sales. About this time, General Rawlings announced a growth goal of 10% per year. And many shared the view that the central focus for expansion should be in *consumer products*, beginning with foods. As an executive commented:

> It made a lot of sense to us. . . . Here was a business—consumer products beginning with family flour, and progressing to cereals, cake mixes, and so on—that had showed a history of steady growth. With our marketing ability, it was obvious that we could control our own destiny to a degree, there. . . . The philosophy was, "We're already there, and obviously we can sell things to the consumer. That's where our strength is."

The company also wanted to expand internationally, but prior to this time nothing much had happened. However, its dual strategies of international growth and expansion into snacks came together in the acquisition of Smith's Potato Crisps, Ltd. of England in early 1966. This was followed in 1967 by 50% of Productos de Trigo, S.A., a Mexican manufacturer of cookies, crackers, and pasta products. Much of the initiative in proposing and closing these acquisitions came from "Bo" Polk,* the flamboyant and controversial executive who headed the finance and controllership areas. Mr. Polk also took over European operations at the time acquisitions spurted there, and is widely credited with many of the successes—and problems—these led to.

General Mills' first non-food consumer acquisition was Rainbow Crafts (a manufacturer of creative toys, including Play Doh), purchased in October 1965. An executive vice president of the Chemicals Division during this period recalled that the "toy and craft" involvement began almost casually, but quickly led to other things:

> It seems to me that somebody came up with the idea that, "Look, there's a little company down in Cincinnati that makes Play Doh, and it's available." To my knowledge, it came to us. I don't think

---

* Louis Polk, Jr., later Financial Vice President. His activities also included new ventures. Mr. Polk was brought in by General Rawlings and stayed with the company until 1968, when he resigned to head MGM.

we found it. Rainbow Crafts just happened to be there, it happened to be a good idea, and we happened to get it. Then we started a real search (internally and externally) into other-than-food consumer areas. These quickly extended into the craft, game, toy, fashion, and jewelry businesses—all broad consumer lines other than food.

As background for this wider diversification program, the Acquisitions Group performed a major review of the consumer product industries of the United States. From this it distilled some six areas of major interest. These were: specialty retailing, restaurants, fashions, furniture, travel, and crafts, games and toys. These investigations helped refine the company's acquisition criteria. Eventually, these criteria became to acquire consumer product or service companies: in low technology fields, with the possibility of a brand franchise, growing faster than gross national product, in fragmented industries, in industries with at least $300 million total potential, and with the possibility of significant earnings-per-share impact. The intention was to build up a position over a period of time through acquisition of smaller units, rather than acquiring large single units.

The acquisition group presented these criteria and candidate industries to the Executive Council in fall 1967. It sanctioned looking into several industries further. The first of these was the fashion industry. The acquisition group then went through a full segmentation of that industry by customer age, type of product, price, style, distribution technique, etc. Following a full field investigation of some 200 companies, a few attractive and available candidates were brought in to top management. Even then, further education was needed. For example: One of the primary fashion candidates quickly left after he was asked in a top management interview to describe his five-year planning processes. He commented, "They really don't understand this industry, do they?" However, within a short while, these sorts of problems receded. One executive later recalled:

As part of the process, we did a very interesting thing, a sort of popularity contest. In effect each member ranked the presented areas in the order they thought we ought to consider them for diversification. As you might expect, the winners of the popularity contest were those most closely related to our existing businesses. The restaurant business got the most votes, the apparel industry very few. The next year was spent studying these industries and developing fairly comprehensive strategies for getting into them. . . . But many of the top managers were still not comfortable with the idea of investing significant amounts of money in unrelated new areas.

Nevertheless, in 1967 Craftmaster Corporation (maker of paint-by-number oil painting sets and other craft and hobby kits) was acquired, as was Kenner Products Corporation (maker of a broad line of innovative toys). Then in 1968, General Mills added Parker Brothers (makers of Monopoly and other games) and Model Products Corporation.

THE McFARLAND YEARS

A prime mover in all this, Mr. James P. McFarland, was named President and Chief Operating Officer in December 1967 to succeed General Rawlings, with Rawlings continuing as CEO. A 40 year veteran with General Mills, Jim McFarland had risen through marketing and general management positions in the Flour, Grocery Products, and later Consumer Products Divisions. The *Wall Street Journal* described him as "a man who had done well in every job he has been given." McFarland continued the strategy of making acquisitions in related areas, with Jesse Jones (maker of sausage and other meat specialties) and Gorton Corporation (a processor of seafoods) in 1968 and other Consumer Foods acquisitions on the Continent, in the U.K., and Canada.

In addition, McFarland created a New Ventures Group "to form entrepreneurial teams that will conceive and develop new areas of profit growth." Acquisitions were stepped up with Monocraft Products (jewelry), Dexter Thread Mills (mail order crafts), Knothe Brothers (sleepwear), Donruss Co. (bubble gum), and David Crystal, Inc. (apparel) being added. Named Chief Executive Officer in 1969, Mr. McFarland could report the largest annual sales increase in the company's history, 18%—and a profit increase of 15%.

Establishing a Corporate Identity

Soon McFarland began a broad based review of the company's overall direction. His own view was that the company should move from the assortment of businesses in which it then operated to "a family of businesses" which would offer more growth potential and possess greater balance. But he decided that the company's key managers should actively participate in this decision.

McFarland began by stating, for the first time, a corporate "mission." He felt that the real talent of the company rested in "its ability to market consumer products and/or services for which a brand franchise could be developed." Although the company had adequate skills in research, manufacturing and technology, its critical edge lay in its marketing capability. The broad mission developed for General Mills became "to discern consumer wants and needs and convert those into products and services for which it could develop markets and a brand franchise."

The next step was to further develop, test, and communicate these concepts within the organization. McFarland took some 30–35 top managers "for a three day retreat up north" which became known as the "goodness to greatness" conference. The company already had some broad financial and growth goals. The whole group first reviewed these and decided they still seemed appropriate. Next Mr. McFarland broke the total unit up into groups of 6 to 8 people. On the first day he asked them to define, "What are the characteristics of a great company?" Each group considered this from the viewpoint of stock-holders, employees, suppliers, the public, and society—and reported back.

> Among characteristics agreed upon as keys to corporate greatness were: "A well-defined corporate purpose"; "A growth corporation in key leading indicators, including particularly earnings per share, sales and an overall increase in market penetration"; "An intense desire for greatness"; "An unusually high degree of creativity and innovation"; "The look of greatness, achieved through flair and imaginative and effective communication"; "Diversification," and "A participative, responsible internal climate."

The second day's discussions were devoted—in the same format—to the company's strengths and weaknesses relative to the defined posture of "greatness." The third day focused on how to overcome the company's weaknesses and move from being a "very good company" toward being a "great company." At the end of each day, the whole group came together and tried to reach a broad consensus through further discussions. The Planning Director then distilled and summarized this consensus for the record. These meetings led to certain fundamental conclusions. In Mr. McFarland's words:

> We had this strong desire to grow. But the feeling was that we were not involved in enough areas of growth—industries or business activities of natural growth. We either had to go against the trends or be absolutely miracle-makers within our fields. Therefore, we decided that we should undertake and develop some new areas of activity. . . . There were also some more subjective elements [in our conclusions]; that we needed more flair in our business, more get up and go, and so on.

The "Comfort Factor"

Until 1969, most acquisitions, domestically and internationally, had been in the foods area. Some non-foods businesses appealed to management

more than others. "The closer an item was to the core of the business, the more comfortable they would feel." Cosmetics were considered closer to foods than apparels. Broadcasting was closer than furniture because the company itself was spending so much on TV advertising. The company justified the consideration of non-food areas because of its deep seated faith in its ability to market consumer products to the homemaker and her family. This perception evolved into a "loose strategy" over a period of time through the interaction of key management personnel. Out of this came two thrusts. One was to expand in food related sectors. The other was to develop new growth centers based on General Mills' marketing skills directed essentially at the homemaker. There was a strong informal feeling that the great majority of the company's resources should be used to expand in the food related areas.

Two Thrusts

Almost the reverse occurred. Over the next five years General Mills invested something like $400 million in new businesses, and the majority were not closely related to foods. A Direct Marketing Division was formed to include LeeWards Creative Crafts, Eddie Bauer (sports equipment and leisure wear), and The Talbots (fine clothing), all with both mail order and retail stores. And General Mills' fashion activities expanded to include Monet costume jewelry; Kimberly Knitwear; Picato; Alligator Company; Lord Jeff Knitting Company; and the Foot-Joy Company.

There were two main reasons why acquisitions were primarily outside the food area. First, the company was unable to continually develop good acquisition candidates in many food related sectors. The field was highly competitive, and acquisition opportunities tended to be marginal—i.e., they either were not market leaders or their cost was prohibitive. Second, when candidate companies were strong in some areas, FTC restrictions prevented the company from acquiring them. In addition, there were two organizations whose sole responsibility was to find and develop new opportunities in the non-food sector. There was a strong bias for these groups to find interesting candidates, and they did.

Still in this same era, General Mills became vitally interested in the ''away-from-home eating'' market. Red Lobster Inns were acquired in January, 1970. Betty Crocker Pie Shops—in the Minneapolis area—opened to feature a broad line of quality, fresh-baked pies. Betty Crocker Tree House restaurants were opened in 4 cities. And General Mills opened fish and chip shops in Arizona and take out chicken shops in Britain. The Corporate Controller commented on General Mills' restaurant activities:

> Data indicated that more and more meals were being eaten away from home. Being a food company, we felt that we should and could participate [successfully] in this segment . . . Red Lobster Inns were acquired on a performance contract basis. And it was one of the best performance contracts we ever had. There were only about 6 outlets in the entire chain and they were all in central Florida. What we really acquired was three people who deeply understood the restaurant business—i.e., the basic mathematics of that business. The real key to satisfactory return is capital turnover. They had built their restaurants so the sales/investment ratio was about 1.5 to 1. With inflation and the more or less sunk cost in invest-

ment, you can't go anywhere but up on returns.

Various executives noted that the company could start small in the restaurant business and use a ''roll out'' concept—i.e., expand successful chains in discreet units, duplicating a local success in new geographical areas, with very little risk after the first few were proved. While the Red Lobster Inns proved successful, other efforts did not. Three of the four chains started internally were liquidated.

A Dazzling Array

By the mid 1970s General Mills businesses had proliferated into a fairly dazzling array. Table 1 shows how rapid growth was and how all this was financed. But some segments were not meeting profit goals. And others were competing for the same markets and resources.

The company had entered five new industries. Simultaneously, rising capital costs and the cash demands of many growing businesses made the Board of Directors and many securities analysts increasingly nervous. The company responded with two major steps: First, management changed its publicly stated strategy to one of consolidating the industries into which it diversified. Second, it placed new emphasis on internal growth as opposed to growth from external sources.

TABLE 1   INCOME STATEMENT (In $ Millions)

	1967	1969	1971	1973	1975	1977
Sales	628	885	1120	1662*	2309*	2909*
COGS	401	579	724	1010	1532	1786
Depreciation	14	23	27	35	42	48
Net Income	30	38	44	66	76	117
Total Assets	367	622	750	909	1206	1447
Long Term Debt	92	214	252	214	305	276
Common Equity	194	281	329	426	560	725

Restated for Pooling of Interest.

Source: Data drawn from various annual reports of General Mills, Inc.

An All Weather Company

Soon, however, acquisitions did continue with Harris Stamp, International Incentives, Feldbacher Backwarenfabrik (Austrian pretzels), David Reid, Bowers and Ruddy Galleries, General Interiors Corp., Clipper Games (Holland), Wallpapers-To-Go, and York Steak House Systems, Inc. becoming major acquisitions. By 1977 General Mills, Inc. (GMI) had some 95 operating subsidiaries in which it held total or major equity positions. Some 30–35% of GMI's business came from non-foods products; its management had decided not to increase the ratio further for fear that General Mills would be considered a "conglomerate" and its P/E ratios would suffer accordingly.

During Mr. McFarland's eight years as Chief Executive Officer the company had grown spectacularly as shown below.

By 1977 top managers were confident that General Mills had developed into an "all weather" company, able—more than ever before—to maintain growth despite the buffets of politics, the economy, or other external environments. In Spring 1977, as Mr. McFarland stepped down as chairman, General Mills signed a letter of intent to sell off its Chemical Division for $75 million, the last of the early post World War II diversifications. Mr. McFarland said:

> We've gone through the wage and price controls period. We've gone through the recession. We went through the boom. We've gone through the energy crisis, and—I think because of our planning process and our understanding of our business—we've been able to maintain

growth. We should constantly position ourselves to be a truly "all weather growth company."

I always believed that one of my greatest responsibilities as Chief Executive Officer was not only to use our physical facilities well, but more importantly, our human resources. For each individual, this meant to make a spot where he could effectively at least start things, implement them, and innovate. The more you use the thoughts of your vital organization, your human resources, the better off you are.

A NEW MANAGEMENT FOR A NEW ERA

E. Robert Kinney became chairman of General Mills in early 1977. Mr. Kinney had come to GMI when it bought Gorton Corp. Prior to that time Kinney had built two small companies into thriving enterprises. Although not in General Mills' Midwest tradition, Kinney's "good gutsy Maine business sense"[1] fit well with General Mills' philosophy. Kinney had moved through several operations positions before becoming its chief financial officer and later president. Although General Rawlings and Mr. McFarland are given most credit for repositioning General Mills, Mr. Kinney continued the entrepreneurial flair that had characterized General Mills' preceding decades. During his five years as CEO, General Mills grew from $2.65 billion to $4.85 billion in sales at an annual average rate of 12.9%. Mr. Kinney further developed the basic strategies of his predecessors—primarily emphasizing and extending the successful and fast growing Consumer

	1977	1969	1977 as % of 1969
Sales	$2,209M	$885M	328
Total Assets	1,447M	662M	232
Net Income	117M	36.2M	323
Earnings Per Share	2.36	.89	265
Stock Prices	$26½–35½	$15¾–21¾	165

Source: Data drawn from company's annual reports and various public sources.

Foods and Restaurant lines. But much also happened in the Toys Group. The company gained the "galaxy-wide" rights to market products based on the Star Wars movies which it parlayed into a $100 million a year enterprise. In another arena, General Mills' Izod line suddenly became fashionable, and sales skyrocketed.

Organizationally, Kinney continued to maintain very loose reins on his subsidiary managements, a policy which was obviously favored by the various entrepreneurs who had sold their burgeoning businesses to General Mills and stayed on to make them grow rapidly with seemingly limitless cash.[2] However, by 1981 many of the original founders of General Mills' subsidiaries had retired, died, or gone on to other endeavors, including Darden of Red Lobster, Chernow of Monet, the Talbots, Feighner of Tom's Foods, the Hoffmans of Wallpapers to Go, Grayson of York Steak Houses, and Gallardo of Casa Gallardo.

After a short but successful reign, in April 1981 Kinney handed the mantle of CEO on to Mr. Bruce Atwater, a 23 year veteran of General Mills and President and COO since 1977. *Forbes*, which had disparaged General Mills' earlier diversification attempts in the mid 1970s as "disastrous," noted that "General Mills had doubled its return on equity and its earnings growth rates to 17.9% and 15.3% respectively, and was now near the top of its industry."[3] While almost half of GMI's sales and earnings in fiscal year 1982 came from its four major areas of diversification— restaurants, toys and crafts, fashion goods, and specialty retailing—45% of its growth over the last decade had come from new products and services developed internally and only 10% from new acquisitions. Between 1967 and 1979 non food acquisitions had cost General Mills some $335 million and 3.5 million shares, about the price of one good-sized acquisition, but in 1981 they contributed $2 billion in sales and $184 million in operating profits.

Interestingly, 13 of GMI's older (over 25 years) food lines had tripled their volume in the same decade to some $2 billion, by responding rapidly and shrewdly to changing consumer tastes (low calorie foods, specialty cake mixes, "healthy" breakfast cereals, and so on). With this strong base, Mr. Atwater predicted sales would double in five years to $8 billion and capital spending would rise to $1.4 billion. "Unlike some consumer companies we have more growth opportunities than we have capital to devote to growth."[3]

Managers and Entrepreneurs

In September 1981, *Business Week* noted:

> This year for the first time, General Mills is imposing stringent financial controls and restrictions in its once nearly autonomous subsidiary chiefs. . . . The corporation has increased internal working capital charges to 13% from 7%. And it has launched a study of the feasibility of taking a "balance sheet approach" to financial management that would look at the cost of financing fixed assets and would force each subsidiary to simulate intracompany dividends. . . . "We want the managers to look at after-tax results, not just pre-tax profits," explains Jane Evans.[2]

With Mr. Atwater firmly in charge, the company was reorganized with two vice-chairmen—one responsible for the Consumer Foods Group and the other the Fashion, Toys, Specialty Retailing, and Restaurant Groups. While wanting to avoid the evils of over-control, Mr. Atwater noted, "You've got to do things differently when you reach a certain size, or you're going to suffer." In the *1981 Annual Report* he noted:

> [Our strategy] demands intelligent and responsive employees who stay in close touch with the consumer. Employees of this calibre are also necessary to support our management philosophy of decentralized growth centers. A combination of decentralized operations, a strong financial reporting system, and heavy emphasis on long range planning are the basic elements of our strategy.

As the entrepreneurial founders of many of General Mills' businesses were replaced—often by managers who had progressed upward through the Consumer Foods Group—the product management system that worked so well in Consumer Foods was being adapted to non-food areas as well. *Fortune* noted some of the impacts as follows, "While the product management system does create champions and encourages or at least rewards risk taking to some degree, it is also a relatively cumbersome process-oriented system in which the annual product plan follows a formula and the most common frustration of product managers themselves is how long it takes to get their proposed actions through the system."[4]

Mr. Atwater emphasized "we're trying to get things done as close to the market as we can. The object is to make running a General Mills Company as much like running a free standing business as possible." Nevertheless, *Business Week* noted in 1981:

> For some of the entrepreneurial managers, the jury remains out on whether General Mills will make good on its implied promise to keep strategic planning within the individual companies' domains. To them, the answer revolves around whether the corporate parent will remain as willing to accept variations in financial goals and performance as it said. "When you were by yourself, you set the standards," sums up Foot-Joy's Tarlow. "Here the standards are set and they're largely General Mills' standards."[2]

But like many other companies, General Mills had its problems with its entrepreneurs, too. When its Kimberly Division's founder had insisted that the division stick with its money-losing knitted products line, there were no experts in General Mills willing to second guess him. Ultimately, General Mills had to liquidate the operation when the division head's "knits strategy" caused excessive losses. In 1985, General Mills' very sophisticated management was still concerned with the problems of how to best utilize, motivate, and control a highly decentralized entrepreneurial management system.

A Long Term Viewpoint

Nevertheless, General Mills had an important tradition of risk taking and patience in developing its enterprises. Tenacity in the face of problems had long permeated the Consumer Foods area where Atwater commented, "We judge people not on whether a product succeeded or failed, but on how well they approached the marketplace."[3] He also said, "We are long-term people . . . when we are convinced that consumer demand exists for a product, we constantly refine the product until it achieves marketing success. We never cut and run."[4] Applied to non-food areas this philosophy led to patience with such troublesome subsidiaries as Ship n' Shore, which plunged into the red in 1979 when it bet wrong on the potential popularity of Qiana, a synthetic silk. "I told them it would take two years to turn around Ship n' Shore, and there was no pressure (to speed that up)," said Stanley Gillette, the subsidiary's President.[2]

Atwater's style brought with it a new dedication to planning, careful market analyses, and targeted acquisitions programs. When *Dun's* selected General Mills as one of its five best managed companies, it stated, "Behind General Mills' success is its mastery of consumer marketing. It exhaustively researches the market potential of every new product considered, and, once the decision to go ahead is made, puts the product in the hands of a product manager whose single assignment is to make it a success. Management plows big bucks into its development and promotion and sticks with it until it turns a profit."[5] But flexibility was also needed. At the 1983 Annual Meeting Mr. Atwater added:

> General Mills intends to continue "our necessarily risk-oriented marketing activities" to execute its strategy of balanced diversification, aggressive consumer marketing, and entry into adjacent businesses. An overly cautious marketing approach would enable our competitors to move ahead more rapidly than General Mills in developing opportunities. On the other hand, a risk-oriented marketing approach

inevitably results in a certain number of initiatives that don't work out. But, what the consumer wants and needs (and competitors' offerings) continually change. This is why it is far more risky to stay with the status quo than to continually experiment with changes and improvements.[6]

THE MID 1980s

1981 through early 1984 were hard years for the U.S. economy. And General Mills whose growth was intimately tied to consumer spending experienced a slower rise in sales. Nevertheless, return on average equity met or exceeded stated corporate goals, dividends per share continued to be raised, and earnings per share continued their 22 year record of increase. Within the five industry groups however, unforeseen problems cropped up and were reflected in group level financial results. (See exhibits for a summary of group performance for the fiscal years 1979 through 1984.)

Consumer Foods led the company forward with its strategy of increased market share and profit growth in its traditional brands, introduction of meaningful new products in established categories, entry or creation of carefully selected new markets through internal development or acquisition, and concentration on productivity improvements in all areas. The other four groups each faltered, leading one analyst to comment that "A principal strength of General Mills has been its ability to diversify outside the consumer food business . . . This diversification is now being tested."[7]

The Restaurant Group which by 1984 accounted for nearly 20% of the company's sales was hard hit by a sudden decline in the Red Lobster chain's popularity and customer counts. As far back as 1982, research indicated to Joe Lee (manager of Red Lobster's first outlet and now the Restaurant Group President) that consumers were interested in a more casual dining experience, as well as lighter fresh food, and a greater variety of price points. "The research was telling

him one thing; the Red Lobster books said something else. Doing very well—in the first year of the recession—hid the believability of the research. With 370 restaurants you didn't want to do the wrong thing," said Lee.[8]

During fiscal 1984 the company began a $100 million chain-wide remodeling program and curtailed further expansion of Red Lobster until the remodeling was finished and earnings improved. The other four restaurants'—York Steak House, Casa Gallardo (Mexican foods), Daryll's (casual style, diverse menu), and Good Earth— concepts were constantly modified during this period with continuous expansion and improving results. Mr. Lee's philosophy—placing maximum responsibility and autonomy close to the restaurant—seemed to pay dividends. "Once Joe approves a plan, he lets the presidents do whatever is necessary to implement it," said one executive. But Lee also held personal quarterly meetings and had short monthly reports from each of his key people. He spent much of his time visiting individual restaurants around the country. "I've got to have a feel of the business myself. I can't get that in an office. I want to see what is actually happening in the restaurants and with the customers." Said an executive, "If Joe heard of a new restaurant concept or a new type of dishwasher, he would go miles out of his way to see it for himself. He almost got killed once when his airplane crash landed in Newfoundland because he wanted to visit his shrimp supplier personally." With high energy and standards, Lee had set a target of doubling his restaurants between 1982 and 1985.[9]

The Toy Group had suffered heavily from Parker Brothers entry into the video game market—which promptly went into a tailspin beginning in 1983. In 1982, its first year in the video business, Parker Brothers racked up earnings of $20 million on sales of $74 million. With such an auspicious start, the company geared up to produce $225 million of cartridges in fiscal 1983. Instead, it had to settle for revenues of $117 million and a loss.[8] Luckily, Parker had adopted basically a "software only" strategy and was able to scale down its operations and stem its losses somewhat. And the success of Star Wars toys and its line of licensed character products, Strawberry Shortcake and the Care Bears, balanced off its video game problems and some currency woes caused by its Mexican operations. In 1985 Parker and the entire Toys Group were trying hard to define how to recapture their lost volume and exploit the complex home entertainment marketplace.

The Fashion Group's Izod/La Coste—while relatively small when acquired—had become the mainstay of GMI's fashion lines. Capitalizing on increased consumer interest in physical fitness, General Mills built Izod's alligator into a highly profitable symbol of quality and broadened its product line into a full range of leisure wear. At first the problem was to produce enough of Izod's classic shirt (the 2058) to meet orders. Izod's Ivy League look became the "sport shirt of choice" in the *Preppy Handbook* craze of the early 1980s, and competition copied the alligator concept and style with wild abandon. But it was Izod's failure to adapt its prep styles into other variations or a total "look" of shirts, pants, accessories (etc.) that gave others a chance to muscle out shelf space in retail stores. Under this impact, the Izod line began a steady decline in 1982. As Jane Evans, then the Executive Vice President of Fashion, said:

"I think it is important to remember that fashion came to Izod. It was not because of anything we did as far as changing the shirt. All of a sudden we were reclassified as being a 'fashion line'. We didn't understand the implications of that." While some 20% of all knit shirts were bought by fad conscious teenage girls, Evans maintained, "Izod had no interest in chasing the juniors." She said flatly, "That is a huge business, it's a dangerous business, and it's not one we'll ever go after."[8]

The mainstream of GMI's David Crystal line—dressy sportswear geared to suburban activities—also proved to be out of tune with apparel market trends, as had Kimberly's double knit and synthetic fabrics.[10] While recognizing General Mills' impressive record and historical strengths, *Wall Street Journal* summarized certain concerns as follows:

The manner in which senior management disclosed Izod's problems also raises questions about how well it tracks General Mills' diverse operating units. Analysts say the Izod episode disclosed other potential problems: (1) Management's staple food heritage may prevent it from adapting to the faster paced marketing needs of nonfoods businesses . . . Fashion isn't like Wheaties and Cheerios. When you turn the key in the morning, you know you're going to sell cereals. But in the rag business, every day is really a new day. (2) The company's formal reporting systems may keep management in the dark until it's too late. And (3) entrepreneurship may be frustrated by great reliance on research and what one analyst calls "a typical large company monthly review that looks at all the numbers. I'm not sure that breeds the kind of creativity you need to run a business," he says.[11]

Specialty Retailing had been developed by General Mills using "consumer trend analysis" to identify new distribution channels for conventional consumer products—chiefly mail order marketing. The Talbots brought GMI into the fashion retailing market with a substantial mail order volume. First The Talbots' mail order sales were extended out of The Talbots' traditional New England markets. Then as new customer loyalties developed, they were exploited with additional retail outlets in selected new areas. Eddie Bauer (quality, down insulated outdoor gear) followed the same strategy. And both brought General Mills into the new telecommunications, computer, and in-home shopping markets.

Overall in Specialty Retailing there were some success stories and some problems. The Talbots, Eddie Bauer, LeeWards retail operations, and Pennsylvania House furniture lines were gradually expanded and doing well. But LeeWards Creative Crafts mail-order business and two other furniture operations experienced serious setbacks and were eventually divested. And overall Specialty Retailing results were hurt by (1) the collapse of the Collectibles business, which was sold in 1983; (2) the sharp downturn in the housing market and hence sales at Wallpapers-to-Go outlets, (these were either sold or remodeled and repositioned as full-service decorating stores); and Wild West Stores' failure to react to changes in jeans fashions (The Wild West stores closed down and reopened as We Are Sportswear outlets in 1982–84).

How Long Is the Primrose Path?

1984 may have been a watershed year for General Mills. Despite selling off its snack foods operation (Tom's Food) which increased its fiscal 1984 operating profits by more than $100 million, net earnings were down $11.7 million from 1983. Earnings per share would have been down also, except that the company bought back 3.2 million shares of common stock on the open market. Security analysts, most of whom had been as confident as management of the company's ability to correct its problems and continue its winning strategy, began in late 1984 to ask such questions as, "How long is the primrose path? Are the problems ahead or being put behind?" At General Mills Annual Meeting in September 1984, Mr. Atwater said that while Izod was troubled, it would "break-even" for the fiscal year ending May 1985. But only a few weeks later he conceded that Izod would have a loss of millions of dollars and could take a 55 cent per share bite out of earnings.[11] This incident created a concern that General Mills might have some fundamental problems to grapple with before it resumed its strong recent growth history.

QUESTIONS

1. Evaluate General Mills implementation of its diversification program. To what extent can such a program be truly planned? How? How permanent can a strategy be in this kind of company? Why?

2. What are the main portfolio issues facing General Mills at the end of the case? What should it do about these?

3. What kind of organization and control systems should General Mills adopt? Why? How should it evaluate and reward managers in its various entrepreneurial endeavors? In its more mature lines?

EXHIBIT 1   GENERAL MILLS, INC.—BUSINESS SEGMENT DATA

Fiscal Year	Sales ($ Million)	Percent of Total Sales	Pre-Tax Operating Profits After Redeployment ($ Million)	Profits As % of Sales	Return on Identifiable Assets	Capital Expenditures ($ Million)	Depreciation Expense ($ Million)
Consumer Foods							
1980	2,218.8	53.2	210.5	9.5	27.7	80.6	33.6
1981	2,514.6	51.8	217.7	8.7	25.9	95.7	40.6
1982	2,707.4	51.0	263.0	9.7	28.9	96.2	46.6
1983	2,792.6	50.3	268.2	9.6	27.3	123.8	51.9
1984	2,713.4	48.4	383.0	14.1	41.0	130.3	53.9
Restaurants							
1980	525.7	12.6	52.7	10.0	19.6	49.8	14.3
1981	704.0	14.5	75.3	10.7	19.9	85.1	19.7
1982	839.4	15.8	79.2	9.4	16.0	122.4	24.4
1983	984.5	17.7	80.0	8.1	14.0	107.6	30.6
1984	1,079.7	19.3	37.3	3.5	6.4	82.3	34.7

EXHIBIT 1 *(Continued)*

Fiscal Year	Sales ($ Million)	Percent of Total Sales	Pre-Tax Operating Profits After Redeployment ($ Million)	Profits As % of Sales	Return on Identifiable Assets	Capital Expenditures ($ Million)	Depreciation Expense ($ Million)
Toys							
1980	647.0	15.5	60.1	9.3	13.6	34.7	19.2
1981	674.3	13.9	70.6	10.5	17.6	28.6	22.9
1982	654.8	12.3	79.2	12.1	19.6	30.6	20.7
1983	728.3	13.1	104.6	14.4	23.2	39.3	22.8
1984	782.7	14.0	51.0	6.5	9.4	36.3	22.2
Fashion							
1980	442.5	10.1	43.7	10.3	18.9	5.2	3.9
1981	580.5	12.0	87.5	15.1	27.0	14.4	5.0
1982	657.3	12.4	101.7	15.5	28.2	13.4	6.0
1983	616.3	11.1	75.9	12.3	21.9	17.3	6.2
1984	587.4	10.5	37.9	6.5	9.7	16.3	7.3
Specialty Retailing							
1980	365.3	8.5	26.4	7.4	14.5	19.3	4.1
1981	379.0	7.8	13.2	3.5	5.5	19.2	5.2
1982	453.2	8.5	(11.9)	-2.6	-4.6	21.8	7.7
1983	429.1	7.7	16.1	3.8	6.7	17.1	9.1
1984	437.6	7.8	(10.9)	-2.5	-5.2	14.3	9.2

Source of Raw Data: General Mills, Inc., *Annual Report,* 1980–84.

EXHIBIT 2 ELEVEN YEAR FINANCIAL SUMMARY—BEFORE RESTATEMENTS (As Reported)

General Mills, Inc., and Subsidiaries

(Amounts in Millions, Except Per Share Data)	May 27, 1984	May 29, 1983	May 30, 1982	May 31, 1981	May 25, 1980
Operating Results					
Earnings per share (a)	$ 4.98	$ 4.89	$ 4.46	$ 3.90	$ 3.37
Return on average equity	19.0%	19.9%	19.1%	18.2%(b)	17.6%(b)
Dividends per share (a)	$ 2.04	1.84	1.64	1.44	1.28
Sales	$5,600.8	5,550.8	5,312.1	4,852.4	4,170.3
Costs and expenses:					
Cost of sales, exclusive of items below	$3,165.9	3,123.3	3,081.6	2,936.9	2,578.5
Selling, general and administrative (c)	$1,841.7	1,831.6	1,635.5	1,384.0	1,145.5
Depreciation and amortization	$ 133.1	127.5	113.2	99.5	81.1
Interest	$ 61.4	58.7	75.1	57.6	48.6
Earnings before income taxes	$ 398.7	409.7	406.7	374.4	316.6
Net earnings	$ 233.4	245.1	225.5	196.6	170.0
Net earnings as a percent of sales	4.2%	4.4%	4.2%	4.1%	4.1%
Weighted average number of common shares (a) (e)	46.9	50.1	50.6	50.4	50.5
Taxes (income, payroll, property, etc.) per share (a)	$ 6.22	5.70	5.88	5.99	4.66
Financial Position					
Total assets	$2,858.1	2,943.9	2,701.7	2,301.3	2,012.4
Land, buildings and equipment, net	$1,229.4	1,197.5	1,054.1	920.6	747.5
Working capital at year-end	$ 244.5	235.6	210.7	337.3	416.3
Long-term debt, excluding current portion	$ 362.6	464.0	331.9	348.6	377.5
Stockholders' equity	$1,224.6	1,227.4	1,232.2	1,145.4	1,020.7
Stockholders' equity per share (a)	$ 27.03	25.68	24.50	22.75	20.32
Other Statistics					
Working capital provided from operations	$ 348.3	401.6	353.6	317.8	262.7
Total dividends	$ 96.0	92.7	82.3	72.3	64.4
Gross capital expenditures	$ 282.4	308.0	287.3	246.6	196.5
Research and development	$ 63.5	60.6	53.8	45.4	44.4
Advertising media expenditures	$ 349.6	336.2	284.9	222.0	213.1
Wages, salaries and employee benefits	$1,121.6	1,115.2	1,028.4	907.0	781.2
Number of employees	80,297	81,186	75,893	71,225	66,032
Accumulated LIFO charge	$ 79.7	79.7	75.5	73.7	60.3
Common stock price range (a)	$ 57⅛– 41⅝	57¾– 38⅝	42⅛– 32⅝	35¾– 23⅜	28¼– 19

(a) Year priors to fiscal 1976 have been adjusted for the two-for-one stock split in October 1975.
(b) Amounts not restated for vacation accrual accounting change made in fiscal 1982.
(c) Includes redeployment gains or losses.
(d) Before discontinued operations.
(e) Years prior to fiscal 1983 include common share equivalents.
(f) In fiscal 1975, we changed from the FIFO to the LIFO method of accounting for selected inventories.

Source: General Mills, Inc., *Annual Report*, 1980–84.

May 27, 1979	May 28, 1978	May 29, 1977	May 30, 1976	May 25, 1975	May 26, 1974
$ 2.92	$ 2.72	$ 2.36	$ 2.04	$ 1.59	$ 1.59
17.0%	17.6%	17.1%	16.7%	14.6%	16.5%
1.12	.97	.79	.66	.58½	.53
3,745.0	3,243.0	2,909.4	2,645.0	2,308.9	2,000.1
2,347.7	2,026.1	1,797.5	1,663.9	1,537.7	1,288.8
1,021.3	883.8	807.9	704.5	546.3	495.4
73.3	58.6	48.1	46.7	41.8	36.3
38.8	29.3	26.7	29.4	36.2	28.5
263.9	245.2(d)	229.2	200.5	146.9	151.1
147.0	135.8	117.0	100.5	76.2	75.1
3.9%	4.2%	4.0%	3.8%	3.3%	3.8%
50.4	49.9	49.6	49.2	47.8	47.3
3.99	3.71	3.43	3.02	2.35	2.36
1,835.2	1,612.7	1,447.3	1,328.2	1,205.6	1,116.9
643.7	587.0	540.1	471.5	441.0	379.4
441.6	285.1	298.2	295.1	276.8	268.1
384.8	259.9	276.1	281.8	304.9	298.2
916.2	815.1	724.9	640.2	560.5	483.4
18.23	16.38	14.60	12.98	11.50	10.26
237.5	197.9	174.2	153.2	124.2	116.2
56.1	48.2	39.1	32.4	27.8	24.4
154.1	140.5	117.1	94.4	99.8	92.2
37.3	30.5	29.9	25.7	22.9	21.6
188.9	170.5	145.6	111.4	70.5	71.5
717.1	622.0	541.2	479.4	402.7	343.7
64,229	66,574	61,797	51,778	47,969	46,398
46.5	29.3	18.7	12.5	15.9	(f)
34⅛–	31½–	35⅜–	34⅛–	27¾–	33¼–
24	26¼	26½	23⅜	14⅛	23¼

EXHIBIT 3   GENERAL MILLS, INC. OPERATING INCOME ($ in millions, except earnings per share)

	1980	% Change	1981	% Change	1982	% Change	1983	% Change	1984E	% Change	1985E
Food Processing											
Cereals and Granola Products	$ 90.0	+ 10.8%	$ 99.7	+ 28.6%	$128.2	+ 2.3%	$131.2	+15.9%	$152.0	+ 8.6	$165.0
Snacks	38.0	+ 5.3	40.0	+ 10.0	44.0	+ 4.6	46.0	−60.9	18.0	+ 16.7	21.0
Flour Baking Mixes and Desserts	55.0	− 5.5	52.0	+ 13.5	59.0	− 3.4	57.0	+ 5.3	60.0	+ 5.0	63.0
Frozen and Refrigerated Products	6.0	− 50.0	3.0	+166.7	8.0	+ 25.0	10.0	+30.0	13.0	+ 30.8	17.0
Consumer Flour and Commercial	21.5	+ 7.0	23.0	+ 4.4	24.0	−0−	24.0	+12.5	27.0	+ 7.4	29.0
Total	$210.5	+ 3.4	$217.7	+ 20.9	$263.2	+ 1.9	$268.2	+ 0.7	$270.0	+ 9.3	$295.0
Restaurants											
Red Lobster	$ 46.0	+ 52.2	$ 70.0	+ 6.0	$ 74.2	− 1.6	$ 73.0	−12.3	$ 64.0	+ 9.4	$ 70.0
York Steak Houses	10.0	+ 10.0	11.0	+ 13.6	12.5	+ 4.0	13.0	+ 7.7	14.0	+ 7.1	15.0
Other	(3.3)	+ 72.7	(5.7)	+ 31.6	(7.5)	− 20.0	(6.0)	−50.0	(3.0)	NM	−0−
Total	$ 52.7	+ 42.9	$ 75.3	+ 5.2	$ 79.2	+ 1.0	$ 80.0	− 6.2	$ 75.0	+ 13.3	$ 85.0
Crafts, Games and Toys											
Parker Brothers	$26.0	+ 7.7	$ 28.0	− 35.7	$ 18.0	+142.2	$ 43.6	−77.1	$ 10.0	+100.0	$ 20.0
Kenner	24.0	+ 8.3	26.0	+ 50.0	39.0	+ 18.0	46.0	+18.0	50.0	+ 20.0	60.0
Fundimensions	−0−	NM	3.0	+ 33.0	4.0	NM	(3.0)	−33.3	(2.0)	NM	3.0
International	10.1	+ 34.7	13.6	+ 33.8	18.2	− 1.1	18.0	−16.7	15.0	+ 13.3	17.0
Total	$ 60.1	+ 17.5	$ 70.6	+ 12.2	$ 79.2	+ 32.1	$104.6	−30.2	$ 73.0	+ 37.0	$100.0
Apparel and Accessories											
David Crystal	$ 31.0	+101.6	$ 62.5	− 4.0	$ 60.0	− 25.0	$ 45.0	−40.0	$ 27.0	− 7.4	$ 25.0
Monet	21.7	+ 15.2	25.0	−0−	25.0	− 12.4	21.9	+ 5.0	23.0	+ 8.7	25.0
Ship n´ Shore and Other	(9.0)	NM	−0−	NM	16.7	− 46.1	9.0	+11.1	10.0	+ 20.0	12.0
Total	$ 43.7	+100.2	$ 87.5	+ 16.2	$101.7	− 25.4	$ 75.9	−21.0	$ 60.0	+ 3.3	$ 62.0
Specialty Retailing	26.4	− 50.0	13.2	NM	(11.9)	NM	16.1	+73.9	28.0	+ 35.7	38.0
Total Operating Profits	$393.4	+ 18.0	$464.3	+ 10.1	$511.4	+ 6.5	$544.8	− 7.2	$506.0	+ 14.6	$580.0
Unallocated Expenses	28.2	+ 14.5	32.3	− 8.4	29.6	+158.1	76.4(1)	−41.1	45.0	+ 11.1	50.0
Interest Expense	48.6	+ 18.5	57.6	+ 30.4	75.1	− 21.8	58.7	+ 2.2	60.0	+ 8.3	65.0
Pretax Income	$316.6	+ 18.3	$374.4	+ 8.6	$406.7	+ 0.7	$409.7	− 2.2	$401.0	+ 15.9	$465.0
Taxes	146.6	+ 21.3	177.8	+ 1.9	181.2	+ 9.2	164.6	+ 2.2	168.3	+ 21.5	204.5
Net Income	$170.0	+ 15.6	$196.6	+ 14.7	$225.5	+ 8.7	$245.1	− 5.1	$232.7	+ 11.9	$260.5
Average Shares (millions)	50.4	−0−	50.4	+ 0.4	50.6	− 1.0	50.1	− 6.2	47.0	− 1.1	46.5
Earnings Per Share	$3.37	+ 15.7	$3.90	+ 14.4	$4.46	+ 9.6	$4.89	+ 1.2	$4.95	+ 13.1	$5.60

E—First Boston Corporation Estimates.

(1) Includes $12 million of TRASOP and $15 million of currency translation losses.

Source: First Boston Corporation, *Research Progress Report,* April 3, 1984.

EXHIBIT 4   FAMILY SPENDING PATTERNS BY INCOME CLASS

Percentage of Average Annual Expenditures by Product Category

Item	Average All Families	Under $5,000	$5,000– 10,000	$10,000– 15,000	$15,000– 20,000	$20,000– 25,000	$25,000 and Over
Food	19.5%	22.3%	20.8%	20.0%	19.3%	18.3%	16.4%
At Home	17.1	20.5	18.7	17.5	16.8	15.7	13.6
Away from Home	2.1	1.4	1.8	2.1	2.4	2.4	2.5
Other	0.3	0.4	0.3	0.4	0.1	0.2	0.3
Alcoholic Beverages	1.0	0.8	1.0	1.0	1.0	0.9	1.1
Tobacco	1.6	2.0	1.9	1.8	1.6	1.4	0.9
Housing	25.4	33.3	27.3	24.8	23.7	22.0	23.0
Shelter	16.3	22.2	17.7	15.8	15.0	13.9	14.4
Utilities	5.3	6.5	5.7	5.4	5.2	4.6	4.3
Other	3.8	4.6	3.9	3.6	3.5	3.5	4.2
Furnishings	5.1	3.8	4.5	4.9	5.5	5.9	5.9
Appliances	1.3	1.3	1.4	1.4	1.4	1.4	1.1
Furniture	1.8	1.2	1.5	1.6	1.9	2.1	2.2
Other	2.0	1.3	1.6	1.9	2.2	2.4	2.6
Clothing & Acc.	8.2	6.7	7.7	7.9	8.3	8.6	9.6
Mens/Boys	2.7	1.7	2.2	2.7	3.0	3.2	3.3
Womens/Girls	3.9	3.1	3.7	3.7	3.9	4.1	5.0
Materials etc.	1.5	1.8	1.8	1.5	1.4	1.3	1.3
Transportation	20.4	15.4	19.9	22.1	21.7	21.6	19.8
Automobile	19.8	14.5	19.2	21.6	21.2	21.1	19.0
Other	0.6	0.9	0.7	0.5	0.5	0.5	0.8
Medical Care	6.1	7.2	7.0	5.9	5.6	5.6	5.5
Health Ins.	2.5	3.4	3.0	2.6	2.1	2.1	1.9
Uninsured Exp.	3.6	3.8	4.0	3.3	3.5	3.4	3.6
Personal Care	1.3	1.2	1.3	1.2	1.2	1.3	1.4
Recreation	8.2	5.3	6.3	7.7	8.6	10.3	11.3
Vacation	3.0	1.9	2.2	2.6	3.1	3.8	4.7
Other	5.2	3.4	4.1	5.1	5.5	6.5	6.6
Reading	1.8	1.0	1.0	1.4	1.9	2.7	3.3
Other	1.3	1.0	1.2	1.3	1.4	1.4	1.9

Source: Equity Research, E.F. Hutton and Company, Inc., May 9, 1983.

EXHIBIT 5 FAMILY SPENDING PATTERNS BY AGE OF HEAD OF HOUSEHOLD

Percentage of Average Annual Expenditures by Product Category

Item	Average All Families	Under 25	25–34	35–44	45–54	55–64	65 and Over
Food	19.4%	11.5%	15.9%	21.6%	20.5%	20.3%	22.8%
At Home	17.0	9.1	13.3	18.7	18.0	18.1	21.1
Away from Home	2.2	1.9	2.3	2.6	2.2	1.9	1.5
Other	0.2	0.5	0.3	0.3	0.3	0.3	0.2
Alcoholic Beverages	1.0	1.2	1.2	0.9	0.9	0.9	0.6
Tobacco	1.6	1.7	1.6	1.6	1.7	1.8	1.2
Housing	25.4	31.4	29.1	23.9	21.8	22.7	28.7
Shelter	16.2	24.5	20.3	15.2	13.4	12.9	15.8
Utilities	5.3	3.4	4.6	5.2	5.2	5.7	7.4
Other	3.9	3.5	4.2	3.5	3.2	4.0	5.5
Furnishings	5.1	5.4	6.1	5.6	4.7	4.3	4.0
Appliances	1.3	1.6	1.5	1.3	1.1	1.1	1.1
Furniture	1.8	2.3	2.4	2.1	1.6	1.2	1.1
Other	2.0	1.5	2.2	2.2	2.0	2.0	1.8
Clothing & Acc.	8.3	8.3	8.6	9.2	8.6	7.7	6.4
Men/Boys	2.7	2.6	3.0	3.3	3.0	2.4	1.5
Women/Girls	4.0	3.4	3.7	4.5	4.3	3.9	3.6
Materials etc.	1.6	2.3	1.9	1.4	1.3	1.4	1.3
Transportation	20.2	25.5	20.1	19.2	22.0	21.3	14.9
Automobile	19.6	25.0	19.6	18.6	21.3	20.7	14.1
Other	0.6	0.5	0.5	0.6	0.7	0.6	0.8
Medical Care	6.1	3.8	5.1	5.1	5.7	7.0	10.2
Health Ins.	2.5	1.6	2.0	1.9	2.2	3.0	4.8
Uninsured Exp.	3.6	2.2	3.1	3.2	3.5	4.0	5.4
Personal Care	1.3	0.5	0.8	1.2	1.4	1.7	1.7
Recreation	8.3	8.6	8.7	8.3	8.0	8.5	7.2
Vacation	3.1	2.0	2.6	2.6	3.1	3.8	4.0
Other	5.2	6.6	6.1	5.7	4.9	4.7	3.2
Reading	1.9	1.1	1.4	1.8	3.1	2.1	0.8
Other	1.3	0.9	1.2	1.4	1.4	1.6	1.4

Source: Equity Research, E.F. Hutton and Company Inc., May 9, 1983.

EXHIBIT 6   ESTIMATED RETAIL FOOD DOLLAR SALES ($ Millions)

Category	Industry			General Mills			Estimated Market Share		
	1982	1981	1980	1982	1981	1980	1982	1981	1980
Dry Packaged Foods									
RTE Cereal	$3,260.0	$3,200.0	$2,420.0	$ 665.0	$ 610.0	$ 490.0	23.0%	19.1%	20.2%
Desserts	1,100.0	1,000.0	828.0	410.0	375.0	300.0	39.3	37.5	36.2
Family Flour	460.0	470.0	427.0	155.0	160.0	180.0	33.7	34.0	42.1
Instant Potatoes	190.0	195.0	140.0	90.0	60.0	50.0	47.4	30.8	35.7
Portable Bars (Granola)	220.0	200.0	104.0	145.0	110.0	45.0	65.9	55.0	43.3
Biscuit Mixes	125.0	110.0	104.0	105.0	100.0	75.0	84.0	90.9	72.1
Helper Dinners & Casseroles	110.0	110.0	84.0	75.0	100.0	58.0	68.2	90.9	69.0
	$5,465.0	$5,285.0	$4,107.0	$1,645.0	$1,515.0	$1,198.0	30.1	28.7	29.2
Frozen Foods									
Processed Fish	650.0	650.0	646.0	130.0	150.0	140.0	20.0%	23.1%	21.7%
Pizza	780.0	950.0	667.0	50.0	40.0	25.0	6.4	4.2	3.7
	$1,430.0	$1,600.0	$1,313.0	$ 180.0	$ 190.0	$ 165.0	12.6	11.9	12.6
Refrigerated									
Yogurt	$ 550.0	$ 525.0	$ 450.0	$ 100.0	$ 80.0	$ 30.0	18.2%	15.2%	6.7%
Total	$7,445.0	$7,410.0	$5,870.0	$1,925.0	$1,785.0	$1,393.0	25.8%	24.1%	23.7%

Note: European, Canadian, Foodservice and Commercial flour and seafood sales represent the remainder of annual sales.

Source: Equity Research, E.F. Hutton and Company, Inc., May 9, 1983.

EXHIBIT 7   OTHER MARKET STATISTICS

SALES OF TOYS/GAMES BY MAJOR CATEGORIES (in Millions of Dollars—Based on Manufacturers' Prices)

Category	1978	1979	1980	1981	1982
Dolls & accessories	308	288	308	395	600
Games & puzzles	534	539	601	634	569
Preschool toys & playsets	365	388	386	404	376
Electronic games (nonvideo)	112	375	476	276	371
Video games	—	—	455	1,090	2,068
Stuffed animals & puppets	243	244	268	307	282
Unpowered toy cars, trucks, boats & planes	155	190	256	331	279
Riding toys (excluding street bicycles)	154	178	176	230	254
Space toys	187	192	167	186	158

Source: Toy Manufacturers of America in "Basic Analysis—Leisure Time," Standard & Poor's *Industry Surveys*, October 13, 1983.

FOOD-AWAY-FROM-HOME MARKET (Food and Drink Sales, in Billions of Dollars)

Market	R1981	R1982	% chg. 1981–82	E1983
Commercial feeding				
Restaurants, lunchrooms	$ 39.3	$ 42.0	6.9%	$ 45.4
Limited menu restaurants	30.8	33.7	9.4	37.3
Bars and taverns	8.3	8.7	4.8	9.2
Hotel and motel restaurants	6.9	7.4	7.2	8.1
Cafeterias	2.3	2.4	4.3	2.6
Other	18.2	18.6	2.2	19.9
Total	105.8	112.8	6.6	122.5
Institutional feeding	18.6	19.6	5.4	20.7
Military feeding	0.7	0.7	—	0.8
Grand total	$125.1	$133.1	6.4%	$144.0

E = Estimated, R = Revised.

Source: National Restaurant Association in "Basic Analysis—Retailing," Standard & Poor's *Industry Surveys*, January 26, 1984.

EXHIBIT 7 *(Continued)*

CHILD POPULATION IN THE U.S. (in Thousands)

Age	1983	1985	% Change 1983–85	1990	% Change 1983–90
Under 5	17,846	18,453	+3.4%	19,198	+7.6%
5–9	15,960	16,611	+4.1%	18,591	+16.5%
10–14	17,768	16,797	−5.5%	16,793	−5.5%

Source: U.S. Department of Commerce, Bureau of the Census in "Current Analysis—Leisure Time," Standard & Poor's *Industry Surveys*, August 9, 1984.

BIRTH STATISTICS (in Thousands)

Year	Number of Births	Number of First Births	First Births as % of Total Births
E1990	3,849,000	—	—
E1985	3,826,000	—	—
E1984	3,788,000	—	—
E1983	3,614,000	—	—
E1982	3,704,000	—	—
1981	3,629,238	1,553,665	42.81
1980	3,612,258	1,545,604	42.79
1979	3,494,396	1,479,260	42.33
1978	3,333,279	1,401,491	42.05
1977	3,326,632	1,387,143	41.70
1976	3,167,788	1,324,811	41.82
1975	3,144,198	1,319,126	41.95
1974	3,159,958	1,314,194	41.59
1973	3,136,965	1,243,358	39.64
1972	3,258,411	1,289,257	39.57
1971	3,555,970	1,375,668	38.69
1970	3,731,386	1,430,680	38.34

Source: U.S. Department of Commerce, Bureau of the Census in "Current Analysis—Leisure Time," Standard & Poor's *Industry Surveys*, August 9, 1984.

EXHIBIT 8   COMPARATIVE FINANCIALS—1982

	Revenues ($ Billions)	Return on Assets	Return on Sales
Food Processing			
Beatrice	9.19	0.9	0.5
Borden Inc.	4.11	6.6	4.0
Campbell Soup	2.95	8.3	5.1
Carnation Co.	3.38	11.4	5.6
Consolidated Foods	6.04	6.6	2.5
Dart & Kraft	10.00	6.9	3.5
General Foods	8.25	6.9	3.5
General Mills	5.55	8.9	4.4
H.J. Heinz	3.74	9.9	5.7
International Multifoods	1.11	7.5	3.2
Kellogg Co.	2.37	17.7	9.6
Nabisco Brands	5.87	8.4	5.4
Pillsbury Co.	3.68	5.8	3.8
Quaker Oats	2.71	8.1	4.4
Ralston Purina	4.80	4.4	1.9
Toys			
Coleco Ind.	0.51	23.3	8.8
Milton Bradley Co.	0.36	6.4	5.3
Restaurants			
Chart House	0.38	6.3	4.9
Denny's Inc.	0.96	6.4	3.8
Victoria Station	0.11	NM	—
Apparel Manufacturers			
Manhattan Ind.	0.40	4.3	1.9
Philips-Van Heusen	0.46	4.1	1.9
Warnaco	0.50	8.5	4.7

Source: Data compiled from various analyses in Standard & Poor's *Industry Surveys.*

AT&T BELL LABORATORIES

Bell Telephone Laboratories was one of the largest and most successful laboratories in the world. Until the court decisions of 1983 and the associated agreements to break up American Telephone and Telegraph Company, the Laboratories had been jointly owned and operated by AT&T Corporation and Western Electric Company. The Laboratories budget was then over $2 billion and its activities had been decentralized to several locations. One of the longer established and more famous locations was at Murray Hill, New Jersey. Here in a "university setting" over 10,000 people were engaged in technical activities ranging from fundamental research to development.* The fundamental research activity (Research Department) was less than $\frac{1}{10}$ the size of the Development Department.

Although relationships between various groups had shifted somewhat from time to time, the basic philosophy, policies, and practices of the Laboratories had been relatively consistent over several decades. Without attempting to reflect their full complexity, some of the most important of these are described briefly below.

---

* *Definitions:*

Fundamental Research *seeks basic principles and relationships underlying physical phenomena without regard to the specific applications of such knowledge.*

Applied Research *further crystallizes fundamental knowledge and demonstrates its potential utility through use of bench scale apparatus.*

Development *applies all available knowledge to the solution of an identified technical problem. The end point of development is reduction to practice in workable prototype form.*

Engineering *refines a prototype (or operating) system or device for commercial exploitation, or other practical end uses.*

Case copyright © 1984 by James Brian Quinn. Research assistant—Allie J. Quinn. The generous cooperation of AT&T Bell Laboratories is gratefully acknowledged.

RESEARCH DEPARTMENT

The Research Department sought further understanding of natural phenomena. The objective of Research was to develop a scientific base for new communication technologies 10–20 years before their ultimate need as system devices. Because the company had defined its activity as that of producing communications services, its knowledge base had to cover all scientific areas which might contribute to a better understanding of human communications and any means for one machine to communicate with another.

The Research Department was "a window between the AT&T–Bell System and the world." Scientists from all over the world were welcomed on visits to the department, and Research Department personnel were welcomed in scientific circles elsewhere. The department's aim was to be in the center of the world's knowledge stream. It kept up with communication technology created elsewhere and was expected to make a "fair share" of the fundamental contributions to the world's communications knowledge. The Research Department felt that it must make its knowledge freely available to other groups if it hoped to be informed of what others were doing. One of the main functions of Research was "to be able to appreciate technology as soon as it became available." This insured that its parent corporations could exploit such knowledge as soon and as intelligently as possible. And no outside group would be able to keep the operating corporations from using important new technologies.

The Research Department was not supposed to create knowledge and technologies only useful in the communications business. The group was not held to any return on investment standard. Instead the parent corporation assumed that if Research produced enough really new knowledge in areas of interest to communications, it would probably pay for itself over a period of time. Several devices resulting from fundamental research had probably more than justified the entire Laboratories' activities for hundreds of years. These included: (1) The photovoltaic effect, (2) the transistor, (3) the MASER (laser), (4) the carrier system for transmission, and (5) "bubble memories" for computers. But Research had produced thousands of other useful principles of greater or lesser value as well.

Research Planning

The heart of research planning at Bell was "to recruit top flight scientists and let them think up something to do." Management's task was not to select problems, but to find areas where knowledge would expand most rapidly. Highly qualified people were hired to work in each such area. These individuals then selected their own problems. Management tried to stimulate and encourage their imaginations and to provide them with the material and personnel backing they needed. Management tried to create an environment in which the individual scientist could be most creative.

The Research Department's organization was flexible. Section heads had to ensure that there were no duplications or gaps in inquiries made in their knowledge fields. But the organization was never used to confine the imaginations of individual researchers. Researchers could pursue their problems into any knowledge area, even though this area might be the primary responsibility of another group. If research developed in certain directions section heads might find they did not have "their people" under their control. Members of one section might work directly with members of other sections whose section heads could become more familiar with their work than their own section heads. The scientists would then look to the former for consultation and guidance.

When Mitchell Marcus, one of the world's leading "speech recognition" scientists, first came to Bell Laboratories he noted, ". . . When

I came for my visit, I was just amazed by the people and the attitude. . . . There was and is a community of people who talk to each other depending only upon what their interests are and not their fields. At a place like M.I.T., for example, psychologists work with psychologists, linguists work with linguists, and computer people work with computer people. They don't get close to each other unless they are writing an interdisciplinary grant proposal. When I came here . . . everyone said you sort of do what you are interested in, and if it's good work, you were fine. . . . It took me a while after I got here to realize that it really is true. The other thing that impressed me about people in this place, and continues to impress me, was, that unlike many people in academic life, people here don't sell themselves constantly. In a very soft spoken way someone will show you something they have built, but only after telling you what the limitations of it are."[1]

No one knew "how much" should be spent in total on fundamental studies, only that Research should do effective work in some selected fundamental fields. Section heads said they did not know within $\pm$ 50% how much effort should be expended in any particular area or precisely what problems should be attacked. Selection of specific scientific problems and approaches was largely left up to individual researchers and their colleagues.

Over a period of time scientists slowly redirected their own researches. They tended to move toward those problems which were most challenging. Since a major program might run over 20 years, time allowed individual researchers to change activities without impairing their freedom to grow in their selected fields. Section heads said that it would be impossible to "direct" fundamental research from above. They pointed out that their scientists knew as much about their chosen fields as anyone in the world. It would, therefore, only be brash for a supervisor to tell them which areas to look into or how to investigate them. Managers were supposed to be able to appreciate research when they saw it, but not to direct research in detail.

As Bela Julesz, world expert on optical information, said, "The tradition at Bell Laboratories has been to help each other. We are employed here not to teach, but rather to consult. There is an artificial emphasis here on cramped space. When I was a visiting professor in Zurich, my office was bigger than this whole corridor. . . . Here the idea is that distances are so constricted that you can, if you have an idea, rush over to someone who is an expert on, say, stochastic processes or invented I don't know what electronic device and consult him. It's so nearby that it takes you less time to go over and see him than to suppress the idea [as you would in a university setting]. . . . Mitchell Marcus said "You discover that a guy you thought was a psychologist is really a physicist by training. People here are sort of widely interested—interested in lots of things—and they collaborate with each other."[1]

But scientists were not allowed to simply wander unchecked. They were expected to be "successful" in handling the problems they chose. Success might be defined as obtaining complete, partial, or indisputably negative answers to major problems or sub-problems. Scientists were informally encouraged to look into those aspects of their problems most applicable to the communications business, but research managers tried to use as few of the pressures of authority as possible. They simply tried to discuss problems with researchers "as one scientist to another." The department's philosophy was that results were determined not by how large a research effort was, but by how smart each of its scientists were. No formal schedule of either effort or intended results existed. Nor were actual results formally compared against any numerical standards.

If scientists' results did not seem to research managers to warrant backing their activities further, they were encouraged in new directions, stimulated to go into other phases of the Laboratories' activities, or motivated to transfer to another company or a university. The standards used in judging a person's work were very subjective. No attempt was made to quantify output standards. The individual's performance was compared against a composite standard of how "a good researcher" would have performed the same task. This standard existed only in the minds of the researcher's supervisors and peers.

In addition, each individual was compared to all other scientists in the department annually. The scientists' performance decile was determined and displayed against their wage decile groupings on an "age-wage" chart. Each individual's salary was reviewed in relation to the wage decile which would correspond to his/her performance decile. The overall wage structure was constantly compared with that of other research groups in the area. As a result of this constant performance evaluation—and the fact that some scientists voluntarily moved out of the department either to follow one of their inventions into development or to accept positions which were more attractive to them personally—only about one in ten of its highly selected scientific group remained in Research permanently.

The limit on how much research was done by the Research Department was established more by the limited availability of highly qualified scientists to do research in chosen areas than by funds limitations imposed by AT&T, Western Electric, or Bell Laboratories.

Sources of Information

Information on technological needs for the communications field flowed to Research from many sources. One source was the set of unsolved problems which were important to Development Department managers. Both formal channels (like memoranda, technical-economic studies, budget evaluations, activities, and technical progress reports) and informal channels (like luncheon or other non-routine get-togethers) were used by research managers to keep abreast of fundamental knowledge needed by operating groups. Research managers were informally "aware" of pressures from Western Electric or Bell System operating divisions to do work in one area vs. another. In addition, Systems Engineering, the long range technological planning section of Bell, tried to foresee the Corporation's technological needs 10–20 years ahead and reported these needs to Research managers. Systems Engineering also watched Research output and tried to see how it could be applied to future problems. Research managers, all top flight scientists themselves, kept an active watch on the literature in their fields and attempted to insure that all pertinent knowledge areas were adequately staffed.

Occasionally, Western Electric or a Bell System operating division would come to the Research Department for an explanation of specific unusual phenomena or to have fundamental technological problems solved. A special aspect was the Engineering Complaint System. If an operating company defined a particular technical operating problem through this system, the Bell Laboratories system had to specify within about 30 days either the problem's solution or how the Laboratories would attempt to solve the problem. Routine follow up occurred until the problem was solved. The degree to which Development and operating engineering groups asked Research to consult was regarded as a measure of the latter's success. Periodic formal "seminars" were held to inform operating technical groups of research progress and to exchange views with these groups. At these seminars research scientists gave technical lectures on their activities and encouraged operating personnel to ask questions. Research personnel also reported their activities in company-wide reports and in formal technical publications at professional meetings or in professional journals.

SYSTEMS ENGINEERING

The Systems Engineering Department acted as a liaison department between Bell Laboratories and the rest of the AT&T, Western Electric, and the Bell System complex. Its specific responsibility was long range technological planning. It discharged this responsibility by obtaining from operating divisions information on their present and future technological needs. To these were added the technical-economic systems problems which Systems Engineers foresaw themselves. Systems Engineering tried to think in terms of system-wide approaches rather than in terms of solutions to local problems.

Desired solutions were expressed as "black boxes" of needed communications gear. How these boxes could be constructed was not a problem for Systems Engineering (S.E.). What the box must do was its province. After recognizing a need, S.E. wrote up an objective specification telling Research and Development what the problem was, what the input and output characteristics were of devices needed to solve it, and sometimes what approaches to the problem looked promising. S.E. estimated the cost, demand, labor savings, dollar savings, improved service benefits, (etc.) the devices might create. If these specifications were approved by top laboratory and corporate management, they were sent to Development to produce prototype devices which were subjected to extensive tests for reliability and systems compatibility before they were accepted for use in the Bell System. Several parallel programs were almost always started for important new technological systems.

Development might in turn look to Research for solutions to basic scientific problems before it could complete its task. Systems Engineering tried to look at least 20 years ahead at all times. Its plans were flexible, but it constantly had to think ahead to the communication systems the next generation would need. Facilities installed today, but useless in the future because of technological changes, could cost the parent corporations billions of dollars in replacement losses. It was Systems Engineering's mission to avoid such waste and to help insure that Bell's operating divisions had available the proper equipment to provide the world's best telephone service.

The Systems Engineering group had access to a great deal of market data drawn up by market research groups of the parent corporations and operating divisions. The number of subscribers, their location, economic status, service requirements, call patterns, etc. were constantly analyzed and forecast by these groups. Systems Engineering was not expected to develop such raw data itself. If it needed figures not presently available, it had to request help from other business research groups in the AT&T-Bell system.

As a result of its forecasts Systems Engineering prepared a booklet of projects with assigned priorities. These proposed projects, and those in process in Development, were reviewed periodically by corporate top management. The status review for each project or "case" examined the information shown in the exhibit below.

No work could begin or continue on a case without approval of its budget by the parent corporations.

SETTING OBJECTIVES AND GOALS

All work in either the Research or the Development Department was carried out under "cases." In Research cases were originated by the scientist and supervisor who were going to perform and oversee the work. The broad objectives of the research, hypotheses to be tested, syntheses or tests to be made, avenues of investigation, etc. might be described in the case write-up. The more basic the research, the more general the write-up. Some cases estimated the applications of the research's results. Others might include a forecast of the economic benefits which might be forthcoming if the project was successful. The latter types of projects were generally in the more applied phases of research. Estimated costs were included with each new case. But this was not an inflexible control limit and might even be expressed as a range of possible costs.

Once inaugurated, cases were formally reviewed annually by Bell Laboratories management, by Western Electric, and by AT&T. For this review the case description included: progress, if any, made in the preceding year; a description of the project objective; and a forecast of activities and costs for the forthcoming year. The case description of the work for the forthcoming year might merely be "investigations will be continued." A summation of the forecast costs of research cases for the forthcoming year equaled the requested budget for the Research Division for that year.

In the early fall advanced copies of cases were sent to AT&T and to Western Electric for review and comments. Plans were revised on the basis of the resulting exchange of views. A final set of cases and summary budget information then went to the Research Committee for final approval. Representatives of the Laboratories, Western Electric and AT&T sat on this committee. Specific cases then were approved by Western Electric and AT&T, funds were allocated by the parent corporations for the forthcoming year's projects and a revised cumulative budget was issued for each case. AT&T allocated its share of Bell Laboratories' basic research costs to Bell System operating divisions through an (approximately) 1% service charge on all revenues. The allowability of this charge as a cost was negotiated

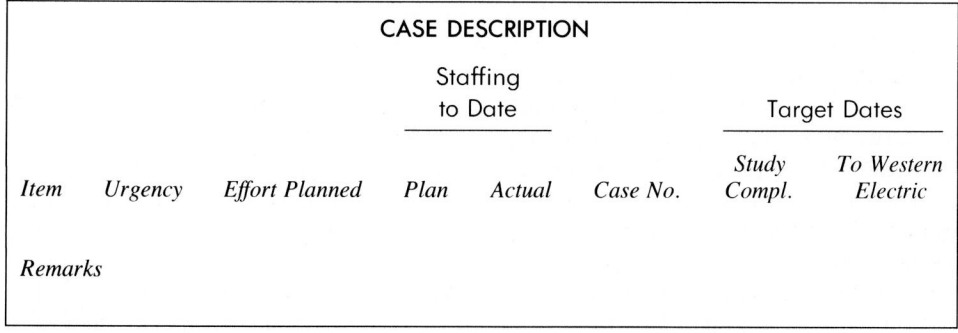

			Staffing to Date			Target Dates	
Item	Urgency	Effort Planned	Plan	Actual	Case No.	Study Compl.	To Western Electric
Remarks							

with each of the rate setting bodies controlling the system's prices.

Budget vs. Actual Expenditures

Individual case budgets were, of course, originated in the Laboratories. The personnel to be assigned to the case were discussed in early fall. To their projected wages were added a stable level of direct charges and any extraordinary costs anticipated for the coming year. At budget reviews actual vs. budgeted costs per case were compared period by period. In addition, a graph compared a cumulative actual vs. budgeted case costs. A good correlation between actual and budget was normally experienced. Since effort, not results, was scheduled in Research, budgets tended to be within 1–2% of actual.

The parent corporations had relatively little to say about the selection of areas for investigation in basic research. In essence, an attempt was made to obtain the most qualified scientists and research administrators. Top corporation executives then relied on these persons to make fundamental inquiries which were of general interest in the communications field. No attempt was made by the parent corporations to dictate fields of inquiry for the Laboratories staff. Corporate officers annually reviewed expenditures for and general fields of basic inquiry, not for the purpose of suggesting new fields but to ensure a balance between fundamental and more applied research expenditures.

EVALUATION OF THE RESEARCH PROGRAM'S PROFITABILITY

AT&T did not make routine financial evaluations of Bell Laboratories' total contributions. The economic studies before program inauguration were the only computed justifications for the various projects of the Laboratories. Some major programs were undertaken upon which no economic justification was attempted.

It was the feeling of many of the AT&T-Bell System executive group that it would be impossible to price out the cost of a given benefit from a research program. "The continuity of a major development defies identification of all of its costs or benefits within any reasonable time span." Developments coming to fruition in 1987 might depend upon the 1910 solution of fundamental mathematical parameters. In turn, a device introduced in 1987 might be improved by further research until the 2005 model bore little resemblance to its 1987 operating counterpart. From conception of a principle to an ultimate operating design is a continuum of joint costs and common benefits. A top financial officer of AT&T said: "From an accounting point of view one simply cannot figure the true cost or benefit of a given development." The parent corporations also had no routine by which they compared the actual benefits of a program with the forecasts of the economic study which might have originally justified it.

Periodically AT&T had been forced by various rate setting groups to justify the charges it made to a regional operating company for Bell Laboratories work. In these cases the corporation had been able to go back over an extensive period of time, list some of the advances the Laboratories had created in that period, estimate the value of these advances to the particular operating company, and prove such an overwhelming margin of contribution that the "Bell Laboratories service charge" had never been disallowed. It was possible that the development of one major technique could have justified the Laboratories' existence in perpetuity. The impact of mechanical dialing, the carrier system, the transistor, or the MASER (laser) were too vast to estimate precisely. Managers felt that over the years the Laboratories had paid its way to the American people with a substantial margin to spare. And they felt that further research efforts should continue to pay large dividends.

The AT&T attitude toward evaluating the results of fundamental research was expressed by one corporate officer as follows: "It would be fruitless for non-technical top managers to try to assess the details of a broad based fundamental research and development program. That is why the company hires research executives.''

However, in evaluating the effectiveness of its overall research program, AT&T management did consider the following questions:

1. Did the Laboratories produce its "fair share" of important discoveries? "Fair share" was defined over a long period of time by management judgment.

2. Did the American telephone system more adequately serve the population than its foreign or domestic counterparts?

3. Were the operating companies buying and satisfied with Western Electric equipment? Operating companies could purchase equipment from any source.

4. Was the patent trading position improving? This was a subjective evaluation.

5. Were the operating divisions and top management personnel satisfied with the technical and administrative efforts of Bell Laboratories?

6. Had there been a satisfactory margin of contribution from the Laboratories over the years? Other than the specific studies for rate setting bodies, no formal quantification of this criterion was attempted. The total value of the contributions was assessed by management judgment.

7. Was better service being provided the American consumer at a comparatively lower cost? Had the quality of U.S. communications service improved more than the cost of the service and at a rate faster (or more timely) than in other countries? This evaluation was again a matter of executive judgment.

THE NEW AT&T

In a series of historic court decisions and out of court agreements, the former Bell Laboratories complex was broken up in 1983. The ''New AT&T'' was freed from many former regulatory constraints and was allowed to compete in world markets on a scale not permitted in the past. Chariman C.L. Brown stated, ''AT&T is in the business of meeting customer needs, worldwide,

for electronic movement and management of information.''

At midnight, December 31, 1983 the Bell System's 22 local operating companies—providing telephone and communications services to individual regions of the U.S.—were grouped into seven regional holding companies quoted separately on the Stock Exchange and managed exclusively by their own officers and boards. These companies would: (1) provide local exchange services, (2) link customers to long distance carriers, (3) handle the ''Yellow Pages'' directories, (4) develop cellular mobile communications services, and (5) market customer premises equipment. Approximately 77% (or $115 billion of AT&T's total $149.5 billion in assets) was assigned to the divested units.

AT&T retained the long distance, R&D (dominantly Bell Laboratories), manufacturing (dominantly Western Electric) and other businesses not assigned to the divested units. On January 1, 1984 AT&T Technologies Inc. assumed the corporate charter of Western Electric and most of the unregulated portions of AT&T's remaining businesses. AT&T Information Systems Inc. began marketing enhanced consumer and business systems on a deregulated basis and took over previously installed equipment leased by specific customers. The Information Systems group was to be a completely independent subsidiary which could not be subsidized by revenues from other elements of the corporation. The group had two divisions: Advanced Information Systems (which would sell business products) and a Consumer Products Division. And AT&T Communications took over responsibility for AT&T's long distance services—which accounted for over half of AT&T's revenues—throughout the U.S. and to the rest of the world. At the start of 1984 AT&T had over $34 billion in assets and some 373,000 employees. While the corporation lost its regulated local businesses, it was free to pursue new opportunities in whatever areas looked promising. Although Western Electric lacked its competitors' experienced marketing groups, it had long term relations with the former Bell operating companies that gave it some initial advantages over others. Still the operating companies were "as free as a pig on ice" to buy from anyone and would doubtless exercise that freedom to their advantage.

AT&T's stated goal was to improve its past 12–13% return on equity for its regulated businesses to the new level of 17.5% approved by FCC. Its unregulated sector goal was "a higher return, as good or better than that realized by other well positioned, high technology companies." AT&T would both manufacture and sell in other countries, as well as the U.S. Its worldwide business interests would be managed by AT&T International. 1984 forecasts in its Prospectus were: $56 billion revenues, $2.1 billion net income (AT), and EPS of $2.02. Other summary financials are in Exhibit 1.

AT&T Bell Laboratories

Although it reported formally through the AT&T Technologies unit to AT&T headquarters, Bell Laboratories was kept essentially intact as a support for all elements in the AT&T complex. In 1984 AT&T expressed its intent "to maintain the funding level for Bell Laboratories research efforts" while aligning development activities more toward its new strategic business units, i.e.: Network Systems (communications switching, transmission, (etc.) systems), Information Systems (blending telecommunications and data processing), Consumer Products (retail sales of multifunctional home telecommunications), Technology Systems (components, electronics, computer, and government activities). Former Western Electric operations were expected to underwrite some 60% of the total Laboratories budget, former Long Lines activities some 30%, and AT&T corporate most of the basic research activities (about 10% of 1984's overall $1.8 billion budget). Some 400 Bell Laboratories people

(mostly engaged in product design and development) were formally shifted to AT&T Information Systems. Another 3000 joined a Central Services Laboratory serving all operating phone companies until 1987, per the divestiture agreement. In 1984 this left some 18,000 people in Bell Laboratories *per se*.

Many changes were expected in Bell Laboratories policies and structures, especially in the patent area where AT&T had operated under a consent decree in 1956. To avoid a breakup of the Bell System at that time AT&T had agreed to provide all U.S. companies with licenses at "reasonable fees". In 1984 Bell Labs held some 31,800 patents (about one per day of its existence) and published some 2,000 articles per year. Licensing brought in about $40 million per year. The divestiture agreement left AT&T with powerful technological capabilities, but it now faced an IBM of greater size than itself and Japanese and European competitors with superb technical skills and a worldwide presence. How AT&T and Bell Labs would prosper in this new environment was an open question. More urgent was what kind of adjustments Bell Laboratories' new president, Ian Ross, would have to make in the posture of one of the world's great laboratories.

QUESTIONS

1. What was the strategic purpose of the Laboratories prior to the breakup of the Bell System? After the breakup?
2. Evaluate the Laboratories past policies and planning systems in light of these goals. What form of management control is appropriate to such creative entities?
3. What must be changed as a result of the AT&T breakup?

EXHIBIT 1   FINANCIAL POSITION AT&T—1983

Dollars in Millions (000,000) Except Per Share Amounts		1983	1982	1981	1980	1979
Revenues	Local service	$ 30,275	$ 28,986	$ 25,553	$ 22,449	$ 20,208
	Toll service	34,529	33,257	30,189	26,051	23,371
	Other (including other income)	5,044	3,514	3,339	3,049	2,604
		69,848	65,757	59,081	51,549	46,183
Expenses	Operating	51,114	45,025	39,346	34,305	30,236
	Income taxes on operations	3,371	4,931	4,119	3,581	3,607
	Other operating taxes	5,309	4,879	4,430	3,928	3,602
	Interest	4,307	3,930	4,363	3,768	3,083
		64,101	58,765	52,258	45,582	40,528
Income before extraordinary charge and cumulative effect of a change in accounting principle		5,747	6,992	6,823	5,967	5,655
Extraordinary charge-net of taxes		(5,498)	—	—	—	—
Prior years cumulative effect of a change in accounting for deferred income taxes		—	287	—	—	—
Net Income		249	7,279	6,823	5,967	5,655
Preferred dividend requirements		127	142	146	150	156
Income applicable to common shares		$ 122	$ 7,137	$ 6,677	$ 5,817	$ 5,499
Earnings per common share		$ .13	$ 8.40	$ 8.47	$ 8.04	$ 8.01
Based on average shares outstanding (in thousands)		936,801	849,550	788,178	723,516	686,109
Amounts before 1983 extraordinary charge and pro forma amounts assuming the 1982 change in accounting for deferred income taxes had been applied retroactively:						
Income applicable to common shares		$ 5,620	$ 6,850	$ 6,726	$ 5,863	$ 5,532
Earnings per common share		$ 6.00	$ 8.06	$ 8.53	$ 8.10	$ 8.06
Total assets		$149,530	$148,186	$137,750	$125,553	$113,444
Long and intermediate term debt		$ 44,810	$ 44,105	$ 43,877	$ 41,255	$ 37,168
Pref. shares sub. to mandatory redemption		$ 1,523	$ 1,550	$ 1,563	$ 1,575	$ 1,588
Conv. pref. shares subj. to redemption		—	$ 301	$ 336	$ 385	$ 433
Dividends declared per common share		$ 5.85	$ 5.40	$ 5.40	$ 5.00	$ 5.00
Ratio of earnings to fixed charges		2.77	3.58	3.26	3.34	3.76
Toll messages for yr. ended Dec. 31 (000,000)		19,732	19,323	18,643	17,457	16,193
WATS mess. for yr. ended Dec. 31 (000,000)		8,159	6,615	5,655	4,874	4,244
Charges for toll messages and WATS messages for the year ended December 31, 1983 account for about 36% and 11%, respectively, of total billed operating revenues.						
Network access lines in serv. at Dec. 31		87	85	84	82	79
Recurring charges—Network access lines in service for the year ended December 31, 1983 account for about 25% of total billed operating revenues.						

Source: AT&T, *Annual Report,* 1983.

EXHIBIT 1 (*Continued*)

STATEMENT OF INCOME AND REINVESTED EARNINGS

Dollars in Millions (Except Per Share Amounts)	Year 1983	Year 1982
OPERATING REVENUES		
Local service		
Service and equipment charges	$25,298.8	$24,633.7
Message charges	2,763.2	2,618.7
Public telephones	1,194.3	946.4
Private lines and other services	1,018.2	787.5
Toll service		
Message charges	23,053.3	23,356.7
WATS	6,825.6	5,565.0
Private lines and other services	4,649.8	4,334.7
Directory advertising and miscellaneous	5,515.8	3,623.7
Provision for uncollectibles	(915.8)	(773.4)
Total operating revenues	69,403.2	65,093.0
OPERATING EXPENSES		
Maintenance	15,548.0	14,986.2
Depreciation	9,854.2	8,734.5
Network and operator services	4,034.9	3,910.2
Marketing and customer services	6,641.1	6,126.6
Financial operations	2,194.8	1,882.0
Directory	1,335.5	1,218.3
Research and systems enginnering	862.2	610.6
Provision for pensions and other employee benefits (D)	5,025.2	5,405.4
Other operating expenses	5,618.0	2,151.5
Total operating expenses	51,113.9	45,025.3
Net operating revenues	18,289.3	20,067.7
OPERATING TAXES		
Federal income taxes (B)	2,888.8	4,411.0
State and local income taxes (B)	482.5	519.3
Property taxes	2,019.1	1,949.4
Gross receipts, payroll-related, and other taxes (O)	3,289.5	2,929.7
Total operating taxes	8,679.9	9,809.4
Operating income	9,609.4	10,258.3
OTHER INCOME		
Western Electric Company net income (G)	50.7	336.7
Interest charged construction	356.8	317.6
Miscellaneous income and deductions-net (B) (E)	36.9	9.4
Total other income	444.4	663.7
Income before interest expense (carried forward)	$10,053.8	$10,922.0

Notes provided in the Annual Report are an integral part of these financial statements.

Source: AT&T, *Annual Report*, 1983.

EXHIBIT 1 (*Continued*)

STATEMENT OF INCOME AND REINVESTED EARNINGS

Dollars in Millions (Except Per Share Amounts)	Year 1983	Year 1982
Income before interest expense (brought forward)	$10,053.8	$10,922.0
INTEREST EXPENSE (O)	4,307.2	3,930.0
Income before extraordinary charge and cumulative effect of a change in accounting principle	5,746.6	6,992.0
Extraordinary charge-net of taxes (A)	(5,497.9)	—
Prior years cumulative effect (through December 31, 1981) of the change in accounting for deferred income taxes (B)	—	286.8
NET INCOME	248.7	7,278.8
Preferred dividend requirements	126.5	141.9
INCOME APPLICABLE TO COMMON SHARES	$ 122.2	$ 7,136.9
EARNINGS PER COMMON SHARE AMOUNTS based on weighted average number of shares outstanding of 936,801,000, 849,550,000 and 788,178,000 in years 1983, 1982, and 1981, respectively:		
Before extraordinary charge and cumulative effect of a change in accounting principle	$ 6.00	$ 8.06
Extraordinary charge (A)	(5.87)	—
Prior years cumulative effect (through December 31, 1981) of the change in accounting for deferred income taxes (B)	—	.34
Earnings per Common Share	$ .13	$ 8.40
REINVESTED EARNINGS		
At beginning of year	$28,888.5	$26,364.9
Add net income	248.7	7,278.8
	29,137.2	33,643.7
Deduct dividends declared:		
Convertible preferred shares subject to redemption:		
$4 Cumulative convertible preferred shares	11.6	25.2
Preferred shares subject to mandatory redemption:		
$3.64 Preferred shares	35.9	36.4
$3.74 Preferred shares	37.4	37.4
$77.50 Preferred shares	41.7	42.6
Common: 1983, $5.85 per share; 1982, $5.40 per share and 1981, $5.40 per share	5,495.9	4,601.0
Miscellaneous-net	7.8	12.6
	5,630.3	4,755.2
At end of year	$23,506.9	$28,888.5

Notes provided in the Annual Report are an integral part of these financial statements.

Source: AT&T, *Annual Report*, 1983.

EXHIBIT 1 (*Continued*)

AT&T 1984 FINANCIAL FORECAST

DOLLARS IN MILLIONS (Except Per Share Amounts)	Post-Divestiture Forecasted Year 1984
Total Operating Revenues	$56,544.1
Depreciation	3,420.2
Other Operating Expenses	48,144.6
Total Operating Expenses	51,564.8
Net Operating Revenues	4,979.3
Federal Income Taxes	1,084.6
Other Operating Taxes	1,764.2
Total Operating Taxes	2,848.8
Operating Income	2,130.5
Other Income	655.6
Interest Expense	676.1
Net Income	2,110.0
Preferred Dividend Requirements	113.4
Income Applicable to Common Shares	$ 1,996.6
Earnings per Common Share	$ 2.02
Weighted Average Number of Shares Outstanding (Million)	989.1

Source: AT&T, *Annual Report*, 1983.

EXHIBIT 2   MISSION STATEMENT: AT&T BELL LABORATORIES

To provide the technology AT&T needs to be a world leader in information systems and services.

AT&T Bell Laboratories is responsible for designing and developing the systems and services needed by AT&T enterprises and for providing the technology base for AT&T's future.

To carry out its design and development responsibilities in partnership with the other AT&T entities, Bell Laboratories will apply systems engineering expertise to help identify the best solutions to customers' needs; help the AT&T enterprises select those projects that profitably service their business objectives and meet their customers' needs; and provide timely, cost-competitive development to support these projects.

To provide the needed technology base, Bell Laboratories will pursue a broad program of research in relevant fields; determine which technologies are essential to AT&T's success; and establish competitive positions in these technologies.

The successful achievement of Bell Laboratories' mission is critically dependent on the contributions of individuals. Therefore, Bell Laboratories will maintain a work climate that will attract and challenge the very best talent from every source and will nurture the careers of all its people.

Source: AT&T, *Supplement to Annual Report*, 1983

EXHIBIT 3 PARTIAL ORGANIZATION CHART: AT&T TECHNOLOGIES, 1984

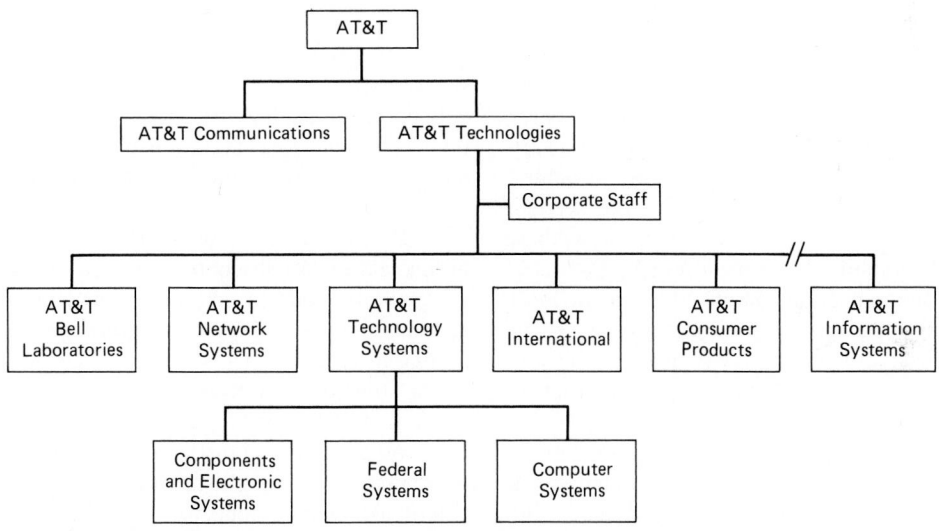

Source: AT&T, *Supplement to Annual Report*, 1983.

┌─ NINE ────────────────────────────────────┐
│ ┌──────────────────────────────────────┐ │
│ │   │ │
│ │   ACHIEVING   │ │
│ │   │ │
│ │   CONFIGURATION   │ │
│ │   │ │
│ └──────────────────────────────────────┘ │
└──┘

This text actually divides into two basic parts. The first, Chapters 1 through 8, introduces a variety of important *concepts*—strategy, structure, process, systems, power, culture. The second, beginning in Chapter 10, considers how these concepts combine to form different major *contexts*: entrepreneurial, mature, diversified, innovation, professional, transition. Serving as the key bridge between these two parts is the idea of *configuration*, which is developed in this chapter.

According to this idea, the various elements of organizations—their strategies, strategy-making processes, structures, support systems, cultures, and so on—tend to cluster together naturally to produce certain relatively distinct overall "configurations" appropriate to particular widely encountered situations, which we call "contexts." We have already seen a good deal of evidence of such clustering into configurations in the earlier chapters: in Mintzberg's three modes of strategy making in Chapter 5, and his six forms of structure in Chapter 6; in Allison's three conceptual models of decision making in Chapter 7; and in Porter's "generic strategies" in Chapter 4. While the complexity of strategy makes it dangerous to push any particular classification scheme too far, some basic differentiations are helpful in establishing starting points for deeper observation and analysis. One does not have to recreate the wheel every time he or she designs a strategy vehicle. Instead,

with an understanding of certain basic configurations, one can concentrate on the nuances that most leverage the particular resources of each organization.

We realize that in devoting the second half of this text to various contexts in which the strategy process tends to take place—and in which distinct configurations tend to form—we are departing from the format of almost all current policy or strategy texts. These usually devote most of the first half of their material to the "formulation" of strategy, and the second half to its "implementation" through structure and systems. Our breakdown into concepts and contexts reflects the fact that formulation and implementation in most complex organizations are intimately intertwined. Strategy drives structure and systems, but the converse is also true. That is why it makes more sense to us to introduce all the concepts related to the strategy process together, and then to consider the various ways in which they might interact in specific situations. In some of these, clear formulation may effectively precede implementation, as the readings will illustrate. But in others it rarely can. In these latter contexts, the words "formulation" and "implementation" themselves often lose meaning—or worse still, mislead one in thinking about how to create an effective strategy. Effective strategic management requires both (1) a recognition that there is no "one best way" to develop a strategy in every situation, and (2) an in depth understanding of the variety of forms and approaches that may be possible in different situations.

SIX IMPORTANT CONTEXTS

The next six chapters examine several of the most important contexts the organizational strategist is likely to encounter. We begin in Chapter 10 with what seems to be the simplest context, certainly one that has had much good press in America since Horatio Alger first went into business—the *entrepreneurial* context. Here a single leader tends to take personal charge or dominate strategy making in a highly dynamic situation. This approach commonly occurs in smaller or newer enterprises. Such situations often involved relatively simple organizational structures and undeveloped or still malleable external environments. But an entrepreneurial context can occur in large organizations too, when the external environment is rapidly changing and an individual has significant personal control over the resources of the enterprise. Thus, a T. Boone Pickens or a Ian Murdock may create effective corporate strategies in much the same fashion, though with considerably greater resources, than a Reuben Mattus building Häagen Dazs.

We next consider a contrasting context that often dominates very large businesses as well as big government departments or quasi public service organizations like utilities or railroads. We label it the *mature* context, although it might equally be referred to as the stable context, or the mass-production or mass-service context. This context tends to lead toward rather formal structures combined with strategy-making processes that are heavily planning- and technique-oriented, in order to wrest the greatest possible marginal gains from external environments that are perceived to be stable, mature, and often competitive as well. What happens to such institutions—as the Royal Bank and GM cases suggest—when the environment changes radically is quite interesting.

Third, we consider the context of the *diversified* organization, which has become increas-

ingly important as waves of mergers have swept across the United States. Because product-market strategies are diversified, these structures tend to be divisionalized, and the focus of strategy shifts to two levels: the corporate or portfolio level and the divisional or business level. A variety of new conflicts, management problems, and strategy approaches naturally tend to emerge. The Continental Group, Pillsbury, Comparative Planning Systems, and General Mills cases offer a sampler of the various possible strategies and structures used to deal with this context.

Our fourth and fifth contexts are those of organizations largely dependent on specialists or experts. These contexts are called *innovation* when the environment is dynamic, *professional* when it is stable. The associated organizations tend to approach strategy in quite unusual ways, at least when compared with the more commonly understood enterepreneurial, mature, and diversified contexts. Responsibility for strategy making tends to diffuse throughout the organization, sometimes even lodging itself at the bottom of the hierarchy. The strategy process itself tends to become rather emergent in nature, both in response to the uncertainty of the environment (in the innovation context) and to the high degree of currency that information must have (in both contexts). Different kinds of expert and innovation situations appear in the AT&T Bell Labs, Pilkington Brothers, Davidson Hospital, Genentech, and Arcop cases.

We complete our discussion of contexts with consideration of the problems of managing *transitions* from one of these contexts to another (a true cultural revolution) or from one major strategy and structure to another *within* a particular context. Transition itself is, of course, a context in its own right.

THE NATURE OF "CONFIGURATION"

But before discussing these various contexts, we should develop further the idea of configuration. The readings of this chapter do that. The first reading, by Miller and Mintzberg of McGill University's Faculty of Management, makes the "case for configuration." It points out why we are often helped in our thinking by considering the world in terms of certain broad types that combine a variety of similar elements. This reading also makes a case for organizational change in "quantum" form—significant shifts in strategies and structures that have to happen suddenly, in revolutionary fashion—as opposed to the view of gradual change, in incremental fashion. Among other things, such quantum leaps may allow organizations to sustain internal consistency and the related benefits of integration rather than having to go through interim states that can confuse customers and employees alike. In effect, when one configuration breaks down sufficiently, the organization may need to leap to another through a kind of strategic revolution.

There would seem to be an evident contradiction between this view and the earlier description of the strategy-formation process as one of "logical incrementalism." But when you think about the two views, they may not be contradictory after all. Consider three things: (1) the specific aspects of the strategy change process that each considers, (2) the time frames of the two viewpoints, and (3) the types of organizations involved. The incrementalist view focuses on the processes going on in strategists' minds as they help create new strategies. Because of the complexities involved, effective strategic thinking requires an incremental, interactive, learning process for all key players. The "quantum change" concept, in contrast, focuses, not on the strategists' intentions, but on the strategies actually pursued by the organization (referred to in Chapter 1 as the realized strategies of the organization). It is these that often seem to change in quantum fashion. It may be, therefore, that managers conceive and sell their intended strategies incrementally, but once that is accomplished they change their organizations in rather rapid, integrated leaps, quantum fashion.

But then again, each of these two approaches may also occur in their own contexts. For example, quantum changes may more easily take place in crisis situations, when top manage-

ments change, or when external environments compress time frames—when technology or regulations suddenly shift, as in the AT&T Bell Labs, Zayre, or Royal Bank of Canada cases. Incremental changes may, in contrast, be more common in large, healthy organizations with multiple power points. The next several chapters will help clarify some of these differences.

The other reading of this chapter reinforces the idea of configuration by presenting a set of specific configurations (a "typology") that has become well known in the strategy literature. It was developed by Miles and his colleagues at Berkeley, and essentially contrasts two basic types of organizations which they label "defenders" and "prospectors." A third type, called "analyzers," is really a hybrid of the first two, while a fourth, "reactors," is a description of what Miles and his colleagues consider to be passive, dysfunctional strategic behavior. Evidence that will enable you to consider the validity and usefulness of the Miles et al. configurations as well as others already introduced will be found throughout the wide variety of cases and readings that follow. These will not try to persuade you of any particular view, but will help you form your own useful typologies and mental images of configurations.

THE CASE FOR CONFIGURATION*

by Danny Miller and Henry Mintzberg

. . . It is generally accepted that we best understand our world by first doing analysis and then synthesis. We divide things up into components, and then put them back together again into some

* Excerpted from a paper published in Danny Miller and Peter H. Friesen, *Organizations: A Quantum View* (Prentice-Hall, 1984) chap. 1; used by permission of the publisher.

form of intelligible composite. The contention in this [reading] is that the methods traditionally favored in the study of organizations, and perhaps the social sciences in general, encourage analysis in the absence of synthesis. Specifically, they tend to focus on simple relationships among few variables in search of direct causation. We wish to advocate an approach here that favors synthesis, developing or isolating composites that take the form of what we have called ''gestalts,'' ''archetypes,'' and ''configurations.'' These can be defined as commonly occurring clusters of attributes or relationships . . . that are internally cohesive. . . .

THE PERSPECTIVE OF SYNTHESIS

. . . In its purest form, the approach of synthesis may combine all five of the attributes discussed below, although the first two are the most critical.

1. *A large number of qualities—ideally, of state, process, and situation—are studied simultaneously in order to yield a detailed, holistic, integrated image of reality. . . .* Studies of the organization need not be restricted to attributes of its structure, but can also consider those of its environment, its technical system, its age and size, its power relationships, its leaders, its strategy, its strategy-making procedures, its flows of information and patterns of communication, its performance and so on.

2. *Data analysis and theory building are geared to finding common natural clusters among the attributes studied. . . .* The objective of the research is to derive theoretical typologies or empirical multivariate taxonomies that discriminate among different configurations of the attributes . . . each configuration revealing its own relationships among the attributes. . . .

3. *Causation is viewed in the broadest possible terms.* The search is not simply for unidirectional causation between pairs of variables or even necessarily for multiple forms of causation. The approach of synthesis is really the search for *networks* of causation. Each configuration has to be considered as

a system in which each attribute can influence many of the others by being an indispensible part of an integrated whole. There are no purely dependent or independent variables in a system; over time, many things depend on many other things. An attribute that drives others at one point will itself be driven by some of those others later; and commonly, attributes drive each other concurrently. . . .

4. *Time and process are taken into account whenever possible.* The approach of synthesis favors longitudinal research where possible, in which processes are studied alongside states. Results from such studies enable the researcher to flesh out his results, helping him to explain leads and lags, and, in general, providing depth to his understanding of why organizations behave as they do. . . .

5. *Despite efforts to measure and quantify, anecdotal data are gathered to help explain the more systematic findings.* Abstract results come to life when put in the context of even one rich, detailed illustration. . . .

Of course . . . the approach of synthesis can be useful only if configurations do in fact reflect reality—that is, only if there occur common, internally homogeneous clusterings of attributes or relationships, a relatively small number of which can account for a large fraction of the population of organizations. Otherwise, far too many types would be needed to explain that population, and the approach of synthesis would become hopelessly inadequate. . . .

SOME REASONS FOR CONFIGURATION

Why should common configurations exist? We propose three main arguments, woven into the following paragraphs, to account for the emergence of organizational configurations.

According to Charles Darwin:

. . . species at any one period are not indefinitely variable, and are not linked together by a multitude of intermediate gradations, partly because the process of natural selection will always be very slow and will act, at any one time, only on a very few forms; and partly because the very process of natural selection almost implies the continual supplanting and extinction of preceding and intermediate gradations (1968: 231).

Hannan and Freeman (1977) have argued that formal organizations may be subject to selection processes similar to those of the biological species. Both survive only if they evolve in ways adapted to their environments. Our first argument, then, is that *Darwinian forces may encourage only relatively few organizational forms to survive in the same setting*, their variety and number circumscribed by the dictates of population ecology. The Darwinian argument is, of course, very tentative as applied to organizations, and we hesitate to make too much of it. It does seem, however, that a type of organizational Darwinism could very well limit the number of viable forms by selecting out those that are relatively weak and those that fail to achieve internal complementarities. The rate of bankruptcies and the relatively young median age of most organizations may indicate that many forms perish before they have a chance to become numerous (Aldrich, 1979). But how orderly and common are the forms that remain, and which forms survive?

Increasingly, researchers and practitioners alike are coming to see the world in "systems" terms. Everything seems to depend on everything else. It used to be fashionable in science and everyday affairs to isolate variables, to catch what has been called "the economist's plague"—holding all other things constant. The trouble is that other things do not remain constant. Things move together because of their interdependencies. And that may be a force for the emergence of configurations in organizations. Our second argument then is that *the organization may be driven toward configuration in order to achieve consistency in its internal characteristics*, *synergy (or mutual complementarity) in its processes, and fit with its situation*. Rather than trying to do everything well, the effective organization may instead con-

centrate its efforts on a theme, and seek to bring all its elements into line with this. Configuration, in essence, means harmony.

Consider the configuration we have called machine bureaucracy, characterized by the following attributes of structure. . . . The organization has highly specialized, routine operating tasks, very formalized procedures, and large units in its operations. The basis for grouping tasks throughout the structure is by function, and coordination is effected by rules and hierarchy. Power for decision making is quite centralized, and there exists an elaborate administrative structure with a clear hierarchy of line authority. Finally, a large contingent of staff analysts is responsible for work flow and production efficiency. Organizations that use this kind of structure tend to emphasize standardization throughout. Rules and regulations permeate their activities and, indeed, reflect an obsession with control; formal communication is favored at all levels; and decision making tends to follow the formal chain of authority. Only at the very top of the hierarchy are the different functional responsibilities brought together; therefore, only at that level can the major decision be made. Hence, the structure is a rather centralized one. The one center of power besides the senior management is the cadre of staff analysts on whom the organization depends for the design of its formalized systems. Such organizations are typically associated with environments that are both simple and stable. The work of complex environments cannot be rationalized into simple operating tasks, and that of dynamic environments cannot be predicted, made repetitive, and thereby standardized. These are typically mature organizations, large enough to have the scale of operations needed for repetition and standardization, and old enough to have been able to settle upon the standards they wish to use. The products or services are usually provided on a repetitive, highly standardized basis, and in mass quantities. External control is sometimes a condition, since that tends to drive an organization toward centralization and bureaucratization. These organizations, in other words, operate as machines, non-adaptive instruments designed to provide standardized outputs at the lowest possible cost.

As can be seen, these attributes are complementary and mutually reinforcing. Many are interdependent, such that a change in one would require a shift in many others. Indeed, one has difficulty determining priority or primacy among them. The stable environment enables the operating procedures to repeat and be formalized, but the existence of formalized procedures causes the organization to search out stable environments. Large size encourages standardization—since procedures tend to repeat, and also because controls must be in large part impersonal. But standardization also encourages growth—to gain economies of scale by increasing the throughput. Likewise, large size encourages the organization to seek out a stable environment, where its inflexibility is less of a weakness, but stability also encourages growth to large size, to take advantage of its opportunities. In other words, each attribute makes sense only in terms of the whole—and together they form a cohesive system. The machine bureaucracy is far from a perfect system; it often abuses its workers, and it suffers serious problems of adaptation. But it (and society) puts up with these as the costs of concentrating its efforts in order to achieve consistency, synergy, and fit. Better to do what it does well—in this case, mass-produce cheaply—than to flounder trying to be all things to all people.

We do not wish to argue that all configurations are successful or even functional. The pursuit of internal harmony and consistency often requires conformity, discouraging diversity of opinion and dissent and prompting excesses. For example, the innovative organization may become reckless, squandering its resources in the pursuit of extravagant novelties. Conservative bureaucracies might, in contrast, move toward complete stagnation. So internal harmony and consistency can be a two-edged sword.

Note our departure in this second point from traditional Darwinian theory, giving rise to the two separate arguments for the emergence of configuration. Our first point argues that it is the environment that causes adaptation *in the long run* by allowing only a limited number of syner-

gistic and compatible organizational forms to survive. Our second point, not inconsistent with the first but departing from the analogy with the biological species, argues that organizations seek to adapt *themselves* to the dictates of consistency, synergy, and fit. They are able to act "morphogenically." Unlike the biological species, which have to wait generations to adapt, organizations have the capacity to adapt themselves within their own lifetimes (Simon, 1969)—for example, by effecting transitions from less to more viable configurations.

And this brings us to our third argument. Were it common for organizations to make such transitions in piecemeal and disjointed fashion, the case for configuration could be weakened. A large number of organizations constantly undergoing piecemeal changes would cause a random cross-section of them to display a great deal of variety. In other words, clustering would break down, and so would our case for configuration. *But the economics of adaptation, as well as some recent empirical evidence, argue for a dramatic quantum approach to organizational change— long periods of the maintenance of a given configuration, punctuated by brief periods of multifaceted and concerted transition to a new one.*

Contingency theory has found that organizations must change their internal attributes— structures, strategies, and processes—to cope with changes in their environments. The question becomes, however, what form does that internal change take? Essentially, the organization has two broad choices. It can try to keep up with changes in its environment by changing itself in piecemeal and perhaps incremental fashion. By so doing, the organization maintains environmental fit, but possibly at the expense of internal consistency. Alternatively, the organization can delay transition until absolutely necessary, thereby better maintaining internal consistency, but at the price of gradually worsening environmental fit. Either choice can damage configuration. But the latter far less than the former, since the interrelationships among the state characteristics and processes—the ways in which the organization functions every day—remain intact.

There are a number of reasons why organizations often opt for the maintenance of internal consistency as long as possible, rather than for continually adapting to the environment. For one thing, environmental change can sometimes prove to be temporary or anomalous. It is sensible then to delay reaction to it, to wait at least until the signals are clear. For another, internal change tends to be costly, involving shifts in established patterns of behavior. It will therefore tend to be resisted, or at least delayed so that many changes can be made at the same time. This is apt to be especially true when a tight integration of structural and process attributes has been achieved. Any change may cause *dis*integration, resulting in discrepancies and disharmonies in the inner workings of the organization (Miller, 1982). Finally, internal change, especially in the face of moderate success, is also resisted for cognitive, political, and ideological reasons. Human cognition is less sensitive to gradual changes in the environment than to pointed discontinuities (Turner, 1976). Adaptation is thus avoided until a major threat is perceived. Also, those in the organization who developed the existing structures and processes—often, the most powerful managers—become enamored of them, blind to their weaknesses, and politically dependent on them. Leaving this point aside, the managers of successful organizations, never sure which of the attributes of their structures and processes lie at the root of that success, will tend to avoid tampering with any one element of their "tried and true" configuration. And when an organization has long been successful, the force of internal ideology tends to impute a mythical quality to its structure and processes, evoking an attitude of conformity that can block not just change but even the perception of the need for it (Starbuck, Greve, and Hedberg, 1978).

Thus, there are a number of reasons why organizations delay adaptation to environmental change, and especially why they try to retain internal configuration as long as possible. But change must, of course, eventually come. As the environment continues to alter and the fit with it worsens, steps must be taken to initiate substantial changes in internal structure and processes. But to evoke such changes in the face of all the forces discussed above would seem to call for virtual revolution. Thus, when such changes do come, they may tend to be pervasive and dramatic, costly and disruptive. The organization is driven to change many of its attributes concurrently, not only to get all of the disruption over with at one time, but, more important, to ensure its attributes are in complementary alignment. In other words, the organization tries to move to a new configuration. And it is driven to execute that move rapidly, to avoid spending too much time in a state of transition. In that state of flux, configuration in the usual sense of the word is absent: The structure and processes lack internal consistency, and the organization is no longer suited to its old environment while not yet adapted to its new one. As the most common pattern of significant adaptation, therefore, we would expect organizations to undergo lengthy periods of the maintenance of a given configuration whenever possible. These periods of relative internal calm and harmony would be interrupted occasionally by brief periods of disruption—of something amounting to internal revolution—during which the move to a new configuration is made (or at least attempted). If this were in fact how organizations change, the chances of finding stable and common configurations would be much enhanced. . . .

CONFIGURATION AND COGNITION

. . . it might be useful before we close the [reading] to argue for the "subjective" or cognitive convenience that configurations offer—for both theoreticians and practicing managers.

Even as untutored visitors to an art museum, we are able to glance at a painting, appreciate its form and structure, and take away impressions of its mood, shape, and perhaps theme. We first appraise our stimulus holistically, roaming over the canvas with our eyes to take in the extensive qualities of the painting. Afterwards, our attention might be directed to appreciating particular areas of the canvas or specific qualities of it—the coarseness of its brushstrokes, the intensity of its hues, the flow of its lines.

In a basic sense then, our first impressions are ones of *synthesis*. That is how we first appreciate a painting, and comprehend its basic message. We are unconsciously effecting a synthesis that employs components or attributes only so far as they configure into a comprehensible whole. Only subsequently might we begin to *analyze* the attributes individually, to consider their role in making up that whole.

If we lived in a world controlled by a malevolent deity, he might have constituted human beings so that analysis would always have to precede synthesis in cognition, even in the viewing of paintings. He might force us to go over a canvas one square inch at a time, and then somehow to combine a myriad of these fragments to obtain some idea of pattern. In such a world, either paintings would be very small or museums very empty.

To be sure, analysis and synthesis are both necessary phases of scientific activity. Analysis defines the components or attributes of a phenomenon and measures them; synthesis combines these into integrated images, conceptions, or configurations, identifying patterns and forming generalizations. Then analysis returns to test these generalizations and deduce their logical consequences. But the purpose of science is insight, much as is the purpose of painting. In other words, just as the painter paints to enlighten the observer, so too does the researcher study to enlighten the practitioner. And we believe that the practitioner—in the case of organization theory, the line manager, staff specialist, or consultant—perceives much as does the visitor to the museum.

Synthesis forms the basis of the practitioner's perception: It must precede, condition, and inform his analysis. Disjointed analysis by itself provides only glimpses of fragments, whose context-free states obscure their meaning. Findings may be statistically significant, but not conceptually so. They become elusive, float away, inhibit rather than foster understanding. The fewer the fragments and the more distant one from another on the invisible canvas, the more difficult it is to get a realistic image of that canvas—to make any sense of things.

Our world of organizations is very complex, and the fragments uncovered by research from the perspective of analysis are very distant from one another. Hence, the images offered to the practitioner have been very incomplete. Our point is that configurations developed from the perspective of synthesis, by providing more complete images of spheres of reality, may be more compatible with patterns of human cognition than are linear relationships, developed from the perspective of analysis, which seek to explain components more than composites. People deal with a complex world by compartmentalizing it in terms of images or clusters, by putting its many attributes into various envelopes, each of which is a convenient storehouse of related information, with its own label. This is what we mean when we use the words *model*, *stereotype*, *kind*, and *type*.

Take, for example, the label "democracy." It could, of course, mean the amount of freedom a citizen has along some continuum, a view compatible with that of analysis. But we suspect that within most minds, the label more accurately represents a configuration of mutually supporting attributes, such as due process, freedom of speech, a free press, universal suffrage, the "social contract," and so on. In the complex world of organizations, populated by practitioners who think in terms of such envelopes, we believe the role of the researcher and theorist is to offer synthesis, holistic concepts, composites and configurations.

The notion of configuration can help us to overcome the problem of the blind men, each of whom touched a different part of the elephant and then argued about the nature of the beast. It can open the eyes of the [observer] to the study of whole beasts, each a logical combination of its own characteristics, similar to all the members of its own species yet fundamentally different from those of other species. . . .

ORGANIZATIONAL STRATEGY, STRUCTURE, AND PROCESS*

by Raymond E. Miles,
Charles C. Snow,
Alan D. Meyer,
and Henry J. Coleman, Jr.

. . . For most organizations, the dynamic process of adjusting to environmental change and uncertainty—of *maintaining an effective alignment with the environment while managing internal interdependencies*—is enormously complex, encompassing myriad decisions and behaviors at several organization levels. But the complexity of the adjustment process can be penetrated: by searching for patterns in the behavior of organizations, one can describe and even predict the process of organizational adaptation. This article presents a theoretical framework that managers and students of management can use to analyze an organization as an integrated and dynamic whole—a model that takes into account the interrelationships among strategy, structure, and process. . . . Specifically, the framework has two major elements: (a) a general model of the process of adaptation which specifies the major decisions needed by the organization to maintain an effective alignment with its environment, and (b) an organizational typology which portrays different patterns of adaptive behavior used by organizations within a given industry or other grouping. . . .

*   Originally published in the *Academy of Management Review* (July 1978); copyright © Academy of Management Review. Reprinted with deletions by permission of the *Academy of Management Review* and the authors.

THE ADAPTIVE CYCLE

We have developed a general model of the adaptive process which we call the *adaptive cycle*. . . . Essentially, [some management writers] argue that organizational behavior is only partially preordained by environmental conditions and that the choices which top managers make are the critical determinants of organizational structure and process. Although these choices are numerous and complex, they can be viewed as three broad "problems" of organizational adaptation: the *entrepreneurial problem*, the *engineering problem*, and the *administrative problem*. In mature organizations, management must solve each of these problems simultaneously, but for explanatory purposes, these adaptive problems can be discussed as if they occurred sequentially.

The Entrepreneurial Problem

The [cycle of adaptation], though evident in all organizations, is perhaps most visible in new or rapidly growing organizations (and in organizations which recently have survived a major crisis). In a new organization, an entrepreneurial insight, perhaps only vaguely defined at first, must be developed into a concrete *definition of an organizational domain*: a specific good or service and a target market or market segment. In an ongoing organization, the entrepreneurial problem has an added dimension. Because the organization has already obtained a set of "solutions" to its engineering and administrative problems, its next attempt at an entrepreneurial "thrust" may be difficult. . . .

In either a new or ongoing organization, the solution to the entrepreneurial problem is marked by management's acceptance of a particular product-market domain, and this acceptance becomes evident when management decides to commit resources to achieve objectives relative to the domain. In many organizations, external and internal commitment to the entrepreneurial solution is sought through the development and projection of an organizational "image" which defines both the organization's market and its orientation toward it (e.g., an emphasis on size, efficiency, or innovation).

Although we are suggesting that the engineering phase begins at this point, the need for further entrepreneurial activities clearly does not disappear. The entrepreneurial function remains a top-management responsibility, although as Bower (1970) has described, the identification of a new opportunity and the initial impetus for movement toward it may originate at lower managerial levels.

The Engineering Problem

The engineering problem involves the creation of a system which *operationalizes management's solution to the entrepreneurial problem*. Such a system requires management to select an appropriate technology (input-transformation-output process) for producing and distributing chosen products or services and to form new information, communication, and control linkages (or modify existing linkages) to ensure proper operation of the technology.

As solutions to these problems are reached, initial implementation of the administrative system takes place. There is no assurance that the configuration of the organization, as it begins to emerge during this phase, will remain the same when the engineering problem finally has been solved. The actual form of the organization's structure will be determined during the administrative phase as management solidifies relations with the environment and establishes processes for coordinating and controlling internal operations. . . .

The Administrative Problem

The administrative problem, as described by most theories of management, is primarily that of reducing uncertainty within the organizational system, or, in terms of the present model, of rationalizing and stabilizing those activites which successfully solved problems faced by the organization during the entrepreneurial and engineering phases. Solving the administrative prob-

lem involves more than simply rationalizing the system already developed (uncertainty reduction); it also involves formulating and implementing those processes which will enable the organization to continue to evolve (innovation). This conception of the administrative problem, as a pivotal factor in the cycle of adaptation, deserves further elaboration.

Rationalization and Articulation In the ideal organization, management would be equally adept at performing two somewhat conflicting functions: it would be able to create an administrative system (structure and processes) that could smoothly direct and monitor the organization's current activities without, at the same time, allowing the system to become so ingrained that future innovation activites are jeopardized. Such a perspective requires the administrative system to be viewed as both a *lagging* and *leading* variable in the process of adaptation. As a lagging variable, it must rationalize, through the development of appropriate structures and processes, strategic decisions made at previous points in the adjustment process. As a leading variable, the administrative system must facilitate the organization's future capacity to adapt by articulating and reinforcing the paths along which innovative activity can proceed. . . .

THE STRATEGIC TYPOLOGY

If one accepts the adaptive cycle as valid, the question becomes: How do organizations move through the cycle? That is, using the language of our model, what strategies do organizations employ in solving their entrepreneurial, engineering, and administrative problems? Our research and interpretation of the literature show that there are essentially three *strategic types* of organizations: Defenders, Analyzers, and Prospectors. Each type has its own unique strategy for relating to its chosen market(s), and each has a particular configuration of technology, structure, and process that is consistent with its market strategy. A fourth type of organization encountered in our studies is called the Reactor. The Reactor is a form of strategic ''failure'' in that inconsistencies exist among its strategy, technology, structure, and process.

Although similar typologies of various aspects of organizational behavior are available (Anderson and Paine, 1975, Ansoff, 1965; Ansoff and Brandenburg, 1971; Miles and Snow, 1978; Rogers, 1971; Segal, 1974), our formulation specifies relationships among strategy, technology, structure, and process to the point where entire organizations can be viewed as integrated wholes in dynamic interaction with their environments. Any typology is unlikely to encompass every form of organizational behavior—the world of organizations is much too changeable and complex to permit such a claim. Nevertheless, every organization that we have observed appears, when compared to other organizations in its industry, to fit predominantly into one of the four categories, and its behavior is generally predictable given its typological classification. The ''pure'' form of each of these organization types is described below.

Defenders

The Defender (i.e., its top management) deliberately enacts and maintains an environment for which a stable form of organization is appropriate. Stability is chiefly achieved by the Defender's definition of, and solution to, its entrepreneurial problem. Defenders define their *entrepreneurial problem* as *how to seal off a portion of the total market in order to create a stable domain*, and they do so by producing only a limited set of products directed at a narrow segment of the total potential market. Within this limited domain, the Defender strives aggressively to prevent competitors from entering its ''turf.'' Such behaviors include standard economic actions like competitive pricing or high-quality products, but Defenders also tend to ignore developments and trends outside of their domains, choosing instead to grow through market penetration and perhaps some limited product development. Over time, a true Defender is able to carve out and maintain a small

niche within the industry which is difficult for competitors to penetrate.

Having chosen a narrow product-market domain, the Defender invests a great deal of resources in solving its engineering problem: *how to produce and distribute goods or services as efficiently as possible*. Typically, the Defender does so by developing a single core technology that is highly cost-efficient. Technological efficiency is central to the Defender's success since its domain has been deliberately created to absorb outputs on a predictable, continuous basis. Some Defenders extend technological efficiency to its limits through a process of vertical integration—incorporating each stage of production from raw materials supply to distribution of final output into the same organizational system.

Finally, the Defender's solution to its administrative problem is closely aligned with its solutions to the entrepreneurial and engineering problems. The Defender's *administrative problem—how to achieve strict control of the organization in order to ensure efficiency*—is solved through a combination of structural and process mechanisms that can be generally described as ''mechanistic'' (Burns and Stalker, 1961). These mechanisms include a top-management group heavily dominated by production and cost-control specialists, little or no scanning of the environment for new areas of opportunity, intensive planning oriented toward cost and other efficiency issues, functional structures characterized by extensive division of labor, centralized control, communications through formal hierarchical channels, and so on. Such an administrative system is ideally suited for generating and maintaining efficiency, and the key characteristic of stability is as apparent here as in the solution to the other two adaptive problems.

Pursued vigorously, the Defender strategy can be viable in most industries, although stable industries lend themselves to this type of organization more than turbulent industries (e.g., the relative lack of technological change in the food-processing industry generally favors the Defender strategy compared with the situation in the electronics industry). This particular form of organization is not without its potential risks. The Defender's *primary risk* is that of *ineffectiveness*—being unable to respond to a major shift in its market environment. The Defender relies on the continued viability of its single, narrow domain, and it receives a return on its large technological investment only if the major problems facing the organization continue to be of an engineering nature. If the Defender's market shifts dramatically, this type of organization has little capacity for locating and exploiting new areas of opportunity. In short, the Defender is perfectly capable of responding to today's world. To the extent that tomorrow's world is similar to today's, the Defender is ideally suited for its environment. . . .

Prospectors

In many ways, Prospectors respond to their chosen environments in a manner that is almost the opposite of the Defender. In one sense, the Prospector is exactly like the Defender: there is a high degree of consistency among its solutions to the three problems of adaptation.

Generally speaking, the Prospector enacts an environment that is more dynamic than those of other types of organizations within the same industry. Unlike the Defender, whose success comes primarily from efficiently serving a stable domain, the Prospector's prime capability is that of finding and exploiting new product and market opportunities. For a Prospector, maintaining a reputation as an innovator in product and market development may be as important as, perhaps even more important, than high profitability. In fact, because of the inevitable ''failure rate'' associated with sustained product and market innovation, Prospectors may find it difficult consistently to attain the profit levels of the more efficient Defender.

Defining its *entrepreneurial* problem as *how to locate and develop product and market opportunities*, the Prospector's domain is usually broad and in a continuous state of development. The systematic addition of new products or markets, frequently combined with retrenchment in other parts of the domain, gives the Prospector's products and markets an aura of fluidity uncharacteristic of the Defender. To locate new areas of opportunity, the Prospector must develop and maintain the capacity to survey a wide range of environmental conditions, trends, and events. This type of organization invests heavily in individuals and groups who scan the environment for potential opportunities. Because these scanning activities are not limited to the organization's current domain, Prospectors are frequently the creators of change in their respective industries. Change is one of the major tools used by the Prospector to gain an edge over competitors, so Prospector managers typically perceive more environmental change and uncertainty than managers of the Defender (or the other two organization types).

To serve its changing domain properly, the Prospector requires a good deal of flexibility in its technology and administrative system. Unlike the Defender, the Prospector's choice of products and markets is not limited to those which fall within the range of the organization's present technological capability. The Prospector's technology is contingent upon both the organization's current *and* future product mix: entrepreneurial activities always have primacy, and appropriate technologies are not selected or developed until late in the process of product development. Therefore, the Prospector's overall engineering problem is *how to avoid long-term commitments to a single type of technological process*, and the organization usually does so by creating multiple, prototypical technologies which have a low degree of routinization and mechanization.

Finally, the Prospector's *administrative* problem flows from its changing domain and flexible technologies: *how to facilitate rather than control organizational operations*. That is, the Prospector's administrative system must be able to deploy and coordinate resources among numerous decentralized units and projects rather than to plan and control the operations of the entire organization centrally. To accomplish overall facilitation and coordination, the Prospector's structure-process mechanisms must be "organic" (Burns and Stalker 1961). These mechanisms include a top-management group dominated by marketing and research and development experts, planning that is broad rather than intensive and oriented toward results not methods, product or project structures characterized by a low degree of formalization, decentralized control, lateral as well as vertical communications, and so on. In contrast to the Defender, the Prospector's descriptive catchword throughout its administrative as well as entrepreneurial and engineering solutions is "flexibility."

Of course, the Prospector strategy also has its costs. Although the Prospector's continuous exploration of change helps to protect it from a changing environment, this type of organization runs the *primary risk of low profitability and overextension of resources*. While the Prospector's technological flexibility permits a rapid response to a changing domain, complete efficiency cannot be obtained because of the presence of multiple technologies. Finally, the Prospector's administrative system is well suited to maintain flexibility, but it may, at least temporarily, underutilize or even misutilize physical, financial, and human resources. In short, the Prospector is effective—it can respond to the demands of tomorrow's world. To the extent that the world of tomorrow is similar to that of today, the Prospector cannot maximize profitability because of its inherent inefficiency. . . .

Analyzers

Based on our research, the Defender and the Prospector seem to reside at opposite ends of a continuum of adjustment strategies. Between these two extremes, a third type of organization is called the Analyzer. The Analyzer is a unique combination of the Prospector and Defender types and represents a viable alternative to these other strategies. A true Analyzer is an organization that attempts to minimize risk while maximizing the opportunity for profit—that is, an experienced Analyzer combines the strengths of both the

Prospector and the Defender into a single system. This strategy is difficult to pursue, particularly in industries characterized by rapid market and technological change, and thus the word that best describes the Analyzer's adaptive approach is "balance."

The Analyzer defines its *entrepreneurial* problem in terms similar to both the Prospector and the Defender: *how to locate and exploit new product and market opportunities while simultaneously maintaining a firm core of traditional products and customers*. The Analyzer's solution to the entrepreneurial problem is also a blend of the solutions preferred by the Prospector and the Defender: the Analyzer moves toward new products or new markets but only after their viability has been demonstrated. This periodic transformation of the Analyzer's domain is accomplished through imitation—only the most successful product or market innovations developed by prominent Prospectors are adopted. At the same time, the majority of the Analyzer's revenue is generated by a fairly stable set of products and customer or client groups—a Defender characteristic. Thus, the successful Analyzer must be able to respond quickly when following the lead of key Prospectors while at the same time maintaining operating efficiency in its stable product and market areas. To the extent that it is successful, the Analyzer can grow through market penetration as well as product and market development.

The duality evident in the Analyzer's domain is reflected in its *engineering* problem and solution. This type of organization must learn *how to achieve and protect an equilibrium between conflicting demands for technological flexibility and for technological stability*. This equilibrium is accomplished by partitioning production activities to form a dual technological core. The stable component of the Analyzer's technology bears a strong resemblance to the Defender's technology. It is functionally organized and exhibits high levels of standardization, routinization, and mechanization in an attempt to approach cost efficiency. The Analyzer's flexible technological component resembles the Prospector's technological orientation. In manufacturing organizations, it frequently includes a large group of applications engineers (or their equivalent) who are rotated among teams charged with the task of rapidly adapting new product designs to fit the Analyzer's existing stable technology.

The Analyzer's dual technological core thus reflects the engineering solutions of both the Prospector and the Defender, with the stable and flexible components integrated primarily by an influential applied research group. To the extent that this group is able to develop solutions that match the organization's existing technological capabilities with the new products desired by product managers, the Analyzer can enlarge its product line without incurring the Prospector's extensive research and development expenses.

The Analyzer's administrative problem, as well as its entrepreneurial and engineering problems, contains both Defender and Prospector characteristics. Generally speaking, the *administrative* problem of the Analyzer is *how to differentiate the organization's structure and processes to accommodate both stable and dynamic areas of operation*. The Analyzer typically solves this problem with some version of a matrix organization structure. Heads of key functional units, most notably engineering and production, unite with product managers (usually housed in the marketing department) to form a balanced dominant coalition similar to both the Defender and the Prospector. The product manager's influence is usually greater than the functional manager's since his or her task is to identify promising product-market innovations and to supervise their movement through applied engineering and into production in a smooth and timely manner. The presence of engineering and production in the dominant coalition is to represent the more stable domain and technology which are the foundations of the Analyzer's overall operations. The Analyzer's matrix structure is supported by intensive planning between the functional divisions of marketing and production, broad-gauge planning between the applied research group and the product managers for the development of new products, centralized control mechanisms in the functional divisions and decentralized control techniques in the product groups, and so on. In sum, the key characteristic of the Analyzer's administrative system is the proper differentiation of the organization's structure and processes to achieve a balance between the stable and dynamic areas of operation.

As is true for both the Defender and Prospector, the Analyzer strategy is not without its costs. The duality in the Analyzer's domain forces the organization to establish a dual technological core, and it requires management to operate fundamentally different planning, control, and reward systems simultaneously. Thus, the Analyzer's twin characteristics of stability and flexibility limit the organization's ability to move fully in either direction were the domain to shift dramatically. Consequently, the Analyzer's *primary risks* are both *inefficiency* and *ineffectiveness* if it does not maintain the necessary balance throughout its strategy-structure relationship. . . .

Reactors

The Defender, the Prospector, and the Analyzer can all be proactive with respect to their environments, though each is proactive in a different way. At the extremes, Defenders continually attempt to develop greater efficiency in existing operations while Prospectors explore environmental change in search of new opportunities. Over time, these action modes stabilize to form a pattern of response to environmental conditions that is both consistent and stable.

A fourth type of organization, the Reactor, exhibits a pattern of adjustment to its environment that is both *inconsistent* and *unstable*; this type lacks a set of response mechanisms which it can consistently put into effect when faced with a changing environment. As a consequence, Reactors exist in a state of almost perpetual instability. The Reactor's ''adaptive'' cycle usually consists of responding inappropriately to environmental change and uncertainty, performing poorly as a result, and then being reluctant to act aggressively in the future. Thus, the Reactor is a ''residual'' strategy, arising when one of the other three strategies is improperly pursued.

Although there are undoubtedly many reasons why organizations become Reactors, we have identified three. First, *top management may not have clearly articulated the organization's strategy*. For example, one company was headed by a "one-man" Prospector of immense personal skills. A first-rate architect, he led his firm through a rapid and successful growth period during which the company moved from the design and construction of suburban shopping centers, through the construction and management of apartment complexes, and into consulting with municipal agencies concerning urban planning problems. Within ten years of its inception, the company was a loose but effective collection of semi-autonomous units held together by this particular individual. When this individual was suddenly killed in a plane crash, the company was thrown into a strategic void. Because each separate unit of the company was successful, each was able to argue strongly for more emphasis on its particular domain and operations. Consequently, the new chief executive officer, caught between a number of conflicting but legitimate demands for resources, was unable to develop a unified, cohesive statement of the organization's strategy; thus, consistent and aggressive behavior was precluded.

A second and perhaps more common cause of organizational instability is that *management does not fully shape the organization's structure and processes to fit a chosen strategy*. Unless all of the domain, technological, and administrative decisions required to have an operational strategy are properly aligned, strategy is a mere statement, not an effective guide to behavior. One publishing company wished, in effect, to become an Analyzer—management had articulated a direction for the organization which involved operating in both stable and changing domains within the college textbook publishing industry. Although the organization was comprised of several key Defender and Prospector characteristics such as functional structures and decentralized control mechanisms, these structure-process features were not appropriately

linked to the company's different domains. In one area where the firm wished to "prospect," for example, the designated unit had a functional structure and shared a large, almost mass-production technology with several other units, thereby making it difficult for the organization to respond to market opportunities quickly. Thus, this particular organization exhibited a weak link between its strategy and its structure-process characteristics.

The third cause of instability—and perhaps ultimate failure—is *a tendency for management to maintain the organization's current strategy-structure relationship despite overwhelming changes in environmental conditions*. Another organization in our studies, a food-processing company, had initially been an industry pioneer in both the processing and marketing of dried fruits and nuts. Gradually, the company settled into a Defender strategy and took vigorous steps to bolster this strategy, including limiting the domain to a narrow line of products, integrating backward into growing and harvesting, and assigning a controller to each of the company's major functional divisions as a means of keeping costs down. Within recent years, the company's market has become saturated, and profit margins have shrunk on most of the firm's products. In spite of its declining market, the organization has consistently clung to a Defender strategy and structure, even to the point of creating ad hoc cross-divisional committees whose sole purpose was to find ways of increasing efficiency further. At the moment, management recognizes that the organization is in trouble, but it is reluctant to make the drastic modifications required to attain a strategy and structure better suited to the changing market conditions.

Unless an organization exists in a "protected" environment such as a monopolistic or highly-regulated industry, it cannot continue to behave as a Reactor indefinitely. Sooner or later, it must move toward one of the consistent and stable strategies of Defender, Analyzer, or Prospector. . . .

## TEN

THE ENTREPRENEURIAL CONTEXT

The entrepreneurial context, at least in its traditional form, encompasses situations in which a single individual, typically with a clear and distinct *vision* of purposes, directs an organization that is structured to be as responsive as possible to his or her personal wishes. Strategy making in this context revolves around a single brain, unconstrained by the forces of bureaucratic momentum. This cohesive center can learn quickly and modify action rapidly as events unfold. Often the vision remains constant, but patterns of action to achieve it may veer sharply in the short run.

Such entrepreneurship is typically found in young organizations, especially ones in new or emerging fields where solutions are as yet unknown, industry structures are still fluid, and new organization forms are still possible. Entrepreneurial vision tends to have a high potential payoff in these situations and may indeed be essential when there are long delays between the initial conception of an idea and its commercial success. In crisis situations, a similar type of strong and visionary leadership may offer the only hope for successful turnaround. And it can thrive as well in highly fragmented industries, where small flexible organizations can move quickly into and out of specialized market niches, respond rapidly to specific or changing customer demands, and can thus outmaneuver bigger bureaucracies.

Another behavior that has more recently been associated with the word entrepreneurship—currently labeled "intrapreneurship"—involves the promotion of strategic change and innovation within larger, more bureaucratic organizations. In these situations, it is often not the boss, but someone in an odd corner of the organization—a "champion" for some technology or strategic issue—who takes on the entrepreneurial role. While intrapreneurship could be treated here, we believe it better fits into our readings about the innovation context.

To describe the structure that seems to be most logically associated with the traditional form of entrepreneurship, we reprint the chapter on Simple Structure from Mintzberg's book *Structure in Fives*. Appended to this reading to illustrate how strategy appears to be made and changed in this context, are some conclusions drawn from a McGill University research project in which the strategies of several entrepreneurial firms were tracked across a number of decades. Then, to investigate the external situations that seem to be most commonly (although not exclusively) associated with the entrepreneurial context, we present excerpts from two chapters of Porter's book *Competitive Strategy*, one on emerging industries, the other on fragmented industries.

Many of our cases deal with entrepreneurship in its classical and turnaround modes. The Genentech and Intel cases deal with some important new ventures of recent years. These involve the kinds of strategies and competitive situations described by Mintzberg and Porter. The Zayre and Pillsbury cases introduce the problems and potentials of the entrepreneurial style during turnarounds in larger organizations. Entrepreneurship provides much of the excitement and glamour of modern business. While we hope these cases and their counterpart readings will make the entrepreneurial juices run strong, we believe they also embrace some much needed caveats for the unwary.

THE SIMPLE STRUCTURE*

by Henry Mintzberg

Consider an automobile dealership with a flamboyant owner, a brand-new government department, a middle-sized retail store, a corporation run by an aggressive entrepreneur, a government headed by an autocratic politician, a school system in a state of crisis. In most ways, these are vastly different organizations. But the evidence suggests that they share a number of basic structural characteristics. We call the configuration of these characteristics the *Simple Structure*.

DESCRIPTION OF THE BASIC STRUCTURE

The Simple Structure is characterized, above all, by what is not—elaborated. Typically, it has little or no technostructure, few support staffers, a loose division of labor, minimal differentiation among its units, and a small managerial hierarchy. Little of its behavior is formalized, and it makes minimal use of planning, training, and the liaison devices. It is, above all, organic. In a sense, Simple Structure is nonstructure: it avoids using all the formal devices of structure, and it minimizes its dependence on staff specialists. The latter are typically hired on contract when needed, rather than encompassed permanently within the organization.

Coordination in the Simple Structure is effected largely by direct supervision. Specifically, power over all important decisions tends to be centralized in the hands of the chief executive officer. Thus, the strategic apex emerges as the key part of the structure; indeed, the structure often consists of little more than a one-person strategic apex and an organic operating core. The chief executive tends to have a wide span of control; in fact, it is not uncommon for everyone else to report to him. Grouping into units—if it exists at all—more often than not is on a loose functional basis, with the coordination between units left to the chief executive. Likewise, communication flows informally in this structure, most of it between the chief executive and everyone else. Thus, a group of McGill MBA students commented in their study of a small manufacturer of pumps, "It is not unusual to see the president of the company engaged in casual conversation with a machine shop mechanic. These types of specialties enable the president to be informed of a machine breakdown even before the shop superintendent is advised."[1] The work flow too tends to be flexible, with the jobs of the operating core being relatively unspecialized and interchangeable.

Decision making is likewise flexible, with the centralization of power allowing for rapid response. Strategy formulation is, of course, the sole responsibility of the chief executive. The process tends to be highly intuitive and nonanalytical, often thriving on uncertainty and oriented to the aggressive search for opportunities. It is not surprising, therefore, that the resulting strategy—seldom made explicit—reflects the chief ex-

---

*   Excerpted from Henry Mintzberg, *Structure in Fives: Designing Effective Organizations* (Prentice-Hall, 1983) chap. 8; used by permission of the publisher.

[1]   *From a paper submitted to the author in Management Policy 701, McGill University, 1970, by S. Genest and S. Darkanzanli.*

ecutive's implicit vision of the place of the organization in its environment. In fact, that strategy is often a direct extrapolation of his personal beliefs, an extension of his own personality.

Handling disturbances and innovating in an entrepreneurial way are perhaps the most important aspects of the chief executive's work. But considerable attention is also given to leadership—a reflection of the importance of direct supervision—and to monitoring for information to keep himself well informed. In contrast, the more formal aspects of managerial work—figurehead duties, for example—are of less significance, as are the need to disseminate information and allocate resources internally, since power and information remain in the strategic apex of the Simple Structure.

Figure 1 shows the Simple Structure symbolically, in terms of our logo, with a wide span of control at the strategic apex, no staff units, and an insignificant middle line.

CONDITIONS OF THE SIMPLE STRUCTURE

Above all, the environment of the Simple Structure tends to be at one and the same time simple and dynamic. A simple environment can be comprehended by a single individual, and so enables decision making to be controlled by that individual. A dynamic environment means organic structure: Because its future state cannot be predicted, the organization cannot effect coordination by standardization. Another condition common to Simple Structures is a technical system that is both nonsophisticated and nonregulating. Sophisticated ones require elaborate staff support structures, to which power over technical decisions must be delegated, and regulating ones call for bureaucratization of the operating core.

Among the conditions giving rise to variants of the Simple Structure, perhaps the most important is stage of development. The *new organization* tends to adopt the Simple Structure, no matter what its environment or technical system, because it has not had the time to elaborate its administrative structure. It is forced to rely on leadership to get things going. Thus, we can conclude that most organizations pass through the Simple Structure in their formative years.

Many *small organizations*, however, remain with the Simple Structure beyond this period. For them, informal communication is convenient and effective. Moreover, their small size may mean less repetition of work in the operating core, which means less standardization. Of course, some organizations are so small that they can rely on mutual adjustment for coordination, almost in the absence of direct supervision by leaders. They constitute a hybrid we can call the *simplest structure*, a Simple Structure with the open lateral communication channels of the Adhocracy.

Another variant—the crisis organization—appears when extreme hostility forces an organization to centralize, no matter what its usual structure. The need for fast, coordinated response puts power in the hands of the chief executive and serves to reduce the degree of bureaucratization as well. (Of course, highly elaborated organizations do not eliminate their technostructures and middle lines when faced with a crisis. But they may temporarily set aside their power over decision making.) James D. Thompson (1967) describes a special case of crisis organization, what he calls the *synthetic organization*. This is temporary, set up to deal with a natural disaster. The situation is new, and the environment is extremely hostile, hence the emphasis on leadership. (Of course, permanent organizations that specialize in disaster work, such as the Red Cross, would be expected to develop standardized procedures

FIGURE 1   THE SIMPLE STRUCTURE

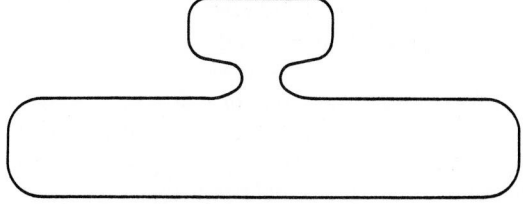

and so to use a more bureaucratic form of structure.)

Personal needs for power produce another variant, which we call the *autocratic organization*. When a chief executive hoards power and avoids the formalization of behavior as an infringement on his right to rule by fiat, he will, in effect, design a Simple Structure for his organization. The same result is produced in the *charismatic organization*, when the leader gains power not because he hoards it but because his followers lavish it upon him. Culture seems to figure prominently in both these examples of Simple Structure. The less industrialized societies, perhaps because they lack the educated work forces needed to man the administrative staff jobs of bureaucratic structures, seem more prone to build their organizations around strong leaders who coordinate by direct supervision. The forces of autocracy or charisma can sometimes drive even very large organizations of developed societies toward the Simple Structure, as in the Ford Motor Company in the late years of its founder.

Another factor that encourages use of the Simple Structure is owner-management, since this precludes outside control, which encourages bureaucratization. The classic case of the owner-managed organization is, of course, the *entrepreneurial firm*. In fact, the entrepreneurial firm seems to be the best overall illustration of the Simple Structure, combining almost all of its characteristics—both structural and situational—into a tight gestalt. The classic entrepreneurial firm is aggressive and innovative, continually searching for the risky environments where the bureaucracies fear to tread. But it is also careful to remain in market niches that the entrepreneur can fully comprehend. In other words, it seeks out environments that are both dynamic and simple. Similarly, the entrepreneurial firm is careful to remain with a simple, nonregulating technical system, one that allows its structure to remain organic and centralized. The firm is usually small, so that it can remain organic and the entrepreneur can retain tight control. Often, it is also young, in part because the attrition rate among entrepreneurial firms is high, in part because those that

survive tend to switch to a more bureaucratic configuration as they age. The entrepreneur tends to be autocratic and sometimes charismatic as well; typically, he has founded his own firm because he could not tolerate the controls imposed upon him by the bureaucracies in which he has worked. Inside the organization, all revolves around the entrepreneur. Its goals are his goals, its strategy his vision of its place in the world. Most entrepreneurs loath bureaucratic procedures—and the technostructures that come with them—as impositions on their flexibility. So their unpredictable maneuvering keeps their structures lean, flexible, and organic.

SOME ISSUES ASSOCIATED WITH SIMPLE STRUCTURE

In the Simple Structure, decisions concerning strategy and operations are together centralized in the office of the chief executive. Centralization has the important advantage of ensuring that strategic response reflects full knowledge of the operating core. It also favors flexibility and adaptability in strategic response: only one person need act. But centralization can also cause confusion between strategic and operating issues. The chief executive can get so enmeshed in operating problems that he loses sight of strategic considerations. Alternatively, he may become so enthusiastic about strategic opportunities that the more routine operations wither for lack of attention and eventually pull down the whole organization. Both problems occur frequently in entrepreneurial firms.

The Simple Structure is also the riskiest of the configurations, hinging on the health and whims of one individual. One heart attack can literally wipe out the organization's prime coordinating mechanism.

Like all the configurations, restricted to its appropriate situation, the Simple Structure usually functions effectively. Its flexibility is well suited to simple, dynamic environments, to extremely hostile ones (at least for a time), and to young and small organizations. But lacking a developed administration, the Simple Structure becomes a liability outside its narrow range of conditions. Its organic state impedes it from producing the standardized outputs required of an environment that has stabilized or an organization grown large, and its centralized nature renders it ineffective in dealing with an environment that has become complex. Unfortunately, however, when structural changes must come, the only person with the power to make them—the chief executive himself—often resists. The great strength of the Simple Structure—its flexibility—becomes its chief liability.

One great advantage of Simple Structure is its sense of mission. Many people enjoy working in a small, intimate organization, where its leader—often charismatic—knows where he is taking it. As a result, the organization tends to grow rapidly, the world being, so to speak, at its feet. Employees can develop a solid identification with such an organization. But other people perceive the Simple Structure as highly restrictive. Because one person calls all the shots, they feel not like the participants on an exciting journey, but like cattle being led to market for someone else's benefit.

As a matter of fact, the broadening of democratic norms beyond the political sphere into that of organizations has rendered the Simple Structure unfashionable in contemporary society. Increasingly, it is being described as paternalistic, sometimes autocratic, and is accused of distributing organizational power inappropriately. Certainly, our description identifies Simple Structure as the property of one individual, whether in fact or in effect. There are no countervailing powers in this configuration, which means that the chief executive can easily abuse his authority.

There have been Simple Structures as long as there have been organizations. Indeed, this was probably the only structure known to those who first discovered the benefits of coordinating their activities in some formal way. But in some sense, Simple Structure had its heyday in the era of the great American trusts of the late nineteenth century, when powerful entrepreneurs personally controlled huge empires. Since then, at least in Western society, the Simple Structure

has been on the decline. Between 1895 and 1950, according to one study (cited in Pugh et al., 1963–64:296), the proportion of entrepreneurs in American industry has declined sharply, whereas that of "bureaucrats" in particular and administrators in general has increased continuously.

Today, many view the Simple Structure as an anachronism in societies that call themselves democratic. Yet it remains a prevalent and important configuration, and will, in fact, continue to be so as long as new organizations are created, some organizations prefer to remain small and informal while others require strong leadership despite larger size, society prizes entrepreneurship, and many organizations face temporary environments that are extremely hostile or more permanent ones that are both simple and dynamic.

STRATEGY FORMATION IN THE SIMPLE STRUCTURE*

How can we characterize the formation of strategy in the simple structure? In "Strategy Making in Three Modes," (Mintzberg, 1973b), we described the entrepreneural mode as follows: power centralized in the hands of the chief executive, whose behavior is dominated by the active search for opportunities, by the pursuit of the goal of growth above all, and by the taking of dramatic leaps forward in the face of uncertainty. That, as noted, is the general view in the literature.

What about entrepreneurship in the real world of simple structures? What does "vision" really mean; where does it come from; how does it change? In the empirical studies of strategy formation carried out at McGill University, in which the strategies of different firms were tracked and studied across several decades of their histories, two exposed entrepreneurship in the simple structure particularly well, a retail chain called

*   This section is adapted from Henry Mintzberg and James A. Waters, "The Mind of the Strategist (s)," in S. Srivastva, ed., The Executive Mind (Jossey-Bass, 1983) and "Tracking Strategies in an Entrepreneurial Firm," Academy of Management Journal (1982), pp. 465–499.

Steinberg's and a manufacturing firm called Cana-delle.

Entrepreneurial Vision at Steinberg's

Steinberg's is a Canadian retail chain that began with a tiny food store in Montreal in 1917 and grew to a sales volume of over a billion dollars by the end of our study period in 1974. Most of that growth came from supermarket operations, although the firm did diversify (primarily into other retailing activities) after 1960. In many ways, Steinberg fits the entrepreneurial mode rather well. Sam Steinberg, who joined his mother in the first store at the age of 11 and personally made a quick decision to expand it two years later, maintained complete formal control of the firm (for example, maintaining personal control of every single voting share; the public stock never had voting rights) to the day of his death in 1978. He also exercised close managerial control over all major decisions, at least until the firm began to diversify.

As for the famous "bold stroke" of the entrepreneur (Cole, 1959), we certainly saw evidence of some rather dramatic changes in the company, for example, a plunge into self-service in the 1930s and into the shopping center business in the 1950s. But for the most part, Sam Steinberg did not plunge until he tested the water. The story of the move into self-service is indicative. To paraphrase from our report (Mintzberg and Waters, 1982), in 1933 one of the company's eight stores "struck it bad," in the chief executive's words, incurring "unacceptable" losses ($125/week). Sam Steinberg closed the store one Friday night, changed its name from "Steinberg's Service Stores" to "Wholesale Groceteria," slashed prices by 15–20%, instituted a form of self-service, printed hand bills, stuffed them into neighborhood mailboxes, and reopened on Monday morning! From that point on, after eventually converting the others, in his words, "We grew like Topsy."

This anecdote tells us something about the bold stroke of the entrepreneur; the term we use

in the article is "controlled boldness." And it also tells us something about the proaction of the entrepreneur. Sam Steinberg was solving a problem, not searching out an opportunity. Indeed, he viewed the situation more as a crisis than a problem. It was this view of things that distinguished his treatment of problems: getting more excited about them than anyone else. Most people would have viewed this as a problem to be solved, likely by doing the obvious—closing the store. By redefining it as a crisis, Sam Steinberg turned it into an opportunity. That was his way of getting energy behind action and of keeping ahead of his competition. He "oversolved" the problem, and remade his company. We refer to this behavior as the "proactive reaction."

Another point about the entrepreneurial mode that came out in this study is that strategy for the entrepreneur is not a formal, detailed plan on paper. It is a personal vision in a brain, a concept of the business. That vision may sometimes get partially articulated, but for the most part it remains locked inside the brain. So long as the entrepreneur is able to make the key decisions for the organization, this of course poses no problem. Indeed, the great advantage of strategy as personal vision is that it can be changed rather easily. A formal plan, in contrast, tends to get widely disseminated in an organization, and so cannot easily be changed.

Knowledge of the Business

A further point that emerged clearly in this study is that the key to generating such a vision, and to changing it at the right time, is intimate, detailed knowledge of the business. In discussing his firm's competitive advantage, Sam Steinberg told us: "Nobody knew the grocery business like we did. Everything has to do with your knowledge." He added:

> I knew merchandise, I knew cost, I knew selling, I knew customers, I knew everything . . . and I passed on all my knowledge; I kept teaching my people. That's

the advantage we had. They couldn't touch us.

This study indicates how effective such knowledge can be when it is concentrated in one individual who is fully in charge (having no need to convince others with different views or degrees of knowledge, neither subordinates below nor superiors at some distant headquarters), and who retains a strong, long term commitment to the organization. So long as the business is simple and concentrated enough to be comprehended in one brain, the entrepreneurial mode is powerful, indeed unexcelled. No other mode of strategy making can provide an equivalent degree of deliberateness and of integration of strategies with each other as well as fit with the environment. None can provide so clear and complete a vision of direction, yet also allow the flexibility to elaborate and rework that vision. The conception of a novel strategy is an exercise in synthesis, which is typically best carried out in a single, informed brain. That is why the entrepreneurial mode is at the center of the most glorious corporate successes.

Embedded in conventional thinking about strategic planning is an implicit image of the strategy maker sitting on a pedestal, being fed aggregate data that he uses to "formulate" strategies to be "implemented" by others. But the history of Steinberg's belies that image. It suggests that clear, imaginative, integrated visions depend on an involvement with detail, an intimate knowledge of specifics (usually associated with implementation). As noted earlier, the ability to be passionately involved at all levels of activity in the business was a striking characteristic of Sam Steinberg.

That this remained possible for such a long period of time, even as the company grew very large, is likely a reflection of the simple and repetitive nature of this business. The same simple transaction repeated itself customer after customer, store after store, thousands of times each day. Once the firm shifted from personalized to self-service (i.e., impersonalized service), then 200 stores were not unlike 20 so long as they were concentrated in a geographical area the leader knew well.

Losing Entrepreneurial Control

The personal touch of the entrepreneur was critical to Steinberg's success. The irony was that it was the very success of the entrepreneurial mode that eventually rendered it unsuitable. When success encouraged the spread of the operations beyond the comprehension of one man—first to expand geographically to regions outside of the leader's personal knowledge, and then to diversify horizontally to new kinds of retailing—a shift in the mode of strategy making became inevitable. No longer could decisions be based on the personalized vision of one individual, because no longer could all the necessary knowledge be brought to a focus there.

Growth and diversification (due to saturation of traditional markets) necessitated the building up of a more formalized structure with divided responsibilities and increased distance between Sam Steinberg and the operations. And that preempted the personal involvement of the leader. The result was a new mode of strategy making, more decentralized, more analytic, in some ways more careful, but at the same time less flexible, less integrated, less visionary, and, ironically, less deliberate.

Back in the entrepreneurial mode, at the height of its success, the genius of a Sam Steinberg, in our view, was that he could pursue one vision for 20 years (from the change to self-service in 1933 until the early 1950's), and then change it when he had to. After spending the 1930s and 1940s perfecting his new retailing formula—worrying about fluorescent lighting and new ways to use cellophane to package meat for self-service, for instance, he was able to shift is thoughts in the 1950's to the impact of the newly arrived shopping centers on overall retailing habits, realizing that he had to redefine the nature of his business. In effect, he was able to detect a major discontinuity in his industry, and to bump his thinking from one level to a wholly different one. We believe such a "gestalt" shift—from cellophane to shopping centers—requires a high degree of sophistication. How does the executive mind function when such a shift becomes necessary?

Shift in Entrepreneurial Vision at Canadelle

Let us turn to our study of Canadelle for some hints at the answer. Canadelle produces women's undergarments, primarily brassieres. It too was a highly successful organization, although hardly on the same scale as Steinberg. Things were going very well for the company in the late 1960s, under the personal leadership of the son of its founder. Suddenly everything changed. To draw from our report (Mintzberg and Waters, 1983): A sexual revolution of sorts was brewing. In sharp contrast to the pointed look that had been so popular for a decade, women wished to appear more natural. "Bra-burning" was a major symbol of the social unheaval of the times, and for a manufacturer of brassieres, the threat was obvious. The mini-skirt dominated the fashion scene, obsoleting the girdle and leading to the development of pantyhose. As the executives of Canadelle put it, "the bottom fell out of the girdle business." Sales dropped by 30% per year, eventually stabilizing at about 5% of the firm's total business. Essentially, it appeared that the whole environment—long so receptive to the company's strategies—had suddenly turned on the company.

We had the good fortune not only to be able to interview the chief executive at length on his response to these changes, but also to include him in our brainstorming team that dealt with these issues in a conceptual way. Let us first describe the events as we saw them in our report and then present our conceptual interpretation of them.

At the time, a French company was promoting in Quebec a light, sexy, molded garment called "Huit" with the theme: "just like not wearing a bra." Their target market was 15–20 year olds. Though expensive when landed in Quebec, and not well-fitting, the product sold well. The

chief executive flew to France in an attempt to license the product for manufacturing in Canada. The French firm refused, but he claimed that what he learned in "that one hour in their offices made the trip worthwhile." He learned that the ostensibly no-bra movement was going to manifest itself primarily as a less-bra movement. What women seemed to want was a more natural look. He also found that the product was being target marketed to younger people.

The second event, shortly after, was a trip to a sister firm in the United States. There, the CEO realized the importance of market segmentation by age and life style. The company then sponsored market research to better understand what women wanted from a brassiere. The results indicated that for the more mature customer, the brassiere was a cosmetic, which she wore to look and feel more attractive. The product had an important sex appeal dimension for these customers. Moreover, it was found that the company's brand had high recognition among these consumers. In contrast, the younger customer wanted to look and feel natural. The sex appeal dimension was considerably less important. Also, in the minds of these consumers, Canadelle's brand name (Wonderbra) was associated with older women. Based on these distinctions, the CEO became convinced that some major product line differentiation was required.

These two events led to a major shift in strategy. The CEO describes it as a kind of revelation—the confluence of different ideas to create a new mental set. In his words, "all of a sudden the idea forms." His groping had led to two new major concepts in the firm's strategy. On the marketing side was market segmentation, specifically the division of market into older and younger customers. And on the technology and manufacturing side was the use of molding to produce seamless brassiere cups.

Canadelle initiated an intensive technology development program to produce its own molded brassiere, stimulated by the recent introduction of new fabrics. The firm introduced a molded garment made of Tricot under their existing brand name for older customers and a stretch garment of Lycra for the younger market (under the name Dici), with a great deal of success.

Three Stage Shift in Vision

On a conceptual level, we can draw on Lewin's (1951) notion of unfreezing, changing, and refreezing to explain this gestalt shift in vision. The process of unfreezing is essentially one of overcoming the natural defense mechanisms to realize that the environment has in fact changed fundamentally. Effective managers, especially effective strategic managers, are supposed to scan their environments continually. One danger of strategic management is that it may encourage managers to be *too* in touch. They may give so much attention to strategic monitoring when nothing important is happening that when something really does change, they may not even notice it. The trick, of course, is to pick out the discontinuities that matter. Many changes are temporary or simply unimportant. Some are consequential and a few, revolutionary. For Canadelle, the changes in the late 1960s were clearly revolutionary.

A second step in unfreezing is the willingness to step into the void, so to speak, for the leader to shed his or her conventional notions of how the business is supposed to function (according to the industry "recipe," as Grinyer & Spender [1979] have termed it), and really open his or her mind to what is happening. Critical is the avoidance of premature closure—not to seize on a new thrust before it is clear what the signals really mean. This takes a special kind of management, one able to live with a good deal of uncertainty and discomfort. The president of Canadelle was able to articulate his feelings about this time: "There is a period of confusion before you know what to do about it . . . You sleep on it . . . start looking for patterns . . . become an information hound, searching for [explanations] everywhere." This stage may be painful, but in our view it is critical to successful strategic reorientation.

Strategic change of this magnitude seems to involve mindset before strategy (or, if you

like "perspective" before "position"), and seems to be essentially conceptual in nature. In other words, the concepts of the strategist—his or her Weltanschauung (worldview)—must change before anything else can change. If this study gives any indication, then while problems and threats in the environment may provoke the unfreezing, it is opportunities that stimulate the process of change. With some idea of what *can* be done, the strategist begins to converge on a new concept of the business—a new strategic vision. Our guess is that what happened here—the presence of one or two basic driving ideas—is typical: in the final analysis, change in mindset is stimulated by a small number of key events, probably one critical incident in most cases. Continuous bombardment of facts, opinions, problems, and so on, may have had to prepare the mind for the change, but one simple insight likely underlies the synthesis—brings all the disparate data together in one sudden "eureka"-type flash.

Once the mind is set, assuming it has read the new environment correctly and has not seized prematurely on trends that have themselves not yet stabilized, then the refreezing step begins. Here the object is not to read the environment, at least not in a global sense, but, in effect, to block it out. This is not the time for the monitoring precepts of strategic management. It is the time to work out the consequences of a new strategic vision.

It has been claimed that obsession is an ingredient in effective organizations (Peters, 1980). For the period of refreezing (not unfreezing or changing), we would agree. What is needed here is not questioning, but the pursuing of the new orientation—the new mindset—with full vigor. When we asked the president how the post 1970 period differed from that of the two previous years, he commented: "Any idea is acceptable so long as its . . ." And he motioned with his hands in two parallel lines to indicate: so long as it is strictly within the bounds of the new vision. A management that was open and divergent in its thinking must now become closed and convergent. We wonder how many executives fail in one or the other side of this problem—

FIGURE 2
LEADERSHIP TAKING THE LEAD
IN SIMPLE STRUCTURE

maintaining set patterns when divergence becomes necessary, or failing to recognize the need to settle down to a convergent pattern after a period of divergence.

While unfreezing was a time of great discomfort, refreezing must be one of great excitement (at least for those who accept the reorientation). The organization now knows where it is going; the object of the exercise is to use all the skills at its command to get there. This is not to say that this is a particularly creative period. Refreezing is characterized more by an analytic orientation, with heavy emphasis on formal evaluation, perhaps closer to the planning mode. Of course, not everyone accepts the new vision; for those steeped in the old strategies, the discomfort now begins, and considerable resistance can arise, forcing the leader to make greater use of the political skills (and powers) at his command. Of course, this problem is relatively minor when structure is simple. [As we shall see in the next text chapter, it is in the mature context that it assumes major proportions.]

Leadership Taking the Lead

To conclude, entrepreneurship in the simple structure is very much tied up with the creation of vision, essentially with *concept attainment*. Since that vision is personal, strategies can be characterized as largely deliberate. But, in the absence of specific plans, the details of these strategies are likely to emerge, so that it is only the broad vision (strategy as perspective) that is really deliberate. And the vision can change too. In other words, the leader is able to adapt en route—he or she can learn, which means new visions can emerge too, although, as we have seen, sometimes rather quickly.

In the entrepreneurial mode, as shown in Figure 2, the focus of attention is on the leader; the organization is malleable and responsive to the leader's initiatives, and the environment for the most part remains benign, the result of the leader selecting (or "enacting") the correct niche for his or her organization. The environment can, of course, flare up occasionally to challenge the organization (the dotted arrow), forcing the leader to seek out a new and more appropriate niche.

COMPETITIVE STRATEGY IN EMERGING INDUSTRIES*

by Michael E. Porter

Emerging industries are newly formed or reformed industries that have been created by technological innovations, shifts in relative cost relationships, emergence of new consumer needs, or other economic and sociological changes that elevate a new product or service to the level of a potentially viable business opportunity. . . .

The essential characteristic of an emerging industry from the viewpoint of formulating strategy is that there are no rules of the game. The competitive problem in an emerging industry is that all the rules must be established such that the firm can cope with and prosper under them.

THE STRUCTURAL ENVIRONMENT

Although emerging industries can differ a great deal in their structures, there are some common structural factors that seem to characterize many industries in this stage of their development. Most of them relate either to the absence of established bases for competition or other rules of the game or to the initial small size and newness of the industry.

Common Structural Characteristics

Technological Uncertainty There is usually a great deal of uncertainty about the technology in an emerging industry: What product configuration will ultimately prove to be the best? Which production technology will prove to be the most efficient? . . .

Strategic Uncertainty . . . No "right" strategy has been clearly identified, and different firms are groping with different approaches to product/ market positioning, marketing, servicing, and so on, as well as betting on different product configurations or production technologies. . . . Closely related to this problem, firms often have poor information about competitors, characteristics of customers, and industry conditions in the emerging phase. No one knows who all the competitors are, and reliable industry sales and market share data are often simply unavailable, for example.

High Initial Costs but Steep Cost Reduction Small production volume and newness usually combine to produce high costs in the emerging industry relative to those the industry can potentially achieve. . . . Ideas come rapidly in terms of improved procedures, plant layout, and so on, and employees achieve major gains in productivity as job familiarity increases. Increasing sales make major additions to the scale and total accumulated volume of output produced by firms. . . .

Embryonic Companies and Spin-Offs The emerging phase of the industry is usually accompanied by the presence of the greatest proportion of newly formed companies (to be contrasted with newly formed units of established firms) that the industry will ever experience. . . .

First-Time Buyers Buyers of the emerging industry's product or service are inherently first-time buyers. The marketing task is thus one of inducing substitution, or getting the buyer to purchase the new product or service instead of something else. . . .

Short Time Horizon In many emerging industries the pressure to develop customers or produce products to meet demand is so great that bottlenecks and problems are dealt with expediently rather than as a result of an analysis of future conditions. At the same time, industry conventions are often born out of pure chance. . . .

Subsidy In many emerging industries, especially those with radical new technology or that address areas of societal concern, there may be subsidization of early entrants. Subsidy may come from a variety of government and nongovernment sources. . . . Subsidies often add a great degree of instability to an industry, which is made dependent on political decisions that can be quickly reversed or modified. . . .

Early Mobility Barriers

In an emerging industry, the configuration of mobility barriers is often predictably different from that which will characterize the industry later in its development. Common early barriers are the following:

- proprietary technology;
- access to distribution channels;
- access to raw materials and other inputs (skilled labor) of appropriate cost and quality;
- cost advantages due to experience, made more significant by the technological and competitive uncertainties;
- risk, which raises the effective opportunity cost of capital and thereby effective capital barriers.

. . . The nature of the early barriers is a key reason why we observe newly created companies in emerging industries. The typical early barriers stem less from the need to command massive resources than from the ability to bear risk, be creative technologically, and make forward-looking decisions to garner input supplies and distribution channels. . . . There may be some advantages to late entry, however. . . .

Strategic Choices

Formulation of strategy in emerging industries must cope with the uncertainty and risk of this period of an industry's development. The rules of the competitive game are largely undefined, the structure of the industry unsettled and probably changing, and competitors hard to diagnose. Yet all these factors have another side—the emerging phase of an industry's development is probably the period when the strategic degrees of freedom are the greatest and when the leverage from good strategic choices is the highest in determining performance.

Shaping Industry Structure The overriding strategic issue in emerging industries is the ability of the firm to shape industry structure. Through its choices, the firm can try to set the rules of the game in areas like product policy, marketing approach, and pricing strategy. . . .

Externalities in Industry Development In an emerging industry, a key strategic issue is the balance the firm strikes between industry advocacy and pursuing its own narrow self-interest. Because of potential problems with industry image, credibility, and confusion of buyers . . . in the emerging phase the firm is in part dependent on others in the industry for its own success. The overriding problem for the industry is inducing substitution and attracting first-time buyers, and it is usually in the firm's interest during this phase to help promote standardization, police substandard quality and fly-by-night producers, and present a consistent front to suppliers, customers, government, and the financial community. . . .

It is probably a valid generalization that the balance between industry outlook and firm outlook must shift in the direction of the firm

as the industry begins to achieve significant penetration. Sometimes firms who have taken very high profiles as industry spokespersons, much to their and the industry's benefit, fail to recognize that they must shift their orientation. As a result, they can be left behind as the industry matures. . . .

Changing Role of Suppliers and Channels Strategically, the firm in an emerging industry must be prepared for a possible shift in the orientation of its suppliers and distribution channels as the industry grows in size and proves itself. Suppliers may become increasingly willing (or can be forced) to respond to the industry's special needs in terms of varieties, service, and delivery. Similarly, distribution channels may become more receptive to investing in facilities, advertising, and so forth in partnership with the firms. Early exploitation of these changes in orientation can give the firm strategic leverage.

Shifting Mobility Barriers As outlined above . . . the early mobility barriers may erode quickly in an emerging industry, often to be replaced by very different ones as the industry grows in size and as the technology matures. This factor has a number of implications. The most obvious is that the firm must be prepared to find new ways to defend its position and must not rely solely on things like proprietary technology and a unique product variety on which it has succeeded in the past. Responding to shifting mobility barriers may involve commitments of capital that far exceed those that have been necessary in the early phases.

Another implication is that the *nature of entrants* into the industry may shift to more established firms attracted to the larger and increasingly proven (less risky) industry, often competing on the basis of the newer forms of mobility barriers, like scale and marketing clout. . . .

Timing Entry

A crucial strategic choice for competing in emerging industries is the appropriate timing of entry. Early entry (or pioneering) involves high risk but may involve otherwise low entry barriers and can offer a large return. Early entry is appropriate when the following general circumstances hold:

- Image and reputation of the firm are important to the buyer, and the firm can develop an enhanced reputation by being a pioneer.
- Early entry can initiate the learning process in a business in which the learning curve is important, experience is difficult to imitate, and it will not be nullified by successive technological generations.
- Customer loyalty will be great, so that benefits will accrue to the firm that sells to the customer first.
- Absolute cost advantages can be gained by early commitment to supplies of raw materials, distribution channels, and so on. . . .

Tactical Moves The problems limiting development of an emerging industry suggest some tactical moves that may improve the firm's strategic position:

- Early commitments to suppliers of raw materials will yield favorable priorities in times of shortages.
- Financing can be timed to take advantage of a Wall Street love affair with the industry if it happens, even if financing is ahead of actual needs. This step lowers the firm's cost of capital. . . .

The choice of which emerging industry to enter is dependent on the outcome of a predictive exercise such as the one described above. An emerging industry is attractive if its ultimate structure (not its *initial* structure) is one that is consistent with above-average returns and if the firm can create a defendable position in the industry in the long run. The latter will depend on its resources relative to the mobility barriers that will evolve.

Too often firms enter emerging industries because they are growing rapidly, because incumbents are currently very profitable, or because ultimate industry size promises to be large. These may be contributing reasons, but the decision

to enter must ultimately depend on a structural analysis. . . .

COMPETITIVE STRATEGY IN FRAGMENTED INDUSTRIES*

by Michael E. Porter

An important structural environment in which many firms compete is the fragmented industry, that is, an industry in which no firm has a significant market share and can strongly influence the industry outcome. Usually fragmented industries are populated by a large number of small- and medium-sized companies, many of them privately held. . . . The essential notion that makes these industries a unique environment in which to compete is the absence of market leaders with the power to shape industry events. . . .

Some fragmented industries, such as computer software and television program syndication, are characterized by products or services that are differentiated, whereas others, such as oil tanker shipping, electronic component distribution, and fabricated aluminum products, involve essentially undifferentiated products. Fragmented industries also vary greatly in their technological sophistication, ranging from high technology businesses like solar heating to garbage collection and liquor retailing. . . .

WHAT MAKES AN INDUSTRY FRAGMENTED?

. . . in many industries there are underlying economic causes [of fragmentation] and the principal ones seem to be as follows:

Low Overall Entry Barriers Nearly all fragmented industries have low overall entry barriers. Otherwise they could not be populated by so many small firms. . . .

Absence of Economies of Scale or Experience Curve Most fragmented industries are characterized by the absence of significant scale economies or learning curves in any major aspect of the business. . . .

High Transportation Costs High transportation costs limit the size of an efficient plant or production location despite the presence of economies of scale. . . .

High Inventory Costs or Erratic Sales Fluctuations Although there may be intrinsic economies of scale in the production process, they may be reaped if inventory carrying costs are high and sales fluctuate. . . . Small-scale, less specialized facilities or distribution systems are usually more flexible in absorbing output shifts than large, more specialized ones, even though they may have higher operating costs at a steady operating rate.

No Advantages of Size in Dealing with Buyers or Suppliers . . . Buyers, for example, might be so large that even a large firm in the industry would only be marginally better off in bargaining with them than a smaller firm. . . .

Diseconomies of Scale in Some Important Aspect [Rapid product changes or style changes, need to maintain low overhead, a highly diverse product line, heavy creative content, need for close local control (as in restaurants), personal service or local image or contacts are key.]

Diverse Market Needs In some industries buyers' tastes are fragmented, with different buyers each desiring special varieties of a product and willing (and able) to pay a premium for it rather than accept a more standardized version. . . .

High Product Differentiation, Particularly if Based on Image . . . Performing artists, for example, may prefer dealing with a small booking agency or record label that carries the image they desire to cultivate.

Exit Barriers If there are exit barriers, marginal firms will tend to stay in the industry and thereby hold back consolidation. . . .

Local Regulation Local regulation, by forcing the firm to comply with standards that may be particularistic, or to be attuned to a local political scene, can be a major source of fragmentation in an industry, even where the other conditions do not hold. . . .

Government Prohibition of Concentration Legal restrictions prohibit consolidation in industries such as electric power and television and radio stations. . . .

Newness An industry can be fragmented because it is new and no firm or firms have yet developed the skills and resources to command a significant market share, even though there are no other impediments to consolidation. . . .

COPING WITH FRAGMENTATION

It takes the presence of only one of these characteristics to block the consolidation of an industry. . . .

In many situations, industry fragmentation is . . . the result of underlying industry economics that cannot be overcome. Fragmented industries are characterized not only by many competitors but also by a generally weak bargaining position with suppliers and buyers. Marginal profitability can be the result. In such an environment, strategic *positioning* is of particularly crucial significance. The strategic challenge is to cope with fragmentation by becoming one of the most successful firms, although able to garner only a modest market share.

Since every industry is ultimately different, there is no generalized method for competing most effectively in a fragmented industry. However, there are a number of possible strategic alternatives for coping with a fragmented structure that should be considered when examining any particular situation. These are specific approaches to pursuing the low cost, differentiate, or focus generic strategies. . . .

Tightly Managed Decentralization Since fragmented industries often are characterized by the need for intense coordination, local management orientation, high personal service, and close control, an important alternative for competition is tightly managed decentralization. Rather than increasing the scale of operations at one or a few locations, this strategy involves deliberately keeping individual operations small and as autonomous as possible. This approach is supported by tight central control and performance-oriented compensation for local managers. . . .

"Formula" Facilities Another alternative, related to the previous one, is to view the key strategic variable in the business as the building of efficient, low-cost facilities at multiple locations. This strategy involves designing a standard facility, whether it be a plant or a service establishment, and polishing to a science the process of constructing and putting the facility into operation at minimum cost. . . .

Increased Value Added Many fragmented industries produce products or services that are commodities or otherwise difficult to differentiate; many distribution businesses, for example, stock similar if not identical product lines to their competitors'. In cases such as these, an effective strategy may be to increase the value added of the business by providing more service with sale, by engaging in some final fabrication of the product (like cutting to size or punching holes), or by doing subassembly or assembly of components before they are sold to the customer. . . .

Specialization by Product Type or Product Segment When industry fragmentation results from or is accompanied by the presence of numerous items in the product line, an effective strategy for achieving above-average results can be to specialize on a tightly constrained group of products. . . . [This] can allow the firm to achieve some bargaining power with suppliers by developing a significant volume of their products. It may also allow the enhancement of product differentiation with the customer as a result of the specialist's perceived expertise and image in the particular product area. . . .

Specialization by Customer Type If competition is intense because of a fragmented structure, a firm can potentially benefit by specialization on a particular category of customer in the industry. . . .

Specialization by Type of Order Regardless of the customer, the firm can specialize in a particular type of order to cope with intense competitive pressure in a fragmented industry. One approach is to service only small orders for which the customer wants immediate delivery and is less price sensitive. Or the firm can service only custom orders to take advantage of less price sensitivity or to build switching costs. Once again, the cost of such specialization may be some limitation in volume.

A Focused Geographic Area Even though a significant industry-wide share is out of reach or there are no national economies of scale (and perhaps even diseconomies), there may be substantial economies in blanketing a given geographic area by concentrating facilities, marketing attention, and sales activity. This policy can economize on the use of the sales force, allow more efficient advertising, allow a single distribution center, and so on. . . .

Bare Bones/No Frills Given the intensity of competition and low margins in many fragmented industries, a simple but powerful strategic alternative can be intense attention to maintaining a bare bones/no frills competitive posture—that is, low overhead, low-skilled employees, tight cost control, and attention to detail. This policy places the firm in the best position to compete on price and still make an above-average return.

Backward Integration Although the causes of fragmentation can preclude a large share of the market, selective backward integration may lower costs and put pressure on competitors who cannot afford such integration. . . .

## ELEVEN

THE
MATURE
CONTEXT

In this chapter, we focus on one of the more common contexts for today's organizations. Whether we refer to this by its form of operations (usually *mass production* or the *mass* provision of *services*), by the form of structure adopted (machine-like *bureaucracy*), by the type of environment it prefers (a *stable* one in a *mature* industry), or by the specific generic strategy it tends to favor (*cost leadership*), the context is quite similar and gives rise to a relatively well-defined configuration.

The readings on what we shall refer to as the *mature* context cover these different aspects and examine some of the problems and opportunities of functioning in this realm. The first reading on "machine bureaucracy" from Mintzberg's book *Structure in Fives*, describes a common structure for this context as well as the environment in which it tends to be found. It also investigates some of the social issues surrounding this particular form of structure.

Appended to this reading is a set of conclusions derived from the McGill University research project on tracking strategy. Here we can see what happens when large organizations accustomed to stability must suddenly change their strategies dramatically. The careful formal planning, on which they tend to rely so heavily in easier times, seems ill suited to dealing with changes that may require virtual revolutions in the organizations' functioning.

We do not use the label machine bureaucracy here as a loaded term, but rather as a description of the type of structure organizations have traditionally moved toward when they were primarily concerned with the attainment of efficiency through standardization of operations. While modern CAD/CAM technologies have changed the output flexibility and the internal work situations of such enterprises enormously, many have yet to convert their structures to adjust to the new potentials. This is one of the challenges posed by the chapter on the *innovative* context and by the cases on General Motors, Exxon, and the Royal Bank.

The second reading is a chapter from Michael Porter's book *Competitive Strategy* on how to deal with the transition to industry maturity. It describes the environment of this context and also probes some of its favored strategies, notably cost leadership.

A particular technique designed for use with this strategy, and the mature context in general, is the subject of the next reading. Called *Cost Dynamics: Scale and Experience Effects* and written by Derek Abell and John Hammond for a marketing textbook, it probes the "experience curve" as developed by the Boston Consulting

Group. This technique, which we first encountered in the Pascale reading on ''The Honda Effect,'' (Chapter 5) became quite popular in the late 1970s. Although its limitations are now widely recognized, it still has certain applicability to firms operating in the mature context.

The reading by William Hall closes the chapter on a different, and optimistic, note. It investigates successful strategies employed by organizations in mature, stagnant industries: cost leadership (aspects of which Hall criticizes) as well as other strategies involving differentiation. It is becoming more widely acknowledged that organizations in mature industries can, by a variety of means, positively manage their way out of what appear to be difficult circumstances. Both service and quality differentiation become key strategies.

THE MACHINE BUREAUCRACY*

by Henry Mintzberg

A national post office, a security agency, a steel company, a custodial prison, an airline, a giant automobile company; all these organizations appear to have a number of structural characteristics in common. Above all, their operating work is routine, the greatest part of it rather simple and repetitive; as a result, their work processes are highly standardized. These characteristics give rise to the *Machine Bureaucracies* of our society, the structures fine-tuned to run as integrated, regulated machines.

BASIC STRUCTURE

A clear configuration of the design parameters has held up consistently in the research: highly specialized, routine operating tasks; very formal-

---

* Excerpted from Henry Mintzberg, *Structure in Fives: Designing Effective Organizations* (Prentice-Hall, 1983), chap. 9; used by permission of the publisher.

ized procedures in the operating core; a proliferation of rules, regulations, and formalized communication throughout the organization; large-sized units at the operating level; reliance on the functional basis for grouping tasks; relatively centralized power for decision making; and an elaborate administrative structure with a sharp distinction between line and staff.

The Operating Core

The obvious starting point is the operating core, with its highly rationalized work flow. As a result of this, the operating tasks are simple and repetitive, generally requiring a minimum of skill and little training—often taking only hours, seldom more than a few weeks, and usually in-house. This leads to a sharp division of labor in the operating core—to narrowly defined jobs, specialized both vertically and horizontally—and to an emphasis on the standardization of work processes for coordination. Thus, formalization of behavior emerges as the key design parameter. Because the workers are left with little discretion in their work, there is little possibility for mutual adjustment in the operating core. The use of direct supervision by first-line managers is limited by the fact that standardization handles most of the coordination. Thus, very large units can be designed in the operating core. . . .

The Administrative Component

The tight regulation of the operating work—in effect, the sealing off of the operating core from disruptive environmental influence—requires that the administrative structure be highly elaborated. First is the middle line, which is fully developed, especially well above the operating core, and is sharply differentiated into functional units. The managers of this middle line have three prime tasks. One is to handle the disturbances that arise among the highly specialized workers of the operating core. Although standardization takes care of most of the operating interdependences, ambiguities inevitably remain, and these give rise to conflicts. These cannot easily be handled by mutual adjustment among the operators, since informal communication is inhibited by the extensive standardization. So they tend to be handled by direct supervision, the orders of first-line managers. And because many of these conflicts arise between operators adjacent to each other in the work flow, the natural tendency is to bring adjacent operators under common supervision—in other words, to group the operators into units that deal with distinct parts of the work flow, which results in the functional basis for grouping operating units. For the same reason, this functional grouping gets mirrored all the way up the hierarchy, from the production and maintenance departments, which look to the plant manager to resolve many of their conflicts, to the manufacturing and marketing vice-presidents, who often expect the same of the company president.

A second task of the middle-line managers, which also explains why they are grouped on functional bases, is to work in a liaison role with the analysts of the technostructure to incorporate their standards down into the operating units. Their third task is to support the vertical flows in the structure—the aggregation of the feedback information up the hierarchy and the elaboration of the action plans that come back down. All these tasks of the middle-line managers require personal contacts—with their subordinates, the analysts, and their own superiors—which limit the number of people they can supervise. Hence, units above the operating core tend to be rather small in size and the overall administrative hierarchy rather tall in shape.

The technostructure must also be highly elaborated. In fact, Stinchcombe identified the birth of this structure in early nineteenth-century industries such as textiles and banking with the growth of technocratic personnel. Because the Machine Bureaucracy depends primarily on the standardization of its operating work processes for coordination, the technostructure—which houses the analysts who do the standardizing—emerges as the key part of the structure. This is so despite the fact that the Machine Bureaucracy sharply distinguishes between line and staff. To the line managers is delegated the formal authority for the operating units; the technocratic staff—officially, at least—merely advises. But without the standardizers—the cadre of work-study analysts, job-description designers, schedulers, quality control engineers, planners, budgeters, MIS people, accountants, operations researchers, and many, many more—the structure simply could not function. Hence, despite their lack of formal authority, considerable informal power rests with the analysts of the technostructure—those who standardize *everyone else's* work.

The informal power of the technostructure is gained largely at the expense of the operators, whose work the analysts formalize to a high degree, and of the first-line managers, who would otherwise supervise the operators directly. Such formalization institutionalizes the work of these managers, removing much of their power to coordinate and putting it into the systems designed by the analysts. The first-line manager's job can, in fact, become so circumscribed that he can hardly be said to function as a manager at all (that is, as someone who is *in charge* of an organizational unit). . . .

The emphasis on standardization extends well beyond the operating core of the Machine Bureaucracy, and with it follows the analysts' influence. In other words, rules and regulations permeate the entire Machine Bureaucracy structure; formal communication is favored at all levels; decision making tends to follow the formal chain of authority. . . .

A further reflection of this formalization is the sharp divisions of labor all over the Machine Bureaucracy. We have already discussed job specialization in the operating core and the sharp division between line and staff. In addition, the administrative structure is sharply differentiated from the operating core. Unlike the case with the Simple Structure, here managers seldom work alongside operators. And the division of labor between the analysts who design the work and the operators who do it is equally sharp. . . . All this suggests that the Machine Bureaucracy is a structure with an obsession—namely, control. A control mentality pervades it from top to bottom. . . . [At] the bottom, consider how a Ford

Assembly Division general foreman describes his work:

> I refer to my watch all the time. I check different items. About every hour I tour my line. About six thirty, I'll tour labor relations to find out who is absent. At seven, I hit the end of the line. I'll check paint, check my scratches and damage. Around ten I'll start talking to all the foremen. I make sure they're all awake, they're in the area of their responsibility. So we can shut down the end of the line at two o'clock and everything's clean. Friday night everybody'll get paid and they'll want to get out of here as quickly as they can. I gotta keep 'em on the line. I can't afford lettin' 'em get out early.
>
> We can't have no holes, no nothing (quoted in Terkel, 1972:186).

. . . [And at the top:]

> When I was president of this big corporation, we lived in a small Ohio town, where the main plant was located. The corporation specified who you could socialize with, and on what level. (His wife interjects: "Who were the wives you could play bridge with.") The president's wife could do what she wants, as long as it's with dignity and grace. In a small town they didn't have to keep check on you. Everybody knew. There are certain sets of rules (quoted in Terkel, 1972:406).

The obsession with control reflects two central facts about these structures: First, attempts are made to eliminate all possible uncertainty, so that the bureaucratic machine can run smoothly, without interruption. The operating core must be sealed off from external influence so that the standard outputs can be pumped off the assembly lines without disruption—hence the need for rules from top to bottom. Second, by virtue of their design, Machine Bureaucracies are structures ridden with conflict; the control systems are required to contain it. The magnified divisions of labor, horizontal and vertical, the strong departmental differentiation, the rigid distinction between line and staff, the motivational problems arising from the routine work of the operating core, all these permeate the structure with conflict. . . . The problem in the Machine Bureaucracy is not to develop an open atmosphere where people can talk the conflicts out, but to enforce a closed, tightly controlled one where the work can get done despite them.

The obsession with control also helps to explain the frequent proliferation of support staff in these structures. Many of the staff services could be purchased from outside suppliers. But that would expose the Machine Bureaucracy to the uncertainties of the open market, leading to disruptions in the systems of flows it so intently tries to regulate. So it "makes" rather than "buys." That is, it envelops as many of these support services as it can within its own boundaries in order to control them, everything from the cafeteria in the factory to the law office at headquarters.

The Strategic Apex

The managers at the strategic apex of these organizations are concerned in large part with the fine-tuning of their bureaucratic machines. . . . Theirs is a perpetual search for more efficient ways to produce given outputs. . . .

But all is not strictly improvement of performance. Just keeping the structure together in the face of its conflicts also consumes a good deal of the energy of top management. As noted earlier, conflict is not *resolved* in the Machine Bureaucracy; rather, it is *bottled up* so that the work can get done. And as in the case of the bottle, the seal is applied at the top; ultimately, it is the top managers who must keep the lid on the conflicts through their role of handling disturbances.

Direct supervision is another major concern of top management. Formalization can do only so much at the middle levels, where the work is more complex and unpredictable than in the operating core . . . the managers of the strategic apex must intervene frequently in the activities of the middle line to effect coordination there. The top managers are the only generalists in the structure, the only managers with a perspective broad enough to see all the functions—the means—in terms of the overall ends. Everyone else in the structure is a specialist, concerned with a single link in the chain of activities that produces the outputs.

All this leads us to the conclusion that considerable power in the Machine Bureaucracy rests with the managers of the strategic apex. That is, these are rather centralized structures; in fact, they are second in this characteristic only to the Simple Structure. The *formal* power clearly rests at the top; hierarchy and chain of authority are paramount concepts. But so also does much of the *informal* power, since that resides in knowledge, and only at the top of the hierarchy does the segmented knowledge come together. The managers of the middle line are relatively weak, and the workers of the operating core have hardly any power at all . . . The only ones to share any real informal power with the top managers are the analysts of the technostructure, by virtue of their role in standardizing everyone else's work. . . .

Strategy Making

Strategy in these structures clearly emanates, from the strategic apex, where the perspective is broad and the power is focused. The process of strategy making is clearly a top-down affair, with heavy emphasis on action planning. In top-down strategy making, all the relevant information is ostensibly sent up to the strategic apex, where it is formulated into an integrated strategy. This is then sent down the chain of authority for implementation, elaborated first into programs and then into action plans.

Two main characteristics of this strategy-making system should be noted. First, it is intended to be a fully rationalized one. . . . All the decisions of the organization are meant to be tied into one tightly integrated system. Exceptions flow up the chain of authority, to be handled at the level at which their effect is contained in a single unit, ultimately at the strategic apex if they cut across major functions. In turn, the resulting decisions flow down the chain for implementation in specific contexts. . . . Second, unique to this structure is a sharp dichotomy between formulation and implementation in strategy making. The strategic apex formulates and the middle line and operating core implement. At least, in theory. We shall come to practice momentarily [in a later section].

Figure 1 shows the Machine Bureaucracy symbolically in terms of [the structuring book's] logo, with a fully elaborated administrative and support structure—both staff parts of the organization being focused on the operating core—and large operating units but narrower ones in the middle line to reflect the tall hierarchy of authority.

CONDITIONS OF THE MACHINE BUREAUCRACY

We began our discussion of the basic structure with the point that the work flow of the Machine Bureaucracy is highly rationalized, its tasks simple and repetitive. Now we can see that such machine bureaucratic work is found, above all, in environments that are simple and stable. The work of complex environments cannot be rationalized into simple tasks, and that of dynamic environments cannot be predicted, made repetitive, and so standardized.

In addition, the Machine Brueaucracy is typically found in the mature organization, large

FIGURE 1   THE MACHINE BUREAUCRACY

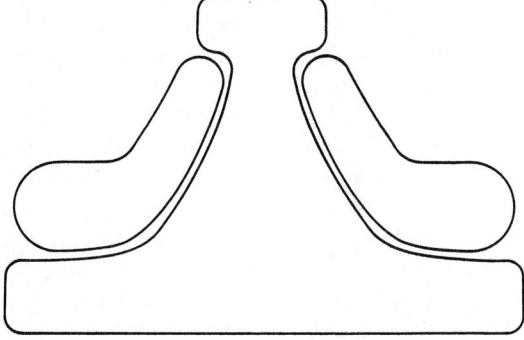

enough to have the volume of operating work needed for repetition and standardization, and old enough to have been able to settle on the standards it wishes to use. This is the organization that has seen it all before and has established a standard procedure to deal with it. . . .

Machine Bureaucracies tend also to be identified with regulating technical systems, since these routinize work and so enable it to be formalized. Such systems cannot be very sophisticated or automated (since either would require decentralization to task specialists in the support staff). . . .

Mass production firms are perhaps the best known Machine Bureaucracies. Their operating work flows from integrated chains, open at one end to accept raw material inputs, and after that functioning as closed systems that process the inputs through sequences of standardized operations until marketable outputs emerge at the other end. . . . Likewise, in process production, when the firm is unable to automate its operations but must rely on a large work force to produce its outputs, it tends to adopt a functional Machine Bureaucratic structure. . . .

In the case of the giant Machine Bureaucracies . . . [which] have great vested interests in environmental stability [without which they cannot maintain their enormous technical systems], where once upon a time they may have bureaucratized because their environments were stable, as they grew large they found themselves having to stabilize their environments because they were bureaucratic. . . . Giant firms in industries such as transportation, tobacco, and metals are well known for their attempts to control the forces of supply and demand—through the use of advertising, the development of long item-supply contacts, sometimes the establishment of cartels, and, as noted earlier, the development of support services. They also adopt strategies of "vertical integration"; that is, they extend their production chains at both ends, becoming their own suppliers and customers. In this way, they are able to bring some of the forces of supply and demand within their own planning processes, and thereby regulate them. . . .

Of course, the Machine Bureaucracy configuration is not restricted to large, or manufacturing, or even private-enterprise organizations. Some small manufacturers—for example, certain producers of discount furniture and paper products—prefer this structure because their operating work is simple and repetitive. Many service firms—what we can call *white-collar bureaucracies*—use it for the same reason, even though their operations are not integrated into single chains. . . .

Another condition often found with many Machine Bureaucracies is external control. . . . Many government agencies—such as post offices and tax collection departments—are bureaucratic not only because their operating work is routine but also because they are accountable to the public for their actions. Everything they do must seem to be fair, notably their treatment of clients and their hiring and promotion of employees. So they proliferate regulations.

Since control is the forte of the Machine Bureaucracy, it stands to reason that organizations in the business of control—regulatory agencies, custodial prisons, police forces—are drawn to this configuration, sometimes in spite of contradictory conditions. . . . Another condition that drives the organization to the machine bureaucratic structure is the special need for safety. Organizations that fly airplanes or put out fires must minimize the risks they take. Hence, [they] formalize their procedures extensively to ensure that these are carried out to the letter. . . . a fire crew cannot arrive at a burning house and then turn to the chief for orders or decide among its members who will connect the hose and who will go up the ladder. . . .

Finally, we note that fashion is no longer a condition that favors the Machine Bureaucracy configuration. This structure was the child of the Industrial Revolution. Over the course of the last two centuries—particularly at the turn of this one—it seems to have emerged as the dominant configuration. But the Machine Bureaucracy is no longer fashionable. As we shall soon see, it is currently under attack from all sides.

SOME ISSUES ASSOCIATED WITH MACHINE BUREAUCRACY

No structure has evoked more heated debate than the Machine Bureaucracy. As one of its most eminent students has noted:

> On the one hand, most authors consider the bureaucratic organization to be the embodiment of rationality in the modern world, and, as such, to be intrinsically superior to all other possible forms of organizations. On the other hand, many authors—often the same ones—consider it a sort of Leviathan, preparing the enslavement of the human race (Cozier, 1964:176).

[Max Weber, who first wrote about these organizations] emphasized the rationality of this structure; in fact, the word *machine* comes directly from his writings. . . . A machine is certainly precise; it is also reliable and easy to control; and it is efficient—at least when restricted to the job it has been designed to do. These are the reasons many organizations are structured as Machine Bureaucracies. . . . When an integrated set of simple, repetitive tasks must be performed precisely and consistently by human beings, the Machine Bureaucracy is the most efficient structure—indeed, the only conceivable one.

But in these same advantages of machine-like efficiency lie all the disadvantages of these structures. Machines consist of mechanical parts; organizational structures also include human beings—and that is where the analogy breaks down. . . .

Human Problems in the Operating Core

James Worthy, when an executive of Sears, Roebuck, wrote a penetrating and scathing criticism of Machine Bureaucracy in his book, *Big Business and Free Men*. Worthy traces the root of the human problems in these structures to the "scientific management" movement [led by Frederick Taylor] that swept America . . . in the first third of this century. . . .

Worthy acknowledges Taylor's contribu-

tion to efficiency, narrowly defined. Worker initiative did not, however, enter into his efficiency equation. . . . Taylor's pleas to remove "all possible brain work" (Worthy, 1959:67) from the shop floor also removed all possible initiative from the people who worked there: ". . . the machine has no will of its own. Its parts have no urge to independent action. Thinking, direction—even purpose—must be provided from outside or above" (p. 79). Treating people as "means," as "categories of status and function rather than as individuals," had the "consequence of destroying the meaning of work itself." And that has been "fantastically wasteful for industry and society" (p. 70). Organizations have paid dearly for these attitudes in the various forms of worker resistance—absenteeism, high turnover rates, sloppy workmanship, strikes, even outright sabotage. . . .

[In fact] some people take to routine work and others abhor it. Some simply appreciate regularity in their work—perhaps . . . because it gives them a chance to get to know it well, or perhaps because it satisfies a need for order and security. But others, either because their need is to do creative, self-actualizing work or because they dislike being told what to do, cannot tolerate the work offered them in Machine Bureaucracies.

As long as everybody can find the work that best suits him or her, there is no problem. But apparently, not everyone can. There appear to be more jobs in the Machine Bureaucracies of our society than people happy to fill them, and too few in the more popular structures. . . .

Taylor was fond of saying, "In the past the man has been first; in the future the system must be first" (quoted in Worthy, 1959:73). Prophetic words, indeed. Modern man seems to exist for his systems; many of the organizations he created to serve him have come to rule him. . . .

[Various of what Thompson (1961) has referred as "bureaupathologies"—dysfunctional behaviors of these structures—] reinforce each other to form vicious circles [in the Machine Bureaucracy]. The displacement of ends in favor of means, the mistreatment of clients, the various manifestations of worker alienation—all lead to tightening of the controls on behavior. The implicit motto of the Machine Bureaucracy seems to be, "When in doubt, control." All problems are to be solved by the turning of the technocratic screws. But since this is what caused the bureaupathologies in the first place, more of it serves only to magnify the problems, leading to the imposition of further controls, and so on. . . .

Coordination Problems in the Administrative Center

Since the operating core of the Machine Bureaucracy is not designed to handle conflict, many of the human problems that arise there spill over into the administrative structure. . . .

It is one of the ironies of the Machine Bureaucracy that to achieve the control it requires, it must mirror the narrow specialization of its operating core in its administrative structure. . . . And this administrative division of labor, in turn, leads to a sharp differentiation of the administrative structure and narrow functional orientations. This in turn means problems of communication and coordination. . . .

The fact, as noted earlier, is that the administrative structure of the Machine Bureaucracy is ill-suited to the use of mutual adjustment. All the communication barriers in these structures—horizontal, vertical, status, line/staff—impede informal communication. "Each unit becomes jealous of its own preogatives and finds ways to protect itself against the pressure or encroachments of others" (Worthy, 1950:176).

Narrow functionalism not only impedes coordination; it also encourages the building of private empires. . . . This encourages the building of top-heavy organizations, often more concerned with the political games to be won than the clients to be served. . . .

But if mutual adjustment does not work—generating more political heat than cooperative light—how does the Machine Bureaucracy resolve its coordination problems in the administration? Instinctively, it tries standardization—for example, by tightening job descriptions or proliferating rules. But standarization is not suited to handling the nonroutine problems of the adminis-

trative center. Indeed, it only makes them worse, undermining the influence of the line managers and increasing the conflict. So to reconcile the coordination problems that arise in its administrative center, the Machine Bureaucracy is left with only one coordinating mechanism, direct supervision. Specifically, nonroutine coordination problems between units are "bumped" up the line hierarchy for reconciliation, until they reach a common level of supervision. This, of course, results in the centralization of power for decision making at the upper levels of the hierarchy, ultimately at the strategic apex. And this in turn results in a host of new problems. In effect, just as the human problems in the operating core become coordination problems in the administrative center, so too do the coordination problems in the administrative center become adaptation problems at the strategic apex [these to be discussed below]. . . .

To conclude, the Machine Bureaucracy is an inflexible configuration. As a machine, it is designed for one purpose only. It is efficient in its own limited domain but cannot easily adapt itself to any other. Above all, it cannot tolerate an environment that is either dynamic or complex. Nevertheless, the Machine Bureaucracy remains a dominant configuration—probably the dominant one in our specialized societies. As long as we demand standardized, inexpensive goods and services, and as long as people remain more efficient than automated machines at providing them—and remain willing to do so—the Machine Bureaucracy, with all its problems, will be with us.

STRATEGY FORMATION IN THE MACHINE BUREAUCRACY*

Earlier we described strategy making in the Machine Bureaucracy *in principle*. And we have just noted the problems of adaptation in this

* This section is adapted from Henry Mintzberg and J. A. Water, "The Mind of the Strategist(s)," in S. Srivastva, ed., The *Executive Mind* (Jossey-Bass, 1983) and Henry Mintzberg, *Structure in Fives* (Prentice-Hall, 1983), chap. 9.

configuration. Now we wish to take up the issue in practice, to find out how strategic change does come about when it becomes necessary. We cite especially the studies in which the McGill group tracked the strategies of Air Canada and Volkswagenwerk, and also the later years of the Steinberg retail chain.

In the Machine Bureaucracy, the process of strategy making, like everything else, is supposed to be formalized, particularly through action planning. Planning was depicted in the "Strategy Making in Three Modes" article (Mintzberg, 1973b) as follows: an emphasis on analysis, especially the assesment of the costs and benefits of competing proposals, a major role for staff personnel, and above all an attempt to formally integrate decisions and strategies.

Planning as Programming in Steinberg

In fact, our best hint of what this might really mean comes from the later years of our study of Steinberg (Mintzberg and Waters, 1982), when we felt that the entrepreneurship of the founder, Sam Steinberg, began to be captured by planning. The Steinberg organization needed to plan more extensively and more formally as it became larger and its operations more dispersed—in other words, as the need for coordination became paramount and less likely to be accomplished successfully in one mind.

One particular event really encouraged the start of the planning mode: the company's entry into capital markets. Months before Steinberg floated its first bond issue (non-voting stock was to come later), Sam Steinberg boasted to a newspaper reporter that "not a cent of any money outside the family is invested in the company." And asked about future plans, he replied: "Who knows? There is so much to do right ahead that it would sound like a wild dream to talk about 10 years from now . . . We will try to go everywhere there seems to be a need for us." A few months later he announced a $5 million dollar debt issue and with it a $15 million 5-year expansion program, one new store every 60 days for a total of 30, the doubling of sales, new stores

to average double the size of existing ones, with parking lots, children's playrooms, and so on. What happened in these few months was the realization in Sam Steinberg's mind that he needed to enter the shopping center business and that he could not do so with the company's traditional methods of short term and internal financing. And no company goes to capital markets without a plan.

But what exactly was that plan? It did not formulate a strategy. Rather it justified, elaborated, and articulated the strategy—in other words, the vision—Sam Steinberg already had. Planning operationalized the strategy, programmed it. It gave order to vision, putting form on it to comply with the needs of the organization and its environment. Thus, planning *followed* the strategy making process, which was essentially entrepreneurial.

But its effect on that process was not incidental. By specifying and articulating the vision, planning constrained it, rendered it less flexible. Sam Steinberg retained formal control of this company to the day of his death. But his control over strategy did not remain so absolute, as change became increasingly difficult to effect. The entrepreneur, by keeping his vision personal, is able to adapt it at will to a changing environment. By being forced to articulate and program it, he loses that flexibility. The danger, ultimately, is that the planning mode forces out the entrepreneurial one; procedure tends to replace vision.

Is there, then, such a thing as a planning mode of strategy making? We suspect not (at least we haven't found it yet). To be more explicit, we do not find major new strategies formulated through any kind of formal procedure. (Of course, not everyone equates planning with formalized procedure; to some people, planning is simply future thinking [see Mintzberg, 1981]; but as Wildavsky (1973) notes in the title of a paper, "If planning is everything, maybe it's nothing.") Rather, the planning mode seems to encourage extrapolation or marginal change in given strategies (or visions), or else the copying of the strategies of other organizations. Planning, in other words, tends to encourage the use of what we are calling "mainline strategies"—standard accepted ones in the industry. The formulation of a dramatic new strategy is essentially the attainment of a new concept. It derives from synthesis, whereas planning tends to be oriented to analysis. Thus, planning seems to be a mode for operationalizing strategy, not for creating it—indeed planning may discourage the creative side of strategy making.

Planning and Strategic Thinking in Air Canada

This seems to come out most clearly in our study of Air Canada (Mintzberg, Brunet, and Waters, 1987). Once the airline was established, around the mid 1950's, particularly once it had developed its basic route structure and established itself as a distinct organization, a number of factors drove it strongly to the planning mode.

Above all was the paramount need for coordination, on two levels. On the operational level, the airline had to coordinate its flight schedules with its aircraft, its crews, and its maintenance. And on the capital level, it had to coordinate the purchase of expensive aircraft with the introduction of new routes or the servicing of existing ones. (Imagine someone calling out in a hanger: "Hey, Fred, this guy says he has two 747's for us; do you know who ordered them?").

Safety is another factor: the intense need for it in the air breeds a mentality of being very careful about what the organization does on the ground too. Other factors include the lead times inherent in key decisions, such as ordering new airplanes or introducing new routes, the sheer cost of the capital equipment, the size of the organization, the airline's status as a government-owned corporation, and the airline's strong influence in its home markets.

In any event, what we find in Air Canada—which we believe is largely the result of the planning orientation—is the absence of a major reorientation of strategy for a good part of our study period (especially the mid 1950s to 1976, when we cut off our study). Aircraft certainly changed—they became larger and faster—but routes did not, nor did markets. Air Canada gave only marginal attention, for example, to cargo, charter, and shuttle operations.

Strategic Change at Volkswagenwerk

How then does the planning-oriented Machine Bureaucracy change its strategy when it has to? Our best indication comes from the study of an organization that had to—Volkswagenwerk (Mintzberg, 1978). We interpret the history of Volkswagenwerk from 1934 to 1974 as one long strategy life cycle. The original "people's car" was conceived by Ferdinand Porsche; the factory to produce it was built just before the war but did not go into civilian automobile production. In 1948 a man named Nordhoff was given control of the organization and under him the firm developed the other necessary components of the strategy, notably those related to service, internal expansion, and so on.

The company enjoyed dramatic success through the 1950s. When problems began to appear, it grafted new pieces onto its existing strategy (a new series of cars, somewhat larger but similar in spirit to the Beetle), without changing its essential concept. Then, when the problems became serious, it reacted almost frantically, conceiving or introducing, under a new leader from outside the business, all kinds of new models with very little sense of its own direction (engines in the front, middle, and rear, air and water cooled, etc.). Finally, under another leader (named Leiding), whose own career developed within the business, it consolidated a new strategy around one of its new models.

What does all this suggest? First, we see the effect of bureaucratic momentum. Even if we leave the influence of planning aside, the effort of setting up assembly lines and creating sales and service networks for a particular automobile locked the company into a certain posture. But bureaucratic momentum here was psychological no less than material. Nordhoff, who had been the driving force behind the development and success of the organization, became a chief impediment to change when the environment demanded it. Leadership had been captured by bureaucratic momentum. Moreover the uniqueness and tight intergration of the strategy—we referred to a "gestalt strategy"—impeded strategic change. Change an element of a tightly integrated gestalt and it *dis*integrates. Thus success can breed failure.

Resistance to Strategic Change

Strategic change in this configuration is also impeded by the very nature of the structure. As long as its environment remains perfectly stable, the Machine Bureaucracy faces no great difficulty of adaptation. Its standard procedures handle the routine problems of coordination, and nonroutine ones do not arise.

But no organization can expect that much stability. Environments inevitably change, generating new nonroutine problems. When these become frequent in the Machine Bureaucracy, the managers at the strategic apex quickly become overloaded. . . . The propensity to pass nonroutine problems up the line hierarchy causes a bottleneck at the top during times of change, which forces the senior managers to make their decisions quickly. But how can they do so when these are decisions that arose elsewhere in the organization, in places where the top managers lack intimate contact?

In theory, the Machine Bureaucracy is designed to account for this problem. It has a management information system (MIS) that aggregates information up the hierarchy, presenting the people at the top with concise summaries of what goes on down below—the perfect solution for the overloaded top manager. Except that much of the information is the wrong kind.

A number of problems arise in the MIS. For one thing, in the tall administrative structure of the Machine Bureaucracy, information must pass through many levels before it reaches the top. Losses take place at each one. Not only natural losses. The fact that the transfers are vertical—between people on different status levels of the hierarchy—means that intentional distortions of information also occur. Good news gets highlighted and bad news blocked on its way up. Probably a greater problem is the MIS's emphasis on "hard" (quantitative), aggregated information. A good deal of evidence suggests that it is not this kind of information top managers need to make their strategic decisions as much as it is soft, specific information.

Often the MIS data are too late as well. It takes time for events to get reported as official "facts," more time for these to get accumulated into reports, and more time still for these to pass up the hierarchy until they finally reach the top manager's desk. In the perfectly stable environment, he can perhaps wait; in a changing one, he cannot. A military commander wants to know about the enemy's movements as they are taking place, not later, when they are reflected in some official measure like casualties in a battle. Likewise, the corporate president wants to be told that his most important customer was seen playing golf yesterday with his major competitor; he does not want to find out about it six months later in the form of a negative variance on a sales report. Gossip, hearsay, speculation—the softest kinds of information—warn the manager of impending problems; the MIS all too often records for posterity that these problems have long since arrived. Moreover, a good deal of important information never even gets into the MIS. The mood in the factory, the conflict between two managers, the reasons for a lost sale—this kind of rich information never becomes the kind of fact that the traditional MIS can handle. So the information of the MIS, by the time it reaches the strategic apex—after being filtered and aggregated through the levels of the administrative hierarchy—is often so bland that the top manager cannot rely on it. In a changing environment, that manager finds himself out of touch.

The obvious solution for the top managers is to bypass the MIS and set up their own informal information systems, ones that can bring them the rich, tangible information they need, quickly and reliably. They are inclined to establish their own networks of contacts and informers, both inside and outside the organization, and expose themselves to as much first-hand information as possible. But getting such information takes time.

And that, of course, was the problem in the first place—the bottleneck at the strategic apex of the Machine Bureaucracy in a changed environment. So a fundamental dilemma faces the top managers of the Machine Bureaucracy as a result of the centralization of the structure and the emphasis on reporting through the chain of authority. In times of change, when they most need to spend time getting the "tangible detail," they are overburdened with decisions coming up the hierarchy for resolution. They are therefore reduced to acting superficially, with inadequate, abstract information.

Formulation-Implementation Dichotomy

The essential problem lies in one of the major tenets of the Machine Bureaucracy, that strategy formulation must be sharply differentiated from strategy implementation. The first is the responsibility of top management; the second is to be carried out by everyone else, in hierarchical order. . . .

The formulation-implementation dichotomy presupposes two fundamental conditions in order to work effectively: that (1) the formulator has full information, or at least information as good as that available to the implementor, and (2) the situation is sufficiently stable or predictable to ensure that there will be no need for reformulation during implementation. The absence of either condition should lead to a collapse of the dichotomy, to proceeding with formulation and implementation concurrently, in an adaptive rather than a planning mode.

The top manager who cannot get the necessary information simply cannot formulate a sensible strategy. The Machine Bureaucracy is designed on the questionable assumption that even in times of change, the MIS will bring the necessary information up to the top of the hierarchy.

The design of the Machine Bureaucracy also assumes that a strategy formulated in one place can later be implemented in another. That is a reasonable assumption under conditions of stability—as long as the world holds still (or at least undergoes predicted changes) while the plan

unfolds. Unfortunately, all too often the world refuses to hold still; it insists on changing in unpredictable ways. This imposes the need to adapt, to alter the strategy as it is being implemented. Under such fluid conditions, either the formulator must implement his own strategy so that he can reformulate it en route—which is what happens in the Simple Structure, which faces a simple, dynamic environment—or else the implementors must take responsibility for the formulation and do it adaptively—which is what happens in the Adhocracy [configuration], which decentralizes power for strategy making in the face of a complex, dynamic environment.

We emerge from this discussion with two conclusions: First, strategies must be formulated outside the machine bureaucratic structure if they are to be realistic. Second, the dichotomy between formulation and implementation ceases to have relevance in times of unpredictable change. Together these conclusions tell us that Machine Bureaucracies are fundamentally nonadaptive structures, ill-suited to changing their strategies. But that should come as no surprise. After all, machines are designed for special purposes, not general ones. So, too, are Machine Bureaucracies.

These are, as Hunt (1970) noted, performance, not problem-solving organizations. Strategic diagnosis is simply not part of their repertoire of standard operating procedures. Machine Bureaucracies work best in stable environments because they have been designed for specific, predetermined missions. Efficiency is their forte, not innovation. An organization cannot put blinders on its personnel and then expect peripheral vision. The managers of the Machine Bureaucracy are rewarded for improving operating efficiency, reducing costs, finding better controls and standards; not for taking risks, testing new behaviors, encouraging innovation. Change makes a mess of the standard operating procedures. In the Machine Bureaucracy, everything is nicely coupled, carefully coordinated. Change a link, and the whole operating chain must be redesigned; change an element in an integrated strategy, and it disintegrates. . . .

When Machine Bureaucracies must change their strategies in important rather than cosmetic ways, their top managers tend to act idiosyncratically; they are not in the habit of making such changes, their MISs have obscured the kind of change that is needed, and their structures are ill-suited to receiving whatever change is eventually proposed. . . .

Strategic Revolutions in Machine Bureaucracy

To return to our original question, how then does the strategy change? Using Miller and Friesen's (1980) term, we believe it does so by "revolution": a new strong leader comes in with a new vision (perhaps because he or she has been closer to the operations, as with Leiding, who turned Volkswagen around), suspends established procedures, ignores staff planners, and consolidates power around him or herself personally, and then does what is necessary. In other words, the Machine Bureaucracy reverts to Simple Structure temporarily, the planning mode to an entrepreneurial mode, in order to realize necessary change. But the large, established organization typically cannot tolerate such personalized control for long, and is likely to spit out its entrepreneur once he or she has rendered the necessary changes (which is exactly what Volkswagen did in 1974). Thus the process of strategic change can be described in terms of Miller and Friesen's (1980) quantum theory—long periods of stability of strategy interrupted occasionally by short bursts of revolutionary change.

Organization Taking the Lead

In Machine Bureaucracy, therefore, as shown in Figure 2, it is the organization that takes the lead over leadership and environment (in contrast to the Simple Structure), with its systems and procedures, its methods of planning and its own

bureaucratic momentum. Of course, an organization cannot undertake massive commitments of resources, such as producing a new model automobile or flying wide-body jets, on a hesitant basis, testing before plunging. Detailed plans and a carefully structured organization are required before proceeding. But the price of such planning and organizing is high.

Later the environment may demand change, especially after the strategy has had some years of success, but the organization inevitably resists. It has been so well programmed to do a given job that it cannot easily adapt itself to another, even if the change seems marginal (from one automobile model to another). Indeed, when a Machine Bureaucracy is especially large and powerful, it is the organization that seeks to impose itself on the environment, for example, by trying to stabilize markets so that they will accept its products. Pfeffer and Salancik (1978) [as we have seen] describe all kinds of methods organizations use to do so—integrating vertically to control suppliers and customers, establishing cartels, developing arrangements with governments, and so on. When response to the environment does become necessary, leadership in the Machine Bureaucracy may try to intervene, encouraging the organization to adapt. But often the leadership gets captured by the forces of organization and momentum (as we saw in Volkswagenwerk), so that reversion to the Simple Structure and the entrepreneurial mode, under a new leader, become a necessary condition for change.

If the strategist of the Simple Structure is a concept attainer, then the one of the Machine Bureaucracy, in its stable, mature condition, is a *planner*, or perhaps more accurately a pigeonholer who slots generic strategies into well defined industry conditions and then hangs on to them for dear life.

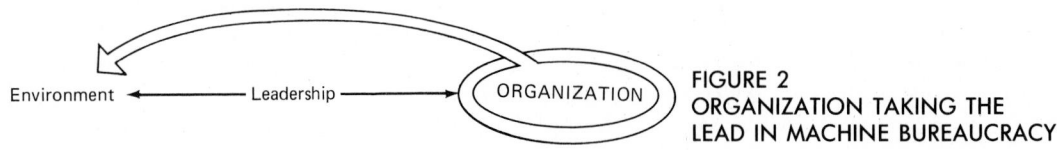

Environment ◄——— Leadership ———► ORGANIZATION

FIGURE 2
ORGANIZATION TAKING THE
LEAD IN MACHINE BUREAUCRACY

THE TRANSITION
TO INDUSTRY MATURITY*

by Michael E. Porter

As part of their evolutionary process, many industries pass from periods of rapid growth to the more modest growth of what is commonly called industry maturity. . . . industry maturity does not occur at any fixed point in an industry's development, and it can be delayed by innovations or other events that fuel continued growth for industry participants. Moreover, in response to strategic break-throughs, mature industries may regain their rapid growth and thereby go through more than one transition to maturity. With these important qualifications in mind, however, let us consider the case in which a transition to maturity is occurring. . . .

INDUSTRY CHANGE
DURING TRANSITION

Transition to maturity can often signal a number of important changes in an industry's competitive environment. Some of the probable tendencies for change are as follows:

1. *Slowing growth means more competition for market share*. With companies unable to maintain historical growth rates merely by holding market share, competitive attention turns inward toward attacking the shares of the others. . . . Not only are competitors probably going to be more aggressive, but also the likelihood of misperceptions and "irrational" retaliation is great. Outbreaks of price, service, and promotional warfare are common during transition to maturity.

2. *Firms in the industry increasingly are selling to experienced, repeat buyers*. The

*   Excerpted with permission of The Free Press, a Division of Macmillan, Inc. from *Competitive Strategy: Techniques for Analyzing Industries and Competitors* by Michael E. Porter. Copyright © by The Free Press.

product is no longer new but an established, legitimate item. Buyers are often increasingly knowledgeable and experienced, having already purchased the product, sometimes repeatedly. The buyers' focus shifts from deciding whether to purchase the product at all to making choices among brands. Approaching these differently oriented buyers requires a fundamental reassessment of strategy.

3. *Competition often shifts toward greater emphasis on cost and service*. As a result of slower growth, more knowledgeable buyers, and usually greater technological maturity, competition tends to become more cost- and service-oriented. . . .

4. *There is a topping-out problem in adding industry capacity and personnel*. As the industry adjusts to slower growth, the rate of capacity addition in the industry must slow down as well or overcapacity will occur. . . . [But the necessary] shifts in perspective rarely occur in maturing industries, and overshooting of industry capacity relative to demand is common. Overshooting leads to a period of overcapacity, accentuating the tendency during transition toward price warfare. . . .

5. *Manufacturing, marketing, distributing, selling, and research methods are often undergoing change*. These changes are caused by increased competition for market share, technological maturity, and buyer sophistication. . . .

6. *New products and applications are harder to come by.* Whereas the growth phase may have been one of rapid discovery of new products and applications, the ability to continue product change generally becomes increasingly limited, or the costs and risks greatly increase, as the industry matures. This change requires, among other things, a reorientation of attitude toward research and new product development.

7. *International competition increases*. As a consequence of technological maturity, often accompanied by product standardization and increasing emphasis on costs, transition is often marked by the emergence of significant international competition. . . .

8. *Industry profits often fall during the transition period, sometimes temporarily and*

sometimes permanently. Slowing growth, more sophisticated buyers, more emphasis on market share, and the uncertainties and difficulties of the required strategic changes usually mean that industry profits fall in the short run from the levels of the pretransition growth phase. . . . Whether or not profits will rebound depends on the level of mobility barriers and other elements of industry structure. . . .

9. *Dealers' margins fall, but their power increases.* For the same reasons that industry profits are often depressed, dealers' margins may be squeezed, and many dealers may drop out of business—often *before* the effect on manufacturers' profits is noticeable. . . . Such trends tighten competition among industry participants for dealers, who may have been easy to find and hold in the growth phase but not upon maturity. Thus, dealers' power may increase markedly.

SOME STRATEGIC IMPLICATIONS OF TRANSITION

. . . Some characteristic strategic issues often arise in transition. These are presented as issues to examine rather than generalizations that will apply to all industries; like humans, all industries mature a little differently. Many of these approaches can be a basis for the entry of new firms into an industry even though it is mature.

Overall Cost Leadership Versus Differentiate Versus Focus—The Strategic Dilemma Made Acute by Maturity

Rapid growth tends to mask strategic errors and allow most, if not all, companies in the industry to survive and even to prosper financially. Strategic experimentation is high, and a wide variety of strategies can coexist. Strategic sloppiness is generally exposed by industry maturity, however. Maturity may force companies to confront, often for the first time, the need to choose among the

three generic strategies described [in Chapter 4 of this text]. It becomes a matter of survival.

Sophisticated Cost Analysis

Cost analysis becomes increasingly important in maturity to (1) rationalize the product mix and (2) price correctly.

Rationalizing the Product Mix . . . a quantum improvement in the sophistication of product costing is necessary to allow pruning of unprofitable items from the line and to focus attention on items either that have some distinctive advantage (technology, cost, image, etc.) or whose buyers are "good" buyers. . . .

Correct Pricing Related to product line rationalization is the change in pricing methodology that is often necessary in maturity. Although average-cost pricing, or pricing the line as a whole rather than as individual items, may have been sufficient in the growth era, maturity often requires increased capability to measure costs on individual items and to price accordingly. . . .

We might summarize this and the other points in this section by saying that an enhanced level of "financial consciousness" along a variety of dimensions is often necessary in maturity, whereas in the developmental period of the industry areas such as new products and research may have rightly held center stage. . . .

Process Innovation and Design for Manufacture

The relative importance of process innovations usually increases in maturity, as does the payoff for designing the product and its delivery system to facilitate lower-cost manufacturing and control. . . .

Increasing Scope of Purchases

Increasing purchases of existing customers may be more desirable than seeking new customers. . . . Such a strategy may take the firm out of the industry into related industries. This strategy is often less costly than finding new customers. In a mature industry, winning new customers usually means battling for market share with competitors and is consequently quite expensive. . . .

Buy Cheap Assets

Sometimes assets can be acquired very cheaply as a result of the company distress that is caused by transition to maturity. A strategy of acquiring distressed companies or buying liquidated assets can improve margins and create a low-cost position if the rate of technological change is not too great. . . .

Buyer Selection

As buyers become more knowledgeable and competitive pressures increase in maturity, buyer selection can sometimes be a key to continued profitability. Buyers who may not have exercised their bargaining power in the past, or had less power because of limited product availability, will usually not be bashful about exercising their power in maturity. Identifying "good" buyers and locking them in . . . becomes crucial.

Different Cost Curves

There is often more than one cost curve possible in an industry. The firm that is *not* the overall cost leader in a mature market can sometimes find new cost curves which may actually make it a lower-cost producer for certain types of buyers, product varieties, or order sizes. This step is key to implementing the generic strategy of focus. . . .

Competing Internationally

A firm may escape maturity by competing internationally where the industry is more favorably structured. Sometimes equipment that is obsolete in the home market can be used quite effectively in international markets, greatly lowering the costs of entry there. . . .

STRATEGIC PITFALLS IN TRANSITION

In addition to failure to recognize the strategic implications of transition described above, there is the tendency for firms to fall prey to some characteristic strategic pitfalls:

1. *A company's self-perceptions and its perception of the industry.* Companies develop perceptions or images of themselves and their relative capabilites ("we are the quality leader"; "we provide superior customer service"), which are reflected in the implicit assumptions that form the basis of their strategies. . . . These self-perceptions may be increasingly inaccurate as transition proceeds, buyers' priorities adjust, and competitors respond to new industry conditions. Similarly, firms have assumptions about the industry, competitors, buyers, and suppliers which may be invalidated by transition. Yet altering these assumptions, built up through actual past experience, is sometimes a difficult process.

2. *Caught in the middle.* The problem of being caught in the middle described [earlier] is particularly acute in transition to maturity. Transition often squeezes out the slack that has made this strategy viable in the past.

3. *The cash trap—investments to build share in a mature market.* Cash should be invested in a business only with the expectation of being able to remove it later. In a mature, slow-growing industry, the assumptions required to justify investing new cash in order to build market share are often heroic. Maturity of the industry works against increasing or maintaining margins long enough to recoup cash investments down the road, by making the present value of cash inflows justify the outflows. Thus businesses in maturity can be cash traps, particularly when a firm is not in a strong market position but is attempting to build a large market share in a maturing market. The odds are against it.

   A related pitfall is placing heavy attention on revenues in the maturing market instead of on profitability. This strategy may have been desirable in the growth phase, but it usually faces diminishing returns in maturity. . . .

4. *Giving up market share too easily in favor of short-run profits*. In the face of the profit pressures in transition, there seems to be a tendency for some companies to try to maintain the profitability of the recent past—which is done at the expense of market share or by foregoing marketing, R&D, and other needed investments, which in turn hurts future market position. . . . A period of lower profits may be inevitable while industry rationalization occurs, and a cool head is necessary to avoid overreaction.

5. *Resentment and irrational reaction to price competition ("we will not compete on price")*. It is often difficult for firms to accept the need for price competition after a period in which it has not been necessary. . . .

6. *Resentment and irrational reaction to changes in industry practices ("they are hurting the industry")*. Changes in industry practices, such as marketing techniques, production methods, and the nature of distributor contracts are often an inevitable part of transition. They may be important to the industry's long-run potential, but there is often resistance to them. . . .

7. *Overemphasis on "creative," "new" products rather than improving and aggressively selling existing ones*. Although past success in the early and growth phases of an industry may have been built on research and on new products, the onset of maturity often means that new products and applications are harder to come by. It is usually appropriate that the focus of innovative activity should change, putting standardization rather than newness and fine tuning at a premium. Yet this development is not satisfying to some companies and is often resisted.

8. *Clinging to "higher quality" as an excuse for not meeting aggressive pricing and marketing moves of competitors*. High quality can be a crucial company strength, but quality differentials have a tendency to erode as an industry matures. . . . Yet it is difficult for many companies to accept the fact that they do not possess the highest quality

product or that their quality is unnecessarily high.

9. *Overhanging excess capacity*. As a result of capacity overshooting demand, or because of capacity increases that inevitably accompany the plant modernization required to compete in the mature industry, some firms may have some excess capacity. Its mere presence creates both subtle and unsubtle pressures to utilize it, and it can be used in ways that will undermine the firm's strategy. . . .

COST DYNAMICS: SCALE AND EXPERIENCE EFFECTS*

by Derek F. Abell and John S. Hammond

Market share is one of the primary determinants of business profitability; other things being equal, businesses with a larger share of a market are more profitable than their smaller-share competitors. For instance, a study by the PIMS Program (Buzzell, Gale and Sultan, 1975) . . . found that, on average, a difference of 10 percentage points in market share is accompanied by a difference of about 5 points in pretax ROI ("pretax operating profits" divided by "long-term debt plus equity"). Additional evidence is that companies having large market shares in their primary product markets—such as General Motors, IBM, Gillette, Eastman Kodak and Xerox—tend to be highly profitable.

An important reason for the increase in profitability with market share is that large-share firms usually have *lower costs*. The lower costs are due in part to economies of scale; for instance,

---

* From Derek F. Abell and John S. Hammond, *Strategic Market Planning: Problems and Analytical Approaches* (Prentice-Hall, 1979), chap. 3; reprinted with deletions by permission of the publisher.

very large plants cost less per unit of production to build and are often more efficient than smaller plants. Lower costs are also due in part to the so-called *experience effect*, whereby the cost of many (if not most) products declines by 10–30 percent each time a company's experience at producing and selling them doubles. In this context *experience* has a precise meaning: it is the cumulative number of units produced to date. Since at any point in time, businesses with large market shares typically (but not always) have more experience than their smaller-share competitors, they would be expected to have lower costs. . . .

This [reading] considers how costs decline due to scale and to experience, practical problems in analyzing the experience effect, strategic implications of scale and experience, and limitations of strategies based on cost reduction. . . .

SCALE EFFECT

As mentioned earlier, scale effect refers to the fact that large businesses have the potential to operate at lower unit costs than their smaller counterparts. The increased efficiency due to size is often referred to as "economy of scale"; it could equally be called "economy of size."

Most people think of economy of scale as a manufacturing phenomenon because large manufacturing facilities can be constructed at a lower cost per unit of capacity and can be operated more efficiently than smaller ones. . . .

Just as they cost less to build, large-scale plants have lower *operating* costs per unit of output. . . . While substantial in manufacturing, scale effect is also significant in other cost elements, such as marketing, sales, distribution, administration, R&D, and service. For instance, a chain with 30 supermarkets in a metropolitan area needs much less than three times as much advertising as a chain with 10 stores. . . . Economies of scale are also achieved with purchased items such as raw material and shipping. . . .

Although scale economies potentially exist in all cost elements of a business in both the

short and long run, large size alone doesn't assure the benefits of scale. It is evident from the above illustrations that size provides an *opportunity* for scale economies; to achieve them requires strategies and actions consciously designed to seize the opportunity, especially with operating costs. . . .

EXPERIENCE EFFECT

The experience effect, whereby costs fall with cumulative production, is measurable and predictable; it has been observed in a wide range of products including automobiles, semiconductors, petrochemicals, long-distance telephone calls, synthetic fibers, airline transportation, the cost of administering life insurance, and crushed limestone, to mention a few. Note that this list ranges from high technology to low technology products, service to manufacturing industries, consumer to industrial products, new to mature products, and process to assembly oriented products, indicating the wide range of applicability. . . .

. . . it is only comparatively recently that this phenomenon has been carefully measured and quantified; at first it was thought to apply only to the labor portion of *manufacturing* costs. . . . In the 1960s evidence mounted that the phenomenon was broader. Personnel from the Boston Consulting Group and others showed that each time cumulative volume of a product doubled, total value-added costs—including administration, sales, marketing, distribution, etc. in addition to manufacturing—fell by a constant and predictable percentage. In addition, the costs of purchased items usually fell as suppliers reduced prices as their costs fell, due also to the experience effect. The relationship between costs and experience was called the *experience curve* (Boston Consulting Group, 1972).

An experience curve is plotted with the cumulative units produced on the horizontal axis, and cost per unit on the vertical axis. An "85 percent" experience curve is shown in Figure 1. The "85 percent" means that every time expe-

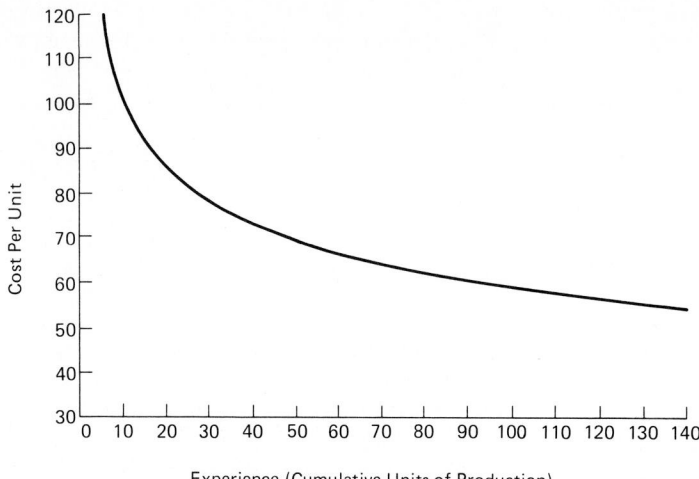

FIGURE 1
A TYPICAL EXPERIENCE
CURVE [85%]

rience doubles, costs per unit drop to 85 percent of the original level. It is known as the *learning rate*. Stated differently, costs per unit decrease 15 percent for every doubling of cumulative production. For example, the cost of the 20th unit produced is about 85 percent of the cost of the 10th unit. . . .

An experience curve appears as a straight line when plotted on a double log paper (logarithmic scale for both the horizontal and vertical axes). Figure 2 shows the ''85 percent'' experience curve from Figure 1 on the double logarithmic scale. . . . Figure 3 provides illustrations for [some specific] products.

SOURCES OF THE EXPERIENCE EFFECT

The experience effect has a variety of sources; to capitalize on it requires knowledge of why it occurs. Sources of the experience effect are outlined below:

1. *Labor efficiency.* . . . As workers repeat a particular production task, they become more dextrous and learn improvements and shortcuts which increase their collective efficiency. The greater the number of worker-paced operations, the greater the amount

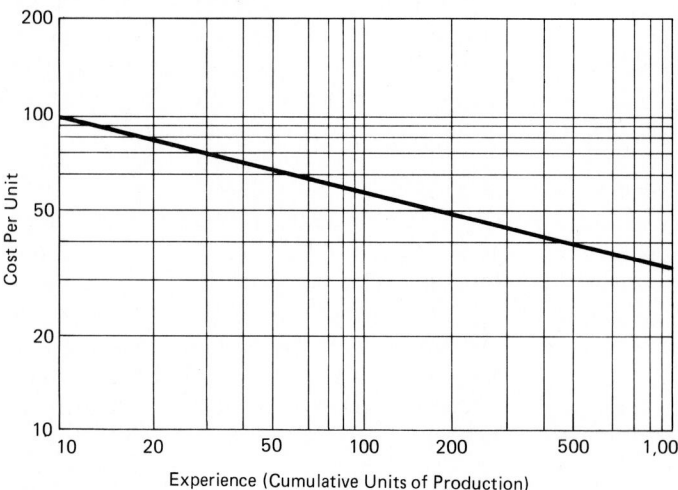

FIGURE 2
AN 85% EXPERIENCE
CURVE DISPLAYED
ON LOG-LOG SCALES

FIGURE 3 SOME SAMPLE EXPERIENCE CURVES

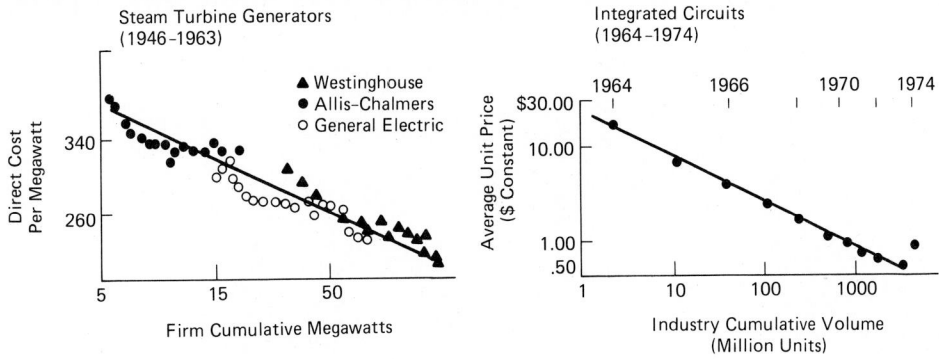

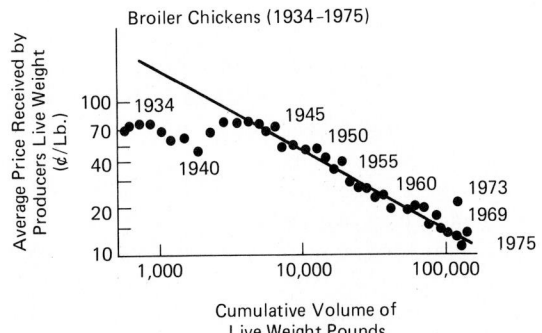

Note: Technically an experience curve shows the relationship between cost and experience. However, cost figures are seldom publicly available; therefore most of the above experience curves show industry price (in constant dollars) vs. experience.

Source: The Boston Consulting Group.

of learning which can accrue with experience. . . .

2. *Work specialization and methods improvements*. Specialization increases worker proficiency at a given task. . . .

3. *New production processes*. Process innovations and improvements can be an important source of cost reductions, especially in capital-intensive industries. . . .

4. *Getting better performance from production equipment*. When first designed, a piece of production equipment may have a conservatively rated output. Experience may reveal innovative ways of increasing its output. . . .

5. *Changes in the resource mix*. As experience accumulates, a producer can often incorporate different or less expensive resources in the operation. . . .

6. *Product standardization*. Standardization allows the replication of tasks necessary for worker learning. Production of the Ford Model T, for example, followed a strategy of deliberate standardization; as a result, from 1909 to 1923 its price was repeatedly reduced, following an 85 percent experience curve (Abernathy and Wayne, 1974). . . .

7. *Product redesign*. As experience is gained with a product, both the manufacturer and customers gain a clearer understanding of its performance requirements. This understanding allows the product to be redesigned to conserve material, allows greater efficiency in manufacture, and substitutes less costly materials and resources, while at the

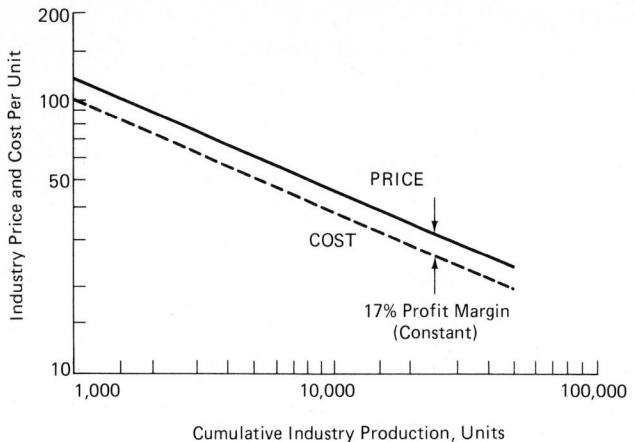

FIGURE 4
AN IDEALIZED PRICE-COST
RELATIONSHIP WHEN PROFIT
MARGIN IS CONSTANT

same time improving performance on relevant dimensions. . . .

The above list of sources dramatizes the observation that cost reductions due to experience don't occur by natural inclination; they are the result of substantial, concerted effort and pressure to lower costs. In fact, left unmanaged, costs rise. Thus, experience does not cause reductions but rather provides an opportunity that alert managements can exploit. . . .

The list of reasons for the experience effect raises perplexing questions on the difference between experience and scale effects. For instance, isn't it true that work specialization and project standardization, mentioned in the experience list, become possible because of the *size* of an operation? Therefore, aren't they each really scale effects? The answer is that they are probably both.

The confusion arises because growth in experience usually coincides with growth in size of an operation. We consider the experience effect to arise primarily due to ingenuity, cleverness, skill, and dexterity derived from experience as embodied in the adages "practice makes perfect" or "experience is the best teacher." On the other hand, scale effect comes from capitalizing on the size of an operation. . . .

Usually the overlap between the two effects is so great that it is difficult (and not too important)

to separate them. This is the practice we will adopt from here on. . . .

PRICES AND EXPERIENCE

In stable competitive markets, one would expect that as costs decrease due to experience, prices will decrease similarly. (The price-experience curves in Figure 3 are examples of prices falling with experience.) If profit margins remain at a constant percentage of price, average industry costs and prices should follow identically sloped experience curves (on double logarithmic scales). The constant gap separating them will equal the profit margin percentage; Figure 4 illustrates such an idealized situation.

In many cases, however, prices and costs exhibit a relationship similar to the one shown in Figure 5, where prices start briefly below cost, then cost reductions exceed price reductions until prices suddenly tumble. Ultimately the price and cost curves parallel, as they do in Figure 4. Specifically, in the development phase, new product prices are below average industry costs due to pricing based on anticipated costs. In the price umbrella phase, when demand exceeds supply, prices remain firm under a price umbrella supported by the market leader. This is unstable. At some point a shakeout phase starts; one pro-

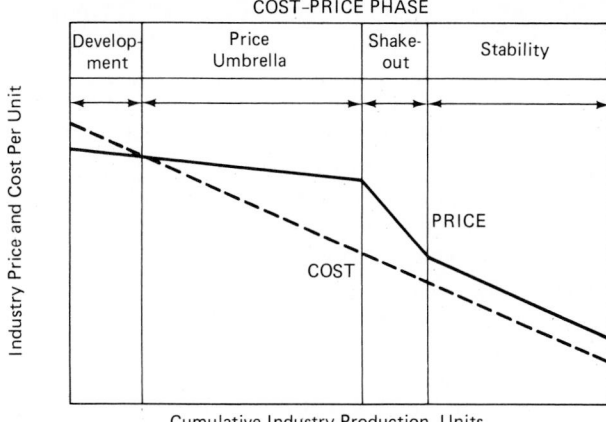

COST-PRICE PHASE

FIGURE 5
TYPICAL PRICE-COST RELATIONSHIP

Source: Adapted from *Perspectives on Experience* (Boston: The Boston Consulting Group, 1972), p. 21.

ducer will almost certainly reduce prices to gain share. If this does not precipitate a price decline, the high profit margins will attract enough new entrants to produce temporary overcapacity, causing prices to tumble faster than costs, and marginal producers to be forced out of the market. The stability phase starts when profit margins return to normal levels and prices begin to follow industry costs down the experience curve. . . .

STRATEGIC IMPLICATIONS

In industries where a significant portion of total cost can be reduced due to scale or experience, important cost advantages can usually be achieved by pursuing a strategy geared to accumulating experience faster than competitors. (Such a strategy will ultimately require that the firm acquire the largest market share relative to competition.).

The dominant producer can greatly influence industry profitability. The rate of decline of competitors' costs must at least keep pace with the leader if they are to maintain profitability. If their costs decrease more slowly, either because they are pursuing cost reductions less aggressively or are growing more slowly than the leader, then

their profits will eventually disappear, thus eliminating them from the market.

. . . the advantage of being the leader is obvious. Leadership is usually best seized at the start when experience doubles quickly (e.g. experience increases tenfold as you move from the 20th to the 2,000th unit, but only doubles as you move from the 2,000th to the 4,000th unit.) Then a firm can build an unassailable cost advantage and at the same time gain price leadership. The best course of action for a product depends on a number of factors, one of the most important being the market growth rate. In fast-growing markets, experience can be gained by taking a disproportionate share of new sales, thereby avoiding taking sales away from competitors (which would be vigorously resisted). Therefore, with high rates of growth, aggressive action may be called for. But, share-gaining tactics are usually costly in the short run, due to reduced margins from lower prices, added advertising and marketing expense, new product development costs, and the like. This means that if it lacks the resources (product, financial, and other) for leadership and in particular if it is opposed by a very aggressive competitor, a firm may find it wise to abandon the market entirely or focus on a segment it can dominate. On the other hand, in no-growth or slowly growing markets it is hard to take share from competitors and the time it takes to acquire superior experience is usually too long and the cost too great to favor aggressive strategies.

In stable competitive markets, usually the firm with the largest share of market has the greatest experience and it is often the case that each firm's experience is roughly proportional to market share. A notable exception occurs when a late entrant to a market quickly obtains a commanding market share. It may have less experience than some early entrants. . . .

EFFICIENCY VS. EFFECTIVENESS: LIMITATIONS TO STRATEGIES BASED ON EXPERIENCE OR SCALE

The selection of a competitive strategy based on cost reduction due to experience or scale often involves a fundamental choice. It is the selection of cost-price *efficiency* over non cost-price marketing *effectiveness*. However, when the market is more concerned with product and service features and up-to-date technology, a firm pursuing efficiency can find itself offering a low-priced product that few customers want. Thus two basic questions arise: 1) when to use an efficiency strategy and 2) if so, how far to push it before running into dangers of losing effectiveness. . . .

Whether to pursue an efficiency strategy depends on answers to questions such as:

1. Does the industry offer significant cost advantages from experience or scale (as in semiconductors or chemicals)?
2. Are there significant market segments that will reward competitors with low prices?
3. Is the firm well equipped (financially, managerially, technologically, etc.) for or already geared up for strategies relying heavily on having the lowest cost . . . ?

If the answer is "yes" to all these questions, then "efficiency" strategies should probably be pursued.

Once it decided to pursue an "efficiency" strategy a firm must guard against going so far

that it loses effectiveness, primarily through inability to respond to changes. For instance, experience-based strategies frequently require a highly specialized work force, facilities and organization, making it difficult to respond to changes in consumer demand, to respond to competitors' innovations, or to initiate them. In addition, large-scale plants are vulnerable to changes in process technology, and the heavy cost of operation below capacity.

For example, Ford's Model T automobile ultimately suffered the consequences of inflexibility due to overemphasizing "efficiency" (Abernathy and Wayne, 1974). Ford followed a classic experience-based strategy; over time it slashed its product line to a single model (the model T), built modern plants, pushed division of labor, introduced the continuous assembly line, obtained economies in purchased parts through high volume, backward integrated, increased mechanization, and cut prices as costs fell. The lower prices increased Ford's share of a growing market to a high of 55.4 percent by 1921.

In the meantime, consumer demand began shifting to heavier, closed-body cars and to more comfort. Ford's chief rival, General Motors, had the flexibility to respond quickly with new designs. Ford responded by adding features to its existing standard design. While the features softened the inroads of GM, the basic Model T design, upon which Ford's "efficiency" strategy was based, inadequately met the market's new performance standards. To make matters worse, the turmoil in production due to constant design changes slowed experience-based efficiency gains. Finally Ford was forced, at enormous cost, to close for a whole year beginning May 1927 while it retooled to introduce its Model A. Hence experience or scale-based *efficiency* was carried too far and thus it ultimately limited *effectiveness* to meet consumer needs, to innovate, and to respond.

Thus the challenge is to decide when to emphasize efficiency and when to emphasize effectiveness, and further to design efficiency strategies that maintain effectiveness and vice versa. . . .

SURVIVAL STRATEGIES IN A HOSTILE ENVIRONMENT*

by William K. Hall

. . . The purpose of this article is to present some preliminary findings from an ongoing research project . . . This project is focusing on two broad questions:

1. How are industry structures in the mature markets evolving in the face of the adverse external pressures of the late 1970s?

2. Given this evolution, what business strategies are appropriate? Which strategic choices give the best chances for survival, growth, and return in the hostile environment ahead?

IN-DEPTH INVESTIGATION

To examine these issues, I selected eight major domestic manufacturing industries for comprehensive study because of their importance to national and/or regional economic development and also because the adverse external trends of the 1970s have been especially severe in their impact on them. As a result, during the 1970s, all eight industries underwent a significant structural change which is expected to continue into the 1980s. Within these industries, I examined the strategies and evolving competitive positions of the 64 largest companies by using a combination of public data sources and field interviews.

In examining the impact of external pressures on these companies, I found that the eight industries either matured during the 1970s or will mature in the 1980s, resulting in lower growth records and growth expectations as shown in Table 1. While the industries (on average) exceeded

national economic growth rates in the 1950s and 1960s, they grew only slightly faster than the GNP in the 1970s, and they are projected to grow significantly more slowly than the U.S. economy in the 1980s.

During this maturation period, these eight industries, which are capital, raw material, and labor intensive, have been subjected to heavy inflationary pressures that cannot easily be price recovered. All are being forced by regulatory agencies to make major investments to comply with new occupational safety and health regulations and with new product safety, performance, and environmental protection standards.

In addition to the domestic pressures, foreign competition has been harsh in the eight basic industries selected for study. . . . Needless to say, the net effect of these adverse trends has made life anything but pleasant for managers and companies in these basic industries. Profitability and sales growth levels have generally fallen to or below the average manufacturing returns in the U.S. economy (Table 2). And industry spokesmen frequently speak out, urging either public assistance or some type of return to the simpler, less painful world of the 1960s. . . .

However, the profiles of basic industry problems and corporate failures tell only part of the story. These "disaster" tales need to be juxtaposed against some success stories to see how some companies have survived and even prospered in the same hostile environment. The resulting comparisons provide important insights into survival strategies and industry dynamics not only for general managers in the eight industries under study but also for managers in other industries as they lead their companies into the new decade. For example, a careful comparison of success and problem strategies in the eight industries in this study demonstrates that:

- Great success is possible, even in a hostile environment.

- Strategies leading to success share common characteristics.

- Successful strategies come from purposeful moves toward a leadership position.

TABLE 1   COMPOUND ANNUAL REAL GROWTH RATES
          IN DEMAND—UNITED STATES

Eight Basic Industries

	1950–1970	1971–1980	1980 Forecast*
Industrial goods			
Primary products			
Steel	4.0%	2.2%	1.5%–2.5%
Tire and rubber	4.2	1.4	1.0–1.5
Intermediate products			
Heavy-duty trucks	7.0	2.8	2.5
Construction and materials handling equipment	7.8	3.6	2.3
Consumer goods			
Durable products			
Automotive	4.8	3.5	2.0–3.0
Major home appliances	6.2	2.9	2.3–2.8
Nondurable products			
Beer	3.1	2.5	2.3
Cigarettes	1.6	1.0	0
Average growth rates— eight industries	4.8%	2.4%	1.9%
Average growth rates— U.S. GNP	3.7%	2.3%	2.5%

* *Based on economic forecasts and industry projections.*

- Problems come from failure to gain or defend a leadership position.
- For a deteriorating position, diversity may not be the proper recovery approach. . . .

I will amplify and discuss each of these insights in subsequent sections of this article.

Great Success Is Possible, Even in a Hostile Environment

When one looks at the eight industries in this study, as well as at other basic manufacturing industries facing the hostile environment of the 1980s, it is easy to slip into generalizations by extrapolating from aggregate industry problems to the individual companies within the industry.

Recent articles in the business press, asking "What Killed the U.S. Steel Industry?", "Is Chrysler the Prototype?", or proclaiming "Tire Industry Goes Flat" or "Last Chances for Cigarette Producers," are typical of those that tend to project adverse trends uniformly onto all competitors in the industry. In fact, however, nothing could be further from the truth. Some of the most vibrant, successful companies in the world reside and prosper in these seemingly hostile industry environments.

If one eliminates from my eight-industry sample of 64 companies all competitors who gain a majority of revenues and profits from diversification efforts outside their basic industry (e.g.,

TABLE 2   FINANCIAL RETURNS AND REVENUE GROWTH RATES,
1975–1979

Eight Basic Industries

	Return on Equity	Return on Capital	EPS Growth	Revenue Growth
Steel	7.1%	5.7%	5.5%	10.4%
Tire and rubber	7.4	5.9	3.9	9.6
Heavy-duty trucks*	15.4	11.6	13.8	13.8
Construction and materials handling equipment	15.4	10.7	16.8	13.0
Automotive*	15.4	11.6	13.8	13.8
Major home appliances	10.1	9.0	3.2	6.8
Beer	14.1	10.2	6.2	12.4
Cigarettes	18.2	10.5	8.9	12.2
Average—eight industries	12.9%	9.4%	9.0%	11.5%
Average *Fortune* "1,000" company	15.1%	11.0%	13.1%	13.1%

* All vehicle manufacturers.

Armco Steel and General Tire), then the most profitable remaining competitors (the industry leaders) in terms of corporate return on equity are those shown in Table 3.

While some variation in returns exists among these leading competitors (Goodyear and Inland had significantly lower returns and growth rates than the other six), the corporate average return on equity earned over the last half of the 1970s easily places these companies in the top 20% of the *Fortune* "1,000" industrials and well ahead of the median *Fortune* company on return on capital and annual growth rate. . . .

Thus even a cursory analysis of leading companies in the eight basic industries leads to an important observation: survival and prosperity are possible even when the business environment turns hostile and industry trends change from favorable to unfavorable. In this regard, the casual advice frequently offered to competitors in basic industries—that is, diversify, dissolve, or be prepared for below-average returns [e.g., Levitt, 1975: 41; Rumelt, 1974: 128–139]—seems oversimplified and even erroneous. A hostile environ-ment offers an excellent basic investment opportunity and reinvestment climate, at least for the industry leaders insightful enough to capitalize on their positions.

Strategies Leading to Success Share Common Characteristics

A more detailed, in-depth examination of the business strategies employed by the top two performing (nondiversified) companies in each of the eight industries sampled reveals that these success strategies share strong common characteristics, irrespective of the particular industry. Indeed, throughout their modern history, all 16 of these leading companies have demonstrated a continuous, single-minded determination to achieve one or both of the following competitive positions within their respective industries:

- Achieve the lowest delivered cost position relative to competition, coupled with both an acceptable delivered quality and a pricing policy to gain profitable volume and market share growth.

TABLE 3   FINANCIAL RETURNS AND GROWTH RATES, 1975–1979

Leading Companies in Eight Basic Industries*

	Average Return on Equity	Average Return on Capital	Annual Revenue Growth Rate
Goodyear	9.2%	7.0%	10.0%
Inland Steel	10.9	7.9	11.4
Paccar	22.8	20.9	14.9
Caterpillar	23.5	17.3	17.2
General Motors	19.8	18.0	13.2
Maytag	27.2	26.5	9.1
G. Heileman Brewing	25.8	18.9	21.4
Philip Morris	22.7	13.5	20.1
Average	20.2%	16.3%	14.7%
Median *Fortune* "1,000" company (same time period)	15.1%	11.0%	13.1%

* Excluding those companies which gained a majority of their returns from diversification efforts.

■ Achieve the highest product/service/quality differentiated position relative to competition, coupled with both an acceptable delivered cost structure and a pricing policy to gain margins sufficient to fund reinvestment in product/service differentiation.

A rough categorization of the strategies employed by these 16 companies, based on selective field studies and observed behavior over time, is shown in Table 4. In most cases, the industry growth and profit leaders chose only one of the two strategic approaches, on the basis that the skills and resources necessary to invest in a low-cost position are insufficient or incompatible with those needed to simultaneously invest in a strongly differentiated position. . . .

However, in at least three cases, the leading companies in my sample chose to combine the two approaches, and each has had spectacular success.

Caterpillar has combined lowest cost manufacturing with higher cost but truly outstanding distribution and after-market support to differentiate its line of construction equipment. As a result,

Caterpillar, ranking as the 24th largest and 39th most profitable company in the United States, is well ahead of its competitors and most of the *Fortune* "500" glamour companies.

Similarly, the U.S. cigarette division of Philip Morris combines the lowest cost, fully automated cigarette manufacturing operation in the world with highest cost, focused branding and promotion to gain industry profit leadership, even without the benefit of either the largest unit volume or segment market share in both domestic and international markets.

And finally, Daimler Benz operates with elements of both strategies but in different segments, coupling the lowest cost position in heavy-duty truck manufacturing in Western Europe with an exceptionally high quality, feature differentiated car line for European and North American export markets. . . .

[An] analysis of business-level returns for all 16 leading competitors in the eight industries (Table 5) indicates some interesting aspects of the respective strategies, as the following comparison reveals:

TABLE 4 COMPETITIVE STRATEGIES EMPLOYED BY LEADING COMPANIES

Eight Basic Industries

Industry	Achieved Low Delivered Cost Position	Achieved "Meaningful" Differentiation	Simultaneous Employment of Both Strategies
Steel	Inland Steel	National	
Tire and rubber	Goodyear	Michelin (French)	
Heavy-duty trucks	Ford	Paccar	
Construction and materials handling equipment		John Deere	Caterpillar
Automotive	General Motors	Daimier Benz (German)	
Major home appliances	Whirlpool	Maytag	
Beer	Miller	G. Heileman Brewing	
Cigarettes	R.J. Reynolds		Philip Morris

- The *lowest delivered cost* leader typically grows more slowly, holding price increases and operating margins down to gain volume, fixed-cost reductions, and improved asset turnover. In addition, this competitor will typically have a lower sales turnover than the differentiated producer, reflecting the higher asset intensity necessary to gain cost reductions in production and distribution.

- The *differentiated position* leader typically grows faster, with higher prices and operating margins to cover promotional, research, and other product/service costs. At the same time, this competitor typically operates with lower asset intensity (higher sales turnover), reflecting both higher prices and a lower cost, "flexible" asset base.

Successful Strategies Come from Purposeful Moves toward a Leadership Position

In examining the business strategies and subsequent performance of the leading competitors, it becomes clear that purposeful movement toward

and defense of a "winning" strategic position—either lowest cost and/or superior, price-justified differentiation—has been the fundamental long-term objective of all 16 high performance companies. There is little doubt that consistency and clarity of purpose have helped to mobilize and coordinate internal resources in gaining and defending a leadership position.

It is important to note that the time-phased pattern of investment decisions used to attain and hold these winning positions was based on "doing the right things" to gain leadership in lowest costs and/or differentiation. As a result, all the high performers in my sample used careful strategic analysis to guide their investments, avoiding simplistic adherence to doctrinaire approaches toward strategy formulation which come from the naive application of tools like:

- Share/growth matrices—planning models which suggest that mature market segments should be "milked" or "harvested" for cash flows.

TABLE 5 BUSINESS LEVEL RETURNS AND REVENUE GROWTH RATES

Leading Industrial Goods Producers* 1978	Operating Margins	Sales Turnover	Operating ROA	Revenue Growth Rates, 1975–1979
Steel				
Inland Steel	8.3%	1.3	10.8%	11.4%
National	12.0	1.5	18.0	12.0
Tire and rubber				
Goodyear	8.6	1.5	12.9	10.5
Michelin	10.0 (est.)	N.A.	N.A.	N.A.
Heavy-duty trucks				
Ford	11.0 (est.)	2.3	25.0 (est.)	12.7
Paccar	12.7	2.4	30.5	15.5
Construction and materials handling equipment				
Caterpillar	15.5	1.8	27.9	14.9
John Deere	10.0	1.3	13.0	17.5
Leading Consumer Goods Producers* 1978				
Automotive				
General Motors	9.6	2.0	19.2%	13.2
Daimier Benz (automotive)	11.0	2.4	26.4	15.1
Major home appliances				
Whirlpool	8.4	1.0	8.4	5.3
Maytag	21.8	1.8	39.2	9.1
Brewing				
Miller	8.2	1.5	12.3	29.2
G. Heileman Brewing	9.5	3.5	33.3	32.2
Cigarettes				
R.J. Reynolds	17.1	2.3	39.3	15.0
Philip Morris	17.7	1.4	24.8	20.1

Lowest delivered cost producer listed first, followed by most differentiated producer.

- Experience curves and PIMS [see Schoeffler, Buzzell and Heany, 1974:137]—planning models which suggest that high market share and/or lowest cost, vertically integrated production are keys to success in mature markets.

Instead, based on a case-by-case analysis, the performance leaders made investment decisions which frequently conflicted with these doctrinaire theories:

- The leadership positions in mature markets were not being milked by any of the 16 competitors, contrary to the advice of consultants who emphasize the portfolio approach to asset management. In fact, the top managers in two of the leading companies I interviewed laughed when they discussed this concept. They pointed out that their future success and growth opportunities were far greater if they aggressively reinvested in their base business than if they redeployed assets into other (diversified) industries.

- Low-cost production is not essential to prosper in mature markets, contrary to the belief of strong proponents of the experience curve. Instead, high sustainable returns also come from reinvesting in an average cost, highly differentiated position, as the data of the previous section and Table 5 demonstrate, and as the ongoing track records of companies like Paccar and Maytag clearly illustrate.

- High market share and accumulated experience are not essential for cost leadership in a mature market, as indicated by proponents of the experience curve and some large-sample empirical studies like PIMS. In fact, four of the eight low-cost producers in this study—Inland Steel, Whirlpool, Miller, and Philip Morris—have achieved their lowest cost positions without the benefit of high relative market shares.

  Rather, these producers have focused their plants by emphasizing modern, automated process technology, and they have heavily invested in their distribution systems to gain scale economies and other cost reductions in their delivery systems.

- Vertical integration is not necessary to exploit cost leadership in mature markets, as suggested by a number of empirical and economic studies. In fact, all of the low-cost producers in the industries under study were less vertically integrated into upstream and downstream activities than at least one other major competitor in their industry.

  Instead of emphasizing vertical integration as a policy, all looked for selective integration into high value-added, proprietary componentry, following the type of integration policy first delineated by General Motors in the 1920s of "not investing in general industries of which a comparatively small part of the product is consumed in the manufacture of cars."

Instead of fully integrating, the low-cost leaders invested to have the most efficient process technology in at least one selective stage of the vertical chain. . . .

Problems Come from Failure to Gain or Defend a Leadership Position

A more detailed examination of the marginal or failing competitors in each of the eight basic industries (Table 6) also reveals some interesting observations:

- The historical strategies and policies pursued by these companies have placed them in an unstable position. All are the high-cost producers in their segments, and all have a product that not only is largely undifferentiated in any meaningful sense but also in many cases is below average in quality and performance.

- The external pressures that these companies complain about—unwarranted regulation and unfair foreign competition—are simply the final blows, sealing a fate that was predestined by improper strategic positioning or repositioning in the 1950s and 1960s, a period when there was still growth and time to maneuver.

- Many of these marginal producers held low-cost or differentiated positions in these earlier years, and made strategic errors in their reinvestment decisions which contributed to their marginal or failing positions today, as the following examples show. . . .

TABLE 6   MARGINAL OR FAILING COMPANIES IN U.S.
           MARKETS

Steel	J&L-Youngstown Kaiser
Tire and rubber	Uniroyal Mohawk Cooper
Heavy-duty trucks	White Motor
Construction and materials handling equipment	Massey-Ferguson Allis Chalmers
Automotive	Chrysler
Major home appliances	Tappan
Beer	Most regional breweries Schlitz
Cigarettes	Liggett & Myers

For A Deteriorating Position, Diversity May Not Be the Proper Recovery Approach

Over the past several years, it has become fashionable to recommend product/market diversification as a way out of an unstable or failing position for mature companies in hostile environments. Unfortunately, in the 64 companies I examined in this research, diversification has "helped" overcome major competitive/performance problems in only three—B.F. Goodrich, General Tire, and Armco Steel (now Armco Group). These three competitors recognized the tenuous nature of their positions early in the maturity cycle and took steps to resegment their base businesses into more advantageous positions by redeploying assets in carefully chosen diversification moves. . . .

On the other hand, efforts to gain meaningful economic diversification have eluded most of the other problem competitors in the eight industries. By waiting too long to begin diversification efforts, most lack the capital and managerial skills to enter new markets and/or to grow businesses successfully in these markets. Thus their diversification efforts to date have been too small or have been managed in too conservative a fashion to obtain sustainable performance improvements. . . .

## TWELVE

THE DIVERSIFIED CONTEXT

A good deal of evidence has accumulated on the relationship between diversification and divisionalization. Once organizations diversity their product or service lines, they tend to create distinct structural divisions to deal with each distinct business. This relationship was perhaps first carefully documented in the classic historical study by Alfred D. Chandler, *Strategy and Structure*: *Chapters in the History of the Great American Enterprise*; Chandler traced the origins of diversification and divisionalization in DuPont and General Motors in the 1920s which were followed later by other major firms. A number of other studies elaborated on Chandler's conclusions; these are discussed in the readings of this chapter.

The first reading, drawn from Mintzberg's *Structure in Fives*, probes the structure of divisionalization—how it works, what brings it about, what intermediate variations of it exist, and what problems it poses for companies and for society at large.

Although this reading ends on a somewhat negative note, the next one presents one of the major challenges of this form of organization and offers a good discussion of how to make a diversification strategy work at the corporate level. This brings us back to a framework discussed in the introduction to Chapter 1, which distinguishes between corporate (or grand) strategies and more discrete business (battle) strategies. Looking be-

yond diversity itself to the synergy that gives the corporation a value beyond the sum of its individual divisions, this chapter from *Strategy in Action* by Boris Yavitz and Bill Newman of the Columbia University Graduate Business School considers how corporate coordination can enhance the overall effectiveness of a company's various divisions. Although experience has proved many forms of synergy difficult to achieve, few would deny its desirability as a goal and the power of its actual accomplishment in specific situations. Synergy comes from corporate "economies of scale" in some companies, while in others it derives from more recently recognized "economies of scope" that use the same management or information systems to deliver a variety of products or services flexibly to a wide range of customers.

As diversification became an especially popular strategy among large corporations in the 1960s and 1970s, a number of techniques were developed to analyze strategies at the corporate level. Among the most widely used were various "portfolio" techniques, which approached the businesses of a diversified company as a portfolio of investments whose return could be optimized by properly balancing their growth and maturity characteristics and by redeploying investments and cash flows among them. Abell and Hammond provide an excellent review of these techniques in *Strategic Market Planning* while John Seeger, of Bentley College, provides a colorful and biting critique of the most famous of these—the Boston Consulting Group's growth-share matrix, with its stable of dogs, wildcats, cash cows, and stars.

Seeger, in fact, has a broader message to convey: "No management model can safely substitute for analysis and common sense." While techniques such as the experience curve and competitive and portfolio analysis can be very useful in understanding critical relationships and in making sure one touches all the right bases, they provide no substitutes for a thorough-going intellectual and intuitive understanding of the full complexity of a company's unique capabilities in its particular environments. Many of these cannot be captured in numerical analyses, but abide in the minds and motivations of the people in the organization. Cases like Pillsbury, General Mills, Continental Group, and Corporative Planning Systems offer opportunities to pursue both the economic issues and human complexities that diversified enterprises present.

THE DIVISIONALIZED FORM*

by Henry Mintzberg

The Divisionalized Form is not so much an integrated organization as a set of quasi-autonomous units coupled together by a central administrative structure. . . . These units are generally called *divisions*, and the central administration, the *headquarters*. . . .

The Divisionalized Form is most widely used in the private sector of the industrialized economy; the vast majority of the *Fortune* 500, America's largest corporations, use this structure or a variant of it. But it is also found in other sectors as well. The multiversity—the multiple

* Excerpted from Henry Mintzberg, *Structure in Fives: Designing Effective Organizations* (Prentice-Hall, 1983), chap 11; used by permission of the publisher.

campus institution—uses a variant of this configuration, as does the hospital system comprising a number of specialized hospitals, and the socialist economy, where state enterprises serve as divisions and the economic agencies of the central government as the headquarters. . . .

THE BASIC STRUCTURE

The Design Parameters

. . . the Divisionalized Form relies on the market basis for grouping units at the top of the middle line. Divisions are created according to markets served and are then given control over the operating functions required to serve these markets, [as shown] in Figure 1. . . . This dispersal (and duplication) of the operating functions minimizes the interdependence between divisions, so that each can operate as a quasi-autonomous entity, free of the need to coordinate with the others. . . .

The structural arrangement naturally leads to pronounced decentralization from the headquarters: each division is delegated the powers needed to make the decisions concerning its own operations. But the decentralization called for in the Divisionalized Form is highly circumscribed—not necessarily more than the delegation from the few managers at headquarters to the few more managers who run the divisions. In other words, the Divisionalized Form calls for decentralization of the parallel, limited vertical variety. In fact, divisionalized structures can turn out to be rather *centralized* in nature. The division managers can hold the lion's share of the power, precluding further vertical decentralization (down the chain of authority) or horizontal decentralization (to staff specialists and operators). . . .

Were the headquarters to delegate *all* its power to the division managers, it would cease to exist, and each division would, in effect, emerge as an independent organization. So some form of control or coordination is required between headquarters and the divisions. . . . In general, the headquarters . . . monitors the re-

FIGURE 1   TYPICAL ORGANIGRAM FOR A DIVISIONALIZED
MANUFACTURING FIRM

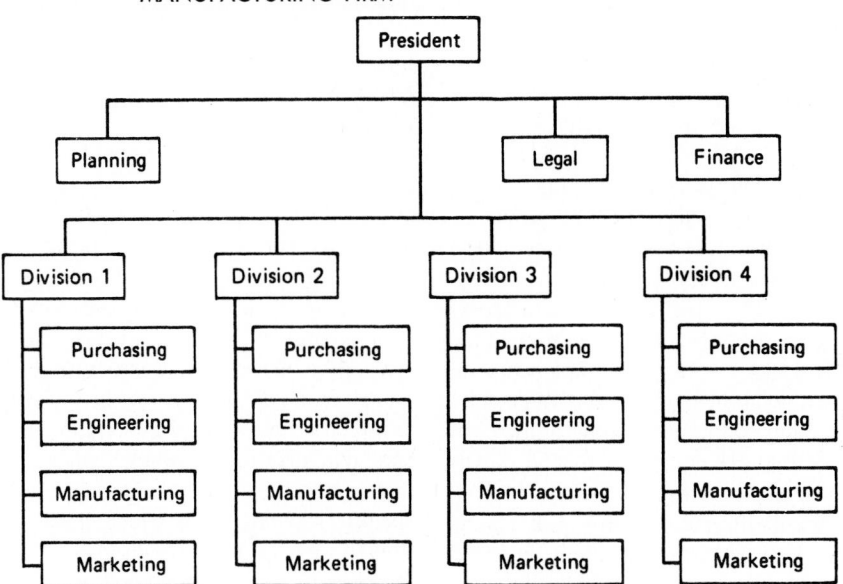

sults of [the divisions'] decisions [through performance control systems]. This monitoring is done after the fact, in specific quantitative terms—in the case of the business corporations, by measures of profit, sales growth, and return on investment. . . . So the prime coordinating mechanism in the Divisionalized Form is the standardization of outputs. . . .

There is [also] a limited role for the two coordinating mechanisms that remain—standardization of skills and direct supervision. The Divisionalized form is dependent for its success on the competence of the divisional managers, to whom much of the decision-making power is delegated. Whereas the managers at the top of the middle line of the other configurations tend to have functional orientations and limited freedom to act independently, those of the Divisionalized Form are ''mini-general managers,'' who run their own operations. That is why the middle line emerges as the key part of this structure. But this characteristic puts the onus on the headquarters to train these division managers as well as it can (in effect, to standardize their managerial skills). Likewise, indoctrination is used to ensure

that the division managers pursue the broader goals of the headquarters instead of the parochial goals of their divisions. Divisional managers are brought back to headquarters periodically for conferences and meetings with the central administrators, and they are sometimes rotated around the different divisions to develop a broad perspective of the organization. Direct supervision serves as a backup mechanism of coordination in the Divisionalized Form. When a division runs into trouble, the headquarters managers may have to step in, perhaps to replace the division manager. So some knowledge of the operations of the division is required, at least to know when to step in, as well as how. . . .

The Structure of the Divisions

. . . In theory, the Divisionalized Form can be superimposed on any of the other configurations. A multiversity or a national accounting firm with regional offices draws a set of Professional Bureaucracies into the Divisionalized Form; a newspaper chain does the same thing with a set of Adhocracies. And a venture capitalist with equity control of entrepreneurial firms may draw a set of Simple Structures into the Divisionalized Form. The divisions of any one organization may also exhibit a variety of structures, as, say, in the case of a municipal government with four "divisions"—a small Simple Structure antipoverty program, a Machine Bureaucracy sanitation service, a Professional Bureaucracy police force, and an Adhocracy urban development group.

But the Divisionalized Form works best with Machine Bureaucracy structures in its divisions and, moreover, drives these structures, no matter what their natural inclinations, toward the Machine Bureaucracy form. The explanation of this important point lies in the standardization of outputs, the key to the functioning of the divisionalized structure. The only way that headquarters can retain control yet protect divisional autonomy is by after-the-fact monitoring of divisional performance. That requires the establishment of clearly defined performance standards, the existence of which depends on two major assumptions. First, each division must be treated as a single integrated system with a single, consistent set of goals. In other words, although the divisions may be loosely coupled with each other, the assumption is that each is tightly coupled within.[1] Second, those goals must be operational ones— in other words, lend themselves to quantitative measures of performance control. In the organic configurations—Simple Structure and Adhocracy, which exist in dynamic environments— such performance standards are difficult to establish. In the Professional Bureaucracy . . . the complexity of the work precludes the establishment of such standards. Moreover, the Professional Bureaucracy is not one integrated system but a collection of individuals with a wide range of goals. That leaves only one configuration that satisfies the assumptions: the Machine Bureaucracy. . . .

Now, what happens when the Divisionalized Form is superimposed on one of the other

three configurations? To make that form work, the assumptions must be made to hold. That is, each division must be made to function as a single integrated system, on which one set of performance measures can be imposed. The division manager, to whom power is delegated from the headquarters, must be able to impose the measures on his division; in other words, he must treat it as a top-down, regulated system. For the Professional Bureaucracy and Adhocracy—in large part bottom-up and nonregulated—that amounts to a pressure to centralize. Moreover, when the division is organized on a functional basis—as it typically is in the Simple Structure, Machine Bureaucracy, and Adhocracy—the division manager is forced to use an action-planning system to ensure that division personnel pursue the performance goals. Action planning imposes ever more specific standards concerning decisions and actions on personnel down the line. That amounts to pressure to formalize (and bureaucratize) the structure of the division. . . . So the Divisionalized Form drives the divisions to be more centralized and more formalized than they would be as independent organizations [and these are the prime characteristics of Machine Bureaucracy]. . . . So we conclude that divisionalization drives the structure of the divisions, no matter what their natural inclinations, toward the Machine Bureaucracy form. . . .

The Powers of the Divisions and the Headquarters

Both communication and decision flows in the Divisionalized Form reflect one central fact: There is a sharp division of labor between the headquarters and the divisions. Communication between the two is circumscribed and largely formal, in good part restricted to the transmission of performance standards down to the divisions and of performance results back up. This is supplemented by personal interchanges between the managers at the two levels, but that is carefully limited. Too much detailed knowledge at the headquarters level can invite meddling in the decisions of the divisions, thereby defeating the very

---

[1] Unless of course, there is a second layer of divisions which simply takes this conclusion down another level in the hierachy.

purpose of divisionalization—namely, divisional autonomy.

In the Divisionalized Form, the divisions are given the power to run their own businesses. They control the operations and determine the strategies for the markets that fall under their responsibility. What powers then are retained by the headquarters? We shall discuss six in all. The first is the formation of the organization's overall product-market strategy. Whereas the divisions determine the strategies for given product markets, the headquarters decides which ones will be given. In effect, the headquarters manages the strategic portfolio, establishing, acquiring, selling, and closing down divisions in order to change its mix of products and markets. . . .

Second, headquarters allocates the overall financial resources. . . . [the divisions] do not pass their work back and forth but do share common financial resources. It is clearly the responsiblity of the headquarters to manage these resources—to draw excess funds from the divisions that do not need them, to raise additional funds in the capital markets when necessary, and to allocate available funds among the divisions that do need them. Headquarters' power over resource allocation also includes the authorization of those divisional capital projects large enough to affect the overall capital budget of the organization. . . .

The key to the control of the divisions in this configuration is the performance control system. Hence, as its third major power, the headquarters designs the performance control system. The managers there, with the aid of their own technostructure, set up the system. They decide on performance measures and reporting periods, establish formats for plans and budgets, and design an MIS to feed performance results back to headquarters. They then operate the system, setting targets for each reporting period, perhaps jointly with the divisional managers, and reviewing the MIS results.

What happens when the MIS signals that a division has run into trouble, that it can no longer meet its performance targets? The management at headquarters must first decide whether the problem lies in conditions beyond the control of the division or in it. If the former—the problem being an economic downturn, the arrival of new competition, or whatever—headquarters basically has the choice of divesting itself of the division or carrying it financially to ride out the trouble. In other words, it acts in terms of one of its first two powers, the management of the strategic portfolio or the allocation of financial resources. But if the problem is perceived to lie in the division, then headquarters draws on its fourth major power. The headquarters replaces and appoints the managers of the divisions. This is a crucial power in the Divisionalized Form, because the structure precludes direct interference by the headquarters managers in the operating affairs of the divisions; the closest they can come is to determine who will run the divisions. To an important extent, therefore, success in the Divisionalized Form depends on this fourth power, on selecting the right people—general managers with the ability to run quasi-autonomous operations effectively, yet in accordance with the goals of the overall organization.

The performance control system may signal a problem in a division, but it is of little help in determining whether that problem is rooted in adverse conditions or incompetent management. Moreover, there are times when the performance control system fails to do a proper job of reporting problems. . . . This leads to the fifth function. The headquarters monitors divisional behavior on a personal basis. . . . Headquarters managers—sometimes called "group executives" and given charge of a number of divisions—visit the divisions periodically to "keep in touch," to get to know them well enough to be able to foresee problems. Such knowledge also enables the headquarters managers to assess requests by divisions for large capital expenditures, and it gives them knowledge of the people in the divisions when replacements must be made. . . .

As its sixth and final power, the headquarters provides certain support services common to the divisions. . . . Services that must be geared to the needs of single divisions, those that must be located in physically convenient places, and those that are relatively easy to duplicate—as in the cases of a marketing research group, a cafeteria, and a public relations unit, respectively—are typically dispersed to the divisions (and are sometimes duplicated at headquarters as well). But coordinated services that must be offered across the range of divisions, or those that must be provided at the common strategic apex, are concentrated in single units at headquarters. Thus, a central finance unit supports the headquarters role of resource allocation; looks after income tax, insurance, pension matters, and the like common to the different divisions; and may also house the technocratic staffers concerned with the performance control system. . . .

To conclude our discussion of the basic structure, Figure 2 shows the Divisionalized Form represented symbolically in terms of our logo. Headquarters is shown in three parts: a small strategic apex of top managers; a small technostructure to the left, concerned with the design and operation of the performance control system as well as some of the management-development programs; and a slightly larger staff support group to the right. Four divisions are shown below the headquarters, with a bulge put in at the level of division manager to indicate that the middle line is the key part of the organization. All four divisions are represented as Machine Bureaucracies to illustrate our point that divisionalization encourages the divisions to use this configuration.

CONDITIONS OF THE DIVISIONALIZED FORM

. . . One situational factor above all drives the organization to use the Divisionalized Form—market diversity. The organization faced with a single integrated market simply cannot split itself into autonomous divisions; the one with distinct markets, however, has an incentive to create a unit to deal with each. . . . [Note also] that divisionalization encourages further diversification. The ease with which headquarters can add new divisions in this structure encourages it to do so; moreover, divisionalization generates a steady stream of general managers who look for more and larger divisions to run. . . .

[There are three main] kinds of market diversity—product and service, client, and region. In theory, all three can lead to divisionalization. . . . Yet, based on client or regional diversification in the absence of product or service diversification, divisionalization often turns out to be incomplete. With identical products or services in each region or for each group of clients, the headquarters is encouraged to centralize a good deal of decision making and concentrate a good deal of support service at the center, to ensure common operating standards for all the divisions. This centralization and concentration of certain functions—some of them critical in formulating product-market strategies—seriously reduces divi-

FIGURE 2   THE DIVISIONALIZED FORM

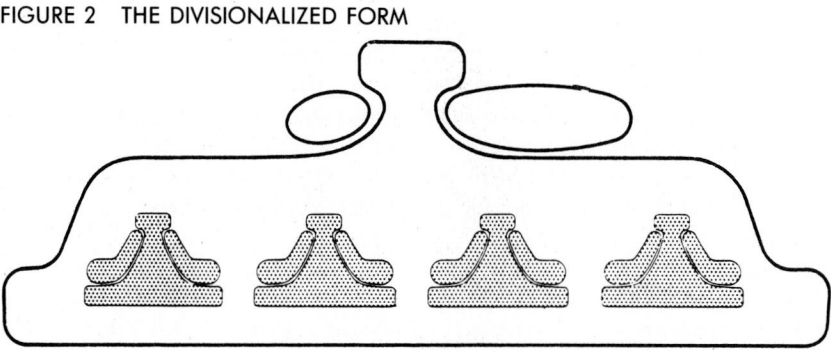

sional autonomy. In effect, the structure is driven toward integrated Machine Bureaucracy, but with one difference: Its operations are divided into distinct market-based units. Thus, one study found that insurance companies concentrate the critical function of investment, and retailers that of purchasing. The headquarters of the latter control sources of supply, product range, pricing, and volume terms, as well as site and property development and merchandising. Day-to-day operations of the retail stores are left to the store managers, who are supervised by a regional hierarchy.

We shall use the term *carbon-copy bureaucracy* for this hybrid of Divisionalized Form and Machine Bureaucracy, the structure that results when an organization sets up identical regional divisions and then concentrates certain critical functions at headquarters. Each division is a replica—a carbon copy—of all the others, performing the same activities in the same ways, unique only in its location. . . . [The carbon-copy bureaucracy is common in retailing], bakeries, breweries, cement producers, and soft-drink bottlers. . . .

[Turning to other conditions], divisionalization is possible only when the organization's technical system can be efficiently separated into segments, one for each division. For example, whereas a geographically diversified cement company can duplicate its processing facilities many times across the face of the nation, a likewise diversified aluminum company with the same sales volume may be unable to if it cannot afford more than one smelter. . . . [Moreover] organizations that must devote huge capital resources to very high fixed-cost technical systems—steel and aluminum producers, and other "heavies" of American industry—tend not to diversify in the first place, and so not to divisionalize. To be more precise, as a group they show little enthusiasm for "horizontal" diversification—into parallel or unrelated product lines. They do diversify "vertically," moving into the product lines at the two ends of their production chains, thereby becoming their own suppliers and customers. But

as we shall see later in this [reading], the strong interdependences between product lines in the same production chain leads to an incomplete form of divisionalization.

. . . the Divisionalized Form [also has] a preferred environment, which it shares with the Machine Bureaucracy. That is because of another condition prerequisite to the use of the Divisionalized Form—outputs (specifically performance criteria) that can be standardized. . . . [This] works best in environments that are neither very complex nor very dynamic; in fact, the very same environments that favor the Machine Bureaucracy. This leads to a rather precise specification of the conditions that most commonly accompany this configuration: the Divisionalized Form is the structural response to a Machine Bureaucracy, operating in a simple, stable environment (typically without huge economies of scale), that has diversified its product or service lines horizontally. . . .

What about the factors of age and size? Although large size itself does not bring on divisionalization, surely it is not coincidental that most of America's largest corporations use some form of this structure. The fact is that as organizations grow large, they become prone to diversify and then to divisionalize. One reason is protection: Large manufacturing firms tend to be organized as Machine Bureaucracies, structures that . . . try to avoid risks. Diversification spreads the risk. Also, the larger a firm becomes vis-à-vis its competitors, the more it comes to dominate its traditional market. Eventually, it simply runs out of room for expansion . . . and so it must find further growth opportunities elsewhere. Thus it diversifies, and later must divisionalize. Moreover, as noted earlier, divisionalization creates a cadre of aggressive general managers who push for further diversification and further growth. . . . The giant corporations—with the few exceptions that remain in one business because of enormously high fixed-cost technical systems—not only require divisionalization but were able to reach their giant size only because of it.

In fact, many corporations have grown so

large and diversified that the simple Divisionalized Form is not sufficient for them. They make
use of a variant we call the *multiple-divisionalized
form*, with divisions on top of divisions. For example, regional divisions may be superimposed
on product divisions, or broad product divisions
(''groups'') may be superimposed on narrower
ones. . . .

Like size, age is also associated with the
divisionalized form. In larger organizations, the
management runs out of places to expand in the
traditional markets; in older ones, the managers
sometimes get bored with the traditional markets
and find diversion through diversification. In other
cases, time brings new competitors into old market niches, forcing the management to look for
new ones with better potential. . . .

[Power is another factor.] Even in the functionally structured organization, the drive by the
aggressive middle manager for more autonomy
amounts to a pull to divisionalize at his level of
the hierarchy. And in the case of the top manager,
the Divisionalized Form is by far the most effective structure by which to increase the power of
his overall organization, since it enables units
to be added with relatively little effort and disruption. . . . Indeed, the waves of conglomerate
diversification in U.S. industry appear to represent a giant power game, with corporate chief
executives vying with each other to see who can
build the largest empire. These same factors of
power have hardly been absent in other spheres
as well, helping to explain the growth in popularity of the Divisionalized Form in unions, school
systems, universities, and especially governments. . . .

As government grows larger . . . it is
forced more and more to revert to a kind of Divisionalized Form. That is, the central administrators, being unable to control all the agencies and
departments (divisions) directly, settle for granting their managers considerable autonomy and
then try to control their performance. One can,
in fact, view the entire government as a giant
Divisionalized Form (admittedly an oversimplification, since all kinds of interdependences exist
among the departments), with its three main coor-

dinative agencies corresponding to three main
forms of control used by the headquarters of
the divisionalized organization. The budgetary
agency, technocratic in nature, concerns itself
with performance control of the departments; the
public service commission, also partly technocratic, concerns itself with the recruiting and training of government managers; and the executive
(or Privy Council) office reviews the major proposals and initiatives of the departments. Perhaps
this concept of the government as a giant Divisionalized Form is taken to its natural conclusion in
the communist state, where public corporations
and other agencies are tightly regulated by planning and control systems operated by a powerful
central technostructure. . . .

STAGES IN THE TRANSITION
TO THE DIVISIONALIZED FORM

We have a good deal of research on the transition
of the corporation from the functional to the Divisionalized form, much of it from the Harvard
Business School, which has shown a special interest in the structure of the large corporation. Figure
3 and the discussion that follows borrow from
these results to describe four stages of that transition. . . .

The Integrated Form

At the top of Figure 3 is the pure functional
form, used by the corporation whose production
activities form one integrated, unbroken chain.
Only the final output is sold to the customers.
The tight interdependences of the different activities make it possible for such corporations to
use the Divisionalized Form—that is, to grant
autonomy to units performing any of the steps
in the chain—and so they organize themselves
as functional Machine Bureaucracies (or Adhocracies, if they face complex, dynamic environments). They typically produce a single product
line, or at least one line dominates. Large firms
using this structure also tend to be vertically integrated and capital-intensive. . . .

FIGURE 3   STAGES IN THE TRANSITION TO THE DIVISIONALIZED FORM

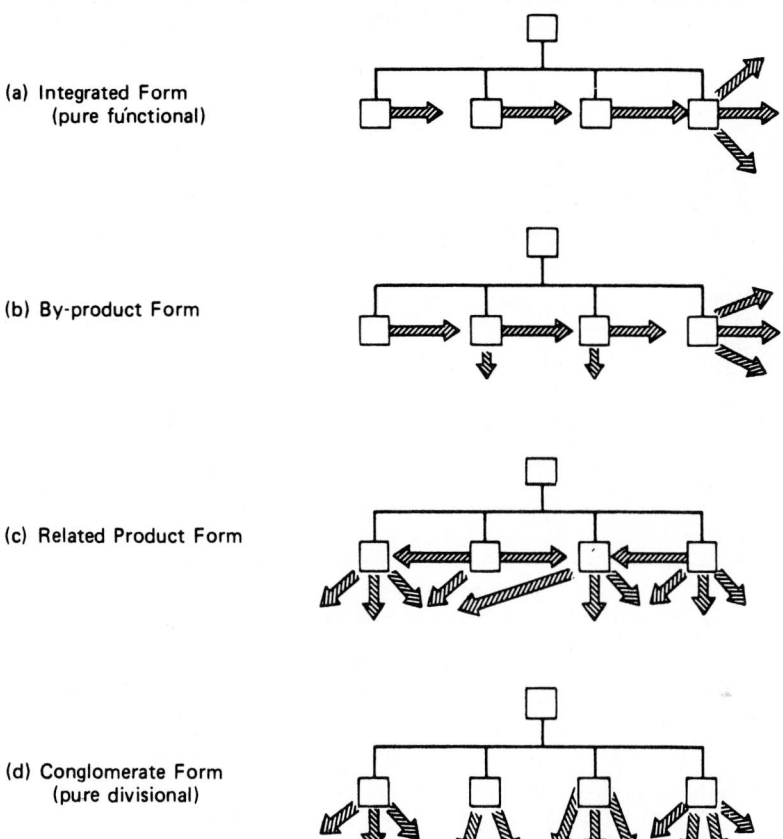

(a) Integrated Form
     (pure functional)

(b) By-product Form

(c) Related Product Form

(d) Conglomerate Form
     (pure divisional)

The By-Product Form

As the integrated firm seeks wider markets; it may choose to diversity its end-product lines and shift all the way over to the pure divisional structure. A less risky alternative, however, is to start by marketing its intermediate products on the open market. This introduces small breaks in its processing chain, which in turn call for a measure of divisionalization in its structure, what can be called the *by-product form*. . . . But because of the processing chain remains more or less intact, headquarters retains considerable control over strategy formulation and some aspects of operations as well. . . .

    Many of the organizations that fall into this category are vertically integrated ones that base their operations on a single basic material, such as wood, oil, or aluminum, which they process to a variety of consumable end products. Figure 4 shows the 1969 processing chain for Alcoa, which earned 69 percent of its revenue from fabricated aluminum end products, such as cookware and auto parts, and 27 percent from intermediate by-products, including cargo space, chemicals, bauxite, and pit and ingot aluminum. (Real estate development—a horizontally diversified service—accounted for the remaining 4 percent.)

The Related-Product Form

Some corporations continue to diversify their by-product markets, further breaking down their processing chain until what the divisions sell on the

FIGURE 4   BY-PRODUCT AND END-PRODUCT SALES OF ALCOA IN 1969

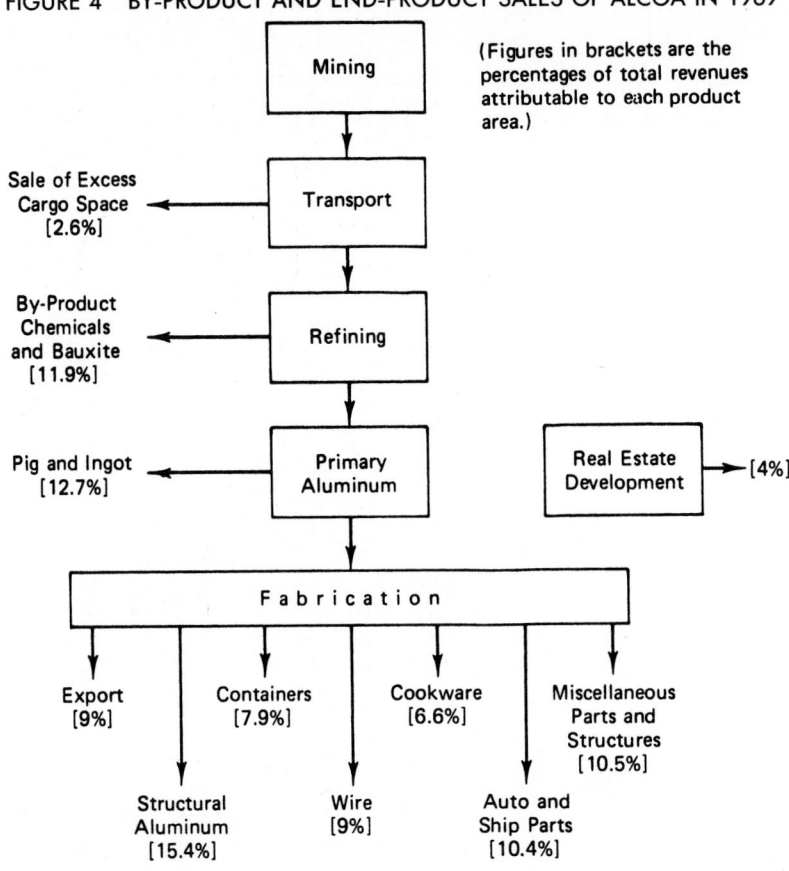

Source: From Rumelt, 1974:21; prepared from data in company's annual reports.

open market becomes more important than what they supply to each other. The organization then moves to the *related-product form*. For example, a firm manufacturing washing machines may set up a division to produce the motors. Eventually, the motor division may become so successful on its own that the washing-machine division is no longer its dominant customer. A more serious form of divisionalization is then called for, to reflect the greater independence of the divisions.

What typically holds the divisions of these firms together is some common thread among their products, sometimes a core skill or technology, sometimes a central market theme. The divisions often sell to many of the same outside customers as well. In effect, the firm retains a semblance of an integrated product-market strategy.

Central planning at the headquarters in the related-product form must be less constraining than in the by-product form, more concerned with measuring performance than prescribing actions. A good deal of the control over the specific product-market strategies must revert to the divisions. But the interdependencies around the central product-market theme encourage the headquarters to retain functions common to the divisions—for example, research and development in the case of a core technology. These central functions are, of course, the "critical" ones for the corporation,

FIGURE 5   ORGANIGRAM OF GENERAL ELECTRIC (CIRCA 1975, USED WITH PERMISSION)

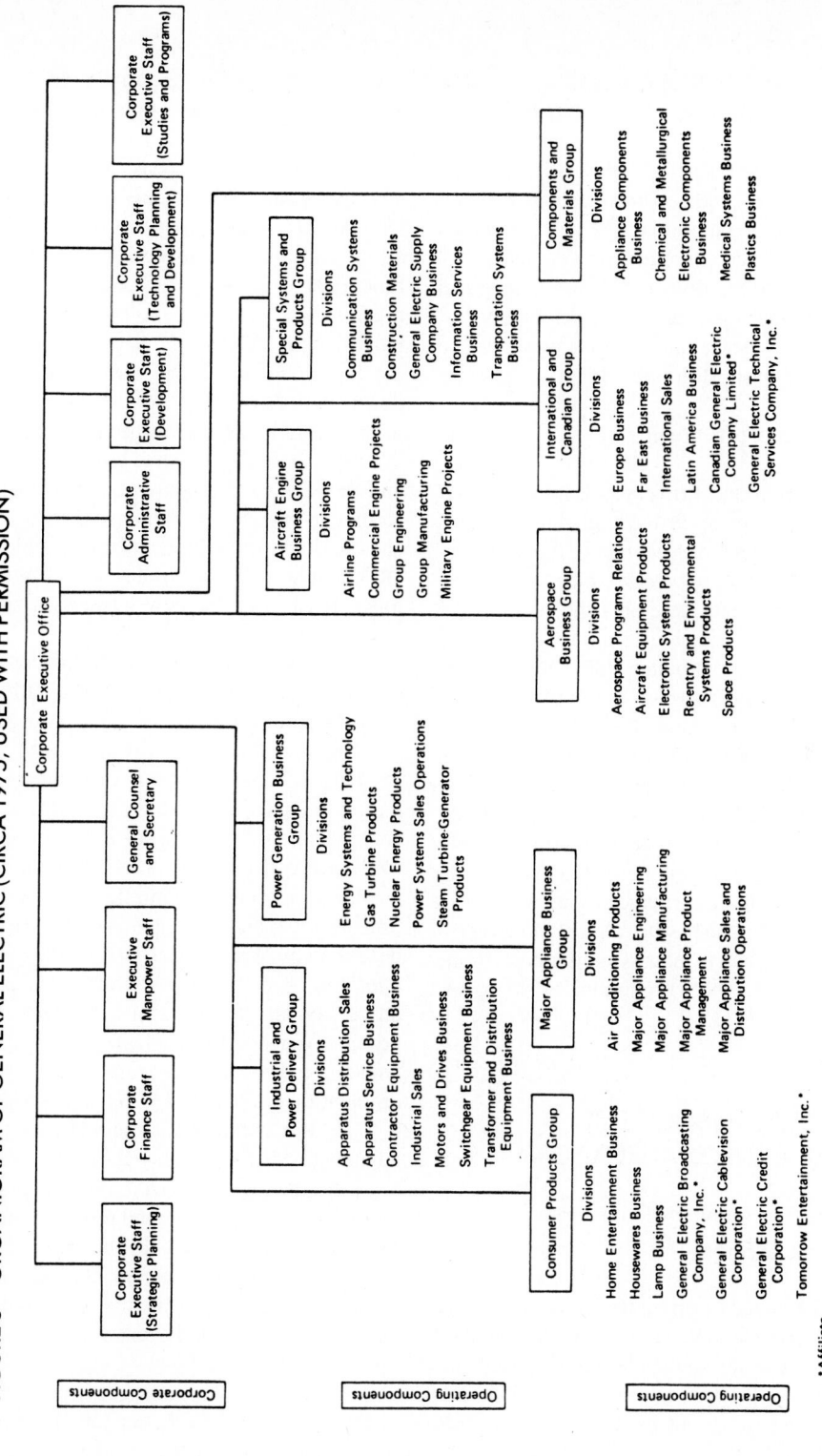

587

so the functional/divisional hybrids—specifically, the ones with *product* or *service* divisions, such as insurance companies that centralize the critical function of investment—would fall into this grouping. So too might a firm such as General Electric, whose organigram (circa 1975) is shown in Figure 5. . . . The structure is divisionalized—in fact . . . multiple-divisionalized—in a typical way, except that there are a greater number of support services at headquarters than we described earlier for the basic structure. . . .

The Conglomerate Form

As the related-product firm expands into new markets or acquires other firms, with less and less regard for a central strategic theme, the organization moves to the *conglomerate form* and adopts a pure divisionalized structure, the one we described earlier . . . Each division serves its own markets, producing product lines unrelated to those of the other divisions—thumbtacks in one, steam shovels in a second, funeral services in a third. In the conglomerate, there are no important interdependences among the divisions, save for the pooling of resources. As a result, the headquarters planning and control system becomes simply a vehicle for regulating performance, specifically financial performance. And the headquarters staff diminishes to almost nothing—a few general or group managers supported by some financial analysts and a minimum of other services. . . .

SOME ISSUES ASSOCIATED WITH THE DIVISIONALIZED FORM

. . . The Economic Advantages of Divisionalization

The Divisionalized Form offers four basic advantages over the functional structure with integrated operations. First, the Divisionalized Form encourages efficient allocation of capital. Headquarters can choose where to put its money, and so can concentrate on its strongest markets, milking the surpluses of some divisions in favor of others. The functional structure has all its eggs in one strategic basket, so to speak. Second, by opening up opportunities to run individual businesses, the Divisionalized form helps to train general managers. In contrast, the middle-line managers of functional structures are locked into dependent relationships with each other, which preclude individual responsibility and autonomy. Third, the Divisionalized Form spreads its risk across different markets. In contrast, one broken link in the operating chain of the functional structure brings the entire system to a grinding halt. Fourth, and perhaps most important, the Divisionalized form is strategically responsive. The divisions can fine-tune their bureaucratic machines while the headquarters concentrates on its strategic portfolio. It can acquire new businesses and divest itself of older, ineffective ones.

But is the functional form the correct basis of comparison? Is it the real alternative to the Divisionalized Form? . . . once an organization is diversified and then divisionalized, there is reason to change the basis of comparison. The real alternative, at least from society's perspective, becomes the taking of a further step along the same path, to the point of eliminating the headquarters and allowing the divisions to function as independent organizations. Textron, as described by Wrigley (1970), had thirty divisions operating in as many different businesses; Beatrice Foods, described in a *Fortune* magazine article (Martin, 1976), had 397. The issue is whether either of these corporations was more efficient than thirty or 397 separate corporations. . . . In this context, we can reconsider the four advantages discussed above.

In the divisionalized organization, headquarters allocates the capital resources among the thirty or 397 divisions. In the case of thirty or 397 independent corporations, the capital markets do the job instead. Which does it better? Two studies suggest that the answer is not a simple one.

Williamson (1975) argues that the Divisionalized Form does the better job. In fact, he describes it as the administrative response to inefficiencies in the capital markets—to idiosyncratic knowledge, opportunistic behaviors, and the like. By virtue of their elaborate performance control systems and their personal contacts, the headquarters managers are better able than the investors to inform themselves of the potential of different businesses—at least, a limited number of businesses. Moreover, the headquarters managers are able to transfer capital between the divisions more quickly and flexibly than can be equivalent market mechanisms. So the Divisionalized Form has "mitigated capital market failures by transferring functions traditionally imputed to the capital market to the firm instead" (Williamson, p. 136).

Williamson's arguments may, in fact, explain why some conglomerate firms have been able to survive and prosper in the economic system. But Moyer in a 1970 paper suggests that these advantages come at a price, specifically that conglomeration—especially by acquisition, the most common way to achieve it—has proven more costly and in some ways, *less* flexible than the market mechanisms:

> An acquiring firm normally pays a 15% premium above the market price of the firm to be acquired in order to consummate a merger. Completely diversified mutual funds can be purchased for a selling charge of 7–9% in the case of "load" funds. . . . Furthermore, an individual stockholder can diversify his own portfolio with brokerage costs averaging only 1.5% to 3.5% of the value of the stock purchased. . . .
>
> Because conglomerate firms have not been required in the past to publish earnings for wholly owned divisions or subsidiaries . . . the stockholder is not in a position to make decisions as to whether subsidiaries which management has seen fit to purchase are enhancing his earning power. An individually diversified portfolio has substantially more flexibility than a conglomerate portfolio. The individual can buy and sell with a minimum of effort depending on the performance of individual stocks. It is a different and more involved matter for a

conglomerate to decide to divest itself or one or more of its subsidiaries (Moyer, 1970:22).

Moyer believes that conglomeration denies the shareholder one of his few remaining prerogatives: the choice of an industry—and a risk level—in which to put his capital. The choice among stocks of different conglomerate firms amounts to the choice among given portfolios—Beatrice Foods instead of Dannon Yogurt.

On the issue of management development, the question becomes whether the division managers receive better training and experience than they would as company presidents. The Divisionalized Form is able to put on training courses and to rotate its managers to vary their experiences; the independent firm is limited in these respects. But if, as the proponents of divisionalization claim, autonomy is the key to management development, then presumably, the more autonomy the better. The division managers have a headquarters to lean on—and to be leaned on by. In Textron, "The price of autonomy is plan achievement. If a division cannot for one reason or another meet its goals, it is subject to close and detailed supervision . . ." (Wrigley, 1970:V–91). In contrast, the company president is on his own, to make his own mistakes and learn from them.

On the third issue, of risk, the argument from the divisionalized perspective is that the independent organization is vulnerable during periods of internal crisis or economic slump; conglomeration provides it with the support to see it through such periods. The counterargument is that divisionalization may conceal bankruptcies, that ailing divisions are sometimes supported longer than necessary, whereas the market bankrupts the independent firm and is done with it. Another point, this one from the perspective of the organization itself, is that just as the Divisionalized Form spreads it risk, so too does it spread the consequences of that risk. A single division cannot go bankrupt; the whole organization is legally responsible for its debts. So a massive enough problem in one division . . . can siphon off the resources of the healthy divisions and even bankrupt the whole organization. *Loose* coupling turns out to be riskier than *no* coupling!

Finally, there is the issue of strategic responsiveness. The loosely coupled Divisionalized Form may be more responsive than the tightly coupled functional form. But the question is, What price even loose coupling? In other words, what effect does conglomeration have on strategic responsiveness? The control system of the Divisionalized Form—which keeps that carrot just the right distance in front of the divisional managers—encourages them to strive for better and better financial performance. At the same time, however, it impedes their ability to innovate. "Textron's management has . . . learned that developing new inventions is not one of its strong points" (quoted in Wrigley, 1970:V–89). Bower explains why:

> . . . the risks to the division manager of a major innovation can be considerable if he is measured on short-run, year-to-year, earnings performance. The result is a tendency to avoid big risky bets, and the concomitant phenomenon that major new developments are, with few exceptions, made outside the major firms in the industry. Those exceptions tend to be single-product companies whose top managements are committed to true product leadership: Bell Laboratories, IBM, Xerox, and Polaroid. These are the top managements that can make major strategic moves for their whole company. Instead, the diversified companies give us a steady diet of small incremental change. (1970:194)

Innovation requires entrepreneurship, and entrepreneurship does not thrive under standardized external control. The entrepreneur takes his own risks to earn his own rewards. . . . Thus, the independent firm appears to be more strategically responsive than the corporate divisions, although perhaps less motivated to achieve consistently high economic performance. Indeed, many divisionalized corporations depend on these firms for their strategic responsiveness, since they di-

versify not by innovating themselves but by acquiring the innovative results of independent entrepreneurs.

The Contribution of Headquarters

To assess the effectiveness of conglomeration, it is necessary to assess what actual contribution the headquarters makes to the divisions. Since the headquarters function of control is supposed to be performed by the board of directors of the independent firm, the question becomes, What does a headquarters offer to the division that an independent board of directors does not?

One thing that neither the headquarters managers nor the board of directors can offer is the management of the individual business. Both are involved with it only on a part-time basis.[2] The management of it is, therefore, logically left to its full-time managers—they have the required time and information. In fact, one issue that faces the Divisionalized Form more than an independent business, because of the closer links between headquarters and divisional managers, is the tendency to forget this point. A strong set of forces [such as the illusion of control provided by an MIS or portfolio technique, as described in a later reading] encourages the headquarters managers to usurp divisional powers, to centralize certain product-market decisions at headquarters and so defeat the purpose of divisionalization. . . .

Among the functions headquarters managers *do* perform are the establishment of objectives for the divisions, the monitoring of their performance in terms of these objectives (an appropriate use for the MIS), the maintenance of limited personal contacts with division managers, and the approval of the major capital expenditures of the divisions. Interestingly, these are also the responsibilities of the board of directors, at least in theory. In practice, however, many boards—notably those of widely held corporations—do these things ineffectively, leaving management carte

---

[2]   *If the directors are full-time, they become, in effect, the management, and there is no formal external control of the firm.*

blanche to do what it likes. Here, then, we seem to have a major advantage of the Divisionalized Form. It exists as an administrative arrangement to overcome another major weakness of the free-market system, the ineffective board. With the attention the headquarters pays to its formal and personal control systems, it induces divisional managers to strive for better and better financial results.

There is a catch in this argument, however, for conglomerate diversification often serves both to diffuse stock ownership and to render the corporation more difficult to understand and control by its board. For one thing, as we saw earlier, diversified corporations are typically large ones and so typically widely held and difficult to understand in any event. For another, the more businesses an organization operates, the harder it is for part-time directors to know what is going on. And finally, as Moyer notes, one common effect of conglomerate acquisition is to increase the number of shareholders, and so to make the corporation more widely held. Thus, the Divisionalized Form in some sense only resolves a problem of its own making. Had the corporation remained in one business, it may have been more narrowly held and easier to understand, and so its directors could have performed their functions more effectively. Diversification helped create the problem that divisionalization solved. Indeed, it is ironic that many a divisionalized corporation that does such an effective job of monitoring the performance of its own divisions is itself so poorly monitored by its board of directors. . . .

What happens when [problems arise]? What can headquarters do about it that a board of directors could not? The chairman of Textron told a meeting of the New York Society of Security Analysts, in reference to the headquarters vice-presidents who oversee the divisions, that "it is not too difficult to coordinate five companies that are well run" (quoted in Wrigley, 1970:V–78). True enough. But what about five that are badly run? What can a staff of thirty administrators at headquarters really do to correct problems in thirty operating divisions? The natural tendency to tighten the control screws does not usually help

once the problem has manifested itself, nor does exercising close surveillance. As noted earlier, the headquarters managers cannot manage the divisions. Essentially, that leaves them with two alternatives. They can replace the division manager, or they can divest the corporation of the division. Of course, the board of directors can also change the management. Indeed, that seems to be its only real prerogative; the management does everything else. . . .

On balance, the case for one headquarters versus a set of separate boards of directors appears to be mixed. It should come as no surprise that one study found that corporations with "controlled diversity" had better profit than those with conglomerate diversity (Rumelt, 1974). Controlled diversity means interdependence among the divisions, which calls for an intermediate, or impure, form of divisionalization, with some critical functions concentrated at headquarters. . . .

Overall [then], the pure Divisionalized Form (that is, the conglomerate form) may offer some advantages over a weak system of boards of directors and inefficient capital markets; but most of those advantages would probably disappear if certain problems in capital markets and boards were rectified. And there is reason to argue that society would be better off trying to correct fundamental inefficiencies in its economic system rather than encouraging private administrative arrangements to circumvent them. In fact, as we now turn from the administrative and economic consequences of the Divisionalized Form to its social ones, we shall see two additional reasons to support this conclusion, one related to the social responsibility of the Divisionalized Form, the other to its tendency to concentrate power in society.

The Social Performance of the Performance Control System

The performance control system of the Divisionalized Form is one of its fundamental design parameters and the chief source of its economic efficiency. Yet this system also produces one of its most serious social consequences.

The Divisionalized Form requires that headquarters control the divisions primarily by quantitative performance criteria, and that typically means financial ones—profit, sales growth, return on investment, and the like. The problem is that these performance measures become virtual obsessions, driving out goals that cannot be measured—product quality, pride in work, customers well served, an environment protected or beautified. In effect, the economic goals drive out the social ones. "We, in Textron, worship the god of Net Worth" (quoted in Wrigley, 1970:V–86).

That would pose no problems if the social and economic consequences of decisions could easily be separated. Governments would look after the former, corporations the latter. But the fact is that the two are intertwined; every strategic decision of the large corporation involves social as well as economic consequences. As a result, the control system of the Divisionalized Form drives it to act, at best socially unresponsively, at worst socially irresponsibly. Forced to concentrate on the economic consequences of his decisions, the division manager comes to ignore their social consequences. . . . Thus, Bower finds that "the best record in the race relations area are those of single-product [nondivisionalized] companies whose strong top managements are deeply involved in the business" (1970:193).

Robert Ackerman (1975), in a study carried out at the Harvard Business School, [investigated this conclusion]. Ackerman found that the benefits of social responsiveness—such as "a rosier public image . . . pride among managers . . . an attractive posture for recruiting on campus" (p. 55)—cannot easily be measured . . . [and so] cannot be plugged into the performance control system. The result is that:

> . . . the financial reporting system may actually inhibit social responsiveness. By focusing on economic performance, even with appropriate safeguards to protect against sacrificing long-term benefits, such a system directs energy and resources to achieving results measured in financial

terms. It is the only game in town, so to speak, at least the only one with an official scorecard. (p. 56)

Headquarters managers, concerned about public relations and corporate liability, are tempted to intervene directly in the divisions' responses to new social issues. But they are discouraged by the Divisionalized Form's strict division of labor; divisional autonomy requires no headquarters meddling in specific decisions. As long as the screws of the performance control system are not turned too tight, the division manager retains some discretion to consider the social consequences of his actions. . . . When the screws are turned really tight, [however], the division manager intent on achieving the standards may have no choice but to act irresponsibly. . . .

The Problems of the Concentration of Power

Earlier we discussed the relationship between size and the Divisionalized Form . . . From society's point of view, we must ask, What price bigness? Clearly there are potential economic costs to bigness, notably the threat to the competitive market. . . .

But the social costs of bigness may be the most serious ones. For one thing, big means bureaucratic. . . . Moreover, there are forces in the Divisionalized Form [reputation concerns, power needs, etc.] that drive it to centralize power not only at the divisional level but also at the headquarters level. In the case of the giant corporation, this results in the concentrating of enormous amounts of power in very few hands. . . .

Paradoxically, the concentration of power within the corporation also leads to conglomeration, divisionalization, and the concentration of power in spheres outside the corporation. Unions federate and governments add agencies to establish countervailing powers—ones to match those of the corporation. . . .

[Ironically] the very arguments used in favor of the Divisionalized Form suggest the way to government intervention [to deal with the problems of social irresponsibility and the concentration of power]. Consider Williamson's key point in this regard, that the administrative arrangements are efficient while the capital markets are not. Why should the government worry about interfering with markets that do not work efficiently? And if the administrative arrangements work as well as Williamson claims, why should government not use them too? If Beatrice Foods really can control 397 divisions, what is to stop Washington from believing that it can control 397 Beatrices? Using the same systems. . . .

Of course, like the corporation, so too would governments be driven to favor economic goals over social ones, as a result of the nature of the control system they would have to use. This means that government control, while perhaps legitimizing the activities of the corporation, would not solve the fundamental social problems raised by divisionalization and would, in fact, aggravate that of the concentration of power in society.

In general, the pure Divisionalized Form does not work effectively outside the private sector. This despite widespread attempts to use it—in school systems, universities, hospitals, government corporations—indeed, in all of them together in one giant public-sector divisionalized monolith.

One problem is that government and sometimes other institutions cannot divest themselves of divisions, or at least, the realities of power are that they seldom do. So there is no vehicle for organizational renewal. Another problem in government is that its civil-service regulations on appointments interfere with the concept of managerial responsibility. . . .

But the most serious problem remains that of measurement: The goals governments and most institutions must plug into the performance control system—basically social goals—do not lend themselves to measurement. And without measurement, the pure Divisionalized Form cannot work. . . . So the choices facing the government—and unions, multiversities, and other federated institutions that try to use the Divisionalized Form in the face of nonquantifiable

goals—are to forget control beyond the appointment of socialized managers, to control machine bureaucratically, or to force in divisionalized control by the imposition of artificial performance standards. . . .

In Conclusion: A Structure at the Edge of a Cliff

Our discussion has led to a "damned if you do, damned if you don't" conclusion. The pure (conglomerate) Divisionalized Form emerges as a configuration symbolically perched on the edge of the cliff, at the end of a long path. Ahead, it is one step away from *dis*integration—breaking up into separate organizations on the rocks below. Behind it is the way back to a more stable integration, perhaps a hybrid structure with Machine Bureaucracy at some intermediate spot along the path. And ever hovering above is the eagle, attracted by its position on the edge of the cliff and waiting for the chance to pull the Divisionalized Form up to more centralized social control, on another, perhaps more dangerous, cliff. The edge of the cliff is an uncomfortable place to be—maybe even a temporary one that must inevitably lead to disintegration on the rocks below, a trip to that cliff above, or a return to a safer resting place on the path behind. . . .

CORPORATE INPUT STRATEGY*

By Boris Yavitz and William H. Newman

Corporate strategy involves more than the choice of a good portfolio. Developing an attractive array of business-units is vital . . . but it is an incom-

* Excerpted with permission of the Free Press, a division of Macmillan, Inc. from *Strategy in Action: The Execution, Politics, and Payoff of Business Planning* by Boris Yavitz and William H. Newman. Copyright © 1982 by The Free Press.

plete view of good corporate strategy. Most corporations do more than make investments and then passively await results. Rather, they seek synergies among the business-units and with the corporation—the progressive corporation does "bring something to the party."

So, a second vital dimension of corporate strategy is: What should be done by the corporation to strengthen its various businesses? Low-cost capital, a supply of outstanding managers, assured access to markets are possibilities. As a result of such inputs from the corporation, most—if not all—of the business-units should gain greater differential advantage than they could muster if they operated independently.

Our focus here is on major inputs. Every corporation provides minor services for its operating units—stockholder relations, filing consolidated reports with governmental agencies, a logo to place on the letterhead are typical examples. But the minor, usually necessary, activities do not significantly affect the fate of the business-units. Even such work as central purchasing or institutional advertising typically is helpful but far from determining the growth or demise of specific business-units. Corporate strategy concentrates on actions that are fundamental to success. It adds yeast, not just seasoning.

The central issues of corporate input strategy are:

1. Selecting a few kinds of contributions the corporation will make to its business-units—contributions of such quality and value that the business-units gain a significant advantage over their competitors.

2. Finding ways to develop a differential advantage in the production or delivery of such services.

3. Integrating these strengths into portfolio selection and corporate mission, and into the design of charters for business-units.

Note that this view supports the concept, already stressed, that business-units are the primary operating segments of a diversified corporation. To the extent it is practical, operating activities should be placed within these business-units.

We would transfer operating activities to another division or to the corporate level only when the benefits of doing so are very high. In this sense, *corporate inputs* run counter to the basic pattern of decentralization. They are exceptions. Nevertheless, experience shows that when wisely selected and carefully administered, corporate inputs can be a powerful asset.

CORPORATE RESOURCE ARSENAL

Diversified corporations can strengthen their business-units primarily in two ways—(a) by providing one or more valuable resources on attractive terms, and/or (b) by central management of synergies among the business-units. The following examples . . . illustrate the possibilities of strategic inputs.

Low-Cost Capital

By far the most widely recognized aid that a parent corporation gives its operating units is growth capital . . . a new business-unit often incurs losses for several years before it can build a profitable niche. And even an established venture needs working capital and fixed capital to grow.

A cash-rich parent is very convenient in such situations. Growth can proceed as rapidly as technology, markets, and environmental conditions warrant. Often a jump on competitors is possible.

The parent corporation need not have cash in the bank (or flowing from owned cash cows), if it can raise new funds at a favorable cost. If its capital structure permits more borrowing and it enjoys a favorable credit rating, interest will be a taxable expense, and thus the net cost of capital will be relatively low for a new venture. Or, if the parent corporation enjoys a high price/earnings (P/E) ratio on its stock, equity capital may "cost" less than the business-unit would have to pay. In this manner financial strategy of the corporation builds a resource that strengthens the business-units.

Of course, not all diversified corporations are in such an enviable condition. They may already be saddled with debt and have a low P/E ratio. Indeed, a large and well-known business-unit with an exciting new product or with extensive collateral may be able to raise capital on better terms than its parent. So, the crux is whether the diversified corporation can and will give its operating units a differential advantage with respect to the supply of capital.

Outstanding Executives

Other corporate inputs may be as invigorating. For instance, a few corporations go to great lengths to develop a pool of unusually well-qualified managers. The high-sounding expression, "Our greatest strength is our people" may be accurate. Selection, training, and know-how are designed to give managers in such corporations a competitive edge. . . .

When a corporation develops enough "depth" of able general managers, it (a) can move immediately instead of searching for an outsider, (b) need not devote time and effort "socializing" a new executive to the corporate culture, (c) doesn't tip off plans to outsiders by searching for a particular kind of manager in the open market, and (d) reinforces the message that this corporation provides great opportunities for its own people.

This is an ambitious strategy. It deals with a soft asset, compared with capital. The people are mobile, and competitors may seduce them. There is doubt about how transferable to other kinds of business some of the skills and know-how will be. Nevertheless, the potential rewards are high. If a corporation does, in fact, succeed in staffing its business-units with executives who can outdistance their competitors, a whole array of other strengths may be promoted.

Corporate R&D

Useful, creative ideas, scientifically tested, are scarce and expensive. For most laboratories to be effective, a "critical mass" (minimum size) is necessary. One way to seek a flow of such ideas and specialized laboratory service, without loading high costs onto each business-unit, is through a centralized R&D division.

For years Bell Laboratories served the various operating companies of the AT&T system in this manner. The worldwide pharmaceutical firms also typically centralize their research work (although separate problems may be studied at separate locations). Other examples are well known. The aim is to create a powerful research group at the corporate level that makes contributions to the operating divisions—contributions that the divisions acting alone would be unable to achieve or even unlikely to investigate.

Centralized R&D has its drawbacks. Lack of responsiveness to operating needs, pursuit of inconsequential questions, reluctance to piggyback on research of competitors, and similar issues are often raised. The more diversified the operating divisions, the more difficult these problems become. Nevertheless, the overall success of such corporations as DuPont with centralized research does indicate that this can be a workable corporate input strategy.

Centralized Marketing

The basic concept of a business-unit places control of major functions—engineering, production, marketing, and the like—within the unit. To a large extent the unit is self-contained and autonomous; it runs its own show. Coordination between the functions and adjustments to the environment of each particular business are decentralized.

Occasionally, however, a corporation seeks strength by defying the usual pattern. One possible exception is to withdraw parts of marketing from the business-units and to perform these particular activities in a corporate marketing division. In fact, this was the original strategy of General Foods Corporation. Each of the several companies that were merged into General Foods—Post Cereals, Jell-O, Maxwell House Coffee, and so on—continued to buy, manufacture, package, price, and ship products as they had previously done. The key contribution of the new corporation was nationwide selling and nationwide promotion for all the products. By combining selling and promotion into a single division, the corporation provided the several operating companies much more complete coverage and skillful promotion than any company could muster when acting separately.

The large Japanese trading companies operate in a roughly similar way for the manufacturing companies they represent, although here the manufacturers maintain a more independent existence.

The Coca-Cola Company, to cite another variation, leaves most marketing functions with its local distributors but it centralizes control over promotion of the trade name. That name is a great corporate resource. Distributors gain a powerful competitive benefit when they are authorized to use this resource.

Such centralized marketing activity creates numerous problems of coordination, adequate attention to each product, and accountability. As the product lines grow in size and diversity, the differential benefit of the pooled service diminishes. But again we observe the corporation searching for some special input it can provide to its business-units so effectively that they enjoy a comparative advantage over competitors.

Note that in each of these examples—low-cost capital, outstanding managers, R&D capability, central marketing—the corporate strategy is to focus on just a few resources. These resources are not complete businesses; instead, they have value only as they are distinctive inputs to the business-units. In effect, the corporation develops an arsenal of exceptional resources. By drawing from that arsenal to supplement their own resources, the business-units gain strengths they cannot muster alone.

Theoretically, corporate input strengths may be so great that they dominate diversification moves. The possibility of benefiting from a particular corporate input may be the prime factor in selecting new businesses to add to the corporate portfolio.

Many diversified corporations, in fact, provide few strategic inputs to their business-units. This is especially true of ''conglomerates''—as-

semblies of already established firms that have little relation to each other and are merely clustered in a passive holding company. The pressure to generate short-term profits and cash flow is often so great that the parent corporation is not even a good source of capital. Moreover, the development of a truly outstanding corporate resource is difficult, time-consuming, and frequently expensive. Long-term commitment to a corporate input strategy is necessary. For these reasons, corporate management must select with care any input resources in which it undertakes to excel.

CORPORATE MANAGEMENT OF SYNERGIES

In addition to providing strategically valuable corporate inputs, diversified corporations may seek differential advantage from synergy among their business-units.

Building synergy is a strategy goal of many diversified corporations. Copper firms combine mining with smelting and extend on into wire drawing. Airlines own resort hotels (often to their regret), and newspapers form ties with local radio stations. The aim . . . is to dovetail operations of two or more business-units in the corporation's portfolio in a way that generates extra benefits.

Of course, in selecting businesses for the portfolio, potential synergies are among the factors considered. However, the actual achievement of synergy usually requires strong guidance. The interaction between business-units has to be shaped so that the desired reinforcement does occur. Corporate strategy sets this direction.

A quick review of several possible sources of synergy among business-units will illustrate the role corporate strategy can play.

Vertical Integration

A corporation that publishes several monthly trade magazines bought out the firm that did most of its printing. The chief aim of the acquisition was to assure fast, adaptable printing service for the magazines—at normal industry prices. Under the guidance of the parent corporation CEO, this service objective is working well. The manager of the printing business, however, is not entirely happy. He is expected to obtain outside business to keep his shop busy when not printing magazines, yet he is not permitted to make major investments in equipment for that purpose unless it can also be used for the magazines. Clearly, in this simple case the corporate strategy to stress vertical integration takes priority over independent operation of the printing business. Although the printing unit is constrained, the total effect on all the business-units combined is a net gain. . . .

Full Utilization of Raw Materials

Related to vertical integration is complete use of raw materials. To paraphrase an old meat-packing quip, synergy comes from utilizing every part of the pig but the squeal. A more recent example is found in the forest-product industry. Peeler logs for plywood come only from the trunk of trees, so a lumber mill is added to use the smaller pieces. Then pulp and papermaking is tied to lumber operations to utilize even smaller pieces, and some of the sawdust finds its way into particle board.

Each of the products—plywood, lumber, pulp and paper, and particle board—may be managed as a separate business-unit. However, the parent corporation is also concerned that the operations be dove-tailed in a way that minimizes raw material costs and maximizes output of the most profitable components of the mix. The corporate task is to make the combined whole more valuable than the sum of the independent parts.

Combined Services

Combined services or products for the consumer are often suggested as a source of synergy. Thus in the household appliance industry the volume leaders have found synergies in selling and servicing a full line (refrigerators, freezers, dishwashers, disposers, ranges, washing machines, and dryers). Each product has its competitors—for example, Maytag in washing machines and Tappan in gas ranges—and its special design issues, but one way to compete in this mature industry is for a corporation to promote full-line service to consumers.

Such synergies are difficult to achieve. The corporate task of coordinating the actions of several business-units is burdensome, and consumers may just not care about the joint effort. Combinations of sewing machines and television sets, for instance, are rare. Fast-food restaurants don't sell groceries. Thus this kind of corporate strategy must be cautiously designed. . . .

A set of combined services . . . normally must be backed up by a series of specialized business-units, each with its own technological and institutional constraints. If these supplying organizations take the limelight or pursue strictly parochial interest, little merging of service will occur. In contrast, if the corporation manages the synchronizing of the services, the strategy has a much better chance of success. . . .

PORTFOLIO ANALYSIS*

by Derek F. Abell and John S. Hammond

. . . A multidivisional, multiproduct company has an important advantage over undiversified firms because of its ability to channel its considerable resources into the most productive units. Instead of the decentralized approach, a number of such companies conduct integrated strategic planning at the corporate or division level to match product potential with resources and to establish the sequence and timing of resource transfers. For example, a diversified conglomerate may de-

* Excerpted from Derek F. Abell and John S. Hammond, *Strategic Marketing Planning: Problems and Analytical Approaches* (Prentice-Hall, 1979), chap. 4; used by permission of the publisher.

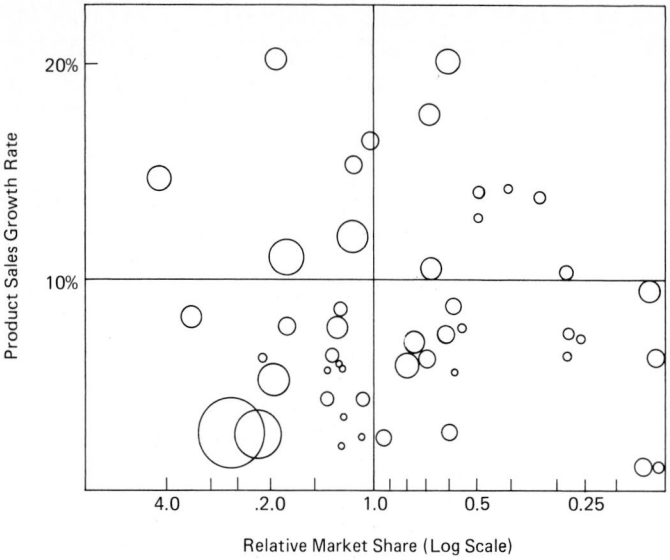

FIGURE 1
A TYPICAL PRODUCT PORTFOLIO CHART [GROWTH-SHARE MATRIX] OF A COMPARATIVELY STRONG AND DIVERSIFIED COMPANY

Source: ©1973, The Boston Consulting Group, Inc. All rights reserved. Published by permission.

cide to slow down the growth of its paper-board division so that it will throw off cash for the expansion of its light aircraft division. Such integrated planning may deliberately suboptimize a division's activities to optimize corporate performance.

The product portfolio approach . . . differs from most other integrative planning techniques in that strategic roles for each product are assigned on the basis of the product's market growth rate and market share relative to competition. These individual roles are then integrated into a strategy for the whole ''portfolio'' of products, taking account of the product portfolios of significant competitors. The differences in growth potential, relative market share, and hence cash flow potential—unique to each product—determine which products represent investment opportunities, which should supply investment funds, and which should be candidates for elimination from the portfolio. The objective is to get the best overall performance from the portfolio, while keeping cash flow in balance.

Several ways have been devised[1] to display relevant information about the firm's portfolio while at the same time reducing the inherent complexity of the problem to somewhat more manageable proportions. It is the creation and interpretation of these displays—for the firm and its competitors—that forms the heart of portfolio analysis. . . .

THE GROWTH-SHARE MATRIX

The most prominent display is the so-called *growth-share matrix* (see Figure 1 for an example), that shows a firm's whole portfolio by giving for each product:

1. Its *dollar sales* (represented by the area of the circle representing it on the matrix).

[1] *These displays and the associated portfolio concept originated with the Boston Consulting Group. See Henderson, 1973; 1970.*

2. Its *market share* relative to the firm's largest competitor (by the horizontal position of the circle on the chart).

3. The *growth rate of the market* (corrected for inflation) in which the product competes (by the position of the circle in the vertical direction).

Relative market share is the ratio of the firm's unit sales of a product to the unit sales of the same product by the firm's largest competitor, which is the same as the ratio of the two companies market shares. . . . A ratio of 1.0 means the firm is tied for the lead. . . . A series of charts made for various points in time will provide a trajectory of each product that indicates both its direction and rate of movement. Superimposing two such charts can dramatize movements over time. Similar charts can be developed for each major competitor.

While we have spoken of "products" (e.g., cross-country ski bindings) as the unit of analysis in portfolio analysis, it is sometimes appropriate to have the unit of analysis be a "business" (e.g., skiing equipment) or even a division (e.g., recreational products). . . . In the meantime the word "product" should be interpreted to mean "appropriate unit of analysis."

PORTFOLIO STRATEGY

Product growth is usually separated into "high" and "low" growth areas by an arbitrary, 10 percent growth line.[2] Similarly, relative market share is usually divided at a relative market share of 1.0, so that "high" share signifies market leadership. There is nothing sacred about either of these dividing lines. The point is to place the lines so that, if they just hold share, most products in the lower left corner of the chart would be cash generators, those in the upper right are cash users,

[2] *Note that market growth rate is a rough proxy for stage in the product life cycle; products above the line can be thought of as in the growth phase, whereas those below can be considered mature.*

and those in the upper left and lower right are roughly in cash balance—neither using nor throwing off significant amounts of cash.

Interpretation of the matrix is based on the following observations:

1. Margins and cash generated increase with relative market share, due to the experience and scale effects. . . .

2. Sales growth requires cash input to finance added capacity and working capital. Thus, if market share is maintained, cash input requirements increase with market growth rate.

3. In addition to the above-mentioned cash input to keep pace with market growth, an increase in market share usually requires cash input to support increased advertising expenditures, lower prices and other share-gaining tactics. On the other hand, a decrease in share may make cash available.

4. Growth in each market will ultimately slow as the product approaches maturity. Without losing market position, cash generated as growth slows can be reinvested in other products that are still growing.

Thus, products to the left of the market share dividing line have strong cash flows from operations due to their good margins and those to the right will have weaker or negative cash flows from operations. Products below the market growth dividing line will need relatively little investment to hold share, whereas those above will need significant investment of cash to keep pace with market growth.

This leads to classification of products into four categories, based on their cash flow characteristics (see Figure 2).

"Cash Cows" (indicated by "$" in the lower left quarter of the chart where they are usually found) are products that characteristically generate large amounts of cash, far more than they can profitably invest. Typically they have a dominant share of slowly growing markets. They are the products that provide the cash to pay interest on corporate debt, pay dividends, cover

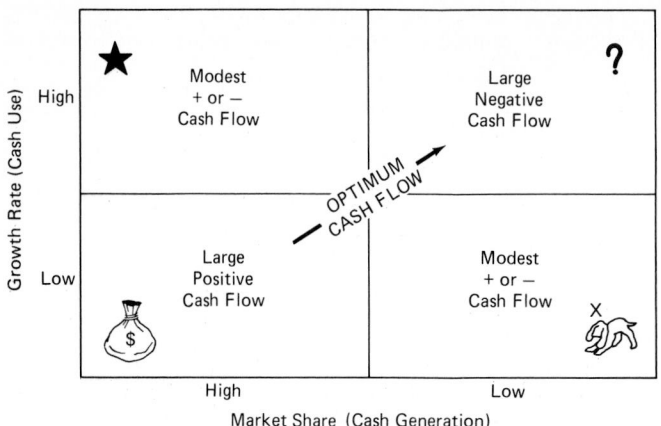

FIGURE 2
PRODUCT CATEGORIES
IN THE PRODUCT PORTFOLIO
CHART

Source: Adapted from "The Product Portfolio," © 1970, The Boston Consulting Group, Inc.

corporate overhead, finance R&D, and help other products to grow.

"Dogs" (indicated by an "x" in the lower right) are products with low share of slowly growing markets. They neither generate nor require significant amounts of cash. Maintaining share usually requires reinvestment of their modest cash flow from operations, as well as modest amounts of additional capital. Because of low share their profitability is poor and they are unlikely to ever be a significant souce of cash; therefore they are often called "cash traps."

"Problem Children" or "question marks" (indicated by a "?" in the upper right) are products with low share of fast-growing markets. Their low share often means low profits and weak cash flow from operations; at the same time because they are in rapidly growing markets, they require large amounts of cash to maintain market share, and still larger amounts to gain share. Hence their name; market growth is attractive, yet large amounts of cash will be required if they will ever gain sufficient share to be strong members of the product portfolio.

"Stars" (indicated by a "*" in the upper left) are high-growth, high-share products which may or may not be self-sufficient in cash flow. This depends on whether their strong cash flow from operations is sufficient to finance rapid growth. Their present, modest cash needs or throw off will change to a large cash throw off in the future, when the growth rate of their market slows.

The location of products on a portfolio chart is indicative of the current health of a portfolio; over time products will move due to market dynamics and to strategy decisions. The object is to analyze the current state and natural dynamics of the portfolio so that decisions yielding a strong portfolio in the future will result.

Movements in the vertical direction, i.e., changes in the rate of market growth, are largely beyond the firm's control (except when their policies influence primary demand . . . and must be anticipated when developing strategic moves. For example, given only a share-maintaining investment, all products will eventually fall vertically to become either "cash cows" or "dogs," depending upon relative market share held prior to the slowing of market growth and product maturity. "Problem children" ultimately become "dogs" unless enough investment is made during the growth phase to shift the product into the "star" area. "Stars" assure the future in that they will become "cash cows" as growth slows and investment needs diminish.

With market growth largely noncontrollable in most instances, portfolio analysis reduces to determining a market share strategy for each product. The foundation of a sound long-term strategy is to use cash generated by "cash cows" to finance market share increases for "problem children" products in which the company has a strong competitive footing (see arrow in Figure 2). If successful, this strategy produces new "stars" which will in turn become "cash cows" of the future. This "success sequence" is shown in Figure 3. The "problem child" product with a weak competitive position is a liability and should be allowed to remain in the portfolio only on a "no cash input" basis, a strategy that will cause it to become a "dog" eventually. "Dogs" should be retained only as long as they contribute some positive cash flow and provided they don't tie up capital that can be used more profitably elsewhere. At some point, many "dogs" become candidates for elimination from the product portfolio. There are many "disaster sequences," for example: allowing a "star's" share to erode to that of a "question mark" and ultimately to a "dog" or allowing the share of a "cash cow" to erode to that of a "dog." Figure 3 illustrates these basic sequences.

Unfortunately many managements pursue strategies other than the success strategies described in the previous paragraph; they overinvest in seemingly safe "cows" and "dogs." They invest less than needed in "question marks," and instead of becoming "stars," these "question marks" ultimately tumble into "dogs." They

spread their resources too thinly among products rather than focusing to achieve outstanding performance from a smaller number, even though that smaller number still provides sufficient diversification from a risk reducing standpoint.

Given these remarks about portfolio strategies, it is easy to see why the portfolio shown in Figure 1 was termed strong and diversified. A large percentage of products are share leaders (relative share greater than 1.0), promising excellent cost positions. Furthermore, these profitable products are among the largest. There are a large number of cash cows to feed the problem children; many of the problem children have good relative market positions; most of the dogs have viable shares; and there are many stars. . . .

TYPES OF STRATEGIES

There are four basic strategies that can be pursued with a given product: building share, holding share, harvesting, or withdrawal. Which is appropriate depends on such factors as a product's present market and cost position, the product's life cycle stage (market growth rate), the firm's resources relative to competitors, its time horizon,

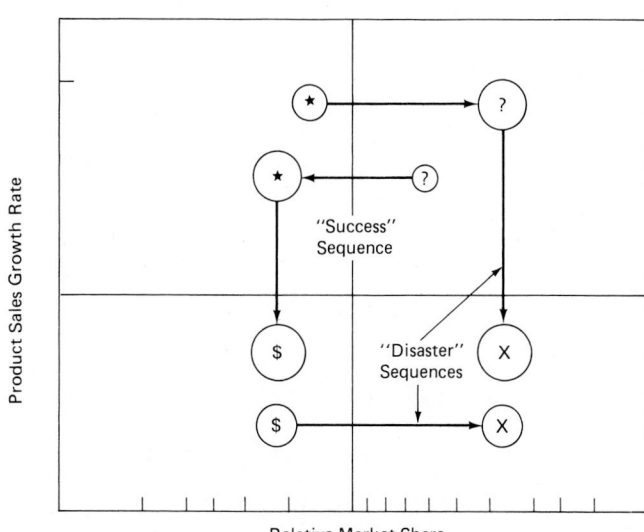

FIGURE 3
PRODUCT DYNAMICS
IN THE PORTFOLIO CHART

Source: Adapted from "The Product Portfolio," © 1970, The Boston Consulting Group, Inc.

its other products, and likely actions and reactions by competitors. The four basic strategies and when each might be appropriate will now be described.

Building Market Share

Sometimes building share is an offensive strategy; firms with a viable share will build to increase their profitability. . . . Sometimes it is defensive; in most industries a minimum relative market share is needed for long-run viability. Firms without this critical share are in an untenable position; they must increase share, or withdraw. (Often the critical share is of the order of $\frac{1}{4}$ of the leader's share.)

The appropriateness of share building depends in part on market growth rate. Unless share leaders are competitively asleep, gaining share in slowly growing, static, or declining markets is difficult and uneconomic. On the other hand, when experience or scale effects are pronounced, when the firm has competitive strength in a product, and when it has the resources to do so, market dominance is the appropriate objective for products in high-growth markets. Market share is usually less expensive to achieve during the rapid growth phase in a product's life cycle because purchase patterns and distribution channels are fluid, and—most importantly—share gains don't have to come from reducing competitor's sales. Instead they can come from capturing a disproportionate share of incremental sales and through sales to new users of the product.

But large share increases are seldom built quickly and they sacrifice short-range profits for profits later. Thus share building is difficult to sell in organizations emphasizing short-run earnings. At the same time, share building is easier to carry out against competitors unwilling to sacrifice short-run profits to hold on to their share.

Share building can be accomplished by price reduction; by improved delivery, quality or product support; or by concentrating on a market segment, isolated in terms of experience, where dominance can be achieved. . . .

Holding Market Share

Holding share is appropriate for mature businesses with leading or strong shares; it is preservation of a desirable status quo. Strongly established products have the advantage of greater experience and consequent lower costs and higher profitability than their rivals with lower shares. Holding share is appropriate for such products, because building share is very costly and time consuming in slowly growing markets. Since increased share must come at the expense of other competitor's sales, it will be resisted strenuously. Furthermore distribution patterns and purchasing relationships are usually stable and difficult to change.

Harvesting

The harvesting strategy purposely allows share to decline to maximize short-term earnings and cash flow (both from operations and freed up working capital). It is especially appropriate for products with poor positions in declining markets. It also may be selected for "problem children" products that have a poor competitive position. The cash generated from harvesting can be used to nurture more promising, growing products. . . .

Withdrawal

When a product has less than the critical share for viability—or, in other words, competition is so far ahead in costs that overwhelming short-run sacrifices would be required to catch up—then withdrawal is appropriate. . . .

REVERSING THE IMAGES OF BCG'S GROWTH/SHARE MATRIX*

by John A. Seeger

. . . Simple concepts can easily be oversimplified, and graphic descriptors can become stereotypes. Few current business concepts are more prone to oversimplification than the growth/share model, with its labelling of products or divisions or whole companies as 'dogs,' 'question marks,' 'stars' or 'cash cows.' Three-quarters of those labels are subject to dangerous misapplication, because popularized versions of the BCG philosophy and its derivatives carry a handy prescription for each category: we should kick the dogs, cloister the cows and throw our money at the stars. Only the question mark category demands management thought.

This commentary attempts to counter these superficial prescriptions by turning the BCG model's own images back upon themselves. If the tendency to oversimplify comes from the language's imagery, then we must make the images do double duty; they must remind the student and manager of the growth/share matrix's pitfalls as well as its presumptions.

EVERY DOG HAS ITS DAY

Consider the 'dogs.' In the BCG model these are the portfolio components which have low market shares and whose markets themselves are matured or shrinking; these are components we should dispose of, for they are going nowhere. The image conveyed by BCG's term is that of a feral beast preying on our resources or of a mangy cur slinking off with our picnic hotdogs.

But there are other kinds of dogs—warm, loving companions of humanity since the time of the caves. These dogs give unquestioning loyalty to their managers, serving as scouts or watchdogs, to spread the alarm if intruders threaten. By establishing a presence—with bared teeth if necessary—these friendly dogs prevent their wild cousins from approaching our picnic at all. They protect our weaker members and occupy the territory so that attackers will keep their distance.

*   J.A. Seeger, "Reversing the Images of BCG's Growth Share Matrix." Originally published in the *Strategic Management Journal* (copyright © 1984 John Wiley & Sons). Reproduced with deletions by permission of John Wiley & Sons Limited.

Our own dogs can repay handsomely a small investment in dog food and flea powder. . . .

'It's a dog,' says [one CEO of his key] retail product line. 'I only wish I could get rid of it.' Such attitudes are easily sensed, by canines or humans. It is predictable that the managers of his company regard its retail division as the least attractive assignment in the company. Good managers do not willingly stay with an organization which is defined in the boss's eyes as hopeless.

Divesting this retail division would be analogous to a fire engine company's disposing of its Dalmation hound. The dog does not contribute much to the direct function of putting out fires. But it looks good in photographs; it makes life more pleasant for the firefighters during their boring waits for alarms; and it keeps other dogs from pissing on the equipment.

WHAT DO YOU GET FROM A CASH COW?

Consider the 'cash cow.' In the BCG model this is a business component which does dominate its market, but whose market is not growing. Since growth cannot logically be expected here, the consultants' advice is to operate the business as a cash flow generator. Management should deny requests for new resources from a cash cow component, and concentrate on milking it for the highest possible returns.

The imagery conveyed by this term is doubly unfortunate. In oversimplified form, the 'cash cow' brand can result in the gradual wastage of both the physical and human resources of an organization, as operating management learns not to request new resources and top management learns not to demand continual replenishment of the unit's productive capacities. Where operations are measured in current profitability and growth aspirations are systematically throttled, it is natural for growth-oriented managers to leave the organization. They are replaced by people content to operate the business as it stands but uninterested and unskilled at changing the business. The creative energy required for continual renewal can decay as natural attrition suits the culture of the organization to its 'cash cow' role.

In effect, classification as a cash cow may be the equivalent, over time, of placing the unit in a cloister where distractions of the outside world are minimized and all attentions are focused on the single goal, generation of high cash flows. 'Milking managers' will be expert at feeding the cow and keeping it healthy in the short run. They may not be adept at maintaining the barn, however. Particularly where large outlays are needed for long term improvements, the cash cow manager is likely to postpone investments which would hurt cash flow in the short run.

Keeping creativity, innovation and energy at high levels in an organization designated as a cash cow is an unsolved problem. One possible solution is suggested by another look at the BCG symbolism. A cow can give more than milk; properly exposed to outside influences and environmental forces, a cow can also give calves.

The investment needed to produce a calf, given that you already have a cow, is incredibly small; without a cow, no amount of investment will do the job. Similarly, the investment needed to produce creative ideas, given a creative workforce, is small; where natural energy has burned out, however, no amount of effort will produce innovation. Recognition of the importance of new projects—even though the business unit itself lacks the resources to exploit them—might help retain the creativity needed in a naturally adaptive organization. Provision of exploitation channels outside the business unit itself—through transfer to other corporate units, new subsidiaries, joint ventures, or entrepreneurial sabbatical leaves— could help the unit's people see the utility of continued idea generation. In a time of diminished general economic growth, no company can afford to reject a good idea because it comes from a unit which is not 'supposed to' grow. Neither can we afford to let the 'cash cow' label stifle the creativity and adaptability which are vital to survival in increasingly competitive times.

The dairying analogy is appropriate for these organizations, so long as we resist the urge to oversimplify it. On the farm, even the best producing cows eventually begin to dry up. The farmer's solution to this is euphemistically called 'freshening' the cow: he arranges a date with a bull; she has a calf; the milk begins flowing again. Cloistering the cow—isolating her from everything but the feed trough and the milking machines—assures that she will go dry.

THE FAULT LIES NOT IN OUR STARS, BUT IN OURSELVES . . .

Consider the 'stars.' In the BCG model, these are the business units with major shares of growing markets. These are the units which need resources and investments in order to exploit their opportunities. These are the units sought by aggressive, ambitious people, who crave the excitement and challenges of growth. It is in the stars that people blaze career reputations and become recognized as winners.

Unfortunately, however, not all stars turn out to be winners over the long term. Current market share and market growth rates are not sufficient criteria to justify investment, although they suffice to label the business unit as a star. Oversimplification of the BCG prescription can result in investing in situations whose growth rates cannot be sustained in the future for a variety of reasons not apparent in backward scanning market analysis. . . .

Investment based on growth rate and share, without regard for environmental constraints or market saturation, is encouraged by the oversimplification inherent in the popular two-by-two matrices.

Still, with proper qualification, the 'star' analogy is appropriate. Think, for example, about the stars themselves. What we know of them is based on old information. When we observe a star through the telescope, we see evidence of an energetic past, but we have no knowledge of whether that same star is still producing energy now. The light we observe has been travelling towards us for aeons—billions of years in some cases—and its source may have long since degenerated into a white dwarf or even a black hole, which would absorb any amount of resources we would care to throw at it without ever permitting any return.

Organizational stars, too, take their place in the BCG matrix based on their past performance. Whether they merit additional investment depends on their future potential, not upon their past.

CONCLUSION

I have no quarrel with the fourth BCG category, the 'question mark' business unit. This unit, a non-dominant participator in a growing market, requires management thought, says the BCG model. All the categories require management thought.

No management model can safely substitute for analysis and common sense. Models are useful to managers, to the extent that they can help provide order to the thinking process. Models are dangerous to managers, to the extent that they bias judgement or substitute for analysis. . . .

┌─ THIRTEEN ─────────────────────────────────┐
│ ┌───┐ │
│ │   │ │
│ │   THE   │ │
│ │   │ │
│ │   INNOVATION   │ │
│ │   │ │
│ │   CONTEXT   │ │
│ │   │ │
│ └───┘ │
└──┘

While most large organizations must draw on a variety of experts to get their jobs done, there has been a growing interest in recent years in those organizations whose work is organized *primarily* around experts. These range from hospitals, universities, and research centers, to consulting firms, space agencies, and high technology biomedical electronics firms. In fact, some evidence cited in one of the readings of this chapter suggests that almost all the major industries that have grown up since World War II fall under this context.

This context is a rather unusual one, at least when judged against the more traditional contexts discussed in previous chapters. Both its strategic processes and its structures tend to take on forms quite different from those presented in Chapters 10–12. Organizations of experts, in fact, seem to divide themselves further into two somewhat different contexts. As indicated in Chapter 6, we shall distinguish between organizations whose experts work in rapidly changing situations that demand a good deal of collaborative innovation (as in the biotechnology or semiconductor fields) and those whose experts work in more stable situations involving slower-changing bodies of skill or knowledge (as in the law, consulting, or accounting). This chapter takes up the first, under the label of the "innovation" context;

Chapter 14 considers the other, as the "professional" context.

Although often seen as a high technology event involving inventor-entrepreneurs, innovation may, of course, occur in high or low technology, product or service, large or small company situations. Innovation may be thought of as the *first reduction to practice* of an idea in a culture. The more radical the idea, the more traumatic and profound its impact will tend to be. But there are no absolutes. Whatever is most new and difficult to understand becomes the "high technology" of its age. As Jim Utterback of MIT is fond of pointing out, the delivery of ice was high technology at the turn of the century, later it was the production of automobiles. By the same token, fifty years from now, electronics and space stations may be considered mundane. Our focus here, however, is on organizations trying to accomplish changes that are sufficiently complex and unstable to require teams of experts—and not just one entrepreneurial individual—to innovate.

The innovation context is one in which the organization often must deal with complex technologies or systems under conditions of dynamic change. Typically, major innovations require that a variety of experts work toward a common goal, often led by a single champion or a small group of committed individuals. Much has been learned from research in recent years on such organizations of experts. While this knowledge seems less structured than that in the previous chapters, several dominant themes have emerged. In the early stages of innovation, highly maneuverable *adhocracies* seem best suited to the purpose.

The first reading, from Mintzberg's *Structure in Fives*, describes this form of structure, with a second section, derived from the strategy tracking studies at McGill University, that look at the strategy-making processes in such organizations. Here we see the full flowering of the "emergent strategy" concept. We also see a strategic leadership less concerned with "formulating and implementing" strategies in the classic sense than with establishing the types of processes in which specific action strategies will grow of their own accord around individual innovations. (Robert Hayes [1985] of Harvard refers to these as "means strategies" as opposed to the "ends strategies" competitive or industry analyses provide.)

In the readings, we see the coming together of several threads that have appeared throughout this text. The concepts of the strategist as managing process more than content, strategy formation as a learning process, the emergence rather than the formulation of strategies, and the emphasis on the mutual interactions of structure, systems, and environments, all flow together into a cohesive approach to the strategy process, another of our configurations.

Of course the emergent view of strategy formation is not restricted to the adhocracy context, as was suggested earlier in the article on the "Honda Effect." It can occur in many contexts—in acquisition (in the diversified context) or overseas penetration strategies (even perhaps in the mature context)—where the number of variables and unknowns is greater than those elements which can be controlled.

The other reading on this context, James Brian Quinn's "Managing Innovation: Controlled Chaos" (winner of the McKinsey prize for the best *Harvard Business Review* article of 1985), suggests how the spirit of adhocracy and strategy formation as a learning process can be integrated with some of the formal strategic processes of large organizations. To achieve innovativeness, other authors have advocated adhocracy with little or no reliance on planning. Quinn suggests that blending broad strategy planning with a consciously structured adhocracy gives better results. This reading also brings back the notion of "intrapreneurship," mentioned in the introduction to Chapter 10 on the entrepreneurial context. When it is successful, intrapreneurship—implying the stimulation and diffusion of innovative capacity throughout a larger organization, with many champions of innovations—tends to follow most of Quinn's precepts. As such, it seems to belong more to this context than the entrepreneurial one, which focuses on organizations highly centralized around the initiatives of their single leaders, whether or not innovative.

A variety of cases support, or offer bases for critiquing, these readings. Chief among these are the Hewlett-Packard, AT&T Bell Labs, Sony, Pilkington Brothers, Matsushita, and Polaroid cases. Many of these allow one to consider the similarities and differences among entrepreneurial and intrapreneurial situations, with varying degrees of innovation.

THE ADHOCRACY*

by Henry Mintzberg

None of the configurations so far discussed is capable of sophisticated innovation, the kind required of a space agency, an avant-garde film company, a factory manufacturing complex prototypes, an integrated petrochemicals company. The Simple Structure can certainly innovate, but only in relatively simple ways. [The Machine Bureaucracy, as well as the Professional Bureaucracy, is a] performance, not a problem-solving, structure. The[se] are designed to perfect standard

* Excerpted from Henry Mintzberg *Structure in Fives: Designing Effective Organizations* (Prentice-Hall, 1983), chap. 12; reprinted by permission of the publisher.

programs, not to invent new ones. And although the Divisionalized Form resolves the problem of strategic inflexibility in the Machine Bureaucracy, as noted in the last chapter, it, too, is not a true innovator. A focus on control by standardizing outputs does not encourage innovation.

Sophisticated innovation requires a fifth and very different configuration, one that is able to fuse experts drawn from different disciplines into smoothly functioning ad hoc project teams. To borrow the word Alvin Toffler popularized in *Future Shock*, these are the *Adhocracies* of our society. . . .

DESCRIPTION OF THE BASIC STRUCTURE

The Design Parameters

In Adhocracy, [again] we have a distinct configuration: highly organic structure, with little formalization of behavior; high horizontal job specialization based on formal training; a tendency to group the specialists in functional units for housekeeping purposes but to deploy them in small, market-based project teams to do their work; a reliance on the liaison devices to encourage mutual adjustment, the key coordinating mechanism, within and between these teams; and selective decentralization to and within these teams, which are located at various places in the organization and involve various mixtures of line managers and staff and operating experts.

To innovate means to break away from established patterns. So the innovative organization cannot rely on any form of standardization for coordination. In other words, it must avoid all the trappings of bureaucratic structure, notably sharp divisions of labor, extensive unit differentiation, highly formalized behaviors, and an emphasis on planning and control systems. Above all, it must remain flexible. . . . A search for organigrams to illustrate this [reading] elicited the following response from one corporation well known for its Adhocracy structure: ". . . we would prefer not to supply an organization chart,

since it would change too quickly to serve any useful purpose."

Of all the configurations, Adhocracy shows the least reverence for the classical principles of management, especially unity of command. The regulated system does not matter much either. In this configuration, information and decision processes flow flexibly and informally, wherever they must, to promote innovation. And that means overriding the chain of authority if need be.

The Simple Structure also retains an organic structure, and so is able to innovate as well. But that innovation is restricted to simple environments, ones that can be easily comprehended by a central leader. Innovation of the sophisticated variety takes place in environments not easily understood. So another kind of organic structure is required, one that relies on the application of sophisticated expertise. The Adhocracy must hire and give power to experts—professionals whose knowledge and skills have been highly developed in training programs. But unlike the Professional Bureaucracy, the Adhocracy cannot rely on the standardized skills of these experts to achieve coordination, because that would lead to standardization instead of innovation. Rather, it must treat existing knowledge and skills merely as bases on which to build new ones.

Moreover, the building of new knowledge and skills requires the combination of different bodies of existing ones. So rather than allowing the specialization of the expert or the differentiation of the functional unit to dominate its behavior, the Adhocracy must instead break through the boundaries of conventional specialization and differentiation. . . . Thus, whereas each professional of the Professional Bureaucracy can operate on his own, in the Adhocracy the professionals must amalgamate their efforts. "Traditional organizations can assume that they know all the problems and the methods. They therefore can assign expertise to a single specialist or compartmentalized, functional group" (Chandler and Sayles, 1970:203). In sharp contrast, in Adhocracies the different specialists must join forces in multidisciplinary teams, each formed around a specific project of innovation.

How does the organization cope with the problem of "uprooting the professional yet allowing him to maintain his ties to his field of expertise" (Chandler and Sayles, 1971 p. 15)? The solution is obvious: The Adhocracy tends to use the functional and market bases for grouping concurrently, in a matrix structure. The experts are grouped in functional units for housekeeping purposes—for hiring, professional communication, and the like—but then are deployed in project teams to carry out their basic work of innovation.

And how is coordination effected in and between these project teams? As noted earlier, standardization is precluded as a major coordinating mechanism. The efforts must be innovative, not standardized. So, too, is direct supervision, because of the complexity of the work. Coordination must be effected by those with the knowledge, the experts who actually do the project work. That leaves mutual adjustment, the prime coordinating mechanism of the Adhocracy. And, of course, with the concentration on mutual adjustment in the Adhocracy comes an emphasis on the design parameter meant to encourage it—namely, the set of liaison devices. Integrating managers and liaison positions are established to coordinate the efforts among and between the functional units and project teams; the teams themselves are established as task forces; and, as noted above, matrix structure is favored to achieve concurrent functional and market grouping. . . .

Thus, managers abound in the Adhocracy—functional managers, integrating managers, project managers. The last-named are particularly numerous, since the project teams must be small to encourage mutual adjustment among their members, and each team needs a designated leader, a "manager." This results in narrow "spans of control" for the Adhocracy, by conventional measures. But that measure has nothing to do with control; it merely reflects the small size of the work units. Most of the managers do not "manage" in the usual sense—that is, give orders by direct supervision. Instead, they spend a good deal of their time acting in a liaison and negotiating capacity, coordinating the work laterally among the different teams and between them and the functional units. Many of these managers are, in fact, experts, too, who take their place alongside the others on the project teams.

With its reliance on highly trained experts, the Adhocracy . . . is decentralized. [Its] experts are distributed throughout the structure, notably in the support staff and managerial ranks as well as the operating core. . . . The decentralization of the Adhocracy is what we [earlier] labeled *selective*, in both the horizontal and vertical dimensions. Decision-making power is distributed among managers and nonmanagers at all the levels of the hierarchy, according to the nature of the different decisions to be made. No one in the Adhocracy monopolizes the power to innovate.

To proceed with our discussion, and to elaborate on how the Adhocracy makes decisions, we must at this point divide it into two types—the Operating Adhocracy and the Administrative Adhocracy.

The Operating Adhocracy

The Operating Adhocracy innovates and solves problems directly on behalf of its clients. Its multidisciplinary teams of experts often work directly under contract, as in the think-tank consulting firm, creative advertising agency, or manufacturer of engineering prototypes. In some cases, however, there is no contract per se, as in the filmmaking agency or theater company.

In fact, for every Operating Adhocracy, there is a corresponding Professional Bureaucracy, one that does similar work but with a narrower orientation. Faced with a client problem, the Operating Adhocracy engages in creative effort to find a novel solution; the Professional Bureaucracy pigeonholes it into a known contingency to which it can apply a standard program. One engages in divergent thinking aimed at innovation; the other, in convergent thinking aimed at perfection. . . . One theater company seeks out new avant-garde plays to perform; another perfects its performance of Shakespeare year after year. In effect, one is prepared to consider an infinite number of contingencies and solutions; the other restricts itself to a few. The missions are the same, but the outputs and the structures that produce them differ radically. . . .

A key feature of the Operating Adhocracy is that its administrative and operating work tend to blend into a single effort. That is, in ad hoc project work, it is difficult to differentiate the planning and design of the work from its execution. Both require the same specialized skills, on a project-by-project basis. As a result, the Operating Adhocracy may not even bother to distinguish its middle levels from its operating core. Managers of the middle line and members of what in other organizations would be called the support staff—typically a highly trained and important group in the Operating Adhocracy—may take their place right alongside the operating specialists on the project teams. And even when distinctions are made, a close rapport must develop between the administrative and operating levels, sometimes to the point where they are able to interchange their roles freely.

Figure 1 shows the organigram of the National Film Board of Canada, a classic Operating Adhocracy (even though it does produce an organigram—one that changes frequently, it might be added). The board is an agency of the Canadian federal government and produces mostly short films, many of them documentaries. The organigram shows a large number of support units as well as liaison positions (for example, research, technical, and production coordinators). The operating core can also be seen to include loose, concurrent functional and market groupings (the latter by region as well as type of film produced).

The Administrative Adhocracy

The second major type of Adhocracy also functions with project teams, but toward a different end. Whereas the Operating Adhocracy undertakes projects to serve its clients, the Administrative Adhocracy undertakes its projects to serve itself. And in sharp contrast to the Operating Adhocracy, the Administrative Adhocracy makes a sharp distinction between its administrative component and operating core. The operating core is truncated—cut right off from the rest of the organization—so that the administrative component that remains can be structured as an Adhocracy.

This truncation may take place in a number of ways. First, when an organization has a special need to be innovative, perhaps because of intense product competition or a very dynamic technology, but its operating core must be machine bureaucratic, the operating core may be established as a separate organization. As we saw [earlier], the social tensions at the base of the Machine Bureaucracy overflow the operating core and permeate the administration. The whole organization becomes ridden with conflict and obsessed by control, too bureaucratic to innovate. By truncating the operating core—setting it up apart with its own administration that reports in at the strategic apex—the main administrative component of the organization can be structured organically for innovation. Second, the operating core may be done away with altogether—in effect, contracted out to other organizations. This leaves the organization free to concentrate on development work. Thus, for the Apollo project, NASA conducted much of its own development work but contracted production out to independent manufacturing firms. A third form of truncation arises when the operating core becomes automated. This amounts to truncation because an automated operating core is able to run itself, largely free of the need for direct supervision or other direct control from the administrative component. The latter, because it need not give attention to routine operating matters, can structure itself as an Adhocracy, concerned with change and innovation, with projects to bring new operating facilities on line.

Oil companies, because of the high automation of their production process, are in part at least drawn toward the Administrative Adhocracy configuration. Figure 2 shows the organigram for one oil company, reproduced exactly as presented by the company (except for modifications to mask its identity, made at the company's request). Note

FIGURE 1   THE NATIONAL FILM BOARD OF CANADA: AN OPERATING ADHOCRACY (CIRCA 1975, USED WITH PERMISSION)

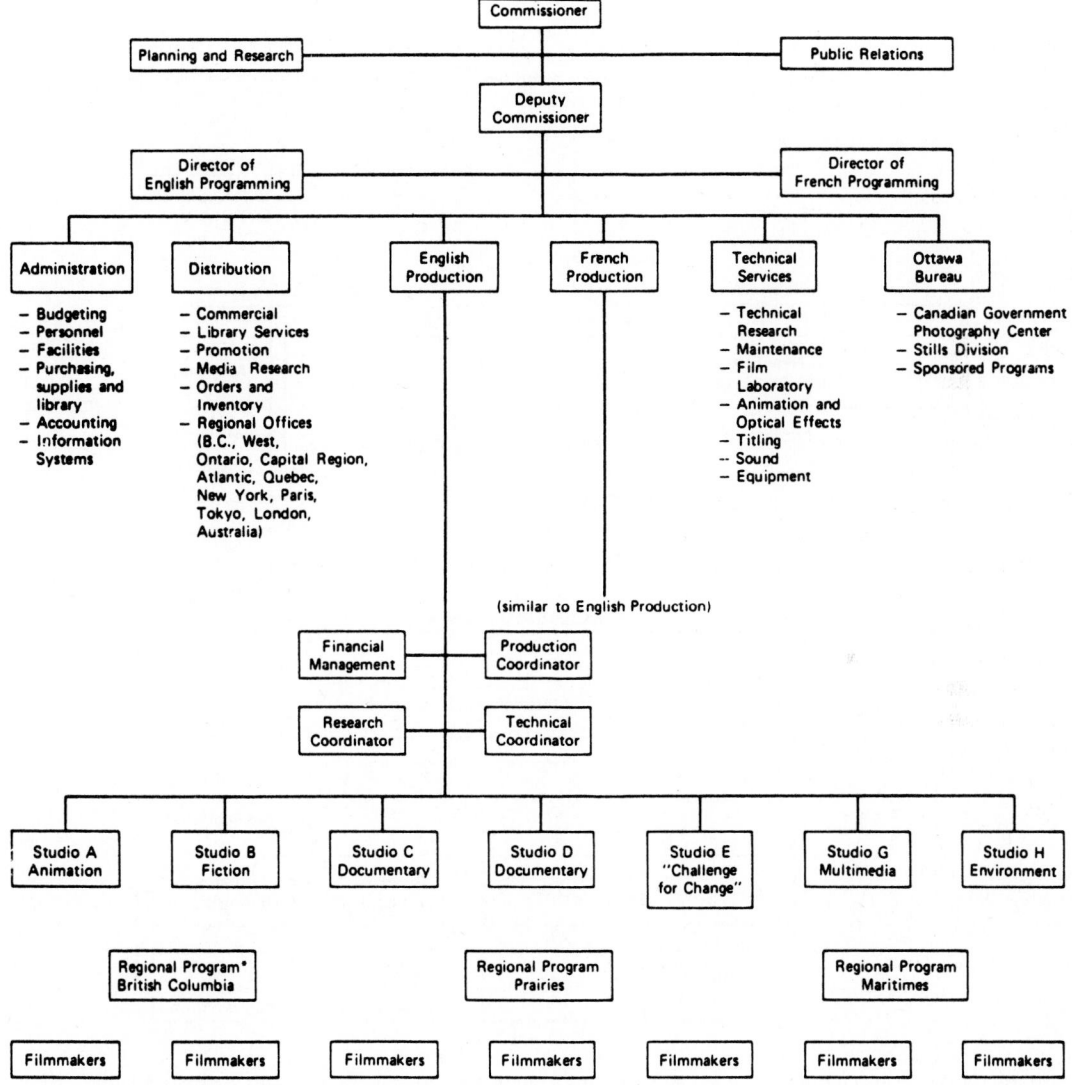

*No lines shown on original organigram connecting Regional Programs to Studios or Filmmakers.

the domination of "Administration and Services," shown at the bottom of the chart; the operating functions, particularly "Production," are lost by comparison. Note also the description of the strategic apex in terms of standing committees instead of individual executives.

The Administrative Component of the Adhocracies

The important conclusion to be drawn from this discussion is that in both types of Adhocracy, the relation between the operating core and the

FIGURE 2   ORGANIGRAM OF AN OIL COMPANY: AN ADMINISTRATIVE ADHOCRACY

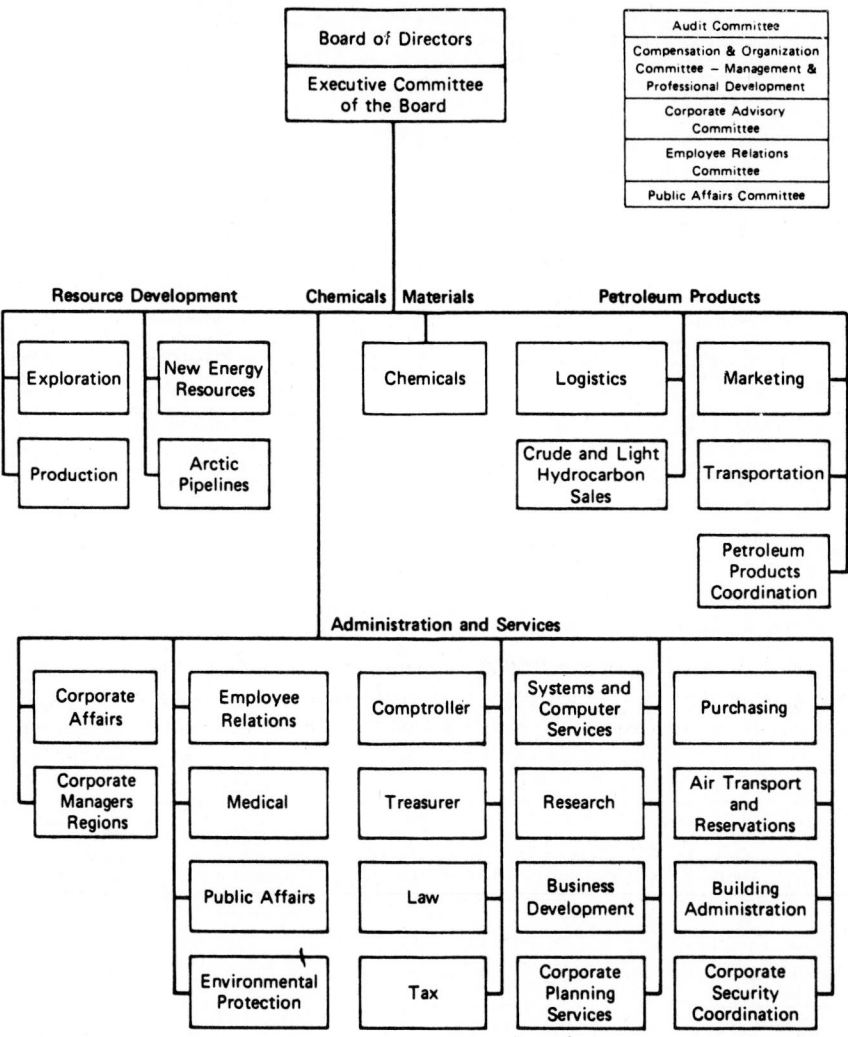

administrative component is unlike that of any other configuration. In the Administrative Adhocracy, the operating core is truncated and becomes a relatively unimportant part of the organization; in the Operating Adhocracy, the two merge into a single entity. In both cases, there is little need for line managers to exercise close direct supervision over the operators. Rather, the managers become functioning members of the project teams, with special responsibility to effect coordi-

nation between them. But in this capacity, they act more as peers than as supervisors, their influence deriving from their expertise and interpersonal skill rather than from their formal position. And, of course, to the extent that direct supervision and formal authority diminish in importance, the distinction between line and staff blurs. It no longer makes sense to distinguish those who have the formal power to decide from those who have only the informal right to advise. Power over decision making flows to anyone in the Adhocracy with expertise, regardless of position.

The support staff plays a key role in the Adhocracy. In fact, it is the key part of the Administrative Adhocracy, for that is where this configuration houses most of the experts on which it is so dependent. The Operating Adhocracy also depends on experts, but since it retains its operating core, it houses many of them there as well as in its support staff. But in both cases, as noted above, much of the support staff is not sharply differentiated from other parts of the organization, not off to one side, to speak only when spoken to, as in the bureaucratic configurations. Rather, the support staff, together with the line managers (and the operators, in the case of the Operating Adhocracy), form part of the central pool of expert talent from which the project personnel are drawn. (There are, of course, exceptions. Some support units must always remain bureaucratic, and apart. Even NASA needs cafeterias.)

Because the Adhocracy does not rely on standardization for coordination, it has little need for a technostructure to develop systems for regulation. The Administrative Adhocracy does employ analysts concerned with adaptation to its external environment, such as marketing researchers and economic forecasters. . . . It does do some action planning, although of a rather general kind. But these analysts do not design systems to control other people so much as take their place alongside the line managers and the support staffers as members of the project teams.

To summarize, the administrative component of the Adhocracy emerges as an organic mass of line managers and staff experts (with operators in the Operating Adhocracy), working together in ever-shifting relationships on ad hoc projects. Figure 3 shows the Adhocracy in terms of our logo, with its parts mingled together in one amorphous mass in the middle. In the Operating Adhocracy, this mass includes the middle line, support staff, technostructure, and operating core. The Administrative Adhocracy includes all of these except the operating core, which is kept apart in a truncated, bureaucratic structure, shown by the dotted section below the central mass.

The reader will also note that the strategic apex of the figure is shown partly merged into the central mass as well. We shall see why in the discussion of strategy formation that follows. . . .

The Roles of the Strategic Apex

The top managers of the strategic apex of the Adhocracy [do] not spend much time formulating explicit strategies, but they must spend a good deal of their time in the battles that ensue over strategic choices, and in handling the many other disturbances that arise all over these fluid structures. The Adhocracy combines organic working arrangements instead of bureaucratic ones, with expert power instead of formal authority. Together these conditions breed aggressiveness and conflict. But the job of the top managers is not to bottle up that aggressiveness, as in the Machine Bureaucracy—that would be impossible in any event—but to channel it to productive ends. Thus, the top managers of the Adhocracy (as well as those in its middle line) must be masters of human relations, able to use persuasion, negotiation, coalition, reputation, rapport, or whatever to fuse the individualistic experts into smoothly functioning mutlidisciplinary teams.

The top managers must also devote a good deal of time to monitoring the projects. Innovative project work is notoriously difficult to control. No MIS can be relied upon to send up complete,

FIGURE 3   THE ADHOCRACY

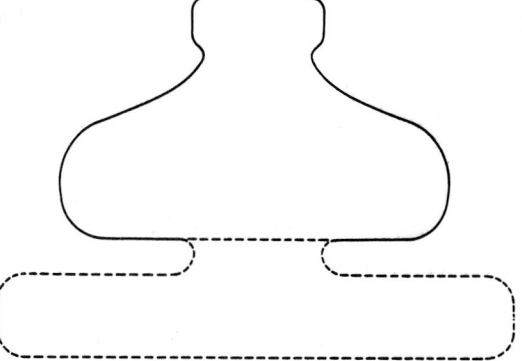

unambiguous results. So there must be careful, personal monitoring of projects to ensure that they are completed according to specifications, on schedule, and at the estimates projected (or, more exactly, not excessively late with too great cost overruns).

But perhaps the most important single role of the top management of Adhocracy (especially Operating Adhocracy) is that of liaison with the external environment. The other configurations tend to focus their attention on clearly defined markets, and are more or less assured of a steady flow of work. Not so in the Operating Adhocracy, which lives from project to project and disappears when it can find no more. Since each project is different, the Operating Adhocracy can never be sure where the next one will come from. . . . So that responsibility often falls on the top managers. In the Operating Adhocracy, therefore, the managers of the strategic apex must devote a great deal of their time to ensuring a steady and balanced stream of incoming projects. That means developing liaison contacts with potential customers and negotiating contracts with them.

Nowhere is this more clearly illustrated than in the consulting business, particularly where the approach is innovative and the structure therefore Adhocracy in nature. An executive once commented to this author that "every consulting firm is three months away from bankruptcy." In other words, three dry months could use up all the surplus funds, leaving none to pay the high professional salaries. And so when a consultant becomes a partner in one of these firms—in effect, moves into the strategic apex—he normally hangs up his calculator and becomes virtually a full-time salesperson. It is a distinguishing characteristic of many an Operating Adhocracy that the selling function literally takes place at the strategic apex.

Project work poses similar problems in the Administrative Adhocracy, with similar results. Reeser asked a group of managers in three aerospace companies, "What are some of the human problems of project management?" Among the common answers were two related to balancing the workload:

- The temporary nature of the organization often necessitates "make work" assignments for its displaced members after the organization has been disbanded. . . .
- Members of the organization who are displaced because of the phasing out of the work upon which they are engaged may have to wait a long time before they get another assignment at as high a level of responsibility. (1969:463)

And so the top managers of the Administrative Adhocracy must also devote considerable attention to liaison and negotiation activities in order to ensure a steady stream of work. . . .

CONDITIONS OF THE ADHOCRACY

. . . The conditions of the environment are the most important ones for this configuration; specifically, the Adhocracy is clearly positioned in an environment that is both dynamic and complex. . . . a dynamic environment calls for organic structure and a complex one calls for decentralized structure. And Adhocracy is the only configuration that is both organic and relatively decentralized. In effect, innovative work, being unpredictable, is associated with a dynamic environment; and the fact that the innovation must be sophisticated means that it is difficult to comprehend— in other words, associated with a complex environment. Thus, we find Adhocracies wherever the conditions of dynamism and complexity together prevail, in organizations ranging from guerrilla units to space agencies. There is no other way to fight a war in the jungle or put the first man on the moon.

As we have noted for all the configurations, organizations that prefer particular structures also try to "choose" environments appropriate to them. This is especially clear in the case of the Operating Adhocracy. As noted earlier, advertising agencies and consulting firms that prefer to structure themselves as Professional Bureaucracies seek out stable environments; those that prefer Adhocracy find environments that are dynamic, where the client needs are unpredictable. . . .

A number of organizations are drawn toward Adhocracy because of the dynamic conditions that result from very frequent product change. The extreme case is the *unit producer*, the manufacturing firm that custom-makes each of its products to order, as in the case of the engineering company that produces prototypes. Because each customer order constitutes a new project, the organization is encouraged to structure itself as an Operating Adhocracy. . . .

Similar to the unit producer is the small high-technology firm, such as those surrounding Boston on Route 128. For the most part, these firms do sophisticated project work—design and sometimes manufacturing—under direct contract to the U.S. government or to the larger corporations in industries such as defense, aerospace, and atomic energy. Their work being complex and their environments dynamic, these firms are dependent on highly trained experts who work in interdisciplinary project teams. But these firms are also small and owned by individual entrepreneurs who maintain personal control. (They are able to do so, of course, only because they are as highly trained as their employees.) So the structure emerges as a hybrid between Operating Adhocracy and Simple Structure, which we call the *entrepreneurial adhocracy*.

Another variant of the unit producer is the newspaper or magazine. From the editorial point of view, every product—that is, every issue—is different. Moreover, the environment is typically very dynamic and often rather complex, especially in the case of daily newspapers and newsmagazines, which must report a vast world of fast-breaking news with very short deadlines. Moreover, the efforts of all kinds of reporters, photographers, editors, and others must be integrated into a single product. So Adhocracy is called for in the editorial department. But from the point of view of the printing and distribution functions, there is great repetition—thousands, sometimes millions of copies of the same issue. And their environment is extremely stable—the

tasks remain unchanged no matter what the content of the issue. So Machine Bureaucracy is called for in these functions. The need for two different structures is, of course, reconciled by truncation. The different functions are kept well separated, with standard outputs serving as the one interface. The Adhocracy editorial department completes its work and then converts it into standardized format—typed copy, page layouts, clipped photographs—which become the inputs to the bureaucratic production process.

Some manufacturers of consumer goods operate in markets so competitive that they must change their products almost continuously. Here again, dynamic conditions, when coupled with some complexity, drive the structure toward the Adhocracy form. An excellent example of what we shall call the *competitive adhocracy* is [a] pop recording company. . . . Its dramatically short product life cycle and fluid supply of recording talent require[s] extremely fast response based on a great deal of inside knowledge. . . . Other examples of competitive adhocracies are found in the cosmetics, pharmaceuticals, and plastics industries.

A number of nonenvironmental conditions are also associated with Adhocracy. One is age— or more exactly, youth—since Adhocracy is not a very stable configuration. It is difficult to keep any structure in that state for long periods of time—to keep behaviors from formalizing and to ensure a steady flow of truly innovative, ad hoc projects. All kinds of forces drive the Adhocracy to bureaucratize itself as it ages. On the other side of the coin . . . young organizations tend to be structured organically, since they are still finding their way and also since they are typically eager for innovative, ad hoc projects on which to test themselves. So we can conclude that the Adhocracy form tends to be associated with youth, with early stages in the development of organizational structures.

The Operating Adhocracy is particularly prone to a short life. For one thing, it faces a risky market, which can quickly destroy it. Unlike the Professional Bureaucracy or Machine Bureaucracy, with their standardized outputs, the Operating Adhocracy can never be sure where its next project will come from. A downturn in the economy or the loss of a major contract can close it down literally overnight.

But if some Operating Adhocracies have short lives because they fail, others have short lives because they succeed. Success—and aging—encourage a metamorphosis in the Operating Adhocracy, driving it to more stable conditions and more bureaucratic structure. Over time, the successful organization develops a reputation for what it does best. That encourages it to repeat certain projects, in effect to focus its attention on specific contingencies and programs. And this tends to suit its employees, who, growing older themselves, welcome more stability in their work. So the Operating Adhocracy is driven over time toward the Professional Bureaucracy to concentrate on the programs it does best, sometimes even toward the Machine Bureaucracy to exploit a single program or invention. The organization survives, but the configuration dies.

Administrative Adhocracies typically live longer. They, too, feel the pressures to bureaucratize as they age. This leads many to try to stop innovating, or to innovate in stereotyped ways, and thereby to revert to more bureaucratic structure, notably of the machine type. But unlike the Operating Adhocracy, the Administrative Adhocracy typically cannot change its structure while remaining in the same industry. In choosing that industry, it chose a complex, dynamic environment. Stereotyped innovation will eventually destroy the organization. Newspapers and plastics and pharmaceuticals companies—at least those facing severe competition—may have no choice but to structure themselves as Adhocracies.

In recognition of the tendency for organizations to bureaucratize themselves as they age, a variant has emerged—"the organizational equivalent of paper dresses or throw-away tissues" (Toffler, 1970:133)—which might be called the *temporary adhocracy*. It draws together specialists from different organizations to carry out a project, and then it disbands. Temporary adhocracies are becoming common in a great many

spheres of modern society: the production group that performs a single play, the election campaign committee that promotes a single candidate, the guerrilla group that overthrows a single government, the Olympic Committee that plans a single Games. A related variant is the *mammoth project adhocracy*, a giant temporary adhocracy that draws on thousands of experts for anywhere from a year to a decade to carry out a single task.

This last variant suggests that size is a less important condition than age for the Adhocracy. Administrative Adhocracies in particular can grow very large indeed. However, Operating Adhocracies tend to be small or middle-sized, constrained by the projects they do, by the number and size of the multidisciplinary teams they can organize, and by their desire to avoid the pressure to bureaucratize that comes from growing large.

. . . Technical system is another important condition in certain cases of this configuration. Although Operating Adhocracies, like their sister Professional Bureaucracies, tend to have simple, nonregulating technical systems, the case for Administrative Adhocracies is frequently quite the opposite. Many organizations use the Administrative Adhocracy because their technical systems are sophisticated and perhaps automated as well. . . . when its technical system is sophisticated, the organization requires an elaborate, highly trained support staff to design or purchase, modify, and maintain it; the organization must give considerable power over its technical decisions to that support staff; and that staff, in turn, must use the liaison devices to coordinate its work. In other words, complex machinery requires specialists who have the knowledge, power, and flexible working arrangements to cope with it. The result is that support staffers emerge as powerful members of the organization, drawing power down from the strategic apex, up from the operating core, and over from the middle line. The organization is drawn to the Administrative Adhocracy configuration.

Automation of a sophisticated technical system evokes even stronger forces in the same direction. . . . the Machine Bureaucracy that succeeds in automating its operating core undergoes a dramatic metamorphosis. The problem of motivating uninterested operators disappears, and with it goes the control mentality that permeates its structure; the distinction between line and staff blurs (machines being indifferent to who turns their knobs), which leads to another important reduction in conflict; the technostructure loses its influence, since control is built into the machinery itself by its designers rather than imposed on workers by the rules and standards of the analysts. Overall, the administrative structure becomes more decentralized and organic, emerging as the type we call the *automated adhocracy*.

Automation is common in the process industries, such as petrochemicals and cosmetics (another reason why firms in the latter industry would be drawn toward Adhocracy). . . . But it should be noted that not all process firms use this configuration. Many are, in fact, far from fully automated, and therefore require large operating work forces that draw them toward Machine Bureaucracy. Steel companies . . . are a case in point. Then there are the process producers that, although highly automated in production, exhibit strong Machine Bureaucracy as well as Administrative Adhocracy tendencies, in some cases because they require large routine work forces for other operating functions (such as marketing in the oil company with many of its own retail outlets). Finally, there are the automated process producers with such simple environments and technical systems—for example, the small manufacturer of one line of hand creams—that the Simple Structure suffices instead of the Administrative Adhocracy.

. . . Fashion most decidedly is [another] condition of Adhocracy. Every characteristic of the Adhocracy is very much in vogue today: emphasis on expertise, organic structure, project teams and task forces, decentralization without a single concentration of power, matrix structure, sophisticated and automated technical systems, youth, and environments that are complex and dynamic. . . .

If Simple Structure and Machine Bureaucracy were yesterday's structures, and Professional Bureaucracy and the Divisionalized Form

are today's, then Adhocracy is clearly tomorrow's. This is the structure for a population growing ever better educated and more specialized, yet under constant exhortation to adopt the "systems" approach—to view the world as an integrated whole instead of a collection of loosely coupled parts. It is the structure for environments that are becoming more complex and demanding of innovation, and for technical systems becoming more sophisticated and highly automated. It is the only structure now available to those who believe organizations must become at the same time more democratic yet less bureaucratic.

Yet despite our current infatuation with it, Adhocracy is not the structure for all organizations. Like all the other configurations, it too has its place. And that place, as the examples of this [reading] make clear, seems to be in the new industries of our age—aerospace, electronics, think-tank consulting, research, advertising, filmmaking, petrochemicals—virtually all the industries that grew up since World War II. . . . Adhocracy [appears to be] the configuration of the last half of the twentieth century.

SOME ISSUES ASSOCIATED WITH ADHOCRACY

[Three] issues associated with Adhocracy . . . merit attention here: its ambiguities and the reactions of people who must live with them, its inefficiencies, and its propensity to make inappropriate transitions to other configurations.

Human Reactions to Ambiguity

Many people, especially creative ones, dislike both structural rigidity and concentration of power. That leaves them only one configuration. Adhocracy is the one that is both organic and decentralized. Thus they find it a great place to work. In essence, Adhocracy is the only configuration for those who believe in more democracy with less bureaucracy.

But not every structure can be an Adhocracy. The organization's conditions must call for it. Forcing Adhocracy on, say, a simple, stable environment is as unnatural—and therefore as unpleasant for the participants—as forcing Machine Bureaucracy on a complex, dynamic one. Furthermore, not everyone shares the same vision of organizational utopia. As we saw in Chapter 9, there are those who prefer the life of Machine Bureaucracy, a life of stability and well-defined relationships. They, in fact, dislike the relationships of Adhocracy, viewing it as a nice place to visit but no place to spend a career. Even dedicated members of the Adhocracies periodically exhibit the same low tolerance for its fluidity, confusion, and ambiguity. "In these situations, all managers some of the time, and many managers all the time, yearn for more definition and structure" (Burns and Stalker, 1961:122–23).

Earlier we discussed two of the common responses Reeser (1969) received when he asked managers in three aerospace companies, "What are some of the human problems of project organization?" Of the other eight responses Reeser reports, six, in fact, relate to structural ambiguities: anxiety related to the eventual phaseout of the projects; confusion of members as to who their boss is, whom to impress to get promoted; low sense of member loyalty owing to frequent transfers between project organizations; a lack of clarity in job definitions, authority relationships, and lines of communication; random and unplanned personal development because of the short time under any one manager; and intense competition for resources, recognition, and rewards.

Reeser's last point raises another major problem of ambiguity, the politicization of the structure. Coupling its ambiguities with its interdependencies, Adhocracy emerges as the most politicized of the five configurations. No structure can be more Darwinian than the Adhocracy— more supportive of the fit, as long as they remain fit, and more destructive of the weak. Structures this fluid tend to be highly competitive and at times ruthless—breeding grounds for all kinds of political forces. The French have a graphic expression for this: *un panier de crabes*—a basket of crabs, all clawing at each other to get up, or out. Take, for example, matrix structure: as noted earlier, what it does is establish an adversary

system, thereby institutionalizing organizational conflict.

There are conflicts that breed politics in the other configurations, too . . . But these conflicts are always contained within well-defined ground rules. In the Simple Structure, the politics that do take place are directed at the chief executive. But his close, personal control precludes much of the political activity in the first place; those who do not like the structure simply get out. And in all the bureaucratic configurations, conflicts and politics are focused on well-defined issues—the power of line versus staff or professional versus nonprofessional, the resistance of workers to the control mentality, the biasing of information sent up to the central headquarters, the ambiguities of pigeonholing, and so on. . . . Not so in the Adhocracy, where specialists from different professions must work together on multidisciplinary teams, and . . . owing to the organic nature of the structure, the political games that result are played with few rules. Adhocracy requires the specialist to subordinate his individual goals and the standards of his profession to the needs of the group . . .

Problems of Efficiency

No structure is better suited to solving complex, ill-structure problems than that of Adhocracy. None can match it for sophisticated innovation. Or, unfortunately, for the costs of that innovation. Adhocracy is simply not an efficient structure. Although it is ideally suited for the one-of-a-kind project, the Adhocracy is not competent at doing ordinary things. It is designed for the *extra*ordinary. The bureaucracies are all mass producers; they gain efficiency through standardization. The Adhocracy is a custom producer, unable to standardize and so to be efficient.

The root of its inefficiency is the Adhocracy's high cost of communication. People talk a lot in these structures; that is how they combine their knowledge to develop new ideas. But that takes time, a great deal. Faced with the need to make a decision in the Machine Bureaucracy, someone up above gives an order and that is that. Not so in the Adhocracy. Everyone gets into the act. First are all the managers who must be consulted—functional managers, project managers, liaison managers. Then there are all the specialists who believe their point of view should be represented in the decision. A meeting is called, probably to schedule another meeting, eventually to decide who should participate in the decision. Then those people settle down to the decision process. The problem is defined and redefined, ideas for its solution are generated and debated, alliances build and fall around different solutions, and eventually everyone settles down to hard bargaining about the favored one. Finally, a decision emerges—that in itself is an accomplishment—although it is typically late and will probably be modified later. All this is the cost of having to find a creative solution to a complex, ill-structured problem.

It should be noted, however, that the heavy costs incurred in reaching a decision are partially recuperated in its execution. Widespread participation in decision making ensures widespread support for the decisions made. So the execution stage can be smoother in the Adhocracy than in the Machine Bureaucracy, where resistance by the operators, not party to the decision, is often encountered.

A further source of inefficiency in the Adhocracy is the unbalanced workloads, as mentioned earlier. It is almost impossible to keep the personnel of a project structure—high-priced personnel, it should be noted—busy on a steady basis. In January, the specialists are playing bridge for want of work; in March, they are working overtime with no hope of completing the new project on time.

The Dangers of Inappropriate Transition

Of course, one solution to the problems of ambiguity and inefficiency is to change the structure. Employees no longer able to tolerate the ambiguity and customers fed up with the inefficiency try to drive the structure to a more stable, bureaucratic form.

That is relatively easily done in the Operating Adhocracy, as noted earlier. The organization simply selects the standard programs it does best and goes into the business of doing them. It becomes a Professional Bureaucracy. Or else it uses its creative talent one last time to find a single market niche, and then turns itself into a Machine Bureaucracy to mass-produce in that niche.

But the transition from Operating Adhocracy into bureaucracy, however easily effected, is not always appropriate. The organization came into being to solve problems imaginatively, not to apply standards indiscriminately. In many spheres, society has more mass producers than it needs; what it lacks are true problem solvers. It has little need for the laboratory that comes up with a modification of an old design when a new one is called for, the consulting firm ready with a standard technique when the client has a unique problem, the medical or university researcher who sees every new challenge in terms of an old theory. The standard output of bureaucracy will not do when the conditions call for the creativity of Adhocracy.

This seems to describe some of the problems of the television networks. Despite their need to be creative, the networks face one irresistible pressure to bureaucratize: the requirement that they produce on a routine basis, hour after hour, night after night, with never a break. One would think they would tend toward Professional Bureaucracy structures, but . . . accounts in the literature suggest strong elements of Machine Bureaucracy. And the results are what one would expect of such structures: stereotyped programming, stale jokes supported by canned laughter, characters in serials that are interchangeable between channels, repetition of the old movies. Interestingly, the two bright spots on TV are the news and the specials, for reasons already suggested in our discussion of Adhocracy. The news department, like the newspaper, faces a truly dynamic environment. The networks can control and therefore stabilize the series, but never the news. Every day is different, and so, therefore, is every program. And the specials really are ad hoc—in this case, by the choice of the networks—and so lend themselves to the creative approach of Adhocracy. But elsewhere the pressures of the routine neutralize creativity, and the result is standardization.

Other organizations face these same dual pressures—to produce routinely yet also be creative. Universities and teaching hospitals must, for example, serve their regular clients yet also produce creative research. Universities sometimes set up research centers to differentiate the research function from teaching activities. These centers enable the professors with the greatest potential for research—often poor teachers—to do it without interruption. In the absence of such differentiation, the organization risks falling into a schizophrenic state, continually wavering between two kinds of structure, never clearly isolating either, to the detriment of both.

The Administrative Adhocracy runs into more serious difficulties when it succumbs to the pressures to bureaucratize. It exists to innovate for itself, in its own industry. The conditions of dynamism and complexity, requiring sophisticated innovation, typically cut across the entire industry. So unlike the Operating Adhocracy, the Administrative Adhocracy cannot often select new clients yet remain in the same industry. And so its conversion to Machine Bureaucracy—the natural transition for the Administrative Adhocracy tired of perpetual change—by destroying the organization's ability to innovate, can eventually destroy the organization itself.

To reiterate a central theme of our discussion throughout this book: in general, there is no one best structure; in particular, there may be, as long as the design parameters are internally consistent and together with the situational factors form a coherent configuration. . . .

STRATEGY FORMATION IN THE ADHOCRACY*

How do organizations with structures resembling Adhocracy go about making their strategies? On first thought, the mode labelled "adaptive" in

* This section is adapted from Henry Mintzberg and James A. Waters, "The Mind of the Strategist(s)," in S. Srivastva, ed., *The Executive Mind* (Jossey Boss, 1983) and Henry Mintzberg and Alexandra McHugh, "Strategy Formation in an Adhocracy," *Administrative Science Quarterly* (1985; pp. 160–197), with portions also from Henry Mintzberg *Structure in Fives* (Prentice-Hall, 1983), chap. 12.

the article "Strategy Making in Three Modes" (Mintzberg, 1973b), would seem to be most appropriate. There it was described as appropriate for the organization that has no clear goals but instead divides its power among members of a complex coalition. Organizations using this mode were characterized as reacting to existing problems rather than searching for new opportunities, and as inclined to make decisions that are disjointed, taken in serial, incremental steps.

Adaptive But . . .

Our research project at McGill, particularly on the tracking of strategies in those organizations strongly reminiscent of Adhocracy—the National Film Board of Canada, a government-owned company that makes mostly short and often innovative films, and Arcop, a small architectural firm well known in Canada for its innovative work—would appear to confirm the flavor of this description although not some of its specific details.

Because the Adhocracy must respond continuously to a complex environment that it cannot predict, it is unable to rely on deliberate strategies. In other words, it cannot predetermine precise patterns in its streams of activities. Rather, many of its actions must be decided upon individually, according to the needs of the moment. And these must be under the control of whoever has the expertise to deal with the issue in question. The result is that power over strategy making in Adhocracy is diffused in ways unheard of in the other types of organizations, such as Simple Structures or Machine Bureaucracies, where the process is clearly top-down, controlled by the strategic apex (and in the divisionalized form, the strategic apexes of the divisions as well). In sharp contrast, control of the strategy formulation process in the adhocracy is not clearly placed, at the strategic apex or elsewhere.

But does continuous and decentralized response to the environment necessarily imply the reaction to problems rather than the proactive search for opportunities? On one hand, the Adhocracies of our studies appeared to be very reactive, continuously trying to read the environment to know which way to go next. On the other hand, they did so to innovate, to create new outputs to serve that environment. So perhaps strategy making in Adhocracy is best described as opportunistic reaction.

That decisions are serial and incremental seems to be true in the sense that many Adhocracies (especially of the operating type) are reluctant to make grand or "strategic" decisions—ones that commit resources and set patterns for long periods of time (and for other decisions). To use the words of Lindblom, they prefer "continual nibbling" to a "good bite" (1968:25). In lieu of strategic-type commitments—what market to enter, what range of products to sell—they tend to make marginal decisions closer to their actions—how to serve *this* customer, how to adapt *that* product. That maintains their flexibility, and hence their creativity.

Here the process is best thought of as strategy *formation*, because strategy in these structures is not so much formulated consciously by individuals as formed implicitly by the decisions they make, one at a time. The concept of the formulation—implementation dichotomy in strategy making—a pillar of the Machine Bureaucracy—loses its meaning in the Adhocracy. It is in the making of specific decisions within and about projects, what would normally be considered implementation, that strategies emerge—that is, are formed—in the Adhocracy. ". . . a single engine fighter plane may evolve into a twin-engine attack bomber; a funding program for exceptional children may become a strategy for integration" (Goodman and Goodman, 1976:496). That is why action planning cannot be extensively relied upon in the Adhocracy. Any process that separates conception from action—planning from execution, formalization from implementation—impedes the flexibility of the organization to respond creatively to its dynamic environment.

Strategy Formation in the Operating Adhocracy

Consider the case of the Operating Adhocracy, a structure never quite sure what it will do next. That depends on what projects come along, which in turn depends partly on how well it does in its current projects. So its strategy never really stabilizes totally, but responds to new projects. Now if strategy evolves continuously according to the projects being done, it stands to reason that strategy formation is controlled by whoever decides what projects are done and how. And in the Operating Adhocracy, that includes line managers, staff specialists, and operators—in other words, potentially almost everyone in the organization.

Take the case of the National Film Board. Among its most important strategies are those related to the content of the one hundred or so mostly short documentary-type films that it makes each year—some about the geography of Canada and the sociology of its peoples, others on pure experimental themes, and so on. Were the Board structured as a Machine Bureaucracy, the word on what films to make would come down from on high. There would be one stable film strategy, formulated at the strategic apex and implemented lower down. (If the Board were structured as the Divisionalized Form, the word would come down from the head of each film division.)

In fact, because it is structured as an Operating Adhocracy, the Board acts otherwise. About one-third of its films are sponsored by agencies of the Canadian government. As long as interested filmmakers can be found, these are accepted, and clients can be thought to impose the strategy. The other two-thirds are proposed by the Board's own employees and are funded from its own general budget. Each proposal is submitted to a standing committee, which at the time of this writing consists of four members elected by the filmmakers, two appointed by the Distribution (marketing) Branch, and the Director of Production and the Director of Programming. The Commissioner—the chief executive—must approve the committee's choices. Thus, operators, middle-line managers, support staffers, and managers at the strategic apex all get involved in the choices of what films to make. But the vast majority of the proposals are initiated by the filmmakers and the executive producers. Each has his own general preferences, whether those be for animated or experimental films, documentaries, or whatever.

But a glance at the Board's catalog invalidates any conclusion about standardization. Certain general themes do develop from time to time. But these also change frequently, according to styles and successes and so on.

The Operating Adhocracy's strategy evolves continuously as hundreds of these kinds of decisions are made each year in complicated ways. Each project leaves its imprint on the strategy. And to return to the basic point being made, so many people at so many levels are involved in these projects—both in deciding which ones to carry out and then in actually carrying them out—that we cannot point a finger at any one part of the organization and say that is where the strategy is formulated. Everyone who gets involved—and that means top- and middle-level managers, staff specialists, and operators, all combined in various task forces and standing committees—has a hand in influencing the strategy that gets formed.

Strategy Formation
in the Administrative Adhocracy

Similar conclusions can be reached about the Administrative Adhocracy, although the strategy-making process is slightly neater there. That is because the Administrative Adhocracy tends to concentrate its attention on fewer projects, which involve more people in interdependent relationships. NASA's Apollo project involved most of its personnel for almost ten years; similarly, the bringing on line of a new processing plant can involve a good deal of the administrative staff of a petrochemical company for years. Moreover, since it carries out its projects only for itself, not for a range of outside clients, the Administrative Adhocracy tends to have a more concentrated product-market sphere of operations. Through the 1960s, for example, NASA focused on the single goal of landing an American on the moon before 1970.

Administrative Adhocracies also need to rely more on action planning, but of a loose kind. The problem with such planning is that although the end or goal of the organization may be known,

the means for reaching it are not. These must be worked out en route, by trial and error. So only a general kind of action planning can take place, one that sets out broad, flexible guidelines within which various project teams can proceed to make their specific decisions. Again, therefore, it is only through the making of specific decisions—namely, those that determine which projects are undertaken and how these projects turn out—that strategies evolve.

The Cyclical Appearance of Strategies
in the National Film Board

To conclude from this, however, that the decisions of Adhocracy (either type) are disjointed—distinct from one another, as described in the adaptive mode—is one assumption that proved overly simple. What happened in our studies proved most interesting. At times decisions and actions showed a definite propensity to converge, that is, to exhibit patterning. In other words, we do find strategies in Adhocracies, indeed even periodic convergence of different strategies around common themes, even though the strategies themselves were typically emergent.

Most surprising in our study of the National Film Board were the ways in which the content of films tended to converge on certain of these themes periodically, and then to diverge, despite a virtually complete absence of direction on film content from the central management. We categorized each of almost 3000 films made at the National Film Board from 1939 to 1976 into 37 categories of content (e.g., experimental, mental health, defense, native people). We then distinguished what we called "focused strategies," where one content category received some sustained attention (essentially five or more films per year for more than two years), from "trickles" (streams with fewer than five films per year), and "blips" (five or more films but only for one or two years).

Figure 4 shows a plot of the percentage of films categorized within the three categories across the 36-year study period. Here we can

FIGURE 4   PROPORTION OF TRICKLES, BLIPS, AND FOCUSED STRATEGIES
AT THE NATIONAL FILM BOARD OF CANADA

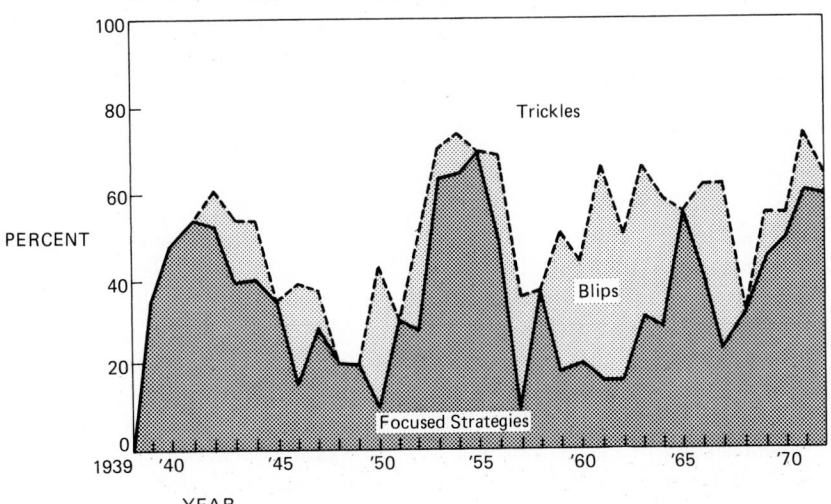

see the tendency to converge around focused strategies and later to diverge periodically, or, as we put it in the report (if we can be forgiven this reference to a film company), the cycling into and out of focus.

The first convergence (about half of all films produced in focused strategy categories) was largely around defense and related films to support the war effort in the early 1940s. Then, until the early 1950s, there was a great deal of divergence, with little focus (usually under 20% of the films produced). The advent of television in Canada captured the Film Board for a few years in the 1950s as no theme ever did before or since (up to more than 3 of every 4 films produced). But that focus ended just as quickly as it began, and was followed by another period of divergence (again usually below 20%). Then, in the mid 1960s, there was a brief period of convergence around the themes of experimentation and social commentary, which was interrupted briefly and then renewed in somewhat modified form in the late 1960s and 1970s around social issues (about 60%).

This cycling of convergence and divergence is quite unlike the patterns of strategic change found in the bureaucratic and entrepreneurial organizations. There, the strength of convergence around given strategic orientations was generally much greater (virtually total in many cases) and the periods of convergence were typically much longer (on the order of fifteen to twenty years), while those of divergence were very brief. In effect, these organizations could not tolerate much divergence; they essentially had to leap from one strategic orientation to another, through what Miller and Friesen (1984) refer to as strategic "revolutions." The Film Board, in contrast, could tolerate such periods of change, at least for a time. It could function without focus; indeed, at times it positively thrived on divergence. (This stands in contrast to a Volkswagenwerk, which went through turmoil when it lacked definition in the late 1960s.) As we noted in our study of Arcop, while strategies may be indispensible in Machine Bureaucracies, they are actually disposable in Adhocracies, where there is little organizational momentum and where so many people get involved in the process of strategy making (Mintzberg et al., 1987). And that means that strategic change need not be revolutionary: the Film Board, for example, seemed to slip into and out of its pervasive television focus of the mid 1950s without missing a step.

The Origins of Strategies in the Film Board

Where do strategies come from in Adhocracy? A few of the patterns in the NFB appeared in the form of conventional, top-down strategies, deliberately imposed by the central management in response to intrinsic needs. Staff cuts, for example, had to be imposed pervasively from the center in response to budget reductions. But such strategies were hardly common in the NFB (unlike the more bureaucratic forms of organization we studied), especially in the important area of film content, the manifestation of the organization's basic mission. Not only was the role of central management apparently minor in this area, but sometimes there was hardly even evidence of strategic decisions per se, by which we mean key decisions taken deliberately to establish major patterns. Yet patterns did form, apparently in response to the needs of a variety of people in the organization as well as forces in the environment.

In a number of important cases, a single, seemingly inconsequential decision, meant to be ad hoc, established a precedent which evoked a pattern. The clearest example was the first series for television which quickly led to the NFB's most dominant film content strategy. When television first came to Canada in 1952, a debate erupted in the NFB about its possible role in the new medium, with some filmmakers anxious to begin producing for it immediately and others (as well as top management) opposed. But after one proposal for a series was accepted and rushed into production, other filmmakers leaped in and the NFB suddenly found itself deeply committed to a major new strategy. Note that this strategy developed purely through mutual adjustment—that is, through filmmakers reacting to each others' actions—and that it developed as a kind of sudden consensus, virtually a spontaneous one.

In some other cases, a pattern formed without even that single decision, as in the appearance of the NFB's feature film strategy. The first feature was made inadvertently, the result of a scheduled shorter film that ran long. But with that precedent set, the strategy followed, as others took advantage of the opening. In other cases, strategies took longer to appear, although the process was similar. A trickle eventually took hold and began to pervade the organization, as in the case of the experimental film focus. All the experimental films produced in the NFB by year are shown in Figure 5. Every one in the figure but

FIGURE 5   EXPERIMENTAL FILMS AT THE NATIONAL FILM BOARD OF CANADA

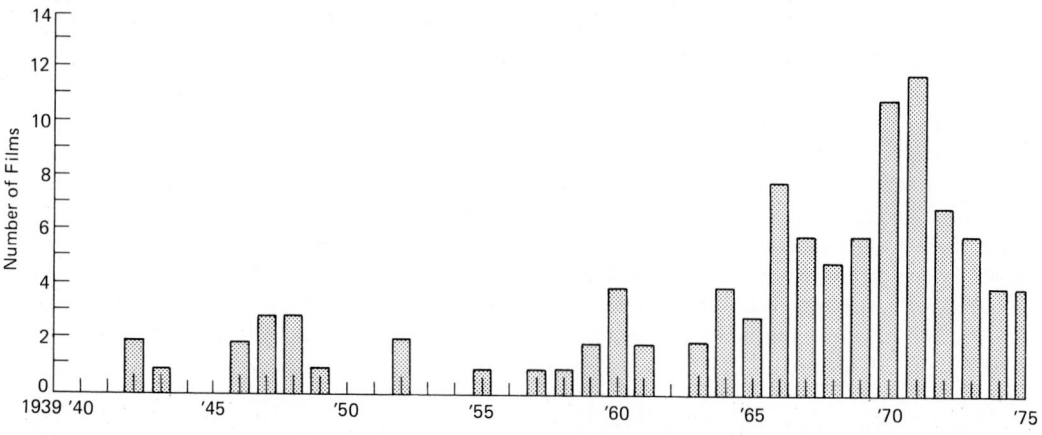

Year

one up to 1960 was made by Norman McLaren, the Board's most celebrated filmmaker; in a sense, the pattern was his and the strategy, a personal one. Only after 1960 did the pattern get adopted by other filmmakers so that the strategy became, in part at least, organizational.

This process of the trickle, or peripheral strategy, eventually evoking a focused strategy is probably a common one in organizations, indeed perhaps the origin of many new strategic perspectives. Someone or some group pursues its own interests for years, in some pocket of the organization. Eventually, casting about for new directions (perhaps the result of a crisis in the established strategies), the organization at large seizes on this peripheral strategy—the marginal product, the unexploited market, the experimental process. In effect, the trickle serves as the feeler or bellwether; *if* it works, and *when* the organization is ready for it, what was a peripheral or auxiliary strategy spreads to become a central one.

Role of Leadership

Where does all this leave the formal leadership, the people who don't make films but sit in executive offices? What role do they play in strategy formation? Must the general managers defer totally to the experts?

The dilemma of management in the Adhocracy lies in trying to exercise influence without being able to rely on formal control. The NFB managers, for example, had their hands on some levers of decision, such as staffing levels and the design of the structure itself, but not others, notably the content of specific films. Trying to manage in this regard is a little like trying to drive an automobile without controlling the steering wheel. You can accelerate and brake, but not determine direction. As we noted in the Arcop study, when you are developing strategies for design, you are not able to design strategies.

In two ways, however, the senior management is able to exercise control. First, it can try to manage the process of strategy making if not the content of strategy. In order words, it can set up the structures to encourage certain kinds of behavior patterns and hire the people who themselves will create those patterns. Had there been no Norman McLaren through the 1950's, for example, there may not have been an experimental film strategy in the 1960's. And second, they can provide general guidelines for strategy, seeking to define certain boundaries outside of which the experts should not take action. We have referred to this [in Chapter 1 of this text] as umbrella strategy.

Umbrella Strategy at Arcop

We saw this form of strategy most clearly in the architectural firm we studied called Arcop. The leadership of this firm always imposed one basic strategic umbrella. Arcop devoted its effort to exciting buildings where it had full control of the design, what it called "public celebration" buildings—unique, visible ones that would have an impact on the community and celebrate its spirit. Within the umbrella, anything went—cultural centers, hotels, office buildings, churches, etc.

Periodically, there was in fact convergence in Arcop's actions, as there was in the National Film Board—at one point, for example, the firm was repeatedly contracted to design performing arts centers. But that convergence was largely emergent—the architects were open to a wide variety of work; they just happened to be most successful in one particular sphere at that particular time. In other words, in some sense the environment (namely the clients) imposed the specific strategy (that is, pattern). Only the umbrella—the broad set of guidelines—was clearly deliberate on the part of the leadership.

Of course, such umbrella strategies can only emanate from leaders who have vision. And that brings us to another strategy making role for management in Adhocracy, perhaps the most critical one—the building of image or ideology, the creation of missionary zeal, in Selznick's (1957) terms, "the embodiment of purpose," "the infusion with value."

A Grass Roots Model of Strategy Formation

To summarize this discussion, we can draw on the conclusion in the study of the National Film Board, where we proposed a "grass roots" model of strategy formation, comprising six points. It serves to contrast especially adaptation in the Adhocracy context with the more conventional views of how strategy is supposed to get made.

1. *Strategies grow initially like weeds in a garden; they are not cultivated like tomatoes in a hothouse.* In other words, the process of strategy formation can be overmanaged; sometimes it is more important to let patterns emerge than to force an artificial consistency upon an organization prematurely. The hothouse, if needed, can come later.

2. *These strategies can take root in all kinds of strange places, virtually wherever people have the capacity to learn and the resources to support that capacity.* Sometimes an individual actor in touch with a particular market niche creates his or her own pattern (or a small, detached subunit does the same thing). Sometimes he or she does not even have to do that, but simply take an initial action which evokes its own pattern. Other times the external environment imposes a pattern on an unsuspecting organization. In some cases, many different actors converge around a theme, perhaps gradually, perhaps spontaneously. Sometimes senior managers fumble into strategies, these in some cases developing gradually in their minds to emerge in a form that makes everyone believe they were deliberately and suddenly designed. The point is that we cannot always plan where the strategies will emerge, let alone plan the strategies themselves.

3. *Such strategies become organizational when they become collective, that is, when the patterns proliferate, to pervade the behavior of the organization at large.* Weeds can proliferate and encompass a whole garden; then the conventional plants may look out of place. The same holds true for emergent strategies. But, of course, what's a weed but a plant that wasn't expected. With a change of perspective, the emergent strat-

egy, like the weed, can become what is valued (just as Europeans enjoy salads of the leaves of America's most notorious weed, the dandelion!).

4. *That process of proliferation may be conscious but need not be; likewise, it may be managed but need not be.* The process by which these initial patterns work their way through the organization need not be consciously intended, by formal leaders or informal ones. Patterns may just spread by collective action, much as plants proliferate themselves. Of course, once the strategies are recognized as valuable, the process of proliferation can be managed, just as plants are selectively propagated.

5. *The pervasion of new strategies, which themselves may be emerging continuously, tends to occur during distinct periods of divergence, that punctuate distinct periods of the convergence of established, prevalent strategies.* Organizations, like gardens, appear to accept the biblical maxim of a time to sow and a time to reap (even though they can sometimes reap what they did not mean to sow). Periods of integrated continuity tend to be interspaced with periods of quantum change, in clear cycles (for reasons cited in Miller and Friesen, 1980, 1984, and Miller and Mintzberg, 1983). In Adhocracies, these cycles tend to be of shorter duration and are more balanced between convergence and divergence, apparently because of the need for distinct periods of experimentation and renewal to work out new strategic themes. But the blurring of the distinction between these two kinds of periods would seem to indicate deterioration in the organization, just as confusion between sowing and reaping would destroy the productivity of a garden.

6. *To manage this process is not to preconceive strategies but to recognize their emergence and intervene when appropriate.* A destructive weed, once noticed, is best unrooted immediately; but one that seems capable of bearing fruit is worth watching, indeed even building a hothouse around. To manage in this context is to create the climate within which a wide variety of strategies can grow (to establish flexible structures and supporting ideologies, to define guiding "umbrella" strategies, etc.), and then to watch

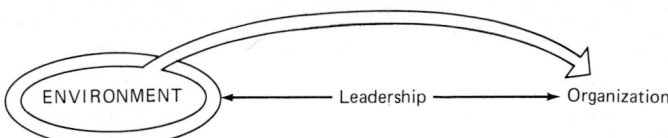

FIGURE 6
ENVIRONMENT TAKING THE LEAD
IN ADHOCRACY

what does in fact come up and not be too quick to cut off the unexpected. While keeping one eye on this process of emergence (the results of which must sometimes be made deliberate), managers must keep the other on the cycle of convergence and divergence, knowing when to promote change for the sake of external adaptation and when to resist it for the sake of internal efficiency. Most important is to avoid the excesses of each—failure to focus or else capture by bureaucratic (or psychological) momentum. In other words, managers have to be able to sense when to exploit an established crop of strategies and when to encourage new strains to displace it.

This "grass roots" model of strategy formation may seem overstated. But it is no more so than the widely accepted conventional model—what we might call the "hothouse," or deliberate, model of strategy formulation. Our theory must encompass both models. No organization can function with strategies that are always and purely emergent: that would amount to a complete abdication of will and leadership, not to mention conscious thought. But none can likewise function with strategies that are always and purely deliberate: that would amount to an unwillingness to learn, a blindness to whatever is unexpected.

Environment Taking the Lead

To conclude, as shown in Figure 6, in Adhocracy it is the environment that takes the lead. It drives the organization, which responds continuously and electically, nevertheless periodically achieving convergence for a time. (We have wondered what the term "organizational intuition" might mean; perhaps the convergence in strategic themes as a result of spontaneous mutual adjustments might be one form of it.) The formal leadership seeks somehow to influence both sides in this relationship, negotiating with the environ-

ment for support and attempting to impose some broad general guidelines (an umbrella) on the organization.

If the strategist of the Simple Structure is a concept attainer and that of the Machine Bureaucracy is a planner, then the strategist of the Adhocracy is a *pattern recognizer*, seeking to detect emerging patterns (inside and outside the umbrella). That way, strategies deemed inappropriate can be discouraged while the apparently more appropriate ones can be encouraged through more conscious attention and concentration of resource—narrowing the umbrella or moving it over. In this last case, we find the paradoxical situation of a leadership changing its intentions to fit the realized behavior of its organization. But that can be a key to successful strategy making in the Adhocracy.

MANAGING INNOVATION: CONTROLLED CHAOS*

by James Brian Quinn

Management observers frequently claim that small organizations are more innovative than large ones. But is this commonplace necessarily true? Some large enterprises are highly innovative. How do they do it? . . . This article [reports on a] 2½ year worldwide study . . . [of] both well-documented small ventures and large U.S., Japanese, and European companies and programs selected for their innovation records. . . . More striking than the cultural differences among these companies are the similarities between innovative small and large organizations and among innovative organizations in different countries. Effective management of innovation seems much the same, regardless of national boundaries or scale of operations.

There are . . . many reasons why small companies appear to produce a disproportionate number of innovations. First, innovation occurs in a probabilistic setting. A company never knows whether a particular technical result can be achieved and whether it will succeed in the marketplace. For every new solution that succeeds, tens to hundreds fail. The sheer number of attempts—most by small-scale entrepreneurs—means that some ventures will survive. The 90% to 99% that fail are distributed widely throughout society and receive little notice.

On the other hand, a big company that wishes to move a concept from invention to the marketplace must absorb all potential failure costs itself. This risk may be socially or managerially intolerable, jeopardizing the many other products, projects, jobs, and communities the company supports. Even if its innovation is successful, a big company may face costs that newcomers do not bear, like converting existing operations and customer bases to the new solution.

By contrast, a new enterprise does not risk losing an existing investment base or cannibalizing customer franchises built at great expense. It does not have to change an internal culture that has successfully supported doing things another way or that has developed intellectual depth and belief in the technologies that led to past successes. Organized groups like labor unions, consumer advocates, and government bureaucracies rarely monitor and resist a small company's moves as they might a big company's. Finally, new companies do not face the psychological pain and the economic costs of laying off employees, shutting down plants and even communities, and displacing supplier relationships built with years of mutual commitment and effort. Such

barriers to change in large organizations are real, important, and legitimate.

The complex products and systems that society expects large companies to undertake further compound the risks. Only big companies can develop new ships or locomotives; telecommunication networks; or systems for space, defense, air traffic control, hospital care, mass foods delivery, or nationwide computer interactions. These large-scale projects always carry more risk than single-product introductions. A billion-dollar development aircraft, for example, can fail if one inexpensive part in its 100,000 components fails.

Clearly, a single enterprise cannot by itself develop or produce all the parts needed by such large new systems. And communications among the various groups making design and production decisions on components are always incomplete. The probability of error increases exponentially with complexity, while the system innovator's control over decisions decreases significantly—further escalating potential error costs and risks. Such forces inhibit innovation in large organizations. But proper management can lessen these effects.

OF INVENTORS & ENTREPRENEURS

A close look at innovative small enterprises reveals much about the successful management of innovation. Of course, not all innovations follow a single pattern. But my research—and other studies in combination—suggest that the following factors are crucial to the success of innovative small companies:

Need Orientation

Inventor-entrepreneurs tend to be "need or achievement oriented." They believe that if they "do the job better," rewards will follow. They may at first focus on their own view of market needs. But lacking resources, successful small entrepreneurs soon find that it pays to approach potential customers early, test their solutions in users' hands, learn from these interactions, and adapt designs rapidly. Many studies suggest that effective technological innovation develops hand-in-hand with customer demand (Von Hippel, 1982:117).

Experts and Fanatics

Company founders tend to be pioneers in their technologies and fanatics when it comes to solving problems. They are often described as ''possessed'' or ''obsessed,'' working toward their objectives to the exclusion even of family or personal relationships. As both experts and fanatics, they perceive probabilities of success as higher than others do. And their commitment allows them to persevere despite the frustrations, ambiguities, and setbacks that always accompany major innovations.

Long Time Horizons

Their fanaticism may cause inventor-entrepreneurs to underestimate the obstacles and length of time to success. Time horizons for radical innovations make them essentially ''irrational'' from a present value viewpoint. In my sample, delays between invention and commercial production ranged from 3 to 25 years.[1] In the late 1930s, for example, industrial chemist Russell Marker was working on steroids called sapogenins when he discovered a technique that would degrade one of these, diosgenin, into the female sex hormone progesterone. By processing some ten tons of Mexican yams in rented and borrowed lab space, Marker finally extracted about four pounds of diosgenin and started a tiny business to produce steroids for the laboratory market. But it was not until 1962, over 23 years later, that Syntex,

the company Marker founded, obtained FDA approval for its oral contraceptive.

For both psychological and practical reasons, inventor-entrepreneurs generally avoid early formal plans, proceed step-by-step, and sustain themselves by other income and the momentum of the small advances they achieve as they go along.

Low Early Costs

Innovators tend to work in homes, basements, warehouses, or low-rent facilities whenever possible. They incur few overhead costs; their limited resources go directly into their projects. They pour nights, weekends, and ''sweat capital'' into their endeavors. They borrow whatever they can. They invent cheap equipment and prototype processes, often improving on what is available in the marketplace. If one approach fails, few people know; little time or money is lost. All this decreases the costs and risks facing a small operation and improves the present value of its potential success.

Multiple Approaches

Technology tends to advance through a series of random—often highly intuitive—insights frequently triggered by gratuitous interactions between the discoverer and the outside world. Only highly committed entrepreneurs can tolerate (and even enjoy) this chaos. They adopt solutions wherever they can be found, unencumbered by formal plans or PERT charts that would limit the range of their imaginations. When the odds of success are low, the participation and interaction of many motivated players increase the chance that one will succeed.

A recent study of initial public offerings made in 1962 shows that only 2% survived and still looked like worthwhile investments 20 years later.[2] Small-scale entrepreneurship looks effi-

---

[1] A study at Battelle found an average of 19.2 years between invention and commercial production. Battelle Memorial Laboratories, "Science, Technology, and Innovation," Report to the National Science Foundation, 1973; also Dean (1974:13).

[2] Business Econon Group, W.R. Grace & Co., 1983.

cient in part because history only records the survivors.

Flexibility and Quickness

Undeterred by committees, board approvals, and other bureaucratic delays, the inventor-entrepreneur can experiment, test, recycle, and try again with little time lost. Because technological progress depends largely on the number of successful experiments accomplished per unit of time, fast-moving small entrepreneurs can gain both timing and performance advantages over clumsier competitors. This responsiveness is often crucial in finding early markets for radical innovations where neither innovators, market researchers, nor users can quite visualize a product's real potential. For example, Edison's lights first appeared on ships and in baseball parks; Astroturf was intended to convert the flat roofs and asphalt playgrounds of city schools into more humane environments; and graphite and boron composites designed for aerospace unexpectedly found their largest markets in sporting goods. Entrepreneurs quickly adjusted their entry strategies to market feedback.

Incentives

Inventor-entrepreneurs can foresee tangible personal rewards if they are successful. Individuals often want to achieve a technical contribution, recognition, power, or sheer independence, as much as money. For the original, driven personalities who create significant innovations, few other paths offer such clear opportunities to fulfill all their economic, psychological, and career goals at once. Consequently, they do not panic or quit when others with solely monetary goals might.

Availability of Capital

One of America's great competitive advantages is its rich variety of sources to finance small, low-probability ventures. If entrepreneurs are turned down by one source, other sources can be sought in myriads of creative combinations.

Professionals involved in such financings have developed a characteristic approach to deal with the chaos and uncertainty of innovation. First, they evaluate a proposal's conceptual validity: If the technical problems can be solved, is there a real business there for someone and does it have a large upside potential? Next, they concentrate on people: Is the team thoroughly committed and expert? Is it the best available? Only then do these financiers analyze specific financial estimates in depth. Even then, they recognize that actual outcomes generally depend on subjective factors, not numbers (Perce, 1982).

Timeliness, aggressiveness, commitment, quality of people, and the flexibility to attack opportunities not at first perceived are crucial. Downside risks are minimized, not by detailed controls, but by spreading risks among multiple projects, keeping early costs low, and gauging the tenacity, flexibility, and capability of the founders.

[LARGE COMPANY] BARRIERS TO INNOVATION

Less innovative companies and, unfortunately, most large corporations operate in a very different fashion. The most notable and common constraints on innovation in larger companies include:

Top Management Isolation

Many senior executives in big companies have little contact with conditions on the factory floor or with customers who might influence their thinking about technological innovation. Since risk perception is inversely related to familiarity and experience, financially oriented top managers are likely to perceive technological innovations as more problematic than acquisitions that may be just as risky but that will appear more familiar (Hayes and Garvin, 1982:70; Hayes and Abernathy, 1980:67).

Intolerance of Fanatics

Big companies often view entrepreneurial fanatics as embarrassments or troublemakers. Many major cities are now ringed by companies founded by these "nonteam" players—often to the regret of their former employers.

Short Time Horizons

The perceived corporate need to report a continuous stream of quarterly profits conflicts with the long time spans that major innovations normally require. Such pressures often make publicly owned companies favor quick marketing fixes, cost cutting, and acquisition strategies over process, product, or quality innovations that would yield much more in the long run.

Accounting Practices

By assessing all its direct, indirect, overhead, overtime, and service costs against a project, large corporations have much higher development expenses compared with entrepreneurs working in garages. A project in a big company can quickly become an exposed political target, its potential net present value may sink unacceptably, and an entry into small markets may not justify its sunk costs. An otherwise viable project may soon founder and disappear.

Excessive Rationalism

Managers in big companies often seek orderly advance through early market research studies or PERT planning. Rather than managing the inevitable chaos of innovation productively, these managers soon drive out the very things that lead to innovation in order to prove their announced plans.

Excessive Bureaucracy

In the name of efficiency, bureaucratic structures require many approvals and cause delays at every turn. Experiments that a small company can perform in hours may take days or weeks in large organizations. The interactive feedback that fosters innovation is lost, important time windows can be missed, and real costs and risks rise for the corporation.

Inappropriate Incentives

Reward and control systems in most big companies are designed to minimize surprises. Yet innovation, by definition, is full of surprises. It often disrupts well-laid plans, accepted power patterns, and entrenched organizational behavior at high costs to many. Few large companies make millionaires of those who create such disruptions, however profitable the innovations may turn out to be. When control systems neither penalize opportunities missed nor reward risks taken, the results are predictable.

HOW LARGE INNOVATIVE COMPANIES DO IT

Yet some big companies are continuously innovative. Although each such enterprise is distinctive, the successful big innovators I studied have developed techniques that emulate or improve on their smaller counterparts' practices. What are the most important patterns?

Atmosphere and Vision

Continuous innovation occurs largely because top executives appreciate innovation and manage their company's value system and atmosphere to support it. For example, Sony's founder, Masaru Ibuka, stated in the company's "Purposes of Incorporation" the goal of a "free, dynamic, and pleasant factory . . . where sincerely motivated personnel can exercise their technological skills to the highest level." Ibuka and Sony's chairman, Akio Morita, inculcated the "Sony spirit" through a series of unusual policies: hiring brilliant people with nontraditional skills (like an opera singer) for high management positions, promoting young people over their elders, designing a new type of living accommodation for workers, and providing visible awards for outstanding technical achievements.

Because familiarity can foster understanding and psychological comfort, engineering and scientific leaders are often those who create atmospheres supportive of innovation, especially in a company's early life. Executive vision is more important than a particular management background—as IBM, Genentech, AT&T, Merck, Elf Aquitaine, Pilkington, and others in my sample illustrate. CEOs of these companies value technology and include technical experts in their highest decisions circles.

Innovative managements—whether technical or not—project clear long-term visions for their organizations that go beyond simple economic measures. . . . Genentech's original plan expresses [such a] vision: "We expect to be the first company to commercialize the [rDNA] technology, and we plan to build a major profitable corporation by manufacturing and marketing needed products that benefit mankind. The future uses of genetic engineering are far reaching and many. Any product produced by a living organism is eventually within the company's reach."

Such visions, vigorously supported, are not "management fluff," but have many practical implications.[3] They attract quality people to the company and give focus to their creative and entrepreneurial drives. When combined with sound internal operations, they help channel growth by concentrating attention on the actions that lead to profitability, rather than on profitability itself. Finally, these visions recognize a realistic time frame for innovation and attract the kind of investors who will support it.

Orientation to the Market

Innovative companies tie their visions to the practical realities of the marketplace. Although each

company uses techniques adapted to its own style and strategy, two elements are always present: a strong market orientation at the very top of the company and mechanisms to ensure interactions between technical and marketing people at lower levels. At Sony, for example, soon after technical people are hired, the company runs them through weeks of retail selling. Sony engineers become sensitive to the ways retail sales practices, product displays, and nonquantifiable customer preferences affect success. . . .

From top to bench levels in my sample's most innovative companies, managers focus primarily on seeking to anticipate and solve customers' emerging problems.

Small, Flat Organizations

The most innovative large companies in my sample try to keep the total organization flat and project teams small. Development teams normally include only six or seven key people. This number seems to constitute a critical mass of skills while fostering maximum communication and commitment among members. According to research done by my colleague, Victor McGee, the number of channels of communication increases as $n[2^{n-1} - 1]$. Therefore:

For team size =	1	2	3	4	5	6
Channels =	1	2	9	28	75	186

7	8	9	10	11
441	1016	2295	5110	11253

Innovative companies also try to keep their operating divisions and total technical units small—below 400 people. Up to this number, only two layers of management are required to maintain a span of control over 7 people. In units much larger than 400, people quickly lose touch with the concept of their product or process, staffs and bureaucracies tend to grow, and projects may go through too many formal screens to survive.

---

[3]   *Thomas J. Allen (1977) illustrates the enormous leverage provided such technology accessors (called "gatekeepers") in R&D organizations.*

Since it takes a chain of yesses and only one no to kill a project, jeopardy multiplies as management layers increase.

Multiple Approaches

At first one cannot be sure which of several technical approaches will dominate a field. The history of technology is replete with accidents, mishaps, and chance meetings that allowed one approach or group to emerge rapidly over others. Leo Baekelund was looking for a synthetic shellac when he found Bakelite and started the modern plastics industry. At Syntex, researchers were not looking for an oral contraceptive when they created 19-norprogesterone, the precursor to the active ingredient in half of all contraceptive pills. And the microcomputer was born because Intel's Ted Hoff "happened" to work on a complex calculator just when Digital Equipment Corporation's PDP8 architecture was fresh in his mind.

Such "accidents" are involved in almost all major technological advances. When theory can predict everything, a company has moved to a new stage, from development to production. Murphy's law works because engineers design for what they can foresee; hence what fails is what theory could not predict. And it is rare that the interactions of components and subsystems can be predicted over the lifetime of operations. For example, despite careful theoretical design work, the first high performance jet engine literally tore itself to pieces on its test stand, while others failed in unanticipated operating conditions (like an Iranian sandstorm).

Recognizing the inadequacies of theory, innovative enterprises seem to move faster from paper studies to physical testing than do noninnovative enterprises. When possible, they encourage several prototype programs to proceed in parallel. . . . Such redundancy helps the company cope with uncertainties in development, motivates people through competition, and improves the amount and quality of information available for making final choices on scale-ups or introductions.

Developmental Shoot-outs

Many companies structure shoot-outs among competing approaches only after they reach the prototype stages. They find this practice provides more objective information for making decisions, decreases risk by making choices that best reflect marketplace needs, and helps ensure that the winning option will move ahead with a committed team behind it. Although many managers worry that competing approaches may be inefficient, greater effectiveness in choosing the right solution easily outweighs duplication costs when the market rewards higher performance or when large volumes justify increased sophistication. Under these conditions, parallel development may prove less costly because it both improves the probability of success and reduces development time.

Perhaps the most difficult problem in managing competing projects lies in reintegrating the members of the losing team. If the company is expanding rapidly or if the successful project creates a growth opportunity, losing team members can work on another interesting program or sign on with the winning team as the project moves toward the marketplace. For the shoot-out system to work continuously, however, executives must create a climate that honors high-quality performance whether a project wins or loses, reinvolves people quickly in their technical specialities or in other projects, and accepts and expects rotation among tasks and groups. . . .

Skunkworks

Every highly innovative enterprise in my research sample emulated small company practices by using groups that functioned in a skunkworks style. Small teams of engineers, technicians, designers, and model makers were placed together with no intervening organizational or physical barriers to developing a new product from idea to commercial prototype stages. In innovative Japanese companies, top managers often worked hand-in-hand on projects with young engineers. Surprisingly, *ringi* decision making was not evident in these situations. Soichiro Honda was known for working directly on technical problems and emphasizing his technical points by shouting at his engineers or occasionally even hitting them with wrenches!

The skunkworks approach eliminates bureaucracies, allows fast, unfettered communications, permits rapid turnaround times for experiments, and instills a high level of group identity and loyalty. Interestingly, few successful groups in my research were structured in the classic "venture group" form, with a careful balancing of engineering, production, and marketing talents. Instead they acted on an old truism: introducing a new product or process to the world is like raising a healthy child—it needs a mother (champion) who loves it, a father (authority figure with resources) to support it, and pediatricians (specialists) to get it through difficult times. It may survive solely in the hands of specialists, but its chances of success are remote.

Interactive Learning

Skunkworks are as close as most big companies can come to emulating the highly interactive and motivating learning environment that characterizes successful small ventures. But the best big innovators have gone even farther. Recognizing that the random, chaotic nature of technological change cuts across organizational and even institutional lines, these companies tap into multiple outside sources of technology as well as their customers' capabilities. Enormous external leverages are possible. No company can spend more than a small share of the world's $200 billion devoted to R&D. But like small entrepreneurs, big companies can have much of that total effort cheaply if they try.

In industries such as electronics, customers provide much of the innovation on new products. In other industries, such as textiles, materials or equipment suppliers provide the innovation. In still others, such as biotechnology, universities are dominant, while foreign sources strongly supplement industries such as controlled fusion. Many R&D units have strategies to develop information for trading with outside groups and have

teams to cultivate these sources. Large Japanese companies have been notably effective at this. So have U.S. companies as diverse as Du Pont, AT&T, Apple Computer, and Genentech.

An increasing variety of creative relationships exist in which big companies participate— as joint venturers, consortium members, limited partners, guarantors of first markets, major academic funding sources, venture capitalists, spin-off equity holders, and so on. These rival the variety of inventive financing and networking structures that individual entrepreneurs have created.

Indeed, the innovative practices of small and large companies look ever more alike. This resemblance is especially striking in the interactions between companies and customers during development. Many experienced big companies are relying less on early market research and more on interactive development with lead customers. Hewlett-Packard, 3M, Sony, and Raychem frequently introduce radically new products through small teams that work closely with lead customers. These teams learn from their customers' needs and innovations, and rapidly modify designs and entry strategies based on this information.

Formal market analyses continue to be useful for extending product lines, but they are often misleading when applied to radical innovations. Market studies predicted that Haloid would never sell more than 5,000 xerographic machines, that Intel's microprocessor would never sell more than 10% as many units as there were minicomputers, and that Sony's transistor radios and miniature television sets would fail in the marketplace. At the same time, many eventual failures such as Ford's Edsel, IBM's FS system, and the supersonic transport were studied and planned exhaustively on paper, but lost contact with customers' real needs.

A STRATEGY FOR INNOVATION

The flexible management practices needed for major innovations often pose problems for established cultures in big companies. Yet there are reasonable steps managers in these companies can take. Innovation can be bred in a surprising variety of organizations, as many examples show. What are its key elements?

An Opportunity Orientation

In the 1981–1983 recession, many large companies cut back or closed plants as their "only available solution." Yet I repeatedly found that top managers in these companies took these actions without determining firsthand why their customers were buying from competitors, discerning what niches in their markets were growing, or tapping the innovations their own people had to solve problems. These managers foreclosed innumerable options by defining the issue as cost cutting rather than opportunity seeking. As one frustrated division manager in a manufacturing conglomerate put it: "If management doesn't actively seek or welcome technical opportunities, it sure won't hear about them."

By contrast, Intel met the challenge of the last recession with its "20% solution." The professional staff agreed to work one extra day a week to bring innovations to the marketplace earlier than planned. Despite the difficult times, Intel came out of the recession with several important new products ready to go—and it avoided layoffs.

Entrepreneurial companies recognize that they have almost unlimited access to capital and they structure their practices accordingly. They let it be known that if their people come up with good ideas, they can find the necessary capital—just as private venture capitalists or investment bankers find resources for small entrepreneurs.

Structuring for Innovation

Managers need to think carefully about how innovation fits into their strategy and structure, their technology, skills, resources, and organizational commitments accordingly. A few examples suggest the variety of strategies and alignments possible:

> Hewlett-Packard and 3M develop product lines around a series of small, discrete, freestanding products. These companies form units that look like entrepreneurial start-ups. Each has a small team, led by a champion, in low-cost facilities. These companies allow many different proposals to come forward and test them as early as possible in the marketplace. They design control systems to spot significant losses on any single entry quickly. They look for high gains on a few winners and blend less successful, smaller entries into prosperous product lines.

> Other companies (like AT&T or the oil majors) have had to make large system investments to last for decades. These companies tend to make longterm needs forecasts. They often start several programs in parallel to be sure of selecting the right technologies. They then extensively test new technologies in use before making systemwide commitments. Often they sacrifice speed of entry for long-term low cost and reliability.

> Intel and Dewey & Almy, suppliers of highly technical specialties to EOMs, develop strong technical sales networks to discover and understand customer needs in depth. These companies try to have technical solutions designed into customers' products. Such companies have flexible applied technology groups working close to the marketplace. They also have quickly expandable plant facilities and a cutting edge technology (not necessarily basic research) group that allows rapid selection of currently available technologies.

> Dominant producers like IBM or Matsushita are often not the first to introduce new technologies. They do not want to disturb their successful product lines any sooner than necessary. As market demands become clear, these companies establish precise price-performance windows and form overlapping project teams to come up with the best answer for the marketplace. To decrease market risks, they use product shoot-outs as close to the market as possible. They develop extreme depth in production technologies to keep unit costs low from the outset. Finally, depending on the scale of the market entry, they have project teams report as close to the top as necessary to secure needed management attention and resources.

> Merck and Hoffman-LaRoche, basic research companies, maintain laboratories with better facilities, higher pay, and more freedom than most universities can afford. These companies leverage their internal spending through research grants, clinical grants, and research relationships with universities throughout the world. Before

they invest $20 million to $50 million to clear a new drug, they must have reasonable assurance that they will be first in the marketplace. They take elaborate precautions to ensure that the new entry is safe and effective, and that it cannot be easily duplicated by others. Their structures are designed to be on the cutting edge of science, but conservative in animal testing, clinical evaluation, and production control.

These examples suggest some ways of linking innovation to strategy. Many other examples, of course, exist. Within a single company, individual divisions may have different strategic needs and hence different structures and practices. No single approach works well for all situations.

Complex Portfolio Planning

Perhaps the most difficult task for top managers is to balance the needs of existing lines against the needs of potential lines. This problem requires a portfolio strategy much more complex than the popular four-box Boston Consulting Group matrix found in most strategy texts. To allocate resources for innovation strategically, managers need to define the broad, long-term actions within and across divisions necessary to achieve their visions. They should determine which positions to hold at all costs, where to fall back, and where to expand initially and in the more distant future.

A company's strategy may often require investing most resources in current lines. But sufficient resources should also be invested in patterns that ensure intermediate and long-term growth; provide defenses against possible government, labor, competitive, or activist challenges; and generate needed organizational, technical, and external relations flexibilities to handle unforeseen opportunities or threats. Sophisticated portfolio planning within and among divisions can protect both current returns and future prospects—the two critical bases for that most cherished goal, high price-earnings ratios.

AN INCREMENTALIST APPROACH

Such managerial techniques can provide a strategic focus for innovation and help solve many of the timing, coordination, and motivation problems that plague large, bureaucratic organizations. Even more detailed planning techniques may help in guiding the development of the many small innovations that characterize any successful business. My research reveals, however, that few, if any, major innovations result from highly structured planning systems. [Why?]. . .

The innovative process is inherently incremental. As Thomas Hughes says, ''Technological systems evolve through relatively small steps marked by an occasional stubborn obstacle and by constant random breakthroughs interacting across laboratories and borders'' (Hughes, 1984:83). A forgotten hypothesis of Einstein's became the laser in Charles Townes's mind as he contemplated azaleas in Franklin Square. The structure of DNA followed a circuitous route through research in biology, organic chemistry, X-ray crystallography, and mathematics toward its Nobel Prize-winning conception as a spiral staircase of [base pairs]. Such rambling trails are characteristic of virtually all major technological advances.

At the outset of the attack on a technical problem, an innovator often does not know whether his problem is tractable, what approach will prove best, and what concrete characteristics the solution will have if achieved. The logical route, therefore, is to follow several paths—though perhaps with varying degrees of intensity—until more information becomes available. Not knowing precisely where the solution will occur, wise managers establish the widest feasible network for finding and assessing alternative solutions. They keep many options open until one of them seems sure to win. Then they back it heavily.

Managing innovation is like a stud poker game, where one can play several hands. A player has some idea of the likely size of the pot at the beginning, knows the general but not the sure route to winning, buys one card (a project) at a time to gain information about probabilities and the size of the pot, closes hands as they become discouraging, and risks more only late in the hand as knowledge increases. . . .

Chaos Within Guidelines

Effective managers of innovation channel and control its main directions. Like venture capitalists, they administer primarily by setting goals, selecting key people, and establishing a few critical limits and decision points for intervention rather than by implementing elaborate planning or control systems. As technology leads or market needs emerge, these managers set a few—most crucial—performance targets and limits. They allow their technical units to decide how to achieve these, subject to defined constraints and reviews at critical junctures.

Early bench-scale project managers may pursue various options, making little attempt at first to integrate each into a total program. Only after key variables are understood—and perhaps measured and demonstrated in lab models—can more precise planning be meaningful. Even then, many factors may remain unknown; chaos and competition can continue to thrive in the pursuit of the solution. At defined review points, however, only those options that can clear performance milestones may continue. . . .

Even after selecting the approaches to emphasize, innovative managers tend to continue a few others as smaller scale "side bets" or options. In a surprising number of cases, these alternatives prove winners when the planned option fails.

Recognizing the many demands entailed by successful programs, innovative companies find special ways to reward innovators. Sony gives "a small but significant" percentage of a new product's sales to its innovating teams. Pilking-ton, IBM, and 3M's top executives are often chosen from those who have headed successful new product entries. Intel lets its Magnetic Memory Group operate like a small company, with special performance rewards and simulated stock options. GE, Syntex, and United Technologies help internal innovators establish new companies and take equity positions in "nonrelated" product innovations.

Large companies do not have to make their innovators millionaires, but rewards should be visible and significant. Fortunately, most engineers are happy with the incentives that Tracy Kidder (1981) calls "playing pinball"—giving widespread recognition to a job well done and the right to play in the next exciting game. Most innovative companies provide both. . . .

MATCH MANAGEMENT TO THE PROCESS

. . . Executives need to understand and accept the tumultuous realities of innovation, learn from the experiences of other companies, and adapt the most relevant features of these others to their own management practices and cultures. Many features of small company innovators are also applicable in big companies. With top-level understanding, vision, a commitment to customers and solutions, a genuine portfolio strategy, a flexible entrepreneurial atmosphere, and proper incentives for innovative champions, many more large companies can innovate to meet the severe demands of global competition.

FOURTEEN

THE PROFESSIONAL CONTEXT

In this chapter we continue to look at organizations that depend primarily on experts to get their work done. Here, although the work is complex (thus requiring experts), it is not dynamic, but is rather stable in nature and slow to change. Accounting and law firms provide excellent examples as do the universities where too often professors lecture from age old notes. Hospitals, too, can reflect these characteristics to a certain extent, since much of what they do has to be tried and true.

The first reading describes a structure that seems well suited to these settings. It is called the "Professional Bureaucracy," and is the last of the configurations described by Mintzberg in *Structure in Fives*. The second reading, by a team of researchers from various Montreal universities, sets forth what strategy means in such a context and how it seems to be made in one typical example of professional bureaucracy, the university setting. Again the process is radically different from conventional business or military notions about how strategies are supposed to be made. Strategies here tend to be more stable than in adhocracies—the article in fact argues that they are remarkably stable. Many of them grow up in the bowels of the organization in response to the professional cultures from which the experts receive their psychic rewards. Strategic processes are often far from being directly controllable by

the senior managers or administrators, and frequently emerge with little relationship to the techniques of formal planning.

This reading helps reinforce the concept of strategy as an emergent pattern of action and commitments. It also provides a clear sense of the dangers of trying to manage strategy making in expert organizations centrally and deliberately. As our society increasingly moves toward a sophisticated "services economy," such professional bureaucracies will increasingly pose strategy challenges to managers and consultants. The Davidson Hospital case offers an opportunity to probe some of the relevant issues in more depth.

THE PROFESSIONAL BUREAUCRACY*

by Henry Mintzberg

. . . Organizations can be bureaucratic without being centralized. Their operating work is stable, leading to "predetermined or predictable, in effect, standardized" behavior. . . . But it is also

* Excerpted from Henry Mintzberg, *Structure in Fives: Designing Effective Organizations* (Prentice-Hall, 1983), chap. 10; used by permission of the publisher.

complex, and so must be controlled directly by the operators who do it. Hence, the organization turns to the one coordinating mechanism that allows for standardization and decentralization at the same time—namely, the standardization of skills. This gives rise to a structural configuration sometimes called *Professional Bureaucracy*, common in universities, general hospitals, school systems, public accounting firms, social-work agencies, and craft production firms. All rely on the skills and knowledge of their operating professionals to function; all produce standard products or services.

THE BASIC STRUCTURE

The Work of the Operating Core

Here again we have a tightly knit configuration of the design parameters. Most important, the Professional Bureaucracy relies for coordination on the standardization of skills and its associated design parameter, training and indoctrination. It hires duly trained and indoctrinated specialists—professionals—for the operating core, and then gives them considerable control over their own work. In effect, the work is highly specialized in the horizontal dimension, but enlarged in the vertical one.

Control over his own work means that the professional works relatively independently of his colleagues, but closely with the clients he serves . . . many doctors treat their own patients, and accountants maintain personal contact with the companies whose books they audit. Most of the necessary coordination between the operating professionals is then handled by the standardization of skills and knowledge—in effect, by what they have learned to expect from their colleagues. During an operation as long and as complex as open-heart surgery, "very little needs to be said [between the anesthesiologist and the surgeon] preceding chest opening and during the procedure on the heart itself: lines, beats and lights on equipment are indicative of what everyone is expected to do and does—operations are performed in abso-

lute silence, particularly following the chest-opening phase" (Gosselin, 1978). The point is perhaps best made in reverse, by the cartoon that shows six surgeons standing around a patient on an operating table with one saying, "Who opens?" Similarly, the policy and marketing courses of the management school may be integrated without the two professors involved having even met. As long as the courses are standard, each knows more or less what the other teaches.

Just how standardized complex professional work can be is illustrated in a paper read by Spencer (1976) before a meeting of the International Cardiovascular Society. Spencer noted that "becoming a skillful clinical surgeon requires a long period of training, probably five or more years" (p. 1178). An important feature of that training is "repetitive practice" to evoke "an automatic reflex" (p. 1179). So automatic, in fact, that Spencer keeps his series of surgical "cookbooks," in which he lists, even for "complex" operations, the essential steps as chains of thirty to forty symbols on a single sheet, to "be reviewed mentally in sixty to 120 seconds at some time during the day preceding the operation" (p. 1182). But no matter how standardized the knowledge and skills, their complexity ensures that considerable discretion remains in their application. No two professionals—no two surgeons or teachers or social workers—ever apply them in exactly the same way. Many judgments are required.

Training and indoctrination are a complicated affair in the Professional Bureaucracy. The initial training typically takes place over a period of years in a university or special institution. Here the skills and knowledge of the profession are formally programmed into the would-be professional. But in many cases, that is only the first step, even if the most important one. There typically follows a long period of on-the-job training, such as internship in medicine and articling in accounting. Here the formal knowledge is applied and the practice of skills perfected, under the close supervision of members of the profession. On-the-job training also completes the process of indoctrination, which began during the formal teaching. Once this process is completed, the professional association typically examines the trainee to determine whether he has the requisite knowledge, skills, and norms to enter the profession. . . . The entrance examination only tests the basic requirements at one point in time; the process of training continues. As new knowledge is generated and new skills develop, the professional upgrades his expertise. He reads the journals, attends the conferences, and perhaps also returns periodically for formal retraining.

The Bureaucratic Nature of the Structure

All this training is geared to one goal—the internalization of standards that serve the client and coordinate the professional work. In other words, the structure of these organizations is essentially bureaucratic, its coordination—like that of the Machine Bureaucracy—achieved by design, by standards that predetermine what is to be done. . . . But the two kinds of bureaucracies differ markedly in the source of their standardization. Whereas the Machine Bureaucracy generates its own standards—its technostructure designing the work standards for its operators and its line managers enforcing them—the standards of the Professional Bureaucracy originate largely outside its own structure, in the self-governing associations its operators join with their colleagues from other Professional Bureaucracies. These associations set universal standards, which they make sure are taught by the universities and used by all the bureaucracies of the profession. So whereas the Machine Bureaucracy relies on authority of a hierarchical nature—the power of office—the Professional Bureaucracy emphasizes authority of a professional nature—the power of expertise.

The other forms of standardization are, in fact, difficult to rely on in the Professional Bureaucracy. The work processes themselves are too complex to be standardized directly by analysts. One need only try to imagine a work-study analyst following a cardiologist on his rounds or observing a teacher in a classroom in order to program

the work. Similarly, the outputs of professional work cannot easily be measured and so do not lend themselves to standardization. Imagine a planner trying to define a cure in psychiatry, the amount of learning that takes place in the classroom, or the quality of an accountant's audit. Thus, Professional Bureaucracies cannot rely extensively on the formalization of professional work or on systems to plan and control it.

Much the same conclusion can be drawn for the two remaining coordinating mechanisms. Both direct supervision and mutual adjustment impede the professional's close relationships with his clients. That relationship is predicated on a high degree of professional autonomy—freedom from having not only to respond to managerial orders but also to consult extensively with peers. In any event, the use of the other four coordinating mechanisms is precluded by the capacity of the standardization of skills to achieve a good deal of the coordination necessary in the operating core.

The Pigeonholing Process

To understand how the Professional Bureaucracy functions in its operating core, it is helpful to think of it as a repertoire of standard programs—in effect, the set of skills the professionals stand ready to use—that are applied to predetermined situations, called contingencies, also standardized. As Weick (1976) notes of one case in point, "schools are in the business of building and maintaining categories" (p. 8). The process is sometimes known as *pigeonholing*. In this regard, the professional has two basic tasks: (1) to categorize the client's need in terms of a contingency, which indicates which standard program to use, a task known as diagnosis; and (2) to apply, or execute, that program. Pigeonholing simplifies matters enormously. "People are categorized and placed into pigeonholes because it would take enormous resources to treat every case as unique and requiring thorough analysis (Perrow, 1970:58). . . . [For example] the management consultant carries his own bag of standard acronymical tricks—

MBO, MIS, LRP, PERT, OD. The client with project work gets PERT; the one with managerial conflicts, OD. Of course, clients often help out by categorizing themselves . . . the student who wants to become a manager registers in the university's business school. . . .

It is this pigeonholing process that enables the Professional Bureaucracy to decouple its various operating tasks and assign them to individual, relatively autonomous professionals. Each can, instead of giving a great deal of attention to coordinating his work with his peers, focus on perfecting his skills. This is not to say that all uncertainty can be removed from the performance of the work, but only that attempts are made to contain whatever uncertainty does remain in the jobs of single professionals. Focusing the uncertainty in this way is one of the reasons the professional requires considerable discretion in his work.

In the pigeonholing process, we see fundamental differences among the Machine Bureaucracy, the Professional Bureaucracy, and the Adhocracy. The Machine Bureaucracy is a single-purpose structure; presented with a stimulus, it executes its one standard sequence of programs, just as we kick when tapped on the knee. No diagnosis is involved. In the Professional Bureaucracy, diagnosis is a fundamental task, but it is circumscribed. The organization seeks to match a predetermined contingency to a standard program. Fully open-ended diagnosis—that which seeks a creative solution to a unique problem—requires . . . Adhocracy. No standard contingencies or programs exist in that configuration.

It is an interesting characteristic of the Professional Bureaucracy that its pigeonholing process creates an equivalence in its structure between the functional and market bases for grouping. Because clients are categorized, or categorize themselves, in terms of the functional specialists who serve them, the structure of the Professional Bureaucracy becomes at the same time both a functional and a market-based one. . . . A hospital gynecology department . . . can be called functional because [it] groups specialists according to the knowledge, skills, and work processes they use, or market-based because [it] deals with its own unique types of clients [namely] women. . . .

Focus on the Operating Core

All the design parameters that we have discussed so far—the emphasis on the training of operators, their vertically enlarged jobs, the little use made of behavior formalization or planning and control systems—suggest that the operating core is the key part of the Professional Bureaucracy. The only other part that is fully elaborated is the support staff, but that is focused very much on serving the operating core. Given the high cost of the professionals, it makes sense to back them up with as much support as possible, to aid them and have others do whatever routine work can be formalized. Thus, universities have printing facilities, faculty clubs, alma mater funds, publishing houses, archives, athletics departments, libraries, computer facilities, and many, many other support units.

The technostructure and middle line of management are not highly elaborated in the Professional Bureaucracy. In other configurations (except Adhocracy), they coordinate the work of the operating core. But in the Professional Bureaucracy, they can do little to coordinate the operating work. Because the need for planning and the formalizing of the work of the professionals are very limited, there is little call for a technostructure (except, as we shall see, in the case of the nonprofessional support staff). . . . Likewise, the middle line in the Professional Bureaucracy is thin. With little need for direct supervision of the operators or mutual adjustment between them, the operating units can be very large, with few managers at the level of first-line supervisor, or, for that matter, above them. . . . The McGill Faculty of Management at the time of this writing functions effectively with sixty professors and a single manager, its dean.

Thus, Figure 1 shows the Professional Bureaucracy, in terms of our logo, as a flat structure with a thin middle line, a tiny technostructure,

FIGURE 1   THE PROFESSIONAL BUREAUCRACY

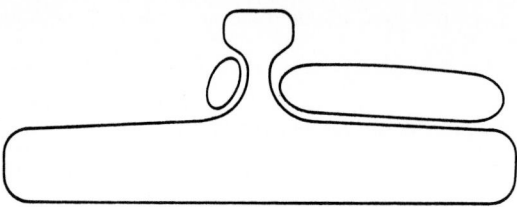

and a fully elaborated support staff. All these characteristics are reflected in the organigram of McGill University, shown in Figure 2.

Decentralization in the Professional Bureaucracy

Everything we have seen so far tells us that the Professional Bureaucracy is a highly decentralized structure, in both the vertical and horizontal dimensions. A great deal of the power over the operating work rests at the bottom of the structure, with the professionals of the operating core. Often, each works with his own clients, subject only to the collective control of his colleagues, who trained and indoctrinated him in the first place and thereafter reserve the right to censure him for malpractice.

The Administrative Structure

What we have seen suggests that the Professional Bureaucracy is a highly democratic structure, at least for the professionals of the operating core. In fact, not only do the professionals control their own work, but they also seek collective control of the administrative decisions that affect them— decisions, for example, to hire colleagues, to promote them, and to distribute resources. Controlling these decisions requires control of the middle line of the organization, which professionals do by ensuring that it is staffed with ''their own.'' Some of the administrative work the operating professionals do themselves. Every university professor, for example, serves on committees of one kind or another to ensure that he retains some control over the decisions that affect his work.

Moreover, full-time administrators who wish to have any power at all in these structures must be certified members of the profession and preferably be elected by the professional operators, or at least appointed with their blessing. What emerges, therefore, is a rather democratic administrative structure.

This administrative structure itself relies largely on mutual adjustment for coordination. Thus, the liaison devices, although uncommon in the operating core, are important design parameters in the middle line. Task forces and especially standing committees abound, as indicated in Figure 2; a number of positions are designated to integrate the administrative efforts, as in the case of the ward manager in the hospital; and some Professional Bureaucracies even use matrix structure in administration.

Because of the power of their operators, Professional Bureaucracies are sometimes called ''collegial'' organizations. In fact, some professionals like to describe them as inverse pyramids, with the professional operators at the top and the administrators down below to serve them— to ensure that the surgical facilities are kept clean and the classrooms well supplied with chalk. Such a description underestimates the power of the *professional* administrator—a point we shall return to shortly—but it seems to be an accurate description of the nonprofessional one—namely, the administrator who manages the support units. For the support staff—often much larger than the professional one, but charged largely with doing nonprofessional work—there is no democracy in the Professional Bureaucracy, only the oligarchy of the professionals. Support units, such as housekeeping or kitchen in the hospital or printing in the university, are as likely as not to be managed tightly from the top. They exist, in effect, as machine bureaucratic constellations within the Professional Bureaucracy.

What frequently emerge in the Professional Bureaucracy are parallel [and separate] administrative hierarchies, one democratic and bottom-up for the professionals, and a second machine bureaucratic and top-down for the support staff . . . as shown in Figure 3.

FIGURE 2   ORGANIGRAM OF McGILL UNIVERSITY (CIRCA 1978)

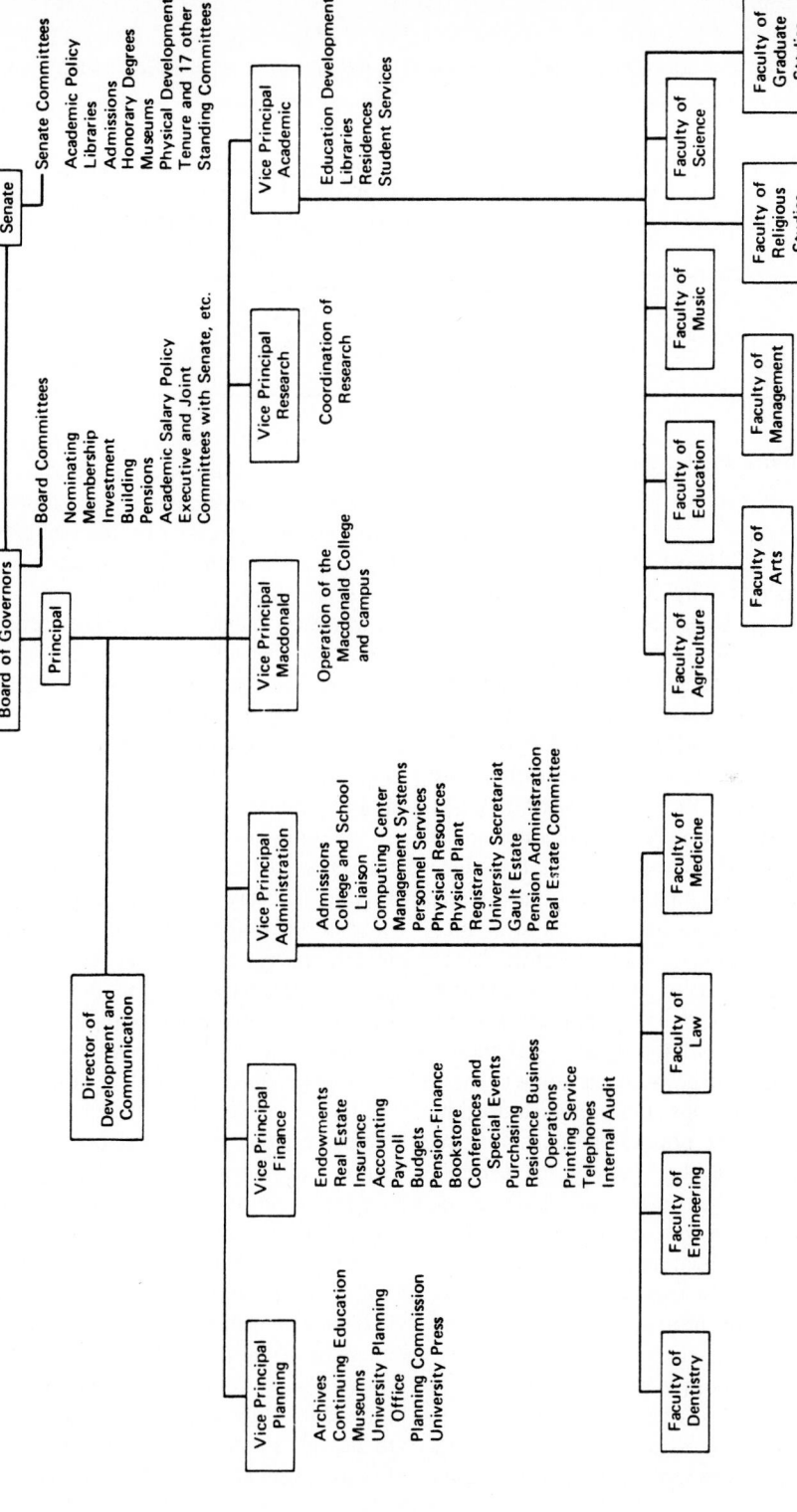

Note: This unofficial organigram was drawn by the author based upon University documents.

FIGURE 3   PARALLEL HIERARCHIES IN THE PROFESSIONAL BUREAUCRACY

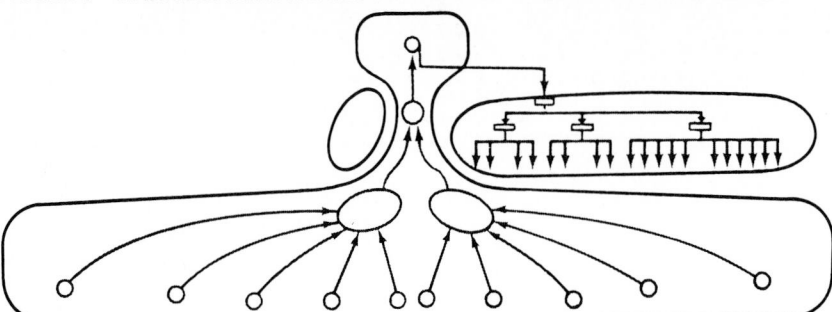

The Roles of the Professional Administrator

Where does all this leave the administrators of the professional hierarchy, the executive directors and chiefs of the hospitals and the presidents and deans of the universities? Are they powerless? Compared with their peers in the Simple Structure and the Machine Bureaucracy, they certainly lack a good deal of power. But that is far from the whole story. The professional administrator may not be able to control the professionals directly, but he does perform a series of roles that gives him considerable indirect power in the structure.

First, the professional administrator spends much time handling disturbances in the structure. The pigeonholing process is an imperfect one at best, leading to all kinds of jurisdictional disputes between the professionals. Who should teach the statistics course in the MBA program—the mathematics department or the business school? . . . Seldom, however, can a senior administrator impose a solution on the professionals or units involved in a dispute. Rather, the unit managers—chiefs, deans, or whoever—must sit down together and negotiate a solution on behalf of their constituencies. Coordination problems also arise frequently between the two parallel hierarchies, and it often falls to the professional administrators to resolve them.

Second, the professional administrators—especially those at higher levels—serve key roles at the boundary of the organization, between the professionals inside and interested parties—governments, client associations, and so on—on the outside. On the one hand, the administrators are expected to protect the professionals' autonomy, to "buffer" them from external pressures. On the other hand, the administrators are expected to woo these outsiders to support the organization, both morally and financially. Thus, the external roles of the manager—maintaining liaison contacts, acting as figurehead and spokesman in a public relations capacity, negotiating with outside agencies—emerge as primary ones in professional administration.

Some view the roles professional administrators are called upon to perform as signs of weakness. They see these people as the errand boys of the professionals, or else as pawns caught in various tugs of war—between one professional and another, between support staffer and professional, between outsider and professional. In fact, however, these roles are the very sources of administrator power. Power is, after all, gained at the locus of uncertainty. And that is exactly where the professional administrators sit. The administrator who succeeds in raising extra funds for his organization gains a say in how these are distributed. Similarly, the one who can reconcile conflicts in favor of his unit or who can effectively buffer the professionals from external influence becomes a valued—and therefore powerful—member of the organization. . . .

We can conclude that power in these structures does flow to those professionals who care to devote effort to doing administrative instead of professional work, especially to those who do it well. But that, it should be stressed, is not laissez-faire power: the professional administrator keeps his power only as long as the professionals perceive him to be serving their interests effectively. . . .

CONDITIONS OF THE PROFESSIONAL BUREAUCRACY

This third configuration appears wherever the operating core of an organization is dominated by skilled workers—professionals—who use procedures that are difficult to learn, yet are well defined. This means an environment that is both complex and stable—complex enough to require the use of difficult procedures that can be learned only in extensive formal training programs, yet stable enough to enable these skills to become well defined—in effect, standardized. Thus, the environment is the chief situational factor in the use of the Professional Bureaucracy. . . .

Technical system is an important situational factor only for what it is not in the Professional Bureaucracy—neither highly regulating, sophisticated, nor automated. The professional operators of this configuration require considerable discretion in their work. It is they who serve the clients, usually directly and personally. So the technical system cannot be highly regulating, certainly not highly automated. The professional resists the rationalization of his skills—their division into simply executed steps—because that makes them programmable by the technostructure, destroys his basis of autonomy, and drives the structure to the machine bureaucratic form.

Nor can the technical system be sophisticated. The surgeon uses a scalpel, the accountant a pencil. Both must be sharp, but they are otherwise simple and commonplace instruments. Yet both allow their users to perform independently what can be exceedingly complex functions. More sophisticated instruments—such as the computer in the accounting firm or the coronary-care unit in the hospital—reduce the professional's autonomy by forcing him to work in multidisciplinary teams, as he does in the Adhocracy. . . .

Thus, the prime example of the Professional Bureaucracy is the *personal-service organization*, at least the one with complex, stable work. Schools and universities, consulting firms, law and accounting offices, and social-work agencies all rely on this configuration as long as they concentrate not on innovating in the solution of new problems, but on applying standard programs to well-defined problems. The same is true of hospitals, at least to the extent that their technical systems are simple. (In those areas that call for more sophisticated equipment—apparently a growing number, especially in teaching institutions—the hospital is driven toward a hybrid structure, with characteristics of the Adhocracy. But this tendency is mitigated by the hospital's overriding concern with safety. Only the tried and true can be used on regular patients. Institutions entrusted with the lives of their clients have a natural aversion to the looser, organic structures such as Adhocracy.) A good deal of the service sector of contemporary society, in fact, applies standard programs to well-defined problems. Hence, the Professional Bureaucracy tends to predominate there. . . .

So far, all our examples have come from the service sector. But Professional Bureaucracies can be found in manufacturing, too, notably where the environment demands work that is complex yet stable, and the technical system is neither regulating nor sophisticated. This is the case of the *craft enterprise*, an important variant of the Professional Bureaucracy. Here the organization relies on skilled craftsmen who use relatively simple instruments to produce standard outputs. The very term *craftsman* implies a kind of professional who learns traditional skills through long apprentice training and then is allowed to practice them free of direct supervision. Craft enterprises seem typically to have tiny administrations—no technostructures and few managers, many of whom, in any event, work alongside the craftsmen.

The Professional Bureaucracy is also occasionally found as a hybrid structure. . . . Consider, for example, the symphony orchestra, an organization staffed with highly skilled musicians who play standard repertoires. Some people have described it as a dictatorship of the conductor. In any event, there is no denying its need for strong leadership, based on direct supervision. [The result is a hybrid of Professional Bureaucracy and Simple Structure.]

SOME ISSUES ASSOCIATED WITH PROFESSIONAL BUREAUCRACY

The Professional Bureaucracy is unique among the five configurations in answering two of the paramount needs of contemporary men and women. It is democratic, disseminating its power directly to its workers (at least those who are professional). And it provides them with extensive autonomy, freeing them even of the need to coordinate closely with their peers, and all the pressures and politics that entails. Thus, the professional has the best of both worlds: he is attached to an organization, yet is free to serve his clients in his own way, constrained only by the established standards of his profession.

As a result, professionals tend to emerge as responsible and highly motivated individuals, dedicated to their work and the clients they serve. Unlike the Machine Bureaucracy, which places barriers between the operator and the client, this configuration removes them, allowing a personal relationship to develop. Here the technical and social systems can function in complete harmony.

Moreover, autonomy allows the professionals to perfect their skills, free of interference. They repeat the same complex programs time after time, forever reducing the uncertainty until they get them just about perfect, like the Provençal potter who has spent his career perfecting the glazes he applies to identical pots. . . .

But in these same characteristics of democracy and autonomy lie the major problems of the Professional Bureaucracy. For there is virtually no control of the work aside from that by the profession itself, no way to correct deficiencies that the professionals themselves choose to overlook. What they tend to overlook are the major problems of coordination, of discretion, and of innovation that arise in these configurations.

Problems of Coordination

The Professional Bureaucracy can coordinate effectively in its operating core only by the standardization of skills. . . . But the standardization of skills is a loose coordinating mechanism at best, failing to cope with many of the needs that arise in the Professional Bureaucracy.

There is, first of all, the need for coordination between the professionals and the support staff. To the professional, that is simply resolved: He gives the orders. But that only catches the support staffer between two systems of power pulling in different ways, the vertical power of line authority above him and the horizontal power of professional expertise to his side. Perhaps more severe are the coordination problems among the professionals themselves. Unlike Machine Bureaucracies, Professional Bureaucracies are not integrated entities. They are collections of individuals who come together to draw on common resources and support services but otherwise want to be left alone. As long as the pigeonholing process works effectively, they can be. But that process can never be so good that client needs do not fall in the cracks between the standard programs. . . .

The pigeonholing process, in fact, emerges as the source of a great deal of the conflict of the Professional Bureaucracy. Much political blood is spilled in the continual reassessment of contingencies, imperfectly conceived, in terms of programs, artificially distinguished.

Problems of Discretion

The assumption underlying the design of the Professional Bureaucracy is that the pigeonholing process contains all the uncertainties in single professional jobs. As we saw above, that assumption often proves false, to the detriment of the organization's performance. But even where it works, problems arise. For it focuses all the discretion in the hands of single professionals, whose complex skills, no matter how standardized, require the exercise of considerable judgment. Such discretion is, perhaps, appropriate for professionals who are competent and conscientious. Unfortunately, not all of them are. And the Professional Bureaucracy cannot easily deal with [these] professionals. . . .

[Sometimes] the professional confuses the needs of his clients with the skills he has to offer them. He simply concentrates on the program that he favors to the exclusion of all the others—perhaps because he does it best or simply enjoys it most. This presents no problem as long as only those clients in need of that favorite program are directed his way. But should other clients slip in, trouble ensues. Thus, we have the psychiatrists who think that all patients (indeed, all people) need psychoanalysis, the consulting firms prepared to design the same planning system for all their clients. . . .

Dealing with this means-ends inversion is impeded by the difficulty of measuring the outputs of professional work. When psychiatrists cannot even define the words *cure* or *healthy*, how are they to prove that psychoanalysis is better for manic-depressives than chemical therapy would be? . . . That is one reason that the obvious solution to the problems of discretion—censure by the professional association—is seldom used. Another is that professionals are notoriously reluctant to act against their own. . . .

Discretion not only enables some professionals to ignore the needs of their clients; it also encourages many of them to ignore the needs of the organization. Professionals in these structures do not generally consider themselves part of a team. To many, the organization is almost incidental, a convenient place to practice their skills. They are loyal to their profession, not to the place where they happen to practice it. But the organization has need for loyalty, too—to support its own strategies, to staff its administrative committees, to see it through conflicts with the professional association. Cooperation, as we saw earlier, is crucial to the functioning of the administrative structure. Yet, as we also saw, professionals resist it furiously. . . .

Problems of Innovation

In these structures, major innovation also depends on cooperation. Existing programs can be perfected by individual specialists. But new ones usually cut across existing specialties—in essence, they require a rearrangement of the pigeonholes—and so call for interdisciplinary efforts. As a result, the reluctance of the professionals to work cooperatively with each other translates itself into problems of innovation.

Like the Machine Bureaucracy, the Professional Bureaucracy is an inflexible structure, well suited to producing its standard outputs but ill-suited to adapting to the production of new ones. All bureaucracies are geared to stable environments; they are performance structures designed to perfect programs for contingencies that can be predicted, not problem-solving ones designed to create new programs for needs that have never before been encountered.

The problems of innovation in the Professional Bureaucracy find their roots in convergent thinking, in the deductive reasoning of the professional who sees the specific situation in terms of the general concept. In the Professional Bureaucracy, this means that new problems are forced into old pigeonholes. . . . Nowhere are the effects of this deductive reasoning better illustrated than in Spencer's (1976) comments, "All patients developing significant complications or death among our three hospitals . . . are reported to a central office with a narrative description of the sequence of events, with reports varying in length from a third to an entire page"; six to eight of these cases are discussed in the one-hour weekly "mortality-morbidity" conferences, including presentation of it by the surgeon and "questions and comments" by the audience (p. 1181). An "entire" page and ten minutes of discussion for cases with "significant complications"! Maybe enough to list the symptoms and slot them into pigeonholes; hardly enough even to begin to think about creative solutions. As Lucy once told Charlie Brown, great art cannot be done in half an hour; it takes at least forty-five minutes!

The fact is that great art and innovative problem solving require *inductive* reasoning—that is, the inference of new general concepts or programs from particular experiences. That kind of thinking is *divergent*—it breaks away from old routines or standards rather than perfecting existing ones. And that flies in the face of everything the Professional Bureaucracy is designed to do.

So it should come as no surprise that Professional Bureaucracies and the professional associations that control their procedures tend to be conservative bodies, hesitant to change their well-established ways. Whenever an entrepreneurial member takes up the torch of innovation, great political clashes inevitably ensue. Even in the Machine Bureaucracy, once the managers of the strategic apex finally recognize the need for change, they are able to force it down the hierarchy. In the Professional Bureaucracy, with operator autonomy and bottom-up decision making, and in the professional association with its own democratic procedures, power for strategic change is diffuse. Everybody, not just a few managers or professional representatives, must agree on the change. So change comes slowly and painfully, after much political intrigue and shrewd maneuvering by the professional and administrative entrepreneurs.

As long as the environment remains stable, the Professional Bureaucracy encounters no problem. It continues to perfect its skills and its given system of pigeonholes that slots them. But dynamic conditions call for change—new skills, new ways to slot them, and creative, cooperative efforts on the part of multidisciplinary teams of professionals. And that calls for another configuration, [the Adhocracy].

What responses do the problems of coordination, discretion, and innovation evoke? Most commonly, those outside the profession—clients, non-professional administrators, members of the society at large and their representatives in government—see the problems as resulting from a lack of external control of the professional and of his profession. So they do the obvious: try to control the work with one of the other coordi-

nating mechanisms. Specifically, they try to use direct supervision, standardization of work processes, or standardization of outputs.

Direct supervision typically means imposing an intermediate level of supervision . . . to watch over the professionals. That may work in cases of gross negligence. . . . But specific professional activities—complex in execution and vague in results—are difficult to control by anyone other than the professionals themselves. . . .

Likewise, the other forms of standardization, instead of achieving control of the professional work, often serve merely to impede and discourage the professionals. And for the same reasons—the complexity of the work and the vagueness of its outputs. Complex work processes cannot be formalized by rules and regulations, and vague outputs cannot be standardized by planning and control systems. . . . Technocratic controls do not improve professional-type work, nor can they distinguish between responsible and irresponsible behavior—they constrain both equally. That may, of course, be appropriate for organizations in which responsible behavior is rare. But where it is not . . . technocratic controls only serve to dampen professional conscientiousness.

Controls also upset the delicate relationship between the professional and his client, a relationship predicated on unimpeded personal contact between the two. . . . The controls remove the responsibility for service from the professional and place it in the administrative structure, where it is of no use to the client. It is not the government that teaches the student, not even the school system or the school itself; it is not the hospital that delivers the baby. . . . These things are done by the individual professional. If that professional is incompetent, no plan or rule fashioned in the technostructure, no order from an administrator can ever make him competent. But such plans, rules, and orders can impede the competent professional from providing his service effectively. . . .

Are there then no solutions to a society concerned about its Professional Bureaucracies? Financial control of Professional Bureaucracies and legislation against irresponsible professional behavior are obviously necessary. But beyond that, must the professional be left with a blank check, free of public accountability? Solutions are available, but they grow from a recognition of professional work for what it is. Change in the Professional Bureaucracy does not sweep in from new administrators taking office to announce major reforms, nor from government technostructures intent on bringing the professionals under their control. Rather, change seeps in by the slow process of changing the professionals—changing who can enter the profession, what they learn in its professional schools (norms as well as skills and knowledge), and thereafter how willing they are to upgrade their skills. Where such changes are resisted, society may be best off to call on the professionals' sense of responsibility to serve the public, or, failing that, to bring pressures on the professional associations rather than on the Professional Bureaucracies.

STRATEGY FORMATION
IN THE UNIVERSITY
SETTING*

by Cynthia Hardy,
Ann Langley,
Henry Mintzberg,
and Janet Rose

It is well-known that strategies are formulated before they are implemented, that planning is the central process by which they are so formulated, and that structures should be designed to implement given strategies. At least this is well known to those who have read the conventional literature on strategy making. In the university setting, these imperatives stand almost totally at

*   Originally published in J.L. Bess, ed., *College and University Organization: Insights from the Behavioral Sciences* (New York University Press, 1984) copyright © Association of Higher Education, 1984; reprinted with deletions by permission of the publisher, and copyright holder.

odds with what really happens, leading to the conclusion either that universities "have it all wrong" or that the strategy theoreticians do. . . .

We . . . believe that the conventional view of strategy—as a plan, or a set of explicit intentions preceding and controlling actions—is too narrow to permit a satisfactory understanding of strategy formation in the university setting (as well as many others). An alternate view of strategy focuses not on *a priori* articulation of *intention*, but on the existence of consistency in the actions and/or decisions emerging from an organization. Specifically, we define strategies as *realized* as patterns in streams of decisions or actions (Mintzberg, 1972, 1978; Mintzberg and Waters, 1983). . . .

Based on this definition, the study of strategy formation in the university setting takes on a new interest. Rather than merely throwing up our hands at the infrequent use or abortive outcomes of explicit strategic planning, or, alternately, going to the other extreme and dismissing universities as "organized anarchies" with strategy making processes as mere "garbage cans" (March and Olsen, 1976), we are able to focus on how decisions and actions order themselves into patterns over time. . . .

Of course, defining strategy as pattern or consistency in actions says nothing about the actions on which to focus. By this definition, universities can have strategies about everything. But the discovery that all the classrooms of a given university are painted beige would seem to pale in comparison to the discovery of a pattern in actions of favouring the sciences over the humanities. Clearly some patterns deserve more attention than others. One danger, however, is to assume that actions are important simply because they come under the control of central administrators, or, more to the point in the university setting, that they are unimportant because they are controlled by individual professors. Indeed, the key area of strategy making in most organizations concerns the elaboration of the basic mission (the products or services offered to the public), and in universities, as we shall argue, this is significantly controlled by individual professors (e.g., in their choices of course materials and research projects). We believe other important areas of strategy include the inputs to the system (notably the choice and subsequent tenuring of academic staff, the determination of student enrollment, and the raising of external funds), the means to perform the mission (the construction of buildings and facilities, the purchase of research equipment etc.), the structure and forms of governance (design of the committee system, the hierarchies, the regulations concerning promotion and tenure, etc.), and the various means of support for the mission (notably the elaboration of the university's support structure, from computers and libraries to alumni offices and printing facilities).

If strategies are taken to be patterns in actions, then to understand strategy formation, we must first consider how actions come about and then consider how these actions converge over time to create patterns. Accordingly, we take up next the issue of how decisions (which are intended to provoke actions or changes in actions) are made in universities, and then consider how they, and the actions that they evoke, form patterns, in order to draw conclusions about the nature of university strategies and the processes by which they are formed.

DECISION-MAKING
IN THE UNIVERSITY SETTING

Were universities to formulate strategies from the conventional perspective, central administrators would develop detailed and integrated plans about the programs to be offered, the courses to be taught, the students to be admitted, the buildings to be built, and so on, much as automobile companies normally work out the design of their product lines and production facilities before they take action. . . . [But universities are different kinds of organizations, namely Professional Bureaucracies.]

Because universities require specialized expertise [and because the work of the different professors are so "loosely coupled"], many of their decisions, and in particular some concerned with the definition of the basic elements of the mission (teaching and research), can only be made by individual professors. Others can in fact come under direct control of central administrators, for example, decisions concerned with the financing of the university and with the provision of many of its support services. Many important decisions, however, can be made neither by individual professors nor by central administrators, but require rather the participation of various actors with different interests and expertise. Decisions in these cases emerge from complex collective and interactive processes. . . . As illustrated in Figure 1, we examine in turn the decisions controlled by individual professionals, by central administrators, and by the collectivity, the latter in terms of four models of decision making: collegial, political, garbage can, and rational analysis.

Decisions Made
by Professional Judgment

In the university setting individual professors have a great deal of autonomy over research and teaching because of the difficulties of supervising or formalizing this work [in turn because of pigeonholing and the emphasis of the standardization of skills for coordination]. Thus, many of the decisions that, in effect, detail the basic missions of the university come under the control of the individual professor. . . . Clear examples, at least when courses are not taught in multiple sections, would seem to be teaching method and materials, course content, books, grades, etc.; likewise for research conducted on an individual basis, topic and methodology, etc. But while that control may seem to be absolute from the perspective of the organization, it is not so from the perspective of external influence. . . . The reason why individual professors are trusted to make their own decisions in the areas listed above is that their skills and knowledge have been standardized through long years of training. In a sense they have been programmed through their own doctoral or professional studies to approach their fields of endeavor in generally accepted ways,

FIGURE 1   THREE LEVELS OF DECISION-MAKING IN THE UNIVERSITY

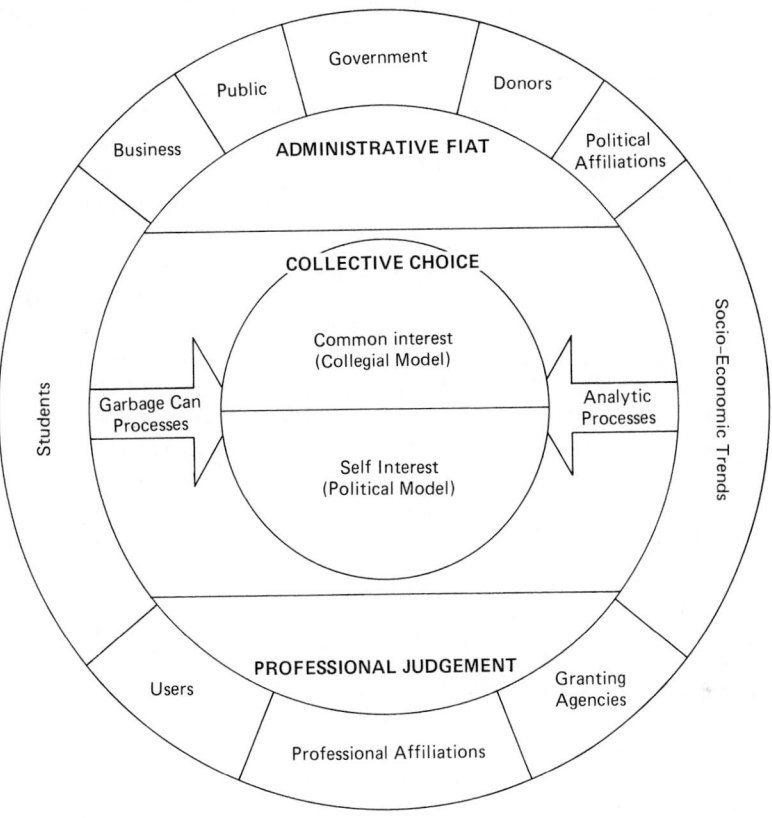

in terms of what they teach, and perhaps how, as well as in terms of how they carry out research, and perhaps on what. . . . Thus professors choose books that tend to be well regarded by their colleagues, they design their courses in ways that reflect their own training, they adopt teaching methods acceptable in their disciplines (and sometimes even sanctioned by professional associations, as in certain practical work in medicine), they research subjects that can be funded by the granting agencies (which in turn are subject to professional influence), and they write articles in styles acceptable to the journals refereed by their peers.

Pushed to the limit, then, "academic freedom" can look like professional control—it may be explicit freedom from administrators, even from peers in other disciplines, but it is not implicit freedom from colleagues in other universities. . . . Thus we have titled this section decision by "professional judgment," the implication being that while judgment may be the mode of choice . . . this is informed judgment, mightily influenced by professional training and affiliation.

Other influences, of course, impinge on the choices of individual professors. Student feedback can modify classroom techniques, demographic factors influence class size that in turn may affect course offerings, corporations can influence research in a field such as engineering by virtue of providing sites for conducting inquiry, and so on. . . . But no force matches that of the implicit and explicit influence of professional affiliation. . . .

Decisions Made by Administrative Fiat

Expertise, professional autonomy, and coordination through standardized skills and knowledge . . . all facilitated by the pigeonholing process, sharply circumscribe the capacity of central administrators to manage the university's professional staff in the ways of conventional bureaucracy—through direct supervision, namely the issuing of direct orders, and through the designation of standards within the organization (e.g., rules, job descriptions, policies). Even the designation of output or performance standards is discouraged by the intractible problem of operationalizing the goals of universities.

To carry this point further, it is in fact the academics who control much of the administration. This they do by staffing the committees and task forces that make many of the key decisions, or by suspending their academic duties to fill administrative posts for a period of time. In other words, the academic staff controls much of the administration by virtue of being seconded to administrative duties for either a few hours or a few years at a time.

While many of the administrative decisions are subjected to collective choice—involving various academics as well as administrators—there are certain ones that fall into the realm of what we are calling administrative fiat. In other words, they are the exclusive prerogatives of the senior administration. . . .

The types of decisions that fall into this realm are rather circumscribed. . . . For example, many financial decisions are made exclusively at this level, although the question of which specific ones varies from one university to another. In general, decisions to invest in stocks . . . buy and sell property, and embark on fund raising campaigns, tend to be taken by central administrators in relative isolation from the remaining members of the organization. . . .

Because many of the support services of the university are organized in a conventional "top-down" hierarchy—machine bureaucratic in nature—they also tend to fall under the control of the central administration. These include, for example, alumni and public relations, athletics

and archives, accounting and payroll, building services and physical plant, and printing and translation services. The specific services may be executed well down in the hierarchy, but decisions concerning their basic orientations—that is, the "strategic" decisions—tend to be controlled well up in the administration. However, power over certain other support services more critical to academic matters—e.g., libraries or computers—tend to fall into the realm of collective decision making, where the central administrators join the academics in the making of choices. . . .

Central administrators may also play a role in determining the procedures by which the collective process functions—what committees exist, who gets nominated to them, and so on. It is the administrators, after all, who have the time to devote to administration. This role can give skillful administrators considerable influence, however indirect, over the strategies developed by others. . . .

In addition, in times of crisis, administrators may acquire more extensive powers in order to deal with the pressing problems of the moment. . . .

A mixture of judgmental and analytic processes may be used to make decisions at the central administration level. It is interesting to note that Cohen and March (1974), in their study of [the university president's] power, found that universities tended to have detailed, explicit plans in precisely those areas in which central administrations had the most influence: capital physical planning and fiscal planning dealing with income uncertainties, cash-flow problems, and short-term investment. It is notable that these plans generally avoided academic issues. . . . the Cohen and March (1974) study suggests that much central university planning in the past has, in fact, been "decorative"—aimed at external public relations rather than internal action.

Decisions Made by Collective Choice

Many decisions in universities are determined neither by administrators nor by sole academics, but evolve out of a variety of interactive processes that occur both within and between departments, and that involve various mixtures of academics as well as administrators from a variety of levels. In our opinion among the most important of these decisions are ones related to the definition, creation, design, and discontinuation of pigeonholes, that is, programs, departments, research centres, and at a lower level, individual courses. Other important decisions that fall into the realm of collective choice include promotion, tenure, and hiring, in some cases, budgeting, and establishing and designing the interactive procedures themselves. . . .

To help understand the roles that various individuals and groups may play in influencing decisions, we can break down the decision making process into three major phases (after Mintzberg, Raisinghani & Théorêt, 1976)—identification, development, and selection (which themselves need not proceed in sequential order, but rather tend to involve complex cycles and interruptions).

The *identification* phase involves the recognition of the need to make a decision, and diagnosis of the situation. . . . [Identification] tends to happen more by individual initiative than by collective interaction. Given the complexity of decision making in universities, and the rigidities that result from the pigeonholing process, change is difficult to imagine without the individual "champion" or "sponsor," who initiates it in the first place and or at least pushes it through the complex interactive process to its completion. . . .

The second stage in decision making, the *development* process, involves the search for and design of alternatives and solutions. In some cases, champions perform this function, proposing rather detailed solutions. In others . . . the issue will tend to be developed by ad hoc groups, or task forces. . . . Administrators may also have substantial influence at this point, through their ability to decide who gets to participate in the task forces, what the mandates of these task forces will be, and what procedures they will use. . . .

The *selection* process involves the screening, evaluation, choice, and authorization of alternatives and solutions. In most universities, this involves several layers of standing committees and individuals, with power of veto or the ability to return issues to lower levels for further development. . . . The structures involved in this stage of decision making in universities are well known for being cumbersome and slow, especially in large institutions. . . .

Thus, to simplify somewhat, in the case of non-routine decisions, we may roughly associate the *identification* of the decision process with individual professors and administrators, the *development* of solutions with ad hoc groups (task forces) interacting "horizontally," and the *selection* of alternatives and solutions with a "vertical" hierarchy of permanent groups (standing committees) as well as administrators and (in public universities), perhaps, government representatives as well. . . .

Models of Interactive Decision Making

How do the individuals participating in these interactive processes in fact perceive and act out their roles. Universities have traditionally been associated with a *collegiality* model, where, in the view of some writers, decisions are made by a "community of individuals and groups, all of whom may have different roles and specialities, but who share common goals and objectives for the organization" (Taylor, 1983: 18). . . . *Common interest* is the guiding force in this view of collegiality, and decision making is, therefore, by consensus (Taylor, 1983). . . .

[Other] authors instead propose a *political* model, in which the irreconcilable differences of interest groups cannot be accommodated by consensus around common goals. Participants thus seek to serve their *self interest*, and political factors become instrumental in determining decision outcomes. . . .

Clearly, neither common interest nor self interest will dominate decision processes all the time. Some combination is naturally to be expected. There may be commitment to certain common goals, but conflict over how they should be achieved; alternatively, consensus can sometimes exist among individuals who wish to pursue different goals—Democrats do, after all, vote with Republicans on many issues in the U.S. Congress.

Decision making is more likely to be political when declining resources intensify competition . . . or when dramatic shifts in the distribution of resources threaten the power positions of particular groups (Pettigrew, 1973; Mumford & Pettigrew, 1975). Collegiality is more likely when there is a commonly accepted ideology or mission, as tends to happen in small, prestigious units, or departments with charismatic leaders, or when there is sufficient slack to accommodate disparate goals. And even when two factions fight politically at one level, other more objective observers may exist at another level who can evaluate cases on their merits. In other words, except in the most polarized situations, politics and some form of collegiality almost inevitably co-exist (Childers, 1981). . . . [In fact] judging by behavior alone, it is difficult to distinguish collegiality from politics. . . . behavior that seems clearly to be the one can sometimes prove to be the other. Thus, successful politics often requires a collegial posture (Pfeffer, 1979a). One must cloak self interest in the mantle of the common good. By the same token, changes that will ultimately benefit the institution at large may sometimes evoke conflict between individuals who have different conceptions of the common good. Furthermore . . . champions may have to resort to the use of power to effect change regardless of whether they are promoting the common interest or their own self-interest. Thus, we distinguish collegiality and politics on the basis of motivation rather than behavior. The former refers to actions which are used to push through decisions that are genuinely considered beneficial for the institution, the latter refers to actions designed to defeat opponents in the pursuit of self-interest . . . .

A third model that has been used to explain decision making in universities, described as "organized anarchies," is the *garbage can*. Here decision making is characterized by "collections of choices looking for problems, issues and feelings looking for decision situations in which they may be aired, solutions looking for issues to which they might be an answer, and decision makers looking for work" (Cohen, March, & Olsen, 1972, p. 1 . . .). Behavior, is, in other words, non-purposive and often random, because goals are unclear and the means to achieve them problematic. Furthermore participation is fluid because of the "cost" of time and energy. . . . Thus, in place of the common interest of the collegial model and the self interest of the political model, the garbage can model offers an active kind of *uninterest*.

The important question is not whether garbage can processes exist—we have all experienced them—but whether they matter. Do they apply to key issues or only incidental ones? . . . Where decisions are important, participation may cease to be fluid because the cost of not participating would outweigh the cost of doing so. Some decisions are important only to individuals (their champions), and so, while their colleagues may play in the garbage can, they play seriously. . . . Other decisions are important to many people, and so all play seriously. Of course, some decisions are not that significant to anyone . . . Such decisions . . . could well end up in the garbage can. There is always someone with free time ("looking for work") willing to challenge a proposal for the sake of so doing, or perhaps to stimulate some academic debate (to "air issues or feelings"), or simply to see if valid arguments underlie the proposal. Thus, like common interest and self interest, uninterest neither dominates decision processes nor is absent from them. In our view, a combination of collegiality and politics will most influence decision making processes that have strategic implications for many actors, while the garbage can model may help describe decision processes that are peripheral, to some actors at least.

Finally, *analysis*, or the "rational actor" (Allison, 1971), may be considered as a fourth model of decision making. Here calculation is used to select the best alternative, or at least to distinguish acceptable from unacceptable proposals. Such an approach seems consistent with machine bureaucracy, . . . [but in] fact, we wish to argue that analysis figures prominently in both collegial and political processes, as well as in garbage can ones. . . . Rational analysis is necessary in universities for a number of reasons. The interactive process itself forces deliberations to be structured and requires that arguments be made explicit for purposes of communication. . . .

Moreover, the hierarchy of selection (particularly authorization) encourages the development of analytic support for proposals, especially when the champion may be denied representation at higher levels. Everything must be made as explicit and rationally persuasive as possible. Also, senior administrators, who often lack direct knowledge about what is going on in many areas of the organization—i.e., lack the ability to develop intuitive perceptions—may request more ''hard'' analytic information on which to support or authorize projects.

Of course, when goals and technology are ambiguous, analytic information inevitably contains logical flaws that can be easily traced by those who are threatened by the information. Detailed responses, also expressed in rationalistic terms (i.e., counter analyses) will therefore often be generated in an attempt to redress the balance. Finally, the democratic nature of universities means that many decisions require the agreement of large numbers of people who are not particularly committed one way or the other *a priori*. These people must be convinced. Of course, the fact that university professors are frequently by nature and experience superb analysts practised in the craft of rational argumentation through their research and teaching also, no doubt, contributes to the tendency to react to issues analytically. . . . In the collegial situation, in which people are assumed to be working in a cooperative manner, analysis will be used mainly to develop understanding, to achieve consensus, to aid communication, and to defend the legitimate interests of the entire group. . . . In the political situation, where self interest dominates, analyses of all kinds are likely to proliferate, directed at persuading the uncommitted. Competition for resources under tight constraints also means that analyses are more likely to be counter-analyzed by affected groups. . . . the benefit of analysis in political situations stems from the picking of holes in the argument of one side by the other: the truth is more likely to emerge and the issue most likely to be understood when opposing analyses, counter-analyses, counter-counter-analyses, etc., are available for the scrutiny of the uncommitted majority. However, in extreme cases, politics can

preclude the effectiveness of analysis too. When an issue is important enough and concerns them directly, the majority of actors may become committed early, and polarization may prevent analysis from being particularly influential unless its conclusions are so overwhelming as to be difficult to refute. . . .

Analysis will even be used in a garbage can situation. It will play the role of focussing attention on issues, problems and solutions. The committee member, described earlier, who in ''looking for work'' challenges proposals for the joy of academic debate, in fact encourages analysis and may thereby play the functional role of forcing out ill-conceived proposals. However, because participation is haphazard and interest low under this model, analyses may tend to go unopposed and errors and biasses may remain undetected. . . .

To conclude, as we showed in Figure 2, we believe the collective sphere of decision making is characterized by combined collegial and political processes, with garbage can influences encouraging a kind of haphazardness on one side due to cognitive and cost limitations (at least for some, less important decisions), and competing analytical influences on the other side encouraging a certain logic or formal rationality (serving as an invisible hand to keep the lid on the garbage can, so to speak!).

STRATEGIES AS PATTERNS EMERGING FROM DECISION PROCESSES

. . . In this concluding section, we draw our findings from the first two sections together in terms of a number of propositions about strategies and their formation as a result of the decision making processes in the university setting. . . .

General Propositions

1. Many different actors are involved in the strategy formation process in universities. As soon as we relax the conventional assumptions of strategies as deliberate and determined centrally, it becomes evident, first, that strategies, as patterns, exist in universities, and, second, that many other actors participate in their formation. . . .

2. Some of the university's strategies pertain to the whole, others to particular parts. Some patterns cut across the entire organization, particularly ones that pertain to facilities, support services, or certain administrative processes (e.g., building campaigns, the provision of library services or athletic facilities, promotion and tenure regulations), while others pertain to particular parts, whether departments (e.g., program design, student selection) or individual professors (e.g., course design, research projects). . . . Thus:

3. We should expect to find a good deal of fragmentation in the strategies pursued by universities. . . . Forces do exist to tie activities together (as we shall discuss later), but many of the strategies are relatively unrelated to each other—hardly even loosely coupled—so that individual ones can be changed without upsetting the system. . . .

4. Control of specific strategies may reside with individual professors, within the administrative structure, or in the collectivity. In other words, decision making at each of the levels we have discussed can lead to important patterns of action, namely strategies. . . .

Propositions about Professional Judgment

5. The mission strategies of the university are largely aggregates of the personal strategies pursued by individual professors, based on professional judgment. . . . It is, of course, the pigeonholing process that allows these personal product/market strategies [about course content, teaching method, research topic and methodology] to develop. But these strategies are not chosen at random:

6. Many of the personal strategies are influenced by, indeed often imported through, professional training and affiliation. Sometimes professional bodies dictate specific orientations

[imposed strategies]. . . . More often, the influence is less direct. The fact that a certain Roger Bennett teaches marketing in McGill University's MBA program by the case method is hardly independent of the fact that he was so trained in Harvard's MBA and DBA programs. And as professional norms change, so too do the strategies: if Bennett's notion that the "marketing concept" has outlived its usefulness catches hold among his marketing colleagues (a process Bennett encourages through his publications in professional journals and his speeches at professional meetings), then the nature of marketing courses all over North America will change. We can say that a new *consensus* strategy will emerge, but across rather than within universities. . . .

7. To a great extent, many important strategies associated with mission cut across universities. Because of the standardization of skills and the sharing of norms, it becomes more accurate to talk of a strategy for teaching marketing than a strategy for teaching at McGill. . . . This is the result of the fact that the range of professional influences is far greater than the more focussed institutional influences, at least in the sphere of the provision of the basic mission.

Propositions about Administrative Fiat

8. In the realm of administrative fiat, central administrators may impose deliberate strategies on the entire organization. Where the administrators have definitive control—portfolio investment, property management, some of the support services—patterns of strategies are not only likely to exist, but to be rather deliberate in nature. . . . [These] show up especially in the formative years of a university. . . .

9. In addition, central administrators seek to exert influence in other spheres through the use of umbrella and process strategies . . . where central administrators cannot act deliberately . . . they try to affect the broad directions [that emergent] patterns may take. . . . For example, while administrators may not be able to dictate course content or teaching methods, they [can construct large classrooms or small ones that encourage lecturing or seminars respectively, and can exercise indirect control over who gets hired in the first place.] . . . Similarly, administrators can use their powers of persuasion within the interactive process to encourage or discourage the projects championed by others or, at the limit, they can evoke their powers of veto to block certain projects. . . .

Likewise, the ability to design the committee structure, and especially to staff the committees, can have a profound influence on the outcome of committee deliberation. The administrator intent on reform in a certain academic sphere may not be able to dictate to a committee, but his power to staff that committee with reformers may be all he needs. . . .

10. Crises enhance the power of central administrators over the formation of strategies. Strategies, as patterns, often emerge from precedent-setting decisions, and these often occur during times of crisis, when radical actions must be taken quickly. . . . Moreover, decisions that would be blocked for years in the interactive process can sometimes be made quickly by administrative fiat in times of crisis. . . .

11. Some strategies resulting from administrative activity are in fact imposed by external influencers. Much as personal strategies may be imposed by professional bodies, so too administrative strategies may be imposed by influential outsiders, such as donors or governmental officials. . . . However, given the decentralization of power over many key strategy areas, external influencers have often been reduced to controlling peripheral strategies (what kind of football team the old alma mater will have) or have been limited to what Cyert and March (1963) call "side payments" (a seat on a weak board, a name on a new building). . . .

Propositions about Collective Choice

12. At one extreme, interactive processes can encourage some loose cohesion in fragmental activities, leading to negotiated departmental or university-wide strategies. When interactive processes are no more than political in nature, we might expect the greatest fragmentation of activities, as each actor seeks to satisfy his own self-interest. But that does not preclude the appearance of consistencies in the actions of the organization over time, which we refer to as *negotiated* strategies . . . At the very least, the negotiated outcomes of interactive decisions—for example, about hiring and promotion, tenure regulations, program development, or enrollment—can lead to a kind of "style" of a given department or of the entire university. Essentially, collective choice means that people from a variety of departments or pigeonholes are committed to the outcome, which can produce patterns across these divisions. . . .

13. At the other extreme, interactive processes can produce strong consistent themes, leading to pervasive ideological strategies. As Clark (1970, 1972) describes the "distinctive colleges," academic institutions sometimes develop powerful and pervasive systems of beliefs which produce strong consistency across all kinds of decisions; we characterize such consistency . . . as an *ideological* strategy. Clark traces the origins of such ideologies to strong leaders in the organization's past . . . By the same token, of course, such leadership can emerge in a department, so that the ideology remains at that level. . . . Note that while the origin of the ideology may be individual—a central administrator or even a single academic who, for example, creates a new pigeonhole—its institutionalization can only occur in the collective process, as a variety of individuals interact to reinforce the new beliefs. . . .

. . . personnel decisions are critical in the development and perpetuation of ideological strategies, especially in universities where the individual professor has so much autonomy. A powerful academic orientation can dominate a department or university only if those invited to join and remain with the group conform to its beliefs. . . . Thus, collegiality reigns supreme in the case of ideological strategy: the emphasis is on unity and the common interest.

14. Between these two extremes, interactive processes create consistencies through formal procedure and implicit habit, leading to (more or less) planned and consensus strategies. Sometimes the interactive processes produce consistency in a formal way, as when a senate enacts new tenure regulations to apply to the whole university. . . . Assuming broad concurrence, the [more or less planned] strategy may also be described as one of explicit consensus.

But *consensus* strategies of an implicit and more emergent nature . . . can also appear out of the interactive process. They develop through precedent and habit, as well as informal mutual adjustment among the different actors in the system. People abide by them, not necessarily out of ideological commitment per se, but more from a sense of how "things are done" in the institution. . . .

To sum up, we have suggested in the last three propositions that the interactive process may produce a range of strategies, from weak negotiated ones to strong ideological ones, with ones of a planned or consensus nature in between.

Concluding Propositions

15. University strategies tend to exhibit a remarkable degree of stability, discouraging any form of strategic "revolution." Were garbage can processes predominant in university decision making, one would not expect stability and patterning, but the reverse: unpredictable, random swings in behavior. Our belief, however, is that this randomness is restricted to relatively minor issues, and tends to balance itself out, so that it appears more in the form of random variations around more stable patterns. Thus, two factions in the medical faculty might fight idiosyncratically about whether or not to admit eight more students, while the overall pattern remains rather stable. It may go up or down by a few students as one side occasionally scores points and then the other. But the pattern will not change unless something fundamental does—like the occurrence of a war or of new restrictions imposed by the local college of physicians and surgeons. In other words, we suspect that garbage can processes create "noise" in the system, and show up as the short-term variations around long term trend lines.

There are many good reasons not only why patterns should appear in universities, but why they should exhibit considerable stability—why strategic "revolutions," when many key strategies change suddenly, should be rare in universities.

Perhaps the most fundamental reason is that responsibility for strategy is divided among so many people: many autonomous individuals are unlikely to change their collective mind, at least not simultaneously, radically, and consistently.

At the individual level, professors who have invested time and effort to learn their standardized skills are unlikely to change them frequently or radically. Hence the mission of the university, represented by the aggregation of the personal strategies based on these skills, is likely to be highly stable. Even the change that does take place is likely to be localized to specific pigeonholes, so that the aggregate mission strategies are hardly affected at any one time. Moreover, the rooting of these personal strategies in professional affiliations makes them even more immutable. Many of these strategies are, after all, established by consensus among professionals flung far and wide, and are upheld by the most respected members of the profession. Forces for change from within an academic institution can, therefore, be countered by the forces of the status quo elsewhere. . . .

Collective decision processes also encourage stability of strategies. We have already noted how staffing decisions can perpetuate established ideologies. In addition, the sheer weight of the interactive processes (especially in the selection phase) is likely to discourage all but the most dedicated and determined champions of change. Moreover, power tends to become institutionalized over time: it is a self-perpetuating phenomenon—those who have it use to get more . . . Another factor is that new members are often selected to fit in with the existing culture of the organization or of a department, and socialization reinforces that tendency.

The strategies that develop through administrative fiat may be more flexible than those emerging from collective choice. This is partly because they tend to be more deliberate and impersonal and are thus more easily confronted than the more emergent strategies of the collectivity. Moreover, these strategies fall under the control of relatively few people. . . . A strategic revolution may, therefore, be conceivable only in the limited spheres of administrative fiat, or only when a severe crisis concentrates more pervasive decision making power in the hands of a few people for a period of time.

What, in our view, typically characterizes university strategy formation, then, is not revolution, nor the randomness of garbage can processes, but a fundamental stability. . . .

16. Changes in university strategies do occur, constantly and gradually, in lagged response to environmental forces, driven by professional judgment, administrative fiat, as well as the collective processes of politics, collegiality, and analysis. While strategic revolution may be rare in universities, we believe gradual, incremental change is endemic. At the broadest level, of mission offerings and ideologies, change may be difficult. But at the narrowest—inside tiny pigeonholes—the "snakelike" development (described in Proposition 7) occurs continuously. Research topics change, new course texts are adopted, course content is updated. . . . Thus, we would expect the university to experience many imperceptible mini-revolutions in place of any overt pervasive ones. In this respect, some of the collective change that does appear may simply be the formal acknowledgment and consolidation of many small individual changes—after the fact. The emergent patterns are thus made deliberate.

Bolder change does, of course, take place on other levels. In the realm of administrative fiat, as noted earlier, change is easier to achieve since the decision making process is so much simpler and more centralized. Thus "revolutions" in support services (say, student residences or the printing service), or in budgeting techniques or fringe benefits, are to be expected occasionally, and these may occur in more academic areas when centralization arises in times of crisis (as when weak departments or programs are terminated). Despite the difficulties, however, collective

processes can also promote strategic change. As power shifts, based on environmental forces—for example, as the sciences gained influence, in the form of greater access to research funding and increased student enrollment, at the expense of the humanities after Sputnik—so too do decisions change, leading to new patterns of behavior. This process is speeded up by individuals who expend energy from political or collegial perspectives to champion new interests. The necessity for them to couch their ideas in analytical terms, and the critical appraisal to which their analyses will be subjected by their opponents, works to produce the rejection of irregular and unjustifiable projects, which in turn enhances stability. But the same forces can also create greater receptivity to those ideas which have a sound underlying rationale.

In all these ways, adaptation to environmental forces can occur gradually and without revolution, although in lagged response to environmental events and trends.

In summary, universities are paradoxically extremely stable at the broadest level and in a state of perpetual change at the narrowest. One may in fact explain the other. Revolutions are perhaps only necessary in organizations that cannot adapt sufficiently at the narrowest level. . . .

To conclude:

17. Strategies abound in universities. If strategies are patterns in activity over time, then much of the literature on the functioning of universities argues against the occurrence of strategies. Planning is discouraged, decision making is fragmented, politics encourages conflict, garbage can processes promote idiosyncrasy.

But our findings are quite to the contrary. Standardization of knowledge and skills together with pigeonholing certainly encourage order and patterning, as does professional affiliation; and analysis encourages stable responses to external needs, while collegiality promotes consistent behavior within the system; even politics works to stop some change and slow the pace of the rest. As for the garbage can model, it may in large part represent the unexplained variance in the system—that is, whatever is not understood might look like organized anarchy. If true, then the more we come to understand strategy formation in the university setting, the less explanatory the garbage can model should become. Our discussion suggests, in fact, that university behavior is epitomized by order and patterning of all sorts—in actions as well as in processes. As soon as strategies are defined from the perspective of realization instead of intention, universities can be seen to have strategies, indeed, when all of the different patterns are considered, to be inundated with strategies!

To close this discussion, we do not wish to leave the reader with the impression that we are totally complacent about strategy formation in the university setting, that is, that we believe universities "have it all right." We too have had our frustrations with the processes described, whether they be fighting to push a Ph.D. program through the collective process, struggling to gain acceptance for unorthodox research, or merely trying to avoid being prematurely pigeonholed! But of one thing we are certain: The problem is not that universities do not have strategies, but that they do—and with a vengeance.

## FIFTEEN

MANAGING TRANSITION

Strategy as a concept tends to be long term, concerned with imposing stable patterns of behavior on the organization. But to manage strategy is frequently to manage change—to recognize when shifts of a strategic nature are possible, desirable, and/or necessary, and then to act. Managing transition is generally far more difficult than it may first appear. The need for really major strategic reorientation occurs rather infrequently in most organizations, and when it does, it usually means moving from a familiar domain into a less well defined future where many of the old organization's rules, concepts, and practices will no longer work. People must often abandon the past roots of their success and develop entirely new skills and attitudes. This is clearly a frightening, threatening event—and often the most difficult challenge a manager can undertake.

The cause of such transitions also vary, from a steady decline in performance which ultimately demands a genuine "turnaround," to a sudden radical shift in a base technology which may require the reconceptualizing of both the product and its production processes; from an organization's gradual shift to the next state in its "life cycle," to the fact that a new chief executive simply wants to put his or her particular stamp on the organization. The resulting strategic alignments may also take on a variety of forms, from a shift of one strategic position to another

within the same industry to the move into several new markets through diversification. Some changes require rapid shifts from one structural configuration to another, while others are accompanied by slower structural change, as when a small entrepreneurial firm grows steadily toward a larger mature company, which may necessitate a shift in perspective from, say, a missionary zeal about innovation and product quality to an obsession with short-term cost leadership. Each transition has its own management prerequisites and problems.

This chapter covers a number of these varying aspects of organizational transition, presenting material on what evokes them in the first place, what forms they can take, and how they can and should be managed in differing situations. We begin with a discussion of transitions in organizational structure and the nature of organizations themselves, and then move on to questions of transitions involving changed technological environments before considering the problems of managing transitions in strategy itself.

The readings appropriately cap the earlier chapters of this book: on strategy and its formation, structure and systems, power and culture, and the various contexts in which these come together. Transitions typically involve them all. Configuration, so carefully nurtured in earlier chapters, turns out to be a double-edged sword, promoting consistency and efficiency on one hand but sometimes discouraging major adaptation on the other.

The first reading, drawn from Mintzberg's book *Structure in Fives* and entitled "Beyond Five," discusses transitions among the various configurations of structure presented in the preceding context chapters. It also seeks to expand the reader's thinking beyond these configurations by noting that while some organizations function effectively by structuring themselves close to one standard configuration, others more appropriately develop hybrids of these configurations or even invent their own unique configurations. We must, in other words, adapt organizations to their own particular needs. Standard approaches suit some organizations, helping us to cope with a complex world, but we must not take them too literally.

The next readings focus our attention on the problems of managing specific transitions. An article by Quinn addresses directly the question of how large organizations can manage complex strategic transitions, especially those which involve a shift in the whole culture of the enterprise. This reading offers a number of useful suggestions on how managers can deal with the practical realities of creating change. Consciously moving incrementally allows them to cope with many of the informational, political, motivational, and commitment problems that often inhibit or prevent change in large organizations. While Quinn's prescriptions do not appear as neat and orderly as those that show up in the "planned change" literature, they have direct relevance to managers who must deal in a complex, somewhat politicized world, i.e., the real world of most large organizations. This reading also closes various loopholes by relating both the emergent and deliberate aspects of strategy formation to the various articles which dealt with the politics and social dynamics of change.

The last three readings focus on the problems of managing two other specific kinds of transitions, those involving "turnarounds" and "technological threats." In his practical and well-organized paper "Designing Turnaround Strategies," Charles Hofer, who teaches policy at the University of Georgia, accomplishes three things. He introduces the typical turnaround situation, where declining performance must be corrected; he makes a key distinction between an operating turnaround and a strategic one, and he discusses various strategies by which each might be achieved.

The reading by Starbuck, Greve, and Hedberg, entitled "Responding to Crises," also considers turnaround situations, but under a different label—crisis. This reading nicely complements Hofer's because it focuses not so much on the *strategies* for achieving turnarounds as on the *processes* necessary for so doing. It also links with our discussion of culture in Chapter 8 in which Hedberg and his colleagues discuss how to change a deeply ingrained culture that is no longer viable. In fact, this reading reflects a most interesting body of research carried out in Sweden in the 1970s on the relationships between culture and strategy. (Two of the authors are Swedish; Starbuck, an American now teaching at the New York University Business School, worked with them in Europe.)

Note how Starbuck and colleagues' ideas link with those of Quinn—how to manage incrementally and above all how to work out difficulties through an interactive learning process. This reading also challenges at every turn many conventional notions in management. For example, its final suggestion is that crises themselves can represent *opportunities* for those organizations prepared to exploit them. Often those who approach crises in this fashion earn critical strategic advantages in the next stage of their industry's development. Consider the emergence of entirely new dominant players in the deregulated transportation and financial services industries. Cases like Federal Express and Royal Bank of Canada offer interesting vehicles for investigating this theme.

The last reading, "Strategic Responses to Technological Threats," is by Arnold Cooper and Dan Schendel of Purdue's Krannert School (the latter the driving force in the field of strategic management, having co-founded both the Society and the Journal by that name). It provides a practical and insightful view on the problems of dealing with dramatic shifts in technology. The article is based on the authors' research into how such changes threaten established organizations and how some have been able to cope with the threats while others have not. The Intel and General Motors cases raise these issues, as do the "Reference Notes" on the semiconductor and financial services industries.

BEYOND FIVE*

by Henry Mintzberg

[In this reading, concluding the discussion of the five structural configurations (Simple Structure, Machine Bureaucracy, Divisionalized Form, Professional Bureaucracy, and Adhocracy)] we go beyond five, in two directions. First we go back to one, and then we go on to six, maybe further. We go back to one by combining our configurations into a single integrated framework, or theory—a system unto themselves. And we go [beyond five] to suggest one last hypothesis on the effective designing of organizations.

THE FIVE CONFIGURATIONS AS ONE SYSTEM

Do any of these configurations really exist? This is a strange question to raise after so many pages of discussion, filled with illustrations. But it is worth asking, in order to draw a tighter line between the five configurations and the reality they purport to describe.

In one sense, the configurations do not exist at all. After all, they are just words and pictures on pieces of paper, not reality itself. Real organizations are enormously complex, far more so than any of these five configurations on paper. What these constitute is a theory, and every theory necessarily simplifies and therefore distorts the

*   Excerpted from Henry Mintzberg, *Structure in Fives: Designing Effective Organizations* (Prentice-Hall, 1983), chap. 13; used by permission of the publisher.

reality. That was why the reader [of the book] was warned at the outset to proceed under the assumption that every sentence in the five [configuration] chapters (including this one) was an overstatement.

But that should not lead to a rejection of the configurations. For the reader's choice is not between theory and reality so much as between alternative theories. No one carries reality around in his head; no head is that big. Rather, we carry around thoughts, impressions, and beliefs about reality, and measures of it we call facts. But all this is useless unless it is ordered in some way, just as a library of books is useless unless the books are catalogued. So, most important, we carry around in our heads comprehensible simplifications—concepts or models or theories—that enable us to catalogue our data and experience. The reader's choice then becomes one of alternative systems of cataloguing—that is, alternative theories.

The reader can trust the theories he builds himself, based on his own experiences, or else he can select from among those offered in books like this one, based on the experiences of the organizations reported in the research (as well as one author's own experiences). Or, more realistically, he selects from among them in building up his own models of reality. His choice of theories is normally based on two criteria: how rich the description is—that is, how powerfully it reflects the reality (or, alternatively, how little it distorts the reality)—and how simple it is to comprehend. The most useful theories are simple when stated yet powerful when applied, like $E = MC^2$.

And so in another sense—at least if I have done my job well—the configurations do indeed exist, in the reader's mind. The mind is where all knowledge exists. . . . The five configurations will . . . exist if they prove to constitute a simple yet powerful theory, more useful in some ways than the others currently available.

To give the theory of the configurations a little push toward that end, this section discusses a number of possible applications of it. First, we discuss it as a set of five pulls acting on

FIGURE 1   THE PENTAGON

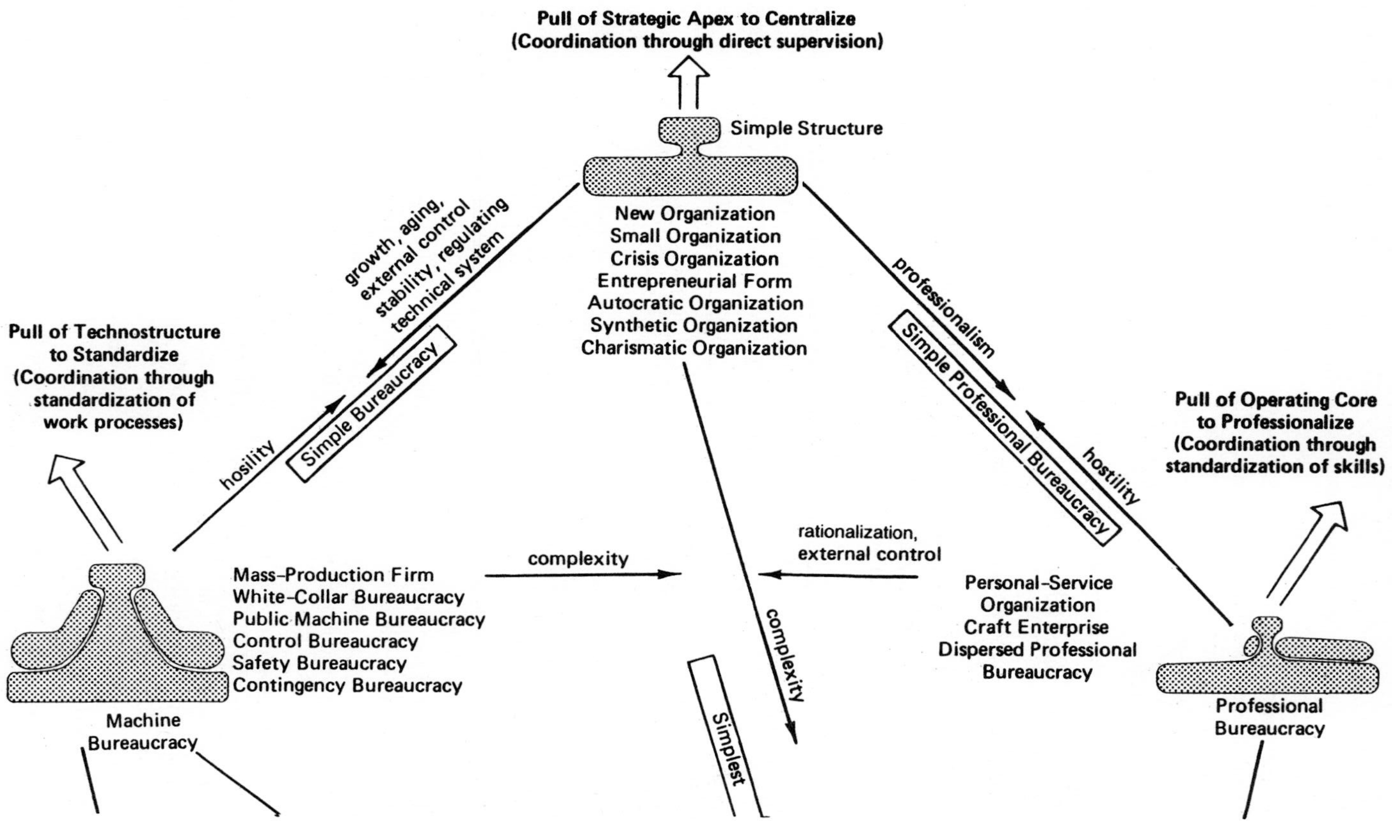

Pull of Strategic Apex to Centralize
(Coordination through direct supervision)

Pull of Operating Core to Professionalize
(Coordination through standardization of skills)

Pull of Technostructure to Standardize
(Coordination through standardization of work processes)

Simple Structure

New Organization
Small Organization
Crisis Organization
Entrepreneurial Form
Autocratic Organization
Synthetic Organization
Charismatic Organization

professionalism

Simple Professional Bureaucracy

hostility

Professional Bureaucracy

Personal-Service Organization
Craft Enterprise
Dispersed Professional Bureaucracy

rationalization, external control

complexity

Simplest

complexity

growth, aging, external control stability, regulating technical system

Simple Bureaucracy

hostility

Mass-Production Firm
White-Collar Bureaucracy
Public Machine Bureaucracy
Control Bureaucracy
Safety Bureaucracy
Contingency Bureaucracy

Machine Bureaucracy

664

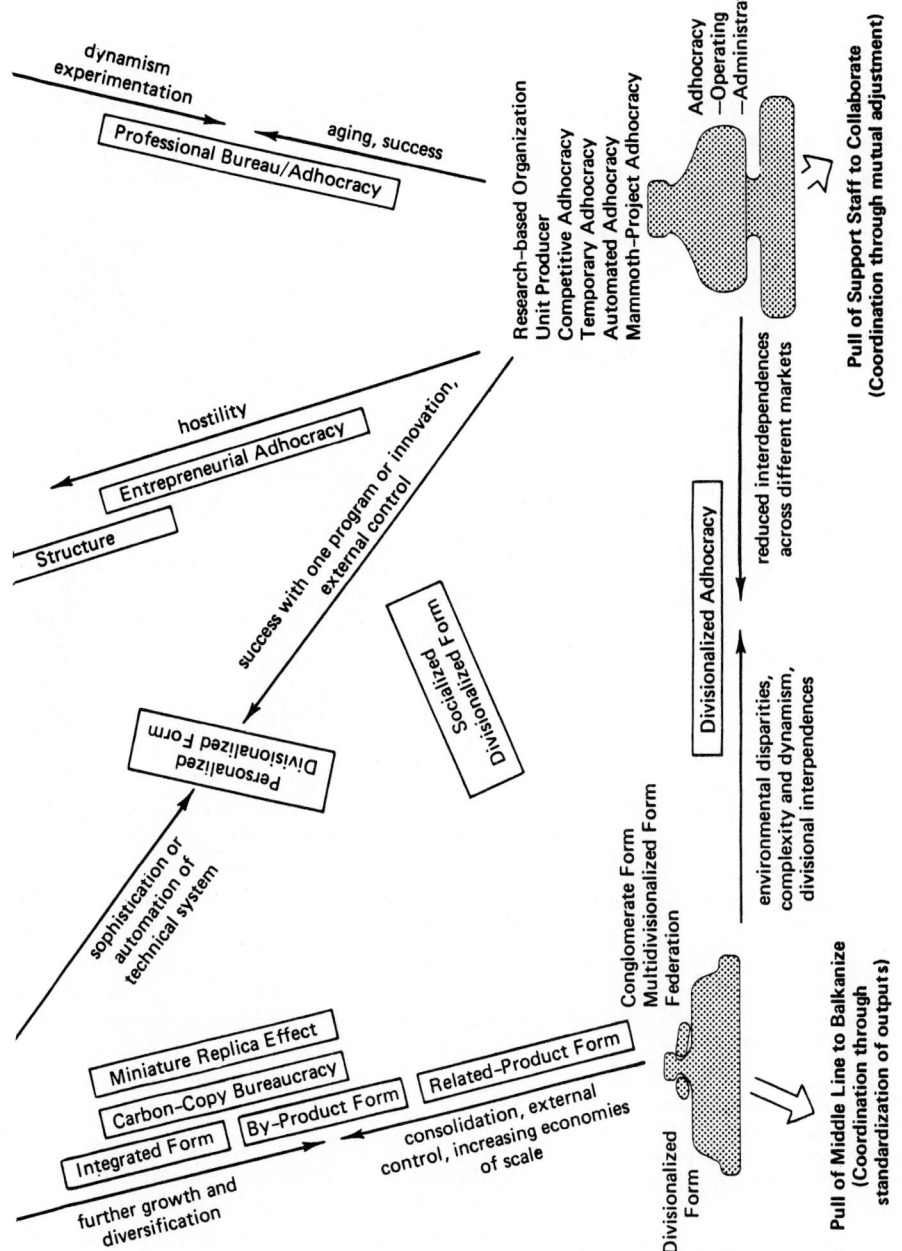

dynamism
experimentation

aging, success

Professional Bureau/Adhocracy

Research-based Organization
Unit Producer
Competitive Adhocracy
Temporary Adhocracy
Automated Adhocracy
Mammoth-Project Adhocracy

Adhocracy
—Operating
—Administrative

Pull of Support Staff to Collaborate
(Coordination through mutual adjustment)

hostility

Entrepreneurial Adhocracy

Structure

success with one program or innovation,
external control

reduced interdependences
across different markets

Socialized Form

Divisionalized Adhocracy

Personalized
Divisionalized Form

sophistication or
automation of
technical system

environmental disparities,
complexity and dynamism,
divisional interpendences

Conglomerate Form
Multidivisionalized Form
Federation

Miniature Replica Effect

Carbon-Copy Bureaucracy

Related-Product Form

By-Product Form

Integrated Form

consolidation, external
control, increasing economies
of scale

further growth and
diversification

Divisionalized
Form

Pull of Middle Line to Balkanize
(Coordination through
standardization of outputs)

almost every organization; second, as a set of five pure types that reflect the structures and situations of many organizations; third, as the basis for describing hybrid structures; and fourth, as the basis for describing transitions from one structure and situation to another. Figure 1 seeks to capture the spirit of these four discussions. Symbolically, it shows the five configurations as forming a pentagon, bounding a reality within which real structures and situations can be found.

Each configuration sits at one of the nodes, pulling real organizations toward it. The Simple Structure, the first stage for many organizations, sits at the top. At the next level, on either side of it, are the two bureaucracies, Machine Bureaucracy on the left and Professional Bureaucracy on the right. Down at the third, bottom level are the two most elaborate configurations, the Divisionalized Form on the left and Adhocracy on the right. Some real organizations fall into position close to one node—one of the pure types—and others fall between two or more, as hybrids, perhaps in transition from one pure type to another.

The Configurations as a Set of Basic Pulls on the Organization

To repeat a point made [earlier], the configurations represent a set of five forces that pull organizations in five different directions. These pulls are shown in the pentagon and are listed below:

- First is the pull exercised by the strategic apex to centralize, to coordinate by direct supervision, and so to structure the organization as a Simple Structure.
- Second is the pull exercised by the technostructure, to coordinate by standardization—notably of work processes, the tightest kind—in order to increase its influence, and so to structure the organization as a Machine Bureaucracy.
- Third is the pull exercised by the operators to professionalize, to coordinate by the standardization of skills in order to maximize

their autonomy, and so to structure the organization as a Professional Bureaucracy.

- Fourth is the pull exercised by the middle managers to Balkanize, to be given the autonomy to manage their own units, with coordination restricted to the standardization of outputs, and so to structure the organization as a Divisionalized Form.
- Fifth is the pull exercised by the support staff (and by the operators as well, in the Operating Adhocracy), for collaboration (and innovation) in decision making, to coordinate by mutual adjustment, and so to structure the organization as an Adhocracy.

Almost every organization experiences all five of these pulls. Take, for example, the case of the theater company, as described by Goodman and Goodman (1972:104). They note "the sense of ownership expressed by the directors," also their power "to a certain extent [to] shape a play into their own image," to choose the team to perform that play, and even to limit the creative contributions of members of that team. All these constitute pulls toward Simple Structure. Of course, put a number of such directors in the same organization and there emerges a pull toward the Divisionalized Form, where each can maximize his autonomy. One director kept "a detailed book which he made and used in the production of a large-scale musical comedy." That book, of course, constituted a pull toward Machine Bureaucracy. Sometimes, however—say, in experimental theater—the "ability to do detailed planning diminishes," the director being "less firm in knowing what he wants" and cuts and additions being more frequent. The pull is toward Adhocracy. The members of theater companies are generally professional and work largely on their own: the "choreographer usually creates a dance sequence to fit music that has already been composed and to fit the space available given the existing set design. The three people need never see or speak to each other and are often working in separate locations. . . ." (p. 496). The pull is toward Professional Bureaucracy.

What structure the organization actually designs depends in good part on how strong each of the pulls turns out to be. As we shall see below, when one dominates, we expect the organization to emerge rather close to one of the pure types of configurations, close to one of the nodes on the pentagon. When two or more pulls coexist in relative balance, we expect a "hybrid" of our configurations to emerge. And as one pull displaces another as dominant, we should be able to describe the organization in a state of transition between two of the configurations.

The Configurations
as a Set of Pure Types

In this second application of the system, the set of configurations is treated as a framework, or typology of pure types, each one a description of a basic kind of organizational structure and its situation.

Our examples throughout [the discussion of the configurations] suggest that a great many organizations, being dominated by one of the five pulls, tend to design structures rather close to one of the configurations. No structure matches any one configuration perfectly, but some come remarkably close—like the small entrepreneurial firm controlled by its president in an almost pure Simple Structure, or the conglomerate corporation that fits virtually all the characteristics of the pure Divisionalized Form.

In the [chapters in each of the configurations in the original book], we . . . labeled and discussed a number of examples and variants of each of the pure types. All these are listed on the pentagon of Figure 1, next to their own configurations. Their number gives some justification for treating the configurations as a typology of pure types.

Support for the notion of a pure type comes from the configuration hypothesis, which was introduced [earlier]: effective structuring requires an internal consistency among the design parameters. In other words, the organization is often driven toward one of the configurations in its search for harmony in its structure. It may experi-

ence pulls toward different configurations but it often exhibits a tendency to favor one of them. Better to be consistent and selective than comprehensive and half-hearted. In fact, we saw in the "extended configuration" hypothesis . . . and in a good deal of evidence presented in the preceding [discussion], that this search for harmony and consistency extends to the situational factors as well. The organization with an integrated structure also favors an environment, a technical system, a size, even an age and a power system consistent with that structure.

Thus, we sometimes find that different organizations in the same industry prefer different configurations, depending on which pull (and segment of the industry) they decide to respond to. To return to the theater company, one may prefer Simple Structure because of a strong-willed director (or Divisionalized Form because of many of them), another Machine Bureaucracy because it chooses to produce musicals by the book, another Professional Bureaucracy in order to perfect its performance of Shakespeare year after year, and a fourth Adhocracy to produce experimental plays. Likewise, the restaurant can structure itself like a Simple Structure, Machine Bureaucracy, Divisionalized Form, or Professional Bureaucracy, depending on whether it wishes to remain a small "greasy spoon," grow larger through the serving of simple basic standards, such as steak and lobster, perhaps even through franchises, or develop the gourmet skills of its chefs through the offering of dishes difficult to prepare but highly standardized. (The restaurant structured as an Adhocracy in order to experiment with each dish it served would probably not attract enough clients to survive!)

The Configurations as a System
for Describing Structural Hybrids

In this third application of the system, the set of five configurations can be treated as the basis for describing structural hybrids.

We have seen in our discussion that not all organizations choose to be consistent in designing their structures, at least not as we have described consistency. They use what we call hybrid structures, ones that exhibit characteristics of more than one configuration. Some of the hybrids we have come across in our discussion seem to be dysfunctional, indications of organizations that cannot make up their minds or, in wanting the best of more than one world, end up with the worst of many. Consider the organization that no sooner gives its middle managers autonomy subject to performance control, as in the Divisionalized Form, than it takes it away by the proliferation of rules and regulations, as in the Machine Bureaucracy. Or the highly regulated Machine Bureaucracy that believes it can give its workers job autonomy, as in the Professional Bureaucracy, through an overambitious quality-of-working-life program. The resulting confusion can render the organization less effective than the pure type of structure, despite its own inherent limitations.

In some cases, however, organizations have no choice: contradictory situational factors over which they have no control force them to adopt dysfunctional hybrids. We saw evidence of this in school systems, police forces, and other organizations with trained operators, that seem to require Professional Bureaucracy yet are driven by concentrated external control (usually governmental) to take on certain characteristics of Machine Bureaucracy, to the detriment of their performance.

But other hybrids seem perfectly logical, indications of the need to respond to more than one valid force at the same time—like the symphony orchestra, a simple professional bureaucracy . . . that hires highly trained musicians and relies largely on their standardized skills to produce its music yet also requires a strong, sometimes autocratic leader to weld them into a tightly coordinated unit. Or the related-product corporation . . . that needs to divisionalize yet also must coordinate certain critical functions near the strategic apex as in functional Machine Bureaucracy. Or the entrepreneurial adhocracy . . . where the chief executive, an expert himself, is able to retain a semblance of central control despite the use of multidisciplinary project teams. All the hybrids discussed in the [original book] are shown on the pentagon of Figure 1, each on a line between the two configurations from which it draws its characteristics.

The hybrids of Figure 1 all involve two configurations. But nothing precludes a combination of the characteristics of three or more configurations. Thus, one McGill student group described an effective church-run convalescent hospital as being tightly controlled by its chief executive—the students referred to her as the "top nun"—yet having a proliferation of its own work rules, and also being dependent on the skills of its medical staff. Here we have a Simple Structure–Machine Bureaucracy–Professional Bureaucracy hybrid. Another McGill group described a subsidiary of a Japanese trading company as "a divisionalized professional machine adhocracy." (Good thing it wasn't simple!)

Does the existence of such hybrids negate the theory? It is certainly true that the more common the hybrids, the more they should be called pure types and the configurations treated as the hybrids. But the presence of hybrids in a typology does not negate it. There is always gray between black and white. The theory remains useful as long as it helps us to describe a wide variety of structures, even hybrid ones. What matters is not that the theory always matches the reality, but that it helps us to understand the reality. That is its purpose. If we can better describe the Japanese trading company by using terms such as *adhocracy*, *machine*, *professional*, and *divisionalized*, then the theory has served us. By identifying its nodes, we are able to map the pentagon.

So far we have talked of the hybrid only as a combination throughout an organization of the design parameters of different configurations. But there is another kind of hybrid as well, the one that uses different configurations in different parts of the organization. In this way, there can be consistency in the structure of each part, if not in the overall organization. We saw an example of this in the case of the newspaper, with its editorial function structured like an Adhocracy and its printing function structured like a Machine Bureaucracy.

Is this notion of different structures in different parts of the organization inconsistent with the theme running through the preceding five chapters, that whole organizations can be described in terms of single configurations? Not necessarily. There are forces that drive a great many organizations to favor one configuration overall. But within these organizations, there are always forces that favor different structures in different places. . . . Each part of the organization strives for the structures that is most appropriate to its own particular needs, in the face of pressures to conform to the most appropriate structure for the overall organization, and it ends up with some sort of compromise. NASA's cafeterias are, no doubt, run as bureaucracies, but they may prove to be more organic than most; likewise, General Motors' research laboratories no doubt favor Adhocracy structure, but they would probably prove to be more bureaucratic than those at NASA. And so, even though the theory may be a convenient tool to describe a whole organization in terms of a pure type, that description should always be recognized as a simplification, to be followed by deeper probes into the structure of each of its component parts.

[It was noted earlier, for example] that Professional Bureaucracy seemed best to describe the overall structure of the general hospital. But we also noted that the support staff tended to be structured along the lines of a Machine Bureaucracy. And . . . we noted [further] that the research function might best be described as an Adhocracy. Professional Bureaucracy, in effect, really applied to the clinical mission, albeit the most critical one. But even when we look deeply within this mission, we find a range of interdependencies, with resulting variations in the use of the design parameters. Hospitals use incredibly complex structures; to understand them fully, we must look intensively at all their component parts—housekeeping and research and clinical medicine, and obstetrics and radiology and surgery, and plastic surgery and cardiovascular surgery and thoracic surgery.

Again, we conclude by emphasizing that the five configurations are meant to be treated not as five mutually exclusive systems, but as

one, as an integrated frame of reference or theory—a pentagon—to guide us in trying to understand and to design complex real-world organizations.

The Configurations as a System for Describing Structural Transitions

The system of the configurations can also be used as a basis to help us to understand how and why organizations undertake transitions from one structure to another. Our discussion of the [configurations] has been laced with comments about such transitions—for example, from Simple Structure to Machine Bureaucracy as an organization ages and grows, or from Operating Adhocracy to Professional Bureaucracy as an organization tires of innovation and seeks to settle down. All the factors discussed in these chapters that cause a transition from one configuration to another are recorded on the pentagon, along arrows running between them.

Two major patterns have appeared among these transitions, both related to stages in the structural development of organizations. The first pattern applies to organizations that begin in simple environments; it flows around the left side of the pentagon starting at the top. Most organizations begin their lives with something close to the Simple Structure. As they age and grow, and perhaps come under external control, they tend to formalize their behaviors and eventually make a first transition toward Machine Bureaucracy. When these organizations continue to grow, they eventually tend to diversify and later may begin a second structural transition, toward the Divisionalized Form. They may stop along the way, with one of the intermediate, hybrid forms—such as the by-product or related-product form—or else go all the way to the pure Divisionalized Form. But as we noted in [the chapter on the Divisionalized Form], this may prove to be an unstable structure, and pressures may arise for another transition. In the recognition of divisional interdependencies, the organization may consolidate back toward Machine Bureaucracy or else establish a new hybrid on the way to Adhocracy.

Of course, a number of other forces can intervene to change this sequence. Should the environment of the new organization become complex or its technical system sophisticated, it will find itself drawn toward Adhocracy instead of Machine Bureaucracy. Likewise, should the organization with a structure like Machine Bureaucracy find itself facing more complexity and less stability, perhaps owing to product competition or the need to use a more sophisticated or even automated technical system, it, too, will tend to shift toward Adhocracy. And should any of the later-stage organizations suddenly find themselves with a hostile environment, they will tend to revert back toward Simple Structure temporarily. Should external control instead become a strong force, the transition will be made back toward Machine Bureaucracy.

The second pattern among the transitions applies to organizations that are born in complex environments. This pattern begins at the bottom right side of the pentagon and then moves up and to the left. In this case, organizations adopt Adhocracy structures soon after birth, eager to develop innovative solutions to wide ranges of contingencies. Sometimes they remain there, perhaps locked in complex, dynamic environments. But many wish to escape, and some in fact are able to. As they age, these organizations become more conservative. In their search for stability, they begin a transition to bureaucracy. Some concentrate on a few contingencies at which they can become expert, and structure themselves like Professional Bureaucracies. Others focus on single, simple contingencies and shift toward Machine Bureaucracy.

Of course, some organizations also begin early with Professional Bureaucracy, imitating the structure of other established professional organizations. They often maintain these structures throughout their lives, unless rationalization of the professional tasks or external control eventually drives them toward Machine Bureaucracy, or the desire for more experimentation on the part of their professional operators, perhaps a reflection of a new dynamism in the environment, drives them toward Adhocracy.

It should be noted that structural transitions often lag the new conditions that evoke them. Structural change is always difficult, necessitating major rearrangements in established patterns of behavior. So there is a tendency to resist it. Such resistance, in fact, explains many of the dysfunctions found in structures—as in the case of the entrepreneur who hangs on to a Simple Structure even though his organization has grown too large for it, or the organization that continues to formalize even though its environment, having grown complex and dynamic, calls for a structure closer to Adhocracy. Their structures may be internally consistent, but they have outlived the conditions that supported them.

As the need for structural change is finally recognized, the organization begins its transition, perhaps gradually to soften the blow. We saw this in the case of the Machine Bureaucracy that diversifies in steps, passing through the by-product and related-product hybrids on its way to the pure Divisionalized Form. But some organizations never complete the transition; they remain in an intermediate, hybrid state because they experience contradictory forces—new ones calling for change, old ones for retention of the current structure. Thus, many corporations remain permanently in the by-product or related-product hybrid: they have diversified, but interdependencies remain among their product lines. But when the forces calling for change are unequivocal, the transition is probably best effected quickly and decisively. Wavering between two configurations—the old, established one no longer appropriate and the new, uncertain one now necessary—leads to a kind of organizational schizophrenia that may be the most damaging state of all.

To conclude, we have seen in this discussion a number of applications of our five configurations as a single system or theory. Together they help us to understand how organizations can be designed for effectiveness. But neither they nor the pentagon that represents them as a system completely bounds our reality—not only of possible organizational designs but also of the means toward organizational effectiveness.

TO SIX . . . AND BEYOND

[Can there be a sixth configuration? Why not? Even a seventh or an eighth. Indeed, we introduced a sixth configuration in the Chapter 6 reading on "The Structuring of Organizations" in this text—the Missionary form—and discussed it briefly in Chapter 8, "Dealing with Culture," even though it was not included within the contexts per se. That would make our pentagon into a hexagon. But why raise such an issue at this point in the discussion. For one simple reason:] because the reader should be left to question one major premise of [*The Structure in Fives*] book. Throughout, we have implied that the effective structuring of organizations is a kind of jigsaw puzzle. "Here are the pieces—the parts of the organization, [the] coordinating mechanisms, [the] design parameters, [the] situational factors. Now let's see how they fit together. Lo and behold, there turn out to be five ways. To design an effective organization, you should select one of these five images. Or at least put together a logical composite of the five of them. You define your situation and then slot right into the pigeonholes (just as the Professional Bureaucracy does with its clients)."

In fact, this makes good sense for many organizations (as it does for most of the clients of Professional Bureaucracies). But not all. Some need to break away from the standard solutions (as must the clients who have unique problems, and so had better find an Adhocracy instead). These organizations must, in other words, create their own configurations—play "Lego" with the pieces instead of jigsaw puzzle—building new, unthought-of, yet equally consistent structures. Thus, we offer a final hypothesis of organizational effectiveness, one that, while compatible with the calls of the others for congruence and consistency, transcends them. We call it the *creation* hypothesis: effective structuring sometimes requires the creation of a new configuration, an original yet consistent combination of the design parameters and the situational factors. Not every organization can create a whole new structural form. But some, to be truly effective, must. That is why those who possess real magic think beyond five.

MANAGING STRATEGIES INCREMENTALLY*

by James Brian Quinn

MANAGING INCREMENTALISM

. . . [A section of the reading on "logical incrementalism" in Chapter 5 of this text states the logic for incremental management of strategies. But specifically] how can one proactively manage in this mode? One executive provided perhaps the most articulate short statement of the overall approach:

> Typically you start with a general concern, vaguely felt. Next, you roll an issue around in your mind until you think you have a conclusion that makes sense for the company. Then you go out and sort of post the idea without being too wedded to its details. You then start hearing the arguments pro and con, and some very good refinements of the idea usually emerge. Then you pull the idea in and put some resources together to study it so it can be put forward as more of a formal presentation. You wait for "stimuli occurrences" or "crises," and launch pieces of the idea to help in these situations. But they lead toward your ultimate aim. You know where you want to get. You'd like to get there in six months. But it may take three years, or you may not get there at all. And when you do get there, you don't know whether it was originally your own idea—or somebody else had reached the same conclusion before you and just got you on board for it. You never know.

Because of differences in organizational form, management style, and the content of individual decisions, no single paradigm holds for all strategic decisions (Quinn, 1977). But my study suggests that [many] executives [in large companies] tend to utilize somewhat similar incremental processes as they manage complex strategy shifts. [Some summary] glimpses follow:

Leading the Formal Information System

Rarely do the earliest signals for strategic change come from the company's formal horizon scanning, planning or reporting systems. Instead, initial sensing of needs for major strategic changes is often described as 'something you feel uneasy about,' 'inconsistencies' or 'anomalies' (Normann, 1977) between the enterprise's current posture and some general perception of its future environment (Mintzberg et al., 1976). Effective managers establish multiple credible internal and external sources to obtain objective information about their enterprise and its surrounding environments (Wrapp, 1967). They use these networks to short-circuit all the careful screens their organizations build up 'to tell the top only what it wants to hear' (Argyris, 1977). They actively search beyond their organization's formal information systems, deeming the latter to be too historical, tradition oriented or extrapolative to pinpoint needed basic changes in time. For example:

> To avoid their own natural biases, executives who are aggressively seeking new potential opportunities or threats make sure their networks include people who look at the world quite differently from the dominating culture of the enterprise. Some companies have structured 'devil's advocates' into their planning processes for this purpose. Others have undertaken 'aggressor company' exercises to stimulate how intelligent aggressors could best attack their patents, markets, or desired future positions. Still others—like Xerox—have commissioned groups of known independent thinkers to make special studies, with the extensive help of

outside consultants and authorities, to ensure top managers view changing environments analytically and creatively.

Building Organizational Awareness

This may be essential when key players do not have enough information or psychological stimulation to voluntarily change their past action patterns or to investigate options creatively. At early stages, successful change managers seem to consciously generate and consider a broad array of alternatives (Wrapp, 1967). While tapping the 'collective wit' of the organization, they try to build awareness and concern about new issues. They assemble objective data to argue against preconceived ideas or blindly followed past practices. Yet they want to avoid prematurely threatening power centers that might kill important changes before potential supporters really know what is at stake and can bring broader interests to bear. At this stage, management processes are rarely directive. Instead they are likely to involve studying, challenging, questioning, listening, talking to creative people outside ordinary decision channels, generating options, but purposely avoiding irreversible commitments (Gilmore, 1973). . . .

Executives may want their colleagues to be more knowledgeable about . . . major issues and help think through ramifications clearly before taking specific actions. They want to avoid being the prime supporter of a losing idea or having the organization attack or slavishly adopt 'the boss's solution' and having to change it as more evidence becomes available. Even though top executives may not have in mind specific solutions to an emerging problem they can proactively guide early steps in intuitively desired directions by defining the issues staffs investigate, selecting the people who make the investigations, and controlling the reporting process. They may not terminate this 'diagnostic phase' (Mintzberg et al., 1976) until they have identified potential proponents and opponents of various positions and are sure that enough people will 'get on board' to make a solution work.

Building Credibility/Changing Symbols

Symbols may help managers signal to the organization that certain types of changes are coming, even when specific solutions are not yet in hand. Knowing they cannot communicate directly with the thousands who must carry out a strategy, many executives purposely undertake a few highly visible symbolic actions which wordlessly convey complex messages they could never communicate as well, or as credibly, in verbal terms. Through word of mouth the informal grapevine can amplify signals of a pending change [with a power] no formal communication could (Rhenman, 1973). . . . Organizations often need such symbolic moves, or decisions they regard as symbolic, to verify the intention of a new strategy or to build credibility behind one in its initial stages. Without such actions people may interpret even forceful verbiage as mere rhetoric and delay their commitment to new thrusts.

Legitimizing New Viewpoints

[Strategy development] will often involve planned delays, since top managers may purposely create discussion forums or allow slack time [so that] their organizations can talk through threatening issues, work out the implications of new solutions, or gain an improved information base that permits new options to be evaluated objectively in comparison with more familiar alternatives. Because of familiarity, solutions which arise out of executives' prior experience are perceived as having lower risks (or potential costs) than newer alternatives that are more attractive when viewed objectively. In many cases, strategic concepts which are at first strongly resisted can gain acceptance and positive commitment simply by the passage of time and open discussion of new information—when executives do not exacerbate hostility by pushing them too fast from the top (Cyert et al., 1958). Many top executives, planners and change agents consciously arrange for such 'gestation periods' and find that the concept itself is

frequently made more effective by the resulting feedback and acceptance. . . . For example:

> When William Spoor took over as CEO at Pillsbury, one of the biggest issues he faced was whether to stay in or get out of the Pillsbury Farms' chicken business. Management was deeply split on the question. Spoor asked all key protagonists for position papers and purposely commissioned two papers on each side for the Board. He invited consultants' views and visited Ralston Purina, which had undergone a similar divestiture. He got an estimate from Lehman Brothers as to the division's value. All this went to the Board which debated the issue for months. A key event occurred when Lehman found a potential European buyer at a good price. Finally, when the vote was taken only one person—Pillsbury Farms' original champion—voted for retention.

Tactical Shifts and Partial Solutions

These are typical steps in developing a new overall strategic posture [when] early problem resolutions [need] to be partial, tentative or experimental. Beginning moves are often handled as mere tactical adjustments in the enterprise's existing posture and as such they encounter little opposition. Executives can often obtain agreement to a series of small programs when a broad objective change would encounter too much opposition. Such programs allow the guiding executive to maintain the enterprise's on-going strengths while shifting momentum—at the margin—toward new needs (Cyert and March, 1963). At this stage, top executives themselves may not yet comprehend the full nature or extent of the strategic shifts they are beginning. They can still experiment with partial new approaches without risking the viability of the total enterprise, while their broad early steps can legitimately lead to a variety of different success scenarios. . . .

As events unfurl, the solutions to several initially unrelated problems tend to flow together into a new synthesis. When possible, strategic logic (risk minimization) dictates starting broad initiatives that can be flexibly guided in any of several possible desirable directions (Wrapp, 1967).

Broadening Political Support

Broadening political support for emerging new thrusts is frequently an essential and consciously proactive step in major strategy changes. Committees, task forces or retreats tend to be favored mechanisms. By selecting such groups' chairmen, membership, timing and agenda the guiding executive can largely influence and predict a desired outcome, yet nudge other executives toward a consensus. The careful executive, of course, still maintains complete control over these 'advisory' processes through his various influence and veto potentials. In addition to facilitating smooth implementation, many managers report that interactive consensus building also improves the quality of the strategic decisions themselves and helps achieve positive and innovative assistance when things otherwise would go wrong. . . . For example:

> Shortly after he became CEO of General Mills, James MacFarland took his 35 top people on a three day retreat to discuss "how to move a good company to greatness." He wanted the views of others in defining greatness and their active participation in achieving it. Working in groups of six to eight, the management team defined what the characteristics of a great company were from various points of view, what General Mills' shortcomings were, and what main thrusts were needed to overcome these. Over time, these broad visions, goals and programs were converted into charters for various divisions and groups. They became the initial guidelines for the company's very successful and flexible development over the next decade.

Overcoming Opposition

Overcoming opposition is almost always necessary at some stage. Careful executives realize that they must deal with the support the preceding strategy had. They try not to unnecessarily alienate managers from the earlier era, whose talents they may need in future ventures, through a frontal assault on old approaches. Instead, they persuade individuals toward new concepts whenever possible, co-opt or neutralize serious opposition if necessary (Sayles, 1964), or move through zones of indifference (Barnard, 1938) where early changes will not be disastrously opposed. Under the best circumstances, they find 'no lose' situations that activate all important players positively towards new common goals. . . .

Successful executives tend to honor [and even stimulate] legitimate differences in views concerning even major directions and note that initial opponents often thoughtfully shape new strategies in more effective directions. Some may become active supporters as new information emerges to change their views. But consensus is not always possible. Strong minded executives sometimes disagree to the point where they must be moved to positions of less influence or stimulated to leave. And timing can dictate very firm top level direction at key junctures.

Consciously Structured Flexibility

Flexibility is essential in dealing with the many 'unknowables' in the total environment. One cannot possibly predict the precise form or timing of all important threats and opportunities the firm may encounter. Logic dictates therefore that managers purposely design flexibility into their organizations and have resources ready to deploy incrementally as events demand. This requires:

1. proactive horizon scanning to identify the general range, scale, and impact of the opportunities and threats the firm is most likely to encounter;

2. creating sufficient resource buffers, or slacks, to respond as events actually do unfurl;

3. developing and positioning 'champions' who will be motivated to take advantage of specific opportunities as they occur;

4. shortening decision lines between such persons and the top for rapid system response.

These—rather than pre-capsuled (and shelved) programs to respond to stimuli which never occur quite as expected—are the keys to real contingency planning. . . . With such flexible patterns designed into the strategy the enterprise is proactively ready to move on those thrusts that by their very nature may have to evolve incrementally.

Trial Balloons and Systematic Waiting

These are often the next steps for prepared strategists. As Roosevelt awaited a critical event like Pearl Harbor, [company] strategists may have to wait patiently for the proper option or precipitating event to appear. For example:

> The availability of desired acquisitions or real estate may depend upon a death, divorce, fiscal crisis, management change or erratic economic break. Technological advances may await new knowledge, inventions or lucky accidents. Or planned market entries may not be wise until new legislation, trade agreements or competitive shake outs occur. Very often the optimum strategy depends on the timing and sequence of such random events. For example the timing and nature of SDS Inc.'s availability was a proximate cause of both the date and results of this first Xerox entry into computers.

Executives may also consciously launch trial concepts . . . [like Mr. Spoor's "Super Box"] in order to attract options and concrete proposals. Usually these trial balloons are phrased in very broad contextual terms. Without making a commitment to any specific solution, the executive activates the organization's creative abilities. This approach keeps the manager's own options open until substantive alternatives can be evaluated against each other and against concrete current realities. And it prevents practical line managers from rejecting desirable strategic shifts because they are forced to compare 'paper options' against what they see as well-defined, urgent needs.

Creating Pockets of Commitment

This may be necessary for entirely new strategic thrusts. The executive may encourage exploratory projects to test options, create necessary skills or technologies or build commitment for several possible options deep within the organization. Initial projects may be kept small, partial, or *ad hoc*, not forming a comprehensive program or seeming to be integrated into a cohesive strategy. At this stage guiding executives may merely provide broad goals, a proper climate and flexible resource support, without being identified with specific projects (Soelberg, 1967). In this way they can avoid escalating attention to any one solution too soon or losing personal credibility if it fails. But they can stimulate those options which lead in desired directions, set higher hurdles for those that do not or quietly have them killed some levels below to maintain their own flexibility. Executives can then keep their own options open, control premature momentum, openly back only winners and select the right moment to blend several successful thrusts into a broader program or concept (Witte, 1972). They can delay their own final decisions on a total thrust until the last moment, thus obtaining the best possible match-up between the company's capabilities, psychological commitments, and changing market needs. . . .

Crystallizing Focus

Crystallizing focus at critical points in the process is, of course, vital. Sometimes executives will state a few key goals at an early stage to generate action or cohesion in a difficult or crisis situation. But for reasons noted, guiding executives often purposely keep early goal statements vague and commitments broad and tentative (Quinn, 1977). Then as they develop information or consensus on desirable thrusts, they may use their prestige or power to push or crystallize a particular formulation. Despite adhering to the rhetoric of specific goal setting, most executives in my study were careful not to state many new strategic objectives in concrete terms until they had carefully built consensus among key players. To do otherwise might inadvertently centralize their organizations, preempt interesting options, provide a common focus for otherwise fragmented opposition, or cause the organization to undertake undesirable actions just to carry out a stated commitment. Because the net direction of an organization's goals ultimately reflects a negotiated balance among the imperatives felt by the dominant executive coalition (Perrow, 1961) and the most important power centers and stakeholders in the enterprise, the last thing an executive wants is to weaken his or her position by creating an unintended counter coalition. When to crystallize viewpoints and when to maintain open options is one of the true arts of strategic management. . . .

Formalizing Commitment

This is the final step in formulation. As partial consensus emerges, the guiding executive may crystallize events by stating a few broad goals in more specific terms for internal consumption. Finally when sufficient general acceptance exists and the timing is right, the decision may appear in more public pronouncements. For example, as General Mills divested several of its major 'old line' divisions its annual reports began to state these as moves 'to concentrate on the company's strengths' and 'to intensify General Mills' efforts in the convenience foods field,' statements which it would have been unwise or impolitic to make until many of the actual divestitures had taken place and a new management coalition and consensus had emerged.

As each major new thrust comes into focus, strategic managers insure that some individual(s) feel responsible for its execution. Plans are locked into programs or budgets, and control and reward systems are aligned to reflect intended strategic emphases (Cohen and Cyert, 1973). Since so much has been written on this subject, I will avoid details here.

Continuing Dynamics and Mutating Consensus

[Unfortunately, old crusades can quickly become a] new conventional wisdom and the organization [can] fail to prepare itself for new concerns and concepts. In trying to build commitment, executives often surround themselves with people who strongly identify with the new strategy. These supporters can rapidly become systematic screens against new views. Even as the organization arrives at its new consensus, guiding executives must move to insure that this too does not become inflexible. Effective strategic managers therefore immediately introduce new foc[i] and stimuli at the top to begin mutating the very strategic thrusts they have just solidified—a most difficult but essential psychological task. . . .

Not a Linear Process

While generation of a strategy generally flows along the sequence presented, stages are by no means orderly or discrete. Few executives manage the process through all phases linearly. . . . The strategy's ultimate development [usually] involves a series of nested partial decisions (in each strategic area) interacting with similar decisions in all other areas and with a constantly changing resource base. Pfiffner (1960) has aptly described the process as "like fermentation in biochemistry, rather than an industrial assembly line." The validity of a strategy lies not in its pristine clarity or rigorously maintained structure, but in its capacity to capture the initiative, to deal with unknowable events, to redeploy and concentrate resources as new opportunities and thrusts emerge and thus to use resources most effectively toward selected goals.

Each major segment of a strategy is likely to be in a different phase of its development—from initial awareness to . . . ultimate commitment—at any given moment. The real integration of all these components into a total enterprise strategy takes place primarily in the minds of individual top executives. Some portions of the strategy may be seen the same way by all, but each executive may legitimately perceive the overall balance of goals and thrusts slightly differently. Some differences may be openly expressed as issues to be resolved when new information becomes available; others may remain unstated, hidden agendas to emerge at later dates: still others may be masked by accepting a broad statement of intention that accommodates many divergent views within its seeming consensus—while a more specific statement might be divisive. Events often move almost imperceptibly from awareness, to concern, to experiments, to options, to partial acceptance, to momenta, to consensus, to formal reinforcement. The process is so continuous that it may be hard to discern the particular point in time when specific clear-cut decisions are made.

INTEGRATING THE STRATEGY

Nevertheless, the total pattern of actions, though incremental, does not remain piecemeal in well-managed organizations. Effective executives constantly reassess the total organization, its capacities and needs as related to surrounding environment. . . .

Concentrating on a Few Key Thrusts

Strategic managers constantly seek to distil out a few (six to ten) 'central themes' that draw the firm's diverse existing activities and new probes into common cause. Once identified, these help maintain focus and consistency in the strategy. They make it easier to discuss and monitor intended directions. In ideal circumstances, these themes can be converted into a matrix of strategic 'thrusts' or 'missions' cutting across divisional plans and dominating other criteria used to rank divisional commitments (see Quinn, 1980). Each division's plans have to show *enough* effort to accomplish its share of each thrust, even though this means overriding short-term present-value

or rate-of-return rankings on projects within the division (Pfeffer et al., 1976). Texas Instruments and General Electric Company have provided some well publicized formal models for doing this. Unfortunately, few companies seem able to implement such complex planning systems without generating voluminous paperwork, large planning bureaucracies and undesirable rigidities in the plans themselves. . . .

Coalition Management

[Nevertheless,] at the heart of all controlled strategy development lies coalition management. Top managers operate at a confluence of pressures from: stockholders, environmentalists, government bodies, customers, suppliers, distributors, producing units, marketing groups, technologists, unions, special issue activities, individual employees, ambitious executives and so on, where knowledgeable people of good will can easily disagree on a proper balance of actions. In response to changing pressures and coalitions among these groups, the top management team continuously forms and reforms its own coalitions aligned around specific decisions. These represent various members' different values and interests concerning the particular issue at hand and are sources of constant negotiations and implied bargains among the leadership group (Sayles, 1964).

Most major strategic moves tend to assist some interests—and executives' careers—at the expense of others. Consequently, each set of interests can serve as a check on the others and thus help maintain the breadth and balance of the overall strategy. Some managements try to insure that all important [polities] have representation or access at the top. And the guiding executive group may continuously adjust the number, power or proximity of these access points to maintain a desired balance and focus (Zaleznik, 1970). People selection and coalition management are the ultimate controls top executives have in guiding and coordinating their companies' strategies. These must be managed with sophistication and care to achieve desired degrees of stimulation, objectivity, cohesion and dynamism. The following quotations, the first by a CEO, the second by Robert Hatfield when Chairman of Continental Group, make the point well:

> If good people share the same values, they will instinctively act together. We must know how people will respond intuitively when they are thousands of miles away. . . . We work hard and consciously to understand each other and where we are going. If we know these things and communicate openly, our actions will be sensible and cohesive. Yet we'll have the flexibility to deal with changing environments. These—and the choice of top-flight people—are our real controls for coordinating strategy development.
>
> How do you manage the strategic process? It all comes down to people: selecting people. First, you look for people with certain general characteristics. They have to be bright, energetic, flexible, with high integrity or they won't be adaptive and last in the long run. Among these, you look for the best people with the kinds of experience and interests likely to lead the company in directions you want it to go. But you have to be careful with this. You don't want just "yes men" on the directions you believe in. You want people who can help you think out new approaches too. Finally, you purposely team people with somewhat different interests, skills, and management styles. You let them push and tug a bit to make sure different approaches get considered. And you do a lot of chatting and informal questioning to make sure you stay informed and can intervene if you have to.

CONCLUSIONS

In recent years, there has been an increasing chorus of discontent concerning corporate strategic planning. Many managers are concerned that despite elaborate strategic planning systems, costly staffs for this purpose, and major commitments of their own time, their most elaborate strategies get implemented poorly, if at all. These executives and their companies have generally fallen into the classic trap of thinking about strategy formulation and implementation as separate sequential processes. . . .

Instead, successful managers who operate logically and proactively in an incremental mode build the seeds of understanding, identity and commitment into the very processes which create their strategies. Careful incrementalism allows them to improve the quality of information used in decisions and deal with the practical politics of change—while they step by step build the organization's momentum toward the new strategy and the psychological motivation to carry it through. . . .

DESIGNING TURNAROUND STRATEGIES*

By Charles W. Hofer

INTRODUCTION

At some time in their history, most successful organizations suffer stagnation or decline in their performance. Such stagnation or decline often causes much management and stockholder anguish in spite of the fact that the continuing emergence of new organizations in a resource-constrained world implies that some older organizations must grow less rapidly than before, or perhaps even stagnate or die. Fortunately, the most typical outcome is that the growth rate of the old organization slows but still remains positive, or, at worst, that the organization ceases growing, but does not decline. Nevertheless, the Western ethic that "one must grow or die" causes psychological problems in such instances, much as the onset of middle age does in many individuals. Once this ethic is recognized for the myth it is, management and stockholders usually adjust to the new situation. Unfortunately, some managements then vegetate rather than realizing that they can only stay in the same place by running faster and faster. That is, they confuse stagnation of outputs (performance) with stagnation of inputs (effort). But as anyone who has tried to row upstream in a swiftly flowing river knows, just maintaining position often requires a lot of effort.

This article will discuss turnarounds and turnaround strategies in business organizations. The topic is an important one, as the number of recent publications on these issues indicates. In spite of such increasing attention, however, no comprehensive, systematic treatment of turnaround strategies has appeared in the literature to date. This article will seek to fill a portion of this gap by examining turnarounds at the business-unit level. Its focus will be prescriptive rather than descriptive. Specifically, it will: (1) analyze the nature of business-level turnaround situations; (2) discuss the types of turnaround strategies that are possible at this level; (3) present an analytical framework for deciding what type of turnaround strategy should be used in particular situations; and (4) discuss how to design and implement the various aspects of the indicated turnaround strategy.

THE NATURE
OF TURNAROUND SITUATIONS

There are two factors that are important in describing turnaround situations. They are (1) the areas of organizational performance affected and (2) the time criticality of the turnaround situation.

In terms of organizational performance, the types of turnarounds that have been pursued and studied most frequently are those involving declines in organizational efficiency and/or profit-

ability. Such declines usually have been measured by declining net income after taxes, although net cash flow and earnings per share have also been used.

The types of turnaround receiving next highest priority have been those involving stagnation or declines in organizational size or growth. The reason for such attention derives partly from the obvious link between size, growth, and net income, partly from the Western myth that one must grow or die, and partly from research findings linking profitability to relative market share. In most of these instances, growth has been measured in absolute terms through an index such as dollar sales. Increasingly though, market share is also being used as a measure of growth at the business-unit level because of the association between market share and profitability.

The third type of turnarounds to receive substantial management attention in the 1980s have been those involving poor organizational asset utilization. Such turnaround efforts have not received as much publicity or research attention as the first two, however, primarily because they have been pursued by firms that are performing reasonably well in terms of profits and growth. Thus, poor performance with respect to asset utilization does not *appear* to pose the same threat to organizational or management survival as poor performance in the former areas. Furthermore, such asset utilization turnaround strategies usually have not been discussed by the firms pursuing them outside of their management councils, primarily for competitive reasons. Asset utilization turnarounds are likely to receive far greater attention from top management in the late 1980's and early 1990s than they have to date, however, because the combination of reasonable profits and poor asset utilization provides an open invitation to corporate takeover and greenmail specialists such as Boone Pickens. Despite (or perhaps because of) such threats, it is still likely that most asset utilization turnaround efforts will continue to be pursued with a low profile.

The second characteristic of turnaround situations that is important to the design of effective turnaround strategies is the time criticality of the firm's current situation. If there is imminent danger to survival, it is almost always necessary to make an operational response to the situation in the near term even though a strategic response may eventually follow. The reason for this is the lengthy time delay that usually exists between the taking of a strategic action and the response that accompanies it. When the threat to organizational survival is not imminent (i.e., when there is some time to respond in a variety of ways), then it is possible to "customize" the turnaround strategy to the specific situation involved.

TYPES OF TURNAROUND STRATEGIES

There are two broad types of turnaround strategies that may be followed at the business-unit level: strategic turnarounds and operating turnarounds.

Strategic turnarounds are of two types: those that involve a change in the organization's strategy for competing in the same business, and those that involve entering a new business or businesses. The latter involve questions of corporation portfolio strategy and will not be discussed further here. Strategies for saving the existing business may be further subdivided according to the nature of the competitive position change desired, and by the core skills and competitive weapons around which the strategy is built. Most such strategic turnarounds can be classified into one of three categories:

1. Those that seek to move to a larger strategic group in the industry involved;

2. Those that seek to compete more effectively within the business' existing strategic group through the use of different (or substantially modified) competitive weapons and core skills; And

3. Those that seek to move to a smaller strategic group in the industry involved.

In terms of competitive weapons and core skills, most strategic turnarounds involve switches in the ways firms seek to achieve differentiation or cost effectiveness, rather than switches from a differentiation strategy to a cost effectiveness strategy, or vice versa.

Operating turnarounds are usually one of four types, none of which involves changing the firm's business-level strategy. These are nonstrategic turnarounds that emphasize: (1) increased revenues; (2) decreased costs; (3) decreased assets; or (4) a balanced combination of two or more of the preceding options. It should be noted that these categories could also be used to describe strategic turnarounds. In strategic turnarounds, though, the focus is on the strategy changes sought, with the performance produced being a derivative of the strategy change. In operating turnarounds, by contrast, the focus is on the performance targets, and any actions that can achieve them are to be considered whether they make good long-run strategic sense or not.

In practice, the distinction between strategic and operating actions and turnarounds becomes blurred because actions that substantially decrease assets also often require a change in strategy to be most effective, and so on. The distinction is still relevant, however, because of the different priorities attached to short-term versus long-term actions and tradeoffs in the two types of strategies.

SELECTING THE TYPE OF TURNAROUND STRATEGY TO BE FOLLOWED

In trying to decide what type of turnaround strategy should be pursued in a particular situation, three questions should be asked:

1. Is the business worth saving? More specifically, can the business be made profitable in the long-run, or is it better to liquidate or divest it now? And, if it is worth saving, then:

2. What is the current operating health of the business?

3. What is the current strategic health of the business?

Although one occasionally encounters turnarounds that involve long time horizons, the vast majority of turnaround situations involve severe constraints on the time available for action. In fact, in most turnaround situations there is some imminent danger to the firm's survival. For this reason, one must first check the current operating health of the business as longer-term considerations will be irrelevant if the firm goes bankrupt in the near-term. For this same reason, the first step in assessing a firm's current operating health is an analysis of its current financial condition. The purpose of such analysis is to determine: (1) how probable it is that the firm may go bankrupt in the near term; (2) how much time it has to make needed changes before it goes bankrupt; (3) the magnitude of the turnaround needed to avoid bankruptcy; and (4) the financial resources that could be raised in the short-term to aid in the battle. Once this analysis is completed, similar analyses must be conducted of the firm's current market, technological, and production positions

in order to complete the determination of its current operating health.

After these analyses are completed, the task of selecting the optimal type of turnaround strategy can begin. In general, such optimal strategies will depend on the firm's current operating and strategic health, as indicated in Figure 1. If both are weak, then liquidation is probably the best option unless the firm has no other businesses in which it could invest. In the latter case, a combined operating/strategic turnaround with very tight controls might be possible. With a weak operating position and a moderate or strong strategic position, an operating turnaround strategy is usually needed, although divesture is also reasonable if the corporation has other businesses in which it might invest.

When the business is strong operationally but weak strategically, then a strategic turnaround is almost always indicated although the firm may have a grace period in which to decide what it will do. When both operating and strategic health

FIGURE 1   SELECTING THE OPTIMAL TURNAROUND STRATEGY

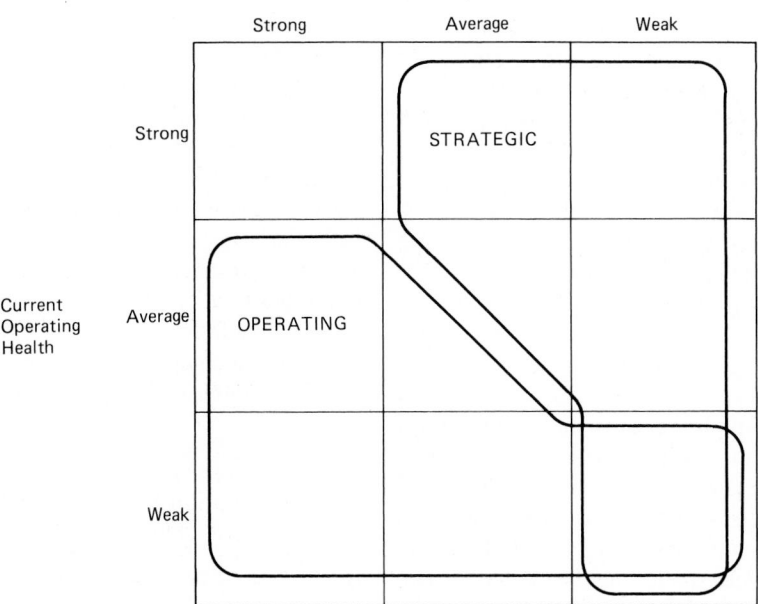

are strong, turnaround strategies are seldom needed unless it is to improve asset utilization, which may sometimes lag. The approach to use for improving asset utilization in such cases will normally depend on the firm's current strategic health.

Once a business has selected the type of broad turnaround strategy it should use, i.e., strategic or operating, it then needs to select the more specific aspects of its turnaround strategy. The details of these action plans will depend, of course, on the exact nature of the industry in which the business competes and on its strengths and weaknesses vis-à-vis its major competitors in that industry.

THE NEED FOR NEW TOP MANAGEMENT

Before discussing any specific turnaround options, though, one nearly universal generalization must be made. It is the "fact" that almost all successful turnarounds require the replacement of the business's current top management. There is, of course, no law written in stone that says a firm's current top management team cannot supervise a successful turnaround. Usually, however, the old management has such a strong set of beliefs about how to run the business in question, many of which must be wrong for the current problems to have arisen, that the only way to get a new view of the situation is to bring in new top management. There will, of course, be some exceptions to this generalization as there are to all generalizations. Nonetheless, in over 95 percent of the cases cited by Kami and Ross (1973) and by Schendel, Patton, and Riggs (1976), a change in top management did accompany a successful turnaround. Thus, one can say that a successful turnaround will require, almost without exception, either a change in top management or a substantial change in the behavior of the existing management team. Moreover, increasing evidence from the experiences of General Electric and other similar multi-industry companies indicate that different general managers are

skilled at different types of tasks. Consequently, the new top management team should be selected to the degree possible with the skills appropriate to the type of turnaround strategy that will need to be followed. For instance, an entrepreneurial strategist should be chosen if a high-growth, strategic turnaround is to be pursued, while a hard-nosed, experienced cost cutter should be selected if an operating turnaround with a major cost-reduction effort is to be pursued.

STRATEGIC TURNAROUNDS

Strategic turnarounds are appropriate when the business has an average or strong current operating position, but a lost position strategically. Although it is possible that the business could be weak in its strategic technological, production, or financial positions (situations which usually produce declines in profits and ROI) but not its market share, such is not usually the case. Instead, most strategic turnarounds involve situations in which there has been a major decline in both sales and share position, and possibly even a change in the strategic group in which the business competes. Consequently, the principal method of differentiating among strategic turnarounds is according to the magnitude of the share reversal or strategic group change sought. Three options are possible: (1) a maintenance of the business's current share and/or strategic group position accompanied by a refocusing of the business on one or more easily defensible product-market segments or niches within the strategic group selected; (2) one-level shifts in share and strategic group position,[1] i.e., movement from a dropout position to a follower position or from a follower position to a competitor position or from a competitor position to a leader position; or (3) two-

---

Theoretically it would be possible, at least in some industries, to make a one-level shift in share position within the same strategic group. Practically, however, almost all efforts to achieve one or two-level shifts in share position require a change in the strategic group in which the business competes.

level shifts in share and strategic group position, i.e., from a dropout position to a competitor position or from a follower position to a leader position.

Usually, however, two-level shifts in share and strategic group position, or even one-level shifts that involve attempting to secure the leadership position, are not possible unless the business has unusual strategic resources that it has failed to exploit as well as access to discretionary strategic funds 50 to 100 percent more than it could normally generate on its own. (One such source is a corporate parent that is willing to fund heavy investments in areas of relative competitive advantage over moderately long periods of time, such as Phillip Morris was willing to do with Miller's.) The only other times when shifts of such magnitude are possible are (1) when the current leader slips, (2) when there is a major change in stage of product-market evolution, or (3) when the turnaround firm is the former leader who had recently fallen.

Normally, therefore, the choice of a strategic turnaround strategy is between a one-level shift in share and strategic group position (which might involve moving from fifth, sixth, or seventh position to a second, third, or fourth position in the industry), and a segmentation or niche strategy within the business' current strategic group. Again, unless the business has unusual resources or there is a shift in stage of product-market evolution, the segmentation/niche type strategy will normally be more profitable in terms of ROI, earnings per share, and other similar asset utilization measures of organizational performance. However, segmentation/niche strategies usually provide little or no opportunity for eventually seizing leadership in the industry involved and will usually produce lower total dollar sales and net income than a successful one-level share and strategic group shifting turnaround strategy—unless the segments selected for the new focus grow substantially. Most businesses, therefore, usually try strategic turnarounds that involve seeking higher dollar sales through one-level shifts in share and strategic group position, with a possible, even though remote, opportunity for seizing

leadership should competitors slip or environmental challenges change.

Optimally, a strategic turnaround should attempt to combine the best features of both these approaches; i.e., it should seek segmentation, but in such a way that overall sales and share would increase because of the strategic position or group change. Such an optimum strategic turnaround is usually not possible, however, unless there is a newly emerging segment to the market, and even then the turnaround business must be able to develop superior products for that segment, as well as upgrading its competences in the other functional areas important for serving that segment. Moreover, to be able to maintain any headstart it might get on its competitors, the firm involved needs to be able to differentiate itself from its key competitors in some relatively enduring way—a most difficult task if its competitors have superior resources.

The major conclusion that can be drawn from industry practice to date is that too much attention is given to strategic turnarounds that involve one-level increases in share and strategic group position, and not enough to strategic turnarounds that involve segmentation and niche hunting.

OPERATING TURNAROUNDS

There are four different types of operating turnaround strategies that are possible:

1. Revenue-increasing strategies
2. Cost-cutting strategies
3. Asset-reduction strategies
4. Combination strategies

While these turnaround strategies might seem to correspond in some ways to the three different types of strategic turnarounds noted above, attempts to make such a correspondence are really misleading since the correspondence is more one of results than of means, and as a consequence, usually exists only in the short-term. A comparison of a typical strategic turnaround involving a one-level shift in the strategic group in which the firm competes with a typical revenue-increasing operating turnaround should help illustrate the differences. In the former instance, the business involved would normally develop a new line of products, alter the basic character of its production system, invest heavily in R&D, possibly even change its methods of distribution, and be slightly overstaffed in anticipation of future growth. In addition, that growth would start slowly since the efforts being undertaken are long-term ones. Later, however, the growth rate would take off for a period of several years before it slowed as the firm reached its new position.

In a typical revenue-generating operating turnaround, however, the firm would keep its existing line of products, although it might supplement these with products that it used to make but had discontinued—provided there was some indication this action would boost current sales. Also, the business might produce some products totally unrelated to its principal business if these required little start-up expense and helped utilize its facilities more fully in the short-term. In addition, both R&D and staffing would be at moderate or low levels relative to sales, while some major marketing efforts, such as price cutting, increased advertising, or increased direct sales calls, would be undertaken to stimulate current sales. One other difference would also exist. In a strategic turnaround designed to move a business to a larger strategic group, few activities would be undertaken that were not directly related to the business's long-term strategic thrust. At the same time, substantial attention would be given to *all* of the key success factors critical to the future health of the business. In a revenue-increasing operating turnaround, by contrast, almost total attention would be focused on short-term, revenue-generating actions with little or no attention to the other areas of the business. Moreover, several of the revenue-generating actions undertaken in such an operating turnaround might have no bearing on the long-term strategic health of the business. In short, strategic and operating turnarounds are really substantially different in

character, even though there sometimes appears to be a similarity in the short-term results they produce.

Because of the primary focus on short-term operating actions, the first step in any operating turnaround should be to identify the resources and skills that the business will need to implement its long-term strategy so that these can be protected in the short-term action program that will follow. Once these resources have been identified, the type of operating turnaround strategy to be followed should be selected based primarily on the firm's current break-even position [Figure 2], with adjustments being made depending on structure of the industry in which it competes and its current financial position.

If the firm is close to its current break-even point (i.e., at 90 percent of more break-even), or if it is in the combination-strategy range, but has high direct labor costs, high fixed expenses, or limited financial resources, then cost-cutting turnaround strategies are usually preferable because moderately large short-term decreases in fixed costs are usually possible and because cost-cutting actions take effect more quickly than revenue-generating actions.

On the other hand, if the business is extremely far below its break-even point (i.e., at less than 33 percent of break-even or lower), then the only viable option is usually an asset-reduction turnaround strategy, especially if the business is close to bankruptcy. In such instances, the principal question is which assets should be sold and which should be kept. The answer depends on the firm's projected future strategy and the saleability of its different assets. As a general rule, the only assets that should be kept are those that the firm will definitely use within the next year or two. Unless bankruptcy is imminent, though, the sale of the firm's remaining non-essential assets should be done with deliberateness rather than haste, because the rushed or forced sale of assets will often reduce the price the seller will get for them by 100 percent or more.

If the firm's sales fall between the above ranges (i.e., in the range of 40 to 70 percent below its break-even point), then the most effec-

FIGURE 2 DECIDING ON THE TYPE OF OPERATING TURNAROUND STRATEGY
TO FOLLOW

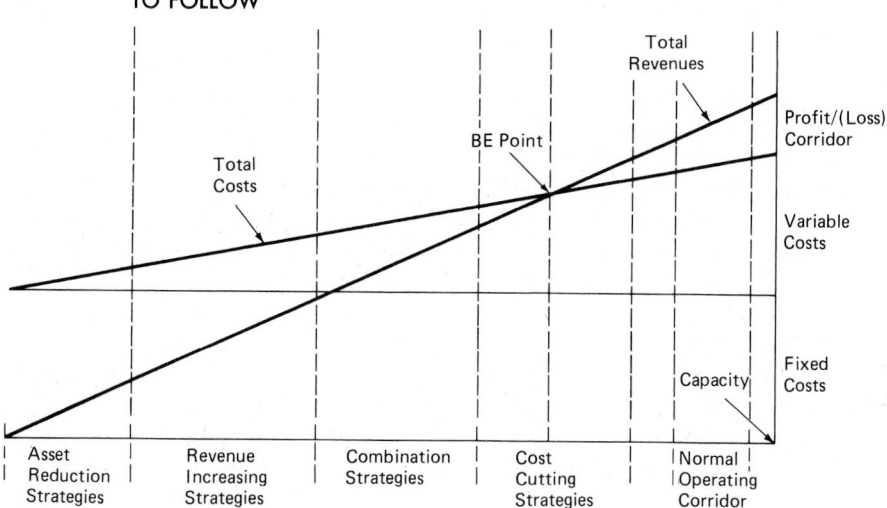

tive operating turnarounds usually involve revenue-generating or asset-reduction strategies, because in such circumstances there is usually no way to reduce costs sufficiently to reach a new break-even, and time and resources are typically not adequate to attempt a combination turnaround strategy. The choice between revenue-generating and asset-reduction strategies in such situations depends primarily on the longer-term potential of the business after turnaround, and the criticalness of the firm's current financial position. If the firm's growth potential is such that its present capacity will be used within a year or two after the start of the turnaround and its finances are not yet desperate, then revenue-generating strategies should be pursued. If its finances are critical but the potential to use its existing capacity is also present, then the firm should follow a combination revenue-generating/asset-reduction strategy. The principal focus, though, should be on revenue generation with the sale of assets limited to the amount needed to meet the firm's cash flow needs for the next three to six months. If the longer-term sales potential is substantially less than the firm's present capacity, though, an asset-reduction strategy should be selected with the

total amount of assets to be sold being determined by the firm's long-term growth potential.

In more immediate positions (i.e., when the business's current sales are between 50 and 80 percent of its current break-even point), combination strategies are usually the most effective, although when fixed costs or direct labor costs are very low, revenue-generating strategies are sometimes even more effective. Under combination strategies, cost-reducing, revenue-generating, and asset-reduction actions are pursued simultaneously in relatively balanced proportions. The rationale for this type of balanced effort is that the cost-benefit ratios for the best cost-reducing and asset-reduction actions are substantially higher than those of the fourth or fifth-best revenue-generating actions, and conversely. Consequently, the cash flow that will be produced by a balanced effort is sufficiently higher than that which would be produced by a single-focus turnaround effort that the greater complexities of managing such a balanced effort are more than compensated for. Such cost-benefit comparisons should be explicitly calculated before beginning a combination strategy, however, because without a substantial dollar advantage, a single-focus turnaround strategy is clearly preferable. The logic behind this preference stems from the magnitude and urgency of the various tasks that must be done in any turnaround situation. There are, quite simply, more things to be done than there is time available to do them. As a consequence, unless there is a clear and ever-present goal to guide one's actions, such as revenue-generation or cost-reduction, it is quite likely (because of past interests or current skills) that one will pursue some profitable tasks substantially beyond the point of diminishing returns. Because of their lack of a single, clear-cut goal, combination strategies are particularly susceptible to this problem. They should, therefore, be pursued only when their payoff more than adequately compensates the firm for the additional managerial complexity and operational difficulties they entail.

No matter what type of operating turnaround strategy is followed, though, the limited financial resources and time urgency associated with most operational turnaround situations require that particular attention be given to all actions that will have a major cash flow impact on the business in the short-term. As a consequence, actions such as collecting receivables, cutting inventories, increasing prices when possible, focusing on high-margin products, stretching payables, decreasing wastage, and selling off surplus assets should almost always be pursued. Some will be a logical extension of the type of turnaround strategy selected. The others should be used only if the timing and total impact of their cash flow contributions warrant taking time away from the firm's chosen turnaround strategy. Among the best tools for addressing the latter questions are sensitivity, variability, and elasticity analyses. Also useful are pro forma cash flow projections and Donaldson's (1969) system for assessing the speed with which various resources can be concerted to cash in financial emergencies.

SUMMARY AND CONCLUSIONS

Before closing, three other points deserve repeating. First, before starting any turnaround, an explicit calculation should be made to determine whether the turnaround effort will be worth it. Too often firms embark on turnaround efforts as a knee-jerk reaction to the myth that nothing can be worse than failure, i.e, liquidation. Such is not the case, though, and in many instances, stockholders, employees, and other organizational stakeholders would be better served if management faced up to the true prospects and benefits of long-run survival and decided to liquidate the business for what it is worth now.

Second, before embarking on a strategic turnaround, an explicit investigation should be made of the conditions in the industry involved, and, in particular, of its competitive structure and stage of evolution. The reason for such analysis is quite simple. It is that industry structure is not uniformly flexible at all points in time. Thus, there are times when strategic changes abound within an industry. During such periods, shifts in relative competitive position occur moderately often. Consequently, during such times strategic turnarounds are relatively easy and inexpensive. At other times, however, it is almost impossible to make major shifts in competitive position with the resources available to most firms in the industry. During these periods, strategic turnarounds should not be attempted unless the organization has access to substantial outside resources or unless there are special circumstances, such as a competitor asleep at the switch, that provide unique opportunities in an otherwise barren situation. Finally, it should be noted that the ideas presented in this article are based on limited research and study. It is, therefore, likely that some of them will be modified (or elaborated on) by future research.

RESPONDING TO CRISIS*

by William H. Starbuck, Arent Greve, and Bo L.T. Hedberg

For nearly fifty years, Facit was regarded as a successful manufacturer of business machines and office furnishings. Facit grew until it operated factories in twenty cities and it maintained sales units in fifteen countries. Employment reached 14,000. Suddenly, this success metamorphosed into impending disaster. For three consecutive years, gross profits were negative and employment and sales declined. Plants were closed or sold. Again and again, top managers were replaced and the managerial hierarchy was reorganized. Consultants were called in: they recommended that more operations should be closed and more employees should be fired. But after numerous meetings, the top managers could not decide whether to do what the consultants recommended. . . .

Facit . . . exemplifies organizations which encounter crises. Crises are times of danger, times when some actions lead toward organizational failure. . . .

Based on several case studies of organizations facing crises, this article explains what makes some organizations especially prone to encounter crises, it describes how organizations typically react to crises, and it prescribes how organizations ought to cope with crises.

WHY DO CRISES OCCUR?

One initial conjecture was that crises originate as threatening events in organizations' environments. A competing conjecture was that crises originate from defects within organizations themselves. Analyses of actual crises suggest that both

* Excerpted from an article originally published in the *Journal of Business Administration* (Spring 1978), pp. 111–178; reprinted with deletions by permission of the *Journal of Business Administration*.

conjectures are partly true and both are partly false. Organizations facing crises do perceive the crises as having originated in their environments. For example, Facit's top managers attributed many difficulties to temporary depressions of the firm's economic environment, and they often complained about the fierceness of market competition. At first, Facit's top managers thought that electronic calculators would replace mechanical calculators only very gradually; later, they saw electronic calculators as a technological revolution that was progressing too quickly for Facit to adapt to it (Starbuck and Hedberg, 1977).

And it was, in fact, true that national economic growth was sometimes faster and sometimes slower. There were indeed competing firms that were wooing Facit's customers. Electronic calculators actually did challenge and ultimately replace mechanical calculators. So the observations of Facit's top managers had bases in reality. But one would have to be quite gullible to accept such reasons as completely explaining Facit's crises.

Organizations' perceptions are never totally accurate. Organizations decide, sometimes explicitly but often implicitly, to observe some aspects of their environments and to ignore other aspects. They also interpret, in terms of their current goals, methods and competences, what they do observe. Such interpretation is evident in the statements about electronic calculators by Facit's top managers.

There are special reasons to question the perceptions of the top managers in organizations facing crises. If crises result partly from defects within organizations, these defects could distort the organizations' perceptions. Because distorted perceptions appear in all organizations, it may be overstatement to say that distorted perceptions are alone sufficient to cause crises. However, perceptual distortions do seem to contribute to crises by leading organizations to take no actions or inappropriate actions. . . .

Defects in organizations not only affect perceptions; they also affect the realities that are there to be perceived. Organizational defects are translated into environmental realities when organizations choose their immediate environments—by choosing suppliers, product characteristics, technologies or geographic locations—or when they manipulate their environments—by advertising, training employees, conducting research or negotiating cooperative agreements (Starbuck, 1976). . . .

Learning to Fail

Talk of organizational defects can, however, easily create misimpressions about the differences between those organizations which encounter crises and those which avoid crises. The organizations which encounter crises do not have qualitatively unusual characteristics, and they are not fundamentally abnormal. Probably the great majority of organizations have the potential to work themselves into crises, and the processes which produce crises are substantially identical with the processes which produce successes (Hedberg *et al.*, 1976).

LEARNING/PROGRAMMING

These ironies arise from how organizations learn and from how they use their successes. The key process for organizational learning is programming: when organizations observe that certain activities appear to succeed, they crystallize these activities as standardized programs. These programs are built into the formalized roles assigned to organizations' members. Both programs and roles make activities consistent across different people and across different times. Programs generate activities that resemble those leading to good results in the past, and they do so efficiently. Organizations respond quickly to most environmental events because these events activate previously learned programs. Programs also loosen organizations' connections to their environments. Because environmental events fall into equivalence classes according to which programs they activate, organizations fail to perceive many of the small differences among environmental events. Because organizations indoctrinate their

members and train them to perform roles, organizations fail to accommodate or utilize many of the differences among members who are recruited at various times in diverse locations (Nystrom *et al.*, 1976).

Programming often facilitates success, and success always fosters programming. Success also produces slack resources and opportunities for buffering—both of which allow organizations to loosen their connections to their environments (Cyert and March, 1963; Thompson, 1967). Customers are clustered into equivalence classes, and products are standardized. Raw materials and products are stored in inventories, work activities are smoothed, and work schedules are stretched out into the future. Programs and roles are added rather frequently and discarded less frequently. Technologies are frozen by means of large capital investments. Such buffers make possible efficiencies that create slack resources, and slack resources can be used to make organizations less dependent upon their environments. Similarly, programming can make it less necessary to expend analytical resources on responses to environmental events, and analytical resources can be used to make organizations less dependent on their environments.

Programming, buffering, and slack resources are tools that cut on two sides. On one side, these tools enable organizations to act autonomously—to choose among alternative environments, to take risks, to experiment, to construct new environmental alternatives—and autonomous actions are generally prerequisites for outstanding successes. But on the other side, these tools render organizations less sensitive to environmental events. Organizations become less able to perceive what is happening, so they fantasize about their environments, and it may happen that realities intrude only occasionally and marginally on these fantasies. Organizations also become less able to respond to the environmental events they do perceive: they too rarely reflect before they act, they believe too strongly in the rightness of their programs, they are too confident of their abilities to act autonomously (Hall, 1976; Starbuck and Hedberg, 1977). Because strategies interact with organizational politics, strategic re-orientations generally induce changes in who holds power, so those people who currently hold power tend to resist strategic reorientations (Normann, 1971; Wildavsky, 1972). . . .

Crises do occur because organizations make mistakes, and these mistakes can be attributed to certain organizational characteristics. For example, . . . Facit . . . sought to remain in obsolete markets; and . . . these strategies were supported by top managers over the protests of managers at low levels and of representatives of the blue-collar workers. The organizations which encounter crises may be marginally extreme: they may allocate too much influence to top managers; they may rely too strongly on formal procedures, formalized communications, and standardized programs; they may feel unwarranted complacency; they may stringently filter their perceptions of their environments; they may have unusually fanciful beliefs about reality; they may initiate imprudent experiments (Grinyer and Norburn, 1975; Hedberg et al., 1976; Miller and Mintzberg, 1974). However, these organizations are marginally extreme at most. Many organizations exhibit these characteristics, all organizations possess some disadvantageous characteristics, and all organizations make mistakes. Environmental events pick out the specific organizations which come face-to-face with their mistakes.

WHAT REACTIONS DO CRISES EVOKE?

Explaining Crises Away

It seems that conventional accounting reports, and the ideology asserting that such reports should be bases for action, are among organizations' major liabilities. The more seriously organizations attend to their accounting reports, the more likely they are to encounter crises, and the more difficulty they have coping with crises.

Accounting reports are intentionally historical: at best they indicate what happened during the previous quarter, and even recent reports are strongly influenced by purchases of goods and equipment dating back many years and by inventories of unsalable products and obsolete components. The formats of accounting reports change very slowly. Accounting reports also intentionally focus upon formalized measures of well observed phenomena; the measures are always numerical, the importances of phenomena are appraised in monetary units, and the observations are programmatic. Much of the content in every report is ritualized irrelevance.

Accounting reports could be more helpful and less misleading, but accounting reports do not themselves cause crises. Rather, concern for accounting reports is one symptom of a generalized pattern of organizational behavior. The organizations which take their accounting reports very seriously are assuming that their worlds change slowly—that precedents are relevant to today's actions, that tomorrow's environments will look much like yesterday's, that current programs and methods are only slightly faulty at most (Hedberg and Jönsson, 1978; Thompson, 1967). Such organizations devote few resources to monitoring and interpreting unexpected environmental events; they do not tolerate redundant, ostensibly inessential activities; they guide their development by means of systematic long-range planning. Concern for formal reports may testify that there is little spontaneous, informal communication: activities are coordinated through planning and programming, performances are evaluated solely by the measures in formal reports, areas of responsibility are clearly demarcated, authority is hierarchically systematic (Miller and Mintzberg, 1974).

All of these characteristics make it difficult for organizations to see unanticipated threats and opportunities. Many unanticipated events are never perceived at all; others are only perceived after they have been developing for some time. Then when unanticipated events are perceived, these characteristics introduce perceptual errors. One consequence is that organizations overlook the earliest signs that crises are developing, because the earliest signs are changes in poorly observed variables and they are communicated orally in informal reports. Another consequence is that, after signs of crises are seen, organizations underestimate the needs for action. Remedies are not attempted when crises are newly born and mild remedies might yet suffice.

Those organizations which are strongly wedded to their pasts, naturally enough, fear rapid changes. They expect abrupt changes to produce undesirable consequences. This logic is often reversed when undesirable events occur: the undesirable events are hypothesized to be the consequences of rapid changes. The early signs of crises are attributed to the organizations' injudicious efforts to change—new markets, capital investments, inexperienced personnel, or product innovations. Such interpretations imply that no remedies are needed beyond prudent moderation, because erformances will improve automatically as operations stabilize.

The idea that organizations ought to be stable structures also fosters another rationalization for early signs of crises—that poor performances result from transient environmental pressures such as economic recessions, seasonal variations in consumption, or competitors' foolish maneuvers. This rationale implies that no major strategic reorientations are called for; to the contrary, the current strategic experiments ought to terminate. Organizations decide that temporary belt-tightening is needed, together with some centralization of control and restraints on wasteful entrepreneurial ventures, but these are portrayed as beneficial changes that focus attention on what is essential (Beer, 1974; Nystrom *et al.*, 1976; Thompson, 1967). . . .

Denials that crises are developing and that strategic reorientations are needed arise, to no small degree, from sincere conviction (Gundhus, 1977). There is widespread endorsement of the idea that actions ought to be determined by rational analyses, and this idea implies that organizations ought to be stable bureaucracies. The managers who rely upon accounting reports really do believe that they should act only on the basis of reliable information and that communications should flow through channels. Of course, manag-

ers who have helped to formulate strategies are likely to be convinced that they have formulated good strategies that should not be changed merely because of transient difficulties. And it is a normal human characteristic to adhere to one's prior beliefs in spite of evidence that they are incorrect.

But not all denials of crises arise from sincere conviction. Managers who have helped to formulate strategies often expect—rightly—that they will be blamed if these strategies are judged faulty. These managers resist strategic reorientations in order to retain power and status, and they try to persuade themselves and others that their strategies are appropriate. Crises induce skilled personnel to depart, financial backers to desert, and suppliers to withhold credit. Anticipating such problems, managers may launch propaganda campaigns that deny the existence of crises. These propaganda efforts always include distortions of accounting reports: accounting periods are lengthened, depreciation charges are suspended, gains from sales or reevaluations of assets are included with operating profits. But it is inconsistent to assert that no crises exist and also to initiate changes that are intended to remedy crises, so to make their propaganda credible, these managers argue that major strategic reorientations are unnecessary.

Facit's top managers made numerous efforts to persuade stockholders, employees, and the public that no crises existed, that the crisis was not serious, or that the crisis had ended. When poor performance first intruded into Facit's accounting reports, the top managers explained that this poor performance was the temporary product of currency devaluations and fierce competition. ''Facit is well equipped to meet future competition. . . . Improvement is underway, but has not affected this year's outcome.'' Later, as the crisis deepened, Facit's managing director was replaced several times: each new managing director reported sadly that the situation was actually worse than his predecessor had publicly admitted, but he was happy to be able to announce that the nadir had been passed and the future looked rosy. Again and again, Facit's top managers announced that their firm was in sound condition and that improved performances were imminent; the chairman of the board and the managing director made such announcements even while they were secretly negotiating to sell the firm. After two years of serious difficulties, when plants were being closed, when hundreds of employees were losing their jobs, and when the top managers were privately in despair, the top managers announced that they intended to expand Facit's product line by sixty percent (Starbuck and Hedberg, 1977).

In many situations, managers find delay to be an effective tactic: delays frequently render overt actions unnecessary, and delays may clarify what actions are desirable. Thus, when managers fail to react to the early signs of crises, they are behaving in a way that would be effective in many situations. But those situations for which delays produce improvements are not crises. In fact, situations are not crises if normal behaviors produce improvements. Crises are dangerous, in part, because normal behaviors make them worse.

Crises call for strategic reorientations, but delays increase both the magnitudes of these reorientations and their urgencies. Reorientations that could have been achieved gradually with moderate stress escalate during delays into major upheavals that are nearly impossible to bring off successfully. Delays are bought at the cost of tight budgets, asset consumption, centralized control, and restrictions on entrepreneurship (Nystrom et al., 1976; Stinchcombe, 1974). But if the top managers who exercise centralized control had the ability to take corrective actions, there would be no crises; so in crises, centralization transfers control to inappropriate people (Starbuck and Hedberg, 1977). Tight budgets and restrictions on entrepreneurship halt strategic experimentation and drive away ambitious, creative managers, with the result that organizations lose both the knowledge to guide reorientations and the people to carry out reorientations. Asset consumption means that organizations have nothing to fall back on when delays fail and needs for action are finally acknowledged.

Living in Collapsing Palaces

The organizations which encounter crises resemble palaces perched on mountaintops that are crumbling from erosion. Like palaces, these organizations are rigid, cohesive structures that integrate elegant components. Although their flawless harmonies make organizational palaces look completely rational—indeed, beautiful—to observers who are inside them, observers standing outside can see that the beauty and harmony rest upon eroding grounds.

Organizational palaces are rigid because their components mesh so snugly and reinforce their neighbors. Perceptions, goals, capabilities, methods, personnel, products, and capital equipment are like stone blocks and wooden beams that interlock and brace each other. There are no chinks, no gaps, and no protruding beams because careful reason has guided every expansion and remodeling. Rationality is solidified in integrated forms that are very difficult to move: the components which blend smoothly in one arrangement fit badly in another, components which mesh tightly must be moved simultaneously, and movements fracture tight junctions. So the inhabitants' first reactions to crises are to maintain their palaces intact—they shore up shaky foundations, strengthen points of stress, and patch up cracks—and their palaces remain sitting beautifully on eroding mountaintops.

However, shoring up affords only temporary remedies against crumbling mountains, and eventually, the palaces themselves start falling apart. People begin to see that the top managers have been making faulty predictions: doubts arise that the top managers know how to cope with the crises, and the top managers usually end up looking like incompetent liars. Idealism and commitments to organizational goals fade; cynicism and opportunism grow; uncertainty escalates (Jönsson and Lundin, 1977; Kahn et al., 1964; Vickers, 1959). But cuts and reorganizations stir up power struggles that undermine cooperation.

These processes of disintegration feedback and reinforce themselves. Organizations' abilities to achieve depend strongly on expectations (King, 1974): when people expect failures, failures become more likely, and expectations of failure multiply. Achievements also depend upon ability and effort. People who see job opportunities elsewhere gain reasons to take them, and the people who are most able are offered more job opportunities, so the average level of ability falls. Those people who remain are told to work harder while taking on unfamiliar tasks and receiving fewer rewards, so their job performances degrade and their satisfactions slide downward. Cynical, opportunistic acts by subordinates elicit exhortations from their superiors—but the exhorters are seen as being untrustworthy cynics. Conflicts and power struggles stimulate additional centralized control by top managers who are themselves seen as grasping power even though they do not know how to use it. . . . Other organizations are unable to help themselves, but they are saved by outside interventions. Facit was such a case.

Two or three years after Facit's crisis became obvious, the top managers reached a state of paralysis. The managerial hierarchy had been reorganized repeatedly. Several small plants had been closed, and the main office-furnishings plant had been sold. But the situation had continued to get worse and worse. . . .

At this point, Electrolux bought Facit and achieved a dramatic turnaround. Eight-hundred employees were laid off right away, but these people were being rehired within three months. It was discovered that Facit possessed a large, unfilled demand for typewriters: a mechanical-calculator plant was converted to typewriters, and the typewriter plants were expanded. The demand for office furnishings was also found to exceed production capacity. Facit's research had developed electronic calculators, small computers, and computer terminals which had never been marketed aggressively; substantial demands existed for these products. During the second year after Electrolux stepped in, Facit's employment went up 10 percent, production increased 25 percent, and Facit earned a profit.

Facit's turnaround was made possible by the disintegration that preceded it. The impedi-

ments to learning usually grow very strong in organizations. Because organizations are intricate, they fear that changes would produce unforeseen disadvantages. Because organizations are logically integrated, they expect changes to initiate cascades of further changes. Because organizations are rational, they buttress their current programs and roles with justifying analyses. These impediments to learning grow strongest in the organizational palaces that emphasize rational analyses, reliable information, and logical consistency. Palaces have to be taken apart before they can be moved to new locations, and organizations have to unlearn what they now know before they can learn new knowledge. Organizations have to lose confidence in their old leaders before they will listen to new leaders. Organizations have to abandon their old goals before they will adopt new goals. Organizations have to reject their perceptual filters before they will notice events they previously overlooked. Organizations have to see that their old methods do not work before they will invent and use new methods (Cyert and March, 1963; Hedberg, 1981; Nystrom *et al.*, 1976).

Unfortunately, crisis-ridden organizations may learn that their old methods do not work, and yet they may not learn new methods which do work.

HOW TO COPE WITH CRISES

Crises are dangerous, by definition. After crises have fully developed, organizations face serious risks of failure. To eliminate these risks is often difficult, and the remedies bring pain to some people. Consequently, the best way to cope with crises is to evade them.

Avoiding Excesses

It is not easy to prescribe how organizations should evade crises. Because crises are partially caused by environmental events that organizations cannot control, events might inflict a crisis upon any organization, and no prescriptions can render crises utterly impossible. Moreover, insofar as crises are caused by defects within organizations, these causes have deep roots: the people in organizations believe that they are using good methods and pursuing sound strategies. Prescriptions advocating different methods are received as advocating poorer methods, and prescriptions of different strategies are received as recommending less sound strategies.

Organizations are right to receive prescriptions skeptically. Their complexities make organizations very difficult to manage as complete systems, whereas prescriptions for managing organizations have to be simple in order to be understandable. When prescriptions describe methods and strategies which are easily translated into actual behaviors, these prescriptions oversimplify, they ignore contingencies, and they state half-truths. When prescriptions specify methods and strategies applying to complete, complex systems, these prescriptions read like poems that express verities but that have obscure applications to actual behaviors. Both kinds of prescriptions induce the people who follow them to misinterpret what is prescribed. Thus organizations should never adhere strictly to any prescription . . . including this one.

Yet, even difficulties created by uncontrolled environmental events need not lead to organizational failures: organizations can pick up and attend to early-warning signals, and so begin remedial actions in time to prevent crises from maturing. And the case studies suggest that many organizations adhere too strictly to those prescriptions which favor rationality, reliability, formality, logical consistency, planning, agreement, stability, hierarchical control and efficiency. All of these properties can bring benefits when they appear in moderation: organizations need some rationality, some formality, some stability, and so on. But excessive emphases on these properties turn organizations into palaces—palaces on eroding mountaintops. Organizations also need moderate amounts of irrationality, unreliability, informality, inconsistency, spontaneity, dissension, instability, delegation of responsibility, and inefficiency. These properties help to keep percep-

tions sharp, they disrupt complacency, and they nurture experimentation and evolutionary change (Hedberg *et al.*, 1976; Miller and Mintzberg, 1974).

One sensible operating rule is that whenever organizations adopt one prescription, they should adopt a second prescription which contradicts the first. Contradictory prescriptions remind organizations that each prescription is a misleading oversimplification that ought not be carried to excess. For example, organizations should work toward consensus, but they should also encourage dissenters to speak out; organizations should try to exploit their strategic strengths, but they should also try to eliminate their strategic weaknesses; organizations should formulate plans, but they should also take advantage of unforeseen opportunities and they should combat unforeseen threats. It is as if each prescription presses down one pan of a balance: matched pairs of prescriptions can offset each other and keep a balance level. There is no evidence in the case studies that these balances have to be exactly level. Small imbalances apparently do not cause serious difficulties, and even large imbalances take long times to produce crises. Organizations err mainly by failing to recognize that good prescriptions become bad prescriptions when they are carried to excess.

But balancing prescriptions is a defensive tactic that cannot rescue the organizations which already face crises. These organizations have been defending themselves—unsuccessfully— too long; they need to go on the offensive. The remainder of this article prescribes how organizations can terminate their crises and begin to rebuild themselves in viable forms.

Replacing Top Managers

When Electrolux took over Facit, it promptly fired all of Facit's top managers. This is exactly what Electrolux should have done. If Electrolux had not taken such drastic action, its intervention would probably have failed. . . .

Indiscriminate replacements of entire groups of top managers are evidently essential to bringing organizations out of crises. The veteran top managers ought to be replaced even if they are all competent people who are trying their best and even if the newcomers have no more ability, and less direct expertise, than the veterans.

By the time crisis-ridden organizations face up to their needs for major, long-run remedies, the organizations are teetering on the brink of failure. They lack disposable assets. No slack remains in their costs, yet they are losing money. Their debts are high, and creditors will lend them no more. Creative, entrepreneurial managers have left. Cooperation has broken down. Subordinates no longer believe what their superiors say. Everyone expects failure. No one has the energy and the enthusiasm to try experiments. There are no resources to support further delays, yet no insiders can argue convincingly that they know what actions should take the place of delays.

Remedies are needed urgently. Perhaps the greatest need is for dramatic acts symbolizing the end of disintegration and the beginning of regeneration. Because propaganda and deceit have been rife, these symbolic acts have to be such that even skeptical observers can see they are sincere acts; and because the top managers represent both past strategies and past attempts to deceive, these symbolic acts have to punish the top managers. In addition, however, the organizations need new perceptions of reality, fresh strategic ideas, and revitalization. Since no one really knows what strategies will succeed, new strategies have to be discovered experimentally. Experimenting depends upon enthusiasm and willingness to take risks; people must have confidence their organizations can surmount new challenges and exploit discoveries. Experimenting also depends upon seeing aspects of reality which have been unseen and upon evaluating performances by criteria that differ from past criteria. Crisis-ridden organizations have already tried those experiments which look promising within their past perceptual frameworks, and the experiments they have not tried are ones they perceive as foolish.

Even crisis-ridden organizations are not undifferentiated wholes. They incorporate multiple,

conflicting perceptions and disparate evaluation criteria. For example, Facit contained many managers and union officers who disagreed with the firm's overall strategic thrust and who were striving to be heard by the top managers. However, such heterogeneities are buried in the lower echelons of hierarchies with monolithic tops. Consensus among top managers is one reason these organizations drift into crises in the first place. Then when crises bring on centralized controls and criticism by outsiders, the top managers coalesce further into unified groups. Dissidents among the top managers rarely dissent publicly. Thus, the top managers filter the heterogeneities out of the ideas, proposals, and opinions of their subordinates.

Before regeneration can proceed, these filters have to be broken up, and replacements of one or two top managers at a time are not enough. Such gradual replacements happen spontaneously while crisis-ridden organizations are disintegrating: if gradual replacements were sufficient to end crises, the crises would already have ended. But when top managers are replaced gradually, the newcomers are injected into on-going, cohesive groups of veterans, and the newcomers exert little influence on these groups, whereas the groups exert much influence on the newcomers.

Group cohesion also impedes the veteran's own efforts to adopt remedies. Each member of a group is constrained by the other members' expectations, and cohesion draws these constraints tight. A group as a whole may bind itself to its current methods even though everyone in the group is individually ready to change; when a group includes one or two members who actively resist change, these resisters can control what happens. . . .

Rejecting Implicit Assumptions

One reason groups of top managers find change difficult is that many of the assumptions underlying their perceptions and behaviors are implicit ones. Explicit assumptions can be readily identified and discussed, so people can challenge these assumptions and perhaps alter them. But implicit assumptions may never be seen by the people who make them, and these unseen assumptions may persist indefinitely. . . .

Experimenting with Portfolios

. . . In order to escape from crises, organizations have to invest in new markets, new products, new technologies, new methods of operating, or new people. Diversification plays the same role in these investments as it does in other investments: expected returns are traded for protection against mistaken predictions.

If an organization had perfect foresight, its optimal strategy would be to invest all of its efforts in a single activity—an activity which is both certain to remedy the crisis quickly and certain to provide a sound basis for future development. However, this single-activity strategy is only optimal for an imaginary organization with perfect foresight. If an organization makes small errors of prediction, it might misjudge the relative merits of several activities that all look good. Such an organization must invest effort in several activities in order to be confident that its portfolio includes the best alternative. If an organization's predictions contain large errors, it might mistakenly invest in activities that look promising but really are not. Such an organization must invest in several activities merely to be confident that its portfolio includes even one good alternative (Landau, 1973). Of course, crisis-ridden organizations have highly distorted perceptions, so they are prone to make enormous errors of prediction.

But crisis-ridden organizations find it difficult to pursue several alternatives simultaneously because they lack resources. Not many organizations start to develop alternatives while they are still [affluent]. . . .

Organizations may have less difficulty obtaining tangible resources than obtaining the equally essential intangible resources, because organizational disintegration subjects people to tremendous stress. Stress amplifies uncertainty (Kahn *et al.*, 1964), and so people have had their fill of uncertainty long before organizations start to investigate alternatives. Consequently,

people want to believe that sure-fire remedies have been found, they do not want to hear about prediction errors, and they do not want to invest themselves in experiments that might fail.

Nevertheless, experimentation is the right theme to engender. Crisis-ridden organizations do not know sure-fire remedies, so they have no choice but to experiment, and some of their experiments will fail. . . .

When people recognize that they are experimenting, they can manage their experiments in ways which cut down the losses that failures would produce. Experimenting people can also accept the inconsistency that they are now searching for remedies among activities that looked unpromising in the frameworks of their organizations' former perceptions and beliefs. Of course, an experimental theme brings the danger that people will not take their activities seriously enough and that experiments will fail solely because people lack faith in them. This danger is serious, but it is a danger arising from realistic skepticism and it can be combatted. Moreover, an experimental theme offers long-run advantages in that experimenting people are unlikely to be satisfied by the first indications of success: they keep on trying for improvements because experiments never come out perfectly (Hedberg *et al.*, 1976; Starbuck and Nystrom, 1977).

Managing Ideology

Top managers are often the villains of crises. They are the real villains insofar as they steer their organizations into crises and insofar as they intensify crises by delaying actions or taking inappropriate actions. And they are symbolic villains who have to be replaced before crises end. But top managers are also the heroes when their organizations escape from crises. They receive the plaudits, and they largely deserve the plaudits because their actions have been the crucial ones.

Sometimes top managers contribute to escapes from crises by inventing new methods and strategies. Top managers have the best chance to do this effectively in small organizations . . . because small organizations do not make sharp demarcations among managers at different levels and they do not sharply distinguish managers from staff analysts. However, even in small organizations, the top managers should beware of relying on their own strategy-making skills. In large organizations where top management is a specialized occupation, it is generally a mistake for the top managers to act as strategy makers.

Especially in large organizations, there are usually staff analysts who are better than the top managers at formulating strategies and inventing new methods. People are promoted to top management partly because they have been given credit for past successes. But these successes are characteristically organizational achievements that blend contributions from several individual people; the leaders of organizational successes often lose their ascribed abilities when their followers change or when their tasks change. The people who have been credited with successes overestimate the generality of their past decision rules and their past analytic techniques, so they underestimate the speed with which their expertise grows obsolete. People are also chosen as top managers partly because they can skillfully manage other people. But managing differs from analyzing, and managers' work is fragmented into brief episodes that leave few opportunities for thoughtful reflection (Mintzberg, 1973a).

Furthermore, when top managers are occupied with strategy-making, they are not doing the more important work which is their special responsibility: managing ideology. The low-level and middle managers do attend to ideological phenomena to some extent, but they focus their attentions upon visible, physical phenomena—the uses of machines, manual and clerical work, flows of materials, conferences, reports, planning documents such as schedules and blueprints, or workers' complaints. Top managers have the complementary responsibility: although they have to attend to visible, physical phenomena to some extent, they should concentrate their attentions on ideological phenomena such as morale, enthusiasm, beliefs, goals, values, and ideas. Managing ideology is very difficult because it is so indi-

rect—like trying to steer a ship by describing the harbor toward which the ship should sail. But managing ideology is also very important because ideological phenomena exert such powerful effects upon the visible, physical phenomena.

Electrolux's turnaround of Facit was wrought almost entirely by managing ideology (Starbuck and Hedberg, 1977). Except for the replacements of top managers, Electrolux left Facit's organization largely alone. Electrolux did loan Facit approximately two million dollars so that actions would not have to be taken solely out of financial exigency, but this was a small sum in relation to the size of the company. What Electrolux did was to reconceptualize Facit and Facit's environment. Electronic calculators were no longer a technological revolution that was leaving Facit behind: Facit was making and selling electronic calculators. Typewriters and office furnishing became key product lines instead of sidelines to calculators. Competition stopped being a threat and became a stimulus. As Electrolux's managing director put it: "Hard competition is a challenge; there is no reason to withdraw." A newspaper remarked: "Although everything looks different today, the company is still more or less managed by the same people who were in charge of the company during the sequence of crises. It is now very difficult to find enough people to recruit for the factories. . . . All the present products emanate from the former Facit organization, but still, the situation has changed drastically". . . .

Facit . . . [is an organization that has] rediscovered the truth of an ancient, Chinese insight. The Chinese symbol for crisis combines two simpler symbols, the symbol for danger and the one for opportunity. Crises are times of danger, but they are also times of opportunity.

Organizations can benefit from crisis if they can perceive their opportunities and can marshall the courage and enthusiasm to pursue them. Whether organizations do this is largely up to their top managers. With little more than words, the top managers can shape ideological settings which reveal opportunities, nurture courage, and arouse enthusiasm. As Edmund Leach rightly observed: "The world is a representation of our language categories, not vice versa."

STRATEGIC RESPONSES TO TECHNOLOGICAL THREATS*

by Arnold C. Cooper and Dan Schendel

Technological innovation can create new industries and transform or destroy existing ones. At any time, many businesses are confronted with a host of external technological threats. Managements of threatened firms realize that many threats may not materialize, at least in the short run. However, one or more of those potential threats may develop in ways that will have devastating impact. Providers of kerosene lamps, buggy whips, rail road passenger service, steam radiators, hardwood flooring, passenger liner service and motion pictures all have had to contend with such threats. Few environmental changes can have such important strategic implications.

A typical sequence of events involving the traditional firm's responses to a technological threat begins with the origination of a technological innovation outside the industry, often pioneered by a new firm. Initially crude and expensive, it expands through successive submarkets, with overall growth following an S-shaped curve. Sales of the old technology may continue to expand for a few years, but then usually decline, the new technology passing the old in sales within five to fourteen years of its introduction.

The traditional firms fight back in two ways. The old technology is improved and major commitments are made to develop products utilizing the new technology. Although competitive positions are usually maintained in the old technology, the new field proves to be difficult. In addition to the major traditional competitors (who are also fighting for market share in the new field), a host of new competitors must be confronted. Despite substantial commitments, the traditional firm is usually not successful in building a long-run competitive position in the new technology. Unless other divisions or successful diversifications take up the slack, the firm may never again enjoy its former success.

Most previous research on technological innovation has been concerned with the practices and problems of innovators. This research is concerned with major technological innovations from the viewpoint of firms in established industries threatened by innovation.

THREATENED INDUSTRIES

The industries and technologies selected for study were the following:

> steam locomotives vs. diesel-electric
>
> vacuum tubes vs. the transistor
>
> fountain pens vs. ball-point pens
>
> boilers for fossil fuel power plants vs. nuclear power plants
>
> safety razors vs. electric razors
>
> aircraft propellers vs. jet engines
>
> leather vs. polyvinyl chloride and poromeric plastics.

Within these traditional industries, twenty-two separate firms were studied, using data available in the secondary literature where over 200 separate sources were examined. The accompanying table lists these firms. Two broad questions are of concern to the study:

> What was the nature of the substitution of the new technology for the old?
>
> What response strategies were used to counter the technological threats?

* A. Cooper and D. Schendel, "Strategic Responses to Technological Threats", *Business Horizons* (February, 1976); reprinted with deletions with the permission of the journal.

TABLE 1   TRADITIONAL INDUSTRIES STUDIED

Firms Studied	Locomotives	Vacuum (Receiving) Tubes	Fountain Pens	Safety Razors	Fossil Fuel Boilers	Propellers	Leather Industry
	American Baldwin	CBS RCA Raytheon Sylvania	Esterbrook Eversharp Parker Sheaffer Waterman	American Gillette	Babcock & Wilcox Combustion Engineering	Koppers Curtiss-Wright United Aircraft	A. C. Lawrence Armour Allied Kid Seton
Sales decline immediately after new technology introduced?	No	No	*	No	No	No	Yes[1]
Sales eventually begin long-term decline?	Yes	Yes	Yes	No	No	Yes	Yes
Time from introduction of new technology until sales of new technology exceeded old.	Fourteen years[2]	Eleven years	Nine years	Twenty-five years[3]	Not during the twenty years since first sale	Five years[4]	†
New markets created by new technology?	No	Yes	Yes	No	No	No	Yes
New technology limited in application or crude at first?	Yes	Yes	Yes	Yes	Yes	Yes	Yes
New technology applied sequentially to submarkets?	Yes	Yes	Yes[5]	No	No	Yes	Yes
First commercial introduction by a firm in traditional industry?	‡	Yes	No	No	§	Yes[6]	No
First commercial introduction by a new firm?	No	No	Yes	Yes	No	No[6]	Yes
Old firms participate in new technology?	Yes	Yes	Yes (4 of 5)	Yes (briefly)	Yes	Yes (2 of 3)	No (1 of 4)[7]
Acquisitions a means of participating in new technology?	No	Yes Raytheon	Yes Parker	Yes Gillette[8]	No	No	Yes Allied Kid
Old technology improved after new technology was introduced?	Yes	Yes	Yes	Yes	Yes	Yes	Yes

Traditional firms involved in improving old technology and in entering new technology?	Yes	Yes	Yes	Yes (4 of 5)	Yes (participation in electric razors short-lived)	Yes	Yes
Attempt to establish barriers to new technology?	No	No	No	No	No	No	No

[1] Production of three of the four types of leather declined in the year after vinyl was first used as a leather substitute.

[2] Available sales data relate to units sold rather than sales dollars, but it appears that diesel-electric sales exceeded steam locomotive sales by 1938, fourteen years after the first diesel-electric switcher was introduced. Subsequently, steam locomotive unit sales exceeded diesel-electric unit sales during World War II, but steam locomotive sales then dropped sharply after the War.

[3] During 1956–1958, electric razor sales exceeded sales of razor blades. Subsequently, however, razor blades regained a sales lead and have maintained it to the time of the study.

[4] Unit production of jet engines exceeded unit production of piston engines during a three-year period in the early 1950s. It appears that the dollar value of jet engines produced exceeded the value of the smaller, less powerful piston engines within about five years of their introduction in the United States.

[5] The pen market is segmented by price. Initially, the ball-point pen was relatively expensive.

[6] Power Jets, a new British firm, developed the first jet engine. General Electric developed and introduced the first American jet engine, relying upon Power Jets' designs.

[7] Allied Kid bought Corfam from DuPont in 1965. Also, all the firms began coating hides with synthetic materials to improve their qualities.

[8] Gillette acquired Braun, A. G., and thereby entered the overseas market for electric razors. Gillette has not reentered the U.S. market since 1938, when its internally developed electric razor was introduced and subsequently withdrawn.

[*] Data were not found to indicate whether sales of fountain pens declined the year the ball-point pen was introduced.

[†] Results are mixed by type of application. By 1950, synthetics had captured 50% of the shoe sole market.

[‡] The first mainline diesel-electric was introduced by General Motors, a firm which never made steam locomotives. However, American Locomotive had earlier introduced an experimental diesel-electric switcher.

[9] The first nuclear power plant was developed by Westinghouse, a firm with a strong position in turbines. However, for the producers of boilers, it was not a traditional competitor which introduced the new technology.

The findings must be regarded as tentative. The data are incomplete in some areas, as should be expected from secondary data [and the number of industries studied small] . . . .

PATTERNS OF SUBSTITUTION

. . . An examination of the sales over time for both the new and old technologies showed variable patterns which do not always duplicate the classical S-shaped pattern. Analysis of this sales data, coupled with extensive examination of other information, leads to a number of conclusions concerning the substitution pattern of new for old technologies.

1. After the introduction of the new technology, the sales of the old technology did not always decline immediately; in four out of seven cases, sales of the old technology continued to expand.

2. In two cases, sales of the old technology continued to expand for the entire period studied, despite growth in sales of the new technology.

3. When sales of the old technology did decline, the time period from first commercial introduction to the time when dollar sales of the new technology exceeded dollar sales of the old ranged from about five to fourteen years.

4. The first commercial introduction of the new technology was, in four out of seven cases, made by a firm outside the traditional industry. It might have been expected that the traditional competitors would have been the logical sources of industry innovation because of their strong customer relationships, well-developed channels of distribution and organizations oriented toward serving those industries.

5. In three of the four industries in which capital requirements were not excessive, new firms were the first to introduce the new technology.

6. The new technology often created new markets which were not available to the old technology. Although the initial ballpoint pens were expensive, low priced pens were later developed which opened up a new market to the "throw away" pen. It was

also estimated that 50% of the applications for the transistor were in equipment made possible by the invention of the transistor. Vinyls were used in floor coverings and building materials, applications not open to leather.

7. The new technology was expensive and relatively crude at first. Often, its initial shortcomings led observers to believe it would find only limited applications. Although the first ball-point pens wrote under water, they blotted, skipped and stopped writing on paper and even leaked into pockets; after an initial fad phase, public disenchantment set in and sales dropped dramatically. The first transistors were expensive and had sharply limited frequencies, power capabilities and temperature tolerance; some observers thought they would never find more than limited application. The jet-powered airplane was initially thought to be suitable only for the military market.

8. The new technology often invaded the traditional industry by capturing sequentially a series of submarkets. Although the new technology was crude it often had performance advantages for certain applications. Some submarkets were insulated from competition for extended periods. General Motors' diesel-electric locomotive first invaded the submarket for passenger locomotives, subsequently the submarket for switcher locomotives, and then freight locomotives— the major submarket—accounting for about 75% of industry sales. The transistor found early application in hearing aids and pocket radios, but not in radar systems and television.

9. The new technology did not necessarily follow the standard S-shaped growth curve. Erratic patterns were caused by abnormal economic and social conditions (World War II in the case of the electric razor, propellers and steam locomotives), by faddish phase of sales (ballpoint pens), and by a newer technology replacing the original new technology (transistors and integrated circuits).

Some Pitfalls of Appraisals

Many factors affect the rate of penetration of a new technology: it does not capture markets overnight. Substantial sales opportunities may exist in the old technology for extended periods. It may be difficult for management in the traditional firms to judge the eventual impact of a developing threat, but at least there is usually time to develop a new strategy.

However, response presumes the ability to recognize and assess the threatening innovation. Intelligence activities focusing only upon traditional competitors are not enough, inasmuch as nontraditional competitors and new firms may be the originators of the threatening technology. It may be necessary to monitor a variety of innovations, many of which may never have significant impact.

Surviving past technological threats does not confer future immunity. In 1934, when General Motors introduced the first mainline diesel-electric locomotive, the producers of steam locomotives could look back upon two earlier threats which they had survived: the electric locomotive, and, in the 1920s, passenger cars with individual gasoline-powered engines. Both of these prior threats captured only small segments of the American locomotive market. There was no indication that the next threat, the diesel-electric, would destroy the traditional industry within fifteen years.

It would be a mistake to wait until decline in sales of the old technology triggered the need for appraisal of the threat. By then, much of the lead time would have passed. However, this means that the new technology must be appraised when it is still relatively crude. In an earlier article, James C. Utterback and James W. Brown (1972) emphasized that hypotheses about directions for change aid in selection of parameters which can be observed and evaluated. For instance, early diesel engines had such a high weight-to-horsepower ratio that a diesel-electric locomotive would have been impossibly large. Managements of steam locomotive firms might have hypothesized that any changes leading to improvements in this weight-to-power ratio were of critical importance and deserved continuous monitoring.

It is not enough to judge that someday a new technology will replace an old one. Rates of penetration must be determined. When the

Baldwin Locomotive Works was founded in 1831, it would have been of little value to tell founders that someday their principal product would be obsolete. However, when Sylvania introduced a new line of vacuum tubes for computers in 1957, the rate of improvement of transistors then taking place was extremely relevant.

The forecaster needs to understand differences in needs of market segments and relate these to probable improvements in the new technology. Some market segments in a traditional industry are threatened earlier and to a greater extent than others. Firms should consider strategies involving emphasis on the less threatened segments.

RESPONSE STRATEGIES

Once the threat has been recognized, what kind of response is made by the traditional firm? If it decides not to participate in the new technology, management might elect one or a combination of the following specific actions.

> Do nothing.
>
> Monitor new developments in the competing technology through vigorous environmental scanning and forecasting activity.
>
> Seek to hold back the new threat by fighting it through public relations and legal action.
>
> Increase flexibility so as to be able to respond to subsequent developments in the new technology.
>
> Avoid the threat through decreasing dependence on the most threatened submarkets.
>
> Expand work on the improvement of the existing technology.
>
> Attempt to maintain sales through actions not related to technology, such as promotion or price-cutting.

A firm might, however, choose to participate in the new technology. The degree of commitment could vary widely, ranging from a token involvement, such as defensive research and development, to seeking leadership in the new technology through major and immediate commitments. Important dimensions of a strategy for participation in the technology include decisions about the level of acceptable risk, the magnitude of commitments to the new technology, the timing of those commitments and the extent of reliance on internal development versus acquisition. Against this background of possible responses, the seven industries were studied to determine the response strategies actually used by the threatened firms. Their strategies are shown in the accompanying table.

Participation in the New Technology

Of the twenty-two firms studied, all but five made at least some effort to participate in the new technology. Fifteen of the firms made major efforts to establish positions in the new technology. Firms with small market shares in the old technology were not the focus of this study. However, it does not appear that they either did not attempt to establish positions in the new technology, or they achieved no visible success. For instance, the hundreds of small razor blade firms never had successful electric razors, and the five smallest locomotive producers never made the transition to diesel-electrics.

Nature of Participation

The timing of traditional firms' entries in the new technology varied widely. Raytheon and RCA vacuum tube producers were among the first to enter the transistor market. By contrast, Parker Pen brought out its first ballpoint pen nine years after its first commerical introduction. Of the nine firms which had traditionally emphasized research and development in their various divisions, six were early entrants in the new technology. By contrast, only two of the firms with a low research and development emphasis were early entrants.

Acquisition was not a widely used means of entry into the new technology. Only four of twenty-two traditional firms used acquisition, and two of these used acquisitions to supplement their internal development. Parker acquired the Writing Division of Eversharp as a means of successfully entering the low-priced ball-point pen market after having first developed a high-priced ball-point pen. Raytheon, having previously made major commitments to germanium transistors, acquired Rheem Semiconductor as a means of entering the silicon transistor field.

Emphasis on Old Technology

In every industry studied, the old technology continued to be improved and reached its highest stage of technical development *after* the new technology was introduced. For instance, the smallest and most reliable vacuum tubes ever produced were developed after the introduction of the transistor. No threatened firm adopted a strategy of early withdrawal from the old technology in order to concentrate on the new. Moreover, all but one of the twenty-two companies continued to make heavy commitments to the improvement of the old technology.

Most of the firms followed a strategy of dividing their resources, so as to participate in a major way in both the old and new technologies. Baldwin Locomotive developed both advanced turbine-powered electric locomotives and diesel-electric locomotives. CBS and Raytheon developed new lines of vacuum tubes and also made major investments in research and development and production facilities for transistors. This dual strategy was not usually successful, particularly in relation to building a strong competitive position in the new technology. There were no apparent actions taken by the traditional firms to create or strengthen the barriers to adoption and diffusion of the innovations.

Firms that pioneered the new technology generally did not enter the old technology. The only exception was BIC, a successful French producer of low-priced ball-point pens, which acquired Waterman, an American fountain pen manufacturer. The acquisition was apparently for Waterman's U.S. distribution system rather than its product line, inasmuch as the fountain pen line was discontinued four years later.

Overall Performance

The new technical innovations did not always lead to immediate financial returns and, in fact, sometimes presented all participants with severe competitive challenges. The nuclear power field involved very heavy investments for many years by all participants before the first profits were earned. The precipitous sales decline, which occurred after the first cycle of ball-point pen sales, drove more than 200 new firms, as well as several established firms, from the market. DuPont's poromeric leather substitute, Corfam, reportedly resulted in losses of $100 million: Goodrich and Armstrong were also entrants who later withdrew from the leather substitute field.

The new technology often evolved rapidly. Transistors, nuclear power plants and jet engines all confronted participants with a succession of decisions about commitments to evolving technologies. Early leaders, such as Raytheon in transistors and Curtiss-Wright in jet engines, lost their competitive positions as the technology changed.

Where the old technology continued to grow, traditional firms were able to maintain their competitive positions and enjoy financial success. But many of the most successful firms in the new technology had never participated in the old technology. In industries in which capital barriers were not great, new firms were among the most successful. Examples of successful new firms were Papermate in ball-point pens, Fairchild Semiconductor in transistors and Schick in electric razors.

Over the long run most of the traditional firms that tried to participate in the new technology were not successful. Of the fifteen firms making major commitments, only two, Parker in ball-point pens and United Aircraft in jet engines, enjoyed long-term success as independent firms participating in the new technology.

Patterns of Commitment

Managers of threatened firms must decide how to allocate resources in choosing between improving the old technology and attempting to establish a competitive position in the new. If sales of the old continue to grow, as in safety razors or fossil fuel power plants, then the strengthening of the firm's position in the business it knows so well can be rewarding. However, if sales of the old technology are declining, heavy, across-the-board commitments seem questionable. Management should carefully segment its markets and identify those which appear protected from the threat. Strategies based upon maintaining strong competitive positions in these segments seem justified.

It is interesting that the traditional firms studied here continued to make substantial commitments to the old technologies, even when their sales had already begun to decline because of the competitive pressures of the new technologies. Perhaps this demonstrates the difficulty of changing the patterns of resource allocation in an established organization. Decisions about allocating resources to old and new technologies within the organization are loaded with implications for the decision makers; not only are old product lines threatened, but also old skills and positions of influence.

It was common for spokesmen for the traditional firms to emphasize the shortcomings of the new technology with comments such as "It is no wonder if the public feels that the steam locomotive is about to lay down and play dead," and "It is certain that substantially all airplanes which operate at speeds of 550 mph or less will use propeller propulsion." The executives who made these statements, conditioned by life-long involvements with the old technology, may have been slower than others to recognize the declining opportunities for their traditional products.

Commitment to the new technology, with its expanding opportunities and lack of entrenched competitors, may seem attractive. Certainly most of the firms studied here made such strategic investments. Yet such decisions are fraught with risk, as evidenced by the traditional firms being relatively unsuccessful in the new fields.

For these companies, the patterns of commitment seem to be related to the firm's characteristics. One group of firms was relatively undiversified and did not have strong research and development orientations. The producers of locomotives, fountain pens, safety razors and two of the leather producers might be so classified. Except for several of the pen companies, these firms usually were *not* early entrants, and furthermore, never captured substantial market shares in the new technologies. It is tempting to conclude that an innovative technical and managerial organization is required to make a successful transition from the old to the new technology.

Another group of firms had relatively strong research and development traditions and were accustomed to managing multibusiness organizations. Most of this group, which included the producers of vacuum tubes, boilers and propellers, made major commitments to the new technologies and in several instances achieved substantial early success. However, these technologies continued to evolve rapidly, so that it was necessary to generate successive generations of successful new products. Here, companies such as Curtiss-Wright in jet engines and RCA and Raytheon in transistors were unable to continue their early successes.

The reasons for these firms' inability to build and maintain strong competitive positions are not obvious. Resource limitations apparently were not a major factor in the transistor industry, inasmuch as a number of new companies were relatively successful. The traditional firms not only had to develop new products based upon different technologies, but also had to adapt to changing methods of marketing, servicing and manufacturing. Their lack of long-term success may be an indication of the relative difficulty of changing organizational strategy successfully. The skills, attitudes and assumptions which undergird successful strategy in a traditional technology may require modification in ways both major and subtle to bring about equivalent success in the new technology. Apparently, many organizations found this difficult to do.

Managers of threatened firms should consider carefully commitments to the new technology. Where such commitments are made, it is desirable to recognize explicitly the different strategic requirements for success in the new field. Acquisition, although not widely used by the firms studied here, merits particular consideration. This may be a way to acquire not only technical capabilities, but also organizations attuned to competition in the new field. There are no easy paths to success when faced with major technological threats. However, the experiences of these firms illustrate some of the approaches and pitfalls which management should consider.

┌─ **SIXTEEN** ─────────────────────────────

THINKING
STRATEGICALLY

We have made no secret of our intention in this text to upset many accepted and cherished notions about how organizations are supposed to work: what their strategies are supposed to be, how they are supposed to be formed, how structure and systems are supposed to coincide with these, how managers are supposed to get their jobs done, and so on. We hope that we have succeeded not only in bringing conventional beliefs into question, but also in helping to replace them with broader, more insightful and useful ways to think about these phenomena.

The articles we bring together here under the title "Thinking Strategically" are lighter and less conceptual than those of the earlier chapters. But they should be no less effective in getting you to think deeply about the strategy process and all that it entails. We hope we have motivated you to think beyond the obvious and to probe deeply the phenomena you will inevitably face in the complex world of organizations; the readings that close this text will leave you on that note.

The first reading is J. Sterling Livingston's classic "The Myth of the Well-Educated Manager," an article as timely today as it was when first published more than a decade ago. Anyone who is in the process of completing a degree program in management or business would do well to contemplate its message about the limita-tions of formal education in this field. Such education can be no more than a start on the road to becoming an effective manager. Speaking from his own experiences as a manager and entrepreneur as well as a professor at the Harvard Business School, Livingston cites evidence on the lack of association between how well a student does in business school and his or her later success on the job. He offers sage advice on how managers can learn their art from their own first hand experiences on the job, and on what kinds of people are suitable to become high performance managers in the first place—a most appropriate note to include in a final chapter of a textbook on general management.

Mintzberg's article on "Planning on the Left Side and Managing on the Right" may help to explain Livingston's findings. Mintzberg brings to bear his own observations from various research studies (including those on managerial work and strategy formation discussed earlier). He suggests that the physiologists' discoveries about the left and right hemispheres of the human brain may shed some light on the management processes we have been considering in this text. Those findings provide a physiological explanation for the sharp contrast between the "hard" analytical views of strategy-making, structure, and systems on the one hand and the "softer" views favoring learning, intuition, and emergent strategy on the other. Ultimately all managers may be heavily influenced by forces that the human intellect has barely begun to investigate. This article serves to reinforce a central theme in this book—that those who would use or develop prescriptive models of complex processes should first of all gain a clear understanding of what is going on in reality, and why; only then can they place any confidence in prescriptions about what should be done.

These two final articles suggest that a great deal remains to be learned about the essential elements that make up the strategy process, and that, in fact, the keys to that learning may be locked deep inside our own physiological (not to mention social) nature. We hope you have learned a great deal from these pages. But we also hope you will leave this book with the humility to keep on learning as you advance in that most fascinating phenomenon—the strategy process.

MYTH OF THE WELL-EDUCATED MANAGER*

J. Sterling Livingston

How effectively a manager will perform on the job cannot be predicted by the number of degrees he holds, the grades he receives in school, or the formal management education programs he attends. Academic achievement is not a valid yardstick to use in measuring managerial potential. Indeed, if academic achievement is equated with success in business, the well-educated manager is a myth.

Managers are not taught in formal education programs what they most need to know to build successful careers in management. Unless they

acquire through their own experience the knowledge and skills that are vital to their effectiveness, they are not likely to advance far up the organizational ladder.

Although an implicit objective of all formal management education is to assist managers to learn from their own experience, much management education is, in fact, miseducation because it arrests or distorts the ability of managerial aspirants to grow as they gain experience. Fast learners in the classroom often, therefore, become slow learners in their executive suite.

Men who hold advanced degrees in management are among the most sought after of all university graduates. Measured in terms of starting salaries, they are among the elite. Perhaps no further proof of the value of management education is needed. Being highly educated pays in business, at least initially. But how much formal education contributes to a manager's effectiveness and to his subsequent career progress is another matter.

Professor Lewis B. Ward (1970) of the Harvard Business School has found that the median salaries of graduates of that institution's MBA program plateau approximately 15 years after they enter business and, on the average, do not increase significantly thereafter. While the incomes of a few MBA degree holders continue to rise dramatically, the career growth of most of them levels off just at the time men who are destined for top management typically show their greatest rate of advancement.

Equally revealing is the finding that men who attend Harvard's Advanced Management Program (AMP) after having had approximately 15 years of business experience, but who—for the most part—have had no formal education in management, earn almost a third more, on the average, than men who hold MBA degrees from Harvard and other leading business schools.

Thus the arrested career progress of MBA degree holders strongly suggests that men who get to the top in management have developed skills that are not taught in formal management education programs and may be difficult for many highly educated men to learn on the job. . . .

UNRELIABLE YARDSTICKS

Lack of correlation between scholastic standing and success in business may be surprising to those who place a premium on academic achievement. But grades in neither undergraduate nor graduate school predict how well an individual will perform in management.

After studying the career records of nearly 1,000 graduates of the Harvard Business School, for example, Professor Gordon L. Marshall concluded that "academic success and business achievement have relatively little association with each other" (Marshall, 1964). In reaching this conclusion, he sought without success to find a correlation between grades and such measures of achievement as title, salary, and a person's own satisfaction with his career progress. (Only in the case of grades in elective courses was a significant correlation found.)

Clearly, what a student learns about management in graduate school, as measured by the grades he receives, does not equip him to build a successful career in business.

Scholastic standing in undergraduate school is an equally unreliable guide to an individual's management potential. Professor Eugene E. Jennings of the University of Michigan has conducted research which shows that "the routes to the top are apt to hold just as many or more men who graduated below the highest one third of their college class than above (on a per capita basis)" (1964:21).

A great many executives who mistakenly believe that grades are a valid measure of leadership potential have expressed concern over the fact that fewer and fewer of those "top-third" graduates from the better-known colleges and universities are embarking on careers in business. What these executives do not recognize, however, is that academic ability does not assure that an individual will be able to learn what he needs to know to build a career in fields that involve leading, changing, developing, or working with people.

Overreliance on scholastic learning ability undoubtedly has caused leading universities and business organizations to reject a high percentage of those who have had the greatest potential for creativity and growth in nonacademic careers.

This probability is underscored by an informal study conducted in 1958 by W.B. Bender, Dean of Admissions at Harvard College. He first selected the names of 50 graduates of the Harvard class of 1928 who had been nominated for signal honors because of their outstanding accomplishments in their chosen careers. Then he examined the credentials they presented to Harvard College at the time of their admission. He found that if the admission standards used in 1958 had been in effect in 1928, two thirds of these men would have been turned down. (The proportion who would have been turned down under today's standards would have been even higher.)

In questioning the wisdom of the increased emphasis placed on scholastic standing and intelligence test scores, Dean Bender asked, "Do we really know what we are doing?"[1]

There seems to be little room for doubt that business schools and business organizations which rely on scholastic standing, intelligence test scores, and grades as measures of managerial potential are using unreliable yardsticks.

Career Consequences

. . . Arrested Progress and Turnover Belief in the myth of the well-educated manager has caused many employers to have unrealistic performance expectations of university graduates and has led many employees with outstanding scholastic records to overestimate the value of their formal education. As a consequence, men who hold degrees in business administration—especially those with advanced degrees in management—have found it surprisingly difficult to make the transition from academic to business life. An increasing number of them have failed to perform up to expectations and have not progressed at the rate they expected.

Quoted in Anthony G. Athos and Lewis B. Ward, "Corporations and College Recruiting: A Study of Perceptions" (unpublished study prepared for the Division of Research, Harvard Business School), p. 14.

The end result is that turnover among them has been increasing for two decades as more and more of them have been changing employers in search of a job they hope they "can make a career of." And it is revealing that turnover rates among men with advanced degrees from the leading schools of management appear to be among the highest in industry.

As Professor Edgar H. Schein of the Massachusetts Institute of Technology's Sloan School of Management reports, the attrition "rate among highly educated men and women runs higher, on the average, than among blue-collar workers hired out of the hard-core unemployed. The rate may be highest among people coming out of the better-known schools" (1969:95). Thus over half the graduates of MIT's master's program in management change jobs in the first three years, Schein further reports, and "by the fifth year, 73% have moved on at least once and some are on their third and fourth jobs" (p. 90).

Personnel records of a sample of large companies I have studied similarly revealed that turnover among men holding master's degrees in management from well-known schools was over 50% in the first five years of employment, a rate of attrition that was among the highest of any group of employees in the companies surveyed.

The much publicized notion that the young "mobile managers" who move from company to company are an exceptionally able breed of new executives and that "job-hopping has become a badge of competence" is highly misleading. While a small percentage of those who change employers are competent managers, most of the men who leave their jobs have mediocre to poor records of performance. They leave not so much because the grass is greener on the other side of the fence, but because it definitely is brown on their side. My research indicates that most of them quit either because their career progress has not met their expectations or because their opportunities for promotion are not promising.

In studying the career progress of young management-level employees of an operating company of the American Telephone & Telegraph Company, Professors David E. Berlew and Douglas T. Hall of MIT found that "men who consistently fail to meet company expectations are more likely to leave the organization than are those who turn in stronger performances" (1964:36).

I have reached a similar conclusion after studying attrition among recent management graduates employed in several large industrial companies. Disappointing performance appraisals by superiors is the main reason why young men change employers.

"One myth," explains Schein, "is that the graduate leaves his first company merely for a higher salary. But the MIT data indicate that those who have moved on do not earn more than those who have stayed put" (p. 90). Surveys of reunion classes at the Harvard Business School similarly indicate that men who stay with their first employer generally earn more than those who change jobs. Job-hopping is not an easy road to high income; rather, it usually is a sign of arrested career progress, often because of mediocre or poor performance on the job.

WHAT MANAGERS MUST LEARN

One reason why highly educated men fail to build successful careers in management is that they do not learn from their formal education what they need to know to perform their jobs effectively. In fact, the tasks that are the most important in getting results usually are left to be learned on the job, where few managers ever master them simply because no one teaches them how.

Formal management education programs typically emphasize the development of problem-solving and decision-making skills, for instance, but give little attention to the development of skills required to find the problems that need to be solved, to plan for the attainment of desired results, or to carry out operating plans once they are made. Success in real life depends on how well a person is able to find and exploit the opportunities that are available to him, and, at the same time, discover and deal with potential serious problems before they become critical.

Problem Solving

Preoccupation with problem solving and decision making in formal management education programs tends to distort managerial growth because it overdevelops an individual's analytical ability, but leaves his ability to take action and to get things done underdeveloped. The behavior required to solve problems that already have been discovered and to make decisions based on facts gathered by someone else is quite different from that required to perform other functions of management.

On the one hand, problem solving and decision making in the classroom require what psychologists call "respondent behavior." It is this type of behavior that enables a person to get high grades on examinations, even though he may never use in later life what he has learned in school.

On the other hand, success and fulfillment in work demand a different kind of behavior which psychologists have labeled "operant behavior." Finding problems and opportunities, initiating action, and following through to attain desired results require the exercise of operant behavior, which is neither measured by examinations nor developed by discussing in the classroom what someone else should do. Operant behavior can be developed only by doing what needs to be done.

Instruction in problem solving and decision making all too often leads to "analysis paralysis" because managerial aspirants are required only to explain and defend their reasoning, not to carry out their decisions or even to plan realistically for their implementation. Problem solving in the classroom often is dealt with, moreover, as an entirely rational process, which, of course, it hardly ever is.

As Professor Harry Levinson of the Harvard Business School points out: "The greatest difficulty people have in solving problems is the fact that emotion makes it hard for them to see and deal with their problems objectively" (1070:109–110).

Rarely do managers learn in formal education programs how to maintain an appropriate psychological distance from their problems so that their judgments are not clouded by their emotions. Management graduates, as a consequence, suffer their worst trauma in business when they discover that rational solutions to problems are not enough; they must also somehow cope with human emotions in order to get results.

Problem Finding

The shortcomings of instruction in problem solving, while important, are not as significant as the failure to teach problem finding. As the research of Norman H. Mackworth of the Institute of Personality Assessment and Research, University of California, has revealed "the distinction between the problem-solver and the problem-finder is vital" (1969: 242).

Problem finding, Mackworth points out, is more important than problem solving and involves cognitive processes that are very different from problem solving and much more complex. The most gifted problem finders, he has discovered, rarely have outstanding scholastic records, and those who do excel academically rarely are the most effective problem finders. . . .

. . . the [skill managers] need cannot be developed merely by analyzing problems discovered by someone else; rather, it must be acquired by observing firsthand what is taking place in business. While the analytical skills needed for problem solving are important, more crucial to managerial success are the perceptual skills needed to identify problems long before evidence of them can be found by even the most advanced management information system. Since these perceptual skills are extremely difficult to develop in the classroom, they are now largely left to be developed on the job.

Opportunity Finding

A manager's problem-finding ability is exceeded in importance only by his opportunity-finding ability. Results in business, Peter F. Drucker reminds us, are obtained by exploiting opportunities, not by solving problems. Here is how he puts it:

"All one can hope to get by solving a problem is to restore normality. All one can hope, at best, is to eliminate a restriction on the capacity of the business to obtain results. The results themselves must come from the exploitation of opportunities. . . . 'Maximization of opportunities' is a meaningful, indeed a precise, definition of the entrepreneurial job. It implies that effectiveness rather than efficiency is essential in business. The pertinent question is not how to do things right, but how to find the right things to do, and to concentrate resources and efforts on them" (1964:5).

Managers who lack the skill needed to find those opportunities that will yield the greatest results, not uncommonly spend their time doing the wrong things. But opportunity-finding skill, like problem-finding skill, must be acquired through direct personal experience on the job.

This is not to say that the techniques of opportunity finding and problem finding cannot be taught in formal management education programs, even though they rarely are. But the behavior required to use these techniques successfully can be developed only through actual practice.

A manager cannot learn how to find opportunities or problems without doing it. The doing is essential to the learning. Lectures, case discussions, or text books alone are of limited value in developing ability to find opportunities and problems. Guided practice in finding them in real business situations is the only method that will make a manager skillful in identifying the right things to do.

Natural Management Style

Opportunities are not exploited and problems are not solved, however, until someone takes action and gets the desired results. Managers who are unable to produce effective results on the job invariably fail to build successful careers. But they cannot learn what they most need to know either by studying modern management theories or by discussing in the classroom what someone else should do to get results.

Management is a highly individualized art. What style works well for one manager in a particular situation may not produce the desired results for another manager in a similar situation, or even for the same manager in a different situation. There is no one best way for all managers to manage in all situations. Every manager must discover for himself, therefore, what works and what does not work for him in different situations. He cannot become effective merely by adopting the practices or the managerial style of someone else. He must develop his own natural style and follow practices that are consistent with his own personality.

What all managers need to learn is that to be successful they must manage in a way that is consistent with their unique personalities. When a manager "behaves in ways which do not fit his personality," as Rensis Likert's managerial research has shown, "his behavior is apt to communicate to his subordinates something quite different from what he intends. Subordinates usually view such behavior with suspicion and distrust" (1969:90).

Managers who adopt artificial styles or follow practices that are not consistent with their own personalities are likely not only to be distrusted, but also to be ineffective. It is the men who display the "greatest individuality in managerial behavior," as Edwin E. Ghiselli's studies of managerial talent show, who in general are the ones "judged to be best managers" (1969:236).

Managers rarely are taught how to manage in ways that are consistent with their own personalities. In many formal education and training programs, they are in fact taught that they must follow a prescribed set of practices and adopt either a "consultative" or "participative" style in order to get the "highest productivity, lowest costs, and best performance" (Likert, 1969:11).

The effectiveness of managers whose personalities do not fit these styles often is impaired and their development arrested. Those who adopt artificial styles typically are seen as counterfeit managers who lack individuality and natural styles of their own.

Managers who are taught by the case method of instruction learn that there is no one best way to manage and no one managerial style that is infallible. But unlike students of medicine, students of management rarely are exposed to "real" people or to "live" cases in programs conducted either in universities or in industry.

They study written case histories that describe problems or opportunities discovered by someone else, which they discuss, but do nothing about. What they learn about supervising other people is largely secondhand. Their knowledge is derived from the discussion of what someone else should do about the human problems of "paper people" whose emotional reactions, motives, and behavior have been described for them by scholars who may have observed and advised managers, but who usually have never taken responsibility for getting results in a business organization.

Since taking action and accepting responsibility for the consequences are not a part of their formal training, they neither discover for themselves what does—and what does not—work in practice nor develop a natural managerial style that is consistent with their own unique personalities. Managers cannot discover what practices are effective for them until they are in a position to decide for themselves what needs to be done in a specific situation, and to take responsibility both for getting it done and for the consequences of their actions.

Elton Mayo, whose thinking has had a profound impact on what managers are taught but not on how they are taught, observed a quarter of a century ago that studies in the social sciences do not develop any "skill that is directly useful in human situations" (1945:19). He added that he did not believe a useful skill could be developed until a person takes "responsibility for what happens in particular human situations—individual or group. A good bridge player does not merely conduct post mortem discussions of the play in a hand of contract; he takes responsibility for playing it" (p. 32).

Experience is the key to the practitioner's skill. And until a manager learns from his own firsthand experience on the job how to take action and how to gain the willing cooperation of others in achieving desired results, he is not likely to advance very far up the managerial ladder.

NEEDED CHARACTERISTICS

Although there are no born natural leaders, relatively few men ever develop into effective managers or executives. Most, in fact, fail to learn even from their own experience what they need to know to manage other people successfully. What, then, are the characteristics of men who learn to manage effectively?

The answer to that question consists of three ingredients: (1) the need to manage, (2) the need for power, and (3) the capacity for empathy. In this section of the article, I shall discuss each of these characteristics in some detail.

The Need to Manage

This first part of the answer to the question is deceptively simple: only those men who have a strong desire to influence the performance of others and who get genuine satisfaction from doing so can learn to manage effectively. No man is likely to learn how unless he really wants to take responsibility for the productivity of others, and enjoys developing and stimulating them to achieve better results.

Many men who aspire to high-level managerial positions are not motivated to manage. They are motivated to earn high salaries and to attain high status, but they are not motivated to get effective results through others. They expect to gain great satisfaction from the income and prestige associated with executive positions in important enterprises, but they do not expect to gain much satisfaction from the achievements of their subordinates. Although their aspirations are high, their motivation to supervise other people is low.

A major reason why highly educated and ambitious men do not learn how to develop successful managerial careers is that they lack the "*will* to manage." The "*way* to manage," as Marvin Bower has observed, usually can be found if there is the "*will* to manage." But if a person lacks the desire, he "will not devote the time, energy and thought required to find the way to manage" (1966:6).

No one is likely to sustain for long the effort required to get high productivity from others unless he has a strong psychological need to influence their performance. The need to manage is a crucial factor, therefore, in determining whether a person will learn and apply in practice what is necessary to get effective results on the job.

High grades in school and outstanding performance as an accountant, an engineer, or a salesman reveal how able and willing a person is to perform tasks he has been assigned. But an outstanding record as an individual performer does not indicate whether that person is able or willing to get other people to excel at the same tasks. Outstanding scholars often make poor teachers, excellent engineers often are unable to supervise the work of other engineers, and successful salesmen often are ineffective sales managers.

Indeed, men who are outstanding individual performers not uncommonly become "do-it-yourself" managers. Although they are able and willing to do the job themselves, they lack the motivation and temperament to get it done by others. They may excel as individual performers and may even have good records as first-line managers. But they rarely advance far up the organizational hierarchy because, no matter how hard they try, they cannot make up through their own efforts for mediocre or poor performance by large numbers of subordinates.

Universities and business organizations that select managerial candidates on the basis of their records as individual performers often pick the wrong men to develop as managers. These men may get satisfaction from their own outstanding

performance, but unless they are able to improve the productivity of other people, they are not likely to become successful managers.

Fewer and fewer men who hold advanced degrees in management want to take responsibility for getting results through others. More and more of them are attracted to jobs that permit them to act in the detached role of the consultant or specialized expert, a role described by John W. Gardner (1965) as the one preferred increasingly by university graduates. . . .

As Charlie Brown prophetically observed in a "Peanuts" cartoon strip in which he is standing on the pitcher's mound surrounded by his players, all of whom are telling him what to do at a critical point in a baseball game: "The world is filled with people who are anxious to act in an advisory capacity." Educational institutions are turning out scholars, scientists, and experts who are anxious to act as advisers, but they are producing few men who are eager to lead or take responsibility for the performance of others.

Most management graduates prefer staff positions in headquarters to line positions in the field or factory. More and more of them want jobs that will enable them to use their analytical ability rather than their supervisory ability. Fewer and fewer are willing to make the sacrifices required to learn management from the bottom up; increasingly, they hope to step in at the top from positions where they observe, analyze, and advise but do not have personal responsibility for results. Their aspirations are high, but their need to take responsibility for the productivity of other people is low.

The tendency for men who hold advanced degrees in management to take staff jobs and to stay in these positions too long makes it difficult for them to develop the supervisory skills they need to advance within their companies. Men who fail to gain direct experience as line managers in the first few years of their careers commonly do not acquire the capabilities they need to manage other managers and to sustain their upward progress past middle age.

"A man who performs nonmanagerial tasks five years or more," as Jennings discovered, "has a decidedly greater improbability of becoming a high wage earner. High salaries are being paid to manage managers (1967:15). This may well explain in part why the median salaries of Harvard Business School graduates plateau just at the time they might be expected to move up into the ranks of top management.

The Need for Power

Psychologists once believed that the motive that caused men to strive to attain high-level managerial positions was the "need for achievement." But now they believe it is the "need for power," which is the second part of the answer to the question: What are the characteristics of men who learn to manage effectively? . . .

Power seekers can be counted on to strive hard to reach positions where they can exercise authority over large numbers of people. Individual performers who lack this drive are not likely to act in ways that will enable them to advance far up the managerial ladder. They usually scorn company politics and devote their energies to other types of activities that are more satisfying to them. But, to prevail in the competitive struggle to attain and hold high-level positions in management, a person's desire for prestige and high income must be reinforced by the satisfaction he gets or expects to get from exercising the power and authority of a high office.

The competitive battle to advance within an organization, as Levinson points out, is much like playing "King of the Hill" (1969:53). Unless a person enjoys playing that game, he is likely to tire of it and give up the struggle for control of the top of the hill. The power game is a part of management, and it is played best by those who enjoy it most.

The power drive that carries men to the top also accounts for their tendency to use authoritative rather than consultative or participative methods of management. But to expect otherwise is not realistic. Few men who strive hard to gain and hold positions of power can be expected to be permissive, particularly if their authority is challenged.

Since their satisfaction comes from the exercise of authority, they are not likely to share much of it with lower-level managers who eventually will replace them, even though most high-level executives try diligently to avoid the appearance of being authoritarian. It is equally natural for ambitious lower-level managers who have a high need for power themselves to believe that better results would be achieved if top management shared more authority with them, even though they, in turn, do not share much of it with their subordinates.

One of the least rational acts of business organizations is that of hiring managers who have a high need to exercise authority, and then teaching them that authoritative methods are wrong and that they should be consultative or participative. It is a serious mistake to teach managers that they should adopt styles that are artificial and inconsistent with their unique personalities. Yet this is precisely what a large number of business organizations are doing; and it explains, in part, why their management development programs are not effective.

What managerial aspirants should be taught is how to exercise their authority in a way that is appropriate to the characteristics of the situation and the people involved. Above all, they need to learn that the real source of their power is their own knowledge and skill, and the strength of their own personalities, not the authority conferred on them by their positions. They need to know that overreliance on the traditional authority of their official positions is likely to be fatal to their career aspirations because the effectiveness of this kind of authority is declining everywhere— in the home, in the church, and in the state as well as in business.

More than authority to hire, promote, and fire is required to get superior results from most subordinates. To be effective, managers must possess the authority that comes with knowledge and skill, and be able to exercise the charismatic authority that is derived from their own personalities.

When they lack the knowledge or skill required to perform the work, they need to know how to share their traditional authority with those who know what has to be done to get results. When they lack the charisma needed to get the willing cooperation of those on whom they depend for performance, they must be able to share their traditional authority with the informal leaders of the group, if any exist.

But when they know what has to be done and have the skill and personality to get it done, they must exercise their traditional authority in whatever way is necessary to get the results they desire. Since a leader cannot avoid the exercise of authority, he must understand the nature and limitations of it, and be able to use it in an appropriate manner. Equally important, he must avoid trying to exercise authority he does not, in fact, possess.

The Capacity for Empathy

Mark Van Doren once observed that an educated man is one "who is able to use the intellect he was born with: the intellect, and whatever else is important" (1967:13). At the top of the list of "whatever else is important" is the third characteristic necessary in order to manage other people successfully. Namely, it is the capacity for empathy or the ability to cope with the emotional reactions that inevitably occur when people work together in an organization.

Many men who have more than enough abstract intelligence to learn the methods and techniques of management fail because their affinity with other people is almost entirely intellectual or cognitive. They may have "intellectual empathy" but may not be able to sense or identify the unverbalized emotional feelings which strongly influence human behavior (Paul, 1967:155). They are emotion-blind just as some men are color-blind.

Such men lack what Normal L. Paul describes as "affective empathy" (p. 155). And since they cannot recognize unexpressed emotional feelings, they are unable to learn from their own experience how to cope with the emotional reactions that are crucial in gaining the willing cooperation of other people.

Many men who hold advanced degrees in management are emotion-blind. As Schein has found, they often are "mired in the code of rationality" and, as a consequence, "undergo a rude shock" on their first jobs (p. 92). After interviewing dozens of recent graduates of the Sloan School of Management at MIT, Schein reported that "they talk like logical men who have stumbled into a cell of irrational souls," and he added:

"At an emotional level, ex-students resent the human emotions that make a company untidy. . . . [Few] can accept without pain the reality of the organization's human side. Most try to wish it away, rather than work in and around it. . . . If a graduate happens to have the capacity to accept, maybe to love, human organization, this gift seems directly related to his potential as a manager or executive" (p. 90).

Whether managers can be taught in the classroom how to cope with human emotions is a moot point. There is little reason to believe that what is now taught in psychology classes, human relations seminars, and sensitivity training programs is of much help to men who are "mired in the code of rationality" and who lack "affective empathy."

Objective research has shown that efforts to sensitize supervisors to the feelings of others not only often have failed to improve performance, but in some cases have made the situation worse than it was before (see Fleishmann et al., 1955). Supervisors who are unable "to tune in empathically" on the emotional feelings aroused on the job are not likely to improve their ability to emphathize with others in the classroom (Paul, pp. 150–157).

Indeed, extended classroom discussions about what other people should do to cope with emotional situations may well inhibit rather than stimulate the development of the ability of managers to cope with the emotional reactions they experience on the job.

CONCLUSION

Many highly intelligent and ambitious men are not learning from either their formal education or their own experience what they most need to know to build successful careers in management.

Their failure is due, in part, to the fact that many crucial managerial tasks are not taught in management education programs but are left to be learned on the job, where few managers ever master them because no one teaches them how. It also is due, in part, to the fact that what takes place in the classroom often is miseducation that inhibits their ability to learn from their experience. Commonly, they learn theories of management that cannot be applied successfully in practice, a limitation many of them discover only through the direct experience of becoming a line executive and meeting personally the problems involved.

Some men become confused about the exercise of authority because they are taught only about the traditional authority a manager derives from his official position—a type of authority that is declining in effectiveness everywhere. A great many become innoculated with an "anti-leadership vaccine" that arouses within them intense negative feelings about authoritarian leaders, even though a leader cannot avoid the exercise of authority any more than he can avoid the responsibility for what happens to his organization.

Since these highly educated men do not learn how to exercise authority derived from their own knowledge and skill or from the charisma of their own personalities, more and more of them avoid responsibility for the productivity of others by taking jobs that enable them to act in the detached role of the consultant or specialized expert. Still others impair their effectiveness by adopting artificial managerial styles that are not consistent with their own unique personalities but give them the appearance of being "consultative" or "participative," an image they believe is helpful to their advancement up the managerial ladder.

Some managers who have the intelligence required to learn what they need to know fail because they lack "whatever else is important," especially "affective empathy" and the need to develop and stimulate the productivity of other people. But the main reason many highly educated men do not build successful managerial careers is that they are not able to learn from their own firsthand experience what they need to know to gain the willing cooperation of other people. Since they have not learned how to observe their environment firsthand or to assess feedback from their actions, they are poorly prepared to learn and grow as they gain experience.

Alfred North Whitehead once observed that "the secondhandedness of the learned world is the secret of its mediocrity" (Whitehead, 1929:79). Until managerial aspirants are taught to learn from their own firsthand experience, formal management education will remain secondhanded. And its secondhandedness is the real reason why the well-educated manager is a myth.

PLANNING ON THE LEFT SIDE AND MANAGING ON THE RIGHT*

by Henry Mintzbeg

In the folklore of the Middle East, the story is told about a man named Nasrudin, who was searching for something on the ground. A friend came by and asked:

> "What have you lost, Nasrudin?"
>
> "My key," said Nasrudin.
>
> So, the friend went down on his knees, too, and they both looked for it. After a time, the friend asked: "Where exactly did you drop it?"
>
> "In my house," answered Nasrudin.
>
> "Then why are you looking here, Nasrudin?"
>
> "There is more light here than inside my own house."

This "light" little story is old and worn, yet it has some timeless, mysterious appeal, one which has much to do with the article that follows. But let me leave the story momentarily while I

* Reprinted with deletions by permission of the *Harvard Business Review* (July-August, 1976). Copyright © by the President and Fellows of Harvard College; all rights reserved.

pose some questions—also simple yet mysterious—that have always puzzled me.

- First: Why are some people so smart and so dull at the same time, so capable of mastering certain mental activities and so incapable of mastering others? Why is it that some of the most creative thinkers cannot comprehend a balance sheet, and that some accountants have no sense of product design? Why do some brilliant management scientists have no ability to handle organizational politics, while some of the most politically adept individuals cannot seem to understand the simplest elements of management science?

- Second: Why do people sometimes express such surprise when they read or learn the obvious, something they already must have known? Why is a manager so delighted, for example, when he reads a new article on decision making, every part of which must be patently obvious to him even though he has never before seen it in print?

- Third: Why is there such a discrepancy in organizations, at least at the policy level, between the science and planning of management on the one hand, and managing on the other? Why have none of the techniques of planning and analysis really had much effect on how top managers function?

What I plan to do in this article is weave together some tentative answers to these three questions with the story of Nasrudin around a central theme, namely, that of the specialization of the hemispheres of the human brain and what that specialization means for management.

THE TWO HEMISPHERES
OF THE HUMAN BRAIN

Let us first try to answer the three questions by looking at what is known about the hemispheres of the brain.

Question One

Scientists—in particular, neurologists, neurosurgeons, and psychologists—have known for a long time that the brain has two distinct hemispheres.

They have known, further, that the left hemisphere controls movements on the body's right side and that the right hemisphere controls movements on the left. What they have discovered more recently, however, is that these two hemispheres are specialized in more fundamental ways.

In the left hemisphere of most people's brains (left-handers largely excepted) the logical thinking processes are found. It seems that the mode of operation of the brain's left hemisphere is linear; it processes information sequentially, one bit after another, in an ordered way. Perhaps the most obvious linear faculty is language. In sharp contrast, the right hemisphere is specialized for simultaneous processing; that is, it operates in a more holistic, relational way. Perhaps its most obvious faculty is comprehension of visual images.

Although relatively few specific mental activities have yet been associated with one hemisphere or the other, research is proceeding very quickly. For example, [an] article in *The New York Times* cites research which suggests that emotion may be a right-hemisphere function (Restak, 1976). This notion is based on the finding that victims of right-hemispheric strokes are often comparatively untroubled about their incapacity, while those with strokes of the left hemisphere often suffer profound mental anguish.

What does this specialization of the brain mean for the way people function? Speech, being linear, is a left-hemispheric activity, but other forms of human communication, such as gesturing, are relational rather than sequential and tend to be associated with the right hemisphere. Imagine what would happen if the two sides of a human brain were detached so that, for example, in reacting to a stimulus, a person's words would be separate from his gestures. In other words, the person would have two separate brains—one specialized for verbal communication, and the other for gestures—that would react to the same stimulus.

This "imagining," in fact, describes how the main breakthrough in the recent research on the human brain took place. In trying to treat certain cases of epilepsy, neurosurgeons found that by severing the corpus callosum, which joins the two hemispheres of the brain, they could "split the brain," isolating the epilepsy. A number of experiments run on these "split-brain" patients produced some fascinating results.

In one experiment doctors showed a woman epileptic's right hemisphere a photograph of a nude woman. (This is done by showing it to the left half of each eye.) The patient said she saw nothing, but almost simultaneously blushed and seemed confused and uncomfortable. Her "conscious" left hemisphere, including her verbal apparatus, was aware only that something had happened to her body, but not of what had caused the emotional turmoil. Only her "unconscious" right hemisphere knew. Here neurosurgeons observed a clear split between the two independent consciousnesses that are normally in communication and collaboration (Ornstein, 1975:60).

Now, scientists have further found that some common human tasks activate one side of the brain while leaving the other largely at rest. For example, a person's learning a mathematical proof might evoke activity in the left hemisphere of his brain, while his conceiving a piece of sculpture or assessing a political opponent might evoke activity in his right.

So now we seem to have the answer to the first question. An individual can be smart and dull at the same time simply because one side of his or her brain is more developed than the other. Some people—probably most lawyers, accountants, and planners—have better developed left-hemispheric thinking processes, while others—artists, sculptors, and perhaps politicians—have better developed right-hemispheric processes. Thus an artist may be incapable of expressing his feelings in words, while a lawyer may have no facility for painting. Or a politician may not be able to learn mathematics, while a management scientist may constantly be manipulated in political situations.

Eye movement is apparently a convenient indicator of hemispheric development. When asked to count the letters in a complex word such as *Mississippi* in their heads, most people will gaze off to the side opposite their most developed hemisphere. (Be careful of lefties, however.) But if the question is a specialized one—for example, if it is emotionally laden, spatial, or purely mathematical—the number of people gazing one way or another will change substantially.

Question Two

A number of word opposites have been proposed to distinguish the two hemispheric modes of "consciousness," for example: explicit versus implicit; verbal versus spatial; argument versus experience; intellectual versus intuitive; and analytic versus gestalt.

I should interject at this point that these words, as well as much of the evidence for these conclusions, can be found in the remarkable book entitled *The Psychology of Consciousness* by Robert Ornstein, a research psychologist in California. Ornstein uses the story of Nasrudin to further the points he is making. Specifically, he refers to the linear left hemisphere as synonymous with lightness, with thought processes that we know in an explicit sense. We can *articulate* them. He associates the right hemisphere with darkness, with thought processes that are mysterious to us, at least "us" in the Western world.

Ornstein also points out how the "esoteric psychologies" of the East (Zen, Yoga, Sufism, and so on) have focused on right-hemispheric consciousness (for example, altering pulse rate through meditation). In sharp contrast, Western psychology has been concerned almost exclusively with left-hemispheric consciousness, with logical thought. Ornstein suggests that we might find an important key to human consciousness in the right hemisphere, in what to us in the West is the darkness. To quote him:

> Since these experiences [transcendence of time, control of the nervous system, paranormal communication, and so on] are, by their very mode of operation, not readily accessible to causal explanation

or even to linguistic exploration, many have been tempted to ignore them or even to deny their existence. These traditional psychologies have been relegated to the 'esoteric' or the 'occult,' the realm of the mysterious—the word most often employed is 'mysticism.' It is a taboo area of inquiry, which has been symbolized by the Dark, the Left side [the right hemisphere] of ourselves, the Night (1975:97).

Now, reflect on this for a moment. (Should I say meditate?) There is a set of thought processes—linear, sequential, analytical—that scientists as well as the rest of us know a lot about. And there is another set—simultaneous, relational, holistic—that we know little about. More importantly, here we do not "know" what we "know" or, more exactly, our left hemispheres cannot articulate explicitly what our right hemispheres know implicitly.

So here is, seemingly, the answer to the second question as well. The feeling of revelation about learning the obvious can be explained with the suggestion that the "obvious" knowledge was implicit, apparently restricted to the right hemisphere. The left hemisphere never "knew." Thus it seems to be a revelation to the left hemisphere when it learns explicitly what the right hemisphere knew all along implicitly.

Now only the third question—the discrepancy between planning and managing—remains.

Question Three

By now, it should be obvious where my discussion is leading (obvious, at least, to the reader's right hemisphere and, now that I write it, to the reader's left hemisphere as well). It may be that management researchers have been looking for the key to management in the lightness of logical analysis whereas perhaps it has always been lost in the darkness of intuition.

Specifically, I propose that there may be a fundamental difference between formal planning and informal managing, a difference akin to that between the two hemispheres of the human brain. The techniques of planning and management science are sequential and systematic; above all, articulated. Planners and management scientists are expected to proceed in their work through a series of logical, ordered steps, each one involving explicit analysis. (The argument that the successful application of these techniques requires considerable intuition does not really change my point. The occurrence of intuition simply means that the analyst is departing from his science, as it is articulated, and is behaving more like a manager.)

Formal planning, then, seems to use processes akin to those identified with the brain's left hemisphere. Furthermore, planners and management scientists seem to revel in a systematic, well-ordered world, and many show little appreciation for the more relational, holistic processes.

What about managing? More exactly, what about the processes used by top managers? (Let me emphasize here that I am focusing this discussion at the policy level of organizations, where I believe the dichotomy between planning and managing is most sharp.) Managers plan in some ways, too (that is, they think ahead), and they engage in their share of logical analysis. But I believe there is more than that to the effective managing of an organization. I hypothesize, therefore, that *the important policy processes of managing an organization rely to a considerable extent on the faculties identified with the brain's right hemisphere.* Effective managers seem to revel in ambiguity; in complex, mysterious systems with relatively little order.

If true, this hypothesis would answer the third question about the discrepancy between planning and managing. It would help to explain why each of the new analytic techniques of planning and analysis has, one after the other, had so little success at the policy level. PPBS, strategic planning, "management" (or "total") information systems, and models of the company—all have been greeted with great enthusiasm; then, in many instances, a few years later have been quietly ushered out the corporate back door. Apparently none served the needs of decision making at the policy level in organizations; at that level other processes may function better.

MANAGING FROM THE RIGHT HEMISPHERE

Because research has so far told us little about the right hemisphere, I cannot support with evidence my claim that a key to managing lies there. I can only present to the reader a "feel" for the situation, not a reading of concrete data. A number of findings from my own research on policy-level processes do, however, suggest that they possess characteristics of right-hemispheric thinking (Mintzbeg, 1973a, [1978]; Mintzberg et al., 1976).

One fact recurs repeatedly in all of this research: the key managerial processes are enormously complex and mysterious (to me as a researcher, as well as to the managers who carry them out), drawing on the vaguest of information and using the least articulated of mental processes. These processes seem to be more relational and holistic than ordered and sequential, and more intuitive than intellectual; they seem to be most characteristic of right-hemispheric activity.

Here are ten general findings:

1. The five chief executives I observed strongly favored the verbal media of communication, especially meetings, over the written forms, namely reading and writing. (The same result has been found in virtually every study of managers, no matter what their level in the organization or the function they supervised.) Of course verbal communication is linear, too, but it is more than that. Managers seem to favor it for two fundamental reasons that suggest a relational mode of operation.

First, verbal communication enables the manager to "read" facial expressions, tones of voice, and gestures. As I mentioned earlier, these stimuli seem to be processed in the right hemisphere of the brain. Second, and perhaps more important, verbal communication enables the manager to engage in the "real-time" exchange of information. Managers' concentration on the verbal media, therefore, suggests that they desire relational, simultaneous methods of acquiring information, rather than the ordered and sequential ones.

2. In addition to noting the media managers use, it is interesting to look at the content of managers' information, and at what they do with it. The evidence here is that a great deal of the manager's inputs are soft and speculative—impressions and feelings about other people, hearsay, gossip, and so on. Furthermore, the very analytical inputs—reports, documents, and hard data in general—seem to be of relatively little importance to many managers. . . .

What can managers do with this soft, speculative information? They "synthesize" rather than "analyze" it, I should think. (How do you analyze the mood of a friend or the grimace someone makes in response to a suggestion?) A great deal of this information helps the manager understand implicitly his organization and its environment, to "see the big picture." This very expression, so common in management, implies a relational, holistic use of information. In effect, managers (like everyone else) use their information to build mental "models" of their world, which are implicit synthesized apprehensions of how their organizations and environments function. Then, whenever an action is contemplated, the manager can simulate the outcome using his implicit models.

There can be little doubt that this kind of activity goes on all the time in the world of management. A number of words managers commonly use suggest this kind of mental process. For example, the word "hunch" seems to refer to the thought that results from such an implicit simulation. "I don't know why, but I have a hunch that if we do x, then they will respond with y." Managers also use the word *judgment* to refer to thought processes that work but are unknown to them. *Judgment* seems to be the word that the verbal intellect has given to the thought process that it cannot articulate. Maybe "he has good judgment" simply means "he has good right-hemispheric models."

3. Another consequence of the verbal nature of the manager's information is of interest here.

The manager tends to be the best informed member of his organization, but he has difficulty disseminating his information to his employees. Therefore, when a manager overloaded with work finds a new task that needs doing, he faces a dilemma: he must either delegate the task without the background information or simply do the task himself, neither of which is satisfactory.

When I first encountered this dilemma of delegation, I described it in terms of time and of the nature of the manager's information; because so much of a manager's information is verbal (and stored in his head), the dissemination of it consumes much of his time. But now the split-brain research suggests that a second, perhaps more significant, reason for the dilemma of delegation exists. The manager may simply be incapable of disseminating some relevant information because it is removed from his verbal consciousness. . . .

4. Earlier in this article I wrote that managers revel in ambiguity, in complex, mysterious systems without much order. Let us look at evidence of this. What I have discussed so far about the manager's use of information suggests that their work is geared to action, not reflection. We see further evidence for this in the pace of their work (''Breaks are rare. It's one damn thing after another''); the brevity of their activities (half of the chief executives' activities I observed were completed in less than 9 minutes); the variety of their activities (the chief executives had no evident patterns in their workdays); the fact that they actively exhibit a preference for interruption in their work (stopping meetings, leaving their doors open); and the lack of routine in their work (only 7% of 368 verbal contacts I observed were regularly scheduled, only 1% dealt with a general issue that was in any way related to general planning).

Clearly, the manager does not operate in a systematic, orderly, and intellectual way, puffing his pipe up in a mountain retreat, as he analyzes his problems. Rather, he deals with issues in the context of daily activities—the cigarette in his mouth, one hand on the telephone, and the other shaking hands with a departing guest.

The manager is involved, plugged in; his mode of operating is relational, simultaneous, experiential, that is, encompassing all the characteristics of the right hemisphere.

5. If the most important managerial roles of the ten described in the research were to be isolated, *leader*, *liaison*, and *disturbance handler* would certainly be among them. (The other seven are *figurehead*, *monitor*, *disseminator*, *spokesman*, *negotiator*, *entrepreneur*, and *resource allocator*, and the last two are also among the most important roles.) Yet these three are the roles least ''known'' about. *Leader* describes how the manager deals with his own employees. It is ironic that despite an immense amount of research, managers and researchers still know virtually nothing about the essence of leadership, about why some people follow and others lead. Leadership remains a mysterious chemistry; catchall words such as *charisma* proclaim our ignorance.

In the *liaison* role, the manager builds up a network of outside contacts, which serve as his or her personal information system. Again, the activities of this role remain almost completely outside the realm of articulated knowledge. And as a *disturbance handler* the manager handles problems and crises in his organization. Here again, despite an extensive literature on analytical decision making, virtually nothing is written about decision making under pressure. These activities remain outside the realm of management science, inside the realm of intuition and experience.

6. Let us turn now to strategic decision-making processes. There are 7 ''routines'' that seem to describe the steps involved in such decision making. These are *recognition*, *diagnosis*, *search*, *design*, *screening*, *evaluation/choice*, and *authorization*. Two of these routines stand out above the rest—the *diagnosis* of decision situations and the *design* of custom-made solutions—in that almost nothing is known of them. Yet these two stand out for another reason as well: they are probably the most important of the seven. In particular, diagnosis seems to be the crucial step in strategic decision making, for it is in that routine that the whole course of decision making is set.

It is a surprising fact, therefore, that diagnosis goes virtually without mention in the literature of planning or management science. (Almost all of the later literature deals with the formal evaluation of given alternatives, yet this is often a kind of trimming on the process, insignificant in terms of determining actual outcomes.) In the study of the decision processes themselves, the managers making the decisions mentioned taking an explicit diagnostic step in only 14 of the 25 decision processes. But all the managers must have made some diagnosis; it is difficult to imagine a decision-making process with no diagnosis at all, no assessment of the situation. The question is, therefore, *where* did diagnosis take place?

7. Another point that emerges from studying strategic decision-making processes is the existence and profound influence of what can be called the *dynamic factors*. Strategic decision-making processes are stopped by interruptions, delayed and speeded up by timing factors, and forced repeatedly to branch and cycle. These processes are, therefore, dynamic ones of importance. Yet it is the dynamic factors that the ordered, sequential techniques of analysis are least able to handle. Thus, despite their importance, the dynamic factors go virtually without mention in the literature of management science.

Let's look at timing, for example. It is evident that timing is crucial in virtually everything the manager does. No manager takes action without considering the effect of moving more or less quickly, of seizing the initiative, or of delaying to avoid complications. Yet in one review of the literature of management, the authors found fewer than 10 books in 183 that refer directly to the subject of timing (Hardwick and Landuyt, 1966). Essentially, managers are left on their own to deal with the dynamic factors, which involve simultaneous, relational modes of thinking.

8. When managers do have to make serious choices from among options, how do they in fact make them? Three fundamental modes of selection can be distinguished—analysis, judg-

ment, and bargaining. The first involves the systematic evaluation of options in terms of their consequences on stated organizational goals; the second is a process in the mind of a single decision maker; and the third involves negotiations between different decision makers.

One of the most surprising facts about how managers made the 25 strategic decisions studied is that so few reported using explicit analysis; only in 18 out of 83 choices made did managers mention using it. There was considerable bargaining, but in general the selection mode most commonly used was judgment. Typically, the options and all kinds of data associated with them were pumped into the mind of a manager, and somehow a choice later came out. *How* was never explained. *How* is never explained in any of the literature either. . . .

9. Finally, in the area of strategy formulation, I can offer only a "feel" for the results since my research is still in progress. However, some ideas have emerged. Strategy formulation does not turn out to be the regular, continuous, systematic process depicted in so much of the planning literature. It is most often an irregular, discontinuous process, proceeding in fits and starts. There are periods of stability in strategy development, but also there are periods of flux, of groping, of piecemeal change, and of global change. To my mind, a "strategy" represents the mediating force between a dynamic environment and a stable operating system. Strategy is the organization's "conception" of how to deal with its environment for a while.

Now, the environment does not change in any set pattern. For example, the environment does not run on planners' five-year schedules; it may be stable for thirteen years, and then suddenly blow all to hell in the fourteenth. And even if change were steady, the human brain does not generally perceive it that way. People tend to underreact to mild stimuli and overreact to strong ones. It stands to reason, therefore, that strategies that mediate between environments and organizational operations do not change in regular patterns, but rather, as I observed earlier, in fits and starts.

How does strategic planning account for fits and starts? The fact is that it does not (as planners were made so painfully aware of during the energy crisis). So again, the burden to cope falls on the manager, specifically on his mental processes—intuitional and experiential—that can deal with the irregular inputs from the environment.

10.   Let me probe more deeply into the concept of strategy. Consider the organization that has no strategy, no way to deal consistently with its environment; it simply reacts to each new pressure as it comes along. This is typical behavior for an organization in a very difficult situation, where the old strategy has broken down beyond repair, but where no new strategy has yet emerged. Now, if the organization wishes to formulate a new strategy, how does it do so (assuming that the environment has stabilized sufficiently to allow a new strategy to be formulated)?

Let me suggest two ways (based on still tentative results). If the organization goes the route of systematic planning, I suggest that it will probably come up with what can be called a "main-line" strategy. In effect, it will do what is generally expected of organizations in its situation; where possible, for example, it will copy the established strategies of other organizations. . . .

Alternatively, if the organization wishes to have a creative, integrated strategy which can be called a "gestalt strategy". . . then I suggest the organization will rely largely on one individual to conceptualize its strategy, to synthesize a "vision" of how the organization will respond to its environment. In other words, scratch an interesting strategy, and you will probably find a single strategy formulator beneath it. Creative, integrated strategies seem to be the products of single brains, perhaps of single right hemispheres.

A strategy can be made explicit, can be announced as what the organization intends to do in the future, only when the vision is fully worked out, if it ever is. Often, of course, it is never felt to be fully worked out, hence the strategy is never made explicit and remains the private vision of the chief executive. (Of course, in some

situations the formulator need not be the manager. There is no reason why a manager cannot have a creative right-hand man—really a left-hand man—who works out his gestalt strategy for him, and then articulates it to him.) No management process is more demanding of holistic, relational, gestalt thinking than the formulation of a creative, integrated strategy to deal with a complex, intertwined environment.

How can sequential analysis (under the label *strategic planning*) possibly lead to a gestalt strategy?

Another "famous old story" has relevance here. It is the one about the blind men trying to identify an elephant by touch. One grabs the trunk and says the elephant is long and soft; another holds the leg and says it is massive and cylindrical; a third touches the skin and says it is rough and scaly. What the story points out is that—

> Each person standing at one part of the elephant can make his own limited, analytic assessment of the situation, but we do not obtain an elephant by adding "scaly," "long and soft," "massive and cylindrical" together in any conceivable proportion. Without the development of an overall perspective, we remain lost in our individual investigations. Such a perspective is a province of another mode of knowledge, and cannot be achieved in the same way that individual parts are explored. It does not arise out of a linear sum of independent observations (Orenstein, 1975:10).

What can we conclude from these ten findings? I must first reemphasize that everything I write about the two hemispheres of the brain falls into the realm of speculation. Researchers have yet to formally relate any management process to the functioning of the human brain. Nevertheless, the ten points do seem to support the hypothesis stated earlier: *the important policy-level processes required to manage an organization rely to a considerable extent on the faculties identified with the brain's right hemisphere.*

This conclusion does not imply that the left hemisphere is unimportant for policy makers. I have overstated my case here to emphasize the importance of the right. The faculties identified with the left hemisphere are obviously important as well for effective management. Every manager engages in considerable explicit calculation when he or she acts, and all intuitive thinking must be translated into the linear order of the left if it is to be articulated and eventually put to use. The great powers that appear to be associated with the right hemisphere are obviously useless without the faculties of the left. The artist can create without verbalizing; the manager cannot.

Truly outstanding managers are no doubt the ones who can couple effective right-hemispheric processes (hunch, judgment, synthesis, and so on) with effective processes of the left (articulateness, logic, analysis, and so on). But there will be little headway in the field of management if managers and researchers continue to search for the key to managing in the lightness of ordered analysis. Too much will stay unexplained in the darkness of intuition.

Before I go on to discuss the implications for management science and planning, I want to stress again that throughout this article I have been focusing on processes that managers employ at the policy level of the organization. It seems that the facilities identified with the right-hemispheric activities are most important in the higher levels of an organization, at least in those with "top-down" policy-making systems.

In a sense, the coupling of the holistic and the sequential reflects how bureaucratic organizations themselves work. The policy maker conceives the strategy in holistic terms, and the rest of the hierarchy—the functional departments, branches, and shops—implement it in sequence. Whereas the right-hemispheric faculties may be more important at the top of an organization, the left-hemispheric ones may dominate lower down.

IMPLICATIONS FOR THE LEFT HEMISPHERE

Let us return to practical reality for a final word. What does all I've discussed mean for those associated with management?

For Planners and Management Scientists

No, I do not suggest that planners and management scientists pack up their bags of techniques and leave the field of management, or that they take up basket-weaving or meditation in their spare time. (I haven't—at least not yet!) It seems to me that the left hemisphere is alive and well; the analytic community is firmly established, and indispensable, at the operating and middle levels of most organizations. Its real problems occur at the policy level. Here analysis must co-exist with—perhaps even take its lead from—intuition, a fact that many analysts and planners have been slow to accept. To my mind, organizational effectiveness does not lie in that narrow-minded concept called "rationality"; it lies in a blend of clear-headed logic *and* powerful intuition. Let me illustrate this with two points.

- *First, only under special circumstances should planners try to plan*. When an organization is in a stable environment and has no use for a very creative strategy . . . then the development of formal, systematic strategic plans (and main-line strategies) may be in order. But when the environment is unstable or the organization needs a creative strategy, then strategic planning may not be the best approach to strategy formulation, and planners have no business pushing the organization to use it.

- *Second, effective decision making at the policy level requires good analytical input; it is the job of the planner and management scientist to ensure that top management gets it.* Managers are very effective at securing soft information; but they tend to underemphasize analytical input that is often important as well. The planners and management scientists can serve their organizations effectively by carrying out ad hoc analyses and feeding the results to top management (need I say verbally?), ensuring that the very best of analysis is brought to bear on policy making. But at the same time, planners need to recognize that these inputs cannot be the only ones used in policy making, that soft information is crucial as well.

For the Teacher of Managers

If the suggestions in this article turn out to be valid, then educators had better revise drastically some of their notions about management education, because the revolution in that sphere over the last fifteen years—while it has brought so much of use—has virtually consecrated the modern management school to the worship of the left hemisphere.

Should educators be surprised that so many of their graduates end up in staff positions, with no intention of ever managing anything? Some of the best-known management schools have become virtual closed systems in which professors with little interest in the reality of organizational life teach inexperienced students the theories of mathematics, economics, and psychology as ends in themselves. In these management schools, management is accorded little place.

I am not preaching a return to the management school of the 1950s. That age of fuzzy thinking has passed, thankfully. Rather, I am calling for a new balance in our schools, the balance that the best of human brains can achieve, between the analytic and the intuitive. In particular, greater use should be made of the powerful new skill-development techniques which are experiential and creative in nature, such as role playing, the use of video-tape, behavior laboratories, and so on. Educators need to put students into situations, whether in the field or in the simulated experience of the laboratory, where they can practice managerial skills, not only interpersonal but also informational and decisional. Then specialists would follow up with feedback on the students' behavior and performance.

For Managers

The first conclusion for managers should be a call for caution. The findings of the cognitive psychologists should not be taken as license to shroud activities in darkness. The mystification of conscious behavior is a favorite ploy of those seeking to protect a power base (or to hide their intentions of creating one); this behavior helps no organization and neither does forcing to the realm of intuition activities that can be handled effectively by analysis.

A major thrust of development in our organizations, ever since Frederick Taylor began experimenting in factories late in the last century, has been to shift activities out of the realm of intuition, toward conscious analysis. That trend will continue. But managers, and those who work with them, need to be careful to distinguish that which is best handled analytically from that which must remain in the realm of intuition, where, in the meantime, we should be looking for the lost keys to management.

CASE III – 1

SONY CORPORATION

Sony Corporation began in the rubble and chaos of Japan at the end of World War II. Its first quarters were a small corner room of a burned out department store in Tokyo's Ginza district. Masaru Ibuka, age 37, had brought along seven young engineers to start "some sort of electronics laboratory or enterprise." His earlier company, Japan Precision Instrument Co., had supplied vacuum tube voltmeters and other instruments to the now defunct war effort, and Mr. Ibuka felt an obligation to provide continued work for his people. "We realized we could not compete against companies already in existence and against products in which they specialized. We started with the basic concept that we had to do something that no other company had done before."

From these inauspicious beginnings sprang one of the world's most innovative companies with worldwide sales in 1982 of $4.53 billion. In a nation not then known for product innovation, what had led to Sony's unique capabilities? Could its successful past policies survive the ferocious competitive atmosphere of the mid 1980s? A brief history of several of Sony's most important innovations provides an interesting basis for analysis.

MEAGER BEGINNINGS

Ibuka wanted to apply a mix of electronics and engineering to the consumer field, but Japan's banks and markets were anything but encouraging

to a tiny upstart with no consumer experience. In August 1945, the group's first problem was to find something to sell. The small group considered anything: bean paste soup, slide rules, an electric rice cooker Ibuka invented. Despite widespread fuel shortages, some electricity existed. Ibuka thought there was a genuine "need" for the innovative aluminum cooker. Technically it worked well—if the water levels and the rice were just right—but none sold. So Ibuka's team began to repair or modify wartime radios for a music and news hungry city. This barely enabled the company to survive as Ibuka slowly depleted his meager savings to keep his people employed during the first arduous year.

Then Akio Morita joined the company. He had been associated with Ibuka on thermal guidance and nocturnal vision projects during the war and had seen an article about his friend's short-wave adaptor and electronic repair business in October 1945. Though there was little money for a salary, Ibuka conveyed his missionary feelings about making electronics technology available to a peacetime civilian Japan. The talented Morita took a faculty appointment at the Tokyo Institute of Technology, but contributed part of his time to Ibuka's small company.

The Young Team

Like Ibuka, Morita had been an inveterate tinkerer as a child and was a descendant of a leading samurai family. As a student at Waseda University, Ibuka had won patents and international awards for a system to transmit sound by modulating neon light. Morita had ghost written articles for his professors at Osaka Imperial University where he had specialized in electronics. But there the similarities ended. Ibuka had failed his employment examination for a large Japanese electric company and only got his first job through

Case copyright © 1986 by James Brian Quinn. Research associates—Penny C. Paquette and Roger Wellington. The generous support of the Adolf H. Lundin Professorship at the International Management Institute, Geneva, Switzerland is gratefully acknowledged. The generous cooperation of Sony Corporation is gratefully acknowledged.

the intervention of a friend. Morita's family company awaited him whenever he was ready.

Ibuka was passionate about invention, a humanist, a dreamer in many ways. Morita was a realist who had been trained in business by his father since birth. Ibuka had little interest in accounting and the intricacies of marketing. Morita was an administrator, as well as an enthusiastic, outgoing man who could charm or spellbind an audience. The two became the closest of friends.

Early Capitalization

When Morita decided to leave the University, Ibuka took an all night train ride to persuade the elder Morita to let his son join the fledgling company. At first the senior Morita was not impressed. Later he not only acquiesced, but invested his own funds in the new firm. The banks were reluctant to lend even short term money, so operating funds were constantly begged from the senior Morita and from personal friends. Eventually the elder Mr. Morita became the company's largest shareholder.

On May 7, 1946, the company was formally incorporated as Tokyo Telecommunications Engineering Co. (TTK being the Japanese acronym). Since companies capitalized at over 200,000 yen encountered more difficult incorporation regulations, TTK listed the company at 198,000 yen—$500–$600 in exchange value—not much of an exaggeration.

The Purposes of Incorporation were listed in the Prospectus along with the new company's "Management Policies." Both of these remarkable statements—little changed since then—are shown in Exhibit 1. In 1983 Sony's Chairman Morita restated some of these basic principles.

> Young people who join our company next year will stay for 25 years. So that means for them the company should be prosperous for that period. All the top people feel responsible that the company live a long, long time, rather than making a big current profit to make a very large bonus. That's why we don't pay bonuses

to executives. We pay bonuses to employees because we like for the employees to feel and participate in the company's results.

> Every year, when we receive our new graduate employees, I like to make a little speech to them. Now you have become a Sony employee. You will spend the most brilliant time of your life here. Nobody can live twice. This is the only life you can have, so I want you to become happy at Sony. If you don't feel happy, you better go out and change your job. But if you decide to stay with us, you must devote yourself to make your life happy and also to make your colleagues happy. People work together here for all of us in mutual benefit, mutual interest.[*]

Expansion with Umbrellas

When TTK surpassed its breakeven volume (primarily making voltmeters), Ibuka poured the cash flows into the introduction of an electrically heated cushion he had invented. TTK sold several hundred. Then Ibuka invented and produced a resonating sound generator that allowed operators trained with military telegraph equipment to hear their usual "dots and dashes" instead of the disconcerting "clicking" of the civilian systems. The American Occupation Forces (rebuilding Japan's destroyed communications systems to American standards) encountered some of TTK's equipment and were so impressed with its sophistication and quality that they began to order from the tiny company. By then TTK had expanded into some shacks in the Shinagawa district that were so dilapidated that executives had to use umbrellas during rainstorms. Nevertheless, Ibuka insisted on such rigorous design and quality standards that TTK—through clever use of a carefully developed supplier network—was soon performing almost all of Japan Broadcasting Network's (NHK's) revisions, converting its equipment to modern standards and building industrial and commercial electronic devices for other companies.

---

[*] *All quotations not footnoted came from personal interviews with Professor Quinn.*

But TTK had no consumer products. Ibuka seriously considered a wire recorder, first introduced by the military in World War II. Japan's Dr. Kenzo Nagai held some key patents on the wire recorder, the device would be unique in consumer markets, and TTK had the proper skills to produce it. Ibuka was just about to commit his best resources to an onslaught on the wire recorder. Then one day as he was visiting the offices of NHK, a member of the Occupation Forces showed him a tape recorder from the U.S., and history was made.

THE TAPE RECORDER

Tape recorders were unheard of in Japan—there wasn't even a word for them. Ibuka's team quickly checked the available patents and found Dr. Nagai held a key one here as well. They rapidly purchased the rights to it, knowing they had the magnetic and electrical skills to make a good machine. But there was little published information about either magnetic tapes or recorders. In Japan there was no plastic available to produce tape and no way to acquire any plastic through Japan's stringent import regulations. The TTK team tried cellophane; it stretched. They tried paper—Ibuka made tapes in his kitchen from rice paper and a paste of boiled rice—its edges caught and broke. Finally, Morita got a cousin in a paper manufacturing company to prepare a batch of specially calendered paper with a slick surface.

Ibuka's group had to develop special techniques to cut the paper, hold it, and coat it uniformly with magnetic powder. They had to compensate for the less controllable paper base by designing extra quality into the circuitry, recording heads, feed systems, and amplifiers in the recorder. It was a great struggle. The accounting manager constantly warned they were spending too much; they could bankrupt the company. Morita kept saying, "Be a little more patient and we will make a fortune." Finally after many months they created not just a new concept in tapes, but a new recorder, a new testing technol-

ogy, and their own complete tape coating machine. Sony became perhaps the first company in the world to make the entire range of products from tapes to recorders, skills involving nearly a dozen basic technologies. In late 1949 they made their first unit, the G type recorder, weighing over 100 pounds and selling for $400.

But would the device sell? Neither Ibuka nor Morita had marketing experience. After many months of effort the first unit was sold to an *oden* shop—a kind of Japanese pub where people came to eat, sing, and talk noisily. Technically the expensive, cumbersome device performed well, but no one quite knew what to do with it. Ibuka's response was to take all his top engineers to an inn and work night and day to reduce the recorder's cost by 50% and to improve its size, weight, and portability. The result was a concept for a suitcase enclosed recorder at a reasonable price—and at less than $\frac{1}{2}$ the G type's weight.

As markets—at first to record NHK's English language programs for use in schools—opened, 3M began to sell its excellent magnetic tape to Japanese broadcasters and other large users. TTK tried to negotiate a license and reached a financially very attractive proposition. But in exchange for the license, 3M insisted that TTK drop its recorder manufacturing. After much consideration Morita and Ibuka said no, wanting no outside control over their product line. But this also meant TTK was now in competition with a much larger and very sophisticated world competitor, a very difficult situation for the young company.

TRANSISTOR RADIOS

In 1952 Ibuka went to the U.S. to explore possible markets for his tape recorder. While he was there, a U.S. friend told him that Western Electric was ready to license its transistor patent for the first time. Ibuka investigated, but when he heard the price was $25,000, he left the U.S. knowing the price was too much for TTK. Ibuka worried as he made the long trip home. He was convinced the transistor would revolutionize electronics, though no one then realized how. As he pondered what to do, another concern came into place. He had hired a number of young physicists. "Would tape recorders be challenge enough for them, motivate them to use their best abilities, or let them grow to their full potentials?" Ibuka was convinced they could not.

"A Pocketable Radio"

By the time Mr. Ibuka reached Tokyo, his questions had crystallized into a strategy to keep his people and his company growing. A short time later he announced, "We're going to use the transistor to make radios small enough so that each individual can carry them for his own use, but with a receiving ability that will enable civilization to reach areas that have no electric power." At that time "portable radios" weighed 10–20 pounds, were briefcase sized, and had batteries that lasted only a few hours. Ibuka spoke of a "pocketable transistor radio." But no one had applied transistors to radios—or much of anything else. The thought of a quality radio the size of a cigarette pack seemed almost beyond belief.

But Kazuo Iwama, a young geo-physicist with no knowledge of transistors, was fired by Ibuka's enthusiasm. He left his job as tape recorder production head to lead the transistor task force. Morita had negotiated a license agreement with Western Electric whereunder the $25,000 patent was credited against potential future royalties. But the Ministry of International Trade and Industry (MITI) had to approve the release of the $25,000 in foreign currency. MITI was furious. If the big Japanese companies weren't interested in transistors, why should MITI support TTK? And why hadn't TTK come to MITI before *any* negotiations? They delayed approval for months until Ibuka's persuasiveness finally prevailed in early 1954.

Ibuka and Iwama immediately left for the U.S., where they found that no one had achieved satisfactory yields on the high frequency transistors needed for radio. Even lower frequency transistors for hearing aids sold for $150–$500. Ibuka and Iwama visited all the U.S. laboratories and plants they could, sending detailed letters to Iwama's task force each night. Months passed as the task force tried to reach the high frequencies needed for radio and the production yields required for commercial exploitation. Again the financial stability of the company was at risk as transistor program costs grew. Only an expanding tape recorder market kept it going.

Shock and a Market

Then came a shock. Texas Instruments announced the world's first transistorized radio, produced for Regency Co. In early 1955 TTK's team pulled out all stops, moving with what they had. In August they put their first radio on display. It was about $4'' \times 8'' \times 1\frac{1}{2}''$. They set a goal of 10,000 transistor radios in the first year and achieved 8,000. "The success of Sony is," said Iwama later, "that we produced a little less than was required. When there is enough, the market is saturated." Still Ibuka wanted a "pocketable radio." Despite the skepticism of marketing experts who thought the product would be too small, squeaky, and unreliable, Ibuka pushed on. TTK's component suppliers refused to modify their standard product lines, which were largely copied from world designs. They too were doubtful of the product's success. Ibuka single-handedly persuaded them to go ahead by offering Sony's technical support and production guidance. It was a momentous change for Japan. Japanese manufacturers had to become truly independent of foreign technology for perhaps the first time. In March 1957 the "pocketable" Type 63 radio was introduced using almost exclusively Japanese know-how. Since the Type 63 was still slightly larger than a shirt pocket, Sony made special shirts into which they would fit. Over a million Type 63s were soon sold.

Once the principle was proved, the bigger companies moved in. TTK changed its name to Sony, derived from the Latin *sonus* (for sound). The name had been carefully chosen to be simple, recognizable, and pronounceable in many languages. The Sony name became almost generic for transistor radios. "Sunny" and "Somy" trade names appeared and were fought off. Meanwhile, Sony had a 2–3 year technology lead and moved on to provide the world's first transistorized short-wave and FM receivers for consumers.

THE SONY SPIRIT

By now Sony was becoming known as a maverick among Japanese companies. It was not bound up in the traditions of older companies and relied as little as possible on the government or banks. Morita and Ibuka could make fast decisions, unhindered by the formalities of the *ringi* method of consensus building found in most larger companies. Over a single lunch Morita reached agreement with CBS for Sony to distribute CBS records in Japan. As the company grew at an amazing pace, it hired senior people away from other concerns—a practice frowned on by more traditional Japanese companies.

Some of the executives' backgrounds were unusual. Ibuka convinced Dr. Kikuchi, Sony's research head, to leave MITI after 26 years there. Shigeru Kobayashi was recruited from the printing industry, given charge of an ailing semiconductor plant, and told "do what you want." Norio Ohga—a music major destined to become a major opera baritone—was recruited upon his graduation from the university. He remained a consultant to Sony as he rose to operatic fame. When he returned from the stage—with no business training—he was made head of the tape recorder plant and rose to be a top board member of Sony. Morita and Ibuka always looked first for talent, not someone "to fill a job." Then with full trust they gave their selections a free hand. "I never knew what hidden abilities I had until I came to Sony," commented one of many so treated.

"Do Something Creative"

Sony's personnel grew over 10 times in the 1950s and four times in the 1960s. Many of its personnel policies derived from its original goal to "establish an ideal factory—free, dynamic, and pleasant." To Ibuka this meant "to have fixed production and budgetary requirements but within these limits to give Sony employees the freedom to do what they want. This way we draw on their deepest creative potentials."[1]

Many more specific policies flowed from the remarkable experiences of Shigeru Kobayashi who took over Sony's Atsugi plant after its brief—and only—strike in 1961. Ibuka told Kobayashi, who knew nothing about semiconductor technology, "You are free to do there whatever you like. Try to do something truly creative." Kobayashi soon concluded the plant's problems derived from people feeling themselves insignificant there, what he called "a small pebble complex." He thought essential trust had been destroyed because management had tried to set up contrived Western methods for measuring output, increasing efficiency, and motivating people.

To eliminate cafeteria lines and to build trust Kobayashi removed all cashier attendants, letting people voluntarily place their meal coupons in appropriate boxes. He shut down the forbidding dormitories used by most Japanese companies then, built small pre-fabricated homes where a few employees could live together, and gave employees full autonomy over their premises. This had never been done in Japan. Next he eliminated time clocks, and created autonomy for Sony's recreation groups, moving away from the carefully controlled company teams so common in Japan.

Cells and Trust

Then Kobayashi developed a series of vertical and horizontal interconnecting teams or "cells" in the plant. Each was a specialized unit that could take charge of its own work. In these small (2 to 20 person) cells, workers could more easily develop a team spirit and help each other. Each cell would respond to input from all other cells above, below, on its sides. The cell would determine what methods to follow and evaluate its own output. Orders did not flow from above. Management's job was to assist the cells, to help them solve problems, to set overall goals, and to praise superior performances, while the cells were to control specific tasks at the workplace and group levels. The specifics of Kobayashi's "cell" system are different in each plant now, but the spirit and values it conveys continue.

In most areas, all new employees—whether

law graduates or finance specialists—must spend several months on the production line learning to appreciate the company's products, practices, and culture. All engineers and scientists hired still must work in sales for several weeks or months. Promising people are shifted every 2–3 years to new areas to expand their knowledge and to identify their abilities for promotion. Typically workers learn several processes and are switched among tasks to keep up their interest. Production lines may be purposely segmented so they can be restructured rapidly if product mixes change. Rewards flow not to individuals, but to groups.

Morita recently said, "The best way to train a person is to give him authority. . . . We tell our young people: don't be afraid to make a mistake, but don't make the same mistake twice. If you think it is good for the company, do it. If something is wrong, I'm the man who should be accused. As CEO it's my job to take on the critics from the outside. For example, this year [1983] our profits are down, I tell my management, don't you worry about that, just do your job right."

Unlike other Japanese companies where seniority determines responsibility, young Sony employees were loaded with work and responsibility. But there was a complex "godfather system" in which a high executive watched over and specifically trained younger talent. A new executive interacted almost daily with his corporate mentor and received sophisticated insights and a corporate perspective. Mr. Morita expressed the overall philosophy this way, "Sony motivates executives not with special compensation systems but by giving them joy in achievement, challenge, pride, and a sense of recognition."

TUMMY AND OTHER TELEVISIONS

As its pocketable radio business boomed, Sony turned to all transistorized television. At first Sony's system could only drive small picture tubes, 5–8 inches across, but not the larger tubes then popular. When Ibuka proposed to introduce a "mini-TV," the market experts again said, "It will never sell. RCA tried it and failed. The market wants big screens." Undeterred, Ibuka introduced an 8 inch set in Japan (May 1960) and in the U.S. (June 1961). Again the road to the marketplace was complex and difficult, but Ibuka's "tummy television" sets became eminently successful.

During this rapid growth period Mr. Morita moved his family to New York so that Sony's top management would know the U.S. market, not through statistics, but through intuition. Although his wife and children could not speak English at first, he insisted that they meet and entertain Americans, enter American camps and schools. Their acculturation was rapid. Morita, himself, often helped sweep out the shabby rat-infested offices of Sony Corp. of America (Sonam), and worked 16 hour days and 7 day weeks. While joining in menial tasks, the distinguished Morita pushed Sonam to be the highest quality U.S. company. He insisted on "establishing proper servicing before distribution" and spent money to import more service engineers, rather than allowing Sonam to move into more acceptable sales headquarters in New York.

When offered a chance by a leading U.S. radio manufacturer to rebrand Sony transistor radios and have them introduced under the American company's well accepted 50 year old name, Morita refused. When asked how he could turn down the benefits of a fast start and 50 years' experience, Morita replied, "This is the first year of our 50 years' experience. If we do not do things ourselves, 50 years from now we will not be a great company like yours today."

"No Fun in Copying"

By 1964 color television had begun to take over the U.S. market. After some diverse experimentation, virtually every color manufacturer operated under RCA's "shadow mask" system using a triangle of 3 electron guns and a grid of tiny color "dots" to create color. But Ibuka said, "I could see no fun in merely copying their excellent system." In 1961 Ibuka had seen the Chromatron tube invented by Dr. O.E. Lawrence (world famous physicist and developer of the first cyclotron). The tube used a series of phosphor "stripes" to generate color, was potentially much simpler to manufacture than the shadow mask, and produced about three times the brightness of the RCA system. Sony had introduced the Chromatron in Japan, but it was plagued with defects, service costs were crushing, and losses were mounting daily on the product. Sonam was stridently pressing for a color system to sell in the U.S.—using the shadow mask.

Then some General Electric representatives came to license Sony a tube with 3 electron guns *in line*, not in the triangular configuration of the shadow mask. No one wanted after all their frustrations to be a mere licensee of a U.S. company, but Sony began investigating this and other possibilities. Engineering morale reached a low in the fall of 1966 after the GE approach. Ibuka came to the labs every day counseling, suggesting, experimenting, encouraging. He started small teams on different approaches in parallel and developed the back up technology for each. He quickly switched engineers from one project to another as roadblocks or leads developed for each alternative.

Ibuka said, "We must produce a product of our own. There is nothing more pitiable than a man who can't or doesn't dream. Dreams give direction and purpose to life, without which life would be mere drudgery." During this difficult period, Morita himself feared for the financial viability of the company, yet he had to calm his dealers. "Business should be considered in ten year cycles," he explained. "If we wait and develop a unique product, we may start several years later, but we will be stronger than all the others in 10 years."

Then toward the end of 1966, a young engineer, Miyaoka, made a mistake while experimenting. Using a single gun and 3 cathodes, he had produced a blurred picture. "But it was a picture"—and a new concept. Intuitively, Ibuka recognized the promise of this approach and said, "This is it. This is the system to go with."

Ibuka became the project manager himself.

His team often worked all night, taking a few hours off to rest on the sofa. By February they thought they had a better picture than the RCA tube, but for months they had problems with electron acceleration and control. Repeatedly experiments failed, and the engineers despaired. Finally, on October 16, 1967 the new "Trinitron" system really worked for the first time. It was a totally unique concept—using phosphor stripes, a one gun, three beam system, and a vertical stripe aperture grille—in a market dominated worldwide by the shadow mask system.

In April Ibuka announced the Trinitron's availability in six months. The program's production head, Yoshida, didn't think that schedule was possible. He pleaded and convinced Ibuka to limit the size of the screen to 12 inches because of fears that the Trinitron's glass bulb might fail in larger sizes. Again teams worked until they lost track of night and day. But after 6 months the first sets rolled off the assembly line. And within a year, the Trinitron dominated the small screen market in Japan. After at first dismissing its added brightness as a function of its small 12-inch size—"a clever marketing ploy" said U.S. competitors—the U.S. market responded. The Trinitron earned the first Emmy in the U.S. ever given to a product innovation. Although named for the prize himself, Ibuka saw that his key engineers shared in it. Sony could not catch up with world demand for the fabulously successful Trinitron until the late 1970s.

VIDEO TAPE RECORDERS

A final example, the video tape recorder (VTR), offers other insights about Sony's management of innovation. The first practical VTR, the Quadruplex, was introduced by Ampex in 1956. It set the standard for commercial television broadcasting for almost 20 years. NHK, Japan's national television network, bought a Quadruplex and (along with MITI) encouraged electronics manufacturers' engineers to become familiar with it. The "Quad" cost about $60,000 and was a complex machine filling several closet-sized equipment racks. In 1958, $3\frac{1}{2}$ months after Mr. Ibuka first saw the Ampex machine, a team under Dr. Nobutshu Kihara and Mr. K. Iwama completed an operating prototype using similar principles.

All the leading (6–7) Japanese consumer electronics companies launched major VTR programs. In the U.S., Ampex expanded its line into professional and industrial units. Philips dominated similar markets in Europe, but ignored consumer markets—perhaps because its VTR business was housed in a division with no consumer lines. No American consumer electronics company invested significantly in VTRs until after 1970, in part because their attention was riveted on surviving the '50s and '60s shakeout in the large U.S. TV market.

Sony Gears Up

Dr. Kihara, who headed Sony's VTR program, would later figure prominently in many of Sony's other famous innovations. When asked how Sony approached such radical innovations Dr. Kihara noted, ''Mr. Ibuka would often come in with the 'seed or hint' of an idea and ask him to 'try it out.' '' For example, shortly after Dr. Kihara had helped build the first VTR prototype (which would have to be priced at about 20 million yen or $55,000) Ibuka said, ''We want to make commercial video recorders, can you develop one that will sell for 2 million yen ($5,500)?'' After Kihara did that, Ibuka said, ''Now can we make a color recorder for the home at 200,000 yen ($550). The complex sequence that ensued led to Sony's early preeminence in the home VTR market.

Sony's first commercial machine (in 1963) lacked Ampex's fidelity, but was $\frac{1}{20}$ of its size and sold for less than $\frac{1}{4}$ of its $60,000 price. By 1965 Sony had the compact CV-2000 for $600, operating reel to reel in black and white to high commercial standards. Its U-Matic machine, the first video cassette recorder, became quite successful in commercial color markets in 1972 at $1100. But Sony's target was the home

market; its product was to be the legendary Betamax.

Early Stages

When did it all start? Mr. Ibuka says, ''Around 1951–52 I started to conceive of something called the video tape recorder; but at that time there was no TV broadcasting in Japan, there was no source to record from. Then we started the transistor radio project, and assigned all our engineers and technicians to it. So we stopped the video tape program until 1958, when Ampex began to deliver its video tape recorder. If we had worked on it steadily, I believe we would have been able to produce the tape recorder first. Within $3\frac{1}{2}$ months (after seeing the Ampex machine) we got an image. Ampex had invented a four head machine. We invented the one head machine. Ampex had studied the rotating head machine. We developed our own system. I specifically ordered Sony engineers *not* to develop a broadcasting machine. Many engineers wanted to imitate the Ampex machine and make a good business in the broadcast field. I strongly ordered that we would make a $500 home machine.''

The first all transistorized VTR was the Sony PV100, a two head 2″ tape machine. The biggest customers were an American medical x-ray company and American Airlines—to monitor landings. In 1965 Sony introduced its first home use VTR, the CV-2000. No formal market research studies were made. ''After our experience with the micro-TV, I didn't believe the marketing research people. Merchandising and marketing people cannot envision a market that doesn't exist.''

Mr. Ibuka continued, ''We decided that the video tape recorder must be a cassette type. Our experience in audio said that open reel types were not good in the home market. We succeeded with the U-Matic, which was the first video cassette recorder in the world. When we decided on the U-Matic (U format) standard, Japan Victor and Matsushita agreed on it. We supplied our technology to both companies. Shortly after, we were able to come up with the Beta form of recording which is a helical system using all the space on the tape. All the relevant technologies were invented by us. We asked Matsushita to join us in that standard. But they had a license to operate with our original patent. So they denied us."

Instead, Matsushita changed the size of their cassettes for their VHS format (which depended in part on Sony's patents) so they could record twice as long, two hours. Other Japanese companies went to potential Japanese and American manufacturers to get them to join in their (VHS) standard, not Beta. They even convinced MITI to ask Sony to make the VHS format the national standard. But Sony already had some 200,000 recorders and many tapes in the marketplace. As one of the many alternatives it had looked at, Sony had actually tried the VHS format and was convinced that its Beta—meaning "full coverage" in Japanese—format was much superior. Sony stayed with the Beta system while many other Japanese companies and American consumer electronic companies adopted VHS. Zenith was the main U.S. exception.

The Design Approach

Dr. Kihara said, "My group started ten different major test options or approaches. Within these we developed two or three alternatives for each subsystem. . . . Much of the development process was trial and error. We did not have formal written plans. . . . For example, we developed a loading system with one reel and a leader, not two reels. We developed another where the wind up drum was inside the cassette. We developed the U-loading system, the M-loading system. We developed single heads, double heads, the skip system, and the asimuth system for reading and writing on the tapes. And so on. By taking the best of each option we ultimately developed Betamax."

In 1982 a development team member said, "Kihara was in charge of what kind of developments would be pursued, what systems to use.

At Sony development moves fast. We make quick—but not rash— decisions. Kihara makes the decisions himself." This was reiterated. "Kihara believes there are only a few people directly involved in a new technology who have adequate information or knowledge about that technology. With new products one must create a new market. Not many people know how these new markets will develop, what a product can do, how well it will function, how it could be used by customers." Says Dr. Kihara, "We have never been told by Morita or Ibuka 'this product's sales will be this big or must make this much money.' "

"In my engineering intuition, something interesting comes to mind. I look at the unique things I can do. . . . I don't want to be a copycat. I want to be first, number one. I don't worry about marketing figures. At other companies, top executives expect their top engineers to do managerial chores. Here they do not. They give me a lot of time for development work."

"Produce Something New, Unique"

Dr. Kihara continued, "Most companies make profit the first priority. Sony's primary mission is to produce something new, unique, and innovative for the enhancement of people's lives. Technical people report right to the top of the organization. There is no formal technical committee, but many joint discussions. I like to make 'surprising reports' to Mr. Morita and Ibuka. If an idea is merely under development, I don't report it. After I obtain a working model, then I report it to Morita and Ibuka. I like to surprise the top. In the early development stages, there are typically only 5 or 6 people involved on a project team; for example in the Mavica camera there were 7 to 8. We work together until we have made a model. After we get the go ahead, the project may be expanded to perhaps 30 people."

At Sony there were no specific budgets for individual projects. Kihara reported to Morita once a year on his total budget. But most individual projects in Kihara's group were kept "beneath the surface," hidden in detail even from Morita and Ibuka. Dr. Kihara met with his younger engineers in a prolonged session at least every two months. Said Kihara, ''I try to transfer my technical knowhow and to cultivate an atmosphere of innovation. The best reward system for a young engineer is the joy he gets from making products that are used and sold. The rate of new products from this area is the highest in the company. This gives the group confidence and satisfaction. Sometimes there may be some bonuses involved, but this is not as important as other things.''

Research to Production

Sony consciously rotates its engineers to other divisions and back to engineering. In many large Japanese companies technology is transferred by drawings, prototypes, or production models. But in Sony people from other areas join the development team directly. They are trained on the spot by Research and Development people. Those most suited for production will go on with the project into production. This practice leaves a vacuum in development which can be filled by new people who infuse the department with fresh blood and ideas.

Dr. Kikuchi, Director of Research, said, ''Everyone at the top has a strong interest in engineering and scientific problems and encourages people below to talk to them. And it is easy for us to talk to them. Even Sony's business people must talk technical languages, not just finance.''

In 1982 Sony's President Iwama and Chairman Morita still visited the R&D labs frequently as did now Honorary Chairman, Ibuka. ''Mr. Morita frequently telephones or brings in ideas from around the world on how to apply physics in new ways. And Mr. Ibuka visits many places in Sony randomly. After playing golf near the research center, he will drop in at the laboratory. He wants to see things, touch things. Recently he went to the laboratory and touched his tongue to a new tape compound, to taste it, to see what it was. He leaves people very excited.''

There were monthly meetings between the top board and the technical section heads. But there was little calculation of projected financial ratios or returns for particular projects. Dr. Kikuchi said, ''We as management must define the problems, but only with sufficient specificity to leave many directions open for technical work. The goal must be clear. It may not be expressed numerically. At first there may not even be a date attached. But it must be clear and not change easily. We let the technical leaders choose the approaches.''

''Periodically, I give a 'crystal award' for highly evaluated work. Even if a team has lost a competition within Sony, we will still give them a crystal award if their quality of work is especially good. . . . We also may give engineers a certain percentage of a new product's first year's sales if their ideas had particular merit. The amount of money is significant, but not huge.''

THE WALKMAN AND MAVICA

Through 1982, Sony continued its innovative ways. In the early 1980s two new products offered interesting examples of Sony's innovation capabilities, the Walkman sound system and the Mavica all electronic still camera system.

As had happened so often before, the idea for Walkman (a compact cassette player with small earphones for highly portable listening) came from Ibuka and Morita. Mr. Morita, who purposely visited places where young people congregated, found that they wanted to listen to music on a very personal basis, especially if the sound was loud rock music. He also thought—as an avid golfer—that sportsmen would like a high quality portable sound system. He gave the engineers a target of developing small high quality earphones and a simple light tape player. When the marketing people heard of the project, they did not think such a system would sell well. They wanted to make the cassette record as well as play. Morita said, ''No. Keep it small and simple.'' Despite marketing's skepticism, Mr. Morita was confident that there was a big market for the new concept. The Walkman sold out instantly upon introduction.

The Mavica Still Camera

In the fall of 1981, Sony had announced its revolutionary Mavica all electronic camera for shooting still pictures. Exhibit 3 describes the way the system operated. The camera used no film or chemical developing processes. Images were recorded on a small magnetic disk called Mavipak and could be viewed immediately on a home TV set through a specially designed playback unit. The system also had a color printer called the Mavigraph which could electronically produce hard copy prints from the video signals developed by the Mavica.

The key technical developments for the system were: (1) an electronic recording technique using very high density magnetic disks (developed in the 1960s by Sony), (2) the development of very high quality charged couple devices (CCDs), which converted the optical image coming through the lens of the camera into a series of electrically charged spots on a semiconductor, and (3) the creation of high density circuit boards small enough to operate the complex camera. Then the problem was to bring these together with optics into a quality system. Again there had been no market analysis on the project. "This was one of my dreams come true," said Kihara, "I wanted it to happen regardless of the marketplace."

Dr. Kihara said, "We got the original idea for the electronic still camera 25 years ago. But the technology did not exist to make it practical." Mr. Iwama, who later became president of Sony, had started the original research on the CCD around 1970. He judged the CCD to be a very important technology and backed it as one of the largest research projects Sony had in the 1970s. By 1982 the CCD was a small semiconductor device (about the size of a fingernail) on which several 100,000 individual pick up dots could convert optically focused light into individual electrical pulses.

Information from the CCD could be transferred directly to a magnetic storage device (disk or semiconductor RAM) from which the original image could be later retrieved, electronically enhanced, or eliminated to make room for another image. The resolution of individual pictures was of course limited by the density of information the camera could pick up and store. A color picture from a regular camera using regular instant film would contain about 100 million bits of information. CCDs in 1981 could pick up about 200,000 bits of information for the same sized black and white picture. But the density of information CCDs could pick up was doubling every 2–3 years, and image processing software could improve the picture's appearance even more. Electronically enhanced pictures from a 600,000 bit source would be difficult for the eye to discern from a regular film photograph.

The Mavica was no larger than a conventional 35 millimeter single-lens reflex camera. Once its pictures were recorded on the Mavipak (or only on part of it), the disk could be removed from the camera and then inserted again with no fear of recording a new picture over a previous picture. Since the Mavipak could be erased, the memory disk could be used repeatedly with no deterioration of picture or color quality. Even small children could load a Mavipak into the camera. In 1982 a Mavipak memory medium could record 50 still color pictures. But this technology was rapidly advancing as well.

Dr. Kihara said, "Although the basic technologies were developed over the last 15 years, the real origin of the Mavica was October 1980. At that time I could see that all the technologies were available to make the idea concrete. We put a small team of 7–8 people on it. In August 1981 we unveiled the product. I did not talk to Mr. Ibuka about the Mavica in concrete form until winter 1980–1981 when I showed him the circuit board. Even then Ibuka didn't think it could be done. But we introduced the product with essentially the same circuit board." At one stage Mr. Ibuka had actually said the project should be stopped, but Dr. Kihara told his team to go ahead anyway. Dr. Kihara said Mr. Ibuka was "very fair" in his appraisal of the ultimate result.

The first official announcement of the Mavica system underlined its radical potentials:

"Sony's new magnetic video still camera uses no photographic film and therefore does not require developing and printing processes which are indispensable to conventional chemical photography. This new still video camera represents an epic making innovation in the history of still photography. For more than 104 years since the invention by Daguerre of France, there has been no fundamental change in the concept and technology of photography."

The Mavica Marketplace

The Mavica camera would move into a marketplace that was yet to be defined. Projected prices in Japan were $650 for the camera, $220 for the playback unit, and $2.60 for each magnetic disk. No price was initially announced for the printer, but it was expected to cost approximately $800–$1,000. The Mavica could also be used as a video camera. By attaching it to a portable Sony video tape recorder, one could make video films. Images could also be transmitted electronically over telephone lines. In addition, the Mavi-graph allowed one to make hard copies of the graphics created on the Sony computer system, other compatible computer systems, and certain imaging equipment like x-rays, CAT scanners, or commercial graphic arts devices. While the initial image on a standard U.S. television set would be limited to the 350 horizontal lines on the tube, high resolution screens of 1,500 lines were expected in the near future.

The investment community responded cautiously, but positively, concerning the product's impact. In its investment report, E.F. Hutton said, "In Hutton's view, the so-called photography industry is in the path of a tidal wave of digital electronic technology. In recent decades, digital electronics has revolutionized many industries that had been based on non-electronic processes. And the processing display of scenes/images may become one of the most important uses of digital electronics yet seen. . . . The lion's share of the [photographic] industry profits have been from the sale of consumables (photographic film, paper, and chemicals) as opposed to hardware. The consumables are chemical based, reasonably pro-

prietary, highly profitable—with film and paper made by the mile and sold by the millimeter."[2]

In its report on the photographic and imaging industry, Smith Barney noted:

- Recent developments, including the rapid growth of electronic home movies, have raised concerns about the impact of electronic imaging on current consumer photographic systems. . . .

- Silver halide technology [which currently dominates consumer imaging] will continue to improve in film sensitivity and sharpness, and hardware will become more compact, reliable, and convenient.

- We expect electronic cameras and other hardware to be more expensive than their silver halide counterparts, but the electronic consumables or recording media will be less costly to use.

- We project a total market for consumer electronic imaging of about $4–5 billion in 1990, accounting for about 29% of total consumer imaging expenditures.[3]

Electronics had already begun to erode the Super 8 movie camera marketplace: Smith Barney summarized shipments of Super 8 movie cameras as follows:

SUPER 8 MM MOVIE CAMERAS

Year	Shipments in Thousands
1962	838
1967	1027
1972	1043
1977	609
1978	525
1979	280
1980	230
1981	180
1982	100 (Est.)

Smith Barney further estimated that "approximately 11.5 billion conventional exposures, including color negative, slide, and black and white films, will require the purchase of about $1.2 billion of conventional film in 1984. Developing and printing will come to about $3 billion in the same year [with reprints and enlargements adding another $.3 billion]. In addition to nearly $150 million for instant cameras, consumers will spend about $700 million in 1984 for 900 million instant exposures. . . . The [total] still photographic market in 1984 [will be] about $8.3 billion.''[3] While the U.S. consumer would expend approximately $9.1 billion in 1984 for still photography and movies (both conventional and video), the worldwide market was estimated to be about $23 billion.

In responding to the Sony announcement, Kodak's president, Mr. Chandler, said, ''People like color prints, . . . more than 85% of the amateur pictures taken are prints, rather than slides, up from about 66% 10 years ago. Traditional still photographs provide better images than those from electronic cameras, which at present can be viewed only over a television screen.''[4] In October 1982, Kodak demonstrated a TV display device for displaying developed negatives from its disc cameras. This unit, informally dubbed the EkTViewer, used a 350,000 element CCD chip and provided a good quality image on television. With a 2–1 zoom device, the unit allowed cropping into any quadrant of the original image with little loss of resolution. Kodak said the display unit would probably be priced around $300–$400. Others speculated that commercial extensions of the EkTViewer could allow zooming, cropping, focus adjustments, contrast changes, and shifts in color balance on the monitor. The commercial units were forecast to handle both disc and 35 millimeter films, but would probably cost well over $1,000.

Polaroid had taken equity positions in a number of smaller companies in the high density magnetic recording, fiber optics, ink jet printing, and continuous tone color film recording fields. Polaroid's Palette, which sold for about $1,500, was the most successful color film recorder/printer introduced in the early 1980s. This system allowed the user to output digital images from IBM, Apple, and DEC PC's and record them on either instant print or 135 film.

Several Japanese competitors were also working on similar electronic camera and print systems, but none would divulge details. Canon said that it might have an electronic camera ''in 2–3 years—but maybe not for 10 years.'' Even Sony's chairman Morita conceded that the initial Mavica posed little threat to conventional 35 millimeter cameras, but thought the Mavica would ''open up a new market.'' Mr. Webster of Kodak further observed, ''If you tie [the Mavica] in with the work that Sony and others are doing in high definition television—with a picture that has twice as many elements in both directions, or 4 times the current resolution—then you would be getting into the realm of what would compete with 35 millimeter and Polaroid cameras.'' In addition, as its resolution problems were resolved, Mavica might offer substantial cost advantages for the consumer. Estimated costs for the Mavica would be only 5–10 cents per picture against 80 cents for a Polaroid shot, or 42 cents for a pocket 110 shot on Kodak film. Even then, such prices assumed that silver costs would stay around $15 an ounce and not suddenly balloon as they recently had to around $48 an ounce.

Estimated U.S. retail still camera sales were as follows:

ESTIMATED DOMESTIC RETAIL STILL CAMERA SALES

(units and $ in millions)

	1984	1983	1984	1983
Disc	5.2	4.9	$ 230	$ 225
Cartridge (110 & 126)	3.2	3.6	65	80
Instant	3.8	3.6	145	125
35 Range-finder	3.0	2.4	375	310
35 SLR	2.6	2.7	585	635
Other	0.1	0.1	80	80
	17.9	17.3	$1480	$1455

Source: P.J. Enderlin, Smith Barney, Harris Upham & Co., Inc., *Electronic Imaging—Impact on Consumer Photography*, December 20, 1984.

The biggest trend in camera sales was the growth of 35 mm cameras from about 3% of the amateur market in the late 1970s to over 50% in the early 1980s. Much of this gain had come at the expense of instant cameras. This reflected the impact of the lower cost, more convenient, more compact, and more reliable equipment introduced and heavily promoted by its Japanese manufacturers. The best 35 mm films far exceeded the resolving power of the human eye—and film performance had recently been accelerating its already impressive historical rate of improvement.

Initially magnetic disks would offer sufficient capability to store electronic images. Kodak's 5.25 inch floppy disk could hold 3.3 megabytes. However, 3M estimated that with magneto-optics, a similar size disk could hold 600 megabytes on each side. This technology was under rapid development. In estimating the potential markets for the Mavica, the sales patterns of video cassette recorders and color video cameras are instructive. See tables below.

U.S. COLOR VIDEO CAMERA MARKET

Year	(units 000)	Year-End Penetration % of Households
1979	61	.1
1980	115	.3
1981	190	.5
1982	296	.9
1983	414	1.3
1984E	500	1.9
1985E	700	2.6

Source: P.J. Enderlin, Smith Barney, Harris Upham & Co., Inc., *Electronic Imaging—Impact on Consumer Photography*, December 20, 1984.

U.S. VIDEO CASSETTE RECORDER MARKET SALES TO DEALERS

(units 000)

Year	Portable —(*)	Table Model	Total	Year-End Penetration % of Households
1975			20	.03
1977			209	.3
1980			805	2.4
1981			1,361	4.0
1982	436	1,599	2,035	6.4
1983	750	3,341	4,091	11.1
1984E	1,000	6,000	7,000	19.1
1985E	1,200	6,800	8,000	28.2

(*) *Includes camcorders.*

Smith Barney estimated the breakdown of the 1984 and 1990 markets as follows:

DOMESTIC CONSUMER ELECTRONIC IMAGING MARKET

($ billions)

	1990	1984
Still Photography		
Silver Halide	$11.0	$8.3
Electronic	1.0	0
Movies		
Silver Halide	0	.1
Electronic	3.5	.7
Total Consumer Imaging	$15.5	$9.1
Total Electronic	$ 4.5	$ .7
% Electronic	29%	8%

Source: P.J. Enderlin, Smith Barney, Harris Upham & Co., Inc., *Electronic Imaging—Impact on Consumer Photography*, December 20, 1984.

As the early 1980s opened, most experts predicted a genuine revolution in the photographic and imaging industries led by new electronic and electro-optical technologies. The question was where Mavica would fit into this revolution and how each of the major players would respond to the challenge?

At this same time Sony was again about to pioneer with the first introduction of a compact disk (laser optical) audio record player which could record 100 billion bits of information on its 5 inch disk and a small 8 mm hand held video camera (CAMCORDER) which could threaten all existing amateur (Super 8) film systems.

ISSUES FOR THE FUTURE

Despite these exciting developments, Sony's financial performance slowed markedly in 1982–83. Mr. Morita, under fire from the press and investment analysts, had to review Sony's posture in the light of changing world electronic markets and determine how to position the company and its newest cluster of revolutionary products for the 1980s. Exhibit 4 summarizes Sony's 1982 financial position and product portfolio. Exhibit

5 shows the basic Mavica system and its potential extensions. The Polaroid case offers additional information on camera and imaging markets.

QUESTIONS

1. What are the most critical policies and practices which made Sony so innovative as a company? Can they be transferred to other companies? What problems do they pose for Sony?
2. How does Sony compare and contrast with conventional views of "the Japanese management style"? How did it compare and contrast with the American approach to "entrepreneurship" when it was a small company?
3. What overall strategy should Sony follow in 1982? Why?
4. How should Mavica fit into that strategy? What should be the specific strategy for introduction of Mavica? Why?

GENERAL SOURCES

"Akio Morita: Chairman and CEO," *Director*, May 1982.

"The Americanization of Sony," *New York Times*, March 18, 1973.

"Another Revolution," *Economist*, June 4, 1983.

"A Diversification Plan Tuned to the People Factor," *Business Week*, February 9, 1981.

Drucker, P., *Management*, Harper and Row, 1974.

P.J. Enderlin, Smith Barney, Harris Upham & Co., Inc., *Electronic Imaging—Impact on Consumer Photography*, December 20, 1984.

"Even Sony Sometimes Stumbles," *Forbes*, April 25, 1983.

"The Giants in Japanese Electronics," *Economist*, February 20, 1982.

"Here Comes Projection Television," *Economist*, October 8, 1977.

"Horatio Alger Story with a Japanese Twist," *New York Times Magazine*, September 10, 1967.

"How to Get Bigger with Smaller Products," *Business Week*, May 25, 1968.

Ibuka, Masaru. "How Sony Developed Electronics for the World Market," *IEEE Transactions on Engineering Management*, Vol. EM-22, No. 1, February 1975.

"An Incongruous Search for Greener Pastures," *Business Week*, February 11, 1980.

Kobayashi, Shigeru. *Creative Management*, American Management Association, 1971.

Lyons, Nick. *The Sony Vision*, New York: Crown Publishers, Inc., 1976.

Morita, Akio. "What Is the Difference Between the Japanese Management and the American?" Chicago, February 17, 1972.

———. "International Marketing of Sony Corporation," monograph, Tokyo, July 14, 1969.

———. "Decision Making in Japanese Business," monograph, Manila, September 30, 1975.

———. "Creativity in Modern Industry," Frank Nelson Doubleday Series, Smithsonian Institution, 1974.

N. Pearlstine, "Blurred Image," *Forbes*, September 4, 1978.

R.D. Schwarz, E.F. Hutton Group, Inc., *Imaging Technology—Industry Report*, June 13, 1985.

"Sony Levels Off," *Forbes*, September 9, 1978.

"Sony's Nearly 40 Years of Making It Better and Smaller," *Broadcasting*, May 16, 1983.

"Sony's Purposeful Dreams," *Fortune*, July 1964.

"Sony's US Operation Goes in for Repairs," *Business Week*, March 13, 1978.

"Talking Business With Akio Morita," *Business Week*, April 18, 1983.

R. Tanner and W. Ouchi. "Made in America: Under Japanese Management," *Harvard Business Review*, September–October 1974.

"Technology vs. Tariffs," *Forbes*, April 15, 1977.

"Video's New Frontier," *Newsweek*, February 9, 1976.

Wall Street Journal, November 2, 1981, p. 23.

EXHIBIT 1 SONY CORPORATION

Purposes of Incorporation

- "The establishment of an ideal factory—free, dynamic, and pleasant—where technical personnel of sincere motivation can exercise their technological skills to the highest levels.

- Dynamic activities in technology and production for the reconstruction of Japan and the elevation of the nation's culture.

- Prompt application of the highly advanced technology developed during the war in various sectors to the life of the general public.

- Making rapidly into commercial products the superior research results of universities and research institutes, which are worth applying to the daily lives of the public."

Management Policies

- We shall eliminate any untoward profit-seeking, shall constantly emphasize activities of real substance, and shall not seek expansion of size for the sake of size.

- Rather, we shall seek a compact size of operation through which the path of technology and business activities can advance in areas that large enterprises, because of their size, cannot enter.

Source: Sony Corporation of America.

- We shall be as selective as possible in our products and will even welcome technological difficulties. We shall focus on highly sophisticated technical products that have great usefulness in society, regardless of the quantity involved. Moreover, we shall avoid the formal demarcation between electricity and mechanics, and shall create our own unique products coordinating the two fields with a determination that other companies cannot overtake.

- Utilizing to the utmost the unique features of our firm, which shall be known and trusted among the acquaintances in the business and technical worlds, we shall open up through mutual cooperation our production and sales channels and our acquisition of supplies to an extent equal to those of large business organizations.

- We shall guide and foster subcontracting factories in directions that will help them become independently operable and shall strive to expand and strengthen the pattern of mutual help with such factories.

- Personnel shall be carefully selected, and the firm shall be comprised of as small a number as feasible. We shall avoid mere formal position levels and shall place our main emphasis on ability, performance, and personal character, so that each individual can show the best in ability and skill.

EXHIBIT 2 MILESTONES IN VTR PRODUCT DEVELOPMENT

Market	Model	Company	Date of Commercial Introduction	Tape Width*	Tape Utilization (sq. ft./hour)	Price (in constant 1967 $)
Broadcast	VR–1000	AMPEX	1956	2″	747	$60,000
Professional	VR–1500	AMPEX	1962	2″	375	12,000
Industrial	PV–100	SONY	1962	2″	212	13,000
Industrial/Professional	EL–3400	PHILIPS	1964	1″	188	3,500
Industrial/Professional	CV–2000	SONY	1965	$\frac{1}{2}$″	90	600
Industrial/Professional	N–1500	PHILIPS	1972	$\frac{1}{2}$″	70	1,150
Industrial/Professional	U–Matic	SONY	1972	$\frac{3}{4}$″	70	1,100
Consumer	Betamax	SONY	1975	$\frac{1}{2}$″	20	850
Consumer	VHS	JVC	1976	$\frac{1}{2}$″	16	790
Consumer	VR2020	PHILIPS	1980	$\frac{1}{2}$″	6	520

From 1972 onward, all models used cassettes instead of open reels and all used high-energy tape.

Source: Sony company records.

EXHIBIT 3 PERSPECTIVE VIEW OF MAVICA

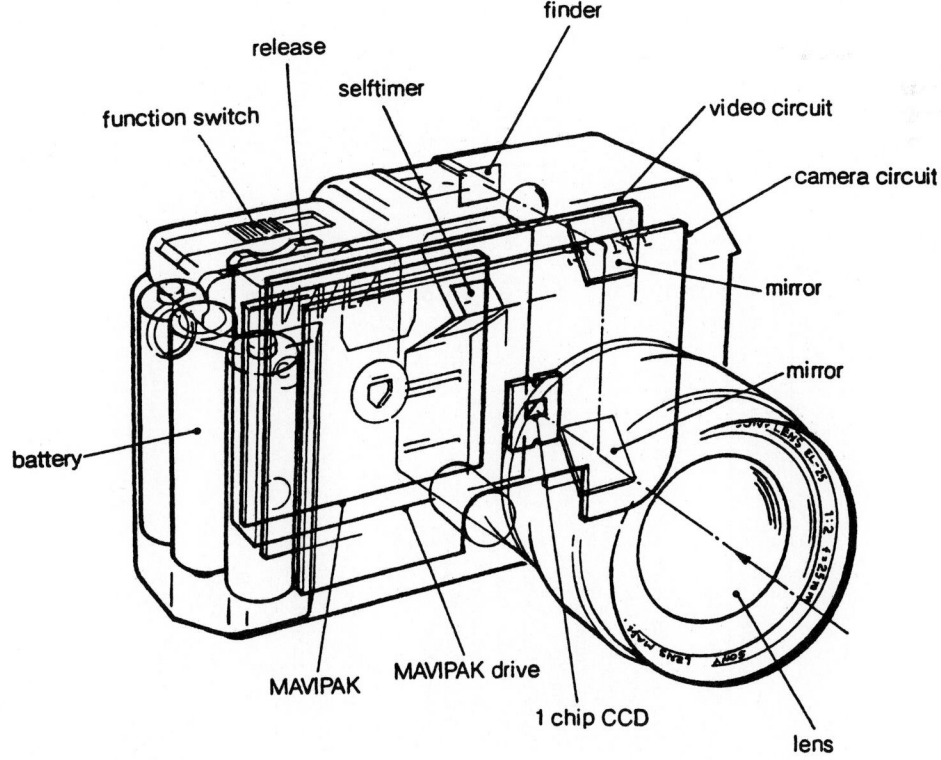

Source: Sony Corporation.

EXHIBIT 4 SONY CORPORATION (Sony Kabushiki Kaisha) FINANCIALS
CONSOLIDATED BALANCE SHEET

Assets	In millions of yen		Translation into thousands of U.S. dollars (Note 3)
	October 31		
	1982	1981 (Restated)	1982
CURRENT ASSETS:			
Cash	33,512	29,436	136,228
Time deposits (Note 7)	109,131	109,399	443,622
Marketable securities, at cost or less which approximates market (Note 6)	34,799	56,183	141,459
Notes and accounts receivable, trade	186,932	184,305	759,886
Notes and accounts receivable, affiliated companies	59,483	69,016	241,801
Allowance for doubtful accounts	(13,751)	(12,025)	(55,898)
Inventories (Note 4)	360,371	322,392	1,464,923
Prepaid expenses and other current assets	35,794	41,922	145,503
Income tax prepayments	47,761	41,754	194,150
Total current assets	854,032	842,382	3,471,674
INVESTMENTS AND ADVANCES:			
Affiliated companies (Note 5)	54,060	44,896	219,756
Directors, officers and employees	4,533	9,290	18,427
Other (Notes 6 and 7)	22,480	22,241	91,382
	81,073	76,427	329,565

Liabilities	In millions of yen		Translation into thousands of U.S. dollars (Note 3)
	October 31		
	1982	1981 (Restated)	1982
CURRENT LIABILITIES:			
Short-term borrowings (Note 7)	306,451	222,020	1,245,736
Current portion of long-term debt	2,129	1,700	8,655
Notes payable, trade	122,597	167,276	498,362
Accounts payable, trade	42,225	61,237	171,646
Notes payable, construction	14,704	20,504	59,772
Notes and accounts payable, affiliated companies	20,706	28,091	84,171
Dividends payable	5,123	4,091	20,825
Accrued income and other taxes	32,612	52,506	132,569
Other accounts payable and accrued liabilities	112,245	103,595	456,279
Total current liabilities	658,792	661,020	2,678,015
LONG-TERM DEBT (Notes 7 and 12)	56,829	20,498	231,012
LIABILITY FOR SEVERANCE INDEMNITIES (Note 8)	39,265	35,973	159,614
ACCUMULATED INCOME TAX REDUCTIONS	10,877	9,399	44,216

PROPERTY, PLANT AND EQUIPMENT (Note 12):

Land	45,599	39,715	185,362
Buildings	151,141	120,035	614,394
Machinery and equipment	259,304	182,584	1,054,081
Construction in progress	14,983	20,084	60,907
	471,027	362,418	1,914,744
Less—Accumulated depreciation	179,768	137,437	730,764
	291,259	224,981	1,183,980

OTHER ASSETS

OTHER ASSETS	13,991	8,865	56,874
	1,240,355	1,152,655	5,042,093

STOCKHOLDERS' EQUITY (Note 10):

Common stock $50 par value			
Authorized — 920,000,000 shares			
Issued: 1982— 230,713,704 shares	11,535	11,531	46,890
1981— 230,625,000 shares			
Capital in excess of par value	91,061	90,755	370,167
Legal reserve	4,854	4,515	19,732
Retained earnings appropriated for special allowances	6,701	5,610	27,240
Retained earnings	350,680	316,439	1,425,528
Cumulative translation adjustment (Note 1)	9,761	(3,085)	39,679
	474,592	425,765	1,929,236

COMMITMENTS AND CONTINGENT LIABILITIES (Note 13)

	1,240,355	1,152,655	5,042,093

The accompanying notes are an integral part of this statement and are provided in the company's annual report.

Source: Sony Corporation, Annual Report, 1982.

EXHIBIT 4 (*Continued*)

SONY CORPORATION (Sony Kabushiki Kaisha) FINANCIALS
CONSOLIDATED TEN-YEAR SUMMARY

Millions of yen except per share amounts (Thousands of U.S. dollars except per share amounts)

	1982	1981	1980	1979	1978	1977	1976	1975	1974	1973
Net sales:										
Overseas	829,665 ($3,372,622)	744,775	610,545	394,554	320,085	310,721	272,455	224,248	198,939	148,653
Domestic	284,157 (1,155,110)	306,266	282,218	248,901	214,832	195,303	191,073	185,362	198,112	165,408
Total	1,113,822 (4,527,732)	1,051,041	892,763	643,455	534,917	506,024	463,528	409,610	397,051	314,061
Operating income	109,584 (445,464)	142,589	117,245	74,719	30,766	56,445	61,974	42,644	53,880	48,079
Income before income taxes	85,542 (347,732)	132,731	116,748	41,272	52,378	64,363	64,388	39,187	46,414	49,159
Income taxes	45,871 (186,468)	69,652	53,026	26,960	29,387	32,985	35,625	22,415	23,693	24,656
Net income	45,820 (186,260)	66,901	68,643	17,716	25,874	34,898	30,926	16,893	22,518	25,134
Per Depositary Share	198.67 (0.81)	291.67	318.34	82.16	120.00	161.85	143.42	78.34	106.55	121.40
Depreciation	48,229 (196,053)	32,421	24,703	20,086	15,844	12,992	10,778	10,850	10,298	7,586

Notes:
1. Each Depositary Share represents 1 share of Common Stock. Per share amounts are based on the average number of shares outstanding during each period, adjusted for all stock distributions.
2. 1981 amounts have been restated using FASB 52, as described in Note 1 of Notes to Consolidated Financial Statements.
3. U.S. dollar amounts for fiscal 1982 are translated for convenience from yen at the rate of Y246 = U.S.$1, the Tokyo foreign exchange market rate as of December 14, 1982, as described in Note 3 of Notes to Consolidated Financial Statements.

Source: Sony Corporation, *Annual Report*, 1982.

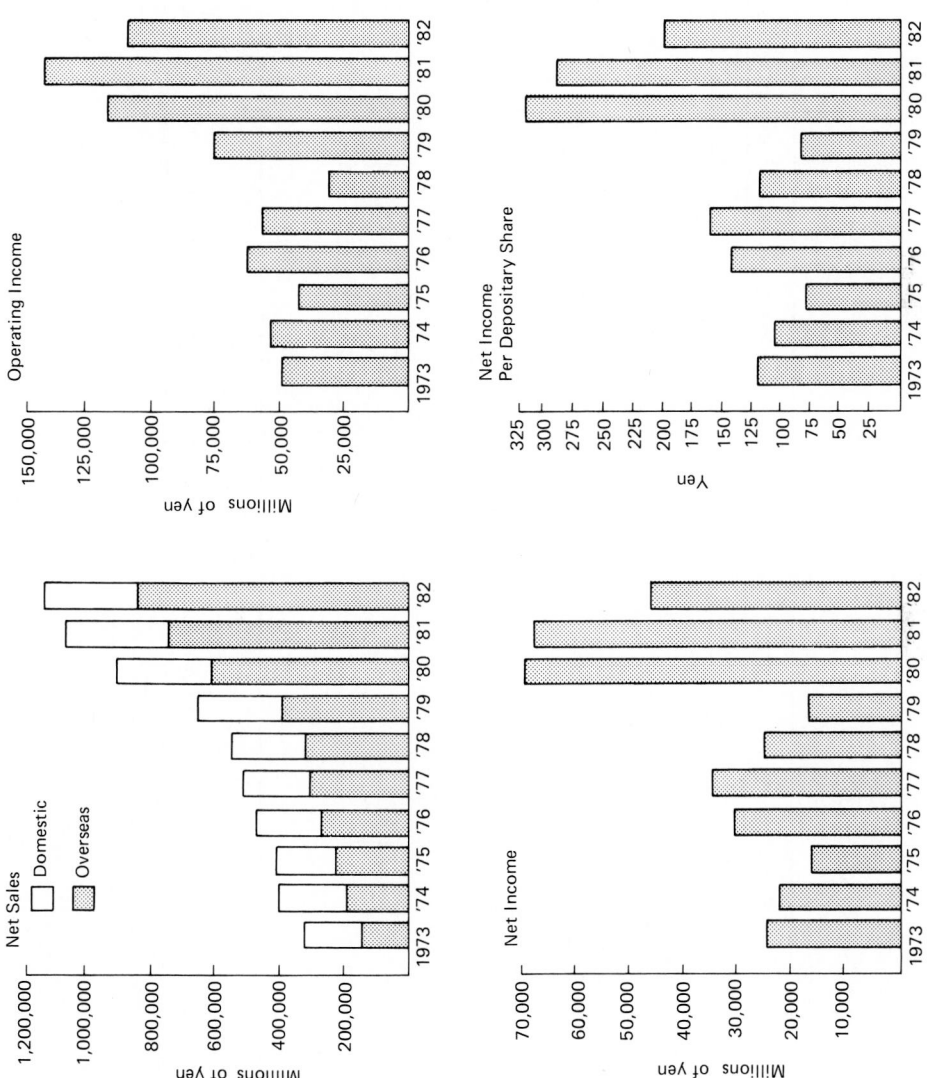

EXHIBIT 4 (Continued)

SONY CORPORATION (Sony Kabushiki Kaisha) FINANCIALS
CONSOLIDATED TEN-YEAR SUMMARY

Millions of yen except per share amounts (Thousands of U.S. dollars except per share amounts)

	1982	1981	1980	1979	1978	1977	1976	1975	1974	1973
Net working capital	195,240 ($793,859)	181,362	137,188	84,265	97,272	89,162	90,840	69,296	64,612	38,892
Capital investment .... (Additions to fixed assets)	112,091 (455,654)	98,089	48,715	38,916	37,604	33,732	16,619	12,468	25,878	35,824
Shareholders' equity	474,592 (1,929,236)	425,765	325,523	263,349	251,024	230,541	201,034	174,421	160,115	119,988
Per Depositary Share	2,057.72 (8.36)	1,856.20	1,509.67	1,221.33	1,164.17	1,069.18	932.33	808.91	757.66	579.56
Total assets	1,240,355 (5,042,093)	1,152,655	877,413	763,907	618,854	552,138	509,859	423,123	416,681	344,194
Average number of shares ... (In thousands of shares)	230,639	229,375	215,625	215,625	215,625	215,625	215,625	215,625	211,328	207,031
Number of issued shares ..... (As of end of fiscal year)	230,714	230,625	215,625	215,625	215,625	215,625	215,625	172,500	172,500	132,500
Number of employees	43,126	38,555	32,821	30,607	27,112	25,881	22,713	22,108	21,635	20,600

Notes:
1. Each Depositary Share represents 1 share of Common Stock. Per share amounts are based on the average number of shares outstanding during each period, adjusted for all stock distributions.
2. 1981 amounts have been restated using FASB 52 as described in Note 1 of Notes to Consolidated Financial Statements.
3. U.S. dollar amounts for fiscal 1982 are translated for convenience from yen at the rate of Y246 = U.S.$1, the Tokyo foreign exchange market rate as of December 14, 1982, as described in Note 3 of Notes to Consolidated Financial Statements.

Source: Sony Corporation, Annual Report, 1982.

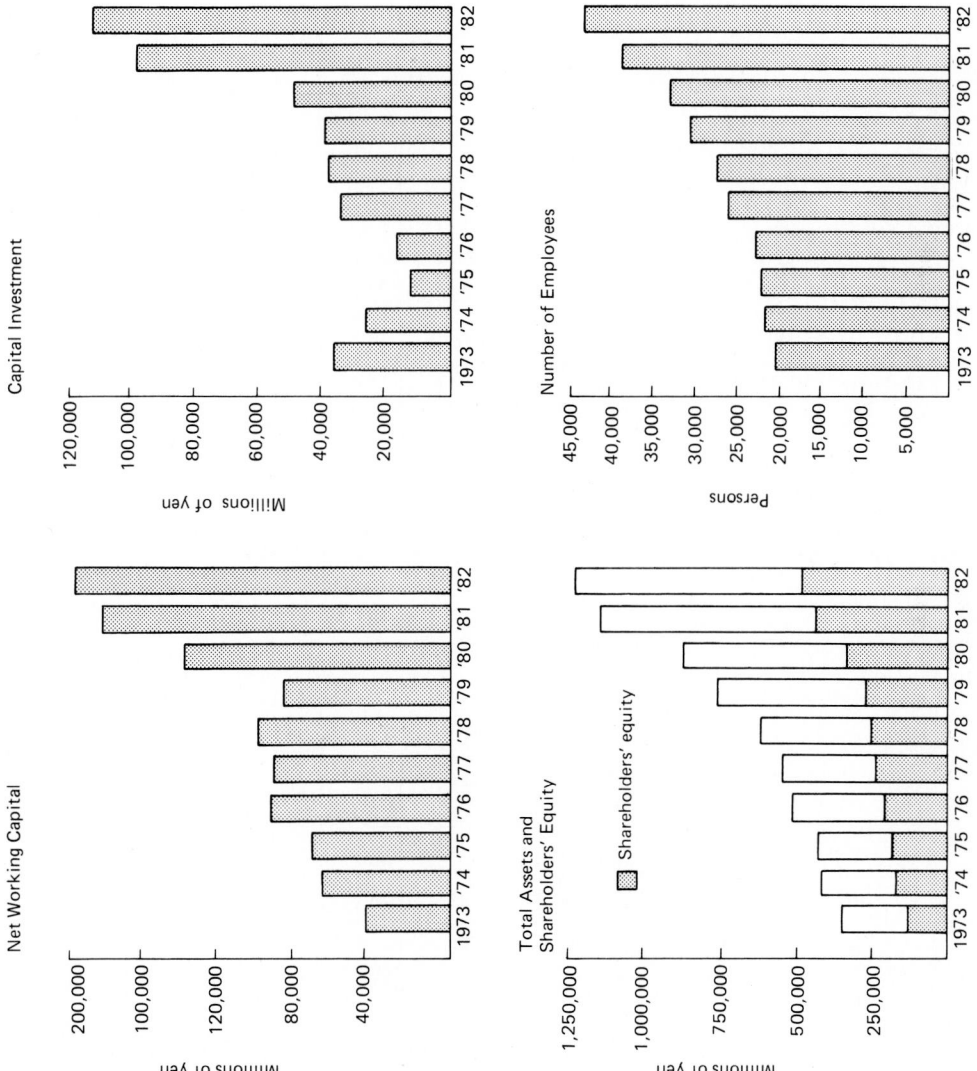

Capital Investment

Millions of yen

120,000 100,000 80,000 60,000 40,000 20,000

1973 '74 '75 '76 '77 '78 '79 '80 '81 '82

Number of Employees

Persons

45,000 40,000 35,000 30,000 25,000 20,000 15,000 10,000 5,000

1973 '74 '75 '76 '77 '78 '79 '80 '81 '82

Net Working Capital

Millions of yen

200,000 100,000 120,000 80,000 40,000

1973 '74 '75 '76 '77 '78 '79 '80 '81 '82

Total Assets and
Shareholders' Equity

Shareholders' equity

Millions of yen

1,250,000 1,000,000 750,000 500,000 250,000

1973 '74 '75 '76 '77 '78 '79 '80 '81 '82

747

EXHIBIT 4 (*Continued*)

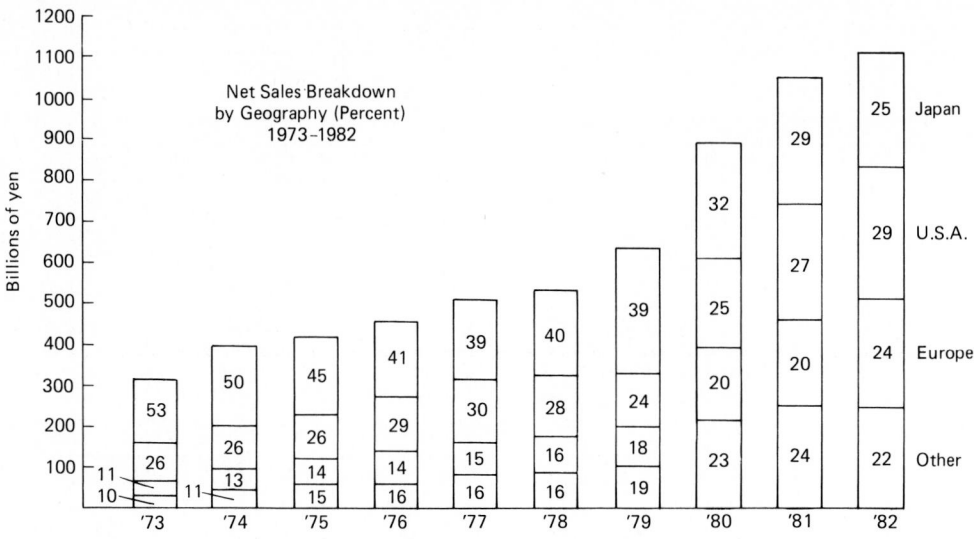

Net Sales Breakdown
by Geography (Percent)
1973–1982

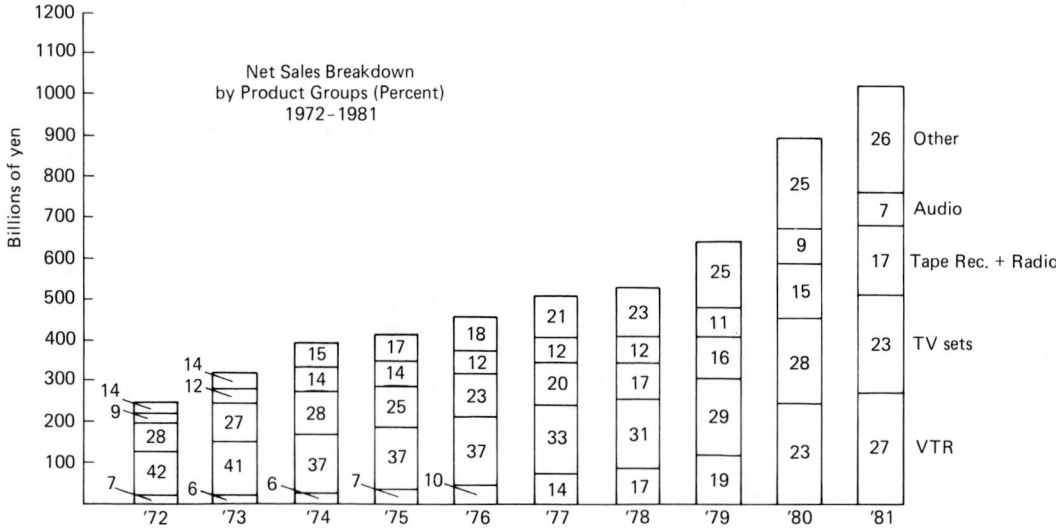

Net Sales Breakdown
by Product Groups (Percent)
1972–1981

Note: In 1982 Sony changed its product groupings as follows: (1) Video Equipment (VTRs, video cameras, video tapes*, etc.); (2) Television Sets (color, black and white, projection*, etc.); (3) Audio Equipment (Hi-Fi audio products, tape recorders and radios, audio tapes*, etc.); (4) Others (Business Machines, etc.). The starred items were previously in the other category. In 1982 Sony provided the following net sales breakdown by product groups:

	Percent of Net Sales			
	Video	TV	Audio	Other
1981	34	26	29	11
1982	43	23	23	11

Source: Sony Corporation, *SEC Form 20F*, 1981 and 1982.

EXHIBIT 5   MAVICA SYSTEM

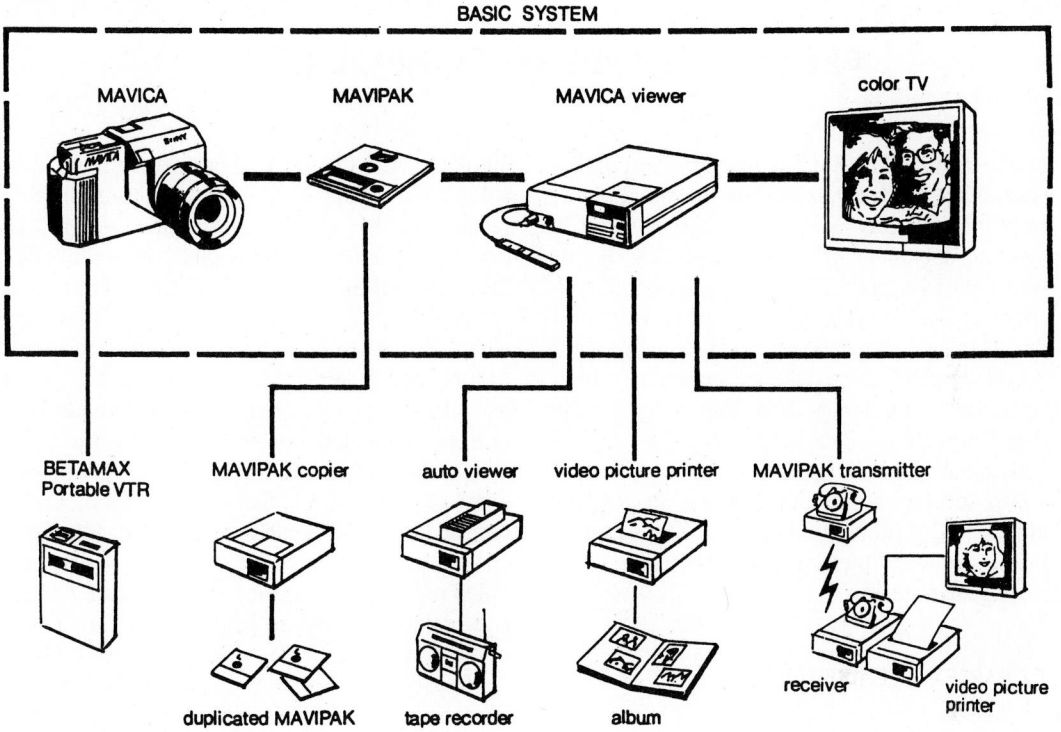

BASIC SYSTEM

MAVICA · MAVIPAK · MAVICA viewer · color TV

BETAMAX Portable VTR · MAVIPAK copier · auto viewer · video picture printer · MAVIPAK transmitter

duplicated MAVIPAK · tape recorder · album · receiver · video picture printer

Source: Sony Corporation

FEDERAL EXPRESS CORPORATION

In the mid 1970s Federal Express Corporation became the largest startup venture capital investment in history. Its success revolutionized package and document delivery in the U.S. By the fall of 1985 Federal's highly entrepreneurial management had built sales to $2 billion and launched the company on a visionary new product concept, ZapMail, which utilized the most modern communications technologies and would potentially dwarf in scale the $96 million investment which had initially gotten Federal Express rolling. In 1986, developing this new concept successfully and relating it properly to the company's existing businesses were forefront issues for Federal's top management team.

COMPLEX BEGINNINGS

The myth is that the Federal Express system sprang full-blown from the head of young Frederick W. Smith in a 1964 Yale term paper for which he received an unappreciating "C" grade. The facts are much more complicated. Although many of the ideas he put forward in that paper were proved correct by later events, it took years to work out the full mechanics of how to provide overnight delivery of packages and documents. First deliveries were not made until the spring of 1973.

In classic style, Fred Smith's entrepreneurial track record probably began when he was 15 and started the Arden Record Company with a high school classmate in Memphis. That same year, Smith also learned to fly, beginning a lifetime fascination with advanced technology and flight. At Yale, he helped revitalize the Yale Fly-ing Club. And his first real business venture after college was selling and repairing aircraft. Smith's father was also a self-made millionaire. He had developed the Dixie Greyhound Co. and founded the Toddle House restaurant chain, a forerunner of today's fast-food outlets. Although he died when Fred was only 4, Fred's father left a sizable fortune and a letter admonishing Fred "to put his inheritance to work and use the funds held in trust as a foundation for greater wealth."[1]

After graduating from Yale and serving two tours of duty in Vietnam as a Marine, Smith returned to the South and purchased a Little Rock company, Arkansas Aviation Sales, which provided maintenance services for corporate aircraft and brokered corporate jets. Despite the success of these ventures, from 1969 until 1971 Smith continued to flesh out the concept of an overnight air delivery service. The Federal Reserve System looked like an ideal first customer for such a service. The cost of the Fed's float of checks in its system was about $3 million per day of delay. Smith took his idea to the Fed, which seemed to respond favorably. When he thought the transaction was set, Smith put up $250,000 of his own funds to start his new company and got his family trust to match his equity investment and to guarantee a $3.6 million bank loan to buy two small Falcon jet aircraft.

A few weeks later the Fed backed out, and Smith had two jets and a rejected concept on his hands. But he had incorporated on June 18, 1971 under the name Federal Express, both to support his proposed relationship with the Federal Reserve and to indicate a developing nationwide service.

The Early 1970s Air Freight Industry

Smith felt a number of U.S. lifestyle and corporate trends strongly supported developing a service for overnight delivery of urgent or high value

Case copyright © 1986 by James Brian Quinn. Case prepared by Penny C. Paquette under the supervision of Professor Quinn. The generous cooperation of the Federal Express Corporation is gratefully acknowledged.

packets. At that time shippers were faced with a variety of choices. They could use the U.S. mails; contract directly with various air or ground carriers; or call air forwarding agents who acted as brokers—arranging trucking to the airport, transport as air cargo on freight or passenger airlines, and truck pickup and delivery at the destination. A typical package went through 5 to 10 different corporate hands. In 1972 the top three domestic air forwarders were Emery, Airborne, and UPS. Regulations prohibited forwarders from operating their own aircraft. For a variety of reasons forwarders' delivery was unreliable and generally took 2 to 4 days. United Parcel Service (UPS) with its huge ground network was more dependable, but could not guarantee delivery in anything less than 2 days. And most air carriers were marginally profitable or losing money on their small package businesses.

Smith spent $150,000 on two different market research studies to investigate his concept. They found the airlines posed particular problems as linkages in the priority parcel delivery system. Over 60% of all airline movements occurred between the 25 largest markets, and only 10% of their fleets were flying after 10:00 P.M. By contrast, over 80% of the small urgent shipments originated or terminated outside the top 25 markets. And the purchase of jumbo aircraft by the major airlines seemed likely to further consolidate routes and decrease the flexibility of the system. As Fred Smith said when he was investigating the Federal Reserve System's possibilities, "[The Fed] gives you in microcosm a picture of the flow of U.S. economic activity. Six thousand pounds of checks a day go from New York City to Chicago, and one pound a day might move randomly from Billings, Montana, to Jacksonville, Florida."[2] In this complexity, Smith saw his opportunity.

A Night to Remember

Still he struggled to find a workable concept which would: (1) meet the market need his research studies said was there, (2) utilize his Falcon aircraft, and (3) fit into the regulatory structures of the CAB. In December 1971 Smith had signed a contract with Pan Am to buy 23 more Falcons, which were available then at a distress price. However, a CAB regulation—Part 298 under which Smith hoped to operate—posed major problems. Part 298 permitted air taxi services to carry people, property, and mail on chartered flights without CAB's prior approval of their specific routes. However, Smith's Falcons exceeded Part 298's allowed gross takeoff weight (including fuel, etc.) of 12,500 pounds, until the regulation was revised in September 1972 to permit "payload weights" of 7,500 pounds. This change, preceded by much lobbying by Smith and substantial opposition from the airlines, made the Falcons viable.

During the fall of 1972 Smith put together a management team for Federal Express and started to design and put in place certain major logistic elements for his system. The crucial determinations made at this time were: (1) to serve only a limited network of cities, (2) to use Memphis, Tennessee as the central sorting point for Federal's proposed "hub and spoke" air system, (3) to establish a van pickup and delivery network to support this system, and (4) to undertake the major modifications to the Falcon aircraft necessary to handle air cargo in volume. As of September 1972, Federal began to fly some contract charters for individual customers, and to service three U.S. mail routes to utilize its aircraft. It also performed several experiments for specific industrial clients to demonstrate that overnight delivery of urgent packages was possible.

Then on March 12, 1973 Federal undertook an operational test with an 11 city network. The results did not bode well for the company, with less than eighteen packages handled—and one of those was a birthday present from Fred Smith to a close friend. Finally the official "first night" for Federal Express occurred on April 17, 1973. But the number of packages handled was still a discouraging 186. By October the nightly count had risen to only 2,000, despite many experiments to improve operations. And keeping the company alive was a full time dilemma.

Charles Lea of New Court Securities said that in September 1973, his company's financial studies had come up with a survival financial package "calling for $52 million: $10 million for operating losses, $40 million for aircraft and equipment, $2.5 million for working capital. Fred Smith had already invested $6–9 million. . . . It would be the largest venture capital deal ever undertaken at that time. . . . The worst case scenario called for losses in the first year of $9.3 million with profits climbing close to $9.5 million by 1976." The major question was how could Smith, who had been working feverishly for years on the project, convince investors to put up such enormous sums for a new company, operating in a new market, with a totally new concept, and hemorrhaging cash and operating losses. At the end of its first fiscal year, May 1974, Federal had revenues of $17.3 million and losses of $13.3 million.

INITIAL STRATEGY POINT

In its initial operations, what crucial issues must Federal Express resolve to be successful? What should its marketing strategy be? What services should it target? Avoid? What major operating problems would you anticipate? How should these be approached? What contingencies must Federal Express be prepared for in its operation? On what basis could Mr. Smith raise essential financing? What organization issues does Federal face? How should these be resolved?

THE INDUSTRY EXPANDS

Through a series of cliffhanging negotiations with banks, venture capitalists, and government regulators Mr. Smith and his team hung doggedly on to their dream and developed a totally new priority delivery system for the U.S. Federal's early financial performance and equity financings are summarized in Exhibit 1. Only those bank financings associated with equity offerings are detailed. What had previously been a relatively diffuse, but homogenous marketplace began a process of segmentation that was accelerated by

the gradual deregulation of the transportation industry and the emergency of a few large competitors.

By 1977 Federal Express' volume had reached a point where within 2 years its future growth would be constrained by the 7,500 pound payload limit set for its aircraft as an air taxi operator. After much more concerted effort by Mr. Smith and others, Washington finally deregulated the air cargo industry as a prelude to the deregulation of the whole airline industry. In January 1978 Federal, along with some 20–30 other carriers, received an All Cargo Air Service Certificate which allowed it to fly any size plane and did not restrict its route system.

In quick succession the Private Express Statute was amended to allow overnight delivery of "extremely urgent" mail without the previous affixing of U.S. postage. This opened the possibility of competing directly with the Postal Service's Express Mail system. The passage of the Motor Carrier Act of 1980 further freed Federal Express and its ground based competitors from regulations. Air carriers had previously been restricted in their ground operations to a defined (35 mile radius) terminal area around an airport. The Act changed that by specifically exempting from federal (ICC) regulations "ground transportation services which were incidental to air transportation services." The same Act also substantially deregulated the small package segment of the trucking industry—allowing ground carriers handling shipments weighing 100 pounds or less to operate without special route certificates.

Federal Express grew rapidly to sales of $160 million in 1978 with profits of $19.4 million. The success of Federal Express had both created a new market and attracted numerous new competitors. An estimated 40% of Federal's volume was made up of items which previously might not have been air shipped at all. Kidder Peabody's Transportation Research Group described the size and characteristics of the "expedited package and document delivery market" in a June 1983 report. Exhibits 2–4 show these findings. The following section briefly describes the way competition was emerging in the late 1970s and early 1980s.

The Early 1980s Marketplace

Emery was the largest and most profitable domestic air freight forwarder with a wide geographical distribution system inside and outside the U.S. Emery had finally responded to Federal's challenge in late 1978 by offering next day delivery using its own planes. It had evolved from using two separate hubs (for small packages and heavier freight) to a single hub in Dayton, Ohio which sorted light and heavy freight at the same time. Emery offered delivery of either kind of package by noon the next day. Although some 60% of its shipments were under 50 pounds, it was still heavily dependent on larger, heavier cargo. Many felt that Emery was using its high margin international business to subsidize its lower margin domestic business in its battle with industry leader, Federal Express.

Airborne, Seattle-based, was the second largest domestic air freight forwarder and by 1982 also held second place in the air express business. Airborne had a wholly integrated air-ground transportation system modeled after Federal's. But 75% of its revenues came from the highly competitive national accounts sector as opposed to lower volume shippers, and it lacked the overall volume to match Federal's position as low-cost producer. Some 20% of its volume came from international operations.

United Parcel Service had revenues of $4 billion in 1980 and shipped more than 1.8 billion packages in that year, all weighing 70 lbs. or less. UPS was privately held by its own management and had some $2 billion in assets. In addition to more than 60,000 ground vehicles driven by 85,000 Teamsters, UPS was the largest single shipper on most railroads and by 1982–83 owned a fleet of planes itself. At the time Federal began offering its overnight service, UPS had only its "Blue Label" service, a second-day delivery commitment. In late 1982 it introduced a "next day by 3 P.M." service (with no "on-call" pickup) for a limited network of cities. Of its daily volume of between 5 and 10 million packages, only about 150,000 of them went by air. UPS concentrated on gaining productivity through the tight management of its people rather than using automation and in 1986 still handled its enormous sorting process by hand.

Purolator Courier was part of a company which also had an armored car division and manufactured automotive products. The Courier division was the company's largest source of revenues. Like UPS, Purolator Courier provided a scheduled pickup and delivery service moving cancelled checks and general commodities of less than 50 lbs. It was the largest and fastest growing non-union trucking concern in North America— four times the size of its nearest non-union ground-based competitor. In 1976, it had started chartering planes for shipments of more than 400 miles, but in the early 1980s approximately 80% of its shipments still moved by surface, which cost $\frac{1}{6}$ of what air transport did. 70% of Purolator's volume was in machine parts, blood plasma, and film for processing. By the early 1980s, it had teamed up with MCI Communications to act as a delivery arm of MCI Mail, and had added on-call pickup services after the trucking industry was deregulated.

FEDERAL'S STRUCTURE IN 1985

By late 1985 Federal Express was offering next day service to more than 40,000 communities, or close to 98% of the U.S. population, through a network of more than 720 Full Service Stations and Business Service Centers in major metropolitan areas. These offered customers access to all of Federal's own services and at one time provided xerographic services for a fee. In addition, Federal maintained more than 5,000 overnight delivery counters or drop boxes and was in the process of opening manned kiosk units in suburban areas. Ground and air transport was provided by a fleet of 12,700 ground vehicles (courier vans, line haul trucks, etc.) and 90 aircraft (11 DC–10s, 53 727s, and 26 Cessna 208 Caravans with individual cargo capacities ranging from 148,000 lbs. down to 2,960 lbs.). The Memphis Superhub with a maximum sorting capacity (for a two hour sort) of 570,000 packages was being augmented by smaller regional hubs in Newark, New Jersey and elsewhere. Express delivery volume for the quarter ending February 28, 1986 was 37 million units.

Federal's major services included three overnight delivery options ("Priority One" for packages weighing up to 150 lbs.; "Courier Pak" for documents, reports, machine parts, etc. generally weighing between 8 ozs. and 6 lbs. in envelopes, boxes, and tubes; and "Overnight Letter" for 9″ × 12″ envelopes holding up to thirty pages). In addition, Federal offered "Standard Air" for packages weighing up to 150 lbs. and scheduled for delivery no later than the close of business on the second day, and "ZapMail" which allowed same-day delivery of documents and graphics via a facsimile transmission network. Federal Express also provided direct service to Canada and "Priority One" and "Courier Pak" services with a second day commitment to major European cities via its European hub in Brussels. A breakdown of operating statistics by each major class of service is provided in Exhibit 5.

By the mid 1980s, the $4.5 billion air express, small package industry was in what one analyst described as "the later stages of the growth phase of its life cycle and was characterized by price discounting, heavy promotion, peaking out of unit profits, and the emergence of many new competitors. . . . Federal Express, however, had not lost any significant market share and continued to show unit volume growth greater than its competitors. In addition, the company (which was the industry's lowest cost producer with an operating profit margin at least twice that of its competitors) continued to lower its costs per package at a rate almost equal to the forecast longer term decline in yield" [i.e. revenues per package].[3] As Mr. Smith commented, "I think in our base business there is about to be an enormous shake out. Not everybody is going to survive. There are 10 competitors in this market, and 2 of them represent 90% of all the growth. You know what that means for the other guys." See the chart below and Exhibit 5 for operating and financial statistics.

Operating Systems and Technology

As one observer commented: "an overnight delivery firm must combine the dispatching capabilities of a nationwide taxi service, the sorting facilities of a postal service without the time margin, the logistics of an airline whose passengers can't get

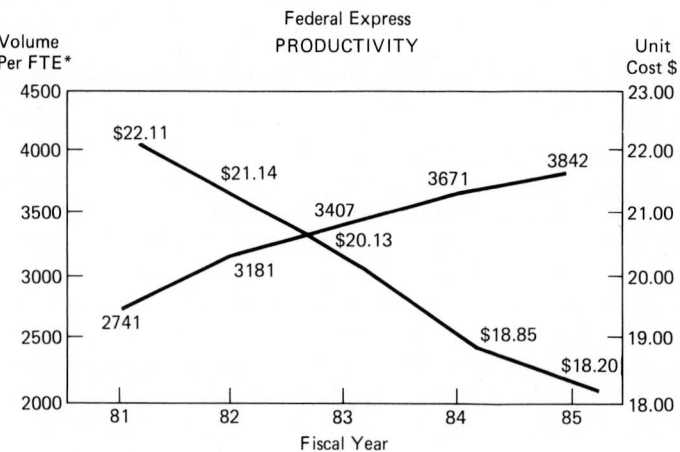

*FTE = Full Time Equivalent Employee

Source: Robinson-Humphrey Company, Inc. Equities Research, *Basic Report-Federal Express Corporation*, Nov. 1, 1985.

themselves on and off the flights and the customer service function of a bank whose customers can demand immediate confirmation of every transaction.''[4] As a consequence, Federal Express had become one of the nation's most highly sophisticated users of electronics and telecommunications technology. As noted by COO James Barksdale, Federal spent between 6% and 7% of its revenues on telecommunications and computing R&D, excluding ZapMail. In the early 1980s Federal had established an Advanced Systems Development group in Colorado Springs to handle the development of its new systems.

Federal's main operating system was called COSMOS for Customer Oriented Service and Management Operating Systems. Information concerning a customer's order was entered into the system at regional customer service centers as the customer called in. Federal's DADS (Digitally Assisted Dispatch System) tied the couriers into local dispatching centers through CRTs in their vans or hand carried lap computers. These allowed couriers to receive, via radio data links, customer pickup information which was sent electronically to their dispatching centers from regional customer service centers. COSMOS was used to track packages at key points in the system and to develop information for control purposes. COSMOS information could be used to respond to customer inquiries (up to 15,000 per day) and provide data for the company's billing system. The information contained in the COSMOS system was also utilized to plan flight operations, monitor activity levels, and manage work flows within the entire Federal network. Federal's data processing center supported one terminal for every two employees and handled a million transactions per hour.

Federal's package and mail sort systems were based on destination zip code information which through 1986 had to be manually entered at the start of the sort process at the Memphis Superhub. This input activated computer controlled conveyor belts and large sweeping arms that, at the right moment, pushed packets off the line and into their destination bins. Federal's new ZODIAC system, due to be introduced in 1987, would allow automated sorting using a camera activated robotic system to read destination zip codes. In addition, Federal operated its own weather analysis, aircraft ground control, and flight simulator facilities. It had equipped its aircraft with the most sophisticated in-flight electronic systems available for commercial aviation. If necessary, each plane could be flown and controlled via onboard computers from take off to touch down at the Memphis Superhub.

Philosophy and Organization

Amidst all this technology Mr. Smith had built what one executive called "A singularly entrepreneurial company." Smith himself was styled, "As close to a true visionary as you can come. He has a tremendous sense of historical perspective, seeing the company in a much bigger and more global way than most senior executives would. Fred sees us playing a key role in the world and in information movement. Any logistical problem or segment for business in those worlds is within our province." The same executive continued:

> Mr. Smith constantly probes the limits of technology and management possibilities by posing "Why can't we" and "What if" questions to the people around him. ZODIAC came about this way. Smith kept saying, "Why can't we do it all electronically? Why not just use bar codes and have a machine to read them?" Once he gets an idea, he's a bulldog; he hangs on until he gets an answer or is convinced it can't be done. But above all, he is concerned about his people, and he generates intense personal loyalties. Some observers have said that if you lined up all Federal Express employees on the bridge across the Mississippi here and Fred said "jump," 99% would leap. He's that kind of person.

In the mid 1980s the Federal Express Manager's Guide instructs every manager to "take care of our people; they, in turn, will deliver the impeccable service demanded by our customers who will reward us with the profitability necessary to secure our future. People-Service-Profit, these three words are the very foundation of Federal Express." Federal's commitment to being a "people-oriented company" goes beyond the lip service paid by many companies. The Senior Vice President and Chief Personnel Officer reports directly to the top. (See Exhibit 6 for a corporate organization chart.) Putting employee considerations first has led Federal to "atomize" stations when they reach 50 vans, rather than to seek greater economies from scale. Its Guaranteed Fair Treatment process means that top executives spend an entire morning most weeks deciding what was "fair" for lower-level employees in what many would consider minor personnel grievances. Every week, the company posts a long list of available positions through its nationwide system. No job can be filled by an outsider unless no one within the company is interested and qualified.

Employee involvement is encouraged by such actions as paying up to $25,000 for productivity improvement suggestions. Candid and extensive communications about every subject are rules at Federal Express, and the philosophy is applied to the financial community as well as employees. Top executives regularly hold brown bag lunches during which they answer employees' questions and listen to suggestions. Every year they hold a company-wide "Family Briefing" to discuss issues of concern to Federal's employees. The atmosphere is informal— everyone calls their CEO "Fred," and top executives make it a point to be visible and accessible. Wages, benefits, and profit-sharing opportunities are outstanding. As the Manager's Guide states, "Our people-first philosophy means Federal Express is dedicated to maintaining an employee relations environment which renders unions unnecessary— not because we are anti-union but because we are totally pro-employee." Considered one of· "The 10 Best Companies in the U.S. to Work For," not a single one of Federal's more than 38,000 employees belongs to a union. Over 75% of its employees are under 35, and the work pace

at its sorting hubs would have made Frederick Taylor beam with pride.

As Jim Barksdale said, "Motivated people move faster. . . . You have to understand our business. Our people philosophy is not out of a spirit of altruism. You have fewer problems and make more money."[5] Federal had invested heavily in training, communications, and management systems to achieve the highest possible service standard, but it also stressed the importance of each individual employee's being committed to that standard. Its Manager's Guide noted harshly, "98% or 99% may be fine for many human endeavors, but our customers expect faultless service — all the time — and there is no acceptable reason in their eyes for our failing to perform in accordance with our commitments."

When asked what the company did internally to foster the spirit of innovation and entrepreneurship which had gotten it to the top of its industry in 1986, Mr. Smith said:

> We try to teach managers that innovation and entrepreneurship at the managerial level is necessary not just to keep everybody interested and to get lots of press. It is essential for the long term success of the organization. I think that is much more important than any particular project or specific thing we might do . . . it's the inculcation of that into the management culture of the company that counts. Another thing that is pretty important is that we let people fail. We give them lots of opportunity to fail and if they do fail, we generally will give them a chance to stay with the company if they want to. We have a fair number of examples of people who have made successful retrograde movements and then gone back up in their careers. We won't kill you if you fail. We won't let you continue in your same position, but we won't fire you. You can't shoot the innovator or you will never develop an entrepreneurial atmosphere inside the company.

"We also just keep pointing out to people that discounted cash flows and rates of return are only as good as the assumptions that are put into them and that qualitative assumptions are often as important as quantitative ones. So we encourage people to advance ideas even if they can't show an immediate payoff and then we make subjective judgments as to whether to adopt them based on our understanding of how the business really works."

THE NEXT GENERATION

As early as 1978/79 Mr. Smith began worrying about the impact the emergence of "electronic mail" might have on the overnight delivery market for documents in which Federal held the dominant position. Said one executive:

> Smith saw electronics as such an important and likely development in the logistics of our business that we should be in the forefront of it. We should lose to ourselves, and not to any competitors. Smith kept saying he wanted the capacity for instantaneous transmission of information in the Federal system, and he saw no reason he couldn't have it. He kept looking for technical people who would say "I can do that." Finally he went outside and hired people who felt that way. He hired Chuck Winston about 1980 from Addressograph Multigraph. Earlier he had bought the heavily computerized insurance division of Cook Industries, a large grain trading company in Memphis that had hit on hard times. This added substantially to the expertise we needed.

Now, Federal could begin more concrete planning for its next generation product, code-named Gemini. Smith hoped Gemini would put Federal Express into the same-day delivery market which he estimated could account for 20–40,000 deliveries per business day in the early 1980s. But its ultimate potentials seemed much larger.

Mr. Smith had seen a facsimile machine designed by AM International (formerly Addres-sograph-Multigraph) for IBM's Satellite Business Systems Division to be used by large companies for overnight intra-company transfers of documents using satellite transmission. The machine helped him crystallize an idea he had been mulling over for some months. This was about the time Federal Express purchased the Cook Industries subsidiary and gained both a future Chief Operating Officer, James Barksdale, and the expertise of some 55 IBM specialists who worked there. Mr. Barksdale joined Federal Express because he was attracted by the challenge of building Federal's existing internal computer systems and people resources into a major new product—first called Gemini, later ZapMail. As Mr. Smith later said,

> We carried more important business correspondence than anybody else in the country . . . so we knew an awful lot about what people were thinking about in terms of their needs for moving high priority documents. In the early part of the 1980s we became very convinced that sometime in the next 10 to 15 years people who had to move documents like that were going to expect to be able to move them from their desk to another instantaneously. You don't have to watch too many episodes of Star Trek and read too many *Business Week* supplements on the office of the future to recognize that technology is going to let you do that.

Developing the Technology

In 1980 Vince Fagan, Federal's Marketing head, was assigned the task of researching the telecommunications industry and its trends. Although Fagan had been a skeptic about "electronic mail," he concluded that from a strategic viewpoint Federal Express had two great strengths to apply in support of the Gemini project. First, its courier network and its COSMOS/DADS systems allowed Federal to offer its customers the instantaneous "connectivity"—the capacity to connect up with virtually anyone anywhere in the country—so critical in telecommunications systems.

Second, the company enjoyed a very advanced expertise in telecommunications, software development, and systems operations.

But Federal had never designed or produced electronic equipment for large volume markets. So, working from specifications developed by Mr. Barksdale and its communications laboratories based at the Colorado Advanced Systems Development group, Federal contracted with Nippon Electric Company (NEC) to develop and produce the ZapMailer—the first computerized "store and forward" facsimile machine which offered a high quality (400 pixel per inch/160,000 pixel per sq. inch) output, high throughput, and complete telephone system compatability.

Mr. Barksdale explained the ZapMailer and its associated systems as follows:

> If you take an image and you digitize that image at a resolution acceptable to the human eye for a business document, you have x black dots and x white dots. For a standard business page, that is 640,000 bits of information. Regular telephone lines allow you to transmit data at a rate of 4,800–9,600 bits per second and special leased circuits permit rates of 56,000 bits per second. Unfortunately, because of expectations about regular photocopiers, the customer wants to scan a page at a rate of about one page every 3 seconds. So the ZapMailer was designed to scan the document at that speed, digitize its image, store it on a magnetic disk drive, and transmit the image through the phone lines as fast as it could—although to date this has been far slower than the rate the ZapMailer could scan and store the information from a page. We then intend to upgrade slower phone lines to our own high speed satellite transmission system.

While the ZapMailer was waiting to transmit, it was to be available for other things—to make other images or to receive incoming images from other ZapMailers. Each machine was to be equipped with multiple ports so it could have this desired flexibility. Finally the ZapMailer was to use plain paper as its output medium, rather than the thermal paper other facsimile machines did. The formidable engineering task to bring this machine into being was given to a small team of highly skilled electronics people headed by Ace McInturff, who had come to Federal Express from AM International. Although the Zap-Mailer development team was in Memphis, the COSMOS group with which it had to coordinate was in Colorado.

THE ZAPMAIL CONCEPT

As the concept for the ZapMailer came into place, Federal Express spent almost $2 million dollars on several market research studies. These studies explained the proposed ZapMail system and its capabilities in detail to various potential customers. The research involved more than 600 users of overnight services and indicated that if such a service existed, demand would be in the tens of thousands of messages per day. 37% of Federal's customers were already using some sort of facsimile transmission equipment, and many of those interviewed indicated they would switch to Gemini. Later when the ZapMail system was publicly announced, the security analysts also responded with enthusiasm. One analyst commented: "Gemini (ZapMail) will quickly set a new standard for fast delivery. Brokerage reports, ad copy, legal briefs, etc. will all be deliverable on a 2 hour basis."[6] Another analyst, for Robinson Humphrey, explained;

> Gemini is a natural extension of Federal's asset base, operational systems, market recognition, and technical expertise. [Although] Gemini startup costs are expected to be $25 to $35 million (including advertising) in fiscal 1984, Gemini leverages Federal's existing assets. The only additional assets required are image transmission machines, packet switching computers and supplementary leased telephone lines.[7]

The company in its meetings with analysts emphasized that Federal was not trying to build a new business with Gemini, but saw it "as a way to launch Federal Express from packages to pages." The range of Gemini services to be offered included: (1) *pickup and delivery* (maximum time elapsed from initial call to delivery would be two hours); (2) *pickup to destination* (Federal would pick up the document and transmit it from a Federal Express office directly to a receiving party who had Federal's image processing equipment on its own premises); (3) *premise to delivery* (customer would originate on its own ZapMailer, send the message to a Federal station, where it would be picked up and delivered by a courier to a customer without its own ZapMailer; and (4) *premise to premise* or *machine to machine* (customer with a ZapMailer would send the message directly to someone else who also had one). See Appendix A for a description of the transmission network and some key issues presented by its technology and operations. Federal Express felt that these services would eventually cannibalize up to 20% of its overnight document volume.

ZapMail Starts Up

As planning for ZapMail progressed, a target date of January 1984 was set for the start of the first phase of service. In the nature of things, McInturff and his small team of electronics specialists had been overwhelmed with the problems of designing the ZapMailer itself and coordinating the initial engineering and production work done at NEC in Japan. Only as January 1984 approached did the operations people—who were busy enough running Federal's rapidly expanding delivery services—get involved in the process. They quickly realized that Federal could not provide sufficient geographical coverage with the 500 ZapMailers NEC was to produce for startup.

In addition, it became clear that Operations couriers could not cover the whole of many cities from Federal's Service Centers or local stations in the prescribed half hour allowed to make pickups or deliveries. The *pickup and delivery mode* concept was $\frac{1}{2}$ hour to pick up, 1 hour to transmit and create remote hard copy, and $\frac{1}{2}$ hour to deliver. Before the official start of service,

NEC had to deliver more than 1,000 machines; and Federal had to establish remote courier sites called "closets" to cover entire cities within half an hour. An experienced management team, made up primarily of Federal Express personnel from its overnight delivery operations, was given the assignment of bringing ZapMail to the market. And the development team went to work on other aspects of the technology.

Service officially started in July 1984, accompanied by an advertising campaign in the Federal Express tradition (see Exhibit 7). In keeping with past practice, the ads emphasized humor and the nature of Federal's service rather than the technology behind it. The financial community responded enthusiastically. Said one analyst, "We believe Federal Express's two hour facsimile service could develop $500 million–$1 billion of revenues five years from now with 35% profit margins, and incremental EPS from this could be $2–$4 per share by 1990. . . . However, (the report warned) the major offering in this market to date, *MCI Mail*, has been notoriously unsuccessful."[8]

ESTIMATED ZAPMAIL PROFITABILITY

Est. Revenue Per Transaction		$40
Costs		
Courier Time	$10	
Postage & Billing	2	
Telecommunications	3	
Management, Supervisory	3	
Subtotal, Incremental Costs		$18
Network: Depr. and Maint.		8
Profit		$14

Source: Rooney Pace, Inc., *Research Report-Federal Express Corporation*, June 18, 1984.

Although Federal had consciously forecast demand on the high side to ensure its ability to meet service commitments, ZapMail volume ran 30 to 60 days behind levels initially projected. Nonetheless, by the 11th week of service, ZapMail's average daily volume was 1,679, which on an annualized basis would give Federal more revenue than MCI's electronic mail service—which had been on the market for more than a year.

The reliability of the ZapMailer machines themselves far exceeded expectations, but there were problems with delays in installing high speed dedicated data lines for some of the ZapMailer machines due to the Bell divestiture. Despite this, service levels (i.e., the percentage of time Federal met its service commitment) quickly went from 70% to more than 90%, and satisfaction levels (as measured by interviews) rose to 95%. An initial breakdown of ZapMail customers by industry indicated that attorneys, ad agencies, real estate firms, and financial service providers were the prime users at this time.

The Second Stage

While the original ZapMailers purchased by Federal were very costly, Federal was able to lower costs rapidly. Costs dropped by a factor of 5 within about two years through increasing volume, falling prices for key technologies, and eliminating some features. Federal was the exclusive marketing agent for the ZapMailer machine for a specified period of time. At first Federal operated only in the pickup and delivery mode. Then, in a second phase rollout, ZapMailers were made available to customers in March 1985. By the middle of September 1985 4,500 machines had been installed, and Federal had firm orders for some 7,000 more. At that point, usage of the ZapMailers by customers who had them in their offices averaged 4.2 pages per ZapMailer day. When machines had been in use for 5 months or more, usage rose to 7.6 pages per day. Although the cost difference between ZapMail and Federal's express document service was minimal for the customer, most ZapMail usage seemed to be in an "emergency" category, and 90% of all volume came from 10% of the customers.

Federal's specified machine-to-machine service standard was originally one hour per 10-page document. But, it soon became clear that although the sender was able to feed the machine at a fast rate and then let the machine deal with the slower rate of transmission, the customer worried about the time it took for the document to arrive at its destination. 25 minutes was about as long as seemed reasonable to users. Conse-

quently, by early 1986 Federal was moving toward a new service standard for 10 pages, of 5 minutes for set-up and 2 minutes to copy and transmit a page. It was meeting this standard about 60% of the time through various adjustments it had made in its telecommunications network. The biggest problems were network hangups. (See Exhibit 8 for details.) Some changes were being planned to deal with the special problems inherent in multi-machine networks within customer companies which had a central location and various branches or local offices.

While the ZapMailers themselves exceeded Federal's reliability and quality expectations, the inconsistent quality of the U.S. telephone system created quality problems which customers blamed on Federal. Satellite quality transmission lines had approximately one bit error for every million bits transmitted, but some local lines in less populated areas had as many as one bit error in every 2,000 bits transmitted.

The tables below give the financial results for the ZapMail project through early 1986.

ZAPMAIL LOSSES AND INVESTMENT

	ZapMail Losses ($ Millions)	Investment in Zap Assets ($ Millions)
FY 1984	$ 24.1	$ 75.0
FY 1985	$125.6	$133.0 (estimate)
FY 1985–Q1	31.3	
FY 1985–Q2	29.6	
FY 1985–Q3	31.6	
FY 1985–Q4	33.1	
FY 1986	$120.2 (estimate)	$200.0 (estimate)
FY 1986–Q1	26.0	
FY 1986–Q2	30.0	
FY 1986–Q3	34.2	
FY 1987	$ 75.0 (estimate)	

Source: Various investment research reports.

ZAPMAIL P&L STRUCTURE

FY 1985 ($ Millions)

Network Expense	$ 23.1
Depreciation and Equipment Leases	12.3
Sales and Service Expense	31.1
Support Operations and Other Exp.	15.7
Total Electronic Products	$ 82.2
Field Operations	$ 18.5
Customer Service and General Support	4.0
Marketing and Advertising	31.9
Total Operating Costs	$136.6
ZapMail Revenues	14.7
Operating Loss	$121.9
Corporation Overhead	3.2
ZapMail Loss	$125.1

Note: Does not include interest expense or tax benefit.

Source: Robinson Humphrey Company, Inc., Equities Research, *Basic Report-Federal Express Corporation*, November 1, 1985.

ZAPMAIL OPERATING DATA

FY 1986 1st Quarter

	ZapMail-Courier	ZapMailer
Volume (thousands)	176	224
Revenue (millions)	$ 6.1	$1.4
Revenue per document	$34.55	$6.42
Pages per document	9.1	4.5

Source: Robinson Humphrey Company, Inc., Equities Research, *Basic Report-Federal Express Corporation*, November 1, 1985.

THE FUTURE

In describing some of the forces shaping the future for Zapmail, Fred Smith noted that the facsimile market itself, telecommunications technologies, and all related costs were changing rapidly. Whereas in the early 1980s only about 10,000 "subminute speed" facsimile machines had been sold each year, in 1985 over 100,000 were sold.

Federal's exclusive marketing agreement with NEC might become a less valuable competitive weapon as other manufacturers developed higher quality machines and as companies marketing facsimile equipment started targeting Federal as a major competitor in that market. Since telecommunications component costs were dropping exponentially, by 1990 Federal hoped to have a very inexpensive ZapMailer available.

Satellite technologies and their related costs were changing also. The G Star3 satellite Federal utilized cost about $3,000 per month in 1986 for each circuit leased. If Federal went ahead with its plan to put up its own satellites in the late 1980s, costs would drop to about $600 per month for each circuit. And advances in satellite architecture or software—particularly demand assigned multiplexing—would make it possible to utilize each circuit's capabilities many times over what had been previously possible. The total cost of Federal's proposed two satellites (plus one ground spare) was estimated at $250 million. Federal had been allocated two satellite "slots" or positions, but had to decide in spring 1986 whether to use them. Earth stations for satellite transmission and reception had cost $25 million five to ten years earlier, but in 1986 they cost as little as $4,500 each and had the ability to transmit at 56,000 bits per second. By 1990 Federal Express expected earth station costs to drop to as low as $1,500.

Federal's use of its telecommunications network was also expanding in leaps and bounds. In addition to using the network for its own operations and for ZapMail, Federal would soon offer its customers the ability to automate their shipping docks by tying them directly into the COSMOS system. The same field service technicians who serviced couriers' radios, DADS computers, (etc.), also serviced customers' ZapMailers and would soon be handling their COSMOS terminals. As Mr. Tom Oliver, Senior V.P., Electronic Products, put the challenge:

> The whole purpose of this thing is to have a network that offers an extremely high speed end-to-end connectivity that is driven over a satellite network, with low

cost but high quality terminals, and low cost satellite earth stations. The output of the machine at the other end of the line must be in a form that is as good as the best xerographic copy you can get today. Perhaps the environment is too difficult to allow one to think through all the things that will be important in advance. Dealing with the unexpected is a part of the process of a large scale innovation like this. Because it is such a complex process— combining leading edge technology and the way the world will be 10 years from now—it is exciting. Things aren't frozen in place. But there is incredible complexity.

But in early 1986, ZapMail's potentials were far from realized, and Federal's management was trying to decide how to best develop ZapMail itself, to relate ZapMail to the rest of Federal's activities. Mr. Smith summarized:

Our feeling is that we are in two super growth businesses. One is the delivery of high priority packages, and the other is the transmission of high priority documents. I think that the forces at work on the high priority packages are as great, if not greater, than they are on the demand for the transmission of documents. Despite our problems so far with ZapMail, I think we as a management group are still very confident about the concept and committed to making sure Federal is a major player in this next crucial development in our industry.

   We have told the stock market that this is an entrepreneurial company, and we've told them what we are trying to do. If people don't like these kinds of uncertainties, they shouldn't own the stock. The company· is very long term oriented, and we've forewarned everyone. We've always said we won't make forecasts. We'll give you all the information and be as candid with you as we can, commensurate with our plans. I feel much more responsible to the employees of the company than I do to most of the outside folks. Most of them are big boys— big investment firms.

   I'm keenly aware of the money that we're socking into our big projects. After all, I'm a big stockholder, too. But I am very confident that if we didn't do these things, come the early 1990s, our base business would have evolved just like any other industry and go down to a marginal rate of return. If our employees and investors want to have their high value added jobs and opportunities, they've got to take some short term hits. That's the price of being an entrepreneurial company.

QUESTIONS

1. What special operations problems does Zap-Mail pose for Federal Express? How should it deal with these?
2. What strategy should Federal Express attempt to utilize in developing ZapMail?
3. How should Federal conceptualize the relationship between ZapMail and its traditional services? Possible future services?
4. What specific actions should Mr. Smith and Mr. Barksdale take in 1986 concerning Zap-Mail? Why?

APPENDIX A

The Zapmail Network

As originally installed, customers' ZapMailers had to be connected into telephone lines leading to one of Federal's 54 "packet switching stations" or "nodes" across the country. Here "packet switching computers" broke the page of data into small packets (of 1,000 bits each) which could be individually identified, transmitted, checked, and reassembled into the original page at its destination. Most often, a message would go from a customer's sending ZapMailer to a "node" over a standard 9600 bit per second (bps) telephone line, be sent over 56,000 bps "trunk line" ground links to the node nearest its destination, then have to go back into a standard 9600 bps telephone line to reach the receiving ZapMailer. Federal started service with a totally ground based network, but soon leased some satellite circuits and by late 1985 had 12 earth stations in place to send and receive messages via satellites between the nodes. Packets could be routed by Federal's computers over ground or satellite circuits independently, so the network could balance itself and adjust for peak loads or failures in the network as necessary.

When Federal's "pick up and delivery" services were used, a courier would take the document(s) to be transmitted to a ZapMailer at the nearest local station, "closet" in a big city, or Service Center—from which it would follow a route similar to the above. If the originating location was also an earth station, its packet switching computer might prepare the packets to be transmitted from a sending "dish" on its grounds or rooftop to a satellite, from which it would be targeted to the right receiving dish at another ground station, and then be sent along ground

links to the local station nearest the intended recipient. Individual ZapMailer machines were too small to contain all the routing information needed to connect directly to receiving machines. Consequently—whether the document was originally scanned in the customer's or Federal's ZapMailer—each ZapMail image went first to a "node." There a packet switching computer broke it into packets, identified each packet as to its recipient and later reassembly needs, found the best route over which to send the packet, and sent it on its way. At the receiving point, a ZapMailer machine would hold the packets for a document until all were in hand and then reassemble and print them with a quality equal to a xerographic copy. (See Diagram.)

By 1986 the network could handle enormous volumes. For example, a large user of packet switched messages might transmit 2 billion packets per month. To maintain the system's in-

1986 ZAPMAIL NETWORK

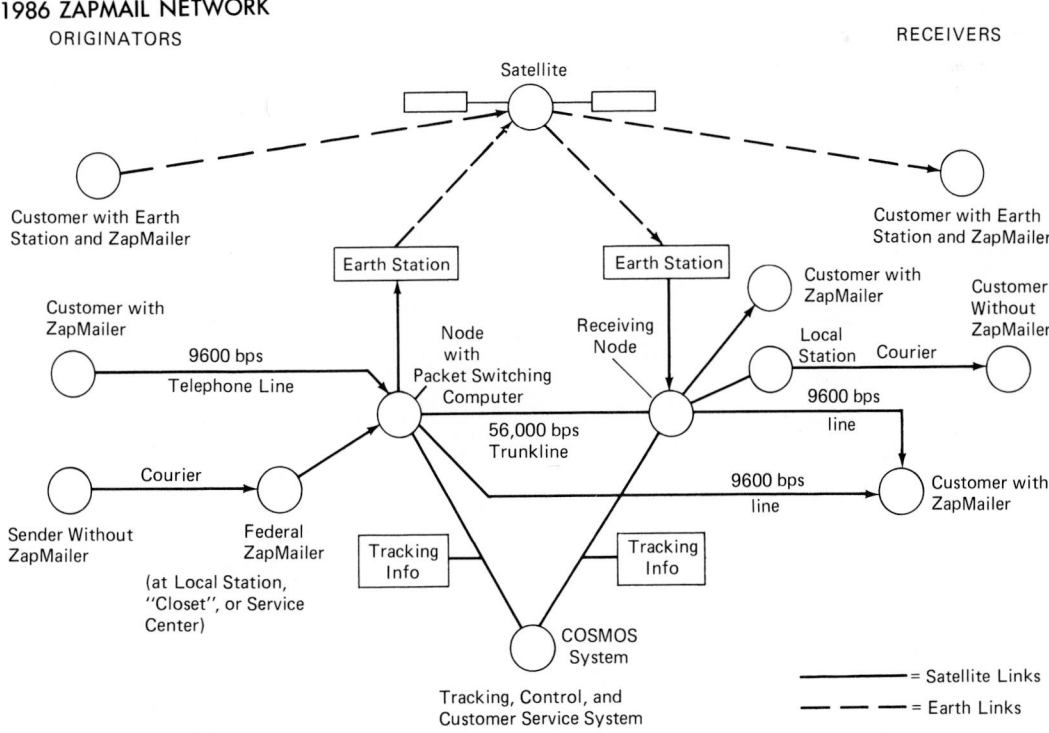

Source: Company interviews.

tegrity despite these volumes, Federal's packet switching computers (designed and built by Tandem) were installed in parallel and with high redundancy. Through clever design the computers could even detect and adjust for a gradual deterioration in their own performance and switch packets elsewhere in the system if necessary. This provided for a "soft fail" as opposed to a "hard fail" capability, crucial to system reliability. As a result, in 1986 Federal's network for ZapMail had not gone "down" since the day it was brought on line (2 years before), despite the fact that it was switching 6 billion packets *a day*.

The combined ground and satellite system was considered a "hybrid system," which Federal hoped to convert into a pure satellite system. Because of new technologies ground station dishes were shrinking in size (and cost) rapidly, with small $4\frac{1}{2}$ foot diameters becoming commercially feasible for high frequency transmission and reception. Even smaller sizes were predicted for the future. Simultaneously, satellite bandwidths (capacities to receive and transmit information per unit of time) were also expanding at exponential rates. Although a ZapMail page con-

tained an enormous amount of information (640,000 bits of electronic data), communication satellites for television could already handle about 100 television channels simultaneously, each with a *6 million bit per second* requirement. And newer satellites were expected to be able to target their transmissions to very small areas (only a few thousand yards in diameter) at the earth's surface, thus increasing their flexibility even further.

Anticipating these changes, Federal's packet switching technique was designed to allow a "Telehub" in Memphis to coordinate the entire ZapMail system when Federal Express moved to its own satellites. The Telehub was: (1) to remember each ZapMailer's unique location, call number, or frequency for transmission and reception; (2) to be directly in touch with all Federal's earth stations; and (3) to pickup, route, and control all Federal packets sent by satellite. Although in 1986 Federal was still leasing satellite space, it hoped that eventually each ZapMailer would be tied to its own earth station or at least have direct access to a 56,000 bps ground line connecting it to an earth station.

EXHIBIT 1   EARLY EQUITY FINANCING HISTORY
FEDERAL EXPRESS CORPORATION

September 1972:	FWS Enterprise Co. (family trust) invests $3.25 million.
February 1973:	(1) FWS invests $2 million. (2) White, Weld & Co. (Brick Meers) agrees to undertake a private placement attempt to raise $20 million. This placement was not successful.
May 1973:	General Dynamics Corp. guarantees $23.7 million loan to FEC from Chase Manhattan Bank (due Sept. 1973). In return, GD received option to acquire 80% of FEC for $16 million. This option was never exercised.
July 1973:	White, Weld and New Court Securities (Charles Lea and Richard Stowe) agree to try another private placement.
October 1973:	Commitments of $23 million secured from venture capitalists. However, Chase Manhattan backed out of loan commitment, thus preventing completion of private placement.
November 1973:	First National Bank of Chicago (Robert Abboud) agreed to replace Chase Manhattan as lead bank in lending pool. First Chicago loans $10 million. Chase lends $10 million, but requires additional $4 million investment from FWS Enterprise Co. This was drawn down as a private placement of $23 million of notes and revolving credit.
March 1974:	(1) 64,000 shares of convertible preferred stock issued to raise $6.4 million. (2) Banks agreed to loan additional $5.1 million in exchange for warrants to purchase 226,190 shares of common stock at an average price of $3.07.

Ownership of FEC

New Court	21%
FWS & FWS Enterp.	19%
Banks	9%
Citicorp Venture Capital	9%
Other	42%

September 1974:	Venture capitalists purchase 1.6 million shares of convertible subordinated notes for $3.9 million.

Ownership of FEC

Lenders/Banks	25%
New Court	16%
Prudential	11%
FWS & FWS Enterp.	9%
Other	39%

Source: Company records.

EXHIBIT 1 (*Continued*)

FEDERAL EXPRESS CORPORATION FINANCIAL HIGHLIGHTS*
(*Fiscal Years 1973–1978*)

	1978	1977	1976	1975	1974	1973
OPERATING RESULTS						
Revenues	$160,301	$ 109,210	$ 75,055	$ 43,489	$ 17,292	$ 6,168
Operating Income (loss)	25,237	13,068	9,845	(4,124)	(8,845)	(2,904)
Pretax Income (loss)	19,544	7,678	3,635	(11,517)	(13,366)	(4,461)
Net Income (loss)	19,498(a)	7,882	3,585	(11,517)	(13,366)	(4,661)
Earnings Per Share	.63(a)	.27	.12			
FINANCIAL POSITION						
Current Assets	$ 30,370	$ 20,349	$ 14,725	$ 9,481	$ 7,981	$ 3,100
Property and Equipment, Net	71,813	53,616	55,297	59,276	59,701	51,487
Total Assets	106,291	75,321	71,229	70,193	70,697	56,771
Current Liabilities	24,315	19,192	12,954	11,818	9,136	44,949
Long Term Debt	30,825	46,229	56,186	59,892	51,605	11,533
Common Stockholders'						
Investment	37,491	(8,488)	(16,561)	(1,517)	(8,694)	289
Ave. Shares Outstanding	11,512	10,292	10,064	1,060	164	100

(a) After tax benefit of loss carryforward.
* $ In thousands except earnings per share.

Source: Company records.

EXHIBIT 2 CHARACTERISTICS OF U.S. INTERCITY EXPRESS PACKAGE/DOCUMENT DELIVERY MARKET

	Urgent (same day)	Priority (next a.m.)		Semipriority (next p.m.)	Nonpriority (next p.m. or 2nd day)
		Under 350 Miles	Over 350 Miles		
Principal transport mode(s)	Van; rail; air	Surface	Air	Air	Air or surface
Size of units (approximate)					
Small packages	NA	15 lbs. (avg)	15 lbs. (avg)	15 lbs. (avg)	15 lbs. (avg)
Envelopes	NA	Under 2 lbs.	Under 2 lbs.	Under 2 lbs.	Under 2 lbs.
Cartons/tubes	NA	Under 6 lbs.	Under 6 lbs.	Under 6 lbs.	Under 6 lbs.
Priority letters	NA	2 to 4 oz.	2 to 4 oz.	2 to 4 oz.	2 to 4 oz.
Illustrative rates (a)					
Small packages	(b)	Surface: $11.35 to $17.40(c) Air: $47.50 to $51.99	Surface: (d) Air: $47.50 to $51.99	Surface: $9.05-to-$19.10(d) Air: Up to $24.00	Surface: $8.25 to $15.39(a) Air: $9.37 to $24.00
Envelopes	(b)	Surface: $13.75 Air: $21.75 to $23.50	Surface: (d) Air: $21.75 to $23.50	Surface: $7.13 to $11.60(e) Air: $9.35 to $12.47	Surface: $2.54 to $13.74(c) Air: $2.70 to $4.00(c)
Cartons/tubes	(b)	Surface: $7.25 to $11.60(c) Air: $34.75 to $36.50	Surface: (d) Air: $34.75 to $36.50	Surface: $7.13 to $10.80(e) Air: $9.35 to $13.44	Surface: $2.54 to $13.74(c) Air: $2.70 to $4.00(c)
Priority letters	(b)	Surface: $8.75 Air: $11.00 to $12.50	Surface: (d) Air: $11.00 to $12.50	Surface: $8.75 Air: $8.75 to $9.35	(e)
Sensitivity	Service	Service	Service	Service, price	Price

NA Not available.
(a) Rates are given for illustrative purposes only. They refer to single units of average weight. They do not reflect volume discounts or any charges that might be added for special services.
(b) It is difficult to categorize same-day delivery rates because they vary with the type of service provided; USPS rates are low ($15.40 for a 14-pound Boston-to-Chicago delivery, for example), but this applies only to airport-to-airport service. Door-to-door pickup and delivery by specialized courier services can easily range up to $100.00, depending on distance.
(c) Depending on distance.
(d) Generally speaking, next-morning deliveries cannot be made by surface to points over 350 miles distant.
(e) Two-ounce letters can move on a 1-to-2 day basis for as little as 37 cents a letter.

Source: U.S. Postal Service, Company Service Guides in Kidder, Peabody & Co., Inc., The Equity Research Department, A. H. Norling, Company Analysis: Federal Express Corp., June 20, 1983.

EXHIBIT 3 ESTIMATED DAILY VOLUME BY CARRIER IN VARIOUS SEGMENTS OF U.S. INTERCITY PARCEL EXPRESS/COURIER EXPRESS PACKAGE/DOCUMENT DELIVERY MARKET (*Units in thousands*)(a)

	Priority Market (E)(b)			Semipriority Market (E)(c)	Nonpriority (E)(d)	Total (E)
	Under 350 Miles(e)	Over 350 Miles(f)	Total			
Small package market						
U.S. Postal Service	(g)	(g)	(g)	30(g)	380	410
United Parcel Service	(g)	(g)	(g)	15	130	145
Purolator	107	10	117	—	(h)	117
Federal Express	6	40	46	22	—	68
Airborne Express	1	12	13	—	—	13
Emery Express	1	12	13	(h)	(h)	13
Burlington Northern	(h)	5	5	—	—	5
United Express	(h)	4	4	—	—	4
Others	1	6	7	—	—	7
Total	116	89	205	67	510	782
Envelope/carton market						
U.S. Postal Service	(g)	(g)	(g)	60(g)	420	480
Federal Express	7	67	74	—	—	74
Purolator	16	7	23	—	(h)	23
Airborne Express	1	10	11	—	—	11
Emery Express	(h)	7	7	—	—	7
United Express	—	1	1	—	—	1
Total	24	92	116	60	420	596
Priority letter market						
U.S. Postal Service	18(i)	48(i)	66(i)	—	—	66
Federal Express	4	36	40	—	—	40
Airborne Express	(g)	3	3	—	—	3
Emery Express (j)	(h)	(h)	(h)	(h)	—	(h)
Purolator (j)	4	1	5	—	—	5
Total	26	88	114	—	—	114

Total market

U.S. Postal Service	18	48	66	90	800	956
Federal Express	17	143	160	22	—	182
Purolator	127	18	145	—	(h)	145
United Parcel Service	—	—	—	15	130	145
Airborne Express	2	25	27	—	—	27
Emery Express	1	19	20	(h)	(h)	20
Burlington Northern	(h)	5	5	—	—	5
United Express	(h)	5	5	—	—	5
Others	1	6	7	—	—	7
Total	166	269	435	127	930	1492

(NA)   *Not available.*
(E)   *Kidder, Peabody & Co. Incorporated estimates.*
(a)   *Average number of shipments per business day (255 days per year).*
(b)   *Next-morning delivery.*
(c)   *Next-afternoon delivery.*
(d)   *Next-afternoon or second-day delivery; all distances; surface or air.*
(e)   *Primarily surface.*
(f)   *Primarily air.*
(g)   *Although some deliveries may be made by noon, service is classified as semipriority because of lack of next morning commitment.*
(h)   *Data either not available or insignificant in volume. Included in other categories.*
(i)   *USPS Express mail letter service is regarded as a priority product despite lack of next morning commitment.*
(j)   *Letter service inaugurated March 1, 1983.*

Source: Kidder, Peabody & Co., Inc., The Equity Research Department, A. H. Norling, *Company Analysis: Federal Express Corp.,* June 20, 1983.

EXHIBIT 4 ESTIMATED CARRIER SHARES IN VARIOUS SEGMENTS OF U.S. INTERCITY EXPRESS PACKAGE/COURIER DELIVERY MARKET, IN TERMS OF REVENUE

Percentage of Small-Package Market

Priority Market Under 350 Miles(a)		Priority Market Over 350 Miles(a)		Semipriority Market(b)		Nonpriority(c)	
Purolator	69.0	Federal	50.4	USPS	42.6	USPS	54.3
Federal	21.7	Emery	14.5	Federal	36.1	UPS	45.7
Airborne	3.1	Airborne	13.7	UPS	21.3	Emery	(d)
Emery	4.5	Purolator	8.4	Emery	(d)	Purolator	(d)
BNAF	(d)	BNAF	4.8				
United	(d)	United	3.0				
All others	1.7	All others	5.2				
Total	100.0	Total	100.0	Total	100.0	Total	100.0
Annual value ($ in millions)	290(E)	Annual value ($ in millions)	830(E)	Annual value ($ in millions)	245(E)	Annual value ($ in millions)	530(E)

Percentage of Envelope/Carton Market

Priority Market Under 350 Miles(a)		Priority Market Over 350 Miles(a)		Semipriority Market(b)		Nonpriority(c)	
Federal	50.7	Federal	76.3	USPS	80.3	USPS	84.4
Purolator	42.3	Airborne	10.1	UPS	19.7	UPS	15.6
Airborne	7.0	Purolator	6.6	Emery	(d)	Emery	(d)
Emery	(d)	Emery	6.2			Purolator	(d)
United	(d)	United	0.8				
Total	100.0	Total	100.0	Total	100.0	Total	100.0
Annual value ($ in millions)	70(E)	Annual value ($ in millions)	455(E)	Annual value ($ in millions)	175(E)	Annual value ($ in millions)	480(E)

Percentage of Priority Letter Market

	%		%
USPS	69.4	USPS	50.0
Federal	17.7	Federal	46.5
Purolator	12.9	Airborne	2.6
Airborne	(d)	Purolator	0.9
Emery		Emery	(d)
Total	100.0	Total	100.0
Annual value ($ in millions)	60(E)	Annual value ($ in millions)	230(E)

Percentage of Total

	%		%
Purolator	56.3	Federal	57.7
Federal	26.0	Airborne	11.0
USPS	10.2	Emery	9.8
Airborne	3.3	USPS	7.5
Emery	3.1	Purolator	6.8
All Others	1.1	BNAF	2.6
		United	1.6
		All Others	3.0
Total	100.0	Total	100.0
Annual value ($ in millions)	420(E)	Annual value ($ in millions)	1510(E)

	%		%
USPS	58.5	USPS	68.6
Federal	20.9	UPS	31.4
UPS	20.6	Emery	(d)
Emery	(d)	Purolator	(d)
Total	100.0	Total	100.0
Annual value ($ in millions)	420(E)	Annual value ($ in millions)	1010(E)

(E) Kidder, Peabody & Co. Incorporated estimates.
(a) Next-morning delivery.
(b) Next-afternoon delivery.
(c) Next-afternoon or second-day delivery.
(d) Data either not available or insignificant in volume. Included in other categories.

Source: Company Service Guides and shareholder reports in Kidder, Peabody & Co., Inc., The Equity Research Department, A. H. Norling, Company Analysis: *Federal Express Corp.,* June 20, 1983.

EXHIBIT 4 (*Continued*)

ESTIMATED CARRIER SHARES IN VARIOUS SEGMENTS OF U.S. INTERCITY EXPRESS PACKAGE/DOCUMENT DELIVERY MARKET, IN TERMS OF UNITS

Priority Market Under 350 Miles(a)		Priority Market Over 350 Miles (a)		Semipriority Market(b)		Nonpriority(c)	
Percentage of Small-Package Market							
Purolator	92.2	Federal	44.9	USPS	44.8	USPS	74.5
Federal	5.2	Airborne	13.5	Federal	32.8	UPS	25.5
Airborne	0.9	Emery	13.5	UPS	22.4	Emery	(d)
Emery	0.9	Purolator	11.2	Emery	(d)	Purolator	(d)
BNAF	(d)	BNAF	5.6				
United	(d)	United	4.5				
All others	0.8	All others	6.8				
Total	100.0	Total	100.0	Total	100.0	Total	100.0
Percentage of Envelope/Carton Market							
Purolator	66.7	Federal	72.8	USPS	100.0	USPS	100.0
Federal	29.1	Airborne	10.9				
Airborne	4.2	Emery	7.6				
Emery	(d)	Purolator	7.6				
United	(d)	United	1.1				
Total	100.0	Total	100.0	Total	100.0	Total	100.0
Percentage of Priority Letter Market							
USPS	69.2	USPS	54.5				
Federal	15.4	Federal	40.9				
Purolator	15.4	Airborne	1.1				
Airborne	(d)	Purolator					
Emery	(d)	Emery	(d)				
Total	100.0	Total	100.0				
Percentage of Total							
Purolator	76.5	Federal	53.2	USPS	70.9	USPS	86.0
USPS	10.8	USPS	17.8	Federal	17.3	UPS	14.0
Federal	10.2	Airborne	9.3	UPS	11.3	Emery	(d)
Airborne	1.2	Emery	7.1	Emery	(d)	Purolator	(d)
Emery	0.6	Purolator	6.7				
BNAF	(d)	BNAF	1.9				
United	(d)	United	1.9				
All others	0.7	All others	2.1				
Total	100.0	Total	100.0	Total	100.0	Total	100.0

Note: *Because of problems in data collection and allocation small differences in estimated market shares may be insignificant or misleading.*
(a) *Next-morning delivery.*
(b) *Next-afternoon delivery.*
(c) *Next-afternoon or second-day delivery.*
(d) *Data either not available or insignificant in volume. Included in other categories.*

Source: Kidder, Peabody & Co., Inc., The Equity Research Department, A. H. Norling, *Company Analysis: Federal Express Corp.*, June 20, 1983.

EXHIBIT 5   FEDERAL EXPRESS CORPORATION PRODUCT LINE STATISTICS

	FY 1981	FY 1982	FY 1983	FY 1984	FY 1985
PACKAGES (000)					
Priority One and Courier Pak	20,117	24,800	29,221	38,080	51,562
Standard Air	2,029	2,207	4,555	11,136	18,932
Overnight Letter	—	5,093	8,830	18,211	33,048
ZapMail	—	—	—	—	554
TOTAL	22,146	32,100	42,606	67,427	104,096
YIELDS					
Priority One and Courier Pak	$26.88	$27.86	$28.25	$28.14	$26.62
Standard Air	21.18	22.15	16.99	13.80	13.45
Overnight Letter	—	10.99	10.76	10.60	10.89
ZapMail	—	—	—	—	27.36
Composite	26.29	24.79	23.42	21.03	19.19
PERCENT OF REVENUES					
Priority One and Courier Pak	91.5%	85.9%	81.9%	74.6%	67.6
Standard Air	7.3	6.1	7.7	10.7	12.5
Overnight Letter	—	7.0	9.4	13.4	17.7
Other	1.2	1.0	1.0	1.3	2.2
TOTAL	100.0%	100.0%	100.0%	100.0%	100.0%
POUNDS/PACKAGE	8.4	6.5	5.8	5.5	5.6
REVENUE/POUND	$3.15	$3.81	$4.02	$3.80	$3.45

Source: Company records.

EXHIBIT 5 (*Continued*)

FEDERAL EXPRESS CORPORATION QUARTERLY PRODUCT LINE STATISTICS

	FY 1985				FY 1986	
	First Quarter	*Second Quarter*	*Third Quarter*	*Fourth Quarter*	*First Quarter*	*Second Quarter*
TOTAL PACKAGES (000)						
Priority One and Courier Pak	11,349	12,319	13,180	14,722	14,488	15,357
Standard Air	4,092	4,487	4,990	5,363	5,317	5,870
Overnight Letter	6,832	7,522	8,513	10,182	10,678	12,075
ZapMail	28	112	168	246	398	629
Total	22,301	24,440	26,851	30,513	30,881	33,931
YIELDS						
Priority One and Courier Pak	$27.08	$26.96	$25.98	$26.56	$26.52	$25.77
Standard Air	13.11	13.97	13.23	13.49	13.27	13.29
Overnight Letter	10.44	10.91	11.02	11.08	11.04	10.97
ZapMail	26.08	30.50	25.19	25.88	18.86	13.15
Composite	19.42	19.65	18.86	19.09	18.79	18.11
PERCENT OF REVENUES						
Priority One and Courier Pak	69.6%	68.5%	66.7%	66.0%	65.2%	63.2%
Standard Air	12.2	12.9	12.9	12.2	12.0	12.5
Overnight Letter	16.2	16.9	18.3	19.0	20.1	21.2
ZapMail	.2	.7	.8	1.1	1.3	1.3
Other	1.8	1.0	1.3	1.7	1.4	1.8
	100.0%	100.0%	100.0%	100.0%	100.0%	100.0%
OPERATING WEEKDAYS	65	63	62	65	64	63
POUNDS/PACKAGE	5.5	5.8	5.5	5.5	5.4	5.4
PAGES/TRANSMISSION	—	—	—	—	6.7	5.6
REVENUE/POUND	$3.52	$3.40	$3.43	$3.47	$3.43	$3.35

Source: Company records.

EXHIBIT 5 (*Continued*)

FEDERAL EXPRESS CORPORATION OPERATING STATISTICS

	FY 1981	FY 1982	FY 1983	FY 1984	FY 1985
TOTAL COSTS ($000)					
Salaries and Employee Benefits	$233,831	$320,345	$419,644	$ 622,675	$ 907,186
Depreciation & Amortization	39,195	56,341	77,421	111,956	172,333
Equipment and Facility Rentals	33,282	44,806	57,751	87,572	146,389
Fuel	57,037	69,282	71,262	93,520	133,473
Maintenance and Repairs	22,286	38,795	44,083	59,482	90,992
Communications	14,382	23,304	27,191	37,370	81,872
Advertising	17,159	25,302	34,558	39,345	60,834
Provision for Uncollectible Accounts	4,290	8,108	11,184	13,927	29,646
Other	68,296	98,166	114,256	205,250	271,213
Total	$489,758	$684,449	$857,350	$1,271,097	$1,893,938
COST PER PACKAGE					
Salaries and Employee Benefits	$10.56	$ 9.98	$ 9.85	$ 9.24	$ 8.71
Depreciation & Amortization	1.77	1.75	1.82	1.66	1.66
Equipment and Facility Rentals	1.50	1.39	1.36	1.30	1.41
Fuel	2.58	2.16	1.67	1.39	1.28
Maintenance and Repairs	1.01	1.21	1.03	.88	.87
Communications	.65	.73	.64	.55	.79
Advertising	.77	.79	.81	.58	.58
Provision for Uncollectible Accounts	.19	.25	.26	.21	.28
Other	3.08	3.06	2.68	3.04	2.61
Total	$22.11	$21.32	$20.12	$18.85	$18.19
COST PER PACKAGE BY DEPARTMENT					
Line Haul Operations	$7.66	$6.79	$5.44	$4.46	$3.62
Package Support Operations	8.58	8.43	8.98	9.26	8.98
Customer Support	1.25	1.59	1.33	1.19	1.10
General Support	1.73	1.33	1.71	1.54	1.38
Advertising & Marketing Support	.99	.98	.95	.70	.66
General and Administrative	1.51	1.75	1.20	1.00	.94
Electronic Products	—	—	.03	.19	.80
Business Service Centers	.21	.21	.24	.31	.44
Provisions for Uncollectible Accounts	.18	.24	.24	.20	.27
	$22.11	$21.32	$20.12	$18.85	$18.19

Source: Company records.

EXHIBIT 5 (*Continued*)

FEDERAL EXPRESS CORPORATION LABOR STATISTICS

FY 1981–FY 1985

	Average Full Time Equivalent Employees					
	FY 1981	FY 1982	FY 1983		FY 1984[1]	FY 1985
Flight Operations	548	574	588	Line Haul	1,458	1,780
Maintenance & Engineering	662	741	791	Field, Sales & Package Support	12,395	19,548
Field	3,864	5,038	6,838	Customer Support	1,962	2,658
Hub & Vehicle Adm.	574	651	792	General and Mktg. Support	1,214	1,756
Package Support	1,084	1,407	1,708			
Marketing, Sales & Advertising	263	308	210	General and Adm.	838	762
General, Administrative and Other	1,085	1,373	1,580	Other	501	562
TOTAL	8,080	10,092	12,507		18,368	27,066

[1] *Classifications reflect a 6/1/83 reorganization.*

Source: Company records.

EXHIBIT 5 (*Continued*)

FEDERAL EXPRESS CORPORATION FINANCIAL HIGHLIGHTS*

(*Fiscal Years 1979–1985*)

	1985	1984	1983	1982	1981	1980	1979
OPERATING RESULTS							
Revenues	$2,030,661	$1,436,305	$1,008,087	$803,915	$589,493	$415,379	$258,482
Operating Income (loss)	136,723	165,208	150,737	119,466	99,735	67,001	40,112
Pretax Income (loss)	83,378	152,260	150,216	131,080	98,044	59,373	33,783
Net Income (loss)	76,077	115,430	88,933	78,385	58,136	37,729	20,383
Earnings Per Share	$1.61	$2.52	$2.03	$1.85	$1.42	$1.00	$ .59
Operating Margin	6.7%	11.5%	15.0%	14.9%	16.9%		
Pretax Margin	4.1%	10.6%	14.9%	16.3%	16.6%		
Excl Aircraft Sales	3.7%	10.4%	14.5%	15.4%	15.3%		
FINANCIAL POSITION							
Current Assets	$ 423,144	$ 328,136	$ 265,171	$ 194,265	$ 166,952	$ 85,454	$ 48,975
Property and Equipment	1,793,016	1,427,281	817,650	603,598	467,194	277,702	123,844
Accumulated Depreciation	(446,993)	(314,642)	(221,258)	(146,026)	(93,944)	395,030	179,823
Property and Equipment, Net	1,346,023	1,112,639	596,392	457,572	373,250		
Total Assets	1,899,506	1,525,805	991,717	730,291	570,112	64,351	43,681
Current Liabilities	316,878	255,910	175,293	114,596	113,846	142,465	45,729
Long Term Debt	607,508	435,158	247,424	223,856	162,705		
Deferred Income Taxes	159,810	112,439	59,094	33,874	13,505		
$9.50 Cumulative Preferred Stock	3,043	4,577	6,112	7,646	9,181		
COMMON STOCKHOLDERS' INVESTMENT							
Common Stock	$ 4,703	$ 4,639	$ 2,197	$ 2,076	$ 1,966		
Add'l. Paid-In Capital	340,753	321,768	222,782	157,489	155,522		
Retained Earnings	466,811	391,314	278,815	190,754	113,387		
Total Common Stockholders' Investment	$ 812,267	$ 717,721	$ 503,794	$ 350,319	$270,875	$ 168,745	$ 74,946

* *$ In thousands except earnings per share.*

Source: Company records.

EXHIBIT 6 FEDERAL EXPRESS CORPORATION 1985 ORGANIZATION

Executive Vice President
Chief Operating Officer
James L. Barksdale

- Ground Operations and Sales
- Telecommunication
- Information Systems
- Central Support Services
- Electronic Products

Senior Vice President
Chief Personnel Officer
James A. Perkins

- Personnel Administration
- Human Resources Analysis
- Human Resource Development
- Corporate Safety, Health, & Fire
- Personnel Information Control Center (PICC)
- Corporate Services

Senior Vice President
Marketing & Customer Service
Carole A. Presley

- Marketing & Customer Service
- Electronic Products
- Express Products
- Customer Service
- Retail Marketing
- Corporate Marketing

Senior Vice President
Chief Financial Officer
David C. Anderson

- Financial Planning
- Revenue & Treasury Operations
- EPD & Telecommunication Finance
- International Audit
- Corporate Finance
- Risk Management
- Controller
- Tax

Senior Vice President
Information Systems
Ron J. Ponder

- Information Systems
- Systems Development
- Operations Research
- Computer Operations (Ground)
- Systems Engineering & Design
- Systems Integration
- Computer Operations

Senior Vice President
Electronic Products
Thomas R. Oliver

- Electronic Products Service
- Electronic Products Sales

Senior Vice President
Group Operations
Fred A. Manske

- Corporate Sales
- International Operations & Customs
- Ground Ops Training & Support Services
- Service Systems

Vice President
Corporate Communications
Daniel N. Copp

- Public Relations
- Employee Communications
- Publishing Services

Senior Vice President
General Counsel
Kenneth R. Masterson

- General Counsel
- Litigation
- Corporate Legal Affairs
- Regulatory Affairs
- Legal
- Corporate Security
- Contracts
- Labor/Employment Law

Senior Vice President
Line Haul Operations
James R. Riedmeyer

- Feeder Aircraft
- Flight Operations & Support
- Maintenance Services
- Corporate Aviation
- Aircraft Acquisition & Sales
- System Control/Scheduling
- Engineering & Quality Assurance

Senior Vice President
Telecommunications
T. Allan McArtor

- stems
- Radio & Voice Systems
- International Telecommunications
- Satellite System Ops & Integration
- Telephone & Radio Systems

Senior Vice President
Central Support Services
Theodore L. Weise

- Sort Systems Development
- Hub Operations
- Properties & Facilities
- BSC/Field Sales & Operations
- Logistics

Source: Company records.

EXHIBIT 7

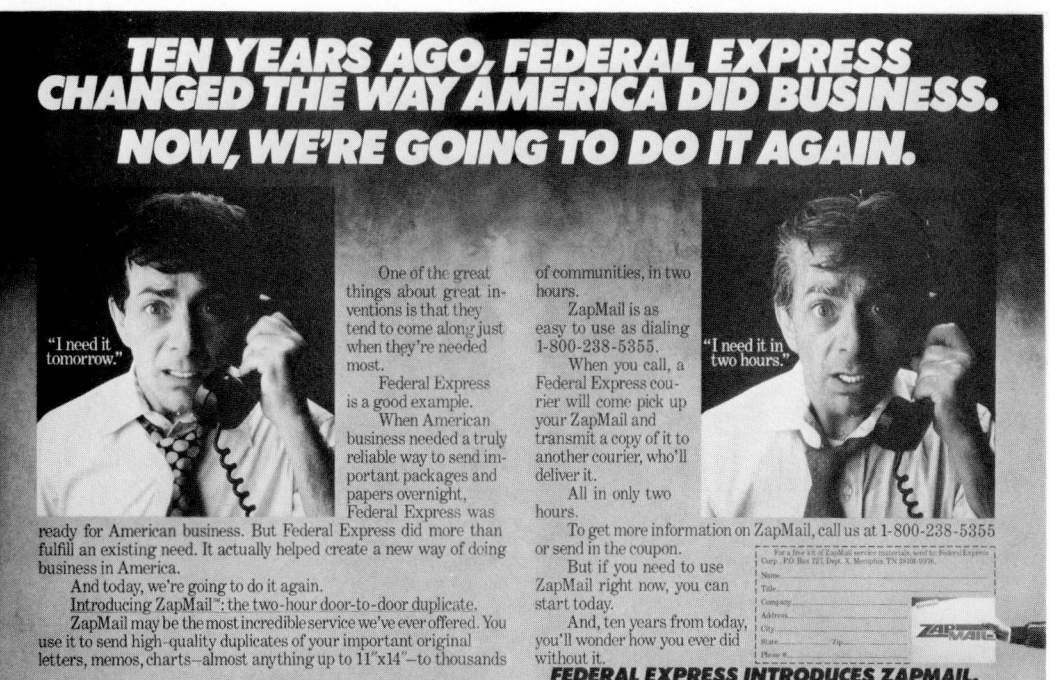

**EXHIBIT 8   NETWORK ANALYSIS REPORT FOR 02/28/86
DOCUMENT FIRST CALL FAILURE TYPES***

Description	Document Count	% of Total Docs With Failures
Destination Busy	1358	53
Machine / Line Down	434	17
Call Drop	746	29
Destination Disk Full	14	1
Total First Call Failures	2552	100%

* Does not include broadcasts

DETAILED ACCOUNT OF ABOVE GROUPS

First Call Type	Document Count	% of Total Docs With Failures
Destination Busy Receiving	1233	48
Dest Busy Transmitting	125	5
All Dest Lines Are Down	40	2
Dial 8 : Connection Failed	363	14
PMX / 2W : No Answer Tone	31	1
Dial 10 : Collision	121	5
No Data for 120 Seconds	199	8
BT: No Call Accepted	23	1
Dial 6 : Request Timeout	21	1
Origin Line Failed	43	2
Dest Line Failed	142	6
Checksum Error On 1st Page	9	0
Other Failures	934	37
No Destination Disk Space	14	1%

Source: Company records.

PILKINGTON BROTHERS P.L.C.

In 1826 William Pilkington—son of a surgeon cum wine and spirit merchant cum apothecary—joined with two well-known glassmakers to form the St. Helen Crown Glass Company and later Pilkington Brothers, Ltd. (1894). The company remained privately held until 1970 when it offered some 5.7 million shares (10%) of its stock to the public. Then in 1973, after being honored as British Businessman of the Year (Sir Harry) Lord Pilkington—the fourth generation direct descendant of the founder to head the company—retired. From 1974–1981 the company's next chairman Sir Alastair Pilkington—scientist, inventor, professional manager, but not a lineal descendant of the ownership group —led the company's transition to a diversified worldwide, technology leading, glass company. In 1981 when Sir Alastair stepped down as CEO, Pilkington's new management team had to design its strategies for a vastly changed world.

EARLY HISTORY

In 1894 Pilkington was the only British producer of both plate and sheet (window) glass, and it had diversified into other flat glasses. Because plate glass processes were so capital intensive, manufacturing was centralized at Pilkington's original St. Helens location, where all needed raw materials— coal, limestone, dolomite, alkali, and iron-free sand—were abundant within reasonable distance.

Case copyright © 1985 by James Brian Quinn. Research assistant—Allie J. Quinn. The generous support of the International Management Institute, Geneva, Switzerland is gratefully acknowledged. The generous cooperation of Pilkington Brothers is gratefully acknowledged.

Flat Glass Technology

The basic processes for making flat glass had remained substantially the same from the 1700s to the early 1900s. *Sheet* glass was drawn into a ribbon through a (slotted) block floating on the surface of the melted glass inside a glass furnace. The ribbon passed vertically upward through asbestos rollers, a lehr which relieved stresses in the glass, and then into a cutting room where the cooled, hardened glass was cut and stacked. The process produced a good inexpensive window glass, but output was limited to relatively thin sheets of glass, subject to inhomogeneities and optical distortion.[1]

These properties were unacceptable for mirrors, automobile windows, and the large windows increasingly used for retail displays and architectural effects. *Plate* glass was required to meet these demands. To make plate, molten glass was rolled into a plate with a waffled surface and then, in a discontinuous process, was ground and polished until both surfaces were smooth and parallel. Grinding required several stages using a series of very large grinding wheels— or discs—with successively finer abrasive surfaces. Polishing was done with buffers and various powdered rouges. Gigantic factories and huge process investments were required. Because of this, plate manufacture slowly became concentrated in the hands of a few producers. And even these could survive only in countries with large markets.

Then in the early 1920s Ford Motor Company began to develop a flow process for continuous rolling of plate. At the same time, and quite independently, Pilkington had developed a continuous grinding process to replace the disk process. Pilkington stepped in to provide the needed technical expertise, joined its development capabilities with Ford, and in 1923— combining continuous rolling with continuous grinding—installed the industry's first continuous plate manufacturing process (at St. Helens). Twelve years later Pilkington pioneered a machine (the "twin") to grind both sides of a plate glass ribbon simultaneously. The machine ranked as one of the world's finest examples of large scale precision engineering and gave Pilkington world technological leadership in the manufacture of quality flat glass.

FLOAT GLASS DEVELOPMENT

Even the twin grinding process for making plate had substantial drawbacks. Tremendous equipment investments (of $30 to $40 million) and sizable markets were required to support a single glass furnace and its associated plate line. Costs of operating and maintaining a grinding and polishing line were very high. Up to 800 people were necessary to keep a line operating continuously. Some 15–20% of the glass ribbon was ground away in the finishing processes. A plant discharged enough abrasives, polishing rouges, and glass to build waste mountains reminding one of the slag heaps of the steel industry. Plants were hundreds of yards long. The noise level of grinders, transfer machinery, and crashing cullet was formidable. And repairs often required costly shut downs or dangerous work in the grinding pits underneath the glass ribbon.

Many dreamed of combining the continuous flow, fire polish, and inexpensiveness of sheet with the distortion-free quality of polished plate. But the secret eluded the industry until the late 1950s when Lionel Alexander Bethune (Alastair) Pilkington[*] developed the float glass process. An intense and impatient but thoroughly gracious man, Alastair had joined the company in 1947 after graduation from Cambridge with a degree in mechanical engineering and service in the Royal Artillery in World War II. He started in the sheet works technical development group, moved into plate works technical development,

---

[*]   Later Sir Alastair Pilkington, F.R.S.

and by 1949 was production manager at the Doncaster works. At Doncaster Sir Alastair started some original experimental work involving interactions of glass and molten metals.

The Invention

Sir Alastair later described how he arrived at the basic idea for float glass:

> One quickly became aware that grinding and polishing was an extremely cumbersome way of making glass free from distortion. [You could see] that the window glass process produced a beautiful surface, which glass naturally has because it is a liquid. What you wanted to do was preserve the natural brilliance of molten glass and form it into a ribbon which was free from distortion. If you could do this you would have done something quite important. . . . A large part of innovation is, in fact, becoming aware of what is really desirable. [Then you] are ready in your mind to germinate the seed of a new idea. . . . You also must want to invent. This is terribly important. I don't know why, but I have always wanted to invent something.
>
> I was able to do some thinking about that time [June 1952] because I was bored. I had been very busy [in production operations at Doncaster and had been] brought back to work under the Technical Director . . . I was actually consciously bored. This gave me time to think about the problem. . . . The idea came to me when I was helping my wife to wash up [dishes], but it had nothing to do with the act of washing up. It was just one of those moments when your mind is able to think and then it was sort of "bang"—like that. Indeed the final solution was very similar to the original idea, though it was an awful long journey from the concept to making salable glass.[2]

Stage I—Experimentation

Alastair quickly drew up some sketches of the new process, which the Engineering Development Group converted into working drawings. The

Board gave verbal approval to the project, and within 3 months a $70,000 pilot plant was built and operational. Fortunately some technical people were available for reassignment just then. Alastair—with a team of several engineers, a foreman, and workman sworn to secrecy— essentially knocked a hole in the side of a remote rolled glass furnace and tried to pour molten glass onto a bed of molten tin. He described this stage as follows:

> We got the cheapest flow of glass we could find in the company. At the earliest possible moment we made a box for the molten tin. The first one leaked like a sieve because we heated the tin by immersed tubes. We had to make gland joints at the end, and I can tell you molten tin goes through any gland joint. It just poured all over the ground. But it showed you could take a ribbon of glass, pass it over tin, at a relatively high temperature, and produce bright parallel surfaces. [The only answer] we wanted out of Stage I was: did the process look promising? Or would we crash up against some basic chemical or physical laws which would prevent the process from operating.
>
> The Pilkington Board decided to give the project the highest possible priority so that either success or failure would be decided as early as possible. My own greatest fear was that float would drag on for years being a near success; interesting enough to justify further work but never quite achieving satisfactory results.[3]

After some six months it appeared that it would be feasible to ''fire finish'' glass by floating it on a bath of molten tin. Once the process could be properly controlled, the bottom surface of the glass should be dead flat because it rested on the flat surface of the liquid tin. Natural forces of gravity and surface tension would tend to make the top surface flat too. And the glass should be of uniform thickness, with both surfaces completely parallel. There appeared to be no insurmountable barriers to achieving such results. But the process was far from producing commercial quality glass.

Still an important choice—that of tin as the support medium—had been made and was never changed. Only gallium, indium, and tin met the strict physical requirements for the process. The support medium had to be liquid from 1100° F to over 1900° F, the range necessary for melting and forming glass. The medium had to be more dense than glass. It needed a low vapor pressure at the 1900° end of the temperature range to avoid excess vaporization and contamination of the glass or the process. Finally the medium must not chemically combine with the glass during processing and had to be available at a reasonable price. Tin was the most attractive alternative on almost all counts. (See Exhibit IA)

Stage II—Pilot Plants

Stage II was to make a ribbon 12 in. wide under controlled atmospheric conditions. The experimental team hoped to learn more about controlling the quality of the glass. A new pilot plant was built in early 1954 to allow long enough runs to analyze and hopefully correct faults in the process. But technological problems were formidable. Upon exposure to the atmosphere the tin oxidized and produced a crystalline scale on the glass' surface. A carefully selected and maintained inert atmosphere slowly began to alleviate this problem. But other technical challenges rose to take its place. Because of the company's expertise in forming a glass ribbon through rollers, the team initially chose this method to flow the molten glass onto the tin surface. (See Exhibit IB) But tin vapors condensed on the water cooled rollers, which then imparted surface imperfections to the tin. Unless the tin was extremely pure it also reacted with the glass. Ultimately the team had to purify the tin well beyond the highest specifications for laboratory quality tin. Finally, the glass source, a rolled glass furnace for making patterned glass, did not provide molten glass of sufficient quality to judge just how well the process was working. Some $46,000 was charged against revenues for the 12″ experimental line, but no commercial quality glass was produced.

Still, progress was encouraging, and the

EXHIBIT I

A. CRITERIA DETERMINING THE CHOICE OF A SUPPORT METAL FOR THE FLOAT BATH

	Melting Point °C	Boiling Point °C	Estimated Density at 1050°C g cm^{-3}	Vapour Pressure at 1027°C Torr
required	< 600	> 1050	>2.5	<0.1
bismuth	271	1680	9.1	27
gallium	30	2420	5.5	7.6×10^{-3}
indium	156	2075	6.5	7.9×10^{-2}
lithium	179	1329	0.5	55
lead	328	1740	9.8	1.9
thallium	303	1460	10.9	16
tin	232	2623	6.5	1.9×10^{-4}

B. THE ROLLER POURING PROCESS

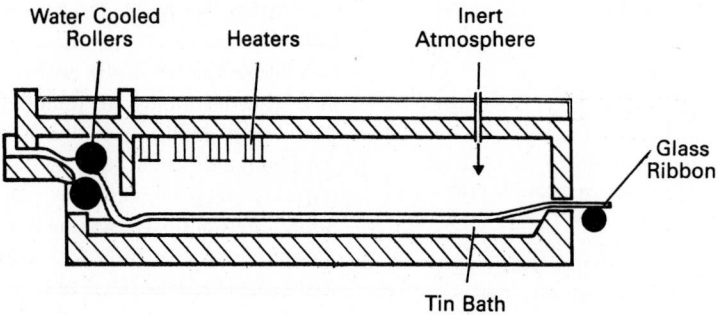

C. DIRECT POURING WITH SPOUT DIPPED INTO THE TIN BATH

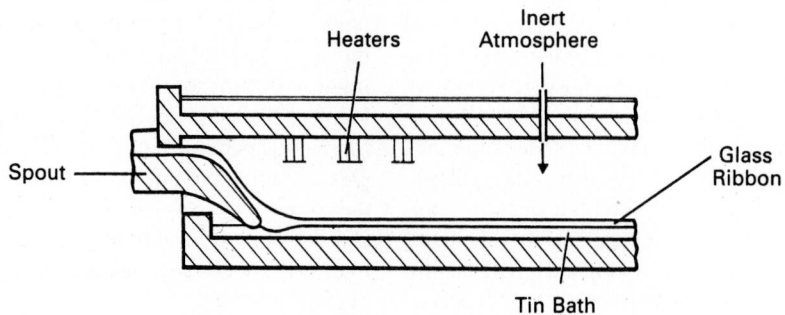

D. DIRECT POURING WITH A FREE FALL FROM THE SPOUT

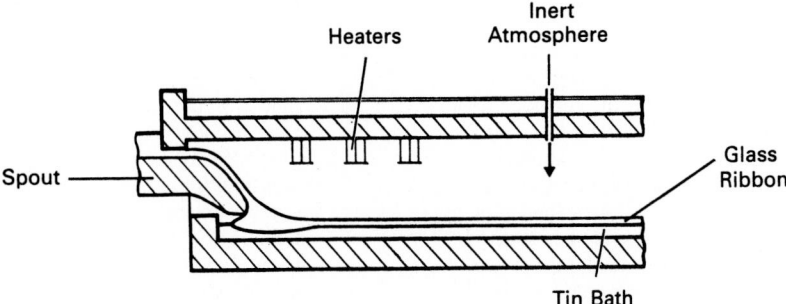

Source: L. A. B. Pilkington, "Review Lecture: The Float Glass Process,"
The Royal Society, 13 February 1969. Reproduced by special permission.

team came upon one substantial bit of good fortune. When the glass was held for one minute at the 1900° F temperature needed to eliminate its surface irregularities, a combination of surface tension and gravity effects caused it to form at an equilibrium thickness of 7 mm (0.275″). By applying a tractive force from the annealing kiln (lehr) the glass might be thinned to 6.5 mm and sold as nominal $\frac{1}{4}$″ glass. As Sir Alastair later said, "This was a fantastic stroke of luck." Some 60% of Pilkington's plate sales at that time were in the $\frac{1}{4}$″ thickness.

In June 1953, upon the retirement of Mr. J. Meikle (former Senior Production Director), Alastair Pilkington at age 33 became head of Pilkington's plate production and a subdirector of the company. He also continued to head the float glass experimental team. Despite the lack of progress in producing commercial quality glass, the board continued its confidence in the project, and in fall 1954 agreed to build a new pilot plant capable of producing a 30″ ribbon of glass. This experimental line was designed and built in the incredibly short span of only 3 months at a cost of $140,000. Molten glass for the line came from the same rolled plate tank as before. The glass made by the process was better than sheet for distortion, but its bubble count would have made it unsalable as plate.

Although roller forming of the glass into a ribbon had appeared more favorable at the outset, the development team continued a parallel project on the alternative possibility of pouring the glass directly onto tin. This approach would avoid roller contamination, but in experimental work tin compounds formed to contaminate the glass. Other major problems of glass flow, ribbon formation, and oxygen and sulfur contamination also persisted. These and high bubble counts from the rolled plate source kept the glass from approaching commercial quality. Nevertheless the technical team's enthusiasm and morale were very high. Sir Alastair said, "It was almost a crusade. Chaps were literally taken off on stretchers from heat exhaustion, yet came back for more. . . . We all thought the major faults in the glass were due to the glass source, not to the float process."

About this time the Board came to a very important decision. Float glass would only be launched on the world if it could replace plate glass. If float merely provided an improved sheet glass, it would occupy a peculiar position between two glasses with well established positions, one of which (sheet) had very low margins. In describing this decision Sir Alastair said:

> The forum for the decision was the Executive Committee of the Board. I was clearly a party to the decision and remember the discussions, but it is difficult to locate an exact moment when the decision was made. It was sometime during the discussions about whether to put down a production scale plant. There were no detailed calculations of such things as the ultimate

capital implications of the process or its effects on our overall capital structure. Nevertheless, over a period of time a consensus crystallized with great clarity. This evolved from a series of formal and informal discussions among the members of the Executive Committee and the Board.

Once arrived at, I don't think anyone had any doubt this was the right decision. On the other hand, as technical director I was very disturbed to be expected to make such a tremendous jump forward in one enormous leap. It would have been easier for the technical group to learn about the process while making a better quality of sheet, then launch ourselves up the ladder from sheet to plate.

Phase III—The 100″ Line

By April 1955 the three small pilot facilities had cost the company some $1.5 million. At this time Alastair Pilkington presented the Board a requisition for another $1.96 million to modify a redundant plate glass furnace and go to a full scale production line capable of producing a 100″ ribbon. On it he hoped to achieve float glass of commercial quality. The cost of operating this full scale line would be £100,000 ($280,000) per month.

At that time 3 mm sheet glass sold for 3.34 pence (3.9¢) per sq ft., while 6 mm plate sold for 21.28 pence (24.9¢) per sq ft. Calculations showed the cost of float, if successful, would be closer to sheet than to plate. Sir Alastair later recalled:

> The early tests had been encouraging on surface quality and parallelism. But we didn't draw up any PERT charts or statements of probability. Nor did we run out detailed financial figures other than project costs. We knew if we could bring it through it would certainly be a world beater. . . . I suppose one should be able to face reality about a major development. But the reality may be difficult to bear in the early stages. You have to live it a bit from year to year.
>
> In the case of float, the figures are intriguing. It eventually took float 12

years to break even on cash flows. At one time it had a negative cash flow of £7 million ($19.6 million). Yet float was a commercial success immediately after we had solved its process problems. That's just how long it takes. If you went to an accountant and said, "I've got a great idea to create a massive negative cash flow for certain, and it may—if it's a great success—break even on its cash flows in 12 years," you wouldn't find many accountants who'd say "that's exactly what I want."

> But you can't look at development only on the basis of cash flows. If your company never does undertake major projects, then your standing is much lower. Some companies make things happen. They take really strategic decisions. Others aren't prepared to take big risks to [possibly] achieve great rewards.

The Board approved the expenditure, and Alastair's team modified an existing plate glass line at the Cowley Hill works. Cowley Hill people were used to change. Many had seen continuous rolling, continuous grinding and polishing, and twin grinding introduced. But the 100″ line immediately encountered enormous troubles. Many of the faults the team had attributed to the poor quality glass source on the 30″ line were actually caused by the float process. The controlled atmosphere then in use still did not maintain a clean glass-tin interface. But the biggest problems occurred in transferring the molten glass onto the tin. Contamination and bubbles plagued the process. Tin oxide condensed on the water cooled surfaces of the rollers metering the glass onto the tin, and this became imprinted on the glass surface. After some time the team made the momentous decision to move to direct pouring, even though this process was still unproved.[4]

In the early experiments with direct pouring the refractory spout dipped into the tin to provide a smooth glass contact. (See Exhibit IC) The chemical erosion on the refractory spout at the glass/tin interface was very rapid and contaminated the process. Glass that had been in touch with the refractory spout and then touched the tin bath created optical distortions called "music lines'' in the glass. Removing the spout from the tin and pouring with a ''free fall'' of glass cured the interface wear problem. (See Exhibit ID) But the ''music lines'' doggedly persisted. Finally the team understood the scientific problems involved and made some key inventions to keep glass which touched the spout from contaminating the whole ribbon.

The team attacked each problem one at a time even though the process might be producing unsalable glass for a half dozen reasons at once. While they slowly solved other contamination problems, bubbles continued to appear in the glass. For 14 months the 100″ line ran 24 hours per day producing useless glass. Every month Alastair had to go to the Board to request another £100,000 ($280,000) to continue. He says of this period, ''One of my records which will never be beaten is that of making more continuously unsalable glass than anyone in the history of the glass industry.''

As technical director, Alastair discussed progress three times daily with the development team. Production executives in the plant were kept well informed. ''We wanted the people who would operate the process to welcome it, not have it landed on them,'' said Sir Alastair. In addition, each morning Alastair would meet with the chief project engineer, Barradell Smith, to lay out strategy for the day:

> I took him away from the noise of crashing cullet so he could have a chance to think. A large pilot plant running 24 hours a day creates great stress and urgency. Glass making goes on around the clock; it never lets up. The heat and crashing glass is unbelievably disconcerting. We would discuss results, what was needed ahead, how the morale of the people was holding up. Every month I would write up a project report for the Board and ask for another £100,000. For 7 years it was an apologia as to why we weren't making salable glass, trying to explain the innumerable faults which occurred. But no single fault persisted. This is why we went ahead. When they would ask, ''Can you make salable glass?'' I would answer: ''I don't

know, but nothing has proved it's impossible.'' I couldn't recommend that we stop, because we had no reason to stop.

> The Board was remarkably understanding throughout all this. But it was very difficult for me at times. As the development leader I had to be an optimist and see problems as challenges to be overcome. I think this is crucial to the success of any development. As a Board member I had to be cold, analytical, and objective. It was hard to fulfill both roles.[5]

Magic and Agony

Finally a magical day came. In mid–1958, the process suddenly made its first salable glass. Unknown to the development team an accident had gone the right way for them. The pouring spout structure was in poor condition. Finally the spout's back broke, and the structure sagged badly in the middle. The bubbles which had plagued the process for 14 long months miraculously disappeared. The result was a beautiful plate of glass, which now came pouring off the line at the rate of roughly a thousand tons a week.

Fortunately, Pilkington could dispose of this vast outpouring. It quickly made arrangements with Triplex—in which Pilkington then owned a substantial interest—to sell the glass as windshields to British automotive companies. Triplex first tested the glass to insure that it met their own strict standards. Then, because the surface characteristics of float plate differed slightly from those of ground plate, Triplex and Pilkington also let a few key procurement and quality control people in the automotive industry know that they were using ''a new process.'' Otherwise the nature of the process was entirely secret. Pilkington actually sold over a million square feet of float glass before it publicly announced the process in January 1959. ''One thing we were good at was security,'' said Sir Alastair. ''People easily fail to understand that the greatest secret about a new process is not how to do it, but that it can be done.'' The process was a complete surprise to the industry. Even after the announcement, there were skeptics in other companies who wouldn't believe what had been accomplished.

Later in 1959 the float line was shut down for long overdue maintenance. The line was then carefully rebuilt with all that had been learned from the experimental line. There was agonizing disappointment when the new line was started up. The bubbles and crystals once again appeared. For several more months the team traced down every possible cause of the problem. Using a model in which silicone oil represented the glass and lead nitrate took the place of tin, they identified certain factors associated with the broken spout as keys to success. With new knowledge of the process the development team both captured the good features of the broken spout and designed a way to feed any contaminated glass to the edges of the ribbon. Although much more work was necessary, the process ultimately became self cleaning and could run continuously for years without a shutdown for repairs.

The company had spent some £7.5 million ($21 million) over 7 years' time. And it had chewed up more than 100,000 tons of glass. But in late 1959 Pilkington could make a glass of quality suitable for the market.

A STRATEGY FOR FLOAT

In October 1958 when the 100″ line was just beginning to produce salable plate, the Board formed a Directors Flat Glass Committee "to consider the broad issues of flat glass policy both in the present and the future." The committee[*] discussed all aspects of flat (rolled, sheet, wired, plate, etc) glass strategy worldwide, but by far the most important issue was float.

The Directors Flat Glass Committee tried to raise all the key issues about float. How should Pilkington use its technological advantage? What would its impact be on existing lines, competition, investments? How would float affect exports, em-

ployment, facilities, depreciation and tax structures, etc.? Not many detailed staff or financial projections were involved at this stage. Instead the Committeee dominantly tried to deal in broad concepts, to identify alternate routes, and think through the potential consequences of each route for some ten years ahead. Sir Alastair later said, "You would be surprised how it sharpens your mind to be told you are only to think about the future." Members consciously tried to bring out different sides of each issue. At one stage, the Committee even hired a second patent attorney, gave him three of the people most knowledgeable about float, and invited him to attack the patent prepared (but not yet submitted) by the company's regular patent counsel. This helped sharpen and strengthen the ultimate application.

An interesting part of the deliberation was a series of process improvements made in the sheet glass division. Goaded by progress on float, sheet glass engineers found a number of ways to improve the quality and lower the cost of their processes. In fact, for a while, the sheet and float glass teams were actively in competition with each other. The Directors Flat Glass Committee had to weigh the potential impact of these and future changes in sheet and plate technology.

They quickly agreed that float would surpass sheet's quality, but that it would not be sufficiently better than existing plate to demand a premium price because of its quality. On the other hand, a float line would ultimately more than halve labor requirements; it would lower energy costs by about 50%; the 15%–25% of glass ground away in earlier processes would be saved, as would be the cost of abrasives and rouges; equipment investment would be about $\frac{1}{3}$ the (then) $40 million cost of a conventional line; production space requirements would drop by over 50%; and process interruption costs would virtually disappear. The Committee could not forecast the exact dimensions of these advantages. But it was clear that the process, if successful, would substantially lower existing plate costs. One director even predicted that float would be cost competitive with sheet by 1967–68, but this opinion was not widely shared.

---

[*] The Committee was composed of all the executive directors associated with float glass: Sir Harry (Lord) Pilkington, Arthur Pilkington, Alastair Pilkington, J.B. Watt, and D.V. Phelps.

DECISION POINT

What should Pilkington's introduction strategy be? Should it license anyone? If so, whom? In what order? If not, how should it exploit float? What should have been the key considerations?

PATENTS AND LICENSING

Pilkington's goal was to see that float occupied its "right place" in the market place, to strengthen Pilkington's own position as a manufacturer, and to consolidate and extend Pilkington's own manufacturing interests throughout the world. Lord Pilkington later described certain key aspects of the resulting strategy as follows:

> We had the great benefit of time to decide upon our strategy. A great deal was said about ethics: that it was not our job to deliberately deny any existing glass competitor the opportunity of living in competition with us. I don't think we were short-sighted or rapacious. . . . There was a great deal of investment worldwide in plate, and people needed to have time to write off this plant or convert over. The alternative was chaotic disruption of a great industry.

Eventually Pilkington decided to license and licensees quickly lined up, until by the mid-1960s substantially all plate manufacturers used the process and royalty income began to roll in to Pilkington. But licensing was not all a bed of roses. Sir Alastair described a chastening experience from this period:

> "In the early sixties I was summoned with great urgency to a licensee's plant where an incredible thing was happening. The whole float bath was bubbling like a saucepan of boiling water. A unit which is normally calmer than a millpond was apparently on the verge of volcanic eruption! [The glass itself resembled swiss cheese.] . . . We were absolutely

> stumped. We had never seen anything like it and had no immediate answer. . . . Eventually we found that a thermal pump had been created in the bath because of the size of the pores in the refractory brick from which the bath was built."[4] Once the refractory brick was replaced the bath quieted down immediately.

After 1962, despite such temporary setbacks, *every new* plate glass facility built in the world used the float process. By 1968 float costs had become competitive with sheet glass in certain thicknesses. But float had much superior quality, and sheet manufacturers began to deluge the company with license applications. Since there were 20 to 30 times as many sheet manufacturers as there were plate producers, this created important policy dilemmas for Pilkington.

By 1974 the float glass process had virtually replaced polished plate glass worldwide. The plate glass industry had invested over £400 million (approximately $1 billion) in the process. 23 manufacturers in 13 countries (including Russia) operated some 51 float plants under Pilkington licenses, and float costs were very sensitive to scale of operations. Plants had to produce at least 2000 tons of glass per week to be economical, and modern plants produced 5000 T/wk. Many of the OPEC countries, possessing sand and fuel, wanted the process. But these and other developing countries did not have large enough national markets to support a plant.

Nevertheless, a long development process was required before float could make a full range of commercial thicknesses. By the mid-1970s float's thickness range was 2.3 mm to 25 mm, with other thicknesses being made experimentally. And float had become cost competitive with sheet in thinner sections. Through 1981 development and experimentation on float continued. Sir Alastair noted:

> Everytime you made a move, you needed to optimize the plant for that particular thickness, width, or speed. It was a long, long learning process. How does the tin flow? How does it return through the bath? How does the constantly changing viscos-

ity of the glass interact with the process? I don't know how many times I heard people over the years say, "We're just about on the limits of speed, or thickness, or something." Most times I said, "Rubbish! What you really mean is you've got to learn more or invent a new technique. You've reached the limits of your experience, not fundamental scientific limits."

Float opened new realms of chemical challenges to Pilkington's glass technologists. For example, they learned to introduce metal ions into the top surface of float glass. During the float process these ions were electrically attracted toward the tin bath. This penetration created a tinted plate extremely valuable in architectural and automotive uses. The technique, called Electrofloat, allowed the process to be switched from clear to tinted glass and back again in a fraction of the time needed for other processes. In 1967, Pilkington's Triplex subsidiary began work on its "Ten-Twenty" laminated glass for automobile windshields. This special plate made up from panels of thin float glass with a plastic interlayer was designed to greatly reduce laceration injuries in accidents. Pilkington hoped it would replace much of the "toughened" glass used for windshields throughout the world. A special high strength, low weight, Ten-Twenty (10/20) was developed for advanced aircraft. This led to Triplex receiving the Queen's Award for Industry in 1974. Sir Alastair later said:

> Through the early 1970s we were concerned dominantly with flat glass. People thought it would take a great deal of resources and effort to pull float through, and we had a prime responsibility to exploit it in the best possible way. We saw ourselves as a glass company. Anything to do with glass would be of interest to us, but we had a special place in safety and flat glass in the British Empire. We were conscious of our vulnerability due to dependence on flat glass. But we had no announced goal of diversification. While it was natural to be involved in other areas, we were drawn into it, rather than taking the lead.

CONSOLIDATION AND DIVERSIFICATION

In 1929 Pilkington and Triplex—the largest British safety glass producer—had formed a joint company, Triplex Northern, to produce laminate glass. In 1955 Pilkington and Triplex Safety Glass agreed that the latter should acquire Pilkington's 51% interest in Triplex (Northern) for which Pilkington received a block of Triplex Safety Glass shares. After 1955 Pilkington purchased Triplex stock at a steady rate as it came on the market, until in February 1965, Triplex became a subsidiary.

By 1967 Triplex controlled 85–90% of the English automotive safety glass market. Its main competitor was British IndesTructo Glass (BIG), which was controlled by four major auto companies. In early 1967 Triplex discussed with BIG's controlling owners the mutual advantages of a merger. Triplex took over BIG, and terminated all production in BIG's works in July 1967. But Pilkington and Triplex agreed with the automobile companies and the British Board of Trade that they would at all times maintain adequate capacity to meet the users' forecast demands.

Optical and Specialty Glasses

Through its acquisition of Chance Brothers (1951) Pilkington had extended its entry into optical glass. In 1957, the optical business of both companies was merged into the Chance-Pilkington Optical Works. In 1966 a further company, Pilkington Perkin-Elmer (later Pilkington P. E., Ltd.) was set up to develop and produce electro-optical systems including specialized glasses for laser optics.

1971 saw the formation of the Chance-Propper Company to manufacture microscope slides, medical, surgical and laboratory equipment. In addition to ophthalmic glasses and lens systems, Chance Brothers had also led the company into television tubes, decorative glassware, and glass tubing for the fluorescent and incandescent light fields. In 1974 Pilkington added the Michael Birch group —lens prescriptions, sunglasses, safety glasses, and a microfilm equipment company. In 1977–78 it acquired Barr and Stroud, a UK maker of periscopes and precision defense products and SOLA, an Australian based maker of plastic opthalmic lenses. But the Monopolies Commission blocked its bid for UK Optical, the dominant British supplier of spectacle frames and glass lenses. In 1980–81, the electro-optical and opthalmic businesses (including Pilkington's successful light sensitive Reactolite spectacles) were thought to each have revenues of over £30 million.

Fiberglass Products

Chance had been making glass fibers near Glasgow since the late 1920s. Pilkington acquired an interest in this activity in 1938 and eventually purchased the company from Chance Brothers. The company, reorganized as Fibreglass Ltd. in 1962–63, extended its operations in the U.K. and abroad. In 1971 Fibreglass Ltd. announced the development of Cem-FIL fiber, the first glass fiber capable of enduring for any period as a reinforcement of portland cement. This product, jointly developed with the British National Research Development Corporation (NRDC), offered the possibility of lightweight, high-strength, concrete construction techniques not hitherto possible. The glass provided the tensile strength concrete lacked, and it avoided the weight, bulk, and chemical-oxidation problems inherent in steel reinforcing. As an alkali resistant fiber, Cem-FIL could replace asbestos in many of its uses. The development was a major breakthrough in glass chemistry, but in 1981 was only slowly working its way into a conservative marketplace.

Many of the above successful diversifications became substantial businesses. But none compared in tonnage with the flat glass field. Here specialized glasses using float were developed for endless new uses: tinted windows, light sensitive panes, special high impact safety glass for vehicles, electro conducting glass for deicing, and specialized glasses for air conditioning uses all entered the market. Perhaps the greatest potential impact lay in architectural glasses. Glass plates could be hung or suspended together to provide a wall with uninterrupted visibility. Pilkington's Armourplate glass was developed for high impact uses like doors or squash court walls. And solar control or insulated glasses provided new opportunities for energy conservation in construction.

The company also had its failures, largely in the field of pressed glass operations. While some were relatively small—pavement lights, glass blocks for buildings, and battery boxes— in 1975 the company had to withdraw from the television tube glass market after considerable investment. A high level of Japanese tube imports and a UK recession were given as the primary causes for withdrawal.

But the biggest disappointment was the late 1970s commercial failure of 10/20 windshield glass. The glass removed about 98% of the risk of lacerations or head injuries from automobile windshield accidents. When hit by an object, the glass broke into fine particles that literally did not cut. Yet the plastic interlayer was strong enough to prevent a body going through the screen, and flexible enough to minimize brain injury. Still Pilkington could not get auto manufacturers to pay the 15% premium price over ordinary safety glass that made it economic to produce 10/20. Safety was not a great selling point, and the oil price increase put a premium on lightness and consequent fuel economy. The manufacturers said they could not pass costs on to consumers. Sir Alastair commented, "The program was one of those clear technical successes, but a commercial failure—most disappointing to all of us."

Geographical Expansion

In 1946 Pilkington had no glass production facilities outside the UK except a partly owned activity in Argentina. The 1950s and 1960s saw a great international expansion abroad. In 1951 Canada and South Africa started sheet production, followed by India (1965), Australia (1963), and New Zealand (1964). Vasa, in Argentina, became a subsidiary. Safety glass plants opened in New Zealand (1953), Australia (1965), Rhodesia

(1961). During the same period the company acquired interests in other companies in Nigeria (1964), Mexico (1965), South Africa (1965), Sweden (1968), Venezuela (1973). And so on. By 1981 Pilkington had nine float plants in other countries (See Exhibit II). It had 25,000 employees and £515 million in sales overseas versus 20,000 people and £377 million in sales in the UK. Approximately $\frac{1}{2}$ of the company's net trading assets were outside the UK. Exhibit II summarizes Pilkington's production operations outside the UK.

MANAGEMENT STYLE CHANGES

Through the 1960s much of St. Helens depended on Pilkington for employment. And the Pilkington family was conscious of this trust. Young Pilkingtons were looked over carefully before they entered the company and, once in, were expected to work doubly hard. Family members developed personal contacts with employees by living in the town and visiting the works regularly. The company had provided pension funds and hospital services, long before these were common in industry. The family also built and endowed theaters and recreation clubs for its employees in St. Helens. There was a personal touch too. For a long while, retired employees had been given vegetable seeds for their gardens and coal to warm them during the harsh midland winters. The company threw an annual employee party complete with dog shows, parachute jumping, and the like which someone described as "the finest blowout north of London."

A strong sense of morality and responsibility pervaded the company. As one director said:

> I think certainly the moral side does weigh with the company. If one runs a business one is to some extent one's brother's keeper. I think the company would still regard itself as being in business for something more than just money making, in the sense that it takes long-term views, and a long-term view is obviously that you have to look after your human capital

as well as your money. It isn't just what you do this year that matters, but what you are working on that is going to bear fruit in ten years' time. It is important that the company is not only profitable, but also has a "heart."[6]

About 1964 – 65 Arthur Pilkington—an elegant, distinguished, formal Sandhurst graduate—who as president under Lord Pilkington had special talents and interests in organizational questions, set out to reorganize and decentralize the company. At the end of 1964 Douglas Phelps, Chairman of the Executive Committee, was to retire, opening the possibility of a number of executive changes. The company was divided into five process-oriented divisions, each with its own board. Each division was to be a profit center and was to run autonomously day-to-day. To ensure coordination, the divisional boards overlapped. With some changes to adapt to new businesses and geographical shifts, this organization continued through the 1970s when the current organization emerged (See Exhibit IV). The top team was determined that managers not sacrifice long term gains for short term profits.

> Divisionalization and the attendant pressure to show results—return on capital, budgets, etc.—make division managers look for the short term. But we are not in business for a quick return. We are concerned that our long-term policies, like education and recreation for the employees, continue. And that needs group control.

Decentralization created many new positions. Some of them were filled by promotions from within. Outside members were beginning to appear on Pilkington's boards. And the company was both making a concerted effort to bring in young managers and supporting four management schools to develop executive talent.

To integrate these new people, corporate management had "one of those weeks in the country to get everyone away from their desks." They catalogued what was and was not working well. Following this Lord Pilkington, at the strong urging of some key executives, wrote down some very broad corporate objectives, and one specific financial objective—a target return on assets. Lord Pilkington was worried that if he wrote too specific goals or policies the organization could not adapt to opportunities. The document was very secret. Detailed time schedules and financial figures were not included. The whole document was some 10 pages long. It was circulated to the board of directors, but not to other line executives. And no specific financial goals were announced to shareholders or set forth for individual divisions. Lord Pilkington was very concerned about the human implications of ''what you do about such goals if you don't reach them.''

Winds of Change

Through the 1960s the company enjoyed smooth relationships with its unions. The unions did not resist the introduction of float glass. Instead workers seemed genuinely proud to be associated with this great innovation. They appreciated that ''St. Helens had become the center of the world's glass industry.'' In a 1968 investigation— despite the company's market dominance—the Monopolies Commission (the British equivalent of the U.S. Federal Trade Commission) had given Pilkington an unprecedented accolade.

> We are satisfied that Pilkington is conscious of its responsibility, as a monopolist, to the public interest. This sense of responsibility may be associated to some extent with the long-established dominance of the Pilkington family within the business. There would, we think, have to be some quite unforeseen change . . . before Pilkington would deliberately set out to exploit its position of strength at the expense of the public interest.[7]

But by 1970, there were some 15,000 people in the St. Helens ''family,'' many of them new members. General Board members were seen less regularly at the works. And lines of communication from shop floor to top management began to seem much longer. Diversification had led to anomalies between workers in different jobs and places.[8] And small incidents sometimes caused irritations. In a small community like St. Helens, one of these suddenly—a man's paycheck had been miscalculated, an error that was quickly corrected—amplified into a strike in early 1970. When management's hurt and shock subsided, the company recovered and learned from the strike. There were more formal procedures for negotiations and wage structures. Industrial relations professionals were brought into the corporate offices of Pilkington. And both union and management groups said relations improved markedly after the confrontation.

Regimes Change

During this difficult period another matter which would vastly affect the company's future had been quietly resolved: Pilkington Brothers became a public company in 1970. As Lord Pilkington said, ''Modern taxation makes it very difficult to either pass on the wealth you have accumulated or keep it in the company. And without a public market for the stock, death duties could place large individual shareholders in an impossible cash bind.''

The basic decision to go public had been made in 1960–61. The crucial dimension was timing. To present the company fairly to the public, the date had to be related to the successful introduction of float. But it could not be too long delayed because key family members were aging. 1970–71 appeared the proper time frame on both counts. These dates were only broadly conceived in the early 1960s. They became more firm as the decade progressed. The 1970 strike caused many second thoughts about the release date. But Lord Pilkington later said, ''We had taken a conscious decision on the issue date, and with good reason. We ultimately decided the reasoning was still sound and that we should go ahead on schedule.''

Lord Pilkington had originally intended to retire on his 65th birthday which occurred in April 1970, right in the middle of the strike. But it was agreed that he should stay in order to pilot the change from private to public status and should retire after the annual meeting in 1973, when Sir Alastair Pilkington became chairman for a period of distinguished leadership, ending in 1981.

Sir Alastair continued the important processes of professionalizing and decentralizing Pilkington's management. Of his era he said:

> I think the company started to take a much wider view of itself in the world—in processes, products, and geography. I think it moved much more consciously to feeling that it could think out the future it wished to have, define what it meant by success in the future, and then lay out a route toward it. The company moved from feeling that it would essentially deal with situations and opportunities as they arose. We felt that we should create the future, rather than react to external circumstances.
>
> I am very strong on people and on success definition. My own feeling is that unless you decide where you want to go, you never arrive there. I don't set goals for other people. That is one of their key jobs—to define their goals, define success. I set goals for myself. I will set goals for the company, but not for other people. I set the company goals in my own mind, and then they come out in discussions. But I don't sort of lay them down. I've never taken a major decision without consulting my colleagues. It would be unimaginable to me, unimaginable. I can't even see any point to it. Firstly, they help me make a better decision in most cases. But secondly, if they know about it and agree with it, they'll back it. Otherwise, they might challenge it, not openly, but subconsciously.

Throughout Alastair wanted to avoid diversifications or any other moves that led to mediocrity. He said, "I'm absolutely obsessional on the subject of excellence. If you are going to work on a worldwide basis, you must have excellence. One of our most important policy statements was that we would only take on things where we intended to match or lead the world's best performers."

The 1981 Situation

By 1981 the company had changed substantially. Like others in the industry, Pilkington's volume had grown throughout the world. Capacity expanded by a factor of 3 times from 1971 to 1981. See Exhibits III and IIIA. Pilkington had large new facilities outside the UK in Germany, Sweden, Australia, and Mexico. While other glass companies conglomerated and diversified into almost anything, in 1980 Pilkington bought Germany's Flachglas for £141M. *The Paper Clip* described how the new partners matched up: Pilkington had sales of £629M for 1980 and 35,000 employees while Flachglas had sales (unconsolidated) of £219M for 1979 from raw glass (approximately 35%) insulating glass (25%), safety glass (25%), plastics and other (approximately 15%) with 7,900 employees. In justifying further acquisitions in the industry, Antony Pilkington, who took over as chairman from Sir Alastair said, "If you are technologically excellent, you can maintain your position in your chosen market. Glass is not as narrow a field as some imagine."

Both parties moved carefully into the merger which had taken 4 years from concept to reality. The specific opportunity ultimately arose when BSN-Gervais-Danone, a French food company, decided to sell a large part of its glass-making operations. Many bizarre twists accompanied the purchase in which Pilkington could not—for competitive reasons— even investigate the facilities it was about to buy. For example, at the last moment due to legal considerations Pilkington had to come up with £28 million extra to up the percentage of stock bought from 55 to 62%. Then Pilkington had to learn to deal with the dual board and labor representation structures of German companies. But benefits accrued within a few months as Flachglas profits helped offset Pilkington's UK trading losses and Pilkington found new work practices to improve the productivity of its domestic plants. One special aspect of the merger was the fit between Pilkington's strength in process research and Flachglas' strength in product development.[9] The acquisition made Pilkington the largest flat glass manufacturer in the world.

This degree of diversification had worked well. License fees and oversees operations—and importantly the Flachglas group's profits—had bolstered Pilkington's lagging fortunes during the sharp downturn in Britain's 1981–82 economy. The company's UK problems were compounded by a flood of glass imports from Europe, and the worldwide recession of those years. Pilkington's share of the UK flat glass market plummeted from 80% to a little over two-thirds in 1981–82.

The European market was rapidly being restructured. Guardian— one of the most efficient operators in the industry—built a new plant in Luxembourg, turning over its stocks 10 times a year and reportedly making 20% on its capital before interest. Asahi Glass of Japan took over BSN's losing Belgium and Dutch plants, and PPG bought its French units. The new structure is outlined in Exhibit IIIA. Much capacity was added while glass industry work forces plummeted— down 4000 for St. Gobain and 3000 for Pilkington in 2 years. Asahi controlled 50% of Japan's glass industry and was as efficient as Guardian. But the marketplace for flat glass in this period was over 50% in building and 20% in automobiles, both industries depressed by high interest rates. Overall demand was growing only 1% per year.

Although only 20% of Pilkington's flat glass output went to other divisions for processing, its optical business had moved steadily "downstream" through acquisitions. This division's growth rate led to its split into two divisions (ophthalmic and electro-optical) of some £30 million sales each in 1981. After 15 years of technical work, fiber optics were slowly working their way into advanced technology applications, and Pilkington's sun-light sensitive Reactolite spectacles were a great market success especially in Japan. Many of these new high technology businesses reported directly to Pilkington's technical board member, Dr. Oliver, who commented that, "Pilkington is still as prepared as ever to commit itself to long cycle developments like 'integrated optics' which may some day provide an optical replacement for silicon chips. Bread on the water for 1995," was the way he described such investments. "Waiting is the name of the game in high technology."[10]

Against this background of great success and increasing pressures, Pilkington's new management team—under tall, elegant, and marketing experienced Antony Pilkington—had to arrive at its new strategies for the 1980s.

QUESTIONS

1. What do you think of the way the float glass development project was managed?
2. What were the critical factors Pilkington should have considered when it arrived at its float strategy? What should it have done about these?
3. What crucial issues face the company at the end of the case? What should Antony Pilkington do?

EXHIBIT II   PILKINGTON FLOAT PLANTS

Location		Date of Start-Up
UNITED KINGDOM	St. Helens	April, 1962
	St. Helens	July, 1963
	St. Helens	September, 1972
	St. Helens	April, 1981
GERMANY	Gladbeck	March, 1974
	Gladbeck	December 1976
	Weiherhammer	October, 1979
SWEDEN	Halmstad	July, 1976
SOUTH AFRICA	Springs	April, 1977
CANADA	Scarborough	February, 1967
(49% owned)		December, 1970
AUSTRALIA	Dandenong	February, 1974
(50% owned)		
ICO	Mexico City,	November, 1981
(35% owned)	Villa de Garcia	

Plants (owned in partnership with others) in Brazil, Venezuela and Taiwan were scheduled to start-up during 1982.

Source: Company records.

EXHIBIT III   CLEAR FLAT GLASS
SALABLE CAPACITY, WORLD, EXCL. COMMUNIST COUNTRIES

('000 Tonnes Per Annum)	1971			1981		
	Float/ Plate	Sheet	Total	Float	Sheet	Total
North America	1,488	714	2,202	3,869	35	3,904
Europe	1,048	1,842	2,890	3,896	588	4,484
Australasia (incl. Japan and India)	280	1,058	1,338	1,301	793	2,094
Africa		68	68	115	37	152
Middle East		114	114		365	365
South America	45	263	308	94	505	599
Total	2,861	4,059	6,920	9,275	2,323	11,598

The 1981 data excludes the three most recently opened float tanks, one in Europe (Luxguard), one in the Middle East (Turkey Sise) and one in Mexico.

Source: Company records supplied during interview.

EXHIBIT IIIA

TWO YEARS OF DRAMATIC CHANGES
IN EUROPE

	Number of Float Lines		Capacity (Tons Per Day)	
Saint-Gobain	11.5	11.5	5,500	6,000
Pilkington	4	8	1,750	4,750
PPG	1	3	500	1,650
Asahi Glass	nil	2	nil	1,300
SIV (Italian Govt.)	1.5	1.5	700	770
Luxguard	nil	1	nil	500
BSN-Gervais-Danone	7	nil	4,150	nil
Total	25	27	12,600	14,970

Source: La Compagnie de Saint-Gobain in *Financial Times*, January 25, 1982.

EXHIBIT IV PILKINGTON BROTHERS P.L.C. 1981

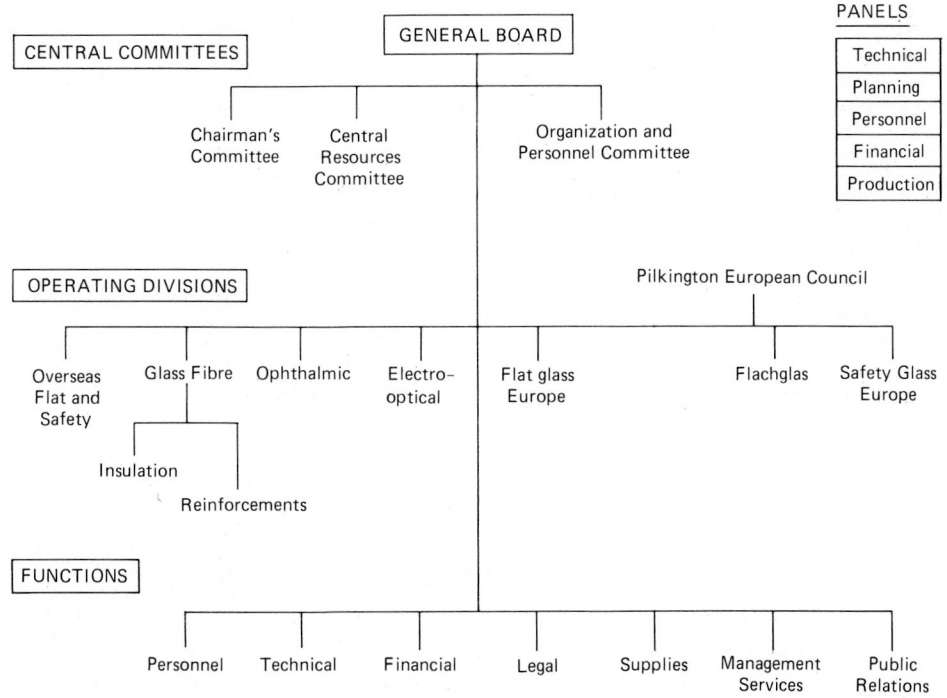

Source: Company records.

EXHIBIT V   PILKINGTON BROTHERS P.L.C.—CHANGES SINCE 1961

	1961	1971	1981
GROUP TURNOVER			
HISTORICAL	£58 MILLION	£123 MILLION	£786 MILLION
IN 1981 MONEY TERMS	£230 MILLION	£300 MILLION	£786 MILLION
		OF WHICH $\frac{2}{3}$ U.K., $\frac{1}{3}$ OVERSEAS	OF WHICH $\frac{1}{3}$ U.K., $\frac{2}{3}$ OVERSEAS
GROUP ASSETS			
HISTORICAL	£36 MILLION	£120 MILLION	£1,200 MILLION
IN 1981 MONEY TERMS	£150 MILLION	£300 MILLION	£1,200 MILLION
		OF WHICH $\frac{3}{4}$ U.K., $\frac{1}{4}$ OVERSEAS	OF WHICH $\frac{1}{2}$ U.K., $\frac{1}{2}$ OVERSEAS

Source: Compiled from company records.

EXHIBIT VI   GROUP FINANCIAL RECORD FOR THE YEARS ENDED 31ST MARCH (£M)

	1978	1979	1980	1981	1982
Sales					
Sales to outside customers	469.5	548.8	629.0	786.8	958.9
Profits					
Trading profit	42.6	50.5	49.0	48.2	26.7
Licensing income	32.8	37.9	37.0	35.3	39.4
Related companies and other income less interest	(3.7)	1.9	5.4	(2.5)	(12.7)
Group profit before taxation	71.7	90.3	91.4	81.0	53.4
Taxation	36.3	42.7	20.5	32.2	49.9
Group profit after taxation	35.4	47.6	70.9	48.8	3.5
Profit attributable to shareholders of Pilkington Brothers P.L.C.	34.1	45.7	68.8	36.3	10.7
Dividends (net of taxation)	7.2	9.8	14.8	17.6	17.6
Profit /(loss) retained in the business	26.9	35.9	54.0	18.7	(6.9)
Assets employed					
Land, buildings, plant and equipment, less depreciation	338.4	385.6	455.3	852.0	924.7
Investments in related and other companies	35.8	49.1	53.1	60.6	70.6
Net current assets (before deducting bank overdrafts)	162.8	193.6	263.4	239.5	262.3
Assets employed	537.0	628.3	771.8	1,152.1	1,257.6
Financed by					
Ordinary share capital	62.2	124.4	155.8	167.7	167.7
Retained profits and reserves	300.9	298.5	426.1	568.4	624.0
	363.1	422.9	581.9	736.1	791.7
Minority interests in subsidiary companies	21.6	20.8	29.5	138.2	120.0
Loan capital and bank overdrafts	129.3	156.2	136.0	235.0	300.5
Deferred taxation and deferred income	23.0	28.4	24.4	42.8	45.4
Total funds invested	537.0	628.3	771.8	1,152.1	1,257.6

EXHIBIT VI   (*Continued*)

	1978	1979	1980	1981	1982
Cash flow					
Operations: funds generated	114.3	143.3	145.1	142.7	181.7
investment in: fixed assets	(38.5)	(44.5)	(69.3)	(127.3)	(94.3)
subsidiary and other companies	(10.8)	(42.4)	4.7)	(151.8)	(47.8)
working capital	(12.5)	(15.3)	(33.2)	(11.7)	(36.7)
taxation and dividends	(29.1)	(46.2)	(50.2)	(53.2)	(53.5)
Share issues, loans and funds brought in by new subsidiaries	(2.3)	11.6	46.3	141.0	19.0
Movement in net liquid funds	21.1	6.5	34.0	(60.3)	(31.6)
Key statistics					
Trading profit before taxation to sales	9.1%	9.2%	7.8%	6.1%	2.8%
Profit attributable to shareholders to average share capital and reserves	9.9%	11.6%	13.7%	5.5%	1.4%
Earnings after taxation per ordinary share (restated to take account of capitalisation share issues)	27.5p	36.7p	52.0p	24.6p	(3.8)p
Dividends per ordinary share (restated to take account of capitalisation share issues)					
Gross, equivalent	8.7p	11.5p	15.0p	15.0p	15.0p
Actual cost to company	5.8p	7.9p	10.5p	10.5p	10.5p
Number of times the dividends are covered by attributable profits	4.7	4.7	4.6	2.1	0.6

Note: *Financial data has not been adjusted for inflation. United Kingdom Retail Price indices for comparison purposes (1978 = 100) are: 1979 = 108.3; 1980 = 125.4; 1981 = 145.9; 1982 = 162.6.*

Source: Pilkington Brothers P.L.C., *Annual Report*, 1982.

EXHIBIT VII   KEY FIGURES FOR PILKINGTON BROTHERS P.L.C.

1981 £M		1982 £M
377.3	Sales: United Kingdom companies	384.3
514.5	Overseas companies	689.5
891.8		1,073.8
105.0	Less sales between Group companies	114.9
786.8		958.9
127.3	Capital expenditure: Land, buildings, plant and equipment	94.3
151.8	Investments in subsidiary and other companies	47.8
279.1		142.1
905.1	Average assets employed excluding investments	1,139.2
40,300	Average number of employees	41,900
6.1%	Trading profit to sales	2.8%
5.3%	Trading profit to average assets employed excluding investments	2.3%
5.5%	Attributable profit after tax to average share capital and reserves	1.4%
24.6p	Earnings after taxation per ordinary share before extraordinary items	(3.8)p
	Dividends per ordinary share	
15.0p	Gross equivalent	15.0p
10.5p	Actual cost to company	10.5p
2.1	Number of times covered by attributable profits after extraordinary items	0.6

Source: Pilkington Brothers P.L.C., *Annual Report*, 1982.

GENERAL MOTORS (B)

The *General Motors Downsizing Decision* case describes the sequence of events leading to the restructuring of the General Motors product line in its automotive marketplace. After an initial strong surge of sales created for General Motors by its new lines, a combination of increasing import sales and a recessionary market made 1980 the worst year for the U.S. auto industry in six decades. General Motors lost over $760 million and many were concerned that the U.S. auto industry would never again be competitive with foreign imports. Various studies showed that Japanese cars enjoyed a $2,000 lower production cost and a better quality performance than most U.S. cars (see Table 1). Average hourly compensation (including fringe benefits) to auto workers in 1981 was $14.71 in the U.S. versus $6.98 in Japan.

MR. SMITH TAKES OVER

Mr. Roger B. Smith took over as Chairman and C.E.O. of G.M. on January 1, 1981. Mr. Smith had joined the company in 1949 as an accounting clerk and—like most of his predecessors as C.E.O.—he had spent most of his career on G.M.'s financial staff. He had a reputation as a dedicated company man who managed by the numbers. Smith went to work immediately, selling the General Motors Building in New York and laying off some 27,000 white collar and 172,000 blue collar workers. These and other cost cutting moves slashed $3 billion from the corporation's budget and (along with other events) produced a profit of $333 million in 1981—for

which Roger Smith received little, if any, praise.

In April 1981, the U.S. had reached a "Voluntary Restraint Agreement" with Japan which was designed to give U.S. auto makers time to adjust their cost structures to the new international competition. While this gave the corporation some breathing room, one analyst pointed out that the four year time frame of the Agreement was not even long enough for the company to design and release a new model. In the meantime, G.M. was haunted by continuing quality problems in the downsized X-car line which was to have been its salvation. In August 1983 the U.S. Department of Justice filed a complaint against G.M. asking for $4 million in civil penalties for its actions concerning a recall of 1.1 million X-cars for brake defect problems. A consent decree settlement of the case led to the establishment of an arbitration process which itself became plagued by delays and other problems. In 1985 G.M. announced it was stopping production of the ill-fated X–cars—a year earlier than planned. In between, General Motors underwent some profound changes. Some of these and the issues they raised are summarized briefly below.

TECHNOLOGY AND CUSTOMER PREFERENCES

Early 1980s competition in automobiles was characterized by two powerful forces: (1) an increasing market fragmentation driven by swiftly changing customer preferences, (2) a much broadened and intensified worldwide cost and technological competition. After years of relatively slow change, technology was forcing rapid adaptations in every aspect of the automotive business. It affected how cars were made, what was put into them, and the way that companies interfaced with their marketplaces.[1]

Case copyright © 1985 by James Brian Quinn. Case prepared by Penny C. Paquette under the supervision of Professor Quinn. Case derived solely from secondary sources.

TABLE 1

ESTIMATED EMPLOYEE COSTS PER VEHICLE

		Ford	Mazda
(1)	Domestic production of cars and trucks (millions)	3.163	0.983
(2)	Total domestic employment		
	Automotive	219,599	24,318
	Nonautomotive	19,876	2,490
(3)	Total domestic employee hours		
	Automotive (millions)	355.75	46.20
(4)	Total employee cost		
	Automotive (millions)	$7794.50	$482.20
(5)	Employee hours per vehicle	112.5	47.0
(6)	Employee cost per vehicle	$2464	$491

Source: *The Competitive Status of the U.S. Auto Industry,* National Academy of Engineering, National Research Council, Washington, DC, 1982.

Flexible Automation

For years auto manufacturing had been based on the traditional economies of scale—high volume, long production runs, rigid product specifications, and hard or fixed automated equipment. Computer based manufacturing allowed production based on short machine set up times, flexible production of a variety of products on the same equipment, and more automated quality control. G.M. launched a large number of initiatives designed to help it adjust to this new reality and to reach its seeming goal of becoming the world's lowest cost producer of high quality cars and trucks through the aggressive application of high technology. The company's expenditures for R&D and new plant and equipment totaled some $32 billion from 1979–1983, contrasted with a similar expenditure of only $15 billion from 1974–1978.[2]

By 1985 G.M. was using some 40,000 computer programmed devices on its plant floors and expected to be using 200,000 of them by 1990. In cooperation with computer, controls, and communications suppliers, G.M. had developed a Manufacturing Automation Protocol (MAP) program which would allow programmable devices to communicate with each other. In 1984, the Advanced Product and Manufacturing Engineering Group which had pushed for investments in artificial intelligence and machine-vision capabilities, proposed a Factory of the Future project. This $52 million project would use 70,000 square feet of an existing plant to test and develop highly flexible, automated production equipment, fully integrated as a system by computer controls. This plant, which would produce steering gears, was expected to perhaps double the cost of producing steering gears—but to speed up the adoption of new automated production technology in G.M. by five years.[3]

In addition, in 1982, G.M. invested $5 million and its own robotics expertise in a 50/50 venture with Fanuc Ltd. of Japan (a leading robot and computer controls manufacturer) to design, manufacture, and sell robotics systems. In 1984 and 1985, G.M. also took minority positions in several supplier companies having expertise in artificial intelligence and specialized areas of machine vision. General Motors saw potential internal applications for some 44,000 machine vision systems in the near future.

The Quality Push

General Motors attacked its problems of quality improvement in a variety of ways. In May 1984 it acquired a 10% interest in Philip Crosby Associ-

TABLE 2

GENERAL MOTORS MINORITY EQUITY INVESTMENT IN TECHNOLOGY FIRMS

Company	Percent Ownership
Teknowledge	13%
Diffracto	30
Robotic Vision Systems	18
View Engineering	15
Applied Intelligent Systems	15
Automatix (option to purchase)	5

Source: "GM Moves Into a New Era," *Business Week*, July 16, 1984 and "High-Tech Drive," *Wall Street Journal*, June 6, 1985.

ates, Inc. (PCA), a recognized quality management training and consulting firm. Together they created the General Motors Quality Institute to train General Motors managers. G.M. implemented statistical process control techniques in many of its plants. This involved rigid control of set ups and processing operations—and checking parts during production rather than randomly after they were finished. In some plants, the previously unthinkable became practice; any worker could halt the production line if defects were spotted. As part of its overall quality improvement program, G.M. demanded higher quality and consistency from its suppliers. Along with other auto makers, General Motors was no longer asking suppliers to "make it to print," but rather "to make it right" and "make it the same every time." In 1984 General Motors revised its General Quality Standard to require suppliers to present a plan for quality improvement, and it established a supplier quality survey program and supplier quality rating system for incoming parts shipments.

As these quality improvement and automation programs came into place, they were expected to affect many aspects of G.M.'s operations and strategy.

ON TO SATURN

General Motors' stated goal of offering a full product line—"a car for every purse and every purpose"—meant that the company had to solve the problem of competing with the Japanese in their stronghold, the subcompact and compact car market. Exhibit 2 outlines the structure of this segment of the U.S. marketplace. It was here also that the Japanese' cost advantages were greatest. In 1981, part way through the development of a new small car (the S-car), which was intended for the 1984 model year, General Motors conducted a detailed cost analysis which concluded that the *same car* could be built by a Japanese auto maker in Japan for *at least* $2,000 less than General Motors could build it. (See Table 3)

G.M.'s detailed figures were developed by its Japanese affiliate, Isuzu.[4] The average robot in a G.M. assembly plant would displace two workers. But in 1983 the Japanese used 6 times as many robots per million vehicles produced as the U.S. industry. Booz Allen & Hamilton also estimated that $800 of the Japanese production cost advantage was due to the simplicity of its product lines. In 1982 the Honda Accord offered 32 option combinations while the Ford Thunderbird offered 69,000.[5] The experts' view on how (on the average) Japanese producers achieved these cost advantages in 1982 is summarized in Table 3. The average cost of shipping a car from Japan to the U.S. in 1982 was about $400, while materials and components supplies cost Japanese producers about $700 less than their U.S. counterparts. American inventory practices were also substantially more costly than the Japanese. (See Table 3A.)

The S-car never went into production. General Motors' X– cars (Citation, Phoenix, Omega, and Skylark) had been introduced in 1979. Its J-cars (Cavalier, 2000, Firenza, Skyhawk, and Cimarron) were added in 1981. G.M.'s share of the small car market rose to 27.9% in 1980 but fell to 23.3% in 1983 despite the introduction of the J-cars and limitations on Japanese imports.[6] Meanwhile G.M. began to plan a totally integrated "Buick City" facility in Flint, Michigan, where steel blanks would enter one end of the line, bodies would be made, vehicles would be assembled, and cars would emerge from the far end.

In the early 1980s, General Motors re-

TABLE 3

FACTORS EXPLAINING THE U.S.–JAPANESE PRODUCTIVITY GAP: RANKINGS AND RELATIVE WEIGHTS FROM EXPERT PANEL

	A		B	C		D	E		Average	
Factor	Rank	Weight[a] (percentage)	Rank	Rank	Weight[a] (percentage)	Rank	Rank	Weight[a] (percentage)	Rank	Weight[a] (percentage)
1. Process yield	1	30	1	1	30	1	1	40	1	30–40
2. Absenteeism	3	20	3	2	30	2	2	25	2.2	20–30
3. Job structure	2	25	2	4	5	5	4	10	3.6	10–25
4. Process automation	6	6	4	3	15	4	3	15	4.0	6–15
5. Quality systems	7	5.5	5	4	10	6	4	10	5.2	5.5–10
6. Product design	4	7	7	4	10	3	7	0	5.0	0–10
7. Work pace	5	6.5	6	7	0	7	7	0	6.4	0–6.5

Panel Members

[a] Fraction of the differential explained by the factor.

Source: The Competitive Status of the U.S. Auto Industry, National Academy of Engineering, National Research Council, Washington, DC, 1982.

TABLE 3A   INVENTORY COMPARISONS — UNITED STATES AND JAPAN

Level/Process	Japan	United States
1. Plant and Process Inventories		
Assembly plant component inventories (equivalent units of production)		
heaters	1 hour	5 days
radiators	2 hours	5 days
brake drums	1.5 hours	3 days
bumpers	1 hour	
Front-wheel-drive transfer case in process parts storage by operation (number of parts)		
mill	7	240
drill	11	200
ream and chamfer	13	196
drill	24	205
mill, washer, test	10	40
assemble	6	96
finish	7	87
Total	79	1064
2. Company Inventories		
Work in process inventories per vehicle		
1979	$80.2	$536.5
1980	$74.2	$584.3
Work in process turns[a]		
1979	40.0	12.1
1980	46.1	13.4

[a] *Defined as cost of goods sold divided by work in process inventories.*

Source: The Competitive Status of the U.S. Auto Industry, National Academy of Engineering, National Research Council, Washington, DC, 1982.

sponded to Japanese competition in several ways. In 1981 G.M. bought 5.3% of Suzuki Motor of Japan for $38 million. And in 1984 G.M. said it would invest another $100 million in a 50/50 joint venture with Korea's Daewoo Group to produce cars for potential import to the U.S. In late 1983 it announced plans to invest some $100 million more in a joint venture with Toyota to build a version of Toyota's popular Corolla to be sold as the Chevrolet Nova. Toyota was the world's lowest cost auto producer, both dominating the Japanese market and reportedly being the only large auto producer to make money there. The deal was approved by the Federal Trade Commission in April 1984, despite protests by Chrysler Corporation. Plans called for production starting in late 1984 at an unused General Motors plant in Fremont (California) of up to 250,000 cars per year for the 12 year duration of the agreement.

The Nova was to fill a gap in G.M.'s product line created by the phasing out of the 10 year old Chevy Chevette. In exchange for wages and fringe benefits close to G.M.'s national new hire rate, the UAW agreed to go along with many of Toyota's labor practices, allowing the use of only 4 classifications of workers—production workers and 3 types of skilled tradesmen. This would allow use of 5 to 10 person production teams within which all workers could rotate jobs regularly and be trained to do everyone else's job. The joint venture would provide jobs for some 12,000 U.S. workers (3,000 at Fremont and 9,000 elsewhere). About 50% of the vehicle's content would be American in origin.

Saturn

In November 1983, General Motors unveiled its most dramatic response to the Japanese challenge—the Saturn Project. Billed as a last ditch effort to build a small car in the U.S. to successfully compete in cost and quality with Japanese small cars, the Saturn line was to begin with basic 2 and 4-door sedans in the $6,000 price range. But it might be expanded later to include liftbacks, station wagons, and possibly mini-vans. Ten percent of General Motors' total R&D budget was devoted to the project.[1] The lessons learned in many of G.M.'s ongoing and planned plant modernizations (e.g. the Flint Assembly Complex, revamped Olds facilities, the Factory of the Future, and the Toyota Joint Venture) were all to be factored into the Saturn project. Although 80% of Saturn's technology was said to be in use somewhere, the rest had to be invented. The program expected to cut the man-hours required to build a small car from 200 to only 40, mainly by pre-assembling such components as doors and front ends and then plugging them together on a production line through "modular assembly."[7]

The Saturn's manufacturing complex was to be located in Spring Hill, Tennessee, less than 50 miles from Nissan's non-union plant in Smyrna. (Nissan had built the plant in response to a U.S. tariff interpretation which moved assembled car bodies and truck cabs from a "components" category (with a 4% tariff) to an "assembly" category (with a 25% tariff.) This would be the most highly integrated and automated car operation in the U.S. Its 6 million square foot complex, containing 150 acres under one roof, would include an assembly plant, stamping plant, engine and transaxle plant, forging operations for the powertrain, some component manufacturing facilities, and Saturn's administrative offices. The complex's projected cost of $3.5 billion (of the Saturn's estimated $5 billion capitalization) made it General Motors most expensive facility. By contrast, a new assembly plant normally cost about $600 million; but Saturn not only included many other operations, it was designed to assemble 500,000 cars per year, nearly double the capacity of a normal assembly plant. Table 4 gives a sense of how manufacturing costs tended to change with volume in conventional plants.

G.M. included the UAW in all of its planning for Saturn. Initially, Saturn would employ about 6,000 workers, some 80% of whom would be protected from lay-offs except in the case of "catastrophic events." Even then a joint committee could reject layoffs in favor of reduced hours or a temporary shutdown. Blue collar workers would be paid *salaries* "equal to 80% of prevailing wages." The remainder of their compensation would be "rewards" tied to productivity targets, quality goals, and Saturn's profits.[8]

As in the Toyota plant, only 4 – 6 job classifications would be used, teaming workers into "work units" of 6–15 people, self managed by an elected UAW "counselor" rather than a company supervisor. Work units would be responsible

TABLE 4

MANUFACTURING-COST CHANGES WITH VOLUME

(*production cost as percent of minimum cost*)

Number of Units	Sub-compact	Compact	Standard
400,000	100.00	100.00	100.00
300,000	104.83	100.98	100.04
200,000	114.68	108.89	101.02
100,000	144.70	133.37	116.50
50,000	204.78	182.31	147.43

Source: J. Hunker, *Structural Change in the U.S. Automobile Industry*, D.C. Heath and Company, Lexington Books, 1983, p. 133—adapted from Eric J. Toder, *Trade Policy and the U.S. Automobile Industry* (New York: Praeger Special Studies, 1978).

for controlling their own variable costs and output quality. If a team came up with a better idea for a process or new piece of equipment, Saturn's finance and purchasing departments "had to respond" and reach a consensus with the team.[9] The contract with UAW also added a grievance system to parallel this consensus-decision making process and tied job security guarantees to seniority. Significantly, to gain final agreement on its Saturn contract, G.M. was forced to cut a mission statement indicating its intention to implement Saturn ideas and methods throughout the company. And UAW's Bieber made it clear that "consideration for granting similar agreements would be limited to high quality, small car plants with high domestic content."[10]

G.M. insisted that Saturn was not just a small car—it was a whole new technology which could eventually be applied to bigger cars as well. Saturn was set up as a separate corporation to negotiate its new labor contracts and to rewrite dealer franchise agreements for its cars. G.M. made the decision to award Saturn franchises separately, rather than simply giving the car to any one of its existing dealer groups, like Chevrolet. Since the Saturn production and distribution system was designed to deliver a car 8 days (instead of 6–8 weeks) after receipt of an order, the relationship between the dealer and General Motors would be much altered.[11] Saturn's designers were given a clean slate and told they could develop all its parts uniquely for the line (if they so desired) without accepting standard corporate components. Saturn's total projected cost was approximately $5 billion.

General Motors domestic competitors lacked the scale and financial resources of General Motors. However, both Chrysler and Ford announced Saturn-like small car projects in 1985. And Chrysler was planning a joint venture with Mitsubishi to build small cars in the U.S. In 1985 Chrysler was already reportedly Detroit's lowest cost producer, in large part because it bought up to 70% of its parts from outside suppliers. G.M. historically bought 10–15% of its standard components outside, while Ford bought 40–50%. See Exhibit 3 for statistics on U.S. passenger car sales and production.

MAJOR DIVERSIFICATIONS

In a market protected from Japanese competition, average auto prices in the U.S. jumped by 50% from 1979 to 1985.[1] U.S. auto producers' profitability exploded, and G.M. built up a huge "war chest" of $8.6 billion in cash. (See Exhibit 4 for detailed financials)

In October 1984 General Motors shocked the U.S. business community by announcing its acquisition of Electronic Data Systems Inc. (EDS) for $2.55 billion financed with a combination of cash and a new class of General Motors' common stock, designated Class E. Holders of EDS stock were given a choice between accepting $44 for each EDS share, or a combination of $35.20 and 0.2 shares of General Motors Class E common, plus a non-transferrable contingent promissory note issued by G.M. Class E's performance was to be linked to the new EDS subsidiary's performance within G.M. EDS, founded in 1962 by H. Ross Perot, was described by General Motors as "a world leader in the design of large scale data processing systems, the operation of cost effective data processing centers and networks, and the integration of large data processing and communications systems." From 1974 to 1984, EDS's revenues had grown from $119 million to $786 million.

BIG THREE NET PROFITS IN MILLIONS

	1980	1981	1982	1983	1984
General Motors	$ (763)	$ 333	963	3,730	4,516
Ford	(1,543)	(1,060)	(658)	1,867	2,907
Chrysler	(1,710)	(476)	(69)	302	1,496

Source: Company annual reports.

EDS FINANCIAL HISTORY ($ million)

	1974	1979	1982	1984
Revenues	$118.7	$274.2	$503.0	$786.1
Net Income	15.3	23.7	75.0	71.1
Earnings Per Share	1.28	1.82	0.86	1.26*
Stock Price Range		$4\frac{5}{8}$–7	$9\frac{1}{2}$–25	$24\frac{1}{4}$–$46\frac{1}{4}$
General Motors EPS	3.27	10.04	3.09	14.22
General Motors Stock Price	$28\frac{7}{8}$–$55\frac{1}{2}$	$49\frac{3}{4}$–$65\frac{7}{8}$	34–$64\frac{1}{2}$	61–$82\frac{3}{4}$

* *Adjusted for 2 for 1 stock splits in 1981 and 1983.*

Source: Compiled from "GM and EDS," *Automotive News*, March 18, 1985 and various other sources.

1984 revenues of EDS were distributed as follows among different client industries as represented by EDS's five groups.

1984 EDS SYSTEMS REVENUE BY GROUP

Industry	Percent
Government	41%
Financial and Industrial	30
Insurance	23
Health Services	4
International	2

Source: Compiled from "GM and EDS," Automotive News, March 18, 1985.

Due to its emphasis on customer satisfaction, EDS had an 85% contract renewal rate and had recently won some extremely large contracts with U.S. military and other governmental agencies. With its business being concentrated mainly in services industries, EDS had little experience in manufacturing-related data processing systems, robotics, or CAD/CAM. Most of its large scale computer integration work had been for the government. Following EDS's acquisition by General Motors, analysts predicted 1985 revenues of $1.8 billion for EDS and $3.6 billion by 1990.[11]

According to G.M. the acquisition of EDS offered "more effective control of health insurance costs, increased data processing capabilities, improved delivery of computer services throughout the corporation, and development of advanced computer systems for manufacturing process-control and order-entry for G.M., its dealers, and suppliers. . . ." A New York Times article said: "Smith had no problem figuring out how EDS could help G.M. What did present a problem was figuring out how to integrate the alien culture into a G.M. monolith without smothering the special qualities that made it successful."[3] Ross Perot had imbued EDS with a strongly individualistic culture. Its motto was "Eagles don't flock, they fly alone." Despite the fact that General Motors, before the merger, was the world's largest corporate user of computers and had some 10,000 data processing employees, one wit said, "EDS merging with G.M. is like a Green Beret

outfit joining forces with the Social Security Administration."[12] Although EDS was set up as a separate, independent subsidiary with Mr. Perot reporting directly to G.M.'s Chairman, many wondered how the potential benefits of a merger could be realized for either party.

Hughes Aircraft

Then in June 1985, in the largest non-oil acquisition in history, G.M. agreed to acquire Hughes Aircraft from its parent, the Hughes Medical Institute, for $2.7 billion in cash plus 50 million shares of G.M. Class H common stock valued at $46 per share. Prior to the acquisition, Hughes stock had been privately held by the Institute and had no established market price. The acquisition created some $4 billion in goodwill, which the SEC insisted be charged against the subsidiary's income rather than against that of G.M. as a whole. The H stock, like its predecessor, Class E stock, was linked to the performance of the newly created G.M. subsidiary which housed it—G.M. Hughes Electronics Corporation. This would include not only Hughes Aircraft, but also Delco Electronics, Delco Systems Operations, and AC Spark Plug's Instrument and Display Systems Group. The combined 1984 sales of these units was estimated to have been $8.7 billion—$5.8 billion for Hughes and the rest for G.M.'s various operations.[13] Credit for engineering G.M.'s acquisition of Hughes went to Roger Smith's protege and heir apparent, F. Alan Smith (E.V.P. Finance) and Courtney Jones (Treasurer).

Hughes Aircraft was the nation's 7th largest defense contractor, deriving about 80% of its sales (versus G.M.'s $1.3 billion) from the Pentagon and enjoying a $12 billion backlog in 1985. Hughes' earnings were $266 million in 1984. Its largest operation, the Ground Systems Group made such things as fire-finder radar sets which pinpointed enemy artillery fire and targeted a response. Other operations included Space and Communications Systems, Electro-Optical and Data Systems, Radar Systems and Missile Systems. The various divisions frequently sold components to one another.[14] Advanced electronics was the fastest growing segment of the U.S. defense budget in 1985.

Hughes had a record of consistently high profitability and unusually low vulnerability to Defense Department program cuts. No single project of its 1,500 major programs accounted for more than 6% of sales, and the 10 largest programs together accounted for less than 40%. Hughes was known for its high concentration of engineering skills—$\frac{1}{3}$ of its 73,000 employees were degreed scientists—and its strengths in systems engineering and artificial intelligence. Hughes had a history of expending large sums of money (some $250 million a year) for R&D, mostly of a high risk nature. It was considered one of the premier high technology companies of the U.S.

G.M.'s spokesman said that Hughes could usefully: (1) contribute its sophisticated technology to a number of advanced G.M. engineering projects including radar based collision-avoidance systems, satellite navigation systems, and advanced composite materials for lightweight vehicle strength; (2) team up with EDS in telecommunications and systems engineering; and (3) be a prime partner in the "Trilby" project to redefine the basic shape and function of post-Saturn cars and trucks "from mechanical products which include a few electrical subsystems to ones with major electromechanical and electronic elements."[15] Skeptics, however, pointed out that Hughes management knew very little about building basic transportation vehicles and that Hughes engineers were accustomed to working on advanced engineering projects like the Stealth Aircraft, the Space Shuttle, Deep Undersea Recovery Vehicles, Strategic Defense Initiative devices, etc.

GMAC Acquisitions

General Motors Acceptance Corporation (GMAC), earning $1 billion per year, was the nation's largest finance company, with over $54 billion in assets and some 300 branches. Its primary function was to arrange financings for pur-

chasers of G.M. cars and trucks. It also had an insurance subsidiary. In 1983, GMAC's profits had been increasing rapidly (46% since 1982) at an essentially non-cyclical pace because of an extensive computerization program and gains in its share of financings.[2] F. Alan Smith (E.V.P. Finance) oversaw GMAC and was given a mandate to seek compatible acquisitions for it. In 1985 GMAC acquired the Colonial Group of 7 mortgage banking and servicing companies (a $7.4 billion portfolio) and the rights to service Norwest Corp.'s $11 billion portfolio of mortgages. These acquisitions provided an expanded customer base and experience in secondary financings.

CAN G.M. DO IT?

While the business press generally responded favorably to General Motors' major moves during the early 1980s, many questioned whether G.M. could manage so much change. The *Wall Street Journal* noted, "No single overriding strategy [seems to] guide all these (technology) programs. Some activities overlap and G.M. is struggling to absorb the lessons learned."[16]

Even in its traditional operations, G.M. had trouble keeping up with demand for some models in 1985, while others languished on its dealers' lots. And the smaller engines G.M. had geared up to build were not well matched to the public's returning desires for greater power. While back in 1979 analysts had predicted that by 1985 as much as 25% of all U.S. passenger cars would be diesel-powered, G.M. had sold only 15,000 diesel cars in 1984. Its diesel engine plant was running at 9% of capacity[17] prior to being shut down in 1985. From 1974 to 1984, G.M. more than doubled the fuel economy of its fleet of cars primarily by expending over $40 billion on new products, plants, and equipment. As a result, it met or exceeded the CAFE Standards from 1979 to 1982. Starting in 1983, however, falling fuel prices changed customer buying habits and G.M. as a full-line manufacturer fell more than 2 m.p.g. below the standards. By 1985, due to the expiration of its accumulated fuel-economy credits, G.M. was at risk for huge fines. The Japanese who, up to this point, had exported mainly fuel efficient subcompacts and compacts, held substantial CAFE credits. By the fall of 1985, G.M. had increased its overall car production capacity by 15% as its new Hamtramck (Detroit) facility and its retooled Flint assembly complex—both geared to making larger cars—came on line. While some analysts predicted falling demand for U.S. made cars in 1986, G.M. expected another boom year. But Japanese capacity had also been rising in recent years. (See Table 5.)

Despite its falling market share, G.M. (which was traditionally the domestic price leader) was planning to increase its base prices on 1986 models by an average of 3% over comparably equipped 1985 models.[18] Mid 1985 earnings at G.M. were 2.3% lower than comparable figures for a year earlier, and the company said it was feeling the impact of costs related to future model programs and its recent acquisition activities. Nevertheless, General Motors was still the largest auto producer on the world scene, dominating not just the U.S., but increasingly the European markets. (See Table 6.)

TABLE 6 CAR PRODUCTION BY MAJOR MANUFACTURER

	1984 (million)
General Motors (U.S.)	6.33
Ford (U.S.)	3.62
Toyota (Japan)	2.49
Nissan (Japan)	2.05
Volkswagen-Audi (W. Ger.)	1.88
Renault (France)	1.55
Peugeot (France)	1.46
Fiat (Italy)	1.39
Chrysler (U.S.)	1.27
Honda (Japan)	1.02
Mazda (Japan)	0.77
Mitsubishi (Japan)	0.59
Daimler-Benz (W. Ger.)	0.48
Austin Rover (U.K.)	0.40

Source: DRI Europe in The Economist, March 2, 1985.

TABLE 5 JAPANESE AUTOMOBILE–PRODUCTION CAPACITY (× 1000 units)

Firm	1979	1980	1981	1982	1983
Toyota	2782	2902	3040	3305	3430
Nissan	2665	2665	2690	2720	2900
Mazda	885	910	960	1070	1250
Honda	770	880	1010	1110	1290
Mitsubishi	1000	1000	1000	1000	1000
Isuzu	320	340	400	520	600
Daihatsu	350	350	350	390	390
Fuji	280	300	320	320	320
Hino	65	66	6	66	66
Nissan diesel	30	35	35	48	50
Grand Total	9147	9363	9871	10,529	11,276

Source: Analysis by the U.S. Department of Transportation based upon published reports and estimates, as cited in U.S. Department of Transportation, The U.S. Automobile Industry, 1980, p. 62.

810

EXHIBIT 1A   OLD ORGANIZATION*

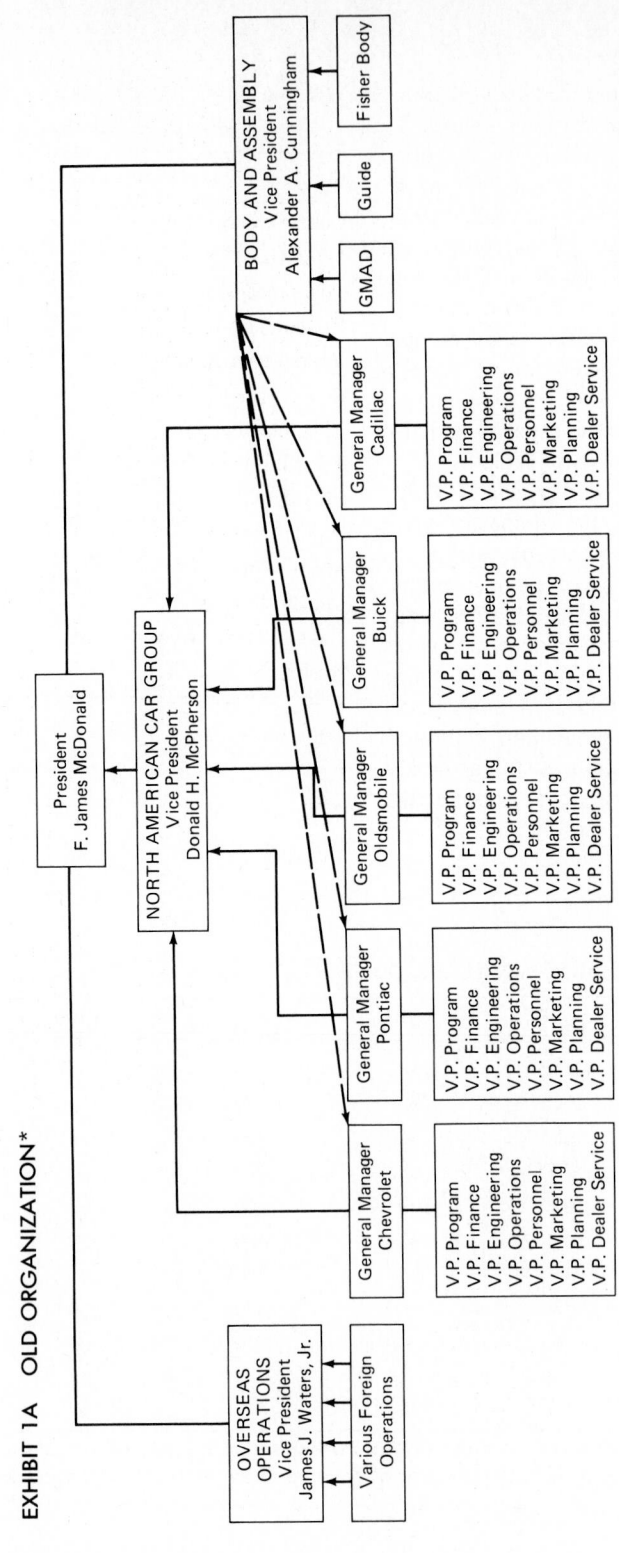

*   *Greatly oversimplified, this diagram depicts former relationships between N.A. car operations and Body and Assembly and the large number of divisional vice presidencies. Solid lines represent direct reporting relationships. Dotted lines represent two-way communications.*

Source: Paine Webber, Inc., Research Report on GM Reorganization, January 20, 1984.

EXHIBIT 1B   NEW ORGANIZATION*

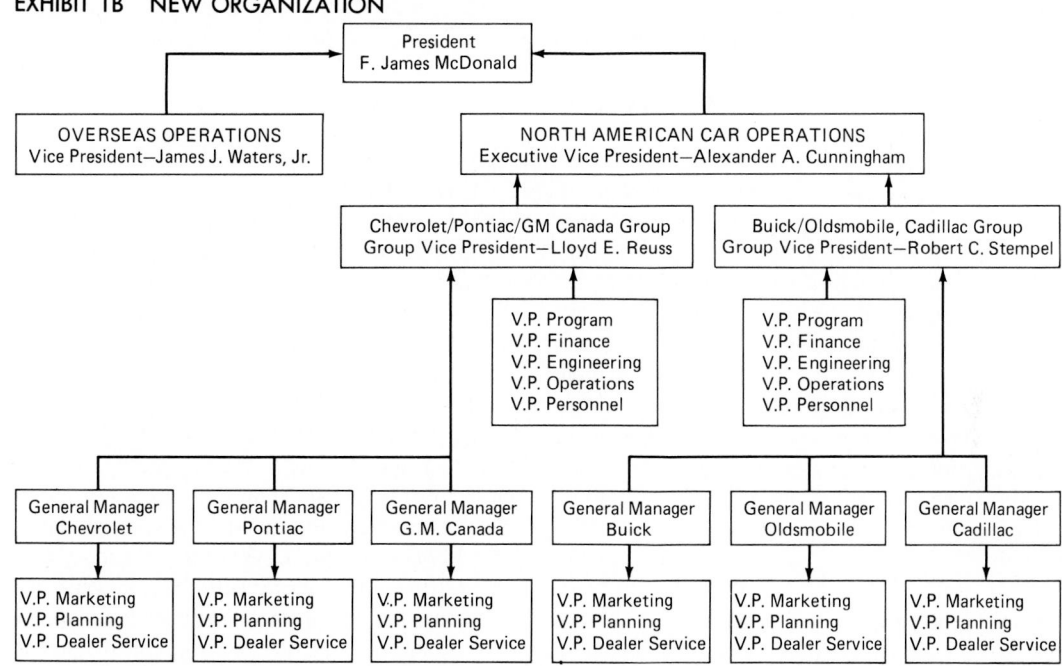

*   *This highly simplified diagram reveals streamlined divisional functions and the eventual absorption of Body and Assembly into N.A. car operations.*

Source: Paine Webber, Inc., *Research Report on GM Reorganization,* January 20, 1984.

Organization Issues

G.M.'s traditional management and decision making style (described in the General Motors Downsizing Decision case) had been one of centralized policy making and decentralized operating management, coupled with a separation of product policy and budgetary powers. G.M.'s key management committee structure consisted of the following: "An Executive Committee which determined which products/programs as well as priorities to recommend to the Finance Committee and the Board; a Finance Committee which established corporate financial goals and determined whether products/programs would receive capital funding before they went to the Board; a Product Policy Committee which made the basic decisions and recommendations regarding development of standard corporate component

hardware and engineering designs; and a Research Policy Committee which (a) developed specific R&D policies and priorities in response to corporate goals established by the Executive Committee and the Board, and (b) reviewed and recommended new basic technologies. The decision making process within committees or groups was described as consensus decision making."[19]

For some years, G.M. had utilized the organization structure described in Exhibit 1A. In January 1984 after an extensive analysis, Mr. Roger Smith announced the organization described in Exhibit 1B. G.M.'s committee structure remained essentially intact. But two separate car groups were established, functioning as fully integrated business units totally responsible for the engineering, manufacturing, and assembly of their products and for the performance and profitability of these products in the marketplace. The

Chevrolet/Pontiac/G.M. of Canada group (CPC) was to target the smaller car, lower cost marketplace, while the Buick/Oldsmobile/Cadillac group (BOC) was to go after larger car and premium price buyers. Robert Stempel and Lloyd Reuss, the two prime contenders to succeed President, F. James MacDonald, were named to head these two major operating groups. Reuss, who had been with Buick, took over CPC while Stempel, who had been with Chevrolet, led BOC. In keeping with these changes, Roger Smith attempted to introduce a "more hands on, more participatory approach for his managers, which included a total reevaluation of their responsibilities, increased authority for middle managers, and a speeded up process for promotions."[20] Mr. Smith's own compensation of $1.5 million in 1984 clearly left some upward mobility for other executives.

In 1985, this complex reorganization was "progressing slowly" and some analysts commented that the white collar workforce appeared to be growing rather than shrinking as predicted. Weaknesses in earnings and sales during the first half of 1985 raised questions about even so seasoned a management as G.M.'s ability to manage all of these transitions simultaneously. While G.M. had made strides in labor relations and productivity within its newer plants, it still faced problems of changing long-standing practices in existing facilities.

Future Issues in the Auto Market

Pressures from imports were growing steadily. Many analysts predicted that sales of imports and cars made in the U.S. by foreign manufacturers would reach 4.5 million or 43% of the U.S. total by 1990.[7] See Exhibit 2 for statistics on U.S. passenger car sales and production. Worldwide sales of automobiles reached 35 million in 1983 and Mr. Smith expected the figure to hit 50 million in the 1990's.[20] Beginning with Honda, the Japanese had started to invest heavily in capacity to build cars in the U.S. By 1990 Japanese production in the U.S. was expected to be at least 1

million cars (300,000 by Honda, 240,000 by Nissan, 250,000 by Toyota, and 240,000 by Mazda). While some observers thought the Japanese were just quota-jumping or attempting to improve trade relations, others believed the Japanese intended to grow into full-fledged U.S. auto companies like G.M.'s Opel or Ford of Europe. Some 30 or so Japanese auto parts suppliers had begun setting up plants in the U.S. While U.S. automakers had record profits during 1984, so had many of the Japanese.

Honda claimed its cost differential between U.S. and Japanese production was only $500 and that it could make money on even its small cars if built in the U.S. Honda had 40% of its sales in the U.S. and derived 65% of its profits there.[21] While some of the Japanese producers had managed to maintain non-union plants, even those that had accepted the UAW enjoyed certain advantages from negotiating entirely new contracts and were not burdened with costs related to older workers and retirees. Despite the end of quotas the Japanese feared a renewal of U.S. protectionism and found it hard and expensive to expand capacity in Japan due to rapidly increasing land costs and scarcity of certain raw materials.

U.S. quotas had forced the Japanese to compete aggressively at home, and they had developed new products with much-improved engines and drivetrains. Given the affluence of the Japanese market, they had progressed quickly down the experience curve for designing and producing intermediate sized cars. Data Resources, Inc. estimated that Toyota and Nissan made $5,800 on each mid-sized car versus $933 for each small car. And Toyota's planned new U.S. factory would build 200,000 intermediate sized cars in 1988. *Business Week* commented: "[As] Japanese car makers face growing pressures to end their dependence on the increasingly cutthroat market for small cars . . . the real competition will be in the market for mid-sized cars."[22] While in the past the Japanese had concentrated on being cost leaders, many felt they were now moving ahead in the development and refining of auto technology. In the future they would rely ever more heavily on new technology they had developed themselves in response to very carefully estimated demands.

QUESTIONS

1. What specific organizational and strategic issues do these major new ventures pose for G.M.?

2. What are the most important external trends it should deal with? How should G.M. as a corporation position itself relative to competitors?

3. What important steps should management take to implement its strategy in the near future?

EXHIBIT 2 U.S. IMPORT SALES BY YEARS, 1984–1973

(Figures Include Dealer Sales and Tourist Deliveries, Cars and Trucks)

Make	1984	1983	1982	1981	1980	1979	1978	1977	1976	1975	1974	1973
Alfa Romeo	3,702	3,002	2,193	2,294	3,007	4,011	6,137	5,505	5,327	5,175	—	—
BMW	70,898	59,243	52,392	41,761	37,017	34,520	31,439	28,776	26,509	19,419	14,693	13,629
Chrysler Total	**143,016**	**137,525**	**142,233**	**144,842**	**189,961**	**185,183**	**106,731**	**121,262**	**78,972**	**60,356**	**42,925**	**40,342**
Dodge Challenger	505	13,171	14,128	12,690	12,617	14,166	17,825	1,832	—	—	—	—
Dodge Colt	36,560	39,158	37,902	42,796	49,798	62,705	45,729	70,679	48,542	60,356	42,925	35,523
Dodge Conquest	3,220	853	—	—	—	—	—	—	—	—	—	—
Dodge Vista	7,805	2,311	—	—	—	—	—	—	—	—	—	—
Plymouth Arrow	—	—	—	—	6,634	21,829	26,825	47,345	30,430	—	—	—
Ply. Colt (Champ)	32,819	34,513	37,129	42,128	47,853	27,031	1,471	—	—	—	—	—
Plymouth Conquest	3,013	805	—	—	—	—	—	—	—	—	—	—
Plymouth Sapporo	331	10,766	13,068	13,326	10,003	12,322	11,737	1,406	—	—	—	4,819
Plymouth Vista	7,465	1,992	—	—	—	—	—	—	—	—	—	—
Trucks	51,298	33,956	40,006	33,902	63,056	47,130	3,144	—	—	—	—	—
DeLorean	—	1,009	3,130	3,012	—	—	—	—	—	—	—	—
Fiat Total	**980**	**7,349**	**15,973**	**34,182**	**40,063**	**61,192**	**63,577**	**69,443**	**65,250**	**102,831**	**72,129**	**58,447**
Ferrari	568	549	686	904	779	656	—	—	—	—	—	—
Fiat	391	6,180	14,113	32,210	37,184	58,934	60,766	63,943	61,540	101,820	72,129	58,497
Lancia	21	620	1,174	1,068	2,100	1,602	2,811	5,500	3,710	1,011	—	—
Ford Total	**—**	**5,657**	**32,967**	**96,781**	**145,970**	**156,197**	**150,781**	**128,762**	**84,493**	**111,148**	**120,981**	**168,203**
Capri	—	—	—	—	—	—	4,079	22,458	29,904	54,585	75,260	113,069
Courier Truck	—	5,657	32,967	63,925	77,375	78,088	70,557	65,755	54,589	56,073	44,491	53,303
Fiesta	—	—	—	32,856	68,595	78,109	76,145	40,549	—	—	—	—
Pantera	—	—	—	—	—	—	—	—	—	490	1,230	1,831
General Motors Total	**14,600**	**15,530**	**22,304**	**61,724**	**88,447**	**114,007**	**86,257**	**96,606**	**56,153**	**83,571**	**89,607**	**107,822**
Buick Opel	—	—	—	—	—	13,815	19,222	29,067	10,483	36,893	59,279	68,400
Chevrolet Spectrum	2,077	—	—	—	—	—	—	—	—	—	—	—

Make												
Chevrolet Sprint	10,927	—	—	—	—	—	—	—	—	—	—	—
Chev. LUV Truck	1,596	15,530	22,304	61,724	88,447	100,192	67,035	67,539	45,670	46,678	30,328	39,422
Honda*	374,819	350,670	365,865	370,705	375,388	353,291	274,876	223,633	150,929	102,389	41,719	38,957
Isuzu	62,612	46,942	33,131	27,764	—	—	—	—	—	—	—	—
Jaguar (BL) Total	**18,044**	**15,815**	**10,349**	**18,921**	**31,949**	**42,306**	**48,068**	**68,476**	**65,164**	**70,839**	**54,870**	**65,948**
Austin	—	—	—	—	—	—	—	75	1,118	13,262	4,761	4,694
Jaguar	18,044	15,815	10,349	4,688	2,951	3,551	4,965	4,349	7,382	6,799	5,299	6,767
Land Rover 4x4	—	—	—	—	—	—	—	—	—	29	690	1,058
MG	—	—	—	3,700	13,688	26,025	26,656	34,794	28,426	27,946	25,034	31,991
Rover	—	—	—	774	480	—	—	—	—	—	—	—
Triumph	—	—	—	9,759	14,830	12,730	16,447	29,258	28,238	22,803	19,086	21,438
Mazda	288,793	249,538	204,679	182,885	170,398	164,832	80,017	56,193	41,179	69,384	75,079	119,004
Mercedes-Benz	79,222	73,692	68,814	67,113	57,941	56,528	48,950	50,692	44,376	42,232	38,826	42,405
Mitsubishi**	56,717	42,072	5,214	—	—	—	—	—	—	—	—	—
Nissan (Datsun)*	593,860	647,542	578,173	584,490	628,136	574,166	432,700	488,217	350,403	331,203	245,273	319,007
Peugeot	20,007	15,687	14,323	16,926	12,930	11,795	9,061	10,295	9,497	11,850	7,948	4,010
Porsche†	19,611	—	—	—	—	—	—	—	—	—	—	—
Renault	12,315	33,361	37,702	31,077	28,294	18,862	15,739	13,198	6,819	5,780	8,756	9,284
Saab	33,631	26,323	18,463	14,613	13,558	15,142	15,662	13,120	9,855	13,542	13,592	17,443
Subaru	157,383	156,840	150,335	152,062	142,968	127,871	103,274	80,826	48,928	41,591	22,980	37,793
Toyota	822,164	726,818	674,554	714,020	713,843	637,891	536,682	576,728	396,723	322,553	269,376	326,844
Volvo	99,541	88,847	72,375	64,477	56,909	56,602	50,880	46,790	43,887	60,338	53,043	60,761
Volkswagen Total	**174,685**	**145,813**	**128,725**	**145,205**	**145,716**	**186,820**	**277,608**	**319,052**	**251,026**	**339,715**	**408,090**	**550,509**
Audi	71,206	47,934	45,954	50,974	42,737	42,709	41,045	36,024	33,316	52,762	50,751	46,136
Porsche†	—	21,831	14,406	11,326	10,597	14,332	17,149	20,096	14,476	18,202	21,082	23,771
Volkswagen	103,479	77,048	68,365	82,905	92,382	129,779	219,414	262,932	203,234	268,751	336,257	480,602
Grand Total	**3,046,600**	**2,850,285**	**2,633,894**	**2,774,854**	**2,882,495**	**2,801,216**	**2,338,439**	**2,397,574**	**1,735,490**	**1,793,916**	**1,579,887**	**1,980,408**

* Honda excludes U.S.-built Accords; Nissan excludes U.S.-built pickups.

** Mitsubishi Motor Corp. established distribution arm independent of Chrysler Corp. in 1982.

† Porsche AG established distribution arm, assuming control from Volkswagen of American Inc., in 1984.

Source: Ward's Automotive Yearbook, 1985.

EXHIBIT 2 (*Continued*)

AUTOMOTIVE NEWS WORLD OUTLOOK

Generated by Data Resources Inc. (In Millions)

	1983	1984	1985	1986	1987	1988	1989	1990
NEW CAR REGISTRATIONS								
Total Western Europe* . .	10,473	10,240	10,391	10,639	10,831	10,852	11,028	11,270
Germany	2,427	2,425	2,495	2,536	2,486	2,547	2,565	2,681
France	2,018	1,810	1,891	1,983	2,065	2,022	2,093	2,162
United Kingdom	1,792	1,733	1,698	1,742	1,782	1,724	1,768	1,809
Italy	1,582	1,629	1,662	1,645	1,676	1,702	1,712	1,693
Total U.S.	9,178	10,640	10,710	10,580	10,483	11,166	11,608	11,839
Asia-Pacific**	1,025	1,159	1,251	1,325	1,367	1,404	1,463	1,521
Japan	3,136	3,228	3,254	3,414	3,362	3,457	3,515	3,617
Total Africa-MidEast . . .	1,271	1,242	1,305	1,450	1,575	1,635	1,603	1,645
Total Latin America	1,401	1,303	1,342	1,445	1,565	1,693	1,847	1,997
Total Eastern Bloc	2,085	2,118	2,155	2,222	2,302	2,366	2,407	2,457
CAR PRODUCTION								
Total Western Europe* . .	11,121	10,772	11,093	11,208	11,393	11,426	11,602	11,845
Germany	3,878	3,677	3,828	3,873	3,880	3,980	4,054	4,193
France	2,961	2,760	2,772	2,818	2,885	2,824	2,830	2,810
United Kingdom	1,045	981	1,016	1,001	1,010	995	1,028	1,050
Italy	1,396	1,493	1,504	1,498	1,518	1,521	1,562	1,594
Total North America	7,746	8,761	8,993	8,361	8,141	8,875	9,206	9,176
Asia-Pacific**	7,909	8,189	8,434	8,752	8,916	9,132	9,327	9,548
Japan	7,152	7,308	7,444	7,630	7,711	7,885	8,051	8,229
Total Latin America	1,113	1,094	1,144	1,247	1,407	1,559	1,670	1,826
Mexico	207	223	242	271	361	431	463	486
NEW TRUCK REGISTRATIONS								
Western Europe***	1,018	983	1,028	1,052	1,060	1,066	1,101	1,129
U.S.	3,161	4,164	4,373	4,342	4,390	4,537	4,624	4,767
TRUCK PRODUCTION								
Western Europe***	1,309	1,233	1,327	1,370	1,385	1,427	1,470	1,495
North America	2,971	4,017	4,166	4,004	3,991	4,122	4,232	4,421

* Includes Germany, France, United Kingdom, Italy, Netherlands, Belgium, Denmark, Ireland, Greece, Sweden, Norway, Finland, Switzerland, Austria, Spain and Portugal.
** Includes Taiwan, South Korea, Peninsular Malaysia, India, Australia and New Zealand but excludes Japan, which is listed separately.
*** Includes Germany, France, United Kingdom, Italy, Spain, Sweden, Netherlands and Belgium.

Source: Automotive News, 1985 Market Data Book Issue, April 24, 1985.

EXHIBIT 2 (*Continued*)

WARD'S IMPORT CAR MARKET SEGMENTATION

	1984		1983	
	Units	% Tot.	Units	% Tot.
MINICOMPACT				
Honda Civic	137,401	5.8	137,747	5.9
Toyota Tercel	103,013	4.4	147,971	6.3
Mazda GLC	45,221	1.9	51,601	2.2
Dodge Colt	36,560	1.6	39,158	1.7
Plymouth Colt	32,819	1.4	34,513	1.5
Chevrolet Sprint	10,927	0.5	—	—
Mitsubishi Mirage	3,101	0.1	—	—
Toyota Starlet	260	0.0	6,717	0.3
Nissan Pulsar	—	—	13,524	0.6
Renault LeCar	—	—	11,148	0.5
Total Regular	**369,302**	**15.7**	**442,379**	**19.0**
Honda CRX	47,445	2.0	—	—
VW Cabriolet	11,068	0.5	9,542	0.4
Fiat X1/9	143	0.0	2,008	0.1
Total Specialty	**58,656**	**2.5**	**11,550**	**0.5**
Total Minicompact	**427,958**	**18.2**	**453,929**	**19.5**
SUBCOMPACT				
Toyota Corolla	157,875	6.7	143,430	6.1
Nissan Sentra	189,488	8.1	209,889	9.0
Subaru	152,543	6.5	150,943	6.5
VW Jetta	37,750	1.6	21,736	0.9
Isuzu I-Mark	4,147	0.2	11,876	0.5
Chevrolet Spectrum	2,077	0.1	—	—
Fiat Strada	40	0.0	659	0.0
Total Regular	**543,930**	**23.2**	**538,533**	**23.0**
Nissan Pulsar NX	37,284	1.6	48,659	2.1
Honda Prelude	66,924	2.9	41,188	1.8
Mazda RX-7	54,310	2.3	52,226	2.2
VW Scirocco	17,138	0.7	13,654	0.5
Alfa Romeo Spider	2,783	0.1	1,931	0.1
Fiat Spider 2000	208	0.0	3,513	0.2
Total Specialty	**178,647**	**7.6**	**161,171**	**6.9**
Total Subcompact	**722,577**	**30.8**	**699,704**	**29.9**
COMPACT				
Honda Accord	123,049	5.2	171,735	7.3
Toyota Camry	93,725	4.0	52,666	2.3
Mazda 626	70,135	3.0	69,561	3.0
Nissan Stanza	44,612	1.9	64,429	2.8
Audi 4000	15,278	0.7	13,166	0.6
Mitsubishi Tredia	13,724	0.6	13,747	0.6
Mitsubishi Cordia	13,194	0.6	12,799	0.5
Dodge Vista	7,805	0.3	2,311	0.1
Plymouth Vista	7,465	0.3	1,992	0.1
Mitsubishi Galant	2,710	0.1	—	—
Ren. Sportwagon (18i)	2,971	0.1	6,053	0.3
Total Regular	**394,668**	**16.8**	**408,459**	**17.6**
Toyota Celica	85,213	3.6	117,836	5.0
Nissan 300 ZX	73,101	3.1	71,144	3.0
Nissan 200SX	63,466	2.7	31,158	1.3
Toyota Supra	29,871	1.3	26,972	1.2
Isuzu Impulse	13,076	0.6	8,855	0.4
Renault Fuego	9,272	0.4	16,028	0.7

	1984		1983	
	Units	% Tot.	Units	% Tot.
Mitsubishi Starion	6,375	0.3	6,209	0.3
Audi 4000 Quattro	3,923	0.2	577	0.0
Dodge Conquest (Challenger)	3,725	0.2	14,024	0.6
Audi Coupe GT	3,508	0.1	3,349	0.1
Plymouth Conquest (Sapporo)	3,344	0.1	11,571	0.5
Total Specialty	**294,874**	**12.6**	**307,723**	**13.1**
Total Compact	**689,542**	**29.4**	**716,182**	**30.7**
MIDSIZE				
Volvo DL/GL	68,610	2.9	60,932	2.6
Nissan Maxima	68,209	2.9	76,209	3.3
BMW 318i	28,661	1.2	34,619	1.5
Toyota Cressida	34,466	1.5	39,755	1.7
Saab 900/900s	18,360	0.8	13,716	0.6
Peugeot 505	19,723	0.8	14,791	0.6
VW Quantum	18,055	0.8	16,343	0.7
Volvo Diesel	5,589	0.2	4,588	0.2
Volvo 740 GLE	1,446	0.1	—	—
Total Regular	**263,119**	**11.2**	**260,953**	**11.2**
Volvo GLT	9,866	0.4	13,198	0.6
Saab 900 Turbo	14,408	0.6	12,117	0.5
Volvo 740 Turbo	47	0.0	—	—
Total Specialty	**24,321**	**1.0**	**25,315**	**1.1**
Total Midsize	**287,440**	**12.2**	**286,268**	**12.3**
LUXURY				
Audi 5000	41,067	1.7	27,735	1.2
Mercedes 300-Series	33,552	1.4	42,765	1.7
Mercedes 190-Series	23,013	1.0	4,180	0.2
BMW 325e	15,772	0.7	—	—
BMW 5-Series	15,409	0.7	16,004	0.7
Jaguar XJ6	14,564	0.6	13,110	0.6
Mercedes 380/500SE	11,692	0.5	5,807	0.3
BMW 7-Series	8,359	0.4	6007	0.3
Volvo 760 GLE/Diesel	7,563	0.3	8,964	0.4
Peugeot 604	284	0.0	450	0.0
Mercedes 240D	26	0.0	9,728	0.4
Total Regular	**171,301**	**7.3**	**134,750**	**5.8**
Porsche	19,611	0.8	21,831	0.9
Mercedes 380 SL	9,288	0.4	9,255	0.4
Audi 5000 Turbo	6,380	0.3	1,928	0.1
Volvo 760 Turbo	4,794	0.2	—	—
Jaguar JX-S	3,480	0.1	2,705	0.1
BMW 633/635 CSi	2,697	0.1	2,613	0.1
Mercedes 500 SEC	1,651	0.1	1,957	0.1
Alfa Romeo GTV-6	919	0.1	1,071	0.1
Ferrari	568	0.0	549	0.0
Audi Quattro Turbo	64	0.0	240	0.0
Lancia	21	0.0	620	0.0
DeLorean	—	—	1,009	0.0
Total Specialty	**49,473**	**2.1**	**43,778**	**1.8**
Total Luxury	**220,774**	**9.4**	**178,521**	**7.6**

Note: Segmentation based on overall car size, marketing intent and price.

Source: Ward's Automotive Yearbook, 1985.

EXHIBIT 2 (*Continued*)

U.S. NEW CAR SALES BY MARKET SEGMENTS (1984–1983 CALENDAR YEARS)

Class/Model	1984	% Share of Segment	1983	% Share of Segment
Subcompact Regular				
Chevette	164,917	13.5	178,759	16.4
1000	28,004	2.3	34,173	3.1
Escort	353,578	28.8	326,333	29.9
Lynx	67,725	5.5	78,876	7.2
Horizon	78,298	6.4	56,763	5.2
Omni	67,933	5.5	50,451	4.6
Renault Encore	69,235	5.6	20,182	1.9
Renault Alliance	100,366	8.2	126,008	11.6
Spirit	—	0.0	4,441	0.4
Golf (Rabbit)	73,844	6.0	85,042	7.8
Class Total	**1,003,900**	**81.8**	**961,028**	**88.1**
Subcompact Specialty				
Fiero	93,485	7.7	22,591	2.1
EXP	31,213	2.5	19,574	1.8
LN7	—	0.0	4,694	0.4
Turismo	47,109	3.8	36,497	3.3
Charger	51,940	4.2	45,975	4.3
Class Total	**223,747**	**18.2**	**129,331**	**11.9**
Total Subcompact	**1,227,647**	**100.0**	**1,090,359**	**100.0**
Compact Regular				
Cavalier	377,545	16.0	259,397	14.2
Citation	92,174	3.9	92,379	5.0
2000	126,916	5.3	88,313	4.8
Phoenix	13,202	0.6	24,362	1.3
Firenza	62,456	2.6	44,753	2.4
Omega	34,103	1.4	49,818	2.7
Skyhawk	121,858	5.1	72,998	4.0
Skylark	104,589	4.4	102,763	5.6

Class/Model	1984	% Share of Segment	1983	% Share of Segment
Intermediate Regular (Con't.)				
LTD	196,907	8.3	165,396	7.6
Granada	—	0.0	3,751	0.2
Marquis	103,722	4.4	65,184	3.0
Cougar '82	—	0.0	906	0.0
Caravelle	9,074	0.4	—	0.0
New Yorker (FWD)	53,698	2.3	50,091	2.3
E-Class	25,870	1.1	35,283	1.6
600 4 Dr.	36,872	1.6	33,882	1.6
Class Total	**1,701,779**	**71.7**	**1,470,082**	**67.8**
Intermediate Specialty				
Monte Carlo	115,930	4.9	105,797	4.9
Grand Prix	71,609	3.0	89,355	4.1
Regal	182,185	7.7	234,035	10.9
Thunderbird	154,865	6.5	134,710	6.2
Cougar	120,964	5.1	87,027	4.0
LeBaron GTS	2,494	0.1	—	0.0
Lancer	1,980	0.1	—	0.0
Cordoba	124	0.0	10,291	0.5
Mirada	250	0.0	4,417	0.2
Eagle	20,654	0.9	31,207	1.4
Class Total	**671,055**	**28.3**	**696,839**	**32.2**
Total Intermediate	**2,372,834**	**100.0**	**2,166,921**	**100.0**
Full-Size				
Chevrolet	258,902	21.6	238,930	24.4
Pontiac	62,084	5.2	26,929	2.8
Oldsmobile 88	258,293	21.6	228,770	23.5
LeSabre	164,314	13.7	151,555	15.6
Ford	169,253	14.2	119,905	12.3

Model	Value	%	Value	%
Tempo	256,532	10.9	136,148	7.5
Topaz	73,454	3.1	41,796	2.3
Fairmont	—	0.0	37,521	2.0
Zephyr	—	0.0	11,583	0.6
Reliant	138,154	5.8	157,247	8.6
Aries	111,984	4.7	119,400	6.5
Concord	—	0.0	11,513	0.6
Accord	133,601	5.6	50,402	2.7
Class Total	**1,646,568**	**69.4**	**1,300,393**	**70.8**
Compact Specialty				
Camaro	202,172	8.5	178,266	9.6
Firebird	101,414	4.3	90,777	4.9
Grand AM	16,751	0.7	—	0.0
Calais	14,881	0.6	—	0.0
Somerset	13,811	0.6	—	0.0
Mustang	138,296	5.8	116,976	6.4
Capri	17,739	0.7	22,708	1.2
Laser	53,131	2.2	11,097	0.6
Daytona	44,717	1.9	8,761	0.5
600 2 Dr.	24,956	1.1	28,593	1.6
LeBaron	98,842	4.2	80,309	4.4
Class Total	**726,710**	**30.6**	**537,487**	**29.2**
Total Compact	**2,373,278**	**100.0**	**1,837,880**	**100.0**
Intermediate Regular				
Celebrity	322,189	13.6	180,627	8.3
Malibu	890	0.0	85,148	3.9
6000	125,823	5.3	92,513	4.3
Bonneville	65,396	2.8	84,122	3.9
Ciera	242,209	10.2	191,720	8.8
Supreme	302,087	12.6	331,179	15.4
Century (FWD)	217,042	9.1	150,280	6.9

Model	Value	%	Value	%
Grand Marquis	143,594	12.0	96,659	9.9
Grand Fury	16,609	1.4	15,101	1.6
Fifth Avenue	94,340	7.9	73,729	7.6
Diplomat	28,623	2.4	22,498	2.3
Total Full-size	**1,196,012**	**100.0**	**974,076**	**100.0**
Luxury Regular				
Oldsmobile 98	34,284	4.4	119,528	16.5
Olds 98 (FWD)	66,135	8.5	—	0.0
Electra	32,578	4.2	80,106	11.0
Electra (FWD)	51,836	6.6	—	0.0
Cadillac (FWD)	77,117	9.9	—	0.0
Cadillac	118,060	15.0	176,003	24.2
Lincoln	90,869	11.6	59,626	8.2
Class Total	**470,879**	**60.2**	**435,263**	**59.9**
Luxury Specialty				
Corvette	30,424	3.9	28,144	3.9
Toronado	41,605	5.3	41,791	5.8
Riviera	53,398	6.8	53,346	7.3
Cimarron	18,014	2.3	19,188	2.6
Seville	36,249	4.6	33,522	4.6
Eldorado	70,577	9.1	71,624	9.9
Continental	31,110	4.0	13,691	1.9
Mark	29,496	3.8	28,257	3.9
Imperial	—	0.0	1,237	0.2
Class Total	**310,873**	**39.8**	**290,800**	**40.1**
Total Luxury	**781,752**	**100.0**	**726,063**	**100.0**
TOTAL DOMESTIC	**7,951,523**	**76.6**	**6,795,299**	**74.1**
TOTAL IMPORT	**2,438,842**	**23.4**	**2,376,056**	**25.9**
GRAND TOTAL	**10,390,365**	**100.0**	**9,171,355**	**100.0**

Note: Segmentation is determined by size, price and marketing intent. With some exceptions, once a car bearing that nameplate and platform is placed in a category, it remains in the group as downsizing occurs unless significant changes are made in size or marketing intent. In general, specialty models are sportier, higher priced cars with separate nameplates. High-line versions of regular cars remain with the regular model. The Cougar name replaced the Monarch in '80–'81, then became the downsized Marquis in '83. The Cougar XR-7 is a specialty car in all model years. Rabbit and Accord are U.S. built models only. Supreme and Regal 4-door models breakout estimated in 1983.

Source: Ward's Automobile Yearbook, 1985.

EXHIBIT 3   G.M. FINANCIAL AND OPERATING SUMMARY

Dollars in Millions Except Per Share and Hourly Amounts

	1984	1983	1982
Sales and Revenues			
United States operations			
Automotive products	$73,053.1	$63,665.0	$47,391.2
Nonautomotive products	2,107.6	1,670.3	2,138.9
Defense and space	1,322.7	826.8	793.8
Computer systems services (since October 18, 1984)	148.7	—	—
Total United States operations	76,632.1	66,162.1	50,323.9
Canadian operations	12,581.6	11,232.4	7,972.6
Overseas operations	11,345.5	11,955.5	12,212.8
Elimination of interarea sales and revenues	(16,669.3)	(14,768.4)	(10,483.7)
Total	$83,889.9	$74,581.6	$60,025.6
Worldwide automotive products	$80,499.3	$71,904.7	$56,676.8
Worldwide nonautomotive products	$ 3,390.6	$ 2,676.9	$ 3,348.8
Worldwide Factory Sales of Cars and Trucks			
(units in thousands)	8,256	7,769	6,244
Net Income			
Amount	$ 4,516.5	$ 3,730.2	$ 962.7
As a percent of sales and revenues	5.4%	5.0%	1.6%
As a percent of stockholders' equity	18.7%	18.0%	5.3%
Attributable to:			
$1-2/3 par value common stock	$ 4,485.3	$ 3,717.3	$ 949.8
Class E common stock (issued in 1984)	$ 18.7	—	—
Earnings per share of common stocks:			
$1-2/3 par value common	$14.22	$11.84	$3.09
Class E common (issued in 1984)	$1.03	—	—
Cash dividends per share of common stocks:			
$1-2/3 par value common	$4.75*	$2.80	$2.40
Class E common (issued in 1984)	$0.09	—	—
Taxes			
United States, foreign and other income taxes (credit)	$ 1,805.1	$ 2,223.8	($ 252.2)
Other taxes (principally payroll and property taxes)	3,572.4	2,675.8	2,470.3
Total	$ 5,377.5	$ 4,899.6	$ 2,218.1
Taxes per share of $1-2/3 par value common stock	$16.98	$15.61	$7.22
Investment as of December 31			
Cash and marketable securities	$ 8,567.4	$6,216.9	$ 3,126.2
Working capital	$ 6,276.7	$ 5,890.8	$ 1,658.1
Stockholders' equity	$24,214.3	$20,766.6	$18,287.1
Book value per share of common stocks:			
$1-2/3 par value common	$72.16	$64.88	$57.64
Class E common (issued in 1984)	$36.08	—	—
Number of Stockholders as of December 31			
(in thousands)			
$1-2/3 par value common and preferred	957	998	1,050
Class E common	623	—	—

EXHIBIT 3 *(Continued)*

	1984	1983	1982
Worldwide Employment (including financing and insurance subsidiaries)			
Average number of employees (in thousands)	748	691	657
Total payrolls (including profit sharing)	$22,505.4	$19,605.3	$17,043.8
Total cost of an hour worked—U.S. hourly employees	$22.60	$21.80	$21.50
Property			
Real estate, plants and equipment—Expenditures	$ 3,595.1	$ 1,923.0	$ 3,611.1
—Depreciation	$ 2,663.2	$ 2,569.7	$ 2,403.0
Special tools—Expenditures	$ 2,452.1	$ 2,083.7	$ 2,601.0
—Amortization	$ 2,236.7	$ 2,549.9	$ 2,147.5
Total expenditures	$ 6,047.2	$ 4,006.7	$ 6,212.1

* *In addition, in December 1984 holders of $1-2/3 par value common stock received one share of Class E common stock for every 20 shares of $1-2/3 par value common stock held.*

Source: General Motors Corporation, *Annual Report*, 1984.

EXHIBIT 3 *(Continued)*

WORLDWIDE FACTORY SALES

(Units in Thousands)

	Cars			Trucks & Buses			Total		
	1984	*1983*	*1982*	*1984*	*1983*	*1982*	*1984*	*1983*	*1982*
United States	4,338	3,996	3,147	1,338	1,123	895	5,676	5,119	4,042
Canada	549	539	335	277	263	230	826	802	565
Overseas†	1,485	1,606	1,388	269	242	249	1,754	1,848	1,637
Total	6,372	6,141	4,870	1,884	1,628	1,374	8,256	7,769	6,244

† *Includes units which are manufactured overseas by other companies and which are imported and sold by General Motors and affiliates.*

PERCENTAGE OF NET INCOME (LOSS) ATTRIBUTABLE TO:

	1984	1983	1982
United States	86%	93%	111%
Canada	17	16	(3)
Overseas	(3)	(9)	(8)
Total	100%	100%	100%
Automotive	100%	102%	101%
Nonautomotive	—	(2)	(1)
Total	100%	100%	100%

PERCENTAGE OF WORLDWIDE DOLLAR SALES AND REVENUES ATTRIBUTABLE TO:

	1984	1983	1982
United States	76%	74%	72%
Canada	13	13	11
Overseas	11	13	17
Total	100%	100%	100%
Automotive	96%	96%	94%
Nonautomotive	4	4	6
Total	100%	100%	100%

Source: General Motors Corporation, *Annual Report*, 1984.

STATEMENT OF CONSOLIDATED INCOME

For the Years Ended December 31, 1984, 1983 and 1982
(Dollars in Millions Except Per Share Amounts)

	1984	1983	1982
Net Sales and Revenues (Note 2)			
Manufactured products	$83,699.7	$74,581.6	$60,025.6
Computer systems services	190.2	—	—
Total Net Sales and Revenues	83,889.9	74,581.6	60,025.6
Costs and Expenses			
Cost of sales and other operating charges, exclusive of items listed below	70,217.9	60,718.8	51,548.3
Selling, general and administrative expenses	4,006.3	3,234.8	2,964.9
Depreciation of real estate, plants and equipment	2,663.2	2,569.7	2,403.0
Amortization of special tools	2,236.7	2,549.9	2,147.5
Amortization of intangible assets (Note 1)	65.8	—	—
Total Costs and Expenses	79,189.9	69,073.2	59,063.7
Operating Income	4,700.0	5,508.4	961.9
Other income less income deductions—net (Note 5)	1,713.5	815.8	476.3
Interest expense (Note 1)	(909.2)	(1,352.7)	(1,415.4)
Income before Income Taxes	5,504.3	4,971.5	22.8
United States, foreign and other income taxes (credit) (Note 7)	1,805.1	2,223.8	(252.2)
Income after Income Taxes	3,699.2	2,747.7	275.0
Equity in earnings of nonconsolidated subsidiaries and associates (dividends received amounted to $706.1 in 1984, $757.3 in 1983 and $412.7 in 1982)	817.3	982.5	687.7
Net Income	4,516.5	3,730.2	962.7
Dividends on preferred stocks	12.5	12.9	12.9
Earnings on Common Stocks	$ 4,504.0	$ 3,717.3	$ 949.8
Attributable to:			
$1-2/3 par value common stock	$ 4,485.3	$ 3,717.3	$ 949.8
Class E common stock (issued in 1984)	$ 18.7	—	—
Average number of shares of common stocks outstanding (in millions):			
$1-2/3 par value common.	315.3	313.9	307.4
Class E common (issued in 1984)	18.2	—	—
Earnings Per Share of Common Stocks (Note 8)			
$1-2/3 par value common	$14.22	11.84	$3.09
Class E common (issued in 1984)	$1.03	—	—

Reference should be made to notes on pages 23 through 30 provided in company's annual report.

Source: General Motors Corporation, *Annual Report, 1984.*

EXHIBIT 3 (*Continued*)

FINANCIALS BY SEGMENT (*Dollars in Millions*)

	United States	Canada	Europe	Latin America	All Other	Total*
1984						
Net Sales and Revenues:						
Outside	$69,355.6	$ 4,411.6	$6,735.7	$1,642.0	$1,745.0	$83,889.9
Interarea	7,276.5	8,170.0	242.2	823.6	401.7	—
Total net sales and revenues	$76,632.1	$12,581.6	$6.977.9	$2,465.6	$2,146.7	$83,889.9
Net Income (Loss)	$ 3,872.0	$ 762.2	$ 291.1	$ 94.4	$ 61.5	$ 4,516.5
Total Assets	$41,692.7	$ 2,833.5	$4,425.7	$2,874.0	$ 932.0	$52,144.9
Net Assets	$22,149.7	$ 1,628.9	($ 439.2)	$1,016.7	$ 41.7	$24,214.3
Average Number of Employees (in thousands)	511	41	122	49	25	748
1983						
Net Sales:						
Outside	$59,668.7	$ 3,866.4	$7,761.7	$1,742.7	$1,542.1	$74,581.6
Interarea	6,493.4	7,366.0	208.6	653.1	295.4	—
Total net sales	$66,162.1	$11,232.4	$7,970.3	$2,395.8	$1,837.5	$74,581.6
Net Income (Loss)	$ 3,469.0	$ 592.3	($ 228.3)	($ 15.0)	($ 91.1)	$ 3,730.2
Total Assets	$34,670.4	$ 2,385.5	$5,379.1	$2,834.3	$ 813.9	$45,694.5
Net Assets	$18,749.3	$ 1,332.9	($ 120.5)	$ 919.6	$ 8.9	$20,766.6
Average Number of Employees (in thousands)	463	39	123	41	25	691
1982						
Net Sales:						
Outside	$45,650.1	$ 2,621.9	$7,150.5	$2,699.5	$1,903.6	$60,025.6
Interarea	4,673.8	5,350.7	234.3	310.2	192.9	—
Total net sales	$50,323.9	$ 7,972.6	$7,384.8	$3,009.7	$2,096.5	$60,025.6
Net Income (Loss)	$ 1,079.3	($ 33.5)	$ 6.2	($ 16.5)	($ 63.2)	$ 962.7
Total Assets	$29,227.4	$ 2,299.0	$5,952.3	$2,973.3	$1,063.5	$41,397.8
Net Assets	$15,756.0	$ 774.7	$ 803.3	$ 894.3	$ 170.7	$18,287.1
Average Number of Employees (in thousands)	441	34	114	38	30	657

* After elimination of interarea transactions.

Source: General Motors Corporation, *Annual Report,* 1984.

EXHIBIT 3 (*Continued*)

CONSOLIDATED BALANCE SHEET

(December 31, 1984 and 1983 Dollars in Millions Except Per Share Amounts)

	1984	1983
ASSETS		
Current Assets		
Cash	$ 467.5	$ 369.5
United States Government and other marketable securities and time deposits—at cost, which approximates market of $8,108.7 and $5,834.6	8,099.9	5,847.4
Total cash and marketable securities	8,567.4	6,216.9
Accounts and notes receivable (including GMAC and its subsidiaries—$3,868.5 and $3,560.7)—less allowances (Note 9)	7,357.9	6,964.2
Inventories (less allowances) (Note 1)	7,359.7	6,621.5
Prepaid expenses and deferred income taxes	428.3	997.2
Total Current Assets	23,713.3	20,799.8
Equity in Net Assets of Nonconsolidated Subsidiaries and Associates (principally GMAC and its subsidiaries—Note 9)	4,603.0	4,450.8
Other Investments and Miscellaneous Assets—at cost (less allowances)	2,344.4	1,221.2
Common Stocks Held for the Incentive Program (Note 3)	144.2	56.3
Property		
Real estate, plants and equipment—at cost (Note 10)	39,354.1	37,777.8
Less accumulated depreciation (Note 10)	21,649.8	20,116.8
Net real estate, plants and equipment	17,704.3	17,661.0
Special tools—at cost (less amortization)	1,697.2	1,504.1
Total Property	19,401.5	19,165.1
Intangible Assets—at cost (less amortization) (Note 1)	1,938.5	1.3
Total Assets	$52,144.9	$45,694.5

824

LIABILITIES AND STOCKHOLDERS' EQUITY

Current Liabilities		
Accounts payable (principally trade)	$ 4,743.5	$ 4,642.3
Loans payable (Note 12)	3,086.0	1,255.2
United States, foreign and other income taxes payable	618.9	202.3
Accrued liabilities (Note 11)	8,988.2	8,809.2
Total Current Liabilities	17,436.6	14,909.0
Long-Term Debt (Note 12)	2,417.4	3,137.2
Capitalized Leases	355.5	384.6
Other Liabilities (including GMAC and its subsidiaries—$300.0 in 1984 and 1983)	5,971.9	4,698.2
Deferred Credits (including investment tax credits—$1,259.9 and $1,281.1)	1,749.2	1,798.9
Stockholders' Equity (Notes 3, 4 and 13)		
Preferred stocks ($5.00 series, $169.8 and $183.6; $3.75 series, $85.8 and $100.0)	255.6	283.6
Common stocks:		
$1-2/3 par value (issued, 317,504,133 and 315,711,299 shares)	529.2	526.2
Class E (issued, 29,082,382 shares in 1984)	2.9	—
Capital surplus (principally additional paid-in capital)	3,347.8	2,136.8
Net income retained for use in the business	20,796.6	18,390.5
Subtotal	24,932.1	21,337.1
Accumulated foreign currency translation and other adjustments (Note 1)	(717.8)	(570.5)
Total Stockholders' Equity	24,214.3	20,766.6
Total Liabilities and Stockholders' Equity	$52,144.9	$45,694.5

*Reference should be made to notes on pages 23 through 30 provided in company's annual report.
Certain amounts for 1983 have been reclassified to conform with 1984 classifications.*

Source: General Motors Corporation, *Annual Report*, 1984.

IBM (C)

The success of the 360 line was greater than anyone had predicted. In 1964 (at the time of the 360 announcement) management expected to place roughly 2,700 of the five largest models by 1970 and projected that only a third of these would be ordered with remote terminal and communications gear. In fact, shipments approached the 5,000 level with more than half demanding extra peripheral equipment. IBM's revenues exploded from $3.5 billion in 1965 to $7.5 billion in 1970. Peripheral equipment represented a large percentage of the customers' hardware dollar in 1970, and the high margins on these sales helped cover further massive R&D expenditures for future mainframes.

IBM has always used very conservative accounting in pricing leases—usually assuming a 4-year life. Hence, a $1 million machine would rent for $250,000 per year. Over the long term, many customers naturally kept their machines longer which provided IBM with huge cash flows that dropped directly to the bottom line. For instance, in 1972 there were still about 3,900 series 1400 computers on rental that were manufactured in the late '50s. But the 360's very success threatened this carefully maintained structure, as independent leasing companies and "plug compatible" peripheral manufacturers (PCMs) moved in for the kill.

One of IBM's major concerns in the early 1970s was that an increasing number of its own customers would come to view IBM merely as another supplier of individual components rather than as a total system provider—an approach that IBM's marketing people had labored assiduously for years to create. To compound problems, on

Case copyright © 1983 by James Brian Quinn. Research associate —Roger Wellington. Case derived primarily from secondary sources.

the last day of the Johnson administration in 1969, the Justice Department filed an anti-trust suit against IBM, charging in part that the entire 360 line represented an effort to reduce competition. The government's goal was nothing less than the breakup of IBM into several separate companies. IBM's response to these various threats had to be handled very carefully and with a long term perspective.

THE 370 RESPONSE

One of its responses was the 370 series of computers. The 370s were designed to be compatible with the 360 machines in terms of software so that the users' huge investments in programming would be protected. Typically a user would invest $3–5 in software for each $1 in hardware. The 370 in essence was intended to make 360 programs run faster, and the transition to the new machines was intended to be painless compared to the disruptive way the 360 had been introduced.

Technical people at IBM would have preferred to equip the whole range of 370 computers with semiconductor memories at introduction. That would have made the 370 series much more versatile, more powerful, and technologically far ahead of any other computer. But IBM's marketing group pressed for earlier introduction with the first available quality product. The ultimate timing decision depended to a large extent on the fact that by 1970 most of the 370's building blocks were in hand, for development had begun as far back as 1965. "We had invested a few hundred million dollars in the 370," said Watson. "We might have been more prudent to upgrade the 360, but we thought a new line would be a stimulant for both the customer and the salesman." Unfortunately, the 370 strategy backfired. Customers often found they could replace two

360's with one 370 and save on monthly rental payments.

To compound difficulties, the medium to large-sized mainframe market began to mature, and hardware prices dropped due to the rapid miniaturization of integrated circuits. To fill the gap in the low end of its line, IBM introduced the System/3, the result of an intensive development effort in the late '60s headed up by the highest ranking line officer at IBM—Frank Cary, who later became IBM's chairman at age 52, when T. Vincent Learson stepped down in 1972. Although the System/3, first shipped in 1970, suffered in the recession of '70–'71 just as the 370 did, it went on to become a best seller with more than 25,000 machines installed. But to achieve the breakthroughs in cost necessary to make it cheap enough for small users, the designers had to sacrifice compatibility with the 360/370 family. The System/3 spawned a new family of machines allowing all its new IBM users to trade up within the line. By 1983, the largest System/3 machines competed in price/performance with the smaller units in the 360/370 series.[1]

THE CARY YEARS

In 1975, an aggressive new company started by one of the designers of the System/360 (Gene Amdahl) and backed by Japan's Fujitsu, became the first to manufacture a "plug compatible" mainframe computer. Amdahl's success in coming up with a cheaper and more sophisticated product targeted at high-powered users forced IBM to reevaluate its policy of introducing products at a controlled pace in order to extract maximum rental revenue from the already installed base.

A New Strategy

Every five or six years IBM had traditionally introduced a new generation of computers that outmoded its existing series. To convince customers to trade up to the new line, the company usually offered new machines with a lot more performance for only a little more money. One rule of thumb used in pricing a new mainframe was that a four-fold improvement in capacity would warrant only a doubling of price. And IBM's long-time pricing policy had been to keep the price/performance ratio constant across the entire line. In keeping with this tradition, IBM's labs developed an entirely new series of machines slated for introduction in 1975 known only by the somewhat cryptic designation "Future System." Future System was to have been a revolutionary technological leap, for the first time breaking away from the architecture of the 360/370 series in the main line of computers.

Future System was perhaps the most formally planned product line development in IBM's history. But it failed to materialize due to massive development difficulties and the prospect that many customers would hesitate to throw away a decade's worth of 360/370 programming investment. IBM had no choice but to extend the life of its existing computers by slightly enhancing them and lowering prices. Demand responded to price cuts more vigorously than IBM planners had assumed. IBM cut prices by one third on two aging models of the System 370, and sales exploded. In some cases, customers' data-processing departments had years of applications programs all coded and ready to run as soon as the cost dropped enough to justify new equipment.

The 4300

The next major step in IBM's product development was the 1979 launch of the 4300, a family of medium-sized computers. According to many estimates, in the first three weeks customers sent in an astounding $10 billion worth of orders for 42,000 machines, twice as many as IBM had expected to manufacture over the entire life of the series. Some customers were assigned delivery dates four years into the future, and places near the head of the line were traded for up to $15,000 each.[2]

The 4300s were priced so low that one model exceeded the computing power of an existing $560,000 machine, yet sold for only $69,-000 —an eight-fold improvement in price/performance ratio. Users of bigger systems who assumed that IBM's future offerings at the high end of the market would be priced according to the same formula canceled orders for IBM's existing big machines, the 3030 series. Instead they turned to short-term leases which they could terminate when the new large-scale 3080 series computers came out.

The result was a terrific cash crunch. Not only did IBM have to fund the production of all those new 4300s, it had to finance $4.2 billion in new leased equipment in 1979 alone—a 55% increase over 1978. Profits in 1979 declined 3.2%—the first such drop in two decades. After trying to repurchase $700 million of its own stock in 1977–78, the company had to go to the bond market in October, 1979 with a $1 billion offering—the largest such public sale in history.

The Mini-Market

"Distributed processing"—connecting large central processors to a series of smaller, special purpose units in a single system— came into vogue in the mid-'60s as small stand-alone machines that could handle limited quantities of information and send it along to a larger central mainframe became available. As they gained popularity, these small units acquired the ubiquitous nickname of "mini-computers," like the mini-skirts that appeared around the same time. The pioneer and leader in mini-computers was Digital Equipment Corp. (DEC), one of the greatest venture capital successes of all time.

Minis were marketed differently from "mainframes." They were sold, not rented, and the purchasers for minis were usually sophisticated companies who didn't need the systems engineers, software packages, and training programs that were IBM's trademark.

As hardware prices and sizes shrank in the 1970s, minis became more powerful, more flexible, and much cheaper. IBM found that many of its customers started practicing a technique called "off-loading." When a large central mainframe was operating at capacity, instead of up-

grading or replacing the existing machine, they pushed off the extra jobs onto minis. This trend finally forced IBM to get serious about this rapidly growing segment. IBM had had small business systems since 1970 when it came out with the System/3, but it didn't announce a true mini-computer until 1976.

DEC, Hewlett-Packard, Data General, Texas Instruments, and others offered quantity discounts on their minis of 30 – 40% to "systems houses"—sophisticated middle-men who bought components in bulk and packaged them into systems for various users. IBM, on the other hand, was used to letting its highly disciplined blue-suited sales force contact and service end users directly and refused to consider discounts of more than 15% for large orders of minis. In the words of a former IBM executive, "You really had to love the machine to take it at that price."

The Office of the Future

As a result of such practices, in 1980 IBM was still fifth in mini-computer sales but was finally learning and moving up fast. Its division responsible for small systems began discounting. And the 4300 series, which was designed with distributed processing applications in mind, helped strengthen IBM's hand. The company also introduced a high level software package called System Network Architecture (SNA) to help link together its minis, mainframes, word processors, smart copiers, and communication devices into the much discussed decentralized "office of the future."

Many firms had entered the battle to become the industry standard for this critical interface. Xerox, DEC, and Intel had teamed up to offer a local network package. And GTE and AT&T were working on global electronic mail and data transmission systems. Sperry and Burroughs were also in the hunt. But IBM's sheer market power if properly focused could ultimately overwhelm many of these efforts. By the end of 1981, 45% of all IBM computer users setting up new information networks had installed SNA. With more than 60% of the worldwide mainframe market in IBM's hands, there was a growing concern that incompatible machines could be frozen out of office network systems.[3]

Linking the World

IBM was also a partner in Satellite Business Systems, a joint venture (with Comsat and Aetna) that had three satellites providing interference free data transmission capabilities. With the deregulation of the communications industry (occurring concurrently with the dropping of the Justice Department's anti-trust suit against IBM in January 1982), IBM was cleared to move further in the direction of total systems services. But, so was the Bell complex.

As a result of its various actions, IBM's market share in minis had risen sharply from roughly 17% in 1980 to almost 25% in 1982. IBM's overall sales were $34.3 billion in 1982— a $5.3 billion increase from the previous year. By comparison, Digital Equipment Corp.'s 1982 revenues *totaled* only $3.8 billion.[4]

THE EIGHTIES AND BEYOND

In 1981, 56-year old John Opel became IBM's fifth Chief Executive Officer. During his years of rising through the corporate ranks from his sales and marketing beginnings, Opel was often frustrated by the centralized management style at IBM. As CEO he promised to remedy that fault. Said Opel, "You have to leave people free to act, or they become dependent. They don't have to be told; they have to be allowed." A quiet, wiry, cerebral executive, who acquired the nickname "the brain" for his searching questions during a stint as Tom Watson Jr.'s assistant during the 1960s, Opel would need all his powers of mind to confront the complex challenges facing IBM in the '80s.

Shrinking Chips

Perhaps the biggest threat to IBM's preeminence came not from any particular competitor, but from changes in the computer technology itself. Integrated circuit (IC) capabilities were radically al-

tering the size, speed, reliability and cost of all computers and accessories. For instance, a circuit package used in a 1983 top-of-the-line machine measured $4'' \times 4'' \times 2''$ and contained over 100 chips interconnected through 33 layers. The same capacity required a space the size of a refrigerator for a 370 System model produced in the early 1970s. Until the 4300 Series, IBM had used ICs that could store 2,000 pieces of information although competitors had gradually introduced 16k chips. The 4300 leapfrogged the competition by using a 64k chip. In 1982, 256k chips were in production and some forecasters believed much denser circuits were feasible. If the automobile industry had developed at the same pace as the computer industry since 1960, a 1982 Rolls Royce would have cost only $2.75 and run 3 million miles on one gallon of gas.

The microprocessor, pioneered by Intel in the early '70s, was the next logical challenge for IBM. Microprocessors were chips that contained both programmable logic and memory circuits as opposed to earlier "single function" chips. The microprocessor was the engine driving the proliferation of electronic devices into home computers, "programmable" microwave ovens, "smart" machines, and so on worldwide. As one of the largest producers of ICs in the world— for its own use—IBM had to consider its possible role in such markets.

$10 Billion in Plant and Equipment

IBM's actions in the early '80s indicated how seriously it took these challenges. Chairman Frank Cary said, "We've got to be price competitive, box by box (machine by machine). Nobody is going to pay us a 20% premium any more." To accomplish this, IBM invested heavily in increased capacity. Between 1977 and 1981 it added 22 million square feet of laboratory and manufacturing space, a staggering $10 billion in plant and equipment. Such additions accounted for roughly two thirds of the gross asset value of plant and other property listed on IBM's balance sheet as of the end of 1982.

But these investments bucked two other important trends. In 1975, according to industry sources, the CPU represented 55% of a system's cost, the rest being terminals, printers, software and other peripherals. By 1980, that share had declined to 35%. Furthermore, systems with big CPUs made up a large but declining share of the market. In 1982 IBM received only 29% of its revenue from the sale or rental of central processors. At the same time, software, which had been only 10% of development costs for early 1960s lines, became some 90% of such costs in the early 1980s.

In a vertically integrated firm like IBM, profits could often be shifted from one segment of the business that was attacked by competitors to areas where the company still retained a significant advantage. Sales and profits on various activities in IBM were heavily influenced by such choices. (Published data on 1982 lines are shown in Exhibit 2.) These same choices could also have devastating impact on smaller competitors— as for example, when IBM lowered the boom on plug compatible memory producers by cutting memory prices while simultaneously increasing its prices on mainframes.

For a long time survival in the plug compatible (PCM) market had depended on producers' ability to adapt swiftly to new offerings by IBM. This pressure made any information of future IBM technology extremely valuable. In 1982, IBM—with the help of the FBI—caught employees of several competing firms stealing proprietary information. Several of the companies involved were Japanese. The trade secrets that allegedly changed hands involved designs for IBM's top of the line 3080 series of central processors.

Organizing for the Future

In a fast changing, high technology industry— where small companies have very real advantages over larger, more bureaucratic firms—IBM was often likened to a whale in a pool with lots of aggressive sharks. IBM had developed some specific techniques for countering a large company's natural propensity to minimize risk. In IBM's early computer years, when Tom Watson Jr. was CEO, he encouraged the fresh thinking of people he called "wild ducks." Bob Evans, said, "Watson Jr. always felt the world is full of people who just don't see it the way most people do. More times than not they are probably wrong, but sometimes they are right, and we ought to have some mechanism for the wild ducks to have their fling. Watson encouraged this 'wild duckism.' He encouraged people, who normally would not be inclined to just go along with a team, to know there was an avenue where—if they wanted to express a different view—they'd be heard and maybe funded to do something by themselves."

To help coordinate its rapidly diversifying lines and complex presence in the marketplace, IBM reorganized in 1981. The most dramatic part of the shake up occurred in IBM's three sales divisions which were folded into one integrated entity called the Information Systems Group. (See Exhibit 1.) This move was prompted in part by the confusion caused by IBM salespeople from different divisions calling on the same company. The change further streamlined IBM's manufacturing operation by grouping all the computer related divisions together. It also set up 14 IBU's (Independent Business Units) and SBU's (Strategic Business Units) that could explore opportunities without the weight of the company's formal bureaucracy to hold them back. This strategy succeeded in shaking up traditional thinking at IBM. An SBU developed and built IBM's entry into the home computer market— the PC (Personal Computer). The rapid acceptance of the IBM PC was largely the result of several critical decisions that were significant departures from past company practice.

While IBM had recently tightened its control over systems software for its large computers (to make it tougher for the plug compatible manufacturers), the PC designers adopted an "open architecture," opening the machines' technical specifications to the public. They commissioned an independent software house (Microsoft) to write the new operating system for the PC and quickly made it public too. Also breaking with tradition, many hardware components were standard units (including an Intel 8088 microprocessor CPU chip) sourced from outside vendors to ensure a faster startup. Finally, instead of relying on IBM's salesforce and 40 odd retail product centers, the PC's marketing people cut a deal with Sears and Computerland to sell IBM machines. The result—IBM's PC garnered 30% of the business micro-computer market in just two years. In late 1983 the PC manufacturing unit was allocating production by shipping only 1 unit for every 7 ordered— despite an assembly line that was so automated it took only 10 minutes of worker time to assemble a unit.[5]

Stiffer Competition

When the government announced settlement of its suits against AT&T and IBM, it provided for the spin-off of the local phone companies from AT&T. But AT&T would retain roughly $40 billion in assets including its long distance lines, its manufacturing divisions (Western Electric), and Bell Laboratories. Many analysts thought AT&T would confront IBM with its first adequately financed, technologically adept competition. Bell Labs built one of the first computers in the 1940s and continued to be a leader in microelectronics development. American Bell, AT&T's recently chartered data-communications subsidiary, would have $5 billion in assets to start with and would be backed up by the world's most advanced global tele-communications system.

IBM also had to deal with the small chip manufacturers who were integrating forward into computers as they developed more powerful microprocessors. But perhaps the biggest threat to IBM's long term dominance in computers might come from the Japanese. By 1983 the Japanese had entered every major segment of the office equipment industry with particular strength in printers and copiers. In addition, Japanese companies held some 10–15% of the worldwide computer market, although their national goal was a 30% share by 1990. Fujitsu, Nippon Electric Co., and Hitachi were the largest computer makers. Fujitsu had surpassed IBM as the #1 computer supplier in Japan. All the Japanese manufacturers

had standardized their current products around IBM 360/370 architecture. Although they sold primarily to their own domestic market, Japanese companies were actively pursuing new world markets through joint ventures and other agreements. Fujitsu was the largest shareholder in Amdahl, which held a 56% share of the IBM plug-compatible mainframe market, and it distributed its own equipment through TRW. Hitachi had a joint distribution agreement with National Advanced Systems, the number 2 PCM.

At the low end of the market, the Japanese presence in desk top computers was small—less than 2% of the U.S. market in 1983. Their products to date had not been very impressive, and their lack of strong dealer networks and brand recognition had limited their sales growth. At the high end, the so-called "Fifth Generation Project" was Japan's attempt to leap-frog established competition and become number one in computer technology by the 1990s. The Japanese envisioned a machine with human-like reasoning capability (called artificial intelligence), and they committed $500 million to start it toward reality. Another related $100 million Japanese program called the National Superspeed Computer Project aimed to produce machines many times faster than 1983's best supercomputers. While many IBM experts doubted that these goals were achievable, they admitted that some major U.S. companies had recently refused to purchase more large IBM computers because they expected the Japanese would eventually dominate the field.

QUESTIONS

1. What should IBM's strategy for the future be? Why? What should be the structure of its portfolio?
2. How should it organize for this?
3. What are the most important changes in its industry IBM must deal with?
4. How should it meet the specific challenge of the Japanese in the future? AT&T? Smaller companies? Anti-trust?

EXHIBIT 1   IBM ORGANIZATION

To conduct its business throughout the world, IBM is organized into the following groups, divisions and wholly owned subsidiaries:

INFORMATION SYSTEMS GROUP

Customer Service Division
Provides maintenance, related support and programming services within the U.S. and its territories for designated systems and products developed primarily by the Information Systems and Communications Group.

Federal Systems Division
Provides specialized information-handling and control systems to the Federal government for seaborne, spaceborne, airborne and ground-based environments. Also participates in applied research and exploratory development.

Field Engineering Division
Provides maintenance and related services within the U.S. and its territories for all current IBM systems and products and designated new systems and products developed primarily by the Information Systems and Technology Group, as well as support for specified IBM program offerings. Has overall responsibility for the distribution of all hardware and software products and related publications. The division also provides maintenance, marketing support and central programming service for assigned products.

National Accounts Division
Has marketing and field administration responsibility within the U.S. and its territories for the full standard line of IBM products. Its assigned customers are selected large accounts with complex information processing needs.

National Marketing Division
Has marketing and field administration responsibility within the U.S. and its territories for the full standard line of IBM products. Its assigned customers are large, medium and small accounts.

Systems Supplies Division
Has responsibility for formulating worldwide business strategy for information processing supplies and accessories; for manufacturing or procurement, and marketing within the U.S. and its territories of IBM supplies and services.

INFORMATION SYSTEMS AND TECHNOLOGY GROUP

Data Systems Division
Has worldwide development and associated programming responsibility for large, complex systems, with primary emphasis on high-performance products, plus U.S. manufacturing responsibility for those systems.

General Products Division
Has worldwide development and U.S. manufacturing responsibility for storage systems, including tape units, disk products and mass storage systems, program products and product-related programming.

General Technology Division
Has worldwide development and product assurance and U.S. manufacturing responsibility for logic, memory and special semiconductor devices and associated packaging. The division also procures components for the IBM World Trade Americas/Far East Corporation and U.S. operating units.

INFORMATION SYSTEMS AND COMMUNICATIONS GROUP

Communication Products Division
Has worldwide development and U.S. manufacturing responsibility for telecommunications systems, office systems, display products, distribution industry systems and related programming. The division serves as the worldwide architectural and systems focal point for office systems and Systems Network Architecture activities.

EXHIBIT 1 (*Continued*)

Information Products Division
Has worldwide development and related
  programming and U.S. manufacturing
  responsibility for typewriters, copiers and
  systems for banking and manufacturing
  industries, and for peripheral equipment,
  including printers, copier systems, keyboards,
  diskettes and associated supplies.

System Products Division
Has worldwide development and U.S.
  manufacturing responsibility for small and
  intermediate-sized general purpose systems,
  robotic systems and related programming. Its
  responsibility for the IBM Personal Computer
  also includes U.S. marketing through retail
  channels.

OTHER DIVISIONS

Real Estate and Construction Division
Manages the selection and acquisition of sites,
  the design and construction of buildings and
  the purchase or lease of facilities for all IBM
  operations in the U.S. The division has
  responsibility for assessing real estate projects
  outside the U.S., as well as for IBM's
  worldwide energy and environmental
  programs. It also provides facility services
  to selected headquarters locations.

Research Division
Brings scientific understanding to bear on areas
  of company interest through basic research
  and development of technologies of potential
  long-range importance.

Source: IBM, *Annual Report*, 1982.

SUBSIDIARIES

IBM Credit Corporation
Offers term leases and finances installment
  payment agreements on IBM information-
  handling equipment in the U.S.

IBM Instruments, Inc.
Has responsibility for IBM's efforts in the
  analytical instruments field, including
  marketing and servicing selected products in
  the U.S.

Science Research Associates, Inc.
Has worldwide development, publication and
  marketing responsibility for a wide range of
  educational and testing materials, services and
  microcomputer software designed for use in
  elementary and secondary schools, colleges,
  businesses and the home.

*IBM World Trade Americas/Far East
Corporation*
With a territory extending across four continents,
  this subsidiary is responsible for IBM
  operations in 46 countries, including
  Australia, Brazil, Canada and Japan.

*IBM World Trade Europe/Middle East/Africa
Corporation*
Through its subsidiary, IBM Europe, located in
  Paris, it is responsible for IBM operations in
  85 countries.

IBM World Trade Corporation
Provides designated support to IBM World Trade
  organizational units.

EXHIBIT 2   IBM FINANCIAL DATA

GROSS INCOME BY SEGMENT††

	1981	1980	1979
	(Dollars in millions)		
Data Processing segment:			
Equipment			
Sales	$ 9,449	$ 7,627	$ 6,335
Rentals	9,660	9,591	8,846
	19,109	17,218	15,181
Maintenance contracts, program products, parts and supplies			
Sales	458	411	385
Rentals	24	25	24
Services	4,482	3,713	2,748
	4,964	4,149	3,157
	24,073	21,367	18,338
Office Products segment:			
Sales	2,245	2,183	2,084
Rentals	1,155	1,253	1,199
Services	819	699	566
	4,219	4,135	3,849
All other segments:			
Sales	749	698	669
Services	29	13	7
	778	711	676
Total	$29,070	$26,213	$22,863

†† This information should be read in conjunction with the Industry Segments notes in the annual report. Gross income from rentals includes maintenance service on rented equipment. Gross income from services consists of maintenance service on sold equipment, program products and other services.

Source: IBM, Annual Report, 1981.

EXHIBIT 2 (*Continued*)

FIVE-YEAR COMPARISON OF SELECTED FINANCIAL DATA

(*Dollars in millions except per share amounts*)

	1982	1981*	1980*	1979	1978
For the year:					
Gross income from sales,					
rentals and services	$34,364	$29,070	$26,213	$22,863	$21,076
Net earnings	4,409	3,610	3,397	3,011	3,111
Per share†	7.39	6.14	5.82	5.16	5.32
Cash dividends paid	2,053	2,023	2,008	2,008	1,685
Per share†	3.44	3.44	3.44	3.44	2.88
Investment in plant, rental					
machines and other property	6,685	6,845	6,592	5,991	4,046
Return on stockholders' equity	23.4%	21.1%	21.1%	21.2%	23.8%
At end of year:					
Total assets	$32,541	$29,107	$26,831	$24,530	$20,771
Net investment in plant, rental					
machines and other property	17,563	16,797	15,200	12,193	9,302
Working capital	4,805	2,983	3,381	4,406	4,511
Long-term debt	2,851	2,669	2,099	1,589	285
Stockholders' equity	19,960	17,676	16,578	14,961	13,494

* *Restated.*

† *Adjusted for 1979 stock split.*

Source: IBM, *Annual Report,* 1982.

EXHIBIT 2 (*Continued*) INDUSTRY SEGMENTS

	1981	1980	1979
	(*Dollars in millions*)		
Information-Handling Business:			
Data Processing			
Gross income— Customers	$24,073	$21,367	$18,338
Operating income	5,832	5,330	4,737
Assets at December 31	23,846	21,088	17,373
Depreciation expense	2,576	2,061	1,683
Capital expenditures	6,094	6,027	5,359
Office products			
Gross income— Customers	4,219	4,135	3,849
Operating income	263	479	566
Assets at December 31	3,495	3,377	3,316
Depreciation expense	306	287	275
Capital expenditures	714	537	608
Federal Systems			
Gross income— Customers	719	647	612
Operating income	56	37	35
Assets at December 31	436	371	329
Depreciation expense	16	13	11
Capital expenditures	37	27	23
Other Business			
Gross income— Customers	59	64	64
Operating income	2	3	6
Assets at December 31	32	36	39
Depreciation expense	1	1	1
Capital expenditures	—	1	1
Consolidated			
Gross income— Customers	$29,070	$26,213	$22,863
Operating income	$ 6,153	$ 5,849	$ 5,344
General corporate and interest expense	(533)	(382)	(240)
Other income, principally interest	368	430	449
Earnings before income taxes	$ 5,988	$ 5,897	$ 5,553
Assets identified to segments	$27,809	$24,872	$21,057
Assets not identified to segments, including marketable securities	1,777	1,831	3,473
Total assets at December 31	$29,586	$26,703	$24,530
Depreciation expense	$ 2,899	$ 2,362	$ 1,970
Capital expenditures	$ 6,845	$ 6,592	$ 5,991

IBM's operations, with very minor exceptions, are in the field of information-handling systems, equipment and services. However, for purposes of segment reporting, IBM's information-handling business has been reported as three segments:

Data Processing consists of information-handling products and services such as data processing machines and systems, computer programming, systems engineering, education and related services and supplies for commercial and government customers.

Office Products consists of information-handling products, systems and services such as electric and electronic typewriters, magnetic media typewriters and systems, information processors, document printers, copiers, and related supplies and services for commercial and government customers.

Federal Systems consists of specialized information-handling products and services for United States space, defense and other agencies and, in some instances, other customers.

Other Business consists of educational, training and testing materials and services for school, home and industrial use.

Intersegment transfers of products and services similar to those offered to unaffiliated customers are not material.

Source: IBM, *Annual Report*, 1981.

EXHIBIT 2 (*Continued*) CONSOLIDATED STATEMENT OF FINANCIAL POSITION AT DECEMBER 31

International Business Machines Corporation and Subsidiary Companies

	(Dollars in millions)			
	1982		1981*	
Assets				
Current Assets:				
Cash	$ 405		$ 454	
Marketable securities, at lower of cost or market	2,895		1,575	
Notes and accounts receivable-trade, less allowance:				
1982, $216; 1981, $187	4,976		4,382	
Other accounts receivable	457		410	
Inventories	3,492		2,803	
Prepaid expenses	789		685	
		$13,014		$10,309
Rental Machines and Parts	16,527		16,599	
Less: Accumulated depreciation	7,410		7,347	
		9,117		9,252
Plant and Other Property	14,240		12,702	
Less: Accumulated depreciation	5,794		5,157	
		8,446		7,545
Deferred Charges and Other Assets		1,964		2,001
		$32,541		$29,107
Liabilities and Stockholders' Equity				
Current Liabilities:				
Taxes	$ 2,854		$ 2,412	
Loans payable	529		773	
Accounts payable	983		872	
Compensation and benefits	1,959		1,556	
Deferred income	402		390	
Other accrued expenses and liabilities	1,482		1,323	
		$ 8,209		$ 7,326
Deferred Investment Tax Credits		323		252
Reserves for Employees' Indemnities and Retirement Plans .		1,198		1,184
Long-Term Debt		2,851		2,669
Stockholders' Equity:				
Capital stock, par value $1.25 per share	5,008		4,389	
Shares authorized: 750,000,000				
Issued: 1982— 602,406,128; 1981—592,293,624				
Retained earnings	16,259		13,909	
Translation adjustments	(1,307)		(622)	
		19,960		17,676
		$32,541		$29,107

The notes on pages 35 through 42 provided in the company's annual report are an integral part of this statement.

* *Restated. See Accounting Change —Foreign Currency Translation note on page 36 of annual report.*

Source: IBM, *Annual Report*, 1982.

EXHIBIT 2 *(Continued)* **GEOGRAPHIC AREAS**

	(Dollars in millions)		
	1982	*1981*	*1980*
United States			
Gross income— Customers	$19,028	$15,088	$12,426
Interarea transfers	1,875	1,857	1,615
Total	$20,903	$16,945	$14,041
Net earnings	2,766	2,094	1,725
Assets at December 31	19,028	16,022	13,737
Europe/Middle East/Africa			
Gross income— Customers	$10,260	$ 9,312	$ 9,932
Interarea transfers	337	383	491
Total	$10,597*	$ 9,695	$10,423
Net earnings	1,196	1,074	1,360
Assets at December 31	9,197	8,981	9,608
Americas/Far East			
Gross income— Customers	$ 5,076	$ 4,670	$ 3,855
Interarea transfers	651	659	450
Total	$ 5,727	$ 5,329	$ 4,305
Net earnings	450	478	388
Assets at December 31	4,925	4,694	4,054
Eliminations			
Gross income	$(2,863)	$(2,899)	$(2,556)
Net earnings	(3)	(36)	(76)
Assets	(609)	(590)	(568)
Consolidated			
Gross income	$34,364	$29,070	$26,213
Net earnings	$ 4,409	$ 3,610	$ 3,397
Assets at December 31	$32,541	$29,107	$26,831

* European operations account for some 95% of this total.

Source: IBM, *Annual Report,* 1982.

EXHIBIT 3   MARKET DATA

WORLDWIDE GENERAL-PURPOSE COMPUTER SHIPMENTS AND INSTALLED BASE—DECEMBER 1981

(U.S.-based manufacturers)

Company	1981 Shipments (Million $)	% Chg. 1980–81	Installed Base Units	Installed Base Value (Million $)
IBM	10,800	+1.4	61,109	74,560
IBM Compatible:				
Amdahl	345	−9.2	650	1,739
National	185	−2.6	702	928
Magnuson	40	+14.3	*	*
IPL	25	+150.0	*	*
Compatible peripherals	1,020	+45.7	*	*
Honeywell	1,590	+2.6	16,934	10,431
Sperry Univac	1,430	+1.4	7,255	8,346
Burroughs	1,190	+19.0	9,361	6,059
NCR	475	−1.0	7,226	2,354
Control Data	420	+5.0	1,272	3,893
Digital Equipment	165	−19.5	1,468	1,203
Cray	135	+170.0	*	*

* Insignificant.

Source: International Data Corp.

GENERAL-PURPOSE COMPUTER SHIPMENTS AND INSTALLED BASE

(U.S.-based manufacturers—in billions of dollars)

	Shipments		Installed Base	
	United States	International	United States	International
E1986	$13.7	$11.0	$68.9	$71.8
E1985	13.0	10.3	65.9	68.2
E1984	12.4	9.7	62.3	64.0
E1983	11.4	8.9	59.0	60.4
E1982	10.3	8.2	56.4	57.2
R1981	9.6	7.7	55.6	54.6
R1980	8.8	7.8	55.0	55.7
1979	7.7	7.6	52.2	45.2
1978	7.5	7.1	48.3	40.1
1977	6.6	5.9	42.9	34.8
1976	5.5	5.3	37.9	30.6
1975	5.6	5.0	33.8	27.4
1974	6.2	4.4	30.2	23.9
1973	5.4	4.0	27.3	21.4
1972	5.0	3.5	24.7	18.8

E-Estimated; R-Revised.

Source: International Data Corporation.

THE CONTINENTAL GROUP, INC.

The Continental Can Company began in 1904 in a former glass factory in Syracuse, New York. In October 1976 its name changed to the Continental Group, Inc. to reflect the shifting focus of its activities over the preceding 25 years. In 1984 its new CEO, Mr. Bruce Smart, after building Continental into a balanced and diversified giant, faced a challenge none of his predecessors had. How did Continental arrive at its current posture? And what should Mr. Smart do about the latest challenge to its existence?

PAST STRATEGIES

Coming out of World War II Continental's president, Hans Eggars, and sales vice president, Tom Fogarty, saw a need to focus on a market segment where the smaller company could distinctly surpass its larger rival, American Can Company. Recognizing an opportunity in the tin shortages of the war period, Eggars had put his research group to work to make beer cans with half the electrolytic plate then used. Customers soon got twice as many cans per pound of allocated tin as American could offer. Exploiting this innovation gave Continental the size and reputation to become an equal supplier with American in the burgeoning beer market of the post war period.

Diversification and Packaging

Continental's next CEO, General Lucius Clay, was a forceful man of great quality and integrity, who saw matters on a grand strategic scale. He set out to make Continental the largest, most

Case copyright © 1985 by James Brian Quinn. Research associate — Penny C. Paquette. The generous cooperation of the Continental Group is gratefully acknowledged.

diversified packaging company in the world, striving as he phrased it within the company's walls "to become the General Motors of packaging." According to Raymond Fisher, later chairman of Continental's Executive Committee, "Clay set out on an acquisition campaign and, lo and behold, well before the end of the fifties Continental Can *was* the largest packaging company in the world. He had a clear and simple goal the organization understood. When people got up in the morning they weren't shocked to find that something had been purchased." During this period Continental acquired its initial entries into markets for: vacuum closures for jars, blow molded polyethylene, flexible plastic packaging materials, and paper packaging products.

"We Were Just Converters"

In its can businesses, the company increasingly found itself pitted squarely against American Can Company and sandwiched between its huge suppliers and its very large customers. Said one discouraged executive, "We were just converters . . . all we did was take a little steel and roll it into little circles." Of the 3 cents a pea can cost in 1961, 2.1 cents went to the steel companies for plate. That left 0.9 cents to fabricate, package, sell, and ship the can. At the other end were the processors and brewers who operated on fractional margins for products which sold in the 100 millions to billions of units per year. These customers often played off one supplier against another with dreadful effect. To minimize the cost of shipping empty cans, both Continental and American located plants near the big buyers, making themselves even more dependent on individual customers' whims. Still, as various customers' own scales of operation grew, they were ever more tempted to make their own cans.

Innovations as basic as slitting one's own steel from coils (instead of sheets) could mean millions of dollars per year in this highly competitive field. And a rivalry approaching a vendetta developed between Continental and American. Modern technologies began to pound out containers faster than a machine gun could fire, at rates that could fill the largest warehouse in a few hours. Cans made from paper, steel, or aluminum began to compete with glass bottles, plastics, and boxes for different applications. And General Clay led Continental into all these fields before returning to public duty, to serve as Commander in Chief of Allied Forces in Berlin in early 1962.

Consolidate and Weed

In September 1961, Tom Fogarty became chief executive and immediately began to consolidate the array of businesses that Clay had acquired and to weed out (or supply new management for) the poorest performers. Mr. Hatfield, Continental's CEO from 1971–1981, later said:

> The need for consolidation was apparent. We had many businesses that were unprofitable and some that were not well managed. During Tom's leadership of the company, there was preoccupation on the can business and with the beer and soft drink markets in particular. This, as far as Mr. Fogarty was concerned, was where the company's future lay . . . his goals of consolidation or concentration. This was something he evolved in his own mind and directed, concentrating his personal energies in these areas. Major diversification into other businesses was frequently discussed, but there was a reluctance to make this a firm objective.

Mr. Fogarty concentrated efforts on the beer and soft drink sectors which were the glamour markets of that era. Mr. Fogarty was described as "more operationally oriented than General Clay had been," his leadership generated excellent financial results for the company. However, during this period the company's markets slowly began to change. As Mr. Hatfield said later, "By 1969 we were all acutely aware of the probable topping out of the beverage market. Self manufacture was in the minds of most of the large buyers. And the two piece can brought new competition with it—Reynolds, Coors, and others."

The Hazard Era

When E.L. ("Hap") Hazard became chairman in January 1969, Mr. Fogarty's emphasis on financial performance had limited investment in paper and forest products where returns were inherently longer term. The company had become heavily dependent on the maturing market for beverage cans, and lighter weight two piece cans were replacing the 3 piece cans on which Continental's capital had been concentrated. On the other hand, the company was cash rich and had a low D/E ratio of only .2 to 1. The linchpins of the Hazard strategy were outlined in a meeting at Phoenix, Arizona, soon after he took office. These were: (1) an improved overseas presence through acquisitions, (2) rebalancing the company's investment mix toward non-metallic containers and forest products, (3) longer term investments in R&D and woodlands, and (4) the Conoweld beverage program (installing new welded Continental lines directly in user-owned plants) to extend the life of the beer and beverage can industry.

Despite the tumult of inner city fires and riots, a conscious decision was made to keep the R&D facility in a run-down area of Chicago to provide jobs there and to demonstrate the company's commitment to the city where its Metals Group was headquartered. With the same long term view Hazard undertook a study of whether to move Continental's headquarters to Westchester County or Connecticut and thus equalize the access of all Continental's operating groups to top management. As another key activity Mr. Charles Stauffacher, Continental's Chief Financial and Administrative Officer, began to look for some very large acquisitions to help rebalance the company's risk portfolio. But as Mr. Hatfield later noted:

I can't say that goals for the acquisition program were spelled out so the organization understood them. . . . Some good sized companies did surface as possible combinations during this period. But it finally came down to the point that the Board wasn't really sympathetic. There was a natural inbred reluctance to contaminate this fine company with anything not allied to the packaging business. So we never really took an aggressive run at them.

THE SPRING FOR EUROPE

Continental had sold technology to European can groups ever since the 1930s. And in a dramatic move at the end of World War II, a Continental executive appeared at these European licensees' doors less than six weeks after the armistice to offer them the technology they had missed for some five years.[1] Through such actions Continental built close personal and business relationships with its European businesses over the years. Continental had licensing agreements with 51 companies and minority interests in 33 companies operating in some 100 countries worldwide. And by the end of the 1960s many of these had become major forces in their individual countries' can industries. Metal Box in Britain was the third largest can company in the world; Schmallbach-Lubeca-Werke (Germany), Carnaud (France), Sabigny (Belgium) and Thomassen & Drijver in Holland were among the strongest companies in their domestic markets. But through the 1960s Continental had invested in them only by invitation.

In a series of moves Continental formed a wholly owned subsidiary, Europemballage, for integrated management of its European operations—Schmallbach (86% owned) and Thomassen & Drijver (91% owned). Carnaud dropped out when a majority stockholder, a French steel company, objected that the takeover would violate the chauvanistic terms of its loan from the French government. Other diversification activities—like Tee Pak (sausage casings), Essco Stamping Products and SKD Manufacturing (both auto parts)

of Canada and expansion of Continental's Canadian operations— complemented these international moves in 1970 –71. Along with other acquisitions in Mexico and expansion of its interests in South America, Continental's international operations grew to 25% of the business in 1971.

Paper Expansion

In the Fogarty era Paper Products had not been heavily supported, with the exception of an expansion of the Augusta mill originally built during General Clay's regime. Recognizing a serious situation developing in the rest of the operation, Bruce Smart, then Assistant General Manager of the Paper Products Group, prepared a Long Range Plan to revitalize the business. But paper is extremely capital intensive. And the demands for funds far exceeded anything members of top management had been used to.

Smart recalls, "I remember presenting that Plan and being shocked by Mr. Fogarty's adverse reaction. It was one of the most vivid experiences of my life because I had got the whole Paper organization behind the Plan. Then, at the formal presentation, he reacted very negatively because of the capital implications. I became aware that the financial dynamics of business varied and that when you were running one unfamiliar to your management you needed to educate before you could sell a key program."

Later, competitors expanded—using capital available through cheap southern industrial development bonds. Continental did not. Many of its best managers left to go to other paper companies "where the action was." While Continental held 1.5 million acres of timberland at a book value of some $66 million and a market value of about $300 million, Paper Products' processing capacity was inefficient and rundown. Smart brought in a new group of young managers and concentrated on reviving the least efficient operations (at Hodge, Louisiana). They chose a $100 million expansion and modernization program over a possible $50 million upgrading of the mill. "We designed this big project and took it to the board. By that time Hazard was in charge. He was conditioned to the fact that we had to stay in the Paper business because he could see the signs of aging in beer cans. And it took 15 minutes to get the project approved."

Mr. Hatfield later said of the European and Forest Products decisions:

> These two moves were independent, logical extensions of what we were doing. Hap, Charlie Stauffacher, and I informally discussed how the resources emanating from the Fogarty era could best be invested to broaden the base of the business. We decided to build on the company's strengths and moved forward again on a very predictable course. I can't say this was a formally planned course. But there wasn't any question in anyone's mind what we were up to.
>
> The more formal planning we were going through at that time did prompt some action. For example, a goal (of $125 to $150 million in revenues) was established to diversify the company in the Housewares market. We consolidated the Glassware business left over from Hazel-Atlas, Bondware (paper plates and cups), and a pantry kitchenware line called Decoware. And we bought a couple of small specialty houseware companies. All these moves proved (which was a valuable lesson) that we did not know how to manage such consumer-oriented businesses, and ultimately we got out of them.

THE HATFIELD ERA BEGINS

In 1971 Mr. Hazard was stricken by a serious illness which forced him to retire. He was succeeded by Robert Hatfield as chairman and CEO. About this time, can demand softened, Paper Products was crippled by oversupply, and the European activity was attacked by the European Economic Commission for its "dominant position in cans for meat, fish, seafood, and caps for glass bottles.[1] In its decision the European Court of Justice exonerated Continental of any wrongdoing, but virtually rewrote Article 86 of the Treaty of Rome to prohibit other corporate actions that might endanger effective competition. Continental was essentially barred from creating the European-wide packaging subsidiary it had once envisioned.

A Metals Strategy

Simultaneously, the domestic can business reached a critical stage. Attacks from conservationists and legislative threats to outlaw non-returnable containers escalated. The beverage market switched to two-piece aluminum cans.[3] And food processors, soft drink manufacturers, and brewers began increasingly to make their own cans. The company moved decisively to shift its investment patterns. Mr. Hatfield said:

> During this period, there was no long-range planning. The immediate task seemed quite clear. The domestic can company facilities had to be rationalized on an urgent time schedule, papermaking and converting facilities had to be brought to competitive positions in cost and product quality, and the efforts of the European can business redirected to the profit motive. After a nine-month study and appraisal, we reached the agonizing conclusion there was no choice but to take a major writeoff.
>
> It was obvious that the job of rationalizing the company's canmaking facilities in keeping with the realities of the marketplace would be frightfully expensive and at best a 3 to 5 year job with enormous dislocation of people and continuing impact on company earnings over this period. To expect the managers of this division to absorb such losses on a year-to-year basis and retain their enthusiasm seemed unrealistic. Having reached this conclusion, [in 1972] we took a one-time $190 million charge against pretax profits to "redo" the can company. And, while we were at it, another $40 million was charged off to cover costs of rationalizing other company facilities.

But a realistic new strategy for the cans activity (now called Metals Group) was not easy. Bruce Smart noted:

We had a devil of a time getting the can business in the U.S. to recognize its maturity, because this was perceived by its management to be an unacceptable situation. . . . This created a number of debates between New York's Corporate Headquarters and Chicago's Metal's headquarters and most specifically between Metals and Hayford (then Financial V.P.) over what was a proper direction for that business. The culmination was a change in management at the division level.

With a younger leadership now under Warren Hayford and Donald Bainton, Domestic Metals began to turn toward cash generation. But maintaining its pride was a difficult task. Later Hayford said, "I didn't care how big we were as long as we were the most profitable company in the field. Once we were most profitable, we'd grow as fast as we could while maintaining that status." Hayford began to discuss this theme with a number of executives and to push the concept of Return on Net Assets (RONA) in informal conversations. He then started a series of analyses, "white papers," to generate discussion on the implications and means of "working assets harder."

Hayford's management group tried to define what performance levels would rank them as "best" in their industry. Slowly it emerged that Crown Cork and Seal repeatedly provided a challenging but realistic performance measure for what could be done. Hayford then established periodic reviews in which his management compared its performance to Crown's and tried to define what was needed to move up to that standard. Hayford said that three policies made the crucial difference: (1) Only one person was to be in charge of each Metals operation, (2) Metals had to outperform Crown Cork and Seal, (3) Managing the group had to be fun. He quickly moved to instill the same concepts in Hatfield's and his subordinates' minds.

Richard Hofmann, later president of the Continental Can Company, said:

Bainton (head of the U.S. can business) determined that the Metals Group did not have a "meaningful competitive advantage." From numerous environmental analyses they also discovered that overhead (fixed costs) varied with net assets. Bainton then determined to force his operating managers to drop assets down. To accomplish this, he encouraged them to project a fall in physical sales. Based on this, assets were shut down or spun out. Then costs genuinely did drop and profits boomed as the lower volume expectations were exceeded.

Hayford said:

You can't run a shrink business on a centralized basis. . . . So we started decentralizing everything down the line. The first thing Bainton did was to cut 25% of his population at headquarters. This was a bigger cut than anyone else took, which made it difficult for anyone else to debate cutting back. . . . Then we got Continental Can USA to come in with an alternative domestic strategy with a 30 million base box goal instead of the 36 million projected. When they saw what the cutback could do for profits they discarded the larger alternative and management approved the lower target. . . . We got lucky. We had a damn good year in 1976 in the market place, and everyone thought our divisional management walked on water. This was great. It meant that the change was dramatic, immediate, and observable. If we'd had a bad year it would have been harder to get the tremendous momentum needed behind the move.

Reinvestment Strategies

As Metals began to generate cash flows, funds became available for other activities. Mr. Smart's new management group now in power drew up a plan to invest some $700 million in Forest Products to utilize its full potentials and to bring better balance to the corporation's total portfolio. Mr. Smart, himself, was in the President's Office, and funds began to flow toward Forest Products. Said Mr. Hatfield:

In capital intensive businesses during a period of heavy investment, the return on total corporate assets is adversely impacted. Our decision to invest in the paper business had the objective of developing a longer-term resource-based diversification for the company. With the other investment programs being undertaken, some financial creativity was required.

Diversified products was another area of investment. Tee Pak (sausage casings) was added to the old Plastics and Closures group, and "Diversified Industries" became a viable third leg for the total operation. This included White Cap (bottle tops), Plastic Containers (plastic bottles), Flexible Packaging (sheet and vacuum sealed plastic wrapping) and Tee Pak. By March 1975 *Business Week* reported Mr. Hatfield as saying, "We're looking to increase the diversity of our business and to broaden our product lines. . . . The biggest challenge is to find the right segments, the right companies, the right time."[2]

Mr. Kenneth Michel, head of Diversified Industries, described how his strategy emerged in this area.

We started analyzing what our strengths and weaknesses were and defining what businesses we were in. We spent almost a year pushing different definitions around. No special categories of businesses fit perfectly, while screening out others that weren't logical and wouldn't fit. We kept coming back to something more basic. Our strategy became to determine how to get a "leg-up" on competition and how to exploit it. If we couldn't get a leg-up we thought in terms of divestiture. To enter a business we had several criteria. It had to be a business we could *understand*, one we could *control*, one that could *hedge* our earnings, and one that would *increase* our earnings. Any business which fit these criteria, we'd be interested in.

Later Diversified Industries came in to the Board with a $30 million acquisition that met its criteria. There was a "mental agreement" with the seller. The price was set. All the homework had been done. But a key board member said, "That's not packaging, it doesn't fit" and got up in arms. According to another person present, "He [fought hard] enough that we decided to turn it down, which was a mistake. Its income the following year was $30 million . . . Today the receptiveness at the top level and the board would be different . . . I don't think they'd ever been persuasively asked to purchase a company outside the packaging field before. It took a little reflecting [at the Board level] on where we were and where we should be."

By the late 1970s Diversified Industries enjoyed some of the most profitable lines in the Continental portfolio and was in a strong net investment (negative cash flow) position. Mr. Michel said:

We did have a five year out "look-see" as to what sales, income, capital requirements, RONA, and cash flow as a group was going to be. That was spelled out from the group to the corporation, and the corporation, of course, had a right to reject it. . . . We in essence set our own goals as to sales, income, and returns about two years ahead, but soon saw we would far exceed them. I think our real goal was to exploit our opportunities to the best of our ability. [Because of this] the fact that we set goals where we did I don't think caused people to make any different decisions. . . . We didn't know what the problems would be. It's illogical to pin a number where you might trip over yourself to get there if you set it too high. And if you set it too low, you're not going to exploit that business to the extent you're capable of. I don't think we're smart enough to stick with specific numbers in an explosive business.

A DIVERSIFICATION STRATEGY

Although there were some acquisitions in the Diversified Industries area, most of the investment action and management focus continued to be packaging oriented. Said Mr. Hofmann:

Over a long period of time there developed a management consensus to diversify, but not where to diversify. Sometime in the mid 1970s, Hatfield came to the conclusion that positive action on diversification was necessary—i.e. a fourth leg was needed. This was much in mind when he hired Donahue from Amax.

Mr. Donahue came on board in 1975 as vice chairman and chief financial officer after building a reputation as the creative deal maker in Amax's rapid expansion. A number of potential large acquisitions were considered by Donahue, Smart, and Hatfield. The planning group participated by breaking down all existing product lines into a matrix with the x axis reading "embryonic, growth, maturing, aging, total;" the y axis calibrating taxable earnings as: "strong, constant, or troubled." They asked Mr. Smart to review this analysis and to estimate where the company would probably be in 1981. Then they tried to provide scenarios for other possibilities. The Chief Planner of that era said "Planning tried to organize the guys who had to make decisions, give them enough information to put their hands on, and find out what they did and didn't react well to." Several very large companies in such diverse areas as natural resources, energy, and insurance were tried on for size and fit. Acquisition of any one of these multibillion dollar companies would have preempted the purchase of the other. And each fitted some rationale as a "fourth leg for the stool" of Continental's stability and future growth.

One of the key managers in this process said:

> Hatfield didn't want to announce goals or strategies. He operated with good people around him. He wanted to listen to them. He melded the views of 5–6 outstanding people. He could get them to come out with a unified, coherent, view. Hatfield only announced "motherhood" goals—"We are a decent company. We don't play dirty football." These became common phrases around the company. He opened by putting forward consensus,

a RONA target of 20%, for example. But he left unsaid when and how this would be met.

Richmond Corporation

When Lazard Freres brokerage firm first brought Richmond Corporation (a $1.1 billion life, title, and casualty insurer) to his attention, Donahue was reportedly cool to the idea, "It certainly wasn't one of our priority areas . . . but the more I thought about it, the more I became convinced that Richmond was the best means of achieving a broader capital base." Mr. Smart perhaps best summarized top management's viewpoint when he said, "I think the growth of any company is best measured by the rate at which it adds to its equity base. Growth is not necessarily some hot new product."[3] The Richmond acquisition was closed in mid 1977 and consolidated with other insurance and real estate activities into Continental's Financial Services organization.

Florida Gas Company

In 1979 Continental made its next major diversifying acquisition, Florida Gas Company, for some $351 million. Various components of this unit, which became Continental Resources Company (CRC), participated in different aspects of the energy field. Florida Exploration had five divisions engaged in exploration, development, and production of oil and gas. Florida Gas Transmission Co. operated an interstate natural gas pipeline system extending from the Texas-Mexico border to the southern tip of Florida. Another unit extracted and sold propane, butane, and natural gasoline. Prior to the acquisition Continental had working interests in offshore and onshore gas and oil properties in the Gulf of Mexico and Mississippi. These were merged into Florida Exploration Company.

Florida Gas Transmission Co. was the sole supplier of natural gas to peninsular Florida and was one of only six U.S. companies selected by PEMEX to purchase gas from that prime source. CRC was investigating several major projects including a 1500 mile slurry pipeline that would transport coal from Eastern Appalachia and the Illinois basin to the Southeast. If approved, this project would call for $2–$3 billion in financing over several years.

NEW STRATEGIES FOR THE 1980s

As the 1980s began, the Continental Group's *Annual Report* offered a concise summary of a decade of change:

> . . . The decade just passed was probably the most eventful in Continental's history. But looking back from the perspective of 1980 it may be a bit difficult to remember the way things were for Continental 10 years ago. Known then as Continental Can, the Company was primarily a domestic can maker. It ended 1969 with earnings of $3.18 per share on sales that were just approaching $2 billion mark.
>
> Continental is still the world's largest diversified packaging company, but now its horizon has broadened to include major interests in financial services and energy, with a new emphasis on natural resources. . . . The upshot of these evolutionary changes is a distribution of earnings contribution as follows: Can Company, 41%; Forest Industries, 19%; Diversified Businesses, 10%; Financial Services, 24%; and Continental Resources Company, 6% (representing only four full months of operation).
>
> . . . The number of employees has actually decreased, down from the 1970 total by 10,000 people to a current payroll of 62,000 and the percentage of sales representing overseas operations is up to 31%, also a major change from 16% a decade ago. . . .

When Mr. Bruce Smart took over from Mr. Hatfield as chairman and CEO, he outlined his goals for Continental in its *1981 Annual Report*:

> (1) to reduce holdings in operations that fall short of performance goals or do not

fit the long-term strategy of the company; a target of realizing $400–500 million from such assets was established, (2) to reinvest these funds in areas promising profitable growth, principally in energy, (3) to improve return on equity over the long term as a consequence of this reinvestment strategy, and (4) to strengthen Continental Group's balance sheet and credit standing.

Divestitures

Continental purposely set out to sell certain businesses and to reduce its equity positions abroad. It took time and effort to find the right buyers and get the highest price possible. Although its original goal was to raise $400–500 million for redeployment, Continental eventually exceeded that goal. It accepted Stone Container's offer to purchase its Brown System mills. Many of these had recently been upgraded and made energy efficient, but Continental had no real competitive edge in this segment of Forest Industries. The sale involved the assumption by Stone Container of some $120 million of debt associated with the divested businesses. More than $100 million of the cash received was used to retire long term debt, significantly reducing the company's interest costs and improving its fixed obligation ratio. Another $220 million of the proceeds went to repurchase 4.6 million shares of common stock, or 14% of those outstanding, at $48 per share further increasing earnings per share and strengthening the balance sheet.

The following table[4] outlines operations sold during this period of "redeployment." The company was committed to "achieving self-sufficiency in each of its subsidiary businesses. Performance in subsidiaries was measured by return on assets, further encouraging management to implement small scale asset redeployment within their segments."[5]

By 1984 these funds were redeployed into Continental's four main business groups, resulting in the strong and balanced 1984 portfolio described below. Chairman Smart stated in the

Operation Divested	Gross Proceeds	After-tax Gain (Loss)
	($ millions)	
1981		
Teepak, Inc.	112	2
Canadian Paper Products	50	(2)
Other (including Morton G. Thalhimer—real estate brokerage)	39	16
	201	16
1982		
Containers Ltd. of Australia (20% equity interest)	45	13
Insurance Management Corp.	17	7
Other	16	8
	78	28
1983		
Brown System	525	80
Canadian Packaging	133	25
Plastic Beverage Bottle	31	(6)
Other	39	(8)
	728	91
	$1,007	$135

1983 Annual Report that Continental was ready to move on to a new phase:

> Our primary task is now the efficient production of quality goods and services within our restructured business competences—packaging, forest products, insurance, and energy. . . . Our overall strategy is to achieve the competitive advantages that can result from increased productivity, market focus, and innovation.

Packaging

In December 1983, Continental Packaging Company had been reorganized to facilitate a new strategy stressing market rather than product orientation. As Mr. Smart then told *New England Business*:

> We will start to look at our franchise not as the manufacture of blow-molded bottles, or two-piece aluminum cans, but as our relationship with the big package group marketers. Hitching Packaging's wagon to big customers like General Foods makes more sense than latching on to a particular technology or shape or structure that will inevitably change.[6]

The new organization operated in three major markets: Food and Beverage, Specialty Packaging, and International. Its cost reduction and productivity programs included closing a number of plants which were unable to meet long term profitability standards, while improving capacity utilization and line efficiencies at other facilities. Basic research expenditures were reduced and emphasis directed towards business development and marketing. Continental Packaging had a major position in the fastest growing segment of the can industry—the two-piece aluminum can. However, the near term results of the packaging business would be determined by: (1) the success of new product introductions, (2) continued emphasis on cost-cutting even after demand reaccelerated, and (3) whether or not metal cans would be besieged by another fundamental change in design.[4]

Forest Products

Smart had told the *Wall Street Journal* at the time of the Brown System sale:

> Our forest products business will be reduced in scale but will now be made up of specialty businesses in which we have world class and to some extent proprietary positions backed by a natural resource of immense and growing value.[7]

Continental was the world's largest producer of bleached folding carton board and ranked fourth in total production of bleached paperboard. Its modern bleached paperboard plant in Georgia had an annual capacity of 430,000 tons and was valued at more than $500 million.[8] It was also a major factor in the production of fiber drums with 12 plants. And it still owned 1.45 million acres of timberland located in the Southeast (of which 868,000 acres were in pine plantation targeted for continuing harvest beginning in 1988), carried on the books at $115 million but with a market value (conservatively) of at least $400 million.[9] Continental's *1983 Annual Report* noted that the timberland which previously supplied the Brown System mills could now be managed as a non-integrated profit center. Forest Products' activities were balanced as follows:[10]

Fibre Drum	25%	Fibre drum shipping containers, steel drums, plastic pails, laminator paper, fibre partition and DualPak (polyethylene bottle in corrugated box) for the chemical, pharmaceutical, plastic, food and other industries.
Bleach System	46%	Bleached folding carton grades for folding carton manufacturers; Coated bleached bristols and cover stock for the domestic and international printing industry; and cup and other stock for the food service industry.
Woodlands	29%	Wood raw materials for paper mills and sawmills.

Financial Services

The Financial Services group had benefited substantially from the early 1980s redeployment program. In early 1981 Continental acquired Investors Mortgage Insurance Company for $85.8 million. The company along with Lawyers Title Insurance Company and Continental Land Title Company formed a core in the real estate-related financial services area. Then in mid 1983 American Agency Life Insurance Company, with its 49 master brokerage general agents and 13,000 independent brokers and agents, was acquired for $32 million, further extending Continental's distribution system for Life of Virginia's successful universal life products. In 1984, Continental Financial Services underwrote insurance in three broad segments: life, real estate, and property and casualty insurance.

Life of Virginia's traditional markets in the Southeast and Midwest had been extended through a network of independent brokers and the acquisition of American Agency. Its universal life policy, the Challenger, had achieved rapid acceptance but was being tested as large competitors introduced their own versions of the plan.

Lawyers Title Insurance, the nation's third largest title insurance company, had concentrated on a broad independent agency network while stimulating productivity through special incentive programs. Investors Mortgage Insurance Company had been quite successful in facilitating innovative mortgage financing and in decentralizing its sales force and operational responsibilities toward local levels.

Western Employers Insurance concentrated on underwriting workers' compensation coverage, but had recently expanded geographically into the Northeast and Southwest and had established a division to sell Directors and Officers, Errors and Omissions, and other related coverages.

Chairman Smart described the Insurance segment as:

> A surprisingly nimble and successful middleweight in the industry. There is no way our insurance division will ever be all things to all people in the sense of a Metropolitan or Prudential. . . . It has to pick its spots geographically, marketwise and productwise and win by wit and innovation.[6]

Energy

The bulk of Continental's redeployment in the early 1980s had been into energy. The company had joined with Shell and Mobil in the construction of a 502 mile carbon dioxide pipeline in which the company had a 13% interest, had begun to convert an 890 mile segment of its 4,300 mile natural gas pipeline to petroleum products (while maintaining its natural gas deliveries to the Florida market), and had participated in four major offshore natural gas pipeline projects in the Gulf of Mexico to connect into the Florida Gas Transmission system.

In Exploration and Production, Continental undertook a joint acquisition (with Applied Corporation) of Supron Energy Corp. at a cost of more than $400 million. This acquisition increased the company's proved reserves of oil and gas by approximately 180% and its undeveloped acreage by 50%. Supron's emphasis on development drilling also complemented Florida Exploration's activities and strengthened its position in domestic natural gas.[11] In joint ventures with Shell Oil, Continental acquired additional offshore leases and participated in extensive exploratory drilling activities. In 1981 it spent some $225 million on exploration, but in 1983, due to changed energy prices, Continental was concentrating more on development of known resources.

Concerning Continental's Energy business, Mr. Smart said:

> Although the company is a baby next to the industry giants, it dominates in the market segments it has chosen to exploit. It is the largest supplier of energy to the State of Florida, one of the nation's fastest growing states. When you're small you've got to focus and that's what we're trying to do in oil and gas.[6]

The company's pipeline operations offered a strong cash flow at relatively low risk, facilitating the expansion of other energy activities that were currently balanced between offshore exploration and development through Unicon Production Company (the operating company for the joint Allied and Continental Supron Energy acquisition).[4] Further details on Continental's posture are contained in the attached operating and financial statements.

SIR JAMES AND THE DEVOURING DRAGON

Just as Continental's long sought goals of balance and competitiveness seemed within reach, a new jolt appeared from out of the blue. In early June,

1984, Sir James Goldsmith, a British financier, offered to buy Continental for about $2.1 billion in cash or $50 per share. Earlier, Goldsmith had made a bid for St. Regis Paper Co. and had lost out to another suitor, but only after realizing a $50 million personal profit in a month's time. Sir James' major American holdings in 1984 included the Grand Union Company (supermarkets) and Diamond International (forest products). He said that he wanted to increase his U.S. holdings and that a diversified company like Continental would be ideal. Analysts thought Continental's 1984 earnings would be up 20–30% over 1983. But the $50 per share offer (on June 6th) contrasted sharply with the stock's price on June 1st of $34 and its book value of $38.75. Although Sir James said that he hoped Continental's management would stay on to manage the company and that he would "leave the company largely intact," *Wall Street Journal* reported management was "adamantly opposed" to the takeover—which at that time would have been the largest private acquisition of a public company in history.[12]

When he made his takeover bid for Continental, Sir James Goldsmith (51) had an intricate web of investments both in the United States and in Europe. The son of a French mother and an English father, he dropped out of Eton at 16 and started an ill-fated pharmaceutical company in France. At 20 he eloped with an heiress to a Bolivian tin fortune and by 1964 he was in England starting to build Cavenham, Ltd., his main British holding company which was primarily in foods and publishing. During the 1970s Sir James shifted control of Cavenham to Occidentale in France and began his moves into the United States—prompted at least in part by Europe's drift towards socialism. In 1973 he purchased Grand Union, the seventh largest U.S. supermarket chain and concentrated on revamping that languishing enterprise.[13]

Then in the late 1970s he began the process of buying Diamond International Corporation, a wood, pulp, and paper firm. By 1980 he held 5% of Diamond and made a tender offer for up to 40% of its shares. The Board, knowing Sir James had a good chance of getting the 40%, negotiated a standstill agreement that prevented him from buying more than that for five years in exchange for seats on Diamond's Board. But the U.S. housing slump changed the situation; and by December 1981, with Diamond's profits at only a third of their 1979 level, the Board was prepared to recommend selling out for $44.50 a share. A year later, in December 1982, Sir James took the company private having financed the purchase by borrowing against the company's own assets. Many of Diamond's divisions were readily saleable and Sir James quickly began the process of dismembering the company to pay off his own and the corporation's debt. By early 1984, basically all that remained of what had been Diamond International was 1.7 million acres of timberland held by Diamond Land, Inc. which had an estimated value of over $700 million.[13] (See Exhibit 2 outlining the break-up of Diamond International.)

Exhibit 3 shows the complexity of Sir James' empire. While his businesses used to be concentrated in Britain and on the Continent, 70 to 80% of his holdings were now in the U.S. Generale Occidentale— Goldsmith's French holding company for Grand Union, Groupe Express (publishing) and his oil venture— earned approximately $29 million on sales of $3 billion in 1983. Basic Resources International was a joint oil-exploration venture with the French and Spanish governments whose Guatemalan oil fields had produced little but strife.[14] In June 1984 financial sources in London maintained that Sir James "owned less than 1% of Continental" and was "highly unlikely" to resort to "greenmail" or to swap any stock he might acquire in Continental for any of Continental's properties.[15]

QUESTIONS

1. Evaluate Continental's past strategies and current strategic posture. What other actions should it have taken in the past? When? Why?
2. What issues does Sir James' offer pose for Continental's management? For other companies' managers? What are management's main strategic options in June 1984?
3. What specific actions does each call for?
4. What should management do? Why?

EXHIBIT 1 FINANCIAL AND OPERATING STATISTICS

CONTINENTAL GROUP: FINANCIAL STATISTICS 1955 to 1983

($ millions)

	'55	'57	'59	'61	'63	'65	'67	'69	'71	'73	'75	'77	'79	'81	'83
OPERATING REVENUES	929.4	1,046.3	1,146.5	1,153.3	1,154.0	1,225.6	1,397.6	1,780.0	2,081.6	2,539.7	3,101.9	3,660.9	4,510.9	5,194.4	4,820
GROSS MARGIN	148.5	149.6	150.8	154.9	171.4	207.8	245.5	312.8	306.9	374.7	396.1	462.4	540.0	650.4	446
NET (AFTER TAX) PROFIT	38.7	41.0	40.0	36.1	40.1	59.2	78.1	90.4	72.9	97.0	107.2	143.8	184.6	234.0	199
TOTAL ASSETS	568.9	664.1	750.7	788.5	811.9	920.9	1,012.6	1,199.5	1,571.1	1,776.9	1,963.1	2,723.8	3,595.3	4,135.9	3,653
LT DEBT/EQUITY	.33	.34	.32	.39	.35	.30	.24	.24	.39	.50	.45	.40	.69	.53	.48
RETURN ON SALES	4.2	3.9	3.5	3.1	3.5	4.8	5.6	5.1	3.5	3.8	3.5	3.9	4.1	4.5	4.1
RETURN ON ASSETS	6.8	6.2	5.3	4.6	4.9	6.4	7.7	7.5	4.6	5.5	5.5	5.3	5.1	5.7	5.4
RETURN ON EQUITY	10.9	10.4	8.9	7.8	8.2	11.3	12.8	12.9	9.3	13.1	12.4	11.2	14.6	14.9	13
SHARE PRICE (Hi-Low)	$29\frac{1}{2}$–24	32–$25\frac{1}{4}$	39–$29\frac{1}{4}$	$32\frac{1}{2}$–$23\frac{1}{4}$	32–$27\frac{1}{8}$	$42\frac{1}{4}$–$32\frac{1}{4}$	$40\frac{5}{8}$–$27\frac{1}{4}$	$52\frac{1}{8}$–$41\frac{3}{8}$	$45\frac{1}{4}$–$26\frac{1}{8}$	$30\frac{7}{8}$–$19\frac{1}{2}$	$29\frac{5}{8}$–$22\frac{5}{8}$	$37\frac{3}{8}$–$30\frac{1}{4}$	$31\frac{7}{8}$–$25\frac{5}{8}$	$40\frac{1}{2}$–$30\frac{1}{4}$	$54\frac{1}{2}$–$32\frac{3}{4}$

Note: *Share Prices adjusted for 100% stock dividend in 1956 and 3 for 2 splits in 1966 and 1970.*

Source: Data drawn from various years of *Moody's Industrial Manual.*

EXHIBIT 1 (*Continued*)

THE CONTINENTAL GROUP, INC. STATEMENT OF CONSOLIDATED EARNINGS

(*in millions, except per share amounts*)

Years Ended December 31	*1983*	*1982*	*1981*
Revenues	**$4,820**	$5,012	$5,194
Other Income	**122**	77	97
	4,942	5,089	5,291
Costs and Expenses			
Cost of goods sold and operating charges	**4,374**	4,427	4,544
Selling and administrative	**309**	323	380
Research and development	**29**	28	41
Interest	**108**	135	123
Interest capitalized	**(30)**	(41)	(26)
Gain on debt retirements	**(5)**	—	(25)
	4,785	4,872	5,037
Earnings Before Income Taxes and Insurance Operations	**157**	217	254
Provision for Income Taxes	**17**	87	69
Earnings Before Insurance Operations	**140**	130	185
Equity Earnings of Insurance Operations	**59**	50	49
Net Earnings	**199**	180	234
Dividends on preferred and preference shares	**23**	23	25
Net earnings applicable to common shares	**$ 176**	$ 157	$ 209
Net Earnings Per Common Share[*]	**$ 3.66**	$ 3.20	$ 4.24

[*] *Restated for three-for-two stock split. See Statement of Significant Accounting Policies and Notes to Financial Statements provided in company's annual report.*

Source: The Continental Group, Inc., *Annual Report*, 1983.

EXHIBIT 1 (*Continued*)

FIVE YEAR SUMMARY

(*dollars in millions, except per share amounts*)

	1983	1982	1981	1980	1979
Results of Operations					
Revenues	**$4,820**	$5,012	$5,194	$5,120	$4,511
Net earnings	**199**	180	234	200	185
Per common share*					
Net earnings	**3.66**	3.20	4.24	3.57	3.42
Dividends	**1.73**	1.73	1.67	1.60	1.50
Financial Position at Year End					
Current assets	**$1,040**	$1,045	$1,249	$1,223	$1,238
Total assets	**3,653**	4,199	4,135	4,086	4,030
Current liabilities	**732**	778	835	870	844
Long-term debt	**726**	1,006	961	962	995
Redeemable preference shares	**249**	275	281	296	296
Common stockholders' equity per share*	**35.99**	33.19	31.87	30.16	28.70
Common shares outstanding (in thousands)	**42,428**	48,940	49,187	49,222	48,990
After-tax return on average common stockholders' equity**	**11.5%**	10.6%	15.0%	13.7%	14.1%
Number of Employees at Year End	**39,700**	46,900	51,400	56,700	59,800

* Restated for three-for-two stock split. In January 1984 Continental Group announced a three-for-two stock split which is reflected in all per share data. Net earnings were $3.66, $3.20 and $4.24 per share in 1983, 1982 and 1981, respectively. Significant asset sales and other major one-time events contributed $.50, $.49 and $53 per share during each of the three years.

** Computed excluding accumulated net unrealized investment gains and foreign currency adjustments from common stockholders' equity.

Source: The Continental Group, Inc., *Annual Report*, 1983.

EXHIBIT 1 (*Continued*)

CONSOLIDATED BALANCE SHEET (in millions)

December 31	1983	1982
Assets		
Current Assets		
Cash	$ 176	$ 66
Receivables	477	540
Inventories, at LIFO cost		
Current cost	642	756
Excess over LIFO cost	(332)	(384)
	310	372
Deferred income taxes and other assets	77	67
	1,040	1,045
Investments and Advances		
Insurance Operations	581	548
Unicon Producing Company	181	154
Other	98	166
	860	868
Property, Plant, and Equipment, at cost		
Buildings and equipment	1,909	2,716
Accumulated depreciation	(1,092)	(1,422)
	817	1,294
Oil and gas properties, net	576	624
Timberlands, net of timber harvested	138	114
Construction in progress	55	72
Land	17	20
	1,603	2,124
Other Assets	150	162
	$3,653	$4,199

Liabilities and Equity	1983	1982
Current Liabilities		
Accounts payable	$ 372	$ 365
Short-term debt	29	32
Taxes payable	36	74
Accrued payrolls and employee benefits	174	160
Other	121	147
	732	778
Long-Term Debt, less current portion	726	1,006
Other Liabilities		
Retirement benefits	276	258
Deferred income taxes	56	162
Other	82	91
	414	511
Redeemable Preference Shares	249	275
Preferred and Common Stockholders' Equity		
$4.25 cumulative preferred stock	5	5
Common stock (issued: 1983— 49,239,000 shares; 1982— 48,940,000 shares adjusted for three-for-two stock split)	49	33
Paid-in surplus	343	347
Common stock in treasury	(219)	—
Net unrealized investment gains	72	40
Foreign currency adjustments	39	55
Retained earnings	1,243	1,149
	1,532	1,629
	$3,653	$4,199

See Statement of Significant Accounting Policies and Notes to Financial Statements provided in Company's Annual Report.

Source: The Continental Group, Inc., Annual Report, 1983.

EXHIBIT 1 (*Continued*)

SEGMENT EARNINGS (in millions)

Years Ended December 31	Packaging	Forest Products	Insurance	Energy — Pipeline Operations	Energy — Exploration & Production	Divested Operations	Combined
1983							
Revenues	$2,885	$517	$702	$722	$90*	$ 606	$5,522
Operating and equity earnings	$ 140	$ 41	$ 69	$ 77	$ 18	$ —	$ 345
Disposals/writedowns	(20)	—	—	—	(95)	111	(4)
Corporate expense	(19)	(4)	(3)	(4)	(2)	(3)	(35)
Realized investment gains, net of tax	—	—	8	—	—	—	8
Segment earnings	$ 101	$ 37	$ 74	$ 73	$(79)	$ 108	$ 314
1982							
Revenues	$2,882	$466	$575	$691	$80*	$ 903	$5,597
Operating and equity earnings	$ 114	$ 41	$ 59	$ 92	$ 19	$ 14	$ 339
Disposals/writedowns	—	—	—	—	—	52	52
Corporate expense	(20)	(5)	(3)	(3)	(1)	(8)	(40)
Realized investment gains, net of tax	—	—	—	—	—	—	—
Segment earnings	$ 94	$ 36	$ 56	$ 89	$ 18	$ 58	$ 351
1981							
Revenues	$2,917	$509	$576	$574	$67*	$1,151	$5,794
Operating and equity earnings	$ 75	$ 68	$ 80	67	$ 28	$ 102	$ 420
Disposals/writedowns	—	—	—	—	—	16	16
Corporate expense	(20)	(5)	(3)	(3)	(1)	(9)	(41)
Realized investment gains, net of tax	—	—	2	—	—	—	2
Segment earnings	$ 55	$ 63	$ 79	$ 64	$ 27	$ 109	$ 397

*Does not include revenues from sales to Pipeline Operations, which were $27 million in 1983, $32 million in 1982 and $22 million in 1981. Divested Operations includes the results from January 1, 1981 through the date of sale for businesses sold as a part of the asset redeployment program.

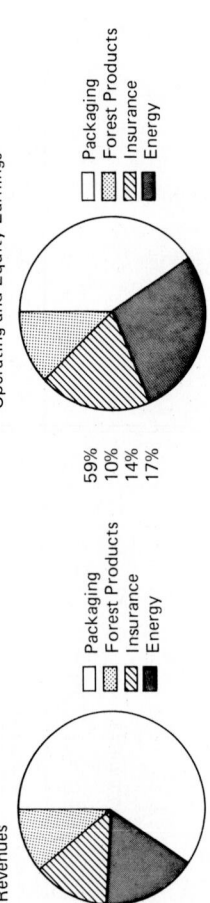

Revenues

Packaging	59%
Forest Products	10%
Insurance	14%
Energy	17%

Operating and Equity Earnings

Packaging	41%
Forest Products	12%
Insurance	20%
Energy	27%

Source: The Continental Group Inc., *Annual Report,* 1983.

EXHIBIT 1 (*Continued*)

OTHER SEGMENT INFORMATION (in millions)

	Packaging	Forest Products	Insurance	Energy: Pipeline Operations	Energy: Exploration & Production	Divested Operations	Corporate*	Consolidated
1983								
Identifiable assets	$1,109	$465		$293	$638	$ —	$320	$2,825
Equity investments	49	2	$581	—	181	—	15	828
Total assets	$1,158	$467	$581	$293	$819	$ —	$335	$3,653
Depreciation, depletion and amortization	$ 78	$ 27		$ 22	$ 66	$ 34	$ 3	$ 230
Capital expenditures	88	54		17	114	23	1	297
1982								
Identifiable assets	$1,158	$426		$285	$690	$645	$179	$3,383
Equity investments	41	20	$548	—	154	—	53	816
Total assets	$1,199	$446	$548	$285	$844	$645	$232	$4,199
Depreciation, depletion and amortization	$ 77	$ 25		$ 21	$ 55	$ 46	$ 3	$ 227
Capital expenditures	81	45		12	214	82	3	437
1981								
Identifiable assets	$1,152	$419		$306	$550	$651	$371	3,449
Equity investments	52	18	$545	—	—	21	50	686
Total assets	$1,204	$437	$545	$306	$550	$672	$421	$4,135
Depreciation, depletion and amortization	$ 80	$ 25		$ 23	$ 39	$ 62	$ 5	$ 234
Capital expenditures	65	37		41	185	62	16	406

* Corporate assets consist principally of cash and deferred income taxes.

Source: The Continental Group, Inc., *Annual Report*, 1983.

EXHIBIT 1 (*Continued*)

INSURANCE–SUMMARY OF OPERATIONS (in millions)

Years Ended December 31	*1983*	*1982*	*1981*
Revenues			
Life insurance	**$372**	$318	$298
Real estate insurance	**228**	163	167
Property and casualty insurance	**97**	100	113
Other	**5**	4	22
	$702	$585	$600
Operating Earnings			
Life insurance	**$ 47**	$ 49	$ 53
Real estate insurance	**18**	2	18
Property and casualty insurance	**4**	7	10
Other	**—**	1	
	69	59	84
Gain on sale of subsidiaries	**—**	9	3
Interest expense[*]	**(17)**	(19)	(24)
Continental Group overhead	**(3)**	(3)	(3)
Earnings before income taxes	**49**	46	60
Income tax benefit (provision)	**3**	4	(13)
Net realized investment gains	**8**	—	2
Net Earnings	**60**	50	49
Dividends on preferred shares	**(1)**	—	—
Company's equity in earnings	**$ 59**	$ 50	$ 49
Dividends Paid to Continental Group	**$ 50**	$ 49	$ 19

[*] *Includes intrasegment interest totaling $14 million in 1983, $17 million in 1982, and $13 million in 1981. The offsetting intrasegment interest income is included in operating earnings.* **Condensed Financial Information** *Insurance includes the accounts of life insurance, real estate insurance, property and casualty insurance, and other operations. This information has been prepared on the basis of generally accepted accounting principles which differ from the statutory accounting practices prescribed by various state regulatory authorities. Net earnings determined in accordance with statutory accounting practices for the insurance subsidiaries were $33 million in 1983, $51 million in 1982, and $55 million in 1981.*

Source: The Continental Group, Inc., *Annual Report*, 1983. Also see notes to table there.

EXHIBIT 1 (*Continued*)   SUPPLEMENTAL OIL AND GAS INFORMATION

(In Millions)	1983	1982	1981	Prior to 1981	Total
Lease acquisition costs	$36	$20	$22	$31	$109
Exploration costs	6	5	—	—	11
Interest capitalized	10	11	7	2	30
	$52	$36	$29	$33	$150

An analysis of Florida Exploration Company's costs of offshore properties not being amortized at December 31, 1983 (by year incurred) appears above.

These offshore properties are part of an ongoing exploration and development program and are expected to be evaluated over the next several years. Onshore properties currently not being amortized were $39 million at December 31, 1983. These properties primarily represent lease acquisition costs in areas where the Company has an active exploration program.

Florida Exploration Company's depletion rate per gross revenue dollar was $.56 in 1983, $.49 in 1982 and $.44 in 1981.

Florida Exploration Company's oil and gas activities are accounted for on the full-cost method. The SEC full-cost accounting rules require that a "ceiling test" be applied to the cost of properties capitalized. The ceiling test limits the amount of costs capitalized to the present value of future new revenues from only proved reserves and the lower of cost or estimated fair value of unproved properties. The present value of future net revenues was computed by applying prices for oil and gas based upon current maker conditions to year-end quantities of proved reserves only, using a 10% discount factor. Future price increases were only considered to the extent they were fixed and determinable. For Florida Exploration Company, curtailments and declining prices in 1983 lowered projected future net revenues and made certain unproved properties uneconomical to develop resulting in a writedown of $95 million ($50 million after tax). Unicon's oil and gas activities are accounted for on the successful efforts method. The amount realizable exceeds the carrying value of the Unicon properties.

Source: The Continental Group, Inc., *Annual Report*, 1983.

EXHIBIT 1 (*Continued*)

SUPPLEMENTAL OIL AND GAS INFORMATION (*Continued*)

Standardized Measure of Future Net Cash Flows from Proved Reserves (*in millions*)

December 31	1983	1982	1981
Estimated future cash flows			
Revenues	$ 606	$724	$599
Production and development costs	(89)	(109)	(111)
	517	615	488
10% discount factor	(145)	(153)	(130)
	372	462	358
Income taxes	(44)	(85)	(51)
Standardized measure of future net cash flows			
Florida Exploration Company	328	377	$307
Company's share of Unicon	299	368	
Combined	$ 627	$745	
The increase (decrease) in standardized measure of future net cash flows was attributable to			
Production	$ (99)	$ (94)	$ (79)
Changes in prices and production costs	(87)	(3)	60
Extensions and discoveries	73	151	74
Revisions of previous quantity estimates	32	39	(37)
Changes in timing of production	(46)	(8)	(36)
Other	(1)	(12)	44
Accretion of discount	38	31	21
Changes in income taxes	41	(34)	51
Florida Exploration Company	(49)	70	$ 98
Unicon	(69)	368	
Combined	$(118)	$438	

Revenues were computed by applying prices for oil and gas based upon current market conditions to year-end quantities of proved reserves. Future price increases were only considered to the extent they were fixed and determinable.

Future production and development costs were based on year-end costs.

Income taxes were computed by applying the statutory income tax rate to the discounted future net cash flows less the year-end tax basis of the proved properties.

Source: The Continental Group, Inc., *Annual Report*, 1983.

EXHIBIT 1 (Continued) OIL AND GAS RESERVES

	1983		1982		1981	
	Oil (In Thousands of Barrels)	Natural Gas (In Millions of Cubic Feet)	Oil (In Thousands of Barrels)	Natural Gas (In Millions of Cubic Feet)	Oil (In Thousands of Barrels)	Natural Gas (In Millions of Cubic Feet)
Proved Reserves						
Florida Exploration Company						
January 1	5,883	123,777	4,342	101,760	4,501	114,525
Revisions of previous estimates	(705)	10,479	942	7,671	(142)	(11,779)
Extensions, discoveries and other additions	1,334	31,686	1,510	35,610	591	20,132
Production	(1,463)	(20,100)	(911)	(21,264)	(608)	(21,118)
December 31	5,049	145,842	5,883	123,777	4,342	101,760
Unicon						
December 31	3,586	202,731	3,908	209,565		
Combined						
December 31	8,635	348,573	9,791	333,342		
Proved Developed Reserves at December 31						
Florida Exploration Company	3,845*	87,476*	5,696	116,349	3,953	83,940
Unicon	2,910	149,034	2,726	155,537		
Combined	6,755	236,510	8,422	271,886		

The Company's reserves are all within the United States and the Gulf of Mexico.
* *Based upon the January 1, 1984 appraisal, 485 thousand barrels of oil and 22,200 million cubic feet of natural gas were reclassified from proved developed to proved undeveloped.*

Source: The Continental Group, Inc., Annual Report, 1983.

EXHIBIT 2   COMPLETED DIVESTITURES OF DIAMOND DIVISIONS

Division	Buyer	Date	Price (millions)
Neekim Can Division	Wearey Corp.	Dec. 1982	$ 98
Escher Wyss GambH	Sulzer Bros. Ltd. (Switzerland)	Feb. 1983	7
Diamond Automation	Leverage buyout by managers of Torok Co.	Mar. 1983	5
Diamond Match	80% sold to assorted investors	Mar. 1983	13
Calmar	83% sold in public offering	June 1983	62
Pulp and Paper	James River Corp. of Virginia	July 1983	149
PENDING SALES			
Retail lumber	Michigan General Corp.		$ 120
Sawmills and millwork plants	Buyer undisclosed		95
Diamond Fiber Products	Buyer undisclosed		38
		SUBTOTAL	$ 587
REMAINING ASSETS (estimated value)			
Timberlands and one sawmill			$ 723
17% of Calmar			13
20% of Diamond Match			3
TOTAL			$1,326
LESS: Goldsmith's cost of acquiring Diamond International			661
Diamond's Corporate Debt (estimated)			162
GOLDSMITH'S POTENTIAL GAIN			$ 503

Source: "Jimmy Goldsmith's U.S. Bonanza," *Fortune*, October 17, 1983.

EXHIBIT 3   THE GOLDSMITH EMPIRE

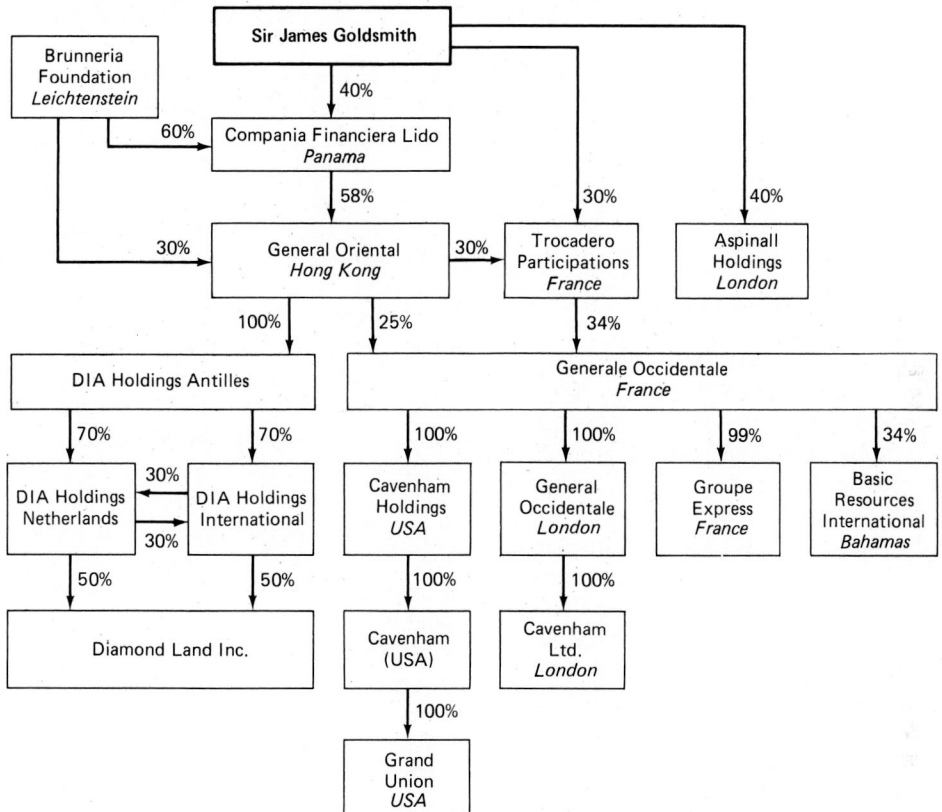

DAVIDSON PSYCHIATRIC HOSPITAL

PRE-1965 TREATMENT AT DAVIDSON

Until 1965, the Davidson Psychiatric Hospital operated in much the same fashion as its sister institutions. It catered to the mentally handicapped in a manner which centered around the dynamic relationship between the physician and patient. Psychiatrists prescribed treatments—usually in the form of drugs, shock therapy and so forth—while the nursing and technical support staff in the hospital performed the variety of maintenance functions necessary to keep the institution in good running order. The latter had little to do with therapeutically helping the patients. Basically then, the Davidson was like any other hospital, the main difference being that it specialized in the treatment of mental illness as opposed to purely physiological disorders.

NEW DEVELOPMENTS IN THE FIELD

Interesting trends had been developing in the way of new mental health treatments since the early 1950s. In England, Maxwell Jones was conducting some fascinating and successful experiments with mental patients. Jones was troubled with the types of therapy which allowed patients to sit idly in their rooms for the greatest part of their stay at an institution. He began to consider the negative effects of isolation upon mental patients. Jones concluded that an increased amount of social interaction among patients would help to give them a more stable and concrete perception of reality.

Interaction between support staff and patients and among the patients themselves was thus encouraged. Treatments which required private sessions between doctor and patient were still to be maintained where necessary, but this was to be supplemented and to some extent supplanted by interaction between the individual and all potentially helpful members of his environment. This afforded a more or less constant form of therapy and the patient's time in the hospital could be more effectively spent.

The benefits of interactive or "milieu" therapy are not confined to the medical or psychiatric realm. The classical, doctor-patient treatment requires large numbers of psychiatrists and as a result is quite costly. On the other hand, interactive therapy was found to be more economical since fewer doctors could deal with more patients. For example, even in the absence of psychiatrists, patients would be able to interact with nursing and technical staff as well as their peers. According to Jones, such interaction could at least to some extent take the place of direct patient-psychiatrist contact.

ORGANIZATION STRUCTURE AND ADMINISTRATIVE CLIMATE

Davidson Psychiatric is run by a staff committee of doctors who are responsible to a board of governors. The latter are charged with approving major allocations of funds and key changes in medical policy. However, since the board is made up mainly of lay personnel, it tends as a rule to go along with the recommendations of the staff committee. Proposals from the committee are usually of such a complex or technical nature that it is difficult for the board to deal with them employing any semblance of rigor. Relationships between the two bodies are characterized by a minimum of conflict.

The staff committee is made up of 12 attending physicians, the director of nursing, and the director of technical and support staff. It is chaired by the current director of the hospital, Dr. Stephenson. The committee is the effective governing body. Issues are decided upon by vote (each member of the committee has one vote). For the most part, the decision-making climate is as democratic as can be with all proposals being subject to the "push and haul of debate."

Dr. Stephenson considers this type of structure to be vital to psychiatric hospitals which hope to keep up-to-date. He claims this is true: "not only because of the technical nature of the matters being discussed but more importantly because of considerations of philosophy and morality which are intertwined with many decisions. In addition, the uncertainty and changefulness inherent in the field make it impossible for one man to play God." Another member of the committee asserted that in psychiatry, "it is impossible to reduce things down to solely hard facts and rigid rules; this is not an exact science."

Dr. Stephenson pointed out that the people who sit on the committee are a very diverse lot of individuals. They are not "organization men" but professionals— each with his own set of interests and competences. The dispositions of these men are nourished not only by the hospital setting but also by their past jobs, educational experiences, professional affiliations, and a host of other factors which make for diversity in professional philosophies.

At Davidson it seems there has developed a polarization among proponents of two schools of psychiatric thought. The first group of psychiatrists are adherents of the traditional approach to therapy. They view psychosis as a disease which must be fought by the physician. The doctor is seen as the principal warrior in the battle and he will use drugs and other techniques at his disposal to combat the illness. The other group of doctors adopt the Jonesian milieu approach to psychiatry and believe that the entire environment of the patient, including his peers, should be enlisted in helping with therapy. These doctors are convinced that group-oriented forms of treatment which maximize the patient's exposure to interpersonal interaction are preferable.

Dr. Stephenson claims that far from reducing the disagreement among these groups, the forum provided by the monthly committee meetings has worked to heighten antagonism. There has emerged increasing polarization between the two factions. What started as a difference of opinion has become a *cause célèbre* which has emanated in increasingly frequent vituperative outbursts at the committee meetings. According to Stephenson, the morale in the hospital is as low as he has ever seen it, and he isn't very optimistic about the future. "We just can't seem to get a meeting of minds anymore."

In order to gain an appreciation of how this situation developed it is important to look at a sequence of events which began as far back as the early days of the hospital.

THE EARLY DAYS: 1949–1960

Davidson Psychiatric was founded in 1949 as a private institution. It had, almost since inception, enjoyed a fine reputation. Its success record, using medical (non-milieu) forms of therapy was very favorable compared to other institutions in its class. Director Richards who had chaired the hospital committee for many years was widely respected for his extensive and innovative publications in the medical area of mental health. He was one of the few select individuals in the medical community whose pioneering ideas and theories had successfully been put into practice. The hospital was well staffed with a full complement of excellent psychiatrists. During the 1950s, the institution was known for the unusual amount of individual attention patients received from the medical staff. All patients were private—there were no public wards.

A DYNAMIC ENVIRONMENT: 1960–1965

During the late 1950s, "society matured to the problems of mental health." As a result, cases which would not have normally come to the attention of a psychiatric hospital were being increasingly referred to such institutions by other hospitals, social agencies, schools and sundry organizations. Davidson became flooded with private patients and there was a good deal of pressure levied against the hospital to open its doors to public patients. It did this first in 1961 by opening a day clinic and soon thereafter by allocating one ward to resident public patients. Since medical types of treatments were used exclusively by the hospital, the professional psychiatric staff became hopelessly overburdened. A meeting of the committee was held to discuss the problem and with only a very few exceptions, everyone agreed that technicians and nurses should begin to play a greater role in administering treatments. By 1963, such staff had taken over a good deal of the work hitherto performed only by psychiatrists.

Because there were inadequate resources available to train technical and nursing personnel in the refinements relevant to their responsibilities, all parties interviewed agreed that the quality of treatment declined very substantially during the period. Two staff members recruited that year had enjoyed extensive experience in "more progressive" institutions in England and the United States and began to complain bitterly about the quality of treatment. They were well aware of the restricted financial resources available to the hospital but felt this was no excuse for the situation. Drs. Theoret and Gosselin, the new recruits, felt that Davidson could make much better use of its resources by commencing, at least in certain wards, milieu therapy. Gosselin claimed that:

> The staff shortage and the belligerence of the old guard to new forms of treatment resulted in the type of environment where for at least 90% of the day, the patient sits around and vegetates. The other 10% of the time he is more often than not

subject to treatment by amateurs. These people try hard—it's just that they aren't sufficiently trained to work in a field that is 30% a science and 70% an art.

The suggestion was defeated after a very emotional discussion between Richards and his eminent colleagues, who were members of the conservative school of medical therapists, and Theoret and Gosselin. The former claimed that the staff shortage was insufficient cause to adopt an unproven mode of therapy and asserted that before this shortage they had enjoyed an excellent reputation using "more acceptable, tried and true" techniques. They agreed, however, that something had to be done to improve patient care and decided to look into a fund-raising campaign that would afford them the resources to hire more staff. Theoret and Gosselin claimed that the committee took a reactionary approach and thought that the "vested psychological interests on the part of the conservative staff to treatments which they themselves helped to develop" were responsible for the "stopgap" approach (fund-raising) to solving the problem. They claimed that clinical-experimental evidence had proven beyond a doubt the superiority of milieu therapy.

By the end of 1964, it became clear that raising additional funds was indeed only a very short-term solution. The number of public patients had increased substantially and two wards had to be devoted to them. The more economically lucrative private patients began to stabilize in number as older members of the staff retired. Funds gathered during 1964 were insufficient to substantially improve treatment.

A CHANGE IN PERSONNEL: 1965–1968

In March 1965 Dr. Richards, age 70, retired. He was replaced by Dr. Stephenson, 42, who was noted for his dynamism and progressiveness at a medium-sized British psychiatric hospital. The latter had worked on applying milieu therapy in England and had witnessed its success in a fairly broad variety of clinical situations. In July 1965 Dr. Stephenson hired three new staff members—each familiar with and a proponent of milieu therapy. Two of the new staff members served as replacements for two members of the retiring personnel. One came to fill a new position created as a result of increased demand and made possible by the fund-raising campaign initiated the year before.

During the committee meeting in September 1965, a real schism between pre-Stephenson staff and the "young turks" became apparent. At that meeting, Stephenson expressed the desire to "bolster the reputation of the Davidson to what it once was." Only one device to accomplish this was proposed: the implementation on a trial basis of milieu therapy.

Immediately, Dr. Silverton, a former close associate of Dr. Richards and an eminent member of the psychiatric community, took objection to Stephenson's approach. He claimed that (1) the past medically oriented therapy was by no means outmoded and was still the most reliable approach; (2) the new unproven types of treatment were employed mainly by "faddist" institutions—usually located in Southern California; and (3) the new director had best turn his attention to getting more "medically competent" personnel. Dr. Silverton's stance was heartily endorsed by six of his pre-Stephenson colleagues who believed that it was time to "put an end to this milieu nonsense once and for all."

Stephenson, Gosselin, and Theoret, as well as the three recently recruited staff members were "visibly shaken" by the reaction of their colleagues and the defeat of the motion to introduce milieu therapy. So were the directors of the nursing and technical staff who sat on the committee *ex officio* on matters directly relevant to the types of medical treatment employed. These individuals had been receiving an increasing number of complaints from their staffs who claimed they were party to a suboptimal effort. In fact, the interviewers learned that the nurses had been performing unconsciously a simplified form of milieu therapy. They "cared for the patients throughout the day and coaxed them into performing some activ-

ity—any activity." They were consequently quite distressed that they saw patients "always alone—as though committed to solitary confinement as a form of punishment."

The meeting was adjourned by Dr. Stephenson who asked all committee members to come to another gathering, three weeks hence, with concrete proposals regarding the improvement of treatment. At that meeting Miss Verdone, the director of nursing, asked for a very small amount of funds to begin conferences and classes to educate the nursing staff about better methods of patient care. When asked to explain the types of courses she had in mind she mentioned that a number of them would be oriented to imparting methods of communicating better with patients so that staff members would be more responsive to their needs and less susceptible to the emotional problems which were such common occupational hazards. The committee almost unanimously agreed that this was a good idea and recommended that it be implemented as soon as possible.

Dr. Stephenson then directed the attention of the committee members to a recent proclamation from a well-respected American body of psychiatrists. It asserted that the refusal to implement milieu therapy is tantamount to malpractice. To bolster his arguments Stephenson and the milieu therapy advocates had prepared a report which outlined a gradual and voluntary scheme for the introduction of the new therapy in the public wards (most of the conventional treatment advocates' patients were private). He mentioned that this was the only possible solution. Meetings with the board of governors, the government and some professional fund-raisers had disclosed that there was no way to obtain enough money to procure the personnel required to effectively pursue old methods of therapy. The suggestion that more psychiatrists be hired was thus shown to be inoperative. In closing, Stephenson mentioned that it should be the right of any doctor who so desires it to prevent his private patients from participating in group therapy. After a good deal of debate the conventional treatment proponents approved the implementation on a trial basis of milieu therapy in the outpatient day hospital only. They insisted on retaining the right to withhold such therapy from their patients in cases where they should deem such action advisable. After the meeting Dr. Stephenson was satisfied that some ("but not nearly enough") progress had been made. The medical therapy advocates, still in the majority, believed and hoped that this would at last "get the adventurers off our backs."

MORE TROUBLE: 1970s

For over three years the hospital was run with milieu therapy being adminstered solely to outpatients. In February 1970 the technical and nursing staff went on strike. As a result, public patients in one ward were sent home. The nursing director summarized the reasons for the strike as follows:

> We (my staff) were doing all we could for the patients. Still, they were confined to restricted areas, usually their rooms, where they whiled away the time staring into space. What a pathetic waste of humanity. We're fully aware of the programs going on at this and other institutions where this type of thing is minimized. It has really begun to grate on our nerves. Something had to be done.

Dr. Stephenson called a committee meeting three days prior to the strike. He asked the nursing director to summarize the reasons for the strike before the committee. It was resolved that committee members should have a week to mull things over and return with some creative suggestions in time for the next meeting. This they did. Dr. Gosselin proposed that since the conventional treatment proponents had little concern for the public ward, they should allow the introduction of milieu therapy to take place at least in this area of the hospital. The vote was close and Gosselin's recommendation was passed—not, however, before the conventional treatment proponents had a chance to stipulate precisely their much anticipated proviso that: "private doctors maintain the right to restrict their patients' group

activities and deny them the chance to take part in milieu therapy."

The nurses returned to work and the technical staff immediately followed suit. All the while animosity was building between the opposite sides of what was becoming an ongoing dispute. The problems were far from over.

THE LAST STRAW: 1970s

In May 1971 Dr. Berg joined the staff. He was another firm believer in milieu therapy. Drs. Theoret, Gosselin, Berg and the balance of the post-Stephenson staff were becoming increasingly incensed at the difficulty they encountered in employing milieu therapy in the public wards. These doctors tried to organize their patients into milieu groups or interaction cells. The tactic met with very limited success since they had to share ward beds with the conventional treatment proponents. As a result, individuals within groups tended to be scattered throughout the hospital's three wards.

During the September 1971 committee meeting, Dr. Silverton commented on the confused and "chaotic" nature of the wards. He mentioned that his patients were being bothered by the milieu therapy staff and that there was far too much activity going on around them. The proponents of milieu therapy retorted that the confused nature of the wards was due to the reactionary veterans whose patients were scattered throughout wards which could otherwise have been effectively organized into interactive cells. Dr. Theoret claimed that this factor was the main obstacle to the effectiveness of the new treatment.

Two weeks after the meeting, Drs. Gosselin and Theoret, who had become very well respected members of the psychiatric community, threatened to resign unless milieu therapy was instituted on a compulsory basis throughout the hospital. The conventional therapy proponents' informal reaction to the joint letter of intended resignation (which was circulated to all staff members on the committee and to the board of governors) was: "it will be good to get things back to normal again after those guys leave.'' Dr. Stephenson was at a loss as to what to do.

QUESTIONS

1. What are the different factors that have led up to the growing conflict between the two groups at Davidson Hospital?

2. What steps, if any, can or should Dr. Stephenson take to help resolve this conflict?

3. What are the strengths and weaknesses of the different approaches which could be taken to resolve this conflict?

4. How does strategy formation in an organization such as Davidson Hospital differ from that in other types of organizations?

BLANCHFLOWER, WHITE AND GREAVES

"The problem we face can be simply described," noted Steven Perryman, managing partner of the law firm of Blanchflower, White and Greaves: "Among all the possible actions, what should we do to maintain and grow our partnership profits? It is reasonably clear that unless we make *some* changes in the way we run our affairs, we will be faced with, at best, flat income levels for the foreseeable future, particularly if you take inflation into account. Few of us in the firm are dissatisfied with our current compensation, but, as individuals, we naturally look forward to some growth in our incomes as our families get larger and as we learn to live up to our incomes. If we are to fulfill our collective income expectations, as well as those of our future partners (our current associates), we must find ways to increase our pool of profits."

Perryman made these comments after reviewing the 1984 Budget and Operating Plan prepared by his executive committee. The plan had projected a continued growth in firm revenues of 8 percent, based in part on adjustments averaging 4.5 percent in the firm's hourly rates. Revenue estimates had been compiled by polling each of the partners of the firm as to their estimates of work forthcoming from existing and new clients. Significant uncertainty existed about these revenue estimates. In recent years, gross fees per lawyer at Blanchflower, White and Greaves had, according to a survey conducted by a public accounting firm, corresponded to the median (approximately $200,000) for firms of its size and

in its city. The executive committee expected that this would also be true in 1984.

Expenses in the 1984 budget were projected to increase by 12 percent, of which over half was attributable to increases in personnel costs, caused by staff increases, built-in salary increases and substantial increases in payroll taxes and health insurance costs. The cost structure of the firm was approximately as follows:

Associate Compensation	27 percent of total costs
Other Employee Costs	38 percent of total costs
Other Operating Costs	35 percent of total costs
Total	100 percent of total costs

Because expenses were projected to rise faster than revenues, the firm's margin (partnership profits as a percent of fees) was projected to decline in 1984, as it had done in each of the last three years. It was projected that over 20 percent of all of the firm's attorney time would, as in past years, be spent on non-billable matters such as administrative activities, leave and holidays, business solicitation, professional development, recruiting, and so on.

Blanchflower, White and Greaves had detected significant fee resistance from its corporate clients. While precise detail was not available, the firm believed its hourly rates were in line with those of other firms in the city, but its billing rates had not risen as rapidly as its expenses. Because of increased competition for the top graduates at the first-tier law schools from which the firm drew its new associates, associate salaries had grown faster than inflation. Occupancy costs had been held at a reasonable level, but there was a threat that these would jump significantly when the firm's lease on its current space expired in eighteen months' time. With the introduction of word processing, computers, extended library resources, and so on, the firm's operating expenses per lawyer had grown rapidly. This not only affected the yearly income statement, but increased the firm's need for capital. In turn, this meant that an increasing percentage of yearly income was retained (and not distributed as partner income) in order to fund the firm's capital needs.

Steve Perryman reflected: "As I contemplated the means by which we could restore and promote the firm's economic health, I decided to sit down and make a list of all the possible actions we could take to improve profitability in both the short and long time-horizons. This exercise yielded the following list. We could:

(1) Raise Our Hourly Rates

"Obviously, this is the action we would do first if we could, but it seems the most unlikely to be successful. However, this may not be the case if we think about raising rates by *restructuring* them. While *some* clients have expressed concern about our fees, this is by no means true of all clients. Clients appear ready to pay top fees for truly superior legal advice: no one has ever complained about the fees charged by our most expert partners. Our hourly billing rates are basically set by seniority: the more senior the partner, the higher the rate. In consequence, all partners of roughly the same seniority bill at the same level. Perhaps we should look at whether this is wise. I have a suspicion that for some of our people we could raise rates fifty percent or more and the clients would never complain because those individuals are so valuable. Other partners may be overpriced at the level they are now at. Perhaps we should be more courageous in raising the rates of our best people. In the same spirit, perhaps we should look a little more carefully at the rates we charge for associates' time. It is there that we think the greatest fee resistance exists, so perhaps those fees could be reduced selectively: kept up for the best associates and reduced for the novices. We see greater demand for partner-intensive work and less for associate-intensive work, so a restructuring of our hourly rates could yield more revenues to the firm.

(2) Change Our Billing Practices

"Fundamentally, continued economic health must come from productivity improvements: accomplishing the same work with fewer resources. For us, this means spending less time to accomplish the same tasks. But since we bill according to the time we spend, better productivity would only mean we would bill less. For example, we could work to find ways to use associates and paralegals to do work now being done by partners. But if we do this, we just get paid less. We need to find some way to profit from any efforts at improved effectiveness or productivity. This would mean experimenting with such things as contingency fees, up-front negotiated flat fees, bonus payments, piece work rates or some form of "value billing." Of course, if we were successful in getting such arrangements with clients, we would then have to work at examining our methods of delivering legal services to indeed become more effective and efficient.

(3) Increase Our Billable Hours for Partners and/or Associates

"In recent years, our average billable hours per attorney have corresponded approximately to medians for firms of our size and location, i.e., in the high 1500s for partners and low 1700s for associates. I really don't know if these numbers can be increased. I suppose there are two basic ways to accomplish this: work more hours in total, or find ways to make more of our work billable. Since partners' billing rates are higher than those of associates, I would guess that working to improve *partner* billable hours is likely to have a bigger impact on our profits: but at what cost? There certainly are lifestyle considerations to take into account here.

(4) Drop Selected Unprofitable Clients

"I am personally convinced that some of our clients are unprofitable. However, I have no way of proving this, since we have never instituted any form of profitability accounting system. Naturally, we do get printouts of fees billed and collected to individual clients, as well as any write-down of hours worked on cases for those clients. However, we do not attempt to allocate any of our fixed costs (such as secretarial, word processing, occupancy, photocopying activities) to individual matters or clients. Similarly, we have no system for estimating the specific cost to us of the lawyer time spent working on cases. For example, not all of our associates are paid the same amount, even those in the same class. Accordingly, an hour of one associate's time does not cost us the same as an hour of some other associate's time. Should we attempt to calculate these costs (and hence profitability) on a case-by-case or client-by-client basis? If so, how? Should we attempt to estimate which clients (or lawyers) are making greatest use of our various fixed facilities and allocate a proportionate share of costs to them? How useful an exercise would this be? After all, even if we could show that some clients were unprofitable measured in this way, I know we'd have lots of fights about both the costing methodology and whether unprofitable clients could one day turn into profitable ones, and hence should be retained.

(5) Drop Selected Unprofitable Types of Work

"The same arguments about dropping unprofitable clients could be made about unprofitable matters. Our accounting system does not record revenues by type of matter, let alone costs. Yet I again suspect that some types of matters we handle are unprofitable. I would foresee that fights over dropping these would be even more rancorous. Should we refuse unprofitable work from otherwise profitable clients? Should we even collect the information in this form?

(6) Reduce Our Overhead

"Since 75 percent of our costs are either non-lawyer compensation costs or other operating ex-

penses, it would seem as if our greatest opportunitie⁀ to keep more of our revenues lie in this area. I can think of at least three major actions:

1. cutting back on occupancy costs (move to less plush quarters);
2. make more efficient use of secretarial and other support staff;
3. get better control of unbilled telephone, photocopying, travel and other expenses.

"In the short term, there is perhaps not a lot we can do about occupancy costs. But our lease will shortly be up, and we do face the decision on what type of space we want to have. In the old days, we always treated ourselves generously in this regard: we have over 600 square feet per lawyer in very comfortable surroundings. But I suspect that the days of 'high living' in this regard are over. Similarly, we have always been generous with secretarial, photocopying and other support personnel, on the theory that to skimp in this area would affect both the quality of our work life and, if we cut back too much, our timely responsiveness to clients. Yet we may be fooling ourselves here: there is probably some 'fat' to be cut. But how do you know when you've trimmed all the fat and started to cut into muscle? In a similar spirit, we have not been too tight-fisted in overseeing cost expenditures such as telephones, taxis, travel and entertainment made by lawyers, especially partners. Again, there is the quality-of-work-life issue. Our business manager (an ex-accountant) keeps proposing all sorts of tight control systems to keep track of these expenses, but I don't want to get to the point of partners having to obtain 'clearance' to spend money. After all, it's *their* firm.

(7) Improve Our Billing and Collection Performance

"At any given point in time, we have about 5 months' worth of 'unbilled work-in-progress' (time charges accumulated to client work but not yet billed). We understand this is in line with other firms, but it is *very* high compared to other professions. Perhaps, by greater use of 'progress billing' (sending bills out prior to the disposition of the matter) we could improve our cash flow. More timely billing might also improve our collections performance, which currently run somewhere between two and three months' worth of our billings. This represents a lot of our money tied up. Yet to accomplish these changes would mean attempting to impose a new 'discipline' on both our billing partners (in getting bills out) and on our clients (paying us more promptly). We have exhorted each other repeatedly on this topic for years, but have not seen much improvement. Are there 'systems' we should consider to help us here?

(8) Reduce Our Write-Offs

"Our write-offs of time worked approximate the averages for firms of our size (five to ten percent, depending upon how you calculate it), but I suspect there is room for improvement here. At the present time, each billing partner makes individual decisions on whether (and how much) to write down our time charges. Officially, they are supposed to consult with our 'Write-Down Committee' if they wish to exceed certain guidelines, but we are having difficulties in enforcing this. I suspect that attacking this problem means more than just exhorting partners. We really should examine *why* we incur write-offs, and attack the problem at its source. Do we staff our cases well? At present, we have a somewhat informal method of assigning associates to projects. Perhaps a more disciplined approach would pay off, as would better oversight on the part of partners as to how well they manage the time billed by associates to their projects.

(9) Increase Our Leverage

"It has always been conventional wisdom that, as partners, we make a lot of our money from our associates. Accordingly, we could try and improve our economic health by reaching for a

higher associate-to-partner ratio. We could do this either by hiring more associates or making fewer partners. This latter solution might involve either just extending the time to partnership (officially or unofficially), or creating a category of principal between partners and associates. Of course, if we *do* increase our leverage, we'd have to go after more leveraged client work, which might not be the sort of work our partners want to do.

(10) Reduce Non-Billable Time

"If we could find a way to reduce our non-billable time, we could free up our partners either to bill more hours or spend more time on business getting. We really do not have a very good handle on where our non-billable time is going. It has been proposed by our business manager that we establish a large number of specific non-billable account numbers for specific activities (e.g., recruiting committee, facilities committee, professional development time, etc.) so that we can better track the time being invested in each of these areas. Presumably, this would also allow us to establish specific time budgets for each activity and hence not only control this time but actually calculate how much each activity is costing us. I'm somewhat afraid of this, because it could become an administrative nightmare keeping track of detailed billing codes. I'm not sure I could force my partners to do it, nor how much it would really help.

(11) Bill Overhead Costs Directly to Clients

"One way to attack our overhead costs would be to bill out to clients more of our secretarial, photocopying and other such costs. The first step would be to improve our controls on making sure we actually bill what we are supposed to. (I'm not sure my partners *are* doing this). The next step would be to consider 'marking up' some of these costs, instead of billing them out at cost. At the highest level, we could start billing out some things that we have traditionally absorbed ourselves.

(12) Get Rid of Non-Productive Partners

"Many of us suspect that this might be the most potent change we could make in affecting the long run health of the firm. However, it is also the least easy to implement.

(13) Reduce Associate Costs

"Naturally, I don't mean cutting the salaries of our current associates. But we could reduce these costs in the long run by changing our recruitment practices. We could go after students at the best schools who are below the first-tier, or go after students at the top of their class at second tier schools."

As he concluded his list, Mr. Perryman reflected: "As you can see, this list is quite varied. Some of the actions represent one-time changes, others are more permanent. Some are easy to implement (in an organizational or political sense), others more difficult. Some will have a quick impact if we can implement them, others will only show benefit over an extended period of time. Some require negotiating new relationships with clients, others are purely internal. Some will require investments to be made, others can be implemented without adding to our costs. I could go on. In fact, I could easily draw up a long list of *criteria* by which we could assess the possible actions. Then we'd have two long lists instead of one! How do we think about this? What should be our plan of attack on this problem?"

QUESTIONS

1. For purposes of discussion and analysis, begin by making assumptions concerning data missing from the case study with respect to (a) the size of this firm (number of lawyers); (b) its associates-to-partner ratio; (c) its profitability margin (ratio of partnership profits to gross fees).

2. Examine the list of potential actions being considered by Steve Perryman. What, if anything, has he left out of his list of ways to improve the economic health of the firm?

3. At the end of the case, Steve Perryman points out that there are a number of criteria by which possible actions can be assessed. Make a list of all the possible criteria he could use in trying to decide which actions to take.

4. What information should Perryman collect to shed light on where economic improvements could best be made?

5. What analyses would you recommend that he make?

6. Which of the various actions being considered by Perryman do you think would be the most fruitful focus of attention in the firm: (a) in the short run; (b) in the long run?

THE HEWLETT PACKARD COMPANY

The Hewlett Packard Company (HP) has been a dynamic business built around innovation. It has traditionally been a fast paced organization characterized by steady growth. From 1957 to 1984, sales increased from $28.1 million to $6 billion, and profits from $2.4 million to $665 million. In 1984 the company had close to 7,000 products on the market, and developed new products at a rate of 300 per year.

HP had become the world's leading manufacturer of electronic test and measurement equipment for engineers and scientists. Besides the electronics industry and scientific research programs, the principal markets for HP instruments included the telecommunications, aerospace, aircraft, and automotive industries. Its principal products were integrated instrument and computer systems, test and measurement instruments, computer systems and peripheral products, medical electronic equipment and systems, instrumentation and systems for chemical analysis, handheld calculators, and solid-state components. HP Laboratories, the company's common research facility, ranked as one of the world's leading electronics research centers.[1] HP was among the world's top ten companies in CAD/CAE/CAM sales. (See Table 1 on page 876.)

Two Talented Co-Founders

The two most influential people in HP's development had been its co-founders, William Hewlett and David Packard—in 1985 Vice Chairman and Chairman of the Board, respectively. Each was

Case copyright © 1986 by Henry Mintzberg and James Brian Quinn. Case prepared by Maria G. Geretto and Penny C. Paquette under the supervision of Professors Mintzberg and Quinn. Case derived solely from secondary sources.

personally responsible for many of the company's most important products and diversification moves. Hewlett was an innovator with great technical expertise; he conceived of product lines and used parts of HP Labs for his own research. Packard was known for his sound business sense and outstanding managerial and administrative skills and was said to be the driving force behind such key decisions as HP's move into medical systems and its efforts to become a major factor in minicomputers.

Doing Things Well

For HP, growth came from doing things well and was not an objective in itself. The company did not stipulate long-term targets for expected profit or market share growth, having explicitly made the decision not to become dependent on such growth. Its focus was on making quality products that commanded a premium price in the marketplace. If it did this job well, the company believed profits would follow. The company's attitude toward long term formal planning was stated by Mr. Hewlett, "We operate on a very short lead time, and don't have a master plan. In terms of next year's detailed plan we try and wait until the last possible moment to get that in place."[2]

How then did HP reach its present position and what challenges did it face in the turbulent electronic markets of the 1980s?

EARLY HISTORY

Hewlett and Packard started what was to become HP in 1938, in a garage behind the Packards' home in Palo Alto, California. The two founders were both graduates of Standard University's engineering program. The company began with an audio oscillator—a high-quality electronic instru-

TABLE 1   THE TOP 10 IN CAD/CAE/CAM WORLDWIDE SALES

Revenue by application ($ million)

Company	Mechanical Engineering	Electronic / Electrical Engineering	Architectural/ Electrical/Civil Engineering	Mapping	Services	Total Revenue
Computervision	272	111	56	6	111	556
IBM	391	13	16	—	109	529
Intergraph	64	20	178	89	52	403
Digital Equipment	107	103	22	32	37	301
Calma Corp. (GE)	70	90	28	—	47	235
McDonnell Douglas	94	—	24	—	16	134
Applicon	62	25	1	—	13	101
Hewlett Packard	45	36	6	—	10	97
Control Data	54	7	9	—	23	93
Prime Computer	53	3	14	—	20	90

Source: International Data Corp. in Paine Webber, Inc., *Hewlett Packard Company Report*, December 2, 1985.

ment for use in developing and testing sound equipment. Among the early customers for their product was Walt Disney Studios. In 1938, Walt Disney asked them to develop eight oscillators having different frequency characteristics and different physical configurations. One result was the HP Model 200A used in developing the soundtrack for the movie "Fantasia."

This large order provided a foundation for the company's early success. But growth was slow during World War II. Hewlett and Packard made a conscious decision not to pursue large military contracts because of their "boom or bust" possibilities. HP accepted only limited government work in microwave technologies and kept itself focused on instrumentation and microwave measurement.[3] HP operated as a partnership until 1947 when it incorporated.

An Expanding Product Line

After World War II the company began to expand its product line significantly and moved from being a focused instrument maker to a more diversi-fied company. In 1957, when the organization reached 1200 employees, this size was considered too large to manage by the informal methods HP had previously used.

For example, early in HP's history, two product development techniques had been prevalent. The first was known as the "next bench syndrome." A central strategy in the early years, this referred to listening to the problems of engineers on the next bench and finding ways to solve them. Since the company was working on the frontiers of its technologies, this approach helped the company identify new technical opportunities and needs; little market research was done, since the company could monitor most market needs internally.[4] A second approach was to design a machine specifically for one customer and then market it to others. This enabled the company to concentrate on products for a few customers, yet produce in volume and charge high margins. Rather than compete on price, the intention was to develop products so advanced and adapted to customers' needs that the market would be willing to pay a premium for HP performance.

Institutionalizing the HP Way

HP's "Corporate Objectives," embracing the company's basic values and philosophy, were put in writing in 1957 and became the "HP Way." (See Exhibit 1.) This same year the first personnel department was created. As Mr. Hewlett noted:

> Contrary to most companies at that time, we did not have a personnel department. We had strong convictions that one of a manager's most important jobs was to deal directly with his employees. We did not want to impose any artificial barriers to hinder direct communication.[3]

Mr. Hewlett later described the important organizational changes which were to occur in 1957 as follows:

> A real turning point for the company occurred in 1957, resulting in changes that would have a profound effect on the company in future years. Up to that time, HP was directed by the owner-founders operating in a single plant in Palo Alto, California. Most of the basic policies that directed the company were firmly in place, and we had a good team of people running the operation.
>
> But there were signs of strain appearing. I think the principal concern Dave and I had was that, as it increased in size, the company might lose the intimacy we felt was so important to the organization. Therefore, in January 1957, Dave and I took the top 10 or 12 people of the organization on a weekend retreat to discuss the future of the company, and to decide what action might be taken to insure its continued success.
>
> Several conclusions were reached. First, we decided to divisionalize the company along product lines. We felt that by reducing the size of the operating units and decreasing the span of control, we would provide an opportunity to recapture the personal touch that everyone felt was so important. The managers of these divisions would assume direct responsibility for the health and welfare of their charge, but they would need some guidance. Sec-

ond, it seemed that this guidance could best be achieved with a simple set of policy statements. In fact, these statements consisted of no more than a codification of past company policies. Coupled with this belief was the conviction that, with these guidelines, local managers could make better decisions than either Dave or me, because—if for no other reason— they would be closer to the problems.[3]

Corporate Culture and Organization

In order to appreciate the culture Hewlett and Packard attempted to foster, it is necessary to understand the founders' own backgrounds and beliefs. As Mr. Hewlett said:

> . . . it is important to remember that Dave and I were products of the Depression. We had observed its effects on all sides, and it could not help but influence our decisions on how a company should be run. Two thoughts were clear from the start. First, we did not want to run a hire and fire operation, but rather a company built on a loyal and dedicated work force. Further, we felt that this work force should be able to share to some extent in the progress of the company. Second, we wished to operate, as much as possible, on a pay-as-you-go basis, that our growth be financed by our earnings and not by debt.[3]

The new organization designed at the weekend retreat in 1957 was called the Product Division Structure. It separated the company into small divisions, which were to become HP's fundamental business units. Each product division became an integrated, self-sustaining organization with a great deal of independence, similar in some ways to a company. Each division had its own engineering, manufacturing, and marketing organization. The divisions had considerable latitude in developing individual products and product line strategies, but they were not permitted to go outside their assigned markets or to raise money outside the corporation.

Technological leadership was to be a major

EXHIBIT 1   THE HP WAY

Business Related

1. Pay as you go —no long-term borrowing
   - Helps to maintain a stable financial environment during depressed business periods.
   - Serves as an excellent self-regulating mechanism for HP managers.

2. Market expansion and leadership based on *new* product contributions
   - Engineering excellence determines market recognition of our new products.
   - Novel new product ideas and implementations serve as the basis for expansion of existing markets or diversification into new markets.

3. Customer satisfaction second to none
   - We sell only what has been thoroughly designed, tested, and specified.
   - Our products have *lasting* value—they are highly reliable (quality) and our customers discover additional benefits while using them.
   - Best after-sales service and support in the industry.

4. *Honesty* and *integrity* in all matters
   - No tolerance for dishonest dealings with vendors or customers (e.g., bribes, kickbacks).
   - Open and honest communication with employees and stockholders alike; conservative financial reporting.

People Related

1. *Belief* in our people
   - Confidence in, and respect for, our people as opposed to depending upon extensive rules, procedures, etc.
   - Depend upon people to do their job right (individual freedom) without constant directives.
   - Opportunity for meaningful participation (job dignity).

2. Emphasis on working *together* and *sharing* rewards (teamwork and partnership)
   - Share responsibilities; help each other; learn from each other; chance to make mistakes.
   - Recognition based on contribution to results—sense of achievement and self-esteem.
   - Profit sharing, stock purchase plan, retirement program, etc.; aimed at employees and company sharing in each other's successes.
   - Company financial management emphasis on protecting employee's job security.

3. A *superior* working environment which other companies seek but few achieve
   - Informality— open, honest communications; no artificial distinctions between employees (first-name basis); management by walking around; and open door communication policy.
   - Develop and promote from within—lifetime training, education, career counseling to help employees get maximum opportunity to grow and develop with the company.
   - Decentralization— emphasis on keeping work groups as small as possible for maximum employee identification with our businesses and customers.
   - Management by objectives (MBO) —provides a sound basis for measuring performance by employees as well as managers and is objective, not political.

Source: The Hewlett Packard Company.

goal for each production division.[1] Operations were pragmatically specialized around the division's technical focus. And what became known as HP's Originator/Producer strategy was introduced to move products to the marketplace. An idea's originator was expected to carry it through all stages of development and into the market if necessary. Bernard M. Oliver, Vice President for R&D (in 1975) said:

> At the time, we split R&D and product engineering. But we discovered that the only way to get things done in a timely fashion was to have the originator of an idea carry it through to the end. We've tried to remove the fences between research and production and make a chute that starts in the lab and ends at the shipping dock.[5]
>
> [To back up this concept] . . . [HP] Product Divisions are purposely kept small, seldom numbering more than 2000 people. This structure spurs entrepreneurship by allowing decisions to be made by the persons most responsible for putting them into action. Compact and action oriented, the HP division combines the flexibility of a small business with the resources of a large corporation.[1]

Key personnel worked together on projects without regard to their status in their own organizations. In developing new products, divisional project engineers organized technical development efforts, but product managers from Marketing joined the team early to provide inputs on design and price. For the most part, the early stage technical work done by the divisions was self-contained, requiring little communication across divisions. And the company tried to keep each division's product-technical-market focus as discrete as possible.

Management by Objectives and Involvement

Mr. Hewlett was later to say of the 1957 reorganization that:

The recommendations of our 1957 meeting were quickly implemented by divisionalization and by wide distribution of the objectives. These objectives had an important role in training and guiding the new management teams. They served to reinforce the principles of cooperative management—the concept of leading, not directing. They stressed a management style that was informal, with give and take discussion, lack of private offices, casual dress and the universal use of first names.

The informal structure of the company led to what was eventually known as its "open door" policy. In a sense this said that any employee who was unhappy could come in and talk with Dave or me or any other senior executive about his problems. Although such a technique could easily be abused, it never was, and it served as an excellent safety valve for the frustrations that occur in any organization.[3]

To back up this philosophy, the organization developed two important policies. The first was Management by Objectives (MBO). Mr. Packard believed this was the most effective way for an innovative company like HP to operate:

> You establish some objectives with people, provide some incentives, and try not to direct the detailed way in which they do their work. We've found you're likely to get a much better performance that way than if you have a more military-type procedure where somebody gives orders and expects them to be followed in every detail.[6]

The second was Management by Walking Around (MBWA), a term later popularized by *In Search of Excellence*. This was an extra step HP took to make sure the open door policy was truly effective. It involved a friendly, unfocused and unscheduled series of interactions with any employee with whom a manager from any level happened to stop by to chat. The result was an implicit invitation to repay this visit and walk through that manager's open door at any time—management by involvement.[4]

Expansion and Diversification

Also in 1957, HP's stock was first made available to the public. One year later the firm made its first acquisition, acquiring F.L. Moseley Co. of Pasadena, a producer of high-quality graphic recorders. By 1964, HP had acquired Sanborn Co. of Waltham, a pioneer in electrocardiography and a supplier of other recording instruments, and F.M. Scientific Corp., a manufacturer of chromatographic devices. Through these acquisitions HP entered medical electronics and analytic chemistry.

The first electronic calculator was designed at HP in 1966. An employee working for one of the calculator companies reportedly brought to HP a concept for an all electronic calculator. An HP team converted this concept into an electronic calculator to compete with the desk top mechanical calculators of that era. HP's calculator had a great deal of power, but was a large device measuring about one square foot.[4] HP successfully directed its early sales efforts toward educational, scientific, and engineering markets, where it was an established supplier of instruments.

Later, in 1972, HP introduced the first scientific handheld calculator, the HP-35. The original HP-35, championed and designed in part by Mr. Hewlett, went into production despite an outside market research study that scoffed at the idea. With no external marketing support, the company managed its own distribution. The HP-35 was introduced at a price of $395. It proved so popular that this price was maintained until mid 1973. The tremendous surge in calculator sales was accompanied by a 33 percent increase in employees as well as a rapid ballooning of inventories.

Complexity and Restructuring

As product complexities grew, in 1970 HP established its first product group structure. Some sales organizations were created at the group level,

separate from those of the product divisions.[7] In years to come, these posed a number of communication and integration issues across divisions, but only within the product group where the units were later coordinated by a vice president or general manager. There was little or no mandated communication across product groups.

HP's first period of significant difficulty occurred in 1970, triggered by economic downturns in both the computer and aerospace industries. The company's sales decreased by nearly $40 million, the first decrease since HP went public. Mr. Hewlett stated how the company dealt with the situation:

> One of the most dramatic examples of working with our employees occurred during the recession in early 1970. It became evident that we had about 10 percent more employees than we needed for the production schedule. Rather than lay off or furlough 10 percent of the work force, we simply decided that everyone in the company would take every other Friday off without pay. It worked very well. Employee after employee commented how much they appreciated the opportunity for continued employment, albeit at a reduced pay rate, when on all sides they saw people who were out of a job. After about six months, we were able to return to a full schedule. We helped our people and we preserved our work force, which was essential for continued development.[3]

Other policies characterized HP's approach to its people. Common coffee breaks were a ritual, and recreational facilities for all employees were available at every plant. Employees at all levels were entitled to use a cottage resort area on HP owned land for vacations free of charge. HP still marks an employee's marriage with the gift of a silver bowl and the birth of a first child with a blanket,[8] and it has long done away with time clocks and rigid hours in favor of Flextime which it finds to be self-policing. Because HP believed that all employees contributed to the success of the organization and should be rewarded in good times, the company also had an attractive bonus plan for all employees. As of June 1985, the company had never had a union or an extensive layoff.

THE 1975 RESTRUCTURING

Mr. Packard began to perceive that HP had grown too fast in the boom years of 1972–73. Business publications noted that inventories and accounts receivables were moving out of control, prices on new products were set too low to generate sufficient cash flows, and products often went into production before development was fully completed. Growth had been pursued vigorously without adequate concerns for profit. For the first time in the company's history, short-term borrowing had increased to the extent that long-term debt was considered.

Shaken by their need, in 1974, to become more personally involved in daily management, Hewlett and Packard wanted to develop an organization structure that could both respond better to growth and diversification needs and provide more effective management of day-to-day operations. Preparing the organization for an orderly management succession also became quite important; Mr. Packard would turn 65 in 1977 and Mr. Hewlett in 1978.

Accordingly, they restructured the organization in 1975. There were three main components to the change: (1) the basic product groups were expanded from four to six, (2) a new management level of top executives was added, and (3) an executive committee was established to oversee the day-to-day operations of the company.

Six Product Groups

Prior to 1975, HP's four product groups had consisted of: Test and Measurement, Data Products, Medical Equipment, and Analytical Instrumentation. The six groups created by the reorganization were: Electronic Test and Measurement Instruments, Computer and Computer Based Systems, Calculators, Solid-State Components, Medical Electronic Products, and Electronic Instrumentation for Chemical Analysis. (See Exhibit 2 for a diagram of the 1975 organization structure.)

Each of the product groups had both its own general manager and a sales service organization serving all the product divisions within that group. The product division marketing departments had as their responsibilities: order processing and shipping, sales engineering and contract administration, service engineering, technical writing, publications, and advertising and sales promotion. In addition, they provided sales forecasts and recommended and reviewed prices.

Nevertheless, because the actual selling and customer service activities were performed at the product group level, each division had to compete for the time of its group's field sales force. The objective of the more centralized sales organization was to increase cooperation and communication between divisional sales teams. Hewlett and Packard insisted that all customers receive similar treatment and be dealt with through consistent policies.[4]

The second element of the reorganization included the appointment of two executive vice presidents jointly responsible for operations— one was John Young who later became president—and a vice president for corporate administration. The new executive committee was made up of these three newly appointed executives and Mr. Hewlett and Mr. Packard. It was to meet weekly to coordinate all aspects of the company's operations.

Loss of Control and Regaining Direction

In early 1974, top management had made some basic strategy decisions. Long-term debt was to be avoided. Short-term debt would be decreased by controlling costs, managing assets and improving profit margins. Most importantly, top management began to realize that the company had somehow allowed market share to emerge as too strong an objective. To remedy this, Hewlett and Packard began a year-long campaign to reemphasize some principles they had developed when the partnership began. Packard was quoted as repeatedly telling company audiences:

> Somewhere we got into the idea that market share was an objective. I hope that is straightened out. Anyone can build market share; if you set your prices low enough, you can get the whole damn market. But I'll tell you it won't get you anywhere around here.[5]

Two further strategies were used to get the company back on track: all prices were increased by 10 percent and R&D by 20 percent from the previous year. The intent was to improve the company's profits, while controlling a rate of growth which had more than doubled sales in three years. By early 1975, profit improvements were dramatic. The reaction to the Hewlett and Packard tour of the divisions was quick: inventories were slashed, accounts receivable tightened, productivity improved, and hiring was dramatically decreased to a total of only 1000 new employees in 1974 down from 7000 in the previous year. From 1973 to 1974 sales increased by $215 million and profits by $33 million.

For a brief period, HP had been the leader in the business and scientific handheld calculator field. In 1974 this market had yielded some 30 percent of the company's profits. However, HP's lead soon fell to competition led by Texas Instruments. HP chose not to compete across the board in calculators. Instead it decided to remain in the specialized upper end of the market. It preferred to develop products so advanced they could command a premium price. HP executives commented publicly that this philosophy fit the company's style of operation. They also indicated that the company was not geared to compete solely on a price basis but wanted to maintain its reputation by adding something that was not already available in competitive products.

To maintain coherence and a sense of personal communication despite the growth that was taking place, HP started an activity in the late 1970s that became known as "communication luncheons." Mr. Hewlett described the purpose and style of these luncheons as follows:

> You simply cannot run an operation and assume that everything is perfect. There are many ways to achieve this feedback. . . . One we have tried and which has been fairly successful, is a technique we call "communication luncheons." A senior executive will visit a division and ask to have lunch with a group of employees, 15 or 20 at most; no supervisors invited. Other employees know in advance who will be attending and very often they pass on their own questions or complaints. . . .
>
> This provides an opportunity to discuss company policy or company problems. . . . Sometimes you detect a pattern of problems—say, for example, inadequate supervisory training. Such problems can be dealt with on a broad company-wide basis. In any event you always learn more about how the company actually operates. Equally important, employees have a chance to hear first-hand what is happening in the company and what management is trying to do.[3]

A NEW ERA

In 1978 when Mr. Hewlett stepped down as CEO, John Young, who had been groomed since 1975 to replace him, was appointed President and CEO. He was to lead HP into the rapidly changing computer marketplace, a relatively new major thrust for the company.

Mr. Young launched several major programs designed to improve HP's planning, to coordinate its marketing efforts, and to strengthen its presence in computer markets. Specific strategy changes supported these important endeavors:

- Mr. Young reorganized HP Laboratories after its R&D chief retired, replacing him with John Doyle, formerly HP's personnel executive. Young felt that the Labs needed management, not science, in its leadership. Doyle was particularly known for his ability to articulate HP's entrepreneurial culture.

- Doyle recruited 220 computer oriented professionals and several key researchers from other successful computer companies.

EXHIBIT 2   SIMPLIFIED ORGANIZATION CHART: 1975

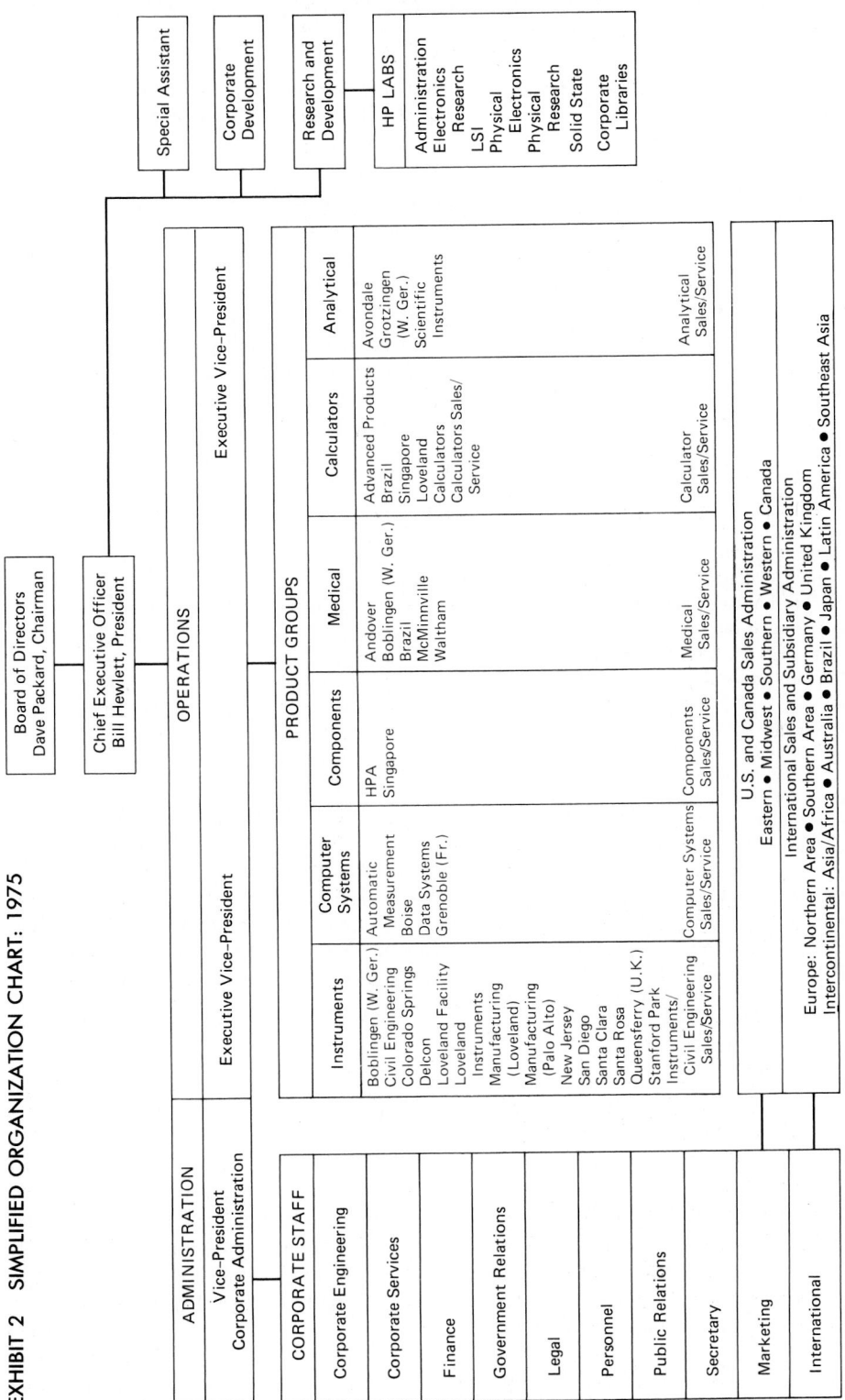

Source: Drawn from "Working Together: The HP Organization," *Measure*, April–May 1975, pp. 16–17. (*Measure* is an HP internal publication.)

- The firm substantially increased its R&D spending.
- For the first time, HP started forming research partnerships with universities.
- The firm worked to couple HP Laboratories more closely to the strategies of its company operating groups.
- HP acquired several small companies to obtain specific applications skills.
- HP set up its first applications marketing division and staffed this with specialists from other industries.

In addition, Mr. Young felt that a focus on quality was one of the best ways to control costs. He said:

> A few years ago, the company did an internal study that had some surprising results. HP had always considered itself a quality leader in the industry—and indeed, it was. The company was therefore somewhat surprised when a study demonstrated that fully 25 percent of its manufacturing costs were involved in responding to bad quality.
>
> A "stretch objective" was announced. Employees were asked to improve on product failure rates by a factor of ten during the decade of the 1980s. . . .
>
> There has been a ripple effect of quality efforts throughout HP. The aggregate impact is large. In 1978, HP's inventory represented about 20.5 percent of sales. In 1983, it was down to 15.9 percent. Much of that reduction can be traced to better quality—less scrap, shorter cycles, and better flow.[9]

Problems with Computers

While these actions were having a positive impact, the effects of a decentralized organization were being adversely felt in its computer markets where HP's products—frequently overlapping and often incompatible in operation—were threatening the firm's fine quality and performance reputation.

HP faced conflicting demands, both within its organization and in the marketplace. In recent years HP had stressed profitability over market share. Of particular importance to HP had been creating unique products that commanded a premium price. HP had never been an organization to create "me-too" products. Said Mr. Young, "We are not in the clone business; we will differentiate our products." But according to *Fortune*, "Hewlett-Packard's traditional approaches were all but useless in creating personal computers. In that business not being a clone—IBM compatible—was a good way to get clobbered in retail stores. . . ."[2]

Yet as one HP corporate executive was quoted by *Forbes*:

> When it comes to the personal computer business, [HP has used] what I would describe as a very opportunistic approach to the marketplace. We have had several organizations in the company that were addressing the market. But none of them had it as their major focus . . . we had over $500 million sales in the personal computer market, which is not bad, but no significant focus on it.[10]

In addition, not many of HP's senior executives had specific experience in computer operations. In fact, most of HP's senior people had started with the organization on the instruments side, including those heading up the computer groups. Some believed this to be a problem, since the requirement of each business was rather distinct.

Past Principles and An Organization for the Future

Following is a 1983 description of the corporate objectives which encompassed HP's most important principles. Although there had been substantial change in the marketplace, few modifications had been made to the company's objectives since they were initially published in 1957.

1. **Profit:** to achieve sufficient profit to finance our company's growth and to provide the

resources we need to achieve our other corporate objectives.

2. **Customers:** to provide products and services of the highest quality and the greatest possible value to our customers, thereby gaining and holding their respect and loyalty.

3. **Fields of Interest:** to build on our strengths in the company's traditional fields of interest, and to enter new fields only when it is consistent with the basic purpose of our business and when we can assure ourselves of making a needed and profitable contribution to the field.

4. **Growth:** to let our growth be limited only by our profits and our ability to develop and produce innovative products that satisfy real customer needs.

5. **Our People:** to help HP people share in the company's success which they make possible; to provide job security based on their performance; to ensure them a safe and pleasant work environment; to recognize their individual achievements; and to help them gain a sense of satisfaction and accomplishment from their work.

6. **Management:** to foster initiative and creativity by allowing the individual greater freedom of action in attaining well-defined objectives.

7. **Citizenship:** to honor our obligations to society by being an economic, intellectual, and social asset to each nation and each community in which we operate.

HP's 1982 organization structure is outlined in Exhibit 3. In 1983 and again in 1984, the company restructured its organization in an attempt to deal with the issues posed by its move into computers. In Mr. Young's announcement of the organization changes of 1984, he spoke of this and previous fundamental reorganizations, ". . . each change has been a logical, evolutionary move that preserved the basic philosophy and integrity of the HP approach to business."[7]

Mr. Young further added:

Becoming a computer company has had a dramatic effect on our company, the biggest challenge is to orchestrate the divisions and provide a strategic glue and direction for the computer effort, while keeping the work units small.

Having small divisions is not the only way to organize a company, but having organizations that people can run like a small business is highly motivational, especially for professionals. Keeping that spirit of entrepreneurship alive is very important to us.[11]

When asked to compare his management style with that of HP's founders, Young said, "Bill is a brilliant engineer and Dave is a great businessman. I stress organization, planning, and the process." He further replied to the question of what he most hoped to achieve, by saying, "To show that it is worth institutionalizing our founders' principles, hopefully by growing some and detracting nothing from the human elements that are so important."[8]

The Program Manager Concept

In response to these issues, a "program manager concept" had come into being at HP. Program managers had broad powers to tap various divisions for necessary support, components, or software. Previously, new products had always come from individual divisions, engineered typically in pursuit of the division's charter to "stay ahead of the game," or from HP Laboratories researchers who had "sold" their ideas and found a divisional sponsor.

The program manager concept was used for a special project called "Dawn." Under the direction of a program manager, half a dozen widely scattered HP divisions were coordinated on a $100 million project. On November 16, 1982, less than two years after "Dawn" began, the HP 9000, considered by many experts to be the ultimate in personal computers, was introduced. To succeed, the activities of the divisions had to be closely coordinated and the divisions' independence limited. As a target market for the HP 9000 (introduced in a remarkably short two years after a program manager was assigned), the company chose manufacturers, since these

EXHIBIT 3   HP ORGANIZATION CHART 1982

ADMINISTRATION	OPERATIONS
Bob Boniface	Paul Ely,
Executive Vice President	Executive Vice President

ADMINISTRATION

Corporate Controller
Jerry Carlson
Controller

Corporate Services
Bruce Wholey
Vice President

General Counsel
and Secretary
Jack Brigham
Vice President

International
Bill Doolittle
Senior Vice President

Government
Affairs
Bob Kirkwood
Director

Patents and Licenses
Jean Chognard
Vice President

Personnel
Bill Craven
Director

Public Relations
Dave Kirby
Director

Marketing
Al Oliverio
Senior Vice President

Treasurer
Ed van Bronkhorst
Senior Vice President

EUROPE

Franco Mariotti
Vice President

Field Sales Regions
France
Germany
Northern Europe
South/East Europe
United Kingdom

Manufacturing
France
Germany
United Kingdom

INTERCONTINENTAL

Alan Bickell
Managing Director

Field Sales Regions
Australasia
Far East
Japan
Latin America
South Africa
Manufacturing
Brazil
Japan
Malaysia
Mexico
Puerto Rico
Singapore

U.S./CANADA SALES

Field Sales Regions
Eastern
Midwest
Neely (Western)
Southern
Canada

Corporate

Marketing
Operations
● Parts Center

COMPUTERS

TECHNICAL COMPUTER GROUP

Doug Chance
Vice President

■ Data Systems
■ Roseville
■ Desktop
  Computer
■ Engineering
  Systems
■ Böblingen
  Desktop
■ YHP Computer
■ Computer I.C.
  ● Cupertino I.C.
  ● Systems
    Technology

COMPUTER PERIPHERALS GROUP

Dick Hackborn
General Manager
■ Boise
■ Disc Memory
■ Greeley
  ● Singapore
■ Vancouver
  ● Bristol

BUSINESS COMPUTER GROUP

Ed McCracken
General Manager
■ Computer Systems
  ● Roseville
■ Information Networks
  ● Office Systems
    Pinewood
  ● Office Systems
    Cupertino
  ● Grenoble
    Datacomm
■ Manufacturing Productivity
  ● Financial
    Systems
■ Böblingen
  General Systems
  ● Information Resources
  ● Guadalajara
    Computer

COMPUTER TERMINALS GROUP

Cyril Yansouni
General Manager
■ Personal Office
  Computer
■ Roseville
  Terminals
■ Grenoble
  ● Puerto Rico

COMPUTER MARKETING GROUP
Jim Arthur, Vice President

■ Computer Support
■ Application Marketing
■ Personal Computer
  Marketing

● Systems
  Remarketing
● Computer
  Supplies

BOARD OF DIRECTORS
Dave Packard, Chairman of the Board
Bill Hewlett, Chairman—Executive Committee

CHIEF EXECUTIVE OFFICER
John Young, President

OPERATIONS
Bill Terry,
Executive Vice President

OPERATIONS
Dean Morton,
Executive Vice President

INSTRUMENTS

MICROWAVE AND COMMUNICATIONS INSTRUMENT GROUP

Hal Edmondson
General Manager
- Colorado Telecom
- Queensferry Telecom
- Stanford Park
- Spokane
- Signal Analysis
- Network Measurements
- Santa Rosa Technology Center

ELECTRONIC MEASUREMENTS GROUP

G. B. Parzybok
General Manager
- Böblingen Instrument
- San Diego
- Colorado Springs
- Logic Systems
- YHP Instrument
- Loveland Instrument
- Lake Stevens Instrument
- New Jersey
- Santa Clara
- Integrated Circuits
  - Santa Clara
  - Loveland
  - Colorado Springs

INSTRUMENT MARKETING GROUP
Bob Brunner, General Manager

- Instrument Support

COMPONENTS GROUP

John Blokker
General Manager
- Microwave Semiconductor
- Optoelectronics
  - Visible Products
  - Interface Products
  - Singapore
  - Malaysia

Compents
Sales/Service

MEDICAL GROUP

Dick Alberding
Vice President
- Andover
- Böblingen Medical
- McMinnville
- Waltham
- Medical Supplies

Medical
Sales/Service

Key
- Division
- Operation (product line/international locations)

ANALYTICAL GROUP

Lew Platt
General Manager
- Avondale
- Scientific Instruments
- Waldbronn

Analytical
Sales/Service

PERSONAL COMPUTATION GROUP

Dick Moore
General Manager
- Corvallis
- Personal Computer
  - Corvallis Components
  - Brazil
  - Singapore

(Computer Marketing Group)

HP LABORATORIES

Research and Development

John Doyle
Vice President

RESEARCH CENTERS

Computer Research

Physical Research

Technology Research

CORPORATE DEVELOPMENT

Dave Sanders
Director

INTERNAL AUDIT
George Abbott
Manager

CORPORATE MANUFACTURING SERVICES

Ray Démeré
Vice President

Source: Hewlett Packard Company.

had been its primary customers for nearly ten years. It also selected four applications areas for focus: planning and control systems, factory automation, office systems, and engineering.

Traditionally, HP had marketed technologically sophisticated products and left applications details to its customers. That strategy worked well for many years because its customers were scientists who were often as sophisticated about applications as HP was. Yet computer customers were no longer necessarily scientists or engineers. As one corporate executive said, "I keep telling my engineers that they now have five minutes to make a sale, not five hours like we used to. We have to focus on apparent user benefits."[2] This executive's own experience typified the problem. While talking to a potential customer

he became a bit rhapsodic about the HP 150's ability to process 2.2 megahertz faster than the IBM PC. "What's a megahertz?" asked the prospect, a lawyer. "I have to get out documents—what can you do for me?"

But technology was rapidly revolutionizing the small computer markets in which HP competed. In 1980 the 64K memory chip had made the desk top microcomputer into one of the fastest growing markets in the U.S. By 1985 the 256K chip allowed production of desk top minicomputers, powerful small lab computers, and engineering and production work stations of great complexity and power. By 1987 new megabit (one million bit) chips would permit mainframe powered computers to be produced in "micro" sizes. Pocket computers, electronic map naviga-

EXHIBIT 4   HEWLETT PACKARD'S MANUFACTURING PRODUCTIVITY NETWORK (MPN)

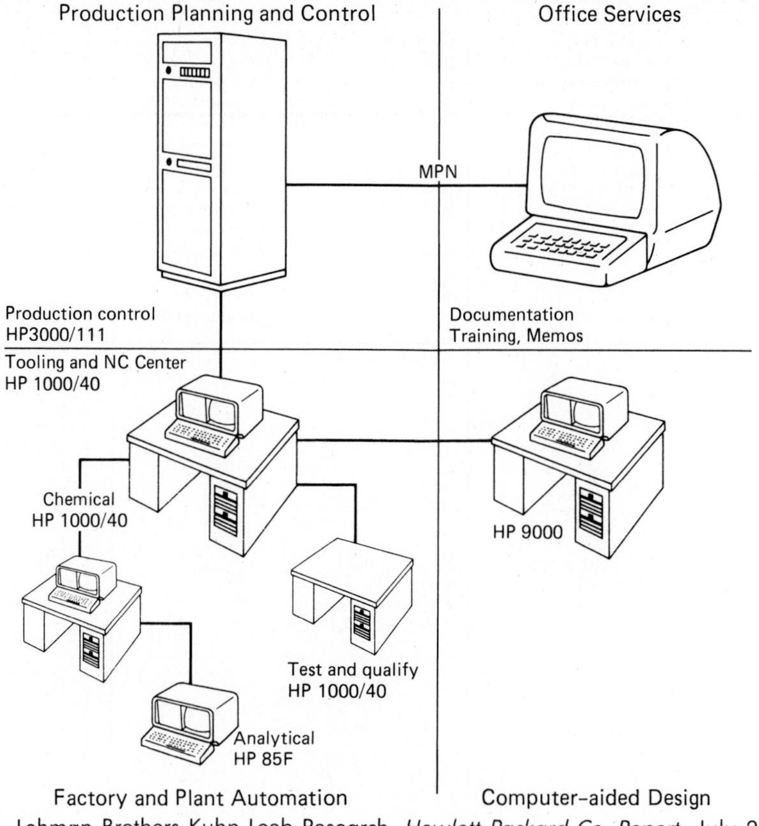

Source: Lehman Brothers Kuhn Loeb Research, *Hewlett Packard Co. Report*, July 26, 1983.

tors, and robots that could see and recognize some natural language commands were in the offing. By 1990 micro-supercomputers based on 4 megabit chips were expected with powers dwarfing all but the largest laboratory models. Yet these remarkable creations were likely to be so inexpensive that they would quickly become ''commodity'' items. Managing this degree of complexity in a commodity marketplace would become a singular challenge.

One analyst had earlier commented that over the past two decades HP had transitioned from a test instrument firm into a major systems company. By 1983 HP was involved in an even more complex shift toward multisystem networks— complete link ups between computers, instruments and peripherals—for laboratory, factory, hospital, or office automation systems.[12] An example of such a multisystem network is outlined in Exhibit 4.

In 1982 HP had over 45 product divisions, of which at least 22 were directly related to computers. But in the burgeoning electronics markets of the mid-to-late 1980s increasing opportunities were appearing to link and relate what previously had been ''stand alone'' sensing, testing, measuring, processing, or controlling units. How HP could respond to these new needs, yet maintain its distinctive entrepreneurial style and culture was a critical issue for its management in the mid 1980s.

QUESTIONS

1. Why has HP been successful in the past? Why was its organization configured the way it was at each major transition point? Evaluate how well its structure and systems were adapted each time for their purposes.

2. What are the critical strategic issues facing HP in the mid 1980s? How should it respond to these? Key financial and operations data appear in the attached exhibits.

3. How should HP organize to meet its future challenges? Why? What changes in management style, control systems, and incentives should accompany these changes?

EXHIBIT 5   HEWLETT PACKARD COMPANY AND SUBSIDIARIES: FINANCIALS

Consolidated Statement of Earnings

For the years ended October 31 (Millions except per share amounts)	1984	1983	1982
Net sales	$6,044	$4,710	$4,189
Costs and expenses:			
Cost of goods sold	2,865	2,195	1,967
Research and development	592	493	424
Marketing	1,066	771	631
Administrative and general	661	523	491
	5,184	3,982	3,513
Earnings before taxes	860	728	676
Provision for taxes	313	296	293
Reversal of DISC taxes[*]	(118)	—	—
	195	296	293
Net earnings	$ 665	$ 432	$ 383
Net earnings per share	$ 2.59	$ 1.69	$ 1.53

* Reversal of DISC taxes accrued prior to 1984 due to a change in U.S. tax law
The accompanying notes provided in the company's annual report are an integral part of these financial statements.

Selected Financial Data

(Millions except per share amounts and employees) For the years ended October 31	1984	1983	1982	1981	1980
Domestic orders	$3,629	$2,901	$2,283	$1,918	$1,517
International orders	2,721	2,021	1,897	1,739	1,570
Total orders	$6,350	$4,922	$4,180	$3,657	$3,087
Net sales	$6,044	$4,710	$4,189	$3,528	$3,046
Earnings before taxes	$ 860	$ 728	$ 676	$ 567	$ 513
Net earnings	$ 665[*]	$ 432	$ 383	$ 305	$ 263
Per share:					
Net earnings	$ 2.59[*]	$ 1.69	$ 1.53	$ 1.24	$ 1.09
Cash dividends	$ .19	$ .16	$ .12	$ .11	$ .10
At year-end:					
Total assets	$5,153	$4,161	$3,470	$2,782	$2,350
Employees (Thousands)	82	72	68	64	57

* Includes a one-time increase in net earnings of $118 million (46 cents per share) resulting from a tax law change.
Source: Hewlett Packard Company, Annual Report, 1984.

EXHIBIT 5 (*Continued*)

Consolidated Balance Sheet

October 31 (millions)	1984	1983	1982
Assets			
Current assets:			
Cash and temporary cash investments	$ 938	$ 880	$ 684
Accounts and notes receivable	1,180	951	773
Inventories:			
Finished goods	373	279	231
Purchased parts and fabricated assemblies	650	469	428
Other current assets	60	53	99
Total current assets	3,201	2,632	2,215
Property, plant and equipment:			
Land	202	167	106
Buildings and leasehold improvements	1,416	1,102	940
Machinery and equipment	1,173	888	714
	2,791	2,157	1,760
Accumulated depreciation and amortization	923	726	589
	1,868	1,431	1,171
Other assets	84	98	84
	$5,153	$4,161	$3,470
Liabilities and shareholders' equity			
Current liabilities:			
Notes payable	$ 217	$ 148	$ 156
Accounts payable	281	203	139
Employee compensation and benefits	398	300	269
Other accrued liabilities	162	103	106
Accrued taxes on earnings	203	112	151
Other accrued taxes	61	54	42
Total current liabilities	1,322	920	863
Long-term debt	81	71	39
Other liabilities	93	46	42
Deferred taxes on earnings	112	237	177
Shareholders' equity:			
Common stock and capital in excess of $1 par value	775	733	587
Retained earnings	2,770	2,154	1,762
Total shareholders' equity	3,545	2,887	2,349
	$5,153	$4,161	$3,470

The accompanying notes provided in the company's annual report are an integral part of these financial statements.
Source: Hewlett Packard Company, *Annual Report*, 1984.

EXHIBIT 5 (*Continued*) **SEGMENT DATA**

Business Segments* (Millions)	1984	1983	1982
Gross sales			
Computer products	$3,269	$2,476	$2,161
Electronic test and measurement	2,289	1,779	1,595
Medical electronic equipment	378	355	323
Analytical instrumentation	229	184	176
	$6,165	$4,794	$4,255
Intersegment sales			
Computer products	73	56	44
Electronic test and measurement	47	26	21
Medical electronic equipment	1	2	1
	121	84	66
Net sales	$6,044	$4,710	$4,189
Earnings before taxes			
Computer products	$ 439	$ 392	$ 370
Electronic test and measurement	514	381	339
Medical electronic equipment	41	61	60
Analytical instrumentation	37	23	28
Eliminations and corporate	(171)	(129)	(121)
	$ 860	$ 728	$ 676

* Sales between affiliates are made at market prices, less an allowance for subsequent manufacturing and/or marketing.

Source: Hewlett Packard Company, *Annual Report*, 1984.

Geographic Areas* (Millions)	1984	1983	1982
Net sales			
United States	$3,527	$2,725	$2,270
Europe	1,620	1,392	1,318
Rest of world	897	593	601
	$6,044	$4,710	$4,189
Earnings before taxes			
United States	$ 768	$ 644	$ 554
Europe	138	148	157
Rest of world	110	59	95
Eliminations and corporate	(156)	(123)	(130)
	$ 860	$ 728	$ 676
Exports from			
United States	$1,420	$1,105	$1,081
Europe	145	100	61
Rest of world	277	160	164

* Net sales are based on the location of the customer. Earnings before taxes reflect the location of the company's facilities. Exports are primarily inter-area transfers to affiliates, which are made at market prices, less an allowance for subsequent manufacturing and/or marketing. Certain amounts have been reclassified to conform to the 1984 format.

EXHIBIT 5 (*Continued*)

Business Segments

Identifiable assets (Millions)	1984	1983	1982
Computer products	$2,182	$1,673	$1,358
Electronic test and measurement	1,379	1,022	903
Medical electronic equipment	268	224	191
Analytical instrumentation	154	133	104
Eliminations and corporate	1,170	1,109	914
	$5,153	$4,161	$3,470

Capital Expenditures (millions)	1984	1983	1982
Computer products	$ 330	$ 248	$ 215
Electronic test and measurement	202	108	104
Medical electronic equipment	27	37	18
Analytical instrumentation	14	18	7
Corporate	88	55	18
	$ 661	$ 466	$ 362

Depreciation and Amortization (Millions)	1984	1983	1982
Computer products	$ 128	$ 105	$ 86
Electronic test and measurement	68	54	46
Medical electronic equipment	11	9	8
Analytical instrumentation	7	6	5
Corporate	23	17	13
	$ 237	$ 191	$ 158

Direct and indirect sales to the U.S. Government amounted to approximately $550 million in 1984, $480 million in 1983 and $420 million in 1982. No other customer accounted for more than 5 percent of net sales.

Source: Hewlett Packard Company, *Annual Report*, 1984.

EXHIBIT 5 (*Continued*)

PRODUCTS AND BUSINESS SEGMENTS

The *Electronic Data Products* segment includes the following product groups: Business Computer, Technical Computer, Computer Peripherals, Computer Terminals, Computer Marketing and Personal Computation Groups. Products include small-to-medium-scale computer systems for business, scientific and industrial applications; desktop, personal and portable computers; personal scientific and business programmable calculators; computer peripherals; and a wide variety of software and support services.

The *Electronic Test and Measurement Products* segment includes the following product groups: Electronic Measurements, Microwave and Communication Instrument, Components, and Instrument Marketing. Products include instruments, systems and components for design, production and maintenance. Products used primarily in the communications, electronics manufacturing and aerospace industries.

Medical Electronic Equipment segment products perform a number of patient-monitoring, diagnostic, therapeutic, and medical and financial data-management functions for health care providers. Included are measurement and computation systems and a wide variety of software and support services and supplies.

Analytical Instrumentation segment products are used primarily to analyze chemical compounds. Products include gas and liquid chromatographs, mass spectrometers, spectrophotometers, laboratory automation systems and integrators.

Source: Hewlett Packard Company, *Annual Report,* 1982.

EXHIBIT 5 (*Continued*)

HEWLETT PACKARD COMPANY ESTIMATED SALES BREAKDOWN

	1982	1983E	1984E	The Market's 5-Yr. Growth
COMPUTERS				
Graphics/CAD	730	900	1090	20%
HP 3000 (MPN)	635	635	750	15%
Peripherals	500	600	750	25%
Calculators	117	90	115	10%
Microcomputers	100	170	215	25%
Software	35	50	70	35%
HP1000 (Factory)	0	12	35	65%
HP 9000 (CAE)	0	30	75	70%
TOTAL	2117	2487	3100	
INSTRUMENTS				
Microwave/Comm.	470	500	590	15%
Elec. Test	835	925	1130	20%
Automatic Test	45	56	70	25%
Components	224	250	285	10%
TOTAL	1574	1731	2075	
MEDICAL				
Patient Monitoring	195	180	205	15%
Diagnostic Instr.	127	150	180	20%
Hospital Mgmt.	0	19	26	30%
TOTAL	322	349	411	
ANALYTICAL				
Gas Chromatographs	45	35	45	15%
Data Stations	105	127	150	20%
UV/Visible Spec.	15	20	25	20%
Liquid Chromatog.	10	12	15	30%
Biotechnology	1	1	5	50%
TOTAL	176	195	240	
COMPANY TOTAL	4189	4762	5826	

Source: E.F. Hutton, Inc., Equity Research, *Hewlett Packard Company Action Report*, June 28, 1983.

EXHIBIT 6   COMPARATIVE FINANCIALS

Electronic Business 200 Rank			Calendar 1984			
1984	*1983*	*Company*	*Electronics Sales ($ Million)*	*Total Sales ($ Million)*	*Net Income ($ Million)*	*Return on Investment (%)*
1	1	IBM	$45,937.0	$45,937.0	$6,582.0	21.8%
2	2	AT&T	17,406.7	33,187.5	1,369.9	5.9
3	3	General Electric	7,210.0	27,947.0	2,280.0	17.0
4	5	Xerox	6,981.0	8,791.6	375.6	6.0
5	4	ITT	6,589.0	12,701.0	302.5	3.4
6	8	Hewlett Packard	6,297.0	6,297.0	564.0	18.2
7	9	Digital Equipment	6,229.6	6,229.6	486.9	7.4
8	6	Honeywell	6,073.6	6,073.6	334.8	10.9
9	10	Texas Instruments	5,741.6	5,741.6	316.0	16.4
10	12	Motorola	5,534.0	5,534.0	387.0	13.7
11	13	RCA	4,945.0	10,111.6	246.4	5.4
12	7	Hughes	4,925.0	4,925.0	300.0	NA
13	11	Burroughs	4,875.6	4,875.6	244.9	8.0
14	15	Sperry	4,648.0	5,370.0	262.2	5.6
15	16	Control Data	3,755.0	5,026.9	31.6	0.4
16	17	NCR	3,728.0	4,074.3	342.6	14.3
17	18	Raytheon	3,454.0	5,995.7	340.1	16.4
18	21	N. A. Philips	3,193.0	4,325.9	130.5	8.7
19	23	TRW	2,904.0	6,061.7	266.8	12.8
20	22	Tandy	2,771.1	2,771.1	234.9	21.1
27	29	Wang	2,421.1	2,421.1	231.0	12.9
31	49	Apple	1,897.9	1,897.9	104.3	13.8
34	38	Zenith	1,717.0	1,717.0	63.6	10.2
41	42	Tektronix	1,419.9	1,419.9	131.5	40.6
49	55	Perkin-Elmer*	1,169.0	1,255.5	79.2	10.2

* *Leader in Analytical Instrumentation.*
NA: Not available.

Source: Electronic Business, July 15, 1985.

Latest Fiscal Year			5-Year Growth (Compounded Growth Rate)		Capital Outlays to Net Cash Flow after Dividends	Debt as % of Total Capital
Cost of Goods as % of Sales	R&D as % of Sales	Net Income per Employee ($ Thousand)	Sales (% per Year)	Net Income (% per Year)		
33.6%	9.1%	$16.7	15.0%	16.9%	83.1%	12.4%
50.5	7.2	3.8	NA	NA	190.1	41.0
69.6	3.7	6.9	4.5	10.1	101.6	6.4
39.4	6.4	3.6	4.6	−7.8	146.4	27.1
76.4	7.7	1.2	−5.9	−4.5	150.0	31.3
45.6	9.8	8.1	20.7	26.8	77.5	3.0
56.0	11.3	3.8	25.4	13.0	77.8	10.0
61.6	6.9	3.6	7.6	6.9	67.7	22.5
68.5	6.4	3.7	12.2	12.8	102.1	19.9
57.9	7.4	3.9	15.3	20.2	128.6	19.1
71.5	2.4	2.3	6.3	−2.8	131.3	41.5
NA	NA	NA	NA	NA	NA	NA
54.9	5.7	3.8	11.5	−4.3	113.4	25.0
59.3	8.4	2.7	3.3	−2.3	103.1	21.0
51.1	6.0	0.6	17.5	−23.2	94.8	76.6
43.7	7.1	5.5	6.3	7.9	61.7	13.1
77.4	3.9	4.6	10.0	11.5	105.7	4.6
74.3	2.3	2.3	12.4	9.8	92.4	34.0
73.3	2.4	2.9	5.9	6.5	113.2	15.7
43.4	0.0	8.3	17.6	27.6	25.1	26.1
47.6	7.3	6.9	46.7	49.0	155.3	23.3
55.5	4.7	11.9	99.5	66.1	38.8	0.0
77.2	5.1	2.2	9.8	27.4	69.5	28.8
50.5	11.2	5.7	11.1	8.9	54.9	68.2
55.3	6.7	4.3	10.0	5.6	68.3	12.9

EXHIBIT 7   REPRESENTATIVE MARKET SHARE DATA FOR HP PRODUCTS

A.   Worldwide 1985 Shares (%) Computers

	Small Systems ($12K-350K)		Microsystems (<$12K)
IBM	20.0	IBM	27.7
DEC	12.7	Apple	9.0
Nixdorf	6.0	Commodore	4.2
HP	5.8	HP	4.2
Wang	4.3	NEC	3.6
NEC	3.1	AT&T	3.5
AT&T	2.4	Wang	2.7

Source: *Wall Street Journal*, April 7, 1986, p. 26.

B.   Test & Measurement Shares (%) 1984

	Logic Analyzers		Universal Microprocessor Development Systems
HP	30	HP	61
Tektronix	29	Tektronix	32
Gould	7	Kontron	4
Phillips NV	7	Millenium	3

Source: F. Eberstadt & Co., Inc., *Test and Measurement Industry Report*, May 20, 1985.

ZAYRE CORPORATION (A)

Discount retailing for broad ranges of non foods merchandise really began in the 1950s. The first stores—like Arlan's, 2 Guys from Harrison, Kings, and J.M. Fields—moved into cheap vacated warehouse or mill spaces. Early discounters tended to be individual entrepreneurs with an intuitive sense of the new U.S. marketplace. Family sizes were exploding in the post war baby boom; U.S. manufacturing efficiencies were creating millions of new jobs; the purchasing power of the working and middle classes had ballooned; national advertising media were stimulating widespread brand recognition and standardized tastes; and the automobile facilitated mobility, suburbanization, and mass purchasing on a scale never possible before. In 1956 Zayre Corporation became the first company to exploit these trends by building a complete newly constructed retail discount store and chain specially designed for self-service sales of general merchandise.

DISCOUNTERS TAKE OVER

The large department stores, which were then the dominant form of retail merchandising, ignored discounters at first. Most responded by upgrading their locations, displays, and services—and raising margins to cover the added costs. The three great national department store chains each reacted differently. Sears undertook an awesome branch rollout into the suburbs, aimed at the price conscious middle income market. J.C. Penney followed suit on a later and smaller scale. Montgomery Ward, anticipating a post war recession, froze its posture, hoarded cash, and went

Case copyright © 1985 by James Brian Quinn. Research associate—Penny C. Paquette. Research assistant—Barbara Dixon. The generous cooperation of the Zayre Corporation is gratefully acknowledged.

into decline. In the early-to-mid 1960s SS Kresge and Woolworth's abandoned their early variety-store formats (open counters, small items in jumbled displays) to build the Kmart and Woolco chains with a larger range of merchandise and more sophisticated presentation. And discount sales boomed:

Year	Number of Stores	Discount Sales
1960	1,329	$ 2 billion
1970	5,000	$19 billion
1980	8,300	$45 billion
1984	8,600	$56 billion

Discounters' 1984 sales represented 48% of all retail general merchandising sales. While there were several major shakeouts on the way, the top 7 chains increasingly concentrated their share of the market from $11 billion in 1974, to $21 billion in 1978, to $34 billion in 1983. In New England, discounting accounted for an incredible 72% of full-line general merchandise sales, with five of the nation's largest 15 discounters headquartered there. Many of the top names of the expansionary 1970s had essentially disappeared—including Woolco, Grants, Korvettes, Mammoth Marts, Two Guys, and Kings. Zayre Corp. had not only survived the rugged shakeout which had occurred, but had enjoyed record breaking growth in the early 1980s, and was positioning itself for the rigorous challenges of the late 1980's. What were the key events in Zayre's recent history? And what should its future strategy be?

ENTREPRENEURIAL TIMES

Mr. Stanley Feldberg, Zayre's first CEO, oversaw his company's growth from its 1950s birth to sales of $1.4 billion in 1978. By then there were

251 Zayre discount stores in major metropolitan areas, mainly east of the Mississippi. Like the discount field itself, Zayre had developed rapidly under the entrepreneurial styles of its founders, mostly Feldberg family members. (See organization chart.) The company had been privately held until it went public in 1962, and was still dominated by the founding group and their scions in the late 1970s. Together they held approximately 30% of Zayre's stock. The organization structure was both a cause and effect of Zayre's growth and management style. In the words of Mr. Stanley Feldberg,

> The original founders had always governed themselves as equal partners, and their successors had been groomed to think the same way. People were careful not to let a single person or position dominate the scene. It was often difficult to get a decision implemented in one area, if the head of that area disagreed. There tended to be management by committee and indeed management by consensus. One of the offshoots of this style was that there was not as much emphasis on profitability or "bottom line" as you might have found elsewhere. Profitability was important but could be sacrificed in the short run while you were seeking expansion opportunities.

Expansion Plans and Complications

Around 1969, Zayre went through a McKinsey & Co. organizational study in concert with a 5 year plan to double its stores (from 125 to 250) and its total volume (from $500 million to $1 billion). McKinsey suggested a much expanded executive force and a restructuring to increase Zayre's managerial depth and diversity. Zayre built up its organization rapidly in anticipation of its planned growth, causing a corresponding short term buildup in overheads. While staying in its traditional market niches, Zayre attempted to decentralize the organization more extensively on a regional basis. Instead of reporting directly to headquarters, district managers began to report to 6 regional managers, who had their own staffs.

These were very large businesses, with some 40–50 stores reporting to each regional manager. While Store Operations decentralized, Merchandising and Real Estate activities stayed centralized. (See organization chart.) And problems soon developed. Said Mr. Stanley Feldberg:

> Frankly, the Merchandising Department had not kept up with our changing customers of the 1960s. We had attempted to keep *absolute* price levels from increasing despite a mild inflation. It finally became impossible to do this and not lose quality in our merchandise lines at the very time our customers' capacity to buy higher quality was steadily growing. We kept advertising prices almost exclusively. In a practice that set my teeth on edge, we sometimes advertised specials with no more than a few days supply on hand to service customers. This brought customers in the door, and kept the store from losing too much on the margins of sale merchandise. But it alienated people who had expected a good buy and couldn't find it.

The merchandising problem was compounded by the fact that Zayre had started to build bigger 80,000 square foot stores (versus 65,000) and to move into suburban areas. Zayre's product lines had to be spread over a larger physical area, creating the impression of thinner inventory coverage. Merchandising techniques of piling goods in aisle bins for quick sale—which had worked so well in lower income areas—failed in the more exclusive suburbs. Ads targeted solely at price didn't bring customers into these stores so readily. And new stores which had been budgeted for $3½ to $4 million volumes, only brought in $1.5–$2 million. Meanwhile Kmart was opening stores budgeted for $9 million sales volumes and had Kresge's massive capital resources to help stock the stores and support them with advertising.

As one executive said, "All this killed our store productivity. As productivity declined, there wasn't enough income to keep the stores current. So we lost more sales. And so on. We wanted

ZAYRE CORPORATION   ORGANIZATION CHART MID–1976

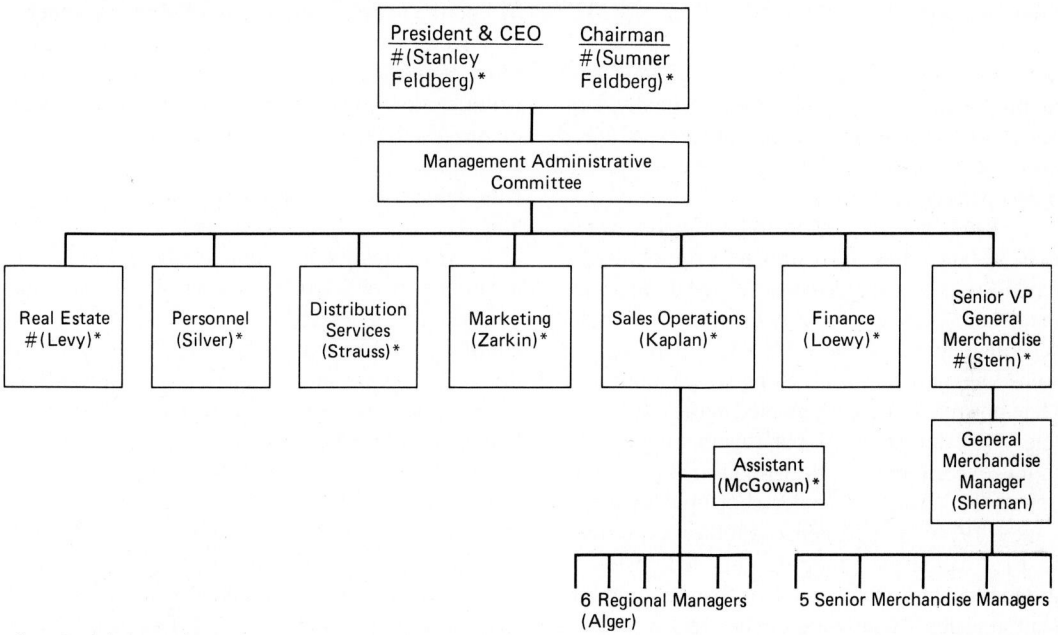

Family members.
* *Member Management Administration Committee.*

Source: Company records.

Race Tracks and Experiments

the stores to look a bit spartan, but soon our parking lots had potholes, maintenance had to be delayed, roofs began to leak, merchandise coverage dropped even more. Top management was deeply aware of the problem, but it was awfully hard to break out. Then along came the oil crisis and the 1974–75 inflation-recession— fiscal 1975 (calendar 1974) earnings dropped to only $835,000.''

Mr. Stanley Feldberg amplified, "As we disappointed customers at a merchandise level, store sales began to dry up, but overhead percentages began to escalate—not uncontrollably, but enough to hurt badly. Our first response was to cut back expenses at the stores, cleaning services, maintenance, even capital and investment payrolls. We cut back support services at home office too. But profits still dropped and we got into a vicious circle where it got even harder to correct things.''

From this low point began one of the greatest turnarounds in retailing history. Zayre's top managers took a long view and began some experiments designed to reposition its stores for the future. They called in a consultant, Alton Doody, who said that while the Zayre Stores' format had been adequate for the 1960s, it was not well tuned to the future. In 1975 Stanley and Sumner Feldberg authorized a series of experimental layouts, presentations, display changes (etc.) that became known as the "Zayre '75" program. Mr. Doody brought in the concept of a "race track aisle" that carried the customers rapidly around the store to various departments. Each department was arranged around this aisle with "windows" on the aisle and "vistas" to invite the customer into the department. And new display techniques were developed to let each department put the "best foot forward" for its merchandise. Some experiments worked; others did not. "Zayre '75" was followed by another series of experiments in "Zayre '76" and again later in "Zayre '77." Sumner and Stanley Feldberg personally supported all these experiments, but they still had to be carried out with limited capital because of tight operating margins.

1976 brought several other major events. *First*, Zayre returned to stronger profitability, as the oil crisis receded. *Second*, Mr. Malcolm Sherman, later president of Zayre Stores, combined several features of the 1975–76 experiments in some Indianapolis stores, along with a more complete inventory showing adapted to the local clientele. He later said, "I put together everything in this experiment I could without making capital demands." And store sales shot upward in this "Indy 1976" experiment. Another experiment in 1977 called the "loop design" led customers around its test stores—rather than through the central aisles—with good effect. And so on. But *third*, and perhaps most importantly, in 1975 Stanley and Sumner Feldberg had begun the search for a CEO to carry Zayre into the 1990s. And for the first time Zayre was looking seriously outside the family's ranks.

A TIME OF CHANGE

After an intensive three year search Mr. Maurice Segall joined Zayre Corp. as its first non-family CEO in February 1978. Mr. Segall was a trained economist who had started his career as chief economist and director of planning and organization at Steinbergs, a large food supermarket operation headquartered in Montreal. He later became director of operations for the Treasure Island Stores chain of J.C. Penney, and finally (1974–78) president of American Express' Credit and Card Division, where he is widely credited with tripling that organization's volume in a series of highly entrepreneurial and insightful moves. Mr. Segall said, "Many people thought I was crazy to go into a family dominated situation in a difficult industry like retail discounting. But I had gotten to know Stanley and Sumner Feldberg very well over the last couple years. I knew they were people of quality and high integrity who would follow through on all commitments made to me—and they would not second guess me. And frankly, while Zayre was a real challenge, I thought it had very high potentials for the future."

Mr. Segall's five year contract called for a base salary of $300,000 a year plus substantial bonuses if he increased net income per share from continuing operations from 10–20% a year in the first 3 years and from 7.5–15% a year in the last two years. It also provided for a signing bonus of $200,000 in the first year, plus deferred compensation of $500,000. In an interview with *Chain Store Age Executive* Mr. Segall said, "The most successful retail executives are people with a real desire for continuing challenge. There are few companies where they can receive such stimulation year in and year out . . . The people who have what it takes, the people who thrive on that challenge, are real risk takers. There are few industries other than retailing which offer these people such opportunities."[1]

First Steps

The Board had placed no constraints or set any specific goals for its new CEO. Mr. Segall immediately began a three month series of travels around to all the stores. Knowing he would be gone constantly, he had kept his family home in Long Island, so his wife would have a familiar environment and close friends nearby while he traveled. In May 1978, Mr. Segall came back to Sumner and Stanley Feldberg and said, "Now I know what I have to do. I like all the experiments. But I want to stop the experiments, put them together, and do the chain."

There were many things that most agreed were crucial to getting Zayre stores back onto their growth curve again. Various executives and outside sources contributed the following composite view:

1. Because of the economic constraints and the corresponding morale problems of the cutback years, many of the stores had become unattractive and some were not well managed at the local level. Frequently, merchandise was not kept neatly arranged. In some cases store cleanliness was even a problem. Many stores did not have complete stock positions, and there was a lot of bickering between the field operations people and the home-office merchants. "When anything was wrong, some other party always seemed at fault."

2. Physically, many stores were in difficult shape. There were numerous stores with leaky roofs and peeling wallboard and plaster. Some of the store fronts were run down and display fixtures were broken or in ill repair. Even stores which had been refurbished were often not properly maintained because of capital constraints. And it would cost millions to bring the chain up to a desired standard.

3. While Zayre had an outstanding financial control system, merchandising control had been a major problem. Merchandising had been centrally managed in detail. Stocking plans for each store were close to identical, even though store sizes and locations varied significantly. Zayre's merchandising group used mainly a "push" system of trying to get good buys on desired merchandise and then pushing goods out through the stores with a standardized plan. This approach had worked well enough when the chain was small, but it began to break down when the company had a complex group of some 250 stores.

4. Many of the stores' presentation techniques in terms of merchandise displays, lighting intensity, wall colors and floor coverings, were not up to date. Long checkout lines and service people not being available to assist on the floors were serious problems. Said one long time Zayre executive, "boxes often littered the floor, and you could look at shelves and see gaps in the merchandise lines. A facelift was necessary both in physical terms and in terms of the morale of employees who had been discouraged during the tight financial period by these surroundings."

Everything at Once

While these were widely recognized issues, action had been difficult to take because of both capital and organizational constraints. Mr. Segall said,

> First, it was evident we had to fix up our physical plant and keep it in shape. We needed enormous amounts of money to do the job. But it's not sufficient just to fix up a store. There are a lot of nice stores that go out of business. You have to update your marketing and advertising for that store, and you have to make sure you get the right merchandise in that store and maintain its stocks. None of this works without good people. The problem is you can't do it one step at a time. This chain had 250 stores, and it would take a lifetime to do it that way.
>
> But we had to do it right. And we didn't have the luxury of time. A key point in all this was to zero in on what our mission was and what our customer definition was. We agreed we should not change the definition of our target customer (the working class customer looking for good value), but would try to get to that customer more effectively. We were not going to suddenly become an upper middle class discount store.

Between May and September, 1978, Mr. Segall—and a few people (notably Malcolm Sherman and Bob Alger) he had identified for their future executive potentials—developed a strategy called the Marketing Development Program (MDP) to present to the Board in September of that year. Before that meeting Mr. Segall decided to reorganize the entire field structure of Zayre Stores. He later said:

> You have to send some messages, and I decided the then executive vice president of Zayre Stores was not the right person to carry this out. There were any number of good people I could have hired from outside. But I decided to look around carefully inside the company and identified

Bob Alger (age 39) as the right person for the job.

We had long discussions about what needed to be done, but I wanted Alger to find the players. Deciding that the whole thing should be done over one weekend, I asked Bob Alger, the V.P. of Personnel, and two promising young executive protégés of Mr. Alger to lock themselves in their hotel rooms at the Logan Hilton for three days and come out with names of all the new district and zone managers for the Zayre chain. It was done in three days without anyone knowing it. Then I asked Mr. Sherman and Mr. Zarkin to develop the kinds of merchandising and advertising strategies we had discussed. All this went into the fall Board presentation.

The proposal asked for $30 million (later $40 million) for a remodeling and updating program and another $25 million for an Electronic Point of Sale (EPOS) program to convert all the cash registers and point of sale controls to a computer basis. Mr. Segall later said, "It was a bet your company strategy. It was either going to work and be successful, or it would drive us into bankruptcy." Exhibits 1–4 set forth some of the key background data for this 1978 strategy meeting.

Zayre Stores was not to change its basic concept. Zayre was to remain a neighborhood, convenience, self-selection, general merchandise, discount department store chain. Its target customer was the lower part of the middle income class and the upper part of the lower income class—the great working class of America. Changes would be made in the stores to reflect the fact that the targeted customers' attitudes and aspirations had changed. Zayre Stores moved to serve their customers' tastes more effectively, rather than to a new customer base.

Other Zayre Operations

In 1976, Sumner Feldberg had been very impressed by the concept of off-price retailing which

he saw at the then young ($120 million volume) Marshall's chain. Off-price stores sold quality brand name merchandise at 20–60% below regular list prices. Zayre tried to buy Marshall's but was outbid by Melville's. Consequently Mr. Feldberg rapidly developed a similar concept for Zayre which became the T.J. Maxx chain, with 10 stores in calendar 1977. T.J. Maxx's target was the middle income customer who wanted a good value at a good price. It appealed to the female homemaker buying for a whole family. As *Forbes* said, "The chain catered to people who were snobby enough to want brand names, but didn't want to pay the full price for them."[2] T.J. Maxx carried brands like Calvin Klein, Gloria Vanderbilt, Liz Claiborne for women; Arrow, Van Huesen, and Ralph Lauren for men; Carter's, Healthtex, and Izod for kids; and a wide selection of branded linens, towels, and housewares. T.J. Maxx stores operated in smaller (25,000 square foot) units in urban and suburban shopping malls. And like most start ups it had lost money in the first few years of operations.

Zayre's other off-price chain was Hit or Miss (H or M), originally acquired as a 10 store Boston chain in 1970, which grew to 17 units by year end. After a promising start, Hit or Miss had begun to top out in the mid 1970s. *Chain Store Age*, said, "In its first eight years, Hit or Miss had become a less than successful teenagers' and low-end girls' apparel chain which emphasized teeny bopper fads, accessories, and fringes."[3] In this very competitive market, H or M had operated 4,000 ft^2 shops in less expensive suburban strip malls where overheads were lower. Its format had been spartan, with bright exposed flourescent lamps, lots of merchandise "up front" on racks, and heavy use of self-service promotional signage. Although by 1978, H or M was targeted more towards the price conscious young woman buying for herself, in the words of *Chain Store Age* "Hit or Miss was missing more than hitting" and was a net money loser for the Zayre Corporation." Although its profitability figures were not broken out in Zayre's published statements, observers said H or M's problems were getting worse in the late 1970s.

The 1978 Competition

The major competitors of Zayre were positioned and moving roughly in the following directions in 1977–78. Traditional department stores had moved to "top of the line" positions in suburban areas or refurbished central cities—or by and large they had failed.

Sears Roebuck. With sales of $17.2 billion and a 6.23% market share of U.S. general merchandise sales in 1977, Sears was the largest of the major chains. Its Annual Report in 1977 stated that its mission was "to provide quality merchandise at competitive prices across the nation." Its current sales distribution was 71% through store outlets, 20% catalog sales, and 9% other. In the late 1960s Sears moved upscale to the middle to upper middle income market vacated by the big full line department stores. Sears anchored its big (up to 200,000 ft^2) full line stores in the more expensive malls and backed its presentations with a greater number of service personnel than most of its chain competitors.[4] Part of the upscale move was toward fashion goods which some thought did not fit too well with Sears' strong (65% of sales) competitive hard goods image.[5] Sears had a strong private label position especially in white goods, and with its high volume Sears could have quality merchandise made inexpensively with the special features it desired.

By 1978 Sears had 366 full line (200,000 ft^2) stores, 371 semi-full-line (78,500 ft^2) stores, and 135 hard line (24,000 ft^2) outlets. Sears also held significant equity in some of its suppliers, and owned 49.9% of a Canadian chain, which had sales of $2 billion. And Allstate insurance contributed some $400 million to profits. Its catalog sales were 55% from in-store centers; only 45% were handled by telephone or through freestanding catalog stores.

Kmart. The second largest chain was Kmart with $9.9 billion in sales, 55% from hard goods and 45% soft lines. Kmart had outlets in 257 of the 275 SMAs of the U.S. Of its 1,395 stores, 795 had been built in the last 5 years and located mainly in high growth suburban areas and smaller industrial or agriculturally based cities. Kmart used a one story format in four basic store types (84,000, 68,000, 55,000, and 45,000 ft^2 formats). These could be "freestanding" stores—not necessarily tied into a shopping center—which could locate in any convenient, available space even in less populated rural or older, high density city markets as well as in the suburbs. Kmart had grown at 20% per year mainly by opening new stores. Kmart had been SS Kresge's vehicle for diversifying out of the maturing variety store business in the 1960s. By 1977 Kmart accounted for 95% of Kresge's sales, and the parent had changed its own name.

J.C. Penney. Nearby was J.C. Penney with its $9.4 billion in sales, 59% from full line stores, and 23% from soft line stores. In 1977 it had 460 full line stores (averaging 88,000 ft^2) mainly in shopping centers of major metropolitan markets. Its 1,226 soft line stores (average 12,000 ft^2) tended to be in the downtown areas of medium sized cities or the "main streets" of smaller communities, where J.C. Penney had built its reputation for reliable quality at a good price. In 1977 its expansion plans were focused around its full line stores, with modernization and some relocation of its soft line outlets. Penney had recently begun a push toward higher profitability by adding more fashionware to its apparel lines and emphasizing home furnishings to combat the competition it faced from department stores in its shopping center locations.[6] Its other operations included 37 freestanding discount stores (the Treasury Stores) which averaged 97,000 ft^2 and were not very successful in 1977. Penney also had 229 drug store outlets (8,000 ft^2) which were performing adequately, a profitable $1 billion catalog business, and a small insurance business which it was just beginning to integrate into its retail outlets.

Wal-Mart. A small but fast growing regional chain was Wal-Mart with $900 million in sales, 68% in hard goods. Wal-Mart had 195 stores in a 10 state area (Texas to North Central states) located within 400 miles of its headquarters and distribution center. Its average store size was

43,000 ft,[2] ranging from 30,000 to 60,000 ft.[2] Wal-Mart was building 30 to 40 new stores a year in standardized formats built around 36 departments. Wal-Mart stressed rock-bottom priced staple goods and emphasized (68% of sales) its hard goods lines.[7] Wal-Mart used a "big frog in little pond" philosophy, preferring to be the largest non-food retailer in the smaller 25,000–30,000 person communities. It targeted county seats where it often edged out older J.C. Penney stores by offering a wider selection with more hard goods.[8] Among discounters, department stores, and variety stores, *Forbes* ranked Wal-Mart first over the past 5 years in average ROE, return on invested capital, sales growth and earnings growth. In its 1978 *Annual Report* CEO Sam Walton said the secret of success was "nothing more than bringing together men and women who are completely dedicated to their jobs, their company and their communities."

QUESTIONS

1. What should the 1978–83 strategy of Zayre Corporation be? What are the critical action sequences?
2. How can Zayre acquire the capital needed for these moves?
3. How should Zayre be reorganized?
4. What other implementing actions must go along with these strategic changes?

EXHIBIT 1 ZAYRE CORPORATION: EXPENSE COMPARISONS WITH CORNELL SAMPLE OF SIMILAR STORES (Fiscal Years 1976–77)

Expense Analysis Percent of Sales
(Excluding Leased or Franchised Departments)

	FYE 1/76		FYE 1/77	
	Cornell Excl. Zayre	Zayre	Cornell Excl. Zayre	Zayre
Total Payroll	12.40%	12.76%	12.79%	12.72%
Supplies	.75	.87	.66	.91
Communications	.23	.78	.25	.40
Travel	.21	.38	.20	.39
Services Purchased	.74	.50	.67	.52
Advertising	2.43	2.93	2.66	3.18
Taxes and Licenses	1.17	1.33	1.12	1.35
Utilities	1.13	1.39	1.13	1.35
Insurance	.57	.70	.66	.71
Property Rentals	3.21	3.36	3.09	3.56
Equipment Rentals	.35	.31	.33	.30
Depreciation & Amort.	.85	1.13	.76	1.00
Repair & Maintenance	.48	.99	.53	1.05
Donations	.01	.02	.02	.02
Professional Services	.24	.17	.22	.18
Unclassified	1.05	1.08	1.09	1.11
Credits and Allowances	(.40)	(.01)	(.22)	—
Total Expense	25.44%	28.39%	25.96%	28.75%

Source: Company records and analyses provided during interview.

Gross Margin, Expense, and Earnings Percent of Sales
(Excluding Leased or Franchised Departments)

	FYE 1/76		FYE 1/77	
	Cornell Excl. Zayre	Zayre	Cornell Excl. Zayre	Zayre
Gross Margin	28.52%	30.15%	28.86%	30.61%
Leased Department Income	.80	.59	.92	.65
Gross Income	29.32	30.74	29.78	31.26
Total Expense	25.44	28.39	25.96	28.75
Net Operating Profit	3.88	2.35	3.83	2.51
Other Income or Deductions	(.23)	(.80)	(.06)	(.69)
Earnings before Income Taxes	3.65	1.55	3.77	1.82
Federal & State Income Taxes	1.84	.78	1.84	.92
Net Earnings After Taxes	1.81%	.77%	1.93%	.90%

Source: Company records and analysis provided during interviews.

EXHIBIT 2   ZAYRE CORPORATION: LOCATION OF OPERATIONS, JANUARY 1978

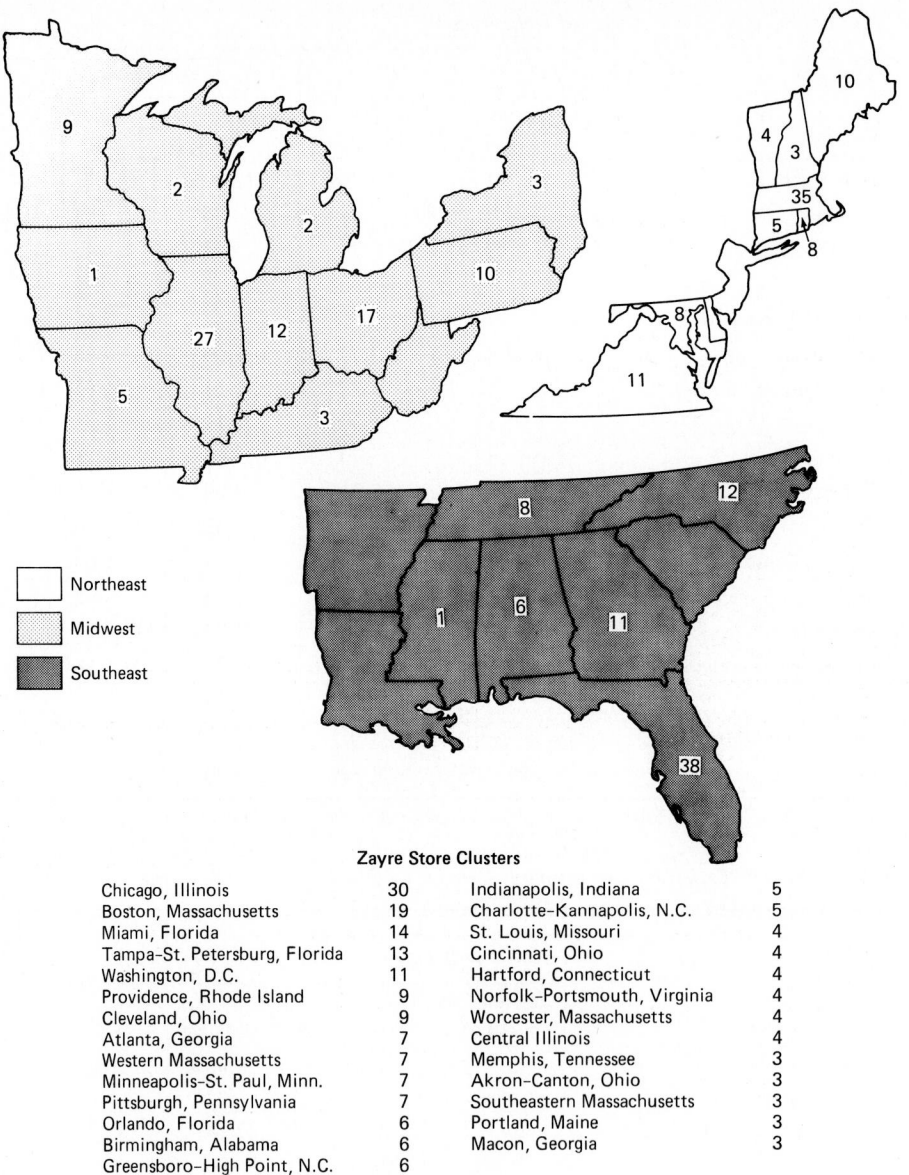

☐ Northeast
▨ Midwest
▨ Southeast

Zayre Store Clusters

Chicago, Illinois	30	Indianapolis, Indiana	5
Boston, Massachusetts	19	Charlotte-Kannapolis, N.C.	5
Miami, Florida	14	St. Louis, Missouri	4
Tampa-St. Petersburg, Florida	13	Cincinnati, Ohio	4
Washington, D.C.	11	Hartford, Connecticut	4
Providence, Rhode Island	9	Norfolk-Portsmouth, Virginia	4
Cleveland, Ohio	9	Worcester, Massachusetts	4
Atlanta, Georgia	7	Central Illinois	4
Western Massachusetts	7	Memphis, Tennessee	3
Minneapolis-St. Paul, Minn.	7	Akron-Canton, Ohio	3
Pittsburgh, Pennsylvania	7	Southeastern Massachusetts	3
Orlando, Florida	6	Portland, Maine	3
Birmingham, Alabama	6	Macon, Georgia	3
Greensboro-High Point, N.C.	6		

Source: Zayre Corporation, *Annual Report,* 1978.

EXHIBIT 3   ZAYRE CORPORATION FINANCIALS*
STATEMENT OF CONSOLIDATED EARNINGS ($ Millions)

	1979	1978	1977	1976	1975	1974
Net sales	$1,394.1	$1,261.3	$1,160.6	$1,084.0	$1,045.5	$996.4
Cost of sales	1,076.7	987.3	907.9	850.7	827.2	777.7
Gross profit	317.5	274.0	252.7	233.3	218.4	218.7
Operating expense	271.5	234.5	212.8	208.1	201.4	190.8
Interest expense	20.0	17.7	18.3	11.1	16.1	12.1
Income before tax	26.9	21.8	21.5	14.1	0.9	15.8
Federal income tax	12.9	10.8	11.3	7.2	0.2	7.2
Net income	14.0	11.0	10.2	4.9	0.8	9.1

CONSOLIDATED BALANCE SHEET ($ Millions)

	1979	1978	1977	1976	1975	1974
ASSETS						
Cash	$ 23.0	$ 23.5	$ 25.9	$ 26.1	$ 38.7	$ 36.6
Accounts receivable	5.5	4.7	4.5	2.8	3.6	5.6
Inventories	254.0	242.3	211.0	187.8	177.6	191.5
Other current assets	19.9	17.9	16.8	15.0	13.6	3.9
Total current assets	302.4	288.5	258.2	231.6	233.5	237.6
Net fixed assets	173.8	168.2	96.0	102.5	112.0	118.5
Total assets	$476.2	$456.8	$354.2	$334.1	$345.4	$356.1
LIABILITIES						
Current installment, LTD	$ 9.2	$ 10.0	$ 11.4	$ 9.8	$ 13.7	$ 9.3
Accounts payable	73.3	76.1	57.6	52.0	60.4	70.6
Accrued expenses, taxes, etc.	62.5	53.7	44.2	35.8	30.5	31.0
Total current liabilities	145.1	139.8	113.1	97.6	104.6	110.9
Long-term debt	188.6	190.0	115.5	122.0	131.3	136.6
Stockholders' equity	142.5	128.0	125.5	114.5	109.5	108.7
Total liabilities and equity	$476.2	$456.8	$354.2	$334.1	$345.4	$356.1

* *Fiscal year ends January of year designated, refers to operations of preceding calendar year.*

Source: Company records.

EXHIBIT 3 (*Continued*)

OPERATING RESULTS OF THE ZAYRE COMPANY BY ITS MAJOR SEGMENTS

| | (Amounts in Thousands) | | | | | |
| | January 27, 1979** | | | January 28, 1978** | | |
	Consolidated	Discount Dept. Stores	Specialty Stores	Consolidated	Discount Dept. Stores	Specialty Stores
Sales & Operating Revenues	$1,394,109	$1,222,900	$171,209	$1,261,301	$1,141,422	$119,879
Operating Income	$ 46,778	$ 38,630	$ 8,148	$ 38,190	$ 33,542	$ 4,648
General Corporate Expense	7,941			6,695		
Interest Expense	11,913			9,653		
Total Income Before Income Taxes	$ 26,924			$ 21,842		
Identifiable Assets	$ 476,243	$ 401,376*	$ 38,214*	$ 456,754	$ 395,561*	$ 25,656*
Depreciation & Amortization	$ 18,941	$ 17,738	$ 1,203	$ 17,561	$ 16,678	$ 883
Capital Expenditures	$ 21,174	$ 17,108	$ 4,066	$ 10,536	$ 5,793	$ 4,743

Identifiable assets are those assets of the Company associated with an industry segment and do not include cash and marketable securities.
**Includes the effect of SFAS 13. "Accounting for Leases." The prior year amounts have been restated accordingly. For further information see notes in company's annual report.*

Source: Zayre Corporation, *Annual Report*, 1978.

EXHIBIT 4   ZAYRE CORPORATION 1978 NUMBER OF RETAIL ESTABLISHMENTS IN OPERATION

| | Reported in January of Year Indicated | | | | | |
	1965	1970	1975	1976	1977	1978
Zayre (discount dept. store)	72	153	258	254	255	252
Hit or Miss (apparel)			62	87	118	173
T.J. Maxx (off-price)						10
On Stage/Nugent's/ Bell (apparel)	43	48	36	34	36	31
Beaconway (fabrics)		7	46	44	42	34
Gasoline stations	2	37	95	95	95	7
Shoppers City (food and non food supermarkets)		8	10	10	10	9
Spree! (discount toy stores)				6	5	

Source: Zayre Corporation, *Annual Report*, 1965, 1970, 1975–78.

ZAYRE CORPORATION (B)

Soon after Mr. Maurice Segall became CEO of Zayre Corporation (see Zayre (A) case) he instituted a number of changes which repositioned Zayre Corporation in its various market places. Critical corrections were made quickly, but "without a bloodbath."

The entire retail environment shifted rapidly in 1978. As the Iranian revolution brought on a tripling of oil prices, rapid inflation and the highest interest rates in history hit the U.S. Many discounters did not survive this difficult period. In 1978 there were over 65 discount chains with volumes over $100 million. Five years later, one third of them did not exist. But Zayre's sales soared to $3.1 billion in 1985 with profits of $80.3 million. (See Exhibit 1.) Bradlee's, Caldor, and Kmart moved toward higher income customers. Zayre Stores stayed with its traditional customers and became one of the few successful chains selling to "center city" populations. Many such areas had strong ethnic preferences. As one Zayre executive said, "We had to solve the problem of maintaining the advantages of chain retailing, yet cater to the needs of individual locations, a really difficult task."

BARRACUDAS OR FOSSILS

By 1983, Chicago was Zayre Stores' biggest market, and sales in the lower-middle income "southside" had grown from $25 million to $100 million in only 5 years. The original remodeling and upgrading budget for Zayre Stores had grown to $100 million. Change was constant during this period. As Malcolm Sherman, Zayre Stores president said, "If ever there was an industry that responds to Darwin's theory of survival of the fittest, it's retailing. A new retailer starts as a young barracuda, and can end up as a fossil 10 years later."

In this respect, off-price merchandising was to the early 1980s what discount stores had been to the 1960s and early 1970s. Off-price chains sprang up all over, specializing in women's apparel, family apparel, shoes, housewares, linens and domestics, and so on. These stores had a special appeal to the "white collar market" to whom brand names and styles were more important. T.J. Maxx boomed in its markets and by 1985 had become the second largest (to Marshall's $1.2 billion) retailer of off-price, brand name apparel in the U.S. according to *Standard & Poors Corporate Descriptions*, December 1984. By 1985 the increased number of Maxx stores had called for a 300,000 ft^2 distribution center in Worcester, Mass. to supplement its original 450,000 ft^2 complex.

Although performance of off-price chains was highly variable, the best such chains achieved some $200 sales per square foot, with an 8–10 times inventory turnover, and net profits before taxes of 5% of sales. *Chain Store Age* estimated total off-price sales of some $17 billion by 1990. Unlike other retail trends started by entrepreneurs, the off-price chains all had big money behind them. U.S. Shoe, Melville, Dayton Hudson, and Zayre were among the big players. In addition to competing with more prestigious retailers like Marshall Field, Lord & Taylor, etc., off-price stores competed directly with the private brands sold by Sears, J.C. Penney, or Montgomery Ward—often made by the same manufacturers to the buyers' specifications. At first, buyers obtained off-price merchandise strictly from manufacturers' overruns, closeouts, returns, previous

Case copyright © 1985 by James Brian Quinn. Research associate—Penny C. Paquette. Research assistant—Barbara Dixon. The generous cooperation of the Zayre Corporation is gratefully acknowledged.

season's merchandise, irregulars (etc.). But increasingly, buyers could obtain excellent prices on large orders placed directly with manufacturers.

Hit or Miss had changed too. It now targeted mid-to-better income females who wanted recognized merchandise at a lower price. It offered current season, first quality women's sportswear (casual pants, shirts, blouses, etc.) and ready-to-wear dresses, coats, and suits in both brand names and private labels at about 50% off regular prices. (Reed Hunter was one of H or M's private labels.) The store focused on the somewhat conservative, youthful, professional, career minded woman, who was very fashion conscious but had to watch costs. Although Hit or Miss had been "repositioned" extensively from 1978–85 and expanded to 356 units in 31 states, the chain seemed to lack a distinctive personality or loyal clientele and was still not a roaring success in 1985.

THE NEW ZAYRE

By 1985, Zayre Corporation had changed markedly. Even with Zayre's powerful recent growth and strong balance sheet, (see Exhibit 1) Mr. Segall was still pointing for new horizons. His goal was a 20% per year compounded growth rate. Despite his easy-to-meet style and great personal charm, he was described by *Forbes* as "all business, clearly a workaholic, but he had to be to bring about such major changes [from 1978–84]. . . . Clear thinking, tough decisions, well executed"[1] were said to be his hallmark. Mr. Segall described his style somewhat differently:

> I want growth in a disciplined fashion.
> . . . Everyone in this company knows what our goals are. We stand up once a year and I talk to 1,500 people—from mail clerks to executive VPs—and they know what our goals are. We don't keep secrets here. We continue to refine our mission statements, our target customers, and so on. We introduced three year plans, which were tied to clear three year in-

come, sales, ROI, and operating objectives. . . . I don't want anything left to chance. I want us to be in control. All of us must execute the basics—not only with the highest of standards, but better than our competitors.

> We have business plans for each segment of the business which pull all these together in a consistent way. We have also developed extensive incentive plans tied directly to these. I believe in incentive plans. Everyone has incentive plans, but ours can be very generous. (See Exhibit 2.) Although I'm well paid, our key people can also make a lot of money, and we have made some millionaires. . . . I think that's great as long as the stockholder makes out better as a result.

Zayre's policy was to pay competitive base salaries, while putting significant emphasis on variable forms of compensation. The exact mix of salary, incentives, and other compensation varied based upon the manager's organization level and job responsibilities. Three objectives underlay the Zayre compensation program: (1) to pay competitive basic and total compensation scales; (2) to reward exceptional individual performance, and (3) to ensure that the compensation program was cost effective by closely tying it to well-communicated business plans. Exhibit 2 summarizes Zayre's basic incentive plans.

In addition, Zayre used four types of long term incentives to retain and reward its key executives: stock options, career shares, restricted stock, and long term cash bonuses. Key executives could buy career shares for book value with a company provided loan. Sale and conversion restrictions lapsed on these at 20% per year. A tax free conversion to common shares could occur on this schedule at a predetermined exchange ratio. Zayre's Long Range Management Incentive Plan (LRMP) was a 3 year cash incentive plan tied to company results for those who could influence intermediate term performance. At the beginning of each 3 year period, a 3 year target was established for Net Income (75%) and Net Income/Sales (25%) at divisional levels and Net

Income (75%) and ROI (25%) at corporate levels. Incentives peaked sharply in a fashion similar to those set forth in Exhibit 2.

Hits and Questions

While T.J. Maxx and Zayre Stores were growing and profitable in 1984–85, Hit or Miss still had problems. Mr. Segall said, "We're not executing properly there. We are currently struggling with the division's real mission. I'm still persuaded there is a market for our kind of store for the career oriented young woman between 20 and 40. But we need a much better distinctive concept and better execution for our present target market. In 3,500 ft² you have very little room to make a statement, and we're making too many statements."

"In the case of T.J. Maxx, we're very pleased with the execution to date, but we're facing a different competitive environment. The T.J. Maxx concept was really designed 8–9 years ago. By definition, that design has to be obsolete now. The problem is how to position this excellent chain for the 1990s and execute that positioning effectively."

Other Ventures

By 1985, Zayre's management had begun to ask itself some very basic questions about the future. "Where do we go from here as a total corporation? What kind of company should we be in the 1990s? Should Zayre start some new ventures or acquire some? We started exploring a wide range of opportunities. When all was said and done we decided to take a crack at BJ's Wholesale Club, which was our version of the Price Club on the west coast. But this is only the beginning."

Self service, cash-and-carry "wholesale clubs" (or warehouses) like BJ's offered a "limited membership" (of small businesses) access to name brand goods at genuine wholesale prices. For an annual fee, a business could buy at posted wholesale prices. Non-commercial buyers could buy under a group membership which involved no annual fee, but required purchase prices 5%

above posted prices. The key to wholesale club operations was abnormally low merchandise margins, extremely efficient operations, in a bare-bones, pseudo-warehouse environment. Mr. Segall noted, "In this kind of operation, there is no room for error. But the concept offers low prices and sound values; and that is what retailing is all about." Sumner Feldberg commented, "It isn't as if we are discovering America here; it happens to be a form of retailing developed over the course of the past few years with which some people have had great success. I'm very impressed with these operations by the remarkable volume they can generate." Sales per square foot of Price Club units were estimated at well over $500.

The Price Club in California had opened its first "wholesale club" warehouse store in 1976 and by 1983 grossed some $630 million and was widely imitated. (See Exhibit 3.) Experts thought this concept would grow to at least $20 billion by 1990.[2] Minimum volumes for early stores were $25–30 million, but some units were selling annual volumes of over $100 million. At first, estimates were that each store needed 400,000–600,000 people in its market area to be profitable, but this could drop as the concept caught on and operations were "debugged." A typical store operated on 10%–11% merchandise margins and sold a major portion of its volume to smaller businesses, restaurants, groceries, drugstores, offices, etc. BJ's units opened with $3–$4 million in inventory each and sought breakevens within one year. Most chains sought 60/40 business/group sales. BJ's Mervin Weich, an MIS data processing expert, noted that inventory turnover goals would be some 16X per year—based on the Price Club experience. Parking for some 400 cars was de rigueur, with start up costs of $5–8 million per store being common. Most wholesale chain clubs targeted staffing levels per store at 70–200 people.

"Deep discounting" at 40–60% off suggested retail prices was also spreading rapidly in drug items, foods, auto parts, books, stationary and so on. There were some 200 such units in 1985, but 1,000 were expected by 1990. They operated in 20-30,000 ft² formats with very restricted lines and inventories purchased mainly on "deals" from suppliers. Direct mail selling was also growing at 10–15% per year. And Zayre was actively expanding its direct mail operation, Chadwick's, begun in 1983. Sumner Feldberg said, "The first catalog effort was terrific and the customer response was excellent. But, Chadwick's is primarily viewed as a means for the company to gain experience in mail order, something we have not been in before, as opposed to our long experience as chain store operators."[3]

1985 Competition

What did Zayre's main competitors look like in 1985?

Sears Roebuck. With $38.8 billion in sales Sears was still the largest retailer by far with a continuing mission "to provide customers with more quality goods and services than any other organization of its kind." Sears sales consisted of $29.5 billion in merchandise, $9.0 billion Allstate Insurance, $2.5 billion Dean Witter financial services, and $1.0 billion from real estate and world trade activities. Sears had developed its "Store of the Future" concept with expanded product lines, more exciting displays and an emphasis on modernized and improved service levels at the point of sale. It had shifted its merchandise mix more to upscale apparel and home furnishings, with relative deemphasis on hard good lines. It was experimenting with smaller (8,000-30,000 ft^2) stores to sell its own franchised products. Sears had also added some specialty stores (100 Business Centers and 4 Paint and Hardware Centers). Its total number of stores was down to 792 from 831 in 1982 with 391 full-line, 355 medium-line, and 52 hard-line stores.

Kmart. Zayre's closest competitor was Kmart with sales of $21.1 billion from 2,400 general merchandise discount stores and 1,120 specialty outlets. Kmart discount stores operated in 48 states with an average 57,000 ft^2 format. Its stated strategy was "to provide a broader offering of brand names, larger assortment of high value goods, and a more contemporary presentation of merchandise" because customers wanted better quality merchandise at lower prices. Its customer mix had moved slightly upscale since 1977. Kmart had diversified *within* retailing into: *Designer Depot*, an off-price family apparel chain following the Marshall's and T.J. Maxx format; *Waldenbooks*, at 900 stores and 5 discount units the largest book retailer in 50 states (acquired for $300 million and expected to sell $1 billion in 1990); *Builders Square*, large (80,000 ft^2) warehouse home centers for contractors and do-it-yourselfers (15 outlets acquired for $88 million); *Pay-Less Drug Stores*, one of the largest retail drug chains (104 units plus discount outlets acquired for $500 million); *Financial Services*, available in 275 Kmarts with 1,000 projected by 1990; *Cafeterias*, 158 units in 2 chains expected to be $1 billion in sales by 1990; *Kmart Trading* for export of U.S. made goods.

J.C. Penney. In metropolitan areas Penney's now had 564 department stores averaging 157,000 ft^2 representing 60% of its sales, and 205 soft-line stores having 7% of sales. It also had 801 small town stores averaging 25,000 ft^2 (13% of sales), catalog sales (14%), and drug stores (14%). It was continuing to expand in fashions using its own designer labels and remodeling its stores accordingly. It was closing down its food, hardware, and car accessory departments.[4] Penney's financial services subsidiary, while still small and primarily involved in insurance sales (now through over 200 in-store centers), also operated the J.C. Penney National Bank and five Financial Centers in California. It had $22 million in net income.

Wal-Mart. Wal-Mart had grown to $4.7 billion in sales with 642 stores in 20 states. Its average store now had 50,000 ft^2 and plans called for 100 new stores in 1985. *Forbes* still showed Wal-Mart as first in its key financial return statistics (See Exhibit 4). Wal-Mart's basic strategy was unchanged, but it had moved into 11 wholesale clubs in 1985, opened its first drug discount store, and was testing a 25,000 ft^2 format for even smaller towns.

The Second Cluster

Among the second cluster of discounters, variety and diversity were most notable. Gemco-Memco stores in California grossed an amazing $23 million per store, including foods. And Target Stores owned by Dayton Hudson averaged $12 million per store. Elsewhere there were numerous local "piperack retailers" who could be successful for short periods of time by selling what the industry considered "schlock" merchandise. These units were very successful in specific locations, but Zayre was distinctly differentiated from these, and was by far the most successful chain with minority customers in the central cities of the U.S. See Exhibit 4 for some comparative data on various chains.

WHERE IS THE FUTURE?

Retailing would undoubtedly undergo many more changes in the late 1980s. See Exhibit 5 for data on some selected trends. Key executives at Zayre added some broad perspectives on how these might fit into their company's future.

Mr. Segall said, "We're all going to have to be sensitive to the extraordinary acceleration in the birth, growth, maturity, and decline cycle of American retailers. The pace is just incredible. The old line retailer is gone, and today's successful patterns will be tomorrow's disasters. For us any aspect of retailing is fair game. The only thing we preclude is non retail—no steelmaking, no broadcasting. Retailing will always be one of the largest business segments in our economy."

But excess capacity and market saturation was a real problem as each major company continued to expand. By 1985 retailing was characterized by "intertype marts with a pharmacy in the rear. Grocery stores carried both pharmacy and general merchandise items. Sears had moved out into financial services, as had Kmart and some J.C. Penney units. And so on. Meanwhile specialized flea markets, off-price catalogs, house-to-house selling, party plans, and telemarketing were expanding at wild rates. And specialized discount retailers—like Toys 'R Us and Bata (shoes)—were establishing a clear presence in their markets.

In March 1985, Mr. Segall noted, "One of the most exciting developments in U.S. retailing in fifty years is the potential purchase by Americans of $100s of billions worth of electronics in the years to come. Increased household formations, a bulge in the educated 25–45 year old group, more use of the home as an entertainment base, the growth of cable communications, new technologies, home computers, (etc.) mean this is the largest single growth category in U.S. retailing." Marketing Science Institute estimated that home appliance, radio, TV, and electronic store sales would grow from $12 billion in 1980 to $52 billion in 1990.

All of these opportunities were being eyed by well-heeled, well-managed, aggressive, large corporations, looking for new entries. Mr. Segall said, "Never before have so many professionals surveyed so many new kinds of developments, ready to pounce on the attractive ones with huge war chests for financing." But each new retailing approach was also reaching maturity faster than ever before, creating ever greater pressure for precise timing, positioning, and care in choosing what directions to pursue.

Macro-Trends

J. Seth in the *Journal of Retailing* cited other macro trends in the field. (1) The U.S. was becoming a very affluent, diverse, adult oriented society with highly individualistic life styles in which time—rather than money—had become the scarce resource. (2) Competition in retailing was becoming more global in both sourcing and distribution. And a changing focus toward deregulation was allowing very large oligopolistic companies to exploit this trend. (3) The single middle class U.S. society was becoming more a dual class, 25% affluent and 60–70% average income society whose basic functional needs were easily met; demand was shifting to psychological satisfactions in products over sheer functionality—to wants over needs. (4) With the emergence of non traditional households with dual or multiple incomes, more goods were being demanded at individualistic, rather than shared levels—with foods, leisure items, clothing, and services all being heavily affected. (5) For demographic and technological reasons, it would be increasingly common not to separate the time and place of work, home, and shopping activities. (6) As technology dropped the relative price of many appliances, the distinction between shopping goods and convenience goods would blur, and customers would increasingly depend on manufacturers as their guarantors of quality.[5]

Another source referred to these trends as "life style retailing" tailored to the life styles of specific target markets, rather than "supplier driven" retailing. Demographically, the 35–45 year old population and the over 80 population were growing most in percentage terms, while the under 20 group was falling in the late 1980s. This bulge represented the best educated, most affluent, and culturally diverse population in U.S. history. During the past 10 years the black U.S. population had grown 17% and the Hispanic population had grown 61%.[6] But Mr. Stanley Feldberg pointed out that there were strongly divergent regional and local trends. For example, the Northeast industrial investment and production base had radically declined and its relative working population had decreased. But the emergence of new and services industries—and transfer payments by government—had given Zayre strong Northeastern sales even in areas where major shutdowns had occurred. He observed, "Our total marketplace is so complex and rapidly changing that we must be constantly ready to adapt to new modes of retailing and specific customer needs as they develop. I doubt that we—or anyone else—can analyze now exactly what the customer will want and what new retailing structures will provide in the early 1990s."

The Retail Revolution

The Retail Revolution cited other powerful trends. Mass advertising and computerized technologies seemed to provide such overwhelming advantages to large retailers that its authors thought that—with few exceptions—the small independent retailer could soon be doomed. Both forces tend to create enormous barriers to entry and to affect margins so substantially that large scale becomes a prerequisite to competitiveness. Large scale and high technologies were already affecting employment skill levels, management sophistication, organizational and cost structures in profound ways—and were likely to be more important in the future. Government policies originally designed to protect small retailers through resale-price-maintenance agreements (allowing producers to fix retail prices on their goods) and Robinson-Patman regulations (producers must be able to justify price differences to customers on the basis of differential costs) had perversely created the very price umbrellas that made bigness possible and indeed essential. All these forces had significantly impacted both the supplier and distribution structure of the retail industry. *The Retail Revolution* ends with a query as to whether these forces will lead in the next 15 years to a point where "a handful of mammoth corporations will be left to constitute the distributive network in the nation . . . Behind the glitter and glamour of modern department stores is a saga of dramatic change and adaptation that we are only beginning to comprehend."[7]

ZAYRE IN THE FUTURE

As Mr. Segall looked to the future he said, "Zayre is almost 30 years old, a maturing young company in its prime. I have tried hard to generate a spirit in the company about itself and the future. This business is all people, and I have a lot of confidence in the people in this company. For the outside world, I only state a few objectives. One is that we are intent on achieving a 20% profit growth per year for many years to come. We intend to keep saying that and to posture ourselves accordingly. Our second goal is the image and reality of a well administered organization and a thoughtful merchant. We must not ever rest on our laurels, but continue to progress with our customers and markets—and to administer competently. The next 5–10 years at Zayre will be exciting, interesting, and challenging. That I can promise you.''

QUESTIONS

1. What should Zayre's 1985 strategy be? Why?
2. How should it position each of its chains relative to each other and competition?
3. What priorities and goals should it set in its growth portfolio? Why?
4. How should it organize for its new strategy? Control each major unit?

APPENDIX A—SOME ORGANIZATIONAL TERMS IN RETAILING

Merchandising involves the entire group of decisions and tasks involved in determining what merchandise is offered, acquiring it, and having it available in the right assortments at the right places to maximize the store's marketing objectives. In many retail operations merchandising includes the functions of buying, receiving, marking, and handling all merchandise as well as controlling inventory levels and mixes in the stores. In some large or complex chains, some of these activities may be split off as specialized functions or be decentralized regionally.

Buying is a major line activity in retailing. Buying decisions include what merchandise should be purchased, in what quantities, at what prices, under what terms, and when it should be purchased and received. In some stores the buyer also determines prices, markups, mark-

downs, and close outs and plans and coordinates a department's special sales. Buying can be organized according to the class of merchandise purchased, store type, or location served. In most department stores buyers are in charge of all merchandising for their particular departments as well as directing the sales force in these departments. In some decentralized operations buying and local sales force management may be separated.

Operations includes all those activities necessary to maintain the quality and appearance of the physical facilities of the enterprise. In some highly decentralized retail concerns, these activities as well as supervision and control of local sales people and inventory handling functions are the responsibility of Operations. Service and support activities locally may report either to Operations or directly to other centralized line or administrative functions.

Sales is the face-to-face presentation of the product to the customer and the first recording of that transaction on the store's books through the cash register, sales slip, or electronic charge system. In some cases salespeople report to the buying or merchandise heads; in others they are separated from these functions and report either through Operations or a centralized sales unit.

Promotion generally includes advertising, publicity, displaying of merchandise, and any tactics (other than merchandise selection and pricing) which will induce profitable sales volume. Special attraction techniques like store signs, catalogs, premiums, trading stamps, and non-recurring interest breaks are considered promotions. Store layout, design, traffic flow planning, rack displays, wall and floor coloring, lighting presentations (etc.) are important aspects of in-store promotion which clearly impact the effectiveness of all other line activities.

EXHIBIT 1   ZAYRE CORPORATION FINANCIALS: SELECTED FINANCIAL DATA

Dollars in Thousands Except Per Share Amounts

Fiscal Year Ended Last Saturday in January	1985	1984	1983	1982	1981 (53 Weeks)
Summary of operations:					
Net sales	$ 3,123,008	$ 2,613,667	$ 2,139,616	$ 1,797,139	$ 1,594,235
Cost of sales, including buying and occupancy costs	2,372,467	1,986,559	1,616,889	1,361,753	1,209,179
Selling, general and administrative expenses	574,599	486,053	425,991	365,611	327,683
Interest costs:					
Debt	17,970	19,709	25,812	25,162	20,950
Capital leases	7,270	7,609	7,095	6,987	7,434
Total expenses	2,972,306	2,499,930	2,075,787	1,759,513	1,565,246
Income before income taxes	150,702	113,737	63,829	37,626	28,989
Provision for income taxes	70,386	52,311	28,653	15,479	11,415
Net income	$ 80,316	$ 61,426	$ 35,176	$ 22,147	$ 17,574
Number of common shares for earnings per share computations:					
Primary	20,108,771	19,254,852	16,286,334	14,335,790	13,795,560
Fully diluted	20,186,983	19,257,456	17,197,673	15,406,211	15,374,975
Net income per common share:					
Primary	$3.99	$3.19	$2.16	$1.53	$1.26
Fully diluted	$3.98	$3.19	$2.05	$1.46	$1.18
Stores in operation—End of year:					
Zayre Discount Department Stores	290	275	264	258	248
Hit or Miss	401	356	267	245	240
T.J. Maxx	156	118	86	64	43
Other financial data:					
Net income as a percent of sales	2.57%	2.35%	1.64%	1.23%	1.10%
Current assets	$ 697,750	$ 563,591	$ 449,246	$ 398,829	$ 347,646
Current liabilities	$ 381,006	$ 298,825	$ 193,735	$ 191,991	$ 148,844
Working capital	$ 316,744	$ 264,766	$ 255,511	$ 206,838	$ 198,802
Total assets	$ 1,108,889	$ 908,005	$ 747,649	$ 643,444	$ 560,737
Long-term obligations, including capitalized leases	$ 217,824	$ 193,434	$ 248,446	$ 245,128	$ 232,426
Shareholders' equity	$ 468,071	$ 395,457	$ 294,762	$ 199,232	$ 174,110
Long-term debt-to-equity ratio, excluding capitalized leases	.31:1	.31:1	.58:1	.87:1	.90:1
Post-tax return on average equity	18.60%	17.80%	14.24%	11.86%	10.62%
Capital expenditures, excluding capitalized leases	$ 98,518	$ 76,279	$ 63,658	$ 54,914	$ 48,279
Number of common shares outstanding at year-end	19,779,981	17,953,297	8,393,173	5,411,615	5,209,166
Equity per common share	$23.66	$20.02	$15.96	$13.70	$12.39
Dividends per common share	$ .39	$ .27	$ .18	$ .15	$ .12

All per share data and number of common shares for earnings per share computations reflect the 10% stock dividend paid May 31, 1984, the two-for-one stock split paid June 29, 1983 and the 20% stock dividend paid June 10, 1982.

Source: Zayre Corporation, *Annual Report*, 1984.

EXHIBIT 1 (*Continued*)

SELECTED INFORMATION: ZAYRE CORP. MAJOR BUSINESS SEGMENTS (In Thousands)

Fiscal Year Ended	January 26, 1985	January 28, 1984	January 29, 1983
Net sales:			
Discount department stores	$2,195,740	$1,902,146	$1,615,999
Specialty stores	927,268	711,521	523,617
	$3,123,008	$2,613,667	$2,139,616
Operating income:			
Discount department stores[a]	$ 122,246	$ 90,847	$ 55,059
Specialty stores	64,156	54,768	46,945
	186,402	145,615	102,004
General corporate expense[b]	17,730	12,169	12,363
Interest expense	17,970	19,709	25,812
Income before income taxes	$ 150,702	$ 113,737	$ 63,829
Identifiable assets:			
Discount department stores	$ 744,630	$ 609,748	$ 555,268
Specialty stores	293,987	257,705	143,843
Corporate (cash and marketable securities)	70,272	40,552	48,538
	$1,108,889	$ 908,005	$ 747,649
Depreciation and amortization:			
Discount department stores	$ 28,754	$ 25,702	$ 24,371
Specialty stores	11,375	8,054	4,007
	$ 40,129	$ 33,756	$ 28,378
Capital expenditures:			
Discount department stores	$ 63,932	$ 43,848	$ 36,331
Specialty stores	34,586	32,431	27,327
	$ 98,518	$ 76,279	$ 63,658

[a] *The discount department stores use the last-in first-out (LIFO) method of valuing hardgoods inventories. (See Note B to the consolidated financial statements for further information.)*
[b] *Expense in fiscal 1983 includes a $1.7 million reserve for certain notes receivable. In fiscal 1984 the Company recovered $1.0 million of the amount reserved. The net results of the Company's test of a new prototype, a wholesale warehouse outlet, are included in general corporate expense.*

Source: Zayre Corporation, *Annual Report*, 1984.

EXHIBIT 1 (*Continued*)

ZAYRE CORPORATION—SEGMENT INFORMATION ($Millions, Except # of Stores)

	Fiscal Year Ending January of					
	1985	*1984*	*1983*	*1982*	*1981*	*1980*
ZAYRE CORPORATION						
Sales Volume	3123	2614	2140	1797	1594	1550
# of Stores	847	749	620	567	531	528
ZAYRE DISCT DEPT STORES*						
Sales Volume	2196	1902	1616	1433	1348	1345
Identif. Assets	745	610	555	506	463	443
Capital Expend.	64	44	36	41	41	37
# of Stores	290	275	264	258	248	254
ZAYRE SPECIALTY STORES*						
Sales Volume	927	712	524	364	246	205
Identif. Assets	294	258	144	115	61	41
Capital Expend.	35	32	27	14	8	4
# of Stores	557	474	353	309	283	274
T.J. Maxx	156	118	86	64	43	30
Hit or Miss	401	356	267	245	240	244

* *Security Analysts estimated that Zayre Stores units averaged about 72,000 ft^2 of space and had sales of about $8 million. They estimated T.J. Maxx averaged some 24,000 ft^2 and $5 million per unit, while Hit or Miss averaged only 3,500 ft^2 and $750,000 per unit.*

Source: Zayre Corporation, *Annual Report,* 1984, 1983, 1981.

STORES LOCATIONS—JANUARY 1985

State	Zayre Stores	T.J. Maxx	Hit or Miss	State	Zayre Stores	T.J. Maxx	Hit or Miss
Alabama	7	6	2	Mississippi	1	0	0
Arizona	0	0	3	Missouri	0	0	1
Colorado	0	3	7	Nebraska	0	1	0
Connecticut	5	8	12	New Hampshire	7	1	1
Washington, D.C.	0	0	2	New Jersey	0	5	32
Florida	63	11	19	New York	7	3	35
Georgia	14	4	12	North Carolina	10	6	7
Illinois	35	16	36	Ohio	17	16	25
Indiana	12	2	7	Oklahoma	0	1	3
Iowa	1	1	4	Pennsylvania	13	8	24
Kansas	0	1	0	Rhode Island	8	1	6
Kentucky	4	3	4	South Carolina	0	2	5
Louisana	0	2	5	Tennessee	9	5	10
Maine	11	1	4	Texas	0	7	28
Maryland	8	0	12	Vermont	4	0	1
Massachusetts	35	14	38	Virginia	11	7	16
Michigan	2	15	25	West Virginia	0	0	2
Minnesota	0	2	7	Wisconsin	6	4	6
					290	156	401

Source: Zayre Corporation, *Annual Report,* 1984.

EXHIBIT 2   ZAYRE CORPORATION—EXAMPLE INCENTIVE PLANS 1985

Recipient	As % of Salary Target/Max.	Performance Criteria	Below Goal Performance/Award	Over Goal Performance/Award	Administration
Store Manager Ass't. Store Mgr.	20%/100% 10%/40%	Controllable Income	99%/95% 98%/80% 95%/30% 90%/0	101%/104% 110%/140% 120%/180% Above = 6% for each 1% improvement	Adjusted for every 1% change in performance
Zone Manager Zone Merch. Mgr. Zone Pers. Mgr.	30%/45% 25%/50% 20%/40%	Net Income and NI/Sales for Zone and Individual goals	Same as Store Managers	+6% for every 1% over goal until 110% Perf. Then +8% per 1% change to 115% Perf.	Award adjusted upward or downward by 6% of the target award per 1% var. in NI/Sales vs. NI beyond a 5% range, but <2x target award. 50% in financial goal, 50% on individual.
Senior Merch. Mgr. Buyer	21%/42% 15%/100%	Sales 25% + Gross Profit 75% + Inventory Levels	−16% per −1% Sales Variance, −11.1% per −1% Gross Profit Variance	+16% per +1% Sales Variance, +11.1% per +1% Gross Profit Variance	Sales award max 106% of Goal. Gross profit award max 109% of goal. Adj. by −2.5% per +1% var. in year end inventory goal if <5%. Max. penalty = 25%.
Zayre Stores Div. Mgt.—Pres. Managers	32.5%/65% 15%/30%	85% 75% NI 25% NI/S 15% Indiv. Perf. goals	−5% per −1% NI below goal	+6⅔% per +1% NI above goal	Adjusted for NI/Sales on same basis if <90% or >105% of goal. Adjusted by performance appraisal vs. individual goals.
Zayre Corp. Mgt.	100%/115–120%	85% 75% NI 25% ROI 15% Indiv. Perf. goals	−5% per −1% NI below goal, −8⅓% per −1% of ROI goal	+5% per +1% NI above goal, +8⅓% per 1% ROI above goal	Awards apply outside ±3% limits on ROI. Adjusted by performance vs. individual goals.

Source: Company records.

EXHIBIT 3   WHOLESALE MEMBERSHIP CLUBS: COMPARATIVE DATA 1984

Company	Current Locations	Proposed Locations	Membership Policy	
			Wholesale	Retail
BJ's Wholesale Club (Zayre)	Hialeah, Fla. Medford, Mass. Johnston, R.I.	Hartford, Conn.	$30 annual fee—up to 2 additional memberships $10 each	5% markup
Club Wholesale (Elixir)	Boise, Idaho Las Vegas, Nev.	2 locations	$25 annual fee	5% markup
Costco	Anchorage, Alaska Clearwater, Fla. Fort Lauderdale Tampa Bay West Palm Beach Portland, Ore. Seattle (3) Spokane Tacoma Salt Lake City	Honolulu (10–12 units)	$25 annual fee	5% markup
Metro Cash & Carry of Illinois	Chicago (3)	No expansion plans	no fee	5% markup
Money's Worth	Greensboro, N.C.	1 in North Carolina	$25 annual fee	5% markup
Pace	Denver (2) Colorado Springs Tampa/St. Petersburg	Denver Tampa/St. Petersburg (2) Jacksonville Atlanta (3) Augusta Des Moines Omaha Greensboro, N.C. Raleigh Chattanooga Knoxville	$25 annual fee	5% markup

			Annual fee	Markup
Price Club	Phoenix Mesa, Ariz. Tucson Los Angeles (5) Orange County, Calif. Sacramento (2) San Diego (4) San Francisco (2) Norfolk, Va. Richmond	Albuquerque	$25 annual fee	$15 fee + 5% markup
Price Savers Wholesale Club	Anchorage, Alaska Salt Lake City Seattle Tacoma	Honolulu	$25 annual fee	5% markup
Sam's Wholesale Club (Wal-Mart)	Birmingham, Ala. Jacksonville, Fla. Kansas City, Mo. St. Louis Oklahoma City Charleston, S.C. Dallas (2) Houston (3)	Atlanta Wichita Louisville Tulsa Knoxville Memphis Nashville	$25 annual fee	5% markup
Warehouse Club (joint partnership W.R. Grace)	Chicago Akron Columbus Dayton Pittsburgh	Detroit	$25 annual fee	5% markup
Wholesale Club	Indianapolis Cleveland Milwaukee	Detroit (4) Cleveland	$30 annual fee	5% markup
Wholesale Plus	Fort Lauderdale	—	$25 annual fee	5% markup
Value Club	Austin El Paso San Antonio (3)	—	$25 annual fee	$5 fee + 5% markup

Source: Reprinted by permission from *Chain Store Age Executive*, November 1984. Copyright © 1984 by Lebhar-Friedman, 425 Park Avenue, New York, NY 10022.

EXHIBIT 4 COMPARATIVE CHAIN PERFORMANCE

	Kmart Corp.	Wal-Mart Corp.	Zayre Corp.
SALES ($ Millions)			
FY ending 1/85	21,096	6,401	3,123
1/81	14,204	1,643	1,594
1/77	8,382	479	1,161
NET INCOME ($ Millions)			
FY ending 1/85	499	271	80
1/81	261	56	18
1/77	262[*]	16[*]	10[*]
TOTAL ASSETS ($ Millions)			
FY ending 1/85	9,262	2,205	1,109
1/81	6,089[*]	592	561
1/77	3,983[*]	168[*]	435[*]
MERCHANDISE INVENTORY ($ Millions)			
FY ending 1/85	4,588	1,104	603
1/81	2,846	280	296
1/77	1,738	89	211
# OF STORES			
FY ending 1/85	3,365[c]	756[a]	847
1/81	2,327[c]	330	531
1/77	1,646	153	451[b]
SQUARE FEET OF SPACE (Millions)			
FY ending 1/85	131.5[f]	41.9[d]	26.6[g]
1/81	114.5[e]	15.5	19.7
1/77	80.3	6.5	19.5

[*] *Restated from original reported figures in later years' annual reports.*
[a] *1984 figure includes 3 wholesale clubs; 1985 figure includes 11 clubs.*
[b] *Figures include On Stage/Nugent/Bell and Beaconway stores but exclude supermarkets and gas stations.*
[c] *Figures include shoe stores, Designer Depots, Waldenbooks, and Builders Square stores but exclude cafeterias.*
[d] *Figures include wholesale club space.*
[e] *Figures include only general merchandise space.*
[f] *Figures include both general merchandise and specialty store space.*
[g] *Rough estimates based on information provided in Annual Reports concerning Zayre Stores, Hit or Miss, and T.J. Maxx.*

Source: Various years' Annual Reports for Wal-Mart Corp., Kmart Corp., and Zayre Corp.

EXHIBIT 4 (Continued)

SELECTED PRODUCTIVITY MEASURES BY RETAILER CLASSIFICATION 1983–84

1983 Estimated Sales per Labor Hour*

	Total (105) %	Discount (17) %	Drug (18) %	Super-market (26) %	Depart-ment (18) %	Home Center (16) %	Specialty (10) %
Less than $25	8	—	6	4	6	6	40
$25–$50	24	29	28	12	33	25	20
$51–$75	15	18	22	4	6	31	20
$76–$100	19	12	17	42	11	6	10
$101 +	5	6	—	12	—	6	—
Refused Comment	13	12	6	15	17	19	10
Don't know/ No answer	16	24	22	12	28	6	—
(MEAN)	$(60.3)	(61.1)	(55.5)	(80.2)	(48.6)	(57.5)	(40.9)

*For chains using this system.

Source: Chain Store Age Executive, September, 1984. Reprinted by permission of Chain Store Age Executive. Copyright 1984 by Lebhar-Friedman, 425 Park Avenue, New York, NY 10022.

1983 Estimated Sales per Net Square Foot*

	Total (78) %	Discount (14) %	Drug (14) %	Super-market (10) %	Depart-ment (27) %	Home Center (6) %	Specialty (7) %
Less than $50	8	—	14	40	—	—	—
$51–$100	13	36	7	—	7	33	—
$101–$150	28	29	29	—	41	17	29
$151–$200	15	14	21	—	18	17	14
$201–$250	5	—	7	10	4	17	—
$251–$300	3	—	—	10	4	—	—
$301–$350	—	—	—	—	—	—	—
$351–$400	—	—	—	—	—	—	—
$401 +	5	7	—	10	—	—	29
Refused Comment	14	14	7	20	11	17	29
Don't know/ No answer	9	—	14	10	15	—	—
(MEAN)	(151.5)	(139.6)	(127.7)	(158.6)	(145.0)	(135.0)	(265.0)

*For chains using this system.

Source: Chain Store Age Executive, September, 1984. Reprinted by permission of Chain Store Age Executive. Copyright 1984 by Lebhar-Friedman, 425 Park Avenue, New York, NY 10022.

1983 Estimated Sales per Gross Square Foot*

	Total (83) %	Discount (13) %	Drug (19) %	Super-market (16) %	Depart-ment (13) %	Home Center (11) %	Specialty (11) %
Less than $50	10	—	5	38	—	—	9
$50–$100	13	23	5	—	15	46	—
$101–$150	24	46	37	—	23	9	27
$151–$200	11	—	21	6	8	18	9
$201–$250	4	—	10	—	8	—	—
$251–$300	2	—	5	6	—	—	—
$301–$350	4	8	5	—	—	—	9
$351–$400	2	—	—	—	—	—	18
$401 +	5	—	—	12	—	9	9
Refused Comment	17	15	5	19	31	18	18
Don't know/ No answer	8	8	5	19	15	—	—
(MEAN)	(160.8)	(130.0)	(161.2)	(159.0)	(132.1)	(144.4)	(235.0)

*For chains using this system.

Source: Chain Store Age Executive, September, 1984. Reprinted by permission of Chain Store Age Executive. Copyright 1984 by Lebhar-Friedman, 425 Park Avenue, New York, NY 10022.

EXHIBIT 4 (Continued)

Sales and Earnings for Quarter Ended in September or October

Chain	1984 Sales (Millions)	1983 Sales (Millions)	% Change
General Merchandise			
Sears[1]	$6,463	$6,190	4.4
Kmart	4,993	4,331	15.3
J.C. Penney	3,211	2,914	10.2
Federated	2,266	2,071	9.4
Dayton Hudson	1,868	1,659	13.0
Woolworth	1,404	1,353	3.8
Wal-Mart	1,584	1,167	36.0
May	1,133	1,003	13.0
Macy	1,011	929	8.8
ADG	951	905	5.0
Allied	932	883	5.5
CHH[2]	906	758	20.0
Zayre	777	659	17.8
Supermarkets and Convenience Stores			
Safeway	4,584	4,300	6.6
Kroger	4,623	4,505	2.6
Southland	3,085	2,430	26.9
Lucky	2,191	2,027	8.1
Winn-Dixie	1,732	1,648	5.1
A&P[3]	1,377	1,192	15.5
Drug Chains			
Walgreen	684	595	15.0
Jack Eckerd	637	543	17.3
Revco	511	453	12.6
Longs	328	291	12.7
Specialty Stores			
Melville	1,066	985	8.2
Tandy	596	583	2.1
U.S. Shoe	416	375	10.9
Limited	349	271	29.0
Toys 'R Us	322	221	45.7
Edison[4]	269	249	7.8
Zale	217	198	9.6

[1] Sears Merchandise Group sales only. Operating profits from this group amounted to $163.8 million, or a 3.1% increase over the $158.9 million of a year earlier.
[2] Actual earnings increased 59%. Earnings per share declined because of actions taken by CHH to fight off a takeover attempt by Limited Inc.
[3] Before extraordinary credits in both years.
[4] Without a nonrecurring after-tax gain from the sale of Handyman Store properties in Texas and Oklahoma, earnings per share would have been 73¢ in the 1984 quarter, a 28.8% decrease.

Source: Chain Store Age Executive, January 1985. Reprinted by permission of Chain Store Age Executive. Copyright 1985 by Lebhar-Friedman, 425 Park Avenue, New York, NY 10022.

EXHIBIT 5 TRENDS IN RETAILING

SALES BY STORE CLASSIFICATION (Yearly Sales in Millions of Dollars)

Type of Store	1972	1976	1977	1979	1980	1981	1982	1983
Food Store	100718	144912	157941	195710	219399	242763	268352	278427
Supermarket	93298	134534	147758	183860	206121	227756	252094	261732
Eating/Drinking Establ.	36885	56852	63276	76751	87310	96417	107484	118935
General Merchandise Store	65065	94748	93948	112400	123157	135518	139654	147354
Department Store	51056	75247	76965	93620	106698	111561	115969	120686
Appliance/Accessory Store	24741	36796	35564	43103	44999	48849	50593	54648
Furn/Home Fnshg/Applce St.	22534	34790	33177	40823	44162	47124	46105	52188
Furn/Home Frnshg Store	14059	21239	20320	25049	26627	28754	27725	30895
Automotive Dealer	90029	123417	149952	175508	169808	182841	172669	203052
Gasoline Service Station	33655	47513	56468	72122	93801	103447	107540	107978
Bldg Matls/Hardware Store	23844	33081	38859	50506	49381	53818	52711	59410
Drugstore	15599	21529	23198	28668	31986	34075	37232	39124
TOTAL RETAIL SALES	459031	661749	723134	887519	965746	1056107	1100750	1186387
EFFECTIVE BUYING INCOME		1176240		1618643	1814167			2329210

SALES BY PRODUCT CLASSIFICATION (Yearly Sales in Millions of Dollars)

Product	1972	1976	1977	1979	1980	1981	1982	1983
Men's/Boys' Clothing	14999	22161	23057	26854	29656	32417	33497	35743
Women's/Girls' Clothing	25923	38110	37055	46278	47612	52052	53758	57502
Footwear	7677	11348	10941	13762	14120	15336	15916	17026
Audio Equ/Music Inst/Supplies			9575		12733	13696	13718	15172
Television	8174	12291	4386	15014	5834	6296	6327	6952
Major Household Appliance	7341	11022	9565	13661	12773	13816	14019	15210
Health and Beauty Aids			11593		15813	17171	18407	19367
Drugs	15660	22021	12703	29175	17475	18710	20257	21362
TOTAL RETAIL SALES	459031	661749	723134	887519	965746	1056107	1100750	1186387

Source: Compiled from Sales and Marketing Management, Survey of Buying Power Data Service, various years.

MOUNTBATTEN AND INDIA

Louis Francis Albert Victor Nicholas Mountbatten, Viscount of Burma, was, at forty-six, one of the most famous men in England. He was a big man, over six feet tall, but not a trace of flab hung from his zealously exercised waistline. . . . Mountbatten knew perfectly well why he had been summoned to London. Since his return from his post as Supreme Allied Commander Southeast Asia, he had been a frequent visitor to Downing Street as a consultant on the affairs of the Asian nations that had fallen under S.E.A.C.'s command. On his last visit, however, the Prime Minister's questions had quickly focused on India, a nation that had not been a part of [Mountbatten's] theater of operations. The young admiral had suddenly had "a very nasty, very uneasy feeling." His premonition had been justified. Attlee intended to name him Viceroy of India. The viceroy's was the most important post in the Empire, the office from which a long succession of Englishmen had held domain over the destinies of a fifth of mankind. Mountbatten's task, however, would not be to rule India from that office. His assignment would be one of the most painful an Englishman could be asked to undertake—to give it up.

A HISTORIC TRAP

Mountbatten wanted no part of the job. He entirely endorsed the idea that the time had come for Britain to leave India, but his heart rebelled at the thought that he would be called on to sever

the ancient links binding England and the bulwark of her empire. To discourage Attlee, he had produced a whole series of demands, major and minor, from the number of secretaries he must be allowed to take with him, to the make of the aircraft, the York MW-102 which had carried him around the world as Supreme Commander Southeast Asia, which would be placed at his disposal. The admiral still hoped somehow to resist Attlee's efforts to force the Indian assignment on him. . . .

There was much more to Mountbatten than his [impeccable] public image reflected; the decorations on his naval uniform were proof of that. The public might consider him a pillar of the Establishment, but the Establishment's members themselves tended to regard Mountbatten and his wife as dangerous radicals. His command in Southeast Asia had given him a vast knowledge of Asian nationalist movements, and there were few Englishmen who could match it. He had dealt with the supporters of Ho Chi Minh in Indochina, Sukharno in Indonesia, Aung San in Burma, Chinese Communists in Malaya, unruly trade unionists in Singapore. Realizing that they represented Asia's future, he had sought accommodations with them rather than try to suppress them as his staff and the Allies had urged. The nationalist movement with which he would have to deal if he went to India was the oldest and most unusual of them all. In a quarter of a century of inspired agitation and protest, its leadership had forced history's greatest empire to the decision that Attlee's party had taken to quit India in good time rather than to be driven out by forces of history and rebellion.

The Sublime Paradox

The Indian situation, the Prime Minister began, was deteriorating with every passing day, and the time for an urgent decision was at hand. It was one of the sublime paradoxes of history that at this critical juncture, when Britain was at last ready to give India her freedom, she could not find a way to do so. What should have been Britain's finest hour in India seemed destined to become a nightmare of unsurpassed horror. She had conquered and ruled India with what was, by the colonial standard, relatively little bloodshed. Her leaving threatened to produce an explosion of violence that would dwarf in scale and magnitude anything she had experienced in three and a half centuries there.

The root of the Indian problem was the age-old antagonism between India's 300 million Hindus and 100 million Moslems. Sustained by tradition, by antipathetic religions, by economic differences subtly exacerbated through the years by Britain's own policy of divide and rule, their conflict had reached a boiling point. The leaders of India's 100 million Moslems now demanded that Britain destroy the unity she had so painstakingly created and give them an Islamic state of their own. The cost of denying them their state, they warned, would be the bloodiest civil war in Asian history. Just as determined to resist their demands were the leaders of the Congress Party, representing most of India's 300 million Hindus. To them, the division of the subcontinent would be a mutilation of their historic homeland, an act almost sacrilegious in its nature.

Britain was trapped between those two apparently irreconcilable demands. Time and again British efforts to resolve the problem had failed. So desperate had the situation become that the present viceroy, an honest, forthright soldier, Field Marshal Sir Archibald Wavell, had just submitted to the Attlee government a final, and drastic, recommendation [called Operation Madhouse]. Should all else fail, he proposed, the British should "withdraw from India in our own method and in our own time and with due regard to our own interests; we will regard any attempt to interfere with our program as an act of war which we will meet with all the resources at our command. . . ."

Each morning brought a batch of cables to the India Office announcing an outburst of wanton savagery in some new corner of the subcontinent. It was, Attlee indicated, Mountbatten's solemn duty to take the post he had been offered. . . . Wavell had all the right ideas, Mountbatten thought. "If he couldn't do it, what's the point of my trying to take it on?" Yet he was beginning to understand that there was no escape. He was going to be forced to accept a job in which the risk of failure was enormous and in which he would easily shatter the brilliant reputation he'd brought out of the war.

Political Conditions

If Attlee was going to drive him into a corner, Mountbatten was determined to impose on the Prime Minister the political conditions that would give him some hope of success. His talks with Wavell had given him an idea what they must be. He would not accept, he told the Prime Minister, unless the government agreed to make an unequivocal public announcement of a precise date on which British rule in India would terminate. Only that, Mountbatten felt, would convince India's skeptical intelligentsia that Britain was really leaving and infuse her leaders with the sense of urgency needed to get them into realistic negotiations.

Second, he demanded something no other viceroy had ever dreamed of asking: full powers to carry out his assignment without reference to London, and above all, without constant interference from London. The Attlee government could give the young admiral his final destination, but he alone was going to set his course and run the ship along the way.

"Surely," Attlee said, "you're not asking for plenipotentiary powers above His Majesty's Government, are you?"

"I am afraid, sir," answered Mountbatten, "that that is exactly what I am asking. How can I possibly negotiate with the Cabinet constantly breathing down my neck?"

A stunned silence followed his words. Mountbatten watched with satisfaction as the nature of his breathtaking demand registered on the Prime Minister's face, and he hoped that it would prompt Attlee to withdraw his offer. Instead, the Prime Minister indicated with a sigh his willingness to accept even that. . . . As he got back into his Austin Princess, a strange thought struck Mountbatten. It was exactly seventy years to the day, almost to the hour, from the moment when his own great-grandmother had been proclaimed Empress of India on a plain outside Delhi. [16–20]

LAST TATTOO FOR A DYING RAJ

George VI, [Lord Mountbatten's cousin] comprehended perfectly well that the great imperial dream had faded and that the grandiose structure fashioned by his great-grandmother's ministers was condemned. But if the empire had to disappear, how sad it would be if some of its achievements and glories could not survive, if what it had represented could not find an expression in some new form more compatible with a modern age. "It would be a pity," he observed, "if an independent India were to turn its back on the Commonwealth."

The Commonwealth could indeed provide a framework in which George VI's hopes might be realized. It could become a multiracial assembly of independent nations, with Britain *prima inter pares* at its core. Bound by common traditions, a common past, by common symbolic ties to his crown, the Commonwealth could exercise great influence in world affairs. If that ideal was to be realized, it was essential that India remain within the Commonwealth when she got her independence. If India refused to join, the Afro-Asian nations, which in their turn would accede to independence in the years to come, would almost certainly follow her example. That would condemn the Commonwealth to becoming just a grouping of the Empire's white dominions instead of the body the King longed to see emerge from the remains of his empire. . . .

Sitting there in their Buckingham Palace sitting room, Victoria's two great-grandsons reached a private decision that January day. Louis Mountbatten would become the agent of their common aspiration for the Commonwealth's future. In a few days Mountbatten would insist that Attlee include in his terms of reference a specific injunction to maintain an independent India, united or divided, inside the Commonwealth if at all possible. In the weeks ahead, there could be no task to which India's new viceroy would devote more thought, more persuasiveness, more cunning than the one conceived that afternoon in George VI's sitting room, that of maintaining a link between India and his cousin's crown. [45–46]

The Coronation

The closing chapter in a great story was about to begin. In a few minutes, on this morning of March 24, 1947, the last Englishman to govern India would mount his gold-and-crimson viceregal throne. Installed upon that throne, Louis Mountbatten would become the twentieth and final representative of a prestigious dynasty, his the last hands to clasp the scepter that had passed from Hastings to Wellesley, to Cornwallis and Curzon. The site of his official consecration was the ceremonial Durbar Hall of a palace whose awesome dimensions were rivaled only by those of Versailles and of the Peterhof of the Tsars. . . .

In Poona, Peshawar and Simla—wherever there was a military garrison in India—troops on parade presented arms as the first gun exploded in Delhi. Frontier Force Rifles, the Guides Cavalry, Hodsons and Skinners Horse, Sikhs and Dogras, Jats and Pathans, Gurkhas and Madrassis poised while the cannon thundered out their last tattoo for the British raj. As the sound of the last report faded through the dome of Durbar Hall, the new viceroy stepped to the microphone. The situation he faced was so serious that, against the advice of his staff, Mountbatten had decided to break with tradition by addressing the gathering before him.

"I am under no illusion about the difficulty of my task," he said. "I shall need the greatest good will of the greatest possible number, and I am asking India today for that good will." As he finished, the guards threw open the massive Assam teak doors of the Hall. Before Mountbatten was the breathtaking vista of Kingsway and its glistening pools, plunging down the heart of New Delhi. Overhead the trumpets sent out another strident call. . . . That brief ceremony, he realized, had turned him into one of the most powerful men on earth. He now held in his hand an almost life-and-death power over four hundred million people, one fifth of mankind. [90–91]

Operation Seduction

India's last viceroy might, as he had glumly predicted at Northolt Airport, come home with a bullet in his back, but he would be a viceroy unlike any other that India had seen. Mountbatten firmly believed ''it was impossible to be viceroy without putting up a great, brilliant show.'' He had been sent to New Delhi to get the British out of India, but he was determined that they would go in a shimmer of scarlet and gold, all the old glories of the raj honed to the highest pitch one last time.

He ordered all the ceremonial trappings that had been suppressed during the war restored— A.D.C.s in dazzling full dress, guard-mounting ceremonies, bands playing, sabers flashing—''the lot.''. . . He intended to replace Wavell's ''Operation Madhouse'' with a kind of ''Operation Seduction'' of his own, a minirevolution in style directed as much toward India's masses as toward their leaders, with whom he would have to negotiate. It would be a shrewd blend of contrasting values, of patrician pomp and a common touch, of the old spectacles of the dying raj and new initiatives prefiguring the India of tomorrow.

Strangely, Mountbatten began his revolution with the stroke of a paint brush. To his aides' horror, he ordered the gloomy wooden panels of the viceregal study, in which so many negotiations had failed, covered with a light, cheerful coat of paint more apt to relax the Indian leaders with whom he would be dealing. He shook Viceroy's House out of the leisurely routine it had developed, turning it into a humming, quasi-military headquarters. He instituted staff meetings,

soon known as ''morning prayers,'' as the first official activity of each day.

Mountbatten astonished his new I.C.S. subordinates with the agility of his mind, his capacity to get at the root of a problem and, above all, his almost obsessive capacity for work. He put an end to the parade of *chaprassis*, who traditionally bore the viceroy his papers for his private contemplation in green leather dispatch boxes. He preferred taut, verbal briefings.

''When you wrote 'May I speak?' on a paper he was to read,'' one of his staff recalled, ''you could be sure you'd speak, and you'd better be ready to say what was on your mind at any time, because the call to speak could come at two o'clock in the morning.''

But it was, above all, the public image Mountbatten was trying to create for himself and his office that represented a radical change. For over a century, the viceroy of India, locked in the ceremonial splendors of his office, had rivaled the Dalai Lama as the most remote god in Asia's pantheon of ruling gods. Two unsuccessful assassination attempts had left him enrobed in a kind of security cocoon isolating him from all contact with the brown masses that he ruled. . . . Hundreds of bodyguards, police and security men followed each of his moves. If he played golf, the fairways of his course were cleared and police were posted along them behind almost every tree. If he went riding, a squadron of the viceroy's bodyguard and security police jogged along after him.

Mountbatten was determined to shatter that screen. He had surrounded himself with the trappings of imperial grandeur that so delighted India's masses with a deliberate calculation. From this pedestal he could make tradition-shattering descents which would have a particular impact on the masses. His first announcement, that he and his wife or daughter would take their morning horseback rides unescorted, sent a shock wave of horror through the house. It took him some time to get his way, but suddenly the Indian villagers along the route of their morning rides began to witness a spectacle so wholly unbelievable as to seem a mirage: the Viceroy and Vicereine of India trotting past them, waving graciously, alone and unprotected.

Then he and his wife made an even more revolutionary gesture. He did something that no viceroy had deigned to do in two hundred years; he visited the home of an Indian who was not one of a handful of privileged princes. To the astonishment of all India, the viceregal couple walked into a garden party at the simple New Delhi residence of Jawaharlal Nehru. While Nehru's aides looked on dumb with disbelief, Mountbatten took Nehru by the elbow and strolled off among the guests casually chatting and shaking hands. The gesture had a stunning impact. "Thank God," an awed Nehru told his sister that evening, "we've finally got a human being for a viceroy and not a stuffed shirt."

Anxious to demonstrate that a new esteem for the Indian people now reigned in Viceroy's House, Mountbatten accorded the Indian military, two million of whom had served under him in Southeast Asia, a long-overdue honor. He had three Indian officers attached to his staff as A.D.C.s. Next, he ordered the doors of Viceroy's House opened to Indians. Only a handful of Indians had been invited into its precincts before his arrival. He instructed his staff that there were to be no dinner parties in the Viceroy's House without Indian guests. And not just a few token Indians. Henceforth, he ordered, at least half the faces around his table were to be Indian.

His wife brought an even more dramatic revolution to the viceregal dining table. Out of respect for the culinary traditions of her Indian guests, she ordered the house's kitchens to start preparing dishes that, in a century of imperial hospitality, had never been offered in Viceroy's House, Indian vegetarian food. Not only that, she ordered the food served on flat Indian trays, with servants holding the traditional wash basins, jugs and towels behind her guests, so that they could, if they chose to, eat with their fingers at the Viceroy's table, then wash their throats with a ritual gargle. . . .

Not long after their arrival, *The New York Times* noted that "no viceroy in history has so completely won the confidence, respect and liking of the Indian people." Indeed, within a few weeks, the success of "Operation Seduction" would be so remarkable that Nehru himself would tell the new viceroy only half-jokingly that he was becoming a very difficult man to negotiate with, because he was "drawing larger crowds than anybody in India." [93–95]

STRAIGHT FOR CIVIL WAR

[But time was short. George Abell, whose reputation for brilliance and understanding of India was unsurpassed] told Mountbatten with stark simplicity that India was heading straight for a civil war. Only by finding the quickest of resolutions to her problems was he going to save her. The great administrative machine governing India was collapsing. The shortage of British officers, which was caused by the decision to stop recruiting during the war, and the rising antagonism between its Hindu and Moslem members meant that the rule of that vaunted institution, the Indian Civil Service, could not survive the year. The time for discussion and debate was past. Speed, not deliberation, was needed to avoid a catastrophe.

Coming from a man of Abell's stature, those words gave the new viceroy a dismal shock. Yet, they were only the first in a stream of reports and actions which engulfed him during his first fortnight in India. He received an equally grim analysis from the man he had hand-picked to come with him as his chief of staff, General Lord Ismay, Winston Churchill's chief of staff from 1940 to 1945. A veteran of years on the subcontinent as an officer in the Indian Army and military secretary to an earlier viceroy, Ismay had concluded that "India was a ship on fire in mid-ocean with ammunition in her hold." The question, he told Mountbatten, was could they get the fire out before it reached the ammunition?

The first report that Mountbatten received from the British governor of the Punjab warned him that "there is a civil-war atmosphere throughout the province." It mentioned [in passing] a recent tragedy in a rural district near Rawalpindi. A Moslem's water buffalo had wandered onto the property of his Sikh neighbor. When its owner sought to reclaim it, a fight, then a riot erupted. Two hours later, a hundred human beings lay in the surrounding fields, hacked to death with scythes and knives because of the vagrant humors of a water buffalo. Five days after the new viceroy's arrival, incidents between Hindus and Moslems took ninety-nine lives in Calcutta. Two days later, a similar conflict broke out in Bombay, leaving forty-one mutilated bodies on its pavements.

Confronted by those outbursts of violence, Mountbatten called India's senior police officer to his study and asked if the police were capable of maintaining law and order in India. "No, Your Excellency," was the reply, "we cannot.". . .

Mountbatten quickly discovered that the government with which he was supposed to govern India, a coalition of the Congress Party and the Moslem League put together with enormous effort by his predecessor, was in fact an assembly of enemies so bitterly divided that its members barely spoke to one another. It was clearly going to fall apart, and when it did, Mountbatten would have to assume the appalling responsibility of exercising direct rule over one fifth of humanity himself, with the administrative machine required for the task collapsing underneath him.

Confronted by that grim prospect, assailed on every side by reports of violence and the warnings of his most seasoned advisers, Mountbatten reached what was perhaps the most important decision he would make in India in his first ten days in the country; it was to condition every other decision of his viceroyalty. The date of June 1948 established in London for the transfer of power, the date that he himself had urged on Attlee, had been wildly optimistic. Whatever solution he was to reach for India's future, he was going to have to reach it in weeks, not months.

"The scene here," he wrote in his first report to the Attlee government on April 2, 1947, "is one of unrelieved gloom . . . I can see little ground on which to build any agreed solution for the future of India." After describing the country's unsettled state, the young admiral issued an anguished warning to the man who had sent him to India. "The only conclusion I have been able to come to," he wrote, "is that unless I act quickly, I will find the beginnings of a civil war on my hands." [95–96]

THE FOUR INDIANS

Because of the urgency of the situation facing him, Mountbatten had decided to employ a revolutionary tactic in his negotiation with India's leaders. For the first time in its modern history, India's destiny was not being decided around a conference table, but in the intimacy of private conversations. . . . Five men would participate in them: Louis Mountbatten and four Indian leaders. The four Indians had spent the better part of their lives agitating against the British and arguing with one another. All were past middle age. All were lawyers who had learned their forensic skills in London's Inns of Court. . . .

In Mountbatten's mind, there was no question what the outcome of that debate should be. Like many Englishmen, he looked on India's unity as the greatest legacy Britain could leave behind. He had a deep, almost evangelical desire to maintain it. To respond to the Moslem appeal to divide the country was, he believed, to sow the seeds of tragedy. Every effort to persuade India's leaders to agree on a solution to their country's problems in a formal meeting had led to a deadlock. [But here in the privacy of his study] he was going to try to achieve in weeks what his predecessors had been unable to achieve in years—get India's leaders to agree on some form of unity. . . .

The Kashmiri Brahman

Nehru was the only Indian leader whom Mountbatten already knew. [At the end of World War II] to the horror of his staff Mountbatten rode through Singapore's streets in his open car with Nehru at his side. His action, his advisers had warned, would only dignify an anti-British rebel.

"Dignify him?" Mountbatten had retorted, "It is he who will dignify *me*. Some day this man will be Prime Minister of India." [97–98]

There was a great deal to bind the scion of a three-thousand-year-old line of Kashmiri Brahmans and the man who claimed descent from the oldest ruling family in Protestantism. They both loved to talk, and they expanded in each other's company. Nehru, the abstract thinker, admired Mountbatten's practical dynamism, the capacity for decisive action that wartime command had given him. Mountbatten was stimulated by the subtlety of Nehru's thought. He quickly understood that the only Indian politician who would share and understand his desire to maintain a link between Britain and a new India was Jawaharlal Nehru.

With his usual candor, the Viceroy told Nehru that he had been given an appalling responsibility and he intended to approach the Indian problem in a mood of stark realism. As they talked, the two men rapidly agreed on two major points: a quick decision was essential to avoid a bloodbath and the division of India would be a tragedy. Then Nehru turned to the actions of the next Indian leader who would enter Mountbatten's study, the penitent Mohandas Gandhi marching his lonely path through Noakhali and Bihar. The man to whom he had been so long devoted was, Nehru said, "going around with ointment trying to heal one sore spot after another on the body of India instead of diagnosing the cause of the eruption of the sores and participating in the treatment of the body as a whole."

In offering a glimpse into the growing gulf separating the Liberator of India and his closest companions, Nehru's words provided Mountbatten with a vital insight into the form that his actions in Delhi should take. If he could not persuade India's leaders to keep their country united, he was going to have to persuade them to divide it. Gandhi's unremitting hostility to partition could place an insurmountable barrier in his path and confront him with a catastrophe. His only hope, then, would be to divorce the leaders of Congress from their aging leader. Nehru would

be the key if that happened. He was the only ally Mountbatten must have; only he might have the authority to stand up against the Mahatma.

Now that words had revealed the discord between Gandhi and his party chief, Mountbatten might be forced to widen and exploit that gap to succeed. He needed Nehru, and he spared no effort to win his support. On none of India's leaders would Operation Seduction have more impact than on the realistic Kashmiri Brahman. . . . Taking Nehru to the door, Mountbatten told him: "Mr. Nehru, I want you to regard me not as the last British viceroy winding up the raj, but as the first to lead the way to a new India." Nehru turned and looked at the man he had wanted to see on the viceregal throne. "Ah," he said, a faint smile creasing his face, "now I know what they mean when they speak of your charm as being so dangerous." [101–102]

The Most Famous Asian Alive

[The next man to see Mountbatten was unique, a saint in his own time. He was Mohandas Gandhi—called Mahatma, meaning "Great Soul."] At every village, his routine was the same. As soon as he arrived, the most famous Asian alive would go up to a hut, preferably a Moslem's hut, and beg for shelter. If he was turned away, and sometimes he was, Gandhi would go to another door. "If there is no one to receive me," he had said, "I shall be happy to rest under the hospitable shade of a tree." Once installed, he lived on whatever food his hosts would offer: mangoes, vegetables, goat's curds, green coconut milk. Every hour of his day in each village was rigorously programmed. Time was one of Gandhi's obsessions. Each minute, he held, was a gift of God to be used in the service of man. . . . He got up at two o'clock in the morning to read his Gita and say his morning prayers. From then until dawn he squatted in his hut, patiently answering his correspondence himself with a pencil, in longhand. He used each pencil right down to an ungrippable stub, because he held that it represented the work of a fellow human being and to waste it would indicate indifference to his labors.

At sunup, Gandhi began to wander the village talking and praying incessantly with its inhabitants. He knew them better than any other man alive. He wanted his independent India built on the foundation of her reinvigorated villages, and he had his own ideas on how to reorder the patterns of their existence. The lessons "which I propose to give you during my tour are how you can keep the village water and yourselves clean," he would tell the villagers; "what use you can make of the earth, of which your bodies are made; how you can obtain the life force from the infinite sky over your heads; how you can reinforce your vital energy from the air which surrounds you; how you can make proper use of sunlight."

The aging leader did not stop with words. Gandhi had a tenacious belief in the value of one concrete act. To the despair of many of his followers who thought a different set of priorities should order his time, Gandhi would devote the same meticulous care and attention to making a mudpack for a leper as preparing for an interview with a viceroy. So, in each village he would go with its inhabitants to their wells. Frequently he would help them find a better location for them. He would inspect their communal latrines, or if, as was most often the case, they didn't have any, he would teach them how to build one, often joining in the digging himself. Convinced that bad hygiene was the basic cause of India's terrible mortality rate, he had inveighed for years against such habits as public defecation, spitting and blowing out one's nostrils on the paths where most village poor walked barefoot. "If we Indians spat in unison," he once said, "we would form a puddle large enough to drown 300,000 Englishmen." [52]

For thirty years [his] battered feet had led the famished hordes of a continent in prayer toward their liberty. They had carried Gandhi into the most remote corners of India, to thousands of villages like those he now visited, to lepers' wading pools, to the worst slums of his nation, to palaces and prisons, in quest of his cherished goal, India's freedom.

Determined to convert [the Congress Party] into a mass movement attuned to his nonviolent creed, Gandhi presented the party a plan of action in Calcutta in 1920. It was adopted by an overwhelming majority. From that moment until his death, whether he held rank in the party or not, Gandhi was Congress's conscience and its guide, the unquestioned leader of the independence struggle. . . . Gandhi's tactic was electrifyingly simple, a one-word program for political revolution: noncooperation. Indians, he decreed, would boycott whatever was British; students would boycott British schools; lawyers, British courts; employees, British jobs; soldiers, British honors. . . .

Above all, his aim was to weaken the edifice of British power in India by attacking the economic pillar upon which it reposed. Britain purchased raw Indian cotton for derisory prices, shipped it to the mills of Lancashire to be woven into textiles, then shipped the finished products back to India to be sold at a substantial profit in a market that virtually excluded non-British textiles. It was the classic cycle of imperialist exploitation, and the arm with which Gandhi proposed to fight it was the very antithesis of the great mills of the Industrial Revolution that had sired that exploitation. It was a primitive wooden spinning wheel. For the next quarter of a century Gandhi struggled with tenacious energy to force all India to forsake foreign textiles for the rough cotton khadi cloth spun by millions of spinning wheels. Convinced that the misery of India's half million villages was due above all to the decline in village crafts, he saw in a renaissance of cottage industry, heralded by the spinning wheel, the key to the revival of India's impoverished countryside. For the urban masses, spinning would be a kind of spiritual redemption by manual labor, a constant, daily remainder of their link to the real India, the India of half a million villages. [61–62]

"The British want us to put the struggle on the plane of machine guns where they have the weapons and we do not," he warned. "Our only assurance of beating them is putting the struggle on a plane where we have the weapons and they have not." Thousands of Indians followed his call, and thousands more went off to jail. The beleaguered governor of Bombay called it "the most colossal experiment in world history and one which came within an inch of succeeding."

It failed because of an outburst of bloody violence in a little village northeast of Delhi. Against the wishes of almost his entire Congress hierarchy, Gandhi called off the movement because he felt that his followers did not yet fully understand nonviolence. Sensing that his change of attitude had rendered him less dangerous, the British arrested him. Gandhi pleaded guilty to the charge of sedition, and in a moving appeal to his judge, asked for the maximum penalty. He was sentenced to six years in Yeravda prison near Poona. He had no regrets. "Freedom," he wrote, "is often to be found inside a prison's walls, even on a gallows; never in council chambers, courts and classrooms." [64]

"A leader," Gandhi replied, "is only a reflection of the people he leads." The people had first to be led to make peace among themselves. Then, he said, "their desire to live together in peaceful neighborliness will be reflected by their leaders." [53]

[Once Winston Churchill had called Mohandas Gandhi "a half-naked fakir."] Now that half-naked fakir was sitting in the viceregal study, "to negotiate and parley on equal terms with the representative of the King-Emperor." He's rather like a little bird, Louis Mountbatten thought, as he contemplated that famous figure at his side, a kind of "sweet, sad sparrow perched on my armchair.". . .

So important had Mountbatten considered this first meeting with Gandhi, that he had written the Mahatma inviting him to Delhi before the ceremony enthroning him as viceroy. Gandhi had drafted his reply immediately, then, with a chuckle, told an aide, "Wait a couple of days before putting it in the mail. I don't want that

young man to think I'm dying for his invitation." That "young man" had accompanied his invitation with one of those gestures for which he was becoming noted and which sometimes infuriated his fellow Englishmen. He had offered to send his personal aircraft to Bihar to fly Gandhi to Delhi. Gandhi had declined the offer. He had insisted on traveling, as he always did, in a third-class railway car.

To give their meeting a special cordiality, Mountbatten had asked his wife to be present. Now, with the famous figure opposite them, worry and concern swept over the viceregal couple. The Mahatma, they both immediately sensed, was profoundly unhappy, trapped in the grip of some mysterious remorse. Had they done something wrong? Neglected some arcane law of protocol? . . .

[Finally] a slow, sorrowful sigh escaped the Indian leader. "You know," he replied, "all my life, since I was in South Africa, I've renounced physical possessions." He owned virtually nothing, he explained—his Gita, the tin utensils from which he ate, mementos of his stay in Yeravda prison, his three "gurus." And his watch, the old eight-shilling Ingersoll that he hung from a string around his waist because, if he was going to devote every minute of his day to God's work, he had to know what time it was.

"Do you know what?" he asked sadly. "They stole it. Someone in my railway compartment coming down to Delhi stole the watch." As the frail figure lost in his armchair spoke those words, Mountbatten saw tears shining in Gandhi's eyes. It was not an eight-shilling watch an unknown hand had plucked from him in that congested railway car, but a particle of his faith. After a long silence, Gandhi began to talk of India's current dilemma. Mountbatten interrupted with a friendly wave of his hand.

"Mr. Gandhi," he said, "first, I want to know who you are." He was determined to get to know these Indian leaders before allowing them to begin assailing him with their minimum demands and final conditions. By putting them at ease, by getting them to confide in him, he hoped to create an atmosphere of mutual confidence and sympathy in which his own dynamic personality could have greater impact. The Mahatma was delighted. He loved to talk about himself, and in the Mountbattens he had found a charming pair of people genuinely interested in what he had to say. He rambled on about South Africa, his days as a stretcher-bearer in the Boer War, civil disobedience, the Salt March. Once, he said, the West had received its inspiration from the East in the messages of Zoroaster, Buddha, Moses, Jesus, Mohammed, Rama. For centuries, however, the East had been conquered culturally by the West. Now the West, haunted by specters like the atomic bomb, had need to look eastward once again. There, he hoped, it might find the message of love and fraternal understanding that he sought to preach. [103–104]

[Much later] India's new viceroy moved into a serious exchange with Gandhi with trepidation. He was not persuaded that the little figure "chirping like a sparrow" at his side could help him elaborate a solution to the Indian crisis, but he knew that he could defeat all efforts to find one. The hopes of many another English mediator had foundered on the turns of his unpredictable personality. It was Gandhi who had sent Cripps back to London empty-handed in 1942. His refusal to budge on a principle had helped thwart Wavell's efforts to untie the Indian knot. His tactics had done much to frustrate the most recent British attempt to solve the problem of liberation. Only the evening before, Gandhi had reiterated to his prayer meeting that India would be divided "over my dead body. So long as I am alive, I will never agree to the partition of India."

If a reluctant Mountbatten was driven to the decision to partition India, he would find himself in the utterly distasteful position of having to impose his will on Gandhi. It was not the elderly Mahatma's body he would have to break, but his heart.

It had always been British policy not to yield to force, he told Gandhi, by way of opening their talks on the right note, but his nonviolent crusade had won, and come what may, Britain was going to leave India. Only one thing mattered

in that coming departure, Gandhi replied. "Don't partition India," he begged. "Don't divide India," the prophet of nonviolence pleaded, "even if refusing to do so means shedding rivers of blood."

Dividing India, a shocked Mountbatten assured Gandhi, was the last solution he wished to adopt. But what alternatives were open to him? Gandhi had one. So desperate was he to avoid partition that he was prepared to give the Moslems the baby instead of cutting it in half. Place three hundred million Hindus under Moslem rule, he told Mountbatten, by asking his rival Jinnah and his Moslem League to form a government. Then hand over power to that government. Give Jinnah all of India instead of just the part he wants, was his nonviolent proposal.

"Whatever makes you think your own Congress Party will accept?" Mountbatten asked.

"Congress," Gandhi replied, "wants above all else to avoid partition. They will do anything to prevent it."

"What," Mountbatten asked, "would Jinnah's reaction be?"

"If you tell him I am its author his reply will be: 'Wily Gandhi,' " The Mahatma said, laughing. [106–109]

The Bully

Why, this man is trying to bully me, an unbelieving Louis Mountbatten thought. His Operation Seduction had come to a sudden, wholly unexpected halt at the rocklike figure planted in the chair opposite his. With his Khadi dhoti flung about his shoulders like a toga, his bald head glowing, his scowling demeanor, his visitor looked to the Viceroy more like a Roman senator than an Indian politician.

Patel was Indian from the uppermost lump of his bald head to the calluses on the soles of his feet. His Delhi home was filled with books, but every one of them was written by an Indian author about India. He was the only Indian leader who sprang from the soil of India. Emotion, one of his associates once observed, formed no part of Patel's character. The remark was not wholly exact. Patel was an emotional man, but he never let those emotions break through the composed facade he turned to the world. If he gave off one salient impression, it was that of a man wholly in control of himself. In a land in which men talked constantly, threw their words around like sailors flinging away their money after three months at sea, Patel hoarded his phrases the way a miser hoarded coins. His daughter, who had been his constant companion since his wife's death, rarely exchanged ten sentences with him a day. When Patel did talk, however, people listened.

Vallabhbhai Patel was India's quintessential politician. He was an Oriental Tammany Hall boss who ran the machinery of the Congress Party with a firm and ruthless hand. He should have been the easiest member of the Indian quartet for Mountbatten to deal with. Like the Viceroy, he was a practical pragmatic man, a hard but realistic bargainer. Yet the tension between them was so real, so palpable, that it seemed to Mountbatten he could reach out and touch it. Its cause was in no way related to the great issues facing India. It was a slip of paper, a routine government minute issued by Patel's Home Ministry dealing with an appointment. But Mountbatten had read it as a calculated challenge to his authority.

Patel had a well-earned reputation for toughness. He had an almost instinctive need to take the measure of a new interlocutor, to see how far he could push him. The piece of paper on his desk, Mountbatten was convinced, was a test, a little examination that he had to go through with Patel before he could get down to serious matters. The Viceroy looked at the note which had offended him, then passed it across his desk to Patel. Quietly he asked him to withdraw it. Patel brusquely refused. Mountbatten studied the Indian leader. He was going to need the support of this man and the machinery he represented. But he was sure he would never get it if he did not face him down now.

"Very well," said Mountbatten. "I'll tell you what I'm going to do. I'm going to order my plane."

"Oh," said Patel, "why?"

"Because I'm leaving," Mountbatten replied. "I didn't want this job in the first place. I've just been looking for someone like you to give me an excuse to throw it up and get out of an impossible situation."

"You don't mean it," exclaimed Patel.

"Mean it?" replied Mountbatten. "You don't think I am going to stay here and be bullied around by a chap like you, do you? If you think you can be rude to me and push me around, you're wrong. You'll either withdraw that minute, or one of us is going to resign. And let me tell you that if I go, I shall first explain to your prime minister, to Mr. Jinnah, to His Majesty's Government, why I am leaving. The breakdown in India which will follow, the blood that will be shed, will be on your shoulders and no one else's." Patel stared at Mountbatten in disbelief. A long silence followed. "You know," Patel finally sighed, "the awful part is I think you mean it." "You're damned right I do," answered Mountbatten. Patel reached out, took the offending minute off Mountbatten's desk and slowly tore it up. [109–111]

The Father of Pakistan

The man who would ultimately hold the key to the subcontinent's dilemma in his hands was the last of the Indian leaders to enter the Viceroy's study. A quarter of a century later, an echo of his distant anguish still haunting his voice, Louis Mountbatten would recall, "I did not realize how utterly impossible my task in India was going to be until I met Mohammed Ali Jinnah for the first time."

Inside the study, Jinnah began by informing Mountbatten that he had come to tell him exactly what he was prepared to accept. As he had done with Gandhi, Mountbatten interrupted with a wave of his hand. "Mr. Jinnah," he said, "I am not prepared to discuss conditions at this stage. First, let's make each other's acquaintance." Then with his legendary charm and verve, Mountbatten turned the focus of Operation Seduction on the Moslem leader. Jinnah froze. To that aloof and reserved man who never unbent, even with his closest associates, the very idea of revealing the details of his life and personality to a perfect stranger must have seemed appalling. Gamely Mountbatten struggled on, summoning up all the reserves of his gregarious, engaging personality. For what seemed to him like hours, his only reward was a series of monosyllabic grunts from the man beside him.

The man who would one day be hailed as the Father of Pakistan had first been exposed to the idea at a black-tie dinner at London's Waldorf Hotel in the spring of 1933. His host was Rahmat Ali, the graduate student who had set the idea to paper. Rahmat Ali had arranged the banquet with its oysters on the half shell and un-Islamic Chablis at his own expense, hoping to persuade Jinnah, India's leading Moslem politician, to take over his movement. He received a chilly rebuff. Pakistan, Jinnah told him, was "an impossible dream." The man whom the unfortunate graduate student had sought to lead a Moslem separatist movement had, in fact, begun his political career by preaching Hindu-Moslem unity. . . . [115]

Like Gandhi, Jinnah had gone to London to dine in the Inns of Court and had been called to the bar. Unlike Gandhi, however, he had come back from London an Englishman. He wore a monocle, superbly cut linen suits, which he changed three or four times a day to remain cool and unruffled in the soggy Bombay climate. He loved oysters and caviar, champagne, brandy and good Bordeaux. A man of unassailable personal honesty and financial integrity, his canons were sound law and sound procedure. He was, according to one intimate, "the last of the Victorians, a parliamentarian in the mode of Gladstone or Disraeli."

A more improbable leader of India's Moslem masses could hardly be imagined. The only thing Moslem about Mohammed Ali Jinnah was the fact his parents happened to be Moslem. He drank, ate pork, religiously shaved his beard each morning, and just as religiously avoided the mosque each Friday. God and the Koran had no place in Jinnah's vision of the world. His political foe Gandhi knew more verses of the Moslem holy book then he did. He had been able to achieve the remarkable feat of securing the allegiance of the vast majority of India's ninety million Moslems without being able to articulate more than a few sentences in their traditional tongue, Urdu.

Jinnah despised India's masses. He detested the dirt, the heat, the crowds of India. Gandhi traveled India in filthy third-class railway cars to be with the people. Jinnah rode first-class to avoid them. Jinnah had only scorn for his Hindu rivals. He labeled Nehru "a Peter Pan;" a "literary figure" who "should have been an English professor, not a politician;" "an arrogant Brahman who covers his Hindu trickiness under a veneer of Western education." Gandhi, to Jinnah, was "a cunning fox," "a Hindu revivalist." The sight of Mahatma, during an interval in a conversation in Jinnah's mansion, stretched out on one of his priceless Persian carpets, his mudpack on his belly, was something Jinnah had never forgotten or forgiven. . . .

His disenchantment with the Congress Party dated from Gandhi's ascension to power. It was not the impeccably dressed Jinnah who was going to be bundled off to some squalid British jail half naked in a dhoti and wearing a silly little white cap. Civil disobedience, he told Gandhi, was for "the ignorant and the illiterate." The turning point in Jinnah's career came after the 1937 elections, when the Congress Party refused to share with him and his Moslem League the spoils of office in those Indian provinces where there was a substantial Moslem minority. Jinnah, a man of towering vanity, took Congress's action as a personal insult. It convinced him that he and the Moslem League would never get a fair deal from a Congress-run India. The former apostle of Hindu-Moslem unity became the unyielding advocate of Pakistan, the project that he had labeled an "impossible dream" barely four years earlier. [116–117]

Mountbatten and Jinnah held six critical meetings during the first fortnight of April 1947. They were the vital conversations—not quite ten hours in length—that ultimately determined the resolution of the Indian dilemma. Mountbatten went into them armed with "the most enormous conceit in my ability to persuade people to do the right thing, not because I am persuasive so much as because I have the knack of being able to present the facts in their most favorable light." As he would later recall, he "tried every trick I could play, used every appeal I could imagine," to shake Jinnah's determination to have partition. Nothing would. There was no trick, no argument that could move him from his consuming determination to realize the impossible dream of Pakistan. . . . He had made himself the absolute dictator of the Moslem League. There were men below who might have been willing to negotiate a compromise, but as long as Mohammed Ali Jinnah was alive, they would hold their silence. . . .

Mountbatten and Jinnah did agree on one point at the outset—the need for speed. India, Jinnah declared, had gone beyond the stage at which a compromise solution was possible. There was only one solution, a speedy "surgical operation" on India. Otherwise, he warned, India would perish. When Mountbatten expressed concern that partition might produce bloodshed and violence, Jinnah reassured him. Once his "surgical operation" had taken place, all troubles would cease and India's two halves would live in harmony and happiness. It was, Jinnah told Mountbatten, like a court case that he had handled, a dispute between two brothers embittered by the shares assigned them by their father's will. Yet, two years after the court had adjudicated their dispute, they were the greatest friends. That, he promised the Viceroy, would be the case in India. . . .

. . . "India has never been a true nation," Jinnah asserted. "It only looks that way on the map. . . . The cows I want to eat, the Hindu stops me from killing. Every time a Hindu shakes hands with me he has to go wash his hands. The only thing the Moslem has in common with the Hindu is his slavery to the British." . . . [118]

For Jinnah, the division that he proposed was the natural course. However, it would have to produce a viable state, which meant that two of India's great provinces, the Punjab and Bengal, would have to be included in Pakistan, despite the fact that each contained enormous Hindu populations. Mountbatten could not agree. The very basis of Jinnah's argument for Pakistan was that India's Moslem minority should not be ruled by its Hindu majority. How then to justify taking the Hindu minorities of Bengal and the Punjab into a Moslem state? If Jinnah insisted on dividing India to get his Islamic state, then the very logic he had used to get it would compel Mountbatten to divide the Punjab and Bengal.

Jinnah protested—that would give him an economically unviable, "moth-eaten Pakistan." Mountbatten, who didn't want to give him any Pakistan at all, told the Moslem leader that if he felt the nation he was to receive was as "moth-eaten" as all that, he would do well to abandon his plan.

"Ah," Jinnah would counter, "Your Excellency doesn't understand. A man is a Punjabi or a Bengali before he is Hindu or Moslem. They share a common history, language, culture and economy. You must not divide them. You will cause endless bloodshed and trouble." "Mr. Jinnah I entirely agree." "You do?" "Of course," Mountbatten would continue. "A man is not only a Punjabi or Bengali before he is a Hindu or a Moslem, he is an Indian before all else. You have presented the unanswerable argument for Indian unity." "But you don't understand at all," Jinnah countered—and the discussion would start again.

Mountbatten was stunned by the rigidity of Jinnah's position. "I never would have believed," he later recalled, "that an intelligent man, well educated, trained in the Inns of Court, was capable of simply closing his mind as Jinnah did. It wasn't that he didn't see the point. He did, but a kind of shutter came down. He was the evil genius in the whole thing. The others could be persuaded, but not Jinnah. While he was alive nothing could be done." [119]

If Louis Mountbatten, Jawaharlal Nehru or Mahatma Gandhi had been aware in April 1947 of one extraordinary secret, the division threatening India might have been avoided. That secret was sealed onto the gray surface of a piece of film, a film that could have upset the Indian political equation and would almost certainly have changed the course of Asian history. Yet so precious was the secret which the film harbored that even the British C.I.D., one of the most effective investigative agencies in the world, was ignorant of its existence. The heart of the film was two dark circles no bigger than a pair of Ping-Pong balls. Each was surrounded by an irregular white border like the corona of the sun eclipsed by the moon. Above them, a galaxy of little white spots stretched up the film's gray surface toward the top of the thoracic cage. That film was an X ray, the X ray of a pair of human lungs.

The damage was so extensive that the man whose lungs were on that film had barely two or three years to live. . . . The lungs depicted on them belonged to the rigid and inflexible man who had frustrated Louis Mountbatten's efforts to preserve India's unity. Mohammed Ali Jinnah, the one unmovable obstacle between the Viceroy and Indian unity, was living under a sentence of death. . . . [124]

Meditating alone in his study after Jinnah's departure, Mountbatten realized that he was probably going to have to give him Pakistan. His first obligation in New Delhi was to the nation that had sent him there, England. He longed to preserve India's unity, but not at the expense of his country's becoming hopelessly entrapped in an India collapsing in chaos and violence. . . .

Military command had given Mountbatten a penchant for rapid, decisive actions, such as the one he now took. In future years, his critics would assail him for having reached it too quickly, for acting like an impetuous sailor and not a statesman, but Mountbatten was not going to waste any more time on what he was certain would be futile arguments with Jinnah. . . . Neither logic nor Mountbatten's power to charm and persuade had made any impact on him. The partition of India seemed the only solution. It now remained to Mountbatten to get Nehru and Patel to accept the principle and to find for it a plan that could get their support.

The Indian Rajahs

Yadavindra Singh presided over the most remarkable body in the world, an assembly unlike any other that man had ever devised. He was the Chancellor of the Chamber of Indian Princes (the

fabled Rajahs). His state of Patiala in the Punjab, was one of the richest in India. He had an army the size of an infantry division, equipped with Centurion tanks to defend it if necessary.

The princes' anachronistic situation dated to Britain's haphazard conquest of India, when rulers who received the English with open arms or proved worthy foes on the battlefield were allowed to remain on their thrones provided that they acknowledged Britain as the paramount power in India. The system was formalized in a series of treaties between the individual rulers and the British Crown. The Princes had recognized the "Paramountcy" of the King-Emperor as represented in New Delhi by the viceroy, and they ceded to him control of their foreign affairs and defense. They received in return Britain's guarantee of their continuing autonomy inside their states. [See map.]

It had once seemed to Rudyard Kipling that Providence had created the maharajas just to offer mankind a spectacle, a dazzling vision of marble palaces, tigers, elephants and jewels. Powerful or humble, rich or poor, they were an extraordinary breed, whose members had fueled those fabled legends of an India now on the brink of extinction. The accounts of their vices and virtues, their extravagant self-indulgences and prodigalities, their follies and their eccentricities had nourished a body of folklore and entranced a world hungry for exotic dreams. They had been the stuff of a myth sweeping disdainfully across the horizon of their impoverished nation on a magic carpet of wealth, leisure and unfettered self-indulgence. . . .

Certain princes like the Nizam of Hyderabad or the Maharaja of Kashmir ruled over states which rivaled in size or population the nations of Western Europe. Others like those in the Kathiawar peninsula near Bombay lived in stables and governed domains no larger than New York City's Central Park. Their fraternity embraced the richest man in the world and princes so poor that their entire kingdom was a cow pasture. Over four hundred princes ruled states smaller than twenty square miles. A good number of them offered their subjects an administration far better than that the British provided. A few were petty despots more concerned with squandering their states' revenues to slake their own extravagant desires than with improving the lot of their peoples. Whatever their political proclivities, however, the future of India's 565 ruling princes, with their average of eleven titles, 5.8 wives, 12.6 children, 9.2 elephants, 2.8 private railway cars, 3.4 Rolls-Royces and 22.9 tigers killed, posed a grave problem in the spring of 1947. No solution to the Indian equation would work if it failed to deal with their peculiar situation. [165,166]

A SUBTLE MOSAIC

Inevitably, Mountbatten's decision would lead to one of the great dramas of modern history. Whatever the manner in which it was executed, it was bound to end in the mutilation of a great nation. . . . To satisfy the exigent demands of Mohammed Ali Jinnah, two of India's most distinctive entities, the Punjab and Bengal, would have to be carved up. The result would make Pakistan a geographic aberration, a nation of two heads separated by 1,500 kilometers (900 miles) of Himalyan mountain peaks, all purely Indian territory. Twenty days, more time than was required to sail from Karachi to Marseilles, would be needed to make the sea trip around the subcontinent from one half of Pakistan to the other. [120]

If the geographical distance dividing the two halves of Pakistan would be great, however, the psychological distance between the two peoples inhabiting them would be staggering. Apart from a common faith in Allah the One, the Merciful, Punjabis and Bengalis shared nothing. They were as different as Finns and Greeks. The Bengalis were short, dark and agile, racially a part of the masses of Asia. The Punjabis, in whose veins flowed the blood of thirty centuries of conquerors, were scions of the steppes of Central Asia, and their Aryan features bore the traces of Turkestan, Russia, Persia, the deserts of Arabia. Neither history, nor language, nor culture

offered a bridge by which those two people might communicate. Their marriage in the common state of Pakistan would be a union created against all the dictates of logic.

The Punjab was a blend as subtle and complex as the mosaics decorating the monuments of its glorious Royal past. To divide it was unthinkable. Fifteen million Hindus, sixteen million Moslems, and five million Sikhs shared the neighborhoods and alleyways of its 17,932 towns and villages. Although divided by religion, they shared a common language, joint traditions, and a great pride in this distinctive Punjabi personality. Wherever the boundary line went, the result was certain to be nightmare for millions of human beings. Only an interchange of populations on a scale never effected before in history could sort out the havoc that it would create. From the Indus to the bridges of Delhi, for over 500 miles, there was not a single town, not a single village, cotton grove or wheat field that would not somehow be threatened if the partition plan were to be carried out.

The division of Bengal at the other end of the subcontinent held out the possibilities of another tragedy. Haboring more people than Great Britain and Ireland combined, Bengal contained thirty-five million Moslems and thirty million Hindus spread over an expanse of land running from the jungles at the foot of the Himalayas to the steaming marshes through which the thousand tributaries of the Ganges and Brahmaputra rivers drained into the Bay of Bengal. Despite its division into two religious communities, Bengal, even more than the Punjab, was a distinct entity of its own. Whether Hindu or Moslem, Bengalis sprang from the same racial stock, spoke the same language, shared the same culture. They sat on the floor in a certain Bengali manner, ordered the sentences they spoke in a peculiar Bengali cadence, each rising to a final crescendo, celebrated their own Bengali New Year on April 15. Their poets like Tabore were regarded with pride by all Bengalis. [122]

A land seared by droughts that alternated with frightening typhoon-whipped floods, Bengal was an immense, steaming swamp, in whose humid atmosphere flourished the two crops to which it owed a precarious prosperity, rice and jute. The cultivation of those two crops followed the province's religious frontiers, rice to the Hindu west, jute to the Moslem east. But the key to Bengal's existence did not lie in its crops. It was a city, the city that had been the springboard for Britain's conquest of India, the second city, after London, of the Empire, and first port of Asia—Calcutta, site of the terrible Hindu-Moslem killings of August 1946.

Everything in Bengal—roads, railroads, communications, industry—funneled into Calcutta. If Bengal was split into its eastern and western halves, Calcutta, because of its physical location, seemed certain to be in the Hindu west, thus condemning the Moslem east to a slow but inexorable asphyxiation. If almost all of the world's jute grew in eastern Bengal, all the factories that transformed it into rope, sacks and cloth were clustered around Calcutta, in western Bengal. The Moslem east, which produced the jute, grew almost no food at all, and its millions survived on the rice grown in the Hindu west. . . .

Yet, no aspect of partition was more illogical than the fact that Jinnah's Pakistan would deliver barely half of India's Moslems from the alleged inequities of Hindu majority rule which had justified the state in the first place. The remaining Moslems were scattered throughout the rest of India so widely that it was impossible to separate them. Islands in a Hindu sea, even after the amputation, India would still harbor almost fifty million Moslems, a figure that would make her the third-largest Moslem nation in the world, after Indonesia and the new state drawn from her own womb. [123]

The Governors

The eleven men seated around the oval table in the conference chamber solemnly waited for Lord Mountbatten to begin the proceedings. They were, in a sense, the descendants of the twenty-four founding fathers of the East India Company, the men whose mercantile appetites had sent Britain along the sea lanes to India three and a half

centuries earlier. . . . Their meeting was an awkward confrontation for Mountbatten. At forty-six, he was the youngest man at the table. . . . He was a comparative stranger in the India to which most of the eleven governors had devoted an entire career, mastering its complex history, learning its dialects, becoming, as some of them had, world-renowned experts on phases of its existence. They were proud men, certain to be skeptical of any plan put before them by the neophyte in their midst. . . . [126]

Mountbatten began by asking each governor to describe the situation in his province. Eight of them painted a picture of dangerous, troubled areas, but provinces in which the situation still remained under control. It was the portrait offered by the governors of the three critical provinces, the Punjab, Bengal, and the Northwest Frontier Province, that sobered the gathering.

His features drawn, his eyes heavy with fatigue, Sir Olaf Caroe spoke first. He had been kept awake all night by a stream of cables detailing fresh outbursts of trouble in his Northwest Frontier Province. The labyrinth grottoes of his mountainous province sheltered scores of secret arms factories, from which flowed a profusion of ornate and deadly weapons to arm Mahsuds, Afridis, Wazirs, the legendary warrior tribes of the Pathans. The situation in the N.W.F.P. was close to disintegrating, he warned, and if that happened, the old British nightmare of invading hordes from the northwest forcing the gates of the Empire might be realized. The Pathan tribes of Afghanistan were poised to come pouring down the Khyber Pass to Peshawar and the banks of the Indus in pursuit of land they had claimed as theirs for a century. "If we're not jolly careful," he said, "we are going to have an international crisis on our hands."

The portrait drawn by Sir Evan Jenkins, the taciturn governor of the Punjab, was even grimmer than Caroe's. . . . Whatever solution was chosen for India's problems, he declared, it was certain to bring violence to the Punjab. At least four divisions would be needed to keep order if partition was decided upon. Even if it was not, they would still face a demand by the

Sikhs for an area of their own. "It's absurd to predict the Punjab will go up in flames if it's partitioned," he said; "it's already in flames." [127]

The third governor, Sir Frederick Burrows of Bengal, was ill in Calcutta, but the briefing of the province's situation as offered by his deputy was every bit as disquieting as the reports from the N.W.F.P. and the Punjab. When those reporters were finally finished, Mountbatten's staff passed out a set of papers to each governor. They carried the details, Mountbatten announced, "of one of the possible plans under examination." It was called, "for easy reference," Plan Balkan, and it was the first draft of a partition plan that Mountbatten had ordered his chief of staff, Lord Ismay, to prepare a week earlier. . . . The plan, aptly named for the Balkanization of the states of Central Europe after World War I, would allow each of India's eleven provinces to choose whether it wished to join Pakistan or remain in India; or, if a majority of both its Hindus and Moslems agreed, become independent. Mountbatten told his assembled governors that he was not going to "lightly abandon hope for a united India." He wanted the world to know that the British had made every effort possible to keep India united. If Britain failed it was of the utmost importance that the world know it was "Indian opinion rather than a British decision that had made partition the choice." He himself thought a future Pakistan was so inherently unviable that it should "be given a chance to fail on its own demerits," so that later "the Moslem League could revert to a unified India with honor."

Those eleven men who represented the collective wisdom of the service that had run India for a century displayed no enthusiasm for the idea that partition might have to be the answer to India's dilemma. Nor did they have any other solution to propose. [128]

Visit to Peshawar

Louis Mountbatten had decided to suspend temporarily the conversations in his air-conditioned office while he, personally, took the political tem-

perature of his two most troubled provinces, the Punjab and the N.W.F.P. The news that he was coming had swept over the Frontier. For twenty-four hours, summoned by the leaders of Jinnah's Moslem League, tens of thousands of men from every corner of the province had been converging on Peshawar. Overflowing their trucks, in buses, in cars, on special trains, chanting and waving their arms, they had spilled into the capital for the greatest popular demonstration in its history.

Now those tall, pale-skinned Pathans prepared to offer the Viceroy a welcome of an unexpected sort to Peshawar. . . . The police had confined them in an enormous low-walled enclosure running between a railroad embankment and the sloping walls of Peshawar's old Mogul fortress. Irritated and unruly, they threatened to drown the conciliatory tones of Operation Seduction with the discordant rattle of gunfire.

They were there because of the anomalous political situation of a province whose population was 93 percent Moslem, but was governed by allies of the Congress Party. . . . Stirred by Jinnah's agents, the population had turned against the Congress leader Ghaffar Khan who supported Gandhi and the government that he had installed in Peshawar. The huge, howling crowd greeting Mountbatten, his wife and seventeen-year-old daughter Pamela was meant to give final proof that it was the Moslem League and not the "Frontier Gandhi" that now commanded the province's support. [129] The crowd, growing more unruly by the hour, threatened to burst out of the area in which the police had herded them and start a headlong rush on the governor's residence. If they did, the vastly outnumbered military guarding the house would have no choice but to open fire. The resulting slaughter would be appalling. It would destroy Mountbatten, his hopes of finding a solution, and his viceroyalty in a sickening blood bath.

There was one way out, an idea condemned by the police and army commander as sheer madness. Mountbatten might present himself to the crowds, hoping that somehow a glimpse of him would mollify them. Mountbatten pondered a few moments. "All right, I'll take a chance and see them.'' To the despair of Caroe and his security officers, Edwina his wife insisted on coming with him. . . . A few minutes later, a jeep deposited the viceregal couple and the governor at the foot of the railway embankment. On the other side of that precarious dike, 100,000 hot, dirty, angry people were shouting their frustration in an indecipherable din. Mountbatten took his wife by the hand and clambered up the embankment. As they reached the top, they discovered themselves only fifteen feet away from the surging waves of a sea of turbans. The ground under their feet shook with the impact of the gigantic crowd stampeding forward in front of them. That terrifying ocean of human beings, incarnated in their shrieks and gesticulations the enormity and the passions of the masses of India. Whirling spirals of dust stirred by thousands of rushing feet clotted the air. The noise of the crowd was an almost tangible layer of air crushing down on them. It was a decisive instant in Operation Seduction, an instant when anything was possible. . . . In that crowd were twenty, thirty, forty thousand rifles. Any madman, any bloodthirsty fool could shoot the Mountbattens ''like ducks on a pond.''

For the first few seconds Mountbatten did not know what to do. He couldn't articulate a syllable of Pushtu, the crowd's language. As he pondered, a totally unexpected phenomenon began to still the mob, stopping perhaps with its strange vibrations an assassin's hand. For this entirely unplanned meeting with the Empire's most renowned warriors, Mountbatten happened to be wearing the short-sleeved, loose-fitting bush jacket that he had worn as Supreme Allied Commander in Burma. Its color, green, galvanized the crowd. Green was the color of Islam, the blessed green of the hadjis, the holy men who had made the pilgrimage to Mecca. Instinctively, those tens of thousands of men read in that green uniform a gesture of solidarity with them, a subtle compliment to their great religion.

His hand still clutching hers, but his eyes straight ahead, Mountbatten whispered to his wife, ''Wave to them.'' Slowly, graciously, the frail Edwina raised her arm with his to the crowd.

India's fate seemed for an instant suspended in those hands climbing above the crowd's head. A questioning silence had drifted briefly over the unruly crowd. Suddenly, Edwina's pale arm began to stroke the sky; a cry, then a roaring ocean of noise burst from the crowd. From tens of thousands of throats came an interminable, constantly repeated shout, a triumphant litany marking the successful passing of the most dangerous seconds of Operation Seduction.

''Mountbatten Zindabad!'' those embittered Pathan warriors screamed, ''Mountbatten Zindabad!'' (''Long live Mountbatten!'') [130–131]

Slaughter at Kahuta

[Soon, however,] a shocked Mountbatten was to get his first direct contact with the horrors sweeping India in the cruel springtime of 1947. The naval officer who had seen most of his shipmates die in the wreck of his destroyer off Crete, the leader who had led millions through the savage jungle war in Burma, was overwhelmed by the spectacle he discovered in that village of 3,500 people, which had once been typical of India's half million villages.

For centuries, Kahuta's dirt alleys had been shared in peace by 2,000 Hindus and Sikhs and 1,500 Moslems. That day, side by side in the village center, the stone minaret of its mosque and the rounded dome of the Sikhs' gurudwara were the only identifiable remnants of Kahuta left on the skyline of the Punjab. Just before Mountbatten's visit, a patrol of the British Norfolk Regiment on a routine reconnaissance mission passed through the village. Kahuta's citizens, as they had been doing for generations, were sleeping side by side in mutual confidence and tranquility. By dawn, Kahuta had for all practical purposes ceased to exist, and its Sikhs and Hindus were all dead or had fled in terror into the night.

A Moslem horde had descended on Kahuta like a wolf pack, setting fire to the houses in its Sikh and Hindu quarters with buckets of gasoline. In minutes, the area was engulfed in fire and entire families, screaming pitifully for help, were consumed by the flames. Those who escaped were caught, tied together, soaked with gasoline and burned alive like torches. Totally out of control, the fire swept into the Moslem quarter and completed the destruction of Kahuta. A few Hindu women, yanked from their beds to be raped and converted to Islam, survived; others had broken away from their captors and hurled themselves back into the fire to perish with their families.

"Until I went to Kahuta," Mountbatten reported back to London, "I had not appreciated the magnitude of the horrors that were going on." This confrontation with the crowd in Peshawar and the atrocious spectacle of one devastated Punjabi village was the last proof Mountbatten needed. Speed was the one absolute, overwhelming imperative if India was to be saved. . . . And if speed was essential, then there was only one way out of the impasse, the solution from which he personally recoiled, but which India's political situation dictated—partition. [131–132]

THE SHATTERED DREAM

The last, painful phase in the lifelong pilgrimage of Mahatma Gandhi began on the evening of May 1, 1947, in the same spare hut in New Delhi's sweepers' colony in which a fortnight before he had unsuccessfully urged his colleagues to accept his plan to hold India together. Crosslegged on the floor, a water-soaked towel plastered once again to his bald head, Gandhi followed with sorrow the debate of the men around him, the high command of the Congress Party. The final parting of the ways between Gandhi and those men, foreshadowed in their earlier meeting, had been reached. All Gandhi's long years in jail, his painful fasts, his hartals and his boycotts had been paving stones on the road to this meeting. He had changed the face of India and enunciated one of the original philosophies of his century to bring his countrymen to independence through nonviolence; and now his sublime triumph threatened to become a terrible personal tragedy. His

followers, their tempers worn, their patience exhausted, were ready to accept the division of India as the last, inescapable step to independence.

Gandhi did not oppose partition simply out of some mystical devotion to Indian unity. His years in the villages of India had given him an intuitive feeling for the soul of his country. Partition, that intuition told him, was not going to be the "surgical operation" Jinnah had promised Mountbatten it would be. It would be a sickening slaughter that would turn friend on friend, neighbor on neighbor, stranger on stranger in thousands of those villages he knew so well. Their blood would be shed to achieve an abhorrent, useless end, the division of the subcontinent into two antagonistic parts condemned to gnaw at each other's entrails. Generations of Indians for decades to come, Gandhi believed, would pay the price of the error they were preparing to commit. Like Mountbatten, Nehru, Patel and the others all felt a catastrophe menaced India, and partition, however painful it might be, was the only way to save the country. Gandhi believed with all his heart and soul that they were wrong. Even if they were right, he would have preferred chaos to partition.

Gandhi's tragedy was that he had that evening no real alternative to propose beyond his instincts, the instincts those men had so often followed before. This night, however, he was no longer a prophet. "They call me a Mahatma," he bitterly told a friend later, "but I tell you I am not even treated by them as a sweeper." Jinnah, he told his followers, will never get Pakistan unless the British give it to him. The British would never do that in the face of the Congress majority's unyielding opposition. They had a veto over any action Mountbatten proposed. Tell the British to go, he begged, no matter what the consequences of their departure might be. Tell them to leave India "to God, to chaos, to anarchy if you wish, but leave.". . .

He was a voice crying in the wilderness. Even his two hand-picked deputies were not ready to heed one last time the voice that had so often given utterance to their joint aspirations. Patel had been prepared to concede partition even before Mountbatten's arrival. He was aging, he had suffered two heart attacks, and he wanted to get on with it, to end these ceaseless debates and get down to the task of building an independent India. Give Jinnah his state, he argued; it wouldn't survive anyway; in five years, the Moslem League would be knocking at their door begging for India's reunification.

Nehru was a torn and anguished man, caught between his deep love for Gandhi and his new admiration and friendship for the Mountbattens. Gandhi spoke to his heart, Mountbatten to his mind. Instinctively, Nehru detested partition; yet his rationalist spirit told him it was the only answer. Since reaching his own conclusion that there was no other choice, Mountbatten and his wife had been employing all the charm and persuasiveness of Operation Seduction to bring Nehru to their viewpoint. One argument was vital. With Jinnah gone, Hindu India could have the strong central government that Nehru would need if he was going to build the socialist state of his dreams. Ultimately, he too stood out against the man he had followed so long. With their two vital voices in favor, the rest of the high command quickly fell in line. Nehru was authorized to inform the Viceroy that while Congress remained "passionately attached to the idea of a united India," it would accept partition, provided that the two great provinces of Punjab and Bengal were divided. The man who had led them to their triumph was left alone with his tarnished victory and his broken dream. [132–134]

"Sheer Madness"

All Mountbatten's hopes had foundered, finally, on the rock of Jinnah's determined, intransigent person. . . . For the rest of his life, Mountbatten would look back on that failure to move Jinnah as the single greatest disappointment of his career. His personal anguish at the prospect of going down in history as the man who had divided India could be measured by a document flown back to London with Ismay in Mountbatten's

viceregal York, his fifth personal report to the Attlee government.

Partition, Mountbatten wrote, "is sheer madness," and "no one would ever induce me to agree to it were it not for this fantastic communal madness that has seized everybody and leaves no other course open. . . . The responsibility for this mad decision," he wrote, must be placed "squarely on Indian shoulders in the eyes of the world, for one day they will bitterly regret the decision they are about to make." [134]

More serious, however, was the real concern which underlay his growing apprehension. If the implications in the plan that he had sent to London were fully realized, the great Indian subcontinent would be divided into three independent nations, not two. Mountbatten had inserted in his plan a clause that would allow the sixty-five million Hindus and Moslems of Bengal to join into one viable country, with the great seaport of Calcutta as their capital.

Contrasted to Jinnah's aberrant, two-headed state, that seemed an entity likely to endure, and Mountbatten had quietly encouraged Bengal's politicians, Hindu and Moslem alike, to support it. He had even discovered that Jinnah would not oppose the idea. He had not, however, exposed it to Nehru and Patel, and it was this oversight that disturbed him now. Would they accept a plan that might cost them the great port of Calcutta with its belt of textile mills owned by the Indian industrialists who were their party's principal financial support? If they didn't, Mountbatten, after all the assurances he had given London, was going to look a bloody fool in the eyes of India, Britain and the world.

A sudden inspiration struck Mountbatten. He would reassure himself privately, informally, with the Indian leader, whom, to the distress of his staff, he had invited to vacation with him in Simla, [Jawaharlal Nehru]. [159] To show the plan to Nehru without exposing it to Jinnah would be a complete breach of faith with the Moslem leader, they pointed out. If he discovered it, Mountbatten's whole position would be destroyed. For a long time, Mountbatten sat silently drumming the tabletop with his fingertips.

"I am sorry," he finally announced, "your arguments are absolutely sound. But I have a hunch that I must show it to Nehru, and I'm going to follow my hunch." That night, Mountbatten invited Nehru to his study for a glass of port. Casually, he passed the Congress leader a copy of the plan as it had been amended by London, asking him to take it to his bedroom and read it. Then perhaps he might let him know informally what reception it was likely to get from Congress. Flattered and happy, Nehru agreed.

[After a few hours], Nehru began to scrutinize the text designed to chart his country's future. He was horrified by what he read. The vision of the India that emerged from the plan's pages was a nightmare . . . an India divided, not into two parts but fragmented into a dozen pieces. Bengal would become, Nehru foresaw, a wound through which the best blood of India would pour. He saw India deprived of the port of Calcutta along with its mills, factories, steelworks; Kashmir, his beloved Kashmir, an independent state ruled by a despot he despised; Hyderabad become an enormous, indigestible Moslem body planted in the belly of India, half a dozen other princely states clamoring to go off on their own. The plan, he believed, would exacerbate all India's fissiparous tendencies of dialect, culture and race to the point at which the subcontinent would risk exploding into a mosaic of weak, hostile states. White-faced, shaking with rage, Nehru stalked into the bedroom of his confidant V. P. Menon, who had accompanied him to Simla. With a furious gesture, he hurled the plan onto his bed. "It's all over!" he shouted. . . .

Mountbatten got his first intimation of his friend's violent reaction in a letter early the following morning. For the confident Viceroy, it was "a bombshell." As he read it, the whole structure he had so carefully erected during the past six weeks came tumbling down like a house of cards. The impression that his plan left, Nehru wrote, was one of "fragmentation and conflict and disorder." It frightened him and was certain to be "resented and bitterly disliked by the Congress Party." Reading Nehru's words, the poised,

self-assured Viceroy, who had proudly announced to England that he was going to present a solution to India's dilemma in ten days' time, suddenly realized that he had no solution at all. The plan that the British Cabinet was discussing that very day, the plan that he had just assured Attlee would win Indian acceptance, would never get past the one element in India that had to accept it, the Congress Party.

Mountbatten's critics might accuse him of overconfidence, but he was not a man to brood at setbacks. Instead of descending into a fit of despondency at Nehru's reaction, Mountbatten congratulated himself on his hunch in showing him the plan, and set out to repair the damage. [161] To redraft his plan, Mountbatten called into his study the highest-ranking Indian in his viceregal establishment. It was a supreme irony that at that critical juncture the Indian to whom Mountbatten turned had not even entered that vaunted administrative elite, the Indian Civil Service. No degree from Oxford or Cambridge graced his office walls. No family ties had hastened his rise. V. P. Menon was an incongruous oddity in the rarefied air of Viceroy's House, a self-made man.

Mountbatten informed Menon that before nightfall he would have to redraft the charter that would give India her independence. Its essential element, partition, had to remain, and it must continue to place the burden of choice on the Indians themselves. Menon finished his task in accordance with Mountbatten's instructions by sunset. Between lunch and dinner, he had performed a tour de force. The man who had begun his career as a two-finger typist had culminated it by redrafting, in barely six hours on an office porch looking out on the Himalyas, a plan that was going to encompass the future of one fifth of humanity, reorder the subcontinent, and alter the map of the world. [162–163]

A DAY CURSED BY THE STARS

[When the day came to approve this plan] the lusterless eyes of Robert Clive gazed down from the great oil painting upon the wall at the seven

Indian leaders filing into the Viceroy's study. Representatives of India's 400 million human beings, those millions whom Gandhi called "miserable specimens of humanity with lusterless eyes," they entered Mountbatten's study on this morning of June 2, 1947, to inspect the deeds that would return to their peoples the continent whose conquest the British general had opened two centuries before. The papers, formally approved by the British Cabinet, had been brought from London by the Viceroy just forty-eight hours before.

One by one, they took their places at the circular table in the center of the room: Congress, represented by Nehru, Patel and its president, Acharya Kripalani; the Moslem League by Jinnah, Liaquat Ali Khan and Rab Nishtar. Baldev Singh was present as spokesman for the six million people who would be more dramatically affected by the words about to be spoken than any others in India, the Sikhs. Against the wall sat Mountbatten's two key advisers Lord Ismay and Sir Eric Mieville. At the center of the table was the Viceroy. . . .

For the first time since he had arrived in Delhi, Mountbatten was now being forced to abandon his head-to-head diplomacy for a round-table conference. He had decided, however, that he would do the talking. He was not going to run the risk of throwing the meeting open for a general discussion that might degenerate into an acrimonious shouting match that could destroy his elaborately wrought plan. Aware of the poignancy and historic nature of their gathering, he began by noting that during the past five years he had taken part in a number of momentous meetings at which the decisions that had determined the fate of the war had been taken. He could remember no meeting, however, at which decisions had been taken whose impact upon history had been as profound as would be the impact of the decision before them.

Briefly, Mountbatten reviewed his conversations since arriving in Delhi, stressing the terrible sense of urgency they had impressed on him. Then, for the record and for history, he formally asked Jinnah one last time if he was prepared to accept Indian unity as envisaged by the Cabinet Mission Plan. With equal formality, Jinnah replied that he was not, and Mountbatten moved on to the matter at hand. Briefly, he reviewed the details of his plan. The dominion-status clause that had ultimately won Winston Churchill's support was not, he stressed, a reflection of a British desire to keep a foot in the door beyond her time, but to assure that British assistance would not be summarily withdrawn if it was still needed. He dwelt on Calcutta, on the coming agony of the Sikhs.

He would not, he said, ask them to give their full agreement to a plan, parts of which went against their principles. He asked only that they accept it in a peaceful spirit and vow to make it work without bloodshed. His intention, he said, was to meet with them again the following morning. He hoped that before that, before midnight, all three parties, the Moslem League, Congress and the Sikhs, would have indicated their willingness to accept the plan as a basis for a final Indian settlement. If this was the case, then he proposed that he, Nehru, Jinnah and Baldev Singh announce their agreement jointly to the world the following evening on All India Radio. Clement Attlee would make a confirming announcement from London.

"Gentlemen," he concluded, "I should like your reaction to the plan by midnight." [191–192]

A Nod of the Head

[That night] in Louis Mountbatten's study the lights still burned, illuminating the last meeting of his harrowing day. He stared at his visitor with uncomprehending disbelief. Congress had indicated in time their willingness to accept his plan. So, too, had the Sikhs. Now the man it was designed to satisfy, the man whose obdurate, unyielding will had forced partition on India, was temporizing. Everything Jinnah had been striving for for years was there, waiting only his acknowledgment. For some mysterious reason, Jinnah simply could not bring himself this night to utter the word that he had made a career refusing to pronounce—"yes."

Inhaling deeply one of the Craven A's that he chain-smoked in his jade holder Jinnah kept insisting that he could not give an indication of the Moslem League's reaction to Mountbatten's plan until he had put it before the League's Council, and he needed at least a week to bring its members to Delhi. All the frustrations generated by his dealings with Jinnah welled up in Mountbatten. Jinnah had gotten his damn Pakistan. Even the Sikhs had swallowed the plan. Everything he had been working for he had finally gotten, and here, at the absolute eleventh hour, Jinnah was preparing to destroy it all, to bring the whole thing crashing down with his unfathomable inability to articulate just one word, "yes."

Mountbatten simply had to have his agreement. Attlee was standing by in London waiting to make his historic announcement to the Commons in less than twenty-four hours. He had gone on the line personally to Attlee, to his government with firm assurances that this plan would work; that there would be no more abrupt twists like that prompted by Nehru in Simla; that this time, they could be certain they had approved a plan that the Indian leaders would all accept. He had, with enormous difficulty, coaxed a reluctant Congress up to this point, and, finally, they were prepared to accept partition. Even Gandhi, temporarily at least, had allowed himself to be bypassed. A final hesitation, just the faintest hint that Jinnah was maneuvering to secure one last concession, and the whole carefully wrought package would blow apart.

"Mr. Jinnah," Mountbatten said, "if you think I can hold this position for a week while you summon your followers to Delhi, you must be crazy. You know this has been drawn up to the boiling point. . . . The Congress has made their acceptance dependent on your agreement. If they suspect you're holding out on them, they will immediately withdraw their agreement and we will be in the most terrible mess."

No, no, Jinnah protested, everything had to be done in the legally constituted way, "I am not the Moslem League," he said. . . .

"Now, now, come on, Mr. Jinnah," said Mountbatten, icy calm, "don't try to tell me that.

You can try to tell the world that. But don't kid yourself that I don't know what's what in the Moslem League. . . . Mr. Jinnah, I'm going to tell you something. I don't intend to let you wreck your own plan. I can't allow you to throw away the solution you've worked so hard to get. I propose to accept on your behalf.

"Tomorrow at the meeting," Mountbatten continued, "I shall say I have received the reply of the Congress, with a few reservations that I am sure I can satisfy, and they have accepted. The Sikhs have accepted. . . . Then I shall say that I had a very long, very friendly conversation with Mr. Jinnah last night, that we went through the plan in detail, and Mr. Jinnah has given me his personal assurance that he is in agreement with this plan.

"Now at that point, Mr. Jinnah," Mountbatten continued, "I shall turn to you. I don't want you to speak. I don't want Congress to force you into the open. I want you to do only one thing. I want you to nod your head to show that you are in agreement with me. . . . If you don't nod your head, Mr. Jinnah," Mountbatten concluded, "then you're through, and there'll be nothing more I can do for you. Everything will collapse. This is not a threat. It's a prophecy. If you don't nod your head at that moment, my usefulness here will be ended, you will have lost your Pakistan, and as far as I am concerned, you can go to hell." [196]

The meeting that would formally record the Indian leaders' acceptance of the Mountbatten plan to divide India began exactly as Mountbatten had said it would. Once again, on the morning of June 3, the Viceroy condemned the leaders to an unfamiliar silence by dominating the conversation himself. As he had expected, he said, all three parties had had grave reservations about his plan and he was grateful that they had aired them to him. Nonetheless Congress had signified its acceptance. So, too, had the Sikhs. He had had, he said, a long and friendly conversation the previous evening with Mr. Jinnah, who had assured him the plan was acceptable.

As he spoke those words, Mountbatten turned to Jinnah, seated at his right. At that instant

Mountbatten had absolutely no idea what the Moslem leader was going to do. The captain of the *Kelly*, the supreme commander who had had an entire army corps encircled and cut off by the Japanese on the Imphal Plain, would always look back on that instant as "the most hair-raising moment of my entire life." For an endless second, he stared into Jinnah's impassive, expressionless face. Then slowly, reluctance crying from every pore, Jinnah indicated his agreement with the faintest, most begrudging nod he could make. His chin moved barely half an inch downward, the shortest distance it could have traveled consonant with accepting Mountbatten's plan. With that brief, almost imperceptible gesture, a nation of forty-five million human beings had received its final sanction.

A Sharp Crack

However abortive its form, however difficult the circumstances that would attend its birth, the "impossible dream" of Pakistan would at last be realized. Mountbatten had enough agreement to go ahead. Before any of the seven men could have a chance to formulate a last reservation or doubt, he announced that his plan would henceforth constitute the basis for an Indian settlement.

While the enormity of the decision they had just taken began to penetrate, Mountbatten had a thirty-four-page, single-spaced document set before each man. Clasping the last copy himself with both hands, the Viceroy lifted it over his head and whipped it back down onto the table. At the sharp crack that followed the slap of paper on wood, Mountbatten read out the imposing title on his equally imposing document—"The Administrative Consequences of Partition."

It was a carefully elaborated christening present from Mountbatten and his staff to the Indian leaders, a guide to the awesome task that now lay before them. Page after page, it summarized in its dull bureaucratic jargon the appalling implications of their decision. None of the seven was in even the remotest way prepared for the shock they encountered as they began to turn the pages of the document. Ahead of them lay a problem of a scope and on a scale no people had ever encountered before, a problem vast enough to beggar the most vivid imagination. They were now going to be called upon to settle the contested estate of 400 million human beings, to unravel the possessions left behind by thirty centuries of common inhabitation of the subcontinent, to pick apart the fruits of three centuries of technology. The cash in the banks, stamps in the post offices, books in the libraries, debts, assets, the world's third-largest railway, jails, prisoners, inkpots, brooms, research centers, hospitals, universities, institutions and articles staggering in number and variety would be theirs to divide.

A stunned silence filled the study as the seven men measured for the first time what lay ahead of them. Mountbatten . . . had forced these seven men to come to grips with a problem so imposing that it would leave them neither the time nor the energy for recrimination in the few weeks of coexistence left to them.

"No Joy in My Heart"

Shortly after seven o'clock on that evening of June 3, 1947, in the New Delhi studio of All India Radio, the four key leaders formally announced their agreement to divide the subcontinent into two separate sovereign nations. As befitting his office, Mountbatten spoke first. His words were confident, his speech brief, his tones understated. Nehru followed, speaking in Hindi. Sadness grasped the Indian leader's face as he told his listeners that "the great destiny of India" was taking shape, "with travail and suffering." Baring his own emotions, he urged acceptance of the plan that had caused him such deep personal anguish, by concluding that "it is with no joy in my heart that I commend these proposals to you."

Jinnah was next. Nothing would ever be more illustrative of the enormous, yet wholly incongruous nature of his achievement than that speech. Mohammed Ali Jinnah was incapable of announcing to his followers the news that he had won them a state in a language that they could understand. He had to tell India's ninety million Moslems of the "momentous decision" to create an Islamic state on the subcontinent in English. An announcer then read his words in Urdu. . . . [197–199]

Gandhi walked into Mountbatten's study at 6 p.m. His prayer meeting was at seven. That left Mountbatten less than an hour in which to ward off a potential disaster. His first glance at the Mahatma told Mountbatten how deeply upset he was. Crumpled up in his armchair "like a bird with a broken wing," Gandhi kept raising and dropping one hand lamenting in an almost inaudible voice: "It's so awful, it's so awful."

In that state Gandhi, Mountbatten knew, was capable of anything. A public denunciation of his plan would be disastrous. Nehru, Patel and the other leaders the Viceroy had so patiently coaxed into accepting it would be forced to break publicly with Gandhi or break their agreement with him. Vowing to use every argument his fertile imagination could produce, Mountbatten began by telling Gandhi how he understood and shared his feelings at seeing the united India he had worked for all his life destroyed by this plan. Suddenly as he spoke, a burst of inspiration struck him. The newspapers had christened the plan the "Mountbatten Plan," he said, but they should have called it the "Gandhi Plan." It was Gandhi, Mountbatten declared, who had suggested to him all its major ingredients. The Mahatma looked at him perplexed.

Yes, Mountbatten continued, Gandhi had told him to leave the choice to the Indian people and this plan did. It was the provincial, popularly elected assemblies which would decide India's future. Each province's assembly would vote on whether it wished to join India or Pakistan. Gandhi had urged the British to quit India as soon as possible, and that was what they were going to do. "If by some miracle the assemblies vote for unity," Mountbatten told Gandhi, "you have what you want. If they don't agree, I'm sure you don't want us to oppose their decision by force of arms."

Approaching seventy-eight, Gandhi was, for the first time in thirty years, uncertain of his grip on India's masses, at odds with the leaders of his party. In his despair and uncertainty, he was still searching in his soul for an answer, still waiting for an illuminating whisper of the inner voice that had guided him in so many of the grave crises of his career. That June evening, however, the voice was silent, and Gandhi was assailed by doubt. Should he remain faithful to his instincts, denounce partition, even (as he had earlier urged) at the price of plunging India into violence and chaos? Or should he listen to the Viceroy's desperate plea for reason? . . .

Less than an hour later, cross-legged on a raised platform in a dirt square in the midst of his Untouchables colony, Gandhi delivered his verdict. Many in the crowd before him had come, not to pray, but to hear from the lips of the prophet of nonviolence a call to arms, a fiery assault on Mountbatten's plan. No such cry would come this evening from the mouth of the man who had so often promised to offer his own body for vivisection, rather than accept his country's division. It was no use blaming the Viceroy for partition, he said. Look to yourselves and in your own hearts for an explanation of what has happened, he challenged. Louis Mountbatten's persuasiveness had won the ultimate and most difficult triumph of his viceroyalty.

As for Gandhi, many an Indian would never forgive him his silence, and the frail old man whose heart still ached for India's coming division would one day pay the price of their rancor. [200]

The Announced Date

For Mountbatten the public announcement was the apotheosis, the consecration of a remarkable *tour de force*. In barely two months, virtually a one-man band, he had achieved the impossible, established a dialogue with India's leaders, set the basis of an agreement, persuaded his Indian interlocutors to accept it, extracted the whole-hearted support of both the government and the opposition in London. He had skirted with dexterity and a little luck the pitfalls marring his route. And as his final gesture he had entered the cage of the old lion himself, convinced Churchill to draw in his claws and left him too, murmuring his approbation.

[As] Mountbatten concluded his talk to the assembled world press [there was] a burst of applause. He opened the floor to questions. He had no apprehension in doing so. "I had been there," he would recall later. "I was the only one who had been through it all, who'd lived every moment of it. For the first time the press were meeting the one and only man who had the whole thing at his fingertips." Suddenly, when the long barrage of questions began to trickle out, the anonymous voice of an Indian newsman cut across the chamber. His final question was the last square left to Mountbatten to fill in the puzzle he had been assigned six months before.

"Sir," the voice said, "if all agree that there is most urgent need for speed between today and the transfer of power, surely you should have a date in mind?"

"Yes, indeed," replied Mountbatten.

"And if you have chosen a date, sir, what is that date?" the questioner asked.

A number of rapid calculations went whirring through the Viceroy's mind as he listened to those questions. He had not, in fact, selected a date. But he was convinced it had to be very soon.

"I had to force the pace," he recalled later. "I knew I had to force Parliament to get the bill through before their summer recess to hold the thing together. We were sitting on the edge of a volcano, on a fused bomb and we didn't know when the bomb would go off." Like the blurred images of a horror film, the charred corpses of Kahuta flashed across Louis Mountbatten's mind. If an outburst of similar tragedies was not to drag all India into an apocalypse, he had to move fast. After three thousand years of history and two hundred years of *Pax Britannica*, only a few weeks remained, the Viceroy believed, between India and chaos. He stared at the packed assembly hall. Every face in the room was turned to his. A hushed, expectant silence broken only by the whir of the wooden blades of the fans revolving overhead stilled the room. "I was deter-

mined to show I was the master of the whole event," he would remember.

"Yes," he said, "I have selected a date for the transfer of power."

As he was uttering those words, the possible dates were still spinning through his mind like the numbers on a revolving roulette wheel. Early September? Middle of September, middle of August? Suddenly the wheel stopped with a jar and the little ball popped into a slot so overwhelmingly appropriate that Mountbatten's decision was instantaneous. It was a date linked in his memory to the most triumphant hours of his own existence, the day in which his long crusade through the jungles of Burma had ended with the unconditional surrender of the Japanese empire. A period in Asian history had ended with the collapse of that feudal Asia of the Samurai. What more appropriate date for the birth of the new democratic Asia arising to take its place than the second anniversary of Japan's surrender? His voice constricted with sudden emotion; the victor of the jungles of Burma, about to become the liberator of India, announced:

"The final transfer of power to Indian hands will take place on August 15, 1947." [201–202]

As soon as the radio announced Mountbatten's date, astrologers all over India began to consult their charts. Those in the holy city of Benares and several others in the South immediately proclaimed August 15 a date so inauspicious that India "would be better advised to tolerate the British one day longer rather than risk eternal damnation."

In Calcutta, Swami Madanananda rushed to his celestial charts as soon as he heard the date announced in a radio broadcast. His calculations foretold disaster. India on August 15 would lie under the Zodiacal sign of Makra (Capricorn), a sign one of whose particularities was its unrelenting hostility to all centrifugal forces, hence to partition. Far worse, India that day would be passing through the influence of Saturn, a notably inauspicious planet, under the star Rahu, the star scornfully labeled by astrologers "the star with no neck," a celestial body whose manifestations were almost wholly malign. From midnight August 14 throughout August 15, Saturn, Jupiter and Venus would all lie in the most accursed site of the heavens, the ninth house of Karamstahn. Like thousands of his colleagues, the young astrologer looked up from his chart overcome by the magnitude of the disaster they had revealed.

"What have they done? What have they done?" he shouted to the heavens whose machinations he interpreted for man. Despite the discipline of his physical and spiritual forces acquired in years of yoga, meditation and tantric studies in a temple in the hills of Assam, the astrologer lost control of himself. Seizing a piece of paper he sat down and wrote an urgent appeal to the man inadvertently responsible for this celestial catastrophe. "For the love of God," he wrote to Mountbatten, "do not give India her independence on August 15. If floods, drought, famine and massacres follow, it will be because free India was born on a day cursed by the stars."

QUESTIONS

1. What were the main forces that Mountbatten had to consider in his handling of the Indian situation?
2. Evaluate the way he handled each critical opponent and situation.
3. Evaluate the overall British strategy in leaving India.
4. What can one conclude about handling negotiation strategies from this case?

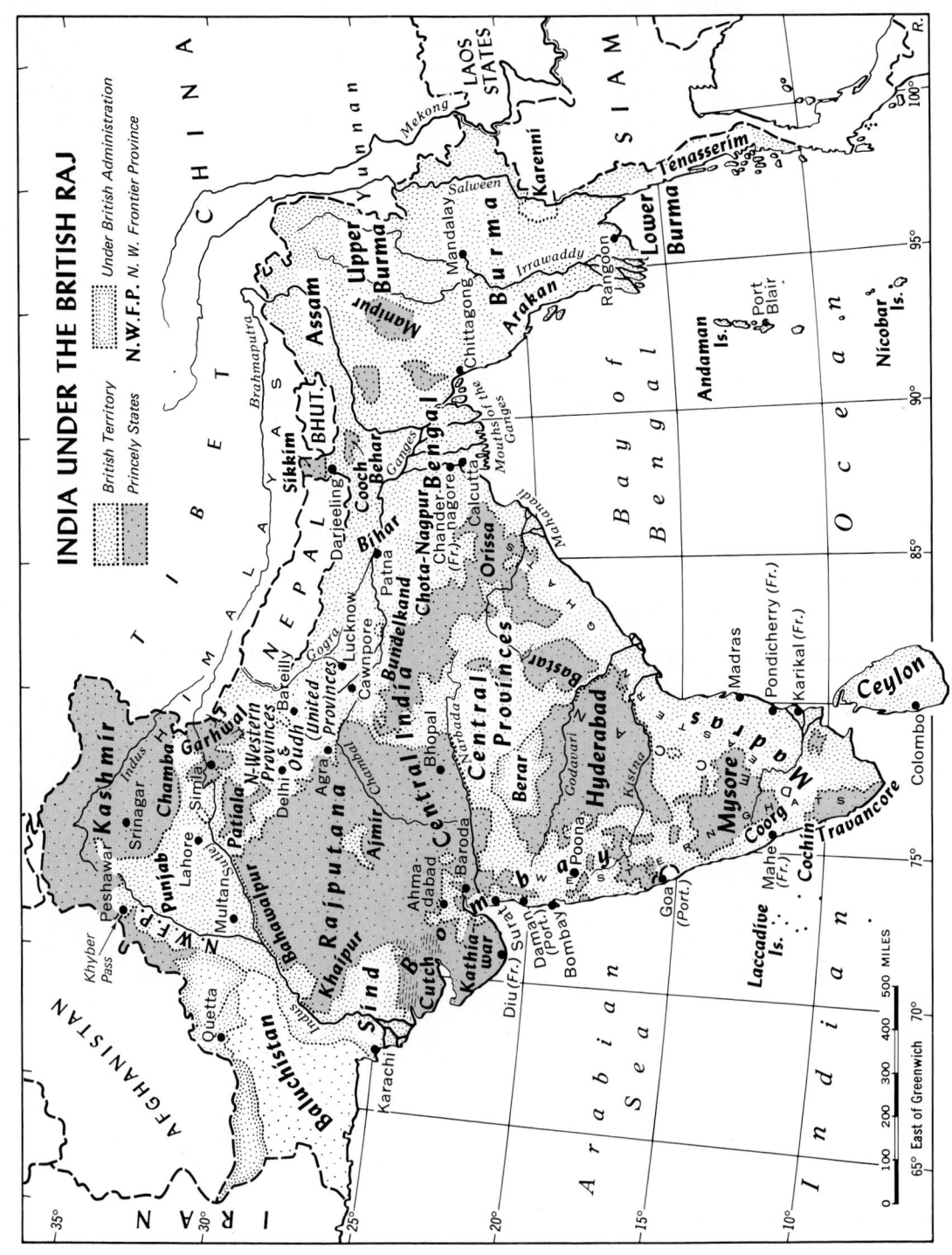

INDIA UNDER THE BRITISH RAJ

British Territory
Princely States
Under British Administration
N.W.F.P. N. W. Frontier Province

CHINA

TIBET

AFGHANISTAN

IRAN

Khyber Pass

Peshawar

N.W.F.P.

Quetta

Baluchistan

Karachi

Indus

Sind

Bahawalpur

Khairpur

Punjab

Lahore

Multan

Patiala

Chamba

Kashmir

Srinagar

Rajputana

Cutch

Kathiawar

Ajmer

Central India

Ahmadabad

Baroda

Surat

Diu (Fr.)

Daman (Port.)

Bombay

Poona

Goa (Port.)

Garhwal

Simla

Delhi

Agra

N-Western Provinces

Oudh

United Provinces

Bareilly

Lucknow

Cawnpore

Chambal

Gogra

Ganges

Bundelkhand

Bhopal

Narbada

Berar

Godavari

Hyderabad

Embay

Mahe (Fr.)

Mysore

Coorg

Madras

Cochin

Travancore

Colombo

Ceylon

Madras

Pondicherry (Fr.)

Karikal (Fr.)

Laccadive Is.

Arabian Sea

Indian Ocean

NEPAL

Brahmaputra

HIMALAYAS

Sikkim

BHUT.

Darjeeling

Cooch Behar

Assam

Manipur

Upper Burma

Mandalay

Yunnan

LAOS STATES

SIAM

Mekong

Salween

Irrawaddy

Burma

Arakan

Karenni

Tenasserim

Lower Burma

Rangoon

Chittagong

Bihar

Patna

Bengal

Chandernagore (Fr.)

Calcutta

Chota-Nagpur

Orissa

Bastar

Central Provinces

Mahanadi

Kistna

Bay of Bengal

Andaman Is.

Port Blair

Nicobar Is.

Indian Ocean

0 100 200 300 400 500 MILES

65° East of Greenwich 70° 75°

35°

30°

25°

20°

15°

10°

100°

95°

90°

85°

95°

954

POSTSCRIPT

In the preface, we stated that we proposed to acknowledge and deal with the *complexity* of a business enterprise. Readers who have progressed through the text probably understand, and hopefully accept, the need to acknowledge complexity. In a very real sense, it is the challenge and complexity of the manager's job that makes a career in business management interesting and fun.

We also expressed our intention to increase the reader's awareness of the various aspects of *judgment* that CEOs are called upon to exercise. The cases have presented many situations, competitive challenges, and dilemmas faced by managers in diverse industries around the world, and the readings have suggested a wide range of perspectives and concepts to help you analyze and exercise judgment on what could otherwise be a confusing mass of observations.

It is now time to take another look at complexity and judgment.

COMPLEXITY

In this text, we have presented a wide range of different contexts, dealt with competitive economics plus the nature of power and politics, discussed structure and systems, and explored the relationship between continuous change in the environment surrounding an enterprise and its efforts to deal with that change by means of strategy. In this way we have tried to impress upon you the inherently complex nature of the strategy process.

Changes in our environment, both outside the firm and within it, are the most significant contributors to complexity. These changes give rise to the need for strategy and that, in turn, generates some of its own change as managers attempt to react constructively to environmental change. But you don't have to look far to find the main generator of change—it is human beings. Just look in a mirror. Aren't your needs and desires changing? And don't overlook generationally induced changes. Do your parents want the same things you want?

Adding to the complexity of this situation are power and politics. These are to be found wherever people are found. People use business enterprises to help them engage in joint and complementary activities. They do so by means of continuous negotiation among themselves. Naturally, this continuous negotiation produces constant changes in the resulting power and political relationships. And, as in all other human institutions, this activity can improve or hurt the fortunes of enterprises. Either way, it adds to complexity.

Furthermore, organizational systems and structures are not simple. Systems may be classified by generally used terms such as planning, control, and payroll among others. Similarly, structures can be classified as line, staff, and matrix among others. However, there is usually very little similarity in the way in which any two different enterprises actually use such systems and structures. Consider control systems as an example: the end results are remedial or compensatory actions based on comparisons of actual accomplishments and budgeted plans year-to-date. Yet each control system must reflect the current focus and particular style of management of its enterprise. And it will change as the enterprise changes. Moreover, structures may be even more likely than systems to be personalized by enterprises.

Finally, context contributes to complexity by making generic problems such as the need for invested capital and customers look very different to the CEO of a giant industrial enterprise in a mature industry than to an entrepreneur in a small high-tech laboratory.

We hope you have learned a great deal about management as a result of placing yourself in various managerial roles in our cases which deal with enterprises in many different contexts. In such roles, you can practice working out appropriate processes for forming and using strategies to further the fortunes of your enterprises.

JUDGMENT

In the preface, we claimed that *judgment* was the most critical attribute for any manager. Judgment directs the thinking process. It illuminates and evaluates the results of thinking and acting. It guides the recall of historical observations from memory and applies to them a set of algorithms, unique to each individual, to generate a framework for evaluating new situations in the future.

The process of judging, while complex in its own right, generally covers three different kinds of activity. The first is recognition of items of interest in the constant stream of newly unfolding phenomena. The second brings into focus selected items from this stream with relevant observations stored from the past. Then, in the third,

an appropriate response is selected and initiated (note that this response can be anything from doing nothing to taking immediate action with monitoring at various levels in between).

But judgment is also very convoluted and complex. For example, judgment is required in the first activity of deciding how to recognize what is of interest and where to search for it. Judgment must also guide the relevance test in the second activity. Finally, judgment is critical in designing and using the decision process for selecting among the response options available in the third activity (how shall one option be selected over the others?).

You should not assume that the judgmental process described above proceeds by the numbers through each of the three activities without backtracking or interruption. Nothing could be less accurate. The process usually moves back and forth among the three activities in a helter-skelter fashion with inductive jumps as judgment on one aspect directs a reconsideration of some previous point.

Actually we are seldom aware of the processes we use when thinking and acting. They are second nature for us. Reflect for a moment on the possible thinking processes of William Spoor, CEO of Pillsbury:

Newly promoted to CEO at Pillsbury, Spoor inherited a flour milling organization that was enmeshed in a commodity market. It had made some attempts to develop value-added products using flour with some success. It had also made several diversifying acquisitions. But stable profits had eluded his predecessors.

His thoughts, as best we can tell, concerned developing and using a strategy that would minimize dependence on selling flour, carefully review the other businesses against desired growth and stable profit goals, and use resources generated by the cutbacks to grow as fast as practical those businesses which the review favored. At the same time, he was well aware of the opinions of the managers of his various business units, his corporate officers and directors, and his customers and ultimately the consumers. He realized that the task facing him had a full measure of dealing with power if he was to change the relative importance of the various businesses in his portfolio.

During the years that were necessary to change Pillsbury's direction, he must have been constantly and relatively unconsciously selecting items of interest to him from the stream of reports, conversations, general business literature that came to his attention, and so on. How did he select what deserved his attention? Certainly, he didn't consciously develop some criteria. Nevertheless, his judgment unconsciously guided him.

His thinking processes assessed the meaning and significance of the selected inputs by associating them with information in his memory that his judgment considered relevant. It also shaped his thinking process in deciding whether any action seemed appropriate based on the insights gained from evaluating the inputs. In doing all of this thinking, it is highly probable that no distinction was consciously made between substance and process—number analysis and power/politics. Little could be gained thereby since each was inextricably bound with the other. Based on this insight, consider how important it is that a CEO have a balanced and inventive judgmental capability.

You may already have guessed our next point. Simply stated, it is that deciding on the process steps—how to take action if action seems appropriate—is not divorced from the earlier decision that some type of action is (or is not) appropriate based on evaluation of environmental changes. Why should it be? Spoor's decision on whether or not to intervene in the stream of events at Pillsbury also involved having to decide on how, when, and where to intervene. These issues depended on what consequences he believed would result from any of the options open to him.

Using judgment in this manner, Spoor managed a process that caused Pillsbury to get out of the chicken raising business, redirect its flour milling activities, divest a number of businesses which did not

fit the new definition of Pillsbury's core businesses (resulting from another Spoor initiative), and plunge deeply into fast food (primarily Burger King). Surely he didn't have all of this in his head the day he became CEO. Using good judgment, he brought along the power holders involved as he guided the process that developed the desire to make these changes.

Consider for a moment how well this free form approach is suited to the interactive negotiating activity with others that stimulates and supports much of our thinking and judging efforts.

This review of Spoor's management of change can help us understand another role of judgment—guiding our thinking processes in deciding on what can be changed and what can't, what can be influenced or even controlled and what can't. This includes evaluating possible changes in terms of questions like: How? How much? In what direction? With what effort? With what likelihood of the expected result? Obviously, a manager cannot change everything. But initial efforts to reach decisions frequently consider options that are not viable and overlook others that are. While many of these types of situations may be obvious, some are not.

Alastair Pilkington was helping his wife with the dishes when the concept of floating molten glass on a bed of molten tin popped into his head. Then as the molten glass cooled and turned to a solid state, he would have flat glass that was distortion free. Surely, this falls under the heading of discovering what can be changed. Why didn't someone else think of this? We will never know. In fact, we probably can never know what prompted Alastair. He says he was bored, that he was aware of the desirability of finding a less expensive process than grinding both sides of a sheet of glass to produce plate glass. Perhaps the soapsuds and scraps of food floating on the dish water triggered his thought.

It is significant that once the notion flashed into his head, his judgment immediately evaluated it as a significant insight. How often do we accept that something can't be changed because it hasn't been, or is against the rule, or was tested some time ago under different circumstances? Necessity may be the mother of invention (and innovation), but intuitive and unstructured but broadly informed thinking and judgment are very likely candidates for the father.

On the other hand, trying to bring innovative judgment to fruition can lead to persistence in trying to bring about a change where it is most unlikely. American efforts to open Japanese markets to American exports through negotiation have produced considerable frustration on both sides, but little progress. Rational changes appear to have inadequate support. Japan is not changing as fast as the United States expects or wishes for reasons that we do not understand or perceive. The fact remains that the cost of trying hardly matches the results gained so far, and the future remains very doubtful given the current American strategy.

By now, it must be apparent that most judgment calls are not simple selections between black and white, but are between subtle shades of gray. This is as true in business as in any other aspect of life. Furthermore, reconsideration and mind changing are usually constant factors:

> Consider the changes in direction at the lower levels of managment in AT&T Bell Laboratories as the tail gets wagged in the Lab's efforts to redefine its mission in supporting the new AT&T. Senior management at the Lab is trying to refocus in support of AT&T's efforts to broaden its interests in communications and electronics. And this effort gets changing signals as AT&T's new thrusts yield results that are better or worse—certainly different—from those anticipated. Therefore, the Lab's middle management can expect high levels of change since they are further out on the tail. This will continue until AT&T gets its new interests into better focus, and it will never return to the controlled and sedate patterns of old. In the meantime, any middle manager's judg-

ment call will have to be a little more gray (tentative) to reflect greater probability of change than in the past.

Judgment is fundamental to all managerial processes because it guides the thinking processes that every manager uses in deciding on:

> What issues to focus on;
>
> What to consider in deciding on whether and, if so, what kind of changes to make in the direction of the business;
>
> What steps to take to bring about those changes; and
>
> What type and degree of monitoring is appropriate.

However, judgment intermingles and retraces these steps in such a continuous manner that they would be hard to recognize, and separate.

> IBM's efforts to develop its 360 line strategy were prompted by a realization that its computer systems in both hardware and software were proliferating out of control. In searching for a viable strategy to check this proliferation while improving the competitiveness of its computer lines, it pursued a number of paths. Eventually, it pruned some and blended others into a strategy that directed all hardware to meet a standard software interface. This freed hardware and software to go their separate ways as long as they did not stray away from the interface. The process of arriving at this strategy (as described in the IBM (A) case) consumed several years, occupied many senior managers and specialists, and vitally affected many careers. A number of large development efforts were turned on, redirected and turned off. Some were restarted with an altered direction only to be changed again. Ultimately, the 360 line resulted.

It would be impossible and unnecessary to pick out instances of any of the steps in using judgment that are listed above. They are listed only to suggest the ways in which judgment is part of the management process. The IBM case shows the process and result.

THE ROLE OF NEGOTIATION IN ENTERPRISES

Putting together complexity and judgment, we can begin to see the manager's role as one of judging how to *negotiate* people through a complex and changing business world.

The changing desires of human beings translate into change for their enterprises because every business enterprise revolves around human beings. This shouldn't surprise us. The business enterprises that we develop are simply one among many types of community activity. We develop them because we want vehicles for enabling some individuals to contribute skills and energy to the production of goods and services in return for compensation. Then, the goods and services can be acquired and used by anyone for a price. In other words, the business enterprises in any community are a significant factor in matching the interests of its people as producers and as consumers.

The development of markets and competition among enterprises and people in all of their various roles in business are natural concomitant developments as business enterprises vie with each other for the attention of producers as well as consumers. The manner in which each enterprise facilitates the matching of the skills and desires of various individuals within a community as described above is quite complex in itself. It is accomplished by means of considerable negotiation between individuals representing themselves and individuals representing the business enterprise—its managers. Individuals representing themselves can be interested in a production role or a consumer role and both roles in many cases.

As part of this negotiation process, each of us takes a unique host of factors and desires

into consideration in guiding our decisions and actions. And as we and our desires change, our enterprises, of necessity reflect those changes. Since no two persons are alike in every respect, each set of negotiations will likely produce widely varying results. Recall the Boehms' problems:

> In the case on Edward Marshall Boehm, we discovered that even the Boehms, husband and wife, did not have totally congruent goals. He had a deep interest in leaving models of wildlife for future generations that were as true and lifelike as he could make them. His wife enjoyed the marketing of his creations. And his distributors wanted to build volume. Obviously, this produced continuous negotiating activity as each party sought to realize more of his or her goals. And this in turn made Boehm a complex enterprise.

The role of enterprise managers in this turbulent current of negotiation is to guide and direct the decisions and actions of people who negotiate for their enterprises. And the importance of this burden on managers increases sharply as we progress from first line supervisors to the CEO. In fact, the CEO must be the focal point for optimizing the long-range health of his or her enterprise. Recall for a moment how Richard Gerstenberg guided the process used by General Motors in reaching its decision to downsize its cars:

> Richard Gerstenberg, GM's CEO, carefully selected among his options step by step and then sequenced and timed them. He responded to the observation by his chief economist that energy costs were in a long term uptrend by forming the Collier taskforce. Then he allowed time to pass while the conclusions in its report were discussed informally throughout GM. This interval permitted the substance of the report to prepare the internal atmosphere at General Motors to accept the process of downsizing its cars.
> Gerstenberg's successor, Tom Murphy, carefully selected among his own options in guiding the downsizing

process step by step. Among them were enhancement of the role of the Project Center, the decision to downsize the big cars first, and the decision to downsize in increments.

Probably now, you are well aware that business enterprises are still developing as a result of innovating adjustments by their members. Recall for a moment the description of how a business enterprise can evolve from a functional to a matrix organization as its product line proliferates. The matrix organizational concept didn't exist forty years ago. Now it can make a manager's world substantially more complex. For example, a marketing manager for a particular product line can find that, as a result of installing a matrix structure, he has a new boss—a newly appointed profit center general manager—in addition to his old boss, the enterprise marketing manager. Now he has two managers pulling him in different directions—marketing at the enterprise level, and profitability at the profit center level.

Certainly his is a more complex world. It is more complex because his CEO believes that the best interests of the whole enterprise are served most effectively when his objectives and activities are balanced between firm-wide marketing and profit for his profit center. And this balance is achieved by reasonable "contention management" between his two bosses, both of whom are responsible to the CEO.

This is a major example of innovative change. Many less significant ones are being conceived and put into use all the time. Nevertheless, this results in more complexity and more demand on judgment in guiding skillful negotiations.

There is nothing permanent about a current pattern of business activity. It can and will adapt to changes in the desires of the people who are involved according to the nature and degree of that involvement. In case after case in this book you have had the opportunity to form your own judgment on how best to adjust an enterprise to its new environment, both external and internal, by inducing desirable forms of change.

CONCLUSION

In this postscript, we have tried to show why we chose to emphasize complexity and judgment throughout the text. We found complexity in the context within which a specific enterprise operates; in the power and political atmosphere surrounding an enterprise; in its systems and structure; and in the constant change taking place all around it. We also found that the most effective means of dealing with all of this complexity is good judgment. Judgment can guide our thinking processes in deciding on which issues to focus; whether change is called for and, if so, what type; how to bring about the change; and how to monitor it if appropriate.

We hope we have left you with a healthy sense of wonder and appreciation for the degree of complexity that any senior manager faces. We also hope you now have a strong desire to further the development of your judgment by becoming personally involved with the challenges and opportunities of the business world.

Only by embracing the complexities of the real world can you experiment with some of the ideas that we hope our book has stimulated, and, in so doing, learn more about yourself. One word of caution! Don't expect everything to work well the first time. Remember, any big league baseball player would be delighted if he hit a home run every 20th turn at bat—he can expect to strike out three times as often. He would still be placed among the batting champions. Don't be afraid to make mistakes as long as you learn from them. After all, the Watsons, Joneses, Gerstenbergs, and Jobs of this world made decisions based on flawed judgments and were occasionally surprised at the results. But their batting averages were well above average. And their judgments were aided by an awareness of their own strengths and weaknesses. They featured their strengths and sought to buttress their weak points by finding and working with trusted individuals whose judgments were superior to their own in those areas. That they could involve such people effectively provides one more group of examples of good judgment on both process and substance.

In short, we have tried to prepare you to use good judgment in dealing effectively with the challenges that await you when you venture forth into the exhilarating game of business life. A willingness to acknowledge that you don't "know it all," but that you are prepared to continue to develop your business judgment first-hand is a great way to start. Your judgment will improve as you apply your observations and experience as guides for future decisions.

GOOD LUCK!

CASE
NOTES

I – 2

1. Summarized from ''A Market Milestone for DNA Research,'' *Business Week*, September 18, 1978.
2. ''Bacteria Make Human Insulin,'' *Chemical and Engineering News*, September 11, 1978.

I – 5

1. Frazier Hunt, *The Untold Story of Douglas MacArthur*. New York, 1954, p. 318.
2. Charles A. Willoughby and John Chamberlain, *MacArthur, 1941–1951*. New York, 1954; Charles A. Rawlings, ''They Paved Their Way with Japs,'' *Saturday Evening Post*, October 7, 1944.
3. Hunt, *Untold*, 318; Douglas MacArthur, *Reminiscences*. New York, 1964, pp. 166–67; Alfred Steinberg, *Douglas MacArthur*. New York, 1961, p. 113; Willoughby and Chamberlain, 105.
4. Richard H. Rovere and Arthur M. Schlesinger, *The General and the President, and the Future of American Foreign Policy*. New York, 1951, pp. 65–66; Willoughby and Chamberlain, 206.
5. Jay Luvaas, ed. *Dear Miss Em: General Eichelberger's War in the Pacific, 1942–1945*. Westport, 1972, p. 75.
6. Gavin M. Long, *MacArthur's Amphibious Navy*. Annapolis, 1969, p. 219; Earl Balik, *The Red Blaik Story*. New York, 1974, p. 501; James M. Burns, *Roosevelt: The Soldier of Freedom, 1940–45*. New York, 1970, p. 488.

7. Daniel E. Barbey, *MacArthur's Amphibious Navy*. Annapolis, 1969, p. 219; Eark Balik, *The Red Blaik Story*. New York, 1974, p. 501; James M. Burns, *Roosevelt: The Soldier of Freedom, 1940–1945*. New York, 1970, p. 488.
8. Author's interviews with Roger Egeberg, October 18, 1976; MacArthur, *Reminiscences*, p. 199; Dorris Clayton James, *The Years of MacArthur, 1941–1945*, Vol. II. Boston, 1975, p. 530; Luvaas, p. 155; William D. Leahy, *I Was There*. New York, 1950, p. 250; Stanley L. Falk, *Decision at Leyte*. New York, 1966, p. 28.
9. Leahy, 251; James, Vol. II, p. 530; MacArthur, *Reminiscences*, p. 197.
10. David J. Steinberg, *Philippine Collaboration in World War II*. Ann Arbor, 1967, p. 101; George C. Kenney, *The MacArthur I Know*. New York, 1951, pp. 155–56; Willoughby and Chamberlain, p. 233.
11. MacArthur, *Reminiscences*, p. 198; Leahy, pp. 250–251.
12. Robert R. Smith, *Triumph in the Philippines*. Washington, 1963, p. 11.
13. John Toland, *The Rising Sun*. New York, 1970, pp. 533–34; Barbey, p. 227; Robert J. Bulkeley, Jr., *At Close Quarters: PT Boats in the United States Navy*. Washington, 1962, p. 376; William F. Halsey, and Joseph Bryan III, *Admiral Halsey's Story*. New York, 1947, p. 199.
14. Halsey and Bryan, pp. 198–201; Henry H. Arnold, *Global Mission*. New York, 1949, pp. 527–

28; James, Vol. II, pp. 537–39; Toland, *The Rising Sun*, p. 534; Kenney, *General*, p. 434.

15. Manuel Quezon, *The Good Fight*. New York, 1946, p. 295; Robert L. Eichelberger, with Milton McKaye, *Our Jungle Road to Tokyo*. New York, 1950, p. 181; J. Griggin, "Philippines," *Holiday*, July 1967.

16. Carlos P. Romulo, *I Saw the Fall of the Philippines*. Garden City, 1942, p. 54; David Steinberg, pp. 104–05.

17. James, Vol. II, pp. 542–43.

18. Carlos P. Romulo, *I See the Philippines Rise*. Garden City, 1946, p. 190; Toland, *Sun*, p. 537; David Steinberg, p. 101.

19. MacArthur, *Reminiscences*, p. 172; Hunt, *Untold*, p. 314.

20. Toland, *Sun*, p. 534; "Promise Fulfilled," *Time*, October 30, 1944.

21. MacArthur, *Reminiscences*, p. 212; Kenney, *Know*, p. 156; Alfred Steinberg, p. 127.

22. Falk, p. 29; Hunt, *Untold*, p. 342.

23. Author's interviews with Egeberg, October 18, 1976; MacArthur, *Reminiscences*, p. 216; James, Vol. II, pp. 554–55; "MacArthur Returns and Returns," *Life*, February 18, 1972; Kenney, *General*, p. 448; Charles A. Lockwood and Hans C. Adamson, *Battle of the Philippine Sea*. New York, 1967, pp. 157–58; "Battle for the Philippines," *Fortune*, June 1945.

24. Author's interviews with Romulo, October 18, 1977; Romulo, *Rise*, p. 3, 94–95; Falk, p. 111.

25. Records of General Headquarters, United States Army Forces, Pacific (USAF-PAC), 1942–1945; Carlos P. Romulo, *I Walked with Heroes*. New York, 1961, pp. 235–36; James, Vol. II pp. 557–58; MacArthur, *Reminiscences*, pp. 216–17; Gavin M. Long, p. 152; Falk, p. 103; David Steinberg, p. 105; Vorin E. Whan, ed., *A Soldier Speaks: Public Papers and Speeches of General of the Army Douglas MacArthur*. New York, 1965, pp. 132–33.

26. Kenney, *General*, p. 452.

27. Romulo, *Rise*, p. 165.

28. Falk, p. 220.

29. Falk, p. 71, 273; James, Vol. II, p. 580; Toland, *Sun*, pp. 576–577.

30. James, Vol. II, p. 585; Eichelberger, *Jungle*, p. 174; Falk, p. 293.

31. James, Vol. II, p. 584; Kenney, *General*, pp.

64–65; Author's interviews with Egeberg, October 18, 1976.

32. Edward M. Flanagan, Jr., *The Angels: A History of the 11th Airborne Division, 1943–1946*. Washington, 1948, pp. 62–63.

33. MacArthur, *Reminiscences*, p. 241; James, Vol. II, p. 621.

34. *New York Times*, January 11, 1945; MacArthur, *Reminiscences*, p. 242.

35. Hunt, *Untold*, p. 365; Bertram C. Wright, comp. *The 1st Cavalry Division in World War II*. Tokyo, 1947, pp. 125–28; Author's interviews with Romulo, October 18, 1977; Flanagan, pp. 77–80; Author's interviews with Egeberg, October 18, 1976; James, Vol. II, p. 641; Romulo, *Rise*, p. 191.

36. MacArthur, *Reminiscences*, pp. 245–46; Luvaas, p. 225.

37. Luvaas, p. 203; Eichelberger, *Jungle*, p. 187; MacArthur, *Reminiscences*, p. 260.

38. Luvaas, p. 203.

39. "In Remembrance of MacArthur," *Life*, April 17, 1964; Luvaas, p. 260; Willoughby and Chamberlain, p. 267.

40. Luvaas, pp. 278–79; Kenney, *General*, pp. 552–53; Kenney, *Know*, pp. 132–33.

41. Hanson W. Baldwin, *Great Mistakes of the War*. New York, 1949, p. 97.

42. Records of General Headquarters, United States Army Forces, Pacific (USAF—PAC), 1942–1945; James, Vol. II, pp. 765–66; Leahy, p. 385; Leslie R. Groves, *Now It Can Be Told*. New York, 1962, pp. 263–64.

43. Hunt, *Untold*, p. 402.

44. James, Vol. II, p. 785; Norman Richards, *Douglas MacArthur*. Chicago, 1967, p. 76; Jules Archer, *Front-Line General: Douglas MacArthur*. New York, 1963, pp. 143–44; Gunther, p. 2.

45. Courtney Whitney, *MacArthur: His Rendezvous with History*. New York, 1955, p. 216; MacArthur, *Reminiscences*, p. 271; "On the Record," *Times*, March 31, 1947; James, Vol. II, pp. 786–87.

46. Collection of Messages (radiograms), 1945–1951; Whitney, pp. 216–17; James, Vol. II, pp. 787–88; MacArthur, *Reminiscences*, pp. 271–72; Craig, pp. 297–98.

47. Toshikazu Kase, *Journey to the "Missouri."* New Haven, 1950, p. 13; MacArthur, *Reminiscences*, pp. 276–77.

I – 6

1. "The Five Best Managed Companies," *Dun's Review*, December 1980.

2. Gene Bylinsky, quoted from *The Innovation Millionaires*. Copyright © 1976, 1974, 1973, 1967 Gene Bylinsky. Reprinted with the permission of Charles Scribner's Sons.

3. *Electronic News*, December 27, 1974.

4. "Meet Bob Noyce," *Computer Decisions*, June 1974.

5. *Wall Street Journal*, October 4, 1969.

6. "Special Report: Where the Action Is in Electronics," *Business Week*, October 4, 1969.

7. *Electronic News*, August 26, 1968.

8. *Electronics*, March 31, 1969.

9. "Why Cores Could Become Just a Memory," *Business Week*, December 26, 1970.

10. "American Industry and What Ails It," *The Atlantic*, May 1980.

11. "Intel Takes Aim at the '80's," *Electronics*, February 28, 1980.

12. "The Micro War Heats Up," *Forbes*, November 26, 1979.

13. "Intel Gambles for Continued Rapid Growth," *International Management*, November 1981.

14. "Creativity by the Numbers," *Harvard Business Review*, May–June 1980.

I – 8

1. Benton Gup, *Financial Intermediaries: An Introduction*, Houghton-Miflin, 1976.

2. "The World is Their Oyster," *Economist*, March 16, 1985.

3. George Benson, *Financial Services: The Changing Institutions and Government Policy*, Prentice-Hall, 1983, pages 252–3.

4. "No Longer a World Apart: A Survey of Wall Street," *Economist*, June 20, 1981.

5. A.D. Little, *Financial Services: A Business in Transaction*, April 1984.

6. *Op. cit.*, Benson, *Financial Services: The Changing.* . . .

7. American Bankers Association, *Statistical Information on the Financial Services Industry*, 3rd Ed. 1984.

8. National Association of Securities Dealers. *1983 NASD Fact Book*.

9. "Banks and Nonbanks: Who's in Control?" *The Bankers Magazine*, September/October 1984, p. 14.

10. "The Future of Private Pension Plans," *Pension World*, August 1980.

11. "An Inflation Scoreboard," *Institutional Investor*, November 1983.

12. "Domestic Financial Statistics," *Federal Reserve Bulletin*, April 1985.

13. McKinsey & Company, Inc. "Discussing the Impact of Deregulating the Commercial Banking Industry," Report to the Office of the Controller of the Currency, June 1982.

14. "Fighting the Fed," *Fortune*, July 8, 1985.

15. "Federal Lawmakers and Regulators Fear States are Going Too Far in Expanding Banks' Powers," *Wall Street Journal*, July 31, 1985.

16. *Federal Reserve Bulletin*, May 1983.

17. "Nationwide Banking: A Welcome Mat, Not a Slammed Door," *Business Week*, June 24, 1985.

18. "A New Awakening: Survey of International Banking," *Economist*, March 24, 1984.

19. "The Revolution in Financial Services," *Business Week*, November 28, 1983.

20. *Euromoney Yearbook 1983*, Credit Suisse—First Boston, Section 1.3.

21. "European Bankers Struggle to Compete in Fast Moving Underwriting Markets," *Wall Street Journal*, August 7, 1985.

22. "The World is Their Oyster," *Economist*, March 16, 1985.

23. "Banking Heads for a New Patch of Thin Ice," *Business Week*, July 29, 1985.

24. K. Cooper and D. Fraser, *Banking Deregulation and the New Competition in Financial Services*, Ballinger Publishing Co., 1984, p. 92.

25. "Bargain Loans," *Wall Street Journal*, June 26, 1985.

26. NASD, *The Financial Services Industry of Tomorrow*, November 1982, p. 17.

27. L. Goldberg and L. White (Eds.), *The Deregulation of the Banking and Securities Industries*, D.C. Heath and Co., 1979.

28. Securities Industry Association, *Securities Industry Yearbook 1984–85*.

29. "Wall Street is Finding . . . It Enjoys Unfixed Rates," *Wall Street Journal*, April 22, 1985, p. 1, 18.

30. SRI, *Success in the New Financial Services Industry*, July 1983.

31. Investment Company Institute, *Mutual Fund Fact Book 1982*.

32. "No Longer a Business Apart: A Survey of Wall Street," *Economist*, June 20, 1981.

33. Robert Perez, *Inside Investment Banking*, Praeger Publishers, 1984.

34. "The World is Their Oyster: A Survey of International Banking," *Economist*, March 16, 1985.

35. "Transformation of Investment Banking," *Harvard Business Review*, January/February 1979.

I – 9

1. "International Report: Canadian Bankers Face Change, A Struggling Economy," *U.S. Banker*, August 1982.

2. "Canada's New Banking Law," *The Banker*, March 1981.

3. "Canada Get to Grips with Deregulation," *Euromoney*, November 1984.

4. "Mulroney Drops a Bombshell," *Business Week*, April 29, 1985.

5. "Merrill Lynch Canada. . . ," *Wall Street Journal*, July 2, 1985, p. 10.

6. "Canada's Banks—A Decade of Change in the Euromarkets," *Euromoney* Supplement July 1985.

APPENDIX A 1 – 9

1. "The Four Pillars," *Canadian Banker*, February 1985.

2. "Where's the Power in the Financial Services Industry?" *Canadian Banker*, June 1985.

3. "Foreign Banks are Hopeful," *Euromoney*, Supplement, July 1985.

4. "An International Banking Centre in Canada," *Canadian Banker*, June 1983.

5. "Reconstruction of the Stockbroking Industry," *Euromoney*, Supplement, July 1985.

6. "Merrill Lynch Canada. . ." *Wall Street Journal*, July 2, 1985, p. 10.

7. "Canada's Fat Cats," *Economist*, July 14, 1984.

8. "Montreal Attempts a Comeback," *Euromoney*, November 1984.

9. *op. cit.*, "Reconstruction of the Stockbroking Industry."

I – 10

1. William B. Harris, "Litton Shoots for the Moon," *Fortune*, April 1958, p. 114.

2. William B. Harris, "Man on the Move," *Forbes*, July 15, 1961, p. 15.

3. William B. Harris, *op. cit.*, p. 116.

4. Carl Rieser, "When the Crowd Goes One Way Litton Goes the Other," *Fortune*, May 1963, p. 117.

5. *Litton Industries Annual Report 1967*, "Letter to Stockholders."

6. Carl Rieser, "What Puts the Whiz in Litton's Fast Growth," *Business Week*, April 16, 1966, p. 179.

7. Litton Industries (BR), Harvard Business School case 9–313–130. Copyright © 1968 by the President and Fellows of Harvard College.

8. Exhibit 2, Litton Industries, Inc. (AR) HBS 9–313–129 provided a partial organization chart.

9. T.L. Stebbins, "Litton Industries, Incorporated," Estabrook & Co., July 25, 1967, p. 5.

10. One source in the company placed the annual telephone bill for corporate headquarters at $7 million.

11. T.L. Stebbins, "What Puts the Whiz in Litton's Fast Growth," *Business Week*, April 16, 1966, p. 176.

12. M.E. Barrett, "The System Texas Instruments Developed to Manage Innovation," *International Management*, May 1984.

13. "Texas Instruments (A): Management and the OST," case prepared by Mariann Jelinek, November 1979. Copyright © 1979 by Texas Instruments Inc.

14. Texas Instruments, Incorporated: Management Systems, Harvard Business School case 9–172–054, prepared by Ronald Hall under the direction of Richard F. Vancil. Copyright © 1972 by the President and Fellows of Harvard College. Used with the permission of the Harvard Business School.

15. Speech by G.A. Dove, London School of Business Studies, May 22, 1970.

16. "Texas Instruments (B): The P&AE System," case prepared by Mariann Jelinek, November 1979, copyright © Texas Instruments Inc.

17. "Texas Instruments (C): The IDEA System," case prepared by Mariann Jelinek, November 1979, copyright © Texas Instruments Inc.

II – 1

1. *The Canadian Architect*, January 1960, p. 51.
2. *Architectural Record*, February 1966, p. 137.
3. *Royal Architectural Institute of Canada Journal*, December 1964, p. 28.
4. *Architectural Record*, December 1967, p. 139.
5. *The Canadian Architect*, September 1966, pp. 46–50.

II – 2

1. "In Light of Polaroid," *Fortune*, September 1938, p. 76.
2. Francis Bello, "The Magic That Made Polaroid," *Fortune*, April 1957, p. 158.
3. Richard Karp, "The Clouded Picture at Polaroid," *Dun's Review*, November 1973, p. 61.
4. Phillip Siekman, "Kodak and Polaroid: An End to Peaceful Coexistence," *Fortune*, November 1970, p. 86.
5. Donald Silverman, "Cash in a Flash?," *Systems Engineering Today*, February 1974, p. 31.
6. Mark Olshaker, *The Instant Image*, Stein and Day, New York 1978, pp. 206–7.
7. "Dr. Land Redesigns His Camera Company," *Business Week*, April 15, 1972, p. 71.
8. Richard Martin, "The Team Builder: Polaroid's New President Faces Problems of Earning Woes and Kodak Competition," *Wall Street Journal*, April 25, 1975, p. 17.
9. *1977 Polaroid Annual Report*, p. 42.
10. "Polaroid's One Step is Stopping Kodak Cold," *Fortune*, February 13, 1978, p. 78.
11. Bernstein, "Polaroid Struggles to Get Back in Focus," *Fortune*, April 7, 1980.
12. H. Weil, "Polaroid and Kodak—Instant Winners," *Financial World*, February 15, 1979.
13. Lehman Brothers, *Research Report*, August 1983.
14. Donaldson, Lufkin, & Jenrette, *Research Report*, December 20, 1982.
15. Dean Witter Reynolds, Inc., *Technology Group Research Note*, August 16, 1982.
16. P. Maher, "Polaroid Seeks Business Focus," *Industrial Marketing*, October 1981.

17. "We Must Broaden our Base, CEO McCune Declares," *Business Week*, March 2, 1981.
18. "Informal, Personal, and Paternalistic," *Business Week*, May 4, 1974, p. 44.
19. See *Polaroid Annual Report*, 1977.
20. See Exhibit VIII for a description of the roles and backgrounds of Polaroid staff members as derived from SEC data and *Who's Who in America*.
21. *Annual Report: Polaroid Corporation*, 1980.
22. Edwin Land, "Thinking Ahead," *Harvard Business Review*, September-October 1959, p. 8.
23. Subrata Chakravarty, "An Interview with Dr. Edwin Land," *Forbes*, June 1, 1975, p. 49.

II – 3

1. *Wall Street Journal*, September 10, 1979, 1;8.
2. *Moody's*, 1970.
3. "The Name of the Game is Still General Mills," *Forbes*, April 1, 1970.
4. "An Unforeseen Succession at the Biggest Miller," *Fortune*, February 1973, p. 18.
5. "Pillsbury Mills Its Future," *Financial World*, February 3, 1971, p. 12.
6. "Pillsbury Turnaround . . ." *Advertising Age*, January 12, 1974.
7. "Pillsbury Mills Its Future," *Financial World*, February 3, 1971, p. 12.
8. *Transcript Consumer Analysts' Meeting*, New York, March 19, 1974.
9. "Recipe at Pillsbury Calls for Pick Results," *Barrons*, July 29, 1974, p. 25.
10. See, T. Hanold, "An Executive View of MIS," *Datamation*, November 1972.
11. "Pillsbury's Winery," *Business Week*, September 8, 1975, p. 32.
12. Mr. W. Scott, Comments before Dain, Kalman & Quail Food Conference, March 1977.
13. "The One Man Show at Pillsbury," *Business Week*, January 19, 1976.
14. W. Kiechel, "Now for the Greening of Pillsbury," *Fortune*, November 5, 1979.
15. Acquired in November 1975 for 516, 175 shares of Pillsbury with about $25 million. *Moody's*, 1976.
16. *Wall Street Journal*, December 6, 1976, p. 24.
17. "William H. Spoor, Pillsbury Co.," *Financial World*, April 1, 1977, p. 20.

18. "Can Pillsbury Rise Above the Defections?" *Business Week*, June 9, 1980.

19. "CBS Chooses Wyman . . ." *Wall Street Journal*, May 23, 1980.

20. "Can Pillsbury Rise Above the Defections?" *Business Week*, June 9, 1980.

21. *Wall Street Journal*, July 20, 1983, p. 16.

22. "Pillsbury Co. Revives . . ." *Wall Street Journal*, November 12, 1984.

23. "Friendly Whopper . . ." *Barron's*, September 10, 1984.

24. "Rising to the Top at Pillsbury," *Business Week*, March 12, 1984.

II – 5

1. A. Sloan, Jr., *My Years with General Motors*, Doubleday, New York, 1972.

2. E. Rothschild, *Paradise Lost: The Decline of the Auto-Industrial Age*, New York: Random House, 1973, pp. 36–37.

3. *Wall Street Journal*, 5/13/69, p. 2:2.

4. *Evaluation of the 1960-1963 Corvair Handling and Stability*, N.H.T.S.A., U.S. Department of Transportation, July 1972.

5. *Wall Street Journal*, 5/13/69, p. 2.

6. 1974 General Motors Report on Programs of Public Interest, Detroit, Michigan, April 1975.

7. Referenced in: *Environmental Quality*: First Report of Council on Environmental Quality, GPO, Washington, D.C., 1970, p. 62.

8. *Wall Street Journal*, 7/30/70, p. 2, 4/8/70, p. 7.

9. *Environmental Quality*, 1970, op. cit., p. 77.

10. *Wall Street Journal*, 11/18/70, p. 8.

11. *Wall Street Journal*, 11/19/70, p. 1.

12. *Wall Street Journal*, 9/17/70, p. 2.

13. *Wall Street Journal*, 11/18/70, p. 2.

14. *Wall Street Journal*, 2/9/70, p. 9.

15. *Wall Street Journal*, 9/10/70, p. 1.

16. "Detroit's Reluctant Ride to Smallsville," *Fortune*, March 1969, pp. 113, 164.

17. *Ward's Automotive Yearbook*, 1972, pp. 26, 111, 119.

18. C. Burck, "How GM Turned Itself Around," *Fortune*, January 16, 1978.

19. *Wall Street Journal*, 5/29/73, p. 1.

20. *Wall Street Journal*, 2/1/74, p. 3.

21. *Wall Street Journal*, 5/28/74, p. 7.

22. *Wall Street Journal*, 3/22/74, p. 1.

23. *Wall Street Journal*, 6/25/74, p. 4.

24. Mr. Terrell is given credit for spotting the program management idea when he was head of the nonautomotive divisions, one of which (Delco) was a NASA supplier. NASA used the system extensively as did the aerospace industry as a whole. *Fortune*, January 16, 1978, *op. cit.*, p. 92.

25. "The GM Efficiency Move that Backfired," *Business Week*, March 25, 1972, p. 46.

26. "DeLorean: Coping with the 70s," *Automotive Industries*, January 15, 1972, p. 19.

27. C.B. Burck, "How GM Turned Itself Around," *Fortune*, January 16, 1978.

28. *Wall Street Journal*, 10/1/74.

29. *General Motors Annual Report*, 1975, p. 4.

30. "This Time They're Remaking the Whole Product Line," *Forbes*, August 15, 1975, p. 23.

31. P. Vanderwicken, "GM: The Price of Being Responsible," *Fortune*, January 1972.

32. *General Motors Annual Report to Stockholders*, 1972, p. 3.

33. "GM in '76: Lighter Cars and Hefty Forecasts," *Industry Week*, September 29, 1975, p. 73.

34. *Wall Street Journal*, 7/23/75, p. 34.

35. *Wall Street Journal*, 1/7/76, p. 1.

36. *Wall Street Journal*, 4/21/76, p. 7.

37. *Wall Street Journal*, 6/14/76, p. 7.

38. *Wall Street Journal*, 11/11/76, p. 3.

39. *Wall Street Journal*, 10/29/76.

40. "The Coming Collision in the Auto Market," *Fortune*, July 1976, p. 101.

41. *New York Times*, October 16, 1977, Section 12, p. 5.

42. C. Burck, "How GM Turned Itself Around," *Fortune*, January 16, 1978, pp. 87–96.

43. *Ibid.*

44. C. Burck, "Will Success Spoil General Motors," *Fortune*, August 22, 1983.

II – 6

1. *Twentieth Century Petroleum Statistics*, by DeGolyer & MacNaughton, 1984.

2. *Oil & Gas Journal*, October 12, November 9, 1981.

3. "More Money Than it Properly Knows What to Do With," *The Economist*, April 18, 1981, p. 70.

4. "Will Norway Face Up to Being Rich?," *Euromoney*, November 1980, p. 42.

5. "Norway: Still Just Crumbs for Foreign Oil Companies," *World Oil*, October 1981.

6. *World Oil*, August 15, 1980, pp. 158 and 160.

7. "Norway: Still Just Crumbs for Foreign Oil Companies," *World Oil*, October 1981.

8. *Ibid*.

9. *World Oil*, March 1981, p. 31.

10. "Why North Sea Oil Gushes, But the Pumps Run Dry," *Economist*, June 16, 1979.

11. "Problems of a European Oil Sheik," *Economist*, January 12, 1980.

12. "U.K. Government Revenues from North Sea Oil," *The Banker*, July 1980.

13. *World Oil*, August 15, 1980, p. 153–56.

14. "U.K. North Sea Expenditures," *Ocean Industry*, November 1980, p. 111–12.

15. "Prospects for the U.K. North Sea Suddenly Become Bleak," *Oil & Gas Journal*, March 23, 1981.

16. "Japan: Long-Term Oil Strategy Succeeding," *Petroleum Economist*, September 1979.

17. "Japanese Adjust to Oil Supply Changes," *Oil & Gas Journal*, January 26, 1981.

18. *Ibid*.

19. "China's Petroleum Surplus May Vanish in the 1980s," *Oil & Gas Journal*, October 6, 1980.

20. "Indonesian Survey," *Euromoney*, January 1979.

21. "Growing Problems Downstream," *Petroleum Economist*, November, 1979.

22. "Indonesia, A Plan Aimed at Cutting Overdependence on Oil," *Business Week*, April 9, 1979.

23. "Heavy Oil Revives Venezuelan Refining," *Oil & Gas Journal*, August 1980.

24. "The Risks in Recharging Venezuela's Economy," *Business Week*, September 1, 1980.

25. "Easy Come, Easy Go," *Forbes*, October 26, 1981.

26. "Nigeria Presses Claim for Reduced State Oil Sales," *Petroleum Economist*, September 1980.

27. "The Disaffection of Nigeria," *Oil & Gas Journal*, August 21, 1978, p. 25.

28. "West African Oil: At Last, an Alternative to the Mideast," *Business Week*, August 10, 1981, p. 52.

29. "Why the Spending Stopped in Nigeria," *Fortune*, July 16, 1979.

II – 7

1. "A Dollop of 'Good, Gutsy Maine Business Sense,' " *Fortune*, July 1976, p. 27.

2. "How to Manage Entrepreneurs," *Business Week*, September 7, 1981, pp. 66-69.

3. "The Second Time Around," *Forbes*, March 2, 1981, p. 70.

4. "The General Mills Brand of Managers," *Fortune*, January 12, 1981.

5. "General Mills: An All-American Marketer," *Dun's Business Month*, December 1981, p. 72.

6. "General Mills Continues to Weed Knits," *Advertising Age*, October 3, 1983, p. 12.

7. Bear Stearns Research Report, September 30, 1982.

8. "When Business Got so Good it Got Dangerous," *Fortune*, April 2, 1983, p. 64.

9. "Farmer to President: Joe Lee of General Mills," *The Cornell Hotel and Restaurant Administration Quarterly*, November 1982.

10. "The Impact of Consumer Trends on Corporate Strategy," Sandra D. Kresch, *Journal of Business Strategy*, Winter 1983.

11. "General Mills' Izod Woes are Said to Reflect Broader Problems of Company Management," *Wall Street Journal*, December 4, 1984.

II – 8

1. J. Bernstein, *Three Degrees Above Zero*, New York: Charles Scribner's Sons, 1984.

III – 1

1. Nick Lyons, *The Sony Vision*, Crown Publishers, New York, 1976, p. 80.

2. R.D. Schwarz, E.F. Hutton, *Imaging Technology—Industry Report*, June 13, 1985.

3. P.J. Enderlin, Smith Barney, Harris Upham & Co., Inc., *Electronic Imaging—Impact on Consumer Photography*, December 20, 1984.

4. "Kodak President Says Concern Could Make Electronic Camera," *Wall Street Journal*, October 29, 1981, p. 38.

III – 2

1. Robert A. Sigafoos, *Absolutely Positively Overnight*, St. Luke's Press, Memphis, 1983, p. 25.
2. "A Business Visionary Who Really Delivered," *Nation's Business*, November 1981.
3. Robinson Humphrey Company, Inc., *Research Report on Federal Express Corporation*, April 1984.
4. "Redefining an Industry Through Integrated Automation," *Infosystems*, May 1985.
5. R. Levering, et al., *The 100 Best Companies to Work for in America*, Addison-Wesley, Reading, Mass., 1984, page 114.
6. Rooney Pace, Inc., *Research Report-Federal Express Corporation*, June 18, 1984.
7. Robinson Humphrey Company, Inc., Equities Research, *Research Report-Federal Express Corporation*, April 1984.
8. Rooney Pace, Inc., *Research Report-Federal Express Corporation*, June 18, 1984.

III – 3

1. L.A.B. Pilkington, "Review Lecture, The Float Glass Process," The Royal Society, London, 13 February 1969.
2. J.J. Ermenc, "Interview with Sir Alastair Pilkington, June 25, 1968," edited transcript, Dartmouth College, Hanover, New Hampshire.
3. Sir Alastair Pilkington, Speech to Toledo Glass & Ceramics Award Ceremony, January 21, 1963.
4. Sir Alastair Pilkington, "Float: An Application of Science, Analysis, and Judgment, Turner Memorial Lecture," *Glass Technology*, August 1971.
5. Interview with James Brian Quinn, Spring 1978. All other quotations from Pilkington employees came from this same series of interviews unless otherwise footnoted.
6. T. Lane and K. Roberts, *Strike at Pilkingtons*, Collins/Fontana, London, 1971.
7. The Monopolies Commission, *Flat Glass: A Report . . .* , HMSO, London, 7 February 1968, p. 89.

8. *Report of Joint Inquiry*, Dept. of Employment and Productivity, HMSO, page 10.
9. *The Paper Clip*, Ford Glass Ltd., Toronto, Ontario, Number 28– 62, June 22, 1982.
10. *Financial Times*, June 11, 1982, p. 16.

III – 4

1. "Another Turn of the Wheel," *The Economist*, March 2, 1985.
2. Research Report on General Motors Corporation, Nomura Securities International, Inc., March 12, 1984.
3. "The Innovator," *New York Times Magazine*, April 21, 1985.
4. General Motors Corporation, *1984 General Motors Public Interest Report*.
5. "Where's the Niche?," *Forbes*, September 24, 1984.
6. Research Report on General Motors Corporation, Duff and Phelps, Inc., April 12, 1984.
7. "Can Detroit Cope This Time?," *Business Week*, April 22, 1985.
8. "GM's Saturn Unit . . . ," *Wall Street Journal*, July 10, 1985.
9. "How Power Will be Balanced on Saturn's Shop Floor," *Business Week*, August 5, 1985.
10. "GM is Expected to Put Saturn Complex in Tennessee . . . ," *Wall Street Journal*, July 29, 1985.
11. "GM and EDS," *Automotive News*, March 18, 1985.
12. "Perot's Singular Style . . . ," *Wall Street Journal*, July 2, 1984.
13. "GM's Purchase of Hughes Aircraft . . . ," *Wall Street Journal*, June 6, 1985.
14. "Pre-Sale Appraisal," *Wall Street Journal*, March 27, 1985.
15. "Can Hughes Advance GM Car Building," *Los Angeles Times*, June 23, 1985.
16. "GM Struggles . . . ," *Wall Street Journal*, June 6, 1985.
17. "Collapse of Diesel Car Market . . . ," *Wall Street Journal*, July 11, 1984.
18. "Why GM is Risking Higher Prices," *Business Week*, September 16, 1985.
19. Harbridge House, Inc., *Corporate Strategies of the Automotive Manufacturers*, D.C. Heath and Company, 1979.

20. "Roger Smith—GM's Big Surprise," *Nation's Business*, February 1985.
21. "Made in the U.S.A.," *Forbes*, April 22, 1985.
22. "Japan vs. Detroit, Round 2: The Midsize Market," *Business Week*, July 22, 1985.

III – 5

1. K.D. Fishman, *The Computer Establishment*, Harper & Row, 1981.
2. "IBM's Battle to Look Superhuman Again," *Fortune*, May 19, 1980.
3. "When IBM 'talks,' Everyone Now Listens," *Business Week*, September 20, 1982.
4. "The Lean, Mean New IBM," *Fortune*, June 13, 1983.
5. *Ibid.*, and "The Colossus That Works," *Time*, July 11, 1983.

III – 6

1. "Continental Can's Continental Tribulations," *Fortune*, August 1973.
2. "How Continental Can is Packaging Growth," *Business Week*, March 3, 1975.
3. "Every Once in a While You Have to Buy a Bank," *Forbes*, September 15, 1976.
4. Donaldson, Lufkin, & Jenrette, *Research Report-Continental Group*, March 22, 1983.
5. Duff & Phelps, *Research Report-Continental Group*, March 3, 1983.
6. "Asset Redeployment Takes Continental Far Afield of Cans," *New England Business*, April 16, 1984.
7. "Major Sale Set of Continental Group Inc. Assets," *Wall Street Journal*, August 31, 1983.
8. "Continental Group Sale . . .," *New York Times*, September 21, 1984.
9. Donaldson, Lufkin, & Jenrette, *Research Report-Continental Group*, March 12, 1983.
10. Duff & Phelps, *Research Report-Continental Group*, September 16, 1983.
11. Butcher & Singer, *Research Report-Continental Group*, February 11, 1982.
12. "Goldsmith: I Wouldn't Cut Up Continental," *Wall Street Journal*, June 1984.
13. "Jimmy Goldsmith's U.S. Bonanza," *Fortune*, October 17, 1983.
14. "How Sir Jimmy Builds His Global Empire," *Business Week*, May 14, 1984.
15. "Continental: Cans and More," *New York Times*, June 6, 1984.

III – 9

1. "Hewlett Packard in Brief," *Company Literature*, 1984.
2. "Hewlett Packard Discovers Marketing," *Fortune*, October 1, 1984.
3. William R. Hewlett, "The Human Side of Management," *Eugene B. Clark Executive Lecture*, March 25, 1982.
4. Thomas L. Wheelen and J. David Hunger, *Strategic Management and Business Policy*, Addison-Wesley Publishing Company, 1983.
5. "Hewlett Packard: Where Slower Growth is Smarter Management," *Business Week*, June 9, 1975.
6. "Hewlett Packard's Calculated Rise," *Management Today*, August 1977.
7. John Young, "HP White Paper on Organization Changes," *Company Literature*, July 19, 1984.
8. Bro Uttla, "Mettle-Test Time for John Young," *Fortune*, April 29, 1985.
9. John A. Young, "The Quality Focus at Hewlett Packard," *Journal of Business Strategy*, Winter 1985.
10. "Back Into the Race," *Forbes*, October 10, 1983.
11. "Can John Young Redesign Hewlett Packard?" *Business Week*, December 6, 1982.
12. E.F. Hutton, Inc., Equity Research, *Hewlett Packard Company Action Report*, June 28, 1983.

III – 10

1. "Turnover at the Top: Cause and Effect," *Chain Store Age Executive*, May 1984.
2. "Making Money at the Low End of the Market," *Forbes*, December 17, 1984.
3. "Hit or Miss on Target with New Look," *Chain Store Age Executive*, February 1983.
4. "Too Big for Miracles," *Forbes*, June 15, 1977, p. 26.
5. "Sears' Strategic About-Face," *Business Week*, January 8, 1979.

6. "J.C. Penney's Fashion Gamble," *Business Week*, January 16, 1978, p. 66.

7. "Wal-Mart: A Discounter Sinks Deep Roots in Small Town, U.S.A.," *Business Week*, November 5, 1979, p. 145.

8. "A Day in the Life of Sam Walton," *Forbes*, January 1, 1977, p. 45.

III – 11

1. Making Money at the Low End of the Market," *Forbes*, December 17, 1984, p. 42.

2. "Membership Retailing Trend Taking Off," *Chain Store Age Executive*, November 1984, p. 17.

3. "Sumner Feldberg: Maxx-imizing Potential," *Chain Store Age Executive*, January 1984, p. 19.

4. "New Fangled Stores for Fussy Buyers: American Retailing," *Economist*, April 30, 1983.

5. J. Seth, "Emerging Trends for the Retailing Industry," *Journal of Retailing*, Fall 1983, p. 6.

6. Blackwell and Talarzyk, "Life-Style Retailing: Competitive Strategies for the 1980s," *Journal of Retailing*, Winter 1983.

7. Bluestone, et al., *The Retail Revolution*, Auburn House Publishing Co., Boston, 1981.

BIBLIOGRAPHY

ABERNATHY, W.J. & K. WAYNE, "Limits on the Learning Curve," *Harvard Business Review*, September–October 1974: 109–119.

ACKERMAN, R.W., *The Social Challenge to Business*. Cambridge, Mass.: Harvard University Press, 1975.

ACKOFF, R.L., *A Concept of Corporate Planning*. New York: Wiley Interscience, 1970.

AGUILAR, F.J., *Scanning the Business Environment*. New York: Macmillan, 1967.

ALDRICH, H.E., *Organizations and Environments*. Englewood Cliffs, N.J.: Prentice-Hall, 1979.

ALLEN, M.P., "The Structure of Interorganizational Elite Cooptation: Interlocking Corporate Directorates," *American Sociological Review*, 1974: 393–406.

ALLEN, S.A., "Organizational Choices and General Management Influence Networks in Divisionalized Companies," *Academy of Management Journal*, 1978: 341–365.

ALLEN, T.J., *Managing the Flow of Technology*. Cambridge, Mass.: M.I.T. Press, 1977.

ALLISON, G.T., *Essence of Decision: Explaining the Cuban Missile Crisis*. Boston: Little, Brown, 1971.

ANDERSON, C.R. & F.T. PAINE, "Managerial Perceptions and Strategic Behavior," *Academy of Management Journal*, 1975: 811–823.

ANSOFF, H.I., *Corporate Strategy: An Analytic Approach to Business Policy for Growth and Expansion*. New York, McGraw-Hill, 1965.

———, & R. BRANDENBURGH, "A Language for Organizational Design," *Managerial Science*, 1971: B717–B731.

ANTHONY, R.N., *Planning and Control Systems: A Framework for Analysis*. Boston: Harvard Business School, 1965.

ARGYRIS, C., "Double Loop Learning in Organizations," *Harvard Business Review*, September–October 1977: 115–125.

ASTLEY, W.G. & C.J. FOMBRUN, "Collective Strategy: Social Ecology of Organizational Environments," *Academy of Management Review*, 1983: 576–587.

ATHOS, A.G. & L.B. WARD, *Corporations and College Recruiting: A Study of Perceptions*. Working Paper, Harvard Business School, no date.

BACON, J. & J.K. BROWN, *Corporate Directorship Practices: Role, Selection and Legal Status of the Board*. New York: The Conference Board, 1975.

BARNARD, C.I., *The Functions of the Executive*. Cambridge, Mass.: Harvard University Press, 1938.

BATY, G.B., W.M. EVAN, & T.W. ROTHERMEL,

"Personnel Flows as Interorganizational Relations," *Administrative Science Quarterly*, 1971: 430–443.

BAUER, R.A., I. POOL, & L.A. DEXTER, *American Business and Public Policy*. New York: Atherton Press, 1968.

BECKER, G., *Human Capital*. New York: National Bureau of Economic Research, 1964.

BEER, S., *Designing Freedom*. Toronto: CBC Publications, 1974.

BENNIS, W.G. & P.L. SLATER, *The Temporary Society*. New York: Harper and Row, 1964.

BERGMANN, A.E., "Industrial Democracy in Germany—The Battle for Power," *Journal of General Management*, Summer 1975: 20–29.

BERLEW, D.E. & D.T. HALL, "The Management of Tension in Organization: Some Preliminary Findings," *Industrial Management Review*, Fall 1964: 31–40.

BERNSTEIN, L., "Joint Ventures in the Light of Recent Antitrust Developments," *The Antitrust Bulletin*, 1965: 25–29.

BETTIS, R. A., "Performance Differences in Related and Unrelated Diversified Firms," *Strategic Management Journal*, 1981: 379–394.

BIERI, J., "Cognitive Structures in Personality" in H.M. Schroder & P. Suedfeld, eds. *Personality: Theory & Information Processing*. New York: Ronald Press, 1971.

BOSTON CONSULTING GROUP, *Perspectives on Experience*. Boston, 1972.

———, *Strategy Alternatives for the British Motorcycle Industry*. London: Her Majesty's Stationery Office, 1975.

BOULDING, K.E., "The Ethics of Rational Decision," *Management Science*, 1966: 161–169.

BOWER, J.L., *Managing the Resource Allocation Process: A Study of Planning and Investment*. Boston: Harvard Business School, 1970a.

———, "Planning within the Firm," *The American Economic Review*, 1970b: 186–194.

BOWER, M., *The Will to Manage*. New York: McGraw-Hill, 1966.

BRAYBROOKE, D., "Skepticism of Wants, and Certain Subversive Effects of Corporations on American Values," in S. Hook, ed., *Human Values and Economic Policy*. New York: New York University Press, 1967.

——— & C.E. LINDBLOM, *A Strategy of Decision: Policy Evaluation as a Social Process*. New York: Free Press, 1963.

BRENNER, S.N. & E.A. MOLANDER, "Is the Ethic of Business Changing?" *Harvard Business Review*, January–February 1977: 57–71.

BURNS, T., "The Directions of Activity and Communication in a Departmental Executive Group," *Human Relations*, 1954: 73–97.

——— & G.M. STALKER, *The Management of Innovation*. London: Tavistock, 1961.

BUZZELL, R.D., B.T. GALE, & R.G.M. SULTAN, "Market Share—A Key to Profitability," *Harvard Business Review*, January–February 1975: 97–106.

BYLINSKY, G., *The Innovation Millionaires*. New York: Charles Scribner's Sons, 1976.

CANTLEY, M.F., "A Long-range Planning Case Study," *OR Quarterly*, 1969: 7–20.

CARZO, R. & J.N. YANOUZAS, "Effects of Flat and Tall Organization Structure," *Administrative Science Quarterly*, 1969: 178–191.

CHANDLER, A.D., *Strategy and Structure: Chapters in the History of the Industrial Enterprise*. Cambridge, Mass.: M.I.T. Press, 1962.

CHANDLER, M.K. & L.R. SAYLES, *Managing Large Systems*. New York: Harper and Row, 1971.

CHEIT, E.F., "The New Place of Business: Why Managers Cultivate Social Responsibility," in E.F. Cheit, ed., *The Business Establishment*. New York: John Wiley, 1964.

CHILDERS, M.E., "What Is Political About Bureaucratic-Collegial Decision Making,'' *Review of Higher Education*, 1981: 25–45.

CHRISTENSON, C.R., K.R. ANDREWS, & J.L. BOWER, *Business Policy: Text and Cases*. Homewood, Ill.: Richard D. Irwin, 1978.

CLARK, B.R., *The Distinctive College: Antioch, Reed and Swarthmore*. Chicago: Aldine, 1970.

———, ''The Organizational Saga in Higher Education,'' *Administrative Science Quarterly*, 1972: 178–184.

CLARK, R.C., *The Japanese Company*. New Haven: Yale University Press, 1979.

COHEN, K.J. & R.M. CYERT, ''Strategy: Formulation, Implementation and Monitoring,'' *The Journal of Business*, 1973: 349–367.

COHEN, M.D. & J.G. MARCH, *Leadership and Ambiguity: The American College President*. New York: McGraw-Hill, 1974.

——— & J.P. OLSEN, ''A Garbage Can Model of Organizational Choice,'' *Administrative Science Quarterly*, 1972: 1–25.

COLE, A.H., *Business Enterprise in Its Social Setting*. Cambridge, Mass.: Harvard University Press, 1959.

COLE, R.E., *Japanese Blue Collar: The Changing Tradition*. Berkeley: University of California Press, 1971.

———, *Work, Mobility and Participation*. Berkeley: University of California Press, 1979.

COLLINS, O.F. & D.G. MOORE, *The Organization Makers: A Behavioral Study of Independent Entrepreneurs*. New York: Appleton-Century-Crofts, 1970.

COPEMAN, G.H., *The Role of the Managing Director*. London: Business Publications, 1963.

CROZIER, M., *The Bureaucratic Phenomenon*. Chicago: University of Chicago Press, 1964.

CYERT, R.M., W.R. DILL, & J.G. MARCH, ''The Role of Expectations in Business Decision Making,'' *Administrative Science Quarterly*, 1958: 307–340.

CYERT, R.M. & J.G. MARCH, *A Behavioral Theory of the Firm*. Englewood Cliffs, N.J.: Prentice-Hall, 1963.

DARWIN, C., *The Origin of Species*. Middlesex, Eng.: Penguin Books, 1968.

DAVIS, R.T., *Performance and Development of Field Sales Managers*. Boston: Harvard Business School, 1957.

DEAN, R.C., ''The Temporal Mismatch: Innovation's Pace vs. Management's Time Horizon, *Research Management*, May 1974: 12–15.

DELBECQ, A. & A.C. FILLEY, *Program and Project Management in a Matrix Organization: A Case Study*. Madison, Wis.: University of Wisconsin, 1974.

DILL, W.R., *GSIA Alumni—Their Progress and Their Goals*. Working paper, Carnegie Institute of Technology, 1962.

DOERINGER, P. & M. PIORE, *Internal Labor Market and Manpower Analysis*. Lexington, Mass.: Lexington Books, 1971.

——— *Strategy of Financial Mobility*. Boston: Harvard Business School, 1969b.

DONALDSON, G., ''Strategy for Financial Emergencies,'' *Harvard Business Review*, November–December 1969a: 67–79.

DORE, R.P., *British Factory—Japanese Factory*. Berkeley: University of California Press, 1973.

DRUCKER, P.F., *The Practice of Management*. New York: Harper and Row, 1954.

———, *Managing For Results*. New York: Harper and Row, 1964.

———, ''Entrepreneurship in Business Enterprise,'' *Journal of Business Policy*, Autumn 1970: 3–12.

———, *Management: Tasks, Responsibilities, Practices*. New York: Harper and Row, 1974.

———, ''Economic Realities and Enterprise Strategy,'' in E.F. Vogel, ed., *Modern Japanese Organization and Decision Making*.

Berkeley: University of California Press, 1975.

———, "Clouds Forming Across the Japanese Sun," *Wall Street Journal*, July 13, 1982.

ECCLES, M.S., *Beckoning Frontiers: Public and Personal Recollections*, edited by S. Hyman. New York: Alfred A. Knopf, 1951.

EDWARDS, J.P., "Strategy Formulation as a Stylistic Process," *International Studies of Management and Organization*, Summer 1977: 13–27.

EPSTEIN, E.M., *The Corporation in American Politics*. Englewood Cliffs, N.J.: Prentice-Hall, 1969.

———, "The Social Role of Business Enterprise in Britain: An American Perspective; Part II," *The Journal of Management Studies*, 1977: 281–316.

ESSAME, H., *Patton: A Study in Command*. New York: Charles Scribner's Sons, 1974.

EVERED, R., *So What Is Strategy?* Working Paper, Naval Postgraduate School, Monterey, 1980.

FARAGO, L., *Patton: Ordeal and Triumph*. New York: I. Obolensky, 1964.

FILLEY, A.C., R.J. HOUSE, & S. KERR, *Managerial Process and Organizational Behavior*. Glenview, Ill.: Scott, Foreman, 1976.

FLEISHMANN, E.A., E.F. HARRIS, & H.E. BURT, *Leadership and Supervision in Industry: An Evaluation of Supervisory Training Program*. Columbus, Ohio: The Ohio State University, 1955.

FOCH, F., *Principles of War*, translated by J. DeMorinni. New York: AMS Press, 1970. First published London: Chapman & Hall, 1918.

FORRESTER, J.W., "Counterintuitive Behavior of Social Systems," *Technology Review*, January 1977: 52–68.

FOURAKER, L.E. & J.M. STOPFORD, "Organizational Structure and Multinational Strategy," *Administrative Science Quarterly*, 1968: 47–64.

FRANKLIN, B., *Poor Richard's Almanac*. New York: Ballantine Books, 1977. First Published, Century Company, 1898.

FRIEDMAN, M., *Capitalism and Freedom*. Chicago: University of Chicago Press, 1962.

——— "A Friedman Doctrine: The Social Responsibility of Business is to Increase its Profits," *The New York Times Magazine*, September 13, 1970.

GALBRAITH, J.R., *Designing Complex Organizations*. Reading, Mass.: Addison-Wesley, 1973.

———, *Organization Design*. Reading, Mass.: Addison-Wesley, 1977.

——— & D. NATHANSON, *Strategy Implementation*. St. Paul, Minn.: West Publishing, 1978.

GARDNER, J.W., "The Anti-Leadership Vaccine," in *Carnegie Corporation of New York Annual Report*, 1965.

GARSON, G.D., "The Codetermination Model of Worker's Participation: Where Is It Leading?" *Sloan Management Review*, Spring 1977: 63–78.

GERTH, H.H. & C.W. MILLS, EDS., *From Max Weber: Essays in Sociology*. New York: Oxford University Press, 1958.

GEZELIUS, G. & L. OTTERBECK, *Kalmar Verkstads AB*, Teaching Case, Institutet för Företagsledning Stockholm School of Economics, 1977.

GHISELLI, E.E., "Managerial Talent," in D. Wolfe, ed., *The Discovery of Talent*. Cambridge, Mass.: Harvard University Press, 1969.

GILMORE, F.F., "Overcoming the Perils of Advocacy in Corporate Planning," *California Management Review*, Spring 1973: 127–137.

GLUECK, W.F., *Business Policy and Strategic Management*. New York: McGraw Hill, 1980.

GOODMAN, L.P. & R.A. GOODMAN, "Theatre as a Temporary System," *Management Review*, Winter 1972: 103–108.

GOODMAN, R.A. & L.P. GOODMAN, "Some Management Issues in Temporary Systems: A Study of Professional Development and Manpower—Theatre Case," *Administrative Science Quarterly*, 1976: 494–501.

GOSSELIN, R., *A Study of the Interdependence of Medical Specialists in Quebec Teaching Hospitals*. Ph.D. thesis, McGill University, 1978.

GREEN, P., *Alexander the Great*. New York: Frederick A. Praeger, 1970.

GRINYER, P.H. & D. NORBURN, "Planning for Existing Markets: Perceptions of Executives and Financial Performance," *Journal of the Royal Statistical Society*, 1975: Series A: 70–97.

―――― & J.C. SPENDER, *Turnaround—Managerial Recipes for Strategic Success*. New York: Associated Business Press, 1979.

GUEST, R.H., "Of Time and The Foreman," *Personnel*, May 1956: 478–486.

GUNDHUS, P., "Bedrift i krise: hvordan avsløres i tide?", *Bedriftsøkonomen*, 1977: 328–331.

HACKMAN, M.R., "Group Influences on Individuals," in M.D. Dunnette, ed., *Handbook of Industrial and Organizational Psychology*, Chicago: Rand McNally, 1976.

HAITANI, K., "Changing Characteristics of the Japanese Employment System," *Asian Survey*, 1978: 1029–1045.

HALL, D.T., *Careers in Organizations*. Pacific Palisades, Calif.: Goodyear, 1976.

HALL, R.H., "Professionalization and Bureaucratization," *American Sociological Review*, 1968: 92–104.

――――, *Organizations: Structure and Process*. Englewood Cliffs, N.J.: Prentice-Hall, 1972.

HALL, R.I., "A System Pathology of an Organization: The Rise and Fall of the Old Satur-

day Evening Post," *Administrative Science Quarterly*, 1976: 185–211.

HAMMOND, P.Y., "Super Carriers and B-36 Bombers" in H. Stein, ed. *American Civil-Military Decisions: A Book of Case Studies*. Birmingham, Ala.: University Press, 1963.

HANNAN, M. & J. FREEMAN, "The Population Ecology of Organizations," *American Journal of Sociology*, 1977: 929–964.

HARBISON, F. & C.A. MYERS, *Management in the Industrial World*. New York: McGraw-Hill, 1959.

HARDWICK, C.T. & B.F. LANDUYT, *Administrative Strategy and Decision Making*. Cincinnati: South Western, 1966.

HART, B.H.L., *Strategy*. New York: Frederick A. Praeger, 1954.

HATTORI, I., "A Proposition on Efficient Decision-Making in Japanese Corporation," *Management Japan*, Autumn 1977: 14–20.

HAYES, R. H., "Strategic Planning—Forward in Reverse?", *Harvard Business Review*, November–December 1985: 111–119.

HAYES, R.H. & W.J. ABERNATHY, "Managing Our Way to Economic Decline," *Harvard Business Review*, July–August 1980: 67–77.

――――. & D.A. GARVIN, "Managing as if Tomorrow Mattered," *Harvard Business Review*, May–June 1982: 70–79.

HAZAMA, H., "Characteristics of Japanese-Style Management," *Japanese Economic Studies*, Spring–Summer 1978: 110–173.

HEDBERG, B.L.T., "How Organizations Learn and Unlearn." in P.C. Nystrom and W.H. Starbuck, eds., *Handbook of Organizational Design*, Volume 1. New York: Oxford University Press, 1981.

――――. & S.A. Jönsson, "Designing Semi-confusing Information Systems for Organizations in Changing Environments," *Accounting Organizations and Society*, 1978: 47–64.

――――, P.C. NYSTROM, & W.H. STARBUCK,

"Camping on Seesaws: Prescriptions for a Self-designing Organization," *Administrative Science Quarterly*, 1976: 41–65.

HENDERSON, B.D., *The Product Portfolio*. Boston: Boston Consulting Group, 1970.

————, *The Experience Curve—Reviewed*. Boston: Boston Consulting Group, 1973.

HIRSCH, P.M., "Organizational Effectiveness and the Institutional Environment," *Administrative Science Quarterly*, 1975: 327–344.

HOFER, C.W. & D. SCHENDEL, *Strategy Formulation: Analytical Concepts*. St. Paul, Minn.: West Publishing, 1978.

HOMANS, G.C., *The Human Group*. New York: Harcourt, Brace and World, 1950.

HOUSE OF REPRESENTATIVES, Staff Report to the Antitrust Subcommittee of the Committee on the Judiciary, *Interlocks in Corporate Management*, Washington, D.C.: U.S. Government Printing Office, 1965.

HUGHES, T., "The Inventive Continuum," *Science 84*, November 1984.

HUNT, R.G., "Technology and Organization," *Academy of Management Journal*, 1970: 235–252.

IRVING, D., *The Trail of the Fox*. New York: E.P. Dutton, 1977.

JACOBS, D., "Dependency and Vulnerability: An Exchange Approach to the Control of Organizations," *Administrative Science Quarterly*, 1974: 45–59.

JAMES, D.C., *The Years of MacArthur, 1941–1945*. Boston: Houghton Mifflin, 1970.

JAMES, R.M., "Effective Planning Strategies," *Human Resource Planning*, vol. 3, no. 1, 1980: 1–10.

JANIS, I.L. & L. MANN, *Decision Making*. New York: Free Press, 1977.

JAY, A., *Management and Machiavelli*. New York: Penguin Books, 1970.

JENKINS, C., *Power at the Top*. Westport, Conn.: Greenwood Press, 1976.

JENNINGS, E.E., *The Mobile Manager*. Ann Arbor: University of Michigan, 1967.

JOHNSON, R.T. & W.G. OUCHI, "Made in the U.S. (Under Japanese Management)," *Harvard Business Review*, September–October 1974: 61–69.

JOMINI, A.H., *Art of War*, translated by G.H. Mendell and W.P. Craighill. Westport, Conn.: Greenwood Press, 1971. Original Philadelphia: J.B. Lippincott, 1862.

JÖNSSON, S.A. & R.A. LUNDIN, "Myths and Wishful Thinking as Management Tools," in P.C. Nystrom and W.H. Starbuck eds., *Prescriptive Models of Organizations*. Amsterdam: North-Holland, 1977.

JORDAN, W.A., "Producer Protection Prior Market Structure and the Effects of Government Regulation," *Journal of Law and Economics*, 1972.

KAHN, R.L., D.M. WOLFE, R.P. QUINN, J.D. SNOEK, & R.A. ROSENTHAL, *Organizational Stress*. New York: John Wiley, 1964.

KAMI, M.J. & J.E. ROSS, *Corporate Management in Crisis: Why the Mighty Fall*. Englewood Cliffs, N.J.: Prentice-Hall, 1973.

KATZ, D. & R.L. KAHN, *The Social Psychology of Organizations*. New York: John Wiley, 1966.

KATZ, R.L., *Cases and Concepts in Corporate Strategy*. Englewood Cliffs, N.J.: Prentice-Hall, 1970.

————, "Time and Work: Towards an Integrative Perspective," in B.M. Staw and L.L. Cummings, eds., *Research in Organizational Behavior*, Vol. 1. Greenwich, Conn.: JAI Press, 1980.

KIDDER, T., *The Soul of a New Machine*. Boston: Little, Brown, 1981.

KING, A.S., "Expectation Effects in Organizational Change," *Administrative Science Quarterly*, 1974: 221–230.

KLAW, S., "The Entrepreneurial Ego." *Fortune*, August 1956: 100 +.

KONO, T., "Comparative Study of Strategy,

Structure and Long-Range Planning in Japan and in the United States," *Management Japan*, Spring 1980: 20–34.

KUHN, T., *The Structure of Scientific Revolutions*. Chicago: University of Chicago Press, 1970.

KURODA, I. & Y. ORITANI, "A Reexamination of the Unique Features of Japan's Corporate Financial Structure," *Japanese Economic Studies*, Summer 1980: 82–117.

LANDAU, M., "On the Concept of a Self-correcting Organization," *Public Administrative Review*, 1973: 533–542.

LEARNED, E.P., D.N. ULRICH, & D.R. BOOZ, *Executive Action*. Boston: Harvard Business School, 1951.

LENIN, V.I., *Collected Works of V.I. Lenin*, edited and annotated. New York: International Publishers, 1927.

LEVINSON, H., "On Becoming a Middle-Aged Manager," *Harvard Business Review*, July–August 1969: 51–60.

———, *Executive Stress*. New York: Harper and Row, 1970.

LEVITT, T., "Why Business Always Loses," *Harvard Business Review*, March–April 1968: 81–89.

———, "Dinosaurs Among the Bears and Bulls," *Harvard Business Review*, January–February 1975: 41–53.

LEWIN, K., *Field Theory in Social Science*. New York: Harper and Row, 1951.

LIKERT, R., *The Human Organization*. New York: McGraw-Hill, 1967.

———, *New Patterns of Management*. New York: McGraw-Hill, 1969.

LINDBLOM, C.E., "The Science of 'Muddling Through,' " *Public Administration Review*, 1959: 79–88.

———, *The Intelligence of Democracy*. New York: Free Press, 1965.

———, *The Policy-Making Process*. Englewood Cliffs, N.J.: Prentice-Hall, 1968.

LITTLE, A.D., INC., "*Transportation Planning in the District of Columbia, 1955–65: A Review and Critique*," Report to The Policy Advisory Committee to the District Commissioners. Washington, D.C.: U.S. Government Printing Office, 1966.

LODGE, G.C., *The New American Ideology*. New York: Alfred A. Knopf, 1975.

LOHR, S., "Japan Struggling With Itself," *New York Times*, June 13, 1982.

MACE, M.L. & G.G. MONTGOMERY, *Management Problems of Corporate Acquisitions*. Boston: Harvard Business School, 1962.

MACHIAVELLI, N., *The Prince, and the Discourses*. New York: Modern Library, 1950.

MACKWORTH, N.H., "Originality," in D. Wolfe, ed., *The Discovery of Talent*. Cambridge, Mass.: Harvard University Press, 1969.

MAGEE, J.F., "Decision Trees for Decision Making," *Harvard Business Review*, July–August, 1964: 126–138.

———, *Desirable Characteristics of Models in Planning*, a paper delivered at the Symposium on the Role of Economic Models in Policy Formulation, sponsored by the Department of Housing and Urban Development, Office of Emergency Planning, National Resource Evaluation Center, Washington, D.C., October, 1966.

MAJONE, G., "The Uses of Policy Analysis," in *The Future and the Past: Essays on Programs*, Russell Sage Foundation Annual Report, 1976–1977.

MAO TSE-TUNG, *Selected Military Writings, 1928–1949*. San Francisco: China Books, 1967.

MARCH, J.G. & J.P. OLSEN, *Ambiguity and Choice in Organizations*. Bergen, Norway: Universitetsforlaget, 1976.

——— & H.A. SIMON, *Organizations*. New York: John Wiley, 1958.

MARSHALL, G.L., *Predicting Executive Achievement*. Ph.D. thesis, Harvard Business School, 1964.

MARTIN, L.C., "How Beatrice Foods Sneaked Up On $5 Billion," *Fortune*, April 1976: 118–129.

MATLOFF, M. & E.M. SNELL, *Strategic Planning for Coalition Warfare (1941–42)*. Washington, D.C.: Office of the Chief of Military History, Department of the Army, 1953.

MAYO, E., *The Social Problems of an Industrial Civilization*. Boston: Harvard Business School, 1945.

MCCLELLAND, D., *The Achieving Society*. New York: Halsted Press, 1976.

MCDONALD, J., *Strategy in Poker, Business and War*. New York: W.W. Norton, 1950.

MILES, R.E. & C.C. SNOW, *Organizational Strategy, Structure, and Process*. New York: McGraw-Hill, 1978.

MILLER, D., "Evolution and Revolution: A Quantum View of Structural Change in Organizations," *Journal of Management Studies*, 1982: 131–151.

——— & P.H. FRIESEN, "Momentum and Revolution in Organizational Adaptation," *Academy of Management Journal*, 1980: 591–614.

———, *Organizations: A Quantum View*. Englewood Cliffs, N.J.: Prentice-Hall, 1984.

MILLER, D. & H. MINTZBERG, *Strategy Formulation in Context: Some Tentative Models*. Working Paper, McGill University, 1974.

———, "The Case For Configuration" in G. Morgan, ed., *Beyond Method: Strategies For Social Research*. Beverly Hills, Calif.: Sage Publications, 1983.

MINTZBERG, H., "Research on Strategy-Making," *Academy of Management Proceedings*, 1972: 90–94.

———, *The Nature of Managerial Work*. New York: Harper and Row, 1973a.

———, "Strategy Making in Three Modes," *California Management Review*, Winter 1973b: 44–53.

———, "The Manager's Job: Folklore and Fact," *Harvard Business Review*, July–August 1975: 49–61.

———, "Patterns in Strategy Formation," *Management Science*, 1978: 934–948.

———, *The Structuring of Organizations: A Synthesis of the Research*. Englewood Cliffs, N.J.: Prentice-Hall, 1979.

———, "What Is Planning Anyway?", *Strategic Management Journal*, 1981: 319–324.

———, J.P. BRUNET, & J. WATERS, "Does Planning Impede Strategic Thinking? The Strategy of Air Canada 1937–1976," in *Advances in Strategic Management*, vol. 4. Greenwich, Conn.: J.A.I. Press, 1986.

———, D. RAÌSINGNANÌ, & A. THÉORÊT, "The Structure of 'Unstructured' Decision Processes," *Administrative Science Quarterly*, 1976: 246–275.

——— & J.A. WATERS, "Tracking Strategy in an Entrepreneurial Firm," *Academy of Management Journal*, 1982: 465–499.

———, "Researching the Formation of Strategies: The History of Canadian Lady, 1939–1976," in R. Lamb, ed., *Strategic Management*. Englewood Cliffs, N.J.: Prentice-Hall, 1983.

———, "Of Strategies, Deliberate and Emergent," *Strategic Management Journal*, 1985: 257–272.

MINTZBERG, H., S. OTIS, J. SHAMSIE, & J.A. WATERS, "Strategy of Design: A Study of 'Architects in Co-Partnership,'" in J. Grant, ed., *Strategic Management Frontiers*, Greenwich, Conn.: JAI Press, 1987.

MONTGOMERY, B.L., *The Memoirs of Field-Marshal The Viscount Montgomery of Alamein*. Cleveland: World Publishing, 1958.

MOORE, D.G., "Managerial Strategies," in W.L. Warner and N.H. Martin, eds., *Industrial Man: Businessmen and Business Organizations*. New York: Harper and Row, 1959.

MORITANI, M., *Japanese Technology: Getting the Best for the Least*. Tokyo: Simul Press, 1981.

MOYER, R.C., "Berle and Means Revisited: The Conglomerate Merger," *Business and Society*, Spring 1970: 20–29.

MUMFORD, E. & A.M. PETTIGREW, *Implementing Strategic Decisions*. London: Longman, 1975.

NADLER, D.A. & E.E. LAWLER, III, "Motivation—A Diagnostic Approach," in J.R. Hackman, E.E. Lawler, III, and L.W. Porter, eds., *Perspective on Behavior in Organizations*. New York: McGraw-Hill, 1977.

NAPOLEON, I., "Maximes de Guerre," in T.R. Phillips, ed., *Roots of Strategy*. Harrisburgh, Pa.: Military Service Publishing, 1940.

NATHANSON, D. & J. CASSANO, "Organization Diversity and Performance," *The Wharton Magazine*, Summer 1982: 18–26.

NEUSTADT, R.E., *Presidential Power: The Politics of Leadership*. New York: John Wiley, 1960.

NORMANN, R., "Organizational Innovativeness: Product Variation and Reorientation," *Administrative Science Quarterly*, 1971: 203–215.

———, *Management for Growth*, translated by N. Adler. New York: John Wiley, 1977.

NYSTROM, P.C., B.L.T. HEDBERG, & W.H. STARBUCK, "Interacting Processes as Organization Designs," in R.H. Kilmann, L.R. Pondy, & D.P. Slevin, eds., *The Management of Organization Design*, Vol. 1. New York: Elsevier North-Holland, 1976.

OHMAE, K., *The Mind of the Strategist*. New York: McGraw-Hill, 1982.

ONO, H., "Nihonteki Keiei Shisutemu to Jinji Kettei Shisutemu," ("Japanese Management System and Personnel Decisions,") *Soshiki Kagaku*, 1976: 22–32.

ORNSTEIN, R., *The Psychology of Consciousness*. San Francisco: W.H. Freeman, 1975.

OUCHI, W.G., "Market, Bureaucracies and Clans," *Administrative Science Quarterly*, 1980: 129–140.

———, *Theory Z*. Reading, Mass.: Addison-Wesley, 1981.

——— & A.M. JAEGER, "Type Z Organization: Stability in the Midst of Mobility," *Academy of Management Review*, 1978: 305–314.

PARSONS, T., *Structure and Process in Modern Societies*. Glencoe, Ill.: Free Press, 1960.

PASCALE, R.T., "Communication and Decision Making Across Cultures: Japanese and American Comparisons," *Administrative Science Quarterly*, 1978: 91–110.

———, "Perspectives on Strategy: The Real Story Behind Honda's Success," *California Management Review*, Spring 1984: 47–72.

——— & A.G. ATHOS, *The Art of Japanese Management*. New York: Simon and Schuster, 1981.

PAUL, N.L., "The Use of Empathy in the Resolution of Grief," in *Perspective in Biology and Medicine*. Chicago: University of Chicago Press, 1967.

PENCE, C.C., *How Venture Capitalists Make Venture Decisions*. Ann Arbor, Mich.: UMI Research Press, 1982.

PERROW, C., "The Analysis of Goals in Complex Organizations," *American Sociological Review*, 1961: 854–866.

———, *Organizational Analysis: A Sociological Review*. Belmont, Calif.: Wadsworth, 1970.

PETERS, T.J., "Symbols, Patterns and Settings: An Optimistic Case for Getting Things Done," *Organizational Dynamics*, Autumn 1978: 2–23.

———, "A Style for All Seasons," *Executive*, Summer 1980: 12–16.

——— & R.H. WATERMAN, *In Search of Excellence: Lessons from America's Best Run Companies*. New York: Harper and Row, 1982.

PETTIGREW, A.M., *The Politics of Organizational*

Decision-Making. London: Tavistock, 1973.

PFEFFER, J., "Size and Composition of Corporate Boards of Directors: The Organization and its Environment," *Administrative Science Quarterly*, 1972a: 218–228.

———, "Merger as a Response to Organizational Interdependence," *Administrative Science Quarterly*, 1972b: 382–394.

———, "Size, Composition and Function of Hospital Boards of Directors: A Study of Organization-Environment Linkage," *Administrative Science Quarterly*, 1973: 349–364.

———, "Administrative Regulation and Licensing: Social Problem or Solution?", *Social Problems*, 1974a: 468–479.

———, "Cooptation and the Composition of Electric Utility Boards of Directors," *Pacific Sociological Review*, 1974b: 333–363.

———, "Power and Resource Allocation in Organizations," in R.H. Miles & W.A. Randolph, eds., *The Organization Game*. Santa Monica, Calif.: Goodyear, 1979a.

———, *Management as Symbolic Action: The Creation and Maintenance of Organizational Paradigms*. Working Paper, Stanford University, 1979b.

——— & H. LEBLEBICI, "Executive Recruitment and the Development of Interfirm Organizations," *Administrative Science Quarterly*, 1973: 449–461.

PFEFFER, J. & P. NOWAK, "Patterns of Joint Venture Activity: Implications for Antitrust Policy," *The Antitrust Bulletin*, 1976a: 315–339.

———, "Joint Ventures and Interorganizational Interdependence," *Administrative Science Quarterly*, 1976b: 398–418.

———, *Organizational Context and Interorganizational Linkages Among Corporations*. Working Paper, University of California at Berkeley, no date.

PFEFFER, J. & G.R. SALANCIK, *The External Control of Organizations: A Resource Dependence Perspective*. New York: Harper and Row, 1978.

——— & H. LEBLEBICI, "The Effect of Uncertainty on the Use of Social Influence in Organizational Decision-Making," *Administrative Science Quarterly*, 1976: 227–245.

PFIFFNER, J.M., "Administrative Rationality," *Public Administration Review*, 1960: 125–132.

PHILLIPS, T.R., ED., *Roots of Strategy*. Harrisburg, Pa.: Military Service Publishing, 1940.

POGUE, F.C., *George C. Marshall: Ordeal and Hope, 1939–1942*. New York: Viking Press, 1966.

PORTER, M.E., *Competitive Strategy: Techniques for Analysing Industries and Competitors*. New York: Free Press, 1980.

———, *Competitive Advantage: Creating and Sustaining Superior Performance*. New York: Free Press, 1985.

POSNER, R.A., "Theories of Economic Regulation," *Bell Journal of Economics and Management Science*, 1974: 335–358.

PRICE, J.L., "The Impact of Governing Boards on Organizational Effectiveness and Morale," *Administrative Science Quarterly*, 1963: 361–378.

PUCIK, V., "Lifetime Employment in Japan: An Alternative to the 'Culture-Structure' Causal Model," *Journal of International Affairs*, 1979: 158–161.

———, "Promotions and Intra-organizational Status Differentiation Among Japanese Managers," *The Academy of Management Proceedings*, 1981: 59–63.

PUGH, D.S., D.J. HICKSON, C.R. HININGS, K.M. MACDONALD, C. TURNER & T. LUPTON, "A Conceptual Scheme for Organizational Analysis," *Administrative Science Quarterly*, 1963–1964: 289–315.

PURKAYASTHA, D., "*Note on the Motocycle In-*

dustry—1975.'' Copyrighted Case, Harvard Business School, 1981.

QUINN, J.B., "Strategic Goals: Process and Politics," *Sloan Management Review*, Fall 1977: 21–37.

———, *Strategies for Change: Logical Incrementalism.* Homewood, Ill.: Richard D. Irwin, 1980.

———, "Managing Innovation: Controlled Chaos," *Harvard Business Review*, May–June 1985: 73–84.

——— & J.A. MUELLER, "Transferring Research Results to Operations," *Harvard Business Review*, January–February 1963: 49–66.

REESER, C., "Some Potential Human Problems in the Project Form of Organization," *Academy of Management Journal*, 1969: 459–467.

REID, S.R., *Mergers, Managers, and the Economy.* New York: McGraw-Hill, 1968.

RESTAK, R., "The Hemispheres of the Brain Have Minds of Their Own," *New York Times*, January 25, 1976.

RHENMAN, E., *Organization Theory for Long-Range Planning.* New York: John Wiley, 1973.

RICKARD, E.B., "The Past is History . . . The Future is Planning," in R.N. Anthony, J. Dearden & R.F. Vancil, eds., *Management Control Systems.* Homewood, Ill.: Richard D. Irwin, 1965.

ROBERTS, K. & C. O'REILLY, "Some Correlates of Communication Roles in Organizations," *Academy of Management Journal*, 1979: 42–57.

ROGERS, E.M., *Communication of Innovations: A Cross-Cultural Approach.* New York: Free Press, 1971.

ROHLEN, T.P., *For Harmony and Strength: Japanese White-collar Organization in Anthropological Perspective.* Berkeley: University of California Press, 1974.

———, " 'Permanent Employment' Faces Recession, Slow Growth and Aging Work Force," *The Journal of Japanese Studies*, 1979: 235–272.

ROSNER, M., *Principle Types and Problems of Direct Democracy in the Kibbutz.* Working Paper, Social Research Center on the Kibbutz, Givat Haviva, Israel, 1969.

ROSS, I., "How Lawless are the Big Companies?", *Fortune*, December 1, 1980: 56–64.

ROSSOTTI, C.O., *Two Concepts of Long-Range Planning.* Boston: The Management Consulting Group, The Boston Safe Deposit & Trust Company, no date.

RUMELT, R.P., *Strategy, Structure and Economic Performance.* Boston: Harvard Business School, 1974.

———, "Evaluation of Strategy: Theory and Models," in D.E. Schendel & C.W. Hofer, eds. *Strategic Management: A New View of Business Policy and Planning.* Boston: Little, Brown, 1979.

———, "A Teaching Plan for Strategy Alternatives for the British Motocycle Industry," in *Japanese Business: Business Policy.* New York: The Japan Society, 1980.

———, "Diversification Strategy and Profitability," *Strategic Management Journal*, 1982: 359–370.

SAKIYA, T., "The Story of Honda's Founders," *Asahi Evening News*, June–August, 1979.

———, *Honda Motor: The Men, The Management, The Machines.* Tokyo, Japan: Kadonsha International, 1982.

SALANCIK, G.R., "Commitment and the Control of Organizational Behavior and Belief," in B.M. Staw and G.R. Salancik, eds., *New Directions in Organization Behavior.* Chicago: St. Clair Press, 1974.

SAYLES, L.R., *Managerial Behavior: Administration in Complex Organizations.* New York: McGraw-Hill, 1964.

SCHEIN, E.H., "Organizational Socialization and the Profession of Management," *Industrial Management Review*, Winter 1968: 1–16.

————, "The Individual, The Organization and The Career: A Conceptual Scheme," *Journal of Applied Behavior Science*, 1971: 401–426.

————, "How Graduates Scare Bosses," *Careers Today*, January, 1969.

SCHENDEL, D.G., R. PATTON, & J. RIGGS, "Corporate Turnaround Strategies: A Study of Profit Decline and Recovery," *Journal of General Management*, Spring 1976: 3–11.

SCHOEFFLER, S., R.D. BUZZELL, & D.F. HEANY, "Impact of Strategic Planning on Profit Performance," *Harvard Business Review*, March–April 1974: 137–145.

SCOTT, W.E., "Activation Theory and Task Design," *Organizational Behavior and Human Performance*, September 1966: 3–30.

SEGAL, M., "Organization and Environment: A Typology of Adaptability and Structure," *Public Administration Review*, 1974: 212–220.

SELZNICK, A., *TVA and the Grass Roots*. Berkeley: University of California Press, 1949.

————, *Leadership in Administration: A Sociological Interpretation*. New York: Harper and Row, 1957.

SHIMADA, H., "The Japanese Employment System," *Japanese Industrial Relations Series*. Tokyo: The Japan Institute of Labor, 1980.

SHUBIK, M., *Games for Society, Business, and War: Towards a Theory of Gaming*. New York: Elsevier, 1975.

SIMON, H.A., *Administrative Behavior*. New York: Macmillan, 1957.

————, "On the Concept of Organizational Goals," *Administrative Science Quarterly*, 1964–1965: 1–22.

————, *The Sciences of the Artificial*. Cambridge, Mass.: MIT Press, 1969.

SMITH, L., "The Boardroom Is Becoming a Different Scene," *Fortune*, May 8, 1978: 150 +.

SOELBERG, P.O., "Unprogrammed Decision Making," *Industrial Management Review*, Spring 1967: 19–29.

SOLZHENITSYN, A., "Why The West Has Succumbed to Cowardice," *The Montreal Star: News and Review*, June 10, 1978.

SORENSEN, T., "You Get to Walk To Work," *New York Times Magazine*, March 19, 1967.

SPENCER, F.C., "Deductive Reasoning in the Lifelong Continuing Education of a Cardiovascular Surgeon," *Archives of Surgery*, 1976: 1177–1183.

STARBUCK, W.H., "Organizations and Their Environments," in M.D. Dunnette, ed., *Handbook of Industrial and Organizational Psychology*. Chicago: Rand McNally, 1976.

————, A. GREVE, & B.L.T. HEDBERG, "Responding to Crises," *Journal of Business Administration*. 1978: 111–137.

STARBUCK, W.H. & B.L.T. HEDBERG, "Saving an Organization from a Stagnating Environment," in H.B. Thorelli, ed., *Strategy + Structure = Performance*. Bloomington: Indiana University Press, 1977.

STARBUCK, W.H. & P.C. NYSTROM, *Pursuing Unknown Goals Through Organizational Designs*, Working Paper, University of Wisconsin-Milwaukee, 1977.

STERN, L.W., B. STERNTHAL, & C.S. CRAIG, "Managing Conflict in Distribution Channels: A Laboratory Study," *Journal of Marketing Research*, 1973: 169–179.

STEVENSON, H.H., "Defining Corporate Strengths and Weaknesses," *Sloan Management Review*, Spring 1976: 51–68.

STEVENSON, W., *A Man Called Intrepid: The Secret War*. New York: Harcourt Brace Jovanovich, 1976.

STEWART, R., *Managers and Their Jobs*. London: Macmillan, 1967.

STIEGLITZ, H., *The Chief Executive and His Job*. New York: National Industrial Conference Board, Personnel Policy Study, 1969.

STIGLER, G.J., "The Theory of Economic Regulation," *Bell Journal of Economics and Management Science*, 1971: 3–21.

STINCHCOMBE, A.L., *Creating Efficient Industrial Administrations*. New York: Academic Press, 1974.

STRAUSS, G., & E. ROSENSTEIN, "Workers Participation: A Critical View," *Industrial Relations*, 1970: 197–214.

SUN TZU, *The Art of War*, translated by S.B. Griffith. New York: Oxford University Press, 1963. Original 500 B.C.

TAIRA, K., *Economic Development and Labor Market in Japan*. New York: Columbia University Press, 1970.

TAKAMIYA, M., "Japanese Multinationals in Europe," *Columbia Journal of World Business*, Summer 1981: 5–17.

TAYLOR, W. H., "The Nature of Policy Making in Universities," *The Canadian Journal of Higher Education*, 1983: 17–32.

TERKEL, S., *Working*. New York: Pantheon, 1972.

THOMPSON, J.D., *Organizations in Action*. New York: McGraw-Hill, 1967.

THOMPSON, V.A., *Modern Organizations*. New York: Alfred A. Knopf, 1961.

TILLES, S., "How to Evaluate Corporate Strategy," *Harvard Business Review*, July–August 1963: 111–121.

TOFFLER, A., *Future Shock*. New York: Bantam Books, 1970.

TREGOE, B., & I. ZIMMERMAN, *Top Management Strategy*. New York: Simon and Schuster, 1980.

TSUJI, K., "Decision-Making in the Japanese Government: A Study of Ringisei," in R.E. Wards, ed., *Political Development in Modern Japan*, Princeton: Princeton University Press, 1968.

TSURUMI, Y., *Multinational Management: Business Strategy and Government Policy*. Cambridge, Mass.: Ballinger, 1977.

TUCHMAN, B.W., *The Guns of August*. New York: Macmillan, 1962.

TURNER, B.A., "The Organizational and Interorganizational Development of Disasters," *Administrative Science Quarterly*, 1976: 378–397.

TUSHMAN, M.L., "Special Boundary Roles in The Innovative Process," *Administrative Science Quarterly*, 1977: 587–605.

URWICK, L.F., "The Manager's Span of Control," *Harvard Business Review*, May–June 1956: 39–47.

UTTERBACK, J.C. & J.W. BROWN, "Monitoring for Technological Opportunities," *Business Horizons*. October 1972: 5–15.

VANCIL, R.F., "Strategy Formulation in Complex Organizations," *Sloan Management Review*, Winter 1976: 1–18.

———— & P. LORANGE, "Strategic Planning in Diversified Companies," *Harvard Business Review*, January–February 1975: 81–90.

VAN DOREN, M., *Liberal Education*, Boston: Beacon Press, 1967.

VARNER, V.J. & J.I. ALGER, EDS., *History of the Military Art: Notes for the Course*. West Point, N.Y.: U.S. Military Academy, 1978.

VICKERS, G., "Is Adaptability Enough?", *Behavioral Science*, 1959: 219–234.

VOGEL, E., *Japan as Number One*. Cambridge, Mass.: Harvard University Press, 1979.

VON BÜLOW, D.F., *The Spirit of the Modern System of War*, translated by C.M. de-Martemont. London: C. Mercier, 1806.

VON CLAUSEWITZ, C., *On War*, translated by M. Howard and P. Paret. Princeton, N.J.: Princeton University Press, 1976.

VON HIPPEL, E., "Get New Products From Customers," *Harvard Business Review*, March–April 1982: 117–122.

VON NEUMANN, J. & O. MORGENSTERN, *Theory of Games and Economic Behavior*. Princeton, N.J.: Princeton University Press, 1944.

WARD, L.B., *Analysis of 1969 Alumni Question-naire Returns*. Unpublished Report, Harvard Business School, 1970.

WATERMAN, R.H., "The Seven Elements of Strategic Fit," *The Journal of Business Strategy*, Winter 1982: 69–73.

WEBER, M., "The Three Types of Legitimate Rule," translated by H. Gerth, in A. Etzioni, ed., *A Sociological Reader on Complex Organizations*. New York: Holt, Rinehart and Winston, 1969.

WEICK, K.E., "Educational Organizations as Loosely Coupled Systems," *Administrative Science Quarterly*, 1976: 1–19.

WHEELWRIGHT, S.C., "Japan—Where Operations Really are Strategic," *Harvard Business Review*, July–August 1981: 67–74.

WHITE, T.H., *In Search of History: A Personal Adventure*. New York: Warner Books, 1978.

WHITEHEAD, A.N., *Aims of Education and Other Essays*. New York: Macmillan, 1929.

WHYTE, W.F., *Street Corner Society*. Chicago: University of Chicago Press, 1955.

WILDAVSKY, A.B., "The Self-evaluating Organization," *Public Administration Review*, 1972: 509–520.

———, "If Planning is Everything, Maybe It's Nothing," *Policy Sciences*, 1973: 127–153.

WILLIAMSON, O.E., *Markets and Hierarchies: Analysis and Antitrust Implications*. New York: Free Press, 1975.

WITTE, E., "Field Research on Complex Decision-Making Processes—The Phase Theorem," *International Studies of Management and Organization*, Summer 1972: 156–182.

WODARSKI, J.S., R.L. HAMBLIN, D.R. BUCKHOLDT, & D.E. FERRITOR, "Individual Consequences versus Different Shared Consequences Contingent on the Performance of Low-Achieving Group Members," *Journal of Applied Social Psychology*, 1973: 276–290.

WORTHY, J.C., "Organizational Structure and Employee Morale," *American Sociological Review*, 1950: 169–179.

———, *Big Business and Free Men*. New York: Harper & Row, 1959.

WRAPP, H.E., "Good Managers Don't Make Policy Decisions," *Harvard Business Review*, September–October 1967: 91–99.

WRIGLEY, L., *Diversification and Divisional Autonomy*. D.B.A. thesis, Harvard Business School, 1970.

YOSHINO, M., *Japan's Managerial System*. Cambridge, Mass.: MIT Press, 1968.

YOUNG, D., *Rommel: The Desert Fox*. New York: Harper & Row, 1974.

ZALD, M.N., "Urban Differentiation, Characteristics of Boards of Directors and Organizational Effectiveness," *American Journal of Sociology*, 1967: 261–272.

ZALEZNIK, A., "Power and Politics in Organizational Life," *Harvard Business Review*, May–June 1970: 47–60.

SUBJECT INDEX

AUTHOR INDEX